LET'S GO:
ISRAEL & EGYPT
(INCLUDING JORDAN) −1 APR 1995

is the best book for anyone traveling on a budget. Here's why:

No other guidebook has as many budget listings.

In Jerusalem we list dozens of places to stay for less than $15 per night; in the countryside, hundreds more for much less. We tell you how to get there the cheapest way, whether by bus, boat, plane, or thumb, and where to get an inexpensive and satisfying meal once you've arrived. There are hundreds of money-saving tips for everyone plus lots of information on special student discounts.

LET'S GO researchers have to make it on their own.

No expense accounts, no free hotel rooms. Our Harvard-Radcliffe student researchers travel on budgets as limited as your own.

LET'S GO is completely revised every year.

We don't just update the prices, we go back to the places. If a charming restaurant has become an overpriced tourist trap, we'll replace the listing with a new and better one.

No other budget guidebook includes all this:

Coverage of both the cities and the countryside; in-depth information on culture, history, and the people; distinctive features like new city and regional maps; tips on work, study, hiking and biking, nightlife and special splurges; and much, much more.

LET'S GO is for anyone who wants to see Israel, Egypt and Jordan on an inflation-fighting budget.

LET'S GO:

The Budget Guide to
ISRAEL
and EGYPT
(INCLUDING JORDAN)

1989

Joel H. Abrams
Editor

Eve. M. Weisberg
Assistant Editor

Written by Harvard Student Agencies, Inc.

PAN BOOKS
London, Sydney and Auckland

Helping Let's Go

If you have suggestions or corrections, or just want to share your discoveries, drop us a line. We read every piece of correspondence, whether a 10-page letter, a postcard, or, as in one case, a collage. All suggestions are passed along to our researcher/writers. Please note that mail received after June 1, 1989 will probably be too late for the 1990 book, but will be retained for the following edition. Address mail to: Let's Go: Israel and Egypt, Harvard Student Agencies, Inc.; Thayer Hall-B; Harvard University; Cambridge, MA 02138; USA.

In addition to the invaluable travel advice our readers share with us, many are kind enough to offer their services as researchers. Unfortunately, the charter of Harvard Student Agencies, Inc. enables us to employ only currently enrolled Harvard students both as researchers and editorial staff.

Published in Great Britain by Pan Books Ltd
Cavaye Place, London SW10 9PG
9 8 7 6 5 4 3 2 1

Published in the United States of America
by St. Martin's Press, Inc.

LET'S GO: ISRAEL AND EGYPT. Copyright © 1989
by Harvard Student Agencies, Inc. All rights reserved.

Maps by David Lindroth, copyright © 1989, 1986 by St. Martin's Press, Inc.

ISBN: 0 330 30550 6

Let's Go: Israel and Egypt is written by Harvard Student Agencies, Inc., Harvard University, Thayer Hall-B, Cambridge, Mass. 02138, USA.

Let's Go ® is registered trademark of Harvard Student Agencies, Inc.

Printed and bound in the United States of America.

Editor	Joel H. Abrams
Assistant Editor	Eve M. Weisberg
Publishing Manager	Mark D. Selwyn
Managing Editors	Alice K. Ma
	Andrea Piperakis
Production/Communications	
Coordinator	Nathanael Joe Hayashi

Researcher/Writers:
Jerusalem (New City), Central and
North Coasts, Golan — Deborah E. Benor
Jordan — J. Carlson
— M. Carlson

Cairo, Mediterranean Coast,
Suez and Red Sea Coast — Paul Caleb Deemer
Nile Valley, Western Desert Oases — Yuly Kipervarg
Jerusalem (Old City), Negev and
South Coast, Sinai, West Bank — Robert G. Morrison

Advertising Manager	Kimberley Harris
Advertising Representatives	Kelly Ann McEnaney
	Charles Emmit Ryan
Legal Counsel	Harold Rosenwald

ACKNOWLEDGMENTS

I greatly enjoyed editing this book. Getting a letter from *Let's Go* inviting me to join the family was similar to being told that "you may have won 10 million dollars." The job evoked warm memories of my time in Israel, and provoked strong desires to visit the many places that I've only read about. I hope you find this guide useful in visiting all these places, and that you take the time to linger and enjoy them.

The first and largest acknowledgment has to go to my Assistant Editor, Eve Weisberg. I made the right choice with Eve, and I have to thank her for the hard work that got the job done. Eve deciphered my red scrawl and tried to make it boldface, made sure we spelled *ḥummus* correctly, and typed from noon until midnight. She also introduced me to *Loxfinger*, the adventures of Israel Bond, Agent Oy-Oy-Seven. Mark Selwyn, another famous resident of Brookline, MA, is responsible for getting me into this and also for helping me successfully get out of this.

Researching for *Let's Go* is fun, but poses special challenges. Pete survived a native traveling companion who was uncommunicative, rigid, wide-eyed, and attracting flies. His clear writing, dry English wit, and diligent research were valuable assets, and as a bonus we got "Godzilla." We had lost hope for my old friend Robert after he researched the West Bank. But this gonzo runner eluded the tear gas and brought back plenty of true stories. Debbie had a yucky time in Tel Aviv, then went on to be a brilliant artist, friend to dogs, and a big smiley-face. As Yuly went down the Nile, he faced the hucksters and the tourist industry—and took action in his own special way. The Carlsons put their previous experiences living in the Middle East to good use as they ventured across the Fertile Crescent from Turkey to Jordan.

Supporting actors as well deserve my gratitude. Numerous other editors and assistant editors helped me along, inspired me, distracted me, and entertained me. Alex Shalaby once more offered his good offices in Cairo. Council Travel arranged flights on esoteric airlines. Prof. Ali Asani and Prof. Carol Zaleski kindly checked the Islam and Christianity sections, respectively. Ken Carr proofread and consulted on Judaism; several other proofreaders and typists polished our pages as well. Ramsses II, our faithful computer, went the whole summer without crashing once. And Ahmed the Camel survived great indignities to offer us his expert opinion.

On a personal level, I'd like to thank Roger, summer roommate, dining companion, and buddy; David, who should have a great time in Paris; Melinda; Ariel; Sarah; Sandra, Tricia, and the rest of the gang; and "My Friend Bob." WHRB occupied my spare time, as I moved from news to classical music, and helped out with the care and feeding of Bessie. Of course, I want to thank Mom and Dad for giving support and bringing me up right.

Eve would like to thank Rachel for tolerating her experiments in Middle Eastern cooking, the Bosserts for generously allowing her to house-sit their mansion, the Yagils for their Israeli hospitality (a long-overdue thanks), Ken for the support, silliness, and diversions he provided, and, of course, Abbott the Dog for keeping her company in the study during those late nights of copyediting.

Lastly, I give thanks for the miracle of finishing this book, and wish all of you healthy and happy travels. Next year in Jerusalem and in Cairo, and in peace.

—Joel Abrams

CONTENTS

x   **Contents**

About Let's Go

In 1960, Harvard Student Agencies, a three-year-old nonprofit corporation established to provide employment opportunities to Harvard and Radcliffe students, was doing a booming business selling charter flights to Europe. One of the extras HSA offered passengers on these flights was a 20-page mimeographed pamphlet entitled *1960 European Guide,* a collection of tips on continental travel compiled by the staff at HSA. The following year, Harvard and Radcliffe students traveling to Europe made notes and researched the first full-fledged edition of *Let's Go: Europe,* a pocket-sized book with a smattering of tips on budget accommodations, irreverent write-ups of sights, and a decidedly youthful slant. The first editions proclaimed themselves to be helpmates to the "adventurous and often pecunious student." Throughout the sixties, the series reflected its era: A section of the 1968 *Let's Go: Europe* was entitled "Street Singing in Europe on No Dollars a Day"; the 1969 guide to America led off with a feature on drug-ridden Haight Ashbury.

During the seventies, *Let's Go* gradually became a large-scale operation, adding regional guides to parts of Europe and slowly expanding into North Africa and nearby Asia. In 1981, *Let's Go: USA* returned after an eight-year hiatus, and in the next year HSA joined forces with its current publisher, St. Martin's Press. Since then, the series has continually blossomed; the additions of *Let's Go: Pacific Northwest, Western Canada, and Alaska* and *Let's Go: California and Hawaii* in 1988 brought the the total numbers of titles to eleven.

Each spring, over 150 Harvard students compete for some 70 positions as *Let's Go* researcher/writers. An editorial staff of 14 carefully reads stacks of 10-page applications and conducts thorough interviews. Those hired possess a rare combination of budget travel sense, writing ability, stamina, and courage. Each researcher/writer travels on a shoestring budget for seven weeks, researching and writing seven days per week, and mailing back their copy to Cambridge—about 500 pages in six installments. Train strikes, grumpy proprietors, noisy hostels, irate tourist officials are all in a day's work, but sometimes things become more serious. The afflictions of the summer of 1988 included one tear gassing, two totaled cars, one concussion, one near-drowning, and, in the most bizarre tale to date, one researcher/writer was chased up a tree by a pack of reindeer.

Back in a cluttered basement in Harvard Yard, an editorial staff of 25 and countless typists and proofreaders spend four months poring over more than 50,000 pages of manuscript as they push the copy through 12 comprehensive stages of intensive editing. In September the collected efforts of the summer are converted from computer diskette to nine-track tapes and delivered to Com Com in Allentown, Pennsylvania, where their computerized typesetting equipment turns them into books in record time. And even before the books hit the stands, the next year's editions are well underway.

LET'S GO: ISRAEL AND EGYPT, including Jordan

General Introduction

The lands of Israel, Egypt, and Jordan have been the setting for visionary dreams, fanatic idealism, and brutal conflict for over two millennia. From the scorched terrain of the Arabian Desert to the snow-covered Golan Heights, tribes and armies have fought bitterly over territory each side feels is rightly their own. Three major world religions stake claims to the same acre of land in Jerusalem. Israeli Jews battle for the same territory on the West Bank that they conquered in biblical times. The conflicts are domestic as well as international: Muslim and Jewish fundamentalists argue with secularists, and everyone wrangles over the best way to create peace. Curiously, while the conflicts are intense, the enemy is often ambiguous. In Israel and the Occupied Territories, the enemy can be a neighbor and often a friend. Although negotiations over peace continue, the religious fervor and intense suffering common to both sides decrease the chances of rational mediation. The way to peace is as tortuous as the alleys of Cairo or Jerusalem.

However, the Middle East is also a land of tradition and hope. An orange grove survives defiantly in the midst of the desert thanks to modern irrigation. A Bedouin tribe invites tourists to experience an evening of traditional food and entertainment. A thirteen-year-old Jew celebrates his Bar Mitzvah at the Western Wall while hundreds of Muslims heed the call of the *muezzin* at the nearby al-Aqsa Mosque. Jordanian students learn technical skills while a kibbutznik teaches her children to till the land.

History unfolds daily, and the contrast between ancient and modern times can be seen everywhere, making the Middle East an exciting place to visit. The remains of the world's first civilization sit barely fifty miles from the world's only vertical linear accelerator. Sights and ruins chronicle the struggles for control of these lands, forming *tels* with layer upon layer of remains from different civilizations. Ancient pyramids, medieval synagogues, Islamic palaces, Crusader cities, and relics from recent wars wait for you to dig in.

Using Let's Go

The timelessness of the Middle East need not leave you penniless, and that's where *Let's Go* helps. *Let's Go* lists economical places to eat and sleep, with accurate reviews of hostels, budget hotels, and inexpensive restaurants in Israel, Egypt, and Jordan. If the manager is grumpy, beds are lumpy, and the hostel is dumpy, we say so. *Let's Go* specializes in sorting out the details, telling you the location of the nearest post office, emergency center, and laundromat. The nitty-gritty, like specific prices and telephone numbers, are included as well. *Let's Go* will orient you, and outline the transportation options to take you to your destination. We note the cheapest places to buy your souvenirs—and tell you how to bargain for them.

Let's Go tells you how to get a job or arrange a study program. Specific information for disabled, senior, and gay travelers is listed. *Let's Go* also gives hints for

1

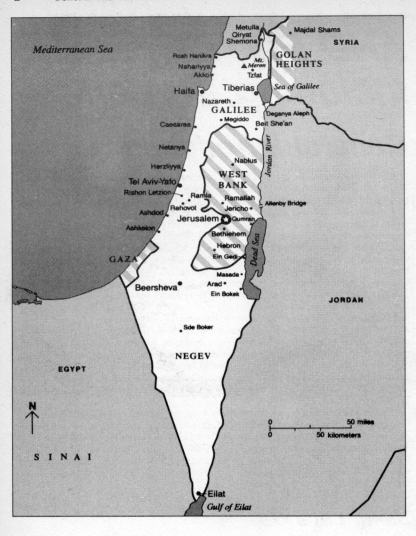

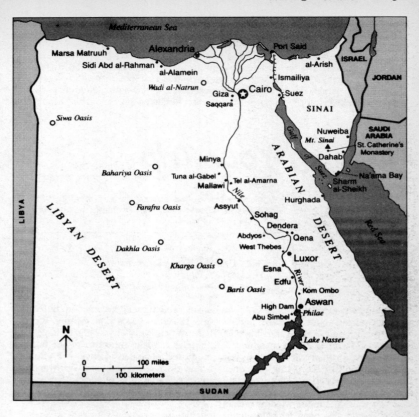

family travel, noting accommodations and activities that are suitable for children. And before you get there, *Let's Go* will advise you on how to arrange passports, visas, and identification cards—whether you're a citizen of America, Australia, Canada, New Zealand, or the U.K. The General Introduction tips you off on what to pack, when to go, and the cheapest way to get there. It will give you the historical and religious background you need to understand the people.

In this book, Israel, Egypt, and Jordan each have their own introductions, which include information on the language, art, architecture, transportation, and lifestyles of the region.

Planning Your Trip

> **Price Warning**
> The information in this book was researched during the summer of 1988. Inflation, though largely stabilized in recent years, will probably have raised some prices since then.

> *Traveling is no fool's errand to him who carries his
> eyes and itinerary along with him.*
> —*Amos Bronson Alcott*

Planning ahead will not only save you considerable time and confusion, but will also educate you about the places and people of the lands you will be visiting. Write a tentative itinerary, but be flexible once there. When every city seems to have 27 museums, 73 archeological sites, and 388 temples to visit, and none of the buses or trains goes in the right direction, relax; don't feel obligated to cover everything your itinerary lists. Keep your eyes open for new discoveries and vary your travels. If ancient ruins begin to look like just some more large piles of rocks, then slow down and do something different. Go to a cafe and people-watch or relax by the banks of the Nile or the Mediterranean.

You should also consider beforehand the amount of money you want to spend during your trip. To help plan your itinerary, take a couple of hours to write to the travel organizations listed in *Let's Go*. Tourism is one of the largest industries in Israel, Egypt, and Jordan; you'll be surprised by the amount of information available.

Useful Organizations and Publications

Research now simplifies travel later. Below are some agencies worth contacting during the planning stages.

Travel Services

Canadian Universities Travel Service Ltd. (TRAVEL CUTS): Canada, 187 College St., Toronto, Ontario M5T 1P7 (tel. (416) 979-2406). Branch offices in Burnaby, Edmonton, Halifax, Montreal, Ottawa, Saskatoon, Toronto, Vancouver, Victoria, and Winnepeg. **U.K.,** 295-A Regent St., London W1R 7YA (tel. (01) 637-3161). Arranges adventure tours and work abroad. Distributes the International Student Identity Card (ISIC), Federation of International Youth Travel Organization (FIYTO), and hostel cards. Prints a free newspaper, which can be found at their offices or at university campuses across Canada.

THE EUROPE SPECIALIST!

- The *lowest* international student/ youth air fares!
- Eurailpasses issued on-the-spot!
- Adventure tours (Europe, U.S.S.R., China, Israel, Egypt & Thailand)
- Travel gear and books
- Youth hostel passes
- International Student I.D. Card issued on-the-spot!
- Work abroad information (Germany, France, Ireland, Jamaica, United Kingdom, New Zealand & Costa Rica)
- International volunteer projects

Council Travel offices located in	
Amherst	413-256-1261
Atlanta	404-577-1678
Austin	512-472-4931
Berkeley	415-848-8604
Boston	617-266-1926
Cambridge	617-497-1497
Cambridge (M.I.T.)	617-225-2555
Chicago	312-951-0585
Dallas	214-350-6166
Evanston	312-475-5070
La Jolla	619-452-0630
Long Beach	213-598-3338
Los Angeles	213-208-3551
Milwaukee	414-332-4740
Minneapolis	612-379-2323
New Haven	203-562-5335
New Orleans	504-866-1767
New York	212-661-1450
	212-254-2525
Portland	503-228-1900
Providence	401-331-5810
San Diego	619-270-6401
San Francisco	415-421-3473
	415-566-6222
Seattle	206-632-2448
Sherman Oaks	818-905-5777
Washington, D.C.	202-337-6464

Council Travel is a travel division of the Council on International Educational Exchange

Free! Student Travel Catalog!
Our fifteenth annual edition. Crammed with helpful hints on study, travel, and work overseas. There are handy order forms for everything including the Int'l Student I.D. Card, railpasses, books and guides, air fare information, etc.

Free! Air Fare Updates!
Need to know the best available student/youth international air fares? Write for a free copy of our air fare update. Just let us know what major U.S. airport you're departing from and when you're leaving.

Return to the office nearest you.
Council Travel

| 205 East 42nd Street | 729 Boylston Street | 919 Irving Street | 831 Foster Street |
| New York, NY 10017 | Boston, MA 02116 | San Francisco, CA 94122 | Evanston, IL 60201 |

Name _____

Address _____

City _____ State _____ ZIP _____

Name of School/University _____

Educational Travel Center (ETC): 438 N. Frances St., Madison, WI 53703 (tel. (608) 256-5551). IYHF (AYH) membership cards, flight information, Eurail and Britrail passes. If you mention *Let's Go,* ETC will send you a free copy of the travel newspaper *Taking Off.*

Federation of International Youth Travel Organizations (FIYTO): 81 Islands Brygge, DK-2300, Copenhagen, Denmark (tel. (01) 54 45 35). Free annual catalog filled with discount airfares for students and youths.

International Student Travel Conference (ISTC): Weimbergstrasse 31, CH-8006 Zurich, Switzerland. **USA,** CIEE/Council Travel Services, 205 E. 42nd St., New York, NY 10017 (tel. (212) 661-1414). **Canada,** Travel CUTS (see address above). **U.K.,** STA Travel (see address below). **Australia,** SSA/STA, 220 Faraday St., Carlton, Melbourne, Victoria 3053 (tel. (03) 347 69 11). **New Zealand,** Student Travel, First Floor, Hope Gibbons Building, 11-15 Dixon St., Wellington (tel. (04) 85 05 61). Issues the International Student Identity Card (ISIC).

International Youth Hostel Federation (IYHF): Midland Bank Chambers, Howardsgate, Welwyn Garden City, Herts, England (tel. (0707) 33 24 87). **USA,** American Youth Hostels, P.O. Box 37613, Washington, DC 20013-7613 (tel. (202) 783-6161). **Canada,** Canadian Hostelling Association, 333 River Rd., Vanier, Ontario, Canada K1L 8H9 (tel. (613) 748-5638). **U.K.,** Youth Hostel Association (YHA), 14 Southampton St., London WC2E 7HY (tel. (01) 836 85 41). **Australia,** Australian Youth Hostel Association (AYHA), 60 Mary St., Surry Hills, Sydney, New South Wales 2010 (tel. (02) 212 11 51). **New Zealand,** Youth Hostel Association of New Zealand, P.O. Box 436, 28 Worcester St., Christchurch, C1 (tel. 79 99 70). IYHF membership costs $20 for those over 18 in the U.S., $10 for those under 18 and over 54; CDN$15 in Canada, CDN$9 for those under 18. Request the *International Youth Hostel Handbook,* Volume 1 ($6 postpaid) for up-to-date listings of hostels in Egypt and Israel. If you arrive without an IYHF card, you may purchase an International Guest Card from the local association or from the larger hostels.

Let's Go Travel Services: Harvard Student Agencies, Inc., Thayer Hall-B, Harvard University, Cambridge, MA 02138 (tel. (617) 495-9649). Student ID cards, American Youth Hostel memberships (valid at all IYHF youth hostels), FIYTO cards for nonstudents, Eurail, Britrail, and France vacancies passes, transatlantic charter flights, maps, travel guides (including the *Let's Go series*), and a new line of budget travel gear—all available on the spot. ISIC, AYH, and FIYTO cards are available by mail (allow 2-3 weeks for delivery). Call or write for the "Bag of Tricks" discount and information packet.

STA Travel: 117 Euston Rd., London NW1 2SX and 74 Old Brompton Rd., London SW7 3LQ (tel. (01) 388 33 61 or 581 10 22). Distributes ISIC and has charter flights to Israel and Egypt.

Student Travel Network: 17 E. 45th St., #805, New York, NY 10017 (tel. (212) 986-9470). Airfares for all youths (under 26) and full-time students under 32.

United States Travel Services (USSTS): 356 W. 34th St., New York, NY 10001 (tel. (212) 947-9533). Write for catalogs on low-cost camping tours and work abroad.

Young Travelers Newsletter: P.O. Box 3887, New Haven, CT 06525. Lists resources, services, bargain airfares, and useful travel tips.

Tourist Offices

Egyptian Tourist Authority: USA, 630 Fifth Ave., New York, NY 10111 (tel. (212) 246-6960); 323 Geary St., San Francisco, CA 94102 (tel. (415) 781-7676); **Canada,** Place Bonaventure, P.O. Box 3O4, Montreal, H5A 1B4 (tel. (514) 861-4420 or 861-4606); **U.K.,** 168 Picadilly, W1 London, England (tel. (01) 493 52 82 or 493 52 83). Write to the New York office for the useful *Travel Guide to Egypt* booklet and student brochures.

Israel Government Tourist Office (GTIO): U.S., 350 Fifth Ave., New York, NY 10118 (tel. (212) 560-0650); 6380 Wilshire Blvd., Los Angeles, CA 90048 (tel. (213) 658-7462); 5 S. Wabash Ave., Chicago, IL 60603 (tel. (312) 782-4306); 4151 Southwest Freeway, #650, Houston, TX 77027 (tel. (713) 850-9341). **Canada,** 180 Bloor St. W., Toronto, Ontario M5S 1M8 (tel. (416) 964-3784). **U.K.,** 18 Great Marlborough St., London W1V 2V6 (tel. (01) 434 36 51). Visit or write for tourist literature, including the helpful *Visitor's Companion.*

Jordan Information Bureau: 2319 Wyoming Ave. NW, Washington, DC 20006 (tel. (202) 265-1606).

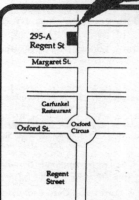
Embassies and Consulates

Egyptian Embassies: U.S., 2310 Decatur Pl. NW, Washington, DC 20008 (tel. (202) 232-5400). **Canada,** 454 Laurier Ave., E. Ottawa, Ontario K1N 6R3 (tel. (613) 234-4931), **U.K.,** 75 South Addly St., London W1 (tel. (01) 499 24 01).

Egyptian Consulates: New York: 110 Second Ave. 10022 (tel. (212) 759-7120). San Francisco: 3001 Pacific Ave. 94115 (tel. (415) 346-9700). Chicago: 505 N. Shore Lake Dr., #6502, 60611 (tel. (312) 670-2633). Other offices in Houston and Montreal.

Israeli Embassies: U.S., 3514 International Drive NW, Washington, DC 20008 (tel. (202) 364-5699); **Canada,** 410 Laurier Ave. W., #601, Ottawa, Ontario K1R 7T3 (tel. (613) 237-6450); **U.K.,** 2 Palace Green, London W8 4QB (tel. (01) 937 80 50); **Australia,** 6 Turrana St., Yarralumia, Canberra, A.C.T. 2600.

Israeli Consulates: New York: 800 Second Ave. 10017 (tel. (212) 351-5200). Los Angeles: 6380 Wilshire Blvd., #1700, 90048 (tel. (213) 651-5700). Chicago: 111 Wacker Dr., #1308, 60611 (tel. (312) 565-3300). Other offices in San Francisco, Boston, Atlanta, Houston, Philadelphia, Miami, Montreal, Toronto, and Sydney.

Jordanian Embassies: U.S., 3504 International Dr. NW, Washington, DC 20008 (tel. (202) 966-2664); **Canada,** 100 Bronson Ave., Ottawa, Ontario K1R 6G8 (tel. (613) 238-8090); **U.K.,** 6 Upper Philimore Gardens, London W8 7HB (tel. (01) 937 36 85).

Work and Study Programs

Council on International Educational Exchange (CIEE): 205 E. 42nd St., New York, NY 10017 (tel. (212) 661-1414). Branch offices in Amherst, Atlanta, Austin, Berkeley, Boston, Cambridge, Chicago, Dallas, Encino, La Jolla, Long Beach, Los Angeles, Minneapolis, Portland, Providence, San Diego, San Francisco, and Seattle. CIEE is one of the broadest ranging student travel organizations and the U.S. representative to the International Student Travel Conference (ISTC). Provides information on low cost travel, educational, and work opportunities. All the usual discount travel cards are available from CIEE, including the International Student Identity Card (ISIC). They will send you the annual Student Travel Catalog for $1, or you can pick it up free at any branch.

Institute of International Education (IIE): 809 United Nations Plaza, New York, NY 10017 (tel. (212) 883-8200). Information on study and teaching opportunities abroad. Write for a list of publications.

International Association for the Exchange of Students for Technical Experience (IAESTE): 10480 Little Patuxent Pkwy., Columbia, MD 21044 (tel. (301) 997-2200). IAESTE operates trainee/intern programs in Israel, Egypt, and Jordan.

Volunteers for Peace: tel. (800) 259-2759. Publishes a guide on current workcamps in Israel. Free newsletter available.

Books

Before ordering books through mail, check your local bookstore to see whether any are in stock. If the books aren't there, ask if the store will order them for you to save yourself the postage and the bother.

Handbook for Women Travellers: Published by Judy Piatkus Ltd., 5 Windmill St., London W1.

The Jewish Travel Guide: Published by Sepher-Hermon Press, 1265 46th St., Brooklyn, New York, NY 11219 (tel. (718) 972-9010). Also from Jewish Chronicle Publications, 25 Furnival St., London EC4A 1JT.

Longman Inc.: 95 Church St., White Plains, NY 10601 (tel. (914) 993-5000). Publishes three historical guides to Upper Egypt, Luxor, and Sakkara and Memphis (each $9.95).

Nomadic Books: 401 NE 45th St., Seattle, WA 98105. Publishes a useful free catalog listing the most recent guidebooks to all parts of the world.

Pilot Books: 103 Cooper St., Babylon, NY 11702 (tel. (516) 422-2225). Publishes several guides with hints for discount travel.

Work, Study, and Travel Abroad: The Whole World Handbook: Published by CIEE (see Work and Study Programs for address). $8.95 plus $1.00 postage.

Documents and Formalities

This can be a hassle. Securing passports, visas, and exiting customs often requires waiting in long, crowded lines. File all necessary applications early, several weeks or even months before your planned departure.

Passports

A valid passport is required to enter Israel, Egypt, and Jordan, and to return to your own country. **U.S. passports** may be obtained at any passport agency; many post offices and courts will also issue them. You may also apply by mail if your most recent passport was issued after your sixteenth birthday and within 12 years prior to the date of the new application. If you are eligible, write to a passport office for form DSP-82. Processing usually takes about two weeks through a passport agency and three to four weeks at a post office.

The passport application must include (1) proof of U.S. citizenship (such as a previous passport, a birth certificate, or a certificate of naturalization) (2) identification (such as a driver's license or old passport), and (3) two identical photographs (two inches square on a white background) taken within six months of the application and signed by you. If you are 18 or over, the fee is $42 for a ten-year passport; those under 18 receive a five-year passport for $27 and must apply in person. Renewals cost $35. For more information write for the pamphlet *Your Trip Abroad* available through the Office of Passport Services, Room 386, Department of State, 1425 K St. NW, Washington, DC 20524, (tel. (202) 532-1355) or call the Washington passport agency's 24-hour number (tel. (202) 783-8200, ext. 5).

Canadian passports may be obtained by mail from the Passport Office, Department of External Affairs, Place du Centre 200, Promenade du Portage, Hull, Quebec K1A 0G3, or in person at one of the 19 regional offices. You must submit (1) a completed application, available at passport and post offices or travel agencies, (2) evidence of Canadian citizenship, and (3) two identical photographs. Your identity must be certified on your application by a "guarantor," someone who has known you for at least two years and who falls into an approved category (including lawyer, mayor, medical doctor, notary public, and police officer). The fee is CDN$25, and normal processing time by mail is two weeks. The passport office recommends that you apply during the winter off-season if possible, and advises that you will receive much faster service (about a week) if you apply in person rather than by mail. Passports are valid for five years and are not renewable. For more information, request the free pamphlets *How to Obtain a Canadian Passport in Canada,* and *Bon Voyage, But . . .* from the passport office.

British passport applications may be picked up at passport offices in London, Liverpool, Newport, Peterborough, Glasgow, or Belfast (open Mon.-Fri. 9am-4:30pm). The completed application must be sent to a passport office along with (1) two recent identical photographs, (2) a birth certificate, (3) a marriage certificate, if relevant, and (4)£15 by check or money order. Completed applications must be countersigned by a professionally qualified person (e.g., doctor, lawyer, teacher) who has known the applicant for at least two years. Children's passports are valid for five years, after which they may be extended for another five years at no extra charge. Passports of those 16 and older are valid for 10 years and are not renewable. Passport extensions for travelers already abroad can be obtained at the nearest British High Commission or Consulate.

Australian passports are available at the local post office or at a passport office (usually located in the provincial capital). Citizens must apply in person with (1) two photographs (45 by 35mm) signed by the applicant and (2) proof of citizenship (an old passport, naturalization or citizenship papers, or a full original birth certificate). For those 18 and older, the passport costs AUS$66 and is good for 10 years. For those under 18, the passport costs AUS$27 but is only valid for five years. All Australian children, including infants, must have their own passports.

New Zealand passports are obtained from the Office of Internal Affairs in Wellington or at the local district agency. Applications may be filed in person or by mail. Documentary evidence of New Zealand citizenship must accompany your application along with NZ$50. Also include a previous New Zealand passport (if relevant), two passport photos (one certified by a friend), and a marriage or birth certificate. The passport is valid for 10 years (five years for those under 10). The renewal procedure is identical to the application process. Children may be included on their parents' passports up to the age of 16. Although two to three weeks are required for processing, the offices can rush in cases of emergency travel.

Whatever your nationality, be sure to record your passport number in a separate place. Memorizing the number is also a wise precaution in case the document should disappear. If you do lose your passport, immediately notify the local police and your embassy or consulate. Embassies can issue temporary passports immediately if you're really in a crunch. It's good practice to carry a second proof of citizenship (birth certificate or driver's license will do) separately from your passport to expedite processing of a new one, should this be necessary.

Visas

A visa is written permission granted by a government to allow foreigners to enter its country. Note that though visas can be obtained abroad, you may save considerable time if you secure them before your trip.

Israel does not require that you obtain a visa beforehand; a tourist visa will be issued free of charge to U.S., British, Australian, New Zealand, and Canadian citizens at the port of entry. However, your passport must be valid at least nine months beyond your time of arrival. These tourist visas are valid for three months, but are extendedable. Study or work visas must be obtained from an Israeli embassy or consulate prior to departure and require proof of employment or acceptance at an educational institution.

Egypt requires a more formal procedure than Israel. Egyptian visas are available by mail or in person at the nearest consulate. You must present (1) your passport, which must be valid at least six months past the date of your planned entry into Egypt, (2) a passport sized photo, and (3) the fee ($11 for U.S. citizens; $19 for Australian, British, Canadian, and New Zealand citizens). Include a stamped, self-addressed envelope if applying by mail, and allow 10 days to receive the visa. If you apply in person, the process usually takes 48 hours. The visa is valid for three months of touring beginning from the date of issue. Although an Egyptian visa can also be issued at the airport in Cairo or at the port of Alexandria, it is strongly recommended that you obtain one in advance. Visas are not available at the borders of Israel (Rafiah and Taba), or Jordan (Suez). A Sinai-only visa, valid for seven days, is available at the Sinai border. An Egyptian visa does not permit the holder to work.

Jordanian visas may be obtained in person or by mail at the Jordanian embassy or at any consulate. It is strongly recommended that you obtain your visa before traveling to Jordan. Jordanian visas are free for U.S. citizens, and are valid for up to four years. Citizens of other countries should contact the Jordanian embassy for their entry fee. A passport valid for at least 6 months past the planned date of entry and a passport-sized photo are required along the visa application. Processing a visa takes about three days.

Sudanese visas are usually issued within one or two days with a letter of recommendation from your embassy (a routine, while-you-wait procedure).

You must register your Egyptian visa with the police within seven days of your arrival or risk a heavy fine (LE25) for noncompliance. This is one part of the bureaucracy that runs smoothly. Ask the tourist office or your hotel manager where to register—frequently the manager will handle the paperwork for you. It's a painless operation, with one form. You may register at a passport office in any regional center: Cairo, Alexandria, Aswan, Luxor, Sharm el-Sheikh, and Marsa Matruuh. You may also register with local police in smaller areas, though this is less reliable and efficient. If you forget, or are unable to register, don't panic: The U.S. embassy issues a free letter of apology for U.S. citizens, with which you may register late at the Mugama Building at Tahrir Square in Cairo.

Once your visa has expired, so has your stay in the country. But **visa extensions** will normally be granted for six months to one year in all three countries. Israeli visa extensions are available at the Ministry of the Interior in Tel Aviv or Jerusalem; Egyptian in Cairo at the Mugama Building; and Jordanian at the Ministry of the Interior in Amman. To apply for an Egyptian visa extension, you must submit (1) a photograph with your passport, and (2) a LE5-6 fee. Applicants must also be able to prove that they have enough foreign currency to cover the expenses of an extended stay. For further information, write for the free pamphlets *Visa Requirements of Foreign Governments* and *Tips for Travelers to the Middle East* from the Department of State, 1425 K St. NW, Washington, DC 20524.

If you don't want to deal with the lines and hassle of securing a visa, **Visa Service Inc.,** 507 Fifth Ave., Suite 904, New York, NY 10017 (tel. (212) 986-0924), will do the dirty work for you. Their fee varies; the average cost of a visa to an American is $10. They will obtain visas for citizens of all nationalities to any country to which travel is permitted.

A Note on Travel to Arab Nations

An Israeli stamp on your passport will prevent you from entering any Arab country except Egypt. Israeli passport officials, however, will give you a detachable visa stamp upon request, eliminating evidence of your presence in the country. Any other evidence that you've been in Israel, such as an Egyptian entry stamp from Rafiah or Taba, will keep you out of Jordan, Syria, and the Sudan. The Egyptians are not as accommodating as the Israelis in providing detachable visas or border stamps. If all else fails, it may be possible to obtain a second passport for limited use. For this option though you had better wear a life-preserver, or you'll drown in red tape.

Customs

Your luggage will be examined—sometimes extremely thoroughly—as you enter and leave Israel, Egypt, and Jordan. Certain items may have to be declared upon entry, including jewelry, typewriters, camera, portable radios, and sports equipment. Normally, these items can be brought in duty-free as long as you take them with you upon departure. It is a good idea to make a list of the serial numbers of all the expensive items you are taking with you and to have it stamped by the customs office upon departure. See the Entry section of the Israel, Egypt, and Jordan introductions for declaration and duty information specific to the country.

You must declare all items acquired abroad upon returning to your own country. **U.S. citizens** may take back a maximum of $400 worth of goods duty-free every 30 days; the next $1000 is subject to a 10% tax. The duty-free goods must be for personal or household use and cannot include more than 100 cigars, 200 cigarettes (one carton), or one liter of wine or liquor (you must be 21 or older to bring liquor into the U.S.). Don't try to bring in 101 cigars.

U.S. customs officials screen out articles such as non-prescription drugs and narcotics, obscene publications, lottery tickets, liquor-filled candies, and most plants. To avoid misinterpretations, be sure that any prescription drugs are clearly marked. A copy of your physician's prescription is helpful. For those planning to import monkeys and other primates, the Customs Department clearly prohibits that too.

Unsolicited gifts may be mailed duty-free from abroad if they're worth less than $50. Spot checks are made on parcels, so write the accurate price and nature of the gift on the package. If you send back parcels worth more than $50, the Postal Service will collect the duty plus a handling charge when delivered. Liquor, perfume, or tobacco may not be mailed into the U.S. If you mail home personal goods of U.S. origin, mark the package "American Goods Returned."

Certain items purchased in Israel, Egypt, and Jordan may be excluded from the U.S. customs tax beyond the normal $400 limit under the Generalized System of Preferences (GSP), a program designed to build the economies of developing nations through export trade. For more information on all aspects of customs, write for the brochure *Know Before You Go* at the Department of the Treasury, U.S. Customs Service, Washington, DC 20229, (tel. (202) 566-8195).

Canadian citizens should identify all valuables on form Y-38 at the Customs Office or point of departure before leaving; these goods may then be reimported duty-free. Citizens may return with a maximum of CDN$20 worth of goods duty-free after 24 hours absence, CDN$100 after 48 hours, or CDN$300 after seven days or more. However, no more than CDN$300 of goods may be imported duty-free per year. The allowance may not include tobacco or alcohol products. You may send gifts valued up to CDN$40 duty-free, but again, no tobacco or alcohol. Anything above the duty-free allowance is taxed at 20% (more if the items are mailed). For more information, write for the pamphlet *I Declare* from the Canadian Department of External Affairs, Ottowa, Ontario, K1A OG2, Canada.

Australian citizens must list the valuables to be taken out of the country on Customs Form B263 upon departure. Listed items can be reimported free. A departure tax stamp available at any office of the Department of Immigration and Ethnic Affairs or the Department of Foreign Affairs is also required to exit Australia. Not more than AUS$5000 may be exported from Australia. Citizens may return with as much as AUS$400 worth of goods duty-free; the next AUS$160 will be taxed at 20%. Australians under 18 are allowed ceilings of AUS$200 and AUS$80, respectively. No more than 250 cigarettes, 250g cigars or 250g tobacco, and one liter of alcohol (for those over 18 only) are permitted. Hatching eggs and articles manufactured from lizards will be quarantined. Personal goods may be mailed home; mark the package "Australian goods returned" to avoid duty. You may mail unsolicited gifts duty-free. For more information, write for the brochure *Australian Customs Information,* Department of Industry and Commerce, Canberra, A.C.T. 2600, Australia.

New Zealand citizens should itemize goods on a Certificate of Export before leaving, which must be signed by a customs officer. Upon returning to New Zealand, citizens are allowed NZ$500 worth of goods duty-free. Articles in excess of NZ$500 are subject fully to duty and in some cases sales tax. Those over 16 are allowed to return with a choice of 200 cigarettes or 250 grams tobacco, 50 cigars, 4.5 liters of wine or beer, or 1125 ml of spirits. Additionally, homemade noodles, dead bees, bird's nests (including soups), and jumping beans are restricted from importation. Turtle shells must be inspected upon arrival. For more information, obtain the pamphlet *New Zealand Customs Guide for Travelers,* available at any embassy.

Identification Cards

The **International Student Identity Card (ISIC)** is the most widely accepted identification to qualify for youth discounts and services. The $10 card can get you discounts at museums, archeological sites, retail stores, flights, trains, buses, and even accommodations. Jordan does not belong to the International Student Travel Conference, so the card is not honored, although you should ask Alia Airlines about reduced fares. To get the most out of your ISIC card, be insistent: Even if signs make no mention of student discounts, produce your card and ask. The card also provides medical insurance up to $2000, plus $100 a day up to 60 days of in-hospital illness. No application form is necessary, but you must supply the following information either in person or by mail: (1) current dated proof of student status (a photocopy of your school ID showing this year's date, a letter on school stationery signed and sealed by the registrar, or a photocopied grade report), (2) a passport-size photo with your name printed on the back, and (3) your birthdate and nationality. The card is valid until the end of the calendar year. Unfortunately for those taking a year off from school, a new card cannot be purchased in January unless you were in school during the fall semester. However, you may be able to purchase the card if you present a letter signed by the your school registrar stating that you intend to return to school. If you have just graduated, you may still obtain an ISIC, valid until December of the same year.

Among the student travel offices that issue the ISIC are the Council on International Educational Exchange (CIEE), International Student Travel Conference (ISTC), Let's Go Travel Services, the Canadian Universities Travel Services (CUTS), SSA/STA, and Student Travel. (See Travel Services above for addresses.) In addition, over 375 travel offices in universities around the United States distribute the ISIC.

If you're not a student, but are under 26, the **Federation of International Youth Travel Organization (FIYTO) card** gives discounts on Dan Tours in Israel and on ferry travel connecting Israel, Egypt, Greece, and Italy. The FIYTO card is available from CIEE, Let's Go Travel, and from agencies within Europe. In the absence of an ISIC or FIYTO card, bring along a high school or college ID card, or show the age on your passport. Your chances of getting student discounts are decreased but not hopeless.

An **International Driving Permit** is required for driving in Israel, Egypt, and Jordan. The permit is available from any local office of the American Automobile Association (AAA) or at the main office, AAA Travel Agency Services, 8111 Gatehouse Rd., Falls Church, VA 22047 (tel. (703) 222-6713). The American Automobile Touring Alliance (AATA), 888 Worcester St., Wellesley, MA 02181 (tel. (617) 237-5200), or the Canadian Automobile Association (CAA, same address as AAA) can also provide the permit. You will need (1) a completed application, (2) two recent passport-sized photos, (3) a valid U.S. or Canadian driver's license (which must always accompany the International Driving Permit), and (4) $5. Applicants for International Driver's Permits must be at least 18 years old.

An **International Insurance Certificate** or "green card" is required to drive in Israel, Egypt, and Jordan. Most rental agencies include this coverage in their prices. Otherwise, obtain this certificate from the dealer from whom you are renting, leasing, or buying. Short term liability insurance may also be purchased from AAA travel services.

International Youth Hostel Federation (IYHF) membership is required to stay in many of Israel and Egypt's hostels. Hostel membership cards are available while-you-wait from budget travel agencies, including CIEE, Let's Go Travel, and Travel CUTS. The cost varies by country ($20 in the U.S., $10 for those under 18 or over 54), and your membership is valid for the calendar year (see Travel Services for addresses in all countries).

Money

Currency and Exchange

The exchange rates valid at press time (Sept. 1, 1988) are listed at the beginning of each country's section; however, rates fluctuate, occasionally dramatically, so check them in the financial pages of a national newspaper when planning your trip. The election and change of government in Israel could cause the shekel to plummet. Before leaving home, buy about $50 in currency of the first country you will visit. This will save you some time at the airport.

Compare rates when exchanging money—banks's commissions can vary greatly. Train stations, luxury hotels, and restaurants generally offer the worst rates. Exchange a sum that you feel comfortable carrying around. Try not to purchase more of a currency than you'll need in a particular country; every time you re-convert money you incur a loss. Avoid keeping all your currency in the same place: Split it up among pockets and bags, or use a moneybelt.

Traveler's Checks

Traveler's checks are the safest way to carry money. Though smaller establishments may not accept them, especially in small towns, traveler's checks are recognized for cash or exchange at almost every bank in the Middle East. Furthermore, if lost or stolen, traveler's checks can be replaced. Checks are available in various currencies; the smallest denomination is usually $20 or equivalent.

Traveler's check companies offer a variety of additional services besides refunding lost or stolen checks, such as medical and legal referrals, emergency message relay, interpretation help, guaranteed hospital entry, and lost document assistance. Some companies will also provide insurance coverage for trip delays, lost luggage, and accident or sickness.

Banks and agencies worldwide sell traveler's checks. Sometimes, you will be charged a commission of about 1-2%, sometimes a set fee, and sometimes no charge at all. You may be able to obtain traveler's checks without a fee from your home-town bank if you have money on deposit there. Listed below are some major traveler's check companies; to find the closest vendor of a particular brand, consult your local telephone book or bank, or call a number listed below.

American Express: tel. (800) 221-7282 from within the U.S. and Canada; from abroad, call collect tel. (801) 968-8300. Checks available in U.S. and Canadian dollars, British pounds, and five other currencies. Three offices in Israel, 11 in Egypt, and two in Jordan. Holders of American Express traveler's checks or credit cards can use American Express offices as a mailing address free of charge.

Bank of America: tel. (800) 227-3460 from within the U.S.; from Canada and abroad, call collect tel. (415) 624-5400. Checks available in U.S. dollars.

Barclays: tel. (800) 221-2426 from within the U.S.; from Canada and abroad, call collect tel. (415) 574-7111. Checks available in U.S. and Canadian dollars and British pounds.

Citicorp: tel. (800) 645-6556 or (800) 523-1199 from within the U.S. and Canada; from abroad, call collect tel. (813) 623-1709. Checks available in U.S. dollars and British pounds.

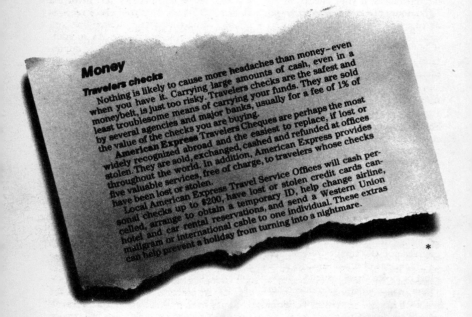

Money

Travelers checks

Nothing is likely to cause more headaches than money–even when you have it. Carrying large amounts of cash, even in a moneybelt, is just too risky. Travelers checks are the safest and least troublesome means of carrying your funds. They are sold by several agencies and major banks, usually for a fee of 1% of the value of the checks you are buying.

American Express Travelers Cheques are perhaps the most widely recognized abroad and the easiest to replace, if lost or stolen. They are sold, exchanged, cashed and refunded at offices throughout the world. In addition, American Express provides five valuable services, free of charge, to travelers whose checks have been lost or stolen.

Local American Express Travel Service Offices will cash personal checks up to $200, have lost or stolen credit cards cancelled, arrange to obtain a temporary ID, help change airline, hotel and car rental reservations, and send a Western Union maligram or international cable to one individual. These extras can help prevent a holiday from turning into a nightmare.

*

Thanks a lot "Let's Go."
We couldn't have said it better ourselves.

Thomas Cook: tel. (800) 223-7373 from within the U.S.; from Canada and abroad, call collect tel. (212) 974-5696. Checks available in U.S., Canadian, and Australian dollars and British pounds.

MasterCard International: tel. (800) 223-9920 in the U.S. and Canada; from abroad, call collect tel. (212) 974-5496. Checks available in U.S. and Australian dollars and British pounds.

Visa: tel. (800) 227-6811 from within the U.S. and Canada; from abroad, call San Francisco collect at tel. (415) 574-7111, London at (01) 937 80 91, or Paris at (14) 60 79 26 55. Checks available in U.S., Canadian, Australian, and New Zealand dollars and British pounds.

American Express, Barclays, and Visa are probably the easiest brands to obtain refunds for in Israel, Egypt, and Jordan; the other companies have you arrange replacement checks through their London offices. In any event, even in the best of circumstances, if your checks are lost or stolen, the refund process may involve a fair amount of red tape and delay. To expedite a refund, separate your check receipts and keep them in a safe place. It is vital that you record check numbers as you cash them so that you can identify exactly which checks are missing. As an additional precaution, leave a list of check numbers with someone at home. Most importantly, keep a separate supply of cash and/or traveler's checks, perhaps in the same place you keep your receipts, for financial emergencies.

Credit Cards

Credit cards are of limited value to the budget traveler because small, inexpensive establishments will not honor them. Credit cards are invaluable, however, in a financial emergency. With major credit cards, such as American Express or Visa, you can receive an instant cash advance as large as your remaining credit line from banks that issue the card. There are 92 **automated teller machines (ATMs)** in Israel and 10 in Jordan at which Visa cardholders can withdraw money at any hour by punching in a personal identification number. If your card doesn't have a number encoded, ask the bank that issued it to provide one.

In Israel, American Express limits you to $1000 cash per 21 days; if you want more than $500 at a time, your card must be confirmed by phone, which can take over an hour. In Egypt and Jordan you will probably be charged a transaction fee. This quick transfusion of cash may be your only source of money, since many traveler's check vendors will not cash a personal check, and transatlantic cables for money take at least 24 hours. For more information, write for the *International Travel Guide,* at Chase Visa, P.O. Box 5111, 1400 Union Turnpike, New Hyde Park, NY 11042. American Express will allow you to use its offices as mailing addresses for free with its card; otherwise, you may have to pay or show American Express traveler's checks to pick up your letters. *The Traveler's Companion,* which lists full-service offices throughout the world, is available from American Express Travel Service Offices. If you're a student or your income level is low, you may have difficulty acquiring an internationally recognized credit card. However, joint-account cards will be issued if someone in your family is already a member. American Express will cheerfully issue an extra green card for $25 per year or an extra gold card for $65 (relax, bills go to your loved ones). Visa charges no fee for additional joint-account cards.

The **Credit Card Service Bureau** (6860 Commercial Drive, P.O. Box 913, Springfield, VA 22150-0913) will provide its members with emergency loans and will insure that your maximum legal liability for unauthorized card use is $50 after 24 hours (no liability before 24 hours). Membership is $5 per year, $36 for three years, and $47.40 for five years.

Sending Money

Sending money overseas is a complicated, expensive, and often extremely frustrating business. Do your best to avoid it: Carry a credit card or a separate stash of traveler's checks.

Money can be sent from your home bank to a branch abroad with a **cable transfer** (in either U.S. or foreign currency) within 24 hours to a major city, a bit longer to a less central location. You pay cabling costs plus the commission charged by your bank (approximately $25 per $1000). Before you leave home, visit your bank to obtain a list of its corresponding banks in Israel, Egypt, and Jordan. This way you'll know where money can be sent. You can also arrange in advance for your bank to send money from your account to foreign banks on specific dates.

Western Union offers a convenient though expensive service for cabling money to Israel. Using MasterCard or Visa, a sender can cable up to $2000 by calling Western Union's toll-free numbers (800) 325-4176 or (800) 325-6000. Without a card, a sender must go in person to a Western Union office with cash or a cashier's check (no money orders accepted) but is not restricted to the $2000 limit. The money will arrive at the central telegram office of the city the sender designates, and may be picked up by showing suitable identification. Money will generally arrive within two to five business days. Unfortunately, Western Union does not cover Egypt and Jordan.

Money cabled through **American Express** offices is guaranteed to arrive within 72 hours. The first $200 will be disbursed in local currency and any amount above that will be in U.S. dollar traveler's checks. The cost to send $500 anywhere in the world is $15.

The **State Department's Citizens Emergency Center** (tel. (202) 647-5225) will deliver money to you if you're in big trouble and you're American. But the water must be really deep for them to help you. The State Department defines emergencies as cases of destitution, hospitalization, or death (in which case you'll have greater problems). The department prefers to send sums not greater than a few hundred dollars. For more information and a complete list of services, write Citizen Emergency Center, Department of State, #4811, 2201 C Street NW, Washington, DC 20520.

If all else falls through and you're desperate for money, consider selling some of your belongings, person, offspring, or siblings. Merchants in the marketplace or other travelers might be interested.

Bargaining

Bargain, bargain, bargain. And when the seller seems to have reached his lowest price, bargain some more. Prices are negotiable in the markets, street stands, small stores, and even in taxis. Do not bargain in the large department stores or better quality shops.

Here are the tricks of the game. Ask the price of the article in a somewhat uninterested fashion. Offer about half the asking price, act firm, and the bidding game begins. Don't be intimidated into paying more than you wish. At the same time, though, be prepared to pay any price you utter. If you give a price and the seller says yes, the article is yours. Even after you leave the store, the seller may follow you into the street—and the game continues.

Safety and Security

Common sense and minimal precautions should carry you safely through your travels. Large cities demand extra caution. Even if the city is familiar, avoid bus and train stations and public parks after dark. Stick to busy, well-lit streets and beware of pickpockets at all times. The managers of your hotel or hostel are good sources of advice on specific areas. You may also feel safer staying in places with a curfew or a night-attendant. If you're in a dormitory-style room, or have no lock on your door, sleep with all valuables on your person or under your pillow; laying your pack alongside the bed is not enough. A money belt or a necklace pouch worn under the shirt are the most theft resistant.

While traveling, steer clear of empty train compartments, particularly at night. Don't check your luggage on trains, especially if are switching en route; luggage is often lost this way. If you plan to sleep outside, or simply don't want to carry everything with you, try to store your gear at a train or bus station. Bomb scares and terrorism are, however, cutting down the availability of these lockers. Thieves who prey on backpackers are exceedingly clever, and crowded youth hostels and overnight trains are favorite hangouts for petty criminals.

Women Travelers

Women may find traveling in Israel, Egypt, and Jordan uncomfortable at times. Israeli standards of dress are more Westernized, and as a woman you will experience less verbal harassment there than in Arab countries. In all three countries, however, women need to be especially sensitive to different cultural traditions. In Arab culture, women are often veiled and secluded in their own homes. Jordan is more conservative than Egypt or the Arab parts of Israel.

Foreign males may not understand that you are irritated or angered by their pursuit. They may confuse the relative freedom of Western women with sexual willingness. American television shows don't exactly help this image. In most cases, the best answer to come-ons is none at all. It may help to wear a Walkman or other device with earphones, as men will be less likely to direct aggressive comments toward you if they think you can't hear them. On the other hand, passivity may be taken as tacit acceptance of the situation. Firmly signaling that you've had enough without being hostile is a good tactic to try when ignoring the offenders doesn't work. Asking an older Egyptian man for assistance may also shame the offending parties into backing down. If a situation becomes genuinely threatening, enter tirade mode. Scream and yell in any language, especially in the presence of onlookers. *Let's Go* lists emergency, police, and consulate phone numbers in most cities.

Most men will treat you with normal respect. While Western women are unfairly stereotyped by Middle Eastern men, so too many Middle Eastern men are stereotyped by Westerners. Standard social practice is to ask guests to tea, and most such invitations are entirely innocent. Realize that some Egyptian men will repeat an invitation continually and be genuinely offended when you decline, but if you don't feel comfortable in the situation, absolutely *do not* give in and go.

Common sense and cultural sensitivity are the best means of avoiding threatening situations in all three countries. In major cities and in major tourist sites, locals are more accustomed to Western codes of dress. Away from the metropolitan areas of Egypt and Jordan, and in both the Orthodox Jewish and Arab sections of Israel, however, it's advisable to emulate the dress and behavior of local women as much as possible. A shawl and a *djellaba* (a long garment with sleeves and a hood) may not make you blend in if your backpack, features, and height give you away first, but the covering allows you to travel more comfortably as a guest in another culture. Also, if you choose to take public transportation, remember to cover up when going from urban areas to tourist sights (such as Saqqara or Dendera in Egypt, or Petra in Jordan), since while en route you will be off the most widely used thoroughfares. Once you arrive, you can peel off your coverings for relief from the heat. Only on or very near the beaches of large tourist resorts are locals used to bathing suits. Don't smoke in public in Arab areas, and avoid sitting alone in cafes.

You will avoid harassment if you look as though you know where you're going—an air of confidence and composure can work wonders. Avoiding eye contact will reduce the chances of an uncomfortable situation. Forego cheaper accommodations in remote areas of town in favor of youth hostels or more centrally located hotels. Stay away from empty train compartments, especially at night. Beware that hostel proprietors have keys to your rooms and often segregate the sexes, so you run risks even if traveling with a man. Never hitchhike—it's especially dangerous in Israel—and beware of cars that may be following you. When riding in cabs, always sit in the back seat, keep your luggage handy, and the door unlocked. Be cautious in crowds or situations in which you find yourself confined with males, such as in an elevator. Strolling arm in arm with another woman, a common European and Middle Eastern practice, may be helpful. Wearing a wedding ring is a good tactic too, especially if you're traveling with a man, since the concept of out-of-wedlock intimacy between the sexes may be perceived as immoral. The *Handbook for Woman Travellers,* (See Books above) provides additional information and accounts about women traveling alone.

Terrorism

The *Jerusalem Post* runs a filler advertisement that reads "Suspicion saves! Beware of suspicious objects." Whether in Israel, Egypt, or Jordan, if you see an unattended package or bag, contact the police immediately, for it could be a bomb. Terrorists often use extremely sophisticated bombs, so that even a wallet or a roll of bills may be an explosive device. Don't take the investigative initiative yourself: Call the police. Similarly, don't ever leave your own belongings unattended. You may return from the bathroom to find the entire area around your unattended backpack roped off by police wearing funny-looking suits. If the police start clearing the area, follow their instructions. Though there has been a perceptible increase in terrorism against Israel associated with the turmoil in the West Bank, attacks against Westerners remain rare.

Insurance

The following firms offer insurance against theft, loss of luggage, or injury. You may buy a policy from them or, in some cases, directly from a travel agent. There are two basic points to remember when buying insurance. First, beware of unnecessary coverage. Check whether your homeowner's insurance (or your family's coverage) provides against theft during travel. University term-time medical plans often include insurance for summer travel. Homeowner's *will* generally cover the loss of travel documents such as passports, plane tickets, rail passes, etc. up to $500. Also note that American Express card holders are often covered. The ISIC card automatically comes with the "Trip Safe" plan (see Identification Cards). In addition, those under 23 should check to see whether their parents have taken out any coverage for them. The second thing to remember is that insurance companies generally require a copy of the police report filed at the time of the theft before they will honor your claim. Similarly, with medical expenses, you must submit evidence that you did indeed pay the charges for which you are requesting reimbursement. The companies listed below can arrange on the spot payment of these bills for you. One final point: Check the time limit on filing to make sure that you will be returning in time to secure reimbursement.

ARM Coverage, Inc.: tel. (800) 645-2424. Provides comprehensive program called "Carefree Travel Insurance." Travel insurance package of cancelation/interruption, medical, baggage, and travel accident coverage. 24-hour hotline. Only cancelation/interruption coverage can be purchased separately.

HealthCare Abroad: tel. (800) 237-6615. Insurance and assistance services from one of the oldest firms in the field. Optional trip cancelation, accidental death, and baggage protection plans.

The Travelers Insurance Co.: tel. (800) 243-3144; in CT, (203) 277-2318. Offers insurance for accidents, sickness, trip cancelation, and emergency medical evacuation. Also offers baggage-only policies, but at steeper rates.

Travel Assistance International/Europ Assistance Worldwide: tel. (800) 821-2828. Probably the most extensive coverage available. Round-the-world assistance programs available 24 hours in the event of financial and medical emergencies. Services include medical coverage, medical evacuation, interpretation, help in locating lost passports and visas, medical and legal referrals, and transmission of urgent messages.

Travel Guard International: tel. (800) 782-5151. Comprehensive package called "Travel Guard." Provides 24-hour hotline for policyholders traveling anywhere in the world.

WorldCare Travel Assistance Association, Inc.: tel. (800) 521-4822; in Washington, DC tel. (202) 293-0335. Provides 24-hour emergency medical hotline with extensive national network. Also offers a ScholarCare program for students and faculty spending a semester or full year abroad.

Drugs

The familiar movie stereotype of abundant hashish in the Middle East is bogus. Don't buy drugs in any country. Israeli, Egyptian, and Jordanian authorities all regard drug possession as an extremely serious offense. If you're lucky, you'll only be kicked out of the country. Other possibilities, which are not shown in the movies, include endless prison stays. Don't expect much consolation from your consulate either. Consular officers can visit the prisoner, provide a list of attorneys, and inform family and friends. They cannot obtain any more lenient treatment than that dictated by the laws of the country.

Likewise, *never* bring drugs across borders. Alcohol is illegal in Saudi Arabia, so don't carry it across either. In some areas, you will find Muslims disapprove of drinking, although alcohol is legal in Israel, Egypt, and Jordan (no drinking age). You and your belongings may be searched thoroughly whether you enter a country by land, sea, or air. Make certain to avoid unintentional involvement by refusing to carry or deliver packages for strangers, however plausible their stories. For more information, send for the brochure *Travel Warning on Drugs Abroad,* Bureau of Consular Affairs, CP/PA #5807, U.S. Department of State, Washington, DC, tel. (202) 647-1488.

Special Considerations For...

Disabled Travelers

Israel, Egypt, and Jordan have in recent years developed facilities to respond to the needs of disabled travelers. **Dr. Sami Bishara** runs a special travel agency in Cairo that advises disabled travelers and organizes tours (see Cairo Practical Information listing). The **Queen Alia Welfare Fund,** established in 1978, is a similar program in Jordan. Double check information from tourist offices to ensure that facilities are equipped for the disabled. The following organizations can also provide you with information.

Access to the World: A Travel Guide for the Handicapped, published by Facts on File Inc., 460 Park Ave. S., New York, NY 10016. $16.95 plus sales tax for New York and California residents.

Evergreen Travel: tel. (800) 435-2288 or (202) 776-1184. Runs Wings on Wheels Tours for the disabled to Israel and Egypt.

Flying Wheels Travel: tel. (800) 533-0363; inside MN, (800) 722-9351. Operates independent and group travel for the disabled.

Mobility International USA (MIUSA): U.S., P.O. Box 3551, Eugene, OR 97403 (tel. (503) 343-1284); **Canada,** Carolyn Maslek, Canadian Bureau for International Education, 141 Laurier Ave. W., Ottawa, Ontario K1P 5J3; **U.K.,** Isobelle McGrath, DIVE, Central Bureau for Educational Visits and Exchanges, Seymour Mews House, Seymour Mews, London W1H 9PE. Provides information on travel programs, international workcamps, accommodations, access guides, and organized tours in 25 countries.

Pauline Hephaistos Survey Projects: 39 Bradley Gardens, West Ealing, London W13, England, (tel. (01) 997 70 55). Publishes an access guide to Israel for the disabled.

Travel Information Service: Moss Rehabilitation Hospital, 12th St. and Tabor Rd., Philadelphia, PA 19141 (tel. (215) 329-5715, ext. 2233). Assists in planning trips and obtaining information about particular countries and cities.

The Royal Association for Disability and Rehabilitation (RADAR): 25 Mortimer St., London, W13 8HE, (tel. (01) 637 54 00). Publishes books on international travel for the disabled.

Twin Peaks Press, P.O. Box 129, Vancouver, WA 98666 (tel. (206) 694-2462). Publishes *Directory of Travel Agencies for the Disabled* and *Travel Guide for the Disabled.*

Whole Persons Tours: P.O. Box 1084, Bayonne, NJ 07002-1084 (tel. (201) 858-3400). Conducts tours and publishes *The Itinerary,* a bimonthly magazine for travelers with physical disabilities.

The Yad Sarah Organization: tel. (02) 24 42 42. Loans medical equipment free of charge in Israel.

Senior Travelers

The following organizations can provide discount information, as well as help for those seniors requiring health assistance. The International Youth Hostel Federation sells membership cards to those over 59 for only $10.

Bureau of Consular Affairs: Dept. of State, 1425 K St. NW, Washington, DC 20524 (tel. (202) 523-1462). Send a postcard for a free copy of *Travel Tips for Senior Citizens,* which provides information on passports, visas, health, and currency for older Americans planning trips abroad.

Elderhostel: 80 Boylston St., #480, Boston, MA 02116 (tel. (617) 426-7788). Offers short-term, residential, academic programs to adults 60 and older and their spouses. No membership dues or formal education needed. $195-$225 weekly fee for room, board, and tuition. Wide variety of subjects.

Mature Outlook: P.O. Box 1205, Glenview, IL 60025 (tel. (312) 291-6534). Membership (ages 50 and over, $7.50 per couple) provides more than 25 benefits and services, including discounts on hotels, rental cars, and tours.

National Council on Senior Citizens 925 15th St., Washington, DC 20005 (tel. (202) 347-8800). Information on discounts and travel abroad.

Pilot Books, 103 Cooper St., Babylon, NY 11702 (tel. (516) 422-2225). Publishes the *1988 Senior Citizens' Guide to Budget Travel.* Send $3.95 plus $1.00 postage.

Gay and Lesbian Travelers

The Middle East is culturally intolerant of gay and lesbian travelers. Homosexuality in all three countries is illegal, and an open lifestyle is taboo. The authorities in Israel, Egypt, and Jordan are not at all sympathetic to homosexual concerns. Although Israel does have official organizations, in Egypt and Jordan gay and lesbian assistance is nonexistent.

The primary organization for gay and lesbian concerns in Israel is the **Society for the Protection of Personal Rights** (Agudat LiShmirat Zechuyot HaPrat), P.O. Box 16151, Tel Aviv 61161 (tel. (03) 510 17 83). Members' club and library with coffee shop is located at 23 Beit Yossef St., Tel Aviv. The society is recognized by the government and has a service, "Israel Hospitality," which supplies information for gay tourists. A free English-language information sheet will be provided upon request. The society also operates a gay and lesbian switchboard, the *White Line* (tel. (03) 62 56 29), open Sunday, Tuesday, and Thursday after 6pm.

The most complete resource for the lesbian traveler is *Gaia's Guide,* which lists bookstores, restaurants, hotels, and meeting places. The annually revised guide is available either in local bookstores or by mail. Contact *Gaia's Guide,* 9-11 Kensington High St., London W8; in Australia or New Zealand, write to *Open Leaves,* 71 Cardigan St., Carlton, Victoria, 3053, Australia.

The best book on gay life around the world is *The Spartacus Guide for Gay Men* by Bruno Gmünder. This guide lists detailed information on bars, discos, beaches, hotels, campgrounds, restaurants, cafes, stores, and book shops for gay men in over 150 countries. The guide is readily available in the U.K. (£12.50), or write Bruno Gmünder, Lützowstrasse 105, P.O. Box 301345, D-1000 Berlin 30, West Germany. In the U.S., contact *Renaissance House,* Box 292 Village Station, New York, NY 10014 (tel. (212) 674-0120).

Traveling with Children

You don't have to abandon budget travel once you decide to bring the children along—it simply requires a little extra planning. An excellent book for tips on everything from airline food to babysitting to toys is *Baby Travel* published by Hippocrene Books, Inc. ($11.95). Most insurance companies offer family plans for travelers with children. Some books that children might enjoy are *Car Tunes,* an activity book and cassette from Random House written by Stephen Elkins; *Emma's First Vacation, First Flight,* and *The Train,* by David McPhail, and *Vacation Surprises,* by Patricia Montgomery.

Think about an itinerary that will appeal to your childrens' interests. A camel ride in Jerusalem, a trip on a Nile *felucca,* or a snorkeling excursion on the Sinai coast may be more engaging for children than museums. *Let's Go* lists several zoos and national parks that also might be of interest. The B'nai B'rith organization sponsors youth tours of Israel, and can also offer advice on family facilities and helpful organizations.

Family accommodations are available in many hostels. Try to book ahead as often as possible. Most of the hostels listed will respond to written requests for reservations, so begin correspondence from home. Once there, check ahead from one hostel to the next.

Vegetarians

The Middle East is a vegetarian's delight. Many of the staple and cheapest foods are vegetables, grains, and fruit. Street food is mostly vegetarian as well. Check under the Food listings for each country for more comprehensive gastronomic information of all kinds. Below are two organizations that publish guides for the vegetarian traveler.

The Vegetarian Society of the U.K.: Parkdale, Durham Rd., Altrincham, Chesire WA 14 4QG (tel. (061) 928 07 93). Publishes *The International Vegetarian Handbook,* listing vegetarian and health conscious restaurants, guesthouses, societies, and health-food stores for travelers in Europe. The book is distributed by Thorson's Publishing Group Ltd., Wellinborough, Northamptonshire (£2.50).

The North American Vegetarian Society: P.O. Box 72, Dolgeville, NY 13329 (tel. (516) 568-7970). Sells the *Handbook* for $8.95 including postage and handling.

Nude Sunbathers

Nude bathing is prohibited in the Muslim countries for cultural and religious reasons. Eilat on the Red Sea, with its discos and miles of beaches, is the St. Tropez of Israel; the absence of a vociferous orthodox community makes Eilat popular with nude bathers. Those wishing exposure to more bare facts should consult **The World Guide to Nude Beaches and Recreation,** published by Harmony Books (tel. (201) 382-7600) for $14.95.

Climate and Health Concerns

Weather

Israel has hot, dry summers and mild, damp winters from its coast inland, an area that includes Jerusalem, Tel Aviv, Haifa, and Hebron. The coastal cities are more humid and rainy than their landlocked counterparts. Because of the sea's moderating influence, winter rarely brings more than a cooling frost. Traveling to the south and particularly to the east of Hebron into the Negev and Jordan Valley introduces you to extreme desert climates. Though pleasantly warm November through March, summer temperatures often venture uncomfortably far above the 33°C mark. Desert nights, however, can be surprisingly cool.

Egypt may be the hottest place regularly visited by tourists. Fortunately, the climate is extremely dry, and the body's cooling system operates miraculously well in low humidity. In the south, temperatures in the summer often reach 49°C and push 54°C. Very hot. Afternoons are best spent sleeping, swimming, or sipping lemonade in a cafe. Cairo itself is only marginally hotter than Tel Aviv or Amman, but the air pollution can make the afternoons uncomfortable. Alexandria is temperate year round, but the humidity is much higher than elsewhere. During the winter the temperature climbs no higher than the low 20s, and nights get much cooler.

Jordan offers the inviting combination of warm days and cool nights in spring and autumn. During the winter, when the mountain regions see snow, Aqaba becomes popular as a sunny resort.

Average Daily Temperatures		
	January	**July**
Alexandria	11-19°C	23-30°C
Amman	4-12°C	18-32°C
Aqaba	10-21°C	30-42°C
Aswan	10-25°C	26-42°C
Cairo	8-19°C	22-36°C
Eilat	10-21°C	30-42°C
Haifa	10-29°C	21-35°C
Jerusalem	6-20°C	19-38°C
Luxor	6-24°C	23-42°C
Tel Aviv	11-20°C	23-30°C

Travel Seasons

Israel has two high tourist seasons. Summer is the favored travel time for North Americans and students; winter is preferred by Europeans who come to bask in the Middle Eastern warmth. **Egypt** has different high and low seasons depending on the region. In Alexandria and Marsa Matruuh, summer (May-Sept.) is the high season; in Cairo, winter is the high season; in the Sinai and around the Dead Sea, winter is the high season, when it's bearable to frolic in the sun. **Jordan** has its peak seasons in spring and autumn.

Off-season travel has its advantages: You will find sparser tourist crowds, lower prices, and greater local hospitality. Air fares, except around major holidays, are also generally cheaper.

Health

The hot temperatures and different foods of the Middle East can make even the most careful traveler sick. Try to eat nutritiously and to avoid overextending yourself physically. The intensity of continual travel may be very stressful; keeping down your daily mileage will help to avoid anxiety. Eschew excessive caffeine and alcohol, both of which cause dehydration. Steer away from dirty restaurants and from street vendors, or your uninitiated stomach may protest vehemently.

Drink plenty of fluids, even when you don't feel thirsty. The sun can dehydrate you quickly and imperceptibly—as much as 10 liters per day may be necessary to replenish you. Be sure to wear a hat when in the sun and a shirt shile snorkeling or swimming or you may find yourself with a blistering sunburn that could keep you in the shade for weeks. Even the already very tan are not exempt. Rule: The desert is not the place to work on a tan.

If you're traveling by car in the desert, carry plenty of extra water for the radiator as well as for drinking. Don't attempt to walk for help in the event of a breakdown; stay put and wait for a passing motorist. Distance and incline can be deceiving, and walking in the heat can fry you sunny-side up. If the car begins to overheat, put the engine in neutral and gun it periodically.

Note that **heatstroke** can occur without direct exposure to the sun. Symptoms include cessation of sweating, increased body temperature, flushed skin, and intense headache. In extreme cases, death can occur. If you suspect you have heatstroke, get out of the heat and sun immediately, cover yourself with wet towels, and drink salted water or fruit juice. If the symptoms continue, get help.

Relying on bottled mineral water is a sensible precaution to take, especially in Egypt and Jordan. To save money you may want to use water-purification tablets instead of bottled water. In some places locals may tell you that the water is safe, but often they have developed antibodies that the tourist has not. Also, heavy chlorination may disturb some stomachs. Anywhere you've been warned not to drink the water, pass up ice cubes, green salad, and unpeeled fruit as well. Sprinkling lime juice on salad may remove some of the bacteria. Always carry a canteen filled with clean water if you plan to spend time outside the cities. Perspiration carries away salt that also must be replaced. It is not necessary to take salt tablets, which sometimes disturb stomachs and cause vomiting. Lightly salting your food occasionally should be adequate.

But, alas, sooner or later, no matter how careful you are, you probably (and in Egypt certainly) will get traveler's diarrhea—affectionately known among its foreign victims as "Pharaoh's Revenge." The dreaded "Revenge" typically strikes 10-12 days after arrival, and lasts 2-4 days if you rest up. The diarrhea is usually accompanied by fever and fatigue. If, or rather, when you get sick, drink plenty of liquids to keep well hydrated. Two domestic remedies are fresh yogurt, and lemon and lime juice into which a small quantity of salt has been dissolved. Commonly recommended American medications for diarrhea are Bactrim, Lomotil, and Pepto-Bismol. Pharmacists can provide a number of locally-produced medicines as well. (Note that Enteriovioform has been banned throughout Europe and the U.S.) If you feel ill for a substantial amount of time, seek medical attention. For more information write the **International Association for Medical Assistance to Travelers (IAMAT),** 417 Center St., Lewiston, NY 14092 (tel. (716) 754-4883) for their pamphlets *How to Avoid Traveler's Diarrhea* and *How to Adjust to the Heat.*

Take extra precaution against **infection** in Egypt and the rural areas of the Jordan Valley. Cuts and bruises must be properly dressed. If you contract an eye infection, see a physician immediately. Take care not to walk barefoot in the mud or on lawns that are wet with Nile River water. Never swim in the Nile. And for heaven's sake, don't drink from it, unless you want a terminal case of "Pharaoh's Revenge."

Travelers with a medical condition requiring medication on a regular basis should consult with their physician before leaving. Diabetics, for example, may need advice on changing insulin levels for flights across multiple time zones. **The American Diabetes Association** (1660 Duke St., Alexandria, VA 22314 (tel. (800) 232-3472)) will provide an ID card and an article with travel tips for 75¢. Carry an ample supply of all medications, since matching your prescription with a foreign equivalent is not always easy. Distribute medication and syringes between carry-on and checked baggage in case one or the other goes astray. Those with medical conditions that cannot be easily recognized (e.g. allergies to antibiotics, contact lenses, diabetes, epilepsy, heart problems) should obtain a **Medic Alert** identification tag, which can communicate vital information in an emergency. The tag also provides the number of Medic Alert's 24-hour hotline, through which attending physicians can obtain information about the member's medical history. Lifetime membership costs $20; telephone (800) IDA-LERT (that's 432-5378).

IAMAT (address above; free membership, but donations encouraged) can provide a worldwide directory of English-speaking physicians whose services are available at fixed and generally reasonable rates. This way you can ensure that the doctor knows that it's your tooth that hurts, not your appendix. The American, Australian, British, Canadian, and New Zealand embassies and consulates, as well as American Express and Thomas Cook offices, can identify English-speaking doctors. The first-aid centers listed for major cities can also be of service.

Although no special **immunizations** are required to travel to Israel, Egypt, or Jordan, you should still check your medical records to ensure that your inoculations are current. Boosters against typhoid, tetanus, and diptheria, as well as a shot of gamma globulin to protect against hepatitis, are wise precautions. Typhoid shots remain good for three years, tetanus for 10. Check with your doctor about incidence of malaria in the areas you intend to visit and take appropriate medication. Egypt and Jordan do require cholera and yellow fever certificates from travelers arriving from countries where these diseases exist. If you don't have the necessary inoculations, you will be put in quarantine for several days, which is as ugly as it sounds. For more information on U.S. public health recommendations, write the Superintendent of Documents, U.S. Government Printing Office, Washington, DC 20402-9325, tel. (202) 783-3238, for their book *Health Information for International Travel* ($5.50).

You might want to bring along a compact traveler's medical kit. It should include a mildly antiseptic soap, vitamins, bandages, a thermometer in a sturdy case, mosquito repellent, motion sickness medicine (such as Dramamine), a pocket knife with tweezers, calamine lotion for sunburn and insect bites, and an antihistamine (the centuries of dust can trigger allergic reactions you never knew you had). Bring a good sunscreen and a lip balm. If you wear glasses or contact lenses, bring an extra pair along. Remember to take contraceptives if needed, since they are not always available or safe in the Middle East. If you are on the Pill, be sure to take time zone changes into account. Also remember that it's more convenient to bring tampons and sanitary supplies than to be stranded without them in a time of need.

An excellent book covering all these concerns, including a special section on AIDS, is *How to Stay Healthy Abroad* by Richard Dawood, published in the U.S. by Viking-Penguin Inc., Direct Order Department, 299 Murray Hill Parkway, East Rutherford, NJ 07072 (tel. (201) 933-1460).

Packing

It's just too hot in the Middle East to be fashion conscious. Pack light. A tried and true method is to set out everything you *think* you'll need for your trip, eliminate half of it, and take more money. Always pack according to the special needs of your journey, but remember that lots of luggage will mark you as a tourist and a heavy bag will create extra transportation needs and costs. Suffice to say that the benefits of traveling light far outweigh the inconvenience of a limited wardrobe. Always test your luggage by trudging around the block with it a few times before you leave. If you can't manage comfortably, start unloading. Having extra room for presents and other purchases is another good reason to begin with a less-than-stuffed bag.

Luggage

Decide first whether a **backpack,** a **light suitcase,** or a **shoulder bag** is most suitable for your travels. If you're planning on covering miles of ground by foot, a sturdy backpack, preferably with an internal frame and several compartments, is hard to beat. With the weight on your back, your hands will be free to handle maps, tickets, and *Let's Go.* Backpacks that convert into soft-sided shoulder bags are another good option. Their versatility enables you to move from urban hotel to countryside camping with ease, and they allow you to fool hotel managers prejudiced against backpackers. Shop or borrow carefully. Knowledgeable salespeople in reputable camping stores are your best source of assistance (see Camping below for more information).

If you use a light suitcase, consider purchasing one with wheels and sturdy straps. Those who wish to travel unobtrusively might choose a large shoulder bag that zips or closes securely.

Regardless of what kind of luggage you choose, a small **daypack** is indispensable for plane flights, sightseeing, and holding your valuables. On short trips, daypacks are useful for carrying your lunch, camera, canteen, and notebook, and can be filled with presents for the trip home. To avoid theft, guard your money, passport, and other important articles in a purse, pouch, or moneybelt. For added security, get

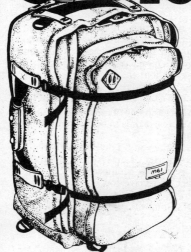

a few combination luggage locks for your bags. Be sure to label all of your luggage inside and out.

Clothing

Natural fibers or **cotton blends** beat synthetics hands down in the heat; better a few creases than polyester suffocation. While dark-colored clothes will hide dirt better, light ones are more comfortable in hot weather. Dark pants or skirts and light-colored tops are probably the best combination. Better yet, do as the locals have done for centuries—wear long, pale, gauzy shirts or skirts. Forego clothes like cut-offs and tank tops that will brand you as the typical out-of-towner and may be culturally offensive. In Egypt, Jordan, and any holy site, both men and women should keep their knees and shoulders covered to avoid offending local standards of modesty. Breaking accepted standards will only draw unwelcome attention to yourself. An economical option that will also ease the transportation burden is to buy more once there; light cotton clothing is available everywhere. When packing, remember that the temperature drops considerably at night, so bring some warmer clothes.

Appropriate **footwear** is crucial and not the place to cut costs. Tennis or well-cushioned running shoes are adequate for walking—be sure they're broken in but not broken down. Buy suitable boots if you plan to do extensive hiking. Israel's famous high quality leather sandals (*sandalim*) are great for short walks or evening idling, but will hurt unaccustomed feet.

Odds and ends

Laundromats are often hard to find, so bring along a supply of mild laundry soap. Dr. Bronner's castile soap (available in camping stores) claims to be good for everything from dish detergent to shampoo to toothpaste.

Electric current in Israel, Egypt, and Jordan is 220 volts. Travelers with appliances designed for 110 volts will either need a converter or must leave behind the hair dryer and electric shaver. A few machines are already equipped with a switch-operated converter, but since outlets are designed to receive round prongs, you'll also need an adapter to change the shape of the plug. Converters and adapters are available in department, hardware, and electrical equipment stores. To order a converter by mail, write Franzus Company, 352 Park Ave. S., New York, NY 10010. For specifics, send a self-addressed stamped envelope to receive their pamphlet *Foreign Electricity Is No Deep Dark Secret.*

Shutterbugs should purchase their **film** before leaving, for it's generally more expensive abroad. You can protect your film from airport X-ray by using a special lead-lined bag available from any photo shop. Arm yourself against the dusty Middle East climate with lens paper, which is not widely available there.

Here's a checklist of other items not to forget:

canteen	sleepsack (sheets for use in hostels)
contact lens solution	soap
contraceptives	string
converter and adaptor	sunglasses
dictionary or phrasebook	sunscreen
first aid kit	tampons
flashlight	toilet paper (instead of the local sandpaper)
needle and thread	travel alarm or watch
paper and pencil	tweezers
plastic bags	waterproof matches
pocket knife	

Weights, Measures, Time Zones, and Arabic Numerals

1 meter(m)=1.09 yards
1 kilometer(km)=about 5/8 mile
1 kilogram(kg)=2.2 pounds
1 liter(l)=1.76 pints beer
F°=9/5C°+32°

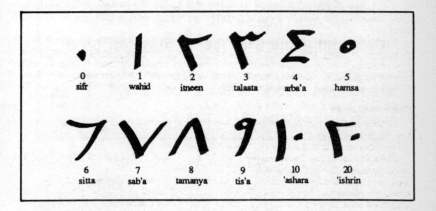

0	1	2	3	4	5
sifr	wahid	itneen	talaata	arba'a	hamsa

6	7	8	9	10	20
sitta	sab'a	tamanya	tis'a	'ashara	'ishrin

The time in Israel, Egypt, and Jordan is six hours ahead of Eastern Standard Time (seven hours ahead in winter) and two hours of Greenwich Mean Time (one hour ahead in winter).

Getting There

By Air

Off-season travelers will enjoy lower fares and a greater availability of inexpensive seats. But you don't have to travel in the dead of winter to save. Peak season rates begin around May and run until about September. Actual dates differ depending on your airline and destination—peak seasons in Israel, for instance, correspond to religious holidays as well as to summer high season. If you arrange your travel dates carefully, you can travel in summer and still save with shoulder or even low-season fares. When planning your trip, try to keep your schedule and itinerary flexible—an indirect flight via Rome or Athens could cost considerably less than a direct flight to Tel Aviv or Cairo. The budget flight plans outlined below differ from one another in economy, flexibility, and security.

With the variety of fares and flights, it's important to find a travel agent who is knowledgable and committed to saving you money. Many agents specialize in a specific area of travel, such as the Middle East. Don't hesitate to shop around—not all travel agents are the same. Commissions are smaller on budget flights, so some agents may not have incentive to search for the cheapest fare. In addition, check the travel section of the Sunday *New York Times* or other major newspapers for bargain fares, and consult CIEE or other student travel organizations—they might offer special deals for students not available to regular travel agents.

Charter flights offer consistently economical airfares. Charters may be booked until the last minute, though most summer flights fill up several months in advance. Later in the season companies often have many empty seats and either offer special prices or cancel flights. Be careful, though: Charters are more of a bargain in high season; during the winter APEX fares (see below) on commercial carriers are competitively priced. Fares advertised in the newspapers are usually the lowest possible; always read the fine print. Charter flights allow you to stay abroad up to one year, and often let you "mix-and-match" arrivals and departures from different cities. Once you have made your plans, however, the flexibility ends. You must choose your departure and return dates when you book your flight, and if you cancel your ticket within 14 or 21 days of departure, you will lose some or all of your money. Travel insurance usually does not cover cancelations for reasons other than serious unforeseen illness, death, or natural disaster.

Although charter flights are cheaper, figure in the cost of being crowded and experiencing delays. You may also not wish to spend so much time waiting in the beautiful airports of the world. Ask a travel agent about the charter company's reliability. Charter companies reserve the right to cancel flights up to 48 hours before departure. Though charters will do their best to find you another flight, the delay could be days, not just hours. The companies also reserve the right to add fuel surcharges even after you have made final payment. To avoid eleventh-hour problems with your reservation, pick up your ticket in advance of the departure date and arrive at the airport several hours before your flight to ensure getting on the plane. Charter companies often have messy reservation systems.

Charter coverage of Israel, Egypt, and Jordan varies from year to year, so consult your travel agent for companies offering flights. Be sure to get the full story about the company's recent record. CIEE and Travel CUTS usually offer flights to the Middle East (see Useful Organizations). If you don't mind leaving home without a return ticket in your pocket, you can try to secure an inexpensive charter flight out of Israel to Europe and North America. **Israel Student Travel Associations (ISSTA)** (see Useful Organizations in the Israel Introduction) has flights from Tel Aviv to London, Paris, and many other European cities for $179-199.

If you choose to fly with a commercial airline, you'll be purchasing greater reliability and flexibility. Note that the **standby** option is no longer available for flights to Israel, Egypt, and Jordan. **Advanced Purchase Excursion Fare (APEX)** provides confirmed reservations and permits you to arrive and depart from different cities. Reservations usually must be made 21 days in advance with 7 to 14 day minimum and 60 to 180 day maximum stay limitations. Beware of hefty penalties for changed reservations and cancelations. For summer travel, book APEX fares early—by mid-May, you may have difficulty getting the departure date you want.

Airline ticket consolidators sell unbooked commercial and charter airline tickets. Most charge a yearly membership fee of about $40 which allows you to book flights with them, but the fares can be extremely cheap. Ask about cancelation fares and advance purchase requirements and, in general, be wary. The details of flight delays and cancelations are beyond the control of these companies, so the traveler is at the mercy of the particular carrier. Some ticket consolidators are Air Hitch (tel. (212) 864-2000), Last Minute Travel Club (tel. (800) 527-8646), and Discount Travel International (tel. (800) 824-4000).

Courier travel is another option. Now Voyager (tel. (212) 431-1616) matches companies that need free-lance couriers to fly to different countries with eager trav-

elers. To book a ticket with Now Voyager, you must visit their New York office in person. All flights originate in New York, and prices vary. Couriers are usually limited to carry-on luggage only. For the names of specific courier companies, check your local yellow pages under "Air Courier Service."

El Al (tel. (800) 223-6700), the national airline of Israel, and **EgyptAir** (tel. (800) 334-6787, and always busy), the airline of Egypt, offer a variety of flights to their respective countries. El Al's peak season (June 24-Aug. 10) APEX fare from New York to Tel Aviv in 1988 was $1099 round-trip, for a 6-day minimum, 2-month maximum, and 14-day advance purchase. In the "shoulder season" (July 11-August 21), the fare was reduced to $999 and the off-season fare to $799. El Al flies to Cairo from Tel Aviv for $124 one way, and if you fly from New York to Tel Aviv with them, you can purchase the "Cairo Extension" fare: round-trip at $130. EgyptAir's APEX round-trip from New York to Cairo during peak season (May 15-Sept. 15) was $1012; the fare drops to $942 for shoulder season (April 1-May 14, Sept. 16-Oct. 31) and to $814 for off-season. EgyptAir originates from most major ports in Europe, Asia, and Africa as well. EgyptAir sometimes offers a $330 fare that can only be reserved 72 hours before the flight. **Alia** (tel. (800) 223-0470), the Jordanian national airline, flies from New York to Amman for $941 peak season (July 1-July 31), $821 off-season. El Al, EgyptAir, and Alia all offer youth and student discounts—ask your travel agent for specifics. Other airlines may be cheaper; you might want to look into Yugoslav Air to Cairo or Amman.

By Land

Trains from many points in Northern Europe can bring you south toward Israel and Egypt—though not all the way. Those under 26 can use **BIJ** (formerly **BIGE**) **tickets** for discounts of up to 50% on regular second-class rail fares on international runs; however, users are restricted to certain trains and hours of travel. BIJ tickets are sold by **Transalpino** and **Eurotrain** at about equal prices. Contact Transalpino Ltd., 71-75 Buckingham Place Rd., London SW1W 0QL (tel. (01) 834 96 56 or 834 62 83). In the US, write to Campus Holidays, 242 Bellevue Ave., Upper Montclair, NJ 07043 (tel. (201) 744-8724). Eurotrain is represented in the U.S. by CIEE Council Travel Offices. CIEE can give you information on routes and sell vouchers for BIJ tickets to and from Britain. For tickets from points elsewhere on the Continent, you must purchase the tickets at Eurotrain offices abroad. When buying a BIJ ticket, you specify both your destination and route, and may take stopovers for up to two months.

Bus travel is another inexpensive overland possibility. **Magic Bus** has cheap, direct service between major cities in Europe—offices are located at 67-68 New Bond Street in London, Rokin 38 in Amsterdam, and Filellinon 20 in Athens. Information on Magic Bus is available from cooperating offices in many other cities as well. **Miracle Bus**, at 408 the Strand, London WC2 (tel. (01) 379 60 55), and **Magic Tours' Budget Bus** are other reasonable coach services running between major cities. Though these bus lines do not travel all the way to Israel, Egypt or Jordan, they can get you to an advantageous point of departure cheaply.

By Sea

Several **ferry lines** sail from Europe to Israel. Fares vary considerably, depending mainly on your discomfort tolerance. Outdoor deck seats may cost as little as $50-60 for a three-day trip, but beware that the last time the public bathrooms were cleaned may have coincided with the building of the pyramids. More comfortable are the three- or four-berth inside cabins that many companies offer at reduced student and youth fares. The following companies service Europe to Haifa:

Afroessa Lines: Israel, c/o Mano Passenger Lines Ltd., 39-41 HaMeginim Ave., Tel Aviv (tel. 53 16 31). **Greece,** 1 Charilaou Tricoupi Street, Piraeus (tel. 418 37 77). Sails the *Paloma*

between Piraeus and Haifa weekly from April 10 through January 6. Leaves Piraeus on Thursday and Haifa on Sunday. The fare for deck seats during high season (June 25-Sept. 16) is $76, and $65 during low. A double berth with a bathroom and shower costs $177 high season, $156 low.

Sol Lines: Israel, 60 Ben Yehuda St., Tel Aviv (tel. 28 21 21). **Greece,** Filellinon 4, Athens (tel. 323 31 76); 11 Amerikis St., Rhodes (tel. 224 60); 140B Franklin Roosevelt St., P.O. Box 1682, Limassol (tel. 69 00 00). The *Sol Phryne* has fares and schedules similar to the *Vergina,* and stops in Rhodes and Limassol on the way to Haifa. The *Sol Olympia* makes the expensive and agonizingly slow voyage from Venice to Haifa every 10 days.

Stability Line: Israel, ℅ Capsi Ltd., 76 Haatzmauth Rd., P.O. Box 27, Haifa (tel. 67 44 44). **Greece,** 11 Sachtouri St., Piraeus (tel. 413 23 92). Operates the *Vergina* between Piraeus and Haifa once per week April 2-October 30. Deck seats one-way during high season (June 25-Sept. 16) $75, and in low season $65.

Ferries also shuttle from **Egypt to Europe.** Note that it may be cheaper to board the ferry from Piraeus to Haifa, and then take a bus to Cairo from Tel Aviv.

Adriatic Line: Egypt, ℅ Menatours, Sa'ad Zaghloul Sq., Alexandria (tel. 80 69 09); also, 14 Talaat Harb St., P.O. Box 1108, Cairo (tel. 74 09 55). **Italy,** ℅ Adriatica di Navigazione, Zattere 1412, P.O. Box 705, 30123 Venezia, Venice (tel. (041) 78 18 66); **Greece,** ℅ Gilnavi Agencies, 97 Akti Miaouli and Favierou, Piraeus (tel. (01) 418 19 01); also ℅ Creta Travel Bureau, 20-22 Epimenidou St., Iraklion (tel. 22 70 02); The *Espresso Egitto* connects Venice, Piraeus, Iraklion, and Alexandria in weekly cruises. Three-berth "youth" cabins from Venice to Alexandria cost $300 during high season, $272 low; from Piraeus to Alexandria the fare is $170 high season, $155 low. Eurailpass holders get a 30% discount. Discounts are also given to seniors and families of four and over. Fares are generally $20-30 more without student or youth cards.

Black Sea Shipping Company: Greece, ℅ CTC Lines, 25 Akti Miaouli St., P.O. Box 80516, Piraeus (tel. 411 87 05); **Egypt,** ℅ Amon Shipping, 71 Nasser Ave., Alexandria (tel. 491 88 72) near the American Consulate; Cyprus, ℅ Francoudi and Stephanou, New Port Rd., P.O. Box 1490, Limassol; **U.S.,** ℅ International Cruise Center, 185 Willis Ave., Mineola, NY 11501; **U.K.,** ℅ CTC Lines, 1-3 Lower Regent St., London, SW14. The uninspiring Russian ships *Adjaria* and *Bashkiria* trace a slow route from Odessa to Istanbul, Piraeus, Larnaca

(Cyprus), Latakia (Syria), and on to Alexandria. Prices are in rubles (about $120 for one bed in a six-bed cabin).

When departing Alexandria, be sure to obtain adequate information on customs regulations from your shipping line. You will almost certainly have to exchange the price of your ticket on the spot and present a receipt to the ticket agent. You may also have to show up 48 hours before departure time at the Maritime Station to deal with the bureaucracy.

Border Crossings

Border crossing policies in the Middle East may change in response to political currents, so be sure to check with travel agents, tourist offices, and the your nation's government for the most up-to-date information. Currently, Arab nations including Jordan, Syria, and the Sudan *refuse* to admit travelers with evidence of a visit to Israel in their passports. If you plan to visit Israel first, and then want to travel to an Arab country, tell the Israeli passport officials when you enter. They are usually understanding and will put your visa stamp on a removable slip of paper, rather than directly in your passport (see Visas).

Since the Camp David Accords in 1977, foreigners have been allowed to travel freely between Israel and Egypt. But if you intend to travel to another Arab country, you should obtain an Egyptian visa outside Israel. Note also that an Egyptian entry or exit stamp from the Israeli border at Taba or Fafiah is a clear indication that you've been in Israel, and thus precludes you from entering other Arab nations.

Between Israel and Egypt

Tour buses are the budget option for travel between Israel and Egypt. Several companies operate out of Tel Aviv, Jerusalem, and Cairo, offering bus transport, three days in a shared room at a tourist-class hotel in Cairo, and an open-ended return ticket. **Mazada Tours,** at 141 Ibn Gvirol St., Tel Aviv (tel. (03) 45 71 84 or 46 30 75) and 20 Shlomzion HaMalka St., Jerusalem (tel. (02) 24 58 97 or 23 37 77) runs round-trip from Tel Aviv or Jerusalem to Cairo for $30 (one way $22); in Egypt, contact Embassy Tours, 8 Boustan St., Cairo (tel. 74 98 06). Mazada offers a 10% youth and student discount. **Neot Hakikar,** at 36 Keren HaYessod St., Jerusalem (tel. (02) 69 93 85), 252 HaYarkon St., Tel Aviv (tel. (03) 46 31 11), is also much cheaper than its well-established rivals, **Galilee Tours** and **Egged Tours.** Neot Hakikar has departures Sunday, Tuesday, and Thursday at 7am ($47); in Egypt, contact Isis Travel, 48 Giza St., Orman Tower Blvd., Cairo (tel. 348 48 21). **United Tours,** at 113 HaYarkon St., Tel Aviv (tel. (03) 29 81 87) and at the King David Hotel, Jerusalem (tel. (02) 22 21 87), offers normal coach transportation between Tel Aviv's Central Station and Cairo's Abbassiya Station (one way $18; round-trip $32). Departure either way 7:30am Sunday, Monday, Wednesday, Thursday; in Egypt, contact East Delta Bus Co., Abbassiya Station, Cairo.

Local buses also travel to the border, and from there another relatively inexpensive bus or taxi will take you across (for example, via bus #15 from Eilat to Taba, or from Gaza to Rafiah via a local bus from the UN Club, seaward from Palestine Sq.).

Flights between Israel and Egypt are offered by Israel's El Al and Egypt's Air Sinai (one way $122). Air Sinai, a sidekick of EgyptAir, was created especially for service to Israel and the Sinai so that EgyptAir would not be denied access to other Arab countries.

You must pay an exit tax (about $7) each time you leave Israel by bus (when you fly, departure tax is normally included in the price of your ticket). Similarly, when leaving Egypt you must pay a $10 exit fee. If you don't already have an Egyptian visa, you can get one at a diplomatic mission in Tel Aviv for $20; processing takes just a few hours (see Tel Aviv Practical Information). You cannot get anything besides a Sinai-only visa at the border.

Between Israel and Jordan

Travel between Israel and Jordan requires sensitivity to the conflict over national claims. Israel and Jordan have been in a declared state of war since 1967. Since Jordan does not recognize the existence of Israel, your passport must be free of any evidence that you've ever been there.

But travel between the two countries is possible. Here's the trick. As far as the Jordanian authorities are concerned, when you cross the King Hussein/Allenby Bridge from the West Bank, you are coming from occupied Jordan since Israel does not exist and cannot have a border. Therefore, Jordanian authorities will allow you to enter, providing your passport does not have an Israeli stamp. Other incriminating evidence includes a visa issued in Israel (including for Egypt), or an Egyptian entry or exit stamp from either Taba or Rafiah on the Egyptian/Israeli border. Remember, unlike Israel, Egyptian authorities do not offer the convenience of giving you an entry stamp on a separate document.

Crossing from Israel to Jordan, proceed approximately as follows. First, purchase some Jordanian dinars ahead of time, for the border exchange facilities are unreliable. Then travel to Jericho, 11km west of the King Hussein/Allenby Bridge. From Jerusalem, take Arab bus #28 at Damascus Gate (NIS1.70), Egged bus #961 or #963 from the central bus station (NIS2.30), or a shared taxi from the stand near Damascus Gate (NIS3.20). Get off the bus in Jericho when you see the large mosque in the city center. Take a right at the mosque to the square where the service taxis wait. The only taxis licensed to go all the way to the bridge (past the first security checkpoint) are those lined up under the big, blue "Jericho Municipality" sign. Others will drop you off at an earlier checkpoint where you'll have to wait for the rare shared taxi with an empty seat.

The King Hussein/Allenby Bridge is open only in the morning (Sun.-Fri. 8am-noon). Arrive as early as possible to ensure that you get through. The bridge is occasionally closed for political or religious events; consular officers, taxi drivers, and bus drivers all keep abreast of the latest developments. The process of crossing between Jordan and Israel is painful for Palestinians, but easy for foreigners with their papers in order. For most foreigners (with the possible exception of Arabs and Jews from any country), the searches are mild, the officers respectful, and the waiting rooms air-conditioned. At the bridge checkpoint, you must pay the exit tax (NIS26.50) and service fee (NIS2.50). After your luggage has been inspected, you'll have to wait for one of the approved buses (JD1.500). You cannot drive a vehicle across the bridge.

Once on the East Bank, you'll be issued a permit saying (in Arabic) that you came over the bridge and are prohibited from returning to Israel. Though you shouldn't lose the evidence that you entered the country legally, don't keep it in an obvious place either, since it announces that you were on the West Bank. This souvenir could prevent you from being issued a West Bank permit later. Note that the Jordanians do not recognize the bridge as an international border, so of course you will not receive an entry or exit stamp in your passport. If you are merely returning over the bridge after a Jordan-based visit to Israel, only your West Bank permit will be stamped. Once on the Jordanian side, you may catch a shared taxi to Amman (JD1.700).

Crossing from Jordan to Israel is relatively hassle-free if you came into Jordan from Egypt, Syria, or elsewhere, and highly problematic if you entered Jordan from Israel. Regardless, you'll need a West Bank permit issued by the Ministry of Interior in Amman (closed on Fri., see Amman Practical Information for details). The process takes three working days and two 50fils revenue stamps, available at post offices or sometimes from a kiosk near the ministry. Preferred religions on the application are Christianity and Islam, but the most difficult application blank will be "port of entry to Jordan." Applicants listing Queen Alia International Airport, Aqaba, or Ramtha (on the Syrian border) have experienced the least problems.

If you came from Israel and indicate the King Hussein/Allenby Bridge as point of entry, however, you are implying that you consider the West Bank to be Israeli territory and will be summarily denied a permit. Write Jerusalem or try leaving the question blank and explaining that you never entered Jordan since the bridge is not an international border. Those trying an Israel-Jordan-Israel itinerary may be denied a permit solely because of an officer's bad mood; try again if you are denied the first time. Many travelers do successfully cross from Israel to Jordan and back again, but don't be assured that you'll be among the lucky.

With West Bank permit in hand, you're free to proceed back to Israel. To reach the King Hussein/Allenby Bridge from Amman, catch a shared taxi from Abdali Station (JD1.700), or reserve a seat on the daily JETT bus (6:30am, one hour, JD2.500). (See Amman Practical Information for more information on transportation) A JETT bus will take you all the way to the Israeli checkpoint. A taxi will take you only as far as the terminal for foreigners; from there, you'll have to take a shuttle bus to the Israeli side (JD1.500). Israeli officials will occasionally ask young travelers for evidence of financial security, and they will always search your luggage thoroughly.

From the border, shared taxis in Israel run to many destinations (Jerusalem, Bethlehem, or Ramallah NIS10; Jericho NIS1.60). The Shaheen Bus Company provides air-conditioned transport roughly on the hour between 11am and 3 or 4pm (to Jerusalem NIS5; Jericho NIS2.10; Hebron NIS6.60). You may pay for transportation on the West Bank with popular Jordanian dinars. (NIS1 is approximately JD2.)

Between Egypt and Sudan

Up the Nile from Egypt lies the **Sudan,** a country undiscovered by tourists. It might be worth a trip for those adventurous souls who can survive a lack of tourist facilities and a rudimentary modern infrastructure. A journey into this underdeveloped nation requires advance planning—you should expect a three-week wait for a **visa.** Apply at the Sudanese Embassy in Cairo (3 al-Ibrahimi St., Garden City; tel. 354 50 43) or, better yet, by mail before you leave (2210 Massachusetts Ave. NW, Washington DC 20008; tel. (202) 338-8565). The three-month visa costs $10 for U.S. citizens, $25 for others, in cash or money order. Include a passport photo (4 if in Egypt). If your passport has an Israeli stamp or an Egyptian stamp from Taba, your application will be denied. You might want to contact the **Sudan Tourist and Hotel Corporation** (P.O. Box 2424, Khartoum; tel. 819 86).

The cheap and interesting way to reach the Sudan is to take the **ferry** across Lake Nasser to **Wadi Halfa.** The ferry leaves from the landing past the Aswan High Dam on Monday and Thursday afternoons, and lasts at least 24 hours. The ferry connects in Aswan with a train from Cairo, and in Wadi Halfa with an extremely crowded train to Khartoum. Tickets can be purchased at the offices of the **Nile Navigation Company** in Aswan (next to the tourist office; open daily 8am-2pm) or in Cairo (office in Ramses Station). Tickets in first class are LE69, in second class LE42. The other option is to **fly** from Cairo to Khartoum. Daily flights are offered by EgyptAir (economy fare LE438, youth fare LE271) and less reliable Air Sudan (economy fare $200; round-trip substantially discounted). EgyptAir has offices throughout Egypt. Air Sudan has one office in Cairo, at 1 el-Bustan St. (tel. 74 72 51 or 74 72 99), and may be impossible to book overseas.

Arab Countries

Traveling among Egypt, Syria, and Jordan should pose few problems. You can obtain visas in the respective capital cities; Syria and Jordan require a letter of introduction from your embassy or consulate. (See Cairo and Amman Practical Information for embassy listings.) Instead of flying between the three countries (an expensive option), take a ferry from Nuweiba in Egypt's Sinai to Aqaba, Jordan (see Nuweiba and Aqaba sections for details), or a comfortable JETT bus from Amman to Damascus, Syria. (See Amman Practical Information for JETT listings.) You may also try your luck at hitchhiking. Jordanian officials at the chaotic Nuweiba-Aqaba checkpoints have been known to overlook Egyptian Taba/Rafiah stamps.

You're likely to encounter hassles if you enter Jordan from Israel and want to go on to Syria. Syria does not follow Jordan's West Bank policy. If you don't have a Jordanian entry stamp, they correctly assume you've entered via the King Hussein/Allenby Bridge, and that therefore you've been in Israel. The Syrians won't be fooled, either, if you "lose" your passport in Jordan, together with whatever entry stamp it may or may not have had. You can obtain a Jordanian entry stamp by taking the ferry from Aqaba to Nuweiba, Egypt, and back. Please note that the Aqaba-Nuweiba-Aqaba ferry scheme, which shows the Syrians that you entered Jordan from Egypt is not a foolproof way of convincing the Jordanians to let you shuttle back to the West Bank; a grumpy official at the Ministry of Interior may have record of your entry at the King Hussein/Allenby Bridge.

Continuing from Syria and Jordan to other Arab countries can be difficult: **Lebanon** is closed to tourists indefinitely; **Iraq** can be visited with a tour group and possibly in transit, although all types of Iraqi visas are difficult to obtain; **Saudi Arabia** remains closed to everyone except workers, Muslim pilgrims, and those travelers with a North Yemen visa who may be allowed to cross Saudi Arabia to South Yemen with a three-day transit visa. Passage from Syria to **Turkey** or **Sudan**, however, should present few difficulties.

Once There

Accommodations

Hotels

Clean, budget hotel accommodations can be found throughout Israel and Egypt, though they are sparse in Jordan. Budget hotels may not offer private bathrooms and may even charge extra for a hot shower. Some hotel owners are hostile to backpackers, though most will be happy to accommodate you and direct you to nearby points of interest. In some areas unmarried couples may have trouble obtaining a room together. Often the quoted room rate at one and two star budget hotels is negotiable, especially during the off-season.

Hostels

Both Israel and Egypt have hostels affiliated with the International Youth Hostel Federation (IYHF) in all major cities and towns. Hostels are great places to meet travel partners and swap tips with people from all over the world. Hostels often serve the cheapest meals in town. Many even provide kitchen facilities, but you may have to supply your own pans and utensils. Most hostels are open to people of all ages, though the majority of travelers are between 17 and 25.

Hostel quality varies widely. Some hostels are strikingly beautiful; others, however, are located in run-down barracks far from the center of town. Most hostels enforce an early curfew—difficult if you want to party late on Ben Yehudah or Dizengoff. Rooms are segregated by sex, and conditions may be cramped or spartan. Sheet sleeping sacks are required at most hostels. Sleeping bags are often not permitted, but most will provide blankets. Israeli hostels do not require that you have an IYHF card, though they will charge extra if you don't. In Egypt you must have an IYHF card to stay at hostels. In addition to official IYHF hostels (marked "IYHF" in our listings), numerous unofficial hostels offer inexpensive lodgings with no membership requirements.

Camping

Israel, Egypt, and Jordan offer an enormous variety of campground settings—from the shores of the Sea of Galilee to the Negev Desert to the beaches of the Mediterranean. The weather is normally warm and dry, and the cost—well, it's the cheapest way to spend a night, besides the old park bench.

Facilities at campsites vary. Some offer electricity, showers, first aid stations, and even a small store. Others will provide nothing more than turf. As a general rule, the more civilized the campground, the more numerous the tourists. Crowds should be expected in the peak seasons. Crowded parks sometimes require advance reservations, so if you don't have one try to arrive early. Many parks shut down entirely in the off-season, or provide only limited services. Some parks limit the number of days that you may stay. Reservation fees depend on the campsite, as do entry fees for vehicles and pedestrians. Wherever possible, *Let's Go* lists available campsites and fees of particular locations.

Avoid the temptation to pitch your tent in an area not designated for camping. First, theft is rife, and police are normally unsympathetic to foreigners on illegal sites. Second, it's always upsetting to drive a stake into a live land mine left from wars past. Acres in the Middle East are roped off because of land mines—don't be tempted by the beauty of the countryside. Lastly, beaches are often closed to camping for security purposes, and the army may swoop down on you and disturb your beauty sleep.

Prepare ahead of time if you intend to camp. It's better to spend the money on good-quality camping gear than hassle with broken equipment in the field. The basic camping ingredients are a sleeping bag, foam pad, and tent (often just a sleeping bag will do). Synthetic-filled sleeping bags are adequate for the mild Middle East, and they're cheaper and more durable than down. Mummy bags (especially appropriate for Egypt) are lighter and more compact than regular bags. Buy your sleeping bag with the worst imaginable weather in mind (see Climate). Synthetic bags usually cost $20-50, while down bags for below-freezing temperatures begin at about $70. Simple Ensolite sleeping pads cost about $6-10; the best air mattress or a sophisticated hybrid such as the Thermarest costs more than $50.

Modern tents are remarkably clever and utterly unlike those canvas contraptions scouts seem to prefer. The best tents are easy to set up, self-supporting (with their own frame and suspension systems), and often don't require staking. When purchasing a tent, make certain it has a rain fly, bug netting, and weighs no more than 3½ kg. Pay attention to the material as well: Synthetic canvas is less expensive, lighter, and more water resistant than cotton canvas, but also is less "breathable." Backpackers and cyclists may wish to pay a bit more for a sophisticated, lightweight tent; some two-person tents weigh only 1kg. Expect to pay at least $70 for a simple two-person tent and over $100 for a serviceable four-person. Sometimes a decent tent can be found for as little as $40, but check it out carefully and be sure you can return it in case of problems.

Other camping basics include a battery-operated lantern (never gas) and a simple plastic groundcloth to protect the tent floor. If you plan on roughing it in extremely primitive areas, water sacks and a solar shower can be very helpful amenities. A small campstove ($20-80), run on butane or white gas, is also very useful, as the Middle East is not filled with firewood. Always bring waterproof matches.

Below are some reputable camping stores in the U.S. All will mail orders overseas.

Campmor: tel. (800) 526-4784.

Eddie Bauer: tel. (800) 426-6253.

L.L. Bean: tel. (800) 341-4341.

Mountain Equipment, Inc. (MEI): tel. (209) 486-8211.

Life in the Middle East

History

Ancient History

The land now occupied by Israel, Egypt, and Jordan was one of the birthplaces of civilization. Our knowledge of this ancient region is derived from a combination of archeological findings, religious materials, and other miscellaneous sources. Artifacts from the **Paleolithic Age** (1 million-70,000 B.C.E.) suggest that a primitive culture of hunters and gatherers may have existed on the banks of the Sea of Galilee during this time. Flint sickles from the **Mesolithic Age** (14,000-7500 B.C.E.), which have been found in present-day Israel provide information about the development of planned cultivation and agriculture there. Remains of the first true cities, built about 5000 years ago, have been located in Jordan. These walled settlements sprung up in the Jordan River Valley and along the Mediterranean Coast, until eventually the larger and more powerful ones grew into city-states and small kingdoms.

Ancient Egypt was one of the first civilizations in the world, and a major power. In the third millennium B.C.E., **Menes,** the semi-mythical first pharoah, united Upper and Lower Egypt to form the **Old Kingdom** (2686-2181 B.C.E.). This was the beginning of the Dynastic Period in Egypt, an era which was to last for thousands of years. During this time, great advances were made in architecture, crafts, and engineering. Writing and papyrus were invented, and a high level of skill was achieved in metal and ivory works. The god-kings were organizing master craftsmen and thousands of laborers to build eternal monuments at a time when even China was just emerging from the Stone Age. It was during this period that the pyramids were built.

During the time of the **Middle Kingdom** (2055-1786 B.C.E.), Egypt's culture flourished and spread. Contact with the southern kingdoms of Nubia and Kush spawned pharaonic cultures there. The Theban god Amon came to be worshiped nationally and religious practices changed so that the afterlife was believed to be open to all, not just kings. By the time the vigorous Eighteenth Dynasty, which included Ramses, brought about the **New Kingdom,** (1587-1085 B.C.E.), pharaonic rule seemed eternal. This was a period of territorial expansion for Egypt, during which spectacular advances were made in mathematics, medicine, astronomy, architecture, and civil government. Great building projects were completed as the wealthy and the powerful strove to ensure their safe passage to the next world.

Near the end of the Middle Kingdom, in the eighteenth century B.C.E., **Abraham,** the first of the Old Testament patriarchs, answered God's call and migrated from Mesopotamia to Canaan, which occupied the Mediterranian coastal plain, part of modern-day Israel. According to the book of Genesis, his descendants, the Hebrews lived a semi-nomadic life, sharing and fighting over the land with neighboring tribes. In the thirteenth or fourteenth century B.C.E., a famine forced them to migrate to Egypt. The Bible tells that pharaoh feared the Hebrews' potential power in numbers, and had them enslaved. In events described in the Hebrew Bible, **Moses** convinced the pharoah (possibly **Ramses II**) to allow the Hebrews to leave Egypt. Under Moses' leadership, the Hebrews crossed the Sinai Peninsula and returned to Canaan, much of which was controlled by the Philistines. Along the way, Moses gave the Israelites the **Torah** (Jewish law), which he received from God on Mt. Sinai. Modern scholars and unbelievers have challenged this account, speculating that only part, or perhaps none, of the Israelite tribes made the exodus.

After Moses' death, **Joshua** led the 12 tribes of Israel across the Jordan and conquered Jericho, on the West Bank. The land they gained was divided among the tribes. Following Joshua's death, the Israelites battled the Philistines for two centuries, finally triumphing under the leadership of **David.** The kingdom reached its height of power under the reigns of David and his son **Solomon.** David conquered Jerusalem, but his son Solomon ordered the building of the Temple, the House of God, in Jerusalem, making it the center for sacrifices to God. Much of the Hebrew Bible is said by scholars to have been written and compiled during the centuries following the construction of the Temple.

After Solomon's death in 922 B.C.E., civil strife arose and the empire was divided into a Northern Kingdom of Israel and a southern kingdom of Judah. In Egypt about the same time, the reign of the boy king **Tut-ankh-amon** marked the beginning of the end. The once vigorous Egyptian society had become corrupt and lethargic. Both countries were weakened and open to invasion.

The Rule of Foriegn Invaders

In the eighth century B.C.E., the **Assyrians** conquered the region, marking the beginning of foreign control. In Israel and Jordan, the **Babylonians** followed close on the heels of the Assyrians in the sixth century. This marked the start of the **Babylonian Exile** for the Jews. When the **Persians** defeated the Babylonians 50 years later and conquered much of the Middle East, the Jews were allowed to return to Jerusalem and build a Second Temple. In Egypt, the Persians established the **27th Dynasty,** the first truly foreign dynasty in Egypt.

Alexander the Great's Greek armies were the next to rule the Middle East, starting in the fourth century B.C.E. Alexander was received as a liberator in Egypt. The oracle of Amon in the Siwa Oasis declared that Alexander was the son of Amon and truly the pharoah. Alexandria was founded and soon became the center of Hellenistic culture in the region.

After Alexander's death in 323 B.C.E., his empire was divided into three parts and **Ptolemy I** assumed control in Egypt. In Judea, the Seleucid Greeks (the Syrian branch) insisted that the Jews worship Greek gods, sowing conflict between themselves and those who supported Hellenization and those who clung to religious law. The Ptolemies controled the region for over 200 years, ruling from Egypt as pharaohs. Their rule continued until they and all the kingdoms of the Mediterranean world fell before the **Roman Empire** just before the start of the Common Era. During the Roman period, ten cities on the East Bank banded together into the Decapolis, while the Nabateans were slowly incorporated into the Empire.

Rise of Christianity and Islam

Around 6 B.C.E., **Jesus Christ** was born in Bethlehem. Jesus claimed he would be the deliverer of the Jews, which the Roman government thought was tantamount to treason. After his crufixion in Jerusalem, his followers were persecuted.

Meanwhile, the Romans continued to try to forcibly assimilate the Jews. The Jews revolted in 66 C.E., but the result was disastrous—in 70 C.E., the Roman general Titus conquered Jerusalem and destroyed the Second Temple. Three years later, the last Jewish holdout in Masada was captured by the Romans, who found that all the defenders had taken their own lives. The Romans exiled most of the Jewish survivors. Judaism was forced into radical changes that laid the groundwork for Judaism as it is known today, as it adapted to life without sacrifice, state, and a focused population.

The **Byzantine** heirs of the Roman Empire adopted and promoted Christianity, making Palestine the holy outpost of the religion. **Coptic Christianity** took root in Egypt and gave rise to a tradition of monasticism, which powerfully influenced subsequent developments in European Christianity deemed heretical by the Roman and Byzantine orthodoxy.

In the seventh century C.E., **Arab** armies intent on spreading Islam, the new religion of **Muhammad,** swept through the region. A few years after the death of Muhammad, the entire Middle East was in Muslim hands; by the next century, Islam pervaded an area greater than that of the Roman Empire at its height. By the end of the **Umayyad Caliphate** (661-750 C.E.), Islam had become established as the primary religion and Arabic as the primary language of the region. The Umayyads were succeeded by the **Abbasid** Dynasty, which ruled until the Mongols conquered most of the Islamic lands in 1252.

The Crusades

In the eleventh century, another of these regional dynasties, the **Seljuks** of Turkey, invaded Palestine. Their rumored brutality toward Christian pilgrims sparked the **Crusades** during which European Christians sought to "liberate" the Holy Land. Acre (Akko) became the Crusaders' capitol as Christians fought Muslims and slaughtered Jews. During the twelfth and thirteenth centuries, the Crusaders continually dominated the Holy Land, leaving behind castles such as Montfort in the Galilee and Shobak in Jordan, subterranean passages in Akko, and churches throughout the land.

The last three centuries of Abbasid rule were marked by the decline of central power. Regional governors established their own autonomous dynasties. One of the most important was the **Fatimid** Dynasty (909-1171), under which Cairo was founded and flourished as a cultural center.

Salah al-Din (known to many as Saladin) expelled the crusaders from Jerusalem and most of Palestine by 1192. The **Ayyubid Dynasty** of his descendants (1171-1250) was followed by the regime of the **Mamluks,** (1250-1516) originally their soldier-slaves. The Mamluks, after their centuries were up, were conquered by the **Ottoman Empire** in the sixteenth century. The sprawling empire was a world pwoer, conquering the remains of the Byzantine Empire in 1453 and almost sweeping into Europe in 1660. Their defeat then at Vienna sparked a long, slow decline before the growing power of the West.

Modern History

European Interests, Zionism, and Arab Nationalism

Egypt's modern history began with the conquest by **Napoleon** in 1798, who tried but failed to conquer Palestine. In 1805, four years after the French occupation ended, a Circassian slave named **Muhammad Ali** became the official ruler of Egypt in the name of the Ottoman Sultan. Although the country was nominally ruled by Muslims, Egypt really belonged to French and later British colonial interests. The construction of the **Suez Canal** in 1869 opened Asia to European domination.

By the end of the nineteenth century, the British were firmly entrenched in Egypt, but there were undercurrents of nationalist sentiment. To perpetuate the guise of democratic self-rule, the British allowed the formation of a nationalist political party called the **Wafd,** but they soon discovered that this party could not be contained effectively. Unable to control the popular unrest, the British granted Egypt political independence and installed **King Fuad** as a constitutional monarch in 1922. However, Britain retained most of its colonial and economic interests in the country, including control over the Canal, which was vital to its empire in India.

Meanwhile, Europeans had also become interested in Palestine. In the late nineteenth century, **Zionism** arose. This idea, first formulated as a modern ideology in *The Jewish State,* a pamphlet written by **Theodore Herzl** in 1896, held that the Jewish people could only be safe from persecution in their homeland. Jews agreed that this should be in the biblical land of Israel. Spurred by late nineteenth century nationalist and socialist ideals, the early Zionist pioneers settled in Palestine and established cooperative agricultural settlements (*kibbutzim*) that later bred reliant leaders. Zionist ideology, along with persecution experienced in Europe, caused increasing numbers of Jews to abandon their countries for Israel. The first and second **Aliyahs,** or waves of Jewish immigration, occurred in 1882 and 1904-14, respectively. By 1914 there were 600,000 Arabs and 100,000 Jews in Palestine.

In order to solicit help to defeat the Ottoman Empire, which was allied with Germany during World War I, the British made promises to both Zionist and Arab nationalist leaders in Palestine. The 1915 **McMahon Letter** promised Hussein ibn

Ali, Sherif of Mecca and later the leader of Jordan, that the British would establish an independent Arab state should the Turks be defeated. Though the Churchill White Paper of 1922 denied that this state was to include Palestine west of the Jordan River, the Arabs insisted that this was the letter's intent. The 1917 **Balfour Declaration** promised that the British would support the establishment of a "national home for the Jewish people," provided that this did not detract from the rights of the non-Jewish communities. Though the **Passfield White Paper of 1930** distinguished between a national home and a sovereign state, the Zionists insisted that the meaning of the document had been to establish the latter.

Arab nationalism also surfaced in Jordan. In 1916, Sherif Hussein led the **Arab Revolt** with the help of British colonel T.E. Lawrence ("Lawrence of Arabia"). In 1917 the Arab and British armies took Jerusalem from the Turks, but British promises of Arab independence turned to compromises, as Palestine and Jordan became subject to British mandate in 1918.

Conflicts were also widespread between Palestinian Arabs and Jewish immigrants. These Arabs, having been subjected to three centuries of debilitating Turkish rule, also hoped for national independence and renaissance in the region. While Transjordan was granted partial independence by Britain in 1923, the British still held the reins. As the twenties, thirties, and forties passed, these conflicting dreams clashed with increasing force. In 1929 and 1936, Arabs rioted against the Jewish population. The rise of **Nazism** in Europe during the thirties brought more Jewish immigrants to Palestine until the **White Paper of 1939** seriously restricted Jewish immigration and land purchases and effectively closed Palestine to refugees from the **Holocaust.** When the Second World War had ended and European Jewry had been shattered, the Zionists were determined to establish a sovereign Jewish State regardless of British intent. The Arabs were equally resolved to prevent its formation.

The War of 1948

In 1946, Britain ended its Mandate over Jordan, and Transjordan was granted full independence under King Abdullah. On November 29, 1947, the United Nations voted to partition Palestine west of the Jordan River into an Arab State and a Jewish State to be economically linked, and to set aside Jerusalem as an international city. While the Jews accepted the partition plan, the Arabs rejected it. Civil war broke out, and Palestinian Arabs and Jews fought throughout the country.

On May 14, 1948, the British Mandate over Palestine ended. Immediately after the Jewish Agency declared the **independence** of the State of Israel, the War of Independence broke out. In the spring of 1949, armistices were signed confirming the results of the fighting—Jordan had taken the West Bank and half of Jerusalem. Israel took the other half and the rest of the area of the Mandate except for the Gaza Strip, which had been captured by Egypt.

Jordan and the West Bank

In 1950, Transjordan joined the West Bank to form the current **Hashemite Kingdom of Jordan.** Although no other Arab country was willing to assume the financial and political burden of assimilating the **Palestinians,** the Jordanians expected to benefit from the political prestige naturally accruing to the state that espoused the Palestinian cause—still inextricably linked to the cause of Arab nationalism. Realizing that peace offered the best hope for Jordan, King Abdullah participated in secret talks with Moshe Dayan, emissary for Israeli Prime Minister David Ben-Gurion. Other Arab governments, threatened by the overtures, let their displeasure be known. In 1951, a Palestinian youth assassinated King Abdullah in Jerusalem. The crown passed to Abdullah's oldest son Talal, who resigned six months later due to health problems. In smooth succsession **King Hussein** assumed control after a one-year regency. Only 18, Hussein embarked on a bold set of programs aimed to raise Jordan's status in the Arab world. He remains one of the Middle East's key players.

The Sinai Campaign/Suez Crisis

Egypt had been left in disarray by the continual struggle between the nationalist and the monarchist factions and by its defeat by Israel in 1948. Into the vacuum stepped a group of young officers led by **Colonel Gamal Abdel Nasser,** who overthrew Fuad's corrupt son King Farouk in a bloodless coup known as the **Revolution of 1952.** After a series of power struggles with his cabinet, Nasser began to pursue an aggressive foriegn policy, aiming to become the leader of the Arab world. When the U.S. withdrew its offer of financing the Aswan Dam, Egypt retaliated by nationalizing the Suez Canal and stating that it would use the revenues to pay for the dam.

Tensions mounted. Nasser signed an arms deal with Russia and blockaded Eilat with Jordanian and Syrian help in 1956. Britain and France worked out a secret plan with Israel to recover control of the Canal. The plan worked at first: Israel invaded the Sinai as a retaliation for the blockade of Eilat. The Anglo-French entered Egypt and began to take the canal, under the pretense of keeping the peace. Israel was accused of collusion with France and Britain by the U.S. and the Soviet Union, who both applied heavy diplomatic pressure and forced Israel, Britain, and France to withdraw their troops.

In 1958, Egypt and Syria formed the United Arab Republic (UAR). The UAR held an anti-West, pro-Communist stance and received Russian support. Although other Arab nations were asked to join, the union gradually fell apart over nationalist disputes. Nevertheless, Nasser continued to direct the course of Arab policy. Nasser hosted two Arab summits in 1964, which inaugurated the **Palestine Liberation Organization (PLO),** an organization that was intended to be the voice of the Palestinian people.

But the addition of a new voice to the chorus did not provide the key to Arab harmony. Egypt and Syria, the PLO's most forceful supporters, pitted themselves against the moderates of Iran and Saudi Arabia. Jordan was caught in the middle. In 1966, it renounced the PLO, and shortly thereafter the PLO and Syria tried to stir up an internal revolt against the Hussein government. The PLO and Israel began a routine of raids and retaliatory raids, increasing tensions and killing civilians.

The 1967 Six Day War

The **Six Day War** was instigated partly by a Soviet claim to Nasser that Israel had activated 11 brigades on the Syrian border. Unknown to Nasser, the allegation was untrue, but he requested that that the U.N. withdraw its buffer-zone troops so as not to lose face. On June 5, Israeli forces launched a preemptive attack against the united threat of some 250,000 Syrian, Jordanian, and Egyptian troops poised at the border. Six days later, a ceasefire was accepted. Israel had retaken the Sinai from Egypt and captured the Golan Heights from Syria, as well as the West Bank from Jordan.

Soon after the ceasefire, Israel began to annex newly-captured East Jerusalem, an effort which was condemned by the UN General Assembly. Roughly 380,000 Palestinian Arabs left their West Bank homes, creating an enormous socioeconomic absorption problem in Jordan. In the years that followed, the U.S. began to supply Israel with arms while the Soviet Union did the same for Egypt.

In Jordan, an internal battle began when King Hussein's government tried to expel the PLO. Coup attemps culminated in the **Civil War of September 1970,** also known as Black September. As injuries and deaths rose into the thousands, Arab leaders pressured Hussein and **Yasir Arafat,** leader of the large al-Fatah faction of the PLO, to come to an agreement. On September 27, a pact was signed to end the Civil War, but the fighting continued sporadically.

The Yom Kippur/October War

Egyptian President Nasser died in September of 1970, and Vice-President **Anwar Sadat** assumed control. In 1971 Sadat openly began preparations to attack Israel. The Soviet Union provided the arms, Saudi Arabia gave the money, and Syria and

Jordan agreed to lend military support. On October 6, 1973, a day when most Israelis were in synagogues observing Yom Kippur, Egypt began its assault. In the war's first three days, Egypt overwhelmed Israel's defenses in the Sinai, and Syrian forces had thrust deep into the Golan and were threatening to break into the Galilee. Israeli reserves were activated, and following weeks of fierce fighting the Israelis managed to push the Egyptians and Syrians back, actually gaining territory. All parties agreed to disengage their forces on January 18 in an agreement negotiated by U.S. Secretary of State Henry Kissinger. Both sides had suffered tremendous losses, and in Israel great public uproar arose against the government's apparent unpreparedness leading to Prime Minister Golda Meir's resignation in April.

King Hussein stayed out of the fray, merely sending an armored brigade to aid the Syrians in the Golan Heights. Jordan refused to consent in September 1974 to Egypt and Syria's declaration that the PLO was the "only legitimate representative of the Palestinian people." However, after 20 Arab states assented to PLO representation at the Arab Summit Conference, Jordan had no other choice but to agree to the plan as well. In November of 1974, the United Nations recognized the PLO as the only genuine Palestinian representative.

Throughout the '70s, more Israelis began to settle on the West Bank. The UN Security Council on November 11, 1976, "strongly deplored" Israel's West Bank operations and demanded Israel follow the rules of the Geneva Convention on the Protection of Civilians in Wartime. Although Prime Minister Yitzhak Rabin (of the leftist Labor party) discouraged moves to make West Bank settlement permanent, the next Israeli government, under Prime Minister Menahem Begin (of the right-wing Likud bloc) pushed vigorously for West Bank settlement.

The Camp David Accords and Sadat's Assassination

In November of 1977, Egypt's President Sadat made a historic visit to Jerusalem, cuasing the other Arab nations to break ties with Egypt. By September of 1978, Prime Minister Begin and President Sadat had forged a two-part agreement with the help of U.S. President Jimmy Carter at Camp David (called, not surprisingly, the **Camp David Accords**). The first part of the treaty stipulated that Arabs living in the West Bank and Gaza would receive autonomy. Under the second part, Israel agreed to relinquish the Sinai in exchange for peace with Egypt. The treaty's second provision has held tenuously; however the guarantee for autonomy in the first part has been a source of continuing controversy. The relationship between Egypt and Israel has been called a "cold peace," which most people agree is better than a cold or hot war.

On July 29, 1980, the UN General Assembly overwhelmingly passed a resolution demanding that Israel immediately withdraw from the territories captured in the Six Day War, including Jerusalem. The next day Israel declared Jerusalem as its "eternal capital," never to be divided again. One week later, Saudi Arabia and Iraq said they would sever all relations with any nation that accepted Jerusalem as Israel's capital. The UN Security Council voted just two weeks later, with the U.S. abstaining, that nations with diplomatic missions in Jerusalem should move them elsewhere in the country.

After the Camp David Accords, Egypt was left isolated in the Arab world and forced to turn to the U.S. for financial support. This displeased Islamic fundamentalists, who expressed their displeasure by assassinating Sadat in October 1981. The Egyptian government acted quickly to regain control, stifling an Islamic riot in Assyut and installing **Hosni Mubarak** as President one week later. Mubarak has worked to reestablish Egypt's status in the Arab world, although his support of various western proposals has upset many Arab states.

The Israeli Invasion of Lebanon and Peace Proposals

On June 6, 1982, Israel invaded Lebanon in an effort to wipe out PLO forces, based in Palestinian refugee camps who had attacked northern Israel. The **Lebanon War** was the first instance of Israel clearly taking the role of the aggressor rather than acting from a defensive position. Although some 6000 PLO members were captured in West Beirut, Israel came under fire from both its own citizens and the world community as the planned invasion extended past the established two-month limit and grew costlier. Condemnation soared when it was revealed that the Israelis were indirectly responsible for a massacre at Sabra and Chatila camps because they had disregarded the Lebanese Christian Phalangists who actually carried out the massacre. The fighting ended in May, 1983, under an agreement negotiated by the U.S. However, Syria refused to leave, so Israel remained as well. The Israelis finally pulled out of Lebanon under the leadership of Prime Minister Shimon Peres in 1985.

Since 1985, King Hussein has attempted to engineer several peace proposals for the Palestinian-Israeli situation. Unfortunately, hard-liners on both sides have refused to accept the other sides' preconditions. Jordan has repeatedly made peace with the PLO and then backed off, as the country sought support for negotiations. At present, Hussein walks a fine line in his efforts to resolve the Palestinian question—the risk of alienating Israel or the U.S. is great, but the risk of alienating the Arab nations and his own population even greater.

Recent Developments

Renewed terrorist attacks in Israel have further impeded the chance for a negotiated peace. In 1986, three Israelis were killed by the PLO's Force 17 in Cyprus, prompting a retaliatory bombing of the organization's Tunis headquarters. A month later, terrorists from the Palestinian Liberation Front hijacked the *Achille Lauro,* killing a Jewish American and dumping him overboard. And in December, Abu Nidal's terrorists opened fire on passengers in the Rome and Vienna airports. Meanwhile, the past several years have seen a disturbing rise in Israeli civilian and military harassment of Arabs living in the West Bank.

In December of 1987, as a result of mounting frustration with the stalemated political situation and Israel's unwillingness to negotiate for Palestinian autonomy, the Palestinians in Gaza and the West Bank began a series of demonstrations. At first Israeli authorities viewed the **Palestinian uprising** (the *intifadah*) as a spontaneous, short-term affair, but it has proved to be a long, bloody battle between Israeli military forces and Palestinian civilians. In August of 1988 the struggle showed few signs of abatement. Israeli government figures recorded over 250 Palestinians killed, 5,000 stone-throwing incidents, and 780 Molotov Cocktails thrown during the first nine months of unrest.

As criticism mounts in Israel and abroad, the Israeli government might be forced to agree to some form of negotiations with Palestinian representatives. U.S. Secretary of State George Shultz has proposed a plan which would involve an international peace conference attended by the permanent members of the UN Security Council, including the Soviet Union, and the parties in conflict. The Palestinians would be represented not by the PLO, but by a joint Palestinian-Jordanian delegation. At the conference, a three-year timetable for deciding the final status of the West Bank and Gaza would be discussed. All those who attended, however, would have to accept UN Resolutions 242 and 338, which call for recognition of Israel and a return to pre-1967 borders. So far, the PLO has rejected the resolutions because they do not call for a Palestinian state, do not specifically name the PLO as the representative of the Palestinians, and do recognize the State of Israel. The Americans and the Israelis, however, refuse to allow the PLO to attend until it accepts the resolutions, renounces violence, and recognizes Israel's right to exist. In the summer of 1988, Jordan appeared to be dropping its claim to represent the Palestinians of the West Bank, making it more difficult to hold negotiations without the PLO. Despite this apparent stalemate, two Middle Eastern leader—Egyptian President Hosni Mubarak and Israeli Foreign Minister Shimon Peres—have publicly endorsed the Schultz Peace Plan. Although the prospect of Middle Eastern peace seems very, very unlikely, there is always a chance that peace will be achieved.

Religion

Judaism

Israel is the world's first and only Jewish state. Judaism provided the reason for the founding of the state and, despite freedom of religion for minorities, is now essentially the state religion.

There are at least two perspectives on Judaism. The Orthodox believer understands the Bible to call for a specific way of life which has been developed from the text by a series of interpreters. These laws are called **halachah** ("the path"). It is a crucial tenet of traditional Judaism that God is behind all of history, the cause and explanation of events both good and bad. Another perspective, however, holds that the Bible is a document written by humans, that *halachah* is custom, and that biblical history is not objective history.

The Bible and History

Genesis says the world began with Adam and Eve; twenty generations later Judaism begins with a man called Abram. God summoned him to "Go forth from thy house, thy father's house, into the land that I will show you" (Genesis 12:1) and put a mark into his name by dubbing him **Abraham.** According to the Bible, Abraham, his son Isaac, and Isaac's son Jacob, whose name was changed to Israel, are the founders of monotheism and worship of the LORD.

After the descendents of Abraham went to live in Egypt and expanded greatly in number, they became slaves of the pharaohs. God then led them out in Exodus to **Mount Sinai.** Tradition holds that during forty days on the mountain, God dictated the **Torah** to Moses. The Torah, comprised of the first five books of the Bible, is what Orthodox Jews consider to be Divine Law, the last word on all issues. Though believers believe this divine origin, non-believing scholars don't. They say the Torah is a composite record of various traditions and legends compiled during the Israelite kingdom centuries later.

The Development of Judaism

Judaism as it is know today began to develop in the context of a cataclysm: the destruction of the Temple in Jerusalem by the Romans in 70 C.E., and the **Exile.** Since God could no longer be worshiped through sacrifices at what was thought literally to be his house, some new way had to be found if the Judean faith was to continue. Lo and behold, one was found: prayer. Coupled with this was study of the ancestral texts, the Bible. These two, **prayer** and **study**, remain the twin pillars of Judaism.

These two paved the way for the entrance of the major figure of Judaism: the **Rabbi.** He evolved from the sage, who probably developed out of the minor priests who roamed the country praying and teaching. The **Mishnah,** a collection of the recorded legal arguments of the Rabbis, has its earliest sources in the Babylonian exile (mid-sixth century B.C.E.), and was finished in 220 C.E. It became the basis in the next two centuries for the **Talmud,** a voluminous commentary on the Mishnah, which is the heart of *halachah.* There are, however, other sources for *halachah,* including later commentators on the Torah, of whom the most famous is Rashi, and the opinions and practices of later rabbis. Other practices of the Orthodox are not technically laws but customs observed like law; one salient example is the black hats and fur coats of many Ultraorthodox, which were the dress of Polish noblemen in the eighteenth century.

There is no one Judaism today. In the 1700s, Eastern European Jewry was split by a new movement called **Hassidism,** which sought to emphasize piety over law. The Hassidim are divided into many different groups; today it is hard to tell them from the regular Orthodox. Another split occurred in the nineteenth century, when some Jews decided that if they were ever to succeed in the world outside the ghettos, they would have to abandon outdated portions of the *halachah.* For instance, they felt that the prohibition against doing work on *shabbat,* which had been expanded in the *halachah* to include activities such as turning on a light, driving, and ringing a doorbell, did not really contribute to the spirit of *shabbat.* This movement, dedicated to finding a way for individuals to live in the modern world while remaining Jewish, is **Reform Judaism.** Another response is found in **Conservative Judaism,** whose adherents try to achieve the same goal without moving outside the *halachah.*

The Synagogue

The major institution of Judaism seen throughout Israel is the **synagogue** or "temple" (in Hebrew *beit knesset,* in Yiddish *shul*). This is the place of communal prayer, which is traditionally held daily, both mornings and evenings. By *halachah,* public prayer does not require a synagogue, or even a rabbi, to be valid; a group of 10 male Jews who are **Bar Mitzvah** ("sons of the commandments," i.e. legally responsible, at age 13) is sufficient. Regardless, in Israel, a synagogue is a neighborhood institution.

Synagogues can come in any shape, size, and color. Prayer is in the direction of Jerusalem. On the wall nearest Jerusalem is the **ark,** usually covered by an ornate curtain, where the Torah scrolls are kept for reading during services on Mondays, Thursdays, and *shabbat.* Over the ark is the *ner tamid* ("eternal lamp"), symbolizing the covenant of the Torah. In the center is the *bimah* ("lectern"), where the Torah is read and prayers are led. The Orthodox have a balcony or partitioned section for women, who are not legally obliged to pray. In Orthodox synagogues, each person goes through the liturgy at his own rate (this is called *davening* in Yiddish), with the leader supplying the first words of each major section.

The **liturgy** is a constant that reached its final form about a century ago but has had the same general outline for over a millennium. The main themes are thanks to God for all the blessings bestowed, especially the covenant; praise for God's greatness and power; supplication for peace, health, wisdom, etc.; and, among the Orthodox, prayer for the coming of the Messiah and the rebuilding of the Temple in Jerusalem. The most important prayer is the **Shema,** which comes from Deuteronomy 6:4:

> *Shema Yisrael, Adonai Eloheinu, Adonai Eḥad*
> *Hear, O Israel: the LORD is our God, the LORD is one.*

For more information and a historical introduction to Judaism, you might read *The Story of Judaism* by Bernard Bamberger. Another good source is *What is a Jew?* by Maurice Kertzer. *Basic Judaism,* by Milton Steinberg, takes a more theological approach.

Islam

"*Bismillah al-Rahmani al-Rahim. In the Name of God, the merciful and the compassionate.*" With this invocation, a Muslim will begin every undertaking in her life. Although traditionally the recipient of bad press in the West, Islam is *not* the fanatical creed of Iranian terrorists and Arab oil moguls. It is a way of life that attempts to bring humanity into harmony with God. The Arabic word *islam* means in its general sense "the act of submission," and Islam the religion is the faithful submission to God's will.

Islam has its roots in the revelation received by the **Prophet Muhammad,** starting during the month of Ramadan in 610 C.E. The piecemeal revelations that came to the Prophet until his death 22 years later form the core of Islam. Collected, they compose the **Koran.** Muslims believe the Arabic text to be perfect, unchanging, and untranslatable—in fact, it is God expressed in human language.

Muhammad slowly gathered followers to his evolving faith. Opposition to his strict monotheism led to persecution in his native city of Mecca in Arabia. In 622, he fled to a nearby city, which asked him to mediate tribal disputes. This event, the **Hijrah** (emigration) is the start of the Muslim calender. After seven years of conflict, he accepted the surrender of Mecca and became a powerful political leader.

Islam continued to grow after the Prophet's death. He was succeeded by the four "rightly-guided caliphs," the last of whom was **Ali.** Ali, Muhammad's son-in-law, was viewed by a segment of the community as his only legitimate successor. The *Shi'at Ali* (Partisans of Ali), known in English as **Shi'ites,** predominate in Iran. Shi'ism is not a creed of fanaticism or fundamentalism, but is rather Islam with a more hierarchical focus.

Pillars of Islam

> *Allahu akhbar. La ilaha il'Allah Muhammadun rasul Allah.*
> *Allah is great. There is no God but God. And Muhammad is*
> *his prophet.*

This call to worship (the *adhan*) sets a rhythm to life in Muslim areas, sounding five times each day from the mosques. It expresses some of Islam's most important beliefs. The first line glorifies God, using the word for God in Arabic, *Allah.* Praise of God and the Prophet is a pious and meritorious action. This phrase is whispered into the ear of newborn babies, and is the last words uttered by dying Muslims. The next lines of the call form the *shahadah,* the declaration of faith. The *shahadah* is the first of the five pillars of Islam. It reflects the **unity of God,** which is Islam's strongest belief, and the special place of Muhammad as God's Messenger.

Testifying to God's unity through the *shahadah* is the only of the **five pillars** of Islam to be an article of belief. Islam is a religion which stresses not faith itself, but correct action as the sign of belief. The second pillar is prayer (*salat*), done five times per day in imitation of the practice of Muhammad. Prayers are preceded by washing, then begin with a declaration of intent, and consist of a set cycle of prostrations. No clergy is necessary to lead prayers—they are often done wherever the Muslim happens to be. On **Fridays,** congregational prayer is encouraged; this is the only special thing about the Muslim "sabbath."

The third pillar is **charity** (*zakat*). Although giving to good causes individually often substitutes, *zakat* is technically an assessed tax on property given to a carefully-regulated communal fund.

Fasting during the month of **Ramadan** is the fourth pillar. Rather than a month without eating, it is a time of daylight fasting and meditation; nights are filled with feasting and partying. During Ramadan (April 6-May 5 in 1989), offices and businesses not catering to tourists may be closed or have shortened hours.

The last pillar, which is required only once in a lifetime, is **pilgrimage** (the *haj*). Each Muslim who can afford it and is physically able should journey to Mecca. In this aspect of Islam, as in many others, the Muslim is imitating the Prophet's actions. Since he was the recipient of God's revelation, he certainly knew the correct way to act. The traditions about his practices, passed on as *sunnah,* are the important norms of society, and the derivation of the name for the majority **Sunni Muslims.** Agreement and social harmony are very important in Islam. Muhammad once said, "My people will not agree on an error," and when consensus is reached, it is seen as correct.

The **sufis** are a mystical movement within Islam, stressing the goal of unity with God. They are organized in orders, with a clear hierarchy from master to disciple.

Mosques

> *Islam has but one pulpit and one stark affirmation—living*
> *or dying, one only—and where men have repeated that in*
> *red-hot belief through centuries, the air still shakes to it.*
> > —*Rudyard Kipling*

Any place where Muslims pray is a *masjid*, a mosque. The word is best translated as "place of prostration." Buildings called mosques are where the community gathers for Friday noon prayers. Beautiful buildings glorify God, and the ban on images has lead to an incredible ingenuity in geometric and calligraphic decoration. The direction facing Mecca, in which all prayer is spoken, is called the *qibla*. It is marked merely by a niche, the *mihrab*. The *imam* (leader of prayer) gives a sermon on Friday from the *minbar* (pulpit). There are two basic designs for mosques: The Arab style, based on Muhammad's house, which has a pillared cloister around a courtyard; and the Persian style, which has a vaulted arch (a *liwan*) on each side. There are no religious restrictions on non-Muslims entering mosques, but they may have been adopted for practical reasons in areas with mobs of tourists. Prayer is not a spectator sport, so try not to visit during times of worship.

For more thorough introductions to Islam, try *An Introduction to Islam* by Frederick Denny or *Ideals and Realities of Islam* by Seyyed H. Nasr. A good sampling of Islamic texts can be found in Kenneth Cragg and marston Speight's *Islam from Within*. If you feel inspired enough to study the Koran, read M. Pickthall's *Meaning of the Glorious Koran* or A.J. Arberry's *The Koran Interpreted*.

Christianity

Christianity began in Palestine with the followers of one man: Jesus; since then, it has grown into a large and powerful faith. The Jesus of history and critical interpretation of the Gospels differs from the Jesus Christ of faith and literal interpretation. While this introduction stresses the former, it should not be forgotten that this Jesus would be unrecognizable to many believers.

The Life of Jesus

The only significant sources on the life of Jesus are the **Gospels.** Scholars agree that the "synoptic gospels" of Mark, Matthew, and Luke were written in that order after 70 C.E., drawing on a "saying source" which recorded the words of Jesus; they were followed by the Gospel of John (after 100 C.E., but having older sources). John deviates from the synoptic gospels, but those three as well represent often-conflicting traditions. Rather than objective history, the sources are history informed by belief in Jesus Christ.

Even the birth of the man regarded by millions as their savior is ambiguous. Various datings of historical events put the birth of Jesus between 4 B.C.E. and 6 C.E. (Use of the dating system "A.D." and "B.C." began only in the Middle Ages and offends many non-Christians.) In Matthew, Bethlehem is the birthplace of Jesus, and Mary and Joseph move to Nazareth to protect him; in Luke, his parents are only temporarily in Bethlehem; and in Mark and John, the birth is not even mentioned. Christians believe that Mary was a virgin, thus showing Jesus as a product of God's creative power and free from humanity's sin. Catholics believe as well in the **Immaculate Conception,** that Mary was conceived without sin. These concepts do not appear directly in the New Testament.

Jesus was baptized (washed in the Jordan River), as a young man by John the Baptist, a religious leader later hailed as the herald of the Messiah. Afterwards, Jesus began **preaching** in the Galilee at places like Capernaum. He helped the common people, healing the sick and throwing out demons. He spoke passionately for the poor and the righteous, most notably in the **Sermon on the Mount.** Twelve **disciples** were attracted to him in this period. Some are obscure, like Thaddeus, but others, like Peter and Judas, are famous names.

After about a year, Jesus went to Jerusalem, where the **Passion,** the story of his death, was played out. The Gospels give unreconcilable accounts, and the story is generally told in a sort of composite. Key events are Jesus throwing the money-changers out of the Temple, being betrayed by Judas, having a Last Supper, being arrested in the Garden of Gethsemane, and being condemned to death by crucifixion by the Jews with Roman assistance. On Good Friday, He carried His cross down the Via Dolorosa, stopping at what became the Stations of the Cross, until he reached Golgotha (or Calvary; now marked by the Church of the Holy Sepulchre). There he died upon the cross. This method of execution was commonly used by the Romans against political opponents, and undermines the New Testament's assertion of Jewish guilt.

History of Christianity

Three days after Jesus was buried, on Easter, it was discovered that he was no longer in his tomb and had been **resurrected.** He appeared to the Disciples and performed sundry miracles. Later, on **Pentecost,** the Disciples were given "tongues of fire," and directed to spread the Gospel (Greek for "good news"). At first, Christianity was a sect of Judaism, accepting the Hebrew Bible and other essential aspects. Gradually, it split further and further, as it proclaimed that Jesus was the Christ (a translation of Messiah) and began accepting uncircumcised members into the faith. The Book of **Acts** documents their actions, and the **Letters of Paul,** which make up most of the rest of the New Testament, were advice to the early communities.

In 325 C.E., the Roman Emperor **Constantine** not only ended persecution and martyrdom of Christians, but also made Christianity the official religion. He convened the Council of Nicea, which came up with an explicit creed. The Church Fathers declared that Jesus Christ was of the same essence of God, and that there were three equal parts to God. This crucial doctrine of the **trinity** holds that the Father, Son, and Holy Spirit are distinct persons but all one God.

The **Church** was called "the body of Christ," and thought to be integral and unsplittable. Nonetheless, the Christian community has suffered numerous schisms. The **Egyptian (Coptic) Church** broke off in the third century. In 1054, the Great Schism split Christiandom into the western **Roman Catholic Church** and the eastern **Greek Orthodox Church.** In 1512, Martin Luther started the Reformation, which began **Protestantism.** Protestantism is itself composed of hundreds of sects, which generally believe in salvation through faith and not through actions. It is only in the 20th century that the ecumenical movement has put all these churches on speaking terms.

Most Christians adhere to a common set of **beliefs.** These include striving to love others and God in the same unconditional manner in which God loves them, expecting nothing material in return. Jesus Christ is regarded as the savior of humanity. According to this belief, individuals are fatally flawed because they are descendents of Adam and Eve, who disobeyed God. Jesus' death, and the rite of Baptism, absolves humankind of this "original sin." Christianity requires a morally disciplined life. The religion differentiates between the base desires of the flesh, which traces from original sin, and the higher needs of the spirit. Traditionally, Christians must avoid promiscuity, adultery, and greed, among other sins. There is also a call to virtuous actions, such as charity and proselytism.

A good introductory book on Christianity is Steven Reynolds's *Christian Religious Tradition.* Another good source are the works of Denise and John Carmody. Reading the *New Testament* will expose you to the core from which Christian belief is derived.

Architecture

The Middle East's architectural remains reveal its history of conquest. While the various conquering peoples held the land, they transported their cultures, including their monumental styles of architecture, to the Middle East. Especially in Israel and Egypt, examples of classic Muslim and Mamluk architecture, as well as buildings from Roman and Crusader times can be found.

The **Egyptians** excelled at architecture and are known as the builders of antiquity. Limestone, granite, and sandstone were employed for tombs and temples, and the Nile allowed for easy transport of building materials. Archeologists have discovered that Egyptians actually used diamond drills to work with granite. Architectural remains today are mainly temples and tombs. The Sun Temple of King Niuserre at Abu Gurab dates from the Old Kingdom. This structure consisted of a spacious court with a large obelisk inside surrounded by covered passages. Reliefs depicting festivities and daily life still cover the walls of the passages. There are only scanty remains of temples from the Middle Kingdom, but they appear to be similar to earlier structures. The temples of the New Kingdom include those of Tuthmosis III and Ramses III, both at Karnak. The earliest tombs were pits covered with a pile of bricks or Nile mud. On the east side of the grave mound stood a *stela,* or gravestone, and a small court where mourners could leave offerings. Dignitaries of the Old Kingdom were buried in *mastabas,* which consisted of a rectangular structure above an underground burial chamber and abutted by a small court for mourners. The royal *mastabas* were later enlarged and surrounded with series of outer casings to produce a step pyramid, forerunner of the true pyramid. At the end of the Fifth Dynasty, the practice of inscribing religious texts on the walls of the pyramids began. Many of these so-called Pyramid Texts can still be viewed today.

The **Israelites** did not build on a similar scale. Nothing remains of Solomon's Temple. Effort was expended on walls and waterworks; King Hezekiah dug a tunnel, which still remains, to channel the only nearby spring into the walls of Jerusalem.

Architecture flourished during the several centuries that the **Roman Empire** controlled the Middle East, especially under King Herod. Most of these structures have since been destroyed or plundered, leaving little but ruined aqueducts and amphitheaters to tell the tale of Roman might. The most impressive remains of this period are the Western Wall in Jerusalem and the ruins of Caesarea. In Jordan, the Romans spent a good part of their four-century rule building the stone cities of the Decapolis. Significant remains lie at Pella, Gedara (Um Qeis), Gerasa (Gerash), and Philadelphia (Amman).

The extant architecture from the **Crusaders,** notably the prison-fortress at Akko, is characterized by its bulk. These structures were built primarily for protection—the Crusader hold over the land was tenuous and had to be continually defended. Castles and fortresses were built in the European style and not modified to suit the climate of the Middle East—the wall are thick, the windows small, and the orientation European. Generally, these structures look as though they were transported from medieval Germany straight to the Middle East. From the **Romanesque** period, only the Church of the Holy Sepulchre and the Church of St. Anne are still in use.

Coptic architecture in Egypt consists mainly of tombs, monasteries, and churches. These structures were constructed of limestone and timber. Granite columns contain detailed reliefs and carvings of crosses, flowers, and other patterns. Two sites at which tombs can be viewed today are the catacombs of Alexandria and the cemetery of El-Bahnasa, at which the form of the small funerary basilica was perfected. The Dayr el-Abyad Monastery, with its decorated niches and frescoes which once covered the whole surface of the walls, is a fine example of early Christian architecture. The churches of Old Cairo have been influenced by both Arab mosques and Western churches.

Muslim architecture tends to vary regionally, as the Muslims adapted the prevailing styles to their own needs as they conquered each new area. The minaret, however, is distinctly Islamic, and along with multiple arches, became a characteristic of the mosque. Many mosques also have domes, which usually rise from square brick bases. The Dome of the Rock in Jerusalem is an unusual structure. Instead of the standard "borrowing" of Roman pillars to form their own archways, the Muslim conquerors copied the Roman and Byzantine rotunda, or circular building plan, in place of their customary square courtyard. The Mosque of Ibn Tulun brought a new style to Egypt, noted for pointed brick arches and arcades. This mosque is now in ruins, but remains one of the great landmarks of Muslim architecture.

The **Mamluk** period is distinguished by an increased richness and variety of crafts and ornamentation. Mamluk architecture is characterized by flat facades with few, if any, projections and sunken panels containing rows of arched windows. The minarets usually have crown-like tops, perched on short, octagonal staffs to which longer circular shafts were later added. Mamluk mosques include ornate *mihrabs* (prayer niches) on the wall, pointing worshipers toward Mecca. **Ottoman** architecture is perhaps best represented by the wall around Jerusalem built under the rule of Suleiman.

Travel Etiquette

Cultural sensitivity requires attention to proper attire: Shorts or sleeveless shirts should not be worn in holy places. Do not visit sanctuaries during services unless you are worshiping, in which case you are always welcome. Remove your shoes before entering a mosque. Always cover your head when visiting a synagogue.

Photography is often forbidden in holy places, archeological sites, and museums. If you are unsure, ask. Photographing is absolutely forbidden at all military installations, including border crossings, railroad stations, bridges, ports, and airfields. If you decide to play secret agent and photograph here, your film will be confiscated and you may be held for questioning.

Itineraries should be arranged with awareness of religious holidays. In Israel, most businesses, transportation, and restaurants close Friday afternoon in expectation of *shabbat,* the Jewish holy day, and do not reopen until Saturday at nightfall. Travelers who drive a car through ultra-orthodox sections of Jerusalem during the *shabbat* may find themselves pelted by a hail of stones. Observant Jews do not drive or operate any equipment on *shabbat*, and the ultra-orthodox are not particularly tolerant. Plan to do like the natives on *shabbat:* Attend a local synagogue, go for a long walk, or simply rest. Businesses are closed on the major Jewish holidays in Israel and during Muslim observances in Egypt, Jordan, and the West Bank.

ISRAEL

US $1 = 1.65 shekels (NIS)	NIS1 = US $0.61
CDN $1 = NIS1.37	NIS1 = CDN $0.73
UK £1 = NIS2.79	NIS1 = UK £0.36
AUS $1 = NIS1.32	NIS1 = AUS $0.76
NZ $1 = NIS1.09	NIS1 = NZ $.92

> For important additional information on Documents and Formalities, Money, Safety and Security, Climate Concerns, Getting There, Border Crossings, History, Religion, and Travel Etiquette, see the General Introduction to this book.

In Israel, in order to be a realist you must believe in miracles.

—*David Ben-Gurion*

Israel is a land of ancient ruins next to cosmopolitan cities, of European culture mingling with Middle Eastern ways, of green fields amidst deserts, and of peaceful parks with burned-out remnants of war among them. News of Palestinian protests has kept many tourists away from Israel, but the country is still very safe; consequently, a tourist industry starved for visitors is sure to offer bargains.

The miracle of Israel is that it has survived all its difficulties. Israel bears the scars but also the splendors of Canaanites, Israelites, Greeks, Romans, Byzantines, Arabs, Crusaders, Mamluks, Ottomans, and Britons. The state of Israel fought off five nations in a war that began even before it declared its independence. Since then, it has fought four more wars, absorbed nearly a million immigrants, and has adjusted to being an occupying power. Currently, Israelis must deal with rioting Palestinians, growing antagonism between ultraorthodox and secular Jews, and a divided electorate. Hebrew has a word to describe the situation: *balagan* (utter chaos).

Yet Israel always seems to muddle its way through all its difficulties. Conflict seems far away to Jews and Arabs who shop side by side in the *shuk*. Tourists may not notice anything but army reservists carrying assault rifles in the streets. Underneath the surface lies a fascinating sociological case-study.

Israel's varied geography generally surprises tourists. Between the parched Negev Desert to the south and the fertile fields of the Upper Galilee, you'll find sun-flooded beaches and even one snow-capped mountain. Its diminutive size, seven hours by bus from Haifa in the north to Eilat in the south, makes Israel easy to explore.

Planning Your Trip

Work

Unemployment in the Israeli economy is about as high as it has ever been. The current rate hovers around 6%. This greatly limits legal employment opportunities for foreigners in Israel. American or European companies with branches in Israel are one possible source of legal employment. Fluent Hebrew, or skills such as carpentry, could also help. If you obtain paid work, your employer must secure a work visa for you through the Ministry of the Interior. Your chances of paid work aren't great, but don't give up hope. Though you may not come away with a profit, the

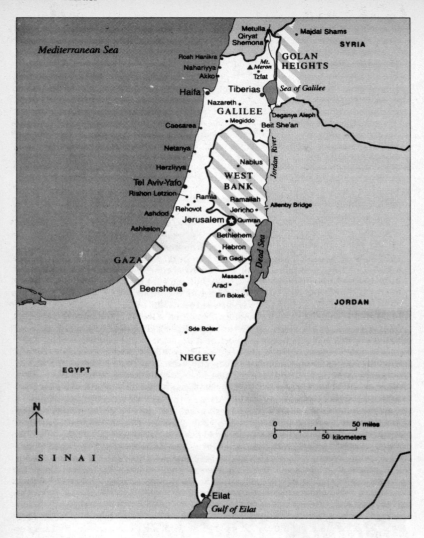

alternative of volunteer work in exchange for room and board is an excellent way to see the country and lend a helping hand too. Below are some options.

Apprenticeships

Israel belongs to the **International Association for the Exchange of Students for Technical Experience (IAESTE).** This organization operates exchange programs for undergraduate and graduate students lasting between two and eighteen months that provide housing, insurance, transportation, visas, and a stipend. Placement depends on the number of companies with openings for interns; you will be expected to help secure job openings. (See Useful Organizations for IAESTE address.) The **Jewish Agency** also offers a six-month internship for young people with experience or education in a specific field. Write to the Center for Ulpanim and Counseling for Young Adults (UCYA), 12 Kaplan St., Tel Aviv (tel. (03) 25 83 11).

Kibbutzim

Israel's 250 *kibbutzim* (sing. *kibbutz*)—communal settlements whose members share the work and profits equally—are always eager for volunteers. *Kibbutzim* vary greatly in size, number of volunteers, and ideological basis. Volunteers generally work six six-hour days per week with several days off per month, and may receive a small monthly allowance in addition to various other benefits. If you're already in Israel, visit the *kibbutz* and talk to other volunteers before you commit yourself for a month or even more. *Kibbutz* life can be seductive in its routine, and many volunteers find themselves staying longer than they had planned. Otherwise, try to get a written promise of placement on a specific *kibbutz* before arriving in Israel. Note that it is much more difficult to arrange *kibbutz* work once you're in Israel than at home.

Jobs for volunteers can be unpredictable. Don't be surprised to find yourself standing among thousands of chickens or turkeys in a coop. You may work in orchards or gardens or end up doing laundry or dishes. Though every effort will be made to rotate work assignments, you should understand that the needs of the *kibbutz* will come before your preferences.

Kibbutz members, accustomed to parades of foreign volunteers passing through the community for a month or two, may not reach out to you unless you make the initial effort to meet them. Remember that you are entering a very tightly knit community, and making friends may be slow and difficult. Try to check out the personality of your *kibbutz* before you commit yourself.

If you wish to combine work with study a suitable option may be the Kibbutz Ulpanim program, available on more than 60 *kibbutzim*. This program provides 24 hours of classroom instruction per week in exchange for 27 hours of work (See Study below).

The **Kibbutz Aliyah Desk,** 27 West 20th St., New York, NY 10011 (tel. (212) 255-1338), has representatives throughout the U.S. and Canada who will help arrange volunteer work. **Project 67,** 36 Great Russell St., London WC1B 3PP (tel. (01) 636 12 62) also places volunteers on *kibbutzim*, as well as on *moshavim* and archeological sites. The **Israel Student Travel Association (ISSTA),** 109 Ben Yehuda St., Tel Aviv 63401, will provide information about the different packages available. Write to them six weeks in advance. Finally, the volunteer department of any Jewish agency should be able to provide you with information.

Once in Israel, you may apply directly to the office of the appropriate kibbutz association in Tel Aviv. Each *kibbutz* is affiliated with a kibbutz association according to political-ideological lines. **Kibbutz Artzi,** 13 Leonardo da Vinci St. (tel. 25 39 05), is affiliated with the left-wing party; **Kibbutz HaDati,** 7 Dubnov St. (tel. 25 72 31), is affiliated with the National Religious Party (only Jews accepted, some religious observance required); and **Takam,** 82 HaYarkon St. (tel. 65 17 10), is affiliated with the Labor Party. Bring your passport and two passport-sized photos with you if you're applying for work on a *kibbutz*.

Moshavim

Moshavim (sing. *moshav*) provide a somewhat different agricultural work experience than *kibbutzim*. *Moshavim* are agricultural communities where almost all farms and homes are privately owned and operated (unlike on *kibbutzim*, where property is communal). You will receive free lodging either with a family on the *moshav* or in a house shared with other workers. Your appointed family will also provide meals or a food allowance. Laundry services, toiletries, and aerograms will be supplied as well. In return, you work a six-day week with a minimum of eight hours per day. Unlike *kibbutz* work, workers are paid, usually about $250 per month. You do not always work with others, but often only on the plot of land owned by your assigned family. A labor shortage at most *moshavim* has made it very easy to find work at one. Applicants must be ages 18 to 35 and be physically fit.

For more information, write the organizations listed above for *kibbutzim*. Once in Israel, contact the **Moshavim Movement,** 19 Leonardo da Vinci St. (tel. 25 84 73), or Steve Jaffe at Unitours, 90A HaYarkon St. (tel. 24 62 61).

Archeological Digs

Working on an archeological dig is another possible way to earn your keep. The work is hard and often monotonous, consisting largely of digging pits, shoveling shards, and hauling baskets of dirt. And you'll do this for between 8 and 10 hours per day, often in searing heat. Work begins at 5am. Don't let dreams of discovering ancient treasures prevent a realistic assessment of your physical stamina and seriousness of interest! Your experience depends not only on these, but on the quality of the dig's findings and how much the leaders care whether you have an inkling of what's developing. In many cases, a dig can be a rewarding educational experience and an excellent way to meet people who share your interests. You will have the opportunity to excavate some of humankind's earliest civilizations, and find sites mentioned in the Bible.

In March, the **Israel Department of Antiquities and Museums,** P.O. Box 586, Jerusalem 91911 (tel. (02) 27 86 03), makes available a list of excavations that are open to volunteers between May and September. Each January, the **Archeological Institute of America,** 675 Commonwealth Ave., Boston, MA 02215 (tel. (617) 353-9361) publishes a thorough listing of digs in its *Archaeological Fieldwork Opportunities Bulletin* ($6). Another good source is the *Biblical Archeology Review* (1317 F St. NW, Washington, DC 20004. Tel. (202) 387-8888.)

Apply directly to the dig leader. Volunteers must be at least 16 (though often 17 or 18, depending on the excavation), in excellent physical condition, and able to work a minimum of two weeks. Be sure to indicate any previous experience or knowledge of archeology, geology, or anthropology in your application, though typically none is required. Many excavations also require an application fee. Volunteers are usually responsible for their own travel arrangements to and from Israel. Most excavations charge for food and accommodations. Accommodations range from camping at the site to a nearby hostel, hotel, or *kibbutz*. The Department of Antiquities recommends that volunteers come fully insured, as most excavations provide only minimal insurance.

Another excavation program is provided through the **Israel Student Travel Association (ISSTA),** which has arrangements with Tel Aviv University for students interested in working on digs. Again the work is long and arduous, and intended only for those seriously interested in the field of archeology.

The "Dig for a Day" program is designed more for the curious tourist. The program includes a 3-hour excavation, seminars on methodology, tools, and history, and a tour of the entire site. The cost for students is about $12. For more information, contact **Archeological Seminars, Inc.,** P.O. Box 14002, Jaffa Gate, Jerusalem 91140 (tel. (02) 27 35 15), from July 1 through September 1.

Volunteers for Israel

The Volunteers for Israel program places participants in non-combat support jobs with the Israeli military. Volunteers began in 1982 during the Lebanon War to give reserve soldiers with businesses and families a chance to return to their domestic affairs. The 23-day program involves menial work, such as washing dishes or packing equipment. Unless your home is encircled with barbed wire and rifle-toting guards, an army base will be a new, though actually dull, environment. You will wear army fatigues, army boots, and sleep in army barracks, but don't expect to carry an Uzi or keep the uniform afterwards. The program offers partially subsidized airfare on El Al or Tower Air, providing you fulfill your commitment. The round-trip ticket is good for 180 days and can be extended once you have finished the program for $50 per 180 days. If you wish to leave early, the airline will charge an additional $50 for your return ticket. There is a special fare for students under 26 with a letter from your university registrar proving enrollment. Write to **Volunteers for Israel,** 40 Worth Street, #710, New York, NY 10013 (tel. (212) 608-4848). Application must include a $45 registration fee.

Study

Israel's full-service European educational system accommodates foreign students. To obtain a **student visa,** you must submit a visa application and medical forms (available from any Israeli embassy or consulate) with two photos and a letter of acceptance from the educational institution you plan to attend.

Ulpanim

An *ulpan* is a short-term study possibility for foreign students that provides intensive study of Hebrew and Jewish culture. Today there are about one hundred *ulpanim* throughout Israel. **Kibbutz Ulpanim** offer 24 hours of classroom instruction per week in return for work. (See Work above.) Studies emphasize conversation and simple reading in Hebrew, and include seminars on current events. Kibbutz Ulpanim run between three and six months. Participants must be between 17½ and 35, single or a couple without children, and in good physical shape. Many American universities recognize Kibbutz Ulpanim for foreign language and elective credits. For more information contact the Kibbutz Aliyah Desk. (See address above under Kibbutzim.)

The **Ulpan Akiva Netanya** runs a series of three- to 20-week study programs in Hebrew and Arabic. The programs include four to five Hebrew study hours per day and cultural activities in the evening, and are open to both Jews and non-Jews from ages 18 to 80. Costs vary according to duration of program. Write to Ulpan Akiva Netanya, P.O. Box 6086, Netanya 42160 (tel. (05) 35 23 12) or the **World Zionist Organization,** 515 Park Ave., New York, NY 10022 (tel. (212) 752-0600).

The Jerusalem municipality also runs very inexpensive *ulpanim.* For information, contact the *ulpan* office in **Beit Ha'Am,** Betzalel St., Jerusalem 94591 (tel. (02) 22 41 56).

Universities

Israel has seven institutions of higher learning, with universities in Tel Aviv, Jerusalem, Ramat-Gan, Haifa, and Be'ersheva, and technical and scientific institutes in Haifa and Rehovot. Programs for foreign students range in length from one summer to four years. **Year-abroad** programs usually begin with a four to nine week *ulpan* to study Hebrew before the semester begins in October, after the Jewish holidays. The courses for these programs are usually in English; if you know Hebrew you have the option to take the regular university courses. Israeli universities also offer full-time **degree programs** on either the undergraduate or graduate level, usually preceded by a *mehina* (see Mehinot below). Admission to undergraduate bachelor programs requires proficiency in Hebrew and at least one year of college. High school students with exceptional backgrounds are also admitted.

Several universities currently operate overseas student programs. You must apply directly to the university through its New York office. Tuition fees are moderate, and scholarships are available. Ask at your university careers office, or write to the **Institute of International Exchange (IIE),** 809 United Nations Plaza, New York, NY 10017 (tel. (212) 888-8200), for their free pamphlet *Basic Facts on Foreign Study* or other helpful publications. The various Friends Committees also offer scholarship assistance. American Guaranteed Student Loans (GSL) may be applied to study in Israel.

Tel Aviv University offers both single-semester and full-year programs for overseas students; the application deadline is June 1 for fall semester or year programs, December 1 for the spring semester. The program is preceded by an *ulpan.* For more information, write to the Office of Academic Affairs, Tel Aviv University, 342 Madison Ave., #1426, New York, NY 10017 (tel. (212) 687-5651).

The **Hebrew University** offers a full-year program in Jerusalem. Applications must be received by April 1. The university also has one-year programs for graduate study. For information on programs and application forms write to the Office of Academic Affairs, Hebrew University, 11 East 69th St., New York, NY 10021 (tel. (212) 472-2288) or Friends of Hebrew University, 3 St. John's Wood Rd., London NW8 8RB (tel. (01) 286 11 76).

For information on the various programs offered by other universities, write to these addresses: **Bar Ilan University,** 130 E. 59th St., New York, NY 10022 (tel. (212) 315-1990); **Ben Gurion University of the Negev,** 342 Madison Ave., #1944, New York, NY 10173 (tel. (212) 687-7721); American Friends of **Haifa University,** 41 E. 42nd St., 24th floor, New York, NY 10017 (tel. (212) 818-9050); **Technion,** 810 7th Ave., New York, NY 10019 (tel. (212) 262-6200).

Summer courses, including Arabic, Hebrew, and Middle Eastern Studies, are offered by Hebrew University of Jerusalem, Tel Aviv University, and Haifa University. The summer courses last about a month, and in 1988 cost between $500 and $700. Language courses, which are taught for the entire summer, cost more. The Hebrew University offers two sessions in July and August. Apply to the various offices of academic affairs or call the Hebrew University Summer Course Department at Mt. Scopus (tel. (02) 88 26 02).

For information about all programs, contact the **Israel Student Authority,** 15 Hillel St., Jerusalem (tel. (02) 24 11 21) or the **Israel University Center,** 515 Park Ave., 10th floor, New York, NY 10022 (tel. (212) 752-0600). More information on study opportunities is available at the Institute of International Exchange and at the New York consulate's Office of Academic Affairs.

Mehinot

Students who do not have the required proficiency in Hebrew but still wish to enter a full undergraduate degree program usually enroll first in *mehinot* (sing. *mehina*) programs. The *mehina* provides a year of intensive Hebrew instruction and a chance to develop study plans as well. *Mehinot* are offered by the universities and other schools of post-secondary education. Note, *mehina* participation does not guarantee acceptance to a university; students still must take entrance examinations. At Hebrew University, Technion, and Practical Engineering Colleges, the *mehina* opens in September or October. The program for Practical Engineers in Be'ersheva begins in August and February. *Mehinot* begin in August at all other schools.

Once There

Entry

Security upon your arrival into Israel is fairly relaxed, especially when compared to the thorough examination your luggage will receive at Ben-Gurion Airport upon your departure. Normally take the "Green Channel" to leave the airport unless you have articles to declare. Any item ordinarily may be brought in duty-free as long as you intend to carry it out upon departure. Take the "Red Channel" to declare articles. Duty must be paid on excessive quantities of perfume, alcohol, and cigarettes. Buses and *sherut* (shared) taxis run regularly to Tel Aviv and Jerusalem.

Useful Organizations

Embassies and Consulates

U.S.: Embassy, 71 HaYarkon St., Tel Aviv (tel. 65 43 38). Consulates, in Tel Aviv, at embassy; in East Jerusalem, 27 Nablus Rd (tel. 23 24 71); in West Jerusalem, 18 Agron Rd. (tel. 28 22 31 or 28 22 32); in Haifa, 12 Jerusalem St. (tel. 67 06 15).

Canada: Embassy, 220 HaYarkon St., Tel Aviv (tel. 22 81 22). Consulate at embassy.

Britain: Embassy, 192 HaYarkon St., Tel Aviv (tel. 24 91 71). Consulate at embassy; in East Jerusalem on Rajib St. near Sheikh Jarrah (tel. 28 24 81 or 28 24 82).

Australia: 37 King Shaul St., 4th floor (tel. 25 04 51).

Tourist and Travel Services

Israel Government Tourist Office (IGTO): Jerusalem, 24 King George St. (tel. 24 12 81); **Tel Aviv,** 7 Mendele St. (tel. 22 32 66); **Haifa,** 18 Herzl St. (tel. 66 65 21). Maps, train schedules, and information on current events. The **Voluntary Tourist Service (VTS)** arranges for tourists to spend evenings with Israeli families.

Israel Youth Hostel Association: 3 Dorot Rishonim St., P.O. Box 1075, Jerusalem 91009 (tel. (02) 22 16 48). Operates 30 hostels. Organizes tours for groups and individuals.

National Parks Authority: 4 Rav Aluf M. Makleff St., P.O. Box 7028, Tel Aviv 61070 (tel. 25 22 81). Material on parks and historical sites. Also sells a 14-day ticket (NIS14.60) covering admission to all sites. Ticket available in Tel Aviv and at major sites.

Society for the Protection of Nature in Israel (SPNI): in Hebrew, *HaHevrah LeHaganat HaTeva. Jerusalem,* 13 Helena HaMalka St.(tel. 22 23 57); **Tel Aviv,** 4 Hashfela St., near the central bus station (tel. (03) 38 25 01); **Haifa,** 8 HaMenahem St. (tel. (04) 66 41 35). Organizes hikes and camping trips. $25 per year dues.

Israel Camping Union: P.O. Box 53, Nahariya 22100 (tel. (04) 92 53 92). Write for information about organized camping tours and a full list of campsites.

Israel Student Travel Association (ISSTA): Jerusalem, 5 Eliashar St. (tel. 22 52 58); **Tel Aviv,** 109 Ben Yehuda St. (tel. 24 43 76); **Haifa,** 28 Nordau St. (tel. 66 91 39). Information about tours, student discounts, and identification.

Safety and Emergency Information

Emergency assistance is available throughout Israel, and most doctors speak English. The **Magen David Adom,** the Israeli Red Cross, provides first aid and other emergency help. Emergency hospitals and pharmacies are open on evenings, *shabbat,* and the holidays. For emergency dental assistance try the Magen David Adom in Jerusalem and in Tel Aviv at 49 Bar Kochba St.

Emergency Numbers in Jerusalem, Tel Aviv, and Haifa

Police..........................100

Magen David Adom.................101

Fire.............................102

Automobile Assistance...........(03) 62 29 61

For other parts of the country, check Practical Information under the appropriate city.

Communication

Mail

Post offices are open from 8am to 12:30pm and from 3:30 to 6pm except Wednesday (8am-2pm) and Friday (8am-1pm), and are closed Saturday and holidays. In the larger cities some offices may keep longer hours. Mail from North America to Israel can take up to two weeks; mail sent from Israel to North America is considerably faster. Be sure to write "Air Mail" on the envelope, or it may take even longer. For some reason, mail from America with five-digit Israeli codes for Jerusalem often goes to Alaska before Israel, delaying its progress. If you need to mail something to North America within 72 hours, the central post offices in Jerusalem, Tel Aviv, and Haifa offer generally reliable International Express Mail service (the hours vary, but are generally Sun.-Thurs. 7:45am-12:30pm and about 4-6pm, Fri. morning only).

Travelers have three means of receiving mail: Poste Restante (*doar shamor* in Hebrew), American Express, and the Israel Student Travel Association (ISSTA). Poste Restante functions in Israel, though you must ask repeatedly to receive all your letters (address them: Name, Poste Restante, name of city, Israel). Have tellers check under both first and last names, and, if possible, check for yourself. Always bring your passport or other proper ID. Lines at American Express are short, and employees often let you check the letter pile. The lines at ISSTA, however, are longer than Israel itself.

Telephone

Public telephones are everywhere. Unfortunately, out-of-order telephones are even more prevalent than sightseers with funny hats. Telephones eat *asimonim* (tokens) for local calls, which are available at post offices, hotel reception desks, and newstands for about NIS.10-.15. Stock up on them whenever you can: They are hard to find, and the insatiable telephones are trained to munch them. English phone directories are available at hotels and the main post offices, or dial 14 for assistance. Avoid calling long distance direct from a pay phone—making a connection may take hours and handfuls of *asimonim*. Instead, use the metered phones at the main post office or at a luxury hotel (though they may charge you double). You can dial direct overseas from central post offices in major cities, which will save both time and money. Dial 00, then the country code (U.S. and Canada code: 1, Great Britain: 44, Australia: 61, New Zealand: 64), area code, and telephone number. For collect and credit card calls, dial 18 for the overseas operator. The Tel Aviv operator (tel. (03) 63 38 81 or 62 28 81) may make your connection more quickly.

The **international phone code** for calling to Israel is 972.

Telegraph

You can phone telegrams by dialing 171. Otherwise, post offices and hotels will send telegrams for you. **Telex** service is available in Tel Aviv at the Mikve Israel post office. (tel. (03) 62 33 09; open 7am-11pm) and in Jerusalem at the central post office.

Currency and Exchange

The primary unit of currency in Israel is the **new shekel (NIS).** Notes come in denominations of NIS100, NIS50, NIS10, and NIS1; coins come in NIS1, NIS.50, 10 agorot, 5 agorot, and 1 agora. The triple-digit hyperinflation of the early 1980s has now been almost completely curtailed as a result of the wage and price freeze instituted during the summer of 1985 (see Economy). That September the new shekel was introduced, equivalent to 1,000 existing shekels and divided into 100 agorot.

Money can be exchanged at any bank or authorized hotel. The hotel rate of exchange is usually slightly worse than that offered by the bank. Bank Leumi will exchange foreign currency for shekels with no commission for a minimum $100 conversion. Shekels can be freely reconverted to a maximum of $100. To change more than $100, show your receipt verifying your original conversion into shekels. (Banks open Sun., Tues., and Thurs. 8:30am-12:30pm and 4-6pm, Mon. and Wed. 8:30am-12:30pm, Fri. and holidays 8:30am-noon. Hotels offer additional hours.)

Use of Foreign Currency

Many services and shops accept U.S., Canadian, and Australian dollars, and Pounds Sterling, but are under no obligation to accept foreign currency. If you do pay in foreign currency (traveler's checks and credit cards included), expect your change to be in shekels. When you use foreign currency, you are exempt from the domestic **Value Added Tax (VAT)** on goods and services. Many shops include VAT in listed prices, so you may have to insist on a discount. VAT refunds can also be obtained by presenting all receipts of purchases made with foreign currency at any export bank upon your departure. Refund will be in the currency used; if the bank cannot make the refund, it will be mailed to your home address. A new policy allows Eurocheques to be written in shekels and count as foreign currency for discounts.

You may bring an unlimited amount of currency, foreign or shekels, into the country in any form. Upon departure, you are permitted to take up to $15,500 and may convert as much as $3,000 worth of shekels back into your own currency. Unless you want to frame them or poster your kitchen, exchange all your shekels before you leave Israel. Few banks are willing to buy them.

Tipping

Do not feel obligated to tip unless in Western-style restaurants, hotels, or in other touristy establishments. Normally a service charge is already included in the bill. If the bill says "service not included," then tipping is customary. Taxi drivers will cheerfully accept tips, but again they are not expected. Israelis usually tip only a barber or hairdresser.

Black Market

Avoid exchanging your money in unofficial, black market booths. They are illegal and hurt Israel's economy. The money-changers are reputed to be con-artists. The hundred new shekels they may seem to be counting out may actually only be ninety-five. So much for the bargain. In any event, the improving performance of the economy has made the premium offered on the black market less significant.

Business Hours

Business hours in Israel are difficult to pinpoint. Because of the variety of religions, different shops close on different days. Most Jewish shops, offices, and places of entertainment are closed early Friday afternoon until after sundown on Saturday for *shabbat*. State-run public transportation, including Egged bus lines, also closes down throughout the country except in Haifa, where the local ruling coalition does not include the religious party. Don't expect to catch a bus after 2pm on Friday. Plan ahead: Israel may be a small country, but it's an awfully long walk from Jerusalem to Tel Aviv. Arab buses continue to run, primarily to the West Bank. Arab-owned concerns close on Fridays; Christian businesses close on Sundays. Usual shopping hours are Monday through Thursday 8am to 1pm and 4 to 7pm, Friday 8am to 2pm.

On the major Jewish holidays (Rosh HaShana, Yom Kippur, Simḥat Torah, Yom HaAtzmaut, and Shavuot; see Holidays) businesses are closed, and have Friday hours the day before. During Succot and Passover, each of which lasts seven days, shops close entirely for the first and last days and are open until early afternoon during intermediate days. Lesser holidays are marked by early closing only. On the West Bank, Gaza, and other predominantly Arab areas, some restaurants close for the entire month of Ramadan, and many others close during the day. Shops close at 3:30pm and reopen from 8-11pm. (See Festivals and Holidays.)

Accommodations

Hostels

Although often crowded in summer, Israel's thirty-three IYHF youth hostels are usually clean and close to historic sites and scenic areas. You can obtain a list of hostels from the **Israel Youth Hostel Association.** (See Useful Organizations.) Hostel locations are also listed on the back of the Government Tourist Office's survey map. Most IYHF hostels accept reservations. They have no age limit, but a few have a maximum stay of three nights. The IYHF hostels are generally more expensive than the unofficial hostels. Overnight fees in 1988 were generally NIS12 for members, NIS14 for nonmembers; breakfast is often included. Individuals 18 and under receive a NIS1 discount. Hostels usually offer lunch and supper for an additional fee. Unfortunately, what you save in money you may lose in convenience. Most hostels have an 11pm curfew, although you can sometimes obtain an extension by special permit in city hostels. In addition, most hostels follow a strict schedule. They are open from 5 to 9pm for check-in, from 7 to 9am for check-out, and are closed the rest of the day, but check the specific listing. There are many excellent unofficial hostels and pensions in Israel. Regardless of whether they are affiliated, hostels are not known for safety. Don't leave valuables lying about, especially while you sleep.

The Israel Youth Hostel Association also offers package tours for individuals and groups. Write to them for information on the "Israel on the Youth Hostel Trail" deals.

Hotels

Hotel accommodations are usually too costly for the budget traveler, though less expensive ones, while rare, do exist. In any case, the time may come when you grow weary of curfews and wish to stay in a more comfortable place. The Ministry of Tourism rates hotels on a five-star basis, with five stars signifying the highest quality and most expensive hotels. Budget travelers will occasionally find reasonably priced one- and two-star hotels in the larger cities; a few have singles for NIS25-30 and doubles for NIS35-40, though most hotels cost more. Prices can often be bargained down substantially when business is slow. Ask at tourist offices for the booklets *Israel: A Youth and Student Adventure* and *Israel Tourist Hotels.*

Camping

Israel's seventeen campsites provide electricity, sanitary facilities, public telephones, first-aid, a restaurant and/or store, and a night guard. Swimming areas are either on the site or nearby. During July and August, most camping places charge NIS10 per night for adults (off-season NIS7). For NIS14 (off-season NIS9) you can get a bed in a rented tent. Another option is to rent a bungalow with two, three, or four beds. This will cost NIS20-25 per person (off-season NIS15-20). For more information, write to the **Israel Camping Union** (see Useful Organizations).

As in other warm countries, you may be tempted to pitch your tent for free in areas not officially designated for camping. Think twice, however, before you unroll your sleeping bag. Certain stretches of beach are off-limits for security reasons (the Mediterranean coast north of Nahariya), and others have a high incidence of robbery (near Haifa, Tel Aviv, and Eilat). Camping on most public beaches is legal. You'll be safest on the more secluded north and south coast beaches near the Sea of Galilee. Don't pitch your tent in illegal areas—encountering a live mine would probably ruin your vacation.

Alternative Accommodations

If you plan to sleep in Bethlehem, Nazareth, or Jerusalem, the three major Christian sites in Israel, consider staying in one of the many **Christian hospices.** There are also hospices on Mount Tabor, in Tiberias, and in Tel Aviv. Most hospices are old monasteries or Franciscan settlements. Officially, they are designed to provide reasonably priced room and board for Christians on pilgrimages to the Holy Land; all the hospices we list, however, welcome tourists and pilgrims alike.

The 39 hospices in Israel are run by organizations representing various Christian denominations and a host of nations. Though prices vary, bed and breakfast costs NIS25-30 per person at most places. Bed only in dormitory rooms can run as low as NIS8. Though austere, the hospices are usually quiet, clean, and comfortable. In addition, most serve cheap, filling meals, and are conveniently located in important religious centers. Unfortunately, the number of rooms is limited, and they can be difficult to obtain in the tourist season. For a list of these hospices, write to the **Ministry of Tourism,** Pilgrimage, Youth and Students Division, P.O. Box 1018, Jerusalem 91009 (tel. (02) 24 01 41).

In some cities (such as Tzfat and Eilat) the cheapest alternative to camping or a youth hostel is a **private home.** The Government Tourist Office and some private travel agencies can arrange accommodations. **Renting Rooms Ltd.,** at P.O. Box 1074, Tel Aviv 61009 (tel. (03) 62 34 11) rents rooms starting at NIS30 with a 10% discount for students. The less expensive alternative is to find a place on your own. Just hang out at the bus station with your bags and someone is bound to find you; this is especially effective in smaller towns. Prices should be no more than what you would pay at the local hostel.

Some *kibbutzim* also offer accommodations called **Kibbutz Inns.** Most of these guest houses are rated three-star by the Ministry of Tourism, and prices run as high as NIS92 for singles and NIS160 for doubles. For more information write Kibbutz Inns, 90 Ben Yehudah St., Tel Aviv 61031, (tel. (03) 24 61 61). Finally, try **ISSTA** (see Travel Services) for cheap package deals on accommodations.

Transportation

Bus

Buses are the most popular and convenient means of traveling around Israel. Except for the Dan Company in Tel Aviv and the Arab buses serving the West Bank and Gaza, **Egged** runs the sole bus service in the country. With over 5000 buses in its fleet, Egged serves nearly every settlement and city in Israel. Several express and local buses travel between the major cities each day. The express buses usually fill up quickly. Buses are generally modern, air-conditioned, and very inexpensive because they are government subsidized. Students receive a 10% discount on all fares with ISIC and passport. Egged offers a card for unlimited travel on both intra- and inter-city buses for NIS70 for one week or NIS110 for two weeks. In addition, Egged issues a day ticket for unlimited bus travel within Jerusalem. Unfortunately, all these offers require far more riding than most travelers could do to get their money's worth.

Buses sometimes become crowded, especially on Saturday nights at the end of *shabbat.* Don't be afraid to push your way in and out of the bus door. Just be sure to preface each push with the word *sliḥa* (excuse me), as do the natives. Adding to the crush is the fact that, for anti-bomb security, luggage compartments are not used on any buses.

Most bus stations have printed schedules—sometimes in English. For express buses, just get in line at the platform (they're always marked) and pay on board. Signs directing you to buy tickets at the ticket window can be safely ignored except for highly traveled, long distance routes (such as Jerusalem-Eilat) for which advance reservations are advisable. When planning your itinerary, remember that only Arab buses run during the *shabbat* (from mid-Friday afternoon to Saturday after sundown). Buses between cities usually leave from the central bus station (*tahanah hamerkazit*).

Many tourists prefer to travel on **Egged tour buses.** Egged offers over a hundred excursion tours to various regions in Israel. Egged tours into the Sinai Desert and along the Red Sea are particularly popular. They're cheaper than the tours run by the Society for the Protection of Nature, though not nearly as good. For more information, check with the Egged tour office in the U.S. by calling (800) 682-3333 or (212) 598-0993 or by writing to their head office at 15 Frischman St., Tel Aviv (tel. (03) 24 22 71).

Taxi

Israeli companies offer both private and less expensive *sherut* (shared) taxis. All city taxis have meters whose use is mandatory, though the drivers often need to be reminded to turn them on. It might be advantageous to bargain if you know how much the ride should cost. Any offers of "special bargains" (translation: no meter and an exorbitant charge) should be refused. Taxis can be phoned as well as hailed on the street.

Sherut taxis hold up to seven people. Certain taxi companies operate *sherut* taxis seven days per week from stations or taxi stands in each city. Inter-city *sherut* taxis operate on loose schedules (ask at stations), except on Saturdays when they simply drive along the roads in search of passengers. Intra-city *sherut* taxis never follow any schedule, but cruise the streets daily. Always fix a price before starting out—it should never be more than 20% higher than the bus fare for the same route. Be particularly insistent about this on Saturdays and late at night when buses don't run and *sherut* drivers may try to rip you off. Most routes, intra-city included, have set fares. Check with Israelis or at the nearest tourist office.

Car

First a caveat: The leading cause of death in Israel is not war. It is automobile accidents. Israeli drivers have a reputation for recklessness. They come closer than tailgating—they practically hitch up. The extensive public transportation makes a car often seem unnecessary. In some cases, however, a car will allow you to reach out-of-the-way places. The brave can drive in Israel with a valid international driver's license (see Identification Cards in the General Introduction). Roads are paved and well-marked, and maps are available at all tourist offices. Israelis drive on the right side of the road. **Hertz, Avis,** and **Eldan** are among the major rental companies in Israel, with offices in all large cities. The cheapest rentals run about $10 per day, plus 22¢ per kilometer, or $32 per day with unlimited mileage. Watch for special deals; Eldan, among others, occasionally offers cut-rate prices. Don't try to save money by not buying insurance. Driving here is just too dangerous.

Train

Rail service in Israel, though very limited, is an alternative for travel between major cities. **Israel Railways** runs a line from Nahariya to Be'ersheva and Dimona in the south that passes through Haifa, Tel Aviv, and major towns along the north coast. Another line from Haifa to Jerusalem passes through the Judean wilderness, some of Israel's more scenic countryside. The Tel Aviv-Jerusalem line is circuitous and slower than travel on the highway.

Like buses, trains cease operation during *shabbat.* Avoid traveling on Friday afternoons because the trains are crowded with people returning home early. It's always safest to reserve seats in advance. Train fares are slightly cheaper than bus fares. Students with an ISIC can obtain a 50% reduction on fare.

Hitchhiking

Israel has marked spots for hitchhikers on main roads and near bus stops. Soldiers always have priority, but tourists should not have much trouble. Don't hesitate to ask military personnel for a ride. Never stick your thumb out in *Let's Go* style when you hitchhike, since in Israel this is equivalent to the American raised middle finger—not the way to get a ride. Instead, point to the side of the road with your index finger. *Women are strongly advised not to hitchhike alone.* The incidence of sexual harassment and assault has increased dramatically in recent years—so much so that female members of the armed forces are forbidden to hitchhike. All solo travelers who accept rides anywhere in the country may be taking a risk.

If you hitchhike in the Negev or the Golan, make sure your ride is going all the way to your destination to avoid becoming stranded (and cooked) in the desert.

Hiking and Biking

Israel's most beautiful scenery is often accessible only by foot. The **Society for the Protection of Nature in Israel (SPNI)** can provide a wealth of hiking suggestions. In general, remember that high altitudes coupled with hot sun may make hiking in midday unsafe; consult with the SPNI for advice. Wear sunscreen, a hat, and drink plenty of water wherever you go. Cyclists should be aware that bicycles are an unfamiliar sight on Israeli roads, and some drivers see them merely as obstacles in the way of their progress. Cycling during the summer may also be dangerous because of the heat. If you decide to cycle, buy proper touring equipment: Riding a bike with a frame pack strapped on it is not quite as safe as pedaling blindfolded over glare ice.

Life in Israel

Religion

Though **Jews** constitute 83% of the population of Israel, freedom of religion has been safeguarded by the state. **Muslims** represent 13% of the population, **Christians** 2.4%, and **Druze** and others 1.6%. Each community operates its own religious courts, funded by the Ministry of Religion, and controls its own holy sites. All religions' days of rest are guaranteed by law.

In a government where four parties representing religious Jews are coaltion partners, it is no surprise that there is a religious bureaucracy. But Israeli Judaism is not monolithic. The head of Jewish religious authority is the Chief Rabbinate, composed of Sephardi and Ashkenazi Chief Rabbis and the Supreme Rabbinical Courts. **Sephardic** Jews are those who emigrated from North Africa, the Middle East, or the Balkan countries; **Ashkenazic** Jews came from Europe. Ethnic and social conflicts tend to overshadow rather small religious differences between them. **Orthodox** Jews themselves are not a solid block, but shade off into the **ultraorthodox.** The latter group are usually recognized by their refusal to wear modern clothing; they vehemently oppose even the smallest perceived violation of Jewish law. The vast majority of Israeli Jews are secular, and generally have little use for religious law. Two groups that are small but growing are the **Reform** (*mitkademet,* or Progressive) and **Conservative** (*masorati*) Jews. These two groups, who believe that Jewish law must be adapted or reapplied to modern life, are unrecognized by the religious bureaucracy and continually harassed by the ultraorthodox.

The *Bene Yisrael,* usually called the **Falashas,** are Jews who recently emigrated in large numbers from Ethiopia to escape famine and persecution. The Falashas follow a Bible in the Ge'ez language, which includes the 24 books of the Bible as well as six additional books outside the canon of other Jews. The Talmud (the compilation of law and commentary on the Bible) never reached Ethiopia, so many practices followed by observant Jews are not recognized by the Falashas. This has been a major problem as the Israeli government attempts to assimilate this new wave of over 15,000 immigrants.

After Mecca and Medina, the most important Muslim holy sites are in Jerusalem—the Dome of the Rock and the al-Aqsa Mosque. The Koran tells of Muhammad's journey from Mecca to al-Asqa ("the farthest") and thence up through the seven heavens to meet with God. There are at least 600,000 Muslims in Israel, not including those in the Occupied Territories.

The Druze, who number almost 50,000 in Israel, are not regarded as Arabs. The friendly relations between Jews and Druze have deteriorated somewhat in the last few years after Israeli annexation of the Golan Heights. All Druze, unlike Muslims, serve in the army. The Druze have their own communal institutions and usually hold one or two Knesset seats. The teachings of the Druze sect are mystical and not revealed to outsiders. They believe that God was incarnated in human forms; the final incarnation was al-Hakim, the founder of the Druze. The religion, which is partly derived from Islam, emphasizes moral principles over ceremony. Prayer services are held in a small structure called a *khalwa.*

Many Christian sects are represented in Israel, including Armenian Orthodox, Abyssinian, Anglican, Coptic (Egyptian), Greek Orthodox, Roman Catholic, and Syrian Orthodox. The nearly 90,000 Christians in Israel account for 14% of the non-Jewish population. While some are immigrants, most are Christian Arabs.

The **Baha'i** religion is centered in Haifa. It was founded in 1862 by Mirza Hussein 'Ali. Baha'is believe that many true prophets exist, the last of whom was Baha'u'llah (Glory of God), another name for the religion's founder. Earlier prophets include Moses, Jesus, and Muhammed. World peace, say the Baha'is, can be achieved through a combination of science and religion. Baha'i holy sites in Israel are the Tomb of the Bab in Haifa and the Tomb of Baha'ullah near Acre. Baha'is have been persecuted in other Middle Eastern countries (such as Iran, Egypt, Syria, and Iraq), but enjoy religious freedom in Israel.

Festivals and Holidays

All Jewish holidays, including *shabbat,* are officially observed. Each holiday begins at sundown the evening preceding its calendar date and ends at sundown. The holidays fall on different days each year with respect to the secular calendar, because their dates are fixed according to the Jewish lunar calendar. On most holidays and the afternoon before, stores, museums, banks, and government-run offices and services are closed in Jewish areas. Interested and modestly dressed observers will be tolerated at the services of the ultraorthodox, but the rites may be incomprehensible.

In 1989 **Rosh HaShana,** the Jewish New Year, will fall on September 30-October 1. Ten days later is **Yom Kippur** (Oct. 9), the most solemn day of the year. On Yom Kippur observant Jews fast in atonement for sins, and Israel shuts down entirely. The mood changes to celebration later in the week with the festival of **Succot** (Oct. 14-21), the Feast of Tabernacles. Open-roofed booths called (surprise!) *succot* (sing. *succah*) are built and decorated with fruits and vegetables, symbolizing both the autumn harvest and the huts of the Israelites during the exodus from Egypt. Seven days after the beginning of Succot falls **Simhat Torah** (Rejoicing of the Law; Oct. 21), when the final chapters of Deuteronomy in the Torah are publicly read and the process starts again in Genesis. Both Jerusalem and Tel Aviv have street festivals.

Hannukah (Dec. 4-11 in 1988, Dec. 23-30 in 1989), the Festival of Lights, is a minor holiday that marks the victory of Jews under Judah Maccabee and the subsequent rededication of the Temple in 164 B.C.E. Only the first and last days are holidays. **Purim** (March 21, 1989), rich in pageantry and skits, celebrates the Jews' salvation from the Persians in the fifth century by Queen Esther. The eight-day holiday of **Passover** (April 20-27) marks the flight of the Jews from slavery in Egypt. During the eight days of Passover, Jews eat *matza* (unleavened bread) to commemorate the Israelites' hurried escape when they did not have enough time to let their bread dough rise. Products made with regular flour and leavening agents (i.e., food you'll be looking for) may be hard to come by during this week in Israel's Jewish areas. Yom HaAtzma'ut (May 10) is a secular holiday, Independence Day. **Shavuot** (June 9) is a joyous harvest festival, celebrated with parties and plays. The fast day of **Tisha B'Av** (July 1) commemorates the destruction of the First and Second Temples.

The most notable holiday observed in predominantly Arab areas and the Occupied Territories is **Ramadan,** a month when the devout fast from dawn to dusk. Some restaurants close for the entire month and many close during the day, but otherwise there are few disadvantages to visiting these areas during Ramadan. In 1989, Ramadan will fall approximately between April 6 and May 5. In the Christian quarters of Israeli cities, major holidays such as the New Year, Easter, and Christmas are celebrated on different days, according to either the Gregorian calendar (observed by Protestants and Catholics) or the Julian calendar (followed by the Greek Orthodox and Armenian churches).

Government

Israel's government is a parliamentary democracy. Though there is no written constitution, a series of Acts of Parliament (1958) serve as the basis for legislation. Israelis do not vote for a candidate in the general election; instead they vote for a list of candidates from one of more than fifteen political parties. The percentage of the popular vote received by a given party is then converted into a proportion of the 120 seats of the Israeli parliament or Knesset. That is, a party receiving 25% of the total vote will get 30 of the 120 Knesset seats. The party with the majority of representatives selects the Prime Minister.

But it's not that simple. Never in Israel's history has a party achieved a majority in a general election. The parties must scramble to form coalitions with others that have similar ideologies. They usually bicker and banter, squabble and scream, cajole and concede for several weeks until agreements are reached. Once enough parties have banded together to form a majority, the game ends and a Prime Minister can be named. Under this election system, even the smallest party can play a significant role in the balance of power and extract concessions: The largest party may need the two or three seats a minor party can provide to achieve the necessary coalition majority.

The two major parties are **Labor** (in Hebrew *Ma'arah*, the Alignment) and **Likud.** Likud (led by Yitzhak Shamir) is the more right-wing of the two, pursuing a hardline approach to the West Bank problem. Labor (led by Shimon Peres), on the other hand, tends to be left-of-center and more willing to make territorial concessions for peace. The practically even split bewteen the two after the August 1984 elections meant that they were forced to share power. Elections scheduled for November 1988, right after *Let's Go* goes to press, will produce a new government.

Israeli parties run the political gamut. The ultra-right wing **Kah,** for example, advocates immediate compensated expulsion of all Arabs from Israel. The far-left **Progressive List for Peace** recommends recognition of the PLO and the creation of a Palestinian state in the West Bank. The ultra-orthodox Jews of Israel are represented by **Shas,** the **National Religious Party,** and **Morasha.** Arguing for religious pluralism and equal rights for women is **Ratz** (the Citizens' Rights Movement). These parties generally hold between one and five seats in the Knesset

Economy

Israel's economy has suffered a long history of instability and inflation. In the past ten years, the currency has been changed from lirot to shekalim (sing. shekel) and from shekalim to new shekalim (NIS) in attempts to control the devaluation of Israeli currency. The new shekel is worth one tenth of an old one, and an old one was worth one thousandth of a lira.

The government's support of the shekel at an artificially high value, in an effort to lower inflation, collapsed in 1983. What followed was a series of devaluations in the shekel, reductions in government spending, and cutbacks in food subsidies. Israelis rushed to buy stable American dollars, and it was even suggested that U.S. dollars be used as legal tender. A new Finance Minister, Yigal Cohen-Orgad, stopped government support of the shekel, and consequently inflation skyrocketed to more than 400%. He lasted less than a year. His replacement tried to solve the problem with an additional billion dollars of American aid, but the government was unable to convince the Histadrut (Federation of Labor) to accept an austerity program and the U.S. withheld the money. Inflation hit a high of 24.3% for October, 1984—an annual rate of 1260%.

In October the government reduced imports and sliced public sector jobs. Unemployment jumped, but inflation dropped to 3.7% in December as a result of a price, wage, tax, and profit freeze. In February 1985, a second economic program was instituted, which dropped many government subsidies and cut spending. Inflation boomed back to 300%. The U.S. appropriated $750 million in emergency aid for 1985-86 and 1986-7.

Social discontent grew as the standard of living fell. In June a series of strikes was held. Wages, prices, and currency exchange rates were frozen until October, and later extended through July 1986. This time, the inflation-reduction methods worked. Israel recorded its first surplus on the current account of the balance of payments in 1985. Today inflation is under 10%, though unemployment is around 6% and the trade deficit is widening.

Kibbutzim and Moshavim

Three percent of the Israeli population lives on *kibbutzim,* which are socialist societies where production is controlled by the entire group. The *kibbutzim* of today, however, barely resemble the fiercely ideological pioneer settlements that began 70 years ago with the founding of Deganya, at the south end of the Sea of Galilee. Then, kibbutzniks were motivated by a pioneering desire to return to the land and achieve both national and socialistic aims. Now most *kibbutzim* are diversified and use state-of-the-art agricultural technology; the Israelis are world leaders in desert irrigation. *Kibbutzim* are responsible for 5% of Israel's industrial and a disproportionate amount of the agricultural production and political leadership. Many *kib-*

butz children now live with their parents, whereas just a decade or two ago nearly all lived in separate dormitories.

Today kibbutzniks face mounting problems, though the experiments in communality have by no means failed. Labor shortages confront *kibbutzim,* as rising numbers of younger members leave the settlements to test their skills elsewhere. Marriage outside the *kibbutz* has drawn away members as well.

Similar to *kibbutzim* are *moshavim,* which provide roughly 40% of Israel's food. Members of a *moshav* typically operate their own piece of land, though the marketing is often done as a collective. Some *moshavim* also have a crop that all members help to manage. *Moshavim* do not have communal dining rooms or separate living quarters for children like *kibbutzim.* Recently, *moshavim* have begun to industrialize as agricultural profits wane.

Language

The contemporary Hebrew language was created from biblical Hebrew by **Eliezer Ben Yehudah,** who compiled the first modern dictionary in the 1920s. Modern Hebrew contains elements of many other European languages. Many words for which no equivalent biblical concept exists have been lifted almost intact from English, such as *psykologia* (psychology), or *cassetta* (cassette). Most Israelis speak some English, and signs are usually written in English as well as Hebrew and Arabic. You may, however, want to learn a few Hebrew phrases so you won't be directed to the *otoboos* (bus) when you want the *sherutim* (bathrooms). For politeness, *todah* is "thanks" and *sliha* is "excuse me." In an emergency, scream *ezrah* (help) or *mishtarah* (police).

Common street names, which go before the name of the street:	
rehov	street
sderot	boulevard
derekh	road
kikar	square

Pronunciation

The letter **H** is a guttural h, as in the German word "ach." Hebrew vowels are also shorter than English ones, which leads to discrepancies in transliteration. Really long vowels are the hallmark of an American accent and make Israelis laugh. Since many Israelis emigrated from Eastern Europe and North Africa, German or French can also be helpful. The best phrasebooks are the Dover publication *Say It in Hebrew* and *Berlitz Hebrew for Travelers* (both about $5). If you intend to spend any time in the Arab towns of the West Bank or the Galilee, try to learn a few Arabic phrases as well as the numerals so you can find the right bus. (See Egypt Introduction.)

Food

> *You shall eat in plenty and be satisfied,*
> *and praise the name of the* LORD *your God.*
> —Joel 2:26

The Israeli diet is governed by the Jewish dietary laws called *kashrut,* a Hebrew word meaning proper or properly prepared. Almost all restaurants in Jewish areas follow the rules of *kashrut,* as do observant Jews in their homes. *Kashrut* (the noun; *kosher* is the adjective) forbids meat or chicken to be eaten with dairy products and prohibits the consumption of food from pigs or shellfish. Consequently, most restaurants serve either meat products or dairy ones; don't expect a glass of milk with chicken. *Kashrut* also requires that animals be killed according to strict, humane guidelines.

The food of Israel is remarkable in its variety. In the gastronomical tug-of-war between Occident and Orient, Israelis lean toward the West, though the raw materials remain stubbornly Middle Eastern. Restaurants run the gamut from Chinese to French, Moroccan to American. Because of the poor quality and high cost of meat, Israelis rely largely on dairy and vegetable products, especially salads and yogurts (try the sweetened fruit yogurt called either *Preely* or *Yogli*). A good way to tell yogurt from sour cream is to look for the percentage milkfat—yogurt will have less than 5%.

> Ah, felafel! Israel's answer to the pizza and hot dog!
> Felafel! He grew nostalgically sick to his stomach with each
> sniff at the counter.
>
> > *Loxfinger* by Sol Weinstein

"Israel's National Food," emblazoned even on postcards, remains **felafel**—pita bread stuffed with deep-fried balls of ground chickpeas and salad and topped with *tahina* sauce. Pizza is a close second, though the crust tastes like the cardboard squares it's served on. *Hoummus* (mashed chickpea, garlic, and lemon dip served with pita) is a spicy alternative, and *shwarma* (chunks of roast lamb and salad wrapped in pita) is a staple among Arabs and Sephardic Jews. The typical Israeli eats a large breakfast, returns home for a big mid-day dinner, and has a light, late supper.

Preparing your own food is very cheap, especially during the summer months when fresh fruits and vegetables abound from *kibbutz* harvests. You can buy groceries inexpensively at the local outdoor markets, at the neighborhood *mahkolet* (small grocery store), or at the Western-style supermarkets in large cities. Market prices for tomatoes fall as low as NIS.60 per kilogram, NIS1.20 per kilogram for apricots (*mish-mish*) and peaches. On hot summer days you'll see street vendors selling what look like hand grenades. Don't worry—these are *sabras* (a prickly cactus fruit), and the inside is edible, although the seeds do not agree with some people.

You may want to carry a canteen filled with water lest you wind up single-handedly subsidizing the Israeli soda industry. Two fruit drinks are sold everywhere that are cheaper than soda and safer than water: *Tapuzim* (orange drink) and *esh-koliot* (grapefruit drink). Israeli sodas tend to taste a bit like motor oil, but Coke, Schweppes, and Royal Crown are available everywhere. Be specific—if you ask for "soda" you'll get club soda. The two most common beers are *Maccabee,* a lager, and *Goldstar,* which is slightly stronger and cheaper. *Nesher* is a very sweet, non-alcoholic malt-beer. Legend claims that if you drink enough *Nesher* on a hot day you'll get slightly high. If you ask for coffee with no specifications, you'll get a small cup of strong, murky Turkish coffee; if you want something resembling American coffee, ask for *nes,* or *nes kafeh,* and you'll get instant coffee. If you want it with milk, ask for it *eem ḥalav.*

The Arts

Literature

The **Hebrew Bible** forms a basis for myth, metaphor, and symbol that is the foundation of much of modern literature. While large parts of the Bible are legal or historical, others are purely literary.

The compilation of the biblical narrative was followed by the age of the Mishnah (100 B.C.E.-700 C.E.) during which *halaḥa* (law derived from the Bible) and *aggada* (elaboration on non-legal biblical aspects) were compiled. This age also saw the growth of the *piyyut* (liturgical poem), composed mainly by cantors. Jewish poetry proliferated in the Middle Ages, such as *Megillat Antiohus* and *Megillat Hannukah*. Narrative prose of the Middle Ages focused on demonological legends.

The increasing revival of Hebrew as a secular language in the **eighteenth century** brought a drastic shift in Hebrew literature. Josef Perl and Isaac Erter parodied Hassidic works in their writings. In tsarist Russia Abraham Mapu, the first Hebrew novelist, wrote *The Hypocrite,* representing the first novel to portray modern Jewish social life in a fictional context. Following generations moved toward realism, often employing the more versatile language of Yiddish.

Around the turn of the **nineteenth century,** Hebrew was revived for literature by Joseph Brenner, whose theme was the tragic, uprooted settler. His works are remarkable not only for their continuing influence on subsequent generations of Israeli writers, but also for their searching and pessimistic depictions of social interaction between Jews and Arabs. In the 1920s and 1930s Nobel Laureate Y.S. Agnon confronted the breakdown of cultural cohesion among modern Jews in his writings. His works include *A Guest for the Night, The Bridal Canopy,* and *Twenty-One Stories.* Lea Goldberg infused the harsh realities of life into her poetry, as in her "Tel Aviv 1935."

Just prior to the creation of the State of Israel, in the **1940s,** a new group of native Hebrew authors arose with a fresh style characterized by a concern for the landscape and the moment. S. Yizhar's *Efrayim Returns to Alfalfa* was a pioneering work showing this new vitality. Beginning in the late **1950s** writers such as Amos Oz and A.B. Yehoshua began to experiment with psychological realism, allegory, and symbolism. The literature of the **1960s** in Israel, reflecting world-wide movements, saw a separation from the traditional ideological patterns of writing. In both prose and poetry, writers experimented with new forms and criticized the provincial realism and didacticism of elder writers. Additionally, new skepticism surfaced over social and political forms. A.B. Yehoshua, for example, wrote about tensions between generations, Arabs and Jews, and Sephardim and Ashkenazim in his "Facing the Forests" and his collection of short stories *Three Days and a Child.* David Shahar has been called the Proust of Hebrew literature for his *The Palace of Shattered Vessels* set in Jerusalem in the 1930s and 40s. Jacob Shabtai's *Past Continuous,* about Tel Aviv in the 1970s, is perhaps one of the best Israeli novels of the decade.

More recently, a number of authors have written fascinating accounts of their experiences in Israel. Amos Oz's *In the Land of Israel* is a series of interviews with native Israelis, including West Bank residents, that documents the wide range of political sentiments. The poet Yehuda Amichai offers insight into the soul of the modern Israeli in his *Selected Poems.* Both books, as with most major Israeli works, have been translated to English. Other personal evaluations of Israel include Saul Bellow's *To Jerusalem and Back* and journalist Lawrence Meyer's *Israel Now.* David Grossman's *Yellow Wind* tells of one Israeli Jew's journey to the West Bank just prior to the uprising. *The West Bank Story* by Rafik Halabi, an Israeli Druze television reporter, is a very informative impartial account. Fawaz Turki's *The Disinherited* offers a thoughtful autobiography of a Palestinian Arab.

For a look backward from the modern day into the past of Jewish experience, read Nobel Laureate Elie Weisel's *Night, Dawn,* or *Souls on Fire.* Aharon Appelfield offers a survivor's account of the Holocaust in *The Age of Wonders* and *Badenheim 1939. Voices Within the Ark* by Howard Schwartz and Anthony Rudolph is an anthology of twentieth century Jewish poetry, much of which derives from the Israeli experience.

Israel's short but tumultuous history has inspired a number of **historical novels.** Consider reading Chaim Potok's *Wanderings,* James Michener's *The Source,* and Leon Uris' *Exodus.* For a more sober textbook history of the land read Barbara Tuchman's *Bible and Sword,* which chronicles Palestine from the Bronze Age to the Balfour Declaration of 1917. The works of Solomon Grayzel are also authoritative and elegant for historical background. An account of Arab Israelis can be found in the dense but provocative *The Arabs in Israel* by Sabri Jiryis. Sacher's *Israel: A History* provides a comprehensive review of the state's history to date.

Music

Music became an organized facet of Israeli culture after World War I, when enthusiastic amateurs and professional musicians assembled chamber groups, a symphony orchestra, an opera company, and a choral society. During the 1930s with the rise of Nazism in Europe, hundreds of Jewish music teachers, students, composers, instrumentalists and singers, and thousands of music lovers, streamed into the country. This influx gave rise to music schools, the Palestine Symphony in 1936 (today the internationally acclaimed Israel Philharmonic Orchestra), and the formation of a radio orchestra (currently the Jerusalem Symphony Orchestra of the Israel Broadcasting Service).

These professional organizations have been joined by the Haifa Symphony Orchestra, the Israel Chamber Orchestra (Tel Aviv) and, in the early 1970s, by the Israel Sinfonietta (Beersheva) and the Netanya Orchestra. Major choral groups include the Tel Aviv Choir (est. 1941) and the Rinat Choir (est. 1955). Seasonal music activities from October into July include the subscription series of the major orchestras, as well as many concerts and recitals by small ensembles and individual performers. Concerts are held in such varied settings as the historic Knight's Hall in the Crusader Castle at Akko to the modern, 3000-seat Mann Auditorium in Tel Aviv.

A uniquely Israeli style of classical music has been slowly evolving. Young Israeli composers must contend with the overwhelming European tradition and, most recently, with the modern and post-modern legacy. A peculiar and singular style has been adopted by some Israeli composers as an attempt to break new ground. The "Mediterranean" style is informed by traditional Eastern and Western melodies, by the cantillation of ancient prayer, and by the dissonant legacy of Schoenberg.

Popular music in Israel is firmly rooted in the lyricism of European folk music. American and British rock and punk are also favorites in Israel, especially in Tel Aviv. American groups often perform in HaYarkon Park in Tel Aviv and Sultan's Pool in Jerusalem, both outdoor areas.

Media

Israelis read newspapers and magazines avidly. Locals and tourists have a choice of 15 Hebrew newspapers, five papers in Arabic, and nine in other languages. The most widely read English language newspaper is the *Jerusalem Post,* availiable at a much lower price than imported American or English papers.

The Israel Broadcasting Authority oversees the **radio** and **television** stations in the country. *Kol Yisrael* (Voice of Israel) runs five stations, each of which appeals to a different audience. There are also multi-language broadcasts that provide information about news and cultural events. *Reshet Gimel* (Station 3) plays Hebrew and English rock music. The Israeli Defense Radio (*Galei Tzahal*) is aimed at the interests of military personnel, including pop music.

Sports and Recreation

Soccer, basketball, and tennis are the most popular sports in Israel. Soccer has become especially popular since the 1976 Olympics in Montreal when the Israeli team made the finals. Thousands come with racket and Spaulding in hand to Ramat HaSharon, just north of Tel Aviv, the tennis center of the country. You may rent tennis courts there, at many luxury hotels, and elsewhere.

Horseback riding clubs abound, with sites in Arad, Beersheba, Caesarea, Eilat, Netanya, and Vered HaGalil. Caesarea even has an eighteen-hole golf course, though a set of clubs is hard to fit into a backpack. Israelis enjoy skiing in the winter on snowy Mt. Hermon. You might wish to rent a sailboat or a sailboard at the Tel

Aviv Marina. Perhaps you want to scuba dive or snorkel in Eilat. Waterskiers and motorboats skim across the Red Sea as well.

For the fleet-footed, there's the eighth-annual Sea of Galilee Marathon in mid-December. You'll run past the Sea of Galilee and across the River Jordan. This is the only marathon in the world run completely below sea level. More sedentary types can just relax on one of Israel's twenty-two supervised beaches.

Jerusalem

> *Upon your walls, O Jerusalem, I have set my watchmen;*
> *All the day and all the night, they shall never be silent.*
> —Isiah 62:6

Posting watchmen on the walls hasn't kept Jerusalem from conquest and reconquest, destruction and reconstruction. The new is built on top of and amidst the old, resulting in a fascinating mixture of ancient, semi-ancient, and modern. Half the population is dedicated to building a new Jerusalem, but another part reveres Jerusalem for its old-style holiness. This is the city where King Solomon built God's House and where the Israelites went to make their sacrifices. Jesus came here to preach, and died on a hill just outside the walls. Muhammad ascended into the Seventh Heaven from Jerusalem on his Night Journey.

Jerusalem's variety and color are spellbinding. Each stone has its own history and legend and grace. And each sunset in the clear air of the Judean hills seems to confirm the ancient legend that when God created the world, nine out of 10 measures of beauty were bestowed on the Land of Israel, and nine-tenths of Israel's beauty given to Jerusalem.

History

Jerusalem's history is a story of conquests, with 18 conquerors in 3000 years leaving their marks on the city. Archeological evidence indicates that Jerusalem was a Canaanite city for 2000-3000 years *before* it was conquered by King David in about 1000 B.C.E. David established Jerusalem as the capital of the Israelite kingdom, and his son Solomon extended the city's boundaries northward from the City of David to include the present-day Temple Mount. There Solomon built the First Temple to house the Ark of the Covenant and to centralize the sacrificial observances.

The Israelite kingdom broke into two shortly after Solomon's death. The Davidic Dynasty continued in the two southern tribes of the Kingdom of Judah, and retained Jerusalem as its capital. Internal strife left the Judahites open to disastrous invasions, and in 586 B.C.E., King Nebuchadnezzer of Babylon burned Jerusalem and the Temple and forced the Jews into exile. In 539 B.C.E., Cyrus of Persia conquered Babylon, and allowed the Jews to return from exile. Reconstruction began in 536 B.C.E. and the Second Temple was completed 20 years later. But Jerusalem was not restored until the court official and prophet Nehemiah rebuilt the city walls in 445 B.C.E. and repopulated the city.

The walls of the city, however, did not prevent 24 more centuries of conquest and domination by various foreign powers. With little opposition, Alexander the Great conquered Jerusalem in 332 B.C.E., and soon Hellenized much of the population. After two centuries of Hellenic rule, and a brief period of Egyptian domination, the Seleucid Empire took Jerusalem in 198 B.C.E. Thirty years later the remaining religious Jews revolted against the king, who had desecrated the rebuilt temple. The rebels, led by Judah Maccabee, occupied and resanctified the temple in 164 B.C.E. and put the priestly hierarchy in secular power over the city.

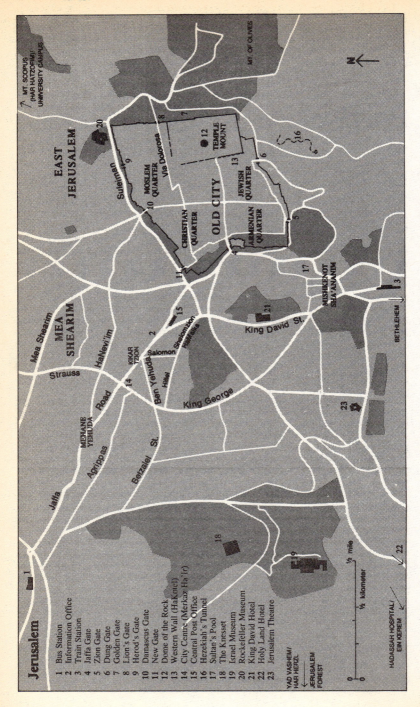

Jerusalem

1 Bus Station
2 Information Office
3 Train Station
4 Jaffa Gate
5 Zion Gate
6 Dung Gate
7 Golden Gate
8 Herod's Gate
9 Lion's Gate
10 Damascus Gate
11 New Gate
12 Dome of the Rock
13 Western Wall (Hakotel)
14 City Centre (Merkaz Ha'ir)
15 Central Post Office
16 Hezekiah's Tunnel
17 Sultan's Pool
18 The Knesset
19 Israel Museum
20 Rockefeller Museum
21 King David Hotel
22 Holy Land Hotel
23 Jerusalem Theatre

In 64 B.C.E., the Roman general Pompey took Jerusalem, ushering in several centuries of Roman rule. The Romans installed Herod the Great, son of a Jewish father and a Samaritan mother, as King of Judea. During his 33-year reign (37-4 B.C.E.), Herod rebuilt the Temple and created the famous Western Wall as part of the supporting structure for the enlarged Temple Mount. In 6 C.E., the Romans turned the governance of the province over to a series of procurators. The fifth procurator, Pontius Pilate, ordered the execution of Jesus in Jerusalem. In 66 C.E. the Jews revolted against Rome; four years later the Roman commander Titus crushed the revolt, destroyed the Temple, and razed Jerusalem. After the Bar Kohba Revolt, which ended in 135, the city was destroyed again by the Emperor Hadrian, and Jews forbidden to reenter.

That same year Hadrian built a new city, "Aelia Capitolina," on the site to serve as a Roman colony. The present-day Old City retains the plan of Hadrian's city in its division into quarters by two major roads and in its north-south orientation. When Constantine converted to Christianity, his mother Helena traveled to the Holy Land, identifying and consecrating sites sacred to Christians. Subsequent Byzantine rulers dedicated themselves to building basilicas and churches to glorify the city's Christian heritage.

After a brief period of Persian rule in the early seventh century, Jerusalem was taken in 638 C.E., six years after the death of Muhammad, by the Muslim Caliph 'Umar (Omar), who cleansed the Temple Mount and dedicated it to Muslim worship. In 691 C.E., his successors completed the Dome of the Rock, often incorrectly referred to as the Mosque of Omar. The Muslims tolerated Christians and Jews as "Peoples of the Book," like themselves.

This period of coexistence ended in the tenth century, when Jerusalem passed into Egyptian control. The Fatimid despots destroyed all synagogues and churches, and passed on their policy of persecuting non-Muslims to their successors, the Seljuk Turks. The reputed closing of pilgrimage routes enraged Western Christians and prompted the Crusades, a series of invasions that culminated in the capture of Jerusalem in 1099. The Latin Kingdom lasted almost 90 years. During this time, churches were built or rebuilt, and hospices, hospitals, and monastic orders were founded. In 1187 Salah al-Din expelled the Crusaders and allowed the resettlement of the city by both Muslims and Jews. Jerusalem became a center for Muslim scholarship from the thirteenth to the fifteenth centuries under the Mamluks.

In 1537, Ottoman Emperor Suleiman the Magnificent set out to rebuild the city walls. The task took four years, and the planners deviated from the older design, leaving Mount Zion and King David's tomb beyond the walls. Enraged by their negligence, Suleiman had the two planners beheaded. Their graves can still be seen just inside Jaffa Gate.

The West made its way into Jerusalem again in the nineteenth century. With the issue of the "Edict of Toleration" for all religions by the sultan of Turkey in 1856, Jews and Christians were once again encouraged to settle within the city. In the 1860s, Sir Moses Montefiore, a British Jew, made several trips to Palestine and founded Jewish settlements outside the walls. Spurred by the first waves of Jewish immigration to Palestine, these settlements quickly developed into bustling neighborhoods, the foundation of Jerusalem's New City.

Both Jews and Arabs resented the increasing British presence in Jerusalem. During World War I, the British made declarations to both Zionists and Arab nationalists implying that each would eventually gain sovereignty over the city, thus securing both Arab and Jewish aid in the British fight against the Ottoman Empire. When the British General Allenby arrived at Jaffa Gate, after having conquered Jerusalem from the Turks, he got off his horse and walked through the gate in the traditional manner of pilgrims. In the end, the British kept Palestine for themselves as a League of Nations mandate.

Jewish settlement in Jerusalem increased sharply in the shadow of World War II, and political tensions increased. The British proposed a partition plan to solve these conflicts. A Zionist resistance movement, including several terrorist groups, was determined to block British policy. In July 1947, Zionist extremists bombed the British headquarters in Jerusalem's King David Hotel. The British announced their intention to withdraw from Palestine and called upon the newly formed United Nations for a settlement. The United Nations voted to partition Palestine into separate Jewish and Arab states and make Jerusalem an international city.

In the War of Independence that followed the 1948 British evacuation, Jews in the New City and the Jewish Quarter were beseiged by the Arabs, who blocked the one road out of the city. The New City held out until the first ceasefire, but the Jewish Quarter of the Old City capitulated to the Jordanian Arab Legion after house-to-house fighting. At the end of the war, the Old City and East Jerusalem were in Jordanian hands, while the newly formed state of Israel held the New City. The two sectors were separated by a no-man's land running through the city. West Jerusalem expanded rapidly during these decades, building new neighborhoods to house immigrants.

Israeli forces captured Jordanian Jerusalem during the whirlwind war of 1967. The Mandelbaum Gate and the walls separating the Israeli and Arab sectors were torn down, and the annexation of East Jerusalem began. Four thousand Arabs were evicted from Jerusalem, and some of their homes destroyed. Israel came under immediate condemnation from the UN General Assembly and Security Council. On June 29 Israel declared Jerusalem to be its "eternal capital." The anniversary, Jerusalem Day, is a great day to be in the New City and an even better time not to be in East Jerusalem. On July 4 and again on July 14, the General Assembly voted unanimously to censure Israel for the annexation and demanded that the city remain untouched. The following May 21, the General Assembly reaffirmed these resolutions. The last reprimand actually accelerated Israel's construction and occupation, as the government sought to create a physical basis to its declared autonomy.

In August 1969, a fire in the al-Aqsa Mosque heightened tensions, as it seemed to substantiate Arabs' fears that their holy sites might be endangered. In fact, the fire was set by an Australian religious fanatic. Housing construction continued as the Israeli government endeavored to double the Jewish population in Jerusalem within ten years. Meanwhile, Muslim and Christian groups protested to UNESCO about Israel's excavations in the Old City, and UNESCO voted to stop financial assistance to Israel.

On June 23, 1980, Israel reaffirmed Jerusalem as its capital, and Prime Minister Begin moved his offices to East Jerusalem. One week later, the UN Security Council voted 14-0 (with the U.S. abstaining) that Israel was not entitled to call Jerusalem its capital. Only Costa Rica has an embassy in Jerusalem. Most other countries, including the United States and the United Kingdom, just have consulates here and their embassies in Tel Aviv. On July 29, the UN General Assembly demanded that Israel pull out of annexed Jerusalem. The next day Israel announced Jerusalem was to be its "eternal capital." Terrorist acts were perpetrated by both Jewish and Arab extremist groups in Jerusalem in the early 1980s. In January of 1984, a group of Jewish terrorists, hoping to rebuild the Temple on the Temple Mount, tried to blow up the al-Aqsa Mosque, but were caught at the last minute. Meanwhile, Arab terrorists carried out numerous bombings in the city and throughout Israel.

In 1988, Jerusalem (along with the West Bank and Gaza) has been hit by the *intifadah,* a Palestinian uprising. The most visible manifestations of the *intifadah* have been riotous protests and the Arab strike, in which Arab businesses open only from 9am-noon. Another dispute, which usually simmers just below violence, is the emnity between secular and ultra-orthodox Jews. Jerusalem's long-time mayor, Teddy Kollek, has struggled to keep the peace.

Orientation

Although many first-time visitors find Jerusalem large and disorienting, it is actually small and disorienting. The city has three main parts: the Old City, East Jerusalem, and the New City (West Jerusalem). The New City and the Jewish Quarter of the Old City are safe. The *intifadah* (uprising)has made East Jerusalem and Arab

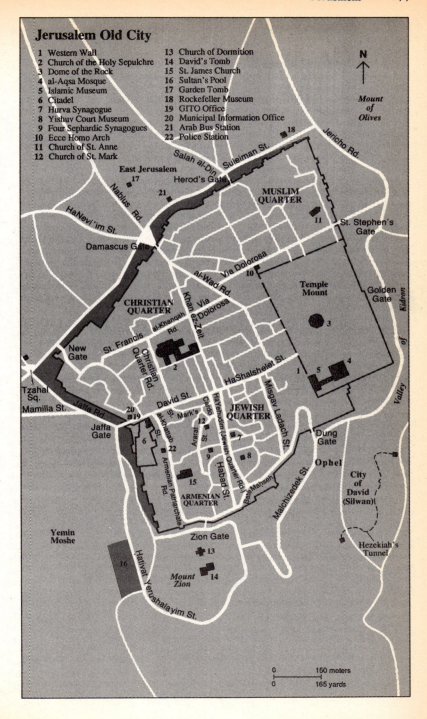

Jerusalem Old City

1 Western Wall
2 Church of the Holy Sepulchre
3 Dome of the Rock
4 al-Aqsa Mosque
5 Islamic Museum
6 Citadel
7 Hurva Synagogue
8 Yishuv Court Museum
9 Four Sephardic Synagogues
10 Ecce Homo Arch
11 Church of St. Anne
12 Church of St. Mark

13 Church of Dormition
14 David's Tomb
15 St. James Church
16 Sultan's Pool
17 Garden Tomb
18 Rockefeller Museum
19 GITO Office
20 Municipal Information Office
21 Arab Bus Station
22 Police Station

N

Mount of Olives

East Jerusalem

Salah al-Din   Suleiman St.

Herod's Gate

Jericho Rd.

Nablus Rd.

HaNevi 'im St.

Damascus Gate

MUSLIM QUARTER

St. Stephen's Gate

Via Dolorosa

al-Wad Rd.

Temple Mount

Golden Gate

Khan ez-Zeit

Via Dolorosa

CHRISTIAN QUARTER

al-Khanqah Rd.

St. Francis

Christian Quarter Rd.

New Gate

Tzahal Sq.

Mamilla St.   Jaffa Rd.

HaShalshelet St.

Misgav Ladach St.

JEWISH QUARTER

David St.

St. Mark's

al-khattab St.

Ararat St.

HaYehudim (Jewish Quarter Rd.)

Bet Mahseh

Jaffa Gate

Armenian Patriarchate Rd.

Habad St.

Malchizedek St.

Dung Gate

Ophel

City of David (Silwan)

ARMENIAN QUARTER

Yemin Moshe

Hativat Yerushalayim St.

Zion Gate

Mount Zion

Hezekiah's Tunnel

Valley of   Kidron

0   150 meters
0   165 yards

parts of the Old City unsafe, depending on political conditions. If a demonstration, or its cousin the riot, breaks out near you, *get away*—it's not a spectator event. The army will tear-gas tourists and protestors alike, and you camera may be impounded.

The **New City**, part of Israel since the foundation of the state, is the administrative and commercial center of Jerusalem, and the seat of the national government. Most of Jerusalem's services and restaurants are located here, as is virtually all of its nightlife. The main street in the New City is **Jaffa Road** (*Derekh Yafo*), which stretches from the central bus station to the Old City's Jaffa Gate. Halfway between the two is Jerusalem's downtown (*Merkaz Ha'Ear*), the area within the triangle formed by the intersections of Jaffa Rd., **King George St.** and **Ben Yehudah St. Zion Square** (Kikar Zion) lies at the intersection of Jaffa and Ben Yehudah. The section of Ben Yehudah between Jaffa Rd. and King George St. is a pedestrian mall. West of the downtown area, between Jaffa Rd. and **Agrippas St.**, is **Mahaneh Yehudah**, the New City's colorful open-air market.

Jerusalem's most important historical and religious sites are located within the walls of the **Old City**, which is still divided into the four quadrants laid out by the Romans in 135 C.E. To get there from the city center, follow Jaffa Rd. past the post office to Jaffa Gate. From there, you can take the promenade around the walls to the other gates. The main avenue in the Old City is **David Street.** whose continuation **Bab el-Silsileh** ("Gate of the Chain") runs to the Western Wall from Jaffa Gate. The **Armenian Quarter** is to your right if you enter by the Jaffa Gate (accessible directly from the Zion Gate). To the left of Jaffa Gate is the **Christian Quarter** (accessible from the New Gate). Approachable from the Damascus Gate, or down David St. and to the left, the **Muslim Quarter** is the most populous. The **Jewish Quarter** faces the Temple Mount and opens on the Dung Gate; it is down David St. and to the right.

Unlike the Old and New Cities, East Jerusalem has a wholly Arab color and flavor. **Suleiman St.** runs in front of the **Damascus Gate.** The Arab bus station, stores, and professional offices are located on Salah al-Din St. Nablus Rd. (*Derekh Shehem*) has the station for buses to the north. **HaNevi'im St.** (*Musrada* in Arabic) has many dry goods stores and hostels. Unlike the tourist-oriented *souk* of the Old City, East Jerusalem is a center of banking and shopping for the local Arab communities.

You can reach any section of the city by bus from the **central bus station.** Egged buses stop along the road outside the station entrance, right across the street or on the street running parallel in front of Binyanei Ha'Ooma (cross the street through the underpass; the stairs are in front of the station). A single ride costs NIS.70. If you'll be in town for more than a week, consider buying a 25-ride punch-card ticket for the price of 20 rides; all drivers sell these. Note that only Arab buses (see Practical Information) run on Saturdays; Egged service stops about 2:30pm on Fridays. The GTIO distributes city maps with bus routes on the back. Below are the most important bus routes.

#5, 6, 13, 18, 20, 21, 35: From the central bus station to the New City center (ask for *merkaz ha'ear*), get off at the intersection of Jaffa Rd. and King George St.

#13, 20, 23: from the central bus station, down Jaffa Rd., to Jaffa Gate by the Old City.

#1: From the central bus station, to Mea Sh'arim, Jaffa Gate, Mt. Zion and the Jewish Quarter in the Old City. This bus route was used to smuggle weapons in 1948.

#9: From the central bus station, skirts the city center, to the Knesset and the Israel Museum, to Mt. Scopus and Hebrew University at Givat Ram.

#27: From the New City center to Damascus Gate and East Jerusalem.

#99: The Jerusalem Circular Line: 34 major tourist sights. Hourly Sun.-Thurs. 9am-5pm, Fri. 9am-2pm. One full circle, including all 34 sights, costs NIS2; 1-day unlimited travel NIS 8.50; 2 days NIS10; students ½ price. For information: tel. 24 81 44 or 24 77 83.

#5, 6, 8, or 21: From the train station to the city center.

The tourist office usually distributes two different maps of the city: the brown Ministry of Tourism map and the pink Gabrieli map. The Gabrieli map is much more detailed, but is only occasionally available at the King George St. office. Aharon Bier's excellent map of the Old City, superimposed on an aerial photograph, shows every courtyard and alley within the city walls. The map is available at the tourist shops inside Jaffa Gate and at the SPNI Bookstore. If you really crave detail, try the Department of Surveys (1 Heshin St., around the corner from the Municipal Tourist Information Office) which sells excellent maps of all sorts.

Practical Information

Government Tourist Information Office (GTIO): Main Office 24 King George St. (tel. 24 12 82), in the New City. This office is not known for friendliness or expertise. More helpful by phone than in person. Branch office inside **Jaffa Gate** in the Old City (tel. 28 22 96) is much better informed and ready to assist. Sets up evenings with Israeli families. Both offices have maps, brochures, bus schedules, a calendar of local events, and a discount ticket for NIS16 that allows admission to 6 major sights. (Students receive discounts anyway by showing ID.) Both open Sun.-Thurs. 8:30am-5pm, Fri. 8:30am-2pm.

Municipal Information Office: 17 Jaffa Rd. (tel. 22 88 44) at Tzahal Sq. Although most of their books are in Hebrew, the staff is friendly and helpful at this uncrowded office. Free Saturday walking tours (10am, destinations posted). Open Sun.-Thurs. 9am-12:30pm, Fri. 9am-noon.

Christian Information Center: Inside Jaffa Gate and to the right (tel. 28 76 47; mailing address P.O. Box 14308). Terrific place for Christian and general information. Lists of Christian hospices, services, and sites in Jerusalem and Israel. Also biblical references for Jerusalem's sights. Map of tour routes NIS1. Schedule of church services for all denominations posted. Open Mon.-Sat. 8:30am-12:30pm and 3-6pm; in winter 8:30am-12:30pm and 3-5:30pm.

Franciscan Pilgrims Office: Same building as Christian Information Center (tel. 28 28 21; mailing address P.O. Box 186). Makes reservations for the masses at Christmas masses, and throughout the year. Pilgrimage certificates available.

Heritage House Jewish Information Office: 5 Tiferet Yisrael St., Jewish Quarter (tel. 28 00 61, evenings 28 79 21), off the main square. The friendly staff is eager to place Jewish travelers in the Heritage House Hostel (see Accommodations) and to provide information about short and long term study programs. Offers a free tour of the Jewish Quarter at noon (Sun.-Thurs.). The office makes dinner arrangements for *shabbat*. Open Sun.-Thurs. 9am-6pm, Fri. 10am-3pm.

Jewish Students Information Center: 5 Beit El, Jewish Quarter (tel. 28 83 38). Similar to the Heritage Center. Has nightly movies, programs, and seminars. There is a library and tape collection as well as a phone message service. Free tours with Jeff Seidel at 3pm on Sun.-Tues., Thurs., and Sat. at 4:45pm. Places travelers in Heritage House as well, and with Jewish families on *shabbat*.

Lifshitz Information Center: above the Cardo in the Jewish Quarter (tel. 28 18 27). Specializes in the Jewish Quarter and Jewish sights in the Old City. Sells Aharon Bier's map (NIS1.50) and the excellent guide, *Quartertour: Walking Tour of the Jewish Quarter* (NIS3.70). Don't buy Amir's map here; get it free at the GTIO. Open Sun.-Thurs. 10am-4pm, Fri. 10am-1pm.

Society for the Protection of Nature (SPN, HaHevra LeHaganat HaTeva): 13 Helena Ha-Malka St. (tel. 22 23 57). "Off-the-Beaten-Track" tours in Jerusalem and the rest of the country as well. Guides speak excellent English, so investigate their field seminars on botany and wildlife. The store sells guidebooks (including *Quartertour*), maps, and camping equipment. Open Sun.-Mon. and Wed. 9am-3:45pm, Tues. 9am-4:45pm, Thurs. 9am-5:45pm, Fri. 9am-12:30pm.

Budget Travel: ISSTA, 5 Eliashar St. (tel. 22 72 57). From Jaffa Rd., turn up Eliashar St. at the bright yellow sign 1 block from Zion Sq. toward the Old City. ISIC costs NIS15; bring proof of student status and a photo from the shop around the corner on Jaffa Rd. Services include student discounts on flights to Europe, buses and flights to Cairo, car rentals, and Eurail passes. Not always the best deal in town. Open Sun.-Tues. and Thurs. 8:30am-1pm and 3-6pm, Wed. and Fri. 8:30am-1pm. Also on Mt. Scopus next to the Rothberg School in the Goldschmidts Building.

Consulates: U.S., 18 Agron St. in New City (tel. 23 42 71) and on Nablus Rd. in East Jerusalem (tel. 28 22 31). Open Mon.-Fri. 8:30-1pm, closed Israeli and U.S. holidays. **U.K.,** Rajib St. near Sheikh Jarrah in East Jerusalem (tel. 28 24 81 or 28 24 82). **Australian and Canadian** embassies in Tel Aviv. No **New Zealand** embassy in Israel.

Banks: Bank Leumi, main office on Jaffa Rd. next to the post office. Open Sun.-Thurs. 8:30am-1:30pm, Fri. 8:30am-noon. Branch offices of **Leumi, HaPoalim,** and **Israel Discount** throughout the city are open Sun., Tues., and Thurs. 8:30am-12:30pm and 4-6pm, Mon. and Wed. 8:30am-12:30pm, Fri. 8:30am-noon. Offices of **First International** are open Sun., Wed.-Thurs. 8:30am-2pm, Mon.-Tues. 8:30am-2pm and 4-7pm, Fri. 8:30am-noon.

American Express: Meditrad, Ltd., 27 King George St. (tel. 22 22 11) at the corner of Ben Yehudah St. You cannot get money wired here. Open Sun.-Tues. and Thurs. 8:30am-1pm and 3:30-6pm, Wed. and Fri. 8:30am-1pm.

Post Office: 23 Jaffa Rd. (tel. 24 47 45). Main section open Sun.-Thurs. 8am-6pm, Fri. 8am-1pm. Poste Restante open Sun.-Thurs. 8am-1pm and 4-6pm, Fri. 8am-noon. **Telegrams** in the main building or dial 171. NIS1.30 per word to U.S., NIS1.10 per word to Britain, NIS1.50 per word to Australia and New Zealand. A letter telegram takes 24 hours instead of 12 hr. but costs half the price. Information desk in main section open 24 hours for express letters (usually very cheap), telegrams and telex for a hefty additional charge. After midnight (except on *shabbat*), ring the doorbell, though it may take a while for someone to wake up. Branch offices throughout the city (ask for the *DOE-ar*). Facsimile and Telex also available. Turn right from main entrance.

Post Office Parcel Service: 23 Jaffa Rd., around the building to the right. Sun., Tues., and Thurs. 7:45am-12:30pm and 3:30-6pm, Mon. and Wed. 7:45am-2pm, Fri. 7:45am-1pm. Special rates for books. Keep boxes open to be searched and bring tape to seal them.

International Telephones: 1 Koresh St., in back of the post office. Open Sun.-Thurs. 7am-8:30pm, Fri. 7am-1:30pm. For collect calls from a pay phone dial (03) 62 28 81, (03) 62 28 82, or (03) 62 28 83. When Jerusalem or any place outside the Tel Aviv (03) area code, give the operator your area code and number. The operator will call you back and take the information (thus you need only 1-2 *asimonim*). From a private phone, dial 18 for operator assisted calls. Don't lose heart if they're all busy.

Telephone Code: 02.

Flight information: for last minute schedule changes on all airlines, call (03) 971 24 84. **El Al** has an advance check-in procedure for Jerusalem: Bags for morning flights can be checked in and inspected the night before. For El Al information and flight confirmation, call 24 67 25. (7:30am-11:30pm) or stop by the office at 12 Hillel St. Buses to Ben Gurion Airport leave from the central bus station, but for early morning flights you may want to pay the extra for a *sherut*.

Central Bus Station (Tahanah Merkazit): Jaffa Rd. (tel. 52 82 31), west of the city center. General information, posted lists of destinations and fares, and ticket windows to the right as you enter. The staff speaks English but is rushed. 10% discount with ISIC and passport. Buses to Tel Aviv (every 10 min., NIS4.80), to Haifa (roughly every 20 min. until 8pm, NIS8.50), to Ben Gurion Airport (every ½ hr. 6am-8pm, NIS4.30), and to Eilat (Sun.-Thurs. 7am, 10:30am, 2pm, and 5pm; Fri. 7am, 10am, and 1pm; NIS15.50, round-trip NIS24.) **Baggage check** across the street, NIS2.50 per item per day. Open Sun.-Thurs. 7am-5pm, Fri. 7am-3pm.

Arab Bus Stations: Suleiman St. Station, in East Jerusalem between Herod's and Damascus Gates, serves routes south. Bus #23 to Hebron (every 10 min. until 8pm, NIS1.50), #22 to Bethlehem (every 15 min. until 7pm, NIS1), #28 to Jericho (every 20 min., NIS1.80), and #36 to Bethany (every ½ hr., NIS.50). **Nablus Rd. Station** serves points north. Bus #18 to Ramallah (NIS1), #23 to Nablus (NIS2.50). On Sat., Arab buses go up Nablus Rd. to Mt. Scopus, and down Hebron and Bethlehem Rd. to the train station, Talpiyot, and Ramat Rahel. Flag down the one you wish to board.

Train Station: Remez Sq. (tel. 71 77 64), just southwest of the Old City at the southern end of King David St. From downtown, take bus #5, 6, or 8. One train per day to Haifa via B'nei Berak, a suburb of Tel Aviv (Sun.-Thurs. 4pm, Fri. 11:30am, NIS7, students NIS5.30).

Taxis (within Jerusalem): Ben Yehudah Taxi, Herbert Samuel St. (tel. 22 55 55), **Citadel Taxi,** Jaffa Gate (tel. 28 43 34), among many others. On the street, hold out your hand horizontally and you should get one.

Intercity *Sherut* Taxis: Intercity rates are fixed between cities for communal *sherut* taxis. 2 pieces of luggage are included in the fare. **HaBirah,** 1 HaRav Kook St. (tel. 22 45 45), and

Kesher-Aviv, 12 Shammai St. (tel. 22 73 66), run taxis Sun.-Fri. afternoons to Kikar Ha-Moshavot in Tel Aviv (NIS5 per person; Fri. nights and Sat. NIS6) and to Haifa (NIS9.50). **Yael Daroma,** next door to Kesher-Aviv (tel. 22 69 85), sends cars to Eilat (NIS20) and Be'ersheva; reservations necessary. Another *sherut* stand at 226 Jaffa Rd. (tel. 53 33 33) behind the central bus station (walk through main station entrance and bear left) sends cars to Tel Aviv and Ashdod. **Nesher,** 21 King George St. (tel. 23 12 31) goes to Ben Gurion Airport. Reserve in advance, and confirm the night before. $4.50 from Nesher, $6.50 from youth hostel, more if paid in shekels. **Parcel delivery** is also available.

English Bookstores: Steimatzky's, 39 Jaffa Rd., 9 King George St., on the Cardo in the Old City, and at 40 Emek Refaim St. Eclectic and extensive selection at import prices. **Yalkut,** 1 Helena HaMalka St. (tel. 22 27 86), has the best selection of used books. Open Sun.-Thurs. 8am-7pm, Fri. 8am-1:30pm. **Sefer VeSefel,** 2 Ya'Avetz St., near corner of 49 Jaffa Rd.; 3rd door on the right and up the stairs. Used and new books and magazines on a variety of topics. Browse on the patio while eating homemade ice cream. Open Sun.-Wed. 8am-10:30pm, Thurs. 8am-11:30pm, Fri. 8am-3pm, and Sat. nights. **The Bookshelf,** 44 Habad St. above the Cardo, Jewish Quarter. Buys and sells English, French, and German used books. Open Sun.-Thurs. 10am-2pm, Fri. 10am-1pm.

Laundromats: Superclean Rehavia, 26 Ussishkin St., in a lovely residential neighborhood. Slightly cheaper than others. Take bus #19 from the city center. **Superclean Geulah,** 1 Ezer Yoldot St., closest to East Jerusalem. Walk west from the intersection of Mea Sh'arim and Strauss; it's in the first alley on the left. **Bakah Washmatic,** 35 Emek Refaim. Take bus #4, 14, or 18 from the city center, get off at the Emek Refaim post office, and cross the street; it's a ½ block farther down. Prices generally NIS4.30 per wash, NIS2 for soap, NIS1.30 per 10 min. of drying. All close early on Fri. for *shabbat*.

Swimming Pools: A list of pools is published in the free *Kol Ha'Ear* newspaper (in Hebrew). The GTIO list is unreliable, so call before you go anywhere. The cheapest pools are **Beit Taylor** (tel. 41 43 62), in Qiryat Yovel, open daily 9am-5pm (bus #18 or 24) and **Jerusalem Swimming Pool,** Emek Refaim St. (tel. 63 20 92), open daily 8am-5pm (bus #4 or 18). Admission at both Sun.-Fri. NIS3, Sat. NIS7.

Film Developing: Photo HaBirah at 91 Jaffa Rd. and **Half Hour Photo** 1 King George St. Both (and most other stores) charge NIS.45 per picture.

Rape Crisis Center: Tel. 24 55 54. 24 hours. English is spoken. They will accompany you to the police and explain procedures.

Mental Health Hotline: Tel. 22 71 71. Called Eran-Emotional First Aid. English is spoken. Assists tourists.

Services for the Disabled: Yad Sarah Organization, 43 Nevi'im St. (tel. 24 42 42). Loans of medical equipment for the disabled. Free, but deposit of full value required. Very helpful.

Ticket Agencies: Cahana, 1 Dorot Rishonim St. (tel. 24 45 77), **Ben Naim,** 38 Jaffa Rd. (tel. 23 12 73), and **Klaim,** 8 Shammai St. (tel. 72 84 63). All sell Sat. tickets to museums and cultural events before *shabbat* begins.

Medical Emergency: Tel. 101. Look for **Magen David Adom** (Israeli Red Cross) next to the central bus station or inside Dung Gate in the Old City (tel. 52 31 33). Newspapers list hospitals and pharmacies on duty for emergencies.

First Aid for Tourists: Bikur Holim, Strauss St., the continuation of King George St. past Jaffa Rd. (tel. 22 67 86). In case of **tear gas** do *not* put water on your face—the chemical reaction will then make your whole face burn, not just your tears.

Tourist Police: Inside Jaffa Gate, to the right (tel. 27 32 22, ext. 33 or 34). English, German, and French are among the languages spoken.

Police: (tel. 100). Russian Compound, off Jaffa Rd. Inside Jaffa Gate to your right in the Old City.

Accommodations and Camping

The accommodation options in Jerusalem are as rich and varied as the city itself. Even if you cannot afford to stay in Henry Kissinger's room at the King David Hotel, you will find plenty of hostels and hospices that will welcome you in all parts of the city. If you want to enjoy Jerusalem's nightlife, you'll need an 11pm curfew at the earliest. Most hostels operate year-round and, though prices do not automatically drop in the off-season, you can bargain more successfully then. If tourism continues to fall, you should have no problem bargaining hotel prices down as well. Accommodations in private houses are another option. Locals may approach you at the bus station, but be aware that their places may not be licensed, and thus not subject to government inspection. As with all Israel, you save the 15% tax if you pay in dollars.

If you'll be living in Jerusalem for over two months, consider renting an **apartment,** especially for July and August when many Israeli students are on vacation. A single room in a shared flat will cost $150 and up per month. The best source of information is the classified section of *Kol Ha'Ear*—find a friend to translate, and submit an ad of your own requesting a flat. Classified ads are free. Also thorough, though more expensive, the **Sh'al Service,** 21 King George St. (tel. 22 44 56 or 22 47 57) grants two months' access to its voluminous listings in English for NIS20 (open Sun.-Thurs. 8:30am-1pm and 4-7pm, Fri. 8:30am-noon). The bulletin boards at Hebrew University and upstairs at the Israel Center on the corner of Strauss and HaNevi'im St. may be helpful as well.

New City

The New City is convenient to the commercial center, and is probably safer. It's also the best place for after-dark entertainment, the streets become one big smorgasbord of eateries, theaters, and cultural centers.

Bernstein Youth Hostel (IYHF), 1 Karen HaYessod St. (tel. 22 82 86), at the corner of Agron, near the Plaza Hotel. A 10-min. walk south on King George St. from the center of town, or take bus #7, 8, or 14 from the central bus station. Reading room, coffeehouse, courtyards, and an air-conditioned dining room that serves large kosher meals. You can work six hours per day in exchange for free bed and meals, but one month commitment is required. Booked solid July through mid-Aug., so call ahead. Office open 7-9am and 5-7pm; luggage check-in during day. No check-out Sat. Curfew 11pm with 20-min. grace period. Members NIS16.50, nonmembers NIS18. Breakfast NIS6 and meals, on request, NIS9.80.

Hotel Zephaniah, 4 Zephaniah St. (tel. 27 27 09 or 28 63 84). From the intersection of Jaffa and King George, walk up Strauss Rd. to Mea Sh'arim Rd. (where Strauss turns into Yehezkel St.), then continue straight 3 blocks to Zephaniah. Or take bus #4 or 9 from the city center or #27 or 39 from opposite the central bus station (6 stops); get off at Yehezkel St. at the Zion orphanage. A converted 3-story apartment building near Mea She'arim in a very Orthodox neighborhood—dress modestly or be harassed. A great area for women who are sick of other types of harassment. Funny, friendly management provides lots of information about getting around the city. Pristine and pleasant, with new bathrooms, refrigerators, color TV room, pay phone, kitchen, storage, and safe. Some doubles have refrigerators. Arrive early to secure a room. Curfew 1am. Dorm beds NIS5-6, doubles NIS27, triples NIS33. Breakfast NIS2.50.

King George Youth Hostel, 15 King George St. (tel. 22 34 98). Soon-to-be the **Arc Hostel,** after a beautiful wall painting in the lounge. Once wild and woolly, this hostel has changed management and style. Where beer once flowed, tea and coffee are now available. Kitchen with pans. Lounge. Clean, but old. Prime location at city center. Dorm beds NIS7 in July-Aug. NIS9. Breakfast NIS2.20. Laundry NIS4.

Edison Youth Hostel, at Yeshayahu and Belilius St. (tel. 38 51 33). From the intersection of Jaffa and King George, walk 1 block up Strauss, take the first left on HaNevi'im, first right up Yeshayahu; hostel is around the second corner on the right, opposite the Edison Cinema. Cramped, but friendly. Refrigerator, safe, bar and free luggage storage for guests. Nightly video movies. Management helps travelers find temporary jobs, and can arrange apartment rentals throughout Jerusalem for longer periods. No curfew. Dorm beds NIS8, doubles NIS32 (bargainable). Breakfast NIS2. Laundry about NIS5.

Jasmine Bed and Breakfast, 3 Even Sapir St. at the corner of Bezalel St. (tel. 23 47 01). Take bus #17 from central bus station. A nice place in a quiet neighborhood right near the center of town. Kitchen with lots of pots. Pleasant coutyard. No curfew; every guest is given a key to the locked front gate. Dorm beds NIS7.

Beit Shmuel Guest House (IYHF), 13 King David St., behind Hebrew Union College (tel. 20 34 55, until 4pm). Designed by renowned architect Moshe Safdie as an international center for the Reform Judaism movement, this two-year-old hostel is really a hotel. Lounges, courtyard, member's kitchen, coffee shop. Disabled access and elevator. A/C. April-Sept. dorm beds NIS30.40, beds in doubles NIS53.20, beds in triples NIS47.50; Oct.-March dorm beds NIS24.70, beds in doubles NIS43.70, beds in triples NIS38.

Hotel Nogah, 4 Bezalel St. (tel. 22 45 90 until 1pm, 66 18 88 after). Bright white sheets and bright white walls. Great location and good facilities: refrigerator, gas range, utensils, sparkling shower, and bath. This small hotel consists of 4 airy rooms and a porch. If you get the porch couch (bathroom attached) it's NIS12 per night. Doubles NIS30, triples NIS40, quads NIS46.

Hotel Eretz Yisrael, 51 King George St. (tel. 24 50 71). Walk out of the center of town on King George, and look for big yellow sign on 2 tree poles with name, just before the Plaza Hotel. Very peaceful. Run by a religious couple who take pride in their hotel's well-deserved reputation as one of the cleanest inexpensive establishments in the New City. Free tea and coffee. Excellent mattresses. Free luggage storage and use of refrigerator, but no kitchen. Unmarried couples will be refused a room. No new guests accepted during *shabbat.* Dorm beds for single-sex groups of 3 or more, NIS17. If you're alone you must pay the price of a single, NIS33. Doubles NIS50.

Geffen Hotel, 4 HaHavatselet St. (tel. 22 40 75 or 22 57 54). Across from Zion Sq. Neat beds in cheerful rooms. Lounge, TV, radio, and refrigerator. Free tea and coffee. Singles NIS33, doubles NIS45, triples NIS60. 10% discount for more than 1 night.

The International Youth Hostel, 35 Ussishkin St. Take bus #17 from central bus station or bus #19 from Jaffa Gate. Close to supermarket and laundromat. TV room, kitchen. Women should not stay here, nor should men who don't want to encourage harassment. The manager, Itzik, was being sued on sexual harassment charges by 3 different women during the summer of 1988. Don't let the beautiful neighborhood and calm exterior fool you. If management changes, this could be a great hostel; it's worth checking. But avoid Itzik (short, dark-skinned, smelling heavily of cologne) at all costs. Curfew 12:30am. Dorm bunks NIS6.

Old City

If there are ongoing protests by Palestinians, it is unwise to stay in Arab areas, but Jerusalem's cheapest and some of its most comfortable hostels are located within the Old City. The views from the rooftops and balconies and proximity to major sights will compensate for the cries of the *muezzins* at the crack of dawn. Lodgings cluster near Jaffa and Damascus Gates. Lodgings in the Jaffa Gate area are cleaner, safer, and more accessible from the New City. Walk down Jaffa Rd. or Agron St. to the end or take bus #1, 3, 13, 19, 20, or 80. The hotels and hostels in the Damascus Gate area are cheaper and livelier because they are in the middle of the Arab *souk.* If business seems slow, and the hostel is empty, you can bargain for a lower price. In the wake of the *intifadah,* this is not the place to announce your support of Israel. You can reach Damascus Gate by walking down to the end of HaNevi'im St. or by taking bus #27. Avoid walking alone through the Damascus Gate area after the markets close, and be cautious about leaving valuables and luggage unattended in Old City hotel rooms. Only the busiest streets in the Old City are lighted at night, and getting lost in the pitch-dark alleys can be alarming, so learn the way back to your hostel during the day.

Near Jaffa Gate

Old City Youth Hostel (IYHF), 2 Ararat St. (tel. 28 86 11). Go down David St. into the market and follow the signs right on St. Mark's Rd., right again across from the Lutheran Hostel, up the narrow street with half-arches. Clean, airy, and safely located in a renovated hospital. Nice lounge and refrigerator but no kitchen. Usually crowded with school groups and soldiers. Check-in 5-9pm, closed 9am-5pm. Strict 11pm curfew. NIS10, breakfast NIS4.50.

Christ Church Hospice, al-Khattab Rd. (P.O. Box 10437; tel. 28 20 82). As you enter Jaffa Gate, take the right around the Citadel; the gate is on your left before the post office. Immaculately neat, and the safest place to stay in the Old City. Dorm rooms of six with adjoining toilets and shower. The Anglican Church gives you a taste of home with bookshelves and drawers under the bed. The peaceful courtyard makes up for the lack of a kitchen. Prices drop during low season (Jan. until Easter), but dorms may close. Children (2-12) stay in parents' room for half price. Outsiders welcome for lunch NIS8, and dinner NIS11. Dorms closed 10am-3pm. Gate locked at 11pm. Dorm beds NIS12.80, singles in guest house NIS28. Breakfast included.

Lutheran Youth Hostel, St. Mark's Rd. (P.O. Box 1405; tel. 28 21 20). Enter Jaffa Gate, cross the square, turn right onto al-Khattab and left onto Maronite Convent Rd.; turn right at St. Mark's Rd., and the hostel is down the road to your left. A superb hostel, with spacious, spotless bedrooms, bathrooms, and kitchen. Friendly, considerate clientele. Fish pond in the lush garden. Arrive early to get a place. Closed 9am-noon. Tight 10:45pm curfew. Dorm beds NIS9, doubles in guest house NIS43. Breakfast included.

Citadel Youth Hostel, St. Mark's Rd. (tel. 28 62 73). Follow direction to Lutheran Hostel; Citadel is before it on your right. Somewhat cramped bedrooms, with a kitchen and TV room. Interesting architecture. A great deal. Open 7am-midnight. Dorm beds NIS5, doubles NIS15.

Alice's Rush Inn Hostel, 42 St. Mark's Rd. (tel. 27 35 29), on the way to the Lutheran Hostel. Beds in cramped bedrooms with equally compact bathrooms and kitchen. The manager may find you at Jaffa Gate. Midnight curfew. Dorm beds NIS5.

New Swedish Hostel, 29 David St. (tel. 85 49 20) Clean, but only one toilet and shower for each sex. Budget boat and plane tickets available. Kitchen and TV room. Women should be careful about staying this deep into the market. Stay six nights and the seventh is free. NIS5, students NIS4.50.

Mr. A's, 27 St. Girges St. (tel. 28 39 82). From Jaffa Gate, take a left onto Greek Patriarchate Rd., then a right onto St. Girges, past the jeweler, shoemaker, and tailor to a small, unmarked brown door on the right. Quiet with a tiny courtyard and a delightful manager who may be waiting on the steps. Laundry, sink, showers, and meager kitchen with a refrigerator. Closed 9am-1pm. 9:30pm curfew, so ask for a key. Bed in a small, cluttered room NIS5.

Knights Palace Hotel, Latin Patriarchate Rd. (tel. 28 25 37). From Jaffa Gate, take your first left; it's a few hundred meters down near New Gate. A converted monastery with large, spotless rooms. Victorian atmosphere with polite management. Singles NIS30, doubles NIS51. Breakfast included.

Lark Hotel, Latin Patriarchate Rd. Compact, but clean. An Armenian restaurant on the first floor is run by the same family. Reception closed on Sunday. Singles, doubles, and triples NIS22.50 per person, students NIS15. Continental breakfast included.

Jaffa Gate Youth Hostel, on al-Khattab St. at the entrance to the market; look for their sign. Cavernous yet crowded rooms with cots. Kitchen, fridge, and lots of showers. Open all day, midnight curfew. Dorm beds NIS5, doubles NIS15.

New Imperial Hotel, near Jaffa Gate (tel. 28 22 61). Take the second left inside the gate—you'll see the sign. Huge, noisy, and cheerless. Oriental rugs and the sitting rooms are a nice touch. Accept the grungy bathrooms and musty odor—you can't beat the price, especially if you bargain. Singles NIS15, doubles NIS30. Breakfast included.

Petra Hostel, on your left on David St., right before you enter the *souk*. Great location with balconies overlooking al-Khattab Sq. Run-down with beat-up foam mattresses. You can do better elsewhere for less. Open 6am-midnight. Dorm beds NIS10. Breakfast NIS2.50.

Near Damascus Gate

Ecce Homo Convent, Eastern Via Dolorosa (tel. 28 24 45). Turn left onto Via Dolorosa from al-Wad Rd.; the small "Notre Dame de Sion" sign is down the road on the door on the left. Beds in cubicles with wooden partitions and curtains. Very clean. Kitchen and study area for guests. Organ music and plain chant reverberate through the stone hallways. Passageway to rooms overlooks the Second Station of the Cross. A quiet and meditative place, undoubtedly the safest hostel for women in the Old City. Cleaning from 10am-noon; you're encouraged to step out then. Strict 10pm curfew. Reception closed Sun. Dorm beds (for women only) NIS8, small singles and doubles for men or women about NIS30 per person. Breakfast included.

Armenian Catholic Patriarchate, al-Wad Rd. (tel. 28 42 62). Enter under the "Armenian Patriarchate" sign just after Via Dolorosa on your left as you walk about 200m down al-Wad from Damascus Gate. Clean, plain, safe, and well-kept. Unmarried couples will be turned away. Open during Christmas. Luggage storage for several days while you travel. From 1-3pm is rest time when you may leave, but cannot enter. Strict 10pm curfew. Dorm beds NIS8. Doubles NIS30, with shower NIS38.

Al-Ahram Hostel, al-Wad Rd. (tel. 28 09 26). Enter Damascus Gate and bear left onto al-Wad at the fork; opposite the third station of Via Dolorosa. Large and fairly comfortable.

Once hectic, but presently calm in the face of recent politics. Kitchen, fridge, and nice rooftop lounge. Midnight curfew. Bed on the roof NIS4.50; dorm beds NIS6. Pleasant private rooms with separate showers NIS25 per person, but bargain down to NIS20.

Al-Arab, Khan ez-Zeit Market Rd. (tel. 28 35 37). From Damascus Gate, bear right onto Khan ez-Zeit; it's on the left, just past the New Hotel. The sign also reads Old City Youth Hostel (but it's not the IYHF Hostel). Colorful interior in the TV and sitting room; stale air in the bedrooms. Kitchen and showers. Midnight curfew. Dorm beds NIS5.

JOC Inn and Teahouse, 21 al-Khanqa St. (P.O. Box 14036; tel. 28 28 65). From Damascus Gate, bear right onto Khan ez-Zeit Market, then turn right onto al-Khanqa St. Dusty bedrooms, banged-up bathrooms, cluttered living room, and a tea room blasting American tunes until the midnight curfew. The minaret next door blasts the call to prayer a few hours later. Dorm beds NIS4.

Tabasco Youth Hostel and Tea Room, 8 Aqabat al-Takiyeh, the first left off Khan ez-Zeit after Via Dolorosa as you walk in from Damascus Gate. Unsafe area for women alone. Clean, slightly musty rooms. Semi-functional bathrooms and no kitchen. Dorm beds NIS7. Free tea.

Jewish Quarter

Heritage House, for men at 10 HaShoarim St. (tel. 28 79 21), for women at 7 HaMalakh St. (tel. 28 18 20). Clean and comfortable, with washing machines and a kitchen, but for Jewish travelers only. Amazingly enough, it's *free*—you just have to put up with proselytism and strict observance of *halachah* (Jewish law). Sun.-Thurs. closed 9am-5pm, midnight curfew (11pm in winter). Fri. closed 9am-2:30pm and 6-9pm, 11pm curfew. Sat. closed 10am-2:30pm, 11pm curfew.

East Jerusalem

East Jerusalem may well be unsafe during times of Palestinian-Israeli tension, but it is ideal for those who want to experience life in an Arab country without leaving Israel. In early summer a large all-night **watermelon market** occupies one side of HaNevi'im St., and the nearby Arab **bakeries** are wonderful for midnight *bagelah* runs and other kinds of snack attacks. Since East Jerusalem lacks the history of the Old City and the conveniences of the New City, good values in accommodations can be found. Women should be careful walking alone at night in East Jerusalem. Four hostels line HaNevi'im St., which intersects with Suleiman St. and Nablus Rd. by the Damascus Gate.

Ramsis Youth Hostel, 20 HaNevi'im St. (tel. 28 48 18). Big windows and high ceilings. Large lounge with TVs. Nice, philosophical manager. Some rooms have balconies. Free storage, fridge, hot pot, and dishes for guests. Dorm beds NIS7, singles NIS15, doubles NIS20.

Faisal Youth Hostel, 4 HaNevi'im St. (tel. 28 21 89). Once a hippie haven, now has new image. Range, fridge, pots, pans, spices, tea, coffee, and storage available for use. Gorgeous view of Damascus Gate from balcony. Clean. Book exchange and Ping Pong. Closed 10:30am-1pm. Midnight curfew. Dorm beds NIS7, singles and doubles a steal at NIS8 per person.

Palm Hotel, 6 HaNevi'im St. Clean rooms, decent beds, and a pleasant lounge full of plants. Minimalist showers. A large collection of Christian books in the living room. Courteous management and a kitchen for guests. No unmarried couples. Dorm beds NIS6, doubles or triples NIS8 per person.

New Raghadan Hostel, 10 HaNevi'im St. (tel. 28 27 25). Easygoing atmosphere with a collection of kitschy art. Cluttered but clean. Balcony, dining and sitting rooms with a TV and VCR, kitchen, and even a washing machine. Curfew 11pm, but keys are available for late nights out. Dorm beds NIS7, singles NIS15, doubles NIS20.

Jerusalem Hotel, 4 Antara Ben Shaddad St. (P.O. Box 20606; tel. 28 32 82). From Damascus Gate, walk up Nablus Rd.; it's the first corner to the left, just past the bus station. Luxurious, modern rooms, pleasant courtyard, and exceptionally friendly management. Luggage and valuables storage for several days. Bargain if business looks slow. Try to reserve in summer. No curfew, but tell the manager if you plan to return late. NIS18 per person with bath. Breakfast included.

Suburbs of West Jerusalem

If you want a quieter, more scenic refuge, there are pleasant IYHF hostels in the hills surrounding Jerusalem. Lodgings listed here are 15 to 30 minutes by bus from the center of town.

Louis Waterman Wise Hostel (IYHF), 8 Pisgah Rd., Bayit VeGan (tel. 42 33 66). Take bus #18 or 20 to Mt. Herzl. A large, clean, beautiful hostel with a good reputation, located in a safe neighborhood. Kitchen, but no utensils. Curfew midnight. Members NIS18.50, non-members NIS20.50. Breakfast included. Highly praised dinners NIS8 (dairy), NIS10 (meat).

Ein Kerem Youth Hostel (IYHF), off Ma'ayan St. (P.O. Box 17013; tel. 41 62 82). Take bus #17 to Ein Kerem, turn left on Ma'ayan St., and hike up the path past Mary's fountain. One of the most beautiful neighborhoods near Jerusalem. You'll be lucky to find a bed here in the summer, but it's worth a try. No curfew, but buses stop running about 11:20pm. Members NIS16, nonmembers NIS18. Breakfast NIS3.30, lunch NIS7, dinner NIS10.

Camping

The campsites around Jerusalem are beautifully situated and have excellent facilities, but they're also expensive. All have hot showers and telephones. Two-to-four person bungalows are available for about NIS15 per person. Although none of the campgrounds has kitchens, all will let you use a camp stove without charge. For more details on camping throughout Israel, pick up the pamphlet "Israel Chalets and Camping" from the tourist office.

Ramat Raḥel Camping, 2km from central Jerusalem (tel. 71 57 12). Take bus #7. Owned by Kibbutz Ramat Raḥel. You must bring a tent. Open 7am-midnight. NIS9 per person. Breakfast NIS5. Use of *kibbutz* swimming pool NIS6.

Beit Zayit Camping, Har Nof (tel. 53 77 17; mailing address: M.P. Harei Yehudah), 6km west of Jerusalem. Take bus #51 (10 per day) direct from the central bus station to Beit Zayit, the last stop. Tell driver you want the pool. To avoid a long wait, take bus #11 or 15A which leave every 15 min. from in front of *Binyene Ha'Ooma* at the central bus station. Ask the driver to tell you when the bus enters Har Nof, and get off at the playground. A sign in English points to a trail that leads to the campsite (10-min. hike). At night, avoid the trail and take bus #51. Free use of refrigerator, very helpful management. Swimming pool NIS4. Camping mid-July-Aug. NIS6 per person, children under 13 NIS3. Off-season NIS4.50 per person, children under 13 NIS1.50. After 4 nights, the pool is free.

Mevo Beitar Camping (tel. 91 24 74 or 91 37 91; mailing address: M.P. Ha'Ela), 15km south-west of Jerusalem. Take bus #93 (7-8 per day) from the central bus station. Owned by Moshav Mevo Beitar. Small mini-market on site, restaurant open all day. Free use of pool. July-Aug: NIS9, children NIS5; Sept.-June NIS5, children NIS3.

Food

Plunge into the spices, aromas, and tastes of the Middle East, Eastern Europe, India, China, Morocco, and Yemen. For Israelis, dining out is a luxury deserving of time and money. If your budget is tight, then felafel may become your staple. Jerusalem caters to the vegetarian with plenty of dairy spots. Many eating places close Friday afternoon and reopen Saturday night, so you may want to join Israelis who stock-up at the markets on Thursday and Friday mornings. **Maḥaneh Yehudah** is an especially lively place. Some restaurants in the New City and many places in East Jerusalem are open Saturday. Pick up the *Jerusalem Post* "Good Food Guide" from the tourist office and ask about dinner with an Israeli family. A new service started in 1988 matches up interested tourists with host families. You'll taste Israeli culture and get a free meal, but you must give tourist office 24 hours notice.

Markets

The most economical way to fill up is to buy your own food at outdoor markets. In the Old City, two cavernous Crusader rooms on the left side of David St., as you walk down from Jaffa Gate, house a 1000-year-old fresh fruit and vegetable market. Stands nearby have platters of Middle Eastern and Turkish candies. Basic provisions such as milk, bread, and chocolate spread may be purchased from small shops that dot the *shuk*. The cheapest food is sold in the New City markets of **Mahaneh Yehudah,** between Jaffa Rd. and Agrippas St., to the west of the city center. Fruit and vegetable stands line the streets, and there's a small grocery store (*mahkolet*) with rock-bottom prices at almost every street corner. The Yemenite section, through the alleys leading east from Mahaneh Yehudah St., is the cheapest for produce, and the stalls along Etz HaHayyim St. sell the best *halvah* (ground sesame seed candy) you'll ever taste. On Agrippas, near the intersection with Mahaneh Yehudah, three *mahkolets* specialize in canned goods. Visit the market at closing time (Sat.-Thurs. 7-8pm, Fri. 3-4pm) when merchants lower their prices shekel by shekel to sell off the day's goods. You can bargain but prices are often so low you won't need to. Thursdays and Friday afternoons are busiest in Mahaneh Yehudah as thousands scramble to obtain the food they need for *shabbat*. If you don't want to spend any money at all, just walk through the meat market in the alleys to the west of Mahaneh Yehuda St.—after looking at the dangling ex-animals, you may not want to eat for days. The Supersol supermarkets (in the basement of the HaMashbir department store at the intersection of King George and Ben Yehudah St., and on the corner of Agron and Keren HaYessod St., among others) have good prices on packaged foods (individual yogurts NIS.40, loaf of bread NIS.60). The **Agron Supermarket** is open Sun.-Tues. 8am-midnight, Wed.-Thurs. all night, and Fri. 8am-2:30pm for those with late-night cravings.

New City

Fast food is ubiquitous in Jerusalem, and tends to be both cheaper and healthier than its American counterpart. The best deals are the self-service felafel joints where you can stuff your pita with as much salad as it will hold. Most of these places are on King George between Jaffa and Ben Yehudah, or in Mahaneh Yehudah. Felafel connoisseurs should stop by the tiny **Merkaz HaFelafel HaTeymani** at 48 HaNevi'im St., your first left off Nathan Strauss if you are coming from Rehov Yafo (Jaffa Road, but no English sign). One of the best and cheapest places for *shwarma* (roast lamb on a spit served in pita) is **Meleh HaShwarma VeFelafel** ("Shwarma and Felafel King") on the corner of King George and Agrippas St., where a serving costs NIS4.

For *shishlik* (cubes of meat on a spit), kebab (ground meat on a spit), or steak, head for the grilled meat joints on Agrippas St. west of Mahaneh Yehuda. Meat usually costs about NIS4 in a pita and NIS8 for a plate with fries or salad. **Simma's** at 82 Agrippas St. serves the best steak around, though it's more expensive than others and often packed. **Ema** and **Makam** nearby are less crowded; try the *me'orav* (mixed grilled meats). For inexpensive and delicious fried meats, turkey roll, and salami, amble over to **Merkaz HaNaknik** ("Sausage Center") on Dorot Rishonim St. off Ben Yehudah near Zion Sq.

Jerusalemites take their *hoummus* as seriously as they do their kebabs, and everyone has a favorite place. **Queen's,** on Helena HaMalka St. (second door on the left as you walk up from Jaffa Rd.), serves excellent *hoummus* with felafel and *fuul* (mashed brown beans) for NIS1.50 in a pita, NIS3 on a plate. The walls here are plastered with pictures of Elvis. **Ta'ami** (no English sign), 3 Shammai St., serves fine kebabs, steaks, and Turkish *moussaka,* as well as some of the best *hoummus* in the city (open for lunch only). **Rahmo,** in Mahaneh Yehuda (up Ha'Armonim St. from Agrippas—the corner store on the right) also has good *hoummus*.

Although popular, Jerusalem's pizza is overpriced and rarely good. **Richie's Pizza** on King George is the best of a limp lot; the joint is a famous hangout for Americans. You can leave messages on the bulletin board for fellow travelers who have no telephones. Israelis prefer the cheesy slabs at **Pizzeria Rimini** on King George or Jaffa Rd. During Passover, *matzah* is substituted for dough. Also try the homemade *borekas* (triangular filo pastries with savory fillings) at a small, smoked-glass window (no sign, so look for the Camel cigarette sticker) underneath the department store on Bezalel St.

For more familiar food, visit one of Jerusalem's delis. **Yosil's**, at 16 King George St., directly above Carvel's, has some of the best corned beef and pastrami in town, though it's fairly expensive. The two delis at the bottom of Shammai St. are much cheaper and quite good.

Israeli ice cream tends to be overly sweet, overpriced, and underscooped. The best Israeli brand is **Snowcrest**, sold everywhere. Americans line up at **Carvel's** on King George St. (near the Mashbir department store, across from Richie's Pizza) for a half-decent taste of home. **Sefer VeSefel**, (see Bookstores in Practical Information) churns up the city's best homemade stuff. Their chocolate chip cookie ice cream sandwich (NIS4.50) will satisfy your cravings for the next millenium. During Hannukah season, street stands begin selling hte holiday treats of *sufganiot* (piping hot jelly donuts) for NIS1. **Don't Pass Me By Tea and Pie** on Maalot Nahalat Shiva St., off Jaffa, serves excellent (you guessed it!) tea and pie in relaxing surroundings. For a different kind of sugar high, try the chocolate chip cookies at **Cookie Craze**, 27 Ben Yehudah St. at the intersection with Shmuel HaNagid (tel. 24 51 15). They'll literally melt in your mouth, at 100g (7 or so cookies) for NIS150. (Open Sun.-Thurs. 9am-9pm, Fri. 9am-3pm, Sat. 9pm-midnight.) Another imported delicacy is the eponymous product of **Cheese Cake**, 23 Yoel Solomon St. on the second floor of an old house (tel. 24 50 82). Flavors range from standby plain to coffee and blueberry. (NIS5 per slice. Open Sun.-Thurs. 10:30am-midnight, Fri. 10:30am-3pm.)

Off the Square, 6 Yoel Salomon St. (tel. 24 25 59), off Zion Sq. Popular garden restaurant with a huge menu including vegetarian taste-like-meat dishes, cheese fondue, and "speecy-spicy" eggplant parmigiani. Yogurt soup NIS4, fruit shakes NIS4.50. Open Sun.-Thurs. noon-midnight, Fri. 11am-2pm, Sat. sundown-midnight. The meat restaurant across the street (tel. 22 77 19) is more elegant and more expensive, but just as popular.

Primus, 3 Ya'Avetz St., off Jaffa and across from Sefer VeSefel (tel. 24 65 65). Yemenite dairy restaurant-bar in a hundred-year-old stone building. Delicious *melawah* (thin fried dough) for NIS5. Open Sun.-Thurs. noon-midnight, Sat. sundown-midnight..

Restaurant-Hen Jerusalem, 30 Jaffa Road (tel. 22 73 17). *Shishlik*, kebab, and Kurdish steak—all delicious and very reasonable. Salads (*hoummus, tahina,* and mixed vegetables) NIS3. Open Sun.-Thurs. 9am-6pm, Fri. 9am-3pm.

Sova, 3 HaHistadrut St. at King George St. (tel. 22 22 66). Zero atmosphere but great food and huge meals. Self-service policy allows you to eat on any budget. Newly-expanded separate dairy and meat sections. Try the chickpea-potato-meat-and-vegetable stew or the tasty gefilte fish. Buy tickets in advance for Friday dinner (served until 8pm). Dairy section open Sun.-Thurs. 11am-11pm, Fri. 11am-3pm. Meat section open Sun.-Thurs. 11am-9pm, Fri. 11am-3pm.

Tiho House, off 7 HaRav Kook St. (tel. 24 41 86). Dairy and veggie restaurant set in the garden of artist Anna Tiho's house and free gallery. Delicious cream cheese and raisin crepes (NIS7), large salads and stuffed mushrooms, eggplants and artichokes with cheese, nuts, and rice (NIS10). Restaurant open Sun.-Thurs. 10am-11:45pm, Fri. 10am-3pm, Sat. sundown-11:45pm. Beautiful Tiho Museum is open Sun.-Mon. and Wed.-Thurs. 10am-5pm, Tues. 10am-10pm, Fri. 10am-2pm.

Beit Ha'Omanim (The Artists' House), 12 Shmuel HaNagid, at Bezalel St. (tel. 23 29 20). A quiet bar and restaurant, popular with Israeli students and artists. Good, light meals served in the courtyard. Omelettes for around NIS10. Open Sun.-Thurs. 10am-2am, Fri. 10am-6pm and 9pm-4am, Sat. 11am-2am.

Home Plus, 9 Helena Hamalka St. at the corner of Horkanus St. (tel. 22 26 12). Never-closed coffee-house, bar, and nouveau dairy-fish restaurant upstairs. Menu features pizza, spaghetti, salads, and sandwiches. Open 24 hours.

Besograyim, 45 Ussishkin St. (tel. 24 53 53). Bracketed by a quiet garden setting in a peaceful neighborhood, with white pebbles underfoot and rustling trees above. This dairy cafe/restaurant offers soups and salads with no question marks for reasonable prices (NIS5-11). The salads are exclamation points (from NIS12.50). The name means "in parentheses." Open Sun.-Thurs. 9am-midnight, Fri. 9am-4pm, Sat. 9pm-midnight.

Tavlin, 16 Yoel Salomon St. (tel. 24 38 47). Piped-in classical music and a wood and stucco interior. Soup, salad, bread, and butter (NIS6), good pot pies (NIS10). Open Sun.-Thurs. noon-midnight, Fri. noon-4pm, Sat. sundown-midnight.

Sheshelly, 17 Bezalel St. (tel. 23 18 88). Brand new Israeli restaurant. Try the ever-popular *couscous* with chicken and vegetables (NIS11). Open Sun.-Thurs. noon-12:30am, Fri. noon-4pm, Sat. sundown-12:30am.

Mama Mia's, 18 Rabbi Akiva St. (tel. 24 80 80), off Hillel St. opposite the Jerusalem Towers Hotel; turn right before the end. A change of pace from budget eating. The owner loves to sing Italian folk songs. Delicious *fettuccini a la Mama Mia* for NIS13 and great homemade ravioli. Open noon-midnight, Fri. noon-4pm.

Csardas, 11 Shlomzion HaMalka St. (tel. 24 31 86). New Hungarian restaurant, complete with wall hangings and red tablecloths. Reasonably priced soups (NIS3.50) and goulash (NIS5.50). Open Sun.-Thurs. 10am-10pm, Fri. 10am-3pm.

Alumah, 8 Ya'avetz St. (tel. 22 50 14), off 49 Jaffa Rd. A quiet natural-food restaurant that serves casseroles, soups, fresh juices, and homemade cakes made from stone-ground whole wheat flour. Open Sun.-Thurs. noon-10pm.

Hameshek Vegetarian Restaurant, 14 Shlomzion HaMalka St. (tel. 22 62 78). Full meals of delicious salads, casseroles, and omelettes NIS5-12. Open Sun.-Thurs. 11am-10pm, Fri. 11am-3pm.

The Dikla Restaurant, first floor of Moriah Hotel on Karen HaYessod St. All-you-can-eat salad bar NIS10, with marinated vegetables, prepared salad spreads, and good breads. Omelettes NIS7. If they ask for your room number in this five-star hotel, don't be fazed. They accept everyone. Salad bar open Sun.-Thurs. noon-3pm and 6-10pm.

The Promenade Cafe and Restaurant, (tel. (05) 02 20 51). Part of the promenade overlooking the Old City. Take bus #8 from Jaffa Rd. Watch a sunset from this place, and you'll love Jerusalem for life. Cafe: watermelon NIS4, avocado salad NIS7. Restaurant: meat meals NIS12-20.

Old City and East Jerusalem

In the summer of 1988, most Arab merchants were complying with calls from Palestinian activists to only open shops and restaurants in the morning. The ever-changing political and economic situation of the Palestinians may have altered listed hours and prices since the time of research.

The Old City and East Jerusalem are full of cheap eateries and fast-food joints serving Middle Eastern fare. Many of these places are excellent, but standards of hygiene and refrigeration vary widely. Look before you bite, and be discriminating, especially in East Jerusalem. **Nasser Eddin Bros.** on Suleiman St., across from Damascus Gate and to the right, is a fairly comprehensive market that stocks everything but fresh produce. (Open Mon.-Sat. 8:30am-8:30pm.) Also convenient is **Herbawi Bros.,** on your left as you enter the Old City through Jaffa Gate. **Salah al-Din Street** is lined with restaurants open on Saturday. Although the lines are gone, **Abu Shakri** (200m in from Damascus Gate on al-Wad Rd.) still serves *hummus* plates that never fail to impress. On Sat., when seating expands into the adjacent garden, you can practice the Israeli art of waiting in line. If this happens, head around the corner to **Linda's,** on Via Dolorosa for an equally scrumptious meal. Linda's *hummus* is tangier, and comes with *fuul*—mashed brown beans. Both charge NIS2.50 per plate and if you want your *hummus* without olive oil, say so. The daring can try the popular chicken restaurants on **Khan ez-Zeit** (look for the massive rotisseries). You can also get good *shwarma* opposite the steps leading up to the Ethiopian monastery on the roof of the Church of the Holy Sepulchre. The pizza-like pastries sold at the corner of Saraya and Khan ez-Zeit, around the corner from the church, are delicious. Khan ez-Zeit is lined with sweet-smelling shops selling honey-soaked Arab pastries. The rectangular ones with the corners folded up around crushed almonds are particularly good. Unrequited chocolate lovers should try the triple-decker *halvah* sold along the streets.

The following restaurants are open on Fridays and during Ramadan:

Sea Dolphin, 21 Al-Rashadiah St., East Jerusalem (tel. 28 27 88). The walls and ceiling are covered with nets, crabs, and other marine objects, as well as their many awards. Mostly tourists. 4 stars for friendliness and 4-star prices. Terrific fish soup NIS5. Entrees NIS18. Open daily noon-4pm and 6-11:30pm, despite the strike.

Abu Saif, (tel. 28 68 12) just inside Jaffa Gate, beyond the tourist office. Don't be put off by the tourist-packed location. Great chicken and a wide range of spicy Middle Eastern dishes (NIS8-10). Try their breakfast special for NIS3. On strike; open mornings.

The Green Door, (name coined by students)—go through Damascus Gate and take a sharp left up an alley where the main road forks. A small, bright green door opens into a dirty, cavernous room. The exceedingly friendly Mr. Muhammad Ali has revolutionized pita pizza. Pizza topped with whatever is available NIS2. Here's your chance to have egg pizza, or anything else you want on your pita. Open daily 4am-11pm.

The Coffee Shop, near Jaffa Gate next to the Christ Church Hospice. The most pristine restaurant in the Old City, with pretty tiles of Jerusalem on the tables and walls. Chow down at the all-you-can-eat salad bar (with bread or soup NIS5, with both NIS8). Homemade brownies or cake for NIS2.50. Look for Majeeb's tomato soup. Open despite strike Mon.-Thurs. 8am-8pm, Fri.-Sat. 8am-9pm.

Abu Ali Restaurant, off Salah al-Din St. in East Jerusalem. Walk up Salah al-Din from Herod's Gate and turn right at the sign for Ibrahim Dandis; Abu Ali's on your left. Terrific Middle Eastern food, especially the *tabouleh;* go into the kitchen and point to what you want, and they'll tell you what it costs. On strike.

Quarter Cafe, above the corner of Tiferet Yisrael and HaShoarim St., Jewish Quarter (look for the sign overhead). Thanks to the miracle of self-service, you can eat *moussaka* while gazing at the Mount of Olives without spending a fortune. Salads and cakes NIS3.50, fish dishes NIS5. Open Sun.-Thurs. 8am-6:30pm, Fri. 8am-3pm.

Cardo Self-Service Restaurant, in the Cardo. Walls feature aerial views of the dishes. Spaghetti NIS3, salads NIS2, fillet of sole NIS6.

Philadelphia, az-Zahra St., off Salah al-Din in East Jerusalem. A favorite of locals and highly recommended. Fish and kebab dishes NIS14. Open daily 1-4pm and 6pm-midnight, despite the strike.

Armenian Sandwiches, 37 Christian Quarter St., the third left off David St. from Jaffa Gate. In a small, clean cave lined with a counter and mirrors, the vivacious owner serves an Armenian pizza with lamb for NIS1.50. Armenian burgers and drinks too. On strike.

Oriental Sweet House, 27 Suleiman St. (tel. 27 20 52). A bakery that serves *nafe* (corn flour, cheese, sugar, and oil), *baklava, borma, burriria, sora* and other delicacies. Take out or sit down. Open daily 7am-6pm. On strike.

Sights

Jerusalem is filled with an amazing variety of historical, archeological, and religious sights. While much of the beauty is readily apparent, the legends and history are often best conveyed through some advance reading or a guided tour. The most interesting, unusual, and easy-to-follow guidebook is *Footloose in Jerusalem* (NIS11) by Sarah Fox Kaminker. In addition to several detailed walks in the New and Old Cities, the book provides excellent maps, good descriptions, important historical background, and illustrations. For a more humorous look at Jerusalem, buy *Marty's Walking Tours of Biblical Jerusalem* (NIS7.50). Marty Isaacs outlines itineraries on the Mount of Olives and through the City of David. *Discovering Jerusalem* (NIS35), by Nahman Avigad is a fascinating description of the most recent digs around the Old City, unfortunately available only in hardback. Nitza Rosovsky's *Jerusalemwalks* (NIS26.90) is by far the most thoughtful guide to the city's lesser known avenues and well-worth the price. *Quartertour Walking Tour of the Jewish Quarter* (NIS3.70) is cheaper, more interesting, and more comprehensive than many of the books that describe guided walking tours. *Guide to the Holy Land* (NIS20 at Christian Information Center), written by a Franciscan monk, describes sites of Christian significance in exhaustive historical detail. Architecture buffs will appreciate *The Holyland* (NIS20.70) by Jerome Murphy O'Connor. Finally, athletes should pick up *Carta's Jogger's Guide to Jerusalem* (NIS16.10). The book details runs (or long walks) through historic areas and sights. Most of these books are available in Steimatzky's and other bookstores throughout the city. (See Bookstores in Practical Information.) **Hebrew Union College,** 13 King David St. (tel. 20 33 33), has an air-conditioned library with the latest and most extensive collection of books about Jerusalem. Seek in the Bible and ye shall find much relevant backround to understand the history and religion of Jerusalem (particularly relevant are II Samuel 5, I Kings 3 and 6, II Kings 24-25, Psalms 122 and 137, and the Gospels).

Every Saturday at 10am the Jerusalem municipal government sponsors an excellent free **Shabbat Walking Tour.** The guides are interesting and well-informed. Meet at 32 Jaffa Rd. at the entrance to the Russian Compound, near Zion Sq. *This Week in Jerusalem* lists the itineraries, which are also posted at the municipal information office at 17 Jaffa Rd. Tours last about three hours and can be very crowded. The **Society for the Protection of Nature in Israel (HaHevrah LeHaganat HaTeva)** offers tours daily. SPNI tours usually cost NIS21 for a full day of hiking in the Judean hills or along unusual routes within the city. SPNI also offers unique field seminars on botany and wildlife. The tour guides on their "Off-the-Beaten-Track Walks" lead perhaps the most interesting excursions in and around Jerusalem. Details, schedules, and pamphlets summarizing all the tours are available at SPNI offices and GTIO offices (see Practical Information). Some *shabbat* tours are free.

Two groups offer excellent, in-depth tours of the Old City: **David's "City of David"** (near the police station at Jaffa Gate) has 12 tours. Most are three hours (cost NIS10-12, students NIS7-9, includes admission to all sites). **Archeological Tours and Seminars** offers tours of the Jewish, Muslim, and Christian Quarters, the Temple Mount, the excavations below the Temple Mount, and the City of David. Tours are preceded by a short seminar; tour and seminar together take about two hours and cost NIS8, with a discount if you sign up for three tours. Meet at 34 Habad St., above the Cardo. The tourist office has schedules for both groups. Free tours of Jewish historic and religious sites are offered by **Jeff Seidel,** who is dedicated to giving young Jewish travelers an awareness of what it means to be Jewish in Jerusalem. Jews and non-Jews are welcome on the fast-moving tours. Meet at the women's water fountain to your right as you face the Western Wall (Sun.-Tues. and Thurs. 3pm, Sat. 4:45pm). Jeff also places Jewish travelers with Orthodox families for *shabbat* meals and encourages them to stay at the Heritage House (see Accommodations). You can get more information about Jeff's tours from the Jewish Student Information Center, 5 Beit-El St. in the Jewish Quarter (tel. 28 83 38).

Upon entering holy places you may be approached by guides who offer their services and expect a fee. To save arguments, set a price first—NIS2 should be the limit. Better yet, just wander over to a group that has an official guide and listen in. Group leaders have all completed a two-year certification program and are usually the best informed. Most appreciate interested listeners, so feel free to ask questions.

Most of the holy places in Jerusalem require modest dress. For women, knees and shoulders should be covered; a good solution is to carry a light blouse and skirt at all times, which can be slipped on over your shorts and T-shirt as needed. Many holy places require men to wear long pants. The combination of hot sun and cool wind can dehydrate summertime walkers. A number of the tours cover areas with no water fountains or merchants, so be sure to bring along a canteen. A hat will also help keep you cool and prevent sunstroke.

Old City

The area enclosed by the city walls is only one square kilometer. Mark Twain remarked in *Innocents Abroad* that a fast walker could walk around the city in an hour. However, among its winding alleys and stone courtyards are many of the holy sites of three of the world's major religions, and relics of 3000 years of crowded living. Even when you've been to the sights and tired of the markets, you'll wander down an alley and discover a forgotten community of icon painters or *yeshiva* students.

The present walls of the Old City were built by Suleiman the Magnificent in 1542 C.E. The city had been without walls since 1219, when el-Muazzan tore down the walls so the Crusaders wouldn't get a fortified city. There are eight gates. The **Golden Gate** has been sealed since 1530, blockaded with Muslim graves. It is thought to lie over the Closed Gate of the First Temple, the entrance through which it is said the Messiah will pass (Ezekiel 44:1-3). The seven other gates open onto completely different parts of the city—try to pass through each one during your stay. **Jaffa Gate** is the most convenient entrance from the New City, and is the traditional entrance for pilgrims, there having been a gate here since 135 C.E. **Damascus Gate** serves East Jerusalem, and **St. Stephen's Gate,** also called the Lion's Gate, is the beginning of the Via Dolorosa. **Dung Gate,** first mentioned in 445 B.C.E. by the prophet Nehemiah, opens near the Western Wall, and **Zion Gate** connects the Armenian Quarter with Mount Zion. **Herod's Gate** stands to the east of Damascus Gate, and the **New Gate,** opened in 1889 to facilitate access to the Christian Quarter, lies to the west.

You can walk on all parts of the wall except those surrounding the Temple Mount. Besides providing a great view of the Old City, this walk will give you an idea of the wall's military importance through the centuries. Clearly labelled near Jaffa Gate are the slits for pouring boiling oil on attackers. You can ascend the "ramparts," as the walkway is called, by purchasing tickets at Damascus or Jaffa Gates (tel. 23 12 21). Each ticket is valid for admission four times within two days of the time stamped on your stub. Once you have a ticket in hand, you don't owe a shekel to the self-appointed "guards" who might approach you along the ramparts. Women should *never* walk alone on the walls, even during the day; many cases of sexual assault have been reported, and there's nowhere to run. (Gates open Sat.-Thurs. 9am-5pm, Fri. 9am-3pm. Section between the Citadel and Zion Gate open Sun.-Thurs. 9am-9:30pm. For walks on Sat. or holidays, purchase tickets in advance. Admission NIS2.10, students NIS1.)

To ascend the ramparts from Damascus Gate, you must enter through the ancient carriageway to the left of the plaza and underneath the gate. The original gateway was much taller and extended far below to the bedrock. The level of the carriageways on either side of you corresponds to the middle Roman period in the second century C.E. At the rampart entrance you can visit the **Roman Square Museum,** which is set among the excavations from *Aelia Capitolina,* as Jerusalem was called when the city served as a garrison for Roman Emperor Hadrian's troops. The museum displays a copy of the sixth-century **Madaba map** from Madaba, Jordan; the map is the earliest extant "blueprint" of the city's layout. Note the huge centipede that seems to crawl from Damascus Gate at the northern tip to Dung Gate at the southern; it's actually a two-dimensional rendition of the **Cardo,** the main thoroughfare, and its "feet" are the Roman columns lining the street. The map has aided archeologists in concluding that the Cardo recently unearthed in the Jewish Quarter is not part of the Roman original, but a Byzantine addition. Scholars also discerned a plaza at the gate's entrance with a statue of Hadrian mounted on a huge column. This image reveals the early origins of the Arabic name for Damascus Gate, *Bab al-Amud,* which means "Gate of the Column." The plaza has been partially uncovered, but the black marble column is missing, so you'll have to settle for the hologram on display. The stones on the floor still have the ruts made by Roman chariots. The room on the left as you enter is set into a Herodian flanking tower, which contains an olive press for extracting oil. At the entrance to the museum is a history of the gate, beginning with the gate's initial construction in 135 C.E. (Museum open Mon.-Sun. 9am-5pm. Admission NIS.90, children NIS.45.)

Another good place for orientation and introduction to the history of the Old City is the **Citadel** complex, sometimes called **Migdal David** (the Tower of David), just inside Jaffa Gate and to the left. The citadel resembles a Lego set of overlapping Hasmonean, Herodian, Roman, Byzantine, Muslim, Mamluk, and Ottoman ruins.

Despite the name, nothing dates from David's time. The Tower of David is the highest point in the citadel and the only survivor of three towers built by Herod. Archeologists have not been able to establish conclusively the exact location of the other two. The citadel is a cultural center with outdoor concerts in summer, several exhibits, and an audio-visual presentation of the city's history and cultural composition. The **Museum of Modern Religious Dress** is an ethnographic fashion show, with mannequins donning the dress of Jerusalem's various cultural, religious, and ethnic groups. Also on display is an Ottoman model of the Holy City, which was discovered in an attic in Geneva; the top of the tower is a wonderful vantage point for surveying the real thing. (Citadel open Sat.-Thurs. 8:30am-4:30pm, Fri. 8:30am-2pm.) A **sound and light show** is presented in English from April to November, Saturday through Thursday at 9:30pm (tel. 28 60 79; admission NIS6).

Markets

When you first walk down David St., the entrance to the Old City's markets nearest Jaffa Gate, you'll warily scan piles of gold pendants, *kaffiyehs,* and T-shirts saying "I got stoned in Gaza." Shopkeepers will call you over to take a closer look. Here, brass pitchers and souvenir trinkets sit side by side with oranges and fragrant spices. Bedouin dresses and harem pants hang from the roofs, and animal carcasses dangle from meat-hooks. And despite the dirt, the beggars, and the crowds, the market (*shuk* in Hebrew, *souk* in Arabic) remains truly intriguing.

Although all of the Old City is infested with shops, there are several highly concentrated commercial thoroughfares. **David Street** (Souk el-Bazaar Rd.), and its continuation, **HaShalshelet Street** (Bab el-Silsileh St.), run from Jaffa Gate to the Temple Mount. Halfway down David St. on the left are two cavernous rooms dating from the Second Crusade that house a **fruit and vegetable market** called *Souk Aftimos.* **Khan ez-Zeit** and the three-laned **Armenian market** extend north from David St. to Damascus Gate over the Roman Cardo Maximus, and south to the Cardo's Byzantine addition. This latter section of the **Cardo** has been reconstructed to house a fashionable shopping district in the Jewish Quarter.

Al-Wad Road ("the valley") is a direct connection to the Western Wall area from Damascus Gate. Along al-Wad you'll find sweet shops, vegetable stands, and bakeries, which provide a refreshing change from the junky tourist trinkets. Coming from Damascus Gate, if you take a right off al-Wad onto **Via Dolorosa,** you'll find small, colorful ceramics shops. **Jerusalem Pottery,** an old company run by an Armenian family, supplies many shops with their wares. Their own shop in the market has a larger, more attractive selection of pieces that sport the company logo on the underside—when buying elsewhere, check for the logo to avoid inferior imitations. Just in from the Temple Mount area on **Souk al-Qattanin Street** off al-Wad Rd. is a large covered market where old and exotic clothing is sold. Shops selling icons fill the tiny streets between **Christian Quarter Road** and the Church of the Holy Sepulchre.

As you walk through the market, look up from time to time. Some of the upper stories of the buildings are beautiful, although the ground floors are often concealed behind plastic icons, crowns of thorns, and postcards. Much of the decorative masonry—stone set within stone over entries and passageways—is characteristic of Mamluk architecture. You may notice doorways adorned with paintings of the Dome of the Rock and the Ka'aba, Islam's most sacred shrine. The painting signifies that a member of the family has made *haj,* the pilgrimage to Mecca, and has been to the holy cities of Medina and Jerusalem as well. For a great free view of the markets, walk down David St. from Jaffa Gate, turn right on **Souk al-Hussor,** and climb the metal staircase to your left. This takes you to the roofs of the market where you can escape the crowds, wander around, and peer down through the skylights at the spectacle below. The roofs also have a wonderful view of the Dome of the Rock and the Mount of Olives. Although less notoriously dangerous than the Ramparts Walk, solo women should not go much farther than the top of the staircase.

Rarely will you find genuine well-made handicrafts in the markets, though you may find beautiful products including inlaid backgammon sets, ceramics, pipes, and metal work. A good price for a large inlaid backgammon set is NIS40; NIS10 for a cheap blouse, NIS25 for a skirt, and NIS4.50 for a glittery scarf. The "rare antiquities" sold in the market are almost always neither, despite claims and appearances. Some are nice, but never buy them as an investment.

Ask around to get an idea of starting prices before you buy, and always bargain, even for food. Merchants usually start by giving you a price two or three times above the sale price, but sometimes up to eight or 10 times true value. As soon as you hear a price, contort your face to express amused disbelief, and state your own figure (a third to a half of his). Remember that you will not be able to go any lower than your first price. When the seller tells you to forget it, walk out of the store. If you are not called back, either the seller has spotted someone else, or your bluff has backfired—hardly a problem since 10 other shops are bound to sell exactly the same item. The secret is to stand firm and avoid appearing attached to an object. Above all, never let yourself be intimidated by the shopkeepers; they will do almost anything to close a sale. Pay in exact change to avoid last minute sleight of hand, or a whole new round of bargaining will begin. ("Well now that I see you have change . . . ") Don't bargain for items that only slightly interest you: The merchants are masters at getting customers hooked. Likewise, do not bargain if you don't intend to buy—you will be thrown out of shops or spat at. And never buy drugs here; dealers and informers are often one and the same. Finally, women should avoid being lured into backrooms to look at a "better selection." Modestly-dressed women will experience less verbal harrassment. The recent Arab strike, which in the summer of 1988 mandated that shops open only 9am-noon, has made merchants desperate for business, so you may have greater success bargaining. If you want to buy something during the afternoon or during a full-day strike, don't despair. Cruise the streets of the market and someone will ask if "you would like to see my shop?"

Temple Mount and Western Wall

In the southeastern corner of the Old City, the **Temple Mount,** about the size of the Muslim Quarter but much less crowded, is holy to Christians, Jews, and Muslims alike. The hill is traditionally identified with biblical Mount Moriah, on which God asked Abraham to sacrifice his son as a test of faith (Genesis 22:2). The First Temple was built here by King Solomon in the middle of the tenth century B.C.E., and destroyed by Nebuchadnezzer in 587 B.C.E. when the Jews were led into captivity in Babylon (I Kings 5-8, II Chronicles 2-7, II Kings 24-25). The Second Temple was built in 516 B.C.E., after the Jews' return from exile (Ezra 3-7). In 20 B.C.E. King Herod rebuilt the temple and enlarged the mount, supporting it with four retaining walls. Parts of the southern, eastern, and western retaining walls still stand. Religious scholars claim that the Holy Ark was located closest to the **Western Wall,** making this wall the holiest site in Judaism.

The Second Temple is remembered by Christians as the backdrop to Jesus' Passion. Like the First Temple, it lasted only a few hundred years. In the fourth year of the Jewish Revolt (70 C.E.) Roman legions ransacked Jerusalem and razed the temple. Attempts to rebuild it during the Bar Koḥba revolt and during the reign of Julian the Apostate failed. Justinian built a chruch here, but the Temple Mount was barren until the arrival of the Muslims in the seventh century. At that time, the Umayyad Caliphs built the two Arab shrines that presently dominate the Temple Mount (*Haram es-Sharif* in Arabic): Israel's holiest, the silver-domed **al-Aqsa Mosque** (built in 715 C.E. and rebuilt several times after earthquakes); and its most magnificent, the **Dome of the Rock** (built in 691 C.E.). A feast for mind and eye, the complex is the third holiest Muslim site, after the Ka'aba in Mecca and the Mosque of the Prophet in Medina. The al-Aqsa Mosque is the point from which God took Muhammad on his mystical Night Journey into heaven (Sura 17, verse 17 of the Koran). It is said that as Muhammad rose to heaven, the rock began to elevate with him, and thus it is possible to go under the rock. The Koran identifies the spot as "the farthest"—**al-Aqsa.** Muhammad originally directed the Muslims to pray facing Jerusalem before he decided on Mecca. The Dome of the Rock is built over a large, famous rock. Muslims say it was here that Abraham almost sacrificed Ishmael, his son by his concubine Hagar, and not Isaac (as the Bible says).

Although the dome was gold once, it was eventually melted down to pay the caliphs' debts. The domes of the mosques and shrines consisted of lusterless lead until the structures received aluminum caps during the restoration work done from 1958 to 1964. The "Jerusalem of Gold" look on the Dome of the Rock was achieved with an aluminum-bronze alloy. Plans for further restoration of both structures are already underway. In a few years, the present coat of the golden dome of the Dome of the Rock is scheduled to be replaced with a copper base gilded with gold leaf. Many of the beautiful tiles covering the walls of the Dome of the Rock were affixed during the reign of Suleiman the Magnificent, who had the city walls built in the sixteenth century. Close examination will distinguish these from the tiles later added by King Hussein of Jordan.

Next to the Dome of the Rock is the much smaller **Dome of the Chain,** where, according to Muslim legend, a chain hung down from heaven to be grasped only by the righteous. The Dome of the Chain, which is presently under renovation, is an exact miniature replica of the Dome of the Rock, except for the dome itself. Between the two mosques lies a *sabil* (fountain) called **al-Kas,** where Muslims must wash before prayer. Built in 709 C.E., the fountain is connected to underground cisterns with a capacity of 10 million gallons. The arches on the Temple Mount, according to Muslim legend, will be used to hang scales to judge the righteous. On the right as you enter the Temple Mount from the ramp is the **Islamic Museum,** which houses a collection of relics taken from the mosques as they were restored. It's a great place to sort out the different types of Arabic calligraphy: Kufic, Maghrebin, and Thuleeth calligraphy are all exhibited in the collection of Korans. Fantasize about boiling your siblings in the huge cauldrons originally used for cooking food for the poor. (Temple Mount open Sat.-Thurs. 8am-3pm; museum open Sat.-Thurs. 9am-4pm. All hours subject to change during Ramadan and other Islamic holidays. Tickets to the mosques and museum available at the booth between al-Aqsa and the museum. Admission NIS5.65, students NIS3.70.) The Mount is periodically closed without notice, and you might for one reason or another be denied entrance. The Mount is supervised by Arab police who speak neither English nor Hebrew, and who are justly annoyed by behavior deemed inappropriate to the holy site. Israeli Druze soldiers may also be posted at the entrance as an extra security measure. Dress modestly, and don't hold hands with members of the opposite sex. Also be aware that many sections considered off-limits by the police are not marked as such. These include the walls around al-Aqsa, the area through the door to the south between al-Aqsa and the museum, and the Muslim cemetery. Once inside al-Aqsa, stay away from areas where Muslims are praying. Observant Jews refrain from visiting the site in order to avoid unwittingly treading upon the Temple's "Holy of Holies."

The 18m tall **Western Wall** (*Hakotel HaMa'aravi* in Hebrew) is part of the retaining wall of the Temple Mount built about 20 B.C.E., and was the largest section of the temple area that remained standing after the destruction in 70 C.E. It was once called the Wailing Wall because Jews, believing that the divine presence lingered here, came to the wall for centuries to mourn the destruction of the First and Second Temples and to tuck written prayers into its crevices. Jews continue to do this every day except Saturday as a means of direct communication with God. The Wall can be reached by foot from Dung Gate, the Jewish Quarter, HaShalshelet St., or al-Wad Rd. (during the day). About 3m off the ground, a gray line marks what was the surface level until 1967. About 20m of Herodian wall still lie below the ground. You can identify the Herodian stones by their carved frames or "dressing"; the stones that lie above were added by Byzantines, Arabs, and Turks. Pre-1948 photos show Orthodox Jews praying at the wall in a crowded alley; after the Six Day War, the present plaza was built as a national gathering place. Israeli paratroopers are sworn in at the Western Wall to recall its capture by the unit in 1967.

Although the Western Wall is not formally a synagogue, the Ministry of Religion has decreed that all rules regarding synagogues apply to the Wall.

The prayer areas for men and women are separated by a screen, and the Torah scrolls are kept in an opening in the connecting building on the men's side of recently excavated sections of the Wall. **Wilson's Arch** (named for the English archeologist who discovered it), located inside this large, arched room, was once part of a bridge that spanned Cheesemakers' Valley, allowing Jewish priests to cross from their Upper City homes to the temple. (Women, unfortunately, cannot enter here.) A peek down the two illuminated shafts in the floor of this room will give you an idea of the wall's original height. If you walk to the far end of the large, vaulted chamber under the arch, you'll find a black door with a slit in it through which you can see more of the wall disappearing into the darkness. The wall continues in this direction through closed tunnels for over ½km. Women and groups can enter the passageways through an archway on the wall to the south near the telephones. (These sites are often closed to the public, but the official hours are Sun. and Tues.-Wed. 8:30am-3pm, Mon. and Thurs. 12:30-3pm, Fri. 8:30am-noon.) Enter through the archway parallel to the row of metal slats, which is in turn parallel to the wall. To the right of the Western Wall, about 10m from the southwest corner, you'll spot the remains of **Robinson's Arch.** This arch was the entrance to the passageway that allowed the royal retinue to pass from the Upper City to the Temple. Below the arch are the ruins of shops and stalls that supported the bridge.

Bar Mitzvahs occur at the Wall on Monday and Thursday mornings—often five or six at once—and are quite a sight, with the women keeping up a steady clamor at the railings and divided screen. Dancing among the crowds is organized by Yeshivat HaKotel to usher in *shabbat* at sundown on Friday. Try to come at least once at night, when the Wall is brightly lit, the air cool, and the area quiet. The plaza has guards posted 24 hours and is safe. Underneath the Western Wall is an underground passage, where Jewish terrorists hid explosives in the early '80s in a plot to blow up the Dome of the Rock. Although this tunnel is closed to the public, "City of David" offers a walking tour of the area and other passages in Jerusalem (tel. 28 78 66; Tues. 9:30am; NIS11, students NIS8).

The excavations at the southern wall of the Temple Mount are known as the **Ophel** region, though "Ophel" technically refers to the hill just outside the southern wall where the City of David is located. The ongoing excavations comprise one of the most important digs in the world. (Open Sun.-Thurs. 9am-5pm, Fri. 9am-3pm.) Archeologists have uncovered 22 layers from 12 periods in the city's development. The Ophel is in the midst of becoming an archeological park with pathways through the site's historical levels. Enter the city walls at the booth to the right of Dung Gate. Of particular interest here are the well-preserved remains of a Byzantine home and its mosaic floor. The cross symbols set in red Eilat tiles and black Golan basalt are unique to the Byzantine period. A tunnel brings you outside the city walls to the foot of the reconstructed steps that lead to the Temple Mount. Right before the steps are the ruins of the ritual baths where pilgrims purified themselves before ascending to the temple. It is difficult to appreciate the Ophel complex without a guide. **Archeological Seminars Ltd.** offers a worthwhile tour starting from the Cardo in the Jewish Quarter. (Tours Sun.-Wed. and Fri. 8:45am, NIS8, 2 hr.)

Jewish Quarter

The Jewish Quarter is in the southeast quadrant of the Old City, the site of the posh Upper City during the Second Temple era. The quarter extends from HaShalshelet Street (Bab el-Silsileh) in the north to the city's southern wall, and from Ararat Street in the west to the Western Wall (*HaKotel*) in the east. You can reach the quarter either by climbing the stairs diagonally across from the Western Wall or by heading down David St. and turning right at the sign for the Cardo Maximus. Jews first settled in this area in the fifteenth century. The Jewish community grew from 2000 in 1800 to 11,000 in 1865, when Jews began to settle outside the walls. Today, about 4000 people live in the Jewish Quarter.

Since the reunification of the Old City in 1967, the Jewish Quarter has been totally rebuilt, repairing the destruction from the house-to-house fighting in 1948 and neglect during the Jordanian occupation. Archeological discoveries at every turn of the shovel slowed the rebuilding and remodeling, though city planners have worked hard to gracefully integrate the ancient remains into the new neighborhood. Wander through the alleys and savor the mixture; it's a remarkably successful bit of unobtrusive modern architecture.

The **Cardo,** Jerusalem's main drag during Roman and Byzantine times, has been excavated and restored. The uncovered section is built over a Byzantine extension of Emperor Hadrian's Cardo Maximus, which ran from Damascus Gate about as far south as David St. Archeologists suspect that Justinian constructed the addition so that the Cardo would extend to the **Nea Church** (below Yeshivat HaKotel). The southern section is less fully restored and remains more authentic. Beneath the Cardo's vaulted roof are ritzy gift shops and art galleries described on a sign as "a continuation of the existing bazaars." Near the entrance to the Cardo, you can climb down to an excavated section of the Hasmonean city walls and remains of buildings from the First Temple period. Farther along the Cardo is an enlarged mosaic reproduction of the Madaba Map, the sixth-century plan of Jerusalem discovered on the floor of a Byzantine church in Jordan. At night the Cardo is open and illuminated for exploring tourists.

The **Yishuv Court Museum,** 6 Or HaHaim St. (tel. 28 46 36), exhibits aspects of life in the Jewish Quarter before its destruction in 1948. The museum is set up as a typical house. To get here, walk up the steps at the southern end of the Cardo, cross over the Cardo on the steps to your left, and look left for the brown and tan sign pointing the way. (Open Sun.-Thurs. 9am-4pm. Admission NIS3.50, students NIS2.50.)

Across Jewish Quarter Rd. from the southern end of the Cardo, a single white stone arch soars above the ruins of the **Hurva Synagogue.** Built in 1700 by the followers of Rabbi Yehudah the Hassid, the synagogue was destroyed by Muslims after only 20 years. In 1856, it was rebuilt as the National Ashkenazic Synagogue, but blown up during the fighting of 1948. To many, the single, sweeping, white arch is a simple reminder of the hope to erect three more arches, which will support the dome of a new synagogue. Adjacent to the Hurva stands the **Heart of the Jewish Quarter (Lev HaRova),** which houses a compelling exhibition of photographs taken during the conquest of the quarter in 1948 and an audio-visual presentation covering the history of the Jewish Quarter from biblical times to the present. (Open Sun.-Thurs. 9am-5pm, Fri. 9am-1pm. Admission NIS1.) The **Ramban Synagogue** next door was named for Rabbi Moshe ben Nahman ("Ramban" is an acronym for his name; he is also known as Nahmanides). Over the years the building has served as a store, a butter factory, and a mosque. Displayed inside is a letter written by the rabbi describing the state of Jerusalem's Jewish community in 1267, the year he arrived from Spain. (Open for morning and evening prayers.)

The **Four Sephardic Synagogues** (the synagogues of Rabbi Yohanan Ben Zakkai and of Elijah the Prophet, the Central Synagogue, and the Istambuli Synagogue) were built by Mediterranean Jews starting in the sixteenth century in conformance to a Muslim law that forbade the construction of synagogues taller than the surrounding houses. To attain loftiness, these synagogues were built in large chambers deep below the surface of the ground. The current structure, though renovated, basically dates from 1835. The synagogues are still the spiritual center of Jerusalem's Sephardic community, and religious services are held here every morning and evening. Of special note are the beautiful Italian Torah arks carved from wood in the Eliyahu HaNavi Synagogue which were brought over from Europe before the Holocaust. In a window of the Yohanan Ben Zakkai Synagogue sits a *shofar* (ram's horn) waiting for the Messiah to use to announce the redemption. To reach the Sephardic Synagogues, walk south on Jewish Quarter Rd. almost to the parking lot, turn left onto HaTuppim St., then left again, and walk down the wooden staircase. (Open Sun.-Thurs. 9am-3pm, Fri. 9am-1pm. Admission NIS1.)

Halfway down Jewish Quarter Rd. is an upturned grinding stone. Beit-El Road runs east from here, winding its way past a small square at **Gal'ed Road,** where a carob tree marks the pre-1967 burial spot of 48 defenders of the Jewish Quarter. A bit farther, by a police station, is **Baté Mahseh Square,** a street of rowhouses built by Dutch and German Jews in the 1800s. The most outstanding building on the street is the **House of Rothschild,** built by the Rothschilds in an attempt to reinvigorate the Jewish Quarter. They invited poor Jewish families to live here for up to three years.

The picturesque ruins of the **Tiferet Yisrael Synagogue,** built by Hassidic Jews during the nineteenth century, are also worth a visit. The synagogue was captured and destroyed in 1948. The upper portions of the ruin have been covered with cement, making it look as if a lumpy, gray mass is consuming it from above. The synagogue is on Tiferet Yisrael Rd., which begins at the northeastern corner of the courtyard behind the Hurva Synagogue.

Farther east on Tiferet Yisrael Rd. is the **Burnt House** (tel. 28 72 11), the remains of the dwelling of a wealthy priest's family in the Second Temple era. In 70 C.E., the fourth year of the Jewish Revolt, the Romans destroyed the Second Temple and, one month later, broke into Jerusalem's Upper City, burning its buildings and killing its inhabitants. The excavation of the Burnt House provided some of the first direct evidence of the destruction of the Upper City: Its charred walls had collapsed, crushing jugs and furniture beneath them, and near a stairwell, the skeleton of an arm was found reaching for a spear. Sound and light shows are set inside the Burnt House, recreating the events of its destruction; the overall effect is impressive. (Open Sun.-Thurs. 9am-5pm, Fri. 9am-1pm. Programs in English at 9:30am, 11:30am, 1:30pm, and 3:30pm. Admission NIS2.50, students NIS1.50.) Attached to the Burnt House is the newly-opened **Herodian Quarter,** consisting of three mansions built for the Second Temple's high priests (*cohanim*). The houses contain mosaics, several ritual baths (*mikvaot*), and stone and pottery dishes found during excavations. (Open Sun.-Thurs. 9am-5pm, Fri. 9am-1pm. Admission NIS3.50, students NIS2.50. Combined ticket to Burnt House and Herodian Quarter NIS3.) Past the Herodian Quarter, on Misgav Ladach St., is the site of the **German Hostel,** built by the Crusaders in the 12th century and predating the IYHF by 800 years. To its right, to the left of the path down to the Wall, is a serene garden amid Crusader vaults.

Taking Plugat HaKotel Road from the Hurva Synagogue Sq. brings you past the **Wide Wall,** remains of the Israelite wall that encircled the City of David, the Temple Mount, and the Upper City. The wall was built by King Hezekiah along with his tunnel (see City of David section for details) to defend the city and ensure water provision during the attacks and sieges of Assyrian King Sennacherib in the eighth century B.C.E.

You can visit some of the small synagogues and *yeshivot* (singular *yeshiva,* Jewish seminary) tucked away in alleys and courtyards throughout the Jewish Quarter. Young men and, in a few places, young women live in these academic institutions for many years as they pursue Judaic learning. Several *yeshivot,* have begun encouraging Jews with little or no religious background to come for short stays. Stop in at **Aish HaTorah**—the guys here are mostly American and welcome visitors, even for only one class. To reach Aish HaTorah from the Western Wall, walk up the stairs to the Jewish Quarter and take your first left onto the street before the covered arcade (Beit HaSho'eva Rd.). They also have a program for women outside the Old City; women should apply to the *yeshiva's* administrative office off Shvut Rd. in the Jewish Quarter. Students' expenses are paid by the *yeshiva.*

Many programs of long and short duration allow Jewish travelers to sample classes or share Jewish holidays in the Old City and throughout Jerusalem. Two information offices are the **Jewish Heritage Information Center,** 5 Tiferet Yisrael St., directed by Rabbi Meir Schuster (open in summer Sun.-Thurs. 10am-10pm; in winter Sun.-Thurs. 10am-6pm, Fri. 10am-1pm) and the **Jewish Student Information Center,** 5 Beit-El (tel. 28 83 38), directed by Jeff Seidel (open 10am to around 6pm). They not only offer useful information about the city and *yeshivot,* but also provide free accommodations for Jewish travelers and arrange *shabbat* stays with Jewish families. Both centers are located near the Hurva Synagogue, in the main courtyard of the Jewish Quarter. Both have helpful staffs with posters and information about programs. The Jewish Student Information Center offers, in addition, a lounge with drinks, videos, and a book and tape library.

Guide yourself through the area with the excellent, detailed *Quartertour Walking Tour of the Jewish Quarter,* available at Steimatzky's or at the Lifshitz Information Center. Two-hour guided tours in English given by **Archeological Seminars Ltd.** start above the information center in the Cardo. (Tours Sun.-Fri. at 11am; check at the tourist information office for schedule changes.)

Christian Quarter and Via Dolorosa

In the northwest quadrant of the Old City, the Christian Quarter surrounds the Church of the Holy Sepulchre, the site traditionally held to be the place of Jesus' crucifixion, burial, and resurrection. Many small chapels and churches of various Christian denominations, all claiming to be significant, lie near the Church of the Holy Sepulchre.

The **Via Dolorosa** (Path of Sorrow) is the route Jesus followed from the site of his condemnation to his grave—from the Praetorium to Calvary. Each stop along the route marks an event, one of the "stations of the cross" on Jesus' final journey according to the accounts given in the Gospels of the New Testament. The present route along Via Dolorosa was established during the Crusader period, but modern New Testament scholars have suggested alternate routes based on more recent archeological and historical reconstruction. One dispute involves establishing exactly where Jesus began his walk. Everyone agrees that Jesus was brought before Pontius Pilate, the Roman procurator, for judgment. A Roman governor ordinarily resided and fulfilled his duties in the palace that was built by Herod the Great and extended south from Jaffa Gate and the Citadel area. This evidence places the starting point on the opposite end of the city from the traditional beginning on Via Dolorosa. On feast days when the temple area was hectic, however, the governor and his soldiers presumably would base themselves temporarily at Antonia's fortress (also built by Herod the Great), to be closer to the Temple Mount. As Jesus was condemned on a feast day (Passover), the **Tower of Antonia,** near St. Stephen's (Lion's) Gate, remains the traditional First Station, although you may see small groups, notably the Catholic Dominican Order, setting out from Jaffa Gate. The placement of the last five stations inside the Church of the Holy Sepulchre is also contested by those who believe that from where Via Dolorosa ends, the route was likely to have continued north toward the skull-shaped Garden Tomb, since the crucifixion took place on a hill called Golgotha, meaning "place of the skull." On Fridays at 3pm (July-Aug. at 4pm), Franciscan monks lead a procession of pilgrims from St. Stephen's (Lion's) Gate. For a superb view of the pilgrims (whom you may join), turn onto Burj Laklak Rd. by the gate and climb the stairs to the ramparts.

Along the Via Dolorosa from St. Stephen's Gate, you'll first see the **Church of St. Anne** on your right. Commemorating the birthplace of Jesus' mother Mary, the church is one of the best preserved and most beautiful examples of Crusader architecture in Israel. The church survived intact throughout the Mamluk period because Salah al-Din used it as a Muslim theological school. That explains the Arabic inscription on the *tympanum* above the church doors. Tradition is deeply rooted here: The simple, solemn, fortress-like structure stands over the ruins of a fifth-century basilica that, in turn, is believed to cover a second- or third-century chapel. You may notice that the church is tilted to one side, symbolizing the crucifixion.

Within the lovely grounds is the **Pool of Bethesda,** which served as the water source for the Temple. Crowds of the sick used to wait beside the pool for an angel to disturb its waters, which was the explanation for the pool's periodic gushing, since the first person to enter the pool after the angel had passed through would be cured. Jesus is believed to have cured a paralytic here as well. The pool is divided into a southern and a northern section, but comprehension of the site is confounded by the remains of a Byzantine cistern and the facade of a Crusader chapel. (Church and grounds open Mon.-Sat. 8am-noon and 2:30-6pm; in winter Mon.-Sat. 8am-noon and 2-5pm. Free.)

Two hundred meters west of St. Stephen's Gate, a ramp on your left leads up to the courtyard of the **el-Omariyeh College,** one site identified as the **first station,** where Jesus was condemned (closed 1-3pm). Opposite the school, from the Via Dolorosa, enter the Franciscan monastery; to your left is the **Condemnation Chapel,** the **second station,** where Jesus was sentenced to crucifixion. On the right is the **Chapel of Flagellation** where he was first flogged by Roman soldiers. Look up to see the crown of thorns adorning the dome, and look around the altar at the mobs clamoring at the windows of the dusk-colored chapel. (Open Mon.-Sat. 8:30am-noon and 2-6pm; in winter Mon.-Sat. 8:30am-noon and 2-5pm.)

Continuing along the Via Dolorosa, you pass beneath the **Ecce Homo Arch,** which tradition maintains was the spot where Pilate looked down on Jesus scourged and uttered "Behold the Man." The arch is actually a part of the triumphal arch that commemorates Emperor Hadrian's suppression of the Bar Kohba revolt in the second century. Adjacent lies the **Convent of the Sisters of Zion,** beneath which excavations have cleared a large chamber thought by some to be the judgment hall, making *it* the first station. Both the convent and el-Omariyeh College fall within the boundaries of the Antonia fortress and can claim with equal certainty to be the first station.

Although the following stations are all marked, and are the destination of millions of pilgrims, they are still difficult to spot. At the **third station,** to the left on al-Wad Rd., Jesus fell to his knees for the first time. A small Polish chapel marks the spot; a relief above the entrance depicts Jesus fallen beneath the cross. At the **fourth station,** a few meters farther, just beyond the Armenian Orthodox Patriarchate, a small chapel commemorates the first fall as Jesus met his mother. Turn right on Via Dolorosa to reach the **fifth station,** where Simon the Cyrene volunteered to take Jesus' cross and carry it for him. Fifty meters farther, the remains of a small column mark the **sixth station,** where Veronica wiped Jesus' face with her handkerchief. The imprint of his face was left on the cloth, which is now on display at the Greek Orthodox Patriarchate on the street of the same name. The **seventh station** marks Jesus' second fall—note the sudden steepness of the road here. In the first century, a gate to the countryside opened here, and tradition holds that notices of Jesus' condemnation were posted on it. Crossing Khan ez-Zeit, ascend Aqabat el-Khanqa and look beyond the Greek Orthodox Convent to the stone and Latin cross that marks the **eighth station.** Here Jesus turned to the women who mourned him, saying "Daughters of Jerusalem, do not weep for me, weep rather for yourselves and for your children" (Luke 23:28). Backtrack to Khan ez-Zeit and ascend the wide stone stairway on the right, and continue through a winding passageway to the Coptic church. The remains of a column in its door mark the **ninth station,** where Jesus fell a third time. Again trace your steps to the main street and work your way through the market to the entrance of the Church of the Holy Sepulchre where the Via Dolorosa ends.

The **Church of the Holy Sepulchre** marks Golgotha, also called Calvary, where Jesus was crucified, buried, and resurrected. The location was first determined by Helena, mother of the Emperor Constantine, during a pilgrimage in 326. Helena thought that Hadrian had erected a pagan temple to Venus and Jupiter on the site in order to divert Christians from their faith. She sponsored excavations which soon uncovered the tomb of Joseph of Arimathea and three crosses, which she surmised had been hastily left there after the crucifixion as the Sabbath approached. Constantine built a magnificent church over the site in 335 C.E., which was later destroyed by the Persians in 614, rebuilt, and again destroyed (this time by the Turks) in 1009. Constantine's church is said to have been magnificent, and part of its original foundations support the present Crusader structure, which dates from 1048. When the present building was conceived, its architects decided to unite under one monumental cross all the oratories, chapels, and other sanctuaries that had cropped up around the site. The project required overextending a transept here and squeezing in an extra chapel there. By 1852, tremendous interfaith conflicts had developed over property rights within the Holy Sepulchre over even miniscule issues such as who had the right to clean the doorstep. The disinterested Ottoman rulers divided the church among the Franciscan order, and the Greek and Armenian Orthodox, Coptic, Syrian, and Ethiopian churches. The first three are the major shareholders, entitled to hold Masses and processions and to burn incense in their shrines and chapels.

One of the most venerated buildings on earth, the church is also one of the most confusing. The diversity of its keepers lends the structure some of its fascination and color, but it also keeps the building in shambles and under perpetual construction. The effects of major fires in 1808 and 1949 and an earthquake in 1927 demanded a level of cooperation and a pooling of resources that the various denominations were unable to muster. Restoration work in any part of the basilica implies ownership, so that each sect is hesitant to assist and eager to hinder the others. The end result is that very little, or nothing at all, is ever accomplished. In 1935 the church was in such a precarious state that, in desperation, the British propped it up with girders and wooden supports. Since 1960 partial cooperation has allowed the supportive scaffolding to be gradually removed, but to this day changing a light-bulb can become a controversy that rages for months.

The sites in the church today bear little resemblance to those described in the Gospels, but discrepancies can be explained. The Gospels place Calvary outside the city walls, but you'll see that it is located on the second floor of the church. At the time of Jesus, according to believers, the basilica's Calvary site was indeed located outside the city walls—the walls there today were built centuries after Jesus' crucifixion and encompass a larger area than the original walls. (Church open daily 4am-8pm; in winter 4am-7pm.) The guards are very strict about modest dress, and they will refuse admission to women with bare shoulders and to men or women in shorts. The first shop outside the eastern entrance to the courtyard rents skirts for NIS1.50; look for the Kodak sign.

As you enter the church you'll face the slab on which Jesus was anointed before he was buried. To continue along the stations, go up the stairs to the right just after you come in. The chapel at the top of the steps is divided into two naves: The right one belongs to the Franciscans, the left to the Greek Orthodox. At the entrance to the Franciscan Chapel is the **tenth station,** where Jesus was stripped of his clothes, and at the far end is the **eleventh,** where he was nailed to the cross. The **twelfth station,** to the left in the Greek chapel, is the unmistakable site of the crucifixion: A life-size Jesus, clad in a metal loincloth, hangs among oil lamps, flowers, and enormous candles. Between the eleventh and twelfth stations is the **thirteenth,** where Mary received Jesus' body. The thirteenth station is marked by a statue, of Mary, adorned with jewels, with a silver dagger stuck in her breast. Below the statue, a portion of the original hillside is visible.

Jesus' tomb is the **fourteenth (final) station.** To find it, return to the ground floor, which is divided into the Greek Orthodox choir (in the center) and the rotunda, which would be on your left if you were entering the church. The **Holy Sepulchre,** in the center of the rotunda, is a large marble structure flanked by absolutely enormous candles. The first chamber in the tomb, the Chapel of the Angel, is named after the angel who announced Jesus' resurrection to Mary Magdalene. A tiny entrance leads from the chapel into the sepulchre itself, an equally tiny chamber lit by scores of candles and guarded by priests. The walls of the tomb have been covered, but the priest in charge will show you a small section of the original wall hidden behind a picture of the Virgin Mary. The raised marble slab in the sepulchre covers the rock on which Jesus' body was laid. Built against the back of the Holy Sepulchre is the tiny Coptic Chapel, in which a priest will invite you to kiss the wall of the tomb, then press a plastic crucifix into your hand, and murmur "donations for the church?" To the right of the Sepulchre, the **Chapel of Mary Magdalene** recalls the place where Jesus appeared to her after the resurrection.

The rest of the church is a dark maze of small chapels, through which priests, pilgrims, and bemused tourists wander. Because a denomination's ability to hang anything on the church's walls indicates possession, the building is full of religious paintings and spidery oil lamps. Near the eastern end, steps lead down to two cavernous chapels commemorating the discovery of the true cross. Notice the Crusader graffiti on the walls beside the steps. In a small chapel on the ground floor just below Calvary, you can see a fissure running through the rock, supposedly caused by the earthquake following Jesus' death. According to legend, Adam was buried beneath Calvary and Jesus' blood dripped through this cleft to anoint him.

St. Alexander's Church, 1 block east of the Church of the Holy Sepulchre on Via Dolorosa, houses the Russian mission in exile. Prayers for Tsar Alexander III are held every Thursday at 7am (the only time the church itself is open). Come to see the excavations downstairs. (Open Mon.-Sat. 9am-1pm and 3-5pm. Admission NIS1.50; ring bell.) Across the street, with its entrance on Muristan St., is the **Lutheran Church of the Redeemer.** Head up the narrow spiral staircase to its bell tower for an incredible view of the city. (Open Mon.-Sat. 9am-1pm and 2-5pm.) The **Greek Orthodox Patriarchate Museum** (tel. 28 40 06), on the street of the same name, is a more recent addition to the Christian Quarter. Under the present Patriarch, Benedictos Papadopoulos, the scattered liturgical riches, gifts of pilgrims, and early printings of the Patriarchate's nineteenth-century press have been spaciously arranged in a reconstructed Crusader building with a lovely garden. Few come here, and a charming elderly monk may follow you from room to room offering his two bits on the collection's pieces. (Open Tues.-Fri. 9am-1pm and 3-5pm, Sat. 9am-1pm. Admission NIS1.)

For something completely different, take a left from the Russian mission onto Khan ez-Zeit to the two-tiered stairway leading to the **Ethiopian Monastery.** At the top of the stairs, go straight and enter the gray door with the green beam over it. The monastery is located over part of the Church of the Holy Sepulchre and is open all day. The Ethiopians have no part of the church itself, so they have become squatters on the roof.

Christian travelers, in particular, should visit the excellent **Christian Information Office,** inside Jaffa Gate to the right (tel. 28 76 77; P.O. Box 14308). They provide a wealth of information about Christian sites, maps, hospices, church services, schools, and institutes. Their list of Christian social services can help you find volunteer work. Religious pamphlets and books link the modern sites to their biblical roots. (Open Mon.-Fri. 8:30am-noon and 3-6pm, Sat. 8:30am-noon; in winter Mon.-Fri. 8:30am-noon and 3-5:30pm.) The **Franciscan Pilgrims Office** (tel. 28 26 21; P.O. Box 186), near the main door, is responsible for the distribution of tickets to St. Catherine's Church in Bethlehem on Christmas Eve. Requests are accepted beginning in October. First priority goes to Roman Catholics.

Armenian Quarter

Lying beside Mount Zion in the southwestern part of the Old City, the Armenian Quarter maintains its cultural identity despite modernization. Aramaic, the ancient language of the Talmud, is spoken both during services and in casual conversation at the **Syrian Orthodox Convent** on Ararat St. The Syrian Church believes this spot to be the site of St. Mark's house and of the Last Supper, while most other Christians recognize the Cenacle on Mount Zion as the hallowed place. To reach the convent, enter Jaffa Gate and walk right along the Citadel onto Armenian Patriarchate Rd. Take a left at St. James Rd. and another left onto Ararat St. The convent is down Ararat St. on the right past the Syrian Orthodox Club. There is a bright new mosaic over the door to the convent. You can visit during the afternoon; if the door is closed, ring the bell.

The **Armenian Compound,** down Armenian Patriarchate Rd., past St. James Rd., is a city within a city, and home to about 1000 Armenians. The compound is privately owned, and is explicitly not a tourist attraction. The compound had been a hospice for Armenian Christian pilgrims, but became permanent residences in 1915 when Armenian refugees and orphans from the Turkish genocide settled there. On your way to the compound, you'll pass the **Seminary of the Armenian Patriarchate,** built in 1975 with funds from an Armenian family in Detroit. Look, because you can't go in. The compound has schools, two libraries, a soccer field, a printing press (Jerusalem's first, dating from 1833), a cathedral, and a monastery. Armenian, an ancient Indo-European language, is spoken within the compound. The Armenians in the compound have friendly liturgical relations with their Syrian neighbors, since they perceive language to be their only difference. Once per year each conducts services in the other's house of worship.

Farther down Armenian Patriarchate Rd. is the entrance to the **Mardigian Museum.** With pictures and scholarly explanations, this museum chronicles the history of Armenia from the beginnings of its Christianization in 46 C.E. to the Turkish genocide of one and a half million Armenians in 1915. Start at room #5, go around and then upstairs, where there are beautiful Arabic manuscripts from the Ottoman period, first editions of books printed on the printing press in the 1950s, and portraits of various patriarchs. After examining the exhibits, you can sit in the courtyard and listen to the liturgical chants played by the underground gatekeepers. (Open Mon.-Sat. 10am-5pm. Admission NIS1.) From either the other end of the museum or to the left of St. James Cathedral you can enter the compound with its wide open courtyards, so uncharacteristic of the Old City. Be discreet, and don't put up a fuss if you're asked to leave. The gates to the compound close at 10pm and do not reopen until 6am, just as the Old City of Jerusalem was locked each night for security under the Turks.

St. James Cathedral is open for services for a half-hour each day. The original structure was built during the fifth century C.E., Armenia's golden age, to honor two St. Jameses. The first martyred Apostle, St. James the Greater, was beheaded in 44 C.E. by Herod Agrippas. St. James the Lesser served as the first bishop of Jerusalem, but was run out of town by Jews who disliked his new brand of Judaism. Under the gilded altar rests the head of St. James the Greater, which tradition holds was delivered to Mary on the wings of angels. St. James the Lesser is entombed in a northern chapel. Persians destroyed the cathedral in the seventh century, Armenians rebuilt it in the eleventh century, and Crusaders enlarged it between 1142 and 1165. The entire church is decked in beautiful ceramic tiles—the Armenians make the tiled street signs for the whole city—and scores of chandeliers, hanging lamps, and censers. Inside there are also canvas and wall paintings from the Middle Ages. Pilgrims have left the votive crosses in the courtyard before the entrance; the oldest cross dates from the twelfth century. Enter the cathedral from Armenian Patriarchate Rd., just past St. James St. (Cathedral open for services Mon.-Fri. 3-3:30pm, Sat.-Sun. 2:30-3:15pm.)

Muslim Quarter

Although the Muslim Quarter contains no official tourist sights, it is worth exploring for its architecture, the most notable of which is from the Mamluk period (1250-1517). Most of these buildings are now residences; none is open to the public. Their facades, however, reflect a former glory. Do not explore the Muslim Quarter during periods of unrest, and do not show off your Hebrew here.

The stretch of Bab el-Silsileh St. running to the Temple Mount features fine architecture. Right after you pass Misgav Ladach Rd., on your right, is the **Tastamuriya Building.** This building contains the tomb of the man of the same name (d. 1384) and was formerly a *madrasa* (Islamic college). Notice the stalactite-decorated niche over the entryway and the interlocking pink and gray stones around the niche. The structure at #118, currently under renovation, has beautiful stonework and inscriptions on its front.

Continuing down Bab el-Silsileh to its intersection with Western Wall St. (HaKotel), you will arrive at the **Kilaniya Mausoleum,** with its characteristically Mamluk stalactite half-dome. The **Turba Turkan Khatun** (Tomb of Lady Turkan) is at #149. The tomb is decorated with repeating patterns, notably the Mamluk blunt star. Look up and observe the rooftop dome on the square base. At the end of Bab el-Silsileh, on your right and often surrounded by tour guides in training, is the **Tankiziya Building.** This venerated structure, on the site of the original seat of the Sanhedrin, is now occupied by the Israelis due to its proximity to the Western Wall and Temple Mount. The Muslim Committee for Jerusalem was based here during the period of Jordanian control. The goblets near the inscription are the coat of arms of Tankiz (d. 1328), signifying that he was a royal cup-bearer. The **Sadiya Building,** on your left before the Tankiziya, has a beautiful marble mosaic over the door.

Some of the "City of David" walking tours (tel. 28 78 66) cover the Muslim Quarter. Also check the posted schedule of the free Saturday 10am walking tours at the municipal information office at 17 Jaffa Rd.

Mount Zion and City of David

Mount Zion stands outside the city walls opposite Zion Gate and the Armenian Quarter. At various times since the Second Temple era, Mount Zion has been enclosed by the city walls. The mount has long been considered the site of the Tomb of David (though recent archeological evidence suggests otherwise), the Last Supper, and the descent of the Holy Spirit at Pentecost. The name, which is applied to Israel as a whole, is thought to be derived from the Jebusite fortress called Zion, which was taken by King David when he conquered the territory to the east. During the siege of the Jewish Quarter in 1948, the area around **Zion Gate** was the scene of some of the fiercest fighting in Jerusalem, as the Haganah tried to break in and relieve the siege of the Jewish Quarter. You can still see the vestiges of fighting around the bombshell-marked gate. The sights by themselves are not very exciting, but guided tours of Mount Zion can elucidate the history and meaning of the area. Buses #1 and 38 run between Mount Zion and Jaffa Gate (#1 goes through Mea Sh'arim to the central bus station; #38 goes to the center of town). To reach the sights on the Mount, leave the Old City through Zion Gate or approach Zion Gate from either Jaffa or Dung Gates. Go straight away from the wall, bearing right at the double door marked "Custodia Terra Sancta," and left at the fork in the road.

A stairway on the left side of the courtyard leads to the **Coenaculum,** identified by most Christians as the site of the Last Supper. Today the walls and stone arches of the Coenaculum are bare; it is the only major Christian site in Jerusalem which is less ornate now than in Jesus' time, when Luke described a large room furnished with couches. One of the reasons for the lack of decoration is that the British passed a law during the Mandate forbidding any changes to be made in the church as it existed at the time, in order to avoid inter-sect disputes. During the fifteenth century, the building was used as a mosque and the prayer niche (*mihrab*) is still visible in the southern wall. To the east, up a few stairs, is a room (usually closed), which some consider the gathering place of the disciples after Jesus' death, when the Holy Spirit descended upon them at Pentecost. (For information about services, call 71 35 91; open 8:30am to sundown.) Below the Coenaculum is the study room of the **Diaspora Yeshiva,** many of whose residents are American. Every Saturday night at 8:30 (July-Aug. 9:30), visitors are welcome to come and bop to live Hassidic rock music. For information, phone 71 68 41.

The entrance to **David's Tomb,** essentially an empty room, is on the other side of the building (go left at the "Custodia Terra Sancta" door). Above the red velvet-covered tomb in the small cave, silver crowns, not always displayed, represent the number of years since Israel gained independence. Archeologists refute the authenticity of the site because Mount Zion was never encompassed by David's walls as was once believed, and it is written that kings and only kings were buried within the city. (Tomb open Sun.-Thurs. and Sat. 8am-5pm, Fri. 8am-2pm. Free.) For a fabulous view of the Old City, walk straight through the greenish courtyard, turn left, and take the stairs up to the top of the minaret.

The **Chamber of the Holocaust,** directly opposite the entrance to David's Tomb, commemorates the Jewish communities destroyed during World War II and displays haunting and ghastly artifacts such as rescued Torah scrolls, ashes, and soap made from human tissue. Open Sun.-Thurs. 8am-5pm, Fri. 8am-1pm. Free. Slide-show at 11:30am, 1:30pm, and 3pm; NIS1.50.) The **Museum of King David,** (tel. 71 68 41), which is an affiliate and practically next door, attempts to convey the spirit and life of David through modern art. The slightly off-the-wall exhibit includes a large oil painting of the 70 musical instruments that David is said to have played. There are also a handful of coins from the Hasmonean period, the period following the Hannukah story. (Open Sun.-Thurs. 8am-5pm, Fri. 8am-2pm, Sat. 8am-5pm. Free.) The **Palombo Museum,** also nearby, displays works of the famous sculptor who crafted the entry gate to the Knesset and contributed works to Yad VaShem. (Open irregular hours, usually in the morning; call 71 09 17. Free.)

The huge, fortress-like **Basilica of the Dormition Abbey** lies off the right fork of the road leading to the Coenaculum. The site has harbored earlier memorials, but the present edifice, commemorating the death of the Virgin Mary, was built at the turn of the century and completed in 1910. Damaged during the battles in 1948 and 1967, parts of the strategically situated basilica have never been repaired. You can descend into the crypt for a glimpse of a figurine of the Virgin. The floor of the ground level is inlaid with symbols of the zodiac from the prophetic tradition. (Open Sept.-June daily 7am-12:30pm and 2-7pm; July-Aug. 8am-1pm and 3-7pm.)

If you have even a mild interest in the biblical history of Jerusalem, the **City of David** is a logical place to begin, since this is where the city did. The quest for the origins of biblical Jerusalem has gone on since 1850 and only recently have the pieces of the puzzle begun to fit. Archeologists confirm that the ridge of Ophel—south of the Temple Mount and outside the city walls—is the site of the Canaanite city captured by King David.

Excavations of the earliest Canaanite walls indicate that the Jebusites were confined to an area of about eight acres. The size and location of the city were precisely chosen above the Qidron Valley so that the inhabitants would have access to the nearby water source (the Gihon Spring), and at the same time remain just high enough on the Ophel's ridge to be adequately defended. In times of peace, townspeople could pass through a "water gate" to bring water into the city. To ensure continued supply during a siege, the Jebusites dug a shaft so they could draw water without leaving the walls. David succeeded in capturing the city only after his soldier, Joab, managed to scale the shaft one night, thus depriving the Jebusites of water. The city was forced to surrender and open its gates to David's forces. In 1867, Warren confirmed this biblical account when he discovered the shaft that now bears his name. In the 1960s Kathleen Kenyon located the 1800 B.C.E. Jebusite city walls which lie just above the Gihon Spring.

King Hezekiah devised a system to prevent a recurrence of David's feat: He built a tunnel to bring the Gihon waters into the city walls and store them in a pool, thus hiding the entrance of the spring and keeping invaders such as the Assyrians from finding water as they camped outside the wall. According to the biblical account, laborers in Jerusalem dug from opposite ends of the tunnel in order to save time as the Assyrian army approached. Minutes before the enemy's arrival, the laborers heard the picks and voices of their companions on the other side just a few meters off the mark (II Chronicles 32). In 1880, a few years after the tunnel was excavated, a local boy exploring the tunnel discovered an inscription carved by Hezekiah's engineers. The Siloam inscription describes the hectic but joyful moment when the construction crews completed the tunnel. (The original inscription is in Istanbul, but a copy is on display at the Israel Museum.)

You can slosh through **Hezekiah's Tunnel** with a flashlight or a candle. The water is about 1m high, and wading the ½km takes about a half-hour. Bathing suits or shorts, and sneakers or waterproof footcovering will do. Start at the Gihon Spring source on Shiloah Way, which branches to the right from Jericho Rd. as you walk down into the Qidron Valley from the bottom of the Mount of Olives. The tunnel ends at the Pool of Shiloah (*Silwan* in Arabic, Siloam in English). You can then walk back to the road to your left and catch an Arab bus up the valley. (Open Sun.-Thurs. 9am-5pm, Fri. 9am-3pm.)

About 100m down from the entrance to the City of David, there's a small museum with photos of the most recent excavations and a spiral staircase that leads down to a tunnel extending into **Warren's Shaft.** If you bring a flashlight, you'll be able to see the entire length of the walls that Joab scaled. (Open Sun.-Thurs. 9am-5pm, Fri. 9am-1pm. Admission NIS2.)

A hundred meters east of the exit to Dung Gate, follow the path which turns right off the road and you'll reach the entrance to the City of David. The excavations in this particular area of the Ophel, called **Section G,** were halted in 1981 when a group of ultra-Orthodox Jews protested that the area might once have been a Jewish cemetery as mentioned in the diaries of several medieval pilgrims. Despite, or maybe because of, the political and sometimes violent hooplah, the Supreme Court of Israel ruled that the site should be closed. As a compromise the Israeli government ordered that digging could continue under rabbinic supervision, but no bones were ever found. Though numbered and labeled, the ruins adjacent to the route are still confusing. You'll see the remains of a tower originally thought to be a Davidic addition to the Jebusite fortifications. The tower is now labeled as a second-century B.C.E. structure, which was built over the ruins of several houses that were destroyed by the Babylonians in 586 B.C.E. You can see the covered remains of one strikingly well-preserved room. Although the site's various levels have been clearly labeled, a guided tour will improve your enjoyment tremendously. The Society for the Protection of Nature, Jerusalem Through the Ages, and Archeological Seminars, Ltd. all offer tours. Check at the tourist office for schedules. If you decide to tour the area alone, bring a copy of *Marty's Walking Tours.* The site is spectacularly illuminated at night. You can get a great view from Ophel Rd., which hugs the southeastern city walls, or from the wall near Dung Gate.

If you follow Shiloah Way down into the Qidron Valley, you will find four tombs to your left. The first, **Absalom's Pillar,** is the legendary tomb of David's favored but rebellious son (II Samuel 15-18). Behind this tomb and to the left is the **Tomb of Jehosaphat.** A dirt path on the left leads to the impressive rock-hewn **Tomb of Bnei Hezir** and the **Tomb of Zechariah.**

East Jerusalem

Although under separate control for less time than now spent under Israeli rule, East Jerusalem feels like a different city from West Jerusalem, only blocks away. This area was the commercial center of Jordanian Jerusalem until 1967, and today many of its Arab residents continue to use Jordanian dinars and Israeli shekels interchangeably. If you're interested in learning about Muslim Arab society, however, you'll have to venture beyond the tourist sights, for they reflect little of the character of the quarter itself.

Midway between Damascus and Herod's Gates in the city walls, **Solomon's Quarries** sink into the city's bowels. The quarries provide a great refuge from the midday heat. Many believe that in these cool caves, which extend about 250m beneath the Old City, workers quarried limestone for the building of ancient Jerusalem during the First Temple period. To separate blocks of stone from the cave walls, wooden planks were set in crevices and soaked with water; as the planks expanded they forced the stone apart. Tradition has it that Zedekiah, Judah's last king, fled the city through a passage to Solomon's quarries when King Nebuchadnezzer of Babylonia invaded in 587 B.C.E. The sign for the quarries reads "Zedekiah's Cave." (Open Sun.-Thurs. 9am-5pm, Fri. 9am-3pm. Admission NIS1.30, students NIS.65.)

Farther east on Suleiman St., opposite the northeastern corner of the city walls, a driveway to the right leads to the **Rockefeller Archeological Museum** (tel. 28 22 51), one of the country's best. The museum's collection records the region's history, beginning with the grisly remains of 100,000-year-old Mt. Carmel Man, and also illustrates the cultural impact of various conquering civilizations. As you enter, turn left and work your way clockwise through the building. The first room includes artifacts demonstrating the influence of the Egyptians in the late Canaanite period. The second room contains the museum's earliest pieces through the Bronze Age. The next room contains beams and panels removed from the al-Aqsa Mosque. The patterns on the wood indicate that the artisans were not Muslims but Byzantine Christians. If you're planning to visit Jericho, pay special attention in the next room, which contains remains of Hisham's Palace (*Khirbet al-Mafjar* in Arabic). The layout of the museum can be confusing—try to visit on a Sunday or Friday morning for the free guided tours at 11am. (Open Sun.-Thurs. 10am-5pm, Fri.-Sat. 10-2pm. Admission NIS6, students NIS4. Take bus #27 or 23.)

A ½ block up Nablus Rd., on Schick St., you'll find a sign pointing toward the **Garden Tomb,** noticed first by Otto Thenius in 1860 and popularized by the British General Gordon. The garden is considered a possible site for Golgotha, site of Christ's crucifixion. The hill does indeed resemble a skull, and some claim a nearby tomb to be that of Joseph of Arimathea, who placed Jesus' body in his own tomb after the crucifixion. (Open Mon.-Sat. 8am-12:30pm and 2:30-4pm. Tours offered in summer.) As you continue along Nablus Rd., stop in at **St. George's Cathedral,** one of the least visited yet loveliest structures in Jerusalem. Consecrated in 1898, St. George's is linked to the British-owned Christ Church in the Old City, but is administered by an Arab bishop. Inside the cathedral is a small exhibit on ancient farming, including a section on brewing. Apparently, Babylonion beer was sour, while Palestinian and Egyptian beer was sweet and spicy.

Beyond the cathedral, past the American Consulate and the intersection with Salah al-Din St. (stay to the right), you'll see the French sign (*Tombeau des Rois*) indicating the gate of the **Tomb of the Kings.** Judean kings were originally thought to be buried here, but recent evidence proves that the tomb was built in 45 C.E. by the Mesopotamian Queen Helena for her family. Enter the huge forecourt, then head into the small opening of the burial chamber. Bring a candle or a flashlight to explore the several tombs, though the inner maze is hardly as large as you might expect, and the rooms are rather plain and uninteresting. (Open daily 8am-12:30pm and 2-5pm. Admission NIS1, students NIS.50.)

The bone-dry slopes of the **Mount of Olives,** to the east of the Old City, are dotted with churches marking the sites of Jesus' triumphant entry into Jerusalem, his teaching, his agony and betrayal in Gethsemane, and his ascension to heaven. That the Mount of Olives has three gardens of Gethsemane and two points of Ascension might cast doubt on the accuracy of the sites, but nothing can detract from the beauty. In Jewish tradition, the Mount of Olives (*Har HaZeitim* in Hebrew) holds importance for the future as well: The thousands buried in the cemetery here will be the first to greet the Messiah on Judgment Day.

A walk down the hill, with stops at the many churches, tombs, and gardens, is most enjoyable in the morning, when the sun shines at your back and permits clear views and photographs of the Old City. Since most churches are closed on Sundays and afternoons from about noon to 3pm, mornings are also the most practical time to come. Arab bus #75 runs from the station across from Damascus Gate to the Mount of Olives. A five-minute walk from the last stop (in the direction the bus was going) will take you to the Intercontinental Hotel, built on bulldozed graves, which offers an incredible view of the Temple Mount. The panorama is also spectacular at night, as you look out at illuminated "Jerusalem of Gold."

Northeast of the Intercontinental Hotel (behind it and to the right), the domineering **Bell Tower** of the Russian convent marks the highest point in Jerusalem. Unfortunately, the entire compound has been closed to the public. South of the hotel along the main road, the **Church of Eleona** and the **Church of the Paternoster** lie behind one gate. Both churches were founded by Queen Helena in the fourth century. The Church of the Eleona stands where Jesus revealed to his disciples the "inscrutable mysteries"—his foretelling of the destruction of Jerusalem and his Second Coming. Destroyed over the years, the church was reconstructed after archeologists uncovered the foundation in 1910. The Church of the Paternoster (Latin for "Our Father"), commemorates the first recital of the Lord's Prayer. Budding linguists can read the prayer in all of the 78 languages, including Esperanto, on the tiled walls. In the midst of the translations is the grotto of the Princess de la Tour d'Auvaigne, who financed and gave 17 years of her own time (1857-74) toward excavations and renovations here. (Open Mon.-Sat. 8:30-11:45am and 3-4:45pm.) Its credibility contested only by the nearby Russian bell tower, the **Chapel of Christ's Ascension** is farther north along the same road. Although the original building was erected in the fourth century, the chapel was converted into a mosque in the twelfth century and is now under Muslim guard. Inside there is a sacred footprint, and you'll probably run into children who will offer a hasty explanation and demand *baksheesh.* (Ring the bell if closed. Admission NIS.50.)

Descending the path which runs down the Mount of Olives from the Intercontinental Hotel, you will see a gate on the left that leads to two tunnels, traditionally identified as the **Tombs of the Prophets** Malahi, Haggai, and Zechariah. Archeological evidence suggests that the graves are far too recent—probably dating from the fourth century C.E. (Open Sun.-Fri. 8am-3pm.) The orange sign with black Hebrew lettering marks the **Common Grave** of all those who died defending the Jewish Quarter in 1948. Next to the Common Grave lies the **National Cemetery,** and farther down the path stretches the immense **Jewish Graveyard,** the largest Jewish cemetery in the world.

The tear-shaped **Basilica of Dominus Flevit** ("the Lord wept"), to the right of the path, was built in 1955 to mark the spot where Jesus wept for Jerusalem. During the construction, which was supervised by the renowned Italian architect Antonio Barluzzi, several unrelated ruins were unearthed. As you enter from the path, you'll pass by some first century Christian tombs. The modern church is built over a seventh century mosaic of fruit. (Open daily 8am-noon and 2:30-5pm; April-Oct. 8am-noon and 2:30-6pm.) Farther down on the right, resembling the Kremlin, is the **Russian Church of Mary Magdalene.** Its seven golden cupolas mark the Mount of Olives in the same way that the Dome of the Rock distinguishes the Temple Mount. In 1885, Tsar Alexander III built the church in the lavish seventeenth-century Muscovite style, and dedicated it to his mother, the Empress Maria Alexandrovna. The crypt houses the body of a Russian grand duchess, smuggled to Jerusalem via Peking after her death in the Russian Revolution. Now a convent, the church assumes the aura of the sacred shrines that surround it, and even claims a part of the Garden of Gethsemane. (Open Tues. and Thurs. 10-11:30am. Call 28 28 97 to be sure it's open.)

At the bottom of the path, deep in the valley, the **Church of All Nations** (Basilica of the Agony) faces west toward the Old City. Enter through the gate for the Garden of Gethsemane, just below the Church of Mary Magdalene. The garden is another reputed Garden of Gethsemane, the place where Jesus spent his last night in prayer and was betrayed by Judas (Mark 14:32-42). The olive grove is one of the oldest and most beautiful in the world. Although the site has been venerated since the fourth century, the present building, also designed by Barluzzi, was built after World War I with international support. Inside, several mosaics show the last days of Jesus' life. In the evening, the beautiful mosaic on the facade, portraying Jesus bringing peace to all nations, shines in the setting sun. The subdued interior is open when the garden is open. (8am-noon and 2:30-6pm; Nov.-March 2:30-5pm.) A quick right at the foot of the road directly ahead of the church leads to the eerie **Tomb of Mary,** which receives light primarily from the door and candles, as there are but two lightbulbs in the whole tomb. Tradition dates this from the fifth century, although the present cavern dates from the Crusader period. Floods have worn away the interior, and there is nothing to see. Greek Orthodox, Armenians, Syrians, and Copts all share the upkeep. (Open Mon.-Sat. 6:30am-noon and 2-5pm.)

New City

Since the first Jewish pioneers timidly moved outside the protective walls of the Old City in the 1860s, the settlements in West Jerusalem have grown into a sprawling modern city. A decree requiring that all buildings be faced with the golden Jerusalem stone guarantees the New City a certain harmony, despite its large population. West Jerusalem may lack the history- and spice-laden atmosphere of the Old City, but the special tastes and feelings of Jerusalem extend far beyond the Old City walls. As you explore outside the city center, you'll discover not only impressive museums, but diverse neighborhoods—the cool, tree-lined streets of Rehavia, the working-class Katamonim, the winding alleys of Nahlaot, and the graceful Arab mansions of Bakah and the German Colony.

One of the outstanding sights in the New City is the **Israel Museum** (tel. 69 82 11), a magnificent collection of diverse exhibits. From the ticket building, walk along the shrub-lined walkway and go up the steps; the main building is straight ahead to your left. On the left as you descend from the main lobby is the section devoted to **archeology,** a meticulously arranged guide to 30,000 years of human habitation in the Fertile Crescent, the arc between ancient Mesopotamia and Egypt. Much of the collection extends from the Canaanite period through the biblical era, including a large assortment of tools and weapons. Straight ahead from the bottom of the steps is the ethnography exhibit, which you should follow clockwise from the left, through the Cycle of Jewish Life. Presenting a sequence of ceremonies from birth onward, each ritual is represented by a different Jewish community. Adjacent is a display of Semitic costumes and an exhibit of traditional Eastern European household and kitchen paraphernalia. Upstairs, the display of Ceremonial Art has the museum's prize pieces of Judaica, up to 400 years old. The largest room is devoted to artifacts that were once profane and later became sacred. This room contains a miniature Buddhist shrine that was severed in two and converted into a *menorah.* On the main wall is a tapestry created from boys' pants. Don't miss the reassembled synagogues at the end of the wing, the first of which is a classically refined Italian original from the eighteenth century.

The museum also displays permanent and traveling art exhibits, from Impressionism to modern Israeli sculpture to ancient Asian and African art. The newest addition to the museum is the **Weisbord Pavilion** right across from the ticket building. The pavilion houses a small permanent collection of Rodin sculptures and early Modern paintings in addition to temporary exhibitions, such as a recent impressive collection of Columbian gold treasures.

Outside, the **Billy Rose Sculpture Garden** contains the works of such modern masters as Henry Moore and Picasso. Pick up a schedule of evening outdoor concerts at the museum, and try to visit on a Tuesday night when the garden is illuminated. Don't forget to visit the **Shrine of the Book,** which displays the Dead Sea Scrolls. The shape of the building resembles, among other things, the covers of the pots in which the scrolls lay hidden for 2,000 years in the Caves of Qumran near the Dead Sea. Dating from the second century B.C.E. to 70 C.E. and belonging to an apocalyptic, monastic sect called the Essenes, some of the scrolls contain versions of the Hebrew Bible almost identical to the books that came down through the hands of countless Jewish scribes, but with important deviations. The Book of Isaiah is the most significant of the scrolls, since it is complete and predates any other known biblical text by 1000 years. On the bottom level of the museum is a collection of letters and relics that predate the destruction of the Second Temple and have been crucial to scholars studying that period. The exhibit is kept dark to protect the scrolls. Free guided tours of the shrine are offered on Sunday at 1:30pm and Tuesday at 3pm.

Take bus #9, 16, or 24 to the Israel Museum. (Open Sun.-Mon. and Wed. 10am-5pm, Tues. and Thurs. 10am-10pm, Fri. 10am-2pm, Sat. 10am-4pm. Sculpture Garden and Shrine open Sun.-Mon. and Wed. 10am-5pm, Tues. and Thurs. 10am-10pm. Guided tours in English Mon. and Wed.-Fri. at 11am, Sun. at 11am and 3pm, Tues. at 4:30pm. Admission to museum only, NIS6; to museum and Shrine, NIS8; students NIS4.) If you're pressed for time one day and you think you'll have to come back, go first to the Dead Sea Scrolls so that you won't have to purchase a complete ticket when you return. Student annual membership costs NIS20 and allows unlimited entrance to Israel, Rockefeller, Tel Aviv, and Haifa Museums, as well as discounts on museum programs. For information about special exhibits, gallery talks, concerts, and events, call 69 82 11.

The **Knesset,** Israel's Parliament, is a five-minute walk from the Israel Museum. To see the Knesset in session, come on Monday or Tuesday from 4 to 7pm or Wednesday from 11am to 7pm and see for yourself just how lively things can get. The debates are in Hebrew or Arabic, and you'll need your passport to enter. On Sunday and Thursday from 8:30am to 2:30pm, you can take a free tour of the building, which includes an explanation of the Israeli system of government and a look at the Chagall tapestry and the mosaics that adorn the building. Take bus #9 or 24 (tel. 55 41 11 for information).

Yad VaShem, meaning "a memorial and a name" (tel. 53 12 02), is the most moving of Israel's Holocaust museums. Using photographs, documents, and artifacts displayed in chronological order, the museum shows Hitler's rise to power, the anti-Semitic laws and pogroms of the 1930s, the deportation of the Jews to the concentration camps, and the destruction of the millions. Part of the museum is devoted to Jewish resistance movements, particularly the Warsaw Ghetto Revolt. The exhibit ends in a simple, powerfully moving memorial. The surrounding gardens were planted in memory of non-Jews who risked their lives to save Jews during World War II. If you enter the grounds on foot, walk to the kiosk and turn left onto the **Avenue of the Righteous among the Nations;** each tree bears a plaque with the names of individual non-Jews who committed themselves to saving Jews. At the end of the avenue, turn right for the museum. The four-part silver mural entitled "The Cry of Silence" contains the essential themes of the entire memorial: From left to right are semi-abstract depictions of cultural and material destruction (candles burning a breast), the struggle to survive (a clutched ladder), the escape to Israel (a boat pointed east), and the Jewish state (in the form of a *sabra* cactus with an arrow of remembrance pointing west). An enormous labyrinthine memorial dedicated to the **Destroyed Communities** is under construction in the valley below and the **Garden of the Children** of the Holocaust is under renovation. (Open Sun.-Thurs. 9am-4:45pm, Fri. 9am-1:45pm. Free.)

Mount Herzl, near Yad VaShem, is a pleasant park and memorial to the founder of modern political Zionism. The **Herzl Museum** (tel. 53 11 08) conveys the energy of a man who made the first modern articulation of Zionism, worked as a newspaper correspondent, and persevered for a Jewish state until his untimely death in 1904 at the age of 44. (Open Sun.-Thurs. 9am-4:45pm, Fri. 9am-12:45pm. Free.) The road to the left when you enter the park continues past the museum to the tomb of Ze'ev Jabotinsky, spiritual leader of the Irgun. The road away from the museum winds through the park to Herzl's grave and to the plots of Levi Eshkol, Golda Meir, and other national leaders. The path ends in a poignant cemetery where Jerusalem's fallen soldiers lie. The cemetery is terraced into a sculptured landscape and each grave is laid out like a bed with the headstone as pillow above a blanket of greenery. Buses #13, 18, 20, 23, 24, 27, and 99 travel to Mount Herzl and Yad VaShem.

The synagogue at the Hadassah Medical Center near Ein Kerem (not to be confused with Hadassah Hospital on Mount Scopus) houses the **Chagall Windows,** which depict the 12 tribes of Israel in enchanting abstract stained-glass designs based on Genesis 49 and Deuteronomy 33. The windows were a gift from the artist in 1962 to Hadassah Hospital. When four of the windows were damaged in 1967, Chagall was sent an urgent cable, to which he replied "You worry about the war, I'll worry about my windows." Two years later he installed four replacements. Three of the windows contain bullet holes recalling the Six Day War. The colors and images chosen from nature and fantasy reflect Jewish history and tradition. The *parohet* (ark curtain) in the center of the room was designed by Aviva Green in 1982 as a textural variation on Chagall's color scheme. Take bus #19 or 27. (Free English tours Sun.-Thurs. 8:30am, 9:30am, 10:30am, 11:30am, 12:30pm, and 2:30pm, Fri. 9:30am, 10:30am, and 11:30am. Synagogue open Sun.-Thurs. 8am-1:30pm and 2-3:45pm, Fri. 8am-12:30pm. Admission NIS4, students NIS2. Call 88 28 19 for updated information.)

Another beautiful stained-glass window is in the imposing **Jerusalem Great Synagogue** (tel. 24 71 12) on King George St., across from the Plaza Hotel. This lavish shrine was built with the money of the Israeli taxpayers. Dress modestly to visit the synagogue, and check out the **Wolfson Museum** next door, on the fourth floor of Hechal Shlomo. The museum contains a large exhibit of Jewish religious and ceremonial objects and one room depicting various scenes from Jewish history in miniature. Major events, from the crossing of the Red Sea to the First Zionist Congress are brought to life in intricate settings peopled by tiny figurines. (Museum open Sun.-Thurs. 9am-1pm, Fri. 9am-noon. Admission NIS2.)

If you take bus #2 from the city center and get off at HaSanhedrin St. off Yam Suf St., you'll find not only a pretty park carpeted with pebbles and pine needles but also the **Tombs of the Sanhedrin.** The Sanhedrin was the high court and senate of ancient times. Composed of esteemed sages and leaders, the Sanhedrin ruled on grave legal matters and even reviewed the case of Jesus. Separate burial areas were designated for the corpses of the members. The tombs are more finely carved than the Tomb of the Kings, but similarly arranged as catacombs. You'll see several tomb-like facades in the park, but the main one has a triangular pediment above and is close to Yam Suf St. (Open Sun.-Fri. 9am-sunset.) Families will enjoy the **Biblical Zoo,** (tel. 82 36 58), which is up HaSanhedrin St. and then right on Bar-Ilan St. Many of the exotic animals here are mentioned in the Bible and the appropriate passages are posted on each cage. To reach the zoo from the center of town, take bus #7, 15, or 27. (Open Sun.-Thurs. 9am-4:30pm, Fri. 9am-1pm, Sat. 9am-3pm. Admission NIS6, students NIS4. Buy tickets for Saturday in advance.)

The **Holyland Hotel** (tel. 63 02 01) has a scholarly and dramatic model of Jerusalem at the time of the Second Temple. Scaled to about one-fiftieth of the city's size, the knee-high model was reconstructed according to historical documents and contains authentic building materials. It offers a good perspective on the Old City's sights and makes the confusing excavations around the Temple Mount easier to understand. Take bus #21 from downtown. (Open daily 8am-5pm; in winter 8am-4pm. Admission NIS3.50, students NIS2.50.)

Tiho House on Tiho St., off HaRav Kook St. near Zion Sq., has an interesting exhibit of life in Jerusalem at turn of the century. Affiliated with the Israel Museum, the building, restaurant (see Food), and gardens are well-kept and make a good mid-city rest-stop. (Open Sun.-Thurs. 10am-5pm, Tues. 10am-10pm, Fri. 10am-2pm.) The **Mayer Institute for Islamic Art** (tel. 66 12 91), 2 HaPalmah St., has a good collection of miniatures, paintings, and artifacts from the Islamic world displayed chronologically. Take bus #15 from the center of town. (Open Sun.-Thurs. 10am-12:30pm and 3:30-6pm, Sat. 10am-1pm. Buy tickets for Saturday in advance. Admission NIS3, students NIS2.)

Three sights in the New City document Israel's twentieth-century struggles. The **Hall of Heroism** (tel. 23 32 09) inside the Russian Compound, Jaffa Rd., commemorates the work of Israel's underground movement in the pre-1948 struggle against British domination. Originally erected by Russian pilgrims, the hall was converted by the British into Jerusalem's desolate main prison. Enter through Heshin St., just off Jaffa Rd. where it splits with Shlomzion HaMalka. Follow the green signs saying "Museum." (Open Sun.-Thurs. 10am-3pm, Fri. 10am-1pm; in summer Sun.-Thurs. 10am-4pm, Fri. 10am-1pm. Admission NIS3, students NIS2.)

The **Tourjeman Post** (tel. 28 12 78) recounts Jerusalem's history from its division in 1948 to its dramatic reunification in 1967. The building withstood severe shelling during the War of Independence and became an Israeli command post when the Jordanian border ran across the street from 1948 to 1967. Nearby stood the now-dismantled Mandelbaum Gate, the only passage across the old Jordanian-Israeli border. To reach the building, follow Shivtei Yisrael St. away from the Old City and turn right onto Hel Handassa St. (the continuation of Shmuel HaNavi St.). The museum will be on your right. (Open Sun.-Mon. and Wed.-Thurs. 9am-4pm, Tues. 9am-6pm, Fri. 9am-1pm. Admission NIS2, students NIS1. Take bus #1, 11, or 27.)

Before the Six Day War, **Ammunition Hill** (*Giv'at HaTahmoshet;* tel. 82 84 42) was Jordan's most fortified strategic position in the city, commanding much of northern Jerusalem. Taken by Israeli commandos in a bloody battle, the hill now serves as a memorial to the soldiers who died in the 1967 conflict. The somber, architecturally striking museum is housed in a reconstructed bunker, and gives a historical account of the 1967 battle using maps, photos, and a Hebrew-English text. You can run through some of the Jordanian trenches. Buses #9, 25, and 28 let you off at the foot of the hill, and there's a great view of the city from the top. (Open Sun.-Thurs. 9am-4pm, Fri. 9am-1pm. Admission NIS2. Accessible to the disabled.)

Mea Sh'arim is the world's only remaining example of the Jewish *shtetl* communities which flourished in Eastern Europe before the Holocaust. The inhabitants of this religious community are devoted to studying and living by the Torah. Most are poor, and living conditions are crowded. Residents still dress in the Eastern European garb of the eighteenth century. In the old section, around the eastern part of Mea Sh'arim St., the houses are arranged in blocks facing inward around central courtyards, originally designed for defense and community insularity.

Although few in number, Mea Sh'arim's extremists are vocal and receive a good deal of publicity. Two sects in particular, the Neturei Carta and the Satmar Hassidim, oppose the Israeli state, believing that Jewish law prohibits the legitimate existence of the state of Israel until the coming of the Messiah. One famous and recurring piece of graffiti states, "Judaism and Zionism are diametrically opposed." These views, nonetheless, do not prevent the most vocal proponents from living in Israel and accepting money and protection from the state.

Signs throughout the neighborhood read, "Daughters of Israel! The Torah requires you to dress modestly," and then proceed to explain exactly what this means. Whether or not you're Jewish, take this seriously: If you dress immodestly, you will not only offend those around you, but risk being chased out of the area. Women must wear long sleeves and skirts; pants are frowned upon and shorts may provoke rock-throwing. Men, too, should wear long pants. Restrain the urge to display affection for your loved one in this part of town, and always ask before you photograph. Many residents consider it a serious invasion of their rights and privacy.

Mea Sh'arim is probably the cheapest place in the world to buy Jewish books and religious items. Bargaining is the rule for religious objects; try the stores on the easternmost stretch of Mea Sh'arim St. For books, look in the small, untouristed shops that sell only literature. The neighborhood also has some of the best bakeries in the city. Most remain open all night on Thursdays, baking *hallah* and cake for the Sabbath. The bakery at 15 Rabbenu Gershom St. (off Yehezkel) bakes great *borekas* and chocolate rolls.

The neighborhoods of **Nahlaot** and **Zihronot,** just south of the Mahaneh Yehudah market, are also crowded and largely religious. Residents are mostly Sephardic Jews from Yemen, Iran, Turkey, and Morocco, and, increasingly, artists and students in search of cheap housing. The narrow, winding alleys and tiny courtyards are festooned with laundry, and in contrast to the bookstores and silversmiths that line the street of Mea Sh'arim, here you'll see barber shops, blacksmiths, and sandalmakers.

On the western edge of the city, the **Jerusalem Forest** is a wonderful place for peaceful walks and picnics. To reach here, take bus #5, 6, 18, or 21, and get off at the Sonol gas station on Herzl Blvd. Walk in the direction the bus was traveling, and take the first right onto Yefe Nof. The second left, Pirhe Hen, leads into the forest. The Jewish National Fund runs a **Plant a Tree with Your Own Hands** program among the groves. (For more information, contact them at 1 Keren Kayemet L'Yisrael St., P.O. Box 283, Jerusalem 91002. Tel. 24 02 51 or 24 17 81, extension 13.) For a beautiful afternoon walk, follow Pirhe Hen to the Youth Center in the middle of the forest. From here you can walk along a shady path to the village of **Ein Kerem** (see Near Jerusalem). Ask for the path at the center; it's easy to find, and Ein Kerem is visible most of the way, but bring a map just in case. From Ein Kerem, you can take bus #17 back to town.

A walk through **Liberty Bell Park (Gan HaPa'amon),** which runs alongside Keren HaYessod St. (reached by buses #5, 6, or 14) will take you to the restored neighborhood of **Yemin Moshe.** It was here that the English Jew, Sir Moses Montefiore, first managed to convince a handful of residents from the Old City's overcrowded Jewish Quarter to spend occasional nights outside the city walls and thus founded the New City. To strengthen the settlers' confidence, Montefiore built a small compound with crenelated walls resembling those of the Old City (*Mishkenot Sha'ananim,* "Tranquil Settlement") and a stone windmill, both of which can be seen today. Inside the windmill, a small museum is dedicated to Montefiore for his persistent efforts. (Open Sun.-Thurs. 9am-4pm, Fri. 9am-1pm. Free.) This beautiful neighborhood of alleyways is now one of the most exclusive in the city, and has become something of an artists' colony, with a number of interesting galleries. In the valley below is the Sultan's Pool, and the Old City is on the valley's opposite bank.

Mount Scopus (Har HaTsofim) lies north of the Mount of Olives, and is the home of both the Hebrew University and the famous Hadassah Hospital. It is worth coming up here just to see the spectacular new **Hecht Synagogue** which overlooks the Old City from the Humanities building; enter via the Sherman Building. (Call 88 38 86 for information about services.) Between 1948 and 1967, Mount Scopus was a garrisoned Israeli enclave in Jordanian territory. Its summit offers magnificent views of Jerusalem, while the university's gorgeous **amphitheater** looks east to Jordan. While you're up there, take advantage of the subsidized cafeterias, especially the **Frank Sinatra** where you can eat a filling meat lunch for a fraction of the cost in the city below. For a lighter meal, try **The Faculty Club** coffee shop where you can munch on a salad while counting Old City steeples from the balcony.

If you feel like you've exhausted the museums and sights in the New City and a large part of your budget, cheer up at, surprisingly enough, the free **Taxation Museum,** 32 Agron St. (tel. 22 89 78). Follow the history of taxes from ancient laws to the modern Israeli "travel tax," which requires any Israeli citizen to pay $150 before leaving the country. The museum consists mainly of documents and pictures, with several mannequins dressed in tax-collectors' uniforms watching your every move. (Open Sun., Tues., and Thurs. 1-4pm; Mon., Wed., and Fri. 10am-noon.)

Entertainment

There are two ways to look at the Jerusalem entertainment scene. You can complain, wear one of the T-shirts that say "Jerusalem nightlife" and have a big black square, and head to Tel Aviv. Or you can accept the fact that the city offers unmatched opportunities for all but the dance-and-drink-all-night crowd. Find a hostel with an 11pm or later curfew, and explore. You'll find the best listings of concerts, exhibits, nightlife, and cultural activities in *Kol Ha'Ear,* a free weekly paper in Hebrew. You might also read the entertainment supplement to Friday's *Jerusalem Post,* the various booklets supplied by the GTIO (such as *This Week in Jerusalem* and *Hello Israel*), and the posters lining the city streets.

Every night, the sixteenth-century ramparts of the Old City are illuminated with a golden hue, transforming the city into a medieval fantasy world. A walk along the walls between Zion Gate and Dung Gate can be spectacular at night, though the path is uneven and you must be careful even when there's a full moon. The walls are absolutely unsafe for women alone. The bar at the Intercontinental Hotel on the Mount of Olives offers a mountaintop view of the walls, the Temple Mount, and the surrounding sprawl of the New City (take Arab bus #75). The terrace of the grand King David Hotel on King David St. offers another lovely view of the walls. Hop on bus #7 to the **Haas Promenade** at Tayelet Har HaNatziv in Talpiyot to view the city from a greater distance. At the end that bus route is Kibbutz Ramat Rahel (tel. 70 25 55), with a sound and light show and *kibbutz*-style evenings of singing and dancing.

For **culture** buffs, the Jerusalem Symphony performs frequently at the plush Jerusalem Theater on David Marcus and Chopin St. (tel. 66 71 67). The theater also hosts numerous plays, dances, lectures, and concerts. Similar events are held at the Israel Museum (tel. 63 62 31), at Binyenei HaOoma across from the central bus station, and at the Hebrew University campuses at both Mount Scopus and Givat Ram. On Saturday nights, there are often recitals of baroque music at the Dormition Abbey on Mount Zion. The Gerard Behar Center (tel. 24 21 57), at 11 Bezalel St., hosts a variety of concerts, including occasional country music.

Built by the Turks in the 1880s as a caravan stop, the **Khan** (tel. 71 82 83), across from the railway station, houses an intimate theater, an art gallery, and an enjoyable nightclub (open until 2am). It's rarely frequented by tourists, but its concerts and plays, some only in Hebrew, are well-known among locals. (Egged buses #6, 7, 8, and 30 or Arab buses #21 and 22 pass by the railway station.) If you have the opportunity, attend a rock, jazz, or classical performance at the **Sultan's Pool,** a beautiful outdoor amphitheater named for Sultan Suleiman the Magnificent, the Ottoman ruler who repaired the ancient aqueduct in 1536. The theater is open only in the summer months. Tickets for American or British rock stars run NIS25-30.

Israeli **folk dancing** conveys some of the city's rhythm; you can either watch or dance almost every night. The Baraton, a club at the top of Hebrew University's Mount Scopus campus, has folk dancing on most Saturday and Wednesday nights at 7:30pm (tel. 88 26 70; bus #9 or 28); the International Cultural Center for Youth (ICCY), 12a Emek Refaim St., offers dancing every Saturday and Tuesday evening at 9pm (tel. 66 41 44; bus #4, 14 or 18); the House for Hebrew Youth (Beit HaNaoar), 105 HaRav Herzog St., conducts classes on Thursdays at 8pm (tel. 66 61 41; bus #19); and outdoor dancing takes place in the Liberty Bell Gardens a bit after *shabbat* ends. All are either free or charge a nominal fee (about NIS.50).

Jerusalem's movie theaters provide a good chance to catch those films you missed last year. Most are in English or have subtitles. Two places screen foreign and American double features: **Cinema One,** Qiryat Yovel (tel. 41 50 67), has interesting programs but is infamous for the poor quality of its projection. Take bus #18, 19, or 20. The real gem is the **Jerusalem Cinemateque,** on Hebron Rd. in the Hinnom Valley (tel. 71 53 98), which screens two repertory films on Friday afternoons, Saturday, Monday, Tuesday, and Thursday nights. A wonderful terrace cafe at the Cinemateque overlooks the Old City walls, and it is one of the only places in the New City where you can get a snack on Friday evenings. Cinemas charge about NIS6, and the Friday supplement of the *Jerusalem Post* has complete listings. Bring your student ID. Native Israeli movies are notoriously bad, so don't bother.

Below are listed some of Jerusalem's lively nightspots for music and dancing.

Tzavta, 38 King George St., behind the parking lot (tel. 22 76 21). A small music-theater club with nightly programs in English. See the schedule of events in front or ask in the GTIO. Visiting musicians and actors are invited to audition. Tickets NIS4-7, discounts for students.

Pargod, 94 Bezalel St. (tel. 23 17 65). A tiny, wonderful club offering a mix of entertainment. Wed. nights and Fri. afternoons are devoted to live jazz. Mon. nights feature local bands (such as "Issy and the Pathologists") at 9:30pm. Open most nights 9pm-12:30am (NIS6 cover), Fri. afternoon 1:30-5:30pm (no cover). Buy tickets before Fri. night.

Asaf's Cave, Mt. Zion Cultural Center (tel. 71 68 41), near David's Tomb. Start of the new week is celebrated Sat. at 9:45pm. The Diaspora Yeshiva Band, with roots in R&B and Talmud, performs in a mixture of English, Hebrew, and Yiddish. Admission NIS11. Wed. nights and Fri. afternoons are devoted to live jazz. Open most nights 9pm-12:30am (NIS6 cover).

Although Jerusalem cafe-sitting does not match Tel Aviv standards, there are some excellent places for food, drink, and taped music in a laid-back atmosphere. Most tourists and a few Israelis congregate at the outdoor cafes along the *midrahov*—the portion of Ben Yehudah St. closed to vehicles and open to overpriced boutiques and underpaid street musicians. **Cafe Akrai,** on A.M. Luntz St. between Jaffa Rd. and Ben Yehudah St., is popular with gay men and women. You might miss their English sign, but the avante-garde interior is unmistakable. The Nahlat Shiva area, off Jaffa Rd. between Rivlin and Yoel Salomon St., is full of small, cozy places to relax over a cup of herbal tea or dessert. **Beit Teh,** 12 Yoel Solomon St., serves 24 different kinds of tea, as well as cake, ice cream, and snacks in a quiet, candlelit, cushion-clad room. (Open until 1am.) All cafes and tea houses close Friday afternoon for *shabbat,* and reopen an hour or two after sundown on Saturday.

Jerusalem's drinking spots come in several shapes and sizes. **The Tavern,** on Rivlin St., is a predominantly English-speaking pub with a dart board in back and live music every Thursday starting at 10pm. (Open nightly until 2am.) **Champs Pub,** on Yoel Salomon St. near Zion Sq., is a crowded but enjoyable bar with a TV and a largely British clientele. (Open Sat.-Thurs. until 12:30am.) The **Little Pub** and **Lalo's Pub,** off 27 Jaffa Rd. east of Rivlin St. (look for the sign), and others around them serve expensive, lousy food, but are open Friday nights and remain popular spots for meeting travelers. **Charlie's Pub** in the Jerusalem Towers Hotel, 23 Hillel St., evokes a Bohemian atmosphere, with its movie posters and '60s music. (Open Sun.-Thurs. 1pm-2am, Fri. from 8:30pm, Sat. sundown-2am.) **Bet Ha'Omanim (The Artist's House),** 12 Shmuel HaNagid St. (tel. 22 36 53), is quieter and attracts more Israelis. (Open every night until 2am.) On Friday nights, the Tavern, Charlie's, and Bet Ha'Omanim are just about the only places to go in the New City center.

The *intifadah* has mellowed the scene in the Old City. The **Coffee Shop** and a few other restaurants in the Jaffa Gate area stay open until a rocking 9pm. In better times, the **Danish Tea House** (down David St. from Jaffa Gate, then left on Muristan Rd.) will play from their American music collection on request (ask to see the list). They're usually open until about midnight. When the political situation cools, the **Open Sesame Cafe,** on al-Wad Rd., will return to being a legendary haven for young tourists. Its wooden walls are covered with messages from passers-through. The **Jewish Student Information Center** (see Practical Information) has nightly speakers, films, and seminars, all with a Jewish bent.

Near Jerusalem

Ein Kerem

A formerly small Arab village on the outskirts of Jerusalem, Ein Kerem ("fountain of vines") is traditionally regarded as the birthplace of John the Baptist. His mother couldn't have chosen a more beautiful spot. Come here for an afternoon, wander through the village's tiny alleys and streets, and escape the tensions of Jerusalem.

The **Church of St. John,** with its soaring tower, marks the spot where John was born. Inside are several beautiful paintings, including the "Decapitation of Saint John." (Open Mon.-Sat. 8am-noon and 3-6pm, Sun. 9am-noon and 3-5pm; Oct.-Feb. Mon.-Sat. 8am-noon and 3-5pm, Sun. 9am-noon and 3-5pm. Dress modestly.) In the **Grotto of the Nativity** below the church, there is a lovely Byzantine mosaic of pheasants—the symbol of the Eucharist. Ask the guardian for a key.

Across the valley, the **Church of the Visitation** recalls Mary's visit to Elizabeth, and contains a rock behind which St. John is said to have been hidden from the murderous Romans when he was a baby. The newer Upper Chapel depicts the glorification of Mary. (Open daily 8am-noon and 3-6pm; Oct.-Feb. daily 8am-noon and 2:30-5pm.) **Mary's Well,** an ancient spring, is a small stone trough below the **Youth Hostel** (see Accommodations, Suburbs) off Ma'ayan St. The pink tower above the hostel belongs to the **Russian Monastery,** which you can visit only by appointment (tel. 22 25 65 or 41 28 87). The two or three cafes in Ein Kerem are expensive for meals but worth a quick stop for coffee and snacks. There is a small **supermarket** across from the post office as you go downhill from the Church of St. John.

To reach Ein Kerem, take city bus #17, which runs every 20-30 minutes from the central bus station and the center of town. Ein Kerem is also a 15-minute walk along a footpath to or from the Hadassah Medical Center and the stop for bus #19.

Bethany

A relatively prosperous Palestinian village, Bethany (or *al-Azariya*) was the home of Lazarus and his sisters Martha and Mary. Jesus is believed to have stayed here when he visited Jerusalem. A **Franciscan Church** built in 1954 marks the spot. The church features several impressive mosaics, including one illustrating the resurrection of Lazarus and another depicting the Last Supper. Outside the church are more mosaics. Three earlier shrines, the earliest built in the fourth century C.E., have been excavated nearby. South of the church you'll find the remains of a vast abbey built in 1143 C.E. by Queen Melisende. Note the enormous olive oil press in the monastery's cavernous interior. (Open daily 7-11:45am and 2-5pm.)

Bethany still contains the first century **Tomb of Lazarus,** which was first enshrined in the fourth century. When the Crusaders arrived, they built a church over it, a monastery over Mary and Martha's house, and a tower over Simon the Leper's (another resident of Bethany cured by Jesus). In the sixteenth century the Muslims erected a mosque over the grotto, and in the following century Christians dug another entrance to the tomb so they too could worship in the grotto. To get there, head for the silver domes of the **Greek Orthodox Church** above the tomb (the Franciscan Church will be just downhill). As you approach the tomb, a lady will come from across the street to show you the light switch (on the right as you enter), and ask for a donation (tomb open daily 8am-6pm). Above the tomb is a small Greek Orthodox Church, also dedicated to Lazarus, but open to the public only on the Saturday Feast of Lazarus in early April. Ten minutes farther along the main road, the **Greek Orthodox Convent** shelters the rock upon which Jesus sat while awaiting Martha from Jericho (ring the bell).

From Jerusalem, take either Egged bus #43 or the more frequent Arab bus #36 (NIS.50) and get off in the town of Bethany, 4km east of Jerusalem (look for the silver-domed church on your left). There are two #36 buses, so ask for *al-Azariye* before embarking. Women in this Arab area of the West Bank should be sure to dress modestly and travel in groups.

Abu Ghosh

Thirteen kilometers west of Jerusalem lies the Arab village of Abu Ghosh, whose inhabitants aided the Jews in the war of 1948 and who speak both Arabic and Hebrew. In the eighteenth century, Sheikh Abu Ghosh required pilgrims to pay a toll here as they traveled to Jerusalem. The town was the last of a series of caravan stops en route to the Holy City. Christians and Jews alike revere Abu Ghosh as the original site of the Ark of the Covenant, which was moved by King David to Jerusalem. The **Notre Dame de L'Arche d'Alliance** (Our Lady of the Ark of the Covenant) was built on the site of the ark—it can't be missed, since it's topped by an enormous statue of Mary holding the infant Jesus. The perimeter of the church is surrounded by barbed wire, making it inaccessible to visitors.

Below the sacred hill stands a magnificently preserved, fortress-like **Crusader Church** built in 1142 and acquired by the French government in 1873. The church now houses six French Benedictine monks and, in an adjacent building, the same number of nuns. Excavations beneath the church have uncovered remains dating back to Neolithic times. The church lies below the main road. Head for the minaret of the attached mosque. (Open Mon.-Wed. and Fri.-Sat. 8:30-11am and 2:30-5:30pm.)

If you're curious about the Benedictine Order, the church is a good place to inquire: Your friendly hosts can explain the importance of the Jewish tradition in Catholic doctrine. A small **hostelry** in the monastery is available for those interested in sharing the monastic life (tel. 33 97 98; donation requested).

A **War Memorial** has been erected at **Kibbutz Qiryat Anavim** near Abu Ghosh in memory of the Palmah soldiers who fell fighting on the road to Jerusalem during the 1948 War of Independence. In this Jewish settlement you'll find the **HaEzrahi Youth Hostel** (tel. 34 27 70; members NIS18, nonmembers NIS20, breakfast included). Three kilometers down the road toward Jerusalem is a **campground** (tel. 53 77 17) run by the *moshav* at Beit Zayit.

To reach Abu Ghosh, take Egged bus #185 or 186 (NIS1.80), which leaves hourly from the central bus station. *Sherut* **taxis** traveling between Jerusalem and Tel-Aviv will stop at the exit, 2km from Abu Ghosh, but you have to pay the full fare to Tel Aviv and walk uphill to Abu Ghosh. To travel from Abu Ghosh to Latrun, you could walk downhill in the direction that the bus was going, take the turn-off for Abu Ghosh, continue down the highway (downhill) to the bus stop at **Shoresh,** and catch a bus there to Latrun. Those who don't like 35 minute walks can take bus #185 or 186 to Shoresh.

Latrun

Located on Jerusalem's vital lifeline, halfway to Tel Aviv, Latrun was the site of fierce fighting during the 1948 War of Independence. From Latrun, Arab forces closed the only road by which food and supplies could have been brought to the besieged inhabitants of Jerusalem. The Arab legion held this crucial junction against numerous Haganah attacks. Eventually the Jews secretly constructed a new section of road, called the Burma Road, outside the range of the Arab guns, to bring food to the starving residents of West Jerusalem. Latrun remained in Arab hands until the Six Day War in 1967. During World War I, the British fought here under General Allenby, and in earlier times, Crusaders, Arabs, Greeks, and Romans also assembled legions here in preparation for their respective assaults on the Holy City. The coveted fort that guards the junction of the Jerusalem-Tel Aviv road with the Ashqelon-Ramallah road is still an Israeli army base.

Across the road from the fort is the **Monastery of Latrun,** built in 1927 by the French Trappist Order on the ruins of a twelfth-century Crusader fortress. The site is presently under excavation and the remains of a Crusader basilica have been unearthed. The trip is also worth it for the wine you can purchase at the monastery (NIS3-13)—it is made by the monks from the local vineyards. This is said to be the site of the home of one of the thieves crucified at the side of Jesus; the name Latrun comes from the Latin *latro,* "thief." (Open daily 10am-12:30pm and 3:30-5:30pm.)

Continuing from the monastery and through the underpass on the road to Ramallah, you will reach a monastery now used by the French Prehistorical Research Center as its base for archeological digs. Below the monastery are the ruins of the **Emmaus Basilica.** Many parts of the church are easily discernible. According to Christian tradition, Jesus appeared to two of his disciples here after his resurrection. (Open 9am-noon, but hours are flexible because the gate to the ruins is the only way for cars to leave the research center. Tel. (02) 22 19 82.)

Canada Park, one of many spots in Israel forested with the help of the Jewish National Fund, is on the edge of the West Bank just north of Emmaus, and contains numerous archeological remains. There is a well-preserved Roman bath at the side of the road near the basilica. Built around 640 C.E., the bath hints at the prosperity of Emmaus during the Roman Byzantine period. Water holes, conduits, and the remains of an amphitheater can also be found in the park. Read the sign overlooking the West Bank Valley of Ayalon—it warns of the precarious security conditions in "Judea and Samaria," or the Occupied Territories.

As you continue north along the edge of the West Bank, you will come to **Modiin,** another interesting archeological site, which features the **Tombs of the Maccabees.** Every year on the first night of Hannukah a team of runners carries a torch, lit near the tombs, to Jerusalem where it is used for the ceremony of lighting the Hannukah candles.

Latrun can be reached by bus #402, 403, 404, or 433 passing between Jerusalem and Tel Aviv every half hour.

Avashalom Stalagmite Cave

The stalagmite and stalactite cave of Avashalom contains amazing speliological structures. Even the ridiculously large numbers of tour groups that converge on this place won't overshadow the beauty of these caverns. If you've never seen such a cave, a visit is a must. Listen to what the guide says about taking pictures; repeated exposure to flashes will damage the formations. Admission (NIS4) includes a slide show and guided tour (tel. 91 11 17).

The cave lies 19km southwest of Jerusalem next to the village of Nes Harim. Take bus #93 or 418 from the central bus station to Nes Harim (5 per day), and walk the 2km to the cave. Unfortunately, tour buses provide the only direct route. (Open Sun.-Thurs. 8:30am-4:30pm, Fri. 8:30am-noon.)

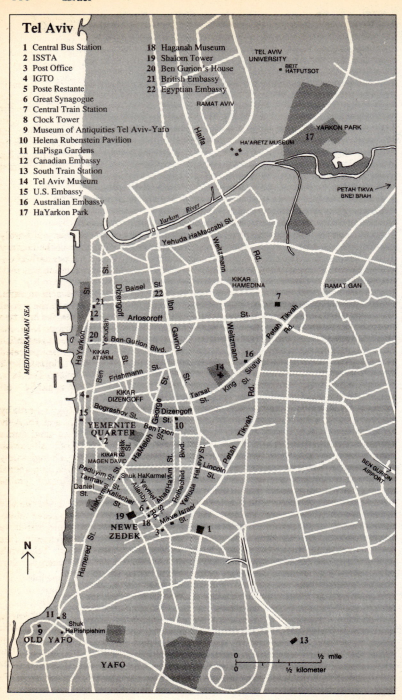

Tel Aviv

1 Central Bus Station
2 ISSTA
3 Post Office
4 IGTO
5 Poste Restante
6 Great Synagogue
7 Central Train Station
8 Clock Tower
9 Museum of Antiquities Tel Aviv-Yafo
10 Helena Rubenstein Pavilion
11 HaPisga Gardens
12 Canadian Embassy
13 South Train Station
14 Tel Aviv Museum
15 U.S. Embassy
16 Australian Embassy
17 HaYarkon Park

18 Haganah Museum
19 Shalom Tower
20 Ben Gurion's House
21 British Embassy
22 Egyptian Embassy

TEL AVIV
UNIVERSITY
BEIT
HATFUTSOT

RAMAT AVIV

YARKON PARK

HA'ARETZ MUSEUM

17

PETAH TIKVA
BNEI BRAH

Yarkon   River

Yarkon River

Yehuda HaMaccabi St.

Haifa

Weizmann

KIKAR
HAMEDINA

Rd.

RAMAT GAN

St.

Dizengoff

Baisel   St.

22

Ibn

7

Arlosoroff

Petah   Tikvah   Rd.

St.

MEDITERRANEAN SEA

21
12

20

Ben-Gurion Blvd.

Gavriel

Weizmann

St.

HaYarkon

KIKAR
ATARIM

Ben

St.

St.

Frishmann

Tarsat

King

St.

St.

St.

Shaul

Rd.

16

14

4

KIKAR
DIZENGOFF

Bograshov St.

George

Dizengoff

15

Ben Izion

St.

St.

10

St.

2

YEMENITE
QUARTER

Bialik

HaMeleh

Petah   Tikvah

BEN GURION
AIRPORT

KIKAR
MAGEN DAVID

St.

St.

Peduyim St.
Tarmav
Daniel

Shuk HaKarmel

Allenby

Ahad Ha'Am

Rothschild

HaLevy

Lincoln

St.

HaKarmel
Kalischer

St.

Rd.

Yehuda

Blvd.

St.

St.

6

19

18

Mikve Israel

NEWE
ZEDEK

3

1

Hameved

St.

N

11 8
Shuk
9   HaPishpishim
OLD YAFO

13

YAFO

½ mile

0

0

½ kilometer

Tel Aviv and the Central Coast

The small bit of Israeli coast stretching from Haifa to Tel Aviv is home to nearly two-thirds of the country's population. The lush, humid coastal plain is Israel's wealthiest and most westernized region. Streamlined steel skyscrapers decorate the Tel Aviv skyline, while farther north tidy *kibbutzim* employ state-of-the-art agricultural techniques to feed the rest of the country. Tel Aviv is also Israel's financial and industrial center. Although many of the resorts on the central coast cater to wealthy vacationers, budget travel is still possible. This bustling and booming region of Israel does inspire emotion: Some visitors fall in love, and some catch the first Egged bus to Jerusalem.

Tel Aviv

Although the Hebrew words *tel aviv* mean "hill of spring," greenery is hardly the first image that is evoked by this urban landscape. In his turn-of-the-century novel *Altneuland,* Theodor Herzl pictured a city which would be established entirely by contemporary Jews in a Jewish homeland; the Hebrew translation was entitled *Tel Aviv.*

The development of Israel's largest city began with Jewish settlement in Jaffa, now its junior partner, in 1820. Jaffa served as Palestine's major port and the arrival point for immigrants. Soon enough Jews had settled in Jaffa to create the first two all-Jewish neighborhoods, **Neveh Tzedek** in 1887 and **Neveh Shalom** in 1891. As the Jewish population in Jaffa continued to increase, the settlers decided to establish a quiet suburb away from the noisy urban port. On April 11, 1909, they parceled out their newly-acquired land north of Jaffa and called the area **Ahuzat Bayit** (Housing Property). One year later, the suburb's name was changed to **Tel Aviv.** Its first main streets included Herzl St., Ahad HaAm St., and Rothschild St.—all still busy thoroughfares.

More and more immigrants continued to arrive and settle in Tel Aviv, until by the 1920s it could no longer be called a suburb of Jaffa. In 1949, Jaffa and Tel Aviv were merged into one city. Tel Aviv's residents quickly transformed sand dunes into a vast landscape of steel, glass, and reinforced concrete. As the only all-Jewish city of its time, Tel Aviv became the center of Jewish art and culture. Though many Israelis swear that nothing could induce them to live in such a noisy, impersonal place, the constant modernization and expansion of Tel Aviv is a vibrant symbol of Israeli determination.

In 1983, the municipality of Tel Aviv put a ban on new office space in the city in an attempt to reduce the flow of Tel Aviv residents outward to the massive suburban area. Various areas, like Neveh Tzedek, are being refurbished into attractive residential and cultural areas, while ethnic areas like the Kerem HaTemanim (the Yemenite Quarter) are preserved with their traditional appeal intact. Tel Aviv's many museums and tourist attractions are slickly presented, and the energy, color, and eclecticism of the city are infectious.

Orientation

Located in the center of Israel's Mediterranean coastline, Tel Aviv is 60km (a 50-min. bus ride) west of Jerusalem, and 90km (a 2½-hr. bus ride) south of Haifa.

Several major streets run parallel through the downtown area. **HaYarkon Street** runs from the northern tip of the city, along the shore, to **Kerem HaTemanim,** (The Yemenite Quarter). **Ben Yehudah Street,** 1 block inland off HaYarkon, contains many restaurants and travel agencies. At November 2 Sq. it becomes **Allenby Road,** and intersects at Magen David Sq. with **King George Street** just south of the **Shuk HaCarmel** (Carmel Market). The cafe-lined **Dizengoff Street,** named for the city's first mayor, parallels Ben Yehudah St. at its northern end, and, at its southern end, turns east-west at **Zina Dizengoff Sq.,** a popular meeting spot. The waterfront at **Yafo** (anglicized as **Jaffa**) lies south, outside the downtown area.

House numbers run from the waterfront to the east, and from south to north. Numbers are posted at street corners on the wall of the nearest house. Be aware that some streets, like Allenby and Dizengoff, make disorienting ninety-degree turns.

The **central bus station,** in the southern part of the downtown area, is spread over several square blocks interspersed with a bustling fruit-fashions-felafel market. Buses to points inside and outside Tel Aviv leave from here, so just keep repeating your destination and sooner or later you'll be steered to the correct bus stand. United Tours, next to the GTIO, sells a detailed map of all bus routes for Tel Aviv and environs (NIS1). The last city bus is 12:30am, and buses do not run on *shabbat.*

The routes of six **urban buses** are important to visitors:

#4: From the central bus station, runs parallel to the coastline up Allenby and Ben Yehudah and back.

#5: From the central bus station, runs north along Rothschild Blvd. and Dizengoff, turns around at Nordau and Yehudah HaMaccabi (2 blocks from the youth hostel), and returns along Dizengoff.

#10: From city hall to Bat Yam via Yafo, returns on Ben Yehudah.

#25: Runs between Tel Aviv University and Bat Yam via Haifa Rd., Yehudah HaMaccabi (near the youth hostel), Shuk HaCarmel (market), and Yafo.

#27: From the central bus station, runs along Petah Tikva Rd. and Haifa Rd. to Tel Aviv University and Bet HaTfutsot, through Tel Baruh and back.

#46: From the central bus station, along Petah Tikva Rd., to Yafo and back.

Intercity buses leave from the seven islands outside the information and ticket counter. If traveling to a major city, avoid the chaos around the counter by finding the right island and purchasing tickets on the bus (usually only possible on buses more than a block from the ticket center). The following departure points are within a few blocks of the station: Buses travel to Ben Gurion Airport (Lod) and Ramla from Finn St.; to Netanya from Hagra St.; to Hadera and Zihron Yaakov from HaNegev St.; to Azor and Bat Yam from the field of Neveh Shaanan; and to Rehovot from HaGedud Ha'Ivri St.

Practical Information

Government Tourist Information Office (GTIO): 7 Mendele St. (tel. 22 32 66 or 22 32 67), off Ben Yehudah, parallel to Frischmann. Maps of Tel Aviv and other cities, schedules of cultural events, and information on hotels in Tel Aviv. Tickets to Israel Philharmonic and other events sold here. On 48 hr. notice, will arrange a visit to meet Israelis in their homes. Open Sun.-Thurs. 8:30am-5pm, Fri. 8:30am-2pm.

Budget Travel (ISSTA): 109 Ben Yehudah St. (tel. 24 71 67), at Ben Gurion St. Cheap plane fares, tours, and information. Will hold mail. For an ISIC, bring a photo, proof of student status, and NIS15. Open May-Sept. Sun.-Tues. and Thurs. 8:30am-6pm, Wed. and Fri. 8:30am-1pm; Oct.-April Sun.-Tues. and Thurs. 9am-1pm and 3-6pm, Wed. and Fri. 9am-1pm.

GSTS International: 57 Ben Yehudah St. (tel. 22 22 63), next to the GTIO. Cheap fares on scheduled airlines, charters, train and boat tickets, car rental and hotel bookings. Open Oct.-May Sun.-Tues. and Thurs. 8:30am-6pm, Wed. and Fri. 8:30am-1pm; June-Sept. Sun.-Tues. and Thurs. 8:30am-2pm, Wed. 3:30-6pm, Fri. 8:30am-1pm.

Embassies: U.S., 71 HaYarkon St. (tel. 65 43 38). Open Mon.-Fri. 8am-4pm. Closed Israeli holidays. **Canada,** 220 HaYarkon St. (tel. 22 81 22). Consular section open Mon.-Fri. 8am-12:30pm. **Australia,** 37 King Shaul St., 4th floor (tel. 25 04 51). **U.K.,** 192 HaYarkon St. (tel. 24 91 71). Consular section open Mon.-Fri. 8am-1pm. **Egyptian,** 54 Basel St. (tel. 22

41 52), just off Ibn Gavirol St. Visa section open Sun.-Thurs. 9-11am. Bring your passport, 2 photos, and $12 (the fee may vary slightly). Get there early—the embassy can be very crowded, and if you haven't made it to the window by 11am, too bad. Pick up your passport with visa at noon. Visa information (tel. 46 41 51).

Banks: Most open Sun.-Tues. and Thurs. 8:30am-12:30pm and 4-5:30pm, Mon., Wed., and Fri. 8:30am-noon. Some banks in hotels may stay open all day. Main bank offices: **Bank Hapoalim,** 104 HaYarkon St.; **Israel Discount,** 16 Mapu St.; **Bank Leumi,** 130 Ben Yehudah St. Branches all over the city and suburbs.

American Express: Meditrad Ltd., 16 Ben Yehudah St. (tel. 29 46 54). Mail held and personal checks approved for card holders (with a passport and 1¼% charge) for up to $500 every 21 days. Larger sums of cash available with telexed approval from a U.S. office. Open Sun.-Tues. and Thurs. 8:30am-1:30pm and 3:30-6pm, Wed. and Fri. 8:30am-1pm.

Post Office: 132 Allenby Rd. **Poste Restante** is two blocks east at 7 Mikve Yisrael St. Both open Sun.-Thurs. 8am-6pm and Fri. 8am-2pm. Tel Aviv has many branch offices that usually close earlier; ask for the nearest *doar.*

Telephones: 7 Mikve Yisrael St., in the post office. You can pay for calls at gate 21, without standing in the long line for the postal bank. To make international calls from outside the phone office, dial 18; for collect calls dial 62 28 81, 62 28 82, or 62 28 83. All three numbers will probably be busy, but keep trying. For directory information dial 14.

Telephone Code: 03.

Airport: Ben Gurion Airport, 22km southeast of Tel Aviv in Lod. For information about flights on all airlines, call 38 11 11. Egged bus #475 leaves from Finn St. near the central bus station every 20 min., Sun.-Thurs. 5:30am-11pm. United Tours bus #222 leaves from the central train station hourly and goes down HaYarkon St. to the airport (Sun.-Fri. 3:45am-11pm, Sat. 11:45am-10:45pm). *Sherut* taxis also available. The ride takes about 45 min.

Buses: For Egged information, call tel. 43 24 14. See above.

Train Station: information tel. 25 42 71. Several trains to Haifa, Netanya, and Nahariya leave from the central train station, Arlosoroff St. across Haifa Rd. Trains to Jerusalem leave at 8:15am from Bnei Brak, returning at 4pm. 20% student discount. Slower, but more pleasant and slightly cheaper than bus travel. You can buy tickets on the train. Take buses #62, 64 from Ben Yehudah to the station. The Hebrew word for train is *rakevet.*

Ferries: J. Kassas Agency, 1 Ben Yehudah St. (tel. 66 49 02). Tickets to Piraeus, Crete or Rhodes in Greece, twice per week, one way $58; 1 stop-over en route to Piraeus $12 extra. **Mano Passenger Lines Ltd.** (tel. 28 21 21, 28 21 22, or 28 21 23), 60 Ben Yehudah St. Books tickets on Afroessa Line ships to Greece. Boats leave Sun. and Thurs. 8pm. Deck chair one way $65 including port tax if under 28 years old; others $78. July-Aug. under 28 $72, others $90. Both offices open Sun.-Tues. and Thurs. 9am-5:30pm, Wed. 9am-2pm, and Fri. 9am-1pm.

Sherut **taxis:** Salomon St., opposite the central bus station, for cars to the suburbs, Haifa, and Jerusalem. Allenby Rd. and HaMoshavot Sq. to most other major cities. These cost roughly 25% more than the buses. *Sherut* taxis run Fri. evenings and Sat., but a *shabbat* surcharge increases fares another 20%.

English Bookstores: Steimatzky's, 103 Allenby St., has the largest selection in Israel. **Pollard's Used Books,** 36 King George St., has a 100-year tradition of buying and selling used books. **2 in 1 Bookstore,** 203 Dizengoff, next to the Greenhouse Hostel, is open 10am-10pm. Good collection of used books; will buy.

Society for the Protection of Nature in Israel (HaḤevrah LeHaganat HaTeveh): 4 Hashfela St. (tel. 38 25 01), near the central bus station. English-guided hiking trips to all parts of the country, year-round. Most tours range far off the beaten tourist track.

Camping Supplies: LaMetayel, Dizengoff Center (tel. 28 68 94). The largest and cheapest camping store in Israel. Books, maps, guides, information, and a full range of equipment. Open Sun.-Thurs. 9:30am-7pm and Fri. 9:30am-1pm. Small store at the **Bnei Dan Youth Hostel (IYHF),** 32 Bnei Dan St., sells packs and some expensive gear.

Kibbutz Offices: Takam (United Kibbutz Movement), 82 HaYarkon St. (tel. 65 17 10). **HaKibbutz Ha'Artzi,** 13 Leonardo da Vinci St. (tel. 25 31 31). Takam and HaArtzi offices open Sun.-Thurs. 8am-2pm. **HaKibbutz HaDati,** 7 Dubnov St. (tel. 25 72 31), religious volunteers only.

Moshav Movement: 19 Leonardo Da Vinci St. (tel. 25 84 73), Sun.-Thurs. 9am-3pm, Fri. 8am-noon, and **Moshav Volunteer Office,** 5 Tiomkin St. (tel. 62 58 06 or 61 53 16), off Yehudah HaLevi St. Office open Sun.-Thurs. 9am-3pm. When applying for work through one of the above offices, bring 2 passport photos and your passport. You must be 18-32 years old and commit for a minimum of 1 month.

Laundromats: 51 Ben Yehudah St. and 45 Bograshov St. Coin-operated washers and dryers. Wash NIS4, soap NIS1, 20 min. drying NIS3. Both open Sun.-Mon. and Wed.-Thurs. 8am-10pm, Tues. and Fri. 8am-2pm.

Crisis Intervention: Telephone counseling, tel. 25 33 11.

Rape Crisis: Tel. 23 48 19, 24 hours.

Committee for Fighting AIDS: Tel. 20 31 21 or 29 01 01, 24 hours. Information in English, Hebrew, and Arabic.

Drug Counseling: Tel. 546 35 87.

Pharmacy: HaGalil Pharmacy, 80 Ben Yehudah St. (tel. 22 33 58). English spoken.

Dental Emergency: Dizengoff Center, Gate 3 (tel. 29 48 69, 28 58 22). Open 24 hours.

First Aid: Tel. 101.

Police, Tel. 100.

Fire, Tel. 102.

Accommodations

Most of Tel Aviv's cheap hotels are located near the beach on or by **Allenby Road, Ben Yehudah Street,** and **HaYarkon Street.** These major roads create quite a racket, so check the noise level before you take any room—the traffic you hear at midday is likely to continue most of the night. Hostels in Tel Aviv fill up quickly, especially during the summer, so try to check in early. Prices drop by about 10% in the off-season. Except during times of increased military tension, sleeping on the beach is tolerated. However, there have been many cases of theft and sexual harassment; single women in particular should not sleep on the beaches. If you must, go as far north as possible (staying south of the port) and sleep on your wallet.

Bnei Dan Youth Hostel (IYHF), 32 Bnei Dan St. (tel. 45 50 42), inconveniently located on the Yarkon River in the northern part of the city. From central bus station take bus #5, get off at Pinkas St., make a left onto Brandeis St., follow Brandeis to the end, make a right onto Bnei Dan St., and walk 2 blocks north. Barracks-style rooms and cramped bungalows. Ask for Yitzhak if you arrive midday and want to register. No transportation on *shabbat.* Light meal NIS5-6, meat meal NIS7-8. Members NIS14, nonmembers NIS16, under 18 NIS5.

The Greenhouse, 201 Dizengoff St. (tel. 23 59 94). Take Bus #5 all the way up Dizengoff. Still the best hostel in Tel Aviv. Clean, airy rooms, kitchen-facilities, spotless showers, friendly management, great location, telephone, and no curfew. Coffee, beer, and soda sold in a pleasant sitting room. Rooftop bar open until 12:30am. Beach campers can use shower and kitchen facilities for NIS3. Dorm beds NIS12.50, doubles NIS26, apartments NIS40, and two-bedroom apartments with kitchen and bath NIS75. Office open 7:30-10am and 2:30pm-midnight.

Hotel Yosef, 15 Bograshov St. (tel. 28 09 55), off Ben Yehudah St. Good location. Nice bar with graffiti-covered walls. Pleasant staff. Information about cheap flights available. Kitchen. Luggage can be checked for no extra charge. Lockout 10am-1pm. Curfew 1am. Dorm beds NIS9. If it's full inside, you can sleep under the stars on the "rooftop lounge" for NIS5.

Back Pack Hostel, 306 Dizengoff St. (tel. 45 83 81 or 44 39 28). Buses #4 or #5 from central bus station, #222 from the airport. Sparkling new hostel in a quiet neighborhood. 2 small kitchens, laundry facilities available, and free tea and coffee in the TV room. No curfew. Dorm beds NIS10, doubles NIS25.

The Hostel, 60 Ben Yehudah St, 4th floor (tel. 28 70 88 or 28 15 00). Excellent location. Newly renovated kitchen and bathrooms. Conscientious manager. Cold drinks and beer available for NIS2. Curfew 2am, but no curfew on Fri. Dorm beds in small room NIS7.50, in large room NIS10. Sheets and hot showers included.

Momo's Hostel, 28 Ben Yehudah St. (tel. 29 74 21 or 28 74 71). Another centrally located hostel with a bar and restaurant downstairs. Ring the bell downstairs if the door is locked. No curfew. Dorm beds with sheets NIS8.

The Top Hostel, 84 Ben Yehudah St. (tel. 23 78 07 or 23 74 19). On the top floor with a great view from the bar. The shabby mattresses are presided over by funky paintings on the walls. Supermarket conveniently located across the street. Curfew 1am. Dorm beds NIS8.

Immanuel House Christian Hospice, 12 Be'er Hoffman St., Yafo (tel. 82 14 59 or 82 47 21), at the corner of Auerbach. Take bus #44 or 46 and get off after the Paz gas station on Eilat St. If you're looking for a neat, friendly, quiet place outside the city center, this is it. Built by Peter Ustinov's father and newly renovated. Curfew 11pm. Dorm beds NIS10, doubles NIS20.

Hotel Riviera, 52 HaYarkon St. (tel. 65 68 70 or 65 38 83), near the beach. Cramped but clean with friendly management. 24-hour cafeteria and late night bar. Singles NIS28, with shower NIS31. Doubles NIS38, with shower NIS46. Breakfast included.

Hotel HaGalil, 23 Beit Yosef (tel. 65 50 36). Turn off Allenby St. between #54 and 56, and follow the signs. Tidy, quiet rooms with private balconies. Excellent location near Shuk Ha-Carmel and Kerem HaTemanim. Closes at midnight, but you can ask for a key to the front door. Singles NIS26, doubles NIS30-40. Triples NIS20 per person.

Hotel Tamar, 8 Gnessin St. (tel. 28 69 97). Follow Mendele St. east from Ben Yehudah all the way to its end. The rooms are silent and spotless, but stuffy; private showers and refrigerator. Decorated in modern Israeli functionalist style. Singles NIS25, doubles NIS35-40.

The Home, 6 Frischmann St., corner of HaYarkon, office #16, (tel. 22 26 95). Rent furnished apartments with small refrigerators and private bathrooms. Ocean views. Per week: Singles $130, doubles $150, triples $200. Per month: $500.

Allenby Street has a row of cheap hotels located near the beach. The area is seedy and probably not safe at night for women alone. During the summer of 1988, the area was in the midst of a major renewal project, indicating that it is soon to become a fancy tourist area. In the meantime, several hotels are still in the budget range. Many of the hotels are undergoing serious renovations.

Bell Hotel, 12 Allenby St. (tel. 65 42 91 or 65 70 11). Clean rooms, each with microscopic bathroom and shower. Friendly manager. A/C, and beautiful ocean views from some rooms. Dorm rooms for groups (men only) NIS20. Singles NIS35, doubles NIS55. Breakfast included.

Monopol Hotel, 4 Allenby St. (tel. 65 59 06). On the beach at HaKnesset Sq. You can see the sunset over the ocean from the large porch attached to beach-front rooms. Undergoing renovation; the old rooms are not dirty but have peeling paint and tiny showers. Singles NIS25, doubles NIS35. Breakfast NIS6.

Migdal David Hotel, 8 Allenby St. (tel. 65 63 92), half a block from the beach. Clean rooms with newly renovated bathrooms that are quickly deteriorating. The rest of the hotel is also being redone, and the new rooms are clean and comfortable. Views of the neighborhood's seedy back alleys. Singles NIS36, doubles NIS70.

Beach Hotel 6 Allenby Rd. (tel. 63 74 63). Clean rooms with small private bathrooms. English not spoken much. Singles NIS30-35, doubles NIS50, triples NIS60.

Hotel Nordau, 27 Nahalat Binyamin (tel. 62 16 12), near Neveh Tzedek. Adequate. Singles NIS30. Doubles NIS50, with bath NIS60. Breakfast included.

Mash House, 4 Trumpeldor St. (tel. 65 76 84), right on the beach between Herbert Samuel St. and HaYarkon St. Rooms and flats with showers and kitchen facilities. Singles NIS27, doubles NIS45, apartments NIS70. Per month: approximately NIS600.

Food

To eat cheaply in Tel Aviv, follow the Israelis to one of the many neighborhoods that specialize in street food. The cheapest places for filling up are the self-service joints on Ben Yehudah St. or the innumerable felafel stands—those around Shuk HaCarmel and along Bezalel St. off Allenby and King George are the spiciest, and stay open the latest. Mix either (but not both) *harif,* the red hot sauce, or the yellow mustard sauce, with lots of *tahina.* One portion (a *manah*) costs about NIS1.50.

The Kerem HaTemanim, between Shuk HaCarmel and the beach, has good, cheap Middle Eastern food. There are a few very cheap workers' restaurants on Peduyim Street. For NIS1-2 you can eat at an *al ha esh* ("on the fire") stand along Kanfe Nisharim St., which runs north-south in the Neveh Tzedek area. Ask around for someone selling homemade *marak basar* (a wonderful Yemenite meat soup) or *melawah* (fried, salted dough dipped in *srug*, *khelbe*, or another sharp sauce). A family's tureens are usually empty by noon or 1pm, so try to eat lunch early.

For a sit-down meal, find an empty seat along **Dizengoff Street,** Tel Aviv's fashion runway. The city's ethnic diversity is revealed in the range of restaurant-cafes with culinary representation by Jewish immigrants from Russia, Argentina, and everywhere in between. Dizengoff St. is also the most likely place to find restaurants open on Saturday. On the northeast side of Dizengoff Sq. there are several good sub shops where you can stuff your own roll with cheese, salads, vegetables, or meat. Avoid the plastic-coated couple, **McDavid's** and **Donald Duck,** unless you're a junk-food junkie suffering from nitrite withdrawal.

For a treat, head north to **Yermiyahu Street,** which runs between Dizengoff and Ben Yehudah just before they intersect. This area is quieter than downtown, and several of its restaurants are superb.

Another alternative is to visit the factories where *bagelahs* are made by hand on primitive equipment; only the hollow center of these large sesame rings resembles American bagels. Sprinkle each bite with the spices contained in the paper twists piled on the counter. There are a handful of *bagelah* bakeries around the central bus station. In the event of a sneak late-night bagel-attack, visit the **all-night bagel factory** at 11 Pines St. The two bagel barns in Yafo, just beyond the old Clock Tower (on the right if you bear left onto Bet Eshel) are a bit more touristy.

For rock-bottom prices, shop at the large, outdoor **Shuk HaCarmel** (Carmel Market). Most of the produce stands are at the southwestern end of the market, west of HaCarmel St. between Tarmav and Kalisher. To catch prices at their lowest, shop an hour or two before the beginning of *shabbat,* when fruit and vegetable vendors cut their prices to sell off their goods. A new renovation project in the Shuk HaCarmel area is rejuvenating "Old Tel Aviv." A block south of the *shuk* is a new pedestrian street with lots of cafes. Farther north (off bus #4), the **Shuk HaTsafon** (Northern Market) is a little more expensive, but cleaner than HaCarmel.

Across Allenby, near King George St. on Bethlehem Rd., there's a row of felafel places that give you pita, which you can fill with felafel, fried eggplant, and dozens of salads. **Felafel Joseph** claims "the best felafel in the world." No kidding. For a quiet alternative to Dizengoff, walk along Shenkin St. (starting from Magen David Sq. across Allenby from the *shuk*). Pubs, galleries, a Russian tea house, and boutiques are opening here, and many university students enjoy the peaceful atmosphere.

No matter where you're going and what you're eating, you'll need to drink plenty of liquids. Practically anywhere in the city, NIS2 will buy a chilled glass of *meets* (fruit juice). Apples, oranges, grapefruit, lemons, bananas, grapes, and coconuts all go through the blender with water or milk.

Zion Restaurant, 28 Peduyim St. Follow HaCarmel, the main *shuk* street, down to Rambam, turn right, and look for narrow Peduyim St. MIxed local and foreign diners in a very Middle Eastern atmosphere. A *hoummus* platter and drink NIS4-5. Open 9am-2pm.

Acapulco, the corner of Dizengoff and Frischmann St. A great spot for people-watching and a cheap kebab dinner. The menu features aerial photos of all the dishes. Main dishes NIS6-7. Open daily 9am-midnight.

Cherry's, Dizengoff at Ben Gurion St. Sidewalk tables and air-conditioned interior. Excellent salads and light meals NIS6-10. Open daily 9am-midnight.

Hungarian Blintzes, 114 Dizengoff St. (tel. 23 05 18). Have your blintzes filled with combinations of cream, chocolate, cinnamon, apples, cheese, nuts, raisins, jam, spinach, and an assortment of other goodies. Two savory blintzes cost NIS6-9.

Domino's, Ben Yehudah St. near Yermiyahu. No relation to the American pizza joint. Sit-down Italian meals NIS8-15. Single serving of pizza NIS2.50, whole pizzas NIS11-15. Open daily noon-2am.

Peking, Dizengoff at Yermiyahu St. (tel. 45 34 23). Serves some of the best Chinese food in Tel Aviv. Soups NIS4-7, hor d'oeuvres NIS4-10, main dishes NIS12-30. Open daily 12:30pm-midnight.

Pirozki, On Dizengoff St. next to Peking. Excellent Russian food and huge salads, indoors or outdoors. Discount lunch menu. Main dishes NIS10-13, desserts NIS5-7. Open daily noon-midnight.

Cafe B'Nordau, 230 Ben Yehudah St. (tel. 44 83 32). This cozy, plant-filled restaurant caters to largely but not exclusively gay clientele. Don't miss its friendly atmosphere and tasty light meals (NIS5-10). Open Sun.-Fri. 9am-1pm, Sat. 11am-1am.

Banana, 334 Dizengoff St. Scrumptious vegetarian fare in a pleasant setting and at reasonable prices. Brown rice and steamed veggies for dinner with dessert will cost you about NIS8-10. Open daily noon-midnight.

Eternity, 6 Kikar Malkei Yisrael St. Run by members of the Black Hebrew sect, a group originally from the midwestern United States who claim to be Jews and have settled in Israel. Their dietary laws prohibit both milk and meat, so you'll find interesting alternatives, from tofu cream pies to vegetarian hot tamales. Full meals NIS10-15. Open Sun.-Thurs. 9am-midnight, Fri. 9am-2pm, and Sat. after sundown.

Sights

The frenzied, chaotic atmosphere of the **Shuk HaCarmel** (Carmel Market) will entertain even the most jaded of tourists. Near the northern entrance to the market, shopkeepers stand behind piles of clothing and footwear. Waving nylon undergarments and red plastic sandals, they bellow their products' virtues. Farther south, near the parking lot, is the bustling produce market, where you can buy fresh fruit and vegetables at the lowest prices in the city. In the meat section on the west side of the market, huge mounds of chickens plucked bare make this area look like the morning after a foul barnyard orgy. The entrance to the *shuk* is at **Magen David Square** at the intersection of Allenby and King George St. The traditionalist community in **Kerem HaTemanim** (the Yemenite Quarter), to the west and north along Allenby, still retains its character despite the number of stores hawking American T-shirts. Take bus #4 from the central bus station and ask the driver to let you off at the *shuk*.

Neveh Tzedek, west of the Shalom Tower, is quickly becoming known as the artists' quarter. Although the streets may be nearly deserted by 7 or 8pm, during the day you can people-watch from cheap cafes and explore the studios of Israel's avant-garde. For an oasis in the asphalt desert, head for the expansive **HaYarkon Park,** in the northern part of the city (take bus #1, 4, or 5), where from 9am-midnight, you can rent a rowboat and cool off on the Yarkon River. Boats can be rented from **Tikva-Dagon** (tel. 41 39 21) or **Irgun HaYarkon** (tel. 44 84 22) near the bridge, where Haifa Rd. crosses the river, at NIS5 an hour for two people, NIS1 extra for each additional passenger. The park also contains a tropical garden and an outdoor amphitheater for concerts. (See Entertainment.)

The numerous exhibits, models, and audio-visual displays at **Beit HaTfutsot** (Museum of the Diaspora) document the Jewish experience in exile. The exhibits show the daily life and religious ritual as well as the history of disparate Jewish communities through movies, slides, maps, and artifacts. For many, the most powerful exhibit is the "Scrolls of Fire," a collection of documents that provide first-person perspectives on massacres from Roman times to the Nazi concentration camps. Mini-cinemas throughout the museum feature documentaries, as well as recordings of dramatized discussions between historical figures. Depending on the extent of your interest, a visit to the museum could take a few hours or a full day. The museum is located on the Tel Aviv University campus in the suburb of Ramat Aviv; take bus #25 from Yafo, Carmel Market, or the IYHF youth hostel, or bus #27 from the central bus station, and get off at gate two of the university. (Open

Sun.-Tues. and Thurs. 10am-5pm, and Wed. 10am-7pm. Admission NIS5, students NIS3. *Chronosphere,* a multi-screen audio-visual display, costs an additional NIS1.)

One kilometer southwest of Beit HaTfutsot on Ha'Universitah St. is the vast **Ha'Aretz Museum Complex,** eight museums built around an archeological site. The most famous attraction here is the **Glass Museum,** containing one of the finest collections of glassware in the world. Exhibits trace the history of glassmaking, from the earliest examples of the craft in the fifteenth century B.C.E. through the Middle Ages. Don't miss the exquisite blue lamp to the left of the entrance, made for a Cairo mosque in the fourteenth century. Across the patio, the **Kadman Numismatic Museum** documents the history of Israel through ancient coins. The **Ceramics Museum** has a rich collection of pottery, especially the Gaza and Akko styles of Ibriq pottery. The **Nechustan Pavilion** houses the rewards of the excavations of the ancient copper industries at Timna, better known as King Solomon's Mines. Walk across the entrance area past the grassy amphitheater to the **Man and His Work Pavilion.**

To the southeast, still in the museum complex, are the **Tel Qasila Excavations,** which have revealed a twelfth-century B.C.E. Philistine port city and ruins dating back to the time of Kings David and Solomon. The Temple area at the top of the hill contains the remains of three separate Philistine temples, built one on top of another. Odd remains of structures from the medieval and Crusader periods also dot the hilltop. Down the hill to the south are smatterings of the residential and industrial quarter of the Philistine town. A good free guide to the *tel* (multi-level site) is available in the small **Tel Qasila Pavilion,** to the east, which contains artifacts found at the site.

Past the Philistine town is the **Folklore Pavilion,** with Jewish religious arts, ceremonial objects, and ethnic costumes. The room at the rear of the pavilion contains a Florentine synagogue's benches, pulpit, and elaborately decorated ark. The Ha'Aretz complex also houses the **Alphabet Museum,** the **Lasky Planetarium,** and the **Museum of Science and Technology.** Take bus #25 from Yafo, Shuk HaCarmel, or the youth hostel; or take #27 from the central bus station. (Complex open Sun.-Fri. 9am-1pm, Tues. 4-7pm, Sat. 11am-2pm and 7-10pm. Admission NIS3, students NIS2.)

Also part of the Ha'Aretz collection, though at a different site, the **Museum of the History of Tel Aviv-Yafo,** 27 Bialik St., off Allenby near Shuk HaCarmel, traces the city's history through photographs, models, tacky dioramas, and a panoramic slide presentation. (Open Sun.-Thurs. 9am-1pm. Admission NIS1.)

The **Tel Aviv Museum,** 27 King Saul Blvd., has split-level galleries and a large collection of Israeli and international modern art. The museum is large, so if your time is limited, head to pavilion #2. In the first half, you will find a wonderful collection of Impressionist art, including canvases by Corot, Renoir, Pissaro, Monet, and Dufy, with some works by Utrillo and a Degas sculpture. The second half features post-Impressionist masters such as Picasso, Juan Gris, Kokoschka, Roualt, and Matisse. Permanent collections and special exhibits celebrating Israeli artists are also on display. Call ahead or pick up a copy of the Friday *Jerusalem Post,* which has a supplementary section listing the museum's exhibits and events. Take bus #18, 19, or 70. (Open Sun.-Thurs. 10am-8pm, Fri. 10am-2pm, Sat. 11am-2pm and 7-10pm. Admission NIS3, students NIS2.)

The ticket for the Tel Aviv Museum also entitles you to enter the **Helena Rubinstein Pavilion,** down the street at 6 Tarsat Blvd., which has changing exhibits, usually on art or history. Take bus #5, 11, or 62. From the Tel Aviv Museum, turn right on King Shaul, left on Ibn Gavirol, right on Dizengoff, and left onto Tarsat. (Open same hours as Tel Aviv Museum.) The **Rubin Museum** at 14 Bialik St., off Ben Yehudah St., houses a permanent exhibition of the Israeli artist Reuven Rubin's painting and drawings. (Open Sun., Mon., Wed., and Thurs. 10am-2pm, Tues. 10am-1pm and 4pm-8pm, Sat. 11am-2pm. Admission NIS1.50, students free.)

Four museums concentrate on the pre-state period that significantly contributed to Israel's present character. The **Haganah Museum,** 23 Rothschild Blvd., houses exhibits tracing the development of the Israeli Defense Force from its beginnings as an underground movement during the British Mandate up to the present. One short video dramatizes "The Night of the Bridges," June 17, 1946, when the Palmah, an elite fighting force, destroyed seven British-maintained bridges in retaliation for the British blockade of ships carrying WWII refugees bound for Palestine. (Open Sun.-Thurs. 8:30am-3pm and Fri. 8:30am-noon. Admission NIS1.) The **Beit Bialik Museum** is the home of Hayim Nahman Bialik, one of Israel's greatest poets, left just as it was when he died. Bialik's manuscripts, paintings, photographs, articles, letters, and 94 books (with translations in 28 languages) are all on display here. (Open Sun.-Thurs. 9am-7pm, Fri. 9am-1pm. Free.) The **Jabotinsky Institute,** 38 King George St., illustrates the career of Za'ev Jabotinsky, the father of the rightwing philosophy of Revisionist Zionism which is the basis of the Likud Party. (Open Sun., Tues., and Thurs. 10am-6pm, Mon. and Wed. 10am-1pm and 6-8pm, Fri. 10am-1pm. Free.) **Ben Gurion's House,** at 17 Ben Gurion Ave., is filled with tributes to Israel's first prime minister by Jews and political leaders from all over the world. (Open Sun.-Thurs. 8am-1pm, Mon. and Thurs. 5-7pm, Fri. 8am-1pm, Sat. 11am-2pm. Free.)

If Tel Aviv has a historical monument, it is the **Great Synagogue** on Ahad Ha'Am St., with its enormous dome and glossy stained-glass windows. Completed in 1926 and renovated in 1970, the synagogue is ancient by Tel Aviv standards. On Friday at sunset, throngs of the faithful make their way toward the synagogue, bringing all traffic to a halt.

At 125m in height, the **Shalom Tower** is the tallest structure in the Middle East and features an observatory with a view of the vast (and monotonous) Tel Aviv area. The price of the elevator ride is also high: NIS5, students NIS3.50. (Open Sun.-Thurs. 9am-7pm, Fri. 9am-2pm). If you think the observatory is worth the price, you'll probably want to visit the **wax museum** on the ground floor. This motley exhibit has Michael Jackson, Charles Manson, and Israeli singer Ofra Haza rubbing sticky elbows with Hansel, Gretel, and Haim Weizmann. Admission, which includes a ticket to the observatory, is NIS7, students NIS5.50. The tower occupies the site of the **Herzliya Gymnasium,** the first school in Israel in which classes were conducted in Hebrew. (Tower and museum open Sept.-May Sun.-Thurs. 9am-4:30pm, Fri. 9am-1:30pm; June-Aug. Sun.-Fri. 9am-6:45pm.) **Safari Park** (tel. 77 61 81) is a 250-acre African animal reserve where wild beasts including giraffes, zebras, ostriches, and elephants roam free. You can get to Ramat Gan and the reserve by bus #30, 35, or 45 and then board one of the three buses that are available for vehicle-less visitors at 10am, noon, and 2pm. (Reserve open Oct.-May Sun.-Thurs. 9am-3pm, Fri. 9am-2pm; June-Sept. Sun.-Thurs. 9am-5pm, Fri. 9am-2pm.)

Entertainment

Tel Aviv's main attraction is its vast, sparkling waterfront. The beaches are fair, though a bit dirty and extremely crowded. Most of the popular beaches are near the Sheraton, Hilton, and Gordon Hotels, while the southern coastline tends to be less packed. Tel Aviv's beaches are rife with theft; if possible, lock your valuables away before you hit the sands. Avoid the grossly overpriced refreshment stands in Atarim Sq. (also known as Namir Sq.); Ben Yehudah St., with bountiful, cheap food and drink, is never more than a two-minute walk from the beach. Near Atarim Sq., a marina rents sailboats, surfboards, and windsurfers. Surfers strut their stuff in the waters between the Carlton and Hilton Hotels. The marina also has an outdoor roller-rink and a municipal pool. The beachside watermelon stands at **Hof HaMa'ariv** (the Western Beach, actually in southern Tel Aviv) are packed in the evening and are often the site of impromptu outdoor dances during the summer.

Tel Aviv is the only city in Israel capable of supporting a real nightlife with a rhythm of its own. Most visitors bask on the beaches during the day, waiting for the city to come alive after nightfall. Tel Aviv's discos open at 10pm, but few really hop before midnight. The **Colosseum,** at Atarim Sq., has the champion light show; **Penguin,** 43 Yehudah HaLevi St., just west of Allenby Rd., and **Liquid,** 18 Montefiore St., are the most popular with the under 20 crowd (there's no minimum drinking age in Israel); both clubs play funk and new wave. Sunday is Gay Night at Liquid. Other gay nightspots include **Attractive,** on Dizengoff St., corner of Arlosoroff, open Mon.-Sat. 11pm-3am, and **Metro,** downstairs from the Sivan movie theater on Allenby St. near the corner of Biyalik and Tchernichovsky Sts., open daily from 9pm. **Sirocco,** 44 Emek Yisrael, is trendy, though the cognoscenti don't arrive until 2am.

The **Kolnoa Dan,** 61 HaYarkon St., at Trumpeldor St., has dancing and, occasionally, live bands. Almost all clubs are closed Mondays; entrance fees range from NIS6 to 13, depending on the evening's program. To party with Israeli college students, head to the disco **Focus** (tel. 42 30 04) at Tel Aviv University on a Friday or Saturday night. Tuesdays starting at 7pm is 60s rock night, while at 7pm on Mondays and Wednesdays the club offers folkdancing.

The Mediterranean art of people-watching is practiced by experts in Tel Aviv's cafes before the discos start up. The best places from which to watch the glittering masses on parade are the tables on **Dizengoff** and **Yermiyahu St. Dizengoff Square** (which is more of a circle) has been spruced up in recent years with a futuristic pedestrian walkway and a fire and water fountain designed by the Israeli artist Agam. On the hour, except at 2 and 3pm, the fountain's colorful triple-tiered circular structure rotates and water and flames flash in synchrony with classical music. Whether you're watching the fountain or the people, you can say in Hebrew *ani mizdangeff* (male) or *ani mizdangeffet* (female), which means "I'm doing/becoming/hanging-out-on Dizengoff."

Just off Dizengoff Sq. in an alley next to the Ester Cinema, **Long John Silver's** plays 60s rock for a friendly, largely English-speaking crowd, and its drinks are less expensive than most in this area. Just behind Long John Silver's, **The Backyard** is popular with young Israelis as a quiet, intimate meeting-spot. At the intersection of Ibn Gavirol and HaShoftim St., **HaShoftim** attracts a funky crowd, as does **The Bistro,** next to the Neveh Tzedek theater in Neveh Tzedek. You'll find the cheapest beer and the liveliest customers at **The Whitehouse,** on HaYarkon St. near Frischmann St. Near Yermiyahu St., **M.A.S.H.** (More Alcohol Served Here), at 275 Dizengoff and **The Bell,** at the junction of Ben Yehudah and Dizengoff St., attract a hippie-ish, backpacking crowd. **The Happy Casserole** at 344 Dizengoff, featuring live music and walls covered with oldies memorabilia, caters more to local Israelis. For jazz, the best options are the Martef Elyon at **Beit Lessin,** 34 Weizmann St. (jazz every Sunday beginning at 10pm) and **Gordon's Pub,** on Gordon St.

Yafo's winding streets, outdoor cafes, and galleries buzz with activity most evenings. One of the city's most popular and packed spots is **Michel's Aladin** at 5 Mifratz Shlomo. The building was built 800 years ago as a Turkish bath. (Weeknights no cover charge, Fri. NIS5, Sat. NIS8, first drink included.) There is an Israeli folk dancing class offered on Sunday nights at 8pm at **Hamlin House,** 30 Weizmann Blvd. The tourist office can tell you about song and folklore sessions nightly at 8:30pm in Kedumim Sq. and occasionally in some of the ritzy hotels in the summer.

Tel Aviv is regarded by Israelis as their country's most cultured city and, indeed, it hosts an assortment of jazz and classical concerts, opera, ballet, and dance performances every night. For an extensive listing of performance schedules and other activities, including folk dancing and singing sessions, see *Events in the Tel Aviv Region, Hello Israel,* and *This Week in Israel,* all free at the GTIO and the more expensive hotels. The ticket office for concerts, plays, and other performances is at 93 Dizengoff St. (Open Sun.-Thurs. 9am-1pm and 5-7pm, Fri. 9am-1pm.) The **outdoor theater** in Neveh Tzedek, 6 Yehieli St., often has concerts and dance performances not listed elsewhere. For schedules, call 65 12 41. The new amphitheater at **HaYarkon Park** features rock and pop performers. For tickets and schedules inquire at Hadran ticket agency, 90 Ibn Gavirol St., north of Malkei Yisrael Sq. (tel. 24 87 87).

Yafo (Jaffa)

The port of Old Yafo is possibly the oldest functioning harbor in the world. The main port through which the first waves of Jewish immigrants arrived in Palestine, Yafo has been relegated by the modern port of Haifa to harboring mainly small fishing boats. Several years ago, Israel undertook a massive renovation project on land, and many of Yafo's convents, mosques, and crusader walls have been cleaned and restored. The lively city center, sidewalk cafes, and art galleries make for an interesting day trip, and the view of Tel Aviv and the Mediterranean from Yafo's landscaped parks is unbeatable.

Yafo, which means "beautiful" in Hebrew, is known in Arabic as Yafa, and in the Bible as Joppa. In the Bible, the reluctant prophet Jonah resisted his calling and fled to Joppa. Here he boarded a ship, from which he was thrown overboard and swallowed by a large fish. According to the New Testament, the Apostle Peter brought the disciple Tabitha back to life here. He then dwelt in the seaside house of the town tanner and received divine instructions to preach to non-Jews. You can visit the supposed house of Simon the Tanner.

The earliest archeological finds in Yafo date from the eighteenth century B.C.E. In 1468 B.C.E., the Egyptians conquered Yafo by hiding soldiers in large, clay jars that were brought in to the city market. King David conquered the city about 1000 B.C.E., and under Solomon it became the main port of Jerusalem, a position it maintained until the rise of Caesarea under King Herod. During the twelfth century, Yafo was taken by the Crusaders, by Salah al-Din, by Richard the Lion-Hearted, by the Muslims, and finally by the Crusaders again, who built magnificent walls and towers, parts of which remain. In 1267 the Mamluks overpowered the city, and from that time on Yafo remained a major Arab stronghold until 1948.

Relations between the Arabs in Yafo and the Jews in Tel Aviv were never good. In 1929, 1936, and 1939, Yafo was the scene of anti-Zionist riots. When the Irgun captured the Arab part of Yafo in 1948, shortly before the creation of the State of Israel, most of Yafo's Arab population—some 70,000 strong—fled the city. Resettled primarily by Jews, Yafo was officially incorporated into the municipality of Tel Aviv in 1949, and today has a large Arab population.

The **Clock Tower of Yafo,** on Yefet St., marks the entrance to the city. Every Wednesday at 9:30am, a free tour of Old Yafo meets here. Next to the clock tower is the minaret of the **el-Mahmudia Mosque,** an enormous structure erected in 1812. Entrance is forbidden to non-Muslims. Down Mifratz Shlomo St. from the mosque, the **Museum of Antiquities of Tel Aviv-Yafo** contains finds from nearby sites in Old Yafo. The columns and capitals scattered about the museum's courtyard date from the first century B.C.E. and were brought here from Caesarea during the last century. (Open Sun., Mon., and Wed.-Fri. 9am-1pm; Tues. 9am-1pm and 4-7pm; Sat. 10am-1pm. Admission NIS1.)

Behind the museum lie the grassy **HaPisga Gardens,** which contain a small, modern amphitheater as well as an archeological site with excavations of an eighteenth-century B.C.E. Hyksos town and a later Egyptian city. A white, gate-like sculpture dominates one hill in the gardens; its three sections depict the fall of Jericho, the sacrifice of Isaac, and Jacob's dream.

From the park, a small wooden footbridge leads to **Kikar Kedumim,** Yafo's tourist center. In 1740, the first Jewish hostel was established on this site. It included two *mikvaot* (ceremonial baths) and a synagogue. Libyan Jews have reopened the synagogue, which is still in use today. After the War of Independence, the beautiful, abandoned Arab stone buildings in this area became home to a large artists' colony. In the late 1950s the government renovated the neighborhood, and today studios, galleries, and cafes lie artfully arranged among the reconstructed buildings. Several interesting sights are located in this quarter, including a small but well-preserved archeological site, the colorful Greek Orthodox **Church of St. Michael,** the Roman Catholic **Monastery of St. Peter,** and the **House of Simon the Tanner.** The nearby clifftops offer splendid views of the Tel Aviv beach front and skyline. **Andromeda's**

Rock, scene of the mythological rescue by the god Perseus, is visible from the light-house a few blocks to the south.

Yafo's large **Shuk HaPishpishim** (Flea Market) retains much of its Middle Eastern charm. One of the most exciting markets in Israel, the covered complex of stalls offers endless delights: Persian carpets, leather goods, used clothes, and brassware of all kinds. Hashish connoisseurs will no doubt be fascinated by the vast selection of enormous *nargilehs,* elaborate Middle Eastern waterpipes. Bargaining is a way of life here, and you should begin by offering no more than half the asking price. To reach the flea market from the clock tower, continue 1 block south down Yefet St. and turn left. The market is sandwiched between Tzion and MeRagusa St., and is closed on *shabbat.*

Not far from the *al ha esh* stands near the clock tower in Yafo, Arabic *mamtekim* sellers hawk their Middle Eastern sweets every few meters. These cakes and pastries, swimming in warm, sticky honey, are especially popular during the nights of Ramadan. Beware of the rubbery, rainbow-colored *rabat lakum;* you'll never survive the sugar rush. But don't miss the *kanafe,* a warm, salty cheese wrapped in pasta and covered with hardened boiled honey. **Dr. Lek's** ice cream and sorbet shop, #8 289th St. (tel. 82 16 47), near Clock Sq., serves delicious desserts.

Between the clock tower and the flea market two stands called **Abu-Lafiah** and **Abu-Limo** sell wonderful homemade pizzas and *borekas* (dough folded over meat, eggs, cheese, or mushrooms), as well as large, soft *bagelahs* dipped in *za'atar,* a sage-like spice. The owners of Abu-Lafiah were so successful at selling this treat that Abu-Limo's (the name is a bizarre hybrid of Arabic and Hebrew) opened next door. The crowds still wisely head for Abu-Lafiah's. For a full seafood meal, try **Fisherman's Restaurant** (Misadat Dagim) on Ha'Aliyah HaShniyah St., southwest of the clock tower. A dinner on the wharf or inside among the stuffed sharks costs NIS10-15.

Near Tel Aviv

Most of Tel-Aviv's suburbs are modern, clean, attractive, and dull. **Petah Tikva** was the site of a raucous conflict in 1984 between Orthodox residents of the town and a movie theater owner who wanted to show films on Friday night. The furor has since subsided and Petah Tikva, like **Holon,** has regained its suburban composure. **Ramat Gan** houses the Tel Aviv stadium, where every four years Jewish athletes from all over the world compete in the Macabiades, patterned after the Olympic Games. **Bat Yam** is a seaside resort with alluring beaches and painfully expensive hotels. **Bnei Brak,** founded in 1924 by Hasidic Jews from Warsaw, is a center of Talmudic scholarship. In the second century C.E. Bnei Brak was the home of Rabbi Akiva's famous yeshiva.

Herzliya Pituaḥ

Herzliya Pituah, the sandy section of the main town of Herzliya, is an unexciting resort town with excellent beaches. Unfortunately, beaches on the weekends charge NIS2 admission and may make you feel like a sandy, suntanned sardine. The area closest to the beach is further cramped by luxury hotels and foreign diplomatic residences, leaving budget travelers in the lurch for lodgings.

Herzliya Pituah does, however, have its merits. One kilometer north of Herzliya's main beach, just beyond the deserted **Sydne Ali** mosque, is the entrance to a beautiful free town beach. Though positively desolate by Herzliya's standards, crowds congregate near the entrance and thin out toward the north. 100m north of the entrance, perched on a ledge above the beach, is an inhabited sandcastle known as the **Hermit's House.** Part of it looks like a boat over which a peacock spreads its fan, part like a gargoyle, and the rest like nothing else you've ever seen. The hermit in question built this fantastic structure with packed sand and decorated it with tires, bottles, broken plates, and anything else that washed ashore. A few years ago he successfully challenged the Israeli government for the right to live in his castle on the sand. Look for his latest creation, the "sand bar" snack stand—he might

be persuaded to give you a tour of his fantastic home and the surrounding caves
he's been digging for the past several years.

On the cliffs above the beach a few hundred meters farther north are the barely
discernable ruins of **Apollonia,** a Roman port fortified by the Crusaders. Huge
chunks of the Crusader walls fell from the cliffs when the city was destroyed and
now lie half-submerged along the beach. Nearby, pieces of Roman glass from an
ancient glass factory can be found on the sand. The glass is green, light blue, and
amber, and generally more opaque than the weathered fragments of Maccabi beer
bottles with which it is often confused.

The ruins of Apollonia are fun to wander around, but not worth a special trip.
To reach Apollonia, take the road east from the beach entrance and turn almost
immediately onto a dirt road. Don't venture too close to the nearby ammunition
factory, which is surrounded by barbed wire. To reach the beach entrance from
Herzliya, walk north along Galei Thelet St., bear left at Golda Meir St. and take
the immediate left onto the dirt road. If in doubt, ask directions to the mosque.
From Tel Aviv, United Bus #90 runs from the Panorama Hotel along Allenby
Rd. and north on Haifa Rd. to the Sharon Hotel in Herzliya. The closest stop from
Dizengoff is on Arlosoroff St. near King Solomon St. The 20-minute ride costs
NIS2. Since the bus runs on *shabbat,* this makes a good Saturday trip when the
weather is pleasant and there's little else to do.

Rehovot and Rishon L'Tzion

Rehovot is a peaceful residential town, best-known for its world-famous **Weizmann Institute of Science.** The institute is named for Israel's first president, Haim
Weizmann, who was also a research chemist. During World War I, Weizmann discovered acetone, which proved essential for the British military effort. Some say
that to express British gratitude, Lord Balfour issued the famous Balfour Declaration of 1917 promising to establish a Jewish National Home. The **Weizmann House**
(tel. 48 32 30 or 48 33 28) and the adjacent burial site are set in a particularly attractive corner of the grounds. (Open Sun.-Thurs. 10am-3:30pm. Admission NIS1.50.)
The institute grounds, once a barren stretch of scrubland, extend over 200 acres
of well-tended subtropical gardens and lawns. The institute's scientific staff of 1800
conduct research on a wide range of subjects. You can find out about the institute
and its projects or pick up maps and brochures at the **Visitors Section** (tel. (08)
48 35 97; #102 in the Stone Administration Building, first building on the left as
you come in the main gate). You can arrange guided tours by calling in advance.
There is a free slide show at the Wix Auditorium, shown Sunday through Thursday
at 11am and 3:15pm and Friday at 11:15am. (Institute open Sun.-Thurs. 8:30am-
3:30pm, Fri. 8:30am-noon.) The main gate to the Weizmann Institute is at the north
end of Herzl St., a 20-minute walk from Bilou St., Manchester Sq., and the central
bus station. Also on Bilou St., you'll find Rehovot's main fruit and vegetable market.
The city's main avenue, Herzl St., is lined with felafel shops and inexpensive restaurants. For authentic, spicy Yemenite dishes, head south along Herzl St. a couple
of blocks from the station, where you'll find a cluster of restaurants. Rehovot has
no cheap accommodations, even at the Institute. Bus #200, which makes the 24km
trip from Tel Aviv, stops 30m beyond the gate of the institute.

One kilometer north of Rehovot, within walking distance (about 20 min.), is a
small new museum at the site of **Giv'at HaKibbutzim** (Kibbutz Hill). The fun museum consists of a reconstructed clandestine bullet factory used by the Haganah
during the British Mandate. Ostensibly a place for orienting groups of soon-to-be-
kibbutz members (hence the name, Kibbutz Hill), movable washing machines covered up the entrances to the underground factory. In the museum you can experience the exciting double existence led by the people of Givat HaKibbutzim. (Tel.
(08) 46 65 52. Open Sun. and Tues.-Fri. 9am-noon, Mon. 9am-noon and 4-7pm,
and Sat. 9am-4pm. Admission NIS1.)

On the way to Rehovot, you'll pass through an older settlement, **Rishon L'Tzion**
(First to Zion). As its name implies, it was one of the first Jewish settlements in
Palestine. Baron Edmond de Rothschild, French benefactor of the Yishuv, gave

the money for its creation amid the newly planted vines in 1882. While Rehovot declined his aid, Rishon L'Tzion might not have survived without it. After planting vines from Bordeaux, Burgundy, and Beaujolais in 1887, he built the winery that is still used by the vineyards of both cities to produce Carmel Mizrahi wine. The winery is the huge building a block south of the central bus station (tel. (03) 941 02). Tours are given irregularly during the day. All the wine you can drink and a small sample bottle cost NIS10. You can also buy wine at a discount after the tour. (Open Sun.-Thurs. 8:30am-3pm.) A small museum of Rishon's history on 2-4 Ahad Ha'Am St. (tel. (03) 94 16 21) contains pictures from the settlement's early days, along with a reconstructed street and school house. (Open Sun. and Tues.-Thurs. 10am-1pm, Mon. 10am-1pm and 4-7pm, and Sat. 6-9pm. Admission NIS1, free on Sat.)

Ramla

Ramla (or "sand" in Arabic) is one of the few cities in Israel that has no ancient roots. Built by the caliph Suleiman in the eighth century, Ramla lay on the strategic road connecting Damascus and Baghdad with Egypt. For 300 years, Ramla was the center of the Muslim community in Palestine, but during the eleventh century, earthquakes and Bedouin looting devastated the city. By the time the Crusaders captured it in 1099, Ramla lay in ruins. In 1267, the Mamluks captured the city, prospering until its conquest by the Turks in the seventeenth century. Ramla deteriorated under Turkish rule, but was gradually revived by Jews escaping persecution in Jerusalem and by Christians serving in the monastery of St. Nicodemus. Ramla became a rest stop for pilgrims on their way to Jerusalem, and Napoleon stayed in the monastery before making his ill-fated attack on Akko.

In the beginning of the twentieth century, Ramla was inhabited mostly by Arabs, and in 1936 anti-Zionist riots caused the Jewish population to flee. When the Israelis attacked Ramla in 1948, the town surrendered immediately and almost all the Arab inhabitants of Ramla, together with those from nearby Lod, were deported by the Israeli army. Today Ramla's population is mostly Jewish and includes 3000 Karaites, a sect that does not recognize the authority of the Talmud or of the oral law.

Of Ramla's four major sights, three can be found by chasing steeples. Just west of the bus station stands the remarkably well-preserved **Omri Mosque,** with its slender white minaret. The mosque was originally a Crusader church built in the twelfth century. The Muslims made only a few changes in the structure, notably in the outer courtyard and the *mihrab,* the niche in the direction of Mecca. The mosque has remained in constant use. (Tel. 22 50 81; open Sun.-Thurs. 8-11am. Modest dress required.)

Farther north on Herzl Boulevard, the square, pointed tower of the **Church of St. Nicodemus and St. Joseph Arimathea** is visible on the left, which commemorates the saints who are said to have taken Jesus off the cross. Though parts of the church were built in the sixteenth century, most was completed in 1902. From Herzl St., turn left on Bialik St., and the entrance is through the first gate on your left. Ring the bell—one of the five monks who live in the monastery's new addition next to the church will show you the main sanctuary. Ask to see Napoleon's room and you'll be taken upstairs, through the corridors of the old monastery to the chambers where Napoleon had his staff headquarters when he unsuccessfully attempted to seize Palestine from the Turks in 1799. (Open Mon.-Sat. 8:30-11am.)

The stubby, square **Tower of the Forty Martyrs** stands alone at the end of Danny Mass St., which branches west off Herzl Blvd., just north of the church. If you're there in the morning, you might be able to find the guard to admit you. Once inside, you can climb up the tower's musty stairs, which seem to be inhabited primarily by winged beasties. The inscription over the tower's entrance says it was built by Muhammad Abu Kalaon in 1318. In the surrounding fields, farther in from the road, you can see the ruins of the **Jamia el-Abiad Mosque,** the White Mosque, built in 716 C.E., for which the tower originally served as a minaret.

The **Pool of St. Helena,** a rain reservoir built in the eighth century for Haroun al-Rashid, a familiar figure from the *Arabian Nights,* was later renamed after Emperor Constantine's mother. It is known as the Pool of el-Anazia in Arabic, and Brehat HaKeshatot (Pool of the Arches) in Hebrew. To reach the pool, walk north on Herzl Blvd. from Danny Mass St. and turn right on Haganah St., just after Bank Hapoalim. The pool is on the right side of the street, opposite the Haganah Gardens. The little building on the left, next to the blue and white murals, has an entrance leading down to the waters. The pools are neither particularly wide nor particularly deep, and there may be no one to admit you. You can rent rowboats here.

Ramla is best visited as a daytrip from Tel Aviv. Buses run between Tel Aviv and Ramla every 15 minutes from 5am to 10:40pm (NIS1). Express buses leave Ramla for Jerusalem about every half hour between 5:50am and 8:20pm. The Ramla **bus station** is on Herzl Blvd., the town's main street.

Netanya

Blessed with good weather year-round and a golden, sandy beach, Netanya is the largest and most famous of Israel's Mediterranean resorts. With a gorgeous wooded path running the length of the waterfront and free entertainment almost every night during the summer, the city is a wonderful place for a relaxing beachside vacation. Walking down the quiet streets near the waterfront, however, you would never guess that this city is also one of Israel's major industrial centers. The diamond-cutting and steel factories have been wisely kept outside the city center.

Unfortunately, because Netanya attracts so many wealthy European tourists, few facilities exist for budget travelers. The hotels and restaurants are not overpriced for what they offer; if anything, they are less expensive than comparable establishments at other Israeli resorts. The problem is simply that there are virtually none of the hostels and self-service restaurants on which budget travelers survive. The town's cultural offerings also reflect its older, wealthier clientele: There is an orchestra, a bridge club, and even a series of meetings for single tourists, but only a handful of cinemas, bars, and discos.

Practical Information

Government Tourist Information Office (GTIO): on the southwestern corner of Ha'Atzma'ut Sq. (tel. 272 86). Helpful and friendly. City maps and lists of upcoming events in Netanya. Open Sun. and Tues.-Thurs. 8:30am-2pm and 4-7pm, Mon. and Fri. 8:30am-2pm.

Banks: Most are open Sun., Tues., and Thurs. 8:30am-12:30pm and 4-6pm; Mon. and Wed. 8:30am-12:30pm; and Fri. 8:30am-noon. Central offices: **Israel Discount Bank** (tel. 33 47 46), 6 Smilansky St.; **First International** (tel. 33 04 44), 25 Zion Sq.; **Bank Hapoalim** (tel. 33 97 41), 11 Ha'Atzma'ut Sq.; **Bank Leumi** (tel. 33 70 71), 5 Herzl St.

Post Office: 59 Herzl St. (tel. 411 09). Branches at 15 Herzl St. and 8 Ha'Atzma'ut Sq. Open Sun.-Tues. and Thurs. 7:45am-12:30pm and 3:30-6pm, Wed. 7:45am-2pm, Fri. 7:45am-1pm.

Bezek (International Phone Calls): 14 Ha'Atzma'ut Sq. Quick and efficient service. Open Sun.-Thurs. 9am-11pm, Fri. 8am-2:30pm.

Telephone Code: 053.

Central Bus Station: 3 Binyamin Blvd. (tel. 33 70 52). Buses to Tel Aviv about every 15 min. (NIS3). Schedule posted on the wall to the left of the information window. **Luggage check** at the far corner of the station away from the information window. Open Sun.-Thurs. 7am-2:30pm, NIS2.50 per day.

Train Station: HaRakevet Rd. (tel. 234 70), outside of town. The Haifa-Jerusalem train stops here once daily (7:50am), as do trains to Nahariya and Tel Aviv (9 per day in each direction).

Taxis: Herzl St. off Zion Sq.

Laundry: 28 Smilansky St., near the corner of Remez St. and a new one at 27 Dizengoff St., corner of Herzl St. (tel. 33 27 35). Wash and dry NIS4.50 each, soap NIS1. Open Sun.-Thurs. 7:30am-8pm, Fri. 7:30am-3pm.

Pharmacies: Herzl St., Weizmann Blvd., and Sha'ar Hagai St. One of the 7 always open; the roster is posted on each door.

Early Closing Day: All shops closed Tues. afternoons.

First Aid: Tel. 233 33.

Police: Tel. 100.

From the bus station on Binyamin Boulevard (which turns into Weizmann Blvd. farther north), walk a block north to **Herzl Sreet,** the town's main shopping avenue. Turn left on Herzl, and after 4 blocks you'll arrive at **Ha'Atzma'ut Square** (Independence Sq.), an attractive park with a fountain. Near the bus station, Sha'ar Hagai Street cuts diagonally from Binyamin Boulevard to Herzl Sreet. Sha'ar Hagai Sreet. has less ostentatious shops, cafes, and bakeries, and a good fruit stand.

Accommodations and Food

Almost all of Netanya's hotels are expensive. Many places lower their prices by 10-15% from November to February, but you should bargain at any time of the year. Make it clear that you're on a tight budget, and remind them that there are many other hotels in town. Camping on the beach is unsafe, especially for single women.

Orit, 21 Hen Ave. (tel. 61 68 18), in the southwestern part of town. A small, cozy hostel. Swedish groups usually fill it during April and Aug.-Nov. Not only the one cheap place to sleep in Netanya, but also scrupulously clean and very friendly. Downstairs are a lovely dining room and lounge, a refrigerator for guests, and current editions of the *Jerusalem Post*. Airy 2-4 person rooms. Singles NIS20, doubles NIS30, students or *kibbutz* volunteers NIS12.

Piroska, 28 Ussishkin St. (tel. 231 77), across the street from "The House." Clean, airy, spacious rooms in apartments with balcony, bath, and fridge. Singles NIS20, doubles NIS30, but prices negotiable.

Hotel Atzmaut, 2 Ussishkin St., 4th floor (tel. 225 62), on Ha'Atzma'ut Sq. Clean, cramped rooms in a convenient location. Singles NIS30, doubles NIS50. Bath and breakfast included.

Hotel Grinstein, 47 Dizengoff St. (tel. 62 20 26), at the corner of Remez St. Clean rooms with balconies in a quiet neighborhood. The manager may tell you there's A/C, referring to the electric fans in some rooms. All rooms with private bathroom. Doubles NIS40, triples NIS55.

Hotel Gal-Yam, 46 Dizengoff St. (tel. 226 03), 2 blocks from Herzl St. Nice, clean rooms with balcony and A/C. NIS25 per person with bath. Breakfast included.

The only way to eat for a reasonable price in Netanya is to buy your own food. Shop at the **open market** around Zangwill St., 2 blocks east of Weizmann Blvd., near the center of town. (Open daily 7am-7pm, Tues. and Fri. 7am-2pm.) The **mini-markets** on HaRav Kook St. sell cheap food and liquor. There are large **supermarkets** on Smilansky and Stamper St. You can buy felafel at one of the stands on Sha'ar Hagai St. (NIS1.50), if you stuff your pita with vegetables from their impressive salad bars, one sandwich will make a filling meal. Unlike most felafel stands, these provide tables for customers, so you needn't eat and run. If you've reached felafel saturation, some of the stands at Ha'Atzma'ut Sq. sell other options for a cheap meal, such as *melawah* (thin fried dough).

The restaurants on Herzl St. between Weizmann Blvd. and Smilansky St. serve grim imitations of American fast food; avoid anything that claims to be pizza or hamburger. If you must eat in a restaurant, order something cheap at one of the restaurants on Ha'Atzma'ut Sq. These are more expensive than the ones closer to Weizmann Blvd., but the portions are large and the food is good. For a much more pleasant meal try the **Mini Golf Restaurant and Pub,** 21 Nice Blvd. (tel. 231 09), perched on the edge of a cliff overlooking the sea. From Ha'Atzma'ut Sq. take King David St. past the Hotel Dan Netanya to Nice Blvd. (also called Nitza Blvd.). A meal of honey-roasted chicken with garlic sauce, rice with raisins, salad, and hot pita costs NIS12. Their grilled and Italian dishes are also excellent. You can play a game of miniature golf here for NIS3 while guzzling a draft beer for the same price. (Open until 4am.) If you can manage dessert, the unnamed *patisserie* at 6 Eliyahu Krause St., one block south of Herzl St. off Smilansky St., serves fresh *challah* and luscious cream pastries at slightly lower prices than its tourist-district counterparts. Don't be seduced by the cakes in Kapulshy's window (Ha'Atzma'ut Sq.)—you'll only find yourself broke.

Sights and Entertainment

You came to Netanya for the **beach.** At the western end of Ha'Atzma'ut Sq. are steps leading to the main one. All Netanya's beaches are free; those to the north, under the small cliffs, are the least crowded.

The Netanya municipality organizes some form of free entertainment almost every night during the summer, and fairly frequently during the winter. From May through October folk dancing is held every Monday and Thursday at 8pm at Beit Yohanan, 4 Raziel St., and every Sunday at 8:30pm in Ha'Atzma'ut Sq. For complete listings of concerts, movies, and a host of other activities, drop by the tourist office and pick up a free copy of their *Program of Events in Netanya.*

The cafe- and pub-lined Herzl St., a pedestrian mall on the two blocks closest to Ha'Atzma'ut Sq. is a people-watching paradise. For some off-the-Biblical-track entertainment, ask the tourist office about visits to a citrus packing house (Dec.-March only), or call the Netanya Diamond Center, 90 Herzl St. (tel. 33 46 24 or 222 33) for information about tours of the city's diamond-cutting factories (sorry, no free samples). The **Abir Brewery** offers free guided tours after which you can buy their beer at a discount. (Open Sun.-Thurs. 10am.) Take bus #601 (the Tel Aviv local) from the central bus station. Netanya's three art galleries are the **Baruh,** 4 Herzl St., open Sun.-Thurs. 9am-1pm and 4-8pm, Fri. 9am-1pm; **Kontiky,** 10 Ha'Atzma'ut Sq., open Sun.-Thurs. 9am-1pm and 4-8pm, Fri. 9am-2pm; and **Gallery 1,** 12 Krause St. Open Sun-Thurs. 9am-1pm and 4-7pm, Fri. 9am-2pm.

Near Netanya

The beautiful **Poleg Nature Preserve,** about 8km south of Netanya, begins where the Poleg River meets the sea. The walk upstream leads past flowering plants and eucalyptus trees planted during the last century to dry up the swamps that once covered the Plain of Sharon. If you're lucky you may see some of the colorful birds that hang out here. A few kilometers south, near **Kibbutz Ga'ash,** seaside cliffs reach almost 61m. During the summer, you can sometimes see hang-gliding here. If you're traveling by bus, just ask the driver to let you off at Nahal Poleg.

Kfar Vitkin, one of the largest *moshavim* in Israel, lies 8km north of Netanya, a five-minute walk from gorgeous, free beaches. The adjoining **Emek Hefer Youth Hostel (IYHF)** (tel. (053) 66 60 32) is very pleasant. (Buses #901 from Tel Aviv, #29, 706, 922 from Netanya, and #901 from Haifa travel here. Ask to get off at *Tsomet Beit Yanney,* then look for the hostel sign.) The site is used as a summer camp for children and occasionally as a training camp for soldiers. The affable manager, Rafi, will be glad to chat and offer advice. A quiet beach, pancake restaurant, and ice cream shop are nearby. (Members NIS12, nonmembers NIS14. Breakfast included. Dinner NIS20, lunch NIS7.)

Caesarea

The ruined city of Caesarea (Kay-SAHR-ya in Hebrew), the Roman capital of Judea and the largest port in Roman Palestine, constitutes one of Israel's finest archeological sites. The extensive remains include a Roman theater, Byzantine mosaics, aqueducts, a Crusader city, and a 2000-year-old harbor with sophisticated engineering rivaling that of any modern Israeli port. It's worth taking the time to visit Caesarea even though it can be difficult to reach without a car. Unfortunately, despite their inaccessibility, the ruins are being commercialized at a frightening rate. Though the sight is not yet ruined, a dozen tacky cafes and gift shops, a beach club, and even a disco have already been built among the ruins, under the supervision of the ominously-named Caesarea Development Authority.

In the fourth century B.C.E., Phoenician travelers established a small settlement and harbor called Strato's Tower on the main trading route between Phoenicia and Egypt. The settlement, along with the rest of the coastal strip, eventually fell into the hands of Caesar Augustus, who granted it to Herod the Great, governor of Judea. Because of its excellent location and harbor, Herod turned Strato's Tower into one of the great cities of the eastern Roman Empire. Construction began in 22 B.C.E., and only 12 years later Strato's Tower was a splendid Roman city flaunting a theater, a hippodrome, aqueducts carrying fresh water from the north, and a harbor capable of accommodating 300 ships. Herod named the new city in honor of Caesar Augustus, and in 6 C.E. Caesarea became the capital of the Roman province of Judea. It remained the seat of Roman power in the area until the downfall of the empire. The Roman prefect of Caesarea from 26 to 36 C.E., Pontius Pilate, ordered the crucifixion of Jesus. The first evidence of Pilate's existence outside the accounts of the Gospels and the historian Josephus was found here in 1961.

In 66 C.E., a riot between Jews and Romans in Caesarea sparked the six-year Jewish Rebellion that led to the destruction of the Second Temple in Jerusalem. When the Romans finally squelched the rebellion in 70 C.E. (except for the holdouts at Masada), they celebrated by sacrificing thousands of Jews in Caesarea's amphitheater. Sixty years later, a second Jewish uprising, the Bar Koḥba Revolt, was also brought to a bitter end. This time the Romans were more selective—10 Jewish sages, among them the famous Rabbi Akiva, were tortured to death in the arena. Ironically, Caesarea later became a center of Jewish and Christian learning. During the Crusades, Caesarea was conquered four times before its capture in 1251 by King Louis IX of France. Louis IX strengthened and expanded the city's fortifications, adding most of the massive ramparts and battlements and the impressive moat, all of which are still in excellent condition. Despite these efforts, Caesarea was captured in 1265 by the Mamluk Sultan Baybars, who destroyed it. The city was never again inhabited.

The ruins at Caesarea consist of an assortment of remains from various historical periods. Very little is left of the Roman city, largely because its magnificent buildings were constantly pillaged by other towns. In Ashqelon or Akko you can now see some of the Roman city's most impressive remains.

To the right as you approach the ticket booth is the dry protective moat, into which part of the guard tower has fallen. The city was further protected by a drawbridge, an iron gate with grooves that are still visible in the stones, and a wooden gate held shut by a pole. To prevent a charging attack, the Crusader city could be entered only by turning two corners. Note the windows above the entrance areas, where archers were stationed to pick off interlopers.

The rest of the site is well-marked. Relics from the Roman period include the main road and several statues; the granaries and residences are Arab remains, while the walls and churches date from the Crusader period. The beach, which is to the left as you enter the city, is pleasant, calm, and of no archeological significance.

Although most of the ruins are within the Crusader walls, the most interesting Roman remnants all lie outside of the site proper. Behind the cafe across from the entrance to the Crusader city is an excavated **Byzantine street,** which contains the most famous finds: colossal Roman statues from the second century C.E., one of red porphyry, the other of white marble. The two headless figures were discovered accidentally by kibbutzniks ploughing their fields. A 1km walk north along either the beach or the road that runs along the Crusader walls leads to Caesarea's town beach and the excellently preserved **Roman aqueduct.**

About 1km east, off a dirt road that begins at the aqueduct, are some splendid Byzantine mosaics. If you walk about 1km south of the Crusader city along either the road or the waterfront, you will reach the enormous and excessively restored **Roman Theater.** Since 1961, it has been used for concerts and dramatic performances. Ask at the ticket office for concert information. Consult GTIO offices in Tel

Aviv or Haifa for more comprehensive listings. Tourists are frequently inspired by the amphitheater to launch impromptu concerts of their own.

About 1km along the main road running east from the theater stands an archway leading to the ruins of the **Roman hippodrome,** now overgrown with banana and orange groves cultivated by the nearby *kibbutz* of Sdot Yam. In its heyday, the race-track could hold 20,000 spectators; it measures 352 by 68 meters. If you want to see the hippodrome and the aqueduct without visiting the theater and the beach, just walk east on the main road from the Crusader city and look for the hippodrome on your right; then turn left at the signposted intersection and follow the signs to the aqueduct. If you get to the Crusader city very early in the morning, you can get in for free—the local fisherfolk leave the gates open. (Site open Sun.-Thurs. 8am-4pm, Fri. 8am-6pm. Admission NIS3, good for Crusader city and theater—other sites free.)

If you're thinking of a quick dip in the ocean, avoid the beach at the ruins unless you crave paying the NIS5 admission charge. Walk south from the theater about 1km to Kayit VeShait resort village, and you'll find a free and wider beach. Pay attention to the "No Bathing" signs posted south along the beach from the amphi-theater to the *kibbutz's* private beach. The tile factory at the *kibbutz* spews rock dust into the ocean, making swimming a health hazard. Where the signs end it is safe to swim, but keep your shoes on, even if you only traipse through the sands. The tar from the oil tankers at the offshore station comes off only after heavy appli-cations of cooking oil or an oil-based moisturizer. If you spend a little time digging in the sand on the beach or at the sand cliffs by the aqueduct you're likely to find bits of pottery, Phoenecian glass, or possibly a Roman coin.

The two hotels on the beach are expensive; head south toward Netanya or Kfar Vitkin for cheaper accommodations. Many visitors to Caesarea simply unroll their sleeping bags on the beach, but devotees of organized **camping** can walk south to Kayit VeShait resort village and occupy a small, sandy corner of their campground. Neither option is safe. Local archeologists have uncovered not only ancient monu-ments, but piles of stolen purses, wallets, and passports. Keep a vigilant eye on your valuables.

If you're **hitching** to Caesarea, get off the Haifa road about 2km north of the Caesarea-Afula interchange where the highway passes over a small road. Although there is no highway exit, you can easily climb down the trestle; Caesarea will be about 1km to the west. Local **buses** running between Tel Aviv or Netanya and Haifa via Hadera stop at the Caesarea exit on the old coastal road. If you're lucky you can catch bus #76 here (9 per day; Fri. last bus 4pm). Walk or hitch the 3½km to the sites. If you're hitching, emphasize that you're going to the ruins (*ha'attikot*) and not to the affluent housing development named Caesaria, 1km closer. To hitch out, head for the old coastal road past the settlement town of Or Akiva. This road is farther from the site, but it's easier to find a ride here.

Near Caesarea

Just outside Moshav Beit Ḥananya on the old coastal road between Caesarea and Ma'agan Mihael are two well-preserved **Roman aqueducts,** believed to have brought water from the Shuni springs northeast of Binyamina down to the ancient city of Caesarea. North of the *moshav,* excavations are continuing at **Tel Mevorah,** where several important Roman artifacts have been found. Two of the marble sarcophagi discovered in the ruins of a Roman mausoleum are on display in the Rockefeller Museum in Jerusalem.

Kibbutz **Ma'agan Mihael** is one of the largest and most beautiful *kibbutzim* in Israel. The large industrial plant at the entrance camouflages fields of cultivation and acres of neat, rectangular fish ponds set between the coastal road and the sea. Part of the *kibbutz* serves as a wildlife preserve with an aviary, and a little museum shelters archeological finds ploughed up in the fields.

There are only two places to stay in the immediate vicinity. The **guest house** run by the *kibbutz* is expensive. The **Beit Sefer Sadeh** (Field Study Center) generally accommodates only pre-arranged tour groups, but you may be able to sleep here if there's room. From the road, walk 1km west to the *kibbutz* entrance and then 1km south, staying close to the highway, to the Beit Safer Sadeh Nature Preserve. It shouldn't be too hard to hitch a ride on this second leg. The preserve runs along the banks of the Nahal HaTaninim (Crocodile River), supposedly the only unpolluted river on the Israeli coast. You can sometimes see large sea turtles there.

The gorgeous beach at **Dor** is protected by four small, rocky islands, each a bird sanctuary, which you can explore at low tide. The **Tel Dor** archeological site is on the hill at the far northern end of the beach; you'll need shoes to walk on the rusty wire-and-sand road. Though the site was probably founded in the fifteenth century B.C.E., most important remains at Dor date from the Hellenistic and Roman periods. The site includes temples dedicated to Zeus and the goddess Astarte, and the ruins of a Byzantine church.

Near the southern end of the beach is a **campsite** (tel. 990 18) run by the Dor Moshav, which was built on the ruins of the Arab village of **Tantura.** (Tent sites open May-Oct. NIS6 per person, 3-person bungalows NIS40.) The caves and ruins make the beach at Tantura a great place to camp. You can reach Dor and Tantura beaches by getting off the highway at the sign for Kibbutz Nahsholim and walking toward the sea, or by hiking 5km north along the beach from Ma'agan Mihael.

About 5km east of Dor on a hill overlooking the fertile coastal plain is **Zihron Ya'akov,** founded in 1882 by Rumanian Jews. The early settlers fought unsuccessfully against malarial swamps until Baron Edmond de Rothschild came to their aid with generous donations. The town's name means "Jacob's Memorial," in honor of the baron's father. Today, Zihron Ya'akov is better known as the home of the **Carmel-Mizrahi Winery,** founded 100 years ago by the baron. The winery now produces most of Israel's domestic wine, as well as a large stock for export. At the end of the free tour, you can sample the finished product. Walk 3 blocks north from the central bus station along HaMeyasdim St. and turn right on HaNadiv St. The winery is the huge building at the bottom of the hill. (Tours every ½ hr. Sun.-Thurs. 9am-12:30pm. Admission NIS3.) The decrepit structure off the shore is the glass factory built by the baron and managed by Meir Dizengoff, the first mayor of Tel Aviv. The factory made bottles for the baron's winery out of the white sand on the coast. The **Rothschild Family Tomb** is nearby. The **Aharonson Museum,** commemorating NILI, an early Zionist paramilitary intelligence unit, is on HaMeyasdim St., just north of the bus station.

Between Dor and the prehistoric caves at **Ein Carmel,** you can turn off the old coastal road to the east for Moshav **Kerem Maharal.** The *moshav* is named after the sixteenth-century Rabbi Judah Loew of Prague, the legendary creator of the *Golem* or Homunculus. From the *moshav,* walk west to a peaceful forest dotted with unmarked ruins.

Haifa and the Northern Coast

> *Your head crowns you like Carmel,*
> *and your flowing locks are like purple.*
> —*Song of Songs 7:5*

The bridegroom's beloved may have hair like purple, but Mount Carmel has the beauty of blue sea, azure sky, green pine trees, and white sandy beaches. While Jerusalem is Israel's most holy city and Tel Aviv the modern metropolis, Haifa is simply a beautiful place to live. Its location on a sheltered bay has helped Haifa become Israel's principal port, and the port has made it an industrial center.

While Theodor Herzl pronounced modern Haifa "the city of the future," the surrounding area contains archeological ruins dating from as far back as the fourteenth century B.C.E. Between these two extremes lie the eerie ancient cemetery at Beit She'arim and the imposing walled Crusader city of Akko. Nearby, two Druze villages on the slopes of Mount Carmel tread a fine line between tradition and tourism; Rosh HaNiqra, at the Lebanese border, attracts visitors to its age-old sea caves. The seaside resort of Nahariya is one of the several Mediterranean beaches—some crowded, others alluringly barren—lining the northern coast.

Haifa

The breeze that blows out of Haifa Bay and up the face of Mount Carmel has lifted the pall of ancient dust from this steeply terraced city. Haifa (pronounced HAY-fah in Hebrew) is clean and spacious, offering the advantages of a prosperous city: It sports spectacular vistas, two universities, and a constantly changing face, as towers replace hovels. At the same time, Haifa does not seem entirely accustomed to its modernity. The rumble of Israel's only subway will be silent until at least 1990 while it undergoes renovation, but buses run up the mountain, several even on Saturdays. Despite its port, through which so many tourists arrive, Haifa has not succumbed to industrial tourism. The cafes and shopping areas travelers enjoy are also frequented by the locals.

The city has long harbored political and religious minorities. Excavations on the Mount have uncovered caves that are believed to have sheltered the elusive Hebrew prophet Elijah from the wrath of King Ahab. Crusaders built the first of several monasteries above Elijah's cave; these passed through the hands of many sects before finally giving shelter to the wandering Carmelite Order. Among the other religious minorities who have found peace in Haifa are German Templars, Muslims, Druze, and Baha'is. In the first flood of Aliyah Bet, the illegal and desperate boat journeys during the 1930s, Jewish immigrants made Haifa their own. The city became the first territory secured after the Israeli Declaration of Independence in 1948. With its port and refineries, Haifa was the early industrial center of the young state, a status that earned it the nickname "Red Haifa"—the workers' city. Old-timers may tell you, with a knowing grin, that "in Jerusalem, *lomdim* (they study), in Tel Aviv, *rokdim* (they dance), but in Haifa, *ovdim!* (they work!)"

While a religiously-observant Jewish community does exist in Haifa, the prevailing tenor of the city is secular. In a country fraught with sectarian squabbles, the comparatively tension-free coexistence of Baha'is, secular and orthodox Jews, Christian and Muslim Arabs, and Druze, makes Haifa Israel's most egalitarian city. If you're looking for traditional Middle Eastern atmosphere, you won't find it in Haifa, but the well-groomed streets and stately residential neighborhoods offer the visitor a good look at modern Israeli society.

Orientation

Haifa, Israel's principal port and the departure and destination point of all passenger ferries, is situated on the Mediterranean coast about 100km south of the Lebanese border and due west of the Sea of Galilee. Rising from the sea, Haifa ascends in three tiers of increasing beauty and affluence. The bustling **downtown** around the **port** is a working area of outdoor stands and small stores. To the west of the port, on the same level, is the central **bus station** and behind it, connected by a tunnel, is the **train station.**

The bus station can be confusing. Like the city itself, the station has three tiers. Out-of-town buses generally drop off passengers on the third level. Local buses leave from the front of the second level, with Egged Information located in the center. Out-of-town buses leave from the lowest level, where the restrooms, luggage storage, and municipal information booth are located. There are many entrances—and many

Haifa

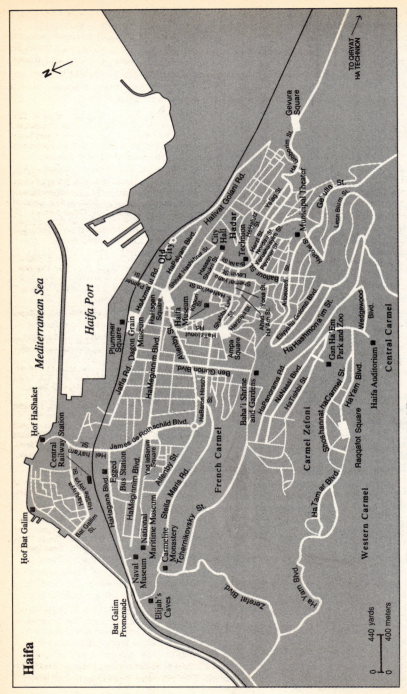

Mediterranean Sea

Haifa Port

Ḥof HaShaket

Ḥof Bat Galim

Bat Galim Promenade

Elijah's Caves

Naval Museum

National Maritime Museum

Carmelite Monastery

Central Railway Station

Egged Bus Station

HaHagana Blvd.

HaMeginim Blvd.

Ḥel HaYam St.

Bat Galim St.

HaShila St.

Yad leBanim Square

Allenby St.

Stella Maris Rd.

Tchernikovsky St.

James de Rothschild Blvd.

HaBaron Hirsch St.

French Carmel

Zerefat Blvd.

Ha Yam Blvd.

HaTam ar Blvd.

Western Carmel

Carmel Zefoni

Shoshannat haCarmel St.

Raqqafot Square

Haifa Auditorium

Central Carmel

Ha Yam Blvd.

HaTishbi St.

HaNassi Blvd.

Gan Ha'Em Park and Zoo

HaPanorama Rd.

Wedgewood Blvd.

Eliyahu Godomi Blvd.

Ha Hashmona'im St.

Ben Gurion Blvd.

Baha'i Shrine and Gardens

HaZiyonut

Ampa Square

Shabtai Levi

Herzl St.

Ha'Am St.

Yona St.

Ahad

HaGefen

Rd.

Masada St.

HaNevi'im St.

Shaar haLevanon

HaWadi St.

Yafo Rd.

Plummer Square

Dagon Grain Museum

Haifa Rd.

Natanzon

HaNegev Square

Haifa Museum

Nordau St.

HaZiyonut Rd.

HaHalutz St.

Pevsner St.

Arlozoroff

Balfour St.

Herzl St.

Sderot HaZiyonut

HaHaluz St.

Hassan Shukri St.

Hashahar St.

Old City

Hativat Golani Rd.

HaAzma ut Rd.

Ha Palyam Blvd.

City Hall

Hadar

Technion

Sderot Jean

Valley St.

Municipal Theater

Gevura Square

Ha Gborim St.

Gelulla St.

Leon Blum St.

Central Carmel

TO QIRYAT
HA TECHNION

Central Post Office

440 yards
0

400 meters
0

people going in circles looking for others. If you plan to meet someone here, specify your meeting place carefully.

The middle tier of Haifa is the **Hadar** district, home to many businesses, cafes, bakeries, and moderately priced hotels. Atop the mountain is **Carmel**, with its beautiful homes, five-star hotels, observation points, restaurants, cafes, and discos. If you want to develop your quadriceps, try the steep climb to the top.

Practical Information

Government Tourist Information Office (GTIO): 20 Herzl St. (tel. 66 65 21 or 66 65 22). Take bus #10 or 12 from the port area or #21 or 28 from the central bus station. Competent, helpful staff with good maps, train schedules, and information on current events. Open Sun.-Thurs. 8:30am-5pm, Fri. 8:30am-2pm. Second office in **Passenger Hall** of the Port; open when ships arrive.

Municipal Information Office: Four offices: **Egged Central Bus Station** (tel. 51 22 08). Conveniently located on lowest level of station. Great assistance. Maps, schedules, lists of clubs and pubs, museums, and accommodations. Even if closed, see information posted on windows and walls outside office. Open Sun.-Thurs. 9am-4pm, Fri. 8am-1pm. Also, at **City Hall,** in Hadar, 14 Hassan Shukri St. (tel. 64 53 59). Open Sun.-Fri. 8am-1pm. Other offices at **23 HaNevi'im St.** (tel. 66 30 56), near the intersection with Herzl St. in the Hadar district (open Sun.-Thurs. 8am-7pm, Fri. 8am-1pm) and **119 HaNassi Blvd.** (tel. 38 36 83) in Carmel (open Sun.-Thurs. 9am-1pm, Fri. 8am-1pm).

Haifa Tourism Development Association: 10 Ahad HaAm St.(tel. 67 16 45), just off HaNevi'im St. Another municipal tourist operation. Open Sun.-Thurs. 8am-3pm, Fri. 8am-1pm.

What To Do in Haifa: In English (tel. 64 08 40).

Budget Travel (ISSTA): 28 Nordau St. (tel. 66 91 39 or 66 04 11). Open Sun.-Fri. 8:30am-1pm; Sun.-Tues. and Thurs. also 4-6pm.

Ticket Offices: Haifa, 11 Be'erwald St. (tel. 66 22 44); **Maccabee,** 20 Herzl St. (tel. 66 46 18); **Garber,** 129 HaNassi Blvd. (tel. 38 47 77); and **Nova,** 15 Nordau St. (tel. 66 52 72).

U.S. Consulate: 12 Yerushalayim St., in Hadar (tel. 67 06 15). Only for commercial matters; in case of lost passport, the GTIO will telephone the Embassy in Tel Aviv for you. Open Sun.-Tues. and Thurs. 8:30am-12:30pm and 3-4:30pm, Wed. and Fri. 8:30am-12:30pm.

Banks: Barclays Discount, 65 Ha'Atzma'ut St. (tel. 53 36 56); **First International,** 3 Banks St. (tel. 52 04 25); **Hapoalim,** 28 HaNevi'im St. (tel. 64 54 31); **Israel Discount,** 47 Ha'Atzma'ut St. (tel. 64 61 11); **Leumi,** 1 Nathanson St. (tel. 64 71 11). Branches located throughout city. General hours 8:30am-12:30pm and 4 or 5 until 5 or 5:30pm. All banks close on Mon. and Wed. afternoons except First International (which closes Tues. and Thurs. afternoons). A bank is open in the Passenger Hall for ships, and in the central bus station. Be wary of wandering people offering exchange.

American Express: Meditrad Ltd., 2 Khayat Sq. (tel. 64 22 67). Entrance in alleyway next to Steimatzky's off Ha'Atzma'ut St., just west of Khayat St. Open Sun.-Tues. and Thurs. 8am-4pm, Wed. and Fri. 8am-1pm.

Post Office: At Shabtai Levi and HaNevi'im St., in Hadar district. Largest and most convenient branch. Also at central bus station and at Palmer and 19 HaPalyam Blvd., in port area. **Poste Restante** services only at HaPalyam branch. HaPalyam office open Sun.-Thurs. 7am-4pm, Fri. 7am-2pm. Hadar office open in winter Sun.-Thurs. 8am-8pm, Fri. 8am-2pm; in summer Sun.-Thurs. 8am-7pm, Fri. 8am-1pm.

International Telephones: At both Palyam and Palmer post offices.

Telephone Code: 04.

Train Station: Bat Gallim (tel. 53 12 11), adjacent and connected by tunnels to central bus station. Trains to Netanya and Tel Aviv every 1-1½ hr. One train per day to Jerusalem at 7am. 20% discount for students with ISIC.

Subway (Carmelite): Closed for renovation until 1990.

Central Bus Station, Yafo St. (tel. 54 91 21 or 54 91 31), at beginning of main road to Tel Aviv. **Baggage check** opposite platform 10, open Sun.-Thurs. 8am-5pm, Fri. 8am-1pm with a noon-12:30pm "Lunch Intermission." Maintains the Lost and Found. **Routes:** Buses heading south leave from here; buses to the north and southeast usually stop in Hadar as well. Last trip on Fri. generally 3-5pm. To Akko and Nahariya (#251 and 271 leaving central bus station via Hadar Daniel St. off HaNevi'im every 15-20 min. from 5:10am-11:30pm, on Sat. every 10-25 min. 9am-midnight. #251 also runs frequently to Akko from bus station and on Sat.); to Tel Aviv (#900 and 901, every 10-20 min. 5:30am-11pm, on Sat. 2:35-11pm); and to Jerusalem (#940 and 966 6:30am-8pm, on Sat. after 5:30pm). Also to Tzfat and to Nazareth.

Ferries: Terminal at the port, next to the train station. Departures for Cyprus, Crete, and mainland Greece, Sun. and Thurs. 8pm. Buy tickets at **Kaspi Travel,** 67 Ha'Atzma'ut St. (tel. 36 74 44), and **Multitour,** 55 HaNamal St. (tel. 66 35 70).

Sherut **Taxis: Tel Aviv** (tel. 66 63 33) to Jerusalem (on the hour Sun.-Fri. 6am-5pm, Sat. 6am-2pm; reservations required), Tel Aviv and Tiberias from 5 Yona St. in Hadar, near the Mashbeer. **Aryeh** (tel. 67 36 66) to Tel Aviv from 9 Be'erwald St. in Hadar. **Amal** (tel. 52 28 28) to Tel Aviv from #6 HeHalutz in Hadar.

Rental Cars: Budget, 145 Jaffa Rd. (tel. 53 85 58); **Eldan,** 117 HaNassi Blvd. (tel. 38 06 39); **Europcar,** 3 Allenby St. (tel. 67 13 48). Same exorbitant rates as you'll find in the rest of the country. Some vehicles with hand controls available.

English Bookstores: Beverly Book, 7 Herzl St. (tel. 93 32 17), ½ block from HaNevi'im St. A great place with a fine selection of fiction and non-fiction, both used and new; average price NIS1.50. Old comics too. Buys and exchanges used books "if they're good." Open Sun.-Mon. and Wed.-Thurs. 9am-1pm and 4-7pm, Tues. and Fri. 9am-1pm. **31 Hehalutz St.,** no English sign, but bookshelves out in front. **Studio 5,** 5 Dereh HaYam St., in Merkaz HaCarmel district, sells (but doesn't buy) used English language books. Open Sun.-Mon. and Wed.-Thurs. 9am-1pm and 4-7pm, Fri. 9am-1pm. **Steimatzky** bookshops are at 82 Ha'Atzma'ut St., near Khayat St.; 16 Herzl St., near GTIO; in the central bus station arcade, and on HaNassi in the Carmel. New books, travel guides, and the excellent 1:250,000 map of Israel.

Society for the Protection of Nature (HaHevra LeHaganat HaTeva): SPNI 8 Menahem St. (tel. 66 41 35), near Nordau St. Helpful, informed staff willing to advise the novice tourist. Brochures and detailed (but expensive) maps available. Open Sun.-Mon. and Wed.-Thurs. 8:15am-3:45pm, Tues. 9:15am-4:45pm, Fri. 8:15am-12:30pm.

Swimming Pools: Maccabee Pool, Bikurim St., in Central Carmel (tel. 38 01 00). Open-air in summer; heated and covered in winter. Admission NIS8. Closes early Fri. afternoon. **Tehnion** pool NIS9. **Dan Panorama Hotel** (tel. 35 22 22) NIS15.

Laundromat: Much to the embarrassment of the tourist office, Haifa does not have a single one.

Information for Gay Travelers: Haifa Hotline (tel. 25 73 19), P.O. Box 45417, Haifa 31453.

Rape Crisis Center: (tel. 38 26 11), 24 hours.

First Aid: 6 Yitzhak Sadeh St. (tel. 101).

Pharmacies: Aliya Pharmacy, 44 Aliya St. (tel. 52 20 62). Open in afternoons. **Carmel Pharmacy,** 133 HaNassi, in Carmel, is friendly and staff speaks English. Open Sun.-Thurs. 8am-1pm and 3:30-7pm, Fri. 8am-2pm. Local pharmacies take turns staying open all night and on *shabbat*. Call **Magen David Adom** (tel. 101) for assistance.

Police: 28 Yafo Rd. (tel. 100).

Accommodations and Camping

Haifa is short on budget hotels, and its youth hostels and campsites, while close to the sea, are not easily accessible from the city. Single rooms start at around NIS25, doubles at NIS35. Most proprietors prefer payment in foreign currency, which will save you the 15% VAT. The Hadar district is cheap and convenient, but noisy. The best nightlife is found in the Carmel, where hotels are plush and expensive.

Carmel Youth Hostel (IYHF), 4km south of the city at Hof HaCarmel (tel. 53 19 44). Closest of 3 IYHF hostels, but still inconvenient. The last stop of bus #43. Last bus leaves Hadar at 6:15pm and central bus station at 6:30pm (Fri. 4pm). If you take buses #45 or 47, which run along the main road by the water (until about 11:15pm), ask to be dropped off at the Sports and Recreation Center (the Youth Hostel stop). Cross the street toward the gas station, turn left just past it, then follow the road as it curves to the right. The hostel is ahead. The path is unlit and can be dangerous at night. The hostel is large with a splendid view, and near a free, uncrowded beach. Only restaurant nearby is the pizza place adjacent to the gas station. Meals available in hostel dining room: light meal NIS6, meat meal NIS8. Bungalows or dorm rooms available (same price). Overrun by children during the summer. Best to make a reservation. Sports center across the street with tennis, squash, and lawn bowling. Basketball court on site. Members NIS12, nonmembers NIS14. Under 18, NIS1 reduction. Breakfast included. Reception open for check-in 5-7pm. No curfew.

Bethel Tourist Hostel, 40 HaGeffen St. (tel. 52 11 10), west of Ben Gurion St. Take bus #22 from central bus station to Ben Gurion St. close to HaGeffen; or walk 15-20 min. up James de Rothschild Blvd., following the curve to the left onto HaBaron Hirsch, which becomes HaGeffen. Friendly, pleasant, and clean. Great place to meet people just off the boat from Greece, or from a *kibbutz.* Lockout 9am-5pm, but new arrivals can leave bags in locked storage and return to register. Lounge with coffee and tea for NIS.50 open all day. Christian books line the walls. On Friday nights partake of dinner (NIS5), songs, and religious discussion. All welcome. Snack shop open for breakfast 7-8:15am. Dorm beds NIS8. Strict 10pm curfew and 7am wake-up. Office open for registration Sat.-Thurs. 5-10pm, Fri. 4-10pm.

Nesher Hotel, 53 Herzl St. (tel. 64 06 44). Fairly ordinary. Good breakfast buffet. Lounge with sometimes-working TV. A/C and fans. 24-hour check-in. Some rooms have private bathrooms. Singles NIS50, doubles NIS69, but try to bargain to NIS55. Breakfast included.

Talpiyyot, 61 Herzl St. (tel. 67 37 53). Very clean and convenient but ask for a room away from the noisy street and with a private bathroom. Fans. Good management. Singles NIS50, doubles NIS75. Buffet breakfast included.

Hotel Aliya, 35 HeHalutz St. (tel. 66 39 18). Decent rooms, with balconies overlooking the tenements in back. Nice manager. No fans. Singles NIS20, doubles NIS40, triples NIS50. No breakfast.

Young Judea Youth Hostel (IYHF), 18km east of Haifa in the village of Ramat Yohanan (tel. 44 29 76). Take bus #66 or 63 from the central bus station to Kfar Ata (runs until 8pm). Primarily for youth groups, which completely fill it June-Sept.; be sure to call ahead. Members NIS12, nonmembers NIS14, family rooms with bath NIS14 per person.

Camping: Kibbutz Ne've Yam (tel. 84 22 40), 18km south of Haifa. Take bus #122 from central bus station. Just off the beach, near the ruins of the Crusader fortress of Atlit (closed to tourists). Excellent facilities, including a small store and restaurant. Only open in summer. Camping with tent, adult NIS10, child NIS5. Bungalows with toilet, shower, and refrigerator cost NIS75 for groups of four. Cooking facilities available. *Kibbutz* pool with waterslide NIS10 per day for camping guests.

Food

You may have a hard time finding cheap accommodations in Haifa, but there's certainly no shortage of low-budget eateries. They cluster in two general areas. The **Hadar** district has a good selection of cheap restaurants, though they vary in quality. Both HaNevi'im and HeHalutz St. are lined with cheap felafel and sandwich stands, some of which are open on Saturday. Sit-down dinners cost NIS4-7 for vegetarian meals and NIS7-12 for meat. On HaNevi'im St., where street vendors often sell *tiras* (corn on the cob), you'll find restaurants offering an eclectic assortment of different cuisines, including Moroccan, Italian, and Rumanian. The main road of the **Merkaz HaCarmel** district, **HaNassi Boulevard,** is dotted with cafes offering light meals and desserts. Many of the cafes, bars, and restaurants in the Carmel are open on Friday nights, but there is no public transportation.

Hadar

At Benny's, 23 HeHalutz St. (tel. 66 03 95), near the intersection with Herzl St. Middle Eastern food. Salads (NIS4) and *shislik* (NIS10).

Tzimhonit Hayim, 30 Herzl St. Old style Jewish dairy restaurant, crowded at lunchtime. A/C. Kreplach, soup, potato blinzes NIS3, stuffed peppers or cabbages NIS2. Name means "Vegetarian Life." Open Sun.-Thurs. 9am-7:30pm, Fri. 9am-1pm.

Bis-Bo Sandwich Bar, 25 HaNevi'im St., bills itself as "the only American-style deli in Haifa." That's stretching it. Good for those feeling hemmed in by the laws of *kashrut*—sample non-kosher exotica such as bacon-cheeseburgers. Burgers NIS4.50 and up, fries NIS2.50, and the special of hamburger, fries, and drink NIS6.30.

Beitteinu, 29 Jerusalem St., inside William Green Cultural Center. Similar fare to the student restaurants below, but a bit more expensive. Full meals with meat NIS7.50. Open for lunch only.

Rimini, 20 HaNevi'im St. Pizza by the slice downstairs, and a fairly clean, popular restaurant upstairs. Pasta NIS5-8, pizza NIS4.50-8, slice NIS1.50.

Bet HaPri (House of Fruit), Shemaryahu Levin St. at Herzl (look for the "Whitman" snowflake logo across from the HaMashbir department store). Any combination of fruits or vegetables is turned into a great shake for NIS2.50. Be creative—it's yummy.

Quick, 15 Nordau St. (tel. 64 48 26). One of the many cafes lining the Nordau pedestrian walkway, but with unusual offerings: NIS11 for half grilled chicken or all the wings you can eat. Open Sun.-Thurs. 9am-midnight, Fri. 9am-3pm, Sat. 5pm-midnight.

Merkaz HaCarmel

The Bank, corner of HaNassi Blvd. and Lebanon Ave. A good place to people-watch. Next to "Cookies." Big salads NIS7-10. Cakes around NIS4. Open on Fri. nights.

Kapulsky's, in Panorama Center. Also 11 Nordau St. Popular with locals and tourists for coffee and cake. Mouth-watering pastries NIS4.50, hot brownie with ice cream and whipped cream NIS7.

Bagel Nash, 135 HaNassi Blvd. at the intersection of Wedgewood St. Omelettes, salads, and you-know-whats. Light dinners around NIS5-10.

The Pub ("HaPub"), on HaNassi Blvd., next to Bank Leumi (look for the wooden benches and tables outside). Light meals NIS4-6, burgers NIS6-10. Open late (past midnight).

Elsewhere

The port area has some real bargains. At 136 Yafo Rd., there is an authentic **pita bakery** where you can buy special extra-large, thin *pitot* fresh from the oven. Bakeries sell 10 rolls for NIS1. Between here and the bus station is a line of good *shwarma* stands.

Sinn-Sinn Chinese Restaurant, 28 Yafo Rd., downtown (tel. 64 22 23). Like most Chinese restaurants in Israel, it's actually run by a Vietnamese family. Vegetarian entrees NIS7, meat entrees NIS10-14.

If you happen to be at the lowest Carmelite station with a few minutes to spare, there is an inexpensive outdoor **fruit and vegetable market** just west of the Paris Sq. station between Nahum and Nathan St. Walking east on Nathanson from here, the shop at #777 sells Arab delicacies. Although the cow spleen is a bit of a splurge at NIS9, the ox testicles are a bargain at a mere NIS3. Adjacent to the fruit market on Nahum St. is the **Shihmona Restaurant,** with some of the best meat prices in the city. (Places generally close here earlier than in the rest of the city.)

Sights

The **Haifa Tourism Development Association,** 10 Ahad Ha'Am St. (tel. 67 16 45), just off HaNevi'im St., offers an excellent free walking tour of Haifa's major attractions every Saturday from 10am to 1pm. The tour leaves from the observation point on the Carmel at the corner of Sha'ar HaLevanon and Ye'fe Nof St. City buses (a few) start running around 9:30am, so you can probably catch one if you are not staying in the Carmel.

Many of Haifa's most interesting museums are in the affluent Carmel district, where elegant homes and luxury hotels grace the Mount's summit. Inexplicably, the Carmel district is called *hamerkaz* or "the center" of the city, though by no stretch of the imagination is it the geographic, business, or government center of Haifa. The 300m ridge offers a gorgeous view of the sea all the way north to the white cliffs of Rosh HaNiqra and south to the ancient fortress of Atlit. Buses #21,

22, 23, 27, and 37 run to Gan Ha'Em, in "Merkaz HaCarmel," the Carmel shopping area.

Gan Ha'Em (Mother's Park) has a delightful municipal zoo. It's not exactly an African game preserve, but kids and adults may be surprised at some of the beasts indigenous to this small country. (Open Sun.-Thurs. 8am-4pm, Fri. 8am-1pm, Sat. 9am-4pm; July-Aug. Sun.-Thurs. 8am-6pm, Fri. 8am-1pm, Sat. 9am-6pm. Admission NIS3, children under 11 NIS2.) Across the park at 124 HaTishbi St. are three museums that offer another perspective on the flora and fauna of northern Israel: the prehistoric **M. Stekelis Museum,** the **Natural History Museum,** and the **Biological Museum.** (All open Sun.-Thurs. 8am-2pm, Sat. 10am-2pm. Admission to zoo includes museums.)

For a taste of nature in the middle of the city, follow the SPNI nature trail that begins in Gan Ha'Em to the right of the shell-shaped stage. Follow the blue signs into the brush. The path will lead you around the zoo and through tangled greenery into a wadi. The trail is 2km long (about 1 hr. walking) and ends in the lower Carmel. (Take buses #3 or 5 to get back uptown).

Ye'fe Nof Rd., popularly called **HaPanorama Rd.,** offers beautiful evening walks. In the daytime, you can visit the **Mané Katz Art Museum,** 89 Ye'fe Nof Rd. (tel. 38 34 82), 1 block west of the Carmelite subway line. The museum displays sculptures and canvases by Mané Katz, a member of the Paris group of Jewish Expressionists that included Modigliani, Chagall, and Cremegne. (Open Sun.-Thurs. 10am-1pm and 4-6pm, Sat. 10am-1pm. Free.) One block farther west, the tiny **Tikotin Museum of Japanese Art,** 89 HaNassi Blvd. (tel. 38 35 54), sells exquisite high-quality posters for NIS4-10. (Open Sun.-Thurs. 10am-5pm, Sat. 10am-2pm.) Near the intersection of HaPanorama and HaTzionut, opposite 135 HaTzionut, you will find a **sculpture garden** with striking bronzes by Ursula Malkin. The new **Panorama Center,** inside the large twin towers, houses a Superkol supermarket, the Shalom Discount Center, a bookstore, and some boutiques. Occasionally, exhibits line the walkways.

At the opposite end of the Carmel ridge, Haifa's two major academic complexes overlook the slopes. To reach **Haifa University,** take bus #24 or 37 from Herzl St. or the central bus station and ask to be let off at the next to last stop. The university's landmark, designed by the renowned architect Niemeier, is the large 25-story **Eshkol Tower,** also known as the "White Elephant." The building is the focus of student activities and always contains art exhibits. From the tower's observatory, Israel itself becomes a work of art: Under a clear sky, the astounding view seems to include the whole country from the Northern highlands to the smogscrapers of Tel Aviv. Notice the Druze Villages on the south slope of the Carmel. Free guided tours of the campus are conducted by students hourly from 9am to 2pm (until noon on Fri.), starting from the main building. (For more information, call 24 00 97.) Various temporary exhibits line the walls of the **Hecht Archeology Museum.** (Open Sun.-Thurs. 10am-5pm, Sat. 10am-1pm. Free.)

The **Technion,** Israel's high-powered scientific academy, is worth visiting primarily for its campus life. The Technion is divided into two campuses: The older one, on Balfour and Herzl St. in Hadar, comprises the school of architecture, while the newer Qiryat HaTechnion (Technion City), on Mt. Carmel, houses the other departments. Take bus #17 from the lower town, #31 from Central Carmel, or #19 from the central bus station or Herzl St. to reach Qiryat HaTechnion. The school has a total enrollment of about 8000, with a faculty of 1500. (Call 29 23 12 for information on occasional guided tours of the new campus.)

Down the slopes of Mt. Carmel to the Hadar district stands the eclectic and engaging **Haifa Museum,** at 26 Shabtai Levi St. (tel. 52 32 55). The museum contains three separate exhibits: Israeli modern art, ancient art, and Jewish ethnology. The ancient art exhibit on the top floor includes beautiful mosaic floors from Shihmona, the archeological site where ancient Haifa was probably located, and an extensive collection of sculptures and figurines from the Canaanite era (eighteenth century B.C.E.) through Greek and Roman times. The informative exhibits give a full account of the special powers, mythological history, and supernatural relatives of many of the ancient deities on display. The collection's highlight is *The Fisherman*, a small masterpiece of Hellenistic sculpture dating from the second or third century B.C.E., housed in the room to the right as you leave the stairs. Also note the second-century B.C.E. Egyptian burial portraits found in Fayyum, near Cairo, which illustrate the wide ethnic variety in the Egyptian community of the period. The ethnology exhibit contains folk costumes, utensils, and musical instruments from Jewish communities around the world. (Open Sun.-Thurs. and Sat. 10am-1pm, Tues., Thurs., and Sat. 10am-1pm and 6-9pm. Admission NIS4, students NIS3.) The ticket is also good for the Prehistory, Japanese Art, and National Maritime Museums. Buses #10, 12, 22, and 28 will get you to the Haifa Museum.

There are two art schools with small galleries half a block past the Haifa Museum at the intersection of HaTzionut Ave. and HaGeffen St. The **Artist's House,** 21 HaTzionut Ave. (tel. 52 23 55), holds local and regional artwork. (Open Sun.-Thurs. 10am-1pm and 4-7pm, Sat. 10am-1pm. Free.) Also stop in at the **Beit HaGeffen Arab/Israeli Cultural Center** at the beginning of HaGeffen St. The center sponsors youth activities and a dance troupe. (Open Sun.-Thurs. 10am-1pm and 4-7pm; Fri. and Sat. 10am-noon.; in winter Sun.-Thurs. 10am-1pm and 4-9pm, Fri. and Sat. 10am-noon. Free.) A few blocks east, the **Technoda** (National Museum of Science and Technology), contains a collection of functional models and demonstrations of the principles of physics. Children and young teenagers especially will enjoy the hands-on exhibits. Take bus #12, 21, 28, or 37. Walk uphill on Balfour St. (from the intersection of Balfour and Herzl St.) to the red-and-white sign on the left pointing out the museum. (Open Mon., Wed., and Thurs. 9am-5pm, Tues. 9am-7pm, Fri. 9am-1pm, Sat. 10am-2pm. Admission NIS2, students NIS1.) The new pedestrian walk on Nordau St., just above Herzl, is lined with cafes and eateries. It's quiet between 2 and 4pm, but lively in the evenings.

Halfway up Mt. Carmel, the golden-domed **Baha'i Temple** is the beautiful shrine of a relatively new religion. Rows of cypress trees surround the temple like sentinels, while palm and eucalyptus flourish in the gardens. Its architecture is a cross between Baroque Christian (the dome) and Moorish (the archways). The temple commands a stunning view of the sprawling municipality below.

The shrine commemorates the Persian Siyyid Ali Muhammad, the first prophet of the rapidly growing Baha'i religion. In 1844 Muhammad declared himself El Bab or "Gateway to God." Before his execution in 1850, he heralded the coming of a new religious teacher and divine messenger. After El Bab's death, his follower Mirza Hussein Ali (also known as Baha'u'llah), was exiled to Akko where he preached non-violence and the unity of all religions. He was the founder of the Baha'i faith; the name of the religion was derived from the first letters of his name. Both founder and prophet-herald are revered by the modern world's four and a half million Baha'is. While Baha'u'llah is buried in the Baha'i gardens in Akko, El Bab's remains, brought to Haifa in 1909, now rest in the Persian gardens next to the temple. Before entering the shrine (no shorts or bare shoulders permitted), remove your shoes and ask for one of the pamphlets explaining the Baha'i faith. As a measure of courtesy, don't turn your back on the sanctuary's interior as you leave, but instead walk out the doorway backwards. The shrine (tel. 52 82 21), located on HaTzionut Ave., can be reached by bus #22 from the central bus station or buses #23, 25, 26, or 32 from HaNevi'im and Herzl St. (Open 9am-noon, gardens open until 5pm. Free.)

Across the street, but inaccessible to tourists are the administrative buildings of the world center of the Baha'i faith. The large white building with the dome that can be seen from the street is the **Universal House of Justice,** whose nine members are chosen every five years by an election of Baha'i leaders. Plans for development here include an International Baha'i Library and a Center for the Study of Sacred Texts. Baha'is believe in the unity of mankind, the oneness of God, and the divine origin of the great religions. They seek the elimination of all forms of prejudice, the advancement of women, the promotion of social and economic justice, and world peace.

In the northwest side of the city, spanning several tiers are **Stella Maris Monastery, Elijah's Caves,** several **museums,** the **cable cars,** and the beginning of **Bat Gallim Promenade.** From the Baha'i shrine, buses #25 and 26 continue up Mt. Carmel to the holy places of yet another religious circle, the Carmelite Order, whose **monastery** stands on a promontory with magnificent views of Haifa Bay. Through the centuries, the Discalced (or barefoot) Carmelite Order, founded in 1150 by a Latin monk named Berthold, was forced to move the site of its cloister by Muslim persecution and various conquests, the most recent of which was Napoleon's siege and loss of Akko in 1799. The monks now live in a relatively new church and monastery complex called **Stella Maris** (Star of the Sea), built in 1836 on the ruins of an ancient Byzantine chapel and a medieval Greek church. The church's dome is crowned by paintings depicting biblical prophets including Elijah rising in his chariot of fire, King David playing his harp, and scenes of the Holy Family. An exquisite statuette of the Virgin Mary (with whom the order is associated), cradling the baby Jesus in her lap, stands inside. No bare knees or shoulders. Next to the Carmelite monastery is a small **museum** containing ruins of former Mt. Carmel cloisters dating from Byzantine and Crusader times. (Open daily 8:30am-1:30pm and 3-6pm. Free.) The convent of the female order of the Carmelites, up the hill from the monastery, is closed to the general public. Sometimes the gates to the convent gardens are opened on special request.

Given the affinity of the Carmelites for Elijah, or Saint Elias, it is no surprise that the **Feast of St. Elias** is a great celebration. Beginning on the evening of July 19, the church remains open until 11pm. Christian Arabs set up booths for food and games, and make a communal party. On the morning of July 20, special masses are celebrated. For more about this festival, see Mukhraqa, listed under Druze Villages.

Across the street from the monastery is the upper station of the **cable car** (*rakhbal*), which runs down the northwestern slope of the Carmel. While the view from the car is striking, the trip is short, and the prerecorded explanation of the view below (given either in English or Hebrew) is rushed and uninformative. The viewing deck at the upper station offers a sweeping view of the bay, port, and northern coastline. At the lower station there is a promenade for quiet seaside strolls. You can board the cars from either the upper station (across from Stella Maris) or the lower station. Reaching the lower station can be a confusing task, although it is only a few blocks from the central bus station. One approach is to take bus #45; get off just after you pass the cable car station on your right. To get there by foot, walk past the central bus station and the train station, turn left on Aliyah HaShniyah St., turn right at Bat-Galim Blvd. toward the sea, and follow the promenade left to the station. A direct bus to the station may be established in the future: Ask at the information stall at the central bus station. (Cable car open Sun.-Thurs. 9am-midnight, Fri. 9am-2pm and 8pm-1am, Sat. 10am-midnight. Round-trip NIS5.)

Opposite the lower cable car station—across the street and tracks—is the **Clandestine Immigration and Naval Museum,** 204 Allenby Rd. (tel. 53 62 49). The museum tells of the exciting exploits behind *Ha'Apala,* the desperate smuggling of immigrants into Israel during the British Mandate. Take bus #5, 43, or 44: Look for the *Af-Al-Pi* ("In spite of"), an old ship used to smuggle immigrants, now sitting atop the museum. (The ship's plank is down Mon. and Wed.-Thurs. 9am-3pm, Sun. and Tues. 9am-4pm, Fri. 9am-1pm. Admission NIS1, children NIS.50).

Just up the street at 198 Allenby is the **National Maritime Museum** (tel. 53 66 22), containing models of seafaring vessels from ancient times to the present, as well as other nautically-oriented exhibits. The prize possession is the bronze bowpiece from a fourth-century C.E. battleship discovered near Atlit in 1980. (Open Sun.-Thurs. 10am-4pm, Sat. 10am-1pm. Admission NIS4, students NIS3.)

The stairs leading to the entrance of **Elijah's Caves** lie just across the street from the naval museum. Like so much of the Holy Land, all three of the country's major faiths revere the spot. In the biblical history of the Israelites, the caves at the base of the mountain sheltered Elijah from the rage of King Ahab and Queen Jezebel after he killed 450 priests of Ba'al at nearby Mukhraqa in the ninth century B.C.E.

(I Kings 17-19). Muslims also revere Elijah as El-Khadar, "the green prophet" of the green mountains. The same caves are said by Christians to have safeguarded the Holy Family upon their return from Egypt. Believers of each faith pray quietly in the dim light. Bus #45 runs to Edmund Fleg St. near the Carmelite Monastery above the caves. If you are approaching from the monastery and have an itch to do some hiking, a difficult path leads down the mountainside beginning near the elbow in the road, across the street from the monastery entrance. Winding down over the ridge toward the sea, the path passes an abandoned chapel halfway down the slope. (Caves open in summer Sun.-Thurs. 8am-6pm, Fri. 8am-1pm; in winter Sun.-Thurs. 8am-5pm, Fri 8am-1pm. Free.) Another place of interest in Haifa is **Wadi Nisnas,** the old Arab Quarter. Between the fork of Wadi Nisnas and Yohanan HaKodesh St. on Nathanson St., the inexpensive Arab **fruit market** does a small but lively business. This bustling area below the Haifa Museum also serves as a gateway to the Hadar district.

On Ha'Atzma'ut St. near Plumer Sq. stands the **Dagon Silo** (tel. 66 42 21), certainly one of the most remarkable granaries ever constructed. This curious edifice, whose asymmetrical twin towers dominate Haifa's waterfront, looks like a modern Crusader fortress. The silo is Israel's only grain-receiving depot, storing 90% of the country's grain. A small archeological exhibit sits in the lobby of the silo's tourist center, just east of the main building on Ha'Atzma'ut St. Take bus #10, 12, or 22. The exhibit and models of the silo's facilities can be seen only when free tours are given (Sun.-Fri. 10:30am). If the silo leaves you hungering for more, visit the new **Israel Edible Oil Museum** nearby in the port area (tel. 67 04 91). Take bus #2 from the central bus station. The museum documents the history and current technology of the vegetable oil industry. (Open Sun.-Thurs. 9am-noon. Free in 1988-89 for its first year of operation.)

To return to the wild, consider a hike or picnic at **Carmel National Park** (called "Little Switzerland"—*Shveytsaria HaK'tana*—by the locals). Take bus #92 from the central bus station, and ask the driver where to get off.

Entertainment

A number of **beaches** along the north coast past the Dagon Silo can provide a welcome diversion on a warm summer day. Hof HaShaket, the most convenient, costs NIS3.50; take bus #41 from the Hadar district. The swimming here is good, and you can rent rafts for use along the breakwater. Hof Bat Galim, near the central bus station, is rocky and unpleasant, and the Olympic-size pool is closed indefinitely. On Saturdays, when the beaches to the north of Haifa are packed, it's worth hitching to the south where you can see the sand between the sunbathers. You can take bus #44 or 45 to free Hof HaCarmel.

When asked about the city's sparse entertainment, Haifa's first mayor is reputed to have pointed to the city's round-the-clock factories and said, "There is our nightlife." Although still a relatively quiet metropolis, Haifa does not lack nighttime entertainment. The GTIO and Municipal Office are both good sources of information. Be sure to pick up the free weekly publication, *Events in Haifa and the Northern Region,* for a complete listing of daily concerts and special events.

A memorable evening activity is a walk along **Ye'fe Nof St.** (HaPanorama). Take the bus to Gan Ha'Em for the view of sparkling city lights. **Gan Ha'Em** is always lively and occasionally has free summer concerts. On Mondays, look for rock concerts at 5:30pm; tickets cost between NIS1 and NIS20. If you don't mind more tourists and higher prices, hike up the street to the **Carmel,** a popular shopping district.

The **Haifa Cinematique,** 104 HaNassi Blvd. (tel. 827 49), a few blocks from Gan Ha'Em, has three or four English movies every night except Friday. Next door is the **Haifa Auditorium,** a beautiful hall where the Israel Philharmonic and distinguished musicians perform regularly. The expensive tickets are usually available the day of performances; inquire at the tourist office in the morning for information.

The **Bat Galim Promenade,** along the shore behind the central bus station and the lower cable car station is lined with places where you can eat, drink, or just watch the waves. **HaSfina** is a large beached boat, open every night for drinking and big band dancing. **Mini and Billy Golf** offers miniature golf and a funny game like it that uses billiard cues. (Open generally 5-10:30pm; each game NIS5, both for NIS8.)

For a very lively evening that may end with your dancing on the tables, hit the **Al Pasha** on Hamman-al-Pasha St., just south of the central post office on Ha'Atzma'ut St. Israeli folksingers perform in this vast Turkish structure turned nightclub (closed Sun.). Farther down near the port, the **London Pride Pub,** 85 Ha'Atzma'ut St. at Khayat Sq. (tel. 66 38 39), is a raucous pick-up joint frequented by sailors. The cover charge is NIS4 on weekdays, NIS6 Fridays and Saturdays, with the first drink included (opens at 9pm).

A few good nightspots are hidden behind the furious, felafel-eating mask of night-time Hadar. **Davka** (tel. 66 99 09), on beautiful Jerusalem St. (downstairs to the left at #23), has evening shows, as well as chamber music on Saturdays at 5pm. Nearby, in the **Binyamin Gardens,** is an expensive restaurant, but don't be tempted: The atmosphere does not warrant a splurge. Instead, enjoy the classical or soft rock music from the bright red, cast-iron carousel in the park. Two local pubs here are **Rodeo** (tel. 67 43 63), 23 Balfour St., and **Studio 46,** 46 Pevsner St. Locals head to the Carmel about 10:30pm. Popular local discos include **Biblos,** 1 Liberia St. (tel. 25 54 81), and **Sunset,** 124 HaNassi Blvd. (tel. 25 69 28). The **Ahuzza Club,** 25 Tchernikovsky (tel. 33 88 37), the **Carmel Pub** (tel. 38 10 82), and **Little Haifa,** 4 Sha'ar HaLevanon St (tel. 38 09 29) are busy pubs. At **Club 120** (*mo'adon meah-esreem* in Hebrew), 120 Ye'fe Nof St. (in Merkaz HaCarmel) there's always a cover (usually NIS4-6), and it's filled to capacity on weekends. There's a 25% student discount on weeknights, and women enter free on Mondays and Wednesdays.

Dances, coffeehouses, and movies at the **Technion** and at **Haifa University** offer good opportunities to meet young Israelis, especially during the school year. Foreign students are welcome at the Technion's nightly dances in July and August. For more information, call 23 41 48; remember to bring your student ID and passport.

On Sunday evenings during the summer Dado Beach hops with free disco **dancing outdoors** from 8pm until midnight. More dancing takes place on Wednesday evenings outdoors at the Carmel Center from 8 to 11pm. On Thursday evenings, on Hassan Shukri St. near Gan HaZikaron, street performers do their tricks by a flower market. At the Rothschild Center, 142 HaNassi Blvd., **folk dancing** begins at 8pm. Films and more folkdancing are offered on Friday nights at the Technion in Ne've Sha'an at 8:30pm (for information call 827 49). On Saturday evenings a free art bazaar is held near the Dan Hotel on Ye'fe Nof St.

If you're a soccer fan, check out Haifa's Qiryat Eliezar field, just south of the central bus station. See the *Jerusalem Post* for game schedules.

Near Haifa

The city of Haifa is a mere spot on the long ridge that is Carmel Mountain. Carmel's slopes produce some of the best vineyards in the Middle East (*Kerem El* means "Vineyard of God"). Plantations of grapevines line the inland foothills (En Hod, Daliyat el-Karmel, Isfiya), the plain of Sharon (Atlit, Ne've Yam, Dor, Zihron Ya'akov, Ma'agan Mihael), the Jezreel Valley (Qiryat Tiv'on, Beit She'arim), and Zevulun Valley (Kfar HaMaccabbi, Akko, Nahariya, the Ahzivs). Many of these places make easy and rewarding daytrips from Haifa. **En Hod,** to the south, is a tiny and intriguing artists' village. The ruins and burial catacombs of **Beit She'arim** offer an eerie, but fascinating insight into the era of Roman-ruled Palestine. The villages of **Isfiya** and **Daliyat al-Karmel** are home to Druze, members of a secretive sect who maintain an ethnic identity separate from the Jews and Muslims around them.

Beit She'arim

Sunk beneath the fertile soil of Carmel, only 19km south of Haifa, the remains of the members of the arcane Hebrew judicial council, the Sanhedrin, rested peacefully for nearly 2000 years. Twenty years ago, excavations at Beit She'arim disturbed their grave when archeologists found an ancient synagogue and the astonishing system of catacombs. Beit She'arim was the gathering place of the Sanhedrin, recognized by the Roman Empire in the second century C.E. as the Supreme Rabbinical Council, the judicial authority over all of world Jewry. Two hundred years later, it had become the sacred and secret burial ground for Jews, victims of the Diaspora, who were barred from Jerusalem. Archeologists have uncovered a vast network of some 20 caves whose walls are lined with dozens of intricately adorned sarcophagi, including one of Rabbi Yehudah HaNassi, first president of the Sanhedrin. The stone-slab covers slide halfway off the rows of coffins that disappear into the dim interiors of the caves around the numerous twists of this underground necropolis. (Open Sat.-Thurs. 8am-4:30pm, Fri. 8am-3:30pm. Admission NIS3, children NIS1.50.)

The archeological site and a museum are located in a park near the town of **Qiryat Tiv'on.** To get to Beit She'arim, take bus #74 or 75 (or #331 to Nazareth) from the central bus station or Herzliyah St. to Qiryat Tiv'on. Buses leave every 20 minutes and the trip takes 40 minutes (last bus leaves Haifa at 11pm, Fri. 3pm). To reach the site from the bus stop, walk down Alexander Said St. (past the hostel), bear left at the supermarket, and then right at the school. Follow this street until the fence (to your right) ends, then take the path on your right down the hill to Beit She'arim antiquities. Ignore the signs pointing out the way to the site; they point to the roads through the hills surrounding the valley and will increase your walking time six-fold. The paved road in front of the entrance to the site leads to an ancient olive press and synagogue. The steps next to the canteen take you to the modern **Alexander Said statue,** on a spot that offers a superb panorama of the surrounding hills. Said was the guardian of these hills during the 1930s until his death in the 1936 uprisings. Because of his good reputation with local Arabs, he served as the mediator among the Arab *chamullas* (extended families) of the area. His descendants fulfill this function today.

Qiryat Tiv'on has an excellent **IYHF Youth Hostel,** 12 Alexander Said St. (tel. 93 14 82), with hospitable management, TV, and nearby swimming pool (NIS3 for hostel guests). After you disembark from the bus, turn right and follow the signs for about 200m. The hostel is often filled with archeological groups, so call ahead before making the trek (members NIS12, nonmembers NIS14; meat meal NIS7-8, dairy meal NIS5). There's a well-stocked **supermarket** down the road to the right; the post office and some kiosks are in **Zionism Square** where the bus stops.

En Hod

In the early 1950s, a group of artists settled in a small, deserted Arab village on a picturesque hill on the western slopes of Mount Carmel and named the village En Hod. The community has subsequently grown into a well-known artists' colony filled with studios, where everything from traditional needle crafts to abstract paintings is created. Many Israelis come here to learn ceramics, weaving, or drawing. Bronze sculptures grace backyards, mobiles swing between trees, and stone figures recline against fences. Some of the old Arab homes are still intact, and the view of the Mediterranean undoubtedly inspires the muse. Although the studios are closed to casual visitors, the large **En Hod Gallery,** run by two friendly, English-speaking women, exhibits works by residents. (Open Sun.-Thurs. and Sat. 9:30am-5pm, Fri. until 4pm. Admission NIS.50.) Across from the gallery is the pretty, though somewhat expensive, **Artists' Inn Cafe** (bacon and eggs NIS6), and nearby is En Hod's **Janco-Dada Museum.** Stop in to look at the works of Marcel Janco, one of the founders of Dadaism and of En Hod. From the top floor porch, gaze down the mountain through the valley to the ancient port of Atlit, now encircled by a military camp. (Open Sun.-Thurs. and Sat. 9:30am-5pm, Fri. 9:30am-4pm. Admission NIS3, students NIS2.)

Across the street next to the restaurant is the blue gate of **Beit Gertrude**, a small museum-memorial to past inhabitants of the village. The former residence of Gertrude Krause, another founder of En Hod, the museum contains artwork by many members of the community and hosts occasional concerts, lectures, and cultural events. (Open Sept.-June, Sat. 11am-2pm, or inquire at the gallery; if it's not too busy, they'll let you in.) Up the road past the restaurant is a small restored Roman **amphitheater**, where there are Israeli rock concerts on Friday evenings (but no Egged bus transportation).

Just up the main road is the settlement on **Yemin Orde**, which commands an even better view. During the summer, more artists are in residence—but so are more tourists. En Hod is 14km south of Haifa. To get there, take **bus** #202, 222, or 922 heading south along the old Haifa-Hadera road. From the En Hod junction where the bus lets you off, the town is a 20-minute walk uphill. Because of the area's large population, **hitching** is relatively easy.

Druze Villages: Isfiya and Daliyat al-Karmel

The faith of the Druze, a staunchly independent religious sect, centers around a hierarchy of elders who are the sole custodians of a religious doctrine hidden from the rest of the world. The Druze believe that the word of God is revealed only to a select few, and these few must be followed to the ends of the earth. Wherever the Druze wander, however, they remain loyal to the country they inhabit. Israel's 60,000 Druze are among its best soldiers, while 500,000 Syrian and 300,000 Lebanese Druze defend Israel's enemies with equal fervor.

Some 17,000 Druze live on Mount Carmel in the colorful villages of **Isfiya** and **Daliyat al-Karmel.** Druze elders are recognizable by their thick mustaches and flowing white *kaffiyehs* (headdresses), and Druze women are distinctive in their black robes and white shawls. Even while hawking their wares, the Druze are extraordinarily generous and warm. If you don't stop to talk to someone yourself, you will probably be approached shortly.

About the only topic the Druze will not discuss is their religion; most of what is known by Westerners comes from British explorers who fought their way into villages and stole holy books. Jethro, father-in-law of Moses, is the most holy prophet. Elijah and the Carmel region also play significant roles. The most important holiday falls on April 25, when Druze from all over Israel gather in the holy village of Hittim, near Tiberias, leaving the other villages somewhat desolate. Devout Druze are forbidden to smoke, drink alcohol, or eat pork, but many young Druze do not adhere strictly to these prohibitions. The book *The Druze in Israel: A Political Study* by Gabriel Ben-Dor, published by Magnes Press, details the ideology, lifestyle, and political situation of the Druze.

The Druze religion was founded in 1017 by an Egyptian chieftain named al-Darazi who drew upon various beliefs current in the Muslim world of the time, especially Shi'ism. But the religion also differs on key tenets from Islam. For instance, Druze are monogamous, while Muslim men may have as many as four wives. The Druze have suffered a history of persecution and repression for their beliefs; hence their attitude of secrecy on the subject.

In the late 1600s, the Druze prospered, and under Emir Fakhir al-Din, the Druze kingdom stretched from Lebanon to Gaza to the Golan Heights. Sixteen villages were built from the Mediterranean Sea to the Jezreel Valley to guard the two major roads on which goods and armies were transported. An unsuccessful rebellion against the Egyptian pasha in 1830 led to the destruction of 14 of the Druze villages in the Carmel; Daliyat and Isfiya are the only two remaining. In the 1860s, when the Turks were anxious to have the Druze as a buffer against the Bedouin and the

Christians who were seeking converts, they welcomed the Druze back to these Carmel villages.

Despite speaking Arabic and living next to Arab Muslims and Christians, the Druze have preserved their ethnic and religious identity for almost 1000 years. Today, however, young Druze are struggling with the conflict between religious tradition and modernization, between staying in the village and leaving for the city. While most older women wear light white veils in public, the younger women are often less strict. Both boys and girls attend school, generally through high school.

In **Daliyat al-Karmel** (25km from Haifa) the bazaar is liveliest on Saturdays, but if you want lower prices and more opportunity to speak with locals, come during the week. You can try to bargain, though vendors know they can extract large sums from most tourists. Beware that most of the clothes and handicrafts are imported from India, while the furniture comes from Gaza.

The Zionist and Christian mystic, Sir Lawrence Oliphant, was one of the few outsiders close to the sect. In the late nineteenth century, he and his wife lived in Daliyat for five years, helping the Druze build their homes. Since 1980, the Israeli Defense Ministry has been paying for the restoration of Oliphant's house on the outskirts of town, as a gesture of gratitude. It is now a memorial to the many Druze soldiers killed in Israel's wars. Although street names are not used, anyone can direct you to the **Beit Oliphant.** Villagers, proud of the memorial, often frequent its gardens. Note the cave between the sculpture garden in the rear and the main house, where Sir Lawrence sheltered Arab and Jewish insurgents against the British. Oliphant's secretary, the Hebrew poet Naftali Hertz Imber, later wrote *HaTikvah,* Israel's national anthem. Next to the house is a new, domed sports complex, which commands a stunning view of the surrounding hills.

Four kilometers up the road from Daliyat al-Karmel, away from Isfiya, is the site where Elijah killed the 450 priests of Ba'al. **Mukhraqa,** the Arabic name, refers to the sacrifice (or "burning") that Elijah offered God from an altar here (I Kings 17). It was from this mount, as well, that Elijah's servant saw the rain cloud that relieved the land's drought. The Carmelites perceive the clouds as a symbol of the Virgin Mary, to whom they are especially devoted. In 1886 they built a small **monastery** here; from the roof on a clear day you can see the snow-capped Mount Hermon on the horizon. (Monastery open daily 8-6pm. Admission to the rooftop viewing area NIS1.) There is no bus service to the monastery, so you'll have to walk, hitch, or hire a taxi in Daliyat al-Karmel. Bear left at the only fork along the way or you'll head toward al-Yakim.

The most exciting day to visit Mukhraqa is July 20, the Feast of St. Elias (Elijah). The park surrounding the monastery fills with Christian Arab families who spread sheets and blankets on the ground and in the trees to form tents. The aroma from many barbeques fills the air. In the small chapel of the monastery, babies wail after baptism. People are friendly, and you may be invited back to a tent to share in the festivities.

Isfiya is 4km closer to Haifa than Daliyat al-Karmel. Isfiya's alleys wind between dusty, sun-baked stone houses, and are filled with boisterous children in the summer. The view from the nearby peaks of Mount Carmel is dazzling: Ridges and forests spread dramatically into the Zevulun valley. Bring a lunch to this picnicker's paradise.

Isfiya has a Christian population of about 1000 Roman Catholics, in addition to the 4000 Druze. A lovely old Catholic church is on the main road. Some members of the church will tell you with pride that their ancestors were Crusaders from Italy. Isfiya houses the excellent **Stella Carmel Hospice** (tel. 78 16 92; P.O. Box 7045, Haifa 31070), run by the Anglican Church and open to all. A converted Arab hotel, the hospice has a lounge filled with magnificent antique Persian rugs. The hospice is to the right of the main road from Haifa, at the entrance to the village. Take bus #192 or 193, or a *sherut* taxi from Haifa University (7 buses per day 10am-4:30pm, last bus on Fri. 2:25pm, last return bus 3pm, on Fri. 1:15pm, in both cases ask the driver for Stella Carmel). Bed and breakfast in the main house is NIS20, half-board NIS27, full board NIS35; bed and breakfast for an outside dorm room

NIS12, half-board NIS20, full board NIS29. Unmarried couples will be offered separate rooms. Management welcomes members of all religions to their scenic, quiet hospice.

The Druze villages make an excellent daytrip. From Haifa, **buses** #192 and 193 leave infrequently from the central bus station and the Hadar district, and stop in both villages on weekdays. Many *sherut* taxis pass and will take you to either village for about NIS2. Prices for this route during the day are equivalent with bus fares. The last bus leaves Daliyat and Isfiya at 3pm, but *sherut* continue to run and stores remain open until about 8pm. To **hitchhike,** start on Abba Khoushy Blvd., which passes Haifa University. From the Haifa-Nazareth road, you must go south at Nesher. The most scenic way to return to Haifa is to hitch in the direction of Kibbutz Bet Oren and the sea. From Daliyat al-Karmel, the road passes Isfiya, then forks right to Haifa and left to Bet Oren. If you go left and left again at the next fork, the road will take you through the beautiful winding valley down to the old coastal road near Atlit. Going south a few kilometers, En Hod is up the next left, and the road to the inviting beach at Neveh Yam is after that on the right.

Akko (Acre)

Just across the mouth of Haifa Bay, Akko is centuries apart from its urban neighbor. Akko, (Acre to English-speakers) is not made up of two cities, as many people believe, but three. Inside a bastion of crumbling walls, the 200-year-old **Arab town** is a labyrinth of alleys and stairwells leading up to ancient Turkish fortifications, only to disappear into the chaos of the streets below. Just outside Arab Akko, a rapidly encroaching **new city** is laying siege to the embattled walls—a familiar struggle throughout Israel. Undisturbed by this contest stands the vast, subterranean **Crusader City,** still only partially excavated, directly underneath old Akko and predating it by 600 years. The airy rooms of this basement city and the network of tunnels lacing through them were fortuitously preserved by the Turks, who found the constructions too solid to raze. They simply filled it in with sand and built their own city on top. The remains appear as an ancient castle, sunk underground and held in perpetual darkness.

The history of this troubled city reflects the ebb and flow of the contending armies that have washed over it, leaving behind their tell-tale architectural jetsam. The Crusaders came to Akko in 1140 on their vainglorious campaign to recapture the Holy Land for Christianity. Failing to take Jerusalem at first, they fell back on peaceful Akko, transforming it into the greatest port of their empire and a worldwide showpiece of culture and architecture. The Mamluks ended Crusader rule in 1290, and almost 500 years later a Bedouin sheikh rebuilt the city. The city that survives today was built by an Albanian adventurer, Ahmed, who ousted the Bedouin and became the Turkish pasha El-Jazzar. Napoleon later claimed, with his typical modesty, that had Akko fallen to him, "the world would have been mine." In the city's final battle, Jewish resistance fighters disguised themselves as British soldiers to lead the 1947 Irgun prison break, a prelude to the War of Independence the following year.

The city may be ancient—some of the houses have been occupied without interruption since the Crusaders built them—but its spirit is still vibrant. Akko was intended for the pedestrian, so allow time to amble about and explore. Some of the Arab residents of the Old City accept tourists easily, while others do not—as you walk through the old town, you may find yourself greeted alternately with smiles and jeers. During school vacations, you may also find yourself awarded an informative, if somewhat tiresome, self-appointed guide. The young men who so boldly approach you are often only interested in practicing their English and impressing their friends, so offering a tip may be taken as an insult. On the other hand, many local men consider picking up foreign women a full-time sport, and what begins as a pleasant conversation may turn into a dangerous encounter. Steer clear of any drugs offered on the streets; the police keep a close watch on dealers and usually lock foreign offenders into the local prison for several very unpleasant days before expelling them from the country. It's best not to prowl the alleys of the Old City after dark.

Practical Information

Municipal Information Office: Tourist Center, El-Jazzar St. (tel. 91 17 64 or 91 02 51), across from the mosque. Friendly and helpful. Information about sites and special events in Akko and a great map of the new and old cities. Open Sun.-Thurs. 8am-4pm, Fri. 8am-noon.

Central Post Office: 11 Ha'Atzma'ut St., next to the municipality building. Open July-Aug. Sun.-Thurs. 8am-2pm, Fri. 8am-noon; Sept.-June Sun., Tues., and Thurs. 8am-12:30pm and 3:30-6pm, Mon. and Wed. 8am-2pm, Fri. 8am-1pm. Smaller office in entrance to Crusader City. **International telephones** and **Poste Restante** are available at Ha'Atzma'ut St.

Banks: in the Old City, **Barclay's Discount,** corner of El-Jazzar and Weizmann St., and the **Arab-Israeli Bank,** around the corner on Weizmann St. Open Sun., Tues., and Thurs., 8:30am-1pm and 4-5:30pm, Mon. and Wed. 8:30am-1pm, Fri. 8:30am-noon. In the new city, banks center around Ben Ami St.

Telephone Code: 04.

Train Station: David Remez St., across from the central bus station (tel. 91 23 50). Haifa-Nahariya and Nahariya-Tel Aviv trains stop here. Last train to Nahariya Sun.-Thurs. 6pm, Fri. 1:58pm. To Tel Aviv last train Sun.-Thurs. 6:45pm, Fri. 2:45pm.

Central Bus Station: HaArba St. in the new town (tel. 91 63 33 for information). Buses #251 and 271 to Haifa and Nahariya. Buses from platform 3 will take weary travelers the short distance to the old city. **Baggage check** open Sun.-Thurs. 7:30am-3pm (NIS3), or in the Old City parking lot in the building with the big car rental signs, open daily 8am-6pm (NIS4).

Taxi: Akko Tzafon, tel. 91 66 66; **Arieh,** tel. 91 33 69.

First Aid: Magen David Adom, tel 101.

Pharmacies: Akko, 35 Ben Ami St. (tel. 91 20 21); **Merkaz,** 27 Ben Ami St. (tel. 91 05 27).

Police: 2 Ben Ami St. (tel. 100).

Orientation

To reach Akko from Haifa or Nahariya, take bus #251 or 271, which depart every 15 minutes. New and old Akko are connected by **Chaim Weizmann Street.** From the central bus station, Herzl Street runs to Weizmann. **HaHaganah Street** hugs the sea to the west from the new city to the lighthouse. On **El-Jazzar Street** are the mosque, Crusader City, information office, and Old City bus stops. On the major street of the new city, **Ha'Atzma'ut,** are the central supermarket, central post office, Wolfson Auditorium, and City Hall. The Old City, located on a peninsula, is riddled with poorly-marked maze-like passages. The famous market winds its way through the middle of the peninsula. The **Southern Promenade** is being developed as a tourist area.

Accommodations and Food

The **Akko Youth Hostel (IYHF)** (tel. 91 19 82), just across from the old lighthouse, has clean, spacious rooms in a 200-year-old building, once the palace of the governor when the Holy Land was a province of the Ottoman Empire. Located in the Crusader City and rarely full, this is one of the finest and most expensive urban hostels in Israel. The airy, spacious lounge and several of the rooms have a mesmerizing view of the sea over the ramparts. There's a helpful map posted in the reception area. To reach the hostel from the bus station, take bus #3 to the Old City, then follow signs through the market to the hostel, or a long walk out of the bus station and turn left, then right at the first corner onto Ben Ami St. Follow Ben Ami to the seashore, turn left onto HaHaganah St. until you reach the lighthouse, and take the alleyway to the left; the hostel will be on your left just past the arch. (11pm curfew. NIS16.50, breakfast included. Dinner NIS9.20, if enough people sign up.)

A private hostel, **Walied's Gate Hostel** (tel. 91 04 10), on Salah al-Din St., next to the Land Gate and parking lot, offers clean, crowded rooms and grubby bathrooms for NIS7 per person, breakfast NIS3. **House Becky** in the small square across from el-Zituneh Mosque, near the exit from the Crusader City, consists of several converted Crusader halls and a pleasant, vine-covered courtyard. The centuries-old rooms were once stables, and still have a stuffy, mildewy smell and dirty bathrooms. Since the rooms have only been partially excavated, the ceilings are low, and add to the general stuffiness. There is a refrigerator, along with other kitchen facilities, in the courtyard. (No curfew. NIS7 per person.) There are other unofficial hostels or rooms for rent in the Old City, but they are not regulated. The port area can be dangerous at night, especially for women alone. Because of Akko's proximity to expensive coastal hotels to the south and the new city developments to the north, beach camping is generally unfeasible.

The **Lighthouse Restaurant,** near the hostel, under the lighthouse, has tables overlooking the water and is a pleasant place for evening idling. Hostel patrons are given a 10% discount. Up the street away from the hostel is the more expensive **Abu Christo** restaurant (tel. 91 00 65). Around the corner from the hostel, heading away from the lighthouse, is the **Pita Bakery**, where hot pita bread is sold for a pittance in the morning. You'll find a number of inexpensive felafel stands near the corner of Weizmann and Ben Ami St. **Abu Elias,** across from the tourist information office, serves a creamy *hoummus* with salad for NIS4. You can buy food at the outdoor market next to the central bus station and at the *shuk* in the Old City. Farther from the hostel are the food stands on Yehosafat St. off Ben Ami St.

Sights and Entertainment

No list or itinerary can do justice to the aura of time and conflict that emanates from the ruins and fortifications of old Akko. To reach the **Old City** from the bus station, walk down Ben Ami St. to Weizmann St. and turn left. The entrance to the old city is just past Eli Cohen Park on the left. As you pass the El-Jazzar well, look for the moat beneath the Burj el-Kommander to the left. The entrance to the **Mosque of El-Jazzar** is to your right on El-Jazzar St. The third largest mosque in Israel, and the most important one outside of Jerusalem, it dominates this city of monuments with its large green dome and sleek minaret. Ahmed El-Jazzar ordered its construction in 1781 on what is believed to have been the site of San Croce, the original Christian cathedral of Akko. As you step through the entrance, you will find yourself in an attractive courtyard with Roman columns taken from Caesarea. The western end of the courtyard rests upon the cellar of a Crusader fortress. The surrounding structures are lodgings for students of the Koran and the personnel of the mosque. The small building in front of the mosque houses the sarcophagi of Ahmed El-Jazzar and his adopted son, Suleiman Pasha. The tower was destroyed by an earthquake in 1927, but promptly restored; the rest of the complex is in magnificent condition.

In front of the mosque sits an octagonal *sabil* (fountain) where the faithful perform *wudhu,* the ritual washing of their heads, hands, and feet before entering the sanctuary. From here, worshipers continue barefoot along the wooden walkway. You will probably be asked to remove your shoes, and you should certainly not set foot on the grass mats (in summer) or the wooden walkway (in winter) that adorn the floor of the mosque's interior. Inside in the green cage on the balcony to the right is a shrine containing a hair from the beard of the prophet Muhammad. As in all mosques, prayers are conducted five times per day, and you will be asked to wait or come back in 20 minutes if you try to enter during prayer time. Around the building to the left you can look through the barred window at a small room containing the sarcophagi of El-Jazzar and his son. El-Jazzar turned the buried Crusader cathedral into an underground water reservoir, filled by rainfall and pipelines. Recently renovated, you can walk on paths elevated above the water. Blouses and skirts are provided for women to cover exposed skin. Well-informed guides will also provide a short tour in return for a small donation. Be sure your guide speaks English. (Open daily 9am-5pm. Admission NIS1.50.)

Behind the tourist office, across from the mosque, are Akko's **Festival Gardens.** The city experimented with a festival of nightly movies and live performances here for NIS4-7 in the summer of 1988. Every Saturday night (6pm-midnight), local artists display their wares in an arts and crafts fair. Ask at the tourist office for a detailed list of events.

Across from the mosque on El-Jazzar St. stands a restored white stone gate, the entrance to the **Subterranean Crusader City.** When first discovered, the rooms were thought to have been built underground, but archeologists have since determined that El-Jazzar found it easier to simply build his own city above them. What is open actually not the entire city, but only the area originally known as the "Hospitaller's Quarter." Excavations were halted for fear that the Arab town above might collapse. In the entrance halls, three enormous pillars are surrounded by a variety of architectural styles. Almost anything in these halls decorated with pictorial representations such as flowers or human forms is the work of the Crusaders, while the more abstract embellishments and the Arabic calligraphy are Ottoman additions. The flowers engraved in several of the columns are among the earliest examples of the *fleur-de-lis,* the French imperial insignia. The elbow joints supporting vaulted arches are thought by some to be an architectural missing link in the progression to the Gothic style. The neighboring halls date from the original twelfth-century Crusader City and were probably part of a hospital complex in which the Hospitaller Order gave medical attention to pilgrims. Sharp eyes will observe that the arches project without bases directly from the floor, indicating that the current foundation is some 4m above the original level. The barrels and girders throughout the complex were placed there recently to support the original walls.

Proceed from the entrance halls to the courtyard where some of the fortifications built by Daher el-Omar are visible. Turn left and enter the Hospitaller's fort through the imposing Turkish gate, directly beneath which stands the original Crusader gate. Turning right from here will bring you to the center of the original Crusader complex. These halls are now used for concerts during July by the Haifa Symphony Orchestra, as well as the annual **Akko Underground Theater Festival.** The festival, a week-long celebration in mid-October, attracts small theater groups from all over Israel. Only a few of the performances are in English. The **Vocalisa Festival,** also called "Voice from the Wall," brings singing groups to these halls from around the world in April. As you leave this area, you may notice a patch of concrete in the ceiling. This covers a hole burrowed by Israeli resistance prisoners in the Citadel above.

Back across the footbridge, follow the halls around and down to the most magnificent and famous of the buried rooms, the **Refectory** or **Crypt of St. John.** In this lofty room supported by three thick columns, the Crusader knights once dined.

Next to the third column in the crypt is a staircase connected to the long underground passageway that leads to six adjacent rooms opening out onto a central courtyard. The passageway may have been dug by the Crusaders as a hiding place in case of attack, or possibly as an elaborate sewage system. It was later restored by El-Jazzar to serve as a means of escape if Napoleon gained entrance to the city walls. The rooms also served as a hospital for wounded knights, and the Turks used it as a post office, naming it al-Posta. The adjacent **Municipal Museum** (just to the right of the Crusader City exit, closed in 1988 for renovations) contains small exhibits covering archeological finds around Akko, Crusader weapons, local folklore, and Islamic art and culture. The building was a Turkish steam bath until 1947. (Crusader City open Sat.-Thurs. 9am-4:30pm, Fri. 9am-2pm. Admission NIS5, students NIS4.) While in the Crusader City, try to see the film "3000 Years: The History of Akko," and "Time Tunnel," a theatrical piece, each of which are shown for organized tour groups.

From the Municipal Museum, take a right turn down the alley to the new **Tourist Center** and continue to the *shuk,* a tumultuous throng of butchers, grocers, bakers, and copper, brass, and leather vendors. Small eateries throughout the *shuk* offer shish kebab, felafel, and sandwiches. (Market open 7am-7pm.) Near the market are several caravanserais (*khan* in Arabic), quadrangular inns with large inner courts where travelers and their caravans once lodged. The most impressive among them is **Khan el-Umdan** (Inn of Pillars), just past the Isnan Pasha mosque and the fishing port. El-Jazzar built this *khan* for Turkish merchants toward the end of the eighteenth century. The lower stories of the courts served as stalls for horses, camels, and other animals, while the upper galleries served as boarding rooms. Note the handsome two-tiered colonnades. The *khan* is marked by a slender, square clock tower with the Turkish half-moon and star. The building was erected in 1906 to celebrate the jubilee of the Turkish Sultan Abdul Hamid, who ruled from 1876 to 1918. The clock is now gone, but you can still climb up the slippery narrow staircase for a stunning view of the city. The tower is open irregular hours (ask at the Old City ticket booth). Inland from the Khan el-Umdan is the Khan el-Shawarda and, a block or so farther, the western sea wall.

Near the Khan el-Umdan is the **Akko Marina.** During July and August, the Arab fishermen will take tourists out in boats for tours of the sea walls and a wonderful view of the city. Set a price before you go (no more than NIS2-3 in a boat with other tourists). Often they will try to sell you "special" private cruises, quoting prices of up to NIS20, but you can bargain them down considerably. If you decide to hire one, watch what kind of boat is brought up: Don't get into a rowboat pulled by children. Women should be on guard against harrassment from adult rowers. You can rent a pedal boat for NIS20 per hour or a motor boat for NIS35 per hour, on Saturdays only, between 9:30am-7pm. (Look for the "Boats for Rent" sign on the small orange dock.)

In the northern part of the Old City, the commanding **Citadel** adjoins the Crusader City on HaHaganah St., opposite the sea wall. This stronghold, used by the British as their central prison, now houses the **Museum of Heroism** (tel. 91 39 00), a monument to Jewish resistance organizations. During the Mandate era, the prison housed about 560 inmates under the guard of about half as many British soldiers. The citadel was erected in the late 1700s on Crusader foundations of the thirteenth century, and was used as a prison by the Turks. The most famous inmate during Turkish rule was Baha'u'llah, founder of the Baha'i faith, who was imprisoned in the second story in 1868. During the British Mandate, members of the Jewish underground, including Ze'ev Jabotinsky, were imprisoned here for terrorism. Jabotinsky was one of the organizers of the Irgun, and founder of what has become the Likud bloc. One particular resistance group, Menahem Begin's Irgun, lost eight members to the citadel's gallows between 1938 and 1947. **The Gallows Room,** now the museum's most sobering exhibit, displays the noose in place, along with photographs of the eight victims. The Irgun retaliated by hanging a British officer. On May 4, 1947, the Irgun outwitted its British captors by staging a spectacular prison break that freed 11 of its members and 255 other inmates. The Haganah, contrary to common belief, took no part in the break, and its members stayed in prison. The event provided material for the escape scene in the movie *Exodus,* which was filmed here. To reach the old museum, follow the stone stairs down to the lower garden, then up the metal stairs and around the side of the prison. (Prison and museum open Sun.-Thurs. 9:30am-5pm, Fri. 9:30am-noon, Sat. 9:30am-4pm. Admission NIS5, students NIS4.)

Across the street from the Museum of Heroism stands the **Burj el-Kuraim** (Fortress of the Vineyards), commonly referred to as the British Fortress, despite its Crusader and Turkish builders. Renowned throughout history as the most inviolable port in the East, Akko remains a city of battlements and bastions. Akko's defense in recent centuries has rested on the **El-Jazzar Wall,** which extends along the northern and eastern sides of the city and is surrounded by a moat of sea water. The best place from which to view the wall is the **Burj el-Kommander** (Commander's Fortress), an imposing Crusader bastion at the northern corner. To enter the watchtower, climb the steps that begin where Weizmann St. crosses the wall. The long, slender cannons along the wall, of French design, are popularly known as "Napoleon's cannons," but inscriptions on some of the barrels indicate that they could not have been brought to Akko before the middle of the last century. The name could be ironically applied to the square, mortar-like Turkish cannons that were used to shoot rocks rather than cannonballs during Napoleon's 1799 siege.

The city walls originally encompassed the entire harbor, but all that remains of the harbor walls is the ruined **Tower of the Flies,** the site of the original lighthouse, standing by itself in the middle of the bay. The original fortifications were toppled by a devastating earthquake in 1837. At the eastern corner near the shoreline is the so-called **Land Gate,** once the only entrance to the city. At the top of the gate, the **Moat's Gardens,** there's a panoramic view of the bay (ascend the unusual double rampway, off the parking lot).

The only part of Akko's new town of interest to tourists is **Hof Argaman** (Purple Beach), where the sand is remarkably white. Some claim that this is the finest beach in Israel. The beach is definitely popular and crowded in summer. (Open June-Oct. 8am-6pm. Admission NIS5. New weight room and sauna NIS4.) To get to Hof Argaman, follow Yonatan HaHashmonai St. from the Land Gate south along the coast for about 10 minutes, taking the detour around the naval school. Dominating the beach are the only hotels in the new town, the Argaman and the Palm Beach, both very expensive. Past the Palm Beach Hotel is a free beach of the same quality as Hof Argaman, but without guards. Just outside the Land Gate, at the less attractive **Walls Beach** (open 7am-6pm, admission NIS3), you can rent sailboards for an inexpensive NIS10 per hour. If you ignore the "bathing prohibited" signs (posted in three languages), none of the several hundred swimmers will ever notice. There's a changing room through the low door across from the beach entrance.

Near Akko

Outside Akko toward Nahariya stands **Loha'me HaGeta'ot,** a *kibbutz* founded by concentration camp and Warsaw Ghetto survivors, many of whom were resistance fighters in the Jewish underground. The **Ghetto Fighters' House** (tel.. 92 04 12), dedicated to the memory of World War II resistance fighters and ghetto rebels, has been given over to answering one of the persistent questions of the Holocaust: Why didn't the Jews fight back? The answer, presented in an impressive display of artifacts, photographs, written testimony, and films, is that when they could, they did, and when they could not, they fought back with their spirit. Not only is the Warsaw Ghetto Uprising considered extensively, but the Nazi atrocities are given graphic treatment. Much of the museum displays the rich and vital cultural life of the Warsaw Ghetto (in particular the poetry of Yitzhak Katzenelson), as well as paintings, drawings, lithographs, sculptures, and prints by prisoners and survivors. To reach the *kibbutz* and museum, take any bus heading for Nahariya; #271 is the most frequent. (Museum open Sun.-Thurs. 9am-4pm, Fri. 9am-1pm, Sat. 10am-5pm. Small donation requested.)

The **Roman aqueduct,** just outside the museum to the south, is remarkably well-preserved—not surprising, given that it's not Roman. El-Jazzar had it built in 1780 to carry water the 15km from the Kabri springs to their stronghold in Akko. Take bus #271, which also runs on Saturday.

Two kilometers south of the *kibbutz* are the beautiful **Baha'i Gardens,** (tel. 81 27 63) arranged in a unique combination of Occidental and Oriental styles. The gardens hold the villa and shrine of Baha'u'llah (Glory of God), the prophet and founder of the Baha'i faith. The villa contains a small collection of religious articles. Baha'i pilgrims from around the world journey to this place, Baha'u'llah's home for the last 12 years of his life. The gardens were planted from 1952-56 to beautify the site. (Shrine open Fri.-Mon. 9am-noon, gardens open daily until 4pm. Free.) The gate on the main road is for Baha'is; all other tourists should get off the bus just north of the gate at the sign for Shomrat. Walk east about ½km, and enter the gate on the right just past the military camp, marked by a small sign. The gardens are on the main Akko-Nahariya road, accessible by bus #271 (about 10-min.).

For a more arduous daytrip, consider the 1km hike through **Nahal Shagur** (also called **Nahal Beit Hakerem**), a tributary of the Hilazon River that extends east of

Akko and is part of the valley dividing the Upper and Lower Galilee. The hike runs along the stone-strewn, deeply-cut riverbed, which is bone dry in summer. During the winter, or even on a very rainy day, this hike is impossible. Steep stone walls and cliffs flank the riverbed, making the hike easy to follow. In addition, the blue-and-white stripe markings guide you along the path. At two points along the path there are steep drops that were once waterfalls. To reach Nahal Shagur, take bus #361 (leaving every ½ hr.) from Akko to Gilon, and get off where the highway meets the road to Gilon. At the intersection you'll see a Hebrew-Spanish sign for "Najal Beit Hakerem." Take the steps near the sign down to the riverbed. A path will lead you out of the *nahal* onto the road between Yasur and Ahihud. Follow the road right to the highway to Akko; you can then turn right (back to Gilon) or hitch to Akko. For a shorter version of the hike, follow the path to the left at the first steep drop, which will lead back to Gilon.

Nahariya

Nahariya has little of historical significance, but does have white sands and golden sun. A sliver of water, the Ga'aton River, around which the town initially developed (*nahar* means "river") runs along the middle of the town's main boulevard. Virtually everyone along this street seems to be going to, or coming from, the beaches. Beyond the cool eucalyptus trees bordering the river, the two sides of HaGa'aton Blvd. are lined with Nahariya's many shops, food stands, businesses, and hotels. On Friday and Saturday nights, parts of the street are blocked to traffic, and tourists and residents emerge to enjoy the cafes, discos, and pubs. Founded in 1934 as a farming village, Nahariya is now a convenient little city with easy access to the beaches that surround it and to the spectacular Rosh HaNiqra caves.

Practical Information

Ten kilometers north of Akko and 10km south of the sea caverns of Rosh HaNiqra, Nahariya is the northernmost town on Israel's coast. The road from Haifa, or the road along the sea, will take you to Ahziv (3km north, a 40-min. walk). Nahariya itself is miniscule: Nearly every service you may need—tourist information, post office, bus station, and food—is located on HaGa'aton Blvd. To reach the beaches, walk a few blocks west on HaGa'aton.

Government Tourist Information Office (GTIO): On the first floor of the municipality building just west of the central bus station on HaGa'aton Blvd., at the end of the square across from the fountain (tel. 92 21 21, ask for ext. 800 or the tourist office). Well-informed, friendly, and helpful. Their map is basic, but it will guide you to the beach and provides information on some nearby sites. Open Sun.-Thurs. 9am-1pm and 4-7pm, Fri. 9am-3:30pm.

Post Office: 40 Ha Ga'aton Blvd. (tel. 92 53 55). Open Sun.-Mon. and Wed.-Thurs. 7:45am-12:30pm and 3:30-6pm, Tues. 7:45am-2pm, Fri. 7:45am-1pm. **International calls** and **Poste Restante** service available. Minimum of 3 minutes per phone call.

Telephone Code: 04.

Banks: Most open Sun., Tues., and Thurs. 8:30am-12:30pm and 4-6pm, Mon. and Wed. 8:30am-12:30pm, Fri. 8:30am-noon. **Barclay's Discount, Leumi,** and **HaPoalim** banks are all on HaGa'aton Blvd. The **First International Bank,** near the bus station, is open Sun., Tues., and Thurs. 8:30am-2pm, Mon. and Wed. 8:30am-2pm and 4-7pm, Fri. 8:30am-noon.

Bus Station: HaGa'aton Blvd. (tel. 92 34 44). Buses #270 and 271 depart for Nahariya from both Haifa (45 min.) and Akko (20 min.). Buses #20 and 22 run to Rosh HaNiqra (6 times daily 9am-5pm; check at station because not all run all the way north). Buses #22, 24, 25, 26 run regularly to Ahziv between 5am and 9pm. #44 travels to Peqi'in.

Train Station: HaGa'aton Blvd., 1 block east (away from the sea) from the bus station. Trains for points south only: Akko, Haifa, Netanya, and Tel Aviv, 6 trains per day 6:30am-6:30pm, last train Fri. 2:35pm.

First Aid: Tel. 92 33 33.

Hospital: Tel. 92 21 01.

Police: HaGa'aton Blvd. (tel. 92 03 44), just east of the Haifa-Nahariya highway.

Accommodations and Food

Nahariya is more accessible to the budget traveler than most of Israel's Mediterranean resorts and offers several reasonably priced hotels. During July and August there is an impressive, if expensive, supply of rooms and bungalows available in private homes. "Rooms to Rent" signs are common on Jabotinsky St.; head down the boulevard to the post office, turn right on Weizmann St., left on HaMeyasdim St. (the next block), and right on Jabotinsky. It's wise to ask to see the room before parting with your money. Because of the unending demand, these rooms are expensive (up to NIS45 or more) in July and August, but polite bargaining may help. The cheapest accommodations remain the Rehayim Hostel and the campground and IYHF hostel nearby in Aḥziv.

Rehayim Youth Hostel, 6 Wolfson St. (tel. 92 05 57), 1 block north of the bus station; cross HaGa'aton Blvd. and turn right on the first unmarked street. The cheapest and nicest place in town. Small dorm rooms and bungalows, a kitchen with utensils, a living room, tables outside in the garden, and clotheslines for bathing suits and laundry. Rent bicycles for daytrips to Aḥziv and Rosh HaNiqra. The manager, Shlomo, lives with his family in the house upstairs. Knock for help. NIS8 per person, NIS1 per sheet. Bike rental NIS7 per day.

Kalman Hotel, 27 Jabotinsky St. (tel. 92 03 55). Very clean, spacious, and pleasant. Currently a 2-star hotel with A/C and showers in every room. Prices listed here will be honored for bearers of *Let's Go.* TV lounge. 1 block from the beach. An excellent place for families. Singles NIS25, doubles NIS40 (July-Aug. NIS29 and NIS50). Big breakfast included.

Motel Arieli, 1 Jabotinsky St. (tel. 92 10 76). Clean rooms with fans in small bungalows and main building. Next to HaGa'aton and the beach. Favorite place among UN soldiers on leave. NIS20 per person.

Hotel Karl Laufer, 31 HaMeyasdim St. Adequate. TV lounge and a nice garden. Singles NIS30, doubles NIS50. Breakfast included, and other meals available.

Beit Erna, 29 Jabotinsky St., 1 block up from the waterfront (tel. 92 01 70). American-motel style as a result of renovations. Nice, but expensive. In high season singles NIS40, doubles NIS59.

Camping: see Aḥziv.

The dozens of restaurant-cafes and felafel stands along both sides of HaGa'aton Blvd. all offer the same food at outrageous prices, although at night they come to life as sunbathers arrive to drink beer and hear music. The **Penguin Cafe** is popular for pizza (NIS8 for a small, 2-person serving). The **Royal Cafe,** west of the Municipality Building on HaGa'aton, has outside seating and offers a breakfast special and omelettes. The **Lahmi Cafe** (tel. 92 34 31), west of the Astor Hotel at 27 HaGa'aton, is clean, air-conditioned, and serves light meals (NIS5-10). Nahariya's beaches and peaceful gardens make delightful picnic grounds; shop at the reasonable **supermarket** on the corner of HaGa'aton and Herzl St. Fruit and vegetable stores dot Herzl between HaGa'aton and HaMeyasdim. A Russian bakery sells several dozen varieties of cookies for NIS5-6 per kilogram, across from Hod theater on Herzl.

Sights and Entertainment

The remains of a 4000-year-old **Canaanite Temple** dedicated to Asherah, the goddess of fertility, were accidentally discovered in 1947 on the hill next to the town's shore. To reach the ruins, walk south along the beach for about 20 minutes. While the site itself is unimpressive, the pleasant walk along the sea is ample compensation. Just walk over the smashed areas of fence.

The 20th-century Municipality Building near the bus terminal contains a **modern art museum** (fifth floor) with very little modern art, a few archeological finds from the area, and a malacological section of pretty seashells. (Open Sun. 10am-noon and 4-6pm, Mon.-Tues. and Thurs.-Sat. 10am-noon, Wed. 10am-noon and 4-6pm. Free.)

Nahariya's *raison d'etre* remains, as always, sun-worship and swimming. The main beach is the crowded **Galei Gallil,** where a lifeguard watches a calm swimming area sheltered by a breakwater. To reach Galei Gallil, walk down HaGa'aton Blvd. and turn right (open 8am-5pm, admission NIS5). Fee covers admission to the heated indoor pool (open year-round), the Olympic-size outdoor pool, and the kiddy pools. All facilities—changing rooms, showers, cafes—are jammed on Saturdays. South of Galei Gallil is a free beach without a breakwater. Farther south is a free municipal beach with lifeguards and dressing rooms, but no shade. As you walk south, you will notice the sculpture dedicated to the refugees who entered Palestine during the British Mandate under the cover of dark. The remains of one ship have been incorporated into the artwork.

Horse-drawn **carriage rides** start from the post office and the eastern end of HaGa'aton. Prices for rides (NIS15, 20 and 30 for 15, 30, and 45 min., respectively) are exorbitant unless you can round up a group or bargain successfully. Each carriage holds 10 people. For entertainment, the **Hod Cinema,** on the corner of Herzl and HaGa'aton, often shows movies in English, as does the **Ron Cinema** on HaGa'aton in the square before the Municipality Building.

No one stays home on Friday or Saturday nights, and entertainment exists for every budget. **The Sleave** is number one for music, drinking, and talking (on HaGa'aton, next to Burger Ranch). Another favorite is **My Pub,** across from the bus station on HaGa'aton (follow the music). **Tropigan** has live music in a garden-atmosphere on a second-floor balcony on HaGa'aton. And for big spenders, or those who can make friends with locals (they all seem to get in free), there's dancing at the **Carlton Hotel** disco, also on HaGa'aton. (Admission NIS20.)

Near Nahariya

Rosh HaNiqra

Despite its uncomfortable position at the border with one of the most war-torn nations in the world, Rosh HaNiqra is a spectacular natural wonder. Throughout the war in Lebanon, the white cliffs and sea caves remained open to tourists. Once you descend into the cool, quiet beauty of the grottos, it's easy to forget altogether the presence of the Israeli border station and UN patrols overhead. Perhaps more fear-inspiring than the heavily-guarded border is the possibility of being swept over the guardrails and into the Mediterranean as you wander through the sea-carved caves. Rosh HaNiqra's caves have been sculpted out of chalk-white cliffs by centuries of lashing waves. These natural grottoes were enlarged when a tunnel, originally intended for a train line between Haifa and Beirut, was dug through the cliffs by the British during World War II.

The nearby *kibbutz,* perceiving the potential for tourism, blasted additional tunnels through the rock to improve access to the sea caves, and topped the cliffs with an observation point and cafeteria that command spectacular panoramas of the northern Israeli coastline. Older Israelis talk of swimming through the strong currents to see the caves years ago. (Open in summer Sun.-Thurs.) The highway from Nahariya ends at the observation point, so the only way down to the caves is by cable car (tel. 85 71 10). (Operates Sun.-Thurs. 8:30am-6pm, Fri. 8:30am-4pm; in winter Sun.-Thurs. 8:30am-4:30pm, Fri. 8:30am-4pm. Adults NIS8.50, students NIS6.50.) Buses #22 and 20 share six trips to this northern point from 9:10am to 5pm, and return 15 minutes later. Many people ride bikes here; start early in the morning, then return via Ahziv for a swim.

Come early, since coach tours and youth groups often invade the caves in the afternoon. The worse the weather, the better the show at Rosh HaNiqra—waves pound against the natural caverns, forming powerful cross-currents and whirlpools, and echoing thunderously through the subterranean tunnels. The eerie blue light reflected off the water bathes the caves in an otherworldly mist. If you decide to take an illegal dip on a calm day and risk joining several dead swimmers already on the sea floor, take care not to venture out into the waters to the north; the Lebanese border guards have no sympathy for even the most ill-informed of illegal immigrants. Photographers should refrain from taking pictures of the border-crossing since their cameras will be seized.

Ahziv

Ahziv beach, which begins about 4km north of Nahariya, is very popular among students and well-equipped with showers and shade, changing rooms and kiosk (admission NIS3). Two roads lead here: The paved road along the coast which ends here, and the noncoastal road where buses stop. Farther north, near Club Med there is an unofficial **nude beach.** On beaches in the area, you'll notice that occasional screams of "meduza" will send everyone running from the water. Then the lifeguard will wade into the water and capture the translucent blue jellyfish; afterwards, everyone will resume swimming. Stinging jellyfish are plentiful along this coast, and occasionally the beach is "closed" because of them.

The historical heart of the area is the **Ahziv National Park,** with its verdant lawns and sheltered beach (complete with showers and changing rooms), on the remains of an eighth-century Phoenician port town. Visible from the beach are the sailboats and beach bungalows of the Club Med to the south. (Park open daily 8am-7pm, Fri. 8am-4pm; in winter daily 8am-4pm. Closed Dec.-Feb. Admission NIS5) Bordering the park on its northern side is **Ahzivland,** a self-proclaimed independent state founded in 1952 by Eli Avivi, who leased the land from the Israeli government. **Eli's Museum,** housed in a deteriorated but beautiful Arab mansion, exhibits his amazingly esoteric collection of implements, statue fragments, and maps, mostly from the Phoenician period. (Open April-Sept. daily 8am-5pm; Oct.-March daily 8am-4pm. Admission NIS3.) The dilapidated sleeping and camping area is reminiscent of an old pirate hide-away. (Sleeping inside NIS12, outside NIS7.50. Use of parking and showers NIS5.)

Across the road is the **Ahziv Diving Center** (tel. 82 36 71), where you can rent a mask for NIS4, snorkel for NIS2, and fins for NIS4 (bargain if demand is low). Diving classes begin on Sunday and run through Saturday ($170). Introductory dives cost $30. Call ahead.

Just north is **Gesher HaZiv,** one of 11 bridges blown up on the evening of June 16, 1946 ("the night of the bridges"), to protest the British government's closure of Israel's ports to Jewish immigrants. The memorial is to 14 young men, members of the Haganah resistance force, who were killed as they tried to blow up a bridge. Following Jewish custom, visitors place small pebbles on the gravestones.

More attractive than Ahzivland by far are the campsite and hostel, both a short distance up the road. The **Ahziv Campground** (tel. 82 39 74) is both pleasant and enormous. It has 250 tent sites, which cost NIS9 per person, NIS5 for children, while two- and four-person bungalows are NIS30 and NIS55 respectively. A locked refrigerator box rents for NIS4.50. On site are a kitchen with gas, a restaurant, and a minimarket. The campground is run by members of Moshav Lehman. (Reception open 7am-7pm.) Another member operates **Ahziv Riding,** with horses for NIS20 per hour, NIS10 per half-hour, and NIS5 for a 15-minute lesson.

Yad Le-Yad Youth Hostel (IYHF) (tel. 82 33 45), ½km farther north along the main road, is huge and rarely full, despite its excellent beachside location. You can buy meals at the bar next door or cook them in the hostel kitchen. (Strict 11pm curfew, but each guest gets a key. Reception open 7am-noon and 3-6pm. Members NIS12, nonmembers NIS14; members under 18 NIS10, nonmembers NIS12. Breakfast included.) About 300m north, on the opposite side of the street, the **Society for the Protection of Nature in Israel** (Hevra LeHaganat HaTeva) offers guided walks in the area (tel. 82 37 62, office open 8am-1pm). You may be able to find someone who can help you in English to find seaside nature paths. You can reach the nature field school, hostel, beach, and campground near Ahziv by bus #22, which departs from Nahariya twice per hour.

Montfort

At the ruined Crusader castle of Montfort, you'll find picturesque ruins, lovely scenery, and a short, challenging hike. Wind-swept and solitary, the fortification poses dramatically, overlooking a deep valley of the western Galilee. The main structure, located near the Lebanese border, was built by the Knights Templar early in the twelfth century and partially destroyed by Salah al-Din in 1187 during his march on Akko. Enlarged and strengthened by the Hospitaller Knights in 1230, the fortress was named Starkenburg ("strong castle" in German), as well as Montfort ("strong mountain" in French). You can still see the impressive 18m-high tower and 20m-long main hall, along with the remains of the fortress complex.

Bus #43 leaves Nahariya for Mi'ilya four times per day. From the bus stop at Mi'ilya, follow the road that ascends from the highway for 2½ km, bearing left at every fork, until it bends sharply to the right and you see the wooden sign for Montfort. Follow the red-and-white-striped blazes along the path another 1½ km; the path to the castle abruptly turns up the rocks to the right, so keep your eyes open.

Descending north from the castle, follow the uphill path to the left at the junction by the ruins of the auxiliary building on the floor of the valley. At the top of the hill is a picnic area. From here, it's a 2km walk to the entrance of the **Keziv Park.** The park lies between the settlements of Goren and Elon on the main road leading west to Rosh HaNiqra. Bus #25 from Nahariya runs to and from Goren several times per day. One kilometer west, the entrance to Kibbutz Elon is a good place to try to hitch out to the coastal road or on to Nahariya.

Both Montfort and **Gadin Castle** at Yeḥiam, 8km to the west by the southern road, were built to protect Akko, the Crusader capital. Though destroyed by the Mamluk Sultan Baybars in 1265, the ruins remain impressive and offer yet another view of the western Galilee highlands. (Castle open Sun.-Thurs. 8am-5pm, Fri. and holidays 8am-4pm. Admission NIS1, students NIS.50.) There are only two buses per day to Yeḥiam from Nahariya, #39 at noon and #42 at 5pm.

Peqi'in

Peqi'in is known as the spot where Rabbi Shimon Bar Yoḥai and his son, Eliezer, fled from a Roman decree prohibiting individuals from studying the Torah. For 13 years, the learned pair hid in a small cave in the hillside, sustained by a miracle that caused a nearby spring to flow and a carob tree to bear fruit. During this time they composed the Zohar, the single most important text of Kabbala (Jewish mysticism). Today the cave is considered holy. To visit, take the winding road from the bus stop to the top of the village. When you reach a marking stone on your right (faintly engraved with a Hebrew map), head downstairs, turning right again through a gap in the stones. Continuing down the steps, choose the downhill fork at every intersection. When you come to a pool fed by Bar Yoḥai's spring, now trickling from a small pipe by the fence, take a right to the road marked by a round red-and-white sign; turn left at the first intersection and follow this curving road down to the white synagogue gate at your right. The synagogue on this site, which stood in the days of Shimon Bar Yoḥai and his son, is now a small **museum.** If the synagogue gate is closed, knock on the door (just opposite the gate and upstairs). Although the museum is technically free, you should leave a small donation in the box on the table with the prayer books.

At the entrance to Peqi'in, near the bus stop, are two small cafes flanking the road. The cafe lower on the hill is run by a friendly Druze man who can provide you with a map of the town's antiquities (in Hebrew). If you ask he'll spread a piece of pita bread with olive oil, dillweed, and a very sour, fermented white cheese, and fold it over 10 times into a delicious sandwich. The Turkish coffee here is fantastic.

Although part of the Galilee, Peqi'in is most accessible from Nahariya. Bus #44 from Nahariya makes the round trip to Peqi'in six or seven times per day; be sure to ask the driver to let you off at Peqi'in Atika (Old Peqi'in), not Peqi'in Hadasha (New Peqi'in), which is one stop earlier. If you ask politely, the driver will drop you off about 3km past Old Peqi'in at Tzomet (junction) Beit Jan. A long walk or hitch will bring you to a small, peaceful Druze village. **Beit Jan** is much less commercialized than Daliyat el-Karmel or Isfiya, and it's not hard to strike up a conversation here. The view of the serene valley is beautiful.

Galilee and Golan Heights

The Galilee is a land of clear air and green hills, and yet also of stormy battles. Jesus of Nazareth wandered this land, preaching and making miracles on the shores of the Kinneret (the Sea of Galilee). Here is where Jewish mystics believed the Messiah would come, and where they wrote the classics of the *kabbalah* (mysticism) while waiting. Yet bordered by Lebanon, Syria, Jordan, and the West Bank, this region has been bitterly contested in the past four decades. Today, iron tanks rust in their tracks as if in imitation of the crumbling stone ruins left by biblical cities.

Several millennia of historic sites are squeezed between the Sea of Galilee and the West Bank. The Lower Galilee, which includes Nazareth and Megiddo (or Armageddon), is marvelous touring country. **Afula** is the transportation hub for the various sights here, but the town itself offers little. Buses to many of the sights in the area run infrequently, so check schedules before you reach Afula to avoid spending the night there.

Whether approached from the dusty Arab villages of the West Bank, the sun-scorched Jordan Valley, or the cool hills of the Upper Galilee, Yam Kinneret is a miraculous sight in this arid land. Hot mineral baths bubble on its shores, and early in the morning, as the sun rises above the distant heights, a single shaft of light knifes across the water. The town of Tiberias on the western shore is a crowded seaside resort, but the setting is spectacular.

Evenings in the Upper Galilee are dramatic. Rocky ridges towering over the valley take their turns in the spotlight of the setting sun before receding into shadow. In daylight, the land here looks almost primeval with waterfalls and hot springs. Dwelling in the dense cedar forests of the nature reserves is the Galilee's exotic wildlife. Perhaps the true miracle of this land lies in the fact that it much of is a creation of human hands, laboriously reclaimed from swampland. It is now Israel's primary agricultural plain, with settlements blending unobtrusively into the serene hills and lush valleys cut by the source waters of the Jordan River. Even the bustling life of the largest town in the Upper Galilee, Qiryat Shmona, is overshadowed by the steep hills that tower over it.

The Golan Heights, stretching from the alligator ponds on the Yarmoukh River in the south to snow-capped Mount Hermon on the Lebanese-Syrian border, lies east of the Kinneret. The area is one of great natural beauty, but is known worldwide for its history of military conflict. The Golan was captured in 1967, when Israel successfully fought an uphill battle against entrenched Syrian troops. The stone trenches and their commanding view of the Galilee are still there for visitors to discover; unfortunately, so are many of the minefields. In 1973, Syria recaptured the Heights but the Israelis successfully counter-attacked. Israel annexed the territory in 1981 and now Jewish settlements are scattered amid ruins and restive Arab villages.

Nazareth

The number of churches, convents, and monasteries in Nazareth reflects the city's importance in Christian tradition, though the perpetual traffic jam on Paul VI St. does not. Enter a church or wander the alleys above town to get a sense of Jesus' hometown. Take a good look around, because you'll lose it in the mass of shops and felafel stands in the main business district.

Practical Information

Government Tourist Information Center (GTIO): Casa Nova St. (tel. 57 30 03 or 57 05 55), near intersection with Paul VI St. From bus station, walk south; an alley to the right, near the Christian Travel Center, connects to Paul VI. GTIO is on the left, across the street. Try to obtain the map at another office before coming to Nazareth. Very helpful staff, but take signs saying "Back Soon" with a grain of salt. Open Mon.-Fri. 8am-5pm, Sat. 8am-2pm. Closed major Christian and Jewish holidays.

Banks: HaPoalim, to the right of the Mashbir department store. Open Mon.-Tues. and Thurs. 8:30am-12:30pm and 4-6pm, Wed. and Sat. 8:30am-12:30pm, Fri. 8:30am-noon. Other banks are on Paul VI St.

Central Post Office: Near Mary's Well, off Paul VI St. Open Mon. and Wed. 7:45am-2pm, Tues. and Thurs.-Fri. 7:45am-12:30pm and 3:30-6pm, Sat. 7:45am-1pm.

Telephone Code: 06.

Central Bus Station: Inter-city buses stop along a stretch of Paul VI St. across from the Mashbir department store. The Egged information office on Paul VI St. is open daily from about 6am-6:30pm. Bus #431 comes from Haifa and continues to Tiberias. Buses #823 and 824 run frequently on the 20-min. trip to Afula, bus hub of the Galilee. **Baggage storage** is next door, NIS2 per piece per day. Open Sun.-Thurs. 7:30am-5pm, Fri. 7:30am-1pm.

Taxis: Ma'ayan, on Paul VI St. (tel. 55 51 05). *Sherut* taxis can be found at the blue signs with the red circle. NIS3 to Tiberias.

Car Rental: Europcar, on Casa Nova St.

First Aid: Tel. 101.

Hospital: Nazareth Hospital, tel. 57 15 01 or 57 15 02.

Pharmacy: Ferah Pharmacy, next to Egged Information.

Police: Tel. 100 or 57 44 44.

Nazareth lies between Haifa (40km northwest) and Tiberias (30km northeast), in the Lower Galilee on a slight elevation north of the Jezreel Valley. The city is made up of two completely different sections. The inhabitants of the old **Arab Town,** where the Christian sites are located, resent the encroaching development of the newer **Natzeret Illit** (Upper Nazareth), where Jewish settlers have built a thriving community. The Arabs here have a strong sense of solidarity with the Palestinians, but the city remains free of tension. Nazareth is marred by a complete lack of street signs. When you get lost in the market, keep walking downhill and you'll eventually come to **Paul VI Street.** This thoroughfare winds uphill from the bus station to Mary's Well and is intersected by **Casa Nova Street.**

Accommodations and Food

The only inexpensive beds in Nazareth are offered by several Christian hospices. Unfortunately, the sisters are frequently in retreat, which puts you on the street. A pristine dormitory with superb facilities is run by the **Religieuses de Nazareth** (tel. 55 43 04, P.O. Box 274), near the basilica (NIS7 per night). Walk up Casa Nova St. and take a left after the Casa Nova Hospice; it will be on the right at #306, just past the pink archway. Cook your meals in the kitchen, eat them in the dining room, and relax in the magazine-filled living room. (Check-in 4pm, but you can leave your pack if you arrive earlier.) If you arrive when the sisters are in retreat, call the **Frères de Betharram** (tel. 57 00 46), whose dormitory beds cost NIS15 per night. The **Sisters of Charles Barrameus** also run a hospice (tel. 55 44 35) behind the Carmelite Convent, with beds for NIS15 per night. The **Casa Nova Hospice** (tel. 71 32 67), on Casa Nova St., is the deluxe option and almost always booked months in advance. (Bed and breakfast NIS25.) The **Galil Hotel,** 6 Paul VI St. (tel. 57 13 11), about a 10-minute walk south of the bus station, has private rooms with showers. (Call ahead. Singles NIS35, doubles NIS63. Breakfast included.)

Felafel stands abound, particularly on Paul VI Street. Scattered throughout the city are numerous cafes specializing in incredibly sweet Middle Eastern desserts. There are plenty of small grocery stores on Paul VI St., on both sides of the central bus station. Buy fruits and vegetables in the produce markets interspersed among the grocery stores. The **Israel Restaurant,** near the corner of Casa Nova and Paul VI St., serves reasonably priced Middle Eastern food (salads NIS3.50, chicken dishes NIS9). Revel in cleanliness and air-conditioning at the **Aljeneenah Restaurant,** just down the street from St. Garbriel Church and the post office (salads NIS3-5, meat dishes NIS15). In the market just past the white mosque in Mosque Sq. and next to a large mural is **El-Hanna,** a good inexpensive Middle Eastern restaurant (meat dishes NIS5).

Sights

Nazareth is a city of churches. The **Basilica of the Annunciation,** which dominates Nazareth's downtown, is a complex of two churches built in 1966 over the remains of older structures and now maintained by Franciscan monks. If you visit during a service, notice how the eerie, high-pitched music from several different parts of the basilica resonates through the immense concrete structure. The artwork in the courtyard was donated by believers in many different countries. Be sure to examine the basilica's huge bronze doors depicting the life of Jesus. The entry level is built on the site of Mary's house, where the archangel Gabriel appeared to Mary to herald the birth of Jesus. To the left of the cave lie excavated ritual baths from a third-century Christian church. Next to the railing is the line of a fourth-century Byzantine church wall; the back wall of the building is from a twelfth-century Crusader church. The church's second level contains an intriguing series of international artistic interpretations of the Annunciation, as well as ceramic reliefs of the stations of the cross molded by Christian Arabs. The excavations of the ancient town of Nazareth lie in an archeological garden underneath the plaza that opens from the upper floor of the church. You can also get glimpses through the hole in the plaza. Ask one of the monks to show you around. Guards at the entrance check that all visitors are dressed modestly. (Open Mon.-Fri. 8:30am-noon and 2-6pm, Sun. and feasts 2-6pm; Oct.-March Mon.-Fri. 9am-noon and 2-5pm, Sun. and feasts 2-5pm.)

Across the plaza stands **St. Joseph's Church,** where you can look down on the cave thought to be Joseph's house. Remnants of an older church lie beneath, and stairs lead down to caves where grain and oil were once stored. The **Greek-Catholic Synagogue Church** in the center of the Arab market is the site of the synagogue where Jesus is believed to have preached as a young man. To get there enter the *shuk* from Casa Nova St., bear left at the first fork, and then take the first right; the entrance will be on your right, at the brown gate. There is a blue star on top that sometimes lights up at night. Climb the stairs on your right for a view of Nazareth's rooftops. Following Paul VI St. uphill from the bus station, you come to **Mary's Well,** reputedly still working. Many believe that the well's water miraculously heals. Veering left and continuing uphill from the well, you come to the **St. Gabriel Greek Orthodox Church,** which stands over the town's original water source. The original church was erected in 356 over the spring where Mary drew water and where the Greek Orthodox believe Gabriel appeared to Mary. The present church, built in 1750, has elaborate Byzantine-style paintings and hangings. Ancient tiles decorate the entrance into the well area. (Open 8am-6pm. The caretaker will open it.) To reach the **Maronite Church,** dating from 1770, follow the road past the Greek-Catholic Synagogue Church, take the first left, and follow the signs. Don't be tempted to take the U-turn. The **Mensa Christi Church** next door allegedly marks the place where Jesus shared a meal with his disciples after the Resurrection. The building surrounds a piece of soft limestone (*mensa*). Although the church is unmarked, the surrounding walls have a colorful mural on them.

For a lovely view over the Galilean hills, hike up to the **Salesian Church** at the top of the natural amphitheater in which the old city is located. (All churches in

Nazareth claim to be open 8:30-11:45am and 2-5pm; in winter 9-11:45am and 2-4:45pm. Many churches close anyway in the afternoon, so visit in the morning. Sunday mornings are reserved for services. Modest dress required at all times.)

Nazareth has a lively **market** (8:30-11:45am and 2-5pm), best reached via Casa Nova St. The variety here is impressive: Toys, clothing, sundry souvenirs, and fruit are all vigorously extolled by proprietors. Women may experience some verbal taunts, but the vendors are generally friendly.

Near Nazareth

Kafr Kanna, a village to the north of Nazareth, is said to be the site of Jesus' miracle of transforming water into wine at the wedding feast (John 2:1-11). The town contains a Franciscan church built in 1881 to commemorate the event. Buses leave for Kafr Kanna every 45 minutes from Mary's Well in Nazareth, or you can take bus #431 to Tiberias, and ask the driver to let you off at Kafr Kanna. Bus #431 leaves every 40 minutes from the main bus station. **Mount Tabor** (588m) is located 33km from Nazareth. Here, churches and a monastery commemorate the Transfiguration of Jesus. This is where Deborah led the Israelites into a victory over Sisera's army (Judges 4-5) and Jesus talked with Moses and Elijah during the Transfiguration (Luke 9: 28-36).

Megiddo (Armageddon)

The settlements at Megiddo were destroyed so many times that its name became synonymous with destruction—hence you'll recognize its Latin name "Armageddon." In the New Testament, Revelation 16:16 tells that at the end of the world demons will go out to all the nations, and they will assemble at Armageddon. It would make a good meeting place, since in ancient times the fortress town of Megiddo bordered the crucial route between Egypt and Mesopotamia that became the Roman Via Maris.

The *tel* (layered hill) at Megiddo was once thought only to date to King Solomon (c. 950 B.C.E.). Excavations in the 1960s revealed remains dating back to the Neolithic Age (c. 3500 B.C.E.) with 20 layers of ruins. The ruins are mostly unreconstructed, except for the grain silo and the water tunnel, but the site is impressive for its sheer vastness. The grain silo was built on the top of the hill to protect stored grain from unnecessary moisture. Because it's difficult to keep all the different sections of the *tel* straight, it's worthwhile to pick up the guide to the site at the ticket window for NIS.20. A small **museum** near the entrance contains exhibits explaining the various layers of excavations and a model of Solomon's chariot town. There are also plans of the town, which show that King Ahab had more stables and chariots than Solomon. There's a list of the many biblical references to Megiddo as well. Try to see the museum between tour groups.

From the observation point at the site, you can look out over the **Valley of Jezreel** (*Emeq Yizre'el*), which was mostly swamp until 1920, when Jewish immigrants drained the land and turned it into Israel's fertile land. The round mountain standing alone in the distance is Mount Tabor.

One of the site's most intriguing features is the tunnel built to hide the city's water source from invaders and to make the water accessible from inside the city walls. The tunnel takes you through a turnstile into the parking lot, so make sure it's your last stop at the site. When you exit, turn right and walk ½km back to the main road. (Site open Sun.-Thurs. 8am-4pm, Fri. 8am-3pm. Admission NIS3, students NIS1.50.) **Bus** #823 leaves Nazareth for Megiddo every hour during the morning, and every 30 minutes from noon to 7:30pm. From Megiddo, buses to Afula, the transportation hub of the Lower Galilee, stop on the south side of the road, while buses to the coast and Tel Aviv stop on the north side, both about every 20 minutes. You can also walk 1km downhill to *tzomet* Megiddo, where you got off the bus, and catch the frequent buses.

Beit She'an, Beit Alpha, Gan HaShlosha, and Belvoir

Along the road from Beit She'an to Afula are many sites of natural and historical interest. In **Beit She'an** you'll find an unreconstructed **Roman amphitheater,** built in 200 C.E. to accommodate 5000 spectators. The stage is still intact. (Open daily 8am-5pm, Fri. 8am-4pm. Admission NIS3, students NIS1.50.) To reach the ruins, turn left (toward the pink felafel stand) as you leave the bus station, and follow the road about 800m. A major excavation is underway, which archeologists antici- pate will reveal an ancient Roman city. The site is in a park called **Gan HaBanim.** The pool is an indulgence only for hot days (NIS5). Beit She'an was bombarded by the Syrians as late as 1975—note the square bomb shelters added onto each house. Buses #415 and 412 leave Afula for Beit She'an every 20 minutes.

Take an afternoon excursion to the lovely park of **Gan HaShlosha** (also known as **Sahne**), which lies 5km northwest of Beit She'an and 1km southeast of Beit Alpha on the road to Afula. It dates back to Roman times and features waterfalls and swimming holes full of crystalline water. There's a snack bar and a restaurant, but bring a picnic instead. Leave your belongings under the lifeguard's chair for safe- keeping. During the summer there is folk dancing on Sundays at 8:30pm. Buses #415 and 412 from either Afula or Beit She'an run to Sahne. (Open daily 7am- 5:30pm. Admission NIS5.) A 10-minute walk along the road behind the park leads to the **Nir David Museum of Mediterranean Archeology,** an extensive collection including some beautiful examples of Hellenistic and Islamic art and pottery. A collection gathered from the area traces the peoples who have lived here, includes remains from a Canaanite temple, an Israelite community, and a Roman weavers' colony. The curator will enthusiastically explain every exhibit to visitors. (Open Sun.-Fri. 8am-1pm, Sat. 10:30am-1pm. You have to pay for the park to see the mu- seum.)

One kilometer northwest of Sahne on the road to Afula within Kibbutz Hepzibah is the sixth-century C.E. synagogue of **Beit Alpha**, with a beautifully preserved mo- saic floor of a zodiac wheel. To reach Hepzibah take bus #415 or 412 from either Beit She'an or Afula. (Open daily 8am-5pm, Fri. 8am-4pm. Admission NIS1.50, students NIS.75.) Do not be misled by the sign for Kibbutz Beit Alpha (1km closer to Beit She'an), which is named after the ancient site.

Another few kilometers closer to Afula on the eastern side of the road is Kibbutz **Ein Harod** with the **Beit Sturman Museum of Natural History.** The museum is devoted to studies of the region, and has an archeological garden with pillars and a sarcophagus. (Open Sun.-Thurs. 8am-1pm and 3-4:30pm, Fri. 8am-noon, Sat. 9:30am-12:30pm. Admission NIS4.50, students NIS2.50.)

Three kilometers down the road to Afula, you can sleep on biblical territory at the **Ma'ayan Harod Youth Hostel (IYHF)** (tel. (06) 53 16 60) and **campground** (tel. (06) 53 16 04), both of which lie 1km off the Afula-Beit She'an road. Bus #35 from Afula, leaving at 6am, noon, and 6pm, will take you directly to the hostel. Buses #412, 402 and 405 bring you to the road leading to the accommodations; the way is marked with orange signs, and the walk is about 1km. The hostel facilities are adequate, the well-stocked kiosk has long hours, and it's the place where Gideon defeated the Midianites (Judges 7). The small cave in the garden contains the grave of one of the Midianite leaders. Families flock to the National Park here, so call ahead in July and August. (Beds in dorms and bungalows NIS12.70, under 18 NIS10.50. Nonmembers NIS2.20 extra. Breakfast NIS6.) The nearby campground (NIS10), unaffiliated with the hostel, has a gargantuan swimming pool (NIS5).

The Tiberias-Beit She'an bus will let you off at the turn-off to **Belvoir,** a twelfth- century Crusader fort which affords spectacular views over the entire Jezreel Valley and, on a clear day, a glimpse of the Kinneret. The castle, (*Kohav HaYarden* in Hebrew, "Star of the Jordan"), overlooked the medieval trade route from Egypt to Damascus. The area was the scene of many battles between the Crusaders and the Muslims, culminating in an 18-month siege of the castle by the Muslims in 1188- 89. The knights finally surrendered, and in acknowledgment of their bravery were permitted to depart unharmed. During the early thirteenth century, the castle was partially destroyed by the sultan of Damascus in order to prevent a Crusader reoccupation of the stronghold. Yet the interior, constructed with massive black blocks of stone and surrounded by a deep moat, is still impressive. Unfortunately, no bus service runs directly to the castle, and it's a very steep 6km uphill walk to the site from the junction where the bus lets you off. The midday summer heat can be murderous, so if you decide to brave the hike (or gamble on a hitch), start early and bring a hat and plenty of water. (Open Sat.-Thurs. 8am-5pm, Fri. 8am-4pm. Admission NIS3.)

Tiberias (Tveria)

Since the Israeli troops took the Golan Heights in 1967, ending the constant shelling of the region, the area around the Kinneret (Sea of Galilee) has become a popular year-round holiday spot. Although tourism has raised prices, it has also brought an abundance of lodgings and a lively weekend nightlife to the area. If you find Tiberias too touristy, raise your eyes to the hills or lower them to the sea. Tiberias is the only major city on the Kinneret and an ideal touring base for the area, though during July and August the city can be extremely humid, due to its location 200m below sea level.

Beneath the party image of this resort beats the heart of a city with a more serious history. Founded in 18 C.E., it was named for the Roman Emperor Tiberias and, according to first-century Jewish historian Josephus, quickly took on its namesake's most salient trait—hedonism. After the Romans destroyed Jerusalem, Tiberias became the center of Jewish life in the Holy Land. It was here around the third century that the *Mishnah* (a collection of Jewish law forming part of the *Talmud*) was codified, the *Talmud* edited, and vowels added to the Hebrew alphabet. The Sanhedrin, the great court of scholars and rabbis, met here. Thus, Tiberias gained the title as one of Israel's four holy cities along with Jerusalem, Hebron, and Tzfat. Under the Byzantines, Jews from Persia and Babylonia came on pilgrimages to Tiberias. Legend has it that the redemption of Israel will begin in Tiberias. Along with most of northern Israel, Tiberias was devastated by an earthquake in 1837. Not until the turn of the century did Jewish immigrants begin to resettle the area. By 1948, when the state of Israel was declared, Tiberias had over 12,000 inhabitants, more than half of them Jewish. The city's population has since doubled.

Practical Information and Orientation

Government Tourist Information Office (GTIO): 8 Alhadef St. (tel. 72 09 92). Head toward the sea from the bus station and turn left on Alhadef St. A daily schedule of events is posted inside. The office will also help find accommodations when the area fills up. Very helpful, but busy. Open Sun.-Thurs. 8:30am-5pm, Fri. 8:30am-2pm.

Central Post Office: HaYarden St. (tel. 72 15 15). Take a right as you exit the bus station onto HaYarden St. and walk toward the sea; the office will be on the left just before Alhadef St. **Poste Restante** at the left-most window. **International phone** services are available through the back entrance, past the pay phones, inside at the glass office immediately to the right. 3-min. minimum. Slightly cheaper rates on Sun. Open Sun.-Tues. and Thurs. 7:45am-12:30pm and 3:30-6pm, Wed. 7:45am-2pm, Fri. 7:45am-1pm.

Telephone Code: 06.

Central Bus Station: HaYarden St. (tel. 79 10 80). To Jerusalem (every 30-45 min. 6am-6pm, NIS7.90), to Tel Aviv (every 30 min. 5:30am-8pm), to Haifa (every 20-45 min. 5:40am-8:30pm). *Sherut* and private taxis can be found on the stretch of HaYarden St. running from the bus station to the water.

Laundry: Panorama, under the Panorama Hotel. 7kg-wash, dry, and fold NIS15. Self-service too. Open Sun.-Fri., sometimes Sat.

Bicycles: Gal Kal, first level of central bus station. Price includes lock, repair kit, and pump. Up to 4 hr. NIS7; 4-24 hours. NIS12. Inner tubes for the lake are NIS5 for 24 hours.

Pharmacy: Center Pharm, at the corner of Bibass St. and HaGalil St. Open Sun.-Fri. 8am-8pm.

First Aid: Tel. 72 01 11 or 79 10 11. Open 24 hours.

Police: Tel. 79 24 44.

Tiberias has three levels. The **old city** is by the water, the **new city** (Qiryat Shmuel) is up the hill (take bus #1 or 5 from the bus station), and the **uptown** is on top of the hill (#7, 8, or 9 from the station). There is little reason to venture above the old city except to see a movie. **HaGalil Street,** running parallel to the water, is the main thoroughfare in Tiberias.

Accommodations and Camping

For a town this size, Tiberias offers an astonishing number of lodging alternatives. All hostels, hospices, and hotels are within several blocks of each other, so you won't have to walk far. Prices rise dramatically during the high season, August and September. The area is also particularly mobbed during the holidays of Passover (April 20-26 in 1989) and the New Year and Sukkot (Sept. 30-Oct. 21 in 1989).

Meyouhas Hostel (IYHF), HaYarden St. (tel. 72 17 75 or 79 03 50). A cavernous, centrally located hostel near the Great Mosque, just west of the road winding along the beaches. Comfortable and safe with a nice TV room. This hostel is extremely busy with groups. IYHF members have priority. Large breakfast NIS6, meat meal NIS12. Check-in 4pm-midnight. Curfew April-Sept. 1am; Oct.-March midnight. Members NIS12.50, under 18 NIS10.50. Nonmembers NIS14.70, under 18 NIS12.70. A/C NIS1.

Church of Scotland Hospice, P.O. Box 104, Tiberias 14100 (tel. 79 10 44 or 79 01 45). A gray stone building to the left of the IYHF hostel, toward the sea. Large private rooms in a lovely setting in the old city. Bath and overhead fans, superb facilities, beautiful garden, and a private beach. Nice management. Fills with groups. Dorm beds in hostel NIS7, breakfast NIS5. Bed and breakfast in hotel NIS29.

Maman Hostel, Atzmon St. (tel. 79 29 86). From HaYarden St. turn south on HaGalil, then bear right on Tavor St.; a sign at the corner of Tavor and Atzmon will direct you to the hostel. Easygoing atmosphere with an attractive, tiny yard. Porch-top lounge with a bar (open 5-11pm) and TV. A/C. Kitchen facilities available. Clean toilets and showers. Dorm beds NIS10.

Nahum Hostel, Tavor St. (tel. 72 15 05). From HaYarden St. turn south on HaGalil, then bear right on Tavor St. about 100m. Fairly clean with kitchens. If you want the building with co-ed rooms, you'll also get lines at the toilet and shower. The rooftop bar with videos is a bonus, as is the egg breakfast for NIS3. Meager ventilation from ceiling fans. Beg for sheets. Dorm beds NIS7.

Castle Inn Hostel, next to the Plaza Hotel (tel. 72 11 75 or 72 18 33). Great location on the wharf with a view of the sea from the terrace. Pleasing rooms with showers and kitchens. A bit pricey. The rooms are hot if you don't buy A/C (NIS5). Closed 1-4pm. Curfew Sun.-Thurs. midnight, weekends 1am. Rooms NIS15.

Hostel Aviv, HaGalil St. (tel. 72 00 31), 1½ blocks south of HaYarden, past Bank HaPoalim. Both a hostel and a hotel. Wide halls, with TV lounge, bar, and kitchen facilities. Noisy because of its location on the street. Small but neat dorm beds NIS7. Doubles in the hostel NIS40, doubles in the hotel NIS60.

Adina's Hostel, 15 HaShiloah St., along the street from the bus station (tel. 72 25 07). Run by a family. Pleasant and clean, with kitchen facilities. Adina is very nice, especially if you speak Hebrew. Open only to Israelis in high season. Dorm beds NIS12, doubles NIS50.

Schweizer Hostel, HaShiloah St. (tel. 72 19 91), at the corner of Bibass St., 200m south of the bus station. Relatively quiet, family-run hostel with TV lounge. Dorm beds NIS15, doubles NIS40. Breakfast NIS4.

Terra Sancta (tel. 72 05 16) upstairs in the Terra Sancta Church, but enter by the stairs on the other side of the building. Dorm beds NIS8.

Lev Hagalil, Habanim St. (tel. 79 26 52), near the IYHF hostel. Efficiency apartments. A/C. Pool. NIS90. Weekly NIS525. Breakfast included.

Camping is the best way to escape the city heat. Though camping in the summer will bring you closer to the crowds, official campsites are often cheaper than hostels. Start by getting information at the stand run by the Ministry of Tourism and the Society for the Protection of Nature (tel. 75 20 56) at Tzemah. This is the junction where the road forks east-west. (Take bus #18, 21, 22, or 24; stand open in summer 8am-5pm.) Their map details the locations of the 25 campsites on the lake. These campsites, marked by a picnic bench and a tree, cost NIS10-15 per carload, regardless of number.

The word for the campgrounds at **Ein Gev** (tel. 75 11 77) is more: more amenities, more expensive, more crowded. Reach Ein Gev by bus #18, 21, or 22; or for four times the price of the bus you can take the ferry run by Kinneret Sailing Company (tel. 72 18 31; open daily 8am-4pm) from the wharf near the Plaza Hotel. There are as many as four trips per day, but be sure to check since schedules vary (one-way NIS8, round-trip NIS12). Camping costs NIS53 for a site for four to five people in high season (bring your own tent) and NIS24 for two people in low season (add NIS11 for each additional adult, NIS9 each additional child). Caravans, small mini-apartments with kitchen, bed, and bathroom, are popular but outrageously expensive at NIS188 for four people. Check-in is at 2pm, check-out at 10am. NIS8 will allow you onto the **beach** for the day. At the beach you can rent paddle boats for NIS18 per hour, and kayaks for NIS10 per hour. There is a comparable free beach just south of the campsite. It's best to wear shoes when going in the water because of the sharp rocks. For campsite reservations in high season (July and Aug.), write at least a month in advance to Ein Gev Camping, Jordan Valley, Israel.

Five kilometers south of Ein Gev is **Ha'On** campsite (tel. 75 75 55 or 75 75 56), accessible by buses #18, 21, and 22 from Tiberias. Ask for the Ha'On bus stop, then take the road toward the sea, on the opposite side of the highway, about 200m through the grove of palm trees. A site for a 4-person tent is NIS30 in high season (50% more on Sat. and Sun.; NIS6 for each additional adult, NIS4.60 for each additional child). Caravans for four (with stove, fridge, and A/C) cost NIS120. The entrance fee to the beach, including the ostrich farm (open 9am-5pm), is NIS8.

Two kilometers southwest of Tiberias lies the **Kfar Hittim** campsite (tel. 79 29 11) in the Hittim Valley. To reach the campsite, take bus #42, which runs from Tiberias (check with bus information for the exact times). Tents and bungalows are available for rent May through October.

Interspersed among the private beaches are stretches of shoreline for **free-lance camping.** You'll need to bring food, water, and insect repellent, but the government has conveniently installed jiffy johns and trash bins at a few of these points. Be wary of theft if you sleep on the beach. Take the Ein Gev bus from Tiberias and get off wherever you see a site, or walk south along the coast past the Tiberias hotsprings.

Food

The afternoon **market** on HaGalil St. (closed Sat.) sells good produce. You can also pick up a light lunch or dinner at one of Tiberias' innumerable felafel stands on HaYarden St., which runs from HaBanim St. toward the bus station (open until about 7pm). The seafood restaurants along the waterfront offer romantic candlelit settings; a good dinner of St. Peter's fish, unique to the Sea of Galilee, costs about NIS17. The cafes and restaurants on HaGalil and HaBonim St. and the squares in between offer cheaper fare, including pizza. For your groceries, there is a **supermarket** in the Great Mosque Plaza across from Meyouhas Hostel, open until 9pm in August and 7:30pm the rest of the year. **HaQishon Street** is a lively nighttime place for pizza and pubs. The restaurant on HaGalil St. with the Donald Duck and red, white, and blue logo is open on Saturday, as are many restaurants on the waterfront.

Egged Bus Station Restaurant. The best deal for a complete meal. Meat dishes NIS6.50, salads NIS1.50. Open Sun.-Fri. for breakfast and lunch.

Avi's Restaurant, HaQishon St., between HaGalil and HaBonim St., a few blocks up from the Plaza. Pizza NIS7-8, cannelloni NIS8. Open daily noon-2am.

Maman Restaurant, HaGalil St. (tel. 72 11 26), at the corner of Bibass St. This place is crammed with Israelis—always a good sign. Middle Eastern food at reasonable prices. A/C. *Ḥoummus* or *taḥina* NIS3, schnitzel NIS10. Open daily 8am-midnight.

Penguin Restaurant, HaQishon St. (tel. 72 03 52), across from Avi's. Good music. Pizza NIS8, salads NIS5, ½ liter draft beer NIS3.

Karamba Vegetarian Restaurant, on Promenade (tel. 79 15 46), take the alley leading to the waterfront from the Meyouhas hostel. Excellent place with an exotic ambience. Salad NIS8, pizza marguereta NIS8, onion quiche NIS12.

Sights

The **old city,** beset by earthquakes and conquerors, has vanished but for a few fragments of the walls scattered throughout the modern town. To get a feeling for its former glory, join the free walking tours offered by the Tiberias Plaza Hotel Saturday at 9:30am (tours leave from the hotel lobby). A seventh-generation Tiberian gives the two-hour tour, pointing out the city's more obscure attractions.

The spruced-up, well-marked **Tomb of Moses Maimonides** on Y. Ben Zakkai St., commemorates the controversial rabbi who attempted to wed Aristotelian and Arabic philosophy to the study of Judaism. According to legend, an unguided donkey carried his coffin straight to Tiberias. To reach the tomb, take HaYarden St. east (toward the water) and turn left on Y. Ben Zakkai St. The tomb is about 2 blocks up on the right. The area has a red fence and black pillars. The white half-cylinder with Hebrew writing is the actual tomb. If you need directions, ask for the tomb of "Rambam," the rabbi's Hebrew acronym (*R*abbi *M*oshe *b*en *M*aimon). The tomb of Rabbi Akiva, for those inspired by the Rambam, is on top of the mountain with a breathtaking panorama. (Take bus #4, and ask for directions.)

Back on the waterfront esplanade, the **Franciscan Terra Sancta Church** stands north of the Plaza Hotel. The church was built in the twelfth century to commemorate St. Peter's role in the growth of Christianity and is thus known as St. Peter's. The apse behind the altar is arched like the bow of a boat, signifying his former profession as a fisherman. In the courtyard is a statue to the Virgin built by Polish troops who were quartered in the church from 1942 to 1945. (Open daily 8-11:45am and 3-5:30pm.)

Tiberias is the site of one of the world's earliest known **hot mineral springs.** One legend maintains that the springs were formed in the great biblical flood when the earth's insides surged upward. Another legend holds that the water was heated by demons under the orders of King Solomon, who then made the demons deaf so that they would never hear of his death and desert their duties. Apparently, they still haven't heard; visitors come here for therapy in the warm flowing waters. During the week you can lie in the pools, too slimy for swimming but very relaxing, and take a cleansing shower afterwards for NIS15 (on Sat. NIS17). A massage is NIS25 (on Sat. NIS29), while a mineral bath is NIS21 (on Sat. NIS25). Also in the complex is an expensive, though excellent, restaurant open for lunch. The springs are 2km south of town on the coastal road. Either walk or catch bus #2 or 5 from the front of central bus station or from HaGalil St. The older building, **Tiberias Hot Springs,** serves those with serious ailments. (Open Sun.-Thurs. 6:30am-4pm, Fri. 6:30am-1pm.) The newer building, **Tiberias Hot Springs Spa** (tel. 79 19 67), serves those seeking a bit of repose. (Open Sun.-Thurs. 8am-8pm, Fri. 8am-2:30pm, Sat. 8:30am-8pm.)

Across the street are ruins of the **Tiberias Hot Springs Synagogue,** actually six ancient synagogues built on top of each other. The highlight of the excavations is a mosaic floor that was part of three separate synagogues. The four upper synagogues were used in the sixth to eighth centuries C.E. A small museum displays other remains. (Site open Sun.-Thurs. 8am-5pm, Fri. 8am-4pm. Admission NIS1.50, students NIS.75.)

Entertainment

There are no free beaches in Tiberias. The shoreline in the city and to the immediate north and south is owned by hotels, which charge admission. All offer changing and shower facilities, boat rentals, and kiosks.

The **Lido Kinneret,** on the left fork down HaYarden St., charges NIS6, on *shabbat* NIS7. NIS40 buys you 15 minutes of waterskiing. (Open daily 8am-6pm.) Just north is **Shell Beach,** where kayaks rent for NIS10 per hour, though student discounts are possible (admission NIS6, *shabbat* NIS7; open 7:30am-9pm). Also to the north are the misnamed **Quiet Beach** (admission NIS5), and **Blue Beach** (NIS10). With some effort, you may find an entrepreneur who will undercut the expensive waterskiing establishments. To the south of Tiberias, about a 15-minute walk, or a short ride on buses #2 or 5, the **Municipal Beach** charges only NIS4. Next to it is the beach of **Hannei Gamat** (admission NIS6, *shabbat* NIS7). Many beaches also have kiddie pools.

Nightlife in Tiberias is limited to either cafe-bars or the few discos in town. **Blue Beach** opens its disco at 8:30pm during the summer—Israeli folkdancing alternates with top-40 hits (admission NIS12). Wear your bathing suit under your party clothes so you can take a dip between sets. You can try to crash the nightclub shows in the hotels. Bop around the lake on nightly **disco cruises** at 9pm run by Kinneret Sailing.

The outdoor cafes along HaGalil St. and the promenade show rock videos or recorded movies. The bars at the Maman and Nahum hostels are pleasant hangouts; both show videos and serve reasonably priced drinks. The **Sea of Galilee Festival,** featuring international folkdancing and singing troupes, usually takes place in Tiberias during the second week of July. Check at the GTIO for details on special events and for information on Ein Gev's Passover music festival.

Slightly south of Tiberias (1km) is **Luna Beach,** with a complex of waterslides. (Open 8am-5pm; admisson NIS20.) The adjacent **Sironit Beach** has only a few slides but is also open 7pm-midnight and is only NIS10.

Near Tiberias

New Testament Sites

The Kinneret was where Jesus walked on water. Appropriately, four of the most significant stories in Christian history are set on the steep hills surrounding the Kinneret's northern coast. The adventurous can tour these sights by bicycle to save the hassle of long walks and waiting for buses. Get a 10-speed mountain bike if possible: The knobby tires will supplement your motocross skills when insane Israeli drivers force you into a roadside ditch. The Kinneret is misnamed as a "sea"; the entire circuit around it is only 58km.

On the **Mount of Beatitudes,** overlooking sea, field, and town, Jesus gave his Sermon on the Mount (Matthew 5). Today, the Mount is one of the most serene, beautiful sanctuaries in Israel. Tour groups flock here but manage to leave the peace undisturbed, perhaps succumbing to the power of the setting. A church, built by Mussolini of all people, now stands on the Mount. The balcony is always cooled by the brisk wind that blows through the hills. Shorts and bare shoulders are not permitted. To reach the Mount, take bus #841 or 459 from Tiberias and get off at the second stop after the bus turns uphill away from the lake. From here, a sign points the way to the church, 1km along a side road. (Church open daily 8am-noon and 2:30-5pm.)

If you take the spectacular path down from the Mount to the coastal road, or get off the bus before it turns up the Mount and hike 3km, you'll find the ancient town of **Capernaum** (*Kfar Nahum*) about 1km to the east, where Jesus healed Simon's mother-in-law and the Roman Centurion's servant (Luke 4:31-37 and 7:1-10). This is also the birthplace of Peter. Franciscans now guard some of the ruins of the ancient city. Shorts are not permitted, and women must cover shoulders and arms. (Open daily 8:30am-4:15pm. Admission NIS1.) Buses #841, 459, 541, and

963 pass the Capernaum junction about once an hour en route to both Tzfat and Tiberias. During the summer, a boat leaves every morning from Lido Beach to Capernaum; round-trip fare is about NIS10, but call ahead (tel. 72 15 38), as the skipper won't sail unless there are enough people. He also won't let you on the boat if you're not properly dressed.

Two kilometers southwest of Capernaum along the coastal road, in **Tabgha,** stands the **Church of the Primacy,** marking the spot where Jesus made Peter "Shepherd of his People." *Tabgha (Tabha* in Hebrew) is an Arabic distortion of the original Greek name for the site, *heptapegon,* meaning seven springs. According to the account in the Book of Luke, after the resurrection, Peter led the apostles on a fishing expedition 100m offshore from Tabgha. A man on shore called to them to throw their nets over the starboard side and assured them of a catch. When the nets hit the water, more fish swam in than they could possibly carry. Jumping off the boat and swimming to shore, Peter found Jesus cooking fish for 12, and when the others sailed in, Jesus conferred primacy on Peter. The 12 celebrated with a feast. The Church of the Primacy is built around a rock said to be the table of this feast. The building itself dates only to the 1930s. On the seaward side of the church are the steps from which Jesus called out his instructions, and on the shoreline is a series of six double or heart-shaped column bases built by early Christians and called the "thrones of the Apostles" (tel. 72 10 61; open 8am-4pm).

Just west of the Church of the Primacy along the northern coast of the sea, lies the **Church of the Multiplication of the Loaves and Fishes.** A mosaic inside relates how Jesus fed 4000 pilgrims with seven loaves and a few small fish (Matthew 15:29-30). A section of the mosaic has been removed so you can see the original fourth century foundations. (Site open April-Sept. 7:30am-6pm; Oct.-March 8am-5pm. Church open 8:30am-5pm. Modest dress required.) Around the right side of the church past the "private" sign and up the stairs is a small **hospice** (tel. 72 10 61), principally for Christian pilgrims but open to everyone. There is a kitchen and a small food store for guests only.

Karei Desheh Youth Hostel (IYHF) (tel. 72 06 01) is about 1km farther east (make a left where the road ends). The hostel has campsites, swimming areas, and peacocks, and is set in a park with eucalyptus trees and a rocky coast. Rooms are air-conditioned. Bring your own food; there is a kitchen. The small market on the grounds or the hostel food are the only other options. (Dorm beds NIS11, bungalows NIS8. Tent camping NIS6. Nonmembers add NIS2.20. Breakfast NIS6, dinner NIS9.80.) One hundred years ago this estate belonged to the German government. In 1987 the Israeli government agreed to return it, but the turn-over date has not been set; call ahead to see if it's still open.

The birthplace of Mary Magdalene, halfway between Tiberias and the Capernaum junction, was a flourishing metropolis during the period of the Second Temple. Only a tiny, white-domed shrine marks where the city of **Migdal** once stood. To reach the shrine, take bus #55 or 54 from Tiberias.

Shores of Yam Kinneret

Horseback is an excellent, if expensive, way to explore the north coast of the lake. The next bus stop after the one for the Hospice of the Beatitudes (bus #459 or 841) will leave you at the road to Korazim, in front of a riding stable called **Vered HaGalil.** A half-day ride through the Galilean hills down to the sea and then up to the Mount of Beatitudes costs NIS45 per person. If you call and ask, the owner, Yehuda Avni, will let you camp free and use shower and toilet facilities the night before your ride. Bring your sleeping bag. There's also a bunkhouse where bed and American breakfast cost NIS25. The restaurant is fairly expensive but the food is great. The stables offer many different kinds of rides, and previous experience isn't necessary. An hour-long rental is NIS18, while a horse for a day is NIS80. (For reservations, write to Vered HaGalil, Korazim or call 93 57 85 or 93 56 09.)

The low level of the Kinneret in 1985-86 had one serendipitous benefit—the discovery of an **ancient boat** off the beach of Kibbutz Ginnosar. The boat was found buried under a segment of newly-exposed lakebed. The boat's wood frame, which had become as porous as a sponge after ages spent sunk in the mud, was encased in a fiberglass frame and hauled on shore. The boat is in near-pristine condition, and has been dated at 100 B.C.E.-100 C.E. It rests in a glass tank filled with water, where it will undergo nine years of chemical treatments. To reach the boat, take bus #841, 459, or 963 from Tiberias to the new Yigal Allon Center (tel. 72 14 95; open Sun.-Thurs. 8am-6pm, Fri. 8am-5pm, Sat. 9am-6pm; admission NIS1.50, students NIS1).

A modern miracle is commemorated near the spot where the Jordan River flows out of the Sea of Galilee about 8km from Tiberias. Founded in 1910, **Deganya Aleph** is Israel's oldest *kibbutz,* the first Jewish settlement in the Jordan Valley, and the birthplace of Moshe Dayan. On May 19, 1948, a few days after the State of Israel was declared, the Syrians took the nearby town of Tzemah and, armed with tanks, tried to overrun Deganya. The settlers, with only small-caliber rifles and Molotov cocktails, held them off until one tank broke through the perimeter. This was stopped by a Deganya settler with a homemade grenade. The other tanks retreated and never returned. The gutted chassis of the Syrian tank resting at an angle on the lawn of the *kibbutz* attests to Deganya's victory. As is the case with many *kibbutzim,* Deganya has become a wealthy, industrial community. Most of its income is generated from its diamond-tool factory. The *kibbutz* also has two small museums at the Beit Gordon, one devoted to the archeology of the Kinneret area, the other to its natural history, with exhibits of stuffed animals. Deganya's size and uniformity make it very easy to get lost. Take a right after the tennis courts and ambulances and ask directions immediately. Next to Beit Gordon is a helpful SPNI office. (Museums open Sun.-Thurs. 9am-4pm, Fri. 8:30am-2pm, Sat. and holidays 9:30am-noon. Admission NIS4, students NIS3.) Deganya can be reached by bus #24 to Hammat Gader; or bus #23, 26, 27, 28, or 29 headed for Beit She'an and the Jordan River Valley.

Eight kilometers southeast of Deganya about one half-hour. from Tiberias, the hot baths of **Hammat Gader** lie on the Jordanian border. Once the site of a large Roman bath complex, the hot sulphur springs have been mostly diverted to a modern pond with a bathhouse. The Roman ruins are partially reconstructed and impressive, with several large bathing areas and a smaller pool that was reserved for lepers. At the southwest corner of the complex is the hottest spring in the area at 51°C. It was named *Ma'ayan HaGehinom* in Hebrew, meaning "Hell's Pool," and *Ain Makleh,* the "Frying Pool" by the Arabs who controlled the baths from 1922 (when they were given them by the British) until 1967. The modern hot pool is crowded with families on outings. There is also an area with black mud that is reputed to cure various skin ailments. Hammat Gader is also the site of an alligator park, where you can observe hundreds of large, somnolent alligators sunning themselves on the banks of their swimming area or cruising slowly though the murky water. Having imported the first generation from Florida, the preserve now raises the young inside a hothouse at the entrance to the ponds. New additions include two waterslides and trampolines as well as a health club with cosmetic treatments and massages.

The park also contains the **ruins** of a fifth-century synagogue, just west of the Roman baths and past the picnic area. The synagogue is at the site of a modern border lookout station; to the northwest, spanning the Yarmoukh River, is a bridge dating from the Ottoman railroad. Admission to the whole Hammat Gader complex is NIS15, students and children NIS12. Bus #24 leaves from Tiberias four times during the morning beginning at 8:30am, 9am, and 10am; the last bus back is at 2:15pm, 12:15pm on Fridays.

Tzfat (Safed)

Anyone who sees the sunset over Mount Meron from Tzfat will understand Tzfat's attraction for generations of scholars, mystics, artists, and dreamers. Set on hazy Mount Canaan, overlooking the Galilean hills and the Sea of Galilee (Yam

Kinneret), Tzfat is a city of serene beauty. Orthodox Jews believe the Messiah will travel from Mount Meron to Tzfat before going to Jerusalem. Some of them here wear buttons that read "We want the Messiah now!"

Although Jewish settlement in Tzfat dates to the time of the Second Temple, the Jewish presence has not been continuous. Plundered first by the Romans and later by the Crusaders, a thriving Jewish community reemerged only in the Middle Ages, when refugees from the Inquisition began to build the synagogues of today's Spanish Quarter. Other mystical and scholarly sects settled in Tzfat as well, among them that of Rabbi Isaac Lourie Ashkenazi, known to his followers as Ha'Ari, "the Lion." Many of the synagogues of these leaders as well as innumerable stories about their great works survive. The Hassidic Jews who live here today are heirs of the mystical Kabbalists who lived in Tzfat during the sixteenth century.

By the late nineteenth century, the town became predominantly Arab, and in the 1948 War of Independence Tzfat was bitterly contested because of its strategic position at the center of northern Galilee. In recent years, Tzfat's beautiful surroundings, serendipitous alleys, and temperate climate have attracted a community of artists and have made it a popular summer resort among Israelis and foreigners alike.

Practical Information

Government Tourist Information Office (GTIO): 23 Jerusalem St. (tel. 93 06 33), a 3-min. walk to the right as you leave the central bus station. The free map is useful, but it's worth buying the new, detailed map for NIS1.50. Very friendly staff. Open Sun.-Thurs. 9am-6pm, Fri. 9am-noon; in winter Sun.-Thurs. 8:30am-12:45pm and 4-6pm, Fri. 9am-noon.

Banks: Leumi, 33 Jerusalem St., **HaPoalim,** 72 Jerusalem St., and **Discount,** 83 Jerusalem St. All open Sun., Tues., and Thurs., 8:30am-noon and 4-6pm, Mon. and Wed. 8:30am-12:30pm, Fri. 8:30am-noon. **First International,** 40 Jerusalem St. open Sun., Tues., and Thurs. 8:30am-2pm, Mon. and Wed. 8:30am-2pm and 4-7pm, Fri. 8:30am-noon.

Central Post Office: HaPalmah St., next to a radar dish visible from the corner of HaPalmah St. at Aliyah Bet. Open Sun.-Fri. 7:45am-2pm; Sept.-June Sun., Tues., and Thurs. 7:45am-2pm and 4-6pm, Fri. 7:45am-noon. The convenient branch on Jerusalem St., near GTIO, has similar hours.

Telephone Code: 06.

Central Bus Station: HaAtzma'ut Sq. (tel. 93 11 22). Bus #459 travels between Tiberias and Tzfat every 1-2 hr. (1 hr). All buses to Qiryat Shmona from Jerusalem and Tel Aviv stop at Rosh Pinna, where you can transfer for a bus to Tzfat, 10km east. There is a direct bus to Jerusalem daily at 7:30am (#964). Buses #361 and 362 travel to and from Haifa through Akko every 20 min. Last bus Sun.-Thurs. 9pm, Fri. 4:45pm. First bus on Sat. at 3pm. **Baggage storage** open Sun.-Thurs. 7am-3pm, NIS3 per piece per day.

Sherut **Taxis:** Tel. 97 07 07. Near the central bus station. Inter-city rides also available from 19 Jerusalem St. (tel. 97 22 72 or 97 29 87).

First Aid: Magen David Adom, (tel. 93 03 33), Aliyah Bet St., near the central bus station.

Police: Tel. 100 in emergencies, otherwise call 93 04 44 or 97 24 44.

Tzfat is arranged in circular terraces of streets descending from the castle ruins in the center. **Jerusalem Street,** the main street, behind the central bus station, makes a complete circle around **Gan HaMetzuda** (Park of the Citadel). **HaPalmah Street,** a second important street, begins off Jerusalem St. near the central bus station and crosses the main street via an arched stone bridge.

Accommodations and Food

Tzfat's youth hostel is well-equipped and only a short ride from the bus station. The other primary option is to sleep in the inexpensive **spare rooms** and separate flats provided by town residents. Most of the rentals are comfortable, with hot showers, living rooms, and separate kitchens for guests. The best way to find one of these places is to let them find you: If you walk around the central bus station holding your luggage, it shouldn't be long before you are approached. Don't pay until you see the quarters. You may also want to stroll up Jerusalem St. and choose one of the places with a "rooms to let" sign (often in Hebrew only). You can ask at the tourist office for the phone numbers listed for rooms to rent. Official prices are NIS20-25, but bargaining, especially during low season, is acceptable. It is wise to check all accommodations for heating and/or blankets; because of the city's altitude and exposed location, nights in Tzfat can be chilly.

Beit Binyamin (IYHF), near the Amal Trade School in South Tzfat (tel. 93 10 86). A 20-min. walk from the bus station, or take bus #2, 2a, or 6. Large, well-equipped hostel with new kitchen and dining room. Breakfast is mandatory, other meals are served only when a group is staying at the hostel. Call ahead. Members NIS12, nonmembers NIS14.

Shoshana Briefer, 2 large apartments off 16 HaPalmah St. Look for Shoshana at the station. She's a small woman with light complexion and thick gray-black hair. To reach the house, follow Jerusalem St. clockwise and pass under a bridge. Take the stairs up to the bridge and cross over, heading away from Gan HaMetzuda. Turn at the first alley to your right and take the alley that runs diagonally in the same general direction as the road. At the bottom of the alley on the left, the large, green metal door is the entrance to one apartment. The other is the gray door on the right, 2/3 of the way down. (It is easiest, however, to ambush, or be ambushed by, Shoshana at the station.) Rooms somewhat dingy, but livable; use of kitchen included. NIS8-15 per person, depending on room size and number of people per room.

Ascent Institute of Tzfat, Bidbaz St. (tel. 97 14 07 or 97 20 87, at night 97 43 90), the street opposite the GTIO. For Jewish travelers, with nightly classes and programs on Tzfat and Kaballah, placement with families on *shabbat*, 3-day hikes to Golan, and walking tours of Jewish sections of the city. Refrigerator available. Call ahead, especially for *shabbat* and the 3-day hikes. Dorm beds NIS10, breakfast NIS3.

Hadar Hotel, Ridbaz St. (tel. 93 00 68), on an alley off Jerusalem St. just past the park. Beautiful, but slightly more expensive. Singles with bath NIS46, doubles with bath NIS60; July-Aug. singles with bath NIS60, doubles with bath NIS88.

The stretch of Jerusalem St. north of the bridge (to #48) is lined with good, cheap felafel stands and expensive sit-down restaurants. **HaMifgash Restaurant** (tel. 93 05 10), 75 Jerusalem St., just opposite the small observation point and park, serves excellent Middle Eastern food. The grilled meat in pita is filling, though a bit expensive. *Shishlik,* kebab, or hamburger sandwiches cost NIS5-7. (Open Sun.-Fri. 9am-11pm.) The **Steakia HaSelah** (no English sign), a tiny grill 2 doors west of the bridge, has some of the best *shwarma* in the country, served in pita with do-it-yourself salads (NIS3). For a slightly fancier, more relaxed atmosphere, try **HaKikar Restaurant** (tel. 93 09 10), at HaMeginim Sq. HaKikar is clean and displays the work of local artists on the walls. Salads with pita cost NIS4, and vegetarian meals run NIS5-8. (Open Sun.-Thurs. 10am-11pm, Fri. 10am-2pm, Sat. 7-11pm.) On Jerusalem St., near the Artists' Quarter is a new pedestrian avenue with many outdoor cafes. The most popular place in the Old City is **The Ice Cream Happening** on Tarpat St., not far from the Ethiopian Gallery (open until midnight during summer, Fri. until 4pm). To reach the fruit and vegetable **market** in front of the post office, take the stairs up to the bridge and walk south (away from Gan HaMetzuda). The market is held every Monday and Tuesday morning. There is also a new **supermarket** on HaPalmah St., above the bus station.

Sights

Be prepared to lose yourself in a maze of antiquity. As with all older cities of Israel, the streets are designed for pedestrians, and have few markings. Think of Tzfat as divided into three semi-distinct sections: the **Park Area,** at the top of the mountain (ringed by Jerusalem St.); the **Artists' Quarter,** southwest and down the hill; and the **Synagogue Quarter** (Old City), immediately to the north of the Artists' Quarter on the other side of Ma'alot Oleh HaGardom.

The meager ruins of a twelfth-century Crusader fortress that once commanded the main route to Damascus grace **Gan HaMetzuda,** a cool, wooded park and a fine spot for a picnic. At the summit stands a monument commemorating the Jews who died here during the 1948 war. The convenient entrance near 41 Jerusalem

St. is across from the Davidka Monument, which commemorates an effective, make-shift weapon used in the War of Independence merely for the frightening noise it made.

The **Israeli Bible Museum** (tel. 97 34 72), just north of the park up the steep stone stairway, displays the work of Phillip Ratner, an internationally known modern American artist. Sculptures, lithographs, graphics, and paintings vividly depict the great biblical personalities. Pick up a list of works along with some relevant newspaper articles from the front desk for use during your visit. (Open Sun.-Thurs. 10am-6pm, Fri.-Sat. 10am-2pm. Free.) The **Shem VaEver Cave,** one of several sacred caves in the region, is believed to be the place where Noah's son and grandson, Shem and Ever, studied the Torah and were later buried. If the caves are locked, try knocking on the door of the small, domed synagogue nearby, and asking the caretaker to open them. The cave is near the top of the bridge off HaPalmah St. Nearby, at the intersection of Jerusalem St. with Arlosoroff St., a forest of English signs will direct you down the hill to the **General Exhibition** near the Artists' Quarter, which is housed in an old mosque. On the way, detour off Arlosoroff into the quarter itself, and gallery-hop through the alleys just south of the Jerusalem-Arlosoroff intersection. Many of the galleries are run by the artists themselves, so hours vary (most are open 10am-1pm and 4-7pm). Those with large displays fronting the street cater mostly to tourists, while those sequestered away and with inconspicuous signs are often more authentic.

Navigating in the snarled streets of the **Synagogue Quarter** (*Qiryat Batei HaKnesset*), also called the Old City, is a matter of luck; resign yourself to getting lost. The Old City's tiny synagogues are its most interesting features. Because Tzfat lies to the north of Jerusalem, their holy arks are placed on the southern rather than the eastern wall. The two most famous are the **Caro Synagogue** and the **HaAri (Ashkenazi) Synagogue.** To reach the Caro Synagogue, take Ma'alot Oleh HaGardom St. off Jerusalem St., and make a right onto Beit Yosef St. Ask to see the remarkable set of old books and Torah scrolls. It was here that Joseph Caro, chief rabbi of Tzfat and author of the vast *Shulhan Aruh* (an extensive and standard guide for daily life according to Jewish law), studied and taught in the sixteenth century. To reach the HaAri Synagogue, follow Beit Yosef until it becomes Alkabetz St., make a right up a stairway with stained glass Stars of David above, and continue straight under the stone arch. The synagogue will be to your right on Najara St. Rabbi Isaac Lourie, nicknamed the Ari (lion), a great Kabbalist, introduced the *Kabbalat Shabbat,* the preparation for the Sabbath, and his student wrote the famous liturgical hymn *Lecha Dodi.* The four pillars that hold up the podium in the middle of the room symbolize the four elements of the world (air, fire, water, and earth) and the four holy cities (Tzfat, Jerusalem, Tiberias, and Hebron). The small hole in the *bimah* (pulpit), directly opposite the door, is the scar of an Arab shell from May, 1948. Although the synagogue was full at the time, no one was hurt, allegedly because of the protection of the ghost of the Rabbi Lourie. A Sephardic synagogue lies farther down the hill near the cemetery. Just downhill from the Caro Synagogue, off Abuhav St. in the Spanish Quarter, stand the **Abuhav** and **Alsheih Synagogues.** Take a left off Beit Yosef St. onto Alsheih St. and then make a sharp right; both buildings will be to your right. The light blue walls of this section are repainted annually before the holiday of *Lag ba'Omer,* and are believed to ward off evil spirits. The blue color symbolizes *malchut* (God's reign) and the also-common green symbolizes *tsmihat hageulah* (the growth of redemption).

Three adjoining **cemeteries** lie on the western outskirts of the Old City, off HaAri St. Follow the path all the way down past the complex of new stone buildings on the left. The small building where the path turns right down the hill into the cemetery is the HaAri synagogue's men's *mikveh,* or ritual bath (women should not enter). The oldest of the cemeteries contains the graves of the most famous Tzfat Kabbalists, as well as a domed tomb built by the Karaites of Damascus (a medieval group of Jewish heretics) to mark the grave of the biblical prophet Hosea. On the wall inside the tomb, you'll find posted an article about an eighth-generation Tzfat resident named Mordechai Shebabo. In the 1970s he began having recurring dreams in which an old, bearded man begged him to restore the badly neglected graves. Shebabo left his position as a national fencer, and single-handedly undertook the restoration of the graves. Any visible grave on the site is the result of this man's work. Shebabo or one of his sons may ask you for a small donation for the upkeep of the cemetery. Legend has it that hidden under this same hill lie Hannah and her seven sons, whose martyrdom at the hands of the Syrians is recorded in the Book of Maccabees. Supposedly you will know that you are walking over their graves by a sudden feeling of fatigue. Also buried near here are the children of Tzfat who were killed in May 1974 on a trip to Ma'alot, when PLO terrorists took over the school in which the children were sleeping. A large memorial service is held for them each year.

The tiny **Ethiopian Folk Art Center and Gallery,** halfway down the Oleh HaGardom steps, is currently the only shop in Israel that features the beautiful and unusual art of Ethiopian Jews. In a project called Operation Moses, which began in 1975 and continued through the mid-1980s, the Israeli government secretly air-lifted Ethiopian Jews out of Ethiopia and away from the religious persecution and starvation they faced. Today this community is struggling to integrate into a reluctant Israeli society, while striving to maintain their own cultural identity. (Gallery open Sun.-Thurs. 9am-6pm; closes early on Fri.) All the way down Oleh HaGardom, **Beit Hameiri** (tel. 97 13 07) contains a museum and an institute for the study of the history of the Jewish settlement in Tzfat. Look for bright orange signs pointing the way here from anywhere in town. (Open Sun.-Fri. 9am-noon. Admission NIS3.50.)

The stories and legends of Tzfat, modern and ancient, are best told by people who live in and love this area. **Shlomo Bar-Ayal** (tel. 97 45 97 or 93 06 33) gives daily tours of the Old City leaving from the GTIO, in such vivid detail that he seems to have lived in Tzfat for centuries. Several nights per week he leads an evening tour starting from the Rimon Inn (2 hr., NIS8.50, students NIS7.50, groups of 5 or more NIS35; call GTIO for times).

If you are stranded in town on Saturday, try the lovely swimming pool and leisure center (tel. 93 02 17) just off Ha'Atzma'ut Rd., behind the central bus station; walk down from the station, turn left, and the turn-off for the swimming pool will be 100m away on the left. (Open in summer only, beginning July, Sun. and Tues. 9am-3pm, Mon., Wed.-Thurs., and Sat. 9am-5pm, Fri. 9am-2pm. Admission NIS6, children NIS4.) Another pool, in the industrial district of south Tzfat (take bus #6 or 7) is heated and open year-round.

Near Tzfat: Meron

Each year on the holiday of *Lag ba'Omer* (May 23 in 1989), thousands of pilgrims converge on the tiny village of Meron, 4km west of Tzfat, site of the tomb of Rabbi Shimon Bar Yohai, the great second-century Talmudic scholar who composed the *Zohar* (the central work of Jewish mysticism) while hiding in a cave in Peqi'in. According to the Kabbalists, Bar Yohai once vowed to God that the Jews would never forget the importance of the Torah. Mindful of this vow, the Tzfat Hassidim dance and sing their way to his tomb in a joyous procession, accompanied by an ancient Torah scroll from the Bana'a Synagogue in the Spanish Quarter. Contact the tourist information office in Tzfat for further details.

Just west of the town is **Mount Meron** (*Har Meron,* with the accent on the "on") the highest mountain in the Galilee at 1208m. An excellent hiking trail offers views of Tzfat and the surrounding countryside, and on clear days you can see Lebanon and Syria to the north, the Mediterranean to the west, and the Sea of Galilee to the southeast. It is possible to ascend the mountain from the town of Meron, but the more pleasant and convenient way is to take bus #43 from Tzfat to Kibbutz Sasa, northwest of the mountain. Buses depart at 7am, 12:30pm, and 5pm, and return around 8am, 1:45pm, and 6:15pm. Catch the early bus to avoid the midday heat. From the *kibbutz,* where the bus turns around, continue 1km to the turn-off on the left for the Beit Sefer Sadeh (Field School; no English sign, but the road is obvious). At the entrance to the field school, there is a hikers information office in an old bus; if the office is closed, ask at the field school for the free map of the trail. The trail begins 100m from the parking lot on the left side of the road, and is indicated by stone markers and black-and-white-striped blazes. A one-hour walk brings you to the summit, where the trail is marked with red-and-white blazes. Stay on the trail, which skirts the summit, since the very top of the mountain is the site of an army radar installation. Twenty minutes farther along the path, you'll approach a picnic site with an asphalt traffic circle on a road; don't cross the road, but follow the road for 20m to the left to where the trail begins again. A long, easy descent, again marked with the black-and-white blazes, ends on a dirt road just above the village of Meron.

The gorgeous 6km hike through **Wadi Ammud** is popular. The clearly marked path begins southwest of Tzfat near Tsomet Meron on the way to Meron village. You can hike down from Tzfat, past the cemeteries and into the wadi or, more conveniently, take a bus toward Meron and tell the bus driver to let you off at Nahal Ammud. This is a particularly difficult trail to navigate. Hike with someone who knows the paths, and be sure to carry a first-aid kit.

Rosh Pinna

Rosh Pinna is an excellent jumping-point to the Golan and Galilee (½ hr. by frequent buses from Tiberias, Qiryat Shmona, Mt. Meron, and the Golan Heights), though it has no sights. The **Rosh Pinna Youth Hostel** (tel. (06) 93 70 86) is located in an 80-year-old school. The dormitory rooms with vaulted ceilings were once the kindergartens. (Members NIS12, nonmembers NIS14. Family rooms NIS15 per person. Breakfast included.) When you get off the bus, follow the signs and climb or hitch up the hill on the left.

Qiryat Shmona

By virtue of its location in the Upper Galilee near the Lebanese border, Qiryat Shmona, until Israel's invasion of Lebanon, was the victim of random acts of PLO terrorism. Many of its buildings bear the scars of these attacks, with bullet-holes or chunks torn from their facades. But violence is not new to the area. Tel Hai, 3km from Qiryat Shmona, was the site of the first armed conflict between Jewish settlers and Arabs in what is now the State of Israel. In 1920, a large band of Arabs gathered around the settlements of Tel Hai, nearby Kfar Giladi, and Metulla to the north (then part of French-administered Syria and Lebanon), and accused Jewish settlers of harboring French soldiers whom the Arabs charged with encroaching on their lands. In an attempt to prove his neutrality, Yosef Trumpeldor, the leader of Tel Hai, allowed four Arabs inside the settlement to search for the French agents. Once inside the complex, the Arabs attacked, killing Trumpeldor and seven others. The six men and two women were buried in Kfar Giladi, where the lion in the Cemetery of the Shomrim ("Guardians") now stands. Trumpeldor's last words, "No matter, it's good to die for our country," have passed into legend. In honor of the eight heroes, the town built on the ruins was dubbed Qiryat Shmona ("town of the eight").

Today, free of strife, Qiryat Shmona has become the administrative and transportation center of the Upper Galilee. It is a quiet, pleasant town, with few noteworthy sites. Buses for the Upper Galilee, the Golan, and Tzfat leave from the **central bus station** (tel. 94 07 40 or 94 07 41), on Tel Hai St. The only place to stay is the four-star North Hotel (tel. 94 47 05, singles NIS60), so head to the cheaper **Tel Hai** or **Rosh Pinna youth hostels.** A cluster of felafel and *shwarma* stands surrounds the intersection of Tel Hai and Tschernikovsky St. On Thursday mornings until noon, an open air *shuk* is located on Tel Hai, just north of the bus station. There's a **post office** south of the bus station on Tel Hai St. that has **international phone call** and **Poste Restante** services. (Open Sun.-Thurs. 7:45am-2pm, Fri. 7:45am-1pm; Sept.-

June Sun. and Wed.-Thurs. 7:45am-12:30pm and 3:30-6pm, Mon.-Tues. 7:45am-2pm, Fri 7:45am-1pm. For **police,** call 94 34 44; **First Aid (Magen David Adom),** dial 94 43 34. The **telephone code** for Qiryat Shmona and the surrounding region is 06.

Near Qiryat Shmona

Tel Hai

Three kilometers to the west, on the outskirts of Qiryat Shmona, Tel Hai sits on a promontory with a breathtaking view of the valley below. First established in 1918 as a military outpost after the withdrawal of British forces from the Upper Galilee, the town has become a symbol of Israel's early pioneer movement and the struggle for the Hula valley region, earlier known as "the Finger of Galilee." A monument to Yosef Trumpeldor, the famous one-armed founder of the Zion Mule Corps, stands on the town's outskirts. The original watchtower and stockade settlement, destroyed by Arabs in 1920, has been reconstructed as a beautiful, little **museum.** Displayed on the neatly kept courtyard of the settlement are the farming tools used by the early settlers. (Open Sun.-Thurs. 8am-1pm and 2-5pm; Sept. 2-May 31 Sun.-Thurs. 8am-4pm, Fri. 8am-1pm, Sat. 9am-2:30pm. Admission NIS3, students NIS2.) An excellent slide show in English will be screened on request for a small group, and an informative brochure is available in English for NIS1.50. Tel Hai is also the home of Israel's northernmost **youth hostel** (tel. 400 43). Just off the main Metulla-Qiryat Shmona road, the hostel is served by bus #20 or 22 from both towns—ask the driver to take you to the youth hostel instead of the archeological site. (Reception open daily 5-7pm. Singles NIS12, doubles NIS35. Breakfast NIS4. Nonmembers same price.)

Just up the road from the hostel is the **military cemetery** containing the graves of the eight heroes of Tel Hai, with a statue of a roaring lion facing the mountains to the east. The cemetery is surrounded by a line of tall pine trees, and inside, colorful flowers and plants are thick around the well-tended graves. Fifty meters up the road, inside the gates of Kibbutz Kfar Giladi, is **Beit HaShomer** ("House of the Guardian"), the IDF (Israeli Defense Force) museum documenting the history of the early settler defense organizations in the Upper Galilee and the exploits of the Jewish regiments in the British Army during World War I. (Open Sun.-Thurs. 8am-noon and 2-4pm, Fri.-Sat. 8:30am-noon. Admission NIS.50.) The *kibbutz* (tel. 414 14) also runs a beautiful but expensive guest house.

Nature Reserves

In a place with a history rich in miracles, the transformation of the Hula Valley, accomplished by Israel's first Jewish pioneers in the 1920s, is still a remarkable achievement. Just south of Qiryat Shmona, the **Hula Nature Reserve** (tel. 93 70 69) thrives where just a few decades ago a vast, stagnant, and dirty swamp festered. The serene 775-acre reserve encompasses dense cypress groves and open fields where pelicans and herons wade in clear pools and water buffalo struggle in vain to stay cool. More exotic wildlife, such as wild boars and mongooses, dwell within the underbrush, but it's rare to see them during the day. The entrance booth rents binoculars for NIS4, which are helpful for those interested in identifying the innumerable birds that wing their way over the papyrus thickets, swamps, and reeds. Try to arrive early: The park becomes progressively less serene as vacationing families with loudly inquisitive children roll in. Bus #841 or 511, leaving hourly from Qiryat Shmona, will take you to a junction 2½km from the entrance to the reserve, and from there you can walk or hitch. (Open Sun.-Thurs. 8am-4pm, Fri. 8am-3pm. Admission NIS3, children NIS1.50. English brochure NIS1. Combination ticket to Hula, Banyas, Gamla, Dan, and 'Ayun Reserves NIS7.20.) Take a hat and water because the observation area has little shade. There's a kiosk and shaded picnic-ground for snacks. A new **visitors center** offers exhibits on flora and fauna, and shows a 15-minute film. (Open Sat.-Thurs. 8am-3pm, Fri. 8am-2pm. Admission NIS2.60.

Huge oak trees, some nearly 2000 years old, can be found in the **Horshat Tal Nature Reserve.** According to a Muslim legend, the trees, which survive nowhere else in Israel, have been preserved due to the 10 messengers of Muhammad who once rested here. Finding not a single tree for shade, nor a hitching post for their camels, they pounded sticks into the earth to fasten their mounts. Overnight the sticks sprouted, and the holy men found themselves in a beautiful forest. The trees now tower over a well-kept, grassy park, crammed on Saturdays with picnicking Israeli families. Especially enticing is the large **swimming pool**—actually the River Dan ingeniously diverted. Its flowing water is always startlingly cold. Ask the bus driver to stop, though he probably will anyway. (Admission NIS4, children NIS1.50.) Buses #25, 26, and 36 from Qiryat Shmona all travel the 9km east through Horshat Tal. Buses run every hour or so, making this an excellent stop for a picnic. About 100m farther along the road is the **Horshat Tal Camping Ground** (tel. 94 04 00), on the banks of the Dan River. The campground is a good jumping-off point for the rest of the Galilee, despite an 11pm curfew; campers must clear out by 1pm. (Tent sites: NIS8, child NIS5; 3-, 4-, and 5-bed bungalows NIS43, NIS55, and NIS65, respectively. Space in a refrigerator for your food NIS4 per night.)

A kilometer down the road, **Kibbutz Sha'ar Yeshuv** hosts the SPNI's field school **Beit Sefer Sadeh Hermon** (tel. 410 91). Accommodations are rarely available here, but you can listen in on a tour group's lectures. Bus #25 from Qiryat Shmona will take you right to the *kibbutz*. The next *kibbutz* to the northeast, **Kibbutz Dan,** is in the midst of the Hula Valley's lushest **nature reserve.** The waters come from the Fountain of Dan at the foot of the large Tel Dan, still under excavation. The many small springs nourish a dense, shady growth of trees and bushes, which grow to record heights. The paths in this small (under 100 acres) but luxuriant reserve offer many opportunities to cool hot, tired feet in the trickling streams. The excavations have revealed the ruins of the ancient Canaanite city of Lahish, which became the capital city of the tribe of Dan, one of the 12 tribes of Israel. A pre-1948 Arab flour mill has also been restored by the park authorities. To reach the reserve take bus #27 or 36 from Qiryat Shmona to Kibbutz Dan, continue up the main road, and turn left at the sign to the reserve. A 3km walk will bring you to the entrance. (Open daily 8am-5pm; in winter daily 8am-4pm. Admission NIS3. The guidebook to the reserve available at the ticket window is worth the NIS.50.) Unfortunately there is no swimming here. The **Beit Ussishkin Museum** of the valley flora and fauna, in the *kibbutz* of the same name, memorializes the former Jewish National Fund director. The *kibbutz* also features a small aviary up the road from the museum. A gate behind the museum leads to the road for the nature reserve; to reach the museum from the reserve you have to go out to the main road and head 1km west to the *kibbutz* entrance. (Museum open Sun.-Thurs. 9am-noon and 1-3pm, Fri. 9am-noon, Sat. 10am-3pm. Admission NIS1, students NIS.80.) Nearby is the spring of Banyas (see Golan Heights below for details).

Metulla

With its well-kept streets and homes, Metulla (9km north of Qiryat Shmona) is a pleasant haven for those in need of a retreat from the frenetic pace and pressures of Israeli cities. In defiance of its location, Israel's largest settlement on the Lebanese border stubbornly maintains its sleepy, small-town mood. Only the rumble of transport trucks, the tufts of barbed wire around the town's perimeter, and the brightly painted bomb shelters serve as reminders of its precarious border location. Bus #20 runs roughly every hour from Qiryat Shmona to Metulla.

Metulla's main attraction is the **Gader HaTovah** (The Good Fence), just west of town, an opening in the border barrier between Lebanon and Israel where Lebanese Christians and Druze are allowed to pass through to obtain free medical services, to visit relatives, and to work in Israel. Israel began passing aid and supplies across the border to Lebanese Christians in 1971, and in 1976 the Good Fence was officially opened. The checkpoint remained open during the war in Lebanon. From the observation point to the right of the snack bars you can see several Lebanese Christian villages, and on the farthest hill to the right (the northwest), the Crusader fortress of Beaufort, which was fortified by the PLO and used as a base for shelling the Israeli border settlements.

The best deal for accommodations in Metulla is the **Hotel Manara** (tel. 94 23 61) at the second bus stop in the town. It's actually a boarding house run by a gracious older couple who are able to speak with you in almost any language but English. (Clean singles NIS15-20.) Just next door is the **Yafeh Pension** (tel. 94 06 17), which has a strange rock garden out front but no English sign (prices vary, around NIS20 for a single, though bargaining may help). Up the road on the right, marked by a wooden sign to the sports center, is a public **swimming pool** (open daily 10am-5pm; admission NIS6). The airy restaurant across from the HaMavri Hotel, marked with a prominent English sign reading "Restaurant," serves good food at surprisingly low prices. If you continue straight on the main road instead of turning left to the Good Fence, you'll come to the small **Ay'un Nature Reserve,** with a picnic area. Through the gate and down the stone steps is a path to the one of the reserve's waterfalls. To reach the Ay'un Stream, continue walking south past the brown sign in the picnic area through the apple groves; the path will lead you right to the river-bed. Unfortunately, in the summer the falls and river run completely dry except for a few stagnant pools. (Reserve open Sat.-Thurs. 8am-4pm, Fri. 8am-3pm. Admission NIS3.)

Just south of Metulla, set back from the road, the cool mountain air is pierced by the mist from the **Tanur Waterfall.** With the 18m drop, the density of mist suggests the image of billowing smoke: *tanur* means "oven." Unfortunately, the fall slows to a trickle after June, but the deep pools at its foot still swarm with darting fish. The Ay'un Stream, fed by the pools, later joins the Jordan on its way south. The water isn't hot, so if you are, jump in. Local bus #20 from Qiryat Shmona will drop you at the turn-off if you ask; from there it's a three-minute walk to the park.

Kfar Blum

This *kibbutz* southeast of Qiryat Shmona has two wonderful attractions: classical music and kayaking. The **Upper Galilee Chamber Music Days** are a week-long series of concerts that feature Israel's famous instrumentalists and vocalists with young, unknown performers. Tickets are fairly expensive (NIS17-22 per concert), and they sell quickly starting in April, but the rehearsals during the day are free. Far from the concert hall, a thrilling 6km kayaking trip costs NIS15 per hour on the water. In summer 1988, there was no shuttle service for returning the kayaks. Call for reservations and information (tel. 94 87 55).

Golan Heights

Armies of many civilizations have struggled over the strategic peaks above the fertile Jordan Valley without regard for their natural beauty. The tradition of military conflict dates back to the Romans, who fought relentlessly to take the town of Gamla, eventually killing all but two of its citizens. In more recent times the Golan Heights passed from Syrian to Israeli control after a two-day campaign during the 1967 war. As a result, the Hula Valley agricultural settlements were relieved from the intermittent shots and shells from the guns of the Syrian troops based above them. In 1973, the Syrians pushed Israeli forces back almost to the pre-1967 borders, only to see Israel reconquer this territory and more the following week. As part of the 1974 disengagement accord worked out in Henry Kissinger's "shuttle diplomacy," Israel returned both this newly-conquered territory and part of the land captured in 1967. In 1981, the Knesset voted to legally annex the rest of the Golan, arousing a storm of international protest as well as unrest among the Golan's sizeable Druze population, who were required to carry passes indicating their Israeli citizenship. For the most part, the annexation has been merely symbolic, but the controversy—both political and military—still flares. Syria claims that the land was seized by an illegal act of aggression, while Israel, having taken the territory after Syrian attack in 1967, counters that Syria's possession of the Heights posed intolerable threats to northern Israeli settlements, pointing to the pre-1967 attacks. From the eastern escarpment you can now look down on Syrian Quneitra in a zone administered by the United Nations; from the western cliffs you can see the bunkers and trenches from which the Syrian armies overlooked large Israeli communities; and from the southern slopes down to the Yarmoukh River you can see the peaceful hills of Jordan.

It is possible to tour most of the Golan by **bus,** but infrequent service along sparsely-traveled roads makes careful planning a necessity. In general, buses to sites near to and east of the Kinneret leave from the central bus station in Tiberias, passing Kibbutz **Sha'ar HaGolan** ("Gateway to the Golan"). The Upper Galilee, Hula Valley, and northern Golan are served by buses from Qiryat Shmona and occasionally from Tzfat as well. The bus from Tzfat crosses the **B'not Ya'akov Bridge** over the Jordan River some 10km from Qazrin. According to legend, this is where Jacob passed with his family when his daughters predicted that they would sell their brother into slavery in Egypt. The name B'not Ya'akov (daughters of Jacob) actually comes from a Crusader order of nuns by the same name. From the bunkers and trenches at Mitzpeh Gadot, Syrian armies once looked down on the strategic bridge, 1km to the west. At the point where the Jordan Valley opens up into the Hula Plain, you will see three-girdered structures, which are tank stoppers repainted by the Israelis after 1973 to complement the large memorial to fallen Israeli soldiers.

Since relatively few cars traverse the Golan, **hitchhiking** requires extreme patience and preparedness. If you do set out on your own, be sure to take a good map, a *kal-kar* (water bottle) and at least a day's worth of food, since eateries are few and far between. *Stay on the paved roads away from leftover Syrian land mines hidden in barren fields.* Any fenced-off area should be avoided whether or not there are warning signs. Mine-sweeping is an arduous seasonal procedure, and many areas are still thickly strewn with the explosives.

Organized **tours** of the area are faster, more convenient, and sometimes less expensive in the long run. However, they can be rushed and usually preclude hiking and swimming. Egged offers full-day tours of the region from Tiberias on Tuesdays, Thursdays, and Saturdays, and manages to provide an excellent overview of the Upper Galilee and Golan Heights region (NIS30, 10% discount with ISIC). There is also a day tour from Tel Aviv (Thurs. and Sat., NIS58), and possible departures from Haifa as well. In addition, Oded Shoshan in Tiberias (tel. 218 12) manages several minibuses and taxis and is very knowledgeable about the Golan. For NIS22 he will take you on a personal tour of the area, with more humor and personality than the Egged guides. The other drivers in his fleet are not as informative as Oded, however, so try to finagle your way into his taxi. The best tours are the two- to four-day camping trips organized by the Society for the Protection of Nature in Israel. Although they are expensive, the trips visit otherwise-inaccessible spots and often include special treats like inner-tubing on the Jordan River. For more information ask for the pamphlet entitled "Off the Beaten Track" at any GTIO.

The only other option is to rent a **car.** While you need a carful of fellow-travelers to make it economical, this is an excellent way to tour the area. You can cover the Golan and Upper Galilee in a day by starting early, although this doesn't leave much time to hike into Gamla or swim in the pools and falls. Unless you find a special package, renting a car may run about NIS60 per day or more (for unlimited mileage). Avis, Budget, and Hertz have branches in most cities. Eldan, an Israeli car rental company, is somewhat cheaper.

Military maneuvers in the Golan may restrict your movement. Roadblocks are usually lifted in a matter of minutes, so if you come upon one, ask how long it will last. In areas near the border, pay strict attention to the requests of soldiers.

Banyas

The Jordan River is the natural boundary of the Holy Land; its main source is the Dan River (the name "Jordan" comes from the Hebrew *yored dan,* "descending from the Dan"). Another important source of the Jordan is the spring of the Banyas, a gushing rock wall at the site of an ancient Greek sanctuary dedicated to Pan, the god of nature and shepherds. Because classical Arabic has no *p* sound, the Arabic version of "Pan's Place" is *banyas.* The prophet Elijah, called *el-Khadar* ("the green one") by Muslims, and venerated as a saint by Christians, also had a shrine by the Banyas. This church was converted into a mosque, which still exists. It was here that Jesus chose his first disciple. The same spot is also sacred to the Alauwy, an Islamic sect whose members live on the banks of the nearby Hatzbani River. Only 1km from the old Syrian border, the area was used as a staging ground for attacks into the Hula Valley until 1967. If you can survive the swelling crowds, try the pita made by local Arab women who bake it over the traditional domed hearth and sell enormous sheets of it for NIS.50, or with *lebenah* (a sour white cheese) for NIS1.

The Banyas is in the Golan Heights, but lies only a few minutes down the road from Dan and Horshat Tal in the Upper Galilee. Although the Banyas is the most popular site in the Upper Galilee-Golan area, the public transportation there is woefully inadequate. Bus #55 travels from Qiryat Shmona through the Golan by way of the Banyas twice per day (1:10pm and 4:15pm), but the last bus back to Qiryat Shmona is at noon. If you want to spend the afternoon at the park, you can try to hitch or walk 5km west to Kibbutz Dan; the last bus (#25, 26, or 36) leaves at 7:35pm. (Park open from 8am-6pm. Admission NIS3. Combination ticket to Banyas, Gamla, Dan, 'Ayun, and Hula Valley Reserves NIS7.20.)

More beautiful than the park is the Banyas waterfall (*mapal banyas*). Just across the stream running through the park is a wooden sign marking the beginning of a path to the waterfall. All subsequent signs are in Hebrew only, but there is only one fork (just past the pita bakery) where it is possible to go wrong; the right branch is the correct one. Across from the pita bakery is a functioning water-driven flour mill. Farther along the path is a clearing that leads to a swimming pool fed by the icy waters of the spring; it was originally constructed for the Syrian officers whose club was housed in what is now a restaurant at the entrance to the park. Just past the pool you emerge into sunlight at the base of a ridge, at the intersection of three paths; the middle and right-hand paths lead to the waterfall, on opposite sides of the stream. Although there are no signs to guide you, barbed-wire fences will keep you on the path. Here, in the largest Israeli-controlled falls in the region, the Banyas crashes over a ledge, forming an icy pool, which is excellent for swimming. Young daredevils leap the 15m from the ledge into the foaming pool below. The falls are surrounded by dense trees, which create a green refuge from the brown hills just above. A nearby *kibbutz* runs a snack bar above the falls. From there the road runs 1km out to the main road, emerging 1km west of the entrance to the park.

On a knobby hill visible through the trees, **Nimrod's Castle** (*Kalat Nimrod*), stands 1½km northeast of the Banyas. According to the biblical table of the descendents of Noah, Nimrod was "the first on earth to be a mighty man" (Genesis 10:8). Legend holds that, as well as building the Tower of Babel, he erected this huge fortress high enough to shoot his arrows up to God. A plaque above one of the many gates reads in Arabic: "God gave him the power to build this castle with his own strength." The strength of his slaves must have been phenomenal as well, judging from the size of the stones they hauled up the steep cliffs. Historians, however, say the fortress was built by the Crusaders during the beginning of the twelfth century. The view from the top of the fortress is unrivaled anywhere in the Upper Galilee or Golan. You can see Mount Hermon to the north and the Hula Valley to the southeast. Small, predominantly Druze villages sleep below the fortress. You can see the tiny shepherds' shacks perched on the mountainside waiting for their Druze owners to return during the three-month grazing season. Keep an eye out for the many oppossums hiding among the fallen stones. The approach to the castle, from which there is a clear view into the tiny Druze village of Ein Qinya, lies just off bus route #55 between Qiryat Shmona and Qazrin; tell the driver you want to climb up to the castle. The castle is also accessible by a footpath from the Banyas, beginning just above the springs. The walk takes about one and a half hours each way and has no shade, so bring a hat and plenty of water.

Qazrin

The young town of Qazrin is the administrative and municipal center of the Golan and an ideal base from which to explore the area. Qazrin enjoys a high standard of living for a young settlement; the town is attractive, if almost numbingly homogeneous with its rows and rows of nearly identical apartment buildings. If you ask, the bus will let you off in front of the **Beit Sefer Sadeh Golan** (Golan Field School, tel. 613 52), an invaluable source of information on the area. They are also very generous about giving lifts in their tour buses when there's room. Their accommodations are often full, but they run an excellent **campground** (tel. 612 34), 500m east along the road in front of the school. Registration is supposed to be open 6:30-11am and 6-9pm, but if no one's there, dump your stuff and ask for Charley, the manager, in the field school. Tent sites NIS7, subject to seasonal variations.

The Golan Archeological Museum and other facilities lie at the north end of town, at the opposite end of Daliyat St. from the field school. Despite its minuteness, the museum is one of the most informative of its kind in the country, with thorough explanations in Hebrew and English accompanying most exhibits. The Golan excavations, largely consisting of engraved artifacts of ancient synagogues and houses, testify to agricultural communities dating back to the New Stone Age. As you look over this pile of rubble, imagine the rumble of Roman chariot wheels and the march of Crusader armies. (Open Sun.-Fri. 9am-2pm, Sat. 10am-2pm. Admission NIS2, students NIS1.) Many of the museum's artifacts come from a site south of the city which displays a large synagogue and other public buildings from the Talmudic era. Ask at the museum for directions to the ruins of the original Qazrin. Next door to the museum there are a **public pool** (open Sun.-Fri. 9am-5pm, Sat. 8am-4pm; admission NIS5), a **supermarket,** and the town's few restaurants; **Orḥa** is pleasant and inexpensive.

Bus #55 makes two trips per day from Qiryat Shmona, approaching Qazrin from the north and going past the towns at the base of Mount Hermon. Alternatively, bus #841 leaves Qiryat Shmona for Rosh Pinna, where you can catch bus #55 or 56 and approach Qazrin from the opposite direction.

A few kilometers north of Qazrin, the road ends in a T heading west to the B'not Ya'akov Bridge or east toward Quneitra. To reach the **Gilabon** and **Dvorah waterfalls** in the **Gilabon Nature Reserve,** head east 1km, then turn left just before the military base. The approach to the reserve begins about 2km down this road. The reserve contains a well-marked, circular path leading to both waterfalls. The pool at the base of the Gilabon, which is the first along the path, is deep and cool. If you swim across the short distance to the fall, you can climb up the slippery rocks and perch behind the shimmering wall of water. To hike the entire trail takes four to five hours, but if you want a shorter route you can hike down to the Gilabon and back without completing the full circle (2-3 hr.).

Breḥat HaMeshushim

A few kilometers southeast of Qazrin, not served by public transportation, is the **Ya'ar Yehudiyya Nature Reserve** and the source of the Zavitan River. From just off the road, you can hike down the river through some of Israel's most spectacular greenery. To reach the hiking path head about 2km southeast along the main highway from Qazrin. Keep your eyes peeled for a small, weather-beaten, orange sign in Hebrew on the right. This sign marks the beginning of the trail. Starting here, you can follow the stream for about two hours through rocky pools, jumping with fish and freshwater crabs during the summer. The trail is clearly marked with red-and-white striped blazes. Before the stream joins the Meshushim stream to the west, the path leads up the steep side of the ravine, across the plateau, and down to Brehat HaMeshushim (Hexagon Ponds). These received their name from the formation of nearly hexagonal columns of rocks at the water's edge. Although the water isn't perfectly clear, it's deliciously refreshing after a hot hike. To leave this area, walk up to the parking area and follow the 5km access road to the main highway, where you can hitch the 17km north to Qazrin. The ponds can also be reached by climbing upriver from the Bet Tzayda Valley (ask for *Tzomet Bet Tzayda*) along the Kinneret or by walking down the path from the deserted village of Jaraba, about 13km south of B'not Ya'akov Bridge off the left side of the road. In addition to many animals, birds, and much flora, you'll see tracks that cross the road or river at right angles, so that tanks can quickly cover these grounds if necessary. The river basin is occasionally closed to through traffic due to military maneuvers in the area. More often, temporary roadblocks are set up while mines go off a few kilometers ahead. Though you'll probably never see the maneuvers, their sounds echo through the hills.

Gamla

For years all that was known about the lost city of Gamla was its remarkable story, as told by the first-century historian Josephus: Somewhere in the Golan existed the remains of an ancient town whose defenders heroically resisted the Roman army during the Great Rebellion, then chose martyrdom (*The Jewish War* Book IV, ch. 1). With the occupation of the Golan Heights in the Six Day War, archeologists seized the opportunity to scour the area for a spot corresponding to the ancient descriptions of the city. Eventually, archeologist Shmaryahu Gutman found the perfect setting at a site 15km southeast of modern Qazrin. On the high escarpments encircling a lonely ridge crowned by the ruins of Gamla stood a battlefield missing only the Roman legions to complete the picture. As further proof, the outline of the hill bore a remarkable likeness to the animal from which Gamla derives its name: The ruins resemble the hump of a camel whose haunches form steep slopes descending into the ravines of two rivers en route to the Kinneret. The only access to its walls is via a narrow strip of land (the camel's tail) connecting it with the higher, surrounding ridges.

At this spectacular site some 2000 years ago, the Romans laid siege to the religious city of Gamla, which was packed with 9000 Jews seeking refuge. After a siege lasting many months, the Romans on the nearby hills led an attack down the corridor of land leading to the city. When the legion managed to pierce Gamla's walls, hordes of Jews were found fleeing up the sides of the hill's ridge. The Romans followed, and on the steep trails beyond the confines of the town, the Jews suddenly turned and massacred the legionnaires. Weeks later, a second attack proved too much to withstand. Rather than suffer slavery at Roman hands, these Jews, like those at Masada, chose death, hurling themselves over the steep rock face of the ridge. Only two women survived. Today Gamla is a serene spot where you may spot a fox, a gazelle, or a hyrax (a relative of the elephant). Among the dry hills and ravines around the ruins, vultures soar during the day.

Getting to Gamla is tricky without a car. If you can catch a ride with a group from the field school you can also benefit from the guide's lecture. Otherwise, hitchhike from Qazrin and walk 1km to the ridge overlooking the ruins. The descent to the ruins along the Roman route takes about 15 minutes, but give yourself time to scramble about the town. The archeologists' camp is at the entrance to the ruins; if they're not too busy, ask someone to show you around the site. If you continue on the path past the ruins, you will reach a lookout point over **Mapal Gamla,** Israel's highest waterfall. The falls are more impressive than the ruins. The path remains above the fall and returns you to the ruins (3 hr.).

Druze Villages: Mas'ada and Majdal Shams

The Druze of the Golan are separated from their Syrian brothers and sisters only by the looming presence of Mount Hermon. By ties of loyalty and affection, these Druze, unlike those on Mount Carmel, bind themselves to Israel's enemy. In 1982, they tore up their Israeli citizenship documents in a feeble rebellion backed by PLO-supplied weapons. Although the Israeli army quickly quashed the revolt, the Druze remain fiercely independent in spirit. The Druze villages of Mas'ada and Majdal Shams are far less accustomed to tourists than those in Carmel, and the atmosphere is more traditional. Women are swathed in black while men wear the traditional black *shirvelas* (low-hanging baggy pants), which date from Ottoman times. Since the Koran describes Muhammad's reemergence in the world as coming through the "bowels of a man," the devout Turkish Muslims wanted to make certain the reborn prophet had enough room in case he arrived unexpectedly. In their odd, ramshackle dwellings—often piles of stone adorned with a splash of green paint and an ornate lattice-work balcony—the Druze continue to cultivate their lands and to practice the secret rituals of their religion, avoiding contact with the outside as much as possible. (For more on Druze history and religion, consult Druze Villages: Isfiya and Daliyat al-Karmel.)

Mas'ada is located at the foot of Mount Hermon, at the intersection of the roads leading south to Qazrin and west to Qiryat Shmona. Mas'ada's farmers cultivate the valley and terrace the low-lying ridges around the mountain. The numerous Israeli flags and pro-Israel murals are the government's rebuke to the town's demonstrators. Down the road 2km is the famous lake, **Birkat Ram.** The perfectly round body of water is something of a geological peculiarity, formed not, as it appears, in a volcano-crater, but by underground water-bearing strata. You'll know you've reached it when you see the parking lot of the two-story Birkat Ram Restaurant. The restaurant is crowded and completely surrounded by fences separating it from the lake. The only decent view is from the porch, and the Druze owners are polite although not overly enthusiastic about gazers. Don't believe the restaurant owner's endorsement of the "beach" below the restaurant, as there is only a stony, muddy shoreline. You can rent a paddleboat for NIS6 per hour, or a sailboard for NIS10 for a half hour, but either way you still have to pay NIS.50 just to walk down to the dock. If you set out to explore the surrounding fields, remember they are owned by Druze citrus farmers who live in nearby villages. Out of the parking lot and to the right, you'll see a picture-postcard view of an immaculate Druze mosque beneath seasonally snowy Mount Hermon.

From Mas'ada to **Majdal Shams** ("tower of the rising sun" in Arabic), the largest town in the Golan (pop. 8000), the road runs 5km along a scenic valley. Two kilometers past Majdal Shams is **Moshav Neveh Ativ,** founded after the mountain was captured from the Syrians in the Six Day War. The *moshav* has been developed into a resort village catering to the ski slopes on the south face of **Mount Hermon** 10km away; call the ski office at 93 11 03. In summer, small two-person bungalows can be rented for NIS36 per night, and lodges for 10-12 people for NIS80 per night. The Alimi family of the *moshav* runs the guest houses from house #19 (tel. 98 13 33). Visitors can hike, swim, or play tennis in the cool mountain air. Bus #55, leaving Qiryat Shmona twice per day, travels to the villages. The last bus from the Druze villages and Neveh Ativ back to Qiryat Shmona runs at noon, and the last to Qazrin at 4pm. Otherwise, it's possible to take a *sherut* taxi from Mas'ada to Qiryat Shmona in the late afternoon. The road from Mas'ada to Qiryat Shmona is particularly beautiful, running west along a deep gorge, and past the hilltop village of Ein Qinya and the silhouette of Nimrod's Castle.

Continuing toward Syria, still higher levels of the Golan can be reached. About 5km before the border are two *kibbutzim,* **Merom Golan** and **Ein Zivan.** Merom Golan ("Golan Heights") was the first Jewish settlement in the Golan, founded a few months after the 1967 war. Nearby, Mount Bental is visible; the peak closer to Ein Zivan, with the radio antennae, is Mount Avital. From the observation point here you can look down into the destroyed city of Quneitra. In 1967, Israel captured the town in fierce fighting, and then returned it to Syria in the 1974 disengagement agreement. Once a city of 30,000 and headquarters of the Syrian Army, Quneitra is now a ghost town in a buffer zone on a tense border. Only an occasional U.N. vehicle disturbs its tense silence.

Negev and South Coast

First-time visitors to Israel might imagine the desert to be just endless, scorching plains of sand. But the Negev's rugged mountainous terrain is dotted with ruins and Bedouin camps, and even gets cool at night. You will be astounded by the fertile, green fields of a *moshav* or *kibbutz* that has somehow been cultivated in the midst of this arid expanse. David Ben-Gurion, "father of the Negev," was the first to promote this region's development.

The main obstacle to Israel's ambitious plan of settling and civilizing the desert, which makes up over half this country, is the lack of water. Water from Lake Tiberias is piped in to irrigate some of the artificial oases, yet most of the Negev remains desolate and wild. But the success that Israel has had in "making the desert bloom" has come to symbolize the country's triumph as a whole.

The **Negev Mountains,** in the southwestern part of the desert bordering on the Sinai, offer the most dramatic scenery, but are almost completely uninhabited. The desert's most striking features are its three enormous (and one tiny) **craters,** formed by erosion over thousands of years. The best and cheapest way to see most of the Negev's natural sights is to join a **Society for the Protection of Nature in Israel** tour (see Useful Organizations in the Israel Introduction). Alternatively, you can travel along the bus routes from Be'ersheva through Mitzpe Ramon. At the western edge of the Negev is Israel's south coast, which offers several historical sites, and five good beaches. To the south of Ashqelon lie the city of **Gaza** and the **Gaza Strip,** a small stretch of coastline that has been under Israeli military administration since 1967. In 1948, the land had been captured by the advancing Egyptian army, but unlike the Sinai, Gaza is not a part of Egypt proper. The Camp David Accords did not return Gaza to Egypt; rather, they vaguely promised negotiated autonomy. Since December, 1987, the hundreds of thousands of Palestinian refugees have been particpating in the *intifidah.* Visiting here would be a bad idea (if foolhardy enough, be sure to inform your embassy of your plans).

Summer visitors to the south coast should be aware that the regions of the Dead Sea and Gaza are among the most humid parts of Israel, a stark contrast to the arid climate just a few miles inland. When in the desert or in the heat of the south coast, drink at least a gallon of liquid daily, wear a hat, get an early start, and try to avoid physical exertion between noon and 3pm (see Health in the General Introduction). Wintertime visitors should bring their warm clothes in preparation for harsh winds and rains.

Partly because of the climate, but mostly because of the political tensions near the Gaza Strip and the scarcity of cars in some areas, hitchhiking is strongly *discouraged;* incidents in recent years have made "tremping" not worth the risk for either men or women. Sleeping on the beach, except very close to the cities of Ashqelon and Ashdod, is definitely out; military patrols comb the beach at night and, especially in the south, often rake the full length of the beach and later check the sand for footprints to prevent terrorist incursions.

Buses to the Negev, particularly to Be'ersheva, Ashqelon, and Eilat, leave frequently from Tel Aviv and Jerusalem. Buses to the Taba (Sinai) and Rafiah (Cairo) borders leave from Jerusalem, Tel Aviv, Ashqelon, and Eilat.

Be'ersheva

Tell any traveler you meet in Israel that you're going to Be'ersheva, and you should expect the response: "Why?" Indeed, Be'ersheva has few historical sites for tourists. Be'ersheva does, however, allow you to experience a large Israeli city not overrun by commercialism. In 1948, when Israel recaptured the city from the Egyptians, Be'ersheva was a village of less than 2000 people. Now, over 120,000 residents—among them Moroccan, Bedouin, Syrian, Iraqi, East European, Russian, and Ethiopian immigrants—have put down roots here.

Be'ersheva means both "well of the oath" and "well of seven" in Hebrew, and the Bible (Genesis 21:25-31) offers both etymologies. The story goes that Abimeleh's servants seized a well that Abraham claimed to have dug. The dispute was ended by a covenant in which Abraham offered seven ewes to Abimeleh in exchange for recognition as the well's rightful owner. The seven ewes were witness to Abraham's oath that it was indeed he who dug the well.

On Thursdays, just south of the bus station, Be'ersheva carries on the ancient tradition of the Bedouin market.There you can purchase everything from Bedouin jewelry, camels, and goats, to American T-shirts and records.

Be'ersheva is an ideal base from which to explore the northern Negev. The transfer point for buses from the north en route to Eilat or the Dead Sea, Be'ersheva is also the transport hub for the Negev. Even a quick stroll between buses gives an unparalleled glimpse of Israeli society in a city that grew from a complete wasteland.

Practical Information

Be'ersheva is located in the middle of the northern Negev, 40km from both the Mediterranean and Dead Seas. To reach the **Old Town,** go out through the main exit of the bus station (next to the information desk), and make a left. Take any bus (signs are in English). Most pass the **shuk** (market) first (with the metal arches), then drive to the Old Town. To walk, continue through the parking lot and make a left onto Ben Tzui St. Make another left onto HaNesi'im Blvd., which turns into Herzl St. and goes right to the Old Town.

Government Tourist Information Office: (tel. 360 01, -02, or -03), across the street from the main entrance to the bus station. Information about accommodations and events. Ask if the large map of the city is available. Open Sun.-Thurs. 8am-7pm, Fri. 8am-1pm.

Banks: Bank Leumi, in the center of the Old Town and at the new mall across the street and to the left of the central bus station. All other major Israeli banks have locations in the Old Town and will change money. Open Sun., Tues., Thurs. 8:30am-12:30pm and 4-6pm, Mon. and Wed. 8:30am-12:30pm, Fri. 8:30am-noon.

Post Office: at the corner of HaNesi'im Blvd. and Ben Zvi St. Open Sun.-Thurs. 7:45am-12:30pm and 3:30-6pm, Fri. 7:45am-1pm. **International telephones** and **Poste Restante** here. There is a smaller branch office in the central bus station.

Telephone code: 057.

Central Bus Station: (tel. 743 41), near the municipal market on the northeastern edge of the Old Town, Be'ersheva's downtown area. Bus #446 runs every ½ hr. to Jerusalem, #393 and 394 run hourly to Eilat until 6:30pm, and #370 runs every 10 min. to Tel Aviv. **Luggage storage** open Sun.-Thurs. 7am-7pm, Fri. 7am-1pm. NIS2.50 per piece per day.

Taxis: YaelDaroma, 19 Keren Kayemet Le'Yisrael St. (tel. 391 44) offers *sherut* taxis to Jerusalem, Eilat, and Tel Aviv. **HaTzvi Taxi** (tel. 393 32), outside the central bus station, travels within the city and the surrounding area.

Car Rental: Hertz (tel. 738 78), next to the tourist office, or **Avis** (tel. 717 77), on Hebron Rd. Rates start at NIS26 plus mileage charges.

English Bookstores: Steimatzky's, 116 Keren Kayemet Le'Yisrael St. Open Sun.-Thurs. 8:30am-1pm and 4:30-7:30pm, Fri. 8:30am-2pm. Also **Minibook** in the alley between Hadassah and Histadrut St. **Books and a Cup of Coffee,** on Smilansky St., inside the courtyard, buys and sells new and used books.

Pharmacy: Yerushalayim (tel. 770 34), on Herzl St. Open daily 9am-noon and 4:30-7pm.

Hospital: Soroka Hospital (tel. 771 11).

First aid: Magen David Adom, 40 Bialik St. (tel. 101 for emergencies, otherwise 783 33).

Police: Herzl St. (tel. 100 for emergencies, otherwise 374 44).

Accommodations

Beit Yatziv Youth Hostel (IYHF), 79 Ha'Atzma'ut St. (tel. 774 44), a few blocks from the Old Town. Bus #13 will take you directly to the hostel from the bus station every 45 minutes, or you can catch any bus to the town center and walk past the Negev Museum on Ha'Atzma'ut St. Best budget beds in Be'ersheva. This 270 bed hostel is almost never full. 24 hour reception. No curfew. NIS11-14 per person. Doubles NIS60. Breakfast included.

Aviv Hotel, Mordei HaGetaot St. (tel. 780 59), off Keren Kayemet Le'Yisrael St. Pristine rooms with balconies, A/C, TV, and shower. Singles NIS30, doubles NIS40, and triples NIS45. Breakfast included.

Arava Hotel, 37 Histadrut St. (tel. 787 92), just off Keren Kayemet Le'Yisrael St. Plain rooms. Friendly and helpful management. Singles with bath NIS31, doubles with bath NIS51-58. Breakfast included.

Hotel HaNegev, 26 Ha'Atzma'ut St. (tel. 770 26). The quality of the rooms varies tremendously, so ask to see a few first. Some rooms have air-conditioning, showers, or TV. Central lounge with TV. Meals available. Doubles NIS47, one triple NIS35.

Food

One of the best places to go for a hot meal is the **self-service cafeteria** in the central bus station: Meat dishes are NIS6, salads NIS1.50. The *hoummus* is lumpy, but the other salads are excellent. Desperadoes for food on McDonald's style trays should head for **Quick Burger** in the mall between Keren Kayemet Le'Yisrael and Ha'Atzma'ut St. Burgers NIS3.20; schnitzel, chips, and salad NIS7. For something lighter, the **snack bar** at the corner of Keren Kayemet Le'Yisrael and HeHalutz St., a few blocks east of Herzl St. in the Old Town, offers grilled meat sandwiches for NIS4.50, *shwarma* for NIS4, and felafel for NIS2. All include self-service salads. The two felafel stands on Keren Kayemet Le'Yisrael St. towards Herzl St. are also quite good. The **bakery** just off Keren Kayemet Le'Yisrael on Shloshet Benei en Harod St. sells piping hot *bagelahs* (NIS.70) and *borekas* (NIS1.30). The cafes and restaurants in the Old Town close down after 10pm. After that, Be'ersheva's most promising places are **Smilansky** and **Trumpeldour Streets,** 4 blocks south of Ha'Atzma'ut, where cafes and art galleries stay open until around midnight. On Friday nights, many of the pubs in this area remain open, serving up food, drinks, and folk music.

Sights

The main attraction in Be'ersheva, besides the Bedouin market on Thursday mornings, is the **Negev Museum** at 18 Ha'Atzma'ut St. (tel. 391 05; take bus #5, 12, or 13 to the last stop). Set in a Turkish mosque, the museum chronicles 5000 years of the history of the Negev. The museum focuses on ancient Be'ersheva (Tel Sheva). The models of the site make the museum a good first stop before visiting the *tel.* The prize of the museum is the **animal mosaic,** a beautiful sixth-century C.E. church floor depicting animals woven together in an intricate geometric design. The center of the museum is devoted to an exhibit on the early, middle, and upper fortresses of Kadesh Barnea (where Moses drew water from a rock). Due to a gruesome accident, the mosque's minaret is closed to visitors. (Open Sun.-Mon. and Wed.-Thurs. 8am-2pm, Tues. and Fri. 8am-12:30pm, Sat. 10am-1pm. Admission

NIS1.50, Sat. free.) The adjacent art gallery has rotating exhibitions of contemporary art. (Open Sun.-Fri. 8:30am-noon, Sat. 10am-1pm.)

Five kilometers northeast of the city are the impressive ruins at **Tel Sheva** (tel. 69 01 03). Bus #055 runs to the site at 2:10pm, 3:15pm, and 5:45pm; on Friday 11:15am and 3pm (NIS1.30). Next to the ruins is a visitors center with a cafeteria, a good but expensive restaurant, and a small, interesting **museum** devoted to the life of the Bedouins. The center is open daily 9am-11pm; the museum is open Sun.-Thurs. 10am-5pm and Fri.-Sat. 10am-1pm (admission NIS2, students NIS1.50); the archeological site is always accessible (free). Unaccompanied women who accept offers of a guided tour of the site by sweet-talking men may find themselves cast in an unpleasant version of "Love Among the Ruins." Everyone should try to join an organized tour group.

Nearby is contemporary Tel Sheva, a village of Bedouin who have been induced by the Israeli government to abandon their nomadic lifestyle and live in Be'ersheva. The residents here wear traditional clothing and retain their native customs. One of these is for women to cover their faces in public. To reach the village of Tel Sheva, stay on bus #55. (Travelers to the archeological site will end up at the village too if they don't make their intentions crystal-clear to the bus driver.) Be'ersheva's other historical attraction is **Abraham's well,** at the corner of Ha'Atzmaut and Hebron St at the southeastern edge of town. The tourist office will insist that it's ancient. (Open daily 8am-7pm.) To get to the well, walk down Ha'Atzma'ut St. through the Old Town.

Be'ersheva's new **Town Hall,** the pride of the city, has an oddly shaped tower that dominates the horizon. The large, white-tiled building next door is **Yad La-Banim,** the **Be'ersheva Museum and Memorial.** The museum has memorial books for inhabitants of Be'ersheva who died in Israel's wars. (Open Sun.-Tues. and Thurs. 9am-12:30pm and 5-8:30pm, Wed. and Fri. 9am-noon, Sat. 10am-1pm. Free.) The modern campus of **Ben-Gurion University,** founded in 1969, lies in the northeastern corner of the city. Free tours of the campus are given if enough people show up (tel. 66 11 11).

Perhaps the most unusual sight in Be'ersheva is the **Memorial of the Negev Palmah Brigade,** located on the eastern outskirts of the city and dedicated to the soldiers who fell in the 1948 campaign to capture the desert. Many of the Hebrew inscriptions give day by day accounts of the battles; the rest explain the significance of the sculptures. Some of the more apparent ones include a watchtower and aqueduct, a lacerated snake representing the defeated enemy forces, and the perforated and split Memorial Dome (free). It's a very long walk to the memorial, and there is no direct public transportation. Bus #55 goes right by the spur road (from there it's a 1km walk), or you can take a taxi for under NIS10. If you make it to the memorial, you'll find a pleasant cafe, open daily.

Thursdays from 6am to 2pm, Be'ersheva hosts the well-known **Bedouin market,** located just south of the municipal market and the bus station, on the road to Eilat. Hundreds of Bedouin, both the semi-settled from around Be'ersheva and the nomads from deep in the desert, gather in the area around Hebron St. to sell sheep, goats, clothes, cloth, jewelry, and even digital watches. By all means get here early and bargain vigorously, or bring some jeans to trade. Try to wade through the plastic garbage and trinkets and seek out some of the beautiful Bedouin crafts such as beaten copperware, embroidered camel bags, and handwoven rugs. The name of the market is misleading, since Israelis and Arabs can also be seen selling T-shirts that tout American pop culture.

The **shuk,** right next to the Bedouin market and easily identifiable by its arched metal rooftops, is primarily a wholesaler's market. A number of stalls deal in Bedouin crafts, and Bedouin women in their beautiful black velvet robes come here to do their shopping.

Entertainment

A determined group of young entrepreneurs are attempting to renovate parts of the Old Town and cultivate an active nightlife. Already, students at Ben Gurion University patronize these pubs and restaurants. Although few of the signs or menus are in English, travelers are welcome.

Trumpeldour Street could be nicknamed Pub Street. **Little Be'ersheva,** at #6 (tel. 757 19), is more of an informal restaurant with pizza, blintzes, and *melawah.* You can sit indoors or out and listen to live music; the drone of the conversation can be heard from far away. **HaSimtas** (the Alley), 16 Trumpeldour St. (tel. 42 33 06) is more crowded and offers live, loud music nightly. Go down the stairs underneath the sign. **Bar Nash,** (tel. 072 43) across the street caters to a teenage crowd. The owner of **Chaplin's** has lined the walls of this club with his collection of original Charlie Chaplin posters. The salads and sundaes look like artwork. Chaplin's offers discounts and '60s music to its members on Tuesday and Thursday evenings, but tourists are always welcome.

For an unusual shopping experience, check out **Scandal Boutique** adjacent to Chaplin's (open most evenings), which sells antique clothing, love gifts, and lingerie. On Saturday, the only places open are the **Jade Palace Chinese Restaurant** (noon-3pm, 7pm-midnight) and **Be'ersheva Ice Cream.**

Near Be'ersheva

Arad

Lovers of pollen-free air should make Arad the next stop on their itinerary. All others know that little else is noteworthy about the town. Founded as a residential settlement in 1961 for laborers from the Dead Sea Works, Arad has grown in importance with the discovery of natural gas nearby. Located halfway between Be'ersheva and Masada, the town serves as a transfer point for buses running to the Dead Sea area. This makes Arad an ideal base for exploring the Dead Sea if you want to escape the searing heat and inflated prices of the Dead Sea region.

Arad's **central bus station** is on Yehudah St. across from the town's commercial center. Many buses (including some to the Dead Sea) leave from the station up the hill on Yerushalayim St. Within the mall is the **tourist office** (tel. 95 81 44), which can supply you with information about the Dead Sea and other nearby areas of interest. (Open Sun.-Thurs. 9am-noon and 5-8pm, Fri. 9am-noon.) The **post office** next door has **international telephones** and **Poste Restante** services. (Open Sun.-Thurs. 7:45am-12:30pm and 3:30-6pm, Fri. 7:45am-1pm.) There is also a **pharmacy** (tel. 95 74 39 in emergencies) as well as a Steimatzky's bookstore.

A local resident comments that there are two of everything in Arad: two bakeries, two grocery stores, and two banks. Most are located in the commercial center. The **banks** are open Sun., Tues., and Thurs. 8:30am-12:30pm and 4-6pm, Mon. and Wed. 8:30am-12:30pm, Fri. 8:30am-noon. If you are stuck in Arad during the day, the first showing at the Oron **Cinema** is NIS5 (the rest are NIS6). **Rachel's Restaurant** (tel. 95 92 19), the oldest restaurant in Arad, has a grill and bar, and serves Middle Eastern food. Main dishes are NIS10 (open noon-midnight). At night, try folkdancing at the cultural center. (Mon. and Sat., NIS2.)

Stay at the quaint **Blau-Weiss Youth Hostel (IYHF)** on Arad St. Walk east on Yehuda St., take a right on Palmach St. past the **police** (tel. 100 or 95 70 44) and **first-aid** (tel. 101 or 95 72 22) stations and follow the signs. (Dorm beds NIS12, under 18 NIS10.50, nonmembers add NIS1.50. Breakfast NIS3, meat meal NIS5, and dairy meal NIS4.) The hostel is closed 9am-5pm, and you can check in between 5-9pm. The rooms are clean, and there is a kitchen for members, but no air-conditioning. You will find many foreign students at the World Union of Jewish Students (WUJS), which sponsors a 6-month intensive *ulpan* in Arad, then places students in professional jobs throughout Israel for another six months.

Arad has tried to make a major tourist attraction out of the archeological site of **Tel Arad,** the ruins of the biblical city of Arad conquered by Joshua, but the ruins are 10km out of town. (Open April-Sept. 8am-5pm; Oct.-March 8am-4pm. Admission 75¢, students 50¢.) The town of Arad itself is mostly residential. It has bus connections to Be'ersheva (#388 every 30-40 min. Mon.-Thurs. 5:45am-10:20pm, Fri. 5:45am-4:30pm, and Sat. 5-11pm), and the Dead Sea (#384, 385, and 386, 7 buses per day, 6:40am-3:45pm; Sat. 4 buses, 7:30am-2:15pm). There are also buses to Tel Aviv (#389, Sun.-Thurs. 6am, 8:30am, and 2pm; Fri. 6am, 8:30am, 12:30pm, and 1:30pm; Sat. 4:30pm and 9pm) and Jerusalem (Sun. 6:45am and Thurs. 8am).

Sde Boqer

One of the most beautiful *kibbutzim* in the Negev, Sde Boqer is truly an oasis in the desert. Olives, apricots, kiwis, and other fruit are produced in its groves for domestic and international markets. Wheat and corn are all grown in its fields, and animals are raised as well. David Ben-Gurion was Sde Boqer's most illustrious member. Ben-Gurion loved the Negev, hated to be torn away from it to serve as Prime Minister, and died here on his beloved *kibbutz.* His home, only slightly larger than the residences of his less famous neighbors, has been left unaltered except for the addition of glass doors separating visitors from the living room and library. The glass does not prevent you from seeing the titles in Ben-Gurion's library like *Judo, Yoga for Americans,* as well as *The Collected Works of Machiavelli.* Books Ben-Gurion wrote are on sale in the living room. (Open Sun.-Thurs. 8:30am-3:30pm, Fri. 8:30am-1pm, Sat. 9am-1pm. Free.) Take bus #60, which runs from Be'ersheva (40km away) 12 times per day Sunday through Thursday and six times on Friday. The stop for the house is one stop after the *kibbutz.* (Ask for *Tsreef Ben-Gurion.*) The forest across the highway is a great picnic spot. To see the tomb of Ben-Gurion, set amidst the desert mountains, continue on bus #60 to Ben-Gurion University and follow the signs.

The **Ben-Gurion University of the Negev** has become a renowned center for desert research and conducts studies ranging from applied geobotanics to desert architecture. Call 353 33 to arrange a visit.

Avdat

The magnificently preserved ruins of a first-century B.C.E. Nabatean city lie 5km south of Sde Boqer in Avdat. On the crossroads of the caravan routes from Petra and Eilat, Avdat once thrived as a stopping point for travelers, and as a base for the the notorious Nabateans' raiding of caravans. From Avdat they could see caravans as far away as Mitzpe Ramon or Sde Boqer. Romans captured the city in the first century B.C.E. and exploited the agricultural skills of its former masters. The city flourished again during the Byzantine period, and a large portion of the visible ruins date from this time. Seventh-century Islamic marauders protected the Roman baths, but not much else. Below the site you'll see the experimental work of Professor Evan-Ari, who has reconstructed the remains of a Nabatean farm. He has unlocked the secret of how the Nabateans were able to cultivate fruit and vegetables without the use of secondary water sources: They channeled all of the rain water from the surrounding hills into one area—a technique known as "run-off farming." The project is organized through Ben-Gurion University at Sde Boqer, and is not ordinarily open to the public.

The archeological site, which is perched high above on a hill, consists of Nabatean remains of an altar and necropolis, enormous water cisterns, Roman baths, most of the columns of a fourth-century Byzantine church, and the city's well-preserved original walls. (Admission NIS3, students NIS.70, but there's nothing to stop you from walking in when the site is closed. Open daily 8am-5pm.) Full meals at the roadside restaurant are NIS10, but schnitzel is only NIS5. Salads and drinks are also sold. Drinking water is available near the bathrooms. Bus #060 runs to Avdat

12 times daily Sunday through Thursday and six times on Friday. Make sure the bus driver lets you off at the archeological site and not at one of the two turn-offs for Ein Avdat, a mid-desert oasis. Bring lots of water for the ascent to the ruins, since there is none at the summit.

Mitzpe Ramon

Until a more direct route to Eilat was built from the Dead Sea about 13 years ago, Mitzpe Ramon (Ramon Observation Point) was the central stop-off en route south. The town began as a camp for highway construction workers in 1954, and developed into a support unit for the military observatory that crowns a hill to the west. Since the return of the Sinai to Egypt, Mitzpe Ramon's importance as a southern tourist and military outpost has grown. Meanwhile new industries in metal and ceramics have been very successful.

Mitzpe Ramon is set 900m above **Maktesh Ramon** (the **Ramon Crater**), the biggest of the four desert craters. A half-kilometer deep, 7km wide, and 40km long, it is the largest single natural pit in the world. Its rock formations are millions of years old, its vegetation comes from four different climatic zones, and evidence of human life in the area predates written history. For obvious reasons, the area has been declared a nature reserve, featuring an archeological-geological-ecological park. There is a brand new **visitors center** (open Sun.-Thurs. 9am-4:30pm, Fri. 9am-2pm; adults NIS4, children NIS3). The center has reconstructions of the rock beds and of the ancient dwellings. A terrific multi-media slide show is presented every 30 minutes. At the top of the center is a panoramic observation window. Next to the visitors center is the new and luxurious, as hostels go, **Mitzpe Ramon Youth Hostel (IYHF)** (tel. 88 25 88 or 888 50). Just finished, this huge hostel, which only admits members, has dorm rooms each with shower and toilet. No curfew, but tell the managers if you will be late. Reception is officially from 5-9pm, but someone is always there. Come early because the hostel fills up. Dorm beds are NIS20, under 18 NIS15. Family rooms with 2-3 single beds are NIS22, under 18 NIS17. Breakfast is included; a meat meal is NIS10, and box lunches are available. Take bus #60 to last stop in Mitzpe Ramon; it lets you off just downhill from both the hostel and visitors center. A flock of ibex may watch you check-in. The **Hotel Nof Ramon,** 7 Nahal Meishar, rents doubles for NIS55.20 and triples for NIS77, with breakfast included. The management also operates a rental car dealership for Avis and Budget.

For **hiking** information, contact the **field school** run by the Society for the Preservation of Nature in Israel. The school endeavors to foster appreciation of the crater among Israelis and tourists. Most of their self-guided tour maps are in Hebrew, but they will go out of their way to translate and suggest paths for you. You may be able to join a group tour. The field school is 3km outside of the town by road, or a ½km hike. Ask someone to point out the Hebrew sign to the road in front of Sharon's Restaurant. Hike past the army installation, and go on to the wide dirt road. Head for the radio antennae of the nearby observatory (off limits). Calling ahead is recommended. The school is hidden in the mountains to avoid disturbing the natural surroundings. A working model of a Nabatean farm farther down the road is under construction, with fruit trees irrigated by the ancient run-off water collection technique. Water is collected from the hills during the one to two rains per year. Nearby, working ovens make clay bricks, and wine and olive presses can are demonstrated. Office hours are 8am-4pm (tel. 886 16 or 886 15). A hostel-like set-up here is designed mainly for school groups. With one or two people, a room is NIS15 per person. With three or more, the price drops a great deal. A kitchen is available, and if a group is having meals prepared you may join them. Nature enthusiasts can volunteer to work four days, then take tours of the crater for three days, and be paid for all seven days.

One street below the youth hostel is a **Co-op Supermarket.** (Open Sun.-Mon. and Wed.-Thurs. 8:30am-1:30pm and 4-7pm, Tues. and Fri. 7am-2pm.) The next street down is Ben-Gurion Blvd. At the far end of the street is a shopping center with a **Bank HaPoalim.** (Open Sun., Tues., and Thurs. 8:30am-noon and 4-6pm; Mon. 8:30am-12:30pm, Wed. and Fri. 8:30am-noon.) In the center is a decent **restaurant** (tuna, hot dogs, or *shwarma* in a pita with salad is NIS3.50). A **delicatessen** sells cheese and salads. Every Monday, in the lot next to the center, is an outdoor fruit and vegetable market. Down the street in the other direction is the **post office.** (Open Sun.-Tues. and Thurs. 7:45am-12:30pm and 3:30-6pm, Wed. 7:45am-2pm, Fri. 7:45am-1pm.) Next door is the **indoor swimming pool.** (Open Sun.-Fri. 8:30-noon and Mon. 4-6pm. Admission NIS5.50, children NIS2.50. On Sat. NIS6, children NIS3.) The adjacent **cultural center** hosts movies and plays.

Sunday through Thursday, from 6:30am to 9:30pm, 11 buses per day run between Mitzpe Ramon and Be'ersheva, with stops at Avdat, Ben-Gurion University, and Sde Boqer; seven buses run on Friday, from 6am to 3:30pm. Bus #392 continues to Eilat at 8:30am, 10:15am, noon, 4:45pm (and on Fri. at 8:30am). Bus #391 to Tel Aviv leaves at 6am.

Dimona and Mamshit

Dimona is a modern Israeli settlement untrampled by tourists. To get there take bus #056 from Be'ersheva (every 20-30 min., NIS2.70). The **central bus station** is on Herzl St. Dimona's main avenues run perpendicular to it on either side. You will find the **post office, cinema, supermarket,** and **shopping center** nearby. There are no accommodations for travelers (the one hotel closed down). Dimona is home to a curious sect called the Black Hebrews whose religious practices are, they claim, based on the Laws of Moses. The Israeli government disagrees, and is trying to deport these English-speaking immigrants from the midwestern United States. If you don't make it to Dimona, you still might encounter members of this sect at the Bedouin market in Be'ersheva.

Next to Dimona is **Mamshit,** a Nabatean city with Roman ruins and Byzantine churches. To reach Mamshit from Dimona, take a bus out to the main road (the *kveesh*) and then catch #392 or 393 toward Eilat; they could also be taken from the route's end in Be'ersheva.

Kibbutz Lahav

Facing Jordanian troops across the border until 1967, Kibbutz Lahav still marks the northern limit of Bedouin desert tents and the southern edge of the *fellaheen* (Arab farmers) villages. In addition to creating one of the largest wheat farms in Israel, members of Lahav built the **Colonel Joe Alon Center** (tel. (057) 74 368 or 74 864) for regional and folkloric studies. The Center houses a small **Archeological Museum** that features inscriptions and pottery from the neighboring digs and *tel.*

More colorful and interesting, however, is the **Museum of Bedouin Culture** (tel. 96 15 97), the largest such museum in the world. (Admission NIS2. Open Sat.-Thurs. 9am-3pm, Fri. 9am-noon.) Bedouin tribespeople, scattered throughout the Negev and Sinai, are undergoing a rapid process of modernization and settlement. Traditional dress, household utensils, jewelry, and tools are fast disappearing, and the museum succeeds in its attempt to preserve artifacts of Bedouin culture. Many Bedouin from the Sinai, the Negev, and even Saudi Arabia (with special governmental permission) have visited and donated family possessions to the museum. The reconstruction of a Bedouin tent is so realistic that Bedouin visitors have fallen asleep in it. Saalem, a Bedouin from the neighboring village of Rahat, often sits just outside the museum in a traditional tent. As he roasts, grinds, and cooks Bedouin coffee for visitors to taste, Saalem explains the extensive network of customs that rule Bedouin life. Saalem speaks only Hebrew and Arabic, but someone is usually there to translate.

Getting to the *kibbutz* can be a problem. Bus #369 runs from Be'ersheva to the Lahav-Devir intersection, but then you must hitch 10km to the *kibbutz*. During the summer, when school buses are not running, this can be a long trek. Bus #042 runs directly to the *kibbutz*, leaving Be'ersheva at 11:50am and 6:50pm Sunday through Thursday. The bus first stops at Devir, so make sure you are getting off at the right settlement. If you notify the museum staff, they will try to find you a ride back to Be'ersheva or the main road with the guides who leave when the museum closes at 3pm.

Outside Kibbutz Lahav is an ongoing excavation of **Tel Harif.** The site is open to participants but not to sightseers. The program is designed for academic credit, with nightly lectures in addition to the work schedule. Summer camp fee for first-time participants is $700. For information contact Dr. Joe Seger, Cobb Institute of Archeology, P.O. Drawer AR, Mississippi State, MS 39762. Excavation dates generally run mid-June to early August.

Eilat

Eilat is an international playground 365 days per year. Even on *shabbat* this city-sized playground is crammed with Israelis, international backpackers, and European gentry—frolicking on the beach by day and in the nightclubs by night. The prevailing cults of sun worship and hedonism have long since erased all memories of the city's biblical and historical significance.

When the Israeli army captured the oasis and revived its biblical name in 1948, Eilat was just a few run down Turkish shacks. About 3000 years earlier, King David built his southernmost defense outpost here; later his son King Solomon realized Eilat's potential as a port for trade with the Far East. Eilat flourished from Solomon's time up until its capture by Saladin in 1167. Under Muslim control, Eilat dwindled to an insignificant oasis and remained a minor military post, until the Israeli capture of the Sinai gave the city enough elbow room to become the country's major resort and a city with 19,000 inhabitants. In the past 10 years, dozens of luxury hotels, restaurants, and tourist shops have sprouted along the beach, which boasts year-round swimming. With the return of the Sinai in 1982, Eilat is once again Israel's southernmost port. It is the natural jumping-off point for excursions into the Sinai Peninsula.

Eilat was declared a free trade zone in 1985. The value added tax (VAT) was abolished, reducing prices for most goods and services by an average of 15%, and placing many of the city's restaurants and accommodations within the hosteler's budget for the first time. All entry and exit taxes at the airport were also eliminated.

The busiest time here is the eight-day holiday of Passover, which will run from April 19 to 27 in 1989. About 100,000 Israelis descend on Eilat, and accommodations are completely booked.

Eilat is a popular stopping point to earn money for travels to Egypt or tickets home. The resorts, hostels, cafes, and discos are often looking for newcomers because of the high turnover. Jobs with hotels and hostels often include lodging. Salaries average $300-400 per month. Unfortunately, most of the jobs are illegal, and payment is under-the-table. The work is often long and hard, and the wages low, but you will join an enthusiastic, international community of travelers.

Practical Information

Eilat is located at the southern tip of the Negev Desert, on a 5km strip of coastline between the Jordanian and Egyptian borders. The city is divided into three major sections: the town itself, on the hills above the sea; the hotel area and Lagoon Beach to the east; and the port to the south. Farther south lie Coral Beach, Taba, and the Egyptian border. At the bottom of HaTmarim Boulevard is Ha'Arava Road, which runs south along the coast to the Egyptian border.

Baggage is a weighty problem in Eilat, where it's too hot to exert yourself much. Since you will only need a shirt, shorts, bathing suit, face mask, snorkel, and canteen, you might consider leaving your pack in the parcel storage at the Egged Bus Station while you tour (terminal open Sun.-Thurs. 8am-6pm, Fri. 8am-1pm;

NIS2.20 per 24 hr.). This is a particularly wise investment if you unwisely intend to sleep on the theft-ridden beach.

Before you hit the beach or head south, obtain a hat and at least one canteen. The dry heat here can dehydrate you quickly with no sweat, so you should drink at least four or five liters of water per day. Since drinking water is often not available, always take some with you. A final word of caution: Eilat's police are particularly severe about jay-walking. Many travelers have been slapped with NIS15 fines. Cross at the pedestrian crossings marked with blue triangles.

Government Tourist Information Office (GTIO): HaTmarim Blvd. (tel. 722 68 or 767 37), ½ block toward the waterfront from the central bus station. One of the most helpful tourist offices in Israel, offering maps, brochures, transportation schedules, and border information. Almost everything you need to know is posted on the walls. They will help find accommodations—a real service when things are full. Open Sun.-Thurs. 8am-6pm, Fri. 8am-1pm.

Municipal Tourist Information: (tel. 742 33), underneath the Neptune Hotel. Good for maps and emergencies. Open Sun.-Thurs. 8am-10pm, Fri. 8am-5pm, Sat. 9am-1pm and 5-10pm.

Egyptian Consulate: 34 Dror St. (tel. 761 15). Walk south on Eilot St., go right at the Moore Center, take the first left, and look for the flag. You may have to enter through the back of the building. Open Sun.-Thurs. 9am-2:30pm. Visas issued on day of application ($10).**British Consulate:** Tel. 723 44.

Banks: Bank Leumi, HaTmarim Blvd. (tel. 741 91), across from the central bus station. Open Mon.-Fri. 8:30am-noon; Sun., Tues., and Thurs. 5-6:30pm. **Israel Discount Bank,** Shalom Shopping Center, toward the beach on HaTmarim Blvd. Open Sun.-Thurs. 8:30am-noon; Sun., Tues., and Thurs. 4-5:30pm. The **International Bank** in Tourist Center is the only bank open on Mon. and Wed. afternoons. Open Sun., Tues., and Thurs. 8:30am-2pm; Mon. and Wed. 8:30am-2pm and 4-7pm; Fri. 8:30am-noon.

Post Office: HaTmarim Blvd., in the Commercial Center. Open Sun.-Tues. and Thurs. 7:45am-12:30pm and 4-6:30pm; Wed. 7:45am-2pm; Fri. 7:45am-1pm. **International telephones** here and local pay phones outside.

Bezeq International Telecommunications: (tel. 721 73). Sun.-Thurs. 7:30am-1pm and 4-10pm, Fri. and holidays 7:30am-1:30pm. Direct and collect phone services available.

Telephone Code: 059.

Airport: At the foot of HaTmarim Blvd. **Arkia** (tel. 721 10) flies to and from Tel Aviv every 90 minutes ($62).

Central Bus Station: HaTmarim Blvd. (tel. 751 61), in the center of town. Buses to Jerusalem via the Dead Sea (Sun.-Thurs. 7am, 10:30am, 2pm, and 5pm; Fri. 7am, 10:30am, and 1pm; Sat. 4pm; NIS15.50. Reserve at least 2 days in advance in high season. If no seats are available, take a bus to Be'ersheva and transfer.); to Tel Aviv via Be'ersheva (Sun.-Fri. 5am-5pm on the hour and 12:30am, Sat. and holidays 1-6pm on the hour and 12:30am; NIS6); to Haifa (Sun.-Thurs. 8:30am, 4pm, and 11:30pm; Fri. 8:30am; Sat. 4pm and 11:30pm; NIS20); to Mitzpe Ramon (Sun.-Thurs. 6:30am, 9am, 1:30pm, 5pm; Fri. 12:30pm; NIS14). 10% student discount with ISIC.

City Buses: #1 and 2 run from the town to the hotel area. #15 runs from the hotel area to the Egyptian border with stops at Coral Beach and Taba, from 7am-9pm every 20-30 minutes.

In-city taxis: Tel. 714 74, 722 12, or 722 13. About NIS8 to Taba and the border.

Intercity *sherut* **taxis:** YaelDaroma, HaTmarim Blvd. (tel. 722 79), at Almogim St. Cars to Be'ersheva, Jerusalem, and Tel Aviv (both via Be'ersheva) 3-4 times per day. Fares slightly higher than the bus, without the hassles. Reserve 2-3 days in advance. Also carries parcels throughout Israel.

Car Rental: Europcar (tel. 769 69) and **Eldan** (tel. 740 27) are in the Shalom Center, **Avis** (tel. 731 65) is next to the airport, and **Budget** (tel. 761 39) is under the Etzion Hotel on HaTmarim Blvd. All have a minimum age requirement of 21. Prices are uniformly high, starting at NIS16 per day without mileage or insurance. You cannot bring a hired car into Egypt.

Bike Rental: By the lagoon in front of the Queen of Sheba Hotel at night. NIS25 for 24 hr.

English Bookstores: Steimatzky's in the central bus station, open Sun.-Thurs. 8:30am-7pm, Fri. 8:30am-2pm. **Book Bar,** (tel. 742 11), corner of Eilot and Yerushalayim. Buys and sells used English books.

Nature Reserves Authority: (tel. 739 88) Information about maps, hiking, and coral reefs.

Birdwatching Center: (tel. 772 36), in the Neot Hakikar office on HaTmarim Blvd. Literature and group tours about migrating birds. Rents field glasses.

Laundromat: Gill Laundromat, just past the corner of Eilot and HaTmarim Blvd. Open Sun.-Thurs. 9am-9pm, Fri. 8:30am-1pm. About NIS9 for wash and dry. Ironing too.

Pharmacy: Eilat Pharmacy, Eilot St. (tel. 750 02), Sun.-Thurs. 8:15am-1pm and 4:30-7pm, Fri. 8am-1:30pm. **Michlin Pharmacy** (tel. 724 34), near the GTIO. Open 8:15am-1:30pm and 4:30-8pm. In an emergency, call 745 54.

First Aid: HaTmarim Blvd. (tel. 101). Magen David Adom (Israeli Red Cross) first aid stations are also located on some beaches.

Hospital: Yotam Rd. (tel. 723 01 or 731 51).

Fire: Tel. 102.

Police: Avdat Blvd. at the eastern end of Hativat HaNegev (tel. 100, for non-emergencies tel. 724 44). "Lost and found" for packs stolen from the beach.

To reach the **Egyptian border,** take bus #15 from a stop across from the central bus station and from stops on HaTmarim Blvd. and Arava Rd. The bus, which does run on *shabbat,* goes all the way to the Sonesta Hotel at Taba, but you'll want to get off just before that at the Israeli checkpoint to obtain your exit visa (look for the Israeli flags marking the station). Or you can take a taxi for NIS8.

For **visits to the Sinai,** you'll need to pay both a departure tax from Israel and an entrance charge to the Sinai. The Israel tax is NIS13. The Egyptian entrance fee of $6 (LE12) must be paid in a foreign currency *other than* shekels. Bring your passport; no advance paperwork is necessary. The Israeli station is open 8am-10pm. This station also issues a one-month visa for travelers coming into Israel from Egypt (free). From this station, bus #15 or taxis will take you to the border or to Eilat.

Buses south into Sinai from the border leave at 10am and 2pm. A bus from St. Catherine's Monastery to the border leaves at noon. Since the trip takes several hours, you will have to stay overnight at St. Catherine's and return the following day. The monastery has a guest house. Similarly, one bus per day leaves the Egyptian border for **Nuweiba** and **Sharm el-Sheikh** and returns from these areas to the border in the morning. Taxis also service the Sinai, with fares slightly higher than the bus but fewer hassles. For taxis to Cairo, you must pay $10 to obtain an Egyptian visa at the consulate in Eilat or Tel Aviv. Bring two photos and arrive early (see Border Crossings in General Introduction).

Accommodations and Camping

The best way to find cheap private rooms in Eilat is to stand around with your pack after you exit the bus. Look lost. Chances are the room-renters will spot you right away. Beware, though, that quality varies tremendously; never pay before you've seen a room. If for some reason you can't find a renter (or a renter can't find you), go to the tourist office, a travel agency, or a real estate office, and they'll find you a place to sleep. Since Eilat is primarily a winter resort, the town bustles from the end of September until the end of April. Accommodations are most difficult to obtain, however, during Sukkot (October 8-19) and Passover (April 19-27), which is also an Israeli school vacation.

Cheap hostels cluster around Hativat HaNegev St.

Youth Hostel (IYHF), just south of the New Tourist Center (tel. 723 58), on a hill across from the Red Rock Hotel. Crowded rooms with 10 beds each and private showers. A/C. Lockers for guests. Under 18 NIS11; 18 and over NIS12. Nonmembers add NIS1.50. Breakfast included. Meat meal NIS7.50, light dairy meal NIS6, Fri. supper NIS8. NIS1 luggage storage charge. Work four hours in exchange for bed and breakfast.

Max and Merran's Youth Hostel, 2 Ofarim St. (tel. 714 08; P.O. Box 1541, Eilat 11611). From the bus station, take HaTmarim Blvd. across Hativat HaNegev, take the first right, and turn left just before the end of the street. The next left is Ofarim. Friendly and clean, but a bit crowded. The legendary Max is less visible than days gone by, but the hostel is still a fun place and rumors of its demise are exaggerated. A safe, cooking facilities, two refrigerators, and a huge collection of video movies. NIS8. Twosomes who arrive early should ask for one of the few double rooms. Closed 9-11am. Midnight curfew. Possibility of work in exchange for room.

Shalom Hostel, Hativat HaNegev St. (tel. 765 44), across the street from the bus entrance to the central bus station—look for red and white sign. Two big hostel rooms. Latecomers tend to be noisy, as reception is open 24 hours (no curfew). Good management and clean rooms with A/C. Immaculate bathrooms, full kitchen facilities, lockers, video games, and color TV. Coveted private rooms. Prices are subject to seasonal "sales." Dorm beds NIS10, doubles NIS55, triples NIS70. For private bathroom, add NIS10. Continental breakfast included.

Taba Youth Hostel, Hativat HaNegev St. (tel. 740 72), next to the Shalom Hostel. Brand new with clean showers, a sitting area, and A/C. The friendly manager advertises its "international standards." Dorm bed NIS12.

Red Mountain Hostel, Hativat HaNegev St. (tel. 749 36), next to Shalom Hostel. This clean and popular hostel features a patio, lockers, and a bar serving light meals. 24-hour check-in. Dorm bed NIS12, single NIS50.

Corinne Room, 413/4 at the corner of Eilot St. and Jerusalem St. (tel. 714 72). Look for their number painted right before the bus stop. Clean, comfortable, and well run. This hotel boasts a kitchen, refrigerator, and TV. Dorms NIS10, doubles with shower NIS30. No curfew.

The Village Youth Hostel, on Hativat HaNegev St. (tel. 713 11). Lots of rooms with A/C, all with private shower and toilet. Lockers available. Satisfied customers. Pub. Dorm beds NIS12, private room NIS40. No curfew. Reception open until 10pm.

Hotel HaDekel, Hativat HaNegev St. (tel. 731 91). From the central bus station, turn right and take your first right again. Breakfast served 8-10am, A/C, and private bath. Friendly management. Clean, but no frills. Singles NIS39, doubles NIS59, triples NIS84. Reception open 24 hours.

Two **camping** alternatives exist in Eilat—official and expensive, or unofficial and free. The latter is by far the more popular. During July and August, literally hundreds of young people ignore the "No Camping" signs and sleep on the public beach. You can take public showers in the adjacent Neptune Cafe during the day for a small charge. Some precautions, however, are in order. Possessions should never be left unguarded, and women alone should join a reliable party. One last problem: rats, attracted by the garbage areas on Lagoon Beach in front of the major hotels.

To avoid these problems, go east of Sun Bay Camping (toward the Jordanian border), or south of the Red Rock Hotel (toward Coral Beach). Sleeping and tent-pitching on these beaches is legal, and there are usable toilets near most of them. By far the best place to camp for free is on the beach at Taba, 8km south of Eilat by the Egyptian border (take bus #15 to the last stop). It's safer than the town beaches, the toilets and outdoor showers are functional, and tent-pitching is possible.

Sun Bay Camping, 750m before the Jordanian border (tel. 731 05). Take bus #1A to the last stop. Bungalows with showers, A/C, and breakfast NIS27 for one, NIS37 for two. Camping on the beach NIS5 per person. Office open 7am-10pm.

Carolina's Camping, at the municipal campground opposite Coral Beach (tel. 719 11 or 792 72). Take bus #15. Clean bathrooms and showers and a compact cafeteria. Small bungalows NIS12 per person with A/C, lights, and electrical outlets (minimum of two people necessary). Camping NIS5 per person. Office open 7am-9pm.

Yigal's Camping, opposite Coral World. Take bus #15 to the observatory, and look for the sign on the right that says "Bedouin Bazaar 30m." Not very polished, but has character. Grounds contain a pool, kitchen, and refrigerator. The manager sells soda, beer (NIS1.80), and wine in an outdoor pub that faces the sea. Bungalows for two NIS37 per person with private shower and toilet; tent pitching NIS5 per night.

Eilat Field School, (tel. 720 21) across from the Coral Beach Reserve. Hostel is often full, but camping is NIS4.50 per person. Toilets and showers included.

Food

Eilat's restaurant fare won't linger in you memory, but there are a few good, clean options. At the **Egged Restaurant** in the central bus station you can buy an omelette, bread, and salad for NIS3 and a full meal for NIS6. The restaurant is clean, and its large windows face the water and Jordan. If you're very hungry and prefer quantity to quality try **The Fisherman House** (tel. 798 30), open 24 hours, adjacent to Coral Beach where all the fish, chips, bread, and salad you can eat costs only NIS13. All the salads (seven offerings) cost NIS6.

The Tourist Center is, well, touristy, but so is all of Eilat. It is the major place, in addition to the Shalom Center, to eat, drink, people-watch, and play guitar. Many restaurants offer full-meal deals for NIS9-11. The new additions here are Mac-Davids and fast-food Chinese. Don't be sucked in by the aggressive restaurant hosts.

Several restaurants in the New Tourist Center and along the waterfront serve the same types of fish you spent the day gaping at underwater. The local bounty is delicious, but expensive. One of the best splurges is **Neviot,** across the bridge to the east of the hotel area. During the day, Neviot is mostly a surfer hangout, but at night the place calms down as customers drift outside to the Bedouin tent where Bedouin coffee is served. The

Family Bakery on HaTmarim Street is open 24 hours per day for delicious late-night snacks. The **Hard Rock Cafe** on Eilot Street is highly recommended by fellow travelers as a good place for food and conversation. Mixed grill is NIS6. (Opens at 5pm.)

Since many accommodations in Eilat provide cooking facilities, you can eat well and inexpensively by purchasing your food at the **supermarket** at Eilot St. and HaTmarim Blvd., 3 blocks inland from the bus station (look for the blue and white squares). (Open Sun.-Thurs. 7:30am-7:30pm and Fri. 7:30am-2pm.) Closer to the center of town is **Eilat Supermarket** in the Rechter Commercial Center across the street from the central bus station. (Open Sun.-Thurs. 7am-8pm, Fri. 7am-6pm, and Sat. 9am-8pm.)

Sights

Spend your days in Eilat underwater. With all the glitzy hotels out of view, you'll find yourself immersed in a dazzling world of coral, butterfly fish, emperor fish, clownfish, lionfish, and many other brilliantly colored species.

The best places to rent scuba and snorkeling equipment are near **Coral Beach,** an underwater nature reserve south of Eilat. To find Coral Beach Reserve, take bus #15 from the central bus station toward the sea (open 8:30am-6pm). The beach is run by the Nature Reserves Authority, and the NIS4 entrance fee helps to preserve the area. Once inside you can rent snorkeling equipment (mask and snorkel NIS2 each, fins NIS3) and follow one of the three "water trails," marked by buoys, through the reef. This is the cheapest way to get close to Eilat's marine life. Other brochures, maps, and books on the coral reef are available at the entrance, or at the **Field School** across the street.

For both novice and advanced scuba diving, look into **Aqua Sport** (tel. 727 88), next to Coral Beach (mask NIS3, fins NIS4.50, snorkel NIS1.50, introductory dive NIS57, class NIS352). They also rent windsurfing equipment for NIS16 per hour. If you plan to do much windsurfing or diving, Aqua Sport will accommodate you in their well-kept, sunny hostel with access to their private beach for NIS16 per person, breakfast included. Other programs include windsurfing, underwater photography courses, diving trips to the Sinai, waterskiing, and small boat rentals. For NIS30, a photographer will take five pictures of your dive. Videos are also available. Classes should be arranged in advance. Call or write Aqua Sport International Ltd. P.O. Box 300, Eilat 88102.

Red Sea Sports Club (tel. 796 85), across the street from Aqua Sport offers night dives for NIS32 and will rent underwater cameras for NIS30-65. Their office on North Beach near the lagoon rents windsurfing boards for NIS13 per hour, and has waterskiing, parasailing, and sailboats for rental.

Coral Beach is the most crowded reef territory on the Red Sea. For more isolated beauty, head south into Sinai.

Before snorkeling, a judicious first stop is the **Coral World Underwater Observatory and Aquarium** (tel. 766 66). The glasswalled underwater observatory lets you examine the coral reefs and fish at close range without even getting your feet wet. The aquarium tanks, in the front of the complex, will especially interest divers—they contain a fabulous collection of fish native to the Red Sea and allow you to identify and learn the names of many of the creatures you will meet in your underwater explorations. There is an enlightening exhibit on luminescent fish and corals. The well-labeled tanks make the guidebook (NIS8) unnecessary. A yellow submarine, soon to arrive, will take passengers on plunges 35m underwater. Take bus #15. Open Sat.-Thurs. 8:30am-4:30pm, Fri. 8:30am-3pm. Admission NIS13. A combination ticket for NIS15.50 includes admission to Hai Bar, Coral Beach, and Timna.

The bus stop just before Coral Beach is the pier for the popular glass-bottom boats run by **Tour Yam Ltd.** (tel. 721 11, 721 12, or 721 13). A 50-minute cruise costs NIS8 (hourly 10am-3pm); three-hour excursions run at 9:30am and 2:30pm. Take the boat ride before snorkeling to ward off total disappointment. A 10pm trip offers a floating casino. Adjacent to **Taba Beach** is the Hotel Sonesta, which both Israel and Egypt claim is within their negotiated borders. The hotel is actually between the two checkpoints on a 100m long stretch of land maintained by the Israelis, and has been a long-standing source of controversy and inconclusive negotiations between the two countries.

Eilat is perfectly positioned for bird watching as migratory groups pass north from Africa, stopping at the salt ponds north of the lagoon and in the northern fields of Kibbutz Eilot from mid-February through May. More than one million birds of thirty different species have been counted in the area. The **International Birdwatching Center** (tel. 772 36) coordinates local tours and educational programs from the GTIO on HaTmarim Blvd.

Entertainment

Rest assured that Eilat offers better entertainment than watching grade-C Kung Fu movies on one of the outdoor VCRs at the New Tourist Center. **Cinema Eilat** (tel. 731 78), next to the post office, features last year's flicks. The major hotels all have discos. The one at the **Americana Hotel** (tel. 751 76) is free, but their special drink prices are for guests only. The liveliest, cheapest, and most international place to park one's elbow is at the **Peace Cafe** (commonly known as the "Piss Bar"), a popular outdoor hangout at the corner of Almogim and Agmonim Sts. around the corner from Max's Youth Hostel. Swap messages with other travelers on the peace board while watching music videos. The **Tropicana** in the Shalom Center features free beer from 9 to 9:10pm (that's right—10 min.) and has a free movie every day at 3pm. The **Red Lion**, in the New Tourist Center, has happy hour from 11:30am to 7:30pm with draft beer for NIS1.50. From 5 to 10pm, buy three drinks and get one free.

The tourist office has information about evening shows and concerts at the **Phillip Murray Cultural Center** (tel. 722 57) on HaTmarim Blvd. near the central bus station. Many of these jazz, classical, rock, and theater performances are worth the charge of NIS6. The center also houses a television, a reading room, and rotating art exhibitions. (Open daily 5-11pm.)

For the very young, there are kiddie rides in front of the Queen of Sheba Hotel. Nearby is a **waterslide.** Two rides cost NIS2 and a one-day ticket is NIS25. For the young at heart, **Promised Land Minigolf** is located next to the Ganei Shulamit Hotel. Play one round for NIS6. Those hungering for spaghetti Westerns can hitch up at the **Texas Ranch** (tel. 731 46) just before Coral Beach. This so-called "American frontier town" is open daily from 9am to 1pm and 3 to 6pm (admission NIS2, children NIS1.60).

Near Eilat

The red granite mountains that tower over Eilat are as beautiful as the coral reefs, but less pleasant to visit. Many tours are organized for hiking and exploring; however, few are available for English-speaking tourists. The field school has maps of paths in Hebrew (NIS1.50) and will help translate if you request.

Sights near Eilat are most easily reached by organized tour or private car. Stunning, rugged desert scenery awaits you to the north of Eilat at **Red Canyon Gorge**. From Red Canyon, tours continue to a lookout above **Moon Valley,** a somber, lunar canyon now controlled by Egypt, and to **Amram's Pillars,** some unusual mid-desert rock formations (half-day tour NIS24 on Egged Tours from the central bus station; tel. 731 48 or 731 49). A Jeep trip is also available for $35 per day through **Johnny Desert Tours** in the Shalom Center.

Timna Valley, a national park that preserves something of the region's Bronze Age history, lies 30km north of Eilat. The 6000-year-old Timna Copper Mines, in the southeast corner of the park, saw their heyday during the Egyptian period. Ruins of eleventh-century B.C.E. workers' camps and cisterns evoke this vital industry. The area still holds significant copper deposits, and mining has continued since 1955. Also in the park, the sandstone **King Solomon's Pillars,** preside over the desert, to a height of 50m. Stop to look at the fourteenth-century B.C.E. **Temple of Hathor** nearby, the remains of an ancient Egyptian sanctuary. United Tours, in the Shalom Center (tel. 742 17), runs tours to Timna Valley. Otherwise you can take any bus that goes to Tel Aviv or Jerusalem and ask the driver to let you off at the sign for Alipaz (not at the Timna Mines signpost) and walk or hitch toward the entrance 2km away. The park is open 7am-dark, admission NIS4, students NIS3.20. *Bring water,* even though there are bathrooms just inside the entrance to the park. There is camping near Timna Lake, an artificial lake created for recreation.

Any northbound bus will also take you to the **Hai Bar Biblical Nature Reserve,** a wildlife park constructed to repatriate animals native to the region in biblical times. (Ask the driver to let you off at Yotvata.) The reserve contains freely roaming gazelles, donkeys, ostriches, and other animals. Large natural enclosures hold eleven species of predators mentioned in the Bible, including leopards, wolves, and striped hyenas. (Open 7:30am-1:30pm, though the look at the animals is 8-11am during feeding time. Admission NIS2.10. Combination ticket that includes the visitor center NIS3.70.) Only closed vehicles are allowed to enter. If you come on foot, come early to wait for a vehicle with space. The entrance to the park is 1½km from Kibbutz Yotvata. Here **Y'elim Camping** (tel. 743 62, check-in time 2pm) has tent space for NIS12, caravans for NIS63, and a swimming pool (admission NIS10, free for guests). A **visitor center** (tel. 760 18), opposite the *kibbutz*, gives out information about the area and shows a film about Negev ecology. The **cafeteria** serves Yotvata's fresh dairy products.

All of the above sights are interesting, but probably not worth the hefty sums charged for tours operated from Eilat by **Egged** (tel. 731 48 or 731 49; 10% student discount), **Dan United** (742 17), and **Neot Hakikar** (tel. 713 29).

Ashqelon

> *And in the houses of Ashqelon*
> *They shall lie down at evening.*
> *For the* LORD *their God will be mindful of them.*
> —Zephaniah 2:7

If God is mindful of you, you'll be able to bask on Ashqelon's 10km of Mediterranean beaches, or camp in its national park amid archeological ruins. Modern residents of Ashqelon proudly declare that they have fulfilled Zephaniah's prophecy that it would be a great city. The area was first settled in the third millenium B.C.E., but flourished as one of the chief cities of the Philistines. The saga of Samson (*Shimshon*), told in Judges chapters 14-16, is just one instance of the centuries of strife between the Israelites and the Philistines.

Ashqelon, now a city of 60,000, was captured in November, 1948, during the War of Independence. The first settlers to come to Ashqelon had hoped to form a *moshav* on the site of then-deserted Migdal. However, in 1952, South African Jews began to plan the plush district of Afridar, initiating modern Ashqelon. You will meet a large number of American, Canadian, Russian, Ethiopian, and European *olim hadashim* (new immigrants); Ashqelon has one of the most important, and probably the most deluxe, absorption center, where immigrants are given special apartments and attend orientation classes during their first three months of residency in Israel. If you speak Spanish, German, or Russian, you'll certainly be able to use it here. Many *olim* are a little homesick, and all have stories to tell about adjusting to life in Israel.

Practical Information

Fifty-five kilometers south of Tel Aviv, Ashqelon is a union of five smaller districts, set in the coastal fertile plain. Each of the neighborhoods retains its own flavor, from the old Arab town of **Migdal** (and its eastern industrial affiliate, **Ramat Eshkol,**) to the snazzy commercial center of **Afridar,** to the flanking residential suburbs of **Barnea, Zion Hills,** and **Shimshon.**

Although the bus station is centrally located, it is far from any of the town's attractions. The public bus system makes it possible to get around without a car. Bus #13 connects the central bus station with the beach; but only in July and August; buses #3 and 9 pass within walking distance of the park behind the beach; and buses #4, 5, and 7 let you off at **Zephaniah Square** in the heart of Afridar. You will know you have arrived when you see the chunky concrete clock tower of the tourist center. The same buses also serve Migdal. Bus #5 continues on to Barnea.

If you do decide to walk, you will benefit from Ashqelon's lack of unmarked, twisting side streets (except in Migdal). Although distances are long, the surroundings make walking quite pleasant. Get oriented with the city map in front of the bus station.

All transportation comes to a grinding halt on *shabbat* and during holidays. You may need to rely on taxis, if you happen to be in Ashqelon for the weekend and want to reach the beach.

Government Tourist Information Office (GTIO): Afridar Center (tel. 324 12). From the central bus station, take bus #4, 5, or 7. The whole staff is helpful. Excellent city maps, information on the national park, buses, hotels, and cultural events. Open Sun.-Thurs. 9am-1pm, Fri. 9am-11pm.

Banks: Israel Discount Bank on Ben-Gurion Blvd., 2 blocks west of the central bus station. Open Sun., Tues., and Thurs. 8:30am-12:30pm and 3:45-6pm, Mon. and Wed. 8:30am-12:30pm, Fri. 8:30am-noon. Like most Israeli towns, Ashqelon suffers no shortage of banks.

Central Post Office: Herzl St. in Migdal. Open Sun.-Thurs. 7:45am-12:30pm and 3:30-6pm, Fri. 7:45am-1pm. **International telephones** and **Poste Restante** here. Branch offices in Afridar Center, Shimshon, and Civic Center (near bus station).

Telephone Code: 051.

Central Bus Station: (tel. 291 11). Information booth provides printed schedules for buses in Ashqelon. To Jerusalem (bus #437, about every hour until 6:30pm, 2:30pm on Fri., 90 min., NIS5); to Tel Aviv (frequently, until 9:30pm, 4:30pm on Fri., NIS3.80); to Be'ersheva (bus #363 or 364 hourly until 7:45pm, 2:30pm on Fri., NIS4); to Gaza Strip (bus #20, at least 3 per day). **Baggage check** open daily 7am-4pm.

Taxis: YaelDaroma on Tzahal St. in Migdal (tel. 223 34), runs *sherut* taxis to Tel Aviv (NIS4) and Gaza (NIS2). You may have to purchase a seat for your pack. Only private taxis operate within Ashqelon and cost up to NIS5 to cross town. Stations are at Kerem Kayemet St. in Shimshon (tel. 222 66), Beit HaMishpat St. in Barnea (tel. 255 55), and opposite the central bus station (tel. 330 77).

Laundry: Orion, 15 Herzl St., Migdal (tel. 234 31). Open Sun.-Thurs. 7am-1pm and 4-7pm, Fri. 7am-1pm.

Pharmacy: Pharmacy Ashqelon across from the GTIO in Afridar (tel. 342 34 in emergencies). Open Sun.-Thurs. 8:30am-1pm and 4:30-7pm, Fri. 8:30am-2pm.

First Aid: Tel. 233 33.

Police: Emergency tel. 100; information tel. 342 22 or 241 44. Located at the corner of HaNassi and Eli Cohen Sts.

Accommodations, Camping, and Food

Ashqelon has one of the best **campgrounds** in Israel, and it is an excellent alternative to the city's high-priced accommodations. To reach the campground, take bus #3 or 9 and ask the driver to let you off at the national park, then follow the small footpath to the campsite. Bear left, toward the ruins. Or take bus #13, get off just before the beach, and walk about five minutes south to the entrance of the park; the campground is a 15-minute walk from the entrance. This route is longer, and you have to pay the park's admission fee of NIS4.50, students NIS2.20. The campground (tel. 367 77), run by the National Parks Authority, offers a variety of lodgings and services. There are beaches, archeological sites, snack bars, restaurants, and lots of picnic space and facilities right on the premises.

Camping facilities are under the management of the Israel Camping Union, so prices are standard: tentsites NIS3 per person, beds in a bungalow NIS25. A caravan with four beds costs NIS100; NIS120 for six beds. This is a good choice if you have enough people. Air conditioning and refrigerators are each available for NIS8 per day. Gas is NIS10 per day. The campground is often full, especially on Saturdays, so call ahead. You can often get away with camping in the park for free, since it's large and crowded, but be sure to guard your possessions. Women should not camp alone.

The GTIO arranges rentals of **private rooms** in homes around the Afridar section of town. The charge is usually NIS20-22, without meals, and quality varies widely. People also solicit boarders at the bus station and campground. They may begin by asking as much as NIS25 per night, but if you mention camping, prices will quickly plummet to NIS8. These rooms are often in Migdal, unmarked, and hard to find.

The only hotel option for budget travelers is the **Samson Gardens,** Sonnabend St. (tel. 346 66) in Afridar. Go through the municipal gardens, turn right onto Drom Africa Blvd., and another right on Sonnabend St. Doubles with air-conditioning and a telephone in the room are NIS35. Triples are NIS40 more. Breakfast is included.

The long beach along the full length of the city, unlike much of the south coast, is not off limits to campers and offers plenty of quiet spots. The worst that can happen is that the military police will chase you up to higher ground. Try not to be too close to the sand, and respect the "separate" Barnea beach during July and August where religious men and women swim separately. Avoid Kibbutz Zikim a few kilometers to the south as well. Don't build fires, and clean up after yourself. The northern beaches might be a little safer, but be extremely wary of thieves on the entire stretch. The black marks on the beaches are from the oil tankers, which you can see unloading their cargo. When the tankers clean their holds with seawater (illegally) instead of with chemicals (expensively), a tar-like substance washes ashore. To get the spots off, use turpentine or cooking oil.

The inexpensive popular restaurants and snack places are all located in Migdal. Take bus #4, 5, or 7 and get off at Migdal Station. **Nitzaḥon** on Herzl St. near the post office has the best selection in town of steaks, *me'orav* (mixed grill), kebab, and stuffed cabbage for NIS6 per plate, and is air-conditioned as well. The restaurant at 70 Herzl St. serves meat sandwiches with hot dogs, schnitzel, or kebab for NIS2.50-4. **Mashehu Mashehu,** located at #49, has similar fare plus *me'orav* (NIS3.50). The nearby cluster of felafel stands have priced each other down to NIS1.50. The **bakery** on Tzahal at the corner of Herzl sells fresh *borekas* (NIS1.30) and *bagelahs* (NIS1-1.50). Shop for fresh produce at the outdoor market (see Sights below). Always an option is the huge **supermarket,** 2 blocks west of the bus station. (Open Sun.-Thurs. 9am-8pm, Fri. 8am-2pm, Sat. 8:30am-10:30pm.)

Sights

Ashqelon's seaside **National Park** (tel. 364 44) is one of the most popular and dramatic in Israel. The park was built on the site of four 1000-year-old Canaanite remains buried under the ruins of Philistine, Greek, Roman, Byzantine, Crusader, and Muslim cities. The ruins offer extensive evidence for Ashqelon's claim to be the oldest city in the world (competition for this title is fierce throughout the Middle East).

While all of Ashqelon's **beaches** sparkle, each has its own particular charms. The National Park's beach at the southernmost edge of the city has a grass lawn and impressive ruins. Delilah Beach faces three small islands within wading and swimming distance. Barnea Beach attracts Ashqelon's wealthier residents. North Beach at the city's edge offers nude bathing but no lifeguards.

Thanks to Ashqelon's native son, Herod the Great, who enlarged and beautified the city that Alexander the Great left behind, the most extensive ruins date from the Roman era. The most compact part of the site, situated in the center of the park, features an imposing Roman colonnade and a haphazard collection of Hellenistic and Roman columns, capitals, and statues, including two magnificent Roman statues of Nike, the winged goddess of victory. The first section of antiquities you see will be the **Bouleuterion,** which was the Council House Square of Ashqelon when it was an autonomous city-state under Severius in the third century C.E. The sunken area with descending steps on the right, which resembles a courtyard, is actually the inside of a Herodian assembly hall. Look down at your sneakers, then up at the pillar reliefs of Nike, one of which is on a globe supported by Atlas. There is also a statue of the goddess Isis with her child-god Horus. These statues, made of marble imported from Italy, were sculpted some time between 200 B.C.E. and 100 C.E.

Along the southern edge of the park are wall segments of the twelfth-century **Crusader city.** The most peculiar parts of the site are the Roman columns sticking out of the ancient Byzantine sea wall on the beach. Originally these columns were used to strengthen the walls, which were destroyed in 1191 by Salah al-Din. Richard the Lion-Hearted rebuilt them, only to have them be obliterated by the Sultan Baybars in 1270.

Outside the park on the northern end of the beach is the splendid **Roman tomb,** believed to have been built for a wealthy Hellenistic family of the third century C.E. The frescoes adorning its interior are in remarkably good condition, and the wall paintings represent scenes from classical mythology: You can see Pan playing his pipes, Demeter, and the snake-haired Gorgons whose portraits were supposed to protect the family from evil. There are also scenes representing the hunt and the grape forest (the squiggly lines underneath are intended to imitate marble). You will have to unbolt a waist-high red iron door to get in. Don't forget to close it on your way out, or sand from the beach will corrode the paintings. (Tomb open Sun.-Fri. 9am-1pm, Sat. 10am-2pm.)

The main attractions in the Afridar section of town are two stunning **Roman sarcophagi,** enclosed in a courtyard along with other Roman sculptures. Both date from the third century C.E. The first depicts the abduction of Persephone to Hades, and the second depicts armor-clad, helmeted Greeks triumphing over naked barbarians. To the left of the first sarcophagus is the basket of flowers Persephone had been picking before her rude kidnapping. The sarcophagi are in the museum court-yard next to the commercial center. (Courtyard open Sun.-Fri 9am-2pm. Free.) On your way out of the GTIO, gawk at Yigal Tumarkin's sculptures of ancient sundials in the Municipal Gardens.

Barnea, Ashqelon's northern and most recently settled sector, contains the ruins of the sixth-century **Byzantine church,** and, nearby, a fifth-century **mosaic floor.** Neither is worth going out of your way to see—after the ruins in the national park, the knee-high pillars and ruined walls are a bit of a let-down, while the design of the floor, none too complex to begin with, has been weathered to an almost uniform pallor. To get there, take bus #5 to Barnea from Afridar or the central bus station, get off at Jerusalem Blvd. and walk half a block to Zvi Segal St. Bus #4 lets you off 1 block farther south at the corner of Jerusalem and Bar Kohba St.

The somewhat shabby but colorful old town of **Migdal** has its own interesting history. After Sultan Baybars destroyed Ashqelon in 1270 C.E., the city was neg-lected for several centuries until, in the nineteenth century, Lady Stanhope claimed to know of a treasure buried here. The ruling Turkish *pashas* of Akko and Jaffa brought Arab slaves to dig for the riches. Although the treasure remains hidden, the Arabs settled here. The huge stones they excavated were shipped to build up Akko and Jaffa. When Israeli forces captured the town in 1948, almost all the Arab population fled to Gaza, where most now live in refugee camps.

With stone houses huddled together, and the occasional minaret and domed roof, Migdal contrasts sharply with the modern, spacious layout of Ashqelon's other dis-tricts. It is now the main shopping quarter of town, featuring a vegetable and fruit **market** on Mondays and Wednesdays, and a lively produce, clothing, and jewelry market on Thursdays. Besides the inexpensive produce, you'll find cheap sand-wiches and snack bars—felafel often costs as little as NIS.80. Walk north on Herzl St. just past Tzahal St., and you'll see the market in the narrow passageway to your left. Bus #4, 5, or 7 will take you to Migdal, although the walk to Migdal down Eli Cohen St. takes 25 minutes and passes through open fields.

Pubs, movies, the beach, people-watching, and the wonders of nature comprise Ashqelon's nightlife. **Bayit HaKfari (The Village House),** in Afridar Sq. next to the clock tower, is the most popular pub among young Israelis, even during the day. The **Rachel Cinema** (tel. 314 29) at Zephaniah Sq. runs English-language films every night at 7:30 and 9:30. **Esther Cinema** (tel. 226 59) in the Zion Hills district also shows films in English. The tourist office has a list of monthly **winter concerts.** There are often sound and light shows near the sarcophagi in Afridar. The nearby Municipal Gardens also hosts outdoor plays and concerts. Tourists and local resi-dents gather on **Delilah Beach** every night around a large beer keg where steak and pizza are also sold. Young Israelis mix at the **Civic Center** on HaNassi St. and on Saturday nights the center features a Youth Disco (small entrance fee). **Bustan HaZeytim (Olive Grove)** (tel. 364 44), in the national park, features dancing, folks-inging, or magicians every Saturday night, and offers food and drink. Most evenings, the fancy hotels, notably the King Shaul and the Shulamit Gardens, sponsor discos or other activities.

Near Ashqelon

Ashdod

In biblical times, Ashdod was one of the five "Cities of Giants," the source of the giant grapes in the Ministry of Tourism's emblem. Although Joshua received accurate information from his spies, he did not conquer Ashdod, and it was here that the Philistines brought the captured Holy Ark. This former city of giants now has 80,000 residents, and is the largest port in Israel, surpassing even Haifa. Its ex-panding industries include everything from cosmetics and textiles to power plants that produce roughly half the nation's electricity. Although Ashdod is on Israel's master agenda for tourist development, the city remains unabashedly ill-equipped to accommodate visitors. The sole accommodations for travelers, the Orly and

MiAmi hotels, are way out of the budget range. Nevertheless, the Israelis who live here are exceptionally friendly and helpful, and their long golden sand beaches, Lido and MiAmi, are soft and clean. Sleeping here is tolerated and quite safe. There are showers, and it's easy to find shade.

After you get off the bus, go next door to the **Bureau of Public Relations** on the seventh floor of the Municipal Building (tel. (055) 523 01). Do what you must to get their excellent, poster-sized city map. Like Ashqelon, Ashdod has plenty of banks. For starters, the two next to the bus station are open Sun., Tues., and Thurs. 8:30am-12:30pm and 3:45-6pm, Mon. and Wed. 8:30am-12:30pm, and Fri. 8:30am-noon. At 25 Rogozim St., down Shapiro St. from the Municipal Building, is a **supermarket.** On Rogozim St. are felafel stands and kiosks. At the end of the street is the main **post office.** (Open Sun.-Tues. and Thurs. 7:45am-12:30pm and 3:30-6pm, Wed. 7:45am-2pm, Fri. 7:45am-1pm.) There is no Poste Restante, but public phones are next door. The police are just off Rogozim St. on Yitzhak HaNassi St. At the end of Rogozim, turn left onto Nordau, and you will come to the beach. For **taxis,** call **Ron** at 221 27. **La Bouquinerie** on Rogozim St. sells English books.

On the southern outskirts of Ashdod lie the remains of a Fatimid fortress (tenth century C.E.) known in Arabic as **Qal'at Al-Mine,** in Hebrew as **Metzudat Ashdod Yam,** and in English as **Fortress of the Port.** Until excavations unearthed bits of ceramic pottery, the site was believed to be more recent. An early Arabic document recounts that Byzantine ships (which were trying to recapture the Holy Land) used to bring in Muslim prisoners to sell to their families. As boats appeared off the coast of Ashdod, the Fatimid fortress would send up smoke signals alerting the townspeople to come at once with their offerings. Thousands brought whatever riches they had, hoping for the return of their loved ones. Qal'at Al-Mine, once part of a chain of coastal fortifications, seems to have served as a focal point for these peaceful, if hectic exchanges. Portions of the four towers remain. To visit the site, take bus #5 south, and ask the driver to let you off at the fortress (at the end of a row of private homes).

The site of the biblical city of **Tel Ashdod,** southeast of the modern city, comprises 23 levels of virtually indistinguishable ruins. The Book of Joshua calls Ashdod a "City of Giants"; nothing of magnitude remains, although excavations continue.

For a striking view of the city and its environs, climb **Yaffa Ben-Ami Memorial Hill,** adjacent to the lighthouse at the end of Ya'ir St. in the northern part of the city. According to Muslim tradition, the ruins mark the tomb of Jonah, who settled on the coast of Ashdod after being ejected from the whale. If you visit Ashdod on a Wednesday, don't miss the colorful **flea market** at Hof Lido (Lido Beach) from 6am until nightfall.

Bus #015 leaves Ashqelon about every hour for Ashdod. Buses #312 and 314 from Tel Aviv run to Ashdod every 10-20 minutes until 8pm, and continue less frequently until 9:50pm.

Yad Mordehai

From May 19 to 24, 1948, during the War of Independence, the 165 members of Kibbutz Yad Mordehai withstood an attack by an Egyptian battalion of 2500. Although the *kibbutz* members eventually had to retreat to nearby G'varam, 300 Egyptians were killed, and the Haganah was given time to regroup and save Tel Aviv. To commemorate this miracle, the *kibbutz* has built a model of the battle on the original site, complete with dummy soldiers, tanks, and weapons. A recorded explanation in several languages recounts the battle and elucidates various parts of the colossal reconstruction. The *kibbutz* is named after Mordehai Anielewicz, leader of the Warsaw Ghetto uprising. A **museum** tells the story of the Jewish resistance movement, and concludes with exhibits about the establishment of the State of Israel and the battle for Yad Mordehai. (Museum open daily 8:30am-4:30pm, battlefield open 8am-5pm. Admission NIS2.50, students NIS2.)

Bus #19 runs from Ashqelon to Yad Mordehai Sunday through Thursday at noon, 2:45pm, and 6pm, and Friday at noon and 4:15pm. Since the last bus returns at 3:10pm (12:40pm Fri.), you'll have to take the noon bus if you don't intend to stay. Catch the bus back from the bus stop on he highway. If you get stuck in the late afternoon, go to the bus stop anyway. Buses from Rafiah pass by, and you may get a ride.

Beit Guvrin, Tel Maresha, and Tel Lakhish

About 22km east of Ashqelon, **Qiryat Gat** is easily accessible from Tel Aviv, Jerusalem, and Ashqelon (bus #025 runs from Ashqelon Sun.-Thurs. every half hour until 8:30pm, Fri. until 2:15pm). From Ashdod, take bus #212 to *tzomet* Ashdod, and then catch a bus heading to Be'ersheva. This small, industrial town is the capital of the Lakhish region—a network of 30 villages established in 1954—and the jumping-off point for exploring several important sites. Tel Gat, the hill to the northeast, was formerly believed to be Gath, one of the five major Philistine cities and the birthplace of Goliath. However, excavations have failed to turn up any evidence of an ancient capital.

Beit Guvrin, a modern *kibbutz,* was built in 1949 on the ruins of the deserted Arab village of Bit Jibrin. The surrounding region is characterized by huge outcroppings of cacti and fig trees, hiding some 4000 caves. Some of the caves were carved naturally, as water carried away the soft limestone. Others were carved by the Phoenicians, who scooped limestone out of gigantic round holes in the earth and used it for the construction of their great port at Ashqelon. As a result, many of the caves have vast bell-shaped rooms with sun roofs. The caves later became natural sanctuaries for hermits and monks of the Byzantine period. St. John and others came here seeking solitary meditation, and often carved crosses and altars into the walls.

At nearby **Tel Sandahanna,** (Arabic for St. John), excavations uncovered beautifully preserved, ornate Byzantine mosaics of colorful birds and flowers. These mosaics, which served as floors in fifth- and sixth-century churches, can be seen near the top of the *tel,* protected by small sheds. Recently a Roman mosaic floor, in even better condition, has been unearthed. (Stones with Hebrew inscriptions from a third-century synagogue, Crusader artifacts, and Greek objects of art from these ruins are on display at the Rockefeller Museum in Jerusalem.) Two of the caves were used for burials, and have niches for the appropriate urns. Since the sites are unmarked and the *tel* is large, you may need to ask for the assistance of one of the kibbutzniks from Beit Guvrin, a 20-minute walk down the hill. Even young children seem to be well-acquainted with the area and can serve as guides.

Getting to and from Beit Guvrin requires advance planning. Bus #011 from Qiryat Gat goes right to the *kibbutz.* (Sun.-Thurs. 6am, 8am, 5:10pm, Fri. 6am, 8am, 2:15pm.) Some of the Qiryat Gat-Hebron buses pass right by Beit Guvrin. Be sure to ask the driver to let you off here since there is no regular stop. Taxis run from the central bus station to Bet Guvrin or Tel Maresha, and to Tel Lakhish. To reach the caves, walk north from the front of the *kibbutz* to the paved road opposite. The first fork bears left to the largest of the Beit Guvrin bell caves.

The right fork leads to **Tel Maresha,** about 3km southeast of Beit Guvrin. The magnificent view from this place makes it worth the trip even if you're tired of ruins. On a clear day, you can see Tel Aviv and the Mediterranean to the west, and the Jordanian hills and the Dead Sea to the east. The ruins here include several Phoenician bell caves, one of which has a stone *calumbarium* with thousands of niches carved into it, two decorated graves, and a Crusader basilica nearby. The 60 caves around the ruins contain colorful wildlife drawings. Try latching onto a tour group to find the occasional artifact on the large *tel.*

Tel Lakhish lies just north of the *moshav* of the same name, 2km south of the Beit Guvrin-Hebron road. Although archeologically more important, Tel Lakhish is not as interesting as Tel Maresha. Because of its strategic location at the intersection of the road to Egypt and the approach to Jerusalem, it was often a scene of conflict in ancient times. It is mentioned in the Bible (Joshua 10:31-32) as one of the Canaanite cities destroyed by the Israelites. Excavations have revealed nine levels of settlements dating as far back as the third millenium B.C.E. There are still remains of graves from the Canaanites and one of their holy sites, but since most of its artifacts have been removed to museums in Jerusalem and Britain, Tel Lakhish is no longer irresistible. In addition, it's also almost inaccessible without a car. Bus #011 does run to the *moshav*. Because of this area's isolation, climate, and proximity to the West Bank, moshavniks strongly discourage camping out in these hills.

Dead Sea

The Dead Sea was given its gloomy name by Christian pilgrims who were disconcerted by the complete absence of any form of life in its waters. At 403m below sea level in the depths of the Afro-Syrian Rift, this is the lowest point in the world. Its Hebrew name, *Yam HaMelah*, which means "the salt sea," is equally appropriate, since the lake has a salt concentration eight times that of ocean water. Swimming in, or rather floating on, the Dead Sea is like nothing else in the world. The high salinity dramatically increases your buoyancy, giving you a unique opportunity to experience life as a human cork. Try to tread water and your body will pop above the surface. If you do the crawl stroke, your legs will refuse to stay underwater, making it impossible to kick. It requires a great deal of exertion to submerge yourself, making the lake paradise for non-swimmers (as long as they stay on their backs).

In ancient times, the Dead Sea was more than a resort. It was a refuge for those in search of religious freedom (the Qumran sect), political freedom (David in hiding at Ein Gedi), or both (the Jewish rebels at Masada). The Dead Sea can also count Jesus, King Herod, and John the Baptist among its temporary residents.

The waters themselves are the subject of controversy: Some swear by their curative properties, others say they're useless, and some don't care. According to a few scientists, and all resort owners, concentrations of bromine, magnesium, and iodine, 10 to 20 times higher than in the ocean, reduce skin allergies, stimulate certain glandular functions, and have a soothing effect on the central nervous system. The sulphur springs at resorts along the coast seem to alleviate the pains of rheumatism and arthritis, but occasionally have an adverse effect on blood pressure. Even the mud is sold for its beneficial beautifying properties.

The high salt content of the Dead Sea, however, is not particularly good for your hair, and if you open your eyes under water, you're in for several minutes of painful blindness. Wash your eyes out immediately in the fresh-water showers found on all beaches. Don't expose any cuts or bruises to the water, which will probably seep into a few minor scrapes you didn't even know you had. Smaller cuts shouldn't prove too painful and may even heal faster, because the salt cleanses the wound and kills bacteria. Don't shave immediately before swimming here. Since you will want to wash off as soon as you get out of the water, you may want to stick to the resorts (Ein Feshka, Ein Gedi, Ein Boqeq, and Neveh Zohar), where showers are available.

The Dead Sea is not an ordinary desert climate—instead of harsh and dry, it's harsh and humid. The humidity, especially in the summer, makes high temperatures barely tolerable. However, athletes will enjoy the 10% increase in oxygen concentration and lack of air pollution, but exertion is only sane in the early morning.

Currently, the Dead Sea is 65km long, up to 18km wide, and with a depth of up to 400m. It won't be for long, as the sea is actually evaporating at an incredible rate and recedes a bit each year. The haze that obscures what would otherwise be a spectacular view of the basin is actually that evaporation. The rift in the Earth's crust which created this place is evident in the jagged wall of cliffs, less than 3km apart, which rise on both the Israeli and Jordanian coasts.

From the central bus station in Jerusalem, several **buses** make frequent trips along the bank of the Dead Sea. Buses #421, 486, and 966 stop at Qumran, Ein Feshka, Ein Gedi, Masada, and Neveh Zohar. Bus #487, also from Jerusalem, runs only to Qumran, Ein Feshka, and Ein Gedi. For those planning to hop on and off the buses, the Jerusalem-Qumran fare is NIS4.80, Qumran-Ein Feshka costs NIS1.40,

Ein Feshka-Ein Gedi costs NIS4, and Ein Gedi-Masada costs NIS2.60. In addition, bus #385 makes about four trips per day (Sun.-Fri.) between Ein Gedi and Be'ersheva. Bus #444 stops at Ein Gedi and Masada en route to Eilat, but only if it's not already full.

If you are going to stay in the Dead Sea area for a while, stock up on food. The only grocery store is at Neveh Zohar, to the south. Elsewhere there are only tourist resorts and *kibbutzim,* and no inexpensive lunches. The searing heat will help you remember that the same rules apply here as in the desert: Bring along a water bottle, drink plenty of fluids, and keep your head covered.

If you really want to get out into the desert, you can take an organized tour. The **Metzokeh Dragot Desert Tour Village** takes you to major sights and through rugged desert terrain. The one-day tour includes refreshments and costs $28. You can be picked up at Ein Gedi or Ein Bokek. For information and reservations call the offices in Jerusalem (tel. (02) 22 81 14) or Kibbutz Mitzpe Shalom (tel. (057) 843 40). **Egged's** tours of the area are cheaper and more popular, though less personalized. The **Society for the Protection of Nature** also offers excellent hiking tours of the area, departing from Jerusalem. **Hitching** through the desert and near the West Bank is inadvisable.

Qumran

In 1947, a young Bedouin shepherd looking for a missing sheep wandered into a remote cliffside cave and stumbled upon a collection of earthenware jars containing parchment manuscripts two thousand years old. These Dead Sea Scrolls have become one of scholars' most important sources on the development of the Bible. The largest, now displayed in the Israel Museum of Jerusalem, was a 7m long ancient Hebrew text of the Book of Isaiah. Encouraged by the initial discovery, archeologists searched the surrounding caves and began excavations at the foot of the cliffs. In 1949, they uncovered the settlement of the sect that wrote the Dead Sea Scrolls.

Archeological evidence suggests that the site was settled as far back as the eighth century B.C.E., was reinhabited in the second century B.C.E., temporarily abandoned during the reign of Herod, and completely deserted after the Roman defeat of the Jewish uprisings in 70 C.E. Historians believe that the authors of the scrolls were the Essenes, a Jewish sect whose members were disillusioned by the corruption and Hellenization of their fellow Jerusalemites, and sought refuge in the sands. These Essenes tried to live according to the pure law, and created their own solar calendar. They expected God's intervention in history to occur soon, and foresaw a struggle between the Sons of Light (themselves and the angels) and the Sons of Darkness (everyone else). The visitor to Qumran who stumbles among the ruins or along the cliffs in the sweltering Dead Sea climate may be moved by a mixture of admiration and incredulity; it took great religious conviction to live in such an unfavorable climate.

The main archeological site is compact and can be viewed without too much exertion. Of special interest are the cisterns and channels that were essential for the efficient storage and passage of water in such an arid climate. Start first at the **watchtower,** which affords an excellent view of the site and is well worth the modest climb. Proceed to the **scriptorium,** the chamber where the scrolls were probably written. The ruins are clearly marked by Hebrew-English signs, and a map of the site is posted just past the entrance. A minor rock climb brings you to the caves themselves. Remember to bring drinking water (available next to the site) and a hat. There is also a cafeteria which sells snacks and reasonably priced light meals, as well as a souvenir shop.

Qumran lies 43km southeast of Jerusalem. The archeological site is located 100m from the coastal highway and is served by buses #486, 421, and 966 from Jerusalem, which let you off at the turn-off, and by buses from Eilat and Ein Bokek to

Jerusalem. Keep your eyes peeled for the sign and ring the bell for the stop. (Open Sun.-Thurs. 8am-5pm, Fri. 8am-4pm. Admission NIS3, students NIS.70.)

Near Qumran: Ein Feshka

Once you've worked up a sweat climbing around at Qumran, take advantage of the salt-water and fresh-water bathing at **Ein Feshka** (Einot Tzukim in Hebrew), 3km south of the ruins. If you have water and don't have a pack to lug, consider walking from Qumran. Unlike other of the desert's respites, where mountain streams trickle from the foot of the Judean Hills and collect in channels along the Dead Sea's flat coast, these springs appear from above, tumble jubilantly downward into small pools, and wind through tangled reeds in a wadi. Herds of ibex and families of hyrax graze in this remarkably fertile desert oasis. Ein Feshka may not have the lush greenery and cascading falls of its southern neighbor, Ein Gedi, but it is never as crowded.

The small beach is fairly quiet, except on weekends. From the beach, a dirt road leads inland to the **nature reserve,** where you can submerge yourself in the thigh-deep pools formed by natural springs. Ein Feshka is the only Dead Sea resort with fresh water ponds adjacent to the swimming area. As the sea level drops, the groundwater level declines as well, bringing plant life eastward in the direction of the receding shoreline. Thus the oasis always maintains its position relative to the sea. Rivulets lace the area, and vacationers lounge about in cakes of reputedly healthful black Dead Sea mud. There are showers, changing rooms, bathrooms, and taps for drinking water. A lifeguard hut separates the beach from the mud area. (Adults NIS5.50, children NIS4. Open April-October 8am-5pm; November-March 8am-4pm.)

Ein Gedi

Along the approach to the Ein Gedi Nature Reserve, which contains the stunning Nahal David wadi, strips of greenery cling to the barren landscape—patches of lushness ascending like vines on a garden wall. Unlike other ordinary oases in this area of the foothills of Judean Hills, Ein Gedi's springs bubble up in the heights and crash down moss-covered grooves into a wadi. The hordes of tourists and herds of ibex attest to the perennial popularity of this remarkable oasis among people and wildlife.

Practical Information

Buses run to Eilat at 8am, 11:30am, noon, 3pm, and 6pm; to Be'ersheva via Arad and Ein Boqeq at 7:45am, 12:30pm, 3:15pm, and 5:45pm; to Tel Aviv at 6am and 2:30pm; to Haifa at 3:30pm; and to Jerusalem 13 times per day. Local buses run to Masada, Ein Boqeq, and Neveh Zohar at 9:30am, 10:15am, 11:15am, 1pm, and 2pm. On Fridays, only the morning buses run; a few buses will run on Saturday nights. Reservations for seats on the Eilat bus cannot be made at Ein Gedi or Masada. During the height of the tourist season, your chances of getting an unreserved seat are good, since Egged often runs two buses at a time to accommodate the crowds. If you want to be on the safe side, buy a seat on a bus to Eilat before you leave Jerusalem. When you get off the bus, follow the signs for **Nahal David,** *not for Ein Gedi,* which is the nearby *kibbutz.* If you continue 500m south along the main road, you'll pass a roadway on your right that leads to the **Arugot Reserve;** 400m farther down from the nature reserve on your left are the **public campgrounds.** Ein Gedi Kibbutz, which houses the major Israeli animation studio, is 1km farther south; a bus runs to and from the site every 30 minutes. There is a **first-aid station** at the campground.

Accommodations

From the road to the reserve, a branch to the right leads to the hostel and to a field school. The prime choice for accommodations in the Dead Sea area is the **Beit Sara Hostel (IYHF)** (tel. 841 65). Although the youth hostel has 206 beds, it is usually crowded, and the management tends to be rather impersonal. The place is clean, the rooms are air-conditioned (between 6pm and 6am), and the cafeteria serves decent meals. The showers are clean and refreshing, but don't drink any of the tap water from the showers or the bathroom; use the drinking fountain instead. If you arrive during the day, buy a token for a luggage locker. (There is free luggage storage at the nature reserve.) The entire hostel is closed from 9am-5pm; check-in is from 5 to 7pm, but get there early or you'll be waiting in line for an hour or two. (Under 18 NIS16.50, 18 and over NIS18; nonmembers add NIS2.20. Breakfast included. Meat or fish hot meals NIS9.80, dairy meals NIS6.) Buy tickets in the kiosk for supper, served 7-8pm.

Diehard campers should head to **Ein Gedi Camping** (tel. 843 03), on a barren, shadeless beach 1km south of the hostel and nature reserve. The campground and other commercial enterprises surrounding it are run by the nearby *kibbutz;* the office next to the snack bar can provide information (office open 7am-10pm). Camping costs NIS10 per person, but since nights at Ein Gedi are almost as hot as the days, you might want to think twice about sleeping without air-conditioning. If you decide to camp, the reception office will guard your valuables. Beach admission is NIS5. Bathrooms and showers are on the beach. The nearby caravans, which accommodate four to six people, offer greater privacy, air-conditioning, refrigerators, bathrooms, towels, and sheets. (NIS75 per night for a couple, NIS23 each additional adult, NIS15 each additional child. If there's an empty caravan, a single person may rent it for NIS55.) The campground also runs an expensive self-service, air-conditioned restaurant (open 8:30am-4:30pm) and a small mini-market (open noon-1pm, 4-5pm). In case you're curious, the heavily advertised guest inn at the *kibbutz* costs (in the words of the campground reception desk) more money than you'll ever have: NIS72 per person in a double. The army discourages free-lance camping.

Sights

Like most places in Israel, if you scratch the surface of Ein Gedi you'll find a biblical story. David fled to this lush oasis to escape the wrath of King Saul (I Samuel 23:29). Ein Gedi is also mentioned in the Song of Songs, where it is referred to as the "Fountain of the Kid," a name that has stuck to this day. In 1953, a few kilometers south of the beach at Ein Gedi, Jewish settlers established a *kibbutz,* which has become well-known for its fruit and for the restored fountain. They also cleared a path for the famous waterfall, replanted palms and reeds in the area, and started a field school for the study of flora and fauna.

Tenuous biblical references aside, the **Ein Gedi nature reserve** is the main reason to come to Ein Gedi. If you're short on time, at least make the 15-minute hike up to **Nahal David** (David's Stream), a beautiful, slender pillar of water dropping the full length of the cliffside to a shallow pool. Abundant pools nourish the area; investigate the little paths that branch off the main trail and disappear into the thicket of giant reeds. You are advised not to drink the water in any of the pools. Try instead to take advantage of the drinking water taps scattered throughout the reserve and at the entrance. Twenty meters below the waterfall on the southern bank of the brook, another trail climbs up the cliffside to **Shulamit Spring.** From the spring you have two options: Continuing up the cliff will bring you to **Dodim (Lovers') Cave,** a marvelously cool, mossy niche, set at the top of the fall (a 30-min. walk). Continuing up to the left, you'll see signs to the fenced in **Calcolithic Temple** (20 min. from Dodim), built 5000 years ago by the first of an almost unbroken chain of settlers in the region. The climb is tiring, but rewarding. Enjoy the solitude and the chance to see a herd of ibex—a strange-looking wild goat. Also watch for the tiny hyrax, which can be found lurking in the reeds—it looks like a small, gray badger without a tail. Zoologists have unconvincingly classified the creature as a relative of the elephant. The exotic plant life includes the Apple of Sodom, with its big leaves and hollow fruit.

From the Calcolithic Temple, either return as you came or make the steep descent along a path to **Ein Gedi Spring** (25 min.). Despite its name, it is merely one of the minor water sources of the oasis. From Ein Gedi Spring a roundabout path runs to Shulamit Spring, from which you can return to the base of the waterfall at Nahal David. Alternatively, continue from Ein Gedi Spring to **Tel Goren** (20 min.), the site of biblical Ein Gedi, where you can visit the remains of a fourth century synagogue discovered in 1970, just 300m to the north of the *tel.* Tel Goren is on the Nahal Arugot Rd. (see Practical Information) 1km from the junction with Rte. 90 at a point 600m south of the entry to the nature reserve. The map in the brochure available at the entrance to the reserve does not help you gauge the ascents and difficulty of the various hikes, but does provide some general orientation. (Reserve open daily 8am-4pm, Fri. until 2pm; don't start the hike up to Dodim Cave later than 2:30pm. Admission NIS3.20. Bags and packs can be left at the entrance for free.)

A fairly difficult climb along **Nahal Arugot,** which begins in the parking lot of the Nahal Arugot Rd. about 2km in from Rte. 90, takes you to the charming "hidden waterfall." It's a good hour-and-a-half walk from the road (look for the sign), but if you follow the course of the stream, you shouldn't have trouble finding it. The pool at the end, considerably deeper than the others, rewards the exertion.

If you are planning on doing any serious hiking in the area, check the public-display maps at the field school. (An overly detailed map is a steep NIS19.) You must register at the field school if you are hiking in the desert interior. There is a small display about the flora, fauna, and archeology of Ein Gedi. South of the *kibbutz,* about 5km from the nature reserve, the **Ein Gedi Spa** has a pleasant beach, a luxurious indoor sulphur bath, and a vegetarian restaurant. Admission to all facilities is NIS14, students NIS12.

Masada

"Masada shall not fall again" is the melodramatic oath of members of the Armored Division of the Israel Defense Force taken yearly at this fortress. The small, lonely rock and its tenacious defense by Jewish rebels has been a symbol for Israelis of their own situation. It's hard to imagine Masada falling at all (except off the cliff)—perched on a flattened mountain, it seems impregnable. The huge fortress (the Hebrew name, *M'tzada,* means fortress) was built as a palace refuge for King Herod from 40 to 4 B.C.E.

In 66 C.E., the Judeans revolted against the dominant Romans. A small band of the rebels, who were the original "Zealots", captured the outpost. The Romans gradually crushed the revolt, taking Jerusalem in 70 C.E. after a siege and destroying the Second Temple. Masada became the last holdout. It was a formidable stronghold; behind its two defense walls were stored many years worth of food, water, and military supplies. The 967 defenders—men, women, and children—held off thousands of Roman legionnaires through a three-year siege. The Romans constructed a wall and camps in a ring around the mount. With patient engineering, they built a stone and gravel ramp up the side of the cliff, and dragged battering rams up it.

When the defenders realized that the Romans would break through the wall the next morning, each man burned his possessions, said farewell to his loved ones, and put them to death. They placed stores of wheat and water in the citadel's courtyard to demonstrate to the Romans that it was not from hunger that they perished. Ten men were chosen by lot to execute the others and check each house to make sure everyone was dead. Lots were drawn again, and one person was selected to take the lives of the other nine, and finally his own. The following morning, when the Romans finally burst in, they encountered a deathly silence. The only survivors, two women and five children, told story of the martyrs of Masada. The story was recorded by Josephus Flavius, a Jewish general in the revolt who had defected to the Romans and become a chronicler. To this day, Masada remains a symbol for those Jews who say that fighting to death is better than surrender.

Practical Information

Masada lies 20km south of Ein Gedi, a few kilometers inland on the road to Arad and Be'ersheva. **Buses** go to Eilat at 8:15am, 11:45am, 12:15pm, 3:15pm, and 6:15pm; to Be'ersheva via Arad at 8am, 11:15am, 12:45pm, 3:30pm, and 6pm; to Haifa at 3:15pm; and to Jerusalem nine times per day from 8:30am to 7:45pm. Take the schedules with a grain of Dead Sea salt—they tend to run late.

There are three ways to reach the ruins—by cable car or by either of two foot paths. The easier of the two trails, the **Roman Ramp,** starts on the west side of the mountain, on Arad Rd., and takes about 30 minutes to climb. However, it is not accessible by public transportation. The walk around the base to the Roman Ramp is extremely arduous and time-consuming. More popular, more scenic, and more difficult is the original **Serpentine Path,** so named for its tortuous bends. The path has only been fixed up a little since the Zealots used it. The hike up takes just under one hour, and if you start early enough (gates open at 4:30am), you will have a breathtaking view from the top—the sun slowly rising over the vast expanse of the Dead Sea some 450m below. It is important to start hiking well before the afternoon, both to avoid the heat and to leave enough time to tour the extensive ruins. If you do come later in the day, listen in on one of the tour groups. Remember to bring water.

The **cable car** stops near the top of Serpentine Path. It starts running at 8am and leaves every 15 minutes for the three-minute ascent; the last cable car up is at 3:30pm, on Friday 1pm. (One way fare is NIS5, students NIS2.60.) Try hiking up the mountain early and then taking the beautiful cable car ride down when it starts to get hot. (Site officially open 4:30am-4pm. Admission NIS3, children NIS1.70.)

Accommodations and Food

The first thing you'll see when you leave the bus is the 150-bed **Taylor Youth Hostel (IYHF)** (tel. 843 49). The hostel has clean rooms and air-conditioning, but becomes crowded since it's the only place around. Watch TV in the coffee shop, where guests may sup for NIS9.80. If you must get into the hostel during the day, try the service gate near the dining room. If you are hiking Masada at 4:30am, tell the management when you arrive and you can take a bag breakfast with you for the following morning. Check-in is between 5-7pm, lock-out 8:30am-4pm. Call between 8am-1pm or 4-8pm. (Members under 18 NIS16.50, over 18 NIS18; nonmembers under 18 NIS18.70, over 18 NIS20.20. Breakfast included.) Next to the hostel are a few overpriced but air-conditioned restaurants.

If you want to sleep outdoors, there is a cement pavilion in front of the hostel. During the day, groups prepare meals there, using the tap and toilet facilities, but at night you may sleep there for free. It may be sold soon. The hostel will allow you to use their showers for NIS2, but they are strict about prohibiting use of other facilities.

The only other accommodations within reach are the **campground** at Neveh Zohar to the south, the **youth hostel** in Arad, and the facilities north at Ein Gedi (see the Near Masada and Arad sections for details). The closest hotels are a few kilometers south at Ein Boqeq.

Someone rolled off Masada while sleeping on the top two years ago, so you can no longer camp out up there. Hikers carrying packs to the top late in the afternoon will be stopped, and people have been brought down by the police. The gates now open at 4:30am for early morning hikers, and after the last cable car up at 3:30pm, you can look around then walk down the path. Watch out for poisonous snakes and scorpions.

Next to the hostel at the base of the mountain is an assortment of outrageously expensive refreshment stands, souvenir shops, and air-conditioned restaurants. The exception is the **snack bar** with large meat sandwiches for NIS3. The shops all feature overpriced copies of archeologist Yigael Yadin's popular book on Masada, which you can buy for far less in Jerusalem. A sound and light show opened in 1988 (NIS10, tel. (057) 95 63 71). Drinking water is available from a number of faucets and hoses; don't take a sip unless it's marked as drinking water (*ma-yeem shteeyah*).

Sights

The ruins at Masada were unearthed in 1963 by a team of archeologists headed by Yigael Yadin. They discovered skeletons of some of the Zealots, as well as numerous dwellings and the structure of Herod's magnificent palaces. Begin your explorations at the entrance to a huge water cistern—one of seven—located to your right near the last flight of stairs to the summit. It is estimated that the defenders were able to store enough water in the cisterns to last eight years. As you enter the site proper, the enormous store-houses stand to your right. Climb up for an aerial view of the palace's impressive layout. About one-third of the ruins is actually restoration work—a black line runs along the walls to distinguish the original from the reconstructed sections. The main attraction of the palace is the Roman-style **bathhouse,** complete with vomitorium, where you can see some of the original frescoes.

At the edge of the northern cliff, with its half-circle patio, lies what archeologists believe was **Herod's private palace.** It was designed to stay cool in the heat of the day. If you follow the steps down along the sheer walls of the cliff you will come to the lower sections of the private palace. In the bathhouse of the lowest section, the skeletons of a man, woman, and child were found, along with a *tallis* (ceremonial prayer shawl). The lower terrace contains a few original frescoes and columns, and affords a spectacular view of Roman General Silva's camp. Traces of all eight Roman camps, appearing as brownish rectangular enclosures, are clearly distinguishable from the mountain summit, and close observance reveals an outline of the wall that connected them.

Climb back up the steps from Herod's palace and turn right as you reach the summit to find the Zealots' **synagogue,** the oldest known synagogue in Israel. Scrolls were found here containing texts from several books of the Bible. Most are now on display in the Shrine of the Book at the Israel Museum in Jerusalem, but a few modest examples can be seen in the museum by the cable car station. (Open only for large tour groups upon request.) Discoveries, such as a ritual bath and remnants of Torah scrolls from around the synagogue and elsewhere, indicate that the community observed all the rituals prescribed by the Jewish orthodoxy of the time despite the hardships of mountain isolation and siege. Continuing still farther along the edge, you will come to the **Western Palace,** which houses splendid Herodian mosaics, the oldest in Israel.

Masada was occupied for a short time in the fifth century C.E. by Christian monks who built the **Byzantine Chapel** next to the Western Palace. Some of the best mosaics are located here. The **Western Gate,** through which you will enter if you climb up the Roman path, offers a view of that route leading up the mountainside. Watchtowers, additional fortifications, and countless Zealot dwellings occupy the rest of the site. Scattered throughout are kegs of drinking water which you should utilize even if you're not thirsty; it is surprisingly easy to become dehydrated.

Near Masada

The excellent beach at **Ein Boqeq** has made the town one of the most popular resorts on the Dead Sea. Located on the southern half of the sea, 15km south of Masada, Ein Boqeq is a good place to stop off for a swim on the way to Arad and Be'ersheva. Showers on the beach allow you to wash off the salt immediately after swimming, as well as some hot mineral springs. **Sidom Apple,** a snack bar, offers expensive meals, drinks, and suntan oil. (Open 8am-midnight.)

A little farther south, within walking distance from **Neveh Zohar,** you'll find a quiet beach, next to the Moriah Hotel, with toilets and outdoor showers. Like the beach at Ein Boqeq, this one is free. **Neveh Zohar Camping** (tel. 843 06) charges NIS6 per person and is a bit barren, but has toilets, showers, refrigerators, and gas. The owner runs a cafeteria and cooks decent meals. There are also two-person bungalows, each with an overhead fan, kitchenette, and private bathroom for NIS20 per person. A small **museum** owned by the Dead Sea Works sits up the street from the campground, on top of the hill. Although the museum has little to offer, the director, Shlomi Droli, is the resident expert on Dead Sea projects and will gladly answer questions. It's essential to call ahead (tel. 66 51 07). The most interesting sights around Neveh Zohar are the fantastic salt formations in the southern regions of the Dead Sea, which seem to float like crystalline icebergs, but are actually rooted to the sea floor.

Traveling south from Neveh Zohar, the road will drop you into searing **Sodom,** where Lot's wife was turned into a pillar of salt. The Hebrew Bible describes Sodom and Gomorrah as the wicked cities of their day upon which God rained fire and brimstone. Only the family of Lot, Abraham's nephew, was spared, and only on the condition that they not look back to witness their neighbors' plight. Out of sympathy or curiosity, Lot's wife snuck the fateful glance back (Genesis 18-19).

In modern Sodom the main attraction is the column of salt that tour guides introduce as Mrs. Lot. Sodom is also the home of the **Dead Sea Works,** which extracts potash and other minerals from the Dead Sea for export. Tours of the factory with a discussion about the Dead Sea as a natural phenomenon and about preservation projects, including an ambitious plan to build a canal from the Mediterranean, can be arranged through the museum in Neveh Zohar, or at the main office in Arad. Most of the workers live in nearby Arad and Dimona because Sodom's heat is intolerable—indisputable evidence, according to some, that it once rained fire and brimstone here. **Buses** #421, 486, and 966 (from Jerusalem) make it as far south as Ein Boqeq, Neveh Zohar, and Sodom.

WEST BANK

Travel in the West Bank is extremely dangerous. The U.S. and U.K. governments officially advise against travel here. For safety, inform your consulate of your plans before you visit.

The towns of the West Bank have always given a physical immediacy to the characters of the Bible and Koran. More recently, West Bank towns have begun to hammer home international headlines and the message of the Palestinian *intifadah* (uprising). While the West Bank contains some interesting sights, Palestinian disturbances and Israeli repression make it dangerous. Visit only with proper planning and precautions.

The relatively sane way to tour the region is in daytrips from Jerusalem. Before you leave Jerusalem, consult with all available sources, including your consulate, the GTIO (see Jerusalem practical information), The Office of Visitor Information of the Civil Administration (212 Jaffa Rd., Jerusalem), local Arabs, and your grandmother. Read a newspaper to keep up-to-date with current happenings in the towns. Be flexible. Don't visit the West Bank if you hear that a general strike has been declared—the area will be paralyzed, including transportation to it, and violence is much more likely. The preferred modes of transportation to the West Bank are Arab buses, Arab *service* (*sherut*), or private taxis. A taxi can drive you right to the sights, often away from the center of town, and wait for you. If you must use a vehicle with yellow (Israeli) license plates, make sure "U.N." or the name of a Christian service agency is printed clearly all over the car. Egged buses are a last resort; take them only to Jewish settlements. Lastly, avoid traveling alone. A group of two to four provides security in numbers.

Unannounced curfews and roadblocks can spring up at any time. They apply to tourists as well, and you risk months in prison if you disobey. Unless you plan to stay with close friends, leave at nightfall.

Occupied by Israel during the 1967 Six Day War, the West Bank is in a state of political limbo, neither granted autonomy, nor annexed outright by Israel. The area is under military administration. Jordan had conquered the territory in 1948, but angered the Palestinians by annexing it instead of creating a Palestinian state. Some refugees from the 1948 and 1967 wars still inhabit the hastily constructed camps at the edge of Hebron, Nablus, and Jericho. The U.N. has repeatedly condemned Israel's occupation of the West Bank, most recently in a July 29, 1980 resolution demanding unconditional withdrawal.

The Israelis fear that to return the Occupied Territories to the Arabs would be to guide the knife to their own throats. It would bring back the days when the 10-mile wide coastal strip, with ¾ of Israel's population, was well within the range of weapons based in the West Bank. Many Israelis dislike the "land-for-peace" formula, since they feel the territory was gained in wars where the Arabs were the aggressors. Eager to establish a friendly buffer against the Arab population, the government has overseen Israeli settlement in the Occupied Territories. Since the early '70s, the material lure of government subsidies and the spiritual attraction of reinhabiting their biblical homeland has drawn over 40,000 Jews to West Bank settlements, who would have to leave their new homes if the land were to be returned.

In December 1987, the Palestinians of the West Bank began the *intifadah.* Frustration about two decades of occupation erupted with a hail of stones and Molotov cocktails, as the generation of Palestinians which has grown up under the occupation began to express itself. The spark was an Arab League summit at which Palestinian concerns were ignored. Coupled with the violence has been non-violent resistance: nonpayment of taxes, resignations from government service, and the formation of independent "popular committees." The Jordanian response has been to abandon claims to the territory, and stop subsidies; the PLO has begun to step into the vaccuum. The Israeli response has been tear gas, detention, and intransigence; so far it has not quelled the uprising.

To minimize hostility toward yourself, be sensitive to the Palestinians and ignore Israel's current control of the West Bank. Say that you are in Palestine, not Israel. Refer to Jerusalem by the Arabic *El-Quds* ("the Holy"). Avoid being seen with Israeli soldiers, except in emergencies. You might want to pick up a copy of Berlitz' *Arabic for Travellers* to keep in plain sight. English-speaking (and even non-English-speaking) Palestinians will be delighted to help you learn Arabic. (For some elementary Arabic phrases, see Language in the Egypt Introduction below.) More importantly, *do not speak Hebrew,* even if it seems to be the easiest method of communication. If you want to travel successfully, respect the customs and traditions of the local populace. Men should always wear long pants and a shirt; women should wear a long skirt and a long-sleeved shirt. In addition, women should not travel alone on the West Bank.

The Jewish holidays and *shabbat* are not observed on the West Bank. The holy month of Ramadan, with its daily fasting and nightly feasting is observed in Muslim West Bank towns. Many restaurants will be closed until sundown (April 7-May 6 in 1989). For more on Islam, see the General Introduction.

Bethlehem

The little pale-white town of Bethlehem is one of the most beautiful and sacred places on the West Bank. It is here that the Bible says that Rachel died, that Ruth fell in love with Boaz, and that shepherd David was plucked from the fields to become king of Israel. But it was the birth of Jesus that transformed Bethlehem into a destination of religious pilgrimage. Micah predicted that the Messiah would come forth "out of Bethlehem"; the gospels claim this city as Jesus' birthplace. Luke 2:1-7 states that Joseph and Mary arrived in Bethlehem and Mary gave birth in a manger. Every Christmas Eve, a solemn procession goes forth from Jerusalem to the Church of the Nativity in Bethlehem to commemorate the birth of Jesus. If you visit Israel in the winter, you'll have three chances to catch the colorful parade: The Catholics and Protestants celebrate Christmas Eve on December 24, the Greek Orthodox on January 6, and the Armenians on January 18.

Bethlehem has not been spared from the tensions of the *intifadah*. However, the large number of souvenir shops, most of which remain open, attest to the fact that Bethlehem is the most touristed town on the West Bank. The Palestinians have become accustomed to invasions of tourists. Tight army security should allow you to tour the birthplace of the "Prince of Peace" in safety.

Practical Information

Government Tourist Information Office (GTIO): Manger Sq. (tel. 74 25 91). Excellent free map of the town (sometimes available at the Jerusalem tourist office), details about special events during Christmas and Easter, and transportation information. They may help you find accommodations when the cheap ones are full. Open Mon.-Fri. 8am-5pm, in winter Mon.-Fri. 8am-4pm, Sat. 8am-1pm. During Ramadan Sat.-Thurs. 9am-2:30pm.

Post Office: Manger Sq., beside the tourist office. Open Mon.-Wed. and Fri.-Sat. 8am-5pm, Thurs. 8am-1pm.

Bus Station: Manger St., 50m northwest of Manger Sq., down the hill and toward Jerusalem. Arab buses from Damascus or Jaffa Gate in Jerusalem: #22, 23 (continues to Hebron), 47 (continues east to Beit Sahur), and 60 (continues past to Abudiye). To Jerusalem (NIS1, ½ hr.) last bus back at around 6pm. Note that the Hebron bus stops only at Rachel's Tomb and at the intersection with Paul VI St., 3km west of Manger Sq.

Minibuses: Dahisheh (#1) from Manger Sq. down from the Palace Hotel, heading north to Rachel's Tomb then south to Dahisheh via the road to Hebron (daily every 30 min., 6:30am-8pm, NIS.50). To Beit Sahur from Cafe Salum on Manger St. between Manger Sq. and bus station.

Service Taxis: From Jaffa or Damascus Gate in Jerusalem to Manger Sq. until about 7pm (NIS1.50).

Banks: Leumi and **Barclay's Discount** in Manger Sq. Open Sun.-Thurs. 8:30am-1pm, Fri. 8:30am-noon.

Police Station: Manger Sq. (tel. 74 15 81).

Telephone Code: 02.

Bethlehem lies only 6km east of Jerusalem. Most of what you'll need in Bethlehem is located on or near **Manger Square,** across from the Basilica of the Nativity. The area enclosed by **Najajreh** and **Star Streets,** both of which begin at Manger Sq., comprises most of the town's shopping district, including the open-air **market.** This part of town has several **pharmacies,** which are permitted to stay open in the after- noon even during the strikes.

Accommodations, Camping, and Food

Although nowadays the town of Bethlehem offers more than mangers, rates and political tensions are much higher than in ancient times. Bethlehem is no longer a pleasant place to spend the night, and you will be hampered by the fact that all sources of food currently close at noon. Unless you are here during Christmas or Easter, stay in a cheap Jerusalem hostel and make Bethlehem a daytrip.

Franciscan Convent Pension, Milk Grotto St. (tel. 74 24 41), on your left past the Milk Grotto. Spotless, well-maintained rooms overlooking the valley. It helps to be able to *parler français ici.* Threesomes should go for the triple at the end of the hall. Curfew 9pm. Bed and breakfast NIS16. Dorm beds NIS8. Sheets NIS1.50. Possibility of floor space at holiday time.

Palace Hotel, Manger St. (tel. 74 27 98), just north of the basilica. Clean rooms. Trees and garden nearby. A good deal, and bargaining could make it better. Singles NIS18, doubles NIS36. Breakfast included.

St. Joseph's Home, Manger St. (tel. 74 24 97), ½km north of Manger Sq., next to the King David Cinema. The sign over the door proclaims "love and peace." Singles NIS35. Breakfast, lunch, and dinner included.

Al-Andalus Hotel, south side Manger Sq. (tel. 74 13 48), upstairs. If nobody is there, go to their restaurant on the side of the building. Green, green rooms. Singles with bath NIS23, doubles with bath NIS45. Bargain down winter price increases.

Ramat Rahel Campground (tel. 71 57 12) is located at a scenic spot midway be- tween Bethlehem and Jerusalem and charges NIS9 per person. Bring your own tent. (Breakfast NIS5.) Take bus #7. You can cool off in the *kibbutz* pool for NIS6.

For felafel fans and transportation enthusiasts, the stands in Manger Sq. and on Manger St. offer the cheapest stomach stuffers and the most accurate information on bus departures. The **Ruins al-Atlal Restaurant,** 1 block from Manger Sq. on Milk Grotto St., features a sit-down environment with neo-Crusader arches and farm im- plements for decor. Twelve kinds of appetizers are NIS3 each, *hoummus* with meat is NIS8, and a hamburger or omelette with salad and potatoes is NIS5. **Da'ana Bak- ery,** on Star St. past the Bethlehem Museum, displays an array of *pitot* and gigantic pancakes, any of which can be supplemented with provisions from one of the super- markets along Manger St. The only food available after noontime during the *intifa- dah* is from the stands outside on Star St., near the Da'ana bakery.

Sights

The massive **Basilica of the Nativity,** on Manger Sq., is a church masquerading as a fortress, which is not surprising if you consider the war-torn history of the re- gion. It is the oldest still-functioning church in the world. The first basilica was erected in 326 over the site of Jesus' birth by Constantine the Great, under the super- vision of his mother Helena. During the Persian invasion in 614, virtually every Christian shrine in the Holy Land was demolished with the exception of this basilica, reputedly spared because it contained a magnificent mosaic of the three wise men in the flowing robes characteristic of the Persian magi. The Crusaders extensively renovated the church, but it fell into disrepair after their defeat at the hands of the Muslims. By the fifteenth century it had become decrepit. Nevertheless, the basilica's importance as a holy shrine never faded, and in the ensuing centuries struggle for its control among Catholic, Greek, and Armenian Christians repeatedly led to bloodshed. Only in the 1840s was the church restored to its former dignity, but squabbles between the various sects over the division of the edifice continue, as the Franciscans and Anglicans joined the fray to secure their own enclaves. In recent years, an elaborate system of arranging schedules for worship has harmonized the competing claims of the different groups, but the confusion and tension after the Greek Orthodox Church refused to accept summer daylight saving time demonstrates the delicate balance of the system.

Despite its history, the Basilica of the Nativity is not very attractive. The lack of awe-inspiring artwork may disappoint the visitor, but the transition from the raucous sunlight to the cavernous interior is nonetheless impressive. The main entrance and windows were blocked up as a safety precaution during medieval times, resulting in the awkward appearance of the facade. To enter, you must bend over and step through the narrow, aptly-named Door of Humility—a reminder of the days when Christians wanted to prevent Muslims from entering the holy place on horseback. Orthodox Jews refuse to enter through this doorway, since it would mean bowing their heads in a Christian shrine. Inside the basilica, whiffs of incense and earthy browns and reds create a solemn atmosphere.

Fragments of beautiful mosaic floors are all that remain of Constantine's church, the original one here. View them beneath the huge wooden trap doors in the center of the marble Crusader floor. The four rows of reddish limestone Corinthian columns and the mosaic fragments along the walls date from Justinian's reconstruction. The oaken ceiling was a gift of England's King Edward IV, while the handsome icons adorning the altar were presented in 1764 by the Russian imperial family.

To reach the **Grotto of the Nativity,** the site of the manger where Jesus is believed to have been born, take one of the staircases on either side of the high altar in the nave on the basilica's main floor. From here, proceed to an underground sanctuary beneath the church. As you enter the dark and womblike grotto, notice the crosses etched into the columns on both sides of the doorway. This religious graffiti is the work of the pilgrims who have come here over the centuries. A star bearing the Latin inscription: *Hic De Virgine Maria Jesus Christus Natus Est* ("Here, of the Virgin Mary, Jesus Christ was born"), marks the spot. The star, first installed by the Catholics in 1717, was removed by the Greeks in 1847 and restored by the Turkish government in 1853. Quarrels over the star supposedly helped start the Crimean War. Don't block access to the star—many pilgrims come to Bethlehem solely to kneel and kiss the sacred spot. (Basilica complex open daily 7am-6pm; in winter 8am-5pm. Sometimes stays open 1 hr. longer. Men must wear long trousers, women long skirts. No bare shoulders.)

Simple, light, and airy, the adjoining **St. Catherine's Church,** built by the Franciscans in 1881, is a welcome contrast to the grim interior of the basilica. You can enter through the separate entrance to the north of the basilica, or you can face the altar in the basilica, and pass through one of the doorways in the wall on your left. There is a garden in the church's courtyard. St. Catherine's is famous as the site from which Midnight Mass is broadcast to a worldwide audience annually on Christmas Eve. Along the walls are superbly detailed wood carvings of the 14 Stations of the Cross. A staircase on the right side of St. Catherine's leads down to the **Tomb of St. Jerome,** but his remains have been removed to Rome. The first room, the **Chapel of St. Joseph,** commemorates the humble carpenter's vision of an angel who advised him to flee with his family to Egypt to avoid Herod's wrath. The burial cave of children slaughtered by King Herod (Matthew 2:6) lies beneath the altar and through the grille in the **Chapel of the Innocents.** Beyond the altar, a narrow passageway leads to the Grotto of the Nativity. The way is blocked by a thick wooden door pierced by a peephole that reveals the grotto. During earlier times of hostility between Christian sects, this glimpse was as close as Catholics could get to the Greek Orthodox-controlled shrine. To the right of the altar, a series of rooms contain the tombs of St. Jerome, St. Paula, and St. Paula's daughter Eustochia. These lead to the spartan cell where St. Jerome produced the Vulgate, the fourth century translation of the Hebrew Bible into Latin that was the standard Christian text throughout the Middle Ages and is still the accepted version for Catholics. Above the altar in this room is a mosaic illustrating this feat of translation.

The daily festivity in Bethlehem is the solemn procession conducted by the Franciscan Fathers to the basilica and underground chapels. To join in the 20 minutes of Gregorian chant and Latin prayer, arrive at St. Catherine's by noon (1pm during daylight saving time). If modern-day Bethlehem has not captured your imagination, this procession can restore a feeling of sanctity. St. Catherine's (and access to the tomb of St. Jerome) is open daily 7am-noon and 2-6pm; in winter 8am-noon and 2-5pm.

A five-minute walk from the Basilica of the Nativity down Milk Grotto St. is the **Milk Grotto Church.** The cellar here is supposedly the cave where the Holy Family hid while fleeing from Herod into Egypt. The cave and church take their names from the original milky white color of the rocks, long since blackened by candle smoke. According to legend, some of Mary's milk fell while she was nursing the infant Jesus, turning the rocks white. Male visitors may feel a bit out of place amid the curious stares of women who come here to pray for fertility. (Open daily 8-11:45am and 2-5pm.) Ring the bell for a monk to admit you.

A ½km north of Manger Sq. along Star St., the three unremarkable restored cisterns of the **Well of David** (tel. 24 77; open daily 7am-noon and 2-7pm) sit in the parking lot of the King David Cinema. When a thirsty David, in battle against the Philistines, was brought water from the enemy's well, he in turn offered it as a sacrifice to God (II Samuel 23:13-17). The cinema (tel. 74 29 39) presents four daily showings of *Jesus,* a tasteful dramatization of Christ's life filmed in Israel under the supervision of a team of historical and biblical scholars. (Showtimes at 10:30am, 2pm, 5pm, and 8:30pm. Admission NIS12.)

The **Tomb of Rachel** is a sacred site for Judaism. Throughout history synagogues have been built and destroyed on the spot, but unless a sense of its religious significance imbues your appreciation, you may find the existing shrine disappointing. A red cloth covers the cenotaph. On one side are fervently praying Hassidic men, and on the other weeping Yemenite women. If you get close to the shrine, be sure you're on the correct side. Rachel died in Bethlehem while giving birth to Benjamin (Genesis 35:19-20), and she became a symbol of maternal devotion and empathetic suffering. Despite her own misfortune, the tomb is revered as the place to pray for a child or for a safe delivery. Men should be sure to don a paper *kippah* (head covering) available at the entrance. The tomb is on the northern edge of town on the road to Jerusalem, at the intersection of Manger St. and Hebron Rd. (Open Sun.-Thurs. 8am-5pm, Fri. 8am-1pm.) All buses between Jerusalem and Bethlehem or Hebron pass the tomb, located 3km north of Manger Sq. Minibus #1 also swings by the tomb.

Bethlehem means "House of Bread" in Hebrew (*Beit Leḥem*) and "House of Meat" in Arabic (*Beit Laḥm*). The bounteous **market,** which clings to the town's steep streets, attests to the accuracy of both names. Unlike the other shops in town, the Bethlehem *souk* makes little attempt to cater to tourists. The Arab women wear intricately embroidered traditional garb, and the men wear the *kaffiyeh,* their traditional headdress. Business is carried on under the shade of tattered burlap and nylon. The market is located up the stairs from Paul VI St. across from the Syrian Church about 2 blocks west of Manger Sq. A few blocks down Paul VI from the market, toward the basilica, is the **Bethlehem Museum,** featuring exhibits of Arab crafts and traditional costumes. (Open Mon.-Sat. 10am-noon and 2:30-5pm.)

Beyond the Arab village of Beit Sahur, on the eastern edge of Bethlehem, is the **Field of Ruth,** believed to be the place where the events in the biblical Book of Ruth occurred. The name of the village in Hebrew is "House of the Shepherds," and

Christian tradition holds that this is Shepherd's Field, where those tending their flocks were greeted by the angel who declared the birth of Jesus (Luke 2:9-11). Take bus #47 from the stop next to the police station in Manger Sq., get off at Beit Sahur, and walk 20 minutes to the site. Otherwise, you can walk the 4km from Bethlehem. Signs will direct you; follow Shepherd's St., starting in Manger Sq. in front the of the basilica. (Open daily 8-11am and 2-5:30pm.)

Four kilometers south of Bethlehem, just off the road to Hebron, stand three large **reservoirs,** clearly great technological feats in their time. Local tradition holds them to be the work of King Solomon, but excavations indicate that the reservoirs might even predate him. They were used by the Romans and even the Turks to supply water for Bethlehem and Jerusalem. The immense, shaded basins make a scenic, restful picnic spot. The small, nearby Turkish fortress dates from the seventeenth century. From Bethlehem, take minibus #1 to Dahisheh. From Damascus or Jaffa Gate in Jerusalem, take Arab bus #23 to Hebron and ask to get off at Dashit (NIS1.50, 40 min.).

Near Bethlehem

Herodian

Rising from the plains of the Judean desert 10km southwest of Bethlehem are the ruins of **Herodian,** a magnificent fortified palace perched atop a conical peak. King Herod, who was haunted by fears of assassination, ordered the construction of this hideout in the first century B.C.E. Enclosed within the massive circular double walls and guarded by four watch towers were all the comforts of Rome: Palace, garden, bathhouse, and "frigidarium" for storage. Fifteen meters below the floor, two giant cisterns were filled with water transported in by donkeys. Originally, a marble staircase provided sole access to the inside. Though engineered to protect the Roman-sponsored ruler from discontented Jews, the palace actually became a rebel stronghold during the Jewish revolts of the first and second centuries C.E. The view from the top is breathtaking—Jerusalem lies to the north, Bethlehem to the west, the Dead Sea is visible to the east in clear weather, and the desolate Judean Desert stretches to the south.

To reach Herodian, take **bus** #47 from Jerusalem or Bethlehem to Beit Sahur and ask someone to show you the unmarked bus stop for Herodian. Buses #52 and 62 also run, but infrequently and irregularly; the locals in Beit Sahur seem to know when the next bus will come. Alternatively, you can continue past Shepherd's Field on the road from Beit Sahur and hike the 7km from the marked turn-off. From the road below the fortress, a 15-minute climb brings you to the top, and provides a firsthand demonstration of the difficulty of a frontal attack. Without bargaining, taxis from Bethlehem will carry six or seven people round-trip for about NIS12. (Open Sat.-Thurs. 8am-6pm, Fri. 8am-5pm. Admission NIS1.50, students NIS.75.)

Monasteries of Mar Saba and St. Theodosius

Even more remarkable and more isolated than Herodian is the **Mar Saba Monastery.** Carved into the walls of a remote canyon, the extensive monastery complex hangs precariously above the sewer-like Qidron River. It was built opposite the cave, marked by a cross, where St. Sabas began an ascetic life in 478 C.E. The monastery was built for his disciples. Sacked by Arabs and Bedouin, the complex has been extensively restored by the Russian Orthodox church. Only 15 monks now live here, though the valley of caves once held 5000 believers. The road running west of the monastery brings you to some of these caves. The bones of St. Sabas are on display in the main church. Women are strictly forbidden to enter and must view the chapels and buildings from the safe distance of a tower near the monastery. Men must wear long pants and long sleeves to be admitted. To enter the monastery, pull the chain on the large blue door. Once inside, you'll be given a five-minute tour in English by one of the monks. The monks occasionally ignore the doorbell on Sundays and late in the afternoon, so try to arrive early on a weekday. There is no entrance fee, but it's customary to make a donation.

The road to Mar Saba passes by the **Monastery of St. Theodosius,** built over a cave reputed to have been the resting place of the Magi on their way from Bethlehem. The sacred cave was also the home of this fifth-century saint, who spent most of his 105 years here after leaving his birthplace of Cappadocia. The tall walls and imposing steel gate were designed to deter unwelcome visitors, but if you persistently rattle the doorbell, one of the monks will eventually admit you. Inside, there is little of interest apart from the seventh-century mosaics and masonry preserved under the shed in the central courtyard.

To reach both monasteries, take **Arab bus** #60, which leaves every couple of hours from the Bethlehem station, to the Arab village of Abusiye; the last bus returns to Bethlehem at 4pm. Bus #60 originates in Jerusalem. St. Theodosius' monastery will be unmistakable on the rise to the left of the road; it overlooks Abusiye. From here it's a 7km, one-and-a-half hour walk to Mar Saba: Continue along the paved road for just under 1km until you reach a fork. The left-hand branch, heading uphill, leads to Mar Saba. Once you leave the *baksheesh*-demanding children of Abusiye behind, the scenic 6km trek provides a glimpse of the silence and serenity that attracted the monks and their followers here. Hitching is not advisable, but if you want to avoid the climb back out of the valley, there is a good chance that you can meet sympathetic tourists at the monastery who will squeeze you in for the return to Bethlehem. Service **taxis** from Manger Sq. won't do the round-trip for under NIS15, though for only a few shekels more you can visit Herodian as well.

Jericho

Descending from Jerusalem into the scorched Jordan River Valley, the centuries peel away until you abruptly reach the refreshing oasis of Jericho, possibly first city in the world. The precious water that still bubbles up from underground springs has historically made Jericho a tempting conquest. Only the vicious heat and humidity remind you of the city's proximity to the Dead Sea and below-sea-level altitude. The greenery of modern Jericho contrasts with the eerie desert to the north. A largely abandoned refugee camp stands darkly on the edge of town as a reminder of the city's twentieth-century battles.

Jericho is best known for the biblical account of its walls, the world's first, which came a-tumblin' down when Joshua sounded the trumpets. According the Bible, two spies sent into town by Joshua, Moses' successor, were sheltered in the house of the harlot, Rahab. In exchange for the deed, her family was to be spared if she marked her house in scarlet. When the tribes of Israel attacked, the entire city was destroyed with the exception of the single house with a scarlet cord dangling from its window (Joshua 2-6).

Practical Information, Accommodations, and Food

Forty kilometers east of Jerusalem, Jericho lies on the road to Amman, Jordan and at the junction of the highway to the Galilee. The King Hussein/Allenby Bridge, located 10km east of Jericho, has served as the only route across the Jordan River since the King Abdullah Bridge to the south was destroyed in wartime.

Arab bus #28 (NIS1.80) from the Damascus Gate station runs to the bus stop on Ein al-Sultan St., 1 block north of the central traffic circle. **Egged buses** #961 and 963 (NIS3.60, 1 hr.) from Jerusalem's central bus station will drop you near the ancient city, as will buses to the Galilee. Arab buses stop running at 5pm, but you can catch Egged buses for Jerusalem until about 7pm from the stop on the corner of Ein al-Sultan and Jaffa St. in Jericho. After that, you may still be able to catch a *sherut* taxi from the taxi stand on the square in front of the municipality building. These shared taxis run frequently between Jericho's main square and the Damascus Gate taxi stand in Jerusalem.

Because of the Israeli military base next to the city, Jericho is one of the safer places to visit on the West Bank. The present town of 7000 Arabs is actually a few kilometers south of the ancient city. Modern Jericho, a pleasant oasis town, offers shady eucalyptus trees, a colorful market, and several streetside cafes. The main square, or traffic circle, is the focus of town life and of the transportation services. Most of Jericho's other services are also located here, including the **police station** (tel. 25 21). The best way to see the sights in Jericho is with a completely cool, multipurpose bicycle. The **bicycle shop,** just off the central square and east of the municipality building, rents balloon-tire bombers for NIS1 per hour. The owner of the shop will ask for a deposit; give him cash so you can save your student ID for discounts at the sights. He may also ask for advance payment—two hours should be enough. On Jericho's flat terrain, cycling is enjoyable and cooling. Be aware that locals bike on the left side of the road. A **taxi** will take you on a loop of the sights for NIS13.

During the summer months, virtually no visitors stay overnight in Jericho, and neither should you. If the temperature and politics cool down in the winter, the only option, **Hisham's Palace Hotel** (tel. 227), is next to the bus stop on Ein al-Sultan St., 1 block north of the main square. It's empty, hot, cavernous, and a bit run-down, but open. (Singles NIS15, doubles NIS30. Bargain heavily.)

Much farther down Ein al-Sultain St. in a residential area is the **Maxim Restaurant.** This clean, attractive eatery offers an all-you-can-eat selection of salads (NIS6.50) and meats (NIS12). Despite its tourist-trap location next to ancient Jericho, the **Mount of Temptation Restaurant** offers identical fare at similar prices. Both restaurants are open in the afternoon.

Sights

Jericho's two most popular sights, Hisham's Palace and ancient Jericho, lie on the outskirts of town. They are best visited in a 6km loop by bicycle or taxi. Since a cluster of restaurants and a cooling spring near the ancient city provide a pleasant rest stop, you might want to visit Hisham's Palace first.

To reach the ruins of **Hisham's Palace,** follow the signs along Qasr Hisham St., which heads north from the eastern side of Jericho's main square. The palace is 3km north on paved roads; look for the turn-off, which leads you 250m from the main road to the palace. Coming from ancient Jericho, head north on the main road leading through the Ein al-Sultan refugee camp. After 1.5km, turn right on the road back to Jericho town; the turn-off to Hisham's Palace will be almost immediately to your left.

The extensive ruin of Hisham's Palace, a splendid example of early Islamic architecture, is an outstanding attraction. Known as *Khirbet al-Mafjar* in Arabic, the palace was designed as a winter retreat from Damascus for the Umayyad Caliph Hisham. The palace was begun in 724 C.E. and completed in 743; only four years later, the building was flattened by an earthquake. The window in the courtyard is in the shape of the six-pointed Umayyad star, and is the site's most renowned feature. The tall pillars on the right mark the pool; nearby is the palace's guest house with the striking "Tree of Life" mosaic covering the dais. Descend into the bath room, with its partially visible mosaic. The small museum by the entrance houses pots and lamps from the site, but the Rockefeller Museum in Jerusalem contains many of the more impressive finds, including a statue believed to represent Caliph Hisham. (Palace open Sun.-Thurs. 8am-4pm, Fri. 8am-3pm. Admission NIS3, students NIS1.50.)

To travel the 2km from Hisham's Palace to ancient Jericho, go back to the main road, continue north (right) for about 50m, then turn left at the intersection with the highway from Jericho to Galilee. Turn south toward Jericho (left), and pass through the Ein al-Sultan refugee camp until you reach ancient Jericho. Since the camp is nearly deserted, it is safe to bike along this road, although exploration is discouraged. This route takes you past a small, modern building housing the mosaic floor of a fifth-century **synagogue.** Under the large menorah depicted in the center of the floor, the Hebrew inscription reads *Shalom al Yisrael* (Peace unto Israel). An orange sign marks the turn-off for the synagogue along a paved road. (Open daily 8am-5pm. Admission NIS1.50, students NIS.75.).

Ancient Jericho is an unmistakable dusty heap of ruined walls rising from the palm groves. Called Tel es-Sultan, the mound contains layer upon layer of remains from ancient cities. The oldest fortifications, 12m down, are 7000 years old. They form the basis of Jericho's claim to be the oldest fortified town in the world. Some of the finds date from the early Neolithic period, including a tower, leading archeologists to suspect that Jericho was inhabited as early as the eighth millennium B.C.E. A limited amount of excavation has exposed many levels of ancient walls, some of them 3.5m thick and 5.5m high. Your imagination will have to substitute for visible splendor at this distinctly unphotogenic site. (Open Sat.-Thurs. 8am-5pm, Fri. 8am-3pm. Admission NIS1.50, students NIS.75.)

To reach ancient Jericho directly from the modern town, follow Ein al-Sultan northwest from the main square. After 1½km, you will reach a cluster of kiosks and restaurants. Turn right on the road toward Galilee to reach the ancient sight that is adjacent to these shops. This trip is an easy walk from the bus stop.

The sea of abandoned huts visible from the *tel* is the **Ein al-Sultan Refugee Camp.** Most of the refugees fled across the Jordan River during the Six Day War, though a few hundred still remain.

Across the street from the ancient city is **Elisha's Spring,** known to the Arabs as *Ein al-Sultan* (Sultan's Spring). Jewish tradition holds this to be the fountain that the people of Jericho required the prophet Elisha to purify (II Kings 2:19-22). Though there isn't much to see apart from the modern pump house, the water is still drinkable and refreshing. Ignore the outdated sign that says "No admittance. United Nations Property."

The imposing Greek Orthodox **monastery** rests precariously on the edge of a cliff among the mountains west of Jericho. The peak on which the monastery stands is believed to be the New Testament's Mount of Temptation. The complex of buildings stands before a grotto, the spot where Jesus is said to have fasted for 40 days and 40 nights after his baptism in the Jordan River (Matthew 4:1-11). Six wizened Greek monks now live in the monastery, which was built in 1895. Ask one to point out the rock where Jesus was tempted by the devil and served by angels. An inscription in ancient Greek describes the event. The road to the monastery heads past the shops near ancient Jericho. The ascent to the monastery, only a few kilometers long, is steep.

The summit of the mountain, named **Qarantal** after the Latin word for "forty," also serves as a pedestal for the Maccabbean **Castle of Dok,** beside which lie the remains of a fourth-century Christian chapel. (Monastery open Mon.-Sat. 8am-5pm; in winter 7am-2pm and 3-4pm. Church often closed by 11am.) Access to the summit of the hill and its ruins is officially blocked, but if you befriend the attendant, he may open the door for you. Another kilometer or so down the road from Qarantal, next to the natural springs of Ein Duq, are the remains of an ancient Jewish settlement and a fifth-century **synagogue** known as Na'Aron. A part of the mosaic floor depicting Daniel in the company of lions was destroyed by iconoclastic Jews who looked on any form of pictorial representation as idol worship; several other sections of the floor seem to have suffered a similar fate. To visit the site, ask for the key in the restaurant at Casino al-Amara in Ein Duq. To reach Qarantal and Na'Aron, take the turn-off to the left just before the site of ancient Jericho.

Near Jericho

The road from Jerusalem to Jericho cuts through the harsh desert landscape of the Judean wilderness. Bedouin camps with their large black tents line both sides. About 8km before Jericho, the **Mosque of Nabi Musa** stands on a hill in the middle of the desert, a short distance from the road. This spot is revered throughout the

Muslim world as the grave of the prophet Moses, and many Muslims wish to be buried next to him. An enormous stone cenotaph marks what is reputed to be his tomb. Islamic tradition holds that Allah carried the bones of the prophet here for the faithful to come and pay their respects. The thirteenth-century Mamluk mosque containing the prophet's tomb is open during Muslim prayer times (dawn, noon, 3:30pm, 7pm, 8:30pm, and Fri. all day). During the month of April, as many as half a million pilgrims from all over the Islamic world make their way to Nabi Musa; throughout this period, only Muslims are admitted.

Depending on which side you talk to, **Ma'ale Adumim** is either the most distant suburb of Jerusalem, or the Jewish settlement closest to the city. Christians hold that the police station here occupies what was originally the site of the Inn of the Good Samaritan.

About 10km east of Jericho is **al-Maghtes,** the spot on the Jordan River where John the Baptist is believed to have baptized Jesus. A nineteenth-century Greek Orthodox monastery marks the spot where Christians still come to immerse themselves. The site remains under military supervision, so in order to visit it, you need a special permit. Ask at the police station for details. To get there from Jericho, take a sharp right at the signpost as you leave the traffic circle, where you would otherwise go straight for Hisham's Palace.

Although the **Jordan River** is Israel's longest (94.8km), most visitors are disappointed by its narrowness. Since 1967, the river has marked the ceasefire line between Israel and Jordan. The **King Hussein/Allenby Bridge** is the only point at which you can cross the river and enter Jordan. (See Border Crossings in the General Introduction.) Because of a special arrangement between Israel and Jordan, Palestinian women and older Palestinian men who live on the West Bank pass back and forth freely to conduct business and visit their families. Young men must secure permission from the Israeli military to leave. Tourists who don't have an Israeli visa in their passport should expect no problems.

Wadi Qelt

To hike through **Wadi Qelt,** (*Nahal Perat* in Hebrew), where the arid Judean desert cracks open to reveal an oasis, is like wandering through a treasure chest. For ages, gleaming diamond springs and emerald foliage have provided a haven for wildlife: Several civilizations, tapping the desert's precious secret, have built aqueducts, palaces, and monasteries. Threading 28km between imperious limestone cliffs and undulating ridges of bone-white chalk, the wadi descends 395m below sea level. Provided that you plan beforehand and take precautions along the way, it's a reasonably safe adventure that offers more drama than the resort oasis at Ein Gedi.

The most interesting and accessible section of the wadi extends from the spring of **Ein Qelt,** past the sixth century **Monastery of St. George,** and down into Jericho, 10km east. The trek takes about four hours, plus time for a picnic, a swim, and a visit to the ruins and caves along the way. The best place to start is at the turn-off from the Jerusalem-Jericho highway, about 9km west of Jericho, marked by the orange sign for "St. George's Monastery." To reach the turn-off and begin the trek, take **Egged bus** #73 from the bus stop, across from the central bus station; buses depart at 6:15am and 2:30pm. For late risers, **Arab bus** #28 to Jericho (leaving hourly) passes the same turn-off. By asking for St. George's Monastery, Ein Qelt, and Mitzpe Yeriho, you can probably convince the driver to let you off at the right place. With either bus, the trip from Jerusalem takes almost an hour. If you're driving, it is possible to skip the hike and drive most of the way to St. George's by following the signs from the turn-off on the highway.

From the turn-off, follow the sign that points out a deteriorating paved road, which forks after a five-minute walk. Another sign indicates the right branch for the monastery, but you'll bypass most of the hike if you go that way. Instead, take the left branch, and after 100m turn right onto the dirt road that heads north.

Twenty minutes of winding your way through the barren rock hills leads you down to the valley, Ein Qelt springs, and the **Wadi Qelt Nature Reserve.** Near the valley floor, an enormous wall on the left once supported the Herodian aqueduct. The aqueduct, restored during the Mandate, conducts water from Ein Fuwar spring, several kilometers west, to the Cypros fort at the mouth of the wadi near Jericho. Climb up the opposite bank of the wadi and turn right onto the path along the modern aqueduct. From this point the trail to Jericho is clearly marked by red blazes. After following the aqueduct for a half-hour, the trail descends to the dry riverbed. As you meander for another 40 minutes, don't be paranoid about being watched from the abandoned grottos and dolomite overhangs. You'll arrive beneath a series of arches built to allow the ancient aqueduct to span the wadi from north to south. Just beyond, a cross carved on the bluff overhead marks the pilgrims' route to St. George's; as you round the next bend, the oversize sandcastle looms into sight.

St. George's Monastery dates from the fifth to sixth centuries C.E. It was built near the cave of Horeb, where the prophet Elijah is said to have hidden to escape the wrath of Jezebel, queen of Samaria (1 Kings 18-19). The floor of St. George's Church is sprinkled with Byzantine mosaics. Look for the likeness of a two-headed eagle, the Byzantine symbol of power. The neighboring St. John's Church houses a spooky collection of skulls and bones of monks who were slaughtered when the Persians swept through the valley in 614 C.E. The Greek Orthodox monks who maintain the monastery can refill your canteen for the rest of the journey into Jericho. (Open Mon.-Sat. 6am-5pm; Nov.-March 7am-3pm, occasionally the door remains open later. Admission NIS.30. Modest dress required.)

When you leave the monastery, stay on the same side of the wadi, as the trail climbs 100m above the bed and passes seemingly inaccessible caves and ruins of monasteries that cling to the gorge's sheer rock faces. After a half-hour, the trail splits; take the right branch, crossing the wadi and climbing the other side into a mostly abandoned refugee camp that lies southwest of Jericho. Follow the dirt road by the mosque with the minaret, through banana plantations and into town. To reach the center of town, turn left when you reach the paved road by the Israeli army installation. The half-hour walk takes you past the archeological site of **Tel Abu Alayiq,** where the Hasmonean, Herodian, and Roman ruins span both banks of the wadi. Particularly impressive is the first-century B.C.E. winter palace where King Herod died. You can also reach the ruins by taking the dirt road that turns off the Jerusalem road between the "Wadi Qelt" restaurant and the Israeli military compound at the southern edge of town.

For those interested in exploring other sections along the wadi and around Jericho, the **Society for the Protection of Nature in Israel** office in Jerusalem sells an excellent detailed Hebrew topographical map of the Judean Desert (NIS12). The staff can also provide information about different routes, though they will probably try to dissuade you from setting off on your own. They organize groups led by English-speaking guides who are well-informed about the wadi's natural and artificial phenomena. However, because of the number (up to 20 people) and diversity of participants, the pace is slow.

For any hike in the wadi, make sure to wear a hat and bring plenty of water. In summer, many of the seasonal waterfalls and pools dry up, but you can splash around in the aqueduct. Drinking from the aqueduct, though preferable to dehydration, is not recommended, and you probably won't be tempted after a few goat droppings float by. In the winter and spring, too much water may be a problem: Storms can arise suddenly and flash floods in the gorge are a real danger. Keep an eye on the weather, and climb to high ground at the first sign of rain.

Hebron (Hevron or el-Khalil)

Hevron comes from the Hebrew word for friend and *el-Khalil ar-Rahman* (the full Arabic name) means "friend of the compassionate." The friend in question is Abraham, the common ancestor of both peoples. Friendship, however, is not the word to describe the Jewish-Palestinian relationship here. The predominantly Arab inhabitants of Hebron harbor fierce resentment over the two decades of Israeli occupation. Arab antipathy has been further strengthened by attempts to reestablish a Jewish quarter within the town and by the proximity of Qiryat Arba, a controversial Jewish settlement.

The only remaining basis for Hebron's name is seen at a small cave. Here, three great religions converge around the haunting tombs of the biblical matriarchs and patriarchs. Mosque and synagogue stand across from one another in a small couryard, and Muslim, Jewish, and Christian chants merge in prayer to common ancestors.

In biblical times, Hebron was known as Qiryat Arba ("District of the Four"). One legend maintains that the "four" referred to four giants who fell from heaven after a revolt against God. In the Book of Numbers, when Moses sent spies to Canaan to bring back a report on the conditions there, the scouts returned with wide-eyed reports of Hebron's giants. As proof, they brought bunches of grapes so large that a single cluster had to be carried by two men; this image is the ubiquitous symbol of Israel's Ministry of Tourism. You can still sample Hebron's grapes; grab a bunch at the entrance to the Oak of Abraham.

Hebron's Jewish population remained small until the nineteenth century when many Hassidic and Russian Jews emigrated here. In 1925, an entire *yeshiva* moved from Russia to Hebron, and a Hadassah medical clinic was opened. The local Arabs took offense, and in the 1929 riots that swept Palestine, virtually the entire Jewish community perished. The British administrators took the survivors to Jerusalem, and Hebron had no Jewish inhabitants until its capture in 1967. Since then, a significant number of Jews have returned to the area, settling outside the town in Qiryat Arba. Nearby Kfar Etzion, destroyed in 1948, has also been resettled. Since then, the city has been guarded round the clock by the Israeli army, and for the past decade outbreaks of revolutionary unrest have frequently made international headlines. Guardhouses that resemble airport control towers are located in front of Jewish buildings in downtown Hebron.

Practical Information

Arabs here carefully distinguish between Israelis and tourists. You can help them and further guarantee your safety by avoiding all things Israeli or Hebrew. If you consult with Israeli soldiers, do it where you won't be seen. Be discreet, but this may be the only place in the world where you should be sure to brand yourself as a tourist. Visitors should make an effort to be respectful of Muslim traditions. An excellent safety precaution is to stay in areas patrolled by Israeli soldiers, such as King David St. and the area around the Cave of Mahpela. But if you are lost, look it—many young Arabs in Hebron love to practice their English by giving meticulous directions.

Leave Hebron well before sunset. Don't even think about investigating the nightlife. This is the most dangerous city in the West Bank. Before you come, check the security situation in the newspapers, at your consulate, the GTIO, and the Office of Visitor Information (212 Jaffa Rd., Jerusalem). You cannot be too careful.

Located a scenic 35km south of Jerusalem on the road to Be'ersheva, Hebron is the only urban center on the West Bank south of Bethlehem. **Egged buses** #34, 440, and 443 come from the Jerusalem central bus station and stop in the main square in front of the Cave of Mahpela after stopping in the Qiryat Arba settlement. Buses run until dark. These buses should be used as a last resort, and then on the way out of the West Bank. **Arab bus** #23 (NIS1.50), which runs frequently from Damascus Gate, is a more diplomatic way to arrive, and will drop you in the city center, where King Faisal, King David, and Khalil ar-Rahman St. converge. From here, a 1km walk along **King David Street** brings you to the tombs; follow the signs east to the Cave of Mahpela.

Service taxis shuttle between Jerusalem's Jaffa and Damascus Gates and Hebron's King David St., near the cave and the old market. Taxis cost about 30%

more than the buses, but they run until later in the evening. The last Arab bus for Jerusalem departs at around 6pm, and stops on **King Faisal Street,** just off the city center. Most of the town's services, including the **post office, bank, hospital** (tel. 97 61 26), and **police station** (tel. 971 44) are also located here.

Most **food** can only be bought at the **market.** Discreetly check with the soldiers at the cave first as to whether this is safe. Here you will find fresh produce, grocery stores, a few cafes, and felafel stands.

The Cave of Mahpela

Abraham chose Hebron, the highest of the four holy cities (at an altitude of 1000m), as the site of his family cemetery. Beginning with his wife, Sarah (Genesis 23:17-19), all the subsequent matriarchs and patriarchs but one were buried here, in the Cave of Mahpela. The exception is Jacob's second wife, Rachel, who died on the way to Bethlehem. *Mahpela* means a double cave, or a cave over a cave. Some claim that Abraham chose the cave because he knew it to be the burial place of Adam and Eve. Consequently, many rabbis explain that Qiryat Arba refers not to four giants, but to the four married couples who are supposedly buried here: Abraham and Sarah, Isaac and Rebecca, Jacob and Leah, and Adam and Eve. The patch of land above the tombs has been bitterly contested throughout history by Crusaders, Muslims, and Jews. Presently, it is the only religious shrine in Israel where both Jews and Muslims worship together. Consider hiring a guide (about NIS5). Not only will a guide be able to point out interesting features of the building, but you may feel more comfortable walking around with an Arab.

The colossal edifice that now stands over the Cave of Mahpela looks more like a fortress than a house of worship. Like many structures in Israel, the shrine's patch-work architecture reflects its rich history. Both Jewish and Muslim traditions attribute the original stonework of the building to King Solomon's reign. The king is said to have enlisted the help of demons to cut and move the large blocks. The oldest surviving sections, forming the base of the 3m thick walls, date archeologically from King Herod's time. The largest stone is 8m wide and weighs 40 tons. Notice that the massive stones were fitted together so precisely that no mortar was necessary. During succeeding centuries the building fell into disrepair, though a small syna-gogue was continually maintained inside the ruins. In 372 C.E., the Byzantines built a roof and used it as a church. During this period, the Byzantines built the shrines over the graves. In 686 C.E., Muslims took over and added a mosque. In 1103, the Crusaders conquered Hebron and promptly transformed the mosque into a church. After they were driven out in turn, the Mamluks added the current mosque and two handsome square minarets. Until 1929, Jews were allowed to stand and pray, but were permitted to ascend only as far as the seventh step, the level of the holy grotto. The Israelis have now dug the steps away, thereby removing the symbol of their former second-class status. On the south side of the building, the steps are still visible. If you look closely, you'll notice that the wall has been blackened by smoke. This marks the spot of the seventh step where certain Orthodox Jews still come to pray and burn candles. Upon entering, male visitors should don a paper *kippah,* available at the top of the staircase.

From the staircase, a long, open hallway, beside a mosque carpeted with gorgeous Persian rugs, leads to a courtyard. Behind gratings in the small synagogue on the right, large cenotaphs (empty tombs) commemorate Jacob and Leah. Across the courtyard, in a second synagogue, two more huge boxes covered with elaborate cal-ligraphy stand above the tombs of Abraham and Sarah. The actual remains lie 18m below, in the Cave of Mahpela. A locked trap-door in the mosque leads down to the cave itself. Oil is lowered in to keep the candles burning in the cave. To find the final pair, pass through the synagogue in the **Great Mosque,** where the ceno-taphs of Isaac and Rebecca each occupy a small hut. The mosque is square, in the style of early Mamluk architecture, and decorated with inlaid wood and mosaic patterns. Be sure to note the thirteenth-century stained-glass window and the ornate walnut pulpit, dating from 1091, next to the *mihrab* (prayer niche) on the south wall. In the small adjoining women's mosque (on your left as you leave the court-yard) is a window containing a stone with an undistinguished imprint. According to legend, this is Adam's footprint, made when he came here after expulsion from Eden. Opposite the courtyard exit, yet another mosque contains a cenotaph dedicated to Joseph. In the Koran, God told Moses to move Joseph's remains to Hebron. For the half-hour following the five daily calls to prayer, and the entire afternoon during Ramadan, the main mosques are closed to non-Muslims, though passage through the surrounding hallways and synagogues remains free. (Open Sun.-Thurs. 7am-7pm, Sat. 11:30am-7pm. Fri. closed to non-Muslims. Modest dress required.)

Other Sights

The remains of Hebron's **Harat al-Yahud** (Jewish Quarter) stand next to the tombs. The sixteenth-century Sephardic **Synagogue Abram Avino** (Our Father Abraham), has been uncovered and reconstructed, along with some of the surrounding ruins. Hidden behind the shops that line Khalil ar-Rahman St., just west of the Cave of Mahpela, you will find **Birket al-Sultan** (Pool of the Sultan). This enormous tank, now filled more with tires than water, was reputedly the spot where David had the slayer of Saul's son hanged. You'll see several heavily guarded buildings sprouting Israeli flags in central Hebron. These are inhabited by diehard Zionist families intent on reclaiming the Jewish Quarter, a policy that the Israeli government has not supported except with army protection. Shops and a *yeshiva* now number among the controversial Jewish holdings here.

Farther along, to the right of the street, sprawls Hebron's **market,** one of the largest and most interesting on the West Bank. Rather than just another tourist bazaar, the Hebron market is distinguished as a place where Arabs and Bedouin do business. The vaulted ceilings and booths indicate the structure is medieval Crusader, but the artifacts sold are distinctly Middle Eastern. Though attractive and unique, the blown glassware, which has been crafted here since the Middle Ages, is too delicate to travel well. In the market you will also find skinned camels hanging upside down and various animal heads. Discreetly ask the Israeli soldiers before entering the area. Stay close to your companions, and remember the route out.

North of the market, endless tunnels and arched passageways run beneath the houses and ruins of this ancient city, forming a vast labyrinth of covered alleys. The tunnels of this *casbah* are a delight to explore, but are very dangerous. Keep a watchful eye on anyone who seems to be following you. Another area where you can roam is the Harat al-Yahud on the south side of the Cave of Mahpela. The multi-storied stone buildings have similar covered passageways and narrow stairways. Arab families occupy a few, but the rest have been neglected since 1929. Skip this if you don't feel lucky. Once again, ask soldiers before exploring unpatrolled areas.

Two kilometers west of the town center, a comparatively safe five-minute walk beyond the Arab bus station, you will find the **Oak of Abraham.** This is the purported site of the biblical Mamre, where Abraham pitched his tent to welcome tired travelers and was visited by three angels who told him of the impending birth of Isaac (Genesis 18). The oak belongs to the Russian Orthodox Church, which built a monastery around it in 1871. According to Christian tradition, the Holy Family rested here on their way back from Egypt. Unfortunately for the tree, travelers since the Middle Ages have removed splinters from it for good luck, and now nails, baling wire, and rusty steel braces have replaced much of the original wood. Despite its convincing decrepitude, some challenge the tree's authenticity and argue that this oak is a mere 600 years old and that the oak referred to in Genesis actually stood at **Bet Ilanim,** north of Hebron, on Keizun al-Rama St. Excavations at this site have also uncovered enormous Herodian walls, as well as traces of Roman temples and a fourth-century Christian chapel. If the front gate is locked, you can walk right in from the other side of the monastery's grounds.

The streets of Hebron are worth exploring, with due care, for their wealth of hidden monuments from past ages. An excellent example of Mamluk architecture is the thirteenth-century minaret of the **Ali Baka Mosque,** on al-Ai Yubi St. Most of the mosque is presently under reconstruction, but the Muslims continue to pray within its half-built walls. In the southwest part of Hebron are the ruins of a Crusader fort (*Deir al-Arbain*). The site is holy to both Jews and Muslims, for beneath the ruins are believed to lie the tombs of Ruth and her grandson Jesse, father of King David. Follow the signs from King David St. for the neighboring Jewish Cemetery, which features a monument to the victims of Hebron's 1929 riots.

Qiryat Arba, less than 1km northeast of the cave, is unusual among West Bank settlements for its proximity to a large Arab population center. Religiously motivated settlers founded Qiryat Arba in 1972 as a compromise with the government, which did not want them in the middle of Hebron. Tall buildings, wide streets, and green parks contrast sharply with the comparative squalor outside the settlement's barbed wire perimeter. Nevertheless, many of the 5000 residents would eagerly trade the suburban living for an opportunity to reestablish the Jewish Quarter in Hebron, a move that the government has continued to oppose. English is widely spoken, and in the parks or *yeshiva* (to the left as you enter) you will undoubtedly meet people willing to explain the ideology that has drawn them here.

It is unsafe to walk to Qiryat Arba. Instead, take a Jerusalem-Hebron **Egged bus,** all of which stop within the settlement.

Ramallah

If you are interested in West Bank politics, Ramallah is the best place to learn the Palestinian perspective. The Palestinians in Ramallah are friendly to tourists, although less willing to discuss politics than before the *intifadah.* Out of politeness and respect, don't argue—just listen.

There are few noteworthy tourist sites in Ramallah. Visit the colorful market, next to the bus station. If you are let off at the less-busy garage at the bottom of the hill, walk back up the hill to reach the market. Ramallah is one of the most beautiful towns on the West Bank; walk around the houses away from the city center. As you approach Ramallah from Jerusalem, you will pass through el-Bireh. The line between the two towns is marked by the beautiful, green-domed **Mosque of Abu Narrer.** If you linger too long at its gate, you will be shooed away. The dome is visible from the market. The inscription over the door reads "There is no God but Allah, and Muhammad is his prophet," the fundamental creed of Islam.

Ramallah lost its Arab tourist clientele following the 1967 occupation; the uprisings have turned away everyone else. There is no longer a tourist office. If the political situation improves, the **Pension Miami** (tel. 95 28 08) on Jaffa Rd. will reopen. On the way to the hotel, at al-Mughtaribeen Sq., is **Naoum's Restaurant.** When it reopens, try the *musakhan,* a half-chicken served on flat bread with spiced onions and pine nuts. For now, there is good *shwarma* and felafel to be had throughout the town. The kiosk on Exhibition St., across from Naoum's, serves excellent, highly spiced rolled felafel sandwiches for only NIS1.

To reach Ramallah, take **Arab bus** #18 from the station on Nablus Rd. just north of Damascus Gate in Jerusalem (40 min., NIS1). Buses to Jerusalem leave from Jaffa Rd. in Ramallah, just off Manara Sq., the main traffic circle. The last leaves at 6pm. *Service* **taxis** from the square run until about 9pm (NIS1.50) and arrive at the taxi stand near Damascus Gate in Jerusalem, 1 block west of the bus station.

Near Ramallah: Beit-El

The peaceful village of **Beit-El,** 5km northeast of Ramallah on the road to Nablus, is marked on pilgrims' maps as the base of Jacob's Ladder. This is reputed to be the spot where Jacob lay down to sleep and dreamed of a ladder ascending to heaven with angels going up and down. On awakening, Jacob built an altar and named the spot Beit-El, "House of God"(Genesis 28:12-19).

Today, Beit-El is the headquarters of the Israeli civilian administration that governs the West Bank. Although the administration delegates limited authority to Arab mayors and other Palestinian leaders, the power remains in the hands of the Israeli officials. The administration center itself is of no interest to tourists, but a visit to the nearby Jewish settlement of Beit-El is worthwhile. Surrounded by tall fences, barbed wire, and guarded by army patrols, the settlement provides a glimpse of life in one of the besieged settlements. Most of the working population commutes to Jerusalem, but there are also a few cottage industries within the settlement, including a workshop that manufactures *t'fillin* (religious articles worn over the head and on the arm by male Jews during prayer). The residents are usually willing to discuss West Bank politics.

Beit-El is accessible by **Egged bus** #70 from Jerusalem or El-Bireh. From Ramallah you can walk, take a taxi, or take the bus to Nablus as far as the administrative center. If you take a taxi, make sure the driver takes you all the way to the town. Think carefully before you try to hitch.

Bir Zeit

Twelve kilometers northwest of Ramallah is the home of the largest and most important **university** on the West Bank. Its 2200 students have a history of opposition to the Israeli government; whenever political turmoil forces the Israeli army to tighten security in the West Bank, Bir Zeit is usually the first institution to be shut down. Ask around in Ramallah to make sure places are open before you make the trip. Specify that you want to visit the university (*jaamiat*) and not the town. Students here are very radical, especially since Jordan's King Hussein will not allow a college on the West Bank. The old campus is next to the last bus stop; the best place to meet students here is in the dining hall. The palatial new campus lies 2km out of town on the road back to Ramallah. The university is in session mid-October through mid-February, and from early March until late June, unless the Israelis close it. **Bus** #19 leaves for Bir Zeit from Radio Blvd. in Ramallah, just off Manara Sq. **Taxis** leave from the same street.

Nablus (Shekhem)

Young Palestinians look upon Nablus (known in the Bible and to many Israelis as Shekhem) as a candidate for the intellectual and administrative capital of their unborn nation. The largest city on the West Bank, it is home to Najah University, the territory's second most important university. When you walk off the bus, you will be struck by the bustling business district set in the picturesque valley. If you wander around, you will be asked by Palestinians about what you're doing and where you're going. If you walk by Israeli army patrols, their heads will turn in unison, but don't stop to talk.Perhaps the most rewarding way to spend your time here is to accept the residents' hospitality and learn something of the life of West Bank Palestinians. No matter what your hosts tell you, Nablus is truly the badlands of the West Bank. Don't forget it. The town may be completely roadblocked on the day you plan to visit.

Practical Information and Accommodations

Nablus lies 63km north of Jerusalem and 46km north of Ramallah. It is not difficult to visit the Nablus area as a daytrip from Jerusalem. The highway from the south passes through gorgeous hill country, where olive groves hide the scars left by fierce hilltop fighting in 1967.

To reach Nablus, take an **Arab bus** from Nablus Rd. in Jerusalem (NIS3.50) or from Ramallah (NIS3). The last bus to Jerusalem from Nablus leaves at 5:30pm. Don't miss it. The bus trip is a grueling two-and-a-half hours. *Sherut* taxis (NIS5.50) are often quicker and always more comfortable. Buses also run from Afula and

Jenin in the north. To visit the university, ask anyone at the station to point out the bus (no number) from central Nablus to the campus, 3km away.

Nablus is no place to be for the night; hotels in the town are currently closed. However, if you're stuck in the future, try the humble **Pension Ramses,** 85 Assakia St., 1 block south of the municipal building. (Not the place for solo women.) The **Palestinian Hotel,** 4 Shwetri St. (tel. 700 40), had pleasant balconies and spacious quarters. From the taxi and bus stations in central Nablus, head west, bearing left, and walk 700m down Ghirnata St. to its end. Bear slightly right onto Shwetri St., and the hotel will be immediately on your left.

Sights

After arriving by bus or taxi in the center of Nablus, wander south into the crowded streets and passageways of the **market.** Paralleling the main road for over 1km, the main market street overflows with Nablus merchants, their Palestinian customers, and tea-sipping onlookers. By walking through the market, you'll catch glimpses of *sheykhs* preparing their mosques for daily prayer, Palestinian women in richly embroidered dresses buying produce for their families, and students conversing on the sidewalks. Savor a piece of the famous, extraordinarily rich *kunafi nablusia.* Nablus turns out uncountable trayfuls of this cheese concoction, which is topped with sweet orange flakes and honey (½ piece NIS1.20, whole piece NIS1.80). During the uprising, the market is open 9am-noon and requires extreme caution.

Throughout the market and everywhere in Nablus, you'll continue to see the smiling image of Dafer Masri, Nablus' Palestinian mayor. A wreathed monument next to the municipality building marks the spot where he was slain in the winter of 1986. More than likely, his assassins were Palestinians who resented his alleged chumminess with Israeli leadership; the killing is remembered with great bitterness here.

To the east, 3km from the town center, lie two famous though unspectacular pilgrimage sights. **Jacob's Well** is now enclosed within a subterranean Greek Orthodox shrine. The well is believed to date from the time when Jacob bought the surrounding land to pitch his tents (Genesis 33:18-19). You can reach the ancient water-hole through the tranquil gardens and court of the Greek Orthodox religious complex. The sprightly caretaker-monk will spill water into the well to demonstrate its 40m depth. He may also point out a battered photograph of the former superior of the shrine, murdered by a Jewish fanatic in 1979 to protest Christian control of the well. (Usually open Mon.-Sat. 8am-noon and 2-5pm; during strike 8-11am.) A few hundred meters north of the well lies the **Tomb of Joseph.** According to the Book of Joshua, the bones of Joseph were carried out of Egypt and buried in Shekhem (Joshua 24:32). The tomb was a Muslim shrine until three years ago, when it was taken over by Jewish authorities. Israeli soldiers now guard the unimpressive velvet-shrouded cenotaph and the adjacent new *yeshiva.* (Open daily 6am-6pm; no shorts or bare shoulders permitted.)

To reach the two sites, walk the 3km from the center of Nablus toward Jerusalem, take a local taxi (NIS.50 per person), or have a bus drop you off. The tomb and well are just northwest of the intersection of the Nablus-Jerusalem highway and the road to Jericho. Traveling from Nablus, you'll find Jacob's Well on your left as you approach the intersection. Joseph's Tomb lies off Amman St., a few hundred meters north of the well. Visitors should take the safer main roads between the two sites, avoiding a shortcut on neighborhood roads through the poverty-stricken **al-Balata Refugee Camp.** Follow the clear signs through the intersection and up Amman St. Near Jacob's Well is an incorrect sign for Joseph's Tomb pointing back to the highway. The Arab bus driver may point out al-Balata ("the Oak") on the way in to Nablus from the south. This large refugee camp was built to house those who fled Israel in 1948, many of them with the intention of returning. The site is identified with the Oak of Moreh, the first place where it is believed that Abraham was promised Canaan for his offspring (Genesis 12:6).

Mount Gerizim, the tree-covered slope just southeast of Nablus, features an excellent view of the green and brown Shomron Valley. Since the fourth century B.C.E., it has been the holy mountain of the Samaritans, who revere it as the spot where Abraham offered to sacrifice his son Isaac. The Samaritans, an Israelite sect who were excommunicated in biblical times, are known for their literal interpretation of certain scriptures. The highlight of the Samaritan observance of Passover is the sacrifice of sheep atop Mount Gerizim. Tourist buses from Jerusalem and Tel Aviv bring visitors to witness the bloody rite. The hike up the mountain is a long one, but taxis can be hired for about NIS15. Taxis will take you around the mountain to ascend its southern flank, reached by an access road off the Nablus-Jerusalem highway.

Near Nablus

An intriguing array of Israelite, Hellenistic, and Roman ruins are sequestered in the multi-colored Shomron Hills, 11km northwest of Nablus. The strategic peak on which the ruins lie was first settled by Omri, King of Israel in the ninth century B.C.E. Under Herod, the city was made the showpiece of the Holy Land to win the favor of the Roman Emperor. The ruins are just above the present-day Arab town of **Sabastiya.** At the base of the site, on the access road that bypasses the town, the majestic columns of a colonnaded street offer some indication of Sabastiya's former opulence. At the entrance to the site itself, the similarly imposing pillars of the basilica stand like a row of thick-trunked trees. The beautifully preserved **Roman theater** farther on is more impressive than its famous counterpart at Caesarea. At the top of the hill, along with a spectacular view of the Shomron Hills, lie the remnants of Israelite and Hellenistic acropolis walls, and a Roman acropolis, dominated by the enormous column bases of the **Temple of Augustus.** The extensive remains of **Ahab's Palace,** built in the ninth century B.C.E., adjoin the temple. (Site open Sat.-Thurs. 8am-5pm, Fri. 9am-4pm. Admission NIS2, students, NIS1.50.) To reach the ruins, get off the bus at the first white "Sabastiye" sign (this road leads through the modern town) or at the second, yellow "Samaria/Sebaste" sign (the route past the colonnaded street), and head uphill.

The village of Sabastiya is worth a moment's attention as well, especially for the ruins of a splendid twelfth-century Crusader **cathedral,** accessible by steps leading down from the main square. The cathedral was built over the remains of an earlier basilica, which was believed to have stood over the sacred tombs of the prophets Elisha and Obadiah and of St. John the Baptist. The ruins are located within the confines of the **Mosque of Nabi Yahya,** the Arabic name for St. John.

To reach Sabastiya, take the Arab bus bound for Jenin from the central bus station in Nablus or hail one of the numerous *sherut* taxis. The bus will take you only as far as one of the turn-offs for Sabastiya, a 2km walk from the village and site.

EGYPT

US $1 = 2.32 Egyptian pounds (LE)	LE1 = US $0.43
CDN $1 = LE1.92	LE1 = CDN $0.52
UK £1 = LE3.92	LE1 = UK £0.26
AUS $1 = LE1.86	LE1 = AUS $0.54
NZ $1 = LE1.54	LE1 = NZ $0.65

> For important additional information on Documents and Formalities, Money, Safety and Security, Climate Concerns, Getting There, Border Crossings, History, Religion, and Travel Etiquette, see the General Introduction to this book.

On top of an astoundingly old civilization grows a nation struggling to be modern. The abundance of history can be overwhelming; modern Egypt is often regarded as a third-world nation squatting on the grounds of an open-air archeological museum that doesn't belong to it. But the contemporary juxtaposition of past and present, of temples and televisions, is a fact of which Egyptians can be proud. Life here is a vibrant affirmation of humankind's ability to take on larger-than-life tasks.

Ignore for a moment the mapped borders of Egypt; they're just the result of recent politics. Egypt is the Nile Valley, a freak product of central African geography and climate that created the most fertile strip in the world right in the middle of a sterile desert. The Nile's gift of life inspired a series of religions, and a parade of invaders from envious empires. The Pharaoh's control of the annual floodwaters was the basis of his power and claim to divinity.

Modern technology boasts of that power now. The Aswan High Dam, near the southern border, remains the most profound demarcation between ancient and modern Egypt. Completed in 1970, the dam put an end to the annual flood of the Nile. Instead, Egypt now relies on irrigation pumps, hydroelectric power, and faith in technology. If the dam goes, Egypt will be washed into the sea like so much Pharaonic flotsam.

The modern Egyptian state emerged from the ruins of Old World empires. Its evolution as an independent state was fueled by a revolutionary vision of Egypt as the vanguard of renewed Arab nationalism, but this vision discounted Egypt's unique character. Although striving to renew damaged ties with other Arab nations, Egypt is also concerned with joining its former adversaries, the Western industrial states and even Israel, in peace and prosperity. In the past few years, religious and political extremists have asserted themselves, but so far they have been contained by the moderate majority. And for all the restrictions on political and civic freedoms, after three decades of autocracy, the Egyptian Republic is taking cautious but progressive steps toward a functional democracy.

Egypt is a budget traveler's paradise. The sights are stunning, the people and the culture are fascinating, you can live comfortably for a few dollars a day, and you'll almost never get caught in the rain. On the downside, the public infrastructure is not nearly so well developed as in Europe, and most tourist facilities are intended for organized excursions. Independent travel in Egypt is difficult; it requires plenty of time, stamina, and an attitude that mixes one tremendous dollop of patience with some philosophical resignation. Adopt the Sphinx of Giza as your mascot: It has suffered every indignity from being buried in the sand to having its nose shot off, yet nothing ever seems to bother it. The rewards of travel in Egypt are worth every irritation.

A comprehensive itinerary of this remarkable country would explore each of its four regions. The first is the **Mediterranean Coast** bounded by Alexandria, Egypt's second capital facing across the sea toward Greece and the faded glory of its Hel-

lenic past; Marsa Matruuh, with inviting beaches; and Siwa Oasis, a far pilgrimage to the west.

The second region, the **Nile Valley,** is the most popular and, in terms of distance and sights, the most tremendous. On one side of the Nile Valley railroad, the landscape explodes with lush groves of date palms, fig, banana, and mango trees, and fields of sugar cane, corn, and squash; on the other side, desolate sand dunes stretch as far as the eyes can see. Lower Egypt includes the Delta and Cairo vicinity, while Upper Egypt is the south, including Luxor and Aswan, and stretching all the way to Abu Simbel.

The third region is the eastern **Red Sea Coast,** the Arabian Desert, and the remarkable, almost alien world of the Sinai Peninsula, returned to Egypt as part of the Camp David Accords. Snorkeling, hiking, windsurfing, and spectacular scenery at Hurghada and the Aqaba Coast will refresh anyone suffering from a museum-befogged mind.

The last region is the least explored. A trip into the **Western Desert Oases** can include visits to the jewel-like waterholes of Bahariya, Farafra, Dakhla, Kharga, and Baris. The Desert Oases present challenging, rare experiences to those travelers willing to make the arduous journey.

If you're short on time, the best way to see Egypt is to start in Cairo and take the train to Luxor or Aswan. Going down the Nile will give you a quick trip backwards through all of Egypt's lengthy history, as you pass the monuments scattered amid the verdant fields. A lengthy visit will give you the luxury of exploring at your own pace and allow you to get to know the Egyptian people.

Planning Your Trip

Work

A good place to start your search for work in Egypt is at a university career library. If you know Arabic you'll have a distinct advantage in trying to secure work with a foreign company here. Although it offers no placement or referral service, ask the **American Chamber of Commerce** in Egypt at the Marriott Hotel (tel. 340 88 88, ext. 1541) for addresses and phone numbers of its member companies. Consult the **Institute of International Education** for details about opportunities for teaching English language in Egypt. Write for their pamphlet *Teaching Abroad* (see address in General Introduction under Useful Organizations). Work permits can be obtained through any Egyptian consulate, or in Egypt from the Ministry of the Interior.

Apprenticeship

The **International Association for the Exchange of Students for Technical Experience (IAESTE)** sponsors traineeships for undergraduate and graduate students in Egypt (see Useful Organizations in General Introduction). IAESTE will provide you with housing, insurance, transportation, visas, and a stipend. Placement depends on available openings, and applicants are expected to help locate prospective employers.

Volunteer

The **Higher Council for Youth and Sport** in Egypt runs voluntary workcamps where students of different nationalities spend two to four weeks working together on agricultural or sociological projects. Room and board is provided. Limited acceptance. Contact the Council at 10 Modiryiat al-Tahrir St., Garden City, Cairo, or the Egyptian Embassy.

Study

University

The **American University in Cairo (AUC)** offers year-abroad, non-degree, degree, summer school, and intensive-Arabic programs for foreign students. Course areas include Arabic language, Egyptology, and Middle East studies. Room and board are arranged by the students themselves with the assistance of the AUC staff. Full year tuition for the 1988-89 year is $6,500; the summer session costs $1,625 for two courses (6 credits). U.S. citizens in AUC degree or certificate programs may apply for guaranteed student loans. AUC is located conveniently in the center of modern Cairo at 113 Kasr al-Aini St., just off Tahrir Sq. (P.O. Box 2511, tel. 354 29 64/65/66). For more information, write to the American University in Cairo, Office of Admissions, 866 United Nations Plaza, #1, New York, NY 10017 (tel. (212) 421-6320).

Four other Egyptian universities—**Cairo, Ein Shams, Alexandria,** and **Al-Azhar**—have programs for foreign students for one or two semesters. These studies are transferable for credit at most universities. For more information, contact the **Egyptian Educational Bureau,** Cultural Counselor, 2200 Kalorama Road NW, Washington, DC 20008.

Language Institute

Several language institutes offer shorter-term studies in colloquial and classical Arabic. The **Ministry of Higher Education** offers free courses in colloquial Arabic at 2 Dareeh Saad St., el-Falaky, Cairo. The **International Language Institute,** Muhammad Bayoumi St., Heliopolis (tel. 66 67 04), offers morning and evening classes at all levels. The **Berlitz School,** 165 Muhammad Farid St., Cairo (tel. 91 50 96), specializes in colloquial Arabic.

Once There

Entry

A **visa** is required to enter Egypt (see Visas in General Introduction). Generally, all personal items brought into the country that will be taken out upon departure are exempt from taxes. However, these articles must be declared on the appropriate form. Valuables are declared on Form D. You may be required to declare on Form D the amount of foreign currency that you are bringing into the country. Be sure to ask if you don't receive a form, and by all means fill it out and keep all currency exchange receipts. Unless you have your currency declaration when you leave Egypt, all your money can be lawfully confiscated.

Most travelers to Egypt arrive via Cairo. The city can be utterly confusing at first (and later on, too). To minimize your confusion, try to plan your route of escape from the airport, train or bus terminal beforehand. Below we list the major means of transportation into and out of the city.

Upon arrival at **Cairo International Airport,** purchase a visa stamp, if you have not done so already. Visa stamps cost $3 or LE5 for U.S. citizens; all other nationalities pay $10 or LE21. These rates may rise suddenly every three months or so. Don't panic if the official disappears with your passport; it will be returned.

As you pass out of customs, you may be approached by individuals who claim to be "tourist agents" or employees of the Ministry of Tourism. They wait for unescorted travelers and, on the pretext of helping you, set you up in their employer's hotels, which are usually not a credit to the industry. Do not let anyone direct you to a hotel or even a cab; only take cabs from the official stand, which is monitored 24 hours by a Tourist Police officer. If you are unlucky enough to arrive late at night and you have no prearranged accommodations, the safest and easiest course is to check in for the night at one of the reputable hotels at the airport. The best option is the Novotel (tel. 67 17 15), which provides a shuttle bus (singles with bath, $50).

To reach the center of town, take red and white **bus #400** from the back of the parking lot directly in front of the terminal to **Tahrir Square.** The bus runs 24 hours, twice per hour during the day and every hour on the hour late at night and early in the morning. The ride to Tahrir Sq., the last stop, takes over an hour and costs 10pt. A **minivan** (#27) runs between the Old Airport and the Mugama building in Tahrir Sq. (24 hours, infrequent at night; 50pt; 45 min.). There's a free airport shuttle between the old and new airport terminals. A **limousine** costs LE8.50 (prices are fixed and posted), but a **taxi** might cost less after some bargaining.

All trains into Cairo stop at **Ramses Station.** There is absolutely no reason to linger about this chaotic place. Black and white taxis to Tahrir Sq. cost about 50pt. Bus #95 runs from the station to Tahrir Sq. To walk, climb the pedestrian overpass in front of the station and walk to the main street on the south, away from the statue of Ramses II. It's about a half-hour trek from the station to Tahrir Sq. Don't offer more than the LE5-6 that the Egyptians pay.

Buses from the Sinai, Israel, and Jordan usually leave you at **Abbassiya Station** in the northern suburb of Abbassiya. To reach Tahrir Sq. from here, hop a southbound black and white cab (LE1-1.50) or walk left down Ramses St. as you leave the station, beyond the overpass, and to the first bus stop on the right. From here most buses pass Ramses Station and many continue to Tahrir Sq. The terminus for all buses from Alexandria is in front of the Nile Hilton in Tahrir Sq. Some buses from Israel also let passengers off at Tahrir Sq. or major hotels.

Useful Organizations

Embassies and Consulates

U.S.: Embassy, 5 Latin America St., Garden City, Cairo (tel. 355 73 71). **Consulate,** 110 al-Hurriya Rd., Alexandria (tel. 482 19 11). Try to use the Cairo embassy for important matters.

Canadian: Embassy, 6 Muhammad Fahmi al-Sayyid St., Garden City, Cairo (tel. 354 31 10).

U.K.: Embassy, 7 Ahmed Ragheb St., south of the U.S. Embassy, Cairo (tel. 354 08 50). **Consulate,** 3 Mena Kafr Abdu St., Alexandria (tel. 84 71 66), in the Roushdi district. Handles affairs of New Zealand as well.

Australian: Embassy, 5th floor, Cairo Plaza 1097 Corniche al-Nil (tel. 77 79 00 or 77 79 94), 4 blocks south of Shepheard's Hotel.

Tourist Services

The **Egyptian General Authority for the Promotion of Tourism (EGAPT)** has offices in all large cities and some small ones. The Egyptian tourist authorities also run a program called **The Association of Tourists' Friends,** which links travelers with the people of the country. For more information, write The Association of Tourists' Friends, 33 Kasr el-Nil Street, P.O. Muhammad Farid 161, Cairo, Egypt (tel. 392 30 36). **The Tourist Police** can offer visitors assistance with any problems. Most speak English, and their 24-hour offices are located throughout the country. Turn to them in any case of loss, theft, or other criminal problem. The Tourist Police normally give travelers the benefit of the doubt. The officers are recognizable by their distinctive uniforms (black in winter, white in summer) with the words "Tourist Police" aptly printed on their red arm bands. *Let's Go* lists the offices of

EGYPT and the Tourist Police wherever possible. Another possible source of information is the **Egyptian Ministry of Antiquities,** Fakhry Abd el-Noor St., Cairo.

Medical Emergencies

The major hotels have resident doctors who can prescribe medicine or, in serious cases, arrange for specialists and hospitals. Telephone directories list doctors according to specialization as well. Several major hospitals provide 24-hour service, including the Coptic Hospital (Cairo), the Anglo-American Hospital (Zamalek), and the es-Salam International Hospital (Maadi).

Pharmacies carry most U.S. and European drugs. Prescriptions are often not needed in Egypt for drugs that would require them in the U.S. The Egyptian Tourist Authority reports that pharmacists may competently perform injections. No promises. Pharmacies are open 9am-1pm and 4-8pm (often 10pm in summer). Dial 123 for emergencies. (See Health in the General Introduction and Practical Information in the city sections for more information.)

Communication

Mail

Egyptian postal service has improved in recent years, but still don't trust the mail with anything important. Double your chances of having your letter reach its destination by sending two copies. An air mail letter to the U.S. or Europe costs 30pt, postcards 25pt. The most reliable place to mail off letters is said to be the mailbox by the reception desk at the Nile Hilton. When sending postcards you will almost always have better success mailing them from a major hotel than from a post office. Most reception desks sell stamps, although a surcharge may be added. Small post offices scattered about sell stamps at face value; a convenient one in Cairo is in the corner of the Egyptian Museum garden. The most dependable place to receive mail is the main American Express office in Cairo, though Poste Restante functions in most major cities as well. Confusion over first and last names can be avoided by just using an initial and your last name. Mail can also be addressed to the American Consulate. As a general rule, mail to Egypt is faster than mail from Egypt. In either case don't hold your breath—two or three weeks delivery time is normal.

The process for sending a package is Byzantine. First you must obtain an export license from the second floor of the tall post office just north of Cairo's Ramses Station (arrive before 1pm for quickest service). Packages require special cloth wrappings available from shopkeepers near the post office. Most souvenir shops will do the dirty-work necessary to mail your packages back home for a fee. In theory, all mail leaving Egypt is opened and checked.

If you must send something to Europe or North America within 72 hours, go to the main post office at Ataba Square, northeast of Tahrir Sq. The **International Express Mail** office at the side entrance is quite efficient. (Open daily 8am-7pm. 100g LE15, 500g LE22.)

Telephone

The Egyptian telephone system can be time-consuming and frustrating—you may never say another bad word about Ma Bell and her kids. Successful connections are a matter of patience, prayer, and luck. Maybe the pharaohs can help. Note: It is *impossible* to place a **collect call** from Egypt. **Long-distance** or **international calls** are best made from large hotels. The reduced wait is well worth the charge of LE3.50-4. The other option is to call from a government telephone office, but be aware that occasionally you may have to wait several hours for successful connections to Europe and the U.S. If you must make an international call from these offices, go either very early in the morning or very late at night when your chances of obtaining a line before you've finished reading the *Alexandria Quartet* are better. The cost for a three-minute call to the U.S. is LE16.50, to Great Britain LE14, and to Canada LE18. At public telephone offices you pay in advance for a specific number of minutes. You'll be abruptly cut off once your alloted time finishes, so err on the generous side. One final problem: If you don't speak Arabic, you may have difficulty communicating your wishes, especially at smaller offices.

The **international phone code** for calling to Egypt is 20.

Local calls can be dialed direct to most of Egypt's larger cities and towns. Public pay phones are not a common sight in Egypt, but local calls can be made from many hotels, restaurants, and cigarette kiosks. Most hotels normally charge 25pt for local calls; outside hotels the cost is usually 15pt. Be wary of using a phone in a private hotel room; proprietors sometimes level exorbitant charges. Again, phoning in Egypt requires patience and perseverance. To maximize your chances of success, perform the following ritual: (1) Pick up the receiver, insert your coin, and listen for a continuous ringing noise. (2) Dial slowly. (3) After the conversation has begun, press the button to release the coin. If you're unlucky on the first try, don't give up—even if you dial faultlessly, you will not necessarily get the correct party. Don't assume that an unanwered ring means that no one is home. Isn't this fun?

Telegraph

The larger telephone offices and hotels usually provide telex and cable services. In Cairo, go to the Ataba Square telegraph office, directly opposite the main post office. Cables to the U.S. cost about 60pt per word and to Europe 40-50pt per word. You can also send cables to Israel. Dial 124 to send a telegram by phone. It is not always possible to send an international telegram from offices outside of Cairo. However, usually at least one major hotel in a town will provide the service. Allow at least two days for the message to reach its destination, not the promised one-day service.

Currency and Exchange

Egypt's once maddeningly complex array of coins and banknotes is gradually becoming simplified as the old bills and coins pass out of circulation. The *ginyh*, or **Egyptian pound (LE)**, is divided into 100 *irsh*, or **piasters (pt)**. Technically, piasters are further divided into 100 *millim*, but almost the only remnant of this minuscule denomination is an extra zero to the right of the decimal point on some posted prices. **Banknotes** are color-coded and printed with Arabic on one side and English on the other, and come in the following denominations: LE20 (green), LE10 (red), LE5 (blue), LE1 (brown), 50pt (red and brown), 25pt (green), 10pt (black), and 5pt (brown). All bills are the same size except for the 10pt and 5pt notes, which are less than half the size of the larger bills. Older banknotes are size-graded throughout, but these are now rare, although still accepted. LE50 and LE100 notes are also issued in the new system, but are rarely found. In fact, make an effort to break your large bills into denominations of LE1 and below, because most taxi drivers, bus conductors, and street vendors can't be expected to make change.

Coins are also becoming increasingly rare, but occasionally pop up to pester the foreigner. You are most likely to encounter 10pt and 5pt coins, which are usually silver colored with ridged edges. However, the copper colored 1pt and ½pt coins are also marked with the Arabic numerals 10 and 5, in this case representing millims. Fortunately, these coins are almost extinct.

The **currency exchange system** has been completely revised to the great advantage of the tourist. Beginning in the winter of 1986, the government decided to destroy the black market by co-opting its business—the new **tourist rate** actually beats the old black market rate. Just to make sure, the government rounded up 500 black market dealers in a series of sweeping arrests. Be sure to keep all exchange receipts. Note that the New Zealand Dollar is not convertable in Egypt.

You must use the official rate, however, to buy **international transportation.** To buy a plane or boat ticket out of Egypt, find out the price in pounds, exchange just that amount at the official rate, and then present your receipt as you buy the ticket. Remember, you are not allowed to carry more than LE20 in or out of Egypt, nor would you want to, so don't exchange more than necessary.

Prices

A lesson in Arabic: After *min fadlak* (please) and *shokran* (thank you) the most important word to know is *khoaga,* because you are one. *Khoaga* means "tourist," with connotations of naiveté and tremendous wealth. No matter how destitute you consider yourself, many Egyptians will see you as a bottomless well of money waiting to be tapped. Most prices outside of hotels and restaurants are not posted, and so *khoagas* may expect to be charged more than an Egyptian. Far more annoying than this unofficial tourist tax is the seemingly endless tricks blithely unscrupulous merchants use to extract whatever they can. Often tourists are taken because they simply could not anticipate such inventive sneakiness. Many is the *khoaga,* for example, who finds himself perched ten feet off the ground on a rented camel, stunned with disbelief that it costs LE5 more to be let down.

Fortunately, such shysters make up only a tiny percentage of the Egyptians you will meet; they are generally extraordinarily generous and hospitable people. Once you get to know them, or even before you do, Egyptians will offer you all sorts of help and hospitality, expecting nothing in return. As for those few who do prey on *khoagas,* most can be simply ignored and the rest foiled by simple precautions. Avoid salespeople and shops near tourist attractions, and look upon any unsolicited offer of goods or services with grave suspicion—even if told there is no charge. Always agree on a price before you accept anything, and do not pay until you receive what you bargained for. Try to ascertain beforehand how much something is really worth, and pay in exact change—you'll be astonished how quickly some can come up with reasons to keep the extra cash. Most importantly, always insist on getting full value, no matter what excuses are offered. Never feel you owe more than the agreed amount no matter how much they squawk, and never be afraid to walk away at any time, or to firmly refuse an invitation, however kindly, if you feel you'll have to pay later.

Museums and sites run by the government have official admission prices ranging from 50-500pt, although these numbers may have nothing to do with what's printed on the ticket. Student discounts of up to 50% apply at almost all official sites. The men and women who work at ticket kiosks are usually scrupulously honest and will charge you the correct fee. However, the guides who may solicit your business at sites and museums should be ignored; usually, they will recite a few memorized phrases in English—"Mask of Tuthankamen, solid gold, mummy of Tuthankamen, solid gold"—and then expect hefty remuneration. Occasionally, even official agency guides will steer your tour to a gift shop or cafe, run by their friends or business associates. If this happens, remember that the shop will probably be no more expensive or offer different wares than any other similar establishment, and you do not have to buy anything.

Shopping in Egypt is an adventure in itself, and one that requires patience and discretion. For staples and necessities, simply go where the Egyptians go and pay what the Egyptians pay; rare is the department store clerk or pharmacy that thrives by ripping off *khoagas.* For souvenirs and native sundries, be wary. Rare and valuable craftwork is out there—along with pyramid paperweights and fake antiques—but you can pay far too much if you're not careful. Avoid all souvenir shops and kiosks near tourist sights. The bazaars in the cities are chaotic but they are the best places to find woodwork, glassware, textiles and other crafts. If you do find something you want, bargain. (See Bargaining in General Introduction.)

If there is ever a problem with hustlers or rip-off men, you can turn to the Tourist Police stationed at every tourist site, most hotels, and the transportation centers. Officers of the Tourist Police are friendly, helpful, and should be consulted if you ever feel you've been ripped off or mistreated.

Tipping and Baksheesh

An important Arabic word for *khoagas* to know is *baksheesh,* the art of tipping. It is an ancient tradition in Islamic societies and went on long before *khoagas* came on the scene. Although *baksheesh* is quite different from simple charity, it grows out of the belief that those who have should give to those who have not, particularly in return for a favor or service. There are three kinds of *baksheesh.* The most common is similar to **tipping**—a small reward for a small service. Tipping waiters and cab drivers is routine, as well as maids and cooks in hotels after long stays. Don't feel obligated to give anything more if a "service charge" is added to your bill, as is becoming increasingly common. Never tip until after a service is performed, but if it is done well and quickly, be generous. Do not let yourself be railroaded into forking over huge sums—if a smiling doorman demands LE5, tell him *anna mish khoaga* ("I'm not a dumb tourist")—and give him the 25-50pt he deserves. *Baksheesh* becomes most useful when used to procure special favors—seeing a site after hours or climbing a minaret that is forbidden to visitors. Almost any minor rule can be broken for *baksheesh,* but be sure to reward such favors generously. If a custodian gives you a private tour of a mosque long after hours, a pound or two is in order. Never expect recipients of *baksheesh* to make change—one more reason to carry small bills. Once again, never be afraid to ignore the demands for more if you feel that you've been fair.

Baksheesh is rarely expected in return for directions or advice; it would be highly inappropriate, for instance, to offer money to an Egyptian businessman or woman who has helped you find your seat on a train. But *baksheesh* in the form of a tip is advisable in almost any situation where you would like to enjoy good service. Judge the person who has helped you; in some places even children have too much pride to accept *baksheesh.*

The second kind of baksheesh is the giving of **alms.** Everywhere in Egypt you will encounter beggars who are willing to bestow highly rhetorical blessings upon you in return for a little charity. Deal with them as you wish, but be careful of those who try to impose some unwanted service and favor, like opening a door before you can get to it, and then demand *baksheesh.* Refuse all such "favors" loudly and firmly, and if they insist on going ahead with it anyway thank them and walk away. Giving people money in return for annoying you is not sound fiscal policy, and may haunt you when they see you coming back.

The final form of *baksheesh* is simply a bribe, and not something to attempt as a tourist. Bribery requires a great deal more delicacy, familiarity with the culture and language, and discretion than an outsider will possess.

Business Hours

On Friday, the Muslim day of communal prayer, most government offices, banks, and post offices are closed (banks remain closed on Saturdays as well). Other establishments, such as restaurants, remain open seven days per week. Store hours are normally Saturday to Thursday 9am to 1pm and 4pm to 8pm (many are open Friday as well). Government offices usually open from 9am to 2pm, observe a siesta for the remainder of the afternoon, and reopen from about 6pm to 8pm. Some important government offices skip the siesta, while less crucial ones never seem to operate after 2pm. Do your government business in the morning, and expect staffers to leave before official closing times. Bank hours are normally Monday through Thursday 8:30am to 12:30pm and Sunday 10am to noon. Foreign banks keep longer hours, usually Monday through Thursday 8am to 2pm and Sunday 10am to noon. Foreign embassies often keep the hours of their own country. Archeological sites and other points of interest are usually open 7am-6pm, though in summer the most important ones in the Nile Valley open at 6am and close in the early afternoon.

During the month of **Ramadan** (April 6-May 5 in 1989), some restaurants close down entirely, while many others open only after sundown when the daytime fast is broken. The streets empty at dusk as everyone sits down to breakfast, after which business resumes. Shops, closed at 3:30pm during Ramadan, reopen from 8pm to 11pm. In the middle of the night, around 2am to 3am, Egyptians sit down for the second daily meal of Ramadan (called *sahur*) before going to sleep. Especially in the Islamic parts of Cairo, the streets are quite active until long after *sahur*. Although traveling during Ramadan can be inconvenient, the excitement of nighttime celebrations tends to offset daytime frustrations.

Accommodations

Hostels

Egypt has 15 youth hostels that vary in quality. Most are bearable, though grungy and crowded, and the unbeatable price (LE1-4 per night) will probably compensate for the less-than-luxurious atmosphere. Keep a careful eye on your valuables and take your passport, visa, and money to bed with you. Advance reservations are usually unnecessary—everyone is admitted, but arrive early just to be safe. A valid IYHF card is not required, though at most hostels it will save you a pound or two. If you decide once in Egypt to purchase an IYHF card, they are available at the Roda Island youth hostel in Cairo (tel. 84 07 29).

Egyptian youth hostels are divided into two classes according to size. The larger hostels are located in Cairo, Alexandria, Luxor, and Port Said; smaller hostels are in Aswan, Assyut, Damanhour, Marsa Matruuh, Fayyum, Hurghada, Ismailiya, Tanta, Sohag, and Suez. The one hostel outside this classification system is the luxurious, air-conditioned Sharm el-Sheikh hostel. Most hostels have kitchen facilities. For more information, write the Egyptian Youth Hostel Association, 7 Abdel Hamid-Said St., Maarouf, Cairo.

Hotels

Egypt's hotels run the gamut from glistening new resort complexes in Cairo, to spartan, dusty dives along busy streets. But don't give up hope, budget travelers: Clean, comfortable, inexpensive hotels do exist. Most towns and cities have lower-range hotels with rooms for LE2-4 per person, as well as a number of middle-range hotels priced at LE6-9 per person. More comfortable hotels in the LE15-25 range provide many of the same services found in the really expensive places. But, if you feel pressed for cash, you can usually squeak by for about LE1.50 per night without having to look very far. Especially in the cheaper hotels, keep all your valuables with you if possible, and sleep with your passport and money close to your body. In any hotel, ask to see the room before you pay, since price does not always indicate quality. There is a hotel tax which varies by location, from 17% in Cairo to 8% in most other places. Unless otherwise noted, the tax should be included.

Prices vary considerably between high and low season. The high season in Alexandria is June to August, in the Nile Valley October to April. If you visit in the high season, expect hotel rates for the Nile Valley (particularly Luxor and Aswan) to be anywhere from 10 to 50% higher than listed here. In Cairo the high season is also in winter, but the discrepancy between seasonal prices tends to be less. (See Off-Season Travel in the General Introduction.)

Finally, be aware that hot water and private baths are luxuries in Egypt, and you won't get them without paying. Still, every hotel in Egypt will offer a free shower which will at least be wet. Don't expect air conditioning, private telephones, and other conveniences. Even higher priced hotels often lack toilet paper. You can guess what that little squirting pipe in the toilet bowl is for, and why eating with the left hand is taboo in Arab and African cultures. For the faint of heart, Egypt's well-stocked pharmacies and street vendors sell toilet paper.

Transportation

Travel Restrictions

Foreigners are officially required to secure permits to travel in the following areas: secondary roads in the Delta; along the Suez Canal between (but not including) Ismailiya and Suez; the coastal road to Libya beyond Marsa Matruuh; the Siwa Oasis; the Red Sea coast between (but not including) Suez and Hurghada; and all areas in the Sinai off the main roads and outside the tourist zone. The Western Desert Oases no longer require a permit.

Enforcement is very lax, and almost all places of interest to tourists are unrestricted so you will seldom need to concern yourself with such travel restrictions. In restricted zones police are allowed to confiscate your passport and hold you for questioning. Sincere apologies and confessions of ignorance may put the matter to rest. To undertake unusual expeditions in a restricted area, you must seek permission from the Travel Permits Department of the Ministry of the Interior. Bring two photos, your passport, and plenty of patience. In Cairo, the office is located at the corner of Sheikh Ridan and Nuban St.; in Alexandria, on Ferrana St. off al-Huriyya St. No matter where you go, especially if you are traveling in a restricted area, always keep your passport with you.

Law also forbids Egyptians from traveling with foreigners without special permission. Travel agent's licenses, marriage or birth certificates, and the like are required for permission to be granted. This regulation, designed to protect travelers, may prevent you from sightseeing with Egyptian friends. To prevent nasty questioning sessions en route, your friend may want to check with the local police before accompanying you.

Train

The Egyptian railway system serves almost all major towns and points of interest in the country. First- and second-class trains are relatively comfortable and surprisingly inexpensive. They are also one of the most popular ways of traveling, which means long lines and crowded cars. Still, trains are probably the best option for long-distance travel. For shorter distances, alternate forms of transportation—particularly service taxis—are much faster and more reliable.

The government has hesitated to advertise its train system to tourists because barely enough trains are available for the Egyptians. Schedules and signs in the anarchic train stations are never in English. The Roman numerals on the trains indicate their class. Fortunately, fellow passengers are generally very helpful in directing you to the correct ticket windows and platforms. Ask at any major station for the invaluable 40-page English-version *Egyptian Railways Timetable* (50pt).

Student discounts on most major routes can be almost 50%. Riding on the unreserved non-air-conditioned second- and third-class trains may be educational, but it's definitely not recommended for the long treks, or for the squeamish. Better to book seats on **air-conditioned second-class** cars from Cairo (LE6.15 to Luxor, LE7.50 to Aswan); air-conditioned first-class is also available, but not worth the extra leg-room probably doesn't justify the extra cost. **Second-class sleeper cars,** available on normal trains, are an excellent deal for travel to Luxor or Aswan (only LE8 in a double), but are nearly impossible to book. Unmarried couples may not be permitted to share a cabin. Student discounts on sleepers are less than on regular seats; you might get no discounts for the luxurious **wagon-lits** (2nd class LE78, 1st class LE124; dinner and breakfast included). You can reserve space on a sleeper at the wagon-lit offices in Cairo, Luxor, Aswan, and Alexandria. Other kinds of train passage can be reserved only at the station of departure, or through a travel agent (for a fee). Be sure to reserve seats between Cairo and Upper Egypt several days in advance.

When you make **reservations,** be insistent about the day on which you would like to travel; sometimes empty seats are hidden in the ticket seller's arcane record books. Since round-trip reservations cannot be arranged at the point of origin, always take care of return reservations as soon as you reach your destination, particularly if you intend to take a sleeper. During the last week of Ramadan, and the entire week thereafter (the first two weeks of May in 1989) as well as before *id al-adha* (which starts July 13 in 1989), reserved seats on all Egyptian trains, especially to Luxor and Aswan, are completely booked. To travel during this period, book your tickets at least a week in advance. At other times, several days in advance is sufficient.

If your train is full and you don't have the time to wait around, don't despair—board the train without buying a ticket. The conductor will sell you a ticket on the train with a small fine (about LE1.50 between Cairo and Luxor and Aswan). Your only problem will be finding a seat or an empty bit of floor. If you are traveling from Cairo to Alexandria or the Delta, you may want to avoid the hassle of waiting in the ticket lines for reserved seating. The trip is short, you may find a seat anyway, and the fine for not having a ticket is only around 25pt.

The cars nearest the entrance tend to fill up first, so try to head for the far end of the platform. Once the panicked crowds have settled down and your train is rolling, the ride can be pleasant. You'll have a rare chance to meet Egyptians from every region of the country. In first- and second-class cars, stewards sell cheap soft drinks and snacks. Toilets and drinking water are provided, but do yourself a favor and carry your own water and toilet paper.

If you miss your train, immediately return to the back of the ticket windows and find the door to the ticket office. Barge in, ask to see the director, act mildly hysterical, show them your tickets, explain you've just missed your train and that you're a poor student. You'll be amazed: The same lethargic bureaucracy that made you wait for hours to buy the ticket often acts like lightning under such circumstances. If you're extremely lucky, you may be issued a ticket on the next train out—even if there are officially no seats available for at least a week! Never try to bribe a train station official; they will be offended, and it will work against your interests.

Finally, don't throw your money away in despair at the labyrinthine bureaucracy of Egyptian railways. It is possible both to return and to change tickets for very little extra cost. If you want to return reserved tickets, go to the station-master's office before the scheduled departure and your money will be refunded minus a 15pt cancelation fee.

Bus

Inter-city buses are an inexpensive but usually uncomfortable way to travel in Egypt. Often you may feel that half the population of Cairo is packed into your bus. Even so, buses prove valuable for short trips, when trains are a hassle. Buses also provide transportation to areas without rail service, like Hurghada, the Sinai, the Oases, and Abu Simbel. Most routes offer a slightly more expensive, air-conditioned bus on one schedule, usually early in the morning. Private companies serve routes frequented by the wealthier Egyptians (such as Cairo to Alexandria) with special air-conditioned, comfortable, no-standing-please buses. Buses in the Sinai, though irregular, are generally comfortable and air conditioned as well. Note that when you book a ticket for an Egyptian bus, you are often assigned a particular seat. Buses traveling between major cities leave frequently throughout the day, although buses to and from the Sinai and the oases often depart only early in the morning. Try to go to the station the day before to confirm departure times.

Numbers and destinations on Egyptian buses are normally written only in Arabic. The conductors who sit at the little kiosks at Tahrir, Ramses, and the other main terminals are usually very helpful in giving directions.

Taxi

Intra-city shared taxis are a cheap, convenient option for traveling around Cairo (where taxis are black and white) and Alexandria (black and orange). Using these taxis, however, requires some practice. (For tips on how to best flag them down and determine correct payment for your destination, see Cairo Transportation.)

Private taxis (called *taxi spécial*) are much more expensive than the collective variety; use them only for late-night or out-of-the-way travel. The taxi drivers are notorious for milking inflated fares from unsuspecting tourists. To decrease your chances of being taken, try to hail a private taxi on the street instead of finding one which is parked, particularly around popular tourist sights and large hotels. If a cabbie approaches you first, turn him down.

Inter-city service taxis connect Cairo with other locations. These large mono-chromatic Peugeot or Mercedes cars seat seven or eight passengers, but sometimes pack in more. Service taxis leave from established places in Cairo for a variety of destinations. The cost of a trip, usually fixed (except in Sinai), is split among the passengers. There is no advance purchase of tickets, and cars leave as soon as they are filled. Usually you won't have to wait more than 15 minutes. The major advantage of service taxis is their flexibility. You won't be cheated since you pay the same as the other passengers. Service taxis can be hired by a group for several hours or for a full day's sightseeing. Tourist offices have the official rates, normally around LE15-20 per taxi for a half-day (depending on the distances involved). One disadvantage of service taxis is that they can be dangerous. Although most drivers are responsible, their competence behind the wheel, their mania for speed, and even their sobriety, vary widely. Use service taxis only when no other alternative exists, as is the case for most short inter-city trips in Upper Egypt, and not at night.

Service taxi stands in large towns are usually well organized, with dispatchers and aluminum roofs. In the villages, stands may be nothing more than a designated parking lot or a stretch of road. When in doubt, go to the bus station; the taxi stand is usually nearby.

Hitchhiking

Hitchhiking is not a common practice in Egypt, but even within cities Egyptians are usually friendly about picking up foreign hitchhikers. Offers of food and invitations home often accompany rides. Rides are particularly easy to obtain in isolated areas, such as along the Great Desert Road or in out-of-the-way parts of the Nile Valley, where ordinary public transportation is difficult to find. Often, however, drivers who pick up hitchhikers will expect a fare comparable to taxi or bus fare, regardless of whether their passenger is Egyptian or foreign. *Caution:* It is so rare for women to hitchhike alone that misunderstandings can easily arise.

Car Rental

Renting a car may be economical if several people travel in a single vehicle since gas is cheap. A car will enable you to visit remote regions such as the oases or the Red Sea coast. Remember to obtain the necessary permits before driving around back roads in the Delta or out to Siwa. Bear in mind there are few places where you can drop off rental cars. An **International Driver's Permit** (see Identification Cards in General Introduction) is required to drive in Egypt. Any insurance you have will not cover you here, so plan to invest in proper coverage. (See Insurance in General Introduction.) Your biggest headache on the road will be the traffic; driving in Egypt demands nerves of steel, especially in unfamiliar cities. In Cairo, the following rental agencies will rent you a car for anywhere from two days to two months. The age requirements are not always strictly enforced.

Avis Rent-A-Car: Airport (tel. 66 77 11); Nile Hilton (tel. 75 06 66); Fiat 128, $43 per day plus 16¢ per km over 100km. Must be 25.

Budget Rent-A-Car: Airport (tel. 66 77 11, ext. 4223); 5 al-Makrizi St., Zamalek (tel. 340 94 74). Fiat 127, LE53 per day, plus 20pt per km over 100km. Must be 28.

Europcar: Marriott Hotel, Zamalek (tel. 340 11 52). Fiat 127 LE42 per day, plus 16pt per km over 100km. Must be 25.

Hertz Rent-A-Car: Airport (tel. 66 66 88); Ramses Hilton (tel. 77 74 44). Fiat 127, LE58 per day, plus 19pt per km over 100km. Must be 21.

Max Rent-a-Car: 27 Lebanon St., Mohandiseen (tel. 347 47 12). In addition to Fiats and Peugeots, rents Jeep CJs with 4-wheel drive, $61 per day, plus 27¢ per km over 100km. Must be 25.

Renting a caravan is an expensive but comfortable alternative for exploring out-of-the-way parts of Egypt. Since you bring your food and lodgings with you, the added independence is not quite as costly as it first appears, especially split among five or six people. **See-Land Caravan Tours,** 47 Falaki St., Bab el-Luq (tel. 354 50 60), rents enormous Chevrolet trucks for LE160 per day, plus 50pt per km over 100km. Each caravan sleeps six, has running water, air conditioning, a fully-equipped kitchen, and can drive on the toughest desert roads. See-Land requires a LE500 deposit but offers a 10% student discount. Read the contract carefully, though, and be sure they don't overcharge you for mileage.

Plane

EgyptAir, the official airline for all domestic flights, serves all major cities out of Cairo International Airport. All prices listed are one way, coach class. The airline has frequent flights from Cairo to Luxor (1 hr., $51); Cairo to Aswan (2 hr., $72); Cairo to Alexandria (30 min., $30 with discounts on round-trip fares); Cairo to Abu Simbel ($101); Cairo to Hurghada ($56). There are also less frequent flights to Minya and Marsa Matruuh. EgyptAir's main office in the U.S. is at 720 Fifth Ave., New York, NY 10019 (tel. (212) 581-5600). There are no student discounts or youth fares on domestic flights.

EgyptAir has several offices in Cairo, some of which are more crowded than others. The following offices have staff members who speak English: No. 16 Adli St., across from the tourist office (tel. 92 09 99), and Nile Hilton, by Tahrir Sq. (tel. 75 98 06). You can reach their central reservations and information service at 74 74 44 or 74 74 17.

Air Sinai, in the courtyard of the Nile Hilton, is a branch of EgyptAir created to serve the Sinai and Israel. Foreigners must pay in U.S. dollars. These are one-way fares; the round trip is probably undiscounted. Air Sinai flies two or three times per week from Cairo to al-Arish ($46), St. Catherine's ($46), and Sharm el-Sheikh ($58). Convenient flights also run from Luxor to Sharm el-Sheikh ($54), and to St. Catherine's ($66), and from Hurghada to Sharm el-Sheikh ($40) and St. Catherine's ($54). Their flights between St. Catherine's and Sharm el-Sheikh cost $37. Air Sinai's most celebrated flight connects Cairo and Tel Aviv (Tues., Fri., and Sat.; $124).

Life in Egypt

The burgeoning population of Egypt is composed of a surprising variety of cultures and classes, from descendents of the Pharoahs to Bedouin to Coptic Christians, all of whom consider themselves wholly Egyptian. The upper classes affect European dress and customs, while members of the educated middle class do what they can to emulate them on civil service salaries. The cheapest commodity in resource-poor Egypt is labor; the great mass of the lower class lives in appalling poverty, relying on a very strong family structure to provide support. The city dwellers are like urbanites anywhere. Along the banks of the Nile, *fellaheen* farm the rich land in much the same way as their direct ancestors did five thousand years ago, but Egypt must now import food.

Generosity and kindness are characteristic among Egyptians of all classes. Even in the incredible chaos of downtown Cairo people are hospitable and friendly to strangers. In Egypt, the greater honor lies with the host; you won't be there long before you are invited to tea, a meal, or an all-night wedding. The traveler quickly learns that the only way to manage is to constantly ask for directions and advice, which are always freely given. Remember that some Egyptians are so eager to help they will give incorrect directions rather than fail to offer assistance. Because of harsh laws and authoritarian government, violent crimes are not common in Egypt, and it is safe to wander in Cairo even late at night and in slums.

Egypt is, however, a conservative, patriarchal society with a very strong religious tradition. Western moral standards do not apply, especially in matters of family and sex. Every now and then you will see a woman entirely covered with black and grey cloth so that not an inch of skin or hair is visible. She will serve as a reminder that, for most of this society, the role of women remains severely proscribed. Western males will sometimes be confronted with lascivious questioning by Egyptian men, frustrated by strict morals, about their exploits. Most Egyptians believe that Western women are free from moral strictures—and will expect you to behave accordingly, or at least hope you will. If you respect their manners and customs, you will enjoy the benefits of traveling in a stable and safe society.

From the Western tourist's point of view, a disconcerting feature seems to unite Egypt's population: the unequivocal lack of concern for time. Travel in Egypt proves frustrating for European and American visitors who approach the country with their own standards of efficiency. To enjoy Egypt, you must accept the fact that the economical use of time is not a concern. Slow down, don't cram too much into your schedule, and savor the relaxed atmosphere. Never set your mind so fixedly on your plans that you can't sit back and sip a leisurely glass of tea if your bus is a few hours behind schedule.

Frustration is most likely to boil over in encounters with Egypt's mind-boggling bureaucracy. You may well feel that you spend more time buying train tickets than exploring ancient temples. Bring the paper to read as you wait in line, and try not to notice how a bureaucrat disappears to drink tea with his buddies just as you approach the window.

Religion

Ancient Religion

The ancient Egyptians believed in immortality. The elaborate funeral rites and structures—mortuary temples, tombs, and cities of the dead—reflect the culture's devotion to life in this world and the next. Great care was taken to preserve the bodies of the deceased in order to maintain the **ka,** or spiritual double of the person. The afterlife, the ancients believed, would be a time of renewal, happiness and rewards. One of the ways by which Egyptians thought that they could help secure their own afterlife was mummification. They went to great lengths to protect the mummy by the construction of massive **pyramids** and elaborate tombs. The ancient Egyptians believed judgment occurred immediately after death. The blessed would live forever with the sun god Ra, while the wicked would be cut by knives and tortured by fire between midnight and sunrise for eternity.

The gods of ancient Egypt represented the cosmos, the natural elements, the animals, and the life cycle. The major Egyptian animals were associated with particular gods. The cow, for example, corresponded to **Hathor,** the cat to **Bast,** and the frog to **Heqt.** The religion centered on the rhythmic events of nature, such as the rising of the sun and the annual flooding of the Nile.

The sun god, **Ra,** was generally the major figure in the Egyptian pantheon. According to Egyptian myth, humans were created from Ra's tears. Ra was normally depicted as a hawk-headed human with a sun disk, sailing a boat in **Nu** (the celestial ocean). Many other important gods descended from the solar deity. Ra's children were **Shu** (air) and **Tefnut** (dew); other solar gods include **Tum** (setting sun), **Bast** (useful solar heat), and **Sekhet** (fierce heat). Shu and Tefnut in turn engendered **Geb,** the earth god, and **Nut,** the sky goddess.

Geb and Nut were the parents of the family of **Osiris,** gods and goddesses most closely associated with the afterlife. Osiris, the ruler of the afterlife, is depicted as a mummy holding a pharaonic staff and flail. Much of ancient Egyptian art is concerned with the judgment that precedes entrance into the world of Osiris, and passages from the *Book of the Dead* were often carved onto the walls of tombs to instruct the deceased how to ensure their own immortality.

Osiris' sister was **Isis** (dawn), the principal mother goddess in the pantheon. Isis and Osiris were brother and sister as well as wife and husband. They produced **Horus,** the falcon responsible for the midday sun and for transporting the dead pharaoh's body and ka to the afterlife. Osiris was murdered by his brother **Seth,** who dismembered his body and scattered the pieces up and down the Nile. Seth's sister and wife **Nephus** is associated with protection of the dead and the sunset.

The concept that the pharoah was divine unified the ancient Egyptian world view. It legitmitized the ruler's awesome power, and he, in turn, assumed cosmic responsibilities for his people. The rituals performed by the pharoah, or the high priest, sustained harmony between the natural and human realms. Pharoahs were worshiped as gods after death as well, and temples throughout Egypt depict these rulers as deities. Ramses the Great's **Abu Simbel** is the most memorable of these temples. Service to the pharoah while he lived took on spiritual significance. Historians speculate that the laborers who built the pyramids and other pharaonic tombs brought a religious fervor to their work—much as European cathedral builders would thousands of years later.

The prestige of a dynasty's favorite gods rose and fell with their fortunes. The famous Theban triad of **Amun,** god of the sun, **Khonsu,** god of the moon, and **Mut,** consort of the sun and vulture goddess, began as tribal deities. When Thebes became a prominent city within ancient Egypt, the triad came to dominate the pantheon. The Karnak Temple complex, one of the most impressive ever built, testifies to their ancient greatness.

The Macedonian **Ptolemies,** who ruled Egypt in the wake of Alexander, sought to become pharaonic god-kings to their subjects. By merging Greek and Egyptian elements in the Serapis cult, and building temples to the ancient gods, they achieved what Assyrian and Persian invaders before them never could: They became spiritual successors of the pharoahs. Many of the great temples of Upper Egypt date to Ptolemaic times, including those dedicated to **Hathor,** the cow-goddess wife of Horus, to **Sobek,** the crocodile god, and to **Isis,** the mother goddess.

If you plan to spend time wandering among Egypt's monuments, temples, and tombs, some knowledge of ancient religion and culture may help. Nagel's *Encyclopedia Guide to Egypt* is a thorough but expensive English guide to the pharaonic monuments. The *Blue Guide* to Egypt offers detailed descriptions and illustrations of sites as well.

Modern Religion

The most common religion in Egypt is Islam. 85% of the population are Sunni Muslims. Most other Egyptians are Christian Orthodox of the Coptic, or Egyptian, Church. Other small religious minorities include Shiite Muslims, Protestants, Roman Catholics, and Jews. For information on the history and practice of these religions, see Religion under Life in the Middle East.

Festivals and Holidays

Of the several **mullids** (birthdays) celebrated throughout the country, the most important is **Mullid an-Nabi,** the birthday of the prophet Muhammad. Smaller, local *mullids* take place in mosques or at the shrines of particular religious figures. The birthday of Rifa'i, celebrated at Cairo's mosque of the same name, is intriguing, and the festival of Sayyida al-Badawi in Tanta is one of the most interesting in the country. Check with tourist offices for details. Also festive are the two Sufi rituals of **Zikr** and **Zahr.** In the former, a rhythmic group dance builds in fervor, resulting in communal trance state. The latter is a group dance performed by women, primarily as an exorcism rite. Both rituals are practiced on Fridays in many populous areas.

During the month of **Ramadan,** devout Muslims do not eat or drink anything during daylight hours. Ramadan culminates in the three-day festival of **Id al-Fitr.** In 1989, Ramadan will fall around April 6-May 5. Muslims also celebrate **Id al-Adha** (July 13-16, 1989), a remembrance of Abraham's intended sacrifice of his son Ishmael (not Isaac, as Jewish tradition holds) which coincides with the *haj* to Mecca, and the New Year (**Ras el-Sana el-Hegira**). Government offices and banks close during the festivals, but tourist facilities remain open.

Sham an-Nissim falls on the first Monday after Coptic Easter. Though its origins are a mixture of Coptic and pharaonic influences, it has developed into a secular holiday. Egyptians traditionally spend the day on a picnic (the pyramids are a favorite spot), eating *fasikh,* a dried, salted fish difficult for most Western palates to appreciate. Evenings are spent strolling along the Nile or sipping tea or coffee in a cafe. The Coptic celebrations of Easter and Christmas are tranquil affairs marked by special church services.

Perhaps the most interesting festivals are Egyptian weddings. Some come complete with golden thrones for bride and groom, belly dancers, live bands, and Arabic singers. Weddings often take place about 9pm or 10pm on Thursdays at large hotels. If you stroll by, you may catch the procession coming down the stairs.

The major national holidays, observed officially by banks and government offices, but without public celebration are **Sinai Day** (April 25), **Labor Day** (May 1), **Revolution Day** (July 23), and **Victory Day** (Dec. 23).

Economy

Egypt's mushrooming population and shortage of arable land greatly inhibit the struggle to improve its Third World status. All but four percent of Egypt is desert, and the little arable land is overcrowded, though extremely fertile. Fifty percent of the Egyptian labor force works in the agricultural sector, growing primarily corn, cotton, rice, fruit, and grain. These workers account for less than a third of the national income. Furthermore, despite the large number of farmers, Egyptian agriculture still cannot supply enough food for the entire population. The government employs the remainder of the labor force, creating a colossal, floundering bureaucracy; according to one study, the average Egyptian public servant works only 27 minutes per day. So as the population grows at nearly three percent per year, more and more educated Egyptians leave to find work in wealthy, neighboring oil states. And the return of some 250,000 Egyptians from Iraq in 1986 has further augmented the bureaucracy instead of fostering growth. Illiteracy remains high, and the typical diet is inadequate.

To help alleviate these problems, Egypt receives vast sums of foreign aid. Through the seventies Saudi Arabia, Qatar, Kuwait, and the United Arab Emirates supplied Egypt with tens of billions in aid, and formed in 1977 the Gulf Organization for the Development of Egypt (GODE). But after the Camp David Accords in 1979, angry Arab states cut off financial support. Under the Carter Plan, the U.S., Western Europe, and Japan agreed to provide Egypt with $12¼ billion over five years. In spring 1984 Jordan and Iraq restored financial ties with Egypt, though Syria and Libya continue to boycott. In 1987 the U.S. alone provided more than $2.2 billion in aid to Egypt.

President Hosni Mubarak has tried to diversify the Egyptian economy, encouraging development in the private sector. Foreign investment has grown steadily in recent years, and Arab capital has more than doubled since 1982. In 1987 foreign projects represented 35% of the total investment. Revenue from the Suez Canal has consistently been around $1 billion per year during this decade. Most of its profits go to purchase foreign grain. The general economic outlook seems optimistic.

Government

According to its September 11, 1971 constitution, Egypt is a "democratic, socialist state," with executive authority residing in the president and his cabinet, but in effect is neither very democratic nor very socialist. It is more of an election-legimated authoritarian regime, although not a "dictatorship." The president serves six year terms but can be reelected for one additional term of office. He appoints the vice president and ministers. The legislative branch consists of the 392-member People's Assembly whose members serve for a period of five years. The assembly must nominate the president by a two-thirds majority, who is then confirmed in a general election. All males over 18 and those women on the register of voters must participate in the election. Two years ago, President Hosni Mubarak was renominated by the People's Assembly for a second term.

Like his predecessor Anwar Sadat, President Mubarak's government has been challenged repeatedly by Islamic fundamentalists. Mubarak's inauguration followed the assassination of Sadat by fundamentalist militants whose greater aim was to overthrow the Western-style Egyptian government and establish an Islamic republic in its place.

Islamic fundamentalists gained parliamentary strength in the May 1984 elections for the People's Assembly. The fundamentalist group, the Muslim Brotherhood, joined with the Wafd Party, and the alliance achieved the necessary eight percent minimum for parliamentary representation. Meanwhile Islamic fundamentalists were elected to university student councils, often gaining majorities and faculty support. To try to quell the Islamic militants, the government acquiesced to several fundamentalist demands. Alcohol was prohibited from EgyptAir flights, and the television program "Dallas" was banned. Furthermore, an element of divorce law declared by Sadat was found unconstitutional by the Supreme Court.

Mubarak has employed various strategies to counter the fundamentalist threat to his government. Early in his administration Mubarak appeased Islamic moderates in order to isolate militants, even initiating an Islamic newspaper, *Al-Liwa'al-Islami.* Just three years later, Mubarak again utilized the government press, but this time to mock Islamic militants, employing intellectuals such as Tewfiq al-Hakim and Yousuf Idris. (See Literature.)

Mubarak has tried to distance Egypt from Israel, recalling Egypt's ambassador when Israel invaded Lebanon and keeping the diplomatic air cool. In 1984, as Mubarak reached out to other countries, Egypt restored relations with the Soviet Union and was readmitted to the Islamic Conference.

Language

The earliest form of Egyptian writing was **hieroglyphics**—stories depicted by figures. Gradually scribes started to abbreviate pictures, retaining only the vital characteristics. Pictoral characters gave way to signs, forming the cursive called **hieratic.** After the twenty-second dynasty, scribes changed the hieratic writing to a form known as **Enchorial** or **Demotic,** used for business and social needs. The *Book of the Dead* was translated into this script. Well before the end of the Roman reign in Egypt, heiroglyphics had been fully replaced by Demotic, Greek, and Latin. Egyptian no longer served as the state language. **Coptic** is a descendant of ancient Egyptian that uses Greek letters and six letters of the Demotic hieroglyphics. Today it is used only in liturgy.

In 1799 the **Rosetta Stone** was discovered by M. Boussardi, providing the necessary clue to interpret ancient Egyptian. The slab contained a decree written in hieroglyphics, Demotic, and Greek. J. Champollion then deciphered the Egyptian alphabet and hieroglyphics. Characters representing intangibles—thoughts, feelings, ideas—are termed ideographs. The Rosetta Stone now resides in the British Museum.

Since the Muslim conquest, the language of Egypt has been Arabic. Modern **Egyptian Arabic** differs from classical, and the dialect varies from that used in Jordan and elsewhere. Classical Arabic (Fusha) is the language of learned and public discourse and liturgy. Evening news broadcasts, political speeches in the Assembly, and religious sermons are all in classical Arabic. Modern written Arabic is also classical in form. But colloquial Arabic is spoken by everyone in daily life, and it is the only language of the mass of uneducated people. Even within Egypt the vernacular varies: Cairo, Lower Egypt, and Upper Egypt each have their own dialects. Note that Arabic numerals are read from left to right while the language is read from right to left.

Islamic scholars consider Arabic the most beautiful and expressive language on Earth; after all, God chose it for the Koran. However, because it is a Semitic language and has nothing in common with European languages, Westerners may have difficulty learning it. Egyptians are aware of this, and any attempts you make to speak Arabic will be greatly appreciated. You may need to speak some Arabic to communicate your wishes outside tourist areas.

In addition to strange and unpredictable grammar, Arabic uses several sounds that are alien to speakers in English. *Kh* is like the German or Scottish *ch*. It represents a glottal stop, as in "co-operate" and indicates a sound made by tightly constricting the back of the throat. In addition, vowels and consonants can be either long or short, in terms of the length of time it takes to say them. You linger an instant more on the vowel in *salaam* (peace) than you do in *ahram* (pyramids). And a long consonant can mean the difference between *haman* (toilets) and *hamman* (pigeons). *R* is pronounced as a rolling growl, as in French. The aspirated h is hissed from the back of the throat. Try to mimic Arabic pronunciation as closely as possible; distinctions imperceptible to you are essential to communication. The definite article is the prefix *al,* which is often written *el.* It is pronounced somewhere in between the two; when before the consonants d, s, or z the *l* is not pronounced.

ahlan or *salaam aleikoom*	hello
ma'a salaama	goodbye
ismaaki	what is your name?
ismi	my name is
bikaam	how much?
fi	is there, there is
fi chai?	do you have tea?
feen	where?
aiwa	yes
la	no
kweis	good
mish kweis	bad
mish mumkin	impossible (shout at anyone who wants to overcharge you)
talib	student (reason you can't pay inflated prices)
mish kedem al-arabi	I don't speak Arabic.
shokran	thank you

min fadlak or *afwan*	please, excuse me
imshi	go away!

The *Cairo Practical Guide* includes a useful list of words; *Berlitz Arabic for Travelers* is helpful if you can master their transliteration system.

Because of Egypt's 150-year colonial history and its tourist trade, more English is written and spoken here than in other Arab countries. Most educated Egyptians speak at least a little English, and some are fluent. French is commonly spoken among the Egyptian upper classes, especially in Alexandria.

Literature

Most of the writings of the **ancient Egyptians** deal with magic and religion. Poetic love songs were written as well. The *Song of the Harper* advises immediate gratification in the face of transitory life. The *Song of Pentaurt* documents Ramses II's defeat of the Kheta. Hymns to the gods and moral aphorisms were also assembled.

Modern literature offers insights into the nation's culture and curiosities. Naguib Mahfouz is considered one of Egypt's premier contemporary novelists; his *Midaq Alley* describes life along the streets of the Fatimid neighborhood in northern Islamic Cairo in the 1960s, and his classic *Children of Jebelaw* chronicles several generations of a poor family from Cairo. Yusuf Idris, a leading short-story writer, offers a witty acount of modern Egyptian middle-class life in his *Cheapest Nights*. Perhaps the finest work by a contemporary Egyptian author is Sunallah Ibrahin's *The Smell of It,* a semi-autobiographical account of the writer's difficulties after his release from prison. Ironically, the only unabridged copy is in English since the Arabic edition has been censored. For a range of Egyptian fiction, read *Arabic Short Stories,* edited by Mahmoud Manzalaoui. The Egyptian theater of the absurd is represented by Tewfik al-Hakim's *The Fate of the Cockroach* and *Other Plays of Freedom.*

Most English translations of modern Egyptian literature are published by **Heinemann Press, Three Continents Press,** or the **American University in Cairo Press.** In the U.S. most of these books are distributed by Three Continents Press, 1636 Connecticut Ave. NW, #501, Washington, DC 20009 (tel. (202) 332-3885). Paperback editions cost between $5 and $8 (with a 20% discount on all orders of two or more books) and will be sent promptly by UPS. These books can also be found in Cairo at Madbuli's bookstore in Taalat Harb Sq.

Several **non-Egyptians** have written accounts of their travels and experiences within the country. In *The Innocents Abroad* Mark Twain describes his misadventures sightseeing on the Mediterranean, in Egypt, and the Holy Land. *Flaubert in Egypt* (edited by Francis Steegmuller) also offers stories of strangers-in-a-strange-land variety. In *Maalesh: A Theatrical Tour of the Middle East,* French playwright Jean Cocteau makes some insightful and humorous observations about Egypt. Probably the standard literary fare for the Westerner in Egypt is Lawrence Durrell's *Alexandria Quartet* of four novels. For an account of early explorers discovering the Nile, read Alan Moorehead's *The White Nile.* The companion volume, *The Blue Nile,* includes fascinating chapters on the French invasion of Egypt and the rise of Muhammad Ali. Another classic for travelers here is Olivia Manning's *Levant Trilogy,* about the wartime marriage of two British citizens who meet in Cairo during the 1940s.

Plenty of **histories** of Egypt have been written, as well as cultural, theological, and archeological studies. For an exhaustive eye-witness account of 1850s Egypt and Arabia, dig into Sir Richard Francis Burton's *Narrative of a Pilgrimage to Mecca and Medina.* In *The Riddle of the Pyramids,* the English physicist Kurt Mendelssohn offers intriguing solutions to archeological puzzles. John Wilson's *Culture of Ancient Egypt* provides an excellent and entertaining overview for pharaonic-era enthusiasts. E.M. Forster's *Alexandria: A History and a Guide* is a comprehensive guide to the city (for greater entertainment read Forster's *Pharos and Pharillon*). E.W. Lane's *Manners and Customs of the Modern Egyptians,* first published in 1836, is a great companion for touring Islamic Cairo. A superb source of inspiration for adventures in Islamic Cairo is Richard Parker and Robin Sabin's *A Practical Guide to Islamic Monuments in Cairo.* Anwar Sadat's autobiography *In Search of Identity* is also intriguing, as is his wife's book *A Woman of Egypt.*

Food

The influence of Greek, Persian, and Turkish cuisine flavors much of Egyptian fare. Since Egyptian food sometimes wreaks havoc with inexperienced digestive systems, it is mistakenly reputed to be strongly flavored and spiced. In fact, the food is often colorless and bland. Many cities and towns abound with cheap, clean restaurants that serve plentiful helpings of Egyptian food for LE2 or less. Stay away from the extremely inexpensive street vendors: Uninitiated stomachs will almost certainly protest energetically within a few hours. If you're in a hurry, catch a quick bite at a snack bar or fast-food restaurant.

Egyptians generally prefer big, hot meals, which are eaten with flat loaves of bread instead of silverware. *Kebab,* for example, consists of meat served roasted on a skewer with salad, dip, and pita bread. *Kufte* is a spiced ground meat wrapped around a skewer and roasted. Chicken is much cheaper and more widely eaten than beef or mutton. But since meat of any sort is a luxury that most Egyptians cannot afford regularly, the most common food is *fuul* (brown or black beans served mashed or whole with oil and sometimes an egg or small pieces of meat) and *kushari* (a mixture of macaroni, rice, lentils, and tomato sauce). For an exclusively Egyptian dish, try *mulakhiya,* a thick, spicy, green stew made from a flat leaf (Jew's Mallow) cooked either by itself or together with pieces of rabbit, chicken, or lamb. Like chicken, *samak* (fish) is an inexpensive alternative to red meat, and both salt water and fresh water types are available. Catfish from Lake Nasser is especially delicious. *Hammam* (pigeon) is also tasty, although you may come away hungry unless you eat two or three.

You can grab a quick meal at one of the many small restaurants and stalls that line the streets of Egyptian cities and towns. *Fuul mudamas* and *tamiya* (small fried patties or balls of mashed beans and vegetable paste), both served either by themselves or in a sandwich, are the main fare of these small restaurants. *Tahina,* a dip made of sesame-seed paste, and *baba ghanoush,* a mixture of tahina and roasted, mashed eggplant, may also be available in these restaurants, and are eaten with pieces of pita bread.

Shopping for yourself in the *souk* (market) is the cheapest alternative, but you must select your food carefully. Bread, subsidized by the government, is available in three types: *Aish baladi* (round unleavened loaves made with coarse flour); *aish shami* (similar to *baladi,* but made with refined white flour); and *aish* (leavened "French" style loaves). Street salesmen offer the flat or pita types while the leavened loaves must be bought directly from bakeries. Cheese comes in two locally produced varieties: *gibna bayda* (white feta cheese) and *gibna rumi* (a hard, yellow cheese with a sharp flavor). You can also purchase imported cheeses at reasonable prices. *Zabadi* (yogurt) comes unflavored and makes a filling addition to any meal, as does *amar ad-din* (apricot jello), which is served frequently during Ramadan.

Egyptian bakers produce a wide range of delicious pastries, including *baklava* (filo dough, honey, and nuts) and *fatir* (pancakes or flake pastry that are filled with anything from eggs to apricot preserves). Although a luxury for natives, fruit and fruit juices are some of the best values in Egypt by Western standards. Small juice stands abound in Egyptian towns, serving fresh fruit drinks in season (mango, strawberry, pomegranate, banana, orange), as well as perennial favorites such as *asab* (sugar cane juice), *tamar hindi* (tamarind), and *subiya* (a drink made from rice and sugar). After you've tried fresh Egyptian grape juice, you'll never go back to Welch's. For juice with more assurance of hygiene, try the *Best* brand of juices, easily recognizable in silver bags. They're fresh, pasteurized, and cheap (35pt). Fresh fruit is available year-round, but is seasonal in variety: Oranges, dates, and bananas are plentiful during the winter, while melons, peaches, plums, and grapes are summer fruits. If you visit Egypt in August or September, try *tin shawki* (cactus fruit).

Egyptians are devotees of coffee and tea. Egyptian tea, similar to the Western variety, is normally enjoyed with plenty of sugar and no milk. Though you may get Western-style coffee, Egyptians prefer *ahwa* (Arabic coffee), which comes in three degrees of sweetness—*ahwa sada* (no sugar), *ahwa mazbut* (medium sugar), and *ahwa ziedda* (very sweet). Especially when you are in Upper Egypt, try *kirkaday,* a refreshing red drink made by brewing the flower of the fuchsia plant and served hot or cold. Egyptian beer, with the brand-name *Stella,* is light and has a lower alcohol content than European beer. It costs between LE1.75 and LE2.50 in restaurants and bars. Egypt produces a selection of red and white wines ranging between LE2 and LE5 a bottle. Sample some before you buy a case—Egypt is not known for its superior vintages.

Although Egyptian popular cuisine reflects traditionally Arab tastes, the country's colonial history also has left its mark on Egypt's food. Restaurants serving European fare are common in Cairo and Alexandria. In recent years, several Western fast-food chains have established themselves in Egypt, and a taste for hamburgers, french fries, and fried chicken is spreading. Their popularity has spawned local imitation chains, but thankfully both they and their big-name precursors are confined to the major cities.

Cairo

> I arrived at length at Cairo, mother of cities and seat of
> Pharoah the tyrant, boundless in multitude of buildings,
> peerless in beauty and splendor, the meeting-place of comer
> and goer, the halting-place of feeble and mighty, whose
> throngs surge as waves of the sea.
>
> —Ibn Battuta

Walking through Cairo, you can see the same throngs and splendor that greeted Ibn Battuta at Cairo in 1326 C.E. The cars and other trappings of modernity seem to barely mask the antiquity underneath. Each of Cairo's conquerors, from the Romans to the Muslims to the British, have left their mark on the city. And you can journey to those eras without ever leaving the comforting squalor of the late twentieth century. Though formally called *al-Qahira,* Cairo is commonly called *Misr,* the same ancient name as Egypt itself.

Do not, however, expect Cairo to be an inhabited museum. The city groans under the weight of its exploding population. The capital of Egypt and the largest city in Africa, Cairo's concern is with the survival of fifteen million people, not with antiquity. No matter how well you've prepared, the noise, the grime, the crowds, and the poverty still shock. Egypt's realignment with the West has brought massive foreign aid for catch-up work on the city's infrastructure, resulting in constant construction and confusion. Cairo now quite literally stinks of modernity: The sky is filled with smog from the throng of cars careening madly through the jammed streets, and the overtaxed water system occasionally spews sewage down the alleyways. In the past few years, services and transportation have improved significantly, but the standards are still far below Western ones. The planners are hindered by a 2.5% population growth each year, and it will take more than infusions of hard currency to organize the city.

Cairo today seems perversely fecund; it threatens to destroy itself with an overabundance of life. It breathes smog and fumes and smells, and judging from the suspicious street stalls, it will eat almost anything. Cairo will be everything expected of it by the traveler, and much more that is unexpected and occasionally unwanted.

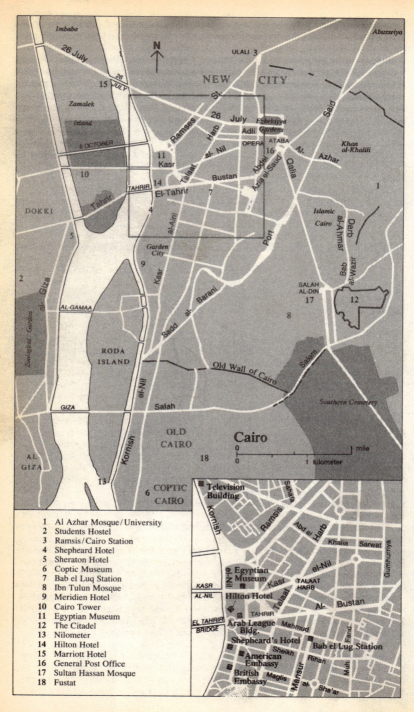

Cairo

0 _____ 1 mile
0 _____ 1 kilometer

1 Al Azhar Mosque/University
2 Students Hostel
3 Ramsis/Cairo Station
4 Shepheard Hotel
5 Sheraton Hotel
6 Coptic Museum
7 Bab el Luq Station
8 Ibn Tulun Mosque
9 Meridien Hotel
10 Cairo Tower
11 Egyptian Museum
12 The Citadel
13 Nilometer
14 Hilton Hotel
15 Marriott Hotel
16 General Post Office
17 Sultan Hassan Mosque
18 Fustat

History

The strategic importance of the stony plateau spreading out from the Nile 12km south of the Delta did not escape the Pharoahs of the Old Kingdom. Their cities of Memphis and Heliopolis, along with the funerary complexes at Saqqara and Giza, were located at the juncture of the newly joined upper and lower lands, right at the throat of the new body politic. Even though the royal capital eventually moved to Thebes and elsewhere, Memphis and Heliopolis remained important political and religious centers until the Ptolemaic period, when Heliopolis and its sun cult faded. Memphis lasted until the beginning of the Christian era, when massive movements of population left only a settlement at Giza and a Roman fort, called Babylon, on the west bank of the river.

When General Amr Ibn al-As conquered Egypt in 641 C.E., he came with specific instructions from the Caliph Uthman to center the new state at Babylon, not Alexandria, which the desert people distrusted because of its Mediterranean culture. Ibn al-As founded the outpost of Fustat, the seed of modern Cairo, on part of the plain due east of the ruins of Babylon. Further political growths and upheavals spread the settlement to the north and northeast, until the Abbasid Governor Ibn Tulun declared Egypt an independent state. He built a palatial new city around his Grand Mosque, modeled on the great cities of Iraq where he had been educated. When the Fatimids came sweeping in from Tunisia (969 C.E.), they took the still empty northern sector of the plain and built a magnificent walled city for the new caliph and his court called al-Qahira, "The Conqueror." Meanwhile, Fustat continued to grow in size and grandeur, becoming known by the old Semitic name for Egypt, Misr. This was the Golden Age in Cairo when, along with Damascus and Baghdad, it was a center of the most advanced culture west of China.

The old city of Fustat burned to the ground not once but twice, so when Salah al-Din overthrew the Fatimids in 1171 there wasn't much left. He opened up the walled enclosure of al-Qahira to the populace and built another fortress, the Citadel, on the hills to the south above the ashes of Fustat. During the short reign of the Ayyubids and the longer but more violent period of the Mamluk Sultans, the city continued to expand, remaining far greater in population and area than any city in Europe throughout the Middle Ages. Almost every sultan or prominent *amir* added a mosque, school, or hospital, usually raiding the Pharaonic ruins for building materials. The casing stones of the Giza Pyramids and Memphis are now strewn all over Islamic Cairo.

The Ottoman conquest of 1516 reduced Cairo to a provincial center, and the city declined and stagnated until the nineteenth century when Napoleon's invasion set off tremors that resulted in the ascendancy of the Turk Muhammad Ali as Khedive. The extravagant royal family built with little regard for Egyptian history, creating Turkish-style mosques and palaces including the huge Mosque of Muhammad Ali, a gaudy echo of the grand mosques of Istanbul. The Khedives, with their European mentors, designed the relatively broad and straight avenues of the New City, built in the lands emptied as the Nile shifted westward. This same geological process also created Gezirah Island.

The early twentieth century saw the creation of a new Heliopolis, planned by the extraordinary Baron Empain as a haven for Europeans. Population pressure has continually necessitated the creation of new suburbs, which appear to have been thrown up overnight. The latest, Madinat Nasr, is built on the edges of the Eastern Desert in an attempt to preserve the precious arable land in the Nile Valley itself. A new program of construction has created satellite cities that speckle the desert near Cairo; 6th of October City is located just beyond the Pyramids, providing still another juxtaposition of old and new.

Orientation

Metropolitan Cairo

Metropolitan Cairo consists of two separate administrative governates: **Cairo,** on the east bank of the Nile, and **Giza,** on the west bank. To the south of **Tahrir Square** in the center of Cairo are the quiet residential streets of **Garden City.** This neighborhood contains foreign embassies and banks, as well as many of the city's best-preserved nineteenth-century colonial mansions. Garden City flanks the west side of one of Cairo's main north-south avenues, **Kasr al-Aini Street.** A large, lower-income neighborhood sprawls to the east and south of Kasr al-Aini, unbroken but for the area just south of the American University, which is occupied by government ministries and the People's Assembly. Farther south, the city becomes steadily more impoverished, reaching the greatest squalor in **Old Cairo,** the historical and spiritual center of the Copts. Two and a half kilometers east of Tahrir Square lies **Islamic Cairo,** densely filled with monuments from all the Islamic periods and the location of Cairo's main *souk* (market) and tourist bazaar. Still farther east on the outskirts of the city lies the **City of the Dead,** the northern half of Cairo's vast Islamic necropolis. Today thousands of people live in and around the mausolea—though before extensive government resettlement, there were about two million. The necropolis extends south to the **Southern Cemetery.** To the northeast, **Ramses Street,** the road to the airport, passes through **Abbassiya** and then through the fashionable residential suburb of **Heliopolis,** replete with colonial architectural extravaganzas that include the residence of President Mubarak. North of downtown Cairo, beyond Ramses St., the lower-middle-class districts of **Bulaq** and **Shubra** gradually fade into the farmlands of the Nile Delta.

The most central bridge across the Nile is the **Tahrir Bridge,** which crosses from Tahrir Sq. to the southern tip of **Gezira Island.** The island's green southern half consists of a large public garden and two private sporting clubs, while the northern half is an upper-middle-class residential area known as **Zamalek;** this name is often applied to the whole island. South of Gezira in the Nile is **Roda Island,** site of Manial Palace and the Nilometer.

The Cairo Sheraton Hotel is on the west bank of the Nile past the Tahrir Bridge. This area of town, known as **Dokki,** is a residential neighborhood with a handful of important embassies. North of Dokki lies **Mohandiseen** ("Engineer's City"), designed in the late 1950s by President Nasser as a neighborhood for engineers and journalists. It is now a middle-class residential area. North of Mohandiseen lies **Imbaba,** which hosts the city's weekly camel market. Beyond spreads a vast, crowded, lower-class urban area and shantytown. South of Dokki at **Giza Square,** just beyond the campus of Cairo Universiy (*not* the American University campus) is the beginning of Pyramids Road, lined with sleazy, overpriced nightclubs. The road ends up at the pyramids of Giza.

Street signs and posted street numbers, in English or in Arabic, are as rare in Cairo as arrests for jaywalking. A good street map is a necessity. A series of folding maps with indexes prepared by Naguib Y. Amin, each covering a different part of Cairo, are particularly useful because they pinpoint the location of businesses that buy advertising space on the map, and the storefronts make good reference points (available at the AUC Bookstore, LE3.50 apiece). The *Blue Guide to Egypt* and the *AUC Practical Guide* also include good maps.

Downtown Cairo

The New City, now the transportation and commercial center of Cairo, was created by the Khedives of the nineteenth century with the British and French colonialists. The layout is much like a European city, with straight avenues radiating from squares (*maydan*) named for national heroes or revolutionary principles. Just east of the Nile, the huge asphalt expanse of **Tahrir Square,** once bedecked with fountains, was torn apart for the construction of the new Metro subway but remains the central hub of the city. Buses leave from two stations on the northern and southern sides to every metropolitan destination. At the north end of Tahrir facing the square is the sandstone **Egyptian Museum;** adjacent to it on the west side is the blue and white Nile Hilton, handy as a temporary haven and mail drop. Pick up a free map at the reception desk. At the southern end of the square is the concave Mugama Building, the Kafkaesque headquarters of the Egyptian bureaucracy. Register your passport here within seven days of arrival (for more details, see Practical Information below). The **American University in Cairo,** directly to the east of the Mugama Building across Kasr al-Aini St., has pleasant gardens filled with English-speaking Egyptians and Arabic-speaking Americans, as well as an excellent bookstore offering a variety of guidebooks and maps. Several metropolitan buses depart from a stop in front of the old Arab League Building, to the west of Mugama along Tahrir St., adjacent to the bridge over the Nile.

Talaat Harb Street runs from the northeast side of Tahrir through Talaat Harb Sq. Ramses Sq. to the north and Ataba Square to the east (both major transportation hubs) form a rough triangle with Talaat Harb, enclosing the main business and shopping district, which is packed with travel agents, banks, restaurants, juice stands, clothing stores, language schools, and budget hotels. Opera Square, on the east side of the triangle near Ataba Sq., was the sight of two great imperialist monuments, now destroyed: The Opera House and Shepheard's Hotel. Only the Azbekiya Gardens, surrounded by bookstalls, remain.

Transportation

For information on getting into Cairo from the principal transportation centers, see the Once There section in the Introduction to Egypt; see Transportation there for general information on transport.

Getting around Cairo can be extremely confusing. There is no shortage of options: Buses, private minibuses, shared taxis, private taxis, streetcars, trains and the new Metro make up the city's tightly-laced, inexpensive transport network.

Bus

The red and white public buses of Cairo run often and everywhere, and they cost practically nothing. But you get what you pay for: They are also shabby, crowded, and uncomfortable. Numbers and all destinations are usually written in Arabic, so you'll need to familiarize yourself with the characters. (See Arabic Numerals in General Introduction.) Most buses run from 6:30am until midnight, and during Ramadan from about 6:30am until 2am with a break from about 6:30 to 7:30pm. Two of Cairo's central bus depots are located in Tahrir Sq. The station opposite the American University and in front of the Mugama serves points south, Giza, and southern portions of Islamic Cairo; the one in front of the Nile Hilton serves points north and the rest of Islamic Cairo. Once you reach the right station, ask someone to point out the correct bus. All buses cost 10pt. The ticket takers on the metropolitan buses are honest; if they're slow to give you change, it's usually because they haven't got it. Try to have change handy. Outside the main stations, catching a bus is often a matter of running it down and properly timing your leap, as they seldom come to a full stop. The entrance is always through the rear door (except at a terminus), and the rear doors have been torn off most buses to facilitate this practice. To disembark, pick a moment when the bus is not moving too rapidly and face the front as you jump off. If you want the bus to come to a full halt at an official bus stop, you must exit through the front door. The front of a bus is generally less crowded than the rear, so it's worth the effort to push your way forward. An emphatic warning: When traveling by bus, keep wallets and valuables securely buried on your person. Deft pickpockets make a living with their acquired talents, practicing almost exclusively on tourists. To avoid other "wandering hands," women should use buses with discretion and should pass up the most crowded. The following are among Cairo's most important bus routes:

From the Mugama Station

#8: Tahrir—Kasr al-Aini—Manial—Giza—Pyramids—Mena House Hotel.

#900: Tahrir—Kasr al-Aini—Manial—Cairo University—Giza—Pyramids—Holiday Inn Hotel (very crowded, except early in the morning).

#82: Mausoleum of Imam al-Shafi'i—Southern Cemetery.

#174: Sayyida Zeinab—Ibn Tulun—Sultan Hasan—Citadel.

#6, 803: Giza Sq.

From the Nile Hilton Station

#50: Abbassiya.

#510: Heliopolis.

#400: Cairo Airport via Heliopolis (Maydan Roxy).

#72: Sayyida Zeinab—Citadel—Mausoleum of Imam al-Shafi'i.

#173, 403: Citadel—Sultan Hasan.

#75: Islamic Museum—Bab Zuwayla.

#63, 66: Al-Azhar—Khan al-Khalili.

#73: Imbaba (camel market).

Buses from Tahrir Sq. to Islamic Cairo are usually extremely crowded. For **Ramses** Station, take any bus from the platform farthest to the east.

From the Arab League Building (on Tahrir St., 50m before Tahrir Bridge)

#13: Zamalek.

#110, 182, 102, 203, 19, 166: Dokki.

Inter-city Buses

Unfortunately, Cairo has no single bus depot. You'll have to search out the various points of departure. The following are most important stations in Cairo:

Tahrir Square (Maydan Tahrir): Most buses leave this confusing hub from stations on the western side of the Nile Hilton. Reserve seats for Alexandria (LE3.50, A/C LE5.50) and Marsa Matruuh (LE7.50, A/C LE12) 24 hours in advance. Buses also leave Tahrir Sq. for Port Said and Ismailia. See Alexandria and Matruuh chapters for details.

Ahmed Himli Square (Maydan Ahmed Himli): Behind Ramses Station, accessible by the vehicle-pedestrian bridge at the southwestern corner of Ramses Sq. and adjacent to the service taxi lot. The Wagh Ibli Company (ticket office near Ramses; tel. 74 66 58 or 60 32 77) serves Upper Egypt, with frequent buses to Fayyum (6:30am-6pm, LE1.50), and 2 to 4 buses per day to Minya (LE3.50), Mallawi (LE3.50), Assyut (LE5.50), Qena (LE9), Luxor (LE11), and Aswan (LE14). Same company also runs to Hurghada—ask for Ghardaka (LE12-15).

Abbassiya Station: Sometimes called Sinai Station. In Abbassiya District, 5km northeast of Ramses Station at the end of Ramses St., near the mental hospital. From Tahrir or Ramses Sq., you can catch local buses (#54, 56, 728) or minibuses (#24, 32). The **Delta Company** (tel. 82 47 53) and the **South Sinai Company** (tel. 83 02 42) run frequent buses to Sinai destinations as well as to Hurghada; see those chapters.

Kolali Square (Maydan Kolali): In Ramses Sq., across from the main train station. Buses for Port Said and Ismailiya; see those chapters.

Giza Station: On Nile St. in Giza. Service taxis and buses depart from here to Fayyum and Nile Valley cities.

Buses traveling between major cities leave frequently throughout the day. Buses to and from the Sinai and the oases often depart only early in the morning. If you can, go to the station the day before to confirm departure times.

Numbers and destinations on Egyptian buses are normally written only in Arabic. If you're in doubt about the bus to take, ask directions. The conductors who sit at the little kiosks at Tahrir, Ramses, and the other main terminals are usually helpful. A temporary bus service connected Cairo to Tel Aviv and Jerusalem (LE57) during the summer of 1988. To inquire if this is still in operation, contact Misr Travel at 1 Talaat Harb St. (tel. 75 00 77).

Minibus

The Cairo municipal government has introduced multi-colored minibuses along many of the same routes served by the larger, older buses. These new vehicles should not be confused with the older, monochromatic taxi-vans that are privately operated (see **Taxi** below). Although more expensive than the regular buses (20-50pt—prohibitively expensive to most Cairenes), the minibuses are far more comfortable. They line up at the Nile Hilton and Mugama Stations; each has a driver and conductor who can direct you to the correct bus. The following are important minibus routes:

From the Mugama Station

#59: Ramses Sq., Tahrir, Old Cairo.

#52, 56: Maadi.

#58: Maadi via Dar es-Salaam.

#83: Dokki, Giza, Maydan et-Ta'awon (al-Ahram St., Pyramids Rd).

#82: Kasr al-Aini, Giza, Faisal Rd., the Pyramids.

From the Nile Hilton

#24: Abbassiya, Roxy.

#27: Masr el-Gadida, Airport.

#39: Hada'iq el-Quba, el-Maza.

#35: Abbassiya, Ismailiya Sq. (Masr el-Gadida).

From the Arab League Building

#77: Bulaq ad-Dakrour.

#76: Ataba, Zamalek, Tahrir, Bulaq ad-Dakrour.

#26: Roxy, Tahrir, Dokki, Giza.

#84: Ataba, Tahrir, Dokki, Giza.

Metro

The new Cairo Metro system, completed in late 1987, is a world apart from the rest of Cairo public transport. Cool, clean, and efficient, the trains run along a single line linking the southern industrial district of Helwan to the workers' homes north of the city, with a number of stops downtown. Trains run every six minutes from 6am to midnight and tickets cost 15-50pt. The downtown stations (look for the enormous red "M" signs) are Mubarak (Ramses Sq.), Orabi (Orabi St. and Ramses St.), Nasser (July 26 St. and Ramses St.), Sadat (Tahrir Sq.), Sa'ad Zaghloul (Mansur St. and Ismail Abaza St.), Sayyida Zeinab (Mansur St. and Ali Ibrahim St.), El Malik el-Saleh (Salah Salem Road) and Mar Girgis (Old Cairo). Because trains are often dangerously packed during rush-hour, you should avoid Metro travel before 9am and between 5 and 7pm.

Taxi

The secret to happiness when traveling within Cairo lies in learning how to take a cab. Never take the large, unmetered, monochromatic Peugeot taxis within the city—they charge LE2-3 for a drive around the corner. Confine your attention instead to the metered **black-and-white taxis** that often carry passengers collectively.

To hail a taxi, pick a major thoroughfare headed in the general direction you wish to travel, stand on the side of the street, stretch out your arm as a taxi approaches, and scream out your destination as it goes by. If the driver is interested in your business, he'll stop and wait for you to run over to his car. Jump in, but don't talk to the driver except to verify your destination. Don't be alarmed if the taxi seems to be going in the wrong direction; drivers sometimes take circuitous routes to avoid traffic-jammed main arteries or take detours to deposit other passengers. If the driver tells you he has to travel a long distance before reaching your destination, refuse the offer and wait for another cab.

New meters have recently been installed in all Cairo taxis, but drivers rarely use them, since passengers jump in and out—haggling only implies that you don't know what you owe. Cairenes simply hail a cab, hop in, and pay what they think is adequate upon arrival. If you follow their example and are firm, the driver will just smile and wish you a nice day.

Once you've used taxis for a while, you'll master the hidden logic of the fares. For journeys of 1km or less, 50pt is usually sufficient. Add 25pt per kilometer thereafter, and about 25% on the entire fare for each additional passenger. You are also expected to pay extra for suitcases and waiting. The fare from Tahrir Sq. to the Northern Cemetery or the Pyramids should be about LE3, and to Khan al-Khalili about LE1.50. Avoid the black-and-white taxis that park in front of major hotels—they're experts at exploiting tourists and often charge as much as limousines.

Do not expect a taxi driver to speak English, or to know the location of every address or street. Try to identify a major landmark or thoroughfare near your destination and learn to pronounce it in Arabic. Street is *sharia,* square is *maydan,* and both words come before the name, e.g. Sharia Talaat Harb, Maydan el-Tahrir. Alternatively, have someone write out the address and directions in Arabic. They'll be glad to do this for you at the tourist office. Communication is fortunately not a problem for most downtown and tourist destinations.

Luggage racks are the only advantage of the expensive, unmetered **Peugeot taxis.** If you're interested in hiring a car for the day, Cairo has a limousine service that rents vehicles with drivers for a daily rate much lower than the cost of a private taxi by the hour. Contact **Limousine Misr** (tel. 259 98 13).

Inter-city service taxis are best for short trips. Catch tehm at Kolali Sq. for Alexandria and the Suez Canal; south to Fayyum and Minya in Giza Sq. by the train station; to the Delta and Port Said in Ahmed Himli Sq. You'll have to hunt for taxis to the Sinai.

You will also see **taxi-vans,** called *arrabeya bil nafar,* all around town. These have the word "taxi" written on the side and carry 12-15 passengers. They function more like buses than taxis, running along fixed routes and often stopping only at certain places. To catch a taxi-van, go to a taxi-van stop and yell out your destination as the van passes. From Ataba Sq. taxi-vans go to Ramses, Tahrir, Northern Cemetery, Zamalek, Islamic Cairo, and Heliopolis. In Tahrir Sq. taxi-vans leave from behind both bus stations and go to Heliopolis, Giza Sq., Dokki, Mohandiseen, and the Pyramids. At the stations, drivers will stand outside their buses and shout out their destinations until the bus fills up. Fares are 20pt for short hauls and up to 50pt for longer trips. Taxi-vans provide the most comfortable means of inexpensive transportation between Cairo and some of the outlying areas, most notably Giza.

River taxis provide an amusing, relaxing, and cheap alternative means of transportation to Old Cairo. Boats run every 30-40 minutes to the Nile barrages, Old Cairo (via Giza), and Imbaba at a cost of 50pt. The departure point is on the corniche in front of the television building about 1km north of Tahrir Sq.

Train

Ticket windows at the chaotic Ramses Station are open from 8am until 10pm. If you have time, go first to the tourist office on Adly St. and have them write out the desired destination and other details in Arabic to avoid confusion. If you don't want to spend a long time waiting in line, come a half hour before opening. Which line you stand in depends upon whether you are reserving a seat in advance or trying to buy a ticket for the same day (often impossible). Women (and men traveling with women) can take advantage of the special women's line that may form at crowded times, which is much shorter and faster than the corresponding men's line. In addition, women are permitted (possibly expected) to push to the front of the line, head held high. They should expect, however, to be pushed and touched themselves. To avoid wasting time, always be sure you are standing in the correct line. If you give up one day and come back the next, don't assume that the same ticket window is the one you want. If you are willing to travel third class, you can buy tickets from the conductor on the train. Third class is a poor idea for women traveling alone; if you have to go this way, try to sit with a group of Egyptian women. Even second class trains can be an alarming experience for women. Traveling first class to avoid this unpleasantness is often worth the price.

The trains enter their berths at least a half hour before departure time, so there should be plenty of time to find your place. None of the train numbers or destinations is in English, but fellow travelers and the Tourist Police will gladly lend a hand. For information at Ramses Station, call 75 35 55. Right next to the sleeper reservation window at the front of the station is an information desk. Cairo's tourist police office doubles as a train information office. For more information on trains, see Transportation in the Egypt Introduction.

Walking

The one positive aspect of Cairo's incredibly packed layout is that almost everything in the city is within easy walking distance of Tahrir Square. While more time-consuming, you can see all the sights of Islamic Cairo, the downtown areas, and Roda and Zamalek Islands without once using mechanized transport (an attractive proposition considering Cairo traffic and driving habits). Biking is not a viable option in Cairo—it would be like trying to cycle blindfolded down the wrong way of a freeway. Many would argue that walking is the *only* way to see the city; on foot, you will undoubtably catch many fascinating glimpses of Cairo life which would go unseen from a bus or car. You will, however, have to get your shoes dirty; don't wear sandals for walks outside downtown areas because the garbage, leaking sewage, and donkey manure are deep.

Traffic will almost always be heavy: The only times the streets are empty are during Ramadan and for important football matches. Take your time and go with the flow of the crowd. Cars reign in Cairo; drivers expect pedestrians to look after themselves. Since pedestrians must often take to the streets, it is wise to walk facing oncoming traffic and heed the horns of oncoming cars. A long, uninterrupted honk usually indicates that the driver is either unwilling or unable to swerve. Some say that in the latest English-Egyptian Arabic dictionary the idiomatic phrase "futile, pathetic gesture at maintaining civilized behavior in the streets" is illustrated by a picture of traffic lights or a traffic cop. Ignore both; everyone else does. Experienced Cairenes warn against being too careful when you cross a street because if you stop short or break into a run you'll throw off the rhythm of the driver bearing down on you, and he just might hit you.

Practical Information

The most comprehensive compendium of useful information on Cairo is *Cairo: A Practical Guide,* which includes a set of city maps. It is published by American University in Cairo Press and is available at most bookstores for LE10. The most reliable telephone directory for goods and services is the *Cairo Telephone List,* published by the Maadi Women's Guild and available for LE10 at the American Chamber of Commerce, Marriott Hotel, Zemalek (tel. 340 88 88, ext. 1541).

Tourist Office: Main Office, 5 Adly St. (tel. 391 34 54). About a 20-min. walk from Tahrir Sq.: Go up Talaat Harb St. past Talaat Harb Sq. and turn right on Adly St. The office is 3 blocks down on the left, marked "Tourist Police." Free map. While the helpful staff is short on actual facts, they can usually steer you in the right direction for more information, and will readily write out questions in Arabic (useful for buying train tickets). Open daily 9am-7pm; during Ramadan 9am-5pm. Other offices at **Cairo International Airport** (tel. 66 74 75) and **Giza** at the Pyramids (tel. 85 02 59).

Passport Office: Mugama Building, south end of Tahrir Sq. Passports must be registered within 7 days of arrival. On the 2nd floor, find the window marked "Information." Registration open Sat.-Wed. 8am-4pm, Thurs. 8am-1:30pm, Fri. 10am-1pm, and every evening 7-9pm. Evening hours are least crowded. Ask at your hotel, and they may register for you.

Ministry of the Interior: Sheikh Ridan and Nuban St., (tel. 355 63 01 or 354 86 61), 2 blocks east of AUC. Apply here for permits to visit Siwa Oasis, secondary roads in the Delta or Sinai, the Suez Canal between Ismailiya and Suez, and the coastal road to Libya beyond Marsa Matruuh. Applications require 2 photos and photocopies of the first 3 pages of your passport and Egyptian entry visa. Processing takes 1 day.

American Embassy: 5 Latin America St. (tel. 355 73 71), 2 blocks south of Tahrir Sq. Lost or stolen passports replaced overnight for LE84; limited passports issued on request for travel to Israel. Passport photographs at the Nile Hilton. Pick up the booklet with advice for American visitors. Open Sun.-Thurs. 8:30am-4pm.

British Embassy: 7 Ahmed Ragheb St. (tel. 354 08 50), south of U.S. Embassy. Open Sun.-Thurs. 7:30am-2pm. Since **New Zealand** has no embassy, the British handle their affairs.

Canadian Embassy: 6 Muhammad Fahmi al-Sayid St., Garden City (tel. 354 31 10 or 354 31 19). Open Sun.-Thurs. 7:30am-3pm.

Australian Embassy: 5th Floor, Cairo Plaza, 1097 Corniche al-Nil (tel. 77 79 00 or 77 79 94), 4 blocks south of Shepheard's Hotel. Open Sun.-Thurs. 8am-3pm.

Israeli Embassy: 6 Ibn al-Malek St., Dokki (tel. 72 60 00). Cross over to Dokki from Roda Island on University Bridge. The street to the right of and parallel to the bridge is Ibn al-Malek. Look up at the top floors for the Israeli flag or for the security guards by the entrance who will ask to see your passport. Open daily 10:30am-12:30pm.

Sudanese Embassy: 3 al-Ibrahimi St., Garden City (tel. 354 50 43). US$10, 4 photos, and a letter of recommendation from your embassy are required for a visa. Open Sun.-Thurs. 8:30am-3pm, visas until noon.

Jordanian Embassy: 6 Gohaina, Dokki (tel. 348 55 66), 2 blocks west of the Cairo Sheraton. Visas require 1 photograph and a letter of introduction, and are free for U.S., Canadian, and Australian passport holders; New Zealand and U.K. passport-holders must pay LE31.50 and LE73.50, respectively. Open Sat.-Thurs. 9am-12:30pm.

Banks: Bank of America, 106 Kasr al-Aini St., Garden City (tel. 354 77 88), and on Sheikh Rihan St. This is the easiest place to obtain advances in Egyptian Pounds with a MasterCard or Visa, but it still may take an hour for telex confirmation. Money can be wired to Egypt through **Citibank,** 4 Ahmed Pasha St., Garden City (tel. 355 18 73), and **Manufacturer's Hanover,** 3 Ahmed Nesim St., Giza (tel. 72 67 03). **Cairo Barclays International Bank,** 12 Sheikh Yusef Sq., Garden City (tel. 354 21 95), 3 blocks south of Tahrir Sq. along Kasr al-Aini St., accepts traveler's checks and has worldwide money transfer services. All banks offer foreign exchange facilities. Open Mon.-Thurs. 8:30am-1:30pm, Sun. 10am-noon; during Ramadan, 10am-1:30pm. Foreign banks are closed on Fri. and Sat., while most Egyptian banks are open Sat. **Bank Misr** at the Nile Hilton is open 24 hours. Banking services in other major hotels are open until 8pm.

American Express: 15 Kasr al-Nil (tel. 75 08 81 or 75 08 92), just off Talaat Harb Sq., toward Ramses St. Best place to have money and mail sent (you must hold their traveler's checks). Open daily 8am-7pm, during Ramadan 8am-6pm. Letter service closed Fri. Other locations: Ramses Hilton (tel. 77 36 90), Nile Hilton (tel. 74 33 83), Marriott Hotel (tel. 341 01 36), Meridien Hotel (tel. 84 40 17), Residence Maadi (tel. 350 78 17), and Sheraton Giza Hotel (tel. 348 89 37). All Cairo offices provide cash dollars or LE for traveler's checks, but you need an American Express card to purchase traveler's checks. Hotel offices provide faster service, but sometimes run out of cash. The office in the Nile Hilton has the longest hours, 8am-7pm.

Travel Agency for the Disabled: Dr. Sami Bishara organizes both individual and group tours to Cairo and Luxor for the mobility-impaired. For brochures and advice, contact him at ETAMS, 99 Ramses St., Cairo (tel. 75 24 62; telex: 22 775 ETAMS).

Post Office: Ataba Sq. Often very crowded. Open Sat.-Thurs. 8am-7pm, Fri. 8am-noon. Other post offices open Sat.-Thurs.. 8:30am-3pm; during Ramadan 9am-1pm. Packages require an export license from Cairo International Airport; major hotels and tourist shops provide this service.**Telephone Office: Main Office,** Ramses St., 1 block north of July 26 St. Other offices on Tahrir Sq., Adly St., and Alfy St., under the Windsor Hotel. All open 24 hours. No collect calls possible anywhere. If you're willing to pay the 25% surcharge, you can make international calls much more easily at the business service offices of the Meridien, Sheraton, and Nile Hilton hotels (24 hours). The Nile Hilton has several local pay phones in the lobby.

Telegraph and Telex Office: Ataba Sq., opposite the main post office. Open 24 hours. Other offices at Tahrir Sq., 26 Ramses St., and Adly St.

Buses, Trains, Metro, Taxis: See respective sections above in "Transportation."

Car Rental: For maniacs willing to risk life and limb to achieve relative freedom of mobility, the following agencies rent cars: **Avis** (tel. 75 06 66), **Europcar** (tel. 340 11 52), **Hertz** (tel. 77 74 44), and **Budget** (tel. 341 37 90). Rates vary, but a Fiat 127 costs around LE60 per day plus 20pt per km over 100km. See Egypt Introduction for more details. You might also want to see hospitals above.

Lockers for storing luggage and valuables are located on the ground floor of Ramses Station, Ramses Sq. They cost 15pt per day for a maximum of 15 days. Walk into the station and ask anyone in uniform, *"Feen el khazanat?"*

English Bookstores: AUC Bookstore, Hill House, American University in Cairo, 113 Kasr al-Aini St., has a wide inventory of English literature, guidebooks, and maps, as well as the highest prices in town. **Anglo-Egyptian,** 165 Muhammad Farid St. (tel. 391 43 37), has new and used English literature at reasonable prices. Open Mon.-Sat. 9am-1:30pm and 5-8pm. **Lehnert and Landrock,** 44 Sharif St. (tel. 74 76 06) also has a wide selection. **Madbuli,** in Talaat Harb Sq., and the bookstores in the **Nile Hilton** and other major hotels have good selections of books on Egypt.

Foreign Newspapers and Magazines: Largest collection at the kiosks along Talaat Harb Sq., or at the intersection of July 26 and Hassan Sabri St., Zamalek.

American Cultural Center: 4 Ahmed Ragheb St., Garden City (tel. 355 05 32), across from the British Embassy. To join, take along your passport (any nationality) and 2 photos. Members can take out books and cassettes from the library. Occasional free films and lectures. Open in summer Mon.-Fri. 10am-4pm; in winter Mon. and Wed. 10am-8pm, Tues., Thurs.-Fri. 10am-4pm.

British Council: 192 el-Nil St., North Dokki (tel. 345 32 81), 1 block south of July 26 St. There is a large library (membership LE10) with books, cassettes, and videotapes. Also sponsors performances by visiting British cultural groups. Open Sun.-Thurs. 8am-2:45pm.

Laundry: Pension Roma, 169 Muhammad Farid St. (tel. 391 10 88; for directions, see listing under Accommodations), charges around 30pt per article, and will have laundry back the next day. If you're really desperate, the **Marriott Hotel,** off July 26 St. in Zamalek, offers a laundry and dry-cleaning service to non-guests which costs about LE2.50 per article. The cheapest way is to buy a bar of soap (20pt) and do it yourself; wet clothes dry in about an hour under the Cairo sun.

Photography and Film Developing: Film and processing is cheaper outside the major hotels. **Actina,** 4 Talaat Harb St. (tel. 75 72 36). Open Mon.-Sat. 10am-4pm. **Kodak,** 20 Adly St. (tel. 74 93 99), opposite the synagogue, has 1-hr. processing (LE1.50 extra). Open Mon.-Sat. 9am-8pm. **Photo Greenwich,** 16 Adly St. (tel. 90 69 90), 1 block east of Kodak, sells cameras, calculators, film, and batteries. Open Mon.-Sat. 9am-8pm. At all of the above, 1 day developing costs around LE1 plus 35pt per print and a roll of Kodachrome film (36 exp.) costs LE5-6.

Swimming Pools: You can pay LE50 per day to live at a major hotel and swim in a deep-blue, Olympic-size pool. Or you can pay LE4 and swim in the less-than-Olympic-size, slightly green (but chlorinated nonetheless) pool on the seventh floor patio of the **Fontana Hotel,** Ramses Sq. (tel. 92 21 45).

24-Hour Pharmacy: First-Aid Pharmacy, corner of July 26 St. and Ramses St. (tel. 74 33 69), northwest side of intersection. This place doesn't look much like a pharmacy. Don't worry: Head pharmacist Dr. Muhammad is competent, speaks fairly good English, and is recommended by foreigners. **Ajaz Khanat Sayfa,** 76 Kasr al-Aini St., Garden City (tel. 354 26 78), several blocks south of Tahrir Sq.

Hospitals: Anglo-American Hospital, Botanical Garden St., Gezira-Zamalek (tel. 340 61 62 or 340 61 63) next to the Cairo Tower. **As-Salam International Hospital,** Corniche al-Nil, Maadi (tel. 84 21 88, 350 71 96, or 350 70 50). **Cairo Medical Center,** Roxy Sq., Heliopolis (tel. 258 02 37 or 258 06 36). In case of emergency, try to reach As-Salam International. Always bring enough cash to pay at the time of treatment.

Private Doctors: General Practice, Dr. Naguib Badir, at Anglo-American Hospital, Zamalek (tel. 340 61 62); **Internal Medicine,** Dr. Victor Fanous, Nile Hilton Hotel Clinic (tel. 74 07 77 or 75 46 23); **Tropical Medicine,** Dr. Zoheir Farid, 16 Abdal Khalak Sarwat St. (tel. 74 50 23 or 74 54 78). **Gynecologist,** Dr. Sherif Gohar, 2 Talaat Harb Sq. (tel. 74 88 08); **Dentist,** Dr. Aida A. Bastawi (tel. 354 75 54).

Medical Emergency: Ambulance (tel. 123 or 77 01 23).

City Ambulance Service: Tel. 77 04 06 or 77 03 65.

Police: Tel. 122.

Accommodations

You can find any of Cairo's many luxury hotels simply by looking for the nearest thirty-story tower done up in pink granite; finding a decent budget hotel is more difficult. Full service hotels can be found for as little as LE25 per night, although the amenities may be less comfortable and clean than you would expect from similar establishments in Europe.

Most of Cairo's inexpensive hotels are in the **New City,** hidden away on the upper floors of downtown office and apartment buildings. Equally inconspicuous are the many hotels along **Talaat Harb Street** between Tahrir Sq. and July 26 St. In summer, the least expensive hotels fill up quickly, but by the end of your walk along this stretch, you will probably find a room. The quality va--- many are run-down and dirty. Be prepared to bargain: It helps if you do not app   -rn out and desperate for sleeping quarters.

Don't shy away from hotels perched on upper floors. Cairo's streets are noisy throughout much of the night and the extra height will make sleeping considerably easier. Be aware, however, that the uppermost floors of downtown buildings often lack both well-functioning elevators and running water. Verify that the elevators and taps work before checking in. Even during the dog days of summer, nights in Cairo are cool enough that air-conditioning isn't necessary, although it will enable you to close the windows and shut out the cacophony of the streets below. Most places also rent fans at reasonable rates and serve tea, coffee, and soft drinks in their lobbies.

The very cheapest places in town can be dangerously unsanitary and uncomfortable. However, for the truly destitute, a mattress can be rented for LE2.50 at the notorious Oxford Guest House, 30 Talaat Harb St. Showers and bedbugs at no extra cost. You may want to get very, very drunk before daring to spend the night here.

Youth Hostel (IYHF), 135 Abdel Aziz al-Saud St., Roda Island (tel. 84 07 29). Take metro to Sayyida Zeinab, and cross the Sayala Bridge. Continue along the road, keeping the Manial Palace gardens to your left, until you come to the hostel across from the Salah al-Din Mosque. Wall-to-wall bunks in spartan but clean rooms. Often very crowded, so call ahead. Lockers in every room, and padlocks available from the warden. Members LE4, nonmembers LE3 extra (after 6 nights you become a full member). Closed 10am-2pm, and also 6-8pm during Ramadan. 11pm curfew.

Downtown and Talaat Harb Street

Windsor Hotel, 19 Alfy Bey St. (tel. 91 58 10 or 91 52 77; telex: 938 39 DOSS UN). Beautiful and clean, in an atmosphere of faded grandeur. Roof garden and restaurant with an opulent bar popular among U.S. and British expatriates. Excellent service. Mr. Doss, the friendly manager, offers a 25% discount on room rates (not including breakfast, tax, or service) to users of *Let's Go.* Singles with bath LE24. Doubles with bath LE30. A/C LE1. Breakfast included.

Pensione Roma, 169 Muhammad Farid St. (tel. 391 10 88 or 391 13 40) 2 blocks south of July 26 St. and east of Talaat Harb St, above the "Gattegno" department store. The proprietor, Mrs. Cressaty, runs a very tight ship. The tastefully decorated rooms are quiet, clean, cool, and airy, and the service here is discreet and professional. This place is no secret, so call ahead. Singles LE9. Doubles LE16, with bath LE17. Breakfast included.

Anglo-Swiss Hotel, 14 Champollion St., 7th floor (tel. 75 14 97), conveniently located 2 blocks west of Talaat Harb Sq. Quiet, secluded, and immaculate, this is the place to calm your shattered nerves after a day of sightseeing. Cool stone floors and conservative decor do actually give it a "European" feel. Singles LE10, doubles LE14. Breakfast included.

Fontana Hotel, Ramses Sq. (tel. 92 21 45), on your left as you leave the station. Although a little shabby, this place has the amenities of a first-class hotel: private baths, phones, rooftop restaurant, disco, pool, and a gift-shop in the lobby. Rooms are clean and comfortable. Singles LE18, doubles LE26. Fans LE2. Breakfast included.

Grand Hotel, 17 July 26 St. (tel. 75 77 00), at the corner of Talaat Harb St. This enormous hotel has sparsely furnished but clean rooms, many with balconies. Singles LE12, with bath LE20. Doubles LE16, with bath LE24. A/C LE1.65. Fans 35pt. Breakfast LE2.

New Hotel, 21 Adly St. (tel. 392 71 76), 2 blocks from Talaat Harb St. Uniformly dark and dingy rooms, but reasonably clean. Main attraction is the location and the atmosphere: This is an Egyptian hotel patronized by Egyptians. Comfortable ground-floor TV lounge. Solo women might feel uncomfortable here. Singles LE13, doubles LE22. No private baths. Breakfast included.

Lotus Hotel, 12 Talaat Harb St. (tel. 75 06 27 or 75 09 66), 1 block from Tahrir Sq. Rooms are large, clean, and well-lit. The enormous tubs are worth the extra LE3. Quiet and relaxed atmosphere. A/C. Singles LE15, with bath LE18. Doubles LE20, with bath LE23. Breakfast included.

Montana Hotel, 25 Sharif St., 7th floor (tel. 74 86 08), 2 blocks south of Adly St. Old but clean rooms. Occasional odor from incense factory nearby (quite pleasant, actually). Singles LE12.50, with shower LE14. Doubles LE18, with shower LE21. Fans LE1.65. Breakfast included.

Capsis Palace Hotel, 117 Ramses St. (tel. 75 42 19), 3 blocks from Ramses Sq. Slightly overpriced with small, but clean rooms in a noisy, somewhat inconvenient location. All rooms with pseudo-A/C. Singles LE16, with bath LE25. Doubles LE31, with bath LE33.

Hotel des Roses, 33 Talaat Harb St. (tel. 75 80 22), 2 blocks north of Talaat Harb Sq. This small, grimy hotel resembles the Oxford Guest House. Rooms reasonably clean, but in a noisy location. Singles LE8, with bath LE10.50. Doubles LE11, with bath LE14.50. Fans LE2. Breakfast included.

Garden City

Garden City House, 23 Kamal ed-Din Salah St. (tel. 354 81 26 or 354 84 00), across from the new Semiramis Hotel. You could not ask for a more central location. The large airy rooms are pleasant, and many have balconies overlooking the scenic Tahrir Sq. bus depot. Singles LE18, with bath LE24. Doubles LE31, with bath LE37. Fans LE1.50. Breakfast, dinner, and all taxes included.

Zamalek

El-Nil Zamalek Hotel, 21 Maahad al-Swissry St. (tel. 340 18 46; international 340 02 20). One of the few budget hotels that actually looks like a hotel. Quiet and secluded, the rooms are spacious, modern, and very clean. All have bath, TV, A/C, and telephone; many also have a balcony overlooking the Nile. The perfect budget honeymoon spot. Singles LE26, doubles LE33.

Balmoral Hotel, 157 July 26 St. (tel. 340 67 61 or 340 05 43), at Maahad al-Swissry St., opposite the Marriott. Located in possibly the noisiest spot in Zamalek. Rooms a little musty, but nice. Singles with bath LE20, doubles with bath LE30. Breakfast included.

Bodmin House, 17 Hasan Sabri St. (tel. 340 28 42), 1 block from July 26 St. Entrance is dark and unpleasant, as are the rooms. Low price is its only virtue. Unaccompanied women should probably avoid this establishment. Singles LE8.50, doubles LE13.50. Breakfast and lunch included.

Khan al-Khalili

El Hussein Hotel, el-Hussein Sq. (tel. 91 84 79 or 91 86 64), next to al-Azhar Sq. Name written in big letters on side of building. This large hotel is well removed from the chaos and confusion of Khan al-Khalili. Rooms are large, clean, and have A/C; many have splendid views. Singles LE12.50, with bath LE18. Doubles LE17, with bath LE24. Breakfast included.

New Rich Hotel, 47 Abdel Aziz St. (tel. 90 01 45), off Ataba Sq. While the gaudy lobby and dreary, but clean, rooms are nothing to write home about, the view from the restaurant is breathtaking, and the hotel's location is perfect for forays into Islamic Cairo. Safer for women (the proprietor is female). Singles LE18, with bath LE25. Doubles LE26, with bath LE33.50. A/C LE1.65. Breakfast included. 15% discount for *Let's Go* users.

Dokki

King Hotel, 20 Abdel Rehim Sabri St. (tel. 71 08 69), about a 15 min. walk from Tahrir. Quiet location. A full-service hotel, with television, refrigerator, and telephone in each room, as well as central A/C. Friendly management and lots of English-speaking tourists. Singles LE35, doubles LE45.

Food

Given a fairly high taste and sanitation tolerance, you'll only need 10pt to fill your stomach in Cairo. The cheapest grub in town is probably *fuul* and *taamiya* (beans and fried vegetable paste), and literally hundreds of *fuul* restaurants litter Cairo. But in the cheapest places, you are really taking chances on bacterial infection. Many *fuul* restaurants also sell fried potato and eggplant sandwiches with pickles (*turshi*)—a real feast. Another inexpensive alternative is *kushari,* a mixture of macaroni, rice, lentils, and fried onions. *Kushari* shops are scattered all over the city and are easy to spot, with the conical piles of rice displayed in their windows. *Kushari* costs as little as 25pt per serving. *Fatir* is a round concoction of flaky dough with a variety of fillings from sausage to sweet jams; like *kushari,* it is sold by numerous shops that display their wares in their windows. Pizza-style *fatir,* with vegetables and meats piled on top as well as stuffed inside, is far tastier than the imitations of Italian pizza in town and at LE2-3, usually much cheaper. At eateries that do not have waiter service, you pay first, obtain a ticket, and then exchange your ticket for food.

Downtown

Felfela, 15 Hoda Sharawy St. (tel. 392 27 51), off Talaat Harb St., 1 block south of Talaat Harb Sq. Excellent Egyptian food and reasonable prices make this one of the best restaurants in Cairo. Try their spiced *fuul* dishes (50-75pt) and *taamiya* (35pt). Also good is *om ali,* a pastry baked with milk, honey, and raisins (LE1.80). Don't be put off by the tacky folkloric decorations. Another entrance on Talaat Harb St. gives access to a self-service take-out counter with cold drinks and a large selection of Egyptian sandwiches for 10-50pt. Open daily 8am-midnight.

Abou Shakra, 69 Kasr al-Aini St. (tel. 84 88 11). Take bus #8 or 900 or the Metro to Sayyida Zeinab; the restaurant is 2 blocks away. The best kebab in town. Order ¼ kilo of meat per person, and they'll bring a selection of salads and dips too. Full meals about LE10. Open daily 1-5pm and 7-11pm.

Doumyati, on the north side of Falaki Sq., near the pedestrian overpass, about 4 blocks east of Tahrir Sq. One of the most popular (and cheapest) *fuul* restaurants in Cairo. *Fuul, taamiya,* salads, bread, and *mahalabiya* (resembling rice pudding) for under LE1. Bring your own drinks. Open 11am-10pm. Closed Friday afternoons.

El Tahrir, on Tahrir St., 3 blocks east of Tahrir Sq. A clean and consistently tasty *kushari* joint. Just sit down and they'll bring you a huge bowl for 50pt. Watch out for the hot sauce in the wine bottles! Open daily 11am-11pm.

El Tahrir Fatatri, on Tahrir St., 2 blocks east of Tahrir Sq. A small savory *fatir* (with meat cheese and sauce, LE2.50) makes a filling meal, and a small sweet (with apple jam and powdered sugar, LE1.50) makes a filling dessert. Open daily 1-11pm.

Zeina, 32 Talaat Harb St., next to the Oxford Guest House. A popular midtown eatery with meals for as little as LE2-3. Excellent *shwarma* sandwiches (55pt), large selection of fruit juices (50pt), cold drinks, and pastries. Open daily 10am-midnight.

El-Guesh, 2 Falaki Sq., at the corner of Tahrir and Falaki St., 4 blocks east of Tahrir Sq. Good kebab (LE6) in a cool, clean restaurant close to the center of town. Open daily noon-10pm.

Alfi Bey Restaurant, 3 Alfy St. (tel. 77 18 88), 1 block north of July 26 St. An old-fashioned restaurant—white plaster walls, wood paneling, and chandeliers—serving traditional Egyptian fare: kebab (LE3.80), pigeon (LE2.80), and macaroni (LE1.10). Open daily 1-5pm and 7:30-10pm.

Riche Restaurant, 17 Talaat Harb St. (tel. 74 87 93), 2 blocks south of Tahrir Sq. Egyptian and Western dishes served on a pleasant patio. Watch the crowds go by and enjoy a cup of coffee or fruit juice (50pt), or a full meal (entrees LE3-5). Popular among younger tourists. Open daily noon-midnight.

Le Carroll, 12 Kasr al-Nil St. (tel. 74 64 34), across from the American Express office. Tasteful decor, excellent service, and delicious French-style food. Meat and seafood entrees are pricey (LE10), but you can get soup and an omelette for under LE6. Better food than Estoril across the street, though a similar menu.

Aly Hassan El Hati, 8 Halim St. (tel. 91 88 29), 1 block south of the Windsor Hotel off July 26 St. A little grimy, but light, airy, and with huge chandeliers. Good kebab (LE3.60), grape leaves (LE2.60), and macaroni with meat sauce (LE1.40), but avoid the rubbery chicken at all costs. Open daily noon-2pm and 7-10pm.

Rex, 14 Sarwat St. (tel. 74 57 63). Turn west off Talaat Harb St., 4 blocks north of Talaat Harb Sq. Small, comfortable restaurant serving Western-style dishes. Try their omelettes (LE1.50) or the delicious baked macaroni with meat sauce (LE2.10). Open Sat.-Thurs. 1-4:30pm and 6-10pm.

Z Cafeteria-Restaurant, On the east side of Tahrir Sq. (tel. 354 42 30). Fast food at the counter, tables on the second floor. Prices are a little steep (*shwarma* and fries LE6). Come here for the air-conditioning. Pleasant, low-ceilinged balcony for contortionists or people less than 4 feet tall. Open daily 10am-9pm.

Aly Baba Cafeteria, on Tahrir Sq., 2 doors away from "Z." More Egyptian fast food. Meals around LE5. Open 10am-10pm.

Fu Ching, 28 Talaat Harb St. (tel. 75 61 84), in a small alley 1 block north of Talaat Harb Sq. Good selection of moderately priced Cantonese food. Delicious spring rolls (dozen LE3.50). Open noon-10pm.

Kentucky Fried Chicken, at 4 locations. The best fast self-service is at 32 Batal Ahmed Aziz St., Mohandiseen. Downtown, at 21 Sarawat St. You'll get the famous Colonel Sanders' recipe or a reasonable facsimile thereof. Hamburgers LE1.50, chicken plates LE3-5. Open 10:30am-1am.

Garden City

Take-Away, Latin America St. (tel. 355 43 41), 1 block south of U.S. embassy. Diner cuisine in a diner atmosphere, with cold beer available. Full meals LE5-8. The breaded chicken "Kentucky" is a bargain at LE3.25. Popular among courting Egyptian couples.

Khan al-Khalili

Dahhan, Husayn Sq., 20m from the end of al-Muski. This dark, smokey hole-in-the-wall serves up some of the best kebab in Cairo (¼ kilo LE5.50). Usually packed with Egyptian families and local traders.

Dahhan Chicken Home, 1 block down al-Muski from Dahlan. Great fried chicken (LE3.75), *shwarma* sandwiches (LE1). The best place to escape the heat and crowds of Khan al-Khalili—A/C and astroturf at no extra price. Open noon-1am.

Mohandiseen

Tandoori Restaurant and Take-Away, 11 Shehab St., Mohandiseen (tel. 348 63 01). Take bus #167 from Tahrir (the Nile Hilton station). Beautiful, brand-new, white marble facade in Moghul style. Pleasant interior decoration, air-conditioned, and very clean. Good service and delicious Indian cuisine for LE6-10. Open noon-11pm.

Taberna Española, 26 Syria St., Mohandiseen (tel. 49 06 61), inside the Cairo Inn. Good *tortillas* for LE4. Restaurant and bar open 24 hours, but the Spanish show takes place only at night. Not recommended for solo women.

Prestige Pizza, 43 Geziret al-Arab (tel. 341 03 83). Remarkably good pizza (LE3-6) and other Italian dishes. Wicker and wood decor, with chairs outside for *al fresco* dining.

Zamalek

Restaurant 5 Bells, 9 el-Adel Abu Baker St. (tel. 340 41 02). Extraordinary establishment serving very good quasi-Italian cuisine. Sit inside by the grand piano or out in the quiet garden by the cherub-bedecked fountains. The entrees are expensive (LE10-15), but you can enjoy a bowl of spaghetti and a beer for LE5. Open noon-1am.

Il Capo, 22 Taha Hussein St. (tel. 341 31 95). Excellent Italian food in an elegant, air-conditioned dining-room. Good spaghetti (LE4) and great pizza (LE8). Come here for dinner, and then head over to **B's Corner** (next door) for music and drinks. Open daily 10am-1:30am.

Tokyo, off Maahad al-Swissry St., 1 block from July 26 Bridge. Sit barefoot on grass mats at low tables, and dine on *yakitori*(LE6), fried prawns (LE8), and other authentic Japanese dishes (around LE10). This is the best Japanese restaurant in Cairo, but be prepared to say *sayonara* to your budget.

Balmoral Hotel Chinese Restaurant, by the corner of Mahhad el-Swissry St. and July 26 St. (tel. 340 67 61). A pleasant restaurant decorated with Chinese antiques, overlooking the gardens of the Palace of Arts. Try the excellent *fu-yung* (Chinese omelette with brown sauce, LE3.50) and sweet and sour dishes (LE9). Most dishes are around LE10, but enjoy a full meal for less. Open daily 11am-11pm.

Hana Korean Restaurant, 21 Maahad al-Swissry St. (tel. 340 18 46), next to the El-Nil Zamalek Hotel. This small, pleasantly-decorated restaurant serves a variety of Asian dishes, reasonably priced at around LE6 each. The *sukiyaki* (a do-it-yourself, stir-fry soup) is delicious, and a huge amound of food for LE12. Open daily noon to midnight.

Roy Rogers, in the Marriott Hotel, by the July 26 Bridge. Good burgers (LE5) and omelettes (LE6), but the main attractions here are the Egyptian waiters, who look quite uncomfortable in cowboy boots, blue-jeans, and ten-gallon hats. Good gosh. Open daily 10am-midnight.

Dokki

Swissair Restaurant (Le Chalet), Nile St. (tel. 72 84 88), 4 blocks north of Gamia Bridge. Come here when you're longing for a taste of home (even if you're not Swiss)—it's easily the best Italian food in town. Delicious lasagna (LE6) and noodles alfredo (LE5), as well as French pastries and a *Herald Tribune* to read while you eat. Open daily 11am-10pm.

Teahouses, Pastry Shops, and Cafes

The favorite pastime of Cairenes is passing time, frittering it away wholesale over a cup of tea or a pastry. Men of the middle and lower classes sit in cafes (*qahwa*) playing backgammon and smoking waterpipes (*sheesha*) for hours at a time. You can find a *qahwa* on almost any street corner east of the Nile, and foreigners are usually welcomed. Egyptian women are never found here, however, and any woman alone will be harassed. Even in the more Western-style establishments, foreign women sitting alone will invariably be approached.

Cairo also offers a variety of teashops, pastry shops, and coffee houses for leisurely caloric intake. In any of the Egyptian pastry shops scattered through downtown (a typical example is the **Haroun al-Rashid,** on Talaat Harb St. across from the Radio Cinema), you select a delicacy, pay for it, and then take a seat.

Groppi, at 3 locations. On Talaat Harb Sq. (tel 743 44), downtown. Formerly a palace of Orientalist delights, famous during the days of the Occupation. Now fairly dull, with only the art-deco decor to remind you of its glory days. The ice creams and pastries are fine, but avoid the overpriced restaurant. Watch out for the LE1 surcharge for sitting down. Other locations at 4 Adly St. (near Opera Sq.) with a pleasant garden, and on al-Ahram St. in Heliopolis. All three open daily 8:30am-10pm.

Riche Cafe, 17 Talaat Harb. An outdoor cafe patronized mostly by young foreigners living in Cairo. The 1952 Revolution is said to have been plotted here. Cold beer, *ouzo,* and other alcoholic drinks available. Open daily 11:30am-10pm. Closed on Fri. and during Ramadan.

La Poire, 1 Latin America St., Garden City, next to Take-Away Restaurant. A certain sweet tooth satisfier: They have the widest selection of Egyptian and French pastries in Cairo, all made on the premises and reasonably priced at 70pt apiece. Open daily 10am-10pm.

Ibis Cafe, Nile Hilton (tel. 74 07 77), on the ground floor. Ideal for breakfast or brunch. Rich tourists in bermudas and Hawaiian shirts, business types with Dior ties, women with purple hair—could this be you? Open buffet from 6-11am. Continental breakfast LE4.50, American brunch LE8.50, plus unlimited salad bar LE3.50.

Brazilian Coffee Shop, 38 Talaat Harb St. Clean white marble counters and shiny old-fashioned coffee mills. Excellent *cafe au lait* (45pt), and cappuccino (45pt) from Brazilian coffee beans. You can also buy unground coffee here. Open daily 7:30am-11:30pm.

La Pergola, Meridien Hotel (tel. 84 54 44), on the corniche. Beautiful *al-fresco* terrace overlooking the Nile. Ideal for watching breathtaking sunsets. Open for snacks 3-7pm. Limit yourself to a fruit-punch or mango juice (LE3) and enjoy the panorama.

Tea Island, in Cairo Zoo, Giza (tel. 98 90 89), at the University Bridge. Open-air cafeteria. Features light snacks (LE1-2) and regular meals (LE3-4). Pleasant environment where you can amuse yourself by throwing bread to the ducks in the pond. Open daily 9:30am-4:30pm.

Khan al-Khalili Coffee Shop, at the Mena House Oberoi Hotel (tel. 85 54 44). Luxurious cafeteria, Oriental decor, and air-conditioning. Snacks and expensive meals. Have a Turkish coffee (LE2) or a glass of mint tea (LE1.50) and enjoy the exotic atmosphere. Open daily 24 hours.

Simmonds Coffee Shop, July 26 St., Zamalek (tel 340 94 36), just east of the intersection with Hasan Sabri St. Excellent cappuccino (35pt), espresso, hot chocolate, or lemonade (30pt). Only a few seats at the counter. Ideal for breakfast, fresh croissants, and *ramequins* (cheese in a mold). Open daily 7:30am-7pm.

Fishawi's Khan al-Khalili, from the square in front of the Husayn Mosque, go to the extreme left side of the Husayn Hotel (on your left). Walk down the left side of the building, turn right into the first alley, and it's straight ahead. A traditional tea-house in the heart of the old bazaar. Nicknamed Cafe des Mirroirs. Furnished in 19th century European style with small hammered brass tables. Enjoy the atmosphere with a pot of mint tea (40pt) and smoke the *sheesha* (water-pipe, 60pt).

In the evenings, you can join the crowd of middle-class Egyptian couples at one of the many cafes, called **casinos,** lining the Nile on Gezirah Island. The **Casino al-Nil,** on the west side of Tahrir Bridge, is one of the best, but take your pick from dozens of others. They range from swank to simple and tend to be jammed on Thursday nights. Another good idea for budget eating is to buy food and drink at a market (a good one runs off Talaat Harb St., 1 block north of July 26 St, open daily until 10pm) and dine outside. Particularly nice spots include the corniche and the Botanical Gardens.

Sights

New City

The overflowing streets of the New City display a fascinating mixture of clashing cultures. During the day, the sidewalks swarm with thousands of people who seem to be going nowhere intently. Street vendors wander about selling plastic gee-gaws from trays and glasses of licorice-drink from silver jugs. Far above the streets, you can pick out baroque remnants of colonial architecture, now with laundry hanging from the cornices. In the evening, Cairenes stroll hand in hand—men with men, women with women—stopping at the many pastry shops and cafes. Every two hours or so the latest kung-fu flick, awkwardly dubbed into Arabic, lets out and hundreds of cinema afficionados explode into the streets. The evening may be the best time to wander—it's much cooler and remarkably safe.

The best place to experience Cairo's daily life is the market. Each market may be known for a different sort of ware, or in a large market, like the one south of Sayyida Zaynab, each alley may be devoted to a different item. Bus #174 runs from Mugama Station in Tahrir Sq. to Sayyida Zaynab. Other major markets are located northeast of Ataba Sq. and in Bulaq (from Tahrir, walk east along Tahrir St. for Ataba Sq.; take bus #46 for Bulaq). **Bab el-Luq Market,** east and south of Tahrir, is renowned for its cheap produce. The **Army Surplus Souk** in Ahmed Hilmi Sq., behind Ramses Station, specializes in inexpensive canteens, excellent military boots, and army fatigues; khaki pants should cost only about LE1. Both markets are open until dusk. While you're in the neighborhood, notice the towering **Statue of Ramses II** in front of the train station. The statue was excavated in 1888 near the remains of the ancient city of Memphis.

Cairo's two main islands are worthy of short visits. **Zamalek** (also called Gezira or "the island") is dominated by the 185m **Cairo Tower.** Early or late in the day, the view from the top of the tower is breathtaking, stretching to the pyramids, the medieval citadel, and the Nile Delta. For LE2 you can take the elevator to the observation deck. Telescopes are available on the sixteenth floor (open 9am-midnight). Though the revolving restaurant is prohibitively expensive, the cafeteria is a good place to sit and contemplate, drink in hand. Just south of where the July 26 Bridge meets the island stands one of Cairo's finest colonial palaces—the **Marriott Hotel.** The hotel was intended to accommodate European guests and was built upon completion of the Suez Canal. The decadent interior is an overwhelming combination of silvered mirrors, gilt-framed canvases, mahogany paneling, and plush carpets. If you entertain fantasies of waltzing silently through an empty ballroom, this is the place to do it. The 1-block stretch around and along Hasan Sabri St. north of July 26 St. is a lively area full of grocery stores specializing in imported foods, as well as colorful shops and pleasant cafes. To the north stretches an area with silent streets, embassies, and foreigners' residences.

A most peculiar sight in Zamalek is the **Safeway Supermarket,** at 29 Ahmed Hishmal St. The child of an Egyptian developer and the Safeway Company of America, the store brings the cool breath of consumerism to the dusty streets of Cairo. Wait until you've been in Cairo a while, and then wander through the four floors of grocery shelves, meat counters, a laundry service, a toy store, and more; listen to the imported Muzak; stare at the bewildered counter-help wearing little name badges saying "Hi! I'm Ahmed!" It will seem like Oz.

On the southern tip of **Roda Island** stands one of central Cairo's most noteworthy ancient monuments. The famous **Nilometer** was designed to measure the height of the river and thereby prophesy the state of the annual harvest. The structure dates from the ninth century C.E., though it was restored and the conical dome was added under Muhammad Ali's reign. The steps descend into a paved pit well below the level of the Nile, culminating in the graduated column that marks the height of the river. The entrance to the Nilometer is often locked, but the custodian lives nearby. If you express interest, one of the local children will run to fetch him. Since the Nilometer lies quite far south, visit it when you tour Old Cairo. The Manial Palace Museum is at the northern edge of the island (see Museum listings below).

Walking west across the island from the palace, and over the Giza Bridge, you will find a lush, green portion of the neighborhood of **Giza**. Straight ahead, at the end of the broad boulevard, looms the handsome campus of **Cairo University.** Along the boulevard to the north stretches **al-Urman Garden (Botanical Gardens)**, the best place in town to toss a frisbee or take refuge under a shady tree. Along the full length of the boulevard to the south and facing the botanical gardens is the **Cairo Zoo.** (Open daily 6am-5pm; crowded on Fri. Admission to either 10pt.)

Heliopolis was one of the most ambitious urban projects carried out during the British colonial period of the late nineteenth and early twentieth centuries. The architecture in this district is a strange mixture of styles; sometimes an Islamic facade has been used to hide a Western structure. Among the best examples of this practice are the palace of Prince Husayn, the palace of Prince Ibrahim, the palace of the Sultana, and the arcades on Abbas Boulevard. The most outrageous example of imported architecture, however, is the Palace of Empain. Known locally as "Le Baron," the palace is a copy of a Hindu temple complete with an electrically controlled rotating tower that allowed Empain to follow the sun through the day. To reach Heliopolis from Tahrir Sq., take bus #400 or 500. A taxi will cost about LE2.50.

One exotic attraction in the New City is the weekly **camel market** at Imbaba. The largest of its kind in the country, the market is held on Fridays from 5 to 10am and is liveliest between 7 and 9am. A few of the camels come from the Western Desert, but most are brought all the way from the Sudan. Some of the Sudanese Bishari tribespeople who bring their camels to market wear traditional dress. Accustomed to a nomadic lifestyle on open desert terrain, they seem noticeably uncomfortable in an urban environment. The camels look so lean because they've been en route for so long—a 30-day march to Aswan precedes the 24-hour truck ride to Cairo. For about LE500 you can ride off on one of the scrawnier beasts. It's a small price to pay to surprise the loved ones back home, though most airlines have very severe penalties for trying to bring a camel aboard. Adjoining the camel enclosure is a livestock market where sheep, goats, donkeys, and water buffalo are sold. To reach the market, take bus #172 or 175 from Ataba Sq., or catch a cab to Imbaba Airport (from there, cross the railroad tracks and turn right). When the market winds down, traffic throughout the shiny boulevards of Mohandiseen comes to a standstill as camels and other creatures are herded along.

Islamic Cairo

Cairo's medieval Islamic district is home to splendid mosques and monuments representing some of the finest Islamic architecture found anywhere in the world. Unlike Damascus and Baghdad, the two other great Middle Eastern capitals of the medieval Islamic world, Cairo was spared the devastation of the Mongol invasions. You can easily imagine the characters of *One Thousand and One Nights* living under the archways. But the monuments are only one part of life here. Once the unrivaled cultural and intellectual center of the Arab world, Islamic Cairo is now a crowded, poverty-ridden neighborhood. Its narrow streets will dazzle your eyes, jangle your ears, and offend your nose. But don't be put off by the dirt, sewage, and garbage; beyond the Islamic city's dingy exterior lies a wealth of ornate decorative friezes, lovely arabesque stucco, finely carved wooden grillwork, vaulted and domed interiors, and countless minarets. Many serve as observation decks, providing a view of Cairo's splendor, impossible to find while embroiled in the city's close, crowded streets. Traveling through Islamic Cairo by car is a bad idea. Streets are narrow, traffic molasses-slow, and parking impossible.

You should leave several hours to thoroughly explore each section of Islamic Cairo on foot. The best time to attempt this is before 9am and between 6 and 8pm, when the narrow streets are coolest and least crowded; bear in mind, though, that the small palaces and museums usually close at 2pm, and during Ramadan many are open mornings only. An excellent guide to the various monuments is Parker and Sabin's *A Practical Guide to Islamic Monuments in Cairo,* which includes a superb set of maps (LE10). Also worth looking into is *The Beauty of Cairo,* by G. Freeman-Grenville, a shorter and more concise guide (LE12), as well as a set of two detailed maps of Islamic Cairo, published by SPARE (Society for the Preservation of Architectural Resources in Egypt) (LE2.50 each). All of these are available from most English language bookstores.

Most of the more important monuments charge admission (50% student discount). You should insist on receiving a ticket to check against the price charged. Caretakers will often serve as tour guides; for ordinary assistance, offer *baksheesh* of about 25pt. If a caretaker holds your shoes or provides shoe-coverings, 20pt is in order. If a door is unlocked for you, or you're shown around in detail, 50pt is appropriate. Bring lots of small bills since asking for change when offering *baksheesh* is awkward and rude. When visiting smaller monuments or when trying to see the interiors of tombs, don't be bashful about hunting down the custodian. Declare your interest to whomever is about and usually the caretaker will be fetched promptly. If you confine your tour of Islamic Cairo to unlocked doors, you will miss many of the city's treasures.

Visitors should take care to dress properly in Islamic Cairo: Revealing clothing will attract a great deal of unsolicited attention to both men and women and will prevent admission to many mosques. Women should wear knee-length skirts or long pants, and shirts with sleeves; in some mosques head coverings are required (these can usually be rented outside for a few piastres).

Most mosques are open all day, but tourists are unwelcome during prayertimes. Wait a few minutes after the congregation has finished before entering. Avoid visiting mosques on Friday afternoon when the Muslim community gathers for afternoon prayer. Certain highly venerated mosques—Sayyidna Husayn, Sayyida Zaynab, and Sayyida Nafisa—are believed to contain the remains of descendents of Muhammad and are permanently closed to the non-Muslim public. An exception is al-Azhar, which remains open to tourists.

Several distinctive architectural features merit special attention in Islamic Cairo. Most prominent are the towering minarets from which the mournful-sounding chants of the *muezzin* (prayer caller) summon the faithful to prayer five times daily. Most mosques are rectangular with cool arcaded porches (*riwaqs*) surrounding a central open courtyard (*sahn*). These usually contain a central covered fountain (*sabil*) for ablutions before prayer. The focus of each mosque is the southeast wall (*qibla*), which holds the prayer niche (*mihrab*) pointing to Mecca in Saudi Araba. Particularly in Mamluk mosques, the *mihrab* and *qibla* are elaborately decorated with marble inlay and Kufic inscriptions. Since Islam forbids the representation of the human form, abstract artwork dominates the mosques' decorations. In the Fatimid period, interlaced foliate patterns in carved stucco and plaster were popular ornamentation. Geometric patterns and elegant calligraphy appeared later in Mamluk times. Particularly beautiful examples of work from this period are found on the pulpits (*minbars*) that usually stand beside the prayer niche. The long wedge-shaped wooden stairways leading to the sermon platform are crafted with interlocking patterns of ivory, walnut, ebony, and other dark woods. (For more information on Islam, see Religion in the General Introduction.)

A good way to start your tour is to walk to the mammoth south gate of Bab Zuwayla. Enter the Mosque of al-Muayyad (the large portal inside on the left) and ask to be taken up to one of the two towering minarets that are perched atop Bab Zuwayla. From there, try to match up your two-dimensional map with the three-dimensional array below by picking out the minarets and domes of the major monuments. If you wish to plunge straight into the fray, take bus #63, 65, or 66 from Tahrir Sq. Alternatively, walk east from Opera Sq. (or Ataba Sq.) on al-Azhar St. Although Islamic Cairo begins at Port Said St., continue on al-Azhar St. about a ¼ mile to al-Muizz al-Din Allah, which runs north-south through the medieval city, connecting its northern and southern gates and providing an excellent place to begin your tour of the district. If you stand on the corner of al-Muizz al-Din

The mausoleum and *madrasa* are now being restored. The square minaret exhibits an exceptional, closely-patterned, carved stucco surface. Next door, to the north along al-Muizz St., is the **Mosque of Sultan Barquq.** Barquq was the first Circassian Mamluk sultan and seized power through a series of brutal assassinations. His mosque was built in 1386, a century later than Qalaun's complex, and the difference in styles is striking. Barquq's minaret is slender and octagonal, and the high, monumental portal is crowned by *muqarnas* (stalactites), one of the distinguishing features of Mamluk architecture. An elaborate silver-inlaid door provides access to the structure. The inner courtyard has four *liwans,* the largest and most elaborate of which doubles as a prayer hall. Its beautiful timber roof has been restored and richly painted in blue and gold. The colorful ceiling is supported by four porphyry columns, quarried in pharaonic times from the mountains near the Red Sea coast. The round disks of marble floor are slices of Greek and Roman columns, used because Egypt has no indigenous marble. (Open daily 9am-4pm. Admission 50pt.)

North of the Mosque of Barquq, al-Muizz St. comes to a fork. The building on the left is all that remains of **Qasr Bishtak,** a lavish palace from the fourteenth century which originally stood five stories high. All floors of the palace had running water, a technological achievement unmatched in Europe for another 300 years. Al-Muizz St. continues to the left into yet another fork marked by the slim eighteenth century **Sabil Kuttab of Abd al-Rahman Kathuda.** Behind the *sabil* (fountain) and *kuttab* (Islamic school for orphans) stands a fourteenth century building. Bear left at the fork and continue north along al-Muizz St. to the end of the next block. On the right stands the small but architecturally important Fatimid **Mosque of al-Aqmar.** Built in 1125, this was the first Cairene mosque to have a stone facade and the shell motif within the keel-arched niche. *Al-Aqmar* means "moonlit," and refers to the way the stone facade sparkles in the moonlight. The facade follows the alignment of the street, while the *qibla* within is oriented toward Mecca. The archway of the northern corner is typical of later Cairene architecture; the height of the cut is just about equal to that of a loaded camel, and the chink was intended to make the turn onto the side street easier to negotiate. The mosque is below the present-day street at the original level of al-Muizz St. (Closed for restoration in the summer of 1988.)

Proceeding north from al-Aqmar Mosque, take the second right and follow the winding alley about 50m down. The doorway on the left marked with a small, green monument plaque is the entrance to Cairo's finest old house, the sixteenth-century **Bayt al-Suhaymi,** a domestic haven with an exquisite reception room on the second floor and a quiet interior courtyard complete with well and garden. (Open daily 9am-4pm. Admission LE1.) Along the same alley, away from al-Muizz St., you will eventually come to al-Gamaliya St. Across the street is the facade of the fourteenth-century *khanqah* (Sufi establishment) of **Baybars al-Gashankir.** Erected in 1310, this building was an abode for mystic Sufis, and is the oldest surviving example of a *khanqah* in Cairo.

Al-Azhar and Khan al-Khalili

The oldest university in the world and the foremost Islamic theological center, the **Mosque of al-Azhar** stands just a few steps from the midpoint of al-Muizz St., at the end of al-Azhar St., facing onto the large square. Al-Azhar University was established in 972 C.E. and rose to preeminence in the fifteenth century as a center for the study of Koranic law and doctrine, a position it still holds. The mosque has been heavily restored and is composed of bits and pieces from various periods. The eighteenth-century western facade is the work of Abd al-Rahman Kathuda. To reach the central court, enter through the double arched gate and pass under the minaret of Qaytbay (1469). Note the restored stucco decoration of the courtyard's facade. The *mihrab* in the central aisle is original. The library, just left of the main entrance, holds over 80,000 manuscripts. The curriculum has remained virtually unchanged since the Mamluk era, although the university now has peripheral faculties in mathematics, physics, and medicine. You can still see the traditional form of instruction, a process of Socratic questioning with groups of students seated around a professor. Some of the 4000 students live year-round on mats in corners of the courtyard. For about 50pt the caretaker will allow you to climb one of the locked minarets for a fantastic view of the complex. Women without headcoverings must don one of the long wraps provided at the entrance. (Open Sun.-Thurs. and Sat. 9am-3pm, Fri. 9-11am and 1-3pm. Admission LE1.)

Across the street, 100m to the north of the main entrance to al-Azhar, stands **Sayyidna Husayn,** Cairo's most venerated Muslim shrine. It is revered throughout the Islamic world as the resting place of the skull of al-Husayn, grandson of the prophet Muhammad. The head is said to have been transported to Cairo in a green silk bag in 1153, almost 500 years after he was killed in the battle of Kerbala (in Iraq). The present edifice is of recent construction, and the gaudy decorations in the interior include large, green neon lights that glow with the name of Allah. Officially, non-Muslims are not allowed to enter, but in Cairo rules were made to be *baksheeshed* into submission. If you express interest, a few piastres will gain entry, but don't try during prayers or on Friday.

On *mullids* (feast days), the president of Egypt traditionally comes to pray at Sayyidna al-Husayn, while racous festivities go on outside in the large square. During Ramadan, this square is the best place to witness the breaking of the fast, signaled by the advent of evening prayers (around 8pm). All the restaurants lay out their fare half an hour before prayers begin, and famished patrons swarm to the tables afterwards. When everyone is stuffed, the square becomes the scene of celebration.

Behind Sayyidna al-Husayn lies the eighteenth-century **Musafirkhana Palace,** a monument well-worth visiting but rather difficult to locate. To reach the palace, walk north down al-Gamaliya St. (toward Bab an-Nasr) until you come to the little fourteenth-century **Mosque of Gamal al-Din al-Ustadar.** The entrance to the palace is 100m east of the mosque. Built during the Ottoman period in imitation of the Mamluk style, the Musafirkhana Palace served as the residence of the Egyptian royal family during the nineteenth and early twentieth centuries. Until the deposition of King Farouk, dignitaries and foreign heads of state were entertained at the palace. The interior has been restored by some of Egypt's leading artisans. If your arrival at the palaces does not coincide with a tour group, you may have difficulty gaining entry. (Officially open Sat.-Thurs. 9am-4pm. Admission LE1.)

Almost all streets south of the palace will lead you back to al-Azhar and Sayyidna al-Husayn. Just turn down any of the little passageways leading west from Sayyidna al-Husayn, and you'll immediately encounter the glittering alleys of **Khan al-Khalili,** the largest tourist bazaar in Egypt. Stretching between Sayyidna al-Husayn and al-Muizz St., this may be the world's most stereotypical, expensive, and tourist-infested Middle Eastern bazaar. As you walk through the labyrinth of twisted alleys, you'll see leather-dyers, carpenters, inlay workers, glass-cutters, and broom-makers. Most of all, you'll see hundreds of tourist shops selling everything from beautiful inlaid and wooden furniture to fake pharaonic antiquities; even the most humble souvenir stands accept all major credit cards. You'll also be accosted in English at every turn with offers to "get special guide," and "just come in and look." Getting a good price in Khan al-Khalili requires patience and ferocious bargaining; many shopkeepers will quote a starting price ten times an object's value. The best strategy is to shuttle back forth between shops and let the shopkeepers bargain each other down. Don't start bargaining for something until you have a sense of its proper value, and never name a price you are not prepared to pay. Some stores post fixed prices that are nothing of the sort. Don't leave the bazaar without admiring the lavish marbel inlay on the Mamluk gates of Sultan al-Ghouri.

Far more colorful, far less touristy, and far less expensive is **al-Muski,** the long bazaar avenue where Egyptians shop for pillowcases, shoes, cloth, tacky furniture, and food. Al-Muski stretches from al-Muizz St. all the way to Port Said St., running parallel and 1 block north of al-Azhar St. If you want to walk between Islamic and downtown Cairo, al-Muski offers the most picturesque route.

Southern al-Muizz Street

In the Fatimid period, al-Muizz Street was the main avenue of the city, running straight through the heart of al-Qahira and connecting the southern and northern entrances, Bab al-Futuh and Bab Zuwayla. Today the street is only a minor thoroughfare bisected by the much larger al-Azhar St. At the southern corners of the intersection of al-Azhar St. and al-Muizz St. stand two impressive Mamluk structures. The **Madrasa of Sultan al-Ghouri** (1503) occupies the southwest corner. Come here for refuge from the noise and crowds and to admire the decorative work on the arches and ceiling. Sometimes a custodian will provide a tour, complete with a climb to the roof and minaret (LE1 *baksheesh* is appropriate). The minaret is square, a reversion from the Mamluk octagonal shape. The *mugarnas* portal invites passersby to enter. The long chains hanging in front of the *mihrab* were used for suspended glass lamps; today a somewhat different effect is achieved with neon. When the sultan built this *madrasa* he placed a talisman to chase away the flies—see for yourself if it still works. The **Mausoleum of Al-Ghouri**, across the street, houses a community center and arts exhibits, and can be explored whenever its doors are open. The dome, once one of the largest in Cairo, is now gone.

The **Wakala of al-Ghouri** is easier to overlook. From the mausoleum, turn left onto al-Azhar St. Then turn right (east) off the street and walk 50m down Sheikh Muhammad Abduh St. On your right, at #3, you will come to a magnificently preserved *wakala* (1505), now transformed into a center for handicrafts and folkloric arts. The courtyard is often used as a theater and concert hall. Originally, the structure served as a commercial hotel with camels, donkeys, and merchandise kept in the courtyard below and merchants living in the rooms above. (Open daily 9am-4pm; during Ramadan 9-11am and 2-4pm. Admission LE1.)

Retracing your steps to al-Muizz St., head south; on your left you will see the eighteenth-century **Fakahani Mosque**. Down the narrow lane behind the mosque is a small doorway overlooked by all but the most vigilant of explorers. It leads into the **House of Gamal al-Din**, an upper-class sixteenth-century mansion. Unhitch the latch and walk in, but be prepared to encounter the watchdog. The house is one of the most splendid of the surviving Ottoman residences in the city, with beautiful wooden ceilings and striking Turkish tiles (open 9am-2pm; admission LE1).

Continuing south down al-Muizz St. to the corner of Ahmad Maher St., you'll find on the left side the entrance to the **Mosque of al-Muayyad** built between 1415 and 1420. Strategically located at Bab Zuwayla and the market area, it is the last of the great open-courtyard congregational mosques. Its presence is announced by the two minarets built on top of the Fatimid gate, its stone-carved dome, and the imposing *muqarnas* portal. The interior has a pleasant garden, and the *qibla-riwaq* (porch along the southeast wall) is covered by an extensively restored ceiling. Notice the great length of the *qibla* wall and the beautiful marble paneling. At the northern end of the *qibla* wall is the mausoleum of Sultan al-Muayyad; its austerity contrasts with the lavish decoration of the main *qibla* wall. The second mausoleum, at the other end of the wall, is an Ottoman addition.

After passing through Bab Zuwayla, turn around to look at this masterpiece of Fatimid architecture. Across the street from Bab Zuwayla, to the right, stands the **Zawiya of Sultan Faraj**, son of Barquq (1408), a small rectangular structure. Notice the remarkable marble lintels above the windows. During the 19th century, execution by strangulation was carried out beside the railings outside. (This was apparently a popular public spectacle at that time.) Access is difficult if you are not Muslim. Opposite this structure, to the left across the street from Bab Zuwayla, stands the small, elegant **Mosque of Salih Talai**, built in 1160. When the mosque was built, the street was at the level of the series of shops standing behind the iron railing. The rent paid by the shopkeepers has helped maintain the mosque. Notice the five keel arches resting on classical columns on the facade. The arches form a remarkable projecting portal, unique in Cairo. The austere yet graceful courtyard is arranged in a compact symmetrical design, opening into a small *qibla riwaq*. The custodian (who will expect *baksheesh*) will show you the way up to the roof. Continuing south on al-Muizz St., you enter a covered bazaar known as the **Street of Tentmakers,** followed a few blocks down by a similar covered alley called the **Street of Saddlemakers.** Turning left as you step out of Bab Zuwayla, you'll find yourself on Darb al-Ahmar St. heading toward the Citadel. A right turn leads to Ahmad Maher St., lined with the shops of carpenters, tombstone-carvers, and metalworkers. The street leads out to Ahmed Maher Sq. on Port Said St., across from the Museum of Islamic Art.

The Citadel

Dominating Islamic Cairo, the lofty Citadel was begun by Salah al-Din in 1178 and has been expanded and modified from then into the twentieth century. To enter the Citadel complex, walk all the way around to the far eastern side, following the road along the southern walls. Don't be misled by the mammoth western gateway of Bab al-Azab across from the Sultan Hasan Mosque—this entrance is kept locked. Admire the Ayyubid and Turkish work of the walls. Enter through the eastern gate of Bab al-Qala. (Open Sun.-Thurs. and Sat. 9am-5pm, Fri. 8:30-11:30am and 1-6pm. Admission LE2, including the Muhammad Ali's Mosque.) To reach the **Mosque of Muhammad Ali,** the main attraction of the complex, follow the road up to the top of the Citadel toward the thin, unadorned Turkish minarets.

During his reign in the first half of the nineteenth century, Muhammad Ali laid the foundations of the modern Egyptian state, sparked the Europeanization of the country, introduced education in the arts and sciences, and paved the way for an independent dynasty. Muhammad Ali leveled the western surface of the Citadel and built a structure intended to serve as a reminder of Turkish dominion. Modeled after the an Ottoman mosque in Istanbul, the edifice is more attractive from a distance; up close, the outline resembles a giant toad. Two years ago, the mosque was refurbished by the Department of Antiquities—its silver domes and marble and alabaster decorations sparkle on the Cairo skyline. The interior is far more dramatic, however, especially just after prayers, when the large chandelier and tiny lanterns are lit. To your immediate right as you enter the prayer hall is the gaudy, gilt **Tomb of Muhammad Ali.** A charming and unexpected French gingerbread clock overlooks the courtyard. King Louis Philippe of France presented the clock in 1848 to reciprocate for Muhammad Ali's gift of the pharaonic obelisk that now stands in Place de la Concorde in Paris.

Directly across from the Muhammad Ali Mosque, merged with the interior fortification walls, is the fourteenth-century **Mosque of al-Nasir Muhammad,** which has recently been restored. Inside, you can see how the various types of columns have been reused. The merlons of the parapet and the pinnacles at the corner are similar to those of the Mosque of al-Maridani. On the southeastern edge of the Mosque of Muhammad Ali, you'll find the steps leading down to **Joseph's Well** (also known as the Well of Saladin), descending 100m to the level of the Nile. The well was dug by Crusader prisoners. To the south of the Muhammad Ali Mosque stand the remains of the Bijou Palace, also built by Muhammad Ali. The famous Mamluk palace known as Qasr al-Ablaq has been recently excavated in this area. The **Military Museum** (open daily 9am-2pm), in the northern part of the Citadel, has a large collection of medieval weaponry and military paraphernalia but is hardly worth the outrageous LE5 admission fee. Near the far eastern end of the northern enclosure is a small, beautiful, domed mosque known as the **Mosque of Suleiman Pasha,** built in 1528.

Central Islamic Cairo

The overwhelming **Mosque of Sultan Hasan,** considered the finest achievement of Mamluk architecture, is despised by devotees of pharaonic art because many of its stones were the exterior casing stones pilfered from the pyramids at Giza. The mosque stands in Salah al-Din Sq., facing the western gate of the Citadel. From downtown, take Muhammad Ali St. from the southern edge of Ataba Sq. and walk east for 2km. Frequent buses also run from Tahrir Sq. Strictly speaking, Sultan Hasan is not a mosque but a combination of a *madrasa* and a mausoleum with an added prayer niche. The ample interior courtyard belongs to the **Madrasa of Sultan Hasan,** surrounded by four enormous vaulted *liwans,* each of which would have housed one of the four schools of judicial thought in Sunni Islam. Notice the beautiful Kufic inscription around the eastern *liwan* (directly across as you enter). Inside the *liwan,* the *mihrab,* is flanked by a pair of Crusader columns. On either side of the eastern *mihrab* bronze doors open into the **Mausoleum of Sultan Hasan.** The huge cenotaph in the center of the mausoleum is frequented by Muslim women who beg Sultan Hasan's assistance in their personal difficulties. (Open 8am-6pm. Admission LE1.)

Directly across the street from the Sultan Hasan Mosque stands the enormous **Rifa'i Mosque,** (1912). Though of little architectural or historical importance, its gargantuan size and polished interior draw every tour group in Cairo. It is the resting place of many Egyptian monarchs and contains the tomb of the Shah of Iran. Both the Rifa'i and Sultan Hasan Mosques are illuminated at night. (Open 8am-6pm. Admission LE1.)

Just around the corner, the small **Mosque of Amir Akhor** has an appealing exterior with a rare double-pinnacled minaret and beautifully carved dome. Facing the mosque, proceed east (to your right) along the walls of the Citadel and turn left up Bab al-Wazir St. You'll soon come to the fourteenth-century **Mosque of Aqsunqur,** more commonly known in guidebooks as the Blue Mosque, after its blue faience-tiled interior. The tiles were imported from Damascus and added in 1652 by a Turkish governor homesick for the grand tiled mosques of Istanbul. Turn right as you leave and continue up the same street; its name changes to Darb al-Ahmar ("Red Way") in memory of Muhammad Ali's massacre of the Mamluk generals here. On your left is the **Maridani Mosque,** which receives few tourists. Notice the beautifully restored *minbar* and *mihrab,* the granite columns that originally belonged to a pharaonic structure, and the large wooden screen separating the courtyard from the prayer hall. Ask the custodian to let you see the *qibla* wall and the *mihrab.*

Continue north along Darb al-Ahmar St.; at the corner where the street veers to the left stands the simple and unobtrusive **Mosque of Qijmas al-Ishaqi.** Don't be deceived by the unremarkable exterior. The light from the stained-glass windows beautifully illuminates the inlaid marble and stucco of the interior. Under the prayer mats in the east *liwan* lies an ornate marble mosaic floor. As you step out, notice the grillwork of the *sabil* (fountain) on your right and the carved stonework of the columns.

Southern Islamic Cairo

If you see only one mosque in Cairo, let it be the **Mosque of Ibn Tulun,** the largest, oldest (879 C.E.), and most harmonious of the city's Islamic monuments. With sweeping contours and a vast courtyard, intricate inscriptions and lacy stuccowork, the mosque is a remarkable blend of simplicity, grandeur, and rich local detail. Ibn Tulun, son of a Turkish slave, was sent to Egypt as governor of al-Fustat in 868 and became governor of the entire province in 879. He declared independence from Baghdad and built a new royal city north of the original capital of al-Fustat. The grand mosque is all that remains of the Tulinid City. Although the structure has undergone restoration on numerous occasions, no essential changes have been made in its overall design or character. To reach the mosque, walk west along Saliba St. from Salah al-Din Sq., by the western gate of the Citadel. The courtyard covers almost seven acres, with intricate stuccowork inside and around the archways and an inscription band of elegant Kufic carved in sycamore wood that runs for over 2km. It is often said (incorrectly) that the entire Koran is inscribed on the mosque walls. The minaret, with an unusual external staircase, was probably built in the thirteenth century to resemble the Ibn Tulun's original tower, which in turn was modeled after the minaret at the Great Mosque of Samarra in Iraq. By walking to the right between the interior and exterior wall of the mosque, you can reach the tower and ascend for view of the courtyard, the city, and the Giza pyramids. (Open 9am-4pm. Admission LE1.) Don't mistake the *madrasa* and Mosque of Sarghatmish, which adjoins the northern side of the Mosque of Ibn Tulun, for Ibn Tulun's entrance; Sarghatmish is closed to non-Muslims.

On the right, as you step out of the main courtyard entrance, you will see the enchanting **Bayt al-Kritiliya** (House of the Cretan Woman), also called the **Gayer-Anderson House.** These two wonderful sixteenth- and eighteenth-century Turkish mansions were merged and refurbished in the 1930s by Major Gayer-Anderson, an English art collector. Today it is a museum containing, among other exhibits, carved wooden *mashrabiyya* screens that allowed women in the harem to see out without being visible from the streets. (Open Sat.-Thurs. 9am-3:30pm, Fri. 9-11am and 1:30-3:30pm. Admission LE1. Ticket valid for the Islamic Museum as well.)

If the Ibn Tulun Mosque is the boldest and most impressive of Cairo's Islamic monuments, then surely the **Madrasa of Qaytbay** is the most delightful and expressive. A short walk to the west of the Gayer-Anderson House, the mosque was built by Mamluk Sultan Qaytbay in 1475 C.E. as a theological college. The beautifully carved *minbar* (pulpit), and the intricate mosaic flooring are some of the finest in Cairo. (The caretaker will unlock it for some *baksheesh.*) Don't let the dust and grime detract from your enjoyment of one of Cairo's most precious monuments. (Open daily 9am-4pm. Admission 50pt.)

Continuing west down Saliba St. you will emerge at the foot of Port Said St., on the edge of Islamic Cairo, by the huge nineteenth-century **Mosque of Sayyida Zaynab.** The shrine houses the tomb of the prophet Muhammad's granddaughter Zaynab, and non-Muslims are forbidden to enter. It's worth glancing in the doorway, especially during prayers. Next to the mosque, the narrow alleys of the **Araz Bazaar** are less touristy but also less hygienic than Khan' al-Khalili.

Old Cairo

Some of Cairo's oldest architectural monuments are in the southern sector of town known as Old Cairo. Nine hundred years before victorious Fatimids founded the city of al-Qahira, the Roman fortress town of Babylon occupied the strategic apex of the Nile Delta just 5km south of the later city site. This outpost became a thriving metropolis during the fourth century C.E., and a number of churches were built within the walls of the fortress. One of the rebuilt churches has survived as a place of worship for the Coptic community. Located outside the walls of the Islamic city, Old Cairo also became the center for Cairo's Jewish community. Although most of the Jewish population of the city fled in 1949 and 1956, a number of Jewish families still inhabit this quarter, worshiping at an ancient synagogue. In addition to a handful of lovely Coptic churches, Old Cairo offers one of the city's finest collections, the **Coptic Museum.**

The easiest way by far to reach Old Cairo is to take the new Metro from Tahrir Sq. to Mar Girgis (about 30pt). Buses #92, 134, 140, and 94 also run from Tahrir Sq., stopping directly in front of the Mosque of 'Amr. If you take a taxi to the outskirts of Old Cairo, tell the driver you want to go to *Masr al-Qadima* or *Jami Amr.*

Coptic Cairo

For most visitors, ancient Egypt is synonymous with towering pyramids, jewel-covered mummy cases, hieroglyphics, and Cleopatra. Many view this pharaonic era as an isolated flowering of civilization that was replaced by the Islamic age of mosques, medieval fortifications, and integration into the Arab world. But for a transition period of several hundred years, beginning in the first century C.E. when the new faith began to take hold in Egypt, Christianity and Hellenistic culture were dominant forces. Egyptian Christianity spread through the Coptic Orthodox Church, which split from the main body of the Christian Church in 451. Both culturally and intellectually, the Coptic period served as a link between the pharaonic and Islamic eras and has left its mark on modern Egypt. The size of the Coptic community today is a subject of heated controversy, with estimates ranging from 6% to 15% of Egyptian population.

"Copt" derives from the Greek word for Egyptian, "Aegyptos," shortened in Egyptian pronunciation to *gibt,* the Arabic word for Copt. Usually, only the appearance of a domed cathedral, or a tiny cross tatooed on a wrist, indicates the presence of this tightly-knit religious minority. Having taken a back seat to the Muslims for centuries, the Copts have emerged in recent years as an independent political and cultural force, causing tension between the Coptic Church and the Egyptian government. On a day-to-day basis, however, centuries of coexistence have instilled mutual tolerance: Egypt's Christians live harmoniously with their Muslim neighbors, especially in small towns.

Christianity's roots in Egypt date from the first century, when a Christian university was founded in Alexandria. In the third century, the Bible was translated into Coptic, the native Egyptian language. In 250, Paul of Thebes, St. Anthony, and St. Pacome (the "Fathers of the Desert") chose a life of solitude in the Egyptian desert, initiating the tradition of Christian monasticism. However, young Christianity did not flourish without internal conflict; a doctrinal dispute arose concerning the interpretation of the Trinity. The doctrine of the Coptic Orthodox Church, monophysitism, recognizes in Christ the simultaneous and indivisible expression of both human and divine natures. In 451, the Alexandrian arm of the Church declared its theological and political independence from Constantinople. Ascending to the throne in the wake of these developments, the Roman Emperor Justinian sought to restore unity by exiling Coptic clergy to isolated desert monasteries. When the Persians captured Egypt in 619, they were welcomed by the rebellious Copts as liberators. During the seventh and eighth centuries, the Egyptian Christians cooperated with their Muslim conquerors, and over the centuries, many Christians converted to Islam. By the ninth century, Christians found themselves a threatened minority once again. They managed to retain conciliatory ties with Rome, though doctrinal differences were never resolved and independence never surrendered. Today, portions of the liturgy are still conducted in Coptic, though most of the service is in Arabic. Coptic Orthodox Masses are held at al-Muallaqa on Friday from 8 to 11am and Sunday from 7 to 10am. Modest dress is required at all times for both men and women.

Built on the site of the Roman Fortress of Babylon, the **Coptic Museum** possesses the world's finest collection of Coptic art. Located in the nineteenth-century Qasr al-Shama, the museum encompasses several peaceful courtyards and gardens. The floors are paved with marble, while a host of elegantly carved wooden *mashrabiyya* adorn the windows. The exhibits, which feature pieces dating from the third through seventh centuries, trace the development of Coptic art. In the earliest works, the predominant mood is pharaonic; in later pieces, a Greco-Roman flavor emerges; and in more recent examples, Islamic influence is apparent. It has been suggested that the Christian cross is derived from the *ankh,* or pharaonic key of life, which evolved into the crucifix shape in Coptic iconography. Coptic art also influenced Islamic architecture, particularly in the development of geometric motifs. Unlike the earlier, monumental art of the pharaohs, Coptic art tended to be a more popular folk medium. Its fanciful and imaginative motifs represent a significant break from the severe styles of the period previous to the third century C.E. The finest exhibits are those of Coptic textiles. The ancient Copts embroidered garments, tablecloths, and curtains with scenes of nymphs, centaurs, hunters, and animals of all kinds, as well as complex geometric patterns. Under the Fatimid and Mamluk Dynasties, Copts provided the garments for the Muslim ruling elite. The museum also houses a variety of architectural fragments brought from the sanctuary of St. Menas at Maryut and the monastery of St. Jeremiahs at Saqqara, as well as illuminated manuscripts and numerous paintings, icons, and ivories. The museum is directly across from the Mar Girgis stop on the Metro. If you arrive by bus or taxi, you'll be let off just outside Old Cairo. Head directly south along the old subway tracks, and the museum will be on your left. (Open Sat.-Thurs. 9am-4pm; Fri. 9-11am and 1-4pm. Admission LE2, students LE1. Cameras prohibited.)

In front of the museum stands Cairo's only substantial classical ruin. The imposing **Roman battlement** originally flanked the main entrance to the Fortress of Babylon. Built in the first century, the fortress overlooked the Nile before the river shifted west. The *castellum* extended over a full acre, and it took invading Muslims more than seven months to overpower the fortifications in the seventh century. The castle's only surviving tower formed part of a massive harbor quay in ancient times. Today a flight of stairs leads down to the foundation of the bastion.

Most of Cairo's Coptic churches do not face directly onto the street. None of the older structures possesses elaborate entrances. They are rectangular in plan and the apse is separated from the main nave by a wooden *iconostasis* (screen of icons) running the length of the room and serving as a partition. Upstairs, the gallery of the nave was reserved for women. Today this upper level has fallen into disuse in most churches, though women and men still sit on opposite sides of the central aisle. Though none of the churches in Coptic Cairo charges admission, all contain donation boxes where you can leave a contribution. The caretaker may not approach you for *baksheesh,* but if you are shown a secluded chapel or crypt, a small tip (25pt) is in order. The churches are open daily from about 9am-4pm. Photographs prohibited in all of the churches.

Standing south of the Coptic Museum, the **Church of al-Muallaqa** (The Hanging Church) was built balanced atop the gate of Babylon Fortress. Known also as the Church of St. Mary, it is perhaps Coptic Cairo's loveliest church and the earliest known Christian place of worship in Egypt. The original elevated building was erected in the late sixth century on the site of a Roman place of worship. Repeated restoration has rendered this early structure all but invisible. Enter al-Muallaqa through the gateway in the walls just south of the museum. A narrow vestibule ends in a flight of stairs leading to a rectangular courtyard filled with icons dating from the seventeenth century. Adjoining the courtyard to the east, the church's facade is carved in intricate high relief. Inside, pointed arches and colorful geometric patterns enliven the main nave. In the center, an elegant pulpit rests on 13 slender columns—one for Christ and each of his disciples. The conspicuous black marble symbolizes Judas. The pulpit is used only once a year, on Palm Sunday. The twelfth-century ebony and ivory *iconostasis* is one of the finest in Coptic Cairo.

North of al-Muallaqa on Mari Girgis St. past the museum, the sixth-century Greek Orthodox **Church of Mari Girgis** (St. George) is a wide, circular building, erected over one of the towers of the Fortress of Babylon. Renovated on several occasions, the present structure, though not very old, preserves the circular plan that was once common in Middle Eastern churches. The serene interior is illuminated by stained glass windows and candles and contains a fine collection of icons.

To the left of St. George's Church on Mari Girgis St., a staircase descends into Old Cairo proper. After entering the city, the first main doorway on the left is marked with a tin plaque indicating the fourteenth-century **Convent of St. George.** The nuns here sometimes enact a traditional Coptic ritual of wrapping a person in chains to symbolize the persecution of St. George by the Romans. Venture farther into Old Cairo and continue to the end of the main alley with the entrance to the convent. Bear right and directly ahead will be Coptic Cairo's most renowned structure, the **Church of Abu Serga** (St. Sergius). A very low archway leads off the main street into a narrow alleyway and the entrance to the church. You can't miss the entrance—there's a conspicuous tourist bazaar across from it. The church, dating from the tenth century, lies several feet below street level. A handsome twelfth-century *iconostasis* separates the sanctuary from the nave, crowned by a series of icons depicting the 12 Apostles. The sanctuary contains an onion-domed altar, supported by four slender columns. (The original altar is on display in the Coptic Museum.) Behind the left side of the *iconostasis* are a set of steps descending to the crypt, where the Holy Family is believed to have rested on their journey into Egypt. Each year on June 1, Mass is celebrated in this tiny chapel to commemorate the event. Rising Nile waters have flooded the crypt in recent years, and it is currently closed to the public. For some *baksheesh* though, the custodian will probably let you have a look.

Leaving the Church of Abu Serga, turn right and head eastward to the end of the alley. Immediately to the left lies the spacious **Church of St. Barbara,** together with a Church of St. Cyrus and St. John dating from the Fatimid era. Legend holds that when the caliph discovered that both Christian churches were being restored, he ordered the architect to destroy one of them. Unable to choose, the architect paced back and forth between the two buildings until he died of exhaustion. Moved by this tragedy, the caliph allowed both churches to stand. The interior of the Church of St. Barbara closely resembles that of its restored cousin. The bones of St. Barbara, who was killed by her father when she attempted to convert him, are said to rest in the tiny chapel reached through a door to the right as you enter the church. The bones of St. Catherine, namesake of the monastery on Mount Sinai, are also rumored to lie here. An inlaid wooden *iconostasis* dating from the thirteenth century graces the church's ornate interior. The main sanctuary contains a series of seven marble steps decorated with black, white, and red stripes leading up to a marble niche that resembles a *mihrab*.

A few meters south of St. Barbara's, a shady garden fronts on the **Ben Ezra Synagogue.** The temple that occupied the site in pre-Christian times was demolished in the first century C.E. to make room for construction of the Roman fortress. Later, a Christian church was built on the spot, and in the twelfth century this building was transformed into the present synagogue. The distinctive Sephardic ornaments and a valuable collection of ancient manuscripts and sixth-century Torah scrolls have been removed until restoration is completed, which will probably take years. Most of the synagogue has been roped off, so you may have to content yourself with limited glimpses of the lovely interior. This synagogue is inhabited by a humorous custodian. Even if you're not interested in seeing the synagogue, it's worth coming just to listen to his spiel.

Fustat

Adjoining Coptic Cairo to the north are the partially excavated remains of Fustat, one of the oldest Islamic settlements and the capital of Egypt during its first two-and-a-half centuries as a Muslim state. The remains consist of a labyrinth of tiny alleys surrounded by low walls. Though the architectural remains of Fustat are insubstantial, a stroll through the site reveals traces of mansions with patios, cisterns, oil presses, water pipes, drains, and cesspits. In the northwest corner of the site, the Mosque of 'Amr, Egypt's first Islamic mosque, has been restored to use. In addition to the architectural fragments, thousands of fine pieces of Islamic pottery and imported Chinese porcelain have been discovered here; they can be seen at the Islamic Museum. In the nearby **pottery district,** you can watch artisans still at work.

To reach Fustat from downtown, take the Metro or a bus to the Mar Girgis station. Head north along Mari Girgis St. and take the first right onto Ain al-Sira St., which leads along the northern edge of Old Cairo. After the first right at the northeastern corner of the wall, turn left and follow the dirt track that leads north through the brick remains of Fustat. The walk takes about 20 minutes. Fustat sprawls over a large area and is never closed. The caretaker at the end of the track charges LE1 admission, 50pt for students, if you wander nearby. If you venture out to this district in the heat of summer, be sure to bring water along. Also beware that the ground near the site is unstable in places, since much of the area was used as a rubbish dump until quite recently. Wild dogs are also known to roam the ruins.

Fustat was the name of a garrison town that some historians maintain derives from the Latin word for camp, *fossatum.* A more romantic account of the founding of Fustat maintains that the conquering general 'Amr sent word to the caliph in Medina that the magnificent Roman port of Alexandria would be the perfect place for the capital of Egypt. To 'Amr's dismay, the caliph preferred to establish his outposts in sand, connected by desert trade routes and invulnerable to naval attack from seafaring Christians. The disappointed general returned to Babylon to find that a white dove had nested in his tent during his absence. Interpreting this as a divine omen, 'Amr founded the new capital of Egypt on the site of his tent, thus dubbed *al-Fustat* (City of the Tent).

One of 'Amr's lasting contributions was Egypt's first mosque, which at the time served as the seat of government, the post office, and *caravanserai,* as well as the city's religious center. The huge, open square was capable of holding nearly 12,000 worshipers (the size of 'Amr's army). Fustat later acquired a large treasury, numerous mansions, and elaborate plumbing and sewage systems, the likes of which were not seen in Europe until the eighteenth century. Fustat remained the capital of Egypt until the conquering Fatimids established the neighboring city of al-Qahira in 969 C.E. By the middle of the twelfth century, however, the Fatimid Dynasty was weakening, and in 1168 Cairo was invaded by Crusader King Amalric of Jerusalem, who fought the Fatimids near Cairo. During the battle, Fustat was burned to the ground to prevent it from falling into the hands of the Crusaders. Except for the great mosque, little survived of the city, and by the end of the fourteenth century Fustat was virtually abandoned.

The present day **Mosque of 'Amr** occupies the site of the original building of 642, which was barely one-fourth the size of the present edifice. Its low roof consisted of thatched palm leaves on a series of palm trunks. The oldest portion of the mosque is its crumbling southeast minaret, added during the Turkish period. The eighteenth-century design of the mosque encompasses a single, spacious courtyard lined on four sides by stately white marble columns, plundered from local Roman and Byzantine buildings during medieval times. The mosque was entirely renovated several years ago.

Near the Mosque of 'Amr is **Dayr Abul'-Safrayn,** a complex of three eighth-century Coptic churches. From the mosque, head north, take the first left, and follow the thoroughfare down to the railroad tracks; the wooden entrance to the churches will be slightly behind you and to the north. Their official hours are 8am to 1pm, but knock loudly to rouse the caretaker if you arrive late. The main attraction is the **Church of St. Mercurius,** dating from the sixth century, but heavily restored during medieval times. The cathedral contains several early icons, as well as a delicate ebony *iconostasis.* In the northern side of the main chamber, an icon picturing St. Barsaum marks the entrance to a tiny vaulted crypt, where the saint is said to have lived for 20 years with his pet snake. Mass is celebrated in the crypt on September 10 to honor St. Barsaum's feast day. Upstairs is another church, comprised of tiny chapels.

Next door is the early seventh-century **Church of St. Shenudi,** the most famous Coptic saint. This chapel contains two fine *iconostases*—one of red cedar and the other of ebony—very similar to Fatimid woodwork. An elegant wooden canopy crowns the altar in the central sanctuary. The smallest of the three main structures at Dayr Abul'-Safrayn is the **Church of the Holy Virgin,** a tiny one-room chapel full of icons and small paintings.

As you leave Old Cairo, heading north by bus or taxi, you will pass the well-preserved fourteenth-century **aqueduct,** erected by Sultan al-Nasir Muhammad to transport water from the Nile to the Citadel.

Cities of the Dead

The vast and forbidding Cities of the Dead, to the northeast and south of the Citadel, contain hundreds of tombs and mausolea from the Mamluk era. Despite the profusion of funerary architecture, the cities remain very much alive. Doubling as a residential district, the area serves as home for hundreds of thousands of Cairenes. In recent decades, vast shanty towns have grown up around the edges of both cemeteries. The modern residents of the medieval necropoli dwell amidst the marble tombs; many households have even incorporated the grave markers into their houses and yards. Labyrinthine networks of narrow alleyways are punctuated by an occasional open square or garden. Far from providing the deceased with a peaceful resting place, the tombs serve as clotheslines, soccer goals, and public benches. On Fridays these quarters come alive with visitors arriving to pay their respects to the deceased. Many of the grave plots are enclosed by walls, encompassing an adjoining chamber and a small house where families pray for their dead relatives on holy days. The Egyptian custom of picnicking at the family tomb on feast days may well be an ancient holdover from pharaonic times, when the corpse was believed to require nourishment to ensure the spirit's well-being in the afterlife. The Cities of the Dead are particularly fascinating on holidays. Visitors are not permitted to enter the mosques on Fridays, or during prayers.

The cemeteries were the burial site of the Mamluk sultans, who spared no expense in the construction of their final resting places. Elaborate tomb complexes, outfitted with domed mausolea, mosques, and adjoining *madrasas*, were erected for Cairo's rulers. Gravestones built for the families of Mamluk nobles vary in size from tiny, tottering tombstones to magnificent mausolea. Cenotaphs of all shapes and sizes dot the crowded thoroughfares of the royal necropoli.

The Mamluk necropolis is divided into two sectors. The **Northern Cemetery,** northeast of the Citadel, is characterized by wide boulevards, quiet gardens, and courtyards. It contains the finer monuments of the two necropoli, with structures dating from the later Mamluk period (fourteenth to sixteenth centuries) to this century. To reach the Northern Cemetery, take one of the several buses departing from Ataba Sq. for Dirasa, a large terminus situated directly west of the necropolis on Salah Salem St., the road to Heliopolis. You can also walk to the cemetery from the al-Azhar Mosque. Head east around the north side of al-Azhar until you reach Bab al-Ghurayyib St. Follow this avenue straight east until you hit Salah Salem St. Dirasa lies ¼ km north (look for the blue overpass). The **Southern Cemetery** is a far more crowded necropolis, housing Ayyubid mausolea and the oldest Mamluk tombs (twelfth to fourteenth centuries). It is located south of the Citadel. Take bus #182 from Tahrir or #81 from Ataba to reach the main thoroughfare, Imam al-Shafi'i St. The Metro also runs to this area from Ataba Sq. (10pt). The Southern Cemetery is accessible by foot from Ibn Tulun, the Sultan Hasan Mosque, or the Citadel. From Ibn Tulun or Sultan Hasan, proceed east to Salah al-Din Sq., just southeast of the Citadel. From here head directly south past the Manshiya Prison, to Imam al-Shafi'i St. The Mausoleum of Imam al-Shafi'i is south of Salah al-Din Sq.

Northern Cemetery

Bordered on the west by Salah Salem St., the Northern Cemetery is a splendid outdoor museum of Mamluk art. Its most illustrious structure is the magnificent fifteenth-century **Mausoleum of Qaytbay.** The gently tapered minaret and ornately carved dome stand directly west of the Dirasa bus stop, clearly visible above the peaks of the surrounding tombs. Approach the structure from the north through the open square to gain the best view of the facade's polychrome striped brickwork. Qaytbay's mausoleum is familiar to every Egyptian as the towering monument pictured on the one-pound note. Qaytbay was a Mamluk slave, purchased for LE130, who rose through the ranks of the army to become leader of Egypt during the closing decades of the fifteenth century. Reigning for 28 years—longer than any other Mamluk except al-Nasir Muhammad—he was a ruthless sultan with a soft spot for beautiful buildings. Enter the complex through the northern doorway, passing through a rectangular sanctuary with four graceful *liwans* capped by a lantern-shaped roof. The mausoleum proper is an airy, domed chamber housing the marble cenotaphs of Qaytbay and his two younger sisters. Also housed in the tomb chamber are two black stones bearing footprints said to be those of the prophet Muhammad. Climb to the top of the triple-tiered minaret for a spectacular view of the Northern Cemetery's crowd of domed mausolea. From here you can also gain a close-up view of the elaborately carved dome. Note how the pieces of the ornamental pattern fit together with unbroken precision. (Admission LE1.)

South of the Mausoleum of Qaytbay are two fourteenth-century monuments constructed for members of the royalty. To reach them, follow the main road south of the mausoleum through the **Gate of Qaytbay,** a stone archway that once guarded the entrance to the tomb complex. When this thoroughfare intersects with a paved road, turn right, and head west toward Dirasa and Salah Salem St. Just beyond the next main street are the remains of the **Tomb of Umm Anuk** (1348), a heavily ribbed dome adjoining a sweeping pointed archway. Umm Anuk was the favorite wife of Sultan al-Nasir Muhammad, and her loving husband presented her with an appropriately lavish tomb. He also constructed the **Tomb of Princess Tolbay** across the way for his principal wife. Muslim law required him to treat the two women equally, but the sultan obeyed only the letter and not the spirit of Koranic law: Judging from the inferior work of the second tomb, it is clear where the sultan's genuine affections lay.

The remaining important tombs in the Northern Cemetery are north of the tombs of the two wives. Follow the cemetery's main north-south boulevard, which runs parallel to Salah Salem St., until you reach the **Tomb of Barsbay al-Bagasi.** Built in 1456, the tomb is decorated with an intricate, geometrical design resembling a tulip, a variation on the Moroccan motif of *dari w ktaf* (cheek and shoulder). About 90 years later, the **Tomb of Amir Sulayman** was built; its dome is carved with a series of zig-zag stripes.

Around the corner to the east is the imposing **Mausoleum of Barquq,** easily identified by its matching pair of ornately sculpted minarets. Built in 1400 for Sultan Barquq by his son, this enormous family plot encompasses a spacious inner court-yard containing the meager remains of a stone fountain and a tamarisk shade tree. The *minbar* beneath the western arcade was donated to the mausoleum by the Mam-luk ruler Qaytbay. Three larger domes grace the western arcade. The smaller, cen-tral peak covers the richly decorated *minbar,* while two matching zig-zag domes—the earliest stone domes in Cairo—shelter the family mausolea located in either corner. Sultan Barquq is interred below the northeast corner of the complex, and the remains of his two daughters occupy the chamber beneath the southeast dome. For a little *baksheesh,* the caretaker will show you around the mausolea and let you climb the minaret. In the northeast corner of the complex, the second story holds the remains of a large *kuttab* and numerous monastic cells that once housed *sufi* mystics. (Admission, excluding the tomb chambers and minaret, 50pt.)

The **Mosque and Mausoleum of Sultan Ashraf Barsbay** are 50m south of the mausoleum of Barquq, along the cemetery's main thoroughfare. Originally intended as a *khanqah,* the fifteenth-century mosque has meticulously fashioned marble mo-saic floors. Lift the protective prayer mats to see the colorful tilework. Adjoining the mosque to the north is the mausoleum, a domed chamber containing a white marble cenotaph, an elaborately decorated *mihrab,* and gleaming mother-of-pearl and marble mosaics. A local tailor has set up shop inside the tomb chamber.

Southern Cemetery

The Southern Cemetery's most impressive edifice is the celebrated **Mausoleum of Imam al-Shafi'i.** The largest Islamic mortuary chamber in Egypt, the mausoleum was erected in 1211 by Salah al-Din's brother and successor in honor of the great Imam al-Shafi'i, founder of one of the four schools of judicial thought of Sunni Islam. In 1178, Salah al-Din erected a large cenotaph over the grave of Imam Shafi'i, which is currently housed within the thirteenth-century mausoleum, now often crowded with Muslims offering prayers. The mausoleum has a graceful dome crowned with a bronze boat. Legend holds that this was intended as a bird feeder, but experts claim the figure is a remnant of the pharaonic tradition, symbolizing the Imam's passage into the afterlife. Built in 1799, the dome consists of two nested wooded shells, painted with a layer of lead. Below, the original edifice shelters the cenotaph and mortuary chamber. The interior of the mausoleum, consisting of a single octagonal room, sparkles with a rainbow of colorfully decorated patterns. In the center is the exquisite teak cenotaph of Imam Shafi'i, one of the finest surviv-ing pieces of Ayyubid wood carving. Although lavishly decorated, the large, original *mihrab* within the mausoleum is not correctly aligned with Mecca. A posted notice indicates the deviance, and nearby is a *mihrab* pointing in the proper direction. In addition to the tomb chamber, the complex contains two mosques, one dating from 1190, the other from 1763. The earlier mosque is closed to non-Muslims. The more recent, open to non-Muslims, remains a vital center of worship. (No admission; 25pt *baksheesh* appropriate.)

The **Mosque of Sayyida Nafisa,** Egypt's third-holiest Islamic shrine, is situated on the western edge of the Southern Cemetery not far from al-Sultaniya, an elegant fourteenth-century tomb. To get there, go to the main intersection southeast of the Citadel and take the major thoroughfare that follows the twelfth-century **Wall of Salah al-Din** in a southwesterly direction. At the end of the wall, bear sharply right and weave westward through a short maze of side streets to reach the entrance. As one of Cairo's three congregational mosques, Sayyida Nafisa is a center of Islamic worship and is off limits to non-Muslims. Pause in the entrance for a glimpse of the interior. The mosque houses a relic of a direct descendant of the prophet Muhammad (*sayyid,* male, or *sayyida,* female). Sayyida Nafisa, the great granddaughter of al-Hasan, a grandson of the Prophet, was venerated during her lifetime. After her death in 824 her tomb attracted throngs of pilgrims. By the tenth century, the original structure proved too small to contain the many worshipers, so successively larger mosques were built. The present structure dates from the nineteenth century. So many mausolea were erected in the immediate vicinity of Sayyida Nafisa's tomb that historians suspect the construction of this sacred shrine sparked the development of the Southern Cemetery. On Fridays, crowds converge on the mosque.

Adjoining the Mosque of Sayyida Nafisa on the eastern side are the thirteenth-century **Tombs of Abbasid Caliphs.** A large gate in the side of the passageway opens into a spacious L-shaped courtyard. The brick and stucco facade of the mausoleum lies on the courtyard's northern side, graced by three delicate pointed arched doorways. At the peak of their authority, the Abbasid caliphs ruled the entire Muslim world (except for Spain) from Baghdad. The last reigning caliph fled from Baghdad in 1258 after invading Mongols toppled the regime. Arriving in Egypt, he was welcomed by the reigning Mamluk sultan, who exalted the deposed caliph in an effort to legitimize his own position. Subsequent Mamluk rulers continued to protect the succession of caliphs without ever allowing the caliphate to gain any degree of effective power. Finally, the sultan in Istanbul declared himself caliph in 1517, thereby consolidating the authority of the Ottoman Sultanate. With Egypt under Ottoman rule, it was impossible for the regional government to protest the abolition of their local charade of religious authority. Though the Abbasid caliphs have been fully deposed, their succession continues to the present day, and members of the family are still buried within the walls of the thirteenth-century mausoleum. Inside are wooden cenotaphs marking the graves of the exiled Abbasid caliphs.

North of the Tombs of the Abbasid Caliphs, along al-Calipha St., lies the **Shrine of Sayyida Ruqayya** (1160), dedicated to the daughter of 'Ali, husband of the Prophet's daughter Fatima, the fourth rightly-guided caliph and a central figure in Shi'a Islam. The central niche of this popular place of worship is embellished with the name of 'Ali, recorded seven times in intricate script.

Across the street lies the **Tomb of Shagarat al-Durr,** the latest Ayyubid building in Cairo (1250) and the final resting place of one of the few women to achieve political power in the history of Islam. Shagarat al-Durr (Arabic for "Tree of Pearls") was a slave who rose to power after marrying al-Salih Ayyub, the final ruling member of Salah al-Din's Ayyubid Dynasty. After her husband's death in 1249, she concealed the sultan's death for three months until her son returned from Mesopotamia to claim the throne. The wily queen soon realized that her frail son would never be able to command a following among Mamluk slave troops, so she promptly engineered his murder. Proclaiming herself Queen, Shagarat al-Durr governed for 80 days until she married the leader of the Mamluk forces. The renegade couple managed to consolidate power over the next several years, but their happy rule ended when the queen discovered that her new husband was considering a second marriage and arranged for his murder. Not to be outdone, his prospective second wife avenged the death of her lover by beating Shagarat al-Durr to death with a pair of wooden clogs and then hurling her body from the top of the Citadel, where it was left to the jackals and dogs. Inside Shagarat al-Durr's mausoleum there is a wooden band around much of the upper chamber wall, carved in heavy Kufic script. Below, the *mihrab* is sparked with a colorful glass mosaic in the Byzantine style.

Museums

Egyptian Museum

In Tahrir Sq. stands the **Egyptian Museum,** the world's unrivalled warehouse of pharaonic treasures. (Open Sat.-Thurs. 9am-4pm, Fri. 9am-noon and 2-4pm. Admission LE3, LE1.50 with student ID.)

Recently renovated, the museum is no longer a dark and cluttered maze, though it lacks meticulous organization. The most conspicuous displays are not always the most interesting, and smaller, hidden rooms should not be overlooked. Come for a few short visits and explore on your own. It was announced in the summer of 1988 that the famed mummy collection, closed in 1981 by President Sadat on religious grounds, would be put on display again in March, 1989, in a special annex to the museum. With special lighting and display cases, this promises to be one of the most fascinating archeological displays in the world.

In the small glass case just inside the entrance, the **Narmer Palette** commemorates the unification of Egypt in 3100 B.C.E. by King Narmer of the First Dynasty. One side of the slate platter depicts the king, in the White Crown of Upper Egypt, striking an enemy from the Delta with a mace, and the other shows the victorious king, in the Red Crown of Lower Egypt, inspecting his fallen foe. From here, the corridors and rooms leading around the central domed court present a chronological sampling of pharaonic art from the Old Kingdom to the Greco-Roman period. Room 42 houses several other masterpieces from the Old Kingdom, widely considered ancient Egypt's finest artistic period. Before you enter, notice the ceramic mosaic scenes that flank the door. These are the earliest known examples of the mosaic technique. Despite the hard diorite stone, the finely molded features of the Fourth Dynasty King Chefren capture an unparalleled air of power and authority. The knotted lotus and papyrus plants on the side of his throne symbolize the pharaoh's sovereignty over a unified Egypt: The lotus, which grows predominantly in Upper Egypt, and the papyrus, which is abundant in the Delta, became common symbols for the joined Upper and Lower Egypt. Note the Horus falcon that cradles the king's head. Because he was a god shared by Upper and Lower Egypt, Narmer diplomatically chose the falcon-god as the symbol of his divine authority. You'll notice that Horus appears frequently throughout Egyptian artwork. In the same room, the naturalistic Fifth Dynasty wooden statue of the portly nobleman called Ka-aper and the painted limestone statue of the casually seated physician Ni-ankh-re demonstrate that convention rather than limited artistic capabilities restricted other royal portraiture to rigid idealization. As you leave the room and continue down the corridor, you will pass by the Fifth Dynasty papyrus stalk columns brought from the funerary complex of Unas (at Saqqara).

The unusually well-preserved paint on Prince Rahotep and his wife Nofret in the next room (#32) conveys the extraordinary realism of these funerary statues sculpted 47 centuries ago. Nofret's skin is a pale yellow, the standard color for women and children, while Rahotep is brownish-orange, to indicate the tan that darkened a man who labored under the sun. To the left, Seneb the dwarf and his wife maintain the conventional balance of a pair of seated figures by using their children as spatial surrogates for Seneb's legs. Nearby stands the world's oldest extant large metal statue, depicting Fourth Dynasty King Pepi I. It was fashioned by beating heated metal sheets around a wooden core.

After the Old Kingdom, Egyptian sculpture suffered a period of decline and mass production. The Middle Kingdom statue of **King Mentuhotep,** to the left of the entrance to room 32, seems crude compared to earlier works. The disproportionately massive legs were probably an awkward attempt to convey a sense of strength. Mentuhotep's skin is black, as it would have appeared after the two-month embalming process, during which the corpse is desiccated with salts and sealed with dark resin. As you continue along the side corridor toward the rear of the museum, notice the arcade of sphinxes and the fluted columns of the Thirteenth Dynasty (Middle Kingdom) with Papyrus capitals. Room 12 holds the burial chamber of King Thutmosis III, with its large dappled bull and star-studded vault.

Proceed to the **Akhnaton room** (#3) at the rear of the museum, which contains statues of the heretical pharaoh who introduced a form of monotheism. He worshiped Aton as the sun god and source of life, representing him as a disk with rays that ended in hands, sometimes holding *ankhs,* the Egyptian symbol for life. Akhnaton also venerated Maat, who was rather indelicately manifested as "truth in artwork." A kind of naturalism replaced the idealization of former eras: Images of Akhnaton, with bulging stomach, voluptuous thighs, and a narrow face with long nose and horse-lips, and of the bulging heads of his daughters, are as grotesque as the images of his wife Nefertiti are lovely and graceful.

Around the corner on the ground floor, objects from the New Kingdom period are displayed in rooms 14 and 24. In room 14 stands the restored Twentieth Dynasty statue of the coronation of Ramses III by the gods Horus and Seth. Also notice the Twenty-Eighth Dynasty landscapes with their vibrantly painted birds and fish. The Ptolemaic, Greco-Roman, and Byzantine exhibits are also on the ground floor. The naturalistic works of the Ptolemaic period displayed in rooms 24 and 25 demonstrate the extent of classical influence. The finest pieces are the colossal bust of Serapis in room 34 and the striking inscribed fragment from the coffin of Petrosirus.

The central courtyard of the museum contains pieces too large to display elsewhere. The highlight is the painted plaster floor from Akhnaton's capital at Tel el-Amarna. The colorful and energetic representations of water scenes are unequaled in Egyptian art.

Collections on the second floor are grouped more haphazardly. The extravagant contents of **Tut-Ankh-Amon's tomb** are surely the most outstanding. Originally squeezed into less than 100 cubic meters, the treasures now occupy an entire quarter of the second level. The eastern corridor contains decorated furniture, golden statues, delicate alabaster lamps, weapons, amulets, and other bare necessities for a king in the underworld. Note the depiction of the *aton* disk on Tut's throne and the resemblance of the inlaid figures to those of the Akhnaton period. Tut was the immediate successor of Akhnaton, and he continued to support the new religion for a short while. Having ascended the throne as a child, however, Tut was easily swayed by the disgruntled priests of Thebes, who convinced him to renounce Aton and embrace the earlier pantheon. Room 4, the most magnificent of all, flaunts the famous coffins and funeral masks, as well as a remarkable collection of jewelry. Outside in the hallway stand four alabaster **canopic jars,** which held the royal liver, lungs, stomach, and intestines—perishable items that were removed during mummification. Considered an insignificant organ, the brain was pulled out through the corpse's nose and discarded. The jars stood with the sarcophagus within four golden shrines that now stretch down the northern corridor.

When you're glutted on gold, check out the rooms opening off the corridor toward the center of the building. Room 34, off the eastern hall, holds a fascinating collection of toys, tools, and household items that reveal how people lived and artisans worked thousands of years ago. Farther down the hall, some exquisite painted panels of mummies from al-Fayyum during the Roman period are hidden in room 14. These unconventional, full-face portraits painted with colors mixed in molten wax display timeless artistic sensitivity. On the northern hall, room 3 is packed with dazzling jewelry from all periods of dynastic history. Room 12, around the corner on the western hallway, holds funerary items from later royal tombs, including an amusing assortment of bushy wigs worn by priests in the Late Period. The vast collection of **cat statues** is displayed in room 19. Don't miss the **figurines** farther along this hall in room 27. During the Old Kingdom, servants were buried alive in order to care for the king in the afterlife, but eventually models proved a more economical and more popular means of providing for the deceased. The new policy was especially appreciated by the servants. The wooden dioramas reveal the methods of butchers, bakers, carpenters, and weavers from the Middle Kingdom across the ages. The clay "soul houses" from lesser burials in the First Intermediate Period provide one of the few extant clues to middle-class domestic architecture. Room 53 holds mummified monkeys, a crocodile, a furry dog, and even a pet gazelle.

The museum giftshop sells maps, books, posters, and postcards (including pictures of the human mummies) at exorbitant prices. One of the best guides available for the Egyptian Museum is the *Blue Guide.* Although expensive, it is much better than the official *Guide to the Egyptian Museum,* which is basically just a catalog of the museum's contents (available from the gift shop, LE3.50). While you can hire a guide outside the building (usually around LE5 per hour), it is easy to discreetly tag along with one of the many tour groups already passing through the museum.

Other Museums

The Museum of Islamic Art, off Ahmad Maher Sq. at the corner of Port Said and Muhammad Ali St., houses one of the world's finest collections of Islamic art. There's a little of everything here, from carpets, glassware, and metalwork, to wood carvings, calligraphy, and pottery. (Since the exhibits have recently been rearranged, make sure any guide to the museum is current before you invest.) The museum is arranged largely by type of craft, so you follow stylistic developments within each medium. Since most tourists concentrate on Cairo's pharaonic attractions, this superb museum is usually quiet and uncrowded. One of the most interesting exhibits features a magnificent collection of ancient Koranic scientific and philosophical manuscripts. Some of the Korans here are engraved in beautiful, fluid Kufic script. Note the stylistic influence of Chinese ceramic work on the Islamic crafts of medieval Persia in the ceramics collection. The museum is about ½ km west of Bab Zuwayla, so it is easily incorporated into a trip to Islamic monuments. To get here from Tahrir Sq., walk east down Tahrir St. all the way to Ahmed Maher Sq. on Port Said St. at the edge of Islamic Cairo. The museum dominates the northern half of Ahmed Maher Sq. (Open Sat.-Thurs. 9am-4pm, Fri. 9-11am and 1:30-4pm. Admission LE2, students LE1. Ticket good for admission to the Gayer-Anderson House on the same day.)

The Mahmud Khalil Museum, 1 Shaykh Marsafy St. in Zamalek opposite the north gate of Gezira Sporting Club, across the street from the Marriott Hotel, contains a fantastic collection of European and Islamic art, including works by Monet, Renoir, Van Gogh, Pisarro, Toulouse-Lautrec, Degas, and Rubens, as well as beautiful Chinese jade carvings and Islamic pottery and tiling. Open Sat.-Thurs. 9am-1:30pm and 5-8pm. Admission LE1, students 50pt. Passport or other ID usually required for admission.

The Museum of Modern Art, 18 Ismail Abu'l-Futuh St. in Dokki, off Finney Sq. at the northern end of al-Sad al-Ali St. The museum features Egyptian paintings from the 1940s to the present. The sculpture garden is filled with scrap-metal creations. Admission LE1, students 50pt. Open Sun.-Thurs. 9am-2pm, Fri. 9am-1pm..

The Mukhtar Museum, just before al-Galaa Bridge in Zamalek (Gezira), was built by Ramses Wissa Wassef and houses the works of Mahmud Mukhtar (1891-1934), one of Egypt's famous sculptors. Admission LE2, students LE1. Open Sat.-Thurs. 9am-1:30pm, Fri. 9-11:30am.

Gezira Museum (tel. 340 51 98) at the Agricultural Society pavilion in Gezira, across from Mukhtar Museum, displays rare paintings, sculptures, and Islamic and Coptic artifacts. Admission 50pt. Open daily 9am-3pm.

Mogamma al-Fenoun (Center of Arts, tel. 340 82 11), is on the corner of Maahad al-Swissry St. and July 26 Bridge. The former residence of Aisha Fahmy, today the center exhibits works by Egyptian and European artists. Among the permanent collection are the works of Abdel Wahab, Muhammad Nagy, and Abdel Hamid Hamdy. European applied arts are on display on the second floor. Free. Open fall-spring Sat.-Thurs. 9am-1pm and 5-8pm.

The Agricultural Museum, at the western end of the October 6 Bridge in Dokki, behind a large, pleasant garden. Contains exhibits on Egyptian agriculture. Also displayed is the only remaining mummified Apis bull from the Serapium at Saqqara. Admission 15pt. Open daily 9am-3pm.

The Manial Palace Museum (tel. 84 26 68) at the northern edge of Roda Island; the entrance is next to the Cairo Youth Hostel on Sayala St., which leads to Cairo University Bridge. Built by Muhammad Ali in the last century, the southern half of the extensive structure now houses a posh Club Med. Visitors have access to the "reception palace," a private mosque, and a small hunting museum with a collection of stuffed birds and other animals. The museum exhibits an interesting collection of Islamic furnishings. Admission LE1. Open daily 9am-2pm.

Dr. Ragab's Papyrus Institute, al-Nil St., Giza (tel. 98 94 76), next to the Yacht Club and south of the Sheraton Hotel. Named after its founder, Dr. Hasan Ragab, a former ambassador to the U.S. who was into processing papyrus and now allows the general public to be. You can (of course!) buy copies of drawings made on papyrus. Admission LE2. Open daily 8:30am-6:30pm.

Entertainment

If, by the end of the day, tomb- and temple-hopping hasn't worn you out, Cairo offers a variety of nighttime entertainments to the intrepid amusement-seeker. The daily English-language newspaper, the *Egyptian Gazette,* is weak on news but lists entertainment and events. *Cairo by Night,* a free weekly periodical available in hotels, occasionally has useful information for nightlife seekers, and *Cairo Today,* a monthly magazine sold at newsstands, runs articles on attractions in the metropolitan area. *Cairoscope,* a guide to "culture and entertainment" in Cairo, lists foreign films, music recitals, and art exhibits; it's available at newsstands and major hotels.

The **sound and light show** at the Giza pyramids is overrated and overpriced. From 7:30-8:30pm in summer, 6:30-7:30pm in winter, the story of the ancient pharaohs is narrated while the Sphinx and the three pyramids are illuminated. "I am the Sphinx! (Ba-doom-doom!) Every morning I greet the dawn!" Tickets go on sale at 6:30pm for a whopping LE10. Arrive early to be assured of a good seat. On Monday, Wednesday, Friday, and Saturday nights, the performance is in English. Organized tours (from American Express or the Hilton) cost LE17, but you can easily take a taxi or bus out to Giza and save the expense. Occasionally, concerts are performed at the pyramids' theater. If you don't mind missing some of the narration (and you shouldn't), you can wander down from the pyramids at dusk and hang out in the empty lot to the right of the auditorium. For even more fun, go on foreign language night ("Ich bin der Sphinx!").

The hot spot for expatriates and the Cairo elite is **The Four Corners,** 4 Hasan Sabri St. in Zamalek, a Western-style complex of two restaurants, a bar, and disco. La Piazza, the "informal" restaurant serves slightly skimpy but delicious light Italian dishes for LE4-6; Matchpoint, the video bar, could easily be in London or New York and has prices to match. Watch for the LE6 minimum—but you will easily spend that much. This is where all the cosmopolitan, Westernized youths at the American University come to hang loose.

B's Corner, 22 Taha Husayn St., Zamalek, a video-bar, offers a host of board games and a constant flow of music. It's a popular hangout with foreigners who live in Cairo and a great place to meet people who know the city well. (Open 8pm-1am.) Take Hasan Sabri St. north of July 26 St. until you come to a square 3 blocks down, then take the fork that runs off to the left; it's 100m down the second street, next to the President Hotel. In the same building is **Il Capo,** a great place for live music. When big-name groups play, you have to consume a minimum of LE10 worth of food and drink; on other nights LE2 worth will suffice. Most bands are scheduled to begin at 10pm, but as everywhere in Egypt, schedules exist to be ignored. The spot often keeps hopping until 5am.

Pub 28, on Shagarat al-Durr St., Zamalek, next to the General Hotel, is popular among gay men and not expensive. (Open 8pm-1am.) **Merryland,** al-Hijaz St., Heliopolis, is a popular nightclub with Asian dancers and a romantic setting. (Open 8pm-1am; crowded on Fri.) Other nightlife options include swank bars, nightclubs, and discos in most of Cairo's fancy hotels, but expect your wallet to be much lighter when you leave. The **Atlas Hotel,** al-Gomhouria St., offers rock music and is popular with gay men and the expatriate crowd on Thursday and Friday nights from 11pm-3am. Though drinks are expensive, there's no cover charge. **Jackie's,** at the Nile Hilton, is Cairo's most exclusive night-spot. Admission is LE10, and smart dress is required (couples only; open 10:30pm-3am). You can gamble at **casinos** in the Nile Hilton, Marriott, and Sheraton hotels, where you must show your passport to enter and do all your gambling in foreign currency. Egyptians are not allowed to waste their money, though they deal, spin, and roll the gambling paraphernalia.

You can enjoy a drink with a panorama overlooking the Nile and the Cairo skyline from the top floor of the **Shepheard's Hotel,** where the small bar features an outdoor terrace. The hotel is in Garden City on the corniche just south of the Kasr al-Nil Bridge. **Club 36** (tel. 744 00), with its breathtaking panoramic view of the Nile and the city from the top floor of the Ramses Hilton, offers a more elegant and more expensive alternative. Jeans and T-shirts are not allowed after 5pm. The Ramses is on the corniche north of the Nile Hilton, through a sea of parking lots from Tahrir.

The most elegant center of Cairo's gay scene among the city's foreign and Egyptian communities is the **Taverne du Champs de Mars** in the Nile Hilton, a *fin-de-siècle* bar transported brick-by-brick from Belgium. It has good piano music, but high prices for food and drink. During Ramadan, **Al-Sokkareya,** near the al-Salam (Hyatt) Hotel at 61 Abdul-Hamid Badawy St., Heliopolis (take bus #50, 128, or 330), offers a wonderful evening in an Egyptian garden setting, with superb singers and musicians, a penny arcade, and fortune tellers. The LE10 entrance fee includes all of your drinks, as well as a *sheesha* (waterpipe). Try *sahlib,* a heavenly concoction of buffalo milk, herbs, spices, raisins, coconut, and nutmeg. (Open 8pm-3am during Ramadan and summer months. Call the Hyatt to confirm.)

In addition to the typical nightclub-style entertainment, some major hotels have shows of Egyptian dancing and music in their ethnic restaurants. The **Felfala** restaurant at the Ramses Hilton serves an excellent but expensive *prix-fixe* dinner (LE24), which includes a terrific display of folk dancing by the Hasan Troupe. Call the Ramses Hilton for times.

Several theater and dance companies perform in Cairo. One of the best is the Egyptian folk dancing **Rida Troupe,** which plays regularly at the **Balloon Theater** on al-Nil St. in Aguza, at the Zamalek Bridge—they're well worth the trip. The Balloon Theater also hosts concerts by famous Arab singers. Check with the tourist office for upcoming events. The **Cairo Circus,** next door to the theater, gives an entertaining one-ring show with lions jumping through burning hoops. Performances are in the evening only. Check with the tourist office for details. There are also performances at the **Gumhurriya Theater** by the **Arabic Music Troupe** and the **Cairo Symphony Orchestra,** usually on Friday evenings, and occasional dance and music concerts at the **Sayyid Darwish Theater,** off Pyramids Rd. on Gamal al-Din al-Afghani St. in Giza. The **Cairo Puppet Theater,** in Azbakiyya Gardens near Opera Sq., offers nightly performances from October to May. Though the shows are performed in Arabic, you can easily understand the colorful musicals.

In the downtown area, Cairo has a handful of **cinemas** that run foreign-language films, usually year-old American flicks. Check the *Egyptian Gazette* for listings. All are on or around Talaat Harb or July 26 St. Ticket prices vary for armchairs, balcony, and orchestra seats but average between 80pt-LE1. Remember that the Egyptian audience doesn't give a hoot about the sound, since they can read the subtitles. Try to sit in the least popular and hence quietest part of the theater—usually the rear of the orchestra. Evening performances begin about 9pm.

The American University in Cairo runs the **Wallace Theater,** featuring two plays per year performed in English, in the New Campus on Muhammad Mahmud St. The university also hosts a variety of concerts from jazz to chamber music. (Open fall-spring.) Check bulletin boards on the buildings of the Old Campus. The **American Cultural Center,** 4 Ahmed Ragheb St., sometimes shows free films on Friday nights. The **British Council,** 192 al-Nil St. (tel. 345 32 81) has a large library, and also sponsors performances by visiting British theatrical and musical groups. The **Italian Cultural Institute,** 3 al-Shaykh Marsafy St. in Zamalek, behind the Marriott Hotel (tel. 340 87 91), the **French Cultural Center** (tel. 354 76 79), at 34 el-Youssef St., east of Kasr al-Aini St., and the **Goethe Institute** (tel. 75 98 77), 5 Abd'l-Selim Arif St. (formerly Bustan St.), all show free foreign and Egyptian films, usually with French subtitles. The **Netherlands Institute,** 1 Mahmud Azmi St. (tel. 340 00 76), Zamalek, offers English lectures about Egypt on Thursdays at 5pm from September through June.

During **Ramadan,** nightlife takes on a whole new meaning in Cairo. All cinemas have performances starting at midnight. Most Cairenes take to the streets around al-Azhar and Husayn Sq. or along the corniche and the bridges across the Nile. Starting at 10-11pm, there are street theater performances, magic shows, and general pandemonium.

You may prefer to spend a more relaxing evening drinking tea or soda at one of the many cafes that line the Nile, an alternative many Egyptians prefer. Or consider relaxing right on the river itself by hiring a *felucca* (sailboat) to take you out. Most *feluccas* can take up to eight people comfortably. The more passengers, the cheaper, but you'll have to do some bargaining for a good rate. *Feluccas* for hire dock just south of the Kasr al-Nil Bridge on the east bank. Across the corniche (on the water) from the Meridien Hotel, a group of boats sails for LE5-6 during the day, LE7 in the evening. The agency across the corniche from the Shepheard's Hotel is always ready to hire out boats; you can wake them up at 4am and they'll happily take you out (LE10 during the day and LE12-15 at night, depending upon your bargaining powers). It's *felucca* etiquette to bring food on board for a picnic and to share it with your driver. Don't go overboard sharing alcoholic beverages, or *you* may go overboard.

For the Young at Heart

For younger travelers who have had their fill of mosques and museums, Cairo offers a number of less serious pursuits in which to indulge. Always popular are the camel rides (or a horseback gallop among the dunes) at the Pyramids in Giza. Following that, a scramble through the insides of the Pyramids themselves is usually enough to wear out even the most energetic child. (For details, see Giza below).

A trip to the top of the **Cairo Tower** in Zamalek (see New City Sights) is always an adventure, and horse-drawn carriages run from its base to the Nile and back (about LE5 for a 15-20 min. ride). Also enjoyable is a ride in a *felucca,* particularly at sunset. Departure points are the Semiramis and Meridien Hotels; see above for details.

The **Cairo Zoo** in Giza has an interesting collection of animals, and there are the lovely **Botanical Gardens** across the street for picnics or running around (see New City Sights). Also interesting is the **Nile Aquarium** on Zamalek Island and the nearby **Cairo Circus,** which has lions jumping through hoops of fire, as well as other attractions. Contact the tourist information office for the circus schedule.

During Ramadan, a variety of puppet shows, magicians, and street performers entertain children in the streets at night.

For the older child, there are frequent afternoon **"tea-dances"** at the Semiramis Hotel (tel. 355 71 71), and at "Jackie's" in the Nile Hilton (tel. 75 06 66).

Near Cairo

The Delta

The most scenic spot in the immediate vicinity of Cairo lies 15km north at the **Nile barrages.** Designed with brightly colored turrets and arches, the barrages were constructed in the first quarter of the nineteenth century in the first large-scale attempt to regulate the flow of water into the Delta. The banks of the Nile are full of outdoor cafes and casinos set in plush gardens where Cairenes and inhabitants of the Delta's larger towns take refuge from urban smog and noise. Avoid visiting on a Friday when the area is especially packed. Next to the barrages, where the Nile reaches one of its widest points, little bridges connect islets.

Immediately past the barrages, the river divides in half, flowing into the Mediterranean at the two ports of **Rosetta** (Rashid) and Damietta. Not coincidentally, Rosetta was where the Rosetta Stone was discovered. The port is a goldmine of Islamic architecture. Scattered throughout the town are dozens of provincial Ottoman mosques and houses from the seventeenth through the nineteenth centuries. The highest concentration lies along Port Said St., opposite the bus stop. About 5km north of Rosetta, the recently restored **Fort of Qaytbay** guards the strategic entrance to the Nile. To visit the peaceful **Mosque of Abu Mandur** perched on the bank of the river, catch one of the southbound taxi boats at the main dock in Rosetta. Many Alexandrians make the two-hour trip just to have a picnic here. Buses run every hour from Alexandria to Rosetta, and stop at the station on the north side of Gomhouriya Sq. (LE2). The train (third-class only) runs from Masr Station (75pt). Visit Rosetta on a day trip—there are no worthwhile accommodations here.

Qanater marks the official beginning of the Delta. Bus #210 runs to Qanater from the front of the Nile Hilton at Tahrir Sq. A small passenger ferry also runs along the Nile between Cairo and Qanater hourly from 6am to 6pm (2 hr., 50pt). Catch the ferry on the west bank of the corniche, north of the Ramses Hilton in front of the Television Building. It's also possible to hire a *felucca,* but the journey to Qanater from Cairo takes a long time since the mast of the boat must be lowered for each bridge.

Farther north begin the flat agricultural lands of the **Nile Delta,** reputed to be the most fertile region in the world. The larger towns are rather unattractive and uninteresting, but the countryside features pleasant farming villages and breathless green landscapes. The best way to enjoy the region is to rent a car or taxi, and drive along the canals and roads winding through the countryside. Tourists are not supposed to leave the main roads, but you probably won't be stopped for a little roaming. If you are stopped, however, don't be surprised if you spend the night doing a little research into the conditions of rural Egyptian jails. Though you'll still catch some of the regional flavor, travel by train or service taxi isn't as scenic, since both forms of transportation serve only the major cities.

The Old Kingdom blossomed primarily in Lower Egypt, and throughout the pharaonic period many fine monuments were erected in the Delta. Due to the looseness and richness of the soil, the deployment of irrigation canals, and the natural fanning out of the river, almost all of the major pharaonic sites in the Delta have been lost. Southeast of **Zagazig** (80 min. from Cairo via any train bound for Port Said, or 1 hr. by service taxi; both LE1.25-1.50), between Mustafa Kamal St. and Bulbais Rd., are the ruins of Bubastis, one of Egypt's most ancient cities and the most accessible of the Delta's pharaonic sites. The name means "house of Bastet" and refers to the handsome cat goddess to whom the main temple was dedicated. Herodotus described the temple as the most pleasurable to gaze upon in all of Egypt. Today it's not, as the sanctuary has become a scattered pile of inscribed blocks. Two hundred meters down the road you can explore the winding underground passages of the **Cat Cemetery,** where numerous celebrated bronze likenesses of Bastet have been uncovered. In Zagazig is the small **Uragi Museum,** which houses local archeological finds. (Open Sat.-Thurs. 9am-1:30pm. Admission 15pt.) The famous Lake Manzalik, the largest in the Delta region, lies 15km from the Ras al-Bahr resort area, not far from Zagazig.

The region's most worthwhile pharaonic site is located far from Cairo in the northeastern corner of the Delta's fertile triangle (4½ hr. by service taxi; no buses). Just outside of the village of **San el-Hagar,** at the junction of Bahr el-Sughir and Bahr Facus, the ruins of ancient **Tanis** are scattered over an area of about 4 square kilometers. They include a royal necropolis, the foundations of several temples, and a pair of sacred lakes.

Helwan and Ma'adi

The suburb of **Helwan** is Egypt's most industrialized and polluted factory town, but it does possess a pair of eccentric sights. You can take the Metro from downtown to Helwan Station (40pt). As you leave the station take a left, and 5 blocks ahead you will find the only **Japanese Gardens** in the Middle East. Constructed in 1918 by an Ottoman subject inspired by his trip to Japan, these sprawling gardens are now in a truly pathetic state of disrepair, and warrant a visit only by those desperate to see something *really* different. Equally decrepit but far more amusing is the nearby **Wax Museum** (Ain Helwan Metro station), with tableaux depicting scenes from Egyptian history, interspersed with assorted executions, disembowelments, and suicides. (Open daily 9am-5pm. Admission 50pt, plus 50pt *baksheesh* for the guide.) In the early part of the century, the elite of Cairo flocked to the Ain Helwan **mineral springs** next door; today the water is dirty and unpleasant.

For 35pt, the Metro toward Helwan takes you to the upper-class residential area of **Ma'adi,** the home of most Americans in Egypt. The Cairo American Primary and Secondary School educates the children of many Americans and other foreign diplomats. On the **Fourth of July,** a homesick American budget traveler's dream comes true, as the school holds a carnival at which over 5000 American citizens consume all the hot dogs, soft drinks, and pot luck food they can put away. Just bring your American accent and an empty stomach—it's all included in your taxes.

Cairo Environs

Most visitors to Egypt spend a few days in Cairo and then immediately head south for Luxor. If you have any time to spare, linger a while longer; the pyramids at **Giza** and at **Saqqara,** the Coptic monasteries of **Wadi al-Natrun,** and the sprawling oasis of **al-Fayyum** are all particularly worthwhile excursions from Cairo.

Giza and the Pyramids

From a distance, they look like the world's largest paperweights, but as you approach, you are seized by (in Napoleon's words), "a sort of stupefaction, almost overwhelming in its effect." Even if you are not as short as Napoleon, the dimensions of the pyramids are sure to impress you. Among the most monumental of human constructions, the pyramids at Giza testify to two of the ancient Egyptians' greatest obsessions: geometry and afterlife. They were labeled one of the seven wonders of the world by the ancient Greeks, and as the only surviving wonder, it is hardly surprising that they remain a great tourist attraction.

Nowhere else in Egypt is the country's booming tourist industry so evident. For a solid mile all around, souvenir shops, alabaster factories, and papyrus museums conspire to pawn off ancient artifacts made a full day ago. At the foot of the pyramids, a sizable army of hustlers will hound you: Bedouin pretenders offer to rent camels and Arabian race horses, hawkers peddle tourist junk at inflated prices, and self-appointed guides approach you at every turn. If you don't show any particular interest, they'll usually move along to a more promising victim. Don't let the racket deter you from spending at least a few hours gawking at the pyramids.

Practical Information

To get to the pyramids (*al-Ahram* in Arabic), take buses #8 or 900 (10pt) from the front of the Mugama Building at Tahrir Sq. in Cairo. The last stop on bus #8 will leave you right near the entrance to the pyramids. Get off the more crowded bus #900 as it turns off just before the Mena House Hotel. Don't jump off as soon as you see the pyramids—they look closer than they are. The more comfortable minibuses in the lot in front and to the right of the Mugama Building also go to the pyramids (35pt). Listen for the drivers shouting "Al-Ahram! Al-Ahram!" Taxis to the pyramids should cost LE3-4 from downtown Cairo.

If you intend to venture into the interior of the pyramids, go early in the morning to beat the crowds and the potentially unbearable heat within. Otherwise, the best time to visit the pyramids is the early evening, a half to one hour after the official closing. Then you will have free access to the entire site, the tourist buses will have left, the hustlers will have begun to pack up and go home, and the sunset at the pyramids makes the sound and light show that follows seem like an array of cheap flashbulbs. If you want to see the show for free, you can sit with the hundreds of Egyptians and watch from anywhere on the site. See if you agree that shining colored lights on the pyramids to make them dramatic is like covering them with moss to make them look old.

Your ticket will admit you to the pyramid interiors and the Sphinx complex. At any time, you may enter the site itself for free. In the summer of 1988, the Sphinx complex was closed for renovations; check before you buy your ticket. (Pyramids open 9am-4pm. Admission LE3, students LE1.50.) You must buy a separate ticket for the Cheops Solar Boat Museum. (Open 9am-4pm. Admission LE5.)

Renting a horse can be enjoyable, though many of the overworked and underfed animals have one hoof in the glue factory. To get a good price it's best to go early in the morning or after 4pm when the crowds are thin. Just stroll into the area between the Rest House and the Cheops Pyramid and look at one horse after another—the owners should eventually bargain each other down to LE3-4 per hour. For longer rides and more reliable mounts, walk down beyond the Sphinx and bear to the right after the Sound and Light Auditorium; there you will find a row of established stables. Examples of reputable establishments are **AA Stables** (tel. 85 05 31) and **S.A. Stables** (tel. 85 93 20; LE5 per hour but negotiable). Camels can be hired for a similar rate. MG Stables, though large and recommended by some guidebooks, is best avoided: They are overpriced and have ripped off customers, refusing to return change from large bills and failing to complete agreed upon routes. If you have any problems, there is a tourist police station adjacent to the ticket office. There are public bathrooms at the Pyramids Rest House (beside the ticket office) and at the Sphinx Rest House (beside the Sphinx).

Accommodations and Food

If you enjoy bedding down amid sun and sand, you can stay at **Salome Campground**, which has fairly clean toilets and showers, and a small restaurant, for LE1.50 per night. To get there, go down Pyramids Rd. until you come to the Maroutiya Canal. Take a left, and head down the road (the campgrounds are sign-posted). There's not much else to do here, however, and the restaurants in the immediate area of the pyramids have prices as outrageous as the claims of the pharaonic relic peddlers. There are only a few exceptions:

Pyramids Shish Kebab Restaurant, 2 blocks from the Sphinx Rest House along the main road from the pyramids. A portion of roast chicken or shish kebab, salad, and bread costs LE5. Open daily 1pm-3am.

Andrea, Maroutiya Canal, about 3km from the intersection with Pyramids Rd. (towards Kardassa). This outdoor restaurant, situated in a vineyard next to the canal, serves excellent roast chicken (LE3) and stuffed vine leaves (LE3), as well as other Egyptian specialties. Cohabiting the site with the restaurant are a number of dogs and cats, who will politely sit by your table growling and licking their chops while you eat. Open daily noon-11pm.

La Rose, next door to Andrea, and serving similar dishes at similar prices. But no animals. Open daily noon-11pm.

Probably the best bet for budget dining in Giza is to buy food and drink from a local shop and picnic among the ruins. A loaf of bread, a jug of *Omar Khayyem* wine (and thou) by the base of the Great Pyramid at sunset is infinitely more romantic than the overpriced, fly-infested restaurants on Pyramids Rd.

Groceries can be purchased at the **El-Helwa Supermarket,** 1 block from the Sphinx Rest House along the main road from the pyramids. (Bread 25pt, cheese 90pt, potato chips 25pt, drinks and mineral water also available. Open 10am-midnight.) Across the street is the **Al-Ahram Supermarket,** which has slightly higher prices and a wider selection. Both are a 10-minute walk from the great pyramid, down past the Sphinx.

Sights

The first pyramids in Egypt were constructed during the thirtieth century B.C.E. Pyramid building reached its zenith in the twenty-sixth century B.C.E., but rapidly declined during the following decades as the pharaohs consolidated their power and became the uncontested rulers of Egypt. The trio of pharaohs interred within the three main pyramids at Giza are Cheops (or Khufu), Chephren (or Khafre), and Mycerinus (or Menkaure). They are the father, son, and grandson who reigned during the twenty-sixth century B.C.E.

Each of the pyramids was once adjoined by its own funerary complex, complete with mortuary temple and riverside pavilion. In the mortuary temple, the pharaoh continued to be worshiped after his death, for the ruler was believed to be a god on a par with the familiar animal-headed deities of pharaonic decorative art. A long, narrow causeway linked the mortuary temple with the neighboring waters of the Nile, culminating in the valley temple, through which the complex proper was reached. The mummy of the deceased ruler was conveyed by boat across the Nile, taken up the causeway in solemn procession, and deposited in its sacred resting place at the heart of the giant pyramid. Unfortunately, most of the smaller structures surrounding the mammoth tombs in Giza proved unable to weather the centuries of quarrying, flooding, and looting. Better preserved funerary complexes can be seen at neighboring Saqqara.

The **Pyramid of Cheops** is the first pyramid you will encounter upon entering the site. When it was completed in 2690 B.C.E., it stood 146m high. Over the course of four-and-a-half millenia its height has decreased by only 3m. The total weight of Cheops is estimated at 6,000,000 tons. To appreciate its mass, crawl through the narrow passageways inside that lead to the king's chamber in the center of the pyramid, probably the most popular place for spelunking in the world. Beware, though: This is an arduous climb, and the faint-hearted or claustrophobic should not attempt it. The highlight of the expedition is the tall, narrow gallery with 9m walls formed from 14 massive slabs of granite. See if you can figure out for yourself when the passageways foresee the end of the world. The king's tomb chamber is a large, square room containing only the cracked bottom half of the sarcophagus. Its most novel feature is the impressive collection of nineteenth-century graffiti. The passageway to the queen's chamber, which starts at the bottom of the gallery, is closed off by an iron grille.

Outside the pyramid, walk around to the southern face of the structure to see the **Solar Boat**, one of the oldest boats in existence, unearthed near the pyramid base in 1954. You can still see the hole from which it was taken. This vessel most likely transported Cheops across the Nile from the "land of the living" on the east bank to his resting place in the "land of the dead" and was buried close to the pharaoh so he could use it to carry him over the ocean of death beneath the earth. A plywood and glass structure that looks like a futuristic ski lodge houses the boat today. Unfortunately, the cost of providing a climate that will prevent Cheops' sacred barge from deteriorating has forced the local authorities to charge a whopping LE5 admission fee. On the east side of the pyramid are the meager remains of the **Mortuary Temple of Cheops.** Besides a few sockets for columns, only the foundations remain.

The middle member of the trio, the **Pyramid of Chephren,** is only 3m shorter than the pyramid of Cheops. Portions of the limestone casing that originally covered the monument still sheathe its apex, making it Egypt's most beautiful pyramid. Another sacred boat was unearthed on its south side, but can be seen only with special permission from the Antiquities Service. The interior of Chephren's tomb is the finest of the three at Giza: The burial chamber still contains Chephren's sarcophagus as well as more nineteenth-century graffiti. The relatively spacious passageways make Chephren the coolest and most comfortable for exploring.

Third in line comes the **Pyramid of Mycerinus,** comparatively small at only 66m. Its burial chamber once contained a magnificent basalt sarcophagus covered with ornate decorative carving. Unfortunately, this treasure was lost at sea en route to the British Museum during the early nineteenth century. Outside, at the northeast corner of the temple, lie the quarried remains of the **Mortuary Temple of Mycerinus.** Farther away, the ruins of the unexcavated Valley Temple of Mycerinus are submerged beneath a blanket of sand.

The smaller pyramids around the big three belonged to the pharaoh's wives and children. Half-buried in the sand throughout the area are fascinating, unmarked tombs of ancient Egyptian nobles. Women alone should be careful.

The famed **Sphinx** crouches downhill to the northeast of the Pyramid of Cheops. Hewn almost entirely from a solid piece of rock, the poised figure is 80m long and gazes out over the world from a height of 22m. Known as *Abu'l-Hul* (father of terror), the mysterious feline man wears a serene and detached expression. Opinion is divided over the Sphinx's identity: Some believe the face is a portrait of Chephren, whose pyramid lies behind it to the northeast, while others maintain that the features represent the local deity, Horan. Its expression and attitude are clearly discernible, though the soft limestone from which it was sculpted has become greatly weathered. Used for target practice during the Turkish Occupation, the Sphinx has lost not only its nose but also its beard (the latter is now in the British Museum). In addition, last year a large chunk of rock fell from its shoulder, threatening to cause extensive damage. A pharaonic nose-job has been prescribed to restore the features and prevent the rest of the face from sliding off, and because of this work the Sphinx complex was closed to tourists in 1988.

At the foot of the Sphinx, just around the corner to the south, is the **Valley Temple of Chephren,** discovered in 1853. Sixteen great pillars support the roof of this edifice, rising to a height of 15m each. The fine grain of the stone will invariably be shown to you by a guide with a candle. *Baksheesh* is expected in return. Directly south, in a tourist complex which originally served as the Rest House of King Farouk, is the **Sphinx House Cafe.** A very cold and welcome bottle of mineral water is yours for LE1.50.

The minor **Pyramid of Abu Ruash,** 7km north of the Giza pyramids, can be reached by foot or hired animal. Service taxis and minibuses also run to the nearby village of Abu Ruash from Giza Square. The pyramid itself is a mound 9m high, only worth a visit to those with a serious interest in Egyptology.

Every year, hundreds of tourists break the law forbidding them to climb the pyramids, and every year a few of them die. The stone is crumbling and the way is far more treacherous than it looks. If you do risk your neck in an ascent, the guards you meet when you come down can usually be pacified with some *baksheesh.* Usually.

Entertainment

When you get tired of staring at the pyramids—if you can get tired of staring at the pyramids—there are a few more options for occupying yourself in the area. The famous **nightclubs** of **Pyramids Road** are notoriously sleazy, and feature scantily clad belly dancers and drunk young Gulf Arabs gawking at them; the bars at the **Mena House Hotel,** although expensive, have live music in a wonderfully ornate setting.

To get away from the crowds, the heat—everything—ride a horse into the desert. The stables next to the Sphinx will happily arrange overnight expeditions or moonlight gallops through the dunes. (See Practical Information.) And for those with fantasies of imperialism, try a round of golf at the **Mena House Golf Club** (tel. 85 54 44) Enter next to the pyramids bus stop. Weekday greens fee is LE13, with club rental for LE4.

Near Giza: Kardassa

On the road from Cairo to Giza, a turn-off to the right at the second canal before the pyramids leads to the village of Kardassa, where the Western Desert and the camel road to Libya begin. The village has become a popular tourist destination because of the quantity of local crafts. Much of what is sold in the tourist shops of Cairo is made in Kardassa. The major products of the village are wool and cotton scarves, *galabiyas* (men's robes), rugs, and Bedouin weavings. The shops are in a sand lot across the canal from the village. The artisans' workshops are usually in the back of the shops or in the side alleys off the main tourist drag. Unfortunately, the influx of tourists to Kardassa has heavily inflated the prices.

Taxis from Giza Sq. to Kardassa cost LE3. Frequent minibuses run to Kardassa from Giza Sq. (25pt), as well as to the turn-off from Pyramids Rd. (15pt).

Saqqara

This ancient necropolis, which spans a 7km stretch of the arid Libyan desert, is teeming with pyramids, tombs, mortuary temples, and other funerary monuments to the pharaohs. Saqqara (pronounced sah-KAH-rah) boasts the world's oldest pyramid, dating from 2700 B.C.E. It took clout to end up here—only the pharaohs, aristocrats, and dozens of mummified Apis bulls were interred at Saqqara. The city, 32km south of Cairo, was the burial ground of the pharaohs who ruled at nearby Memphis, the capital of Egypt during the Old Kingdom. This was a glorious period of unification, a process commenced by Menes, founder of the first of Egypt's 30 dynasties, and completed by Zoser in the Third Dynasty. Although not quite as polished as their pointed cousins at Giza (these have a stepped exterior), the pyramids here have an equally powerful visage. They are less frequented by tourists and are situated squarely in the desert, with nothing but endless stretches of sand in all directions.

Saqqara consists of a cluster of five different archeological sites scattered over a large area. The primary destination for most people is **North Saqqara,** site of the funerary complex and the great Step Pyramid of Zoser I. The three pyramids of **Abu Sir** lie 6km north of North Saqqara, only a few kilometers from the tiny village of Abu Sir. The two pyramids and the funerary complex of **South Saqqara** are about 4km south of the site at North Saqqara. **Dahshur,** in a military zone and closed to tourists in the summer of 1988, lies another 3km to the south. The historically significant but scanty ruins of the ancient city of **Memphis** are farther from the necropolis of Saqqara, located next to the Nile, just south of the village of Mit-Rahine.

It takes time to travel around the sites at Saqqara. Get a very early start. The summer afternoon sun can be immobilizing, so be sure to bring water and wear a hat. Lighting inside some of the tombs is poor—a flashlight (which you can either bring or rent for LE1) will enhance your trip. If you're planning on spending the day at Saqqara, bring your own food.

Practical Information

Start your journey through the ruins at **North Saqqara.** Short of hiring a taxi, however, there is no simple way to reach here. The cheapest and most pleasant way is to take a **minibus** bound for the village of Abu Sir (35pt). The minibus starts running at 6am from Giza Sq. You can also catch it at the second canal before the Giza pyramids, where there's a turn-off marked with a sign that says "Saqqara 22 kilometers." All pyramid-bound transportation from Tahrir passes this turn-off and will leave you there. About 6km before the entrance to the site of North Saqqara, the bus turns off the paved road. You can get off here and try to hitch a ride to the entrance (usually easily), or wait until the last stop at Abu Sir. From there the pleasant 3 km walk to the entrance takes about an hour. Walk south (to the left as you arrive) along the canal just before the village. You can't get lost—just keep following the dirt road by the canal until you reach the paved road. The walk passes through farmland where it's possible to hitch a ride with a pickup truck for most of the way. Turn right at the paved road, and it's only 200m to the site entrance. You can hire a pickup truck at the canal in Abu Sir (about LE1) to take a group to the site.

The most popular way to reach Saqqara from Cairo is to take the milk **train** from Ramses Station to either al-Badrshin or Dahshur, then catch a cab to Saqqara (about LE2). Though you must plan your schedule around that of the trains, this is one way to stretch your Egyptian pounds. You can also take the Metro from Tahrir Sq. to Helwan (the end of the line; 50pt), and catch a cab there to al-Badrshin across the river (LE2-3), then on to Memphis and Saqqara. This eliminates scheduling problems.

A **taxi** is a good option for a large group. You'll save money if you hunt the cab down by the second canal before the pyramids (or at least at Giza Sq.). If you want the taxi to wait for you, it will cost about LE15-30, depending upon how much of the day you spend there. (See Cairo Transportation.) As usual, make sure you have a firm agreement before you set off. Don't pay until you've returned, when an additional tip might be in order. Getting back from Saqqara is slightly easier, since you can usually find a cab at the site and split the cost with other tourists, or hitch a ride from visitors at the site.

A simple but expensive option to reach Saqqara is to join an organized tour. Such tours spend only a few hours at the site, ignoring most of the monuments—but they do get you there and back with a minimum of fuss and a maximum of comfort. **American Express** (tel. 75 06 66) runs a daily tour for LE30; you can sign on at their offices at the Nile Hilton, Ramses Hilton, Marriott, and Cairo Sheraton hotels. **Misr Travel** (tel. 75 00 77) runs a Saqqara-Memphis tour on Thursdays (LE20), leaving from their office at 7 Talaat Harb St. On Tuesday, Friday, and Saturday, they offer full-day tours that combine Memphis and Saqqara with the Giza pyramids. (LE30, including lunch).

Those who indulge in Lawrence of Arabia fantasies can hire a **camel, donkey,** or **horse** for the three-hour ride from Giza to Saqqara. Although a horse is most comfortable, even this can be rough on the inexperienced—especially the surprise galloping. The desert ride will take you past Zawiyyat al-Aryan Pyramid, the site of the sun temple of Abu Gurab, and the three ruined pyramids of Abu Sir. (See Giza Practical Information for stables.) Be careful: The stable may expect you to ride back as well, in which case you'll have to pay for the time you stay at the site. A group of several people can get a good price and split the added cost of the guide. The trip from the Giza pyramids to Saqqara should cost approximately LE12 per person by camel (a camel costs about LE25 for the trip, but carries two), or LE20 by horse. A donkey can cost as little as LE7 per person, but they are harder to find and a bit slow.

Several more pyramids are at **Dahshur,** a restricted military zone closed to tourists in the summer of 1988. Contact the tourist information office in Cairo for more recent information. Ignore the camel-rental characters who will tell you how wonderful Dahshur is and offer to rent you their animals. They take out uninformed tourists and feign astonishment upon arrival at the military establishment, kindly telling their clients the Arabic equivalent of "that's the way the cookie crumbles." The paved road to North Saqqara passes the Pyramid of Zoser, the serapeum, and South Saqqara, on its way to Dahshur.

The only way to reach **South Saqqara** and **Abu Sir** without wheels is by hired animal or on foot. Contrary to what the boys who rent the camels will tell you, it is perfectly possible to **walk** from North Saqqara to Abu Sir or South Saqqara. Either hike takes an hour to an hour and a half. (The distance is a little longer than it seems because the desert terrain is hilly.) It's a marvelous walk through a silent, spectacular landscape, with the pyramids gradually looming larger and larger. There is no chance of getting lost, since both sets of pyramids are easily visible from the serapeum. If you hire an **animal,** bargaining is in order. The proper price per person from the Rest House next to the serapeum to Abu Sir and back is LE3 by donkey, LE5 by camel, and LE7 by horse. Prices to South Saqqara and back are the same or slightly less than to Abu Sir. Chances are you will have the stamina to walk to only one place, so rent an animal to South Saqqara and make your desert hike to the pyramids of Abu Sir. From there it is only a 2km hike to the village of Abu Sir, where you can get a minibus (35pt) back to Giza Sq.

To reach the village of **Abu Sir** from the pyramids outside it, just walk to the clearly visible green belt of fields, and bear right along the canal to the canal village. The best way to pick up the road to the canal is to zero in on the dense grove of palm trees visible from the pyramids. The guards at the pyramids will point out the way. If you came through the village of Abu Sir on the way to North Saqqara, you will have walked south from the village to reach the entrance of North Saqqara; once you've made your way to the pyramids of Abu Sir, however, you will be *north* of the village of Abu Sir and must walk south along the canal in order to return to it. At this point, you will have made a full circle. If you are finished touring South or North Saqqara and want to reach the village of Abu Sir to catch the minibus back to Giza, walk back to the entrance and along the paved road until you come to a bridge. Cross the bridge, turn left, and follow the dirt road along the canal (3km).

All the sites are officially open 9am-4pm, but you can always view the monuments from the outside. Most guards start locking up the doors at the antiquities around 3:30pm, especially in summer and definitely during Ramadan. Save the pyramids of Abu Sir for the end of your visit since there's nothing inside them. Admission to North Saqqara is LE3, students LE1.50. The ticket is good for all Saqqara sites, though unnecessary for Abu Sir.

Sights

North Saqqara

The dominant edifice of Saqqara is the mountainous **Step-Pyramid** built by Imhotep, chief architect to the Pharaoh Zoser, in about 2650 B.C.E. This was the first of Egypt's pyramids. By breaking with the traditional pattern of constructing a small surface tomb for the pharaoh, Imhotep inspired all of Egypt's subsequent architectural achievements, including the Giza pyramids. Like most pharaonic structures, the Step-Pyramid was built as part of a funerary complex. Most experts believe the tomb began as a *mastaba* (literally "bench," the simple flat brick mortuary structure of the Old Kingdom) and was augmented five separate times, until the present six-level building was completed.

The entrance to the Step-Pyramid complex is on the eastern side of the limestone enclosure wall, a bastioned, paneled barrier designed to reproduce the appearance of mud-brickwork, emulating the fortifications typically used to surround cities and palaces of the period. Plunging into the complex itself, you pass through a hallway with a stone ceiling that mimics the palm log rafters of earlier wooden construction. Two fixed stone panels, carved to resemble a massive wooden doorway, open off the hallway onto an impressive 40-pillared colonnade. The walls and roof have been restored as part of a lifetime project of reconstruction undertaken by the French archeologist Jean-Phillippe Lauer. The Egyptian pillars, ridged to create the stylized effect of a bundle of papyrus stems, are probably the world's first stone columns. This imposing corridor culminates in the **Hypostyle Hall,** a fledgling version of the great hallways found at Karnak and Abydos. Its roof is supported by four stately bundle columns slightly smaller than their counterparts in the adjoining colonnade. Beyond this lies the **Great South Court,** a magnificent open yard flanking the southern side of Zoser's stepped tomb. A piece of cobra frieze that once adorned the upper portion of the enclosure wall has been restored in the court's corner. Beside the court, on the southern side, a large shaft drops 28m into the soft desert floor. This huge rectangular pit once contained an extensive collection of sacred funerary jars.

If you climb up the steps to the right of the pit and over the enclosure wall into the southern portion of the site, you'll see the massive **Pyramid of Unas** to the west. Unas was the last pharaoh of the Fifth Dynasty. You can spelunk in the interior burial chamber of the ruined monument. If the door to the pyramid is closed, a guard will come to unlock it shortly. Although the passage into the tomb is uncomfortably low at points, the central burial chamber is airy and light. Its walls consist of huge slabs of white alabaster inscribed with hieroglyphics. These ancient carvings, known as the **Pyramid Texts,** were discovered in 1881 and constitute the earliest known example of decorative hieroglyphic writing on the walls of a pharaonic tomb chamber. Carefully etched into the shiny alabaster, the well-preserved texts record hymns, prayers, and articles necessary for the afterlife. On the western edge of the main chamber sits the basalt sarcophagus of Unas, with its lid on the ground beside it. Above, the ceiling glows with a multitude of five-pointed stars, still shining with traces of their original bright blue coloring.

Opposite the south face of the Pyramid of Unas, an unlikely looking shack covers the shaft that leads to three of Egypt's deepest subterranean burial chambers, the **Persian Tombs,** belonging to three Persian nobles named Psamtik, Zenhebu, and Peleese. A dizzying spiral staircase drills its way 25m into the ground, terminating in the burial area, which consists of three vaulted chambers linked by narrow passageways. Inside, decorative carvings, enlivened with traces of bright paint, cover the walls of the tombs. According to the ancient inscriptions, Zenhebu was a famous admiral and Psamtik a chief physician of the pharaoh's court. Unless you have brought your own source of light, a guard will show you around with a lantern.

To the southwest of the Pyramid of Unas, a 100m path leads out through the desert to the unfinished **Pyramid of Sekhemkhet,** a meager pile of rubble unearthed in 1951. This pyramid was originally intended as an imitation of its giant neighbor, the Pyramid of Zoser. Construction was abandoned after its walls reached a height of only 3m. Underground passageways, one containing an unused alabaster sarcophagus, are buried beneath the rubble foundations but are closed to the public because of the fragile condition of the roofing and corridor walls. East of the Pyramid of Unas, running down the hill, is a long, narrow causeway, smoothly paved and walled in. Nearly 1km long, this originally linked the Pyramid of Unas with a lower valley temple at the banks of the river. Strewn by the sides of the causeway are the **Old Kingdom Tombs.** Over 250 *mastabas* have been excavated here, though only a few of the larger and best-preserved tombs are open to the public. Although the low, rectangular *mastabas* are dwarfed by the towering pyramids, the best ones contain fascinating, delicate bas-reliefs.

The lovely Sixth Dynasty **Mastaba of Idut,** adjacent to the southern enclosure wall of Zoer's funerary complex and just east of the Pyramid of Unas, is comprised of 10 chambers. An entrance chamber leads into a roomy apartment decorated with scenes of Idut watching a hippopotamus hunt. Next door, in the chapel, the eastern wall is embellished with a beautiful depiction of oxen, gazelles, and ibex, as well as the sacrificial slaughter of cattle. Nearby, the **Mastaba of Mehu** and the **Mastaba of Queen Nebet** both have interiors painted with naturalistic scenes of birds, cattle, and other sacrificial animals. South of the causeway is a fabulous pair of enormous **Boat Pits,** side by side next to the causeway just 100m east of the pyramid of Unas. There is some speculation as to whether the pits were intended merely to house the royal barques (as at Giza) or whether these finely sculpted trenches of stone were meant as simple representations of boats. Directly across from the causeway is the **Tomb of Nebkau-her,** a large, well-preserved structure with a beautiful interior. (Closed to the public since 1985.) Rounding a slight bend in the causeway and continuing east, you'll reach the **Mastaba of Nefer-her-ptah,** situated directly south of the causeway. Known as the "tomb of the birds," this *mastaba* contains remarkable half-completed scenes of birds: The sculptor abandoned the project to a skillful painter halfway through. (Closed to the public since 1985.)

At the end of the substantial remains of the causeway, head uphill southward to the **Monastery of St. Jeremiahs,** fewer than 150m away. Built in the fifth century C.E., this structure has been devastated several times, starting in 950 when invading Arabs ransacked the entire edifice. More recently, the Antiquities Service has removed all decorative carvings and paintings to the Coptic Museum in Cairo. Completing this process, a thick layer of sand now covers the monastery's scanty remains, and little of the original structure remains visible. The monastery is best reached by car or horse, since it's usually too hot to walk.

Head back up to the causeway and round the corner to return to the Great South Court of Zoser's mortuary complex. In the northern end, at the base of the Step

Pyramid, are the remains of the *mastaba* that was the seed of Zoser's tomb. In the center of the pyramid's south face is an entrance to the tomb's interior. This long passageway, the **Saite Gallery,** offers stunning views of the interior frame of the pyramid. (Special permission from the Antiquities Service is required to gain entrance.) To the east, the **Heb-Sed Court** runs the length of one side of the courtyard. The building replicates in stone the pavilion employed at the Heb-Sed Jubilee—a festival during which the king demonstrated his vigor by completing a ritual race around the courtyard. The festival may have been derived from an earlier age when kings periodically had to prove their strength or perish. The Heb-Sed Court in the funerary complex, and the panels inside the pyramid that depict Zoser running the race, were supposed to ensure his eternal rejuvenation.

The more substantial **House of the South** stands next door, on the eastern side of Zoser's Pyramid. Its facade is enhanced by stately, proto-Doric columns. Inside, the walls are inscribed with some very ancient tourist graffiti left by a visiting Egyptian in the twelfth century B.C.E. The messages, expressing admiration for King Zoser, were hastily splashed onto the walls with dark paint, scrawled in a late cursive style of hieroglyphics. Heading north, you'll come to the **House of the North,** its facade similarly decorated with a row of three engaged papyriform columns. Nearby, directly in front of the Step-Pyramid's northern face, is the most haunting spectacle at Saqqara, the **Statue of King Zoser,** in a slanted stone hut pierced by two tiny apertures through which the pharaoh can stare fixedly at you. This small structure, known as the **Sardab,** was designed to enable the spirit of the pharaoh to communicate with the outside world. The striking figure is only a plaster copy of the original, which has been removed to the Egyptian Museum in Cairo. Just behind the Sardab is the original entrance to the Step Pyramid. (Closed to the public since 1985.)

To the west, toward the edge of the Step Pyramid complex, a raised patch of desert commands a clear view of the western edge of North Saqqara. If you have a car, you can return to the entrance of Zoser's mortuary complex and drive around to the western portion of the site. Or you can hike five minutes across the desert to reach the **Tomb of Akhti-Hotep and Ptah-Hotep,** halfway between the Step-Pyramid and the canopied Rest House. This remarkable double tomb housed the bodies of a father and son, inspectors of the priests who served the pyramids. The pair designed their own mortuary complex. The structure, which contains some of Saqqara's finest reliefs, is accessible through a long corridor, culminating in the burial chamber of Akhti-Hotep. Just around the corner is the undecorated pillared hall, leading on to a rather dim chapel covered with delightful scenes depicting Akhti-Hotep in various poses in the marshes—constructing boats, fighting off enemies, and fording a river. To the south of the pillared hallway, the tomb of Ptah-Hotep also contains fine reliefs: Animals cavort across the splendid walls with hunters hot on their trail, fowlers cast their nets, and people fishing enjoy a healthy meal.

West of the Tomb of Akhti-Hotep and Ptah-Hotep is a shady **Rest House,** where cold drinks and hot tea can be purchased at monumental prices (soft drinks LE2!). Farther along the highway, where the road jogs sharply to the west, an area has been cleared to reveal badly weathered **Greek statues** said to represent Homer (in the center), Pindar (at the west end), and Plato (at the east end).

The **Serapeum,** a few hundred meters west of the Rest House at the terminus of the main road, was discovered in 1854. It is Saqqara's most visually stunning monument. An eerie subway system lit only by tiny lanterns, this surrealistic mausoleum houses the **Tombs of the Apis Bulls,** where 25 sacred oxen were embalmed and placed in enormous sarcophagi of solid granite. Only one of the bulls was discovered (the rest had been stolen) and is now displayed in Cairo's Agricultural Museum. The same archeologist also discovered a meter-high gold statue of a bull, now in the Louvre in Paris.

The Serapeum is the sole legacy of a mysterious bull-worshiping cult that apparently thrived during the New Kingdom. Little is known about the cult's history or beliefs. Work on the main portion of the underground complex was begun in the seventh century B.C.E. by Psammetichus I and continued through the Ptolemaic era, though much older tombs adjoin this central set of chambers. In the oldest portion of the Serapeum, two large gold-plated sarcophagi and several canopic jars containing human heads were found, as well as the undisturbed footprints of the priests who had laid the sacred animals to rest 3000 years before. (This portion of the tomb is no longer accessible.) Recessed tomb chambers flank the main corridor on both sides, each containing a monolithic sarcophagus. It's difficult to imagine these mammoth coffins being transported to the confines of the cave—their average weight is 65 tons. At the final tomb along the passageway stands the largest sarcophagus of all. Hewn from a single piece of black granite, the coffin is covered with hieroglyphic inscriptions. Clamber down into the chamber for a close-up view. At the far end of the Serapeum, an equally enormous pink granite sarcophagus is decorated with a number of fine reliefs.

The **Tomb of Ti,** 300m north of the Serapeum, was excavated in 1865 and has since been one of the primary sources of knowledge about both daily and ceremonial life during the Fifth Dynasty (toward the end of the Old Kingdom, approximately 2400 B.C.E.), when Ti was a high-ranking court official. Serving under three pharaohs, Ti must have been quite a power-broker: His titles included Overseer of the Pyramids and Sun Temples at Abu Sir, Superintendent of Works, Scribe of the Court, Royal Counselor, and even Lord of Secrets. His rank was considered so lofty that he was allowed to marry a princess, Nefer-Hotep-S, and his children were ranked as royalty. In the tomb paintings, the children wear braided hairpieces, the sign of a contender for the throne. Note also how the children depicted on the bas-reliefs almost invariably have fingers in their mouths, a stylization widely used in Old Kingdom artwork to represent childhood. The bas-reliefs here are among the artistic masterpieces of Egypt's Old Kingdom.

In keeping with the ancient Egyptian belief that death is an extension of life and that the *ka* (spiritual double) has needs analogous to the living body, there arose the practice of depicting scenes from the daily life of the deceased on the walls of the funerary chamber. Tomb walls depict hunts, battles, barter, athletic contests, and domestic life. From the eastern wall of the Tomb of Ti, you can learn about a typical harvest, as well as about shipbuilding; the southern wall provides information about various types of food consumed by wealthy Egyptians, as well as about the harsh system of tax collections; the northern wall demonstrates how linen was woven and fish were caught. All around are scenes from upper-class family life.

Although now entirely buried in sand, an **Avenue of Sphinxes** once ran the full width of the site, commencing near the Tomb of Ti, paving a straight course east past the Step Pyramid complex, and ending at the river's edge near the **Pyramid of Titi.** This weather-beaten pyramid can now be reached by following the east-west highway past the Rest House to the fork and heading a short distance north. The interior of Titi's tomb has several interesting, sacred inscriptions but is usually closed to the public. The 30 rooms comprising the magnificent **Tomb of Mereruka,** just next door to the Pyramid of Titi, are open for visitors to explore. Notice the hippopotami depicted on the opposite wall near the door as you enter. The hippopotamus was worshiped as a benevolent goddess called Thoeris, the patron of women in childbirth. Here, the hippos are depicted not as deities, but as the Nile's hefty river horses, complete with gaping jaws and curly tusks. The naturalistic portrayal of wildlife found inside the **Tomb of Mereruka** has enabled scientists to reconstruct ancient Egyptian fauna. Various species of fish can be differentiated thanks to the minutely detailed work of the artists. If you want to see what actually lay at the heart of all these tombs, one of the caretakers here will gladly (with a little monetary prompting of LE1) show you a **mummy.** Though probably from later burials, the desiccated corpses look old enough to be original.

Farther east is the neighboring **Tomb of Ankhma-Hor.** Though the decorations are relatively sparse, there are several representations of medical operations, including a circumcision and toe surgery. To the left of the entrance are scenes of mourning. One noted Egyptologist has asserted that the Sixth Dynasty tendency to depict funerary scenes indicates a growing pessimism among Egyptians about the afterlife as the Old Kingdom went into its final decline.

South Saqqara

The most interesting funerary monument at South Saqqara is the **Tomb of Chepsekaf** (popularly known as Mastabat Faraun), an enormous stone structure shaped like a sarcophagus and topped with a rounded lid. The great mausoleum was erected for Shepseskaf, the son of Mycerinus (whose pyramid stands at Giza). Though Shepseskaf reigned for only three or four years, his brief stint on the throne was long enough to qualify him for a magnificent tomb. Originally covering 7000 square meters, the Mastabat Faraun is a unique edifice—neither a *mastaba* nor a pyramid. The interior of the tomb consists of long passageways and a burial chamber containing fragments of a huge sandstone sarcophagus. Find a guard to admit you.

Just northwest of the Mastabat Faraun are the ruins of the **Mortuary Temple of Pepi II.** A central colonnade gives way to a tiny chamber housing five empty statue niches. The remains of the sanctuary beyond are still visible. This edifice originally adjoined the pyramid on the west end and was linked to the east with a large valley temple of which little remains today. The **Pyramid of Pepi II** was the culmination of a long processional causeway that joined the valley and mortuary temples. Its interior contains some fine hieroglyphic texts. Two other royal tombs, the **Pyramid of Queen Apuit** and the **Pyramid of Queen Neith,** lie immediately northwest of the Pyramid of Pepi II. Both imitate the plans of the pharaoh's grand funeral complexes on a smaller scale.

The **Pyramid of Djekare-Ises,** which locals call *Haran esh-Shawaf* (Pyramid of the Sentinel), lies north of Pepi II's Mortuary Temple. It rises to a height of 25m and can be entered from the north side via a tunnel.

Abu Sir

The pyramids of Abu Sir are romantically isolated in the Eastern Desert just north of Saqqara. You can enjoy them without hordes of camera-clicking companions, since no tour buses make it here. Accessible only on foot or animal, the pyramids (6km from North Saqqara and 2½km from the village of Abu Sir) are surrounded by an ocean of sand dunes.

The most imposing of the three main pyramids, clearly visible from North Saqqara, the **Pyramid of Neferirkare** stands 68m high. The structure originally had a stone facing like its neighbors at Giza, but the casing has completely deteriorated and the exterior now resembles a step pyramid. Nevertheless, this pyramid is one of the best preserved monuments in the Saqqara area. The **Pyramid of Niuserre** is the most dilapidated of the group, but has an interesting causeway running to the remains of a funerary temple to the southeast. It is possible to enter the **Pyramid of Sahure,** the northernmost member of the group, on its north face. One of the custodians at the site will show you the entrance, which is about ½m high and 2m long and requires a challenging belly-crawl along the sand floor. The small chamber inside served as the pharaoh's tomb. More pyramids are visible from here than from any other site in the country; you'll be able to distinguish at least 10 on the horizon. The custodians here are desperate for business, and one of them will probably show you around with enthusiasm and offer you water from an adjoining spring. If you intend to walk on to the village of Abu Sir, have the guards point out the route. Finding your way to North Saqqara is easy thanks to the immense triangle of King Zoser's pyramid.

If you are traveling by animal between Abu Sir and Giza, have your guide stop off on the way at the Fifth Dynasty **Sun Temple of Abu Gurab,** about 1½km north of the Pyramid of Sahure. Located on the fringe of cultivated fields, the temple was built by King Niuserre in honor of the sun god Ra and features an impressive altar constructed from five huge blocks of alabaster.

Memphis

As late as the thirteenth century, Arab historians wrote with awe of the remnants of the Old Kingdom capital at Memphis. The brick houses of this city of 500,000 inhabitants had returned to mud, but many of the stone monuments were not destroyed until much later, when they were used as construction material in Cairo. Only the ancient canal responsible for the lush vegetation and a few exhibits housed in the modern **museum** in the village of **Mit-Rahine** remain. A limestone colossus of Ramses II, which lay for years in the wet earth, now lies prone in a two-level gallery for your viewing pleasure. In the enclosure where the museum is located you'll find the famous alabaster sphinx measuring 4¼m by 8m. This sphinx probably stood at the south entrance of the Temple of Ptah. (Museum open 9am-4pm. Admission 50pt.)

Wadi al-Natrun

For the past 1500 years, the monasteries of Wadi al-Natrun constituted the backbone of the Coptic community in Egypt, and the four that remain today continue to serve the spiritual needs of Egypt's large Orthodox population. While at one time bolted doors and walls 3m thick greeted uninvited visitors, mainly marauding Bedouin, the intrepid traveler who ventures out to these tiny green islands in the sea of sand will be met with warmth and hospitality unequaled almost anywhere. If the buzzing crowds of downtown Cairo made you think that all of Egypt is a three-ring circus, come to Wadi al-Natrun. The quiet, austere surroundings restore serenity to even the most shattered nerves.

The word "Copt" is a corruption of *ghibt,* the Egyptian word for "Egyptian," but over time came to designate Christian Egyptians specifically. The Orthodox Copts introduced the tradition of monasticism; the first Christian monastery was established in Egypt's Eastern Desert by St. Anthony the Great (250-355 C.E.). In 330, one of Anthony's disciples began monastic life in Wadi al-Natrun. The routine of the monks has hardly changed since then. Over 50 monasteries have been founded in the Natrun valley, of which only four still exist. In the 1980s, Coptic monasticism has again been on the upswing, and new cells have been added to accommodate the monks living in the Natrun valley. The vast majority of these monks practice cenobitic, or communal, monasticism. Although each monk has his own *laura* (cell) and retreats for periods of complete seclusion, they eat meals together at the refectory and attend daily communal prayer services. The majority of the modern monks are young, college-educated Egyptians.

The monks begin their day in church at 3am. Amid billows of incense, wide-eyed icons, and flickering candlelight, they chant the haunting Coptic liturgy for six hours. The service is punctuated by triangle and cymbal music. (Come before 9am to attend.) Non-Christians must sit at the back; Christians may sit in front.) The monks are cloaked from head to foot in black. This signifies, as they will tell you, that they are symbolically dead. When a new monk is initiated, he "dies" to his former self and the world of corporeal desires. The Copts also wear a black hood on which 12 crosses are embroidered, each representing one of Christ's 12 disciples. The hood is said to symbolize the "helmet of salvation" (Ephesians 6).

Practical Information

The safest, and possibly the only, way to reach Wadi al-Natrun is on a journey between Cairo and Alexandria. The West Delta Bus Co. runs hourly **buses** between the two cities; the cheap non-air-conditioned version stops at the Wadi al-Natrun Rest House, 10km from three of the monasteries. In Cairo, the buses leave from in front of the Arab League Building; in Alexandria, from Sa'ad Zaghoul Sq. every hour between 6:30am and 6:30pm. Most buses travel the desert route and stop at the Rest House, 10km from three of the monasteries. The trip costs about LE5; make sure the driver is going to stop at Wadi al-Natrun. From Cairo you should also reserve a seat from Wadi al-Natrun to Alexandria on a later bus. Getting on the bus for Alexandria at Wadi al-Natrun without a ticket is nearly impossible, since most seats are sold a day or two ahead. To make the trip in the opposite direction, simply buy both tickets several days in advance in Alexandria. From the Rest House you can hire a **taxi** for the trip to the monasteries. Round-trip fare should be about LE8-10. On Fridays, there are enough visitors to the monasteries to make **hitchhiking** feasible. Thursday and Friday are the best days to go; you may not be allowed into the monasteries during other days of the week.

It's best to start your journey early if you plan to return to Cairo or Alexandria in the evening. Since the Rest House no longer offers accommodations, there is no place to stay in Wadi al-Natrun town. Men are sometimes permitted to stay overnight in the monasteries (particularly at Dayr Baramus), but must first get written permission from the office of the Patriarchate. To obtain permission, visit the Coptic Orthodox Patriarchate in Alexandria on Nabi Danial St.; in Cairo, you can get permission at the Coptic Orthodox Patriarchate, Ramses St., Anba Reuis Building, adjacent to St. Mark's Church, in Abbassiya. If you are allowed to stay, it is appropriate to offer a donation of LE5-10.

The pickings on the food front are equally slim. The **Rest House Cafeteria** in town has small sandwiches and cold drinks (all around 50pt). It's probably a good idea to bring your own food, especially if you plan to stay at one of the monasteries, where only boiled water is provided for guests. The monks strictly observe the five seasons of fasting: 43 days before the Nativity, three days commemorating Jonah in the Whale, 55 days preceding Lent, the fast of the Holy Apostles (from Pentecost until July 12), and 15 days in commemoration of the Assumption of the Virgin Mary (Aug. 7-22). During these times visitors are not permitted to enter. Evelyn White's *The Monasteries of the Wadi'n Natrun* (1932) provides a history of the formation of the four monasteries of Lower Egypt.

Sights

Although each monastery is slightly different, all four conform to a standard architectural plan. Each is surrounded by a massive wall 13m high and from 3-4m thick, which until the beginning of this century protected the inhabitants from frequent Bedouin attacks. Inside the walls is the **keep**: a huge, block-like structure built in Roman style where the monks took refuge during sieges. Entered by a narrow wooden drawbridge that connected it to the rest of the monastery, the keep consisted of storerooms, air vents, wells, a bakery, a kitchen, and a chapel. In the middle of the monastery, the church and its various chapels are entered through low doors—so low, in fact, that you must stoop to get inside, thereby demonstrating your humility. Be sure to remove your shoes before you enter, just as you would when entering a mosque, and remember that you must dress correctly: No shorts or sleeveless shirts permitted. Do not enter the church eating or chewing gum.

Coptic churches are divided into three chambers on the inside. The **sanctuary** (*haikal*) containing the altar lies behind a curtain or wooden screen (*iconostasis*) inlaid with ivory, and always faces east. You are not allowed to enter the sanctuary, but ask the monk who shows you around if you can peek inside. The next chamber, the **choir**, is the section reserved for Coptic Christians. Behind the choir is the **nave**, which consists of two parts, the first of which is reserved for the *catechumens* (those who are preparing to convert). The back of the nave is for the so-called weepers, or sinners. These Christians, having willfully transgressed, were formerly made to stand at the very back of the church. All the churches have interesting icons and beautifully carved *iconostases*. Three of the churches have frescoes dating from the fourth and fifth centuries—many of them are so dark from centuries of accumulated candle smoke and soot that you can barely make out the shapes and colors.

Dayr al-Suryan (the Monastery of the Syrians), named for the Syrian monks who once inhabited it, lies 50m northwest of the Monastery of St. Bishoi and is easily reached (Thurs.-Fri. are best). The monastery was established when a group of monks broke away from the Monastery of St. Bishoi following a sixth-century theological dispute about the nature of the Mother of God. When the dispute ended, however, this alternative monastery no longer had a purpose. In the beginning of the eighth century it was purchased by a Syrian merchant for use by Syrian monks, the first of whom arrived at the beginning of the ninth century. The monastery was prominent throughout the tenth century, and, by the eleventh, housed the largest community in Wadi al-Natrun. The design of Dayr al-Suryan is believed to be based on the model of Noah's Ark.

Be sure to ask to see the **Door of Prophecies** in the Church of the Virgin Mary. The doors consist of eight ebony leaves, each inlaid with eight ivory panels. The uppermost panels depict disciples, while the panels below depict the seven epochs of the Christian era. The domes of the church are covered with frescoes of the Annunciation, the Nativity, and the Ascension of the Virgin. On the floor of the nave stands a marble basin, which the abbot uses to wash the feet of 12 other monks on Maundy Thursday in emulation of the acts of Jesus during Passion week. The *haikal* of the church is decorated with stucco ornamentation in the Tulinid style. This rare stucco work is extremely important for Islamic art historians. At the back of the church is a low, dark passageway leading to the private cell of St. Bishoi. The monks will show you an iron staple and chain dangling from the ceiling and explain how St. Bishoi would fasten it to his beard, thereby maintaining himself in a standing position lest he fall asleep during his night-long prayer vigils.

Dayr Anba Bishoi (the Monastery of St. Bishoi) is probably the most accessible to visitors. This monastery, 5km from the Rest House and 500m from Dayr al-Suryan, is usually open on Thursdays and Fridays from 10am to 4pm. Like the three other monasteries, this one has suffered from numerous attacks by Bedouin tribes. There are five churches in the monastery: The Church of St. Bishoi, the Church of St. Iskhiron, the Church of the Holy Virgin, the Church of St. George, and the Church of St. Michael. The Church of St. Bishoi has three *haikals* and is part of the most ancient section of the monastery, dating from the ninth or tenth century. Set in the floor at the western end of the church is the *lakan* (marble basin), which is used in the Maundy Thursday Rite of the Foot-washing. The church has undergone several restorations and was completely redecorated in 1957. The entry to the keep is on the first story through a drawbridge that rests on the roof of the gatehouse. Climb to the Church of St. Michael in the tower; from the rooftop you can watch the sun set behind the dunes. The church downstairs, rebuilt in 444 after being sacked by barbarians, contains the remains of St. Bishoi, still believed to perform miracles for the faithful. Nearby, three other groups of cell-buildings have recently been constructed. The building farthest away, with numerous domes, is the residence of Pope Shenuda.

Dayr Abu Maqar (the Monastery of St. Maccarius) lies roughly 8km southeast of Dayr Anba Bishoi and can be seen to the west of the Cairo-Alexandria desert road (from a point about 129km from Alexandria or 86km from Cairo). Visitors are not usually permitted to enter, unless they have letters of recommendation from the Patriarchate. The foundation of Dayr Abu Maqar is associated with the life of St. Maccarius the Great (300-390 C.E.) and marks the beginning of monastic life in Wadi al-Natrun. It is believed that St. Maccarius was led by an angel to a rock and ordered to build a church there. In spite of the monastic community that he founded, St. Maccarius remained an anchorite (solitary monk) throughout his life and lived in a cell connected by a tunnel to a small cave. Virtually no part of the original building remains after numerous sacks. In the beginning of the eleventh century, the monastery became the refuge of many monks fleeing from Muslim persecution. Since then, it has become the residence of the Coptic Patriarch. During the Middle Ages, the monastery was famous for its library, which remained intact until European bibliophiles discovered the treasures in the seventeenth century and decided to move them to European libraries.

Dayr Anba Baramus (The Monastery of the Virgin Mary) is about 4km northwest of the Monastery of St. Bishoi, accessible by taxi from Wadi al-Natrun town. The monastery's Church of St. Mary has a fine *iconostasis*. The wooden doors exhibit carved panels dating from the eleventh century. Relics of St. Moses and St. Isidore are kept in the first section of the old church, currently undergoing renovation. Tradition holds that a crypt under the altar contains the remains of Maximus and Domidius, sons of the Roman Emperor Valentinus (later St. Valentine) who both dwelt here as monks and received annual cards from their dad. The oldest architectural element in the church is the fourth-century column of St. Arsanious. The church of St. John the Baptist was built by the Copts only one century ago. Although renovated in 1981, the beautiful *iconostasis* remained untouched. The keep has cells on the second floor and a chapel on the third floor. The monastery houses a library, unfortunately closed to the public, that contains thousands of rare books and manuscripts.

al-Fayyum Oasis

In the Fayyum, you can get a glimpse of a quieter, rural Egypt most tourists never see, caught as they are behind a wall of Pharaonic monuments and camel-ride hucksters. A little more than 100km from Cairo, al-Fayyum is a large, fertile oasis spreading west and north of the Nile Valley along an offshoot of the river. Although occasionally victim to the same crises of crowding and hurried modernization you find almost everywhere in Egypt, the Fayyum depression remains primarily agricultural, producing everything from cotton to flowers. Devotees of the pastoral will find an overnight stay pleasant; others can easily visit as a daytrip from Cairo or as a stopover on a journey south or north. One warning: The worthwhile destinations in al-Fayyum are spread about outside the main city, so you will need the better part of a day to enjoy them.

Unlike the other oases of Egypt, al-Fayyum shares in the life and culture of the Nile, as it has since its first development by the rulers of the Twelfth Dynasty (nineteenth and twentieth centuries B.C.E.). The Ptolemies, through the construction of canals and irrigation, made it into a rich province with its capital at Crocodopolis (near the site of modern al-Fayyum), the center of a cult that worshiped Sobek and other reptilian deities. The Roman conquerors, all hedonists, used it as a vacation resort as well as one of the primary granaries of the empire. Relatively remote from potential persecution, the oasis was an early center of Coptic Christianity; it also sheltered a large population of exiled Jews in the 3rd century C.E. The Muslims believed the extensive canals and agriculture to be the work of the biblical Joseph during his stay in Egypt; the main waterway, the Bahr Yusef, is named for this wily interpreter of dreams. Although Lake Qaruun to the north is a popular beach resort, the local government is enthusiastically attempting to develop the rest of the area for tourism. Look for their earnest but poorly spelled signs labeling suggestion boxes.

Orientation and Practical Information

Al-Fayyum is a roughly triangular area, about 90km east to west. The eastern edge is bordered by the Nile. The fresh water **Lake Qaruun,** 40km by 8km, separates the northwest edge from the sandy plateau of the Western Desert. The principal city, called simply **Fayyum,** is almost in the center and is the transportation hub for the whole oasis. The city is aligned along the **Bahr Yusef,** which flows west from the Nile; at the center of town the **Bahr Sinnur** leaves the Bahr Yusef at a right angle and flows northward toward the farmlands. The **tourist information office** (tel. 225 86), which doubles as the town **post office,** is a small pre-fab box, situated on the Bahr Yusef beside the cafeteria al-Madinat, 50m east of the juncture of the two canals. The four working waterwheels next to the information office are unique to the Fayyum and are the symbol of the oasis. The helpful staff can direct you to all the sights of the Fayyum, as well as to transportation. The **bus station** is located on the Bahr Yusef about 50m east of the tourist information office. Buses leave for the three-hour trip to Cairo every 10 minutes until 6:30pm (LE1.50). Faster **service taxis** also leave here for Giza Sq. in Cairo all day and night (LE2.50-3). Across the parking lot is the **train station,** but the trains go nowhere of interest. Buses and service taxis serving Beni Suef, al-Minya, and points south stop at **Hawatem Square;** to reach it walk to the third bridge over the canal west of the tourist office, turn left, and walk 1km south. The **police emergency number** is 123.

The best budget bed in Fayyum city is at the **Montaza Hotel** (tel. 32 46 33). Clean, comfortable and well-run, with fans and refrigerators for guests, its only drawback is an out-of-the-way location: Walk north along the left side of Bahr Sinnuris from Bahr Yusef. Take a left at the railroad tracks, and then cross them at the first opportunity (50m ahead). Continue along the railroad tracks for 6 blocks, and take a right; the hotel is on your right, 3 blocks ahead. (Singles LE7. Doubles LE11, with bath LE13.) Across Bahr Yusef and a short distance to the west of the tourist information office is the **Palace Hotel** (tel. 32 36 41), where you'll pay LE7 (singles) or LE12 (doubles) for smaller rooms, slightly grimy toilets, and a central location. For those determined to spend the least amount of money possible, the **IYHF youth hostel** (tel. 36 82) is 1km east of the information office, in the northeast corner of town. Look for the signs or ask for the *Bayt al-Shibab* (LE1 per night, opens at 2pm).

Mokhimar Restaurant, 100m west of the tourist information office, serves up excellent chicken and *tahina* (LE2) and kebab with salad (LE3) from 9am to 3am daily. Bring your own drinks. The plague of locusts in biblical times is quaintly reenacted by the swarms of flies infesting the **Cafeteria al-Madinat,** beside the four waterwheels in the center of town. If the insect-life doesn't deter you, the prices (LE6-8 for a meal) probably will, although this may be the only place in town for breakfast (LE3). *Kushari* and *fuul* stands line the street leading south to Hawatem Sq., along with fresh produce and juice stands.

Sights

Within Fayyum city, there are few sights of importance or interest other than the multitudes of Egyptians living their lives far from the infectious influence of tourism. Visitors who were not sated with Islamic architecture in Cairo can visit the Mamluk **Mosque of Khawand Asal-Bay,** about 1km west of the town center along the canal. The restored mosque was named for the favorite concubine of the Sultan Qaytbay. The interior features some original pieces, including marble pillars and a beautiful teak *mihrab*. For a quick introduction to the rural life of the Fayyum, or simply for a pleasant evening's walk, head north out of town along the Bahr Sinnuris. You will pass farms and green fields stretching in all directions, and after about 2km you will reach the first of the seven **waterwheels,** still functioning in the irrigation system. Unlike Western versions, these great wooden constructions are not used to power mills or pumps but are pumps themselves, ingeniously using the flow of the stream to lift the water to a higher level. They moan as they turn, and four working together make an eerie chorus.

The **Ain Sileen,** (Sileen Springs), are 9km north of town and therefore the easiest to reach of the area's attractions. Fresh water springs bubble out of the ground here amidst a small park. Two restaurant-cafes provide a place to sit and sip tea or soft drinks as the streams burble by. At the end of the short road leading into the area, the final spring spurts out of two concrete pipes in a wall decorated with plaques that list the water's mineral content and its beneficient effects. Bring a bottle or drinking cup only if you want to do battle with Hercules the Microbe. A small swimming pool, crowded with frolicking Egyptian children, is fed by the springs. Foreigners bathing here will create a sensation; foreign women will cause widespread apoplexy. (Free. Open until the late evening.) The **Ain Sileen Hotel,** at LE16.50 for a somewhat grungy single with no fan or air-conditioning, is overpriced, but has pleasant terraces.

Fifteen kilometers farther north is **Lake Qaruun,** the south side of which is lined with beaches, casinos, and at least one luxury hotel. You can sit on the veranda of the **Auberge de Fayyum Hotel,** a former royal hunting lodge, but be prepared to pay LE1.25 for a lemonade as you watch the blue waves lap at the desert on the other side. A cheaper option is the **Gabal al-Zina Casino,** 1km west of the Auberge, which is still overpriced but bearable, and right next to a pleasant beach. Swimming in the lake is refreshing, but there are no showers in the area. To reach Ain Sileen, Lake Qaruun, or any other place north of Fayyum, walk north from the information stand to the railroad tracks, which run parallel to Bahr Yusef. Turn left and walk west to the fourth crossing, cross over, and you will find yourself in the midst of a taxi stand filled with covered pickup trucks. The trucks shuttle between Fayyum and Ain Sileen (30pt) and Lake Qaruun (50pt). It may be necessary to change taxis at the village of Sanhur to reach the lake; the total price should be the same.

The best historical site in the Fayyum is the **Pyramid of al-Lahun,** near the village of that name, to the southeast of Fayyum city. To reach the pyramid, take a service taxi from Hawatem Sq. to the village and hike 3km out to the site, easily visible from the village. This pyramid, built by Senusert II of the Twelfth Dynasty, has been robbed of its stone casing but is still a moderately interesting Pharaonic ruin.

Nile Valley

If there were no Nile, there would be no Egypt. Except for Alexandria and a few oases, all of Egypt's millions huddle within a few miles of this mighty waterway. The world's longest river starts in far-off Lake Victoria, winds through Uganda and the Sudan, then cuts its way through Upper and Lower Egypt. It took the huge Aswan High Dam to tame the Nile, but the structural changes wrought by modern engineering seem to have barely disturbed the surface of the muddy brown waters.

The Egypt of the pharaohs took root and blossomed in the fertile land stolen from the desert by the Nile. Artifacts from the time of the Old Kingdom, almost five thousand years ago, to the empire's end three millennia later line the entire length of the river. Traveling south from Cairo, you move against the Nile's stream, but with the flow of ancient Egyptian history. Leaving the predynastic and Old Kingdom monuments behind at Giza, Memphis, and Saqqara, you come to the Middle Kingdom sites around Minya and Mallawi—most notably the tombs at Beni Hassan. Farther south, magnificent tombs and temples at Luxor and West Thebes recall the capital of the New Kingdom. From Abydos to Abu Simbel, the pharaohs of the New Kingdom adorned the Nile with unforgettable monuments. Rebellious Akhnaton fought New Kingdom traditions, moving the capital south to Tel el-Amarna for one brief, shining period. As you head south from Luxor toward Aswan, the procession of temples at Esna, Edfu, Kom Ombo, and Kalabsha recall the Ptolemaic and Roman eras. In those times, Egypt's leaders sought to reflect some of the pharaonic glory onto themselves.

Before you set off to join the multinational throng of tourists visiting the temples and mausoleums, remember that despite its spectacular remnants of vanished civilizations, the Nile Valley is far more than an ancient cemetery. It is the nourisher of a venerable people. Unlike Westernized Cairo, the villages and towns along the river represent the true national character. Venturing off the tourist trails is a challenge, as fewer people speak English and tourist facilities are spotty. But if you do make an effort to meet the people of the Nile away from the manic marketplace of tourist resorts, you will find them more than willing to greet you with genuine kindness and hospitality—not an outstretched palm. Don't make the mistake of spending most of your time at the ancient temples and missing out on one of the most exotic and vibrant regions of the world.

Getting Around

In the bygone days of British colonial control, a slow, romantic cruise down the Nile was an aristocratic indulgence. Times haven't changed that much. Many companies offer unforgettable luxury cruises at unforgettable prices. Most of the steamers run between Aswan and Luxor, stopping briefly at the antiquities along the way, and charging at least several hundred pounds per person. The most prestigious tours are run by the Hilton and Sheraton hotels; the alternative ones are only a shade cheaper. **Pyramid Travel Agency** (tel. 75 87 16), 1 Talaat Harb St. in Cairo sends the *Ramses, Tut-Ankh-Amon,* and *Queen Cleopatra* between Luxor and Aswan for three-night cruises (LE350 for a double berth) or six-night cruises (LE580 for a double). Fares with **Eastmar** (tel. 75 32 16), 13 Kasr el-Nil St. in Cairo, start at LE250 per person for a three-day cruise. It can be difficult for individuals to book places on these cruises once in Egypt; you might want to make arrangements with a travel agent in Europe or the U.S.

You'll spend much less money for a group cruise on a *felucca,* one of the simple sailboats which ply the river, and probably have just as much fun. (See Between Luxor and Aswan section for details.)

The inexpensive **Cairo-Aswan train** stops at points all along the Nile Valley, and is the most comfortable alternative for traveling between Cairo and either Luxor or Aswan. Reserve your seats several days in advance. For shorter distances, trains are slow, unreliable, and less convenient than service taxis. (See the Egypt Introduction and Luxor or Aswan sections for more information. Note that you should book seats or sleepers in advance.) Most tourists don't take advantage of **service taxis** because they fear they'll be cheated. The trick is to know the proper fare from one town to the next and simply pay the appropriate amount upon arrival. The correct fares for most connections are noted under each city; for others, find out at the tourist office in Luxor or Aswan, or ask other passengers how much they have paid as they get out of the cab. Don't travel in a *taxi spéciale* (private taxi), or you'll pay 10 times as much. The best time to travel is early in the morning, since by mid-afternoon you'll have to wait an hour or more before a service taxi going your way fills up with the requisite seven passengers. Once underway, the taxis are remarkably cool. **Buses** are somewhat safer than service taxis, and somewhat less expensive. The Cairo-Luxor express bus is air-conditioned and reasonably speedy; and unlike almost any other bus, this one allows you to absorb the sights of the Nile Valley. See the individual chapters below for details on schedules and prices for these various modes of transportation.

It's a good idea to bring food with you to towns such as Esna, Edfu, and Kom Ombo, which are too small to have any real restaurants. Roadside kiosks are everywhere, but before you dine at these places, be sure your intestines have already been initiated. Some foreigners can eat at these places all the time without so much as a rumble of the stomach, while others are sent right to the bathroom. Mineral water is available almost everywhere, and you can safely rely on the ubiquitous softdrinks, although it sometimes seems that Egypt is secretly controlled by PepsiCo.

In summer, plan to do most of your sight-seeing between 6 and 11am, before temperatures soar above 43°C. Many of the pharaonic monuments consist of either tombs or well-preserved temples, so much of your sight-seeing will take place out of the sun. From November to May, temperatures are much more comfortable, but because this is Egypt's tourist season, the sights will be a lot more crowded.

Minya and Mallawi

The Upper Egyptian sister cities of Minya and Mallawi lie along a major canal west of the Nile. Minya, the provincial capital and a university town, is the more cosmopolitan of the two. Though graced with public squares and one of the few riverfront parks in Egypt, Minya still has the hectic markets and roadways of a commercial center. Mallawi is slower, sleepier, and dirtier. Together these two make good bases for daytrips to the archeological sites at **Beni Hassan, Hermopolis, Tuna el Gabel,** and **Tel el-Amarna.** Minya, though less convenient to most sites than Mallawi, is more accustomed to accommodating travelers.

Few independent travelers bother to visit this middle section of the Nile Valley. Exploring this region on your own demands more time and energy than the standard jaunts to the Luxor or Aswan areas, and the sites are not as exciting. Yet if you have more than a casual interest in Egyptology and want to leave the crowds behind, the Minya and Mallawi area will be worth the substantial effort.

Practical Information

Minya lies 250km south of Cairo, on the west side of the Nile; Mallawi is 45km farther south, also on the western bank. The trip from Cairo's Ramses Station by train to Minya takes three to four hours; fare in air-conditioned second class is LE3.20 (students LE2.45). **Service taxis** leave regularly for Minya from Giza Station (one way LE3.10); the 250km trip takes about five hours, depending on traffic. It's best to avoid the dangerous service taxis, however, unless you're within 150km of Minya (from Beni Suef, Mallawi, or Assyut); the fare should be a little more than 1pt per kilometer. Minya and Mallawi can also be reached by bus from the Ahmed Himli Station, located next to Ramses Station (LE3.60 to Minya or Mallawi). In Minya itself, the main **taxi and bus station** is located next to a bridge 500m south of the train station; here you can find transportation to major cities both south and north of Minya. Another small station, 300km farther south and across from the small, white Habaski Mosque, has minibuses serving Abu Qurqas. The Minya **Tourist Information Office** is on the Nile; walk due east from the train station through the town square, then turn left on the corniche and continue for 3 blocks. The staff is helpful, but speaks better German than English (tel. 32 01 50, open 8:30am-2pm). **Currency** can be exchanged at the Alexandria Bank and National Bank, both on the corniche. The main **post office** is located near the Habaski Mosque next to an Omar Effendi store.

You can reach **Mallawi** by train from Cairo or Luxor; the trip from Cairo takes about five hours on the air-conditioned, second-class **train** (LE3.60). **Service taxis** from Minya cost 50pt; the fare from Assyut is LE1.10. The **train station** in Mallawi is on the eastern bank of the canal across from town. South of the terminal is the **taxi station** serving points south of Mallawi; 200m north of the train station, past a white mosque across the canal, is another taxi station serving points north. A small bridge spans the canal, leading to the main paved strip of the town. This is Essim St., which runs all along the waterfront. The **police station** is a few blocks down Bank al-Misr St., just north of the second taxi station. You can exchange money at **Cairo Bank,** 100m past the taxi station (open 8:30am-1:30pm and 5-8pm).

You can shuttle between the two cities by bus or taxi, both of which run fairly constantly and take about an hour. In Minya, go to the station next to the bridge; in Mallawi, across from the mosque. Third-class trains run between the cities (and all the villages) all day as well. Although they take 15 minutes longer than the bus or taxi, they are cheaper (20pt, students 15pt) and may be more comfortable when uncrowded.

Accommodations and Food

The choice for budget travelers in Minya is the **Palace Hotel** (tel. 32 70 71), in the centrally located town square 2 blocks away from the train station. A day-glo portrait of Nefertiti greets you in the tiled foyer; a grand colonial staircase leads up to an airy lobby ringed by rooms just dilapidated enough to be funky. Watch outdoor movies on one side, or stay on the other side and get to sleep early. (Singles and doubles LE4.50, with bath LE7.50. Good breakfast with rolls, jam, and omelette LE1.50.) For a few more amenities, try the **Beach Hotel,** between the town square and the Nile, where very clean, carpeted rooms rent for singles LE12.50, doubles LE14.50, both with bath. The **Lotus Hotel,** 1km north of the train station on Sa'ad Zaghloul Rd., has clean, carpeted rooms with bath. (Singles LE13.30, doubles LE18.50, triples LE24. Breakfast included.) Many of Minya's inhabitants sleep outside on the corniche during Ramadan.

For **food** in Minya, try the restaurant on the top floor of the **Lotus Hotel,** which offers a commanding view of the town below. Meals of soup, rice, fish, salad, and dessert cost LE6.40 and a large Stella beer is LE2.60. Though lacking English signs, **Restaurant Sheraton** and **Restaurant Kabage** (on Husseini St., 100m past the town square) are immaculate and serve full meals for LE2-3. Sheraton's owner, Farouk Mahmoud Ahmed, is particularly attentive and knows basic English. For entertainment, try taking a horse-drawn carriage (most destinations within the town will be LE1-1.25).

Most of **Mallawi's** hotels and restaurants are located along Essim St., the garbage-strewn main thoroughfare. The **Samir Amis Hotel and Restaurant** (tel. 29 55) is on the west bank of the canal just north of the train station, but on the other side of the canal. (Singles LE2, doubles LE3, triples LE4.) It's the only hotel in town allowed to take Westerners. Shoo the cockroaches before diving inside the sheets. If the hotel is full, try having a drink at the restaurant and asking the restaurant owner to arrange a room. The restaurant offers the most filling meals in town. (Meat or chicken with rice, vegetables, beans, and salad about LE3; beer LE1.50.) Various cafes and shish kebab places are sprinkled throughout town, especially along Bank al-Misr St. These are best reserved for those whose digestive tracts are already accustomed to Egypt's sidewalk grub.

Sights

A word to the weary: Don't try to see too much in a day in the Minya and Mallawi area. Allow yourself a day for each of the major sites: Beni Hassan and Tuna al-Gabel (highest priority), Hermopolis (lower priority but close to Tuna al-Gabel), and Tel el-Amarna (high priority). A tiny **archeological museum** in Mallawi houses artifacts unearthed at the local sites. (Open Sat.-Thurs. 9am-1pm, Fri. 9-11am. Admission 50pt, students 25pt.)

Beni Hassan

The rushing waters of an angry mountain stream apparently destroyed the ancient village of Beni Hassan, but the neighboring necropolis, housing 39 pharaonic rock tombs, remains securely on the map as one of the finest Middle Kingdom sites in Upper Egypt. These two bedroom apartments for the afterlife, dating from the Eleventh and Twelfth Dynasties (2000-1800 B.C.E.), have colorful wallpaper paintings that still retain a touch of their original vibrancy, though the ruinous effects of 4000 years of earthquakes and vandalism are evident.

Halfway between Minya and Mallawi, Beni Hassan can be reached by service taxi from either town to the sizable village of Abu Qurqas. The fare is 25pt from Minya, 30pt from Mallawi. Next to the bridge spanning the canal in the center of town, you'll see a sign indicating the road to the antiquities. Walk the 3km east to the Nile bank, or take one of the covered pickup trucks that leave from the east side of the bridge (10pt). Private taxis cost LE1. From the government office at the riverside, you can buy one ticket for transportation and admission to the site. This includes boat fare to cross the Nile (LE2.75, six or more, LE1.25 each) and a mini-bus from the dock on the far side to the tombs, 500m inland. The tombs are open daily from 6am to 7pm. Admission to the tombs is LE1, students 50pt. Permission to take photos costs LE5, and use of a flash is prohibited.

The **Tomb of Kheti** (#17) originally contained six lotus columns hewn from solid rock. Two of these graceful supports still adorn the interior, and decorative scenes on the southern wall depict Kheti accompanied by his various servants—a fan-bearer, a sandal-bearer, and a gnarled dwarf. The northern wall depicts colorful birds: One roosts in a tree, another flies free above an open trap, and a third is caught in a snare. Nearby, women dance in long lines apart from the men, while above them two cattle are caught copulating.

Kheti's father, Baket, was responsible for the construction of one of the necropolis' most lavish burial places. The **Tomb of Baket** (#15) features scenes of Egyptians at work. Look for the hairdresser, laundryman, painter, goldsmith, and angler. On the rear wall, wrestlers demonstrate nearly 200 different moves; the positions are more than mildly erotic. On the southern wall, a thief is beaten by angry citizens, while on the northern a theme from Kheti's tomb is repeated, this time with two copulating gazelles. Also notice a primitive Coptic cross on the front inside wall, evidence of the period when the tombs were used as dwellings and churches by the

Copts. The rounded mud dwellings closest to the foot of the mountain are Coptic graves.

The **Tomb of Khumhotep** (#3) was built for one of the province's most prestigious officials, the ruler of the province of Antelope and governor of the Eastern Desert. The base of one 16-sided proto-Doric column remains, and the ceiling anticipates a triple vault. On the walls, Khumhotep inspects the various activities of his province, including the arrival of the Semitic Amo tribe from Syria. Hieroglyphics outline the history of Khumhotep's family. The tomb features extraordinarily rich colors, especially a lovely aquamarine around the entrance to the inner chamber.

In the neighboring **Tomb of Amenemhat** (#2), a checkerboard pattern enlivens the vaulted ceiling, while the upper walls display yet more wrestlers and fighting soldiers. Four 16-sided proto-Doric columns remain standing. The cows on the northern wall look as if they were transplanted from the hills of Vermont or Guernsey. A badly damaged statue of Amenemhat with his wife and mother rests at the rear of the tomb chamber. From the northernmost tomb you can see the adjacent mud villages of **Diaba** (large and Muslim) and **Qibti** (small and Christian).

Hermopolis and Tuna al-Gabel

The appeal of these two sites lies chiefly in the peculiar history and myth that surround them, and not in their surviving remnants. In one ancient Egyptian creation story, the sun god sprang from a cosmic egg on the hillock at Hermopolis. Although the mound no longer exists, remains of the ancient city of Hermopolis survive 10km northwest of Mallawi. Twelve kilometers farther west, isolated in an arid plain at the foot of the Western Desert hills, lie the ruins at Tuna al-Gabel. This necropolis features a bizarre collection of funerary remains, including an enormous underground burial area where thousands of sacred baboons and ibises were mummified and interred. Egyptologists suspect that Tuna al-Gabel served as the Hermopolitan cemetery. At any rate, the two can be visited in a single trip. Unfortunately, public transportation won't take you all the way to either site. You should be able to persuade the driver of a pick-up truck to do the entire route in a half-day excursion from Mallawi for LE10, a good deal for groups. The alternatives, finding local pickup truck-taxis and walking, can easily wear you out.

In order of importance and interest, go to **Tuna al-Gabel** first. Bring a flashlight for the tombs and an ample supply of water; the site is awash in desert sands. For 30pt you can take a service taxi or pick-up truck from Mallawi to the town of Tuna al-Gabel, which is 5km from the necropolis. From here try to hitch a ride with a truck carrying workers to a local quarry (pay about 25pt per person). From the turn-off to the quarry, it's a 2km hike to the site—this is where you might wish you had hired a private taxi. A truck in the village may take you out and back for about LE2. The site is open daily from 6am to 5pm. Admission is LE1, plus a 25pt toll to enter the desert. The **ticket office**lies near the village.

The necropolis at Tuna al-Gabel has been excavated recently, and almost everything of interest removed. Nevertheless, the isolation of the site, the rustle of the desert sand, and the eerie silence of the caves lend an air of mystery to the ruins. The most unusual attraction is **al-Sarad-eb** (The Galleries), the series of mysterious underground catacombs where sacred animals were buried during the Ptolemaic and Roman periods. All along the ¼ mile catacomb are broken remnants of the two million pots used to house the ibises. Don't be alarmed by the larger-than-life baboon statue 100m inside the catacomb on your left. Only a few of the mummified creatures remain on the site; above the cemetary is a small enclosure where some of the better preserved remains are kept.

Farther into the desert on the narrow stone walkway is the **City of the Dead,** filled with royal mausolea laid out like a town, with houses, streets, and walkways. Most of the tombs here show the influence of Hellenistic style—they look more like people you might know. The finest structure is the **Tomb of Petosiris,** high priest of the Temple of Thoth. Inside, a vestibule opens up into the central chamber, where a square shaft plummets to the burial chamber. The decorative bas-reliefs on the walls, dating from around 300 B.C.E., depict pharaonic deities in typical Hellenic

poses. Behind this edifice sits the **Tomb of Isadora,** a young woman from An-
tinopolis. Isadora's mummy is on display inside a glass case: Teeth, fingernails, and
even traces of hair can still be detected on the corpse, an accomplishment stemming
from 2000 years of desert air, not embalming skill.

Slightly south of the Tomb of Isadora, a stone walkway branches north toward
al-Sakiya (The Well), a huge circular brick shaft that once supplied the necropolis
and its sacred aviary with fresh water. The water wheel, built in 300 B.C.E., pumped
water up from 70m below the desert floor. For some *baksheesh,* the guard will open
it up, and you can climb down to the well's bottom after shooing the bats away.
The walkway to the ancient well passes through the remains of a great **Temple to
Thoth,** which once dominated the entire necropolis. A few of the massive facade
columns remain, along with a series of pillars that once enclosed the forecourt.

To visit **Hermopolis,** you need to reach **Ishmunin,** a 20-minute drive from Mallawi. (All the locals know Ishmunin, but have not heard of Hermopolis.) Just outside Ishmunin is the turnoff, which goes only to Hermopolis and not Tuna al-Gabel
despite the claims of the blue sign.

Two huge sandstone baboons facing east are all that remain of the ancient city
of Khnum. Called Hermopolis by its Ptolemaic Greek citizens, the city dates from
at least the nineteenth dynasty. The two apes once supported the ceiling of a great
temple; the unfortunate creatures had their erect phalluses hacked off by later generations of prudish Egyptians. The temple served as cult center for Thoth, an enigmatic god who had the body of a man and the head of an ibis; the baboon was one
of his sacred animals. The Egyptians revered him as scribe of the divine court, inven-
tor of writing, and patron of wisdom. The Greeks, arriving in the fifth century
B.C.E., associated this learned deity with their own messenger god, Hermes, and
named their metropolis in his honor. Farther along the road, across a lush green
field, stand the slender rose granite columns of a **Greek agora.**

Tel al-Amarna

Among the eternal procession of ancient Egyptian rulers, one pharaoh has earned
a special place in the modern imagination: Akhnaton. Rebelling against the old
order of political and religious power at Thebes, Akhnaton abandoned the Karnak
Temple to venerate a single god named Aton. Aton was represented by a brilliant
sun disk whose rays terminated in outstretched palms, often holding an *ankh*—the
circle-topped cross symbolizing eternal life. Akhnaton took his court out of Thebes
and built a new capital far to the north, at Tel al-Amarna. Here Akhnaton dreamed
of worshiping Aton and living in peace with his beloved wife Nefertiti. The idyll
lasted long enough to produce the naturalistic "Amarna style" of art and the beginnings of a new city. But the spark of individualism was soon extinguished: At the
age of 35, Akhnaton followed his children and Nefertiti to the grave and the old
powers quickly retook Egypt. With Akhnaton's new city razed, the capital moved
back to Thebes and Tel al-Amarna was declared unholy ground. Paradoxically, the
taboo helped preserve the remains of Akhnaton's home, since no later civilization
would build over the home of this proto-monotheistic heretic. The still-beautiful
necropolis of Tel al-Amarna, 12km south of Mallawi on the east bank of the Nile,
houses five rock-hewn tombs from Akhnaton's reign.

To reach Tel al-Amarna, take one of the local pickup trucks from the depot south
of the Mallawi train station (25pt). The trucks leave from the parking lot at the
end of the bridge crossing into town; you'll be dropped off at the bank of the Nile
where you can take a ferry to the site for 25pt. Smaller motorboats which transport
the locals are 50pt. (Last ferry 6pm; avoid the *feluccas,* LE3). Alternatively, hire
a motorboat for about LE5 and share among a group. Once across, you must purchase an admission ticket to the area at a small office (25pt), then hire a donkey
or a tractor to bring you to the antiquities. At a booth about 2km outside of the
village, you must purchase another admission ticket for the tombs. (LE1, students
50pt. Site open daily 7am-5pm.)

There are two groups of tombs: Of the six in the northern group (all nearby),
#1, 3, and 4 are most worth a visit; a couple of the southern tombs are interesting,

but unless you're a die-hard it's probably not worth the 10km round-trip trek through the desert. A tour of the #1-6, the northern group, on a **donkey** costs LE2, and takes four hours. If you're not insistent, you'll be shown only #3-5, as the others are a bit of a detour. **Tractors,** which pull covered wagons, are faster, but cost LE4 for up to four people. A van can also be rented for LE5 during the low season. A visit to the southern tombs costs LE10 for four people on a half-day's journey by tractor. A donkey ride costs LE2.50 and takes about eight hours. The villagers at Tel al-Amarna, famous for their orneriness and monopoly on donkeys, may demand double these prices, especially for the difficult trip south. The donkey drivers may refuse to do the southern route during the summer. If you are young, strong, and gung-ho you can walk to the northern tombs, about 4km through the desert and then up the mountain. Be sure you bring water if you don't want to pay four times standard prices. The lights in the tombs are often out of order, so bring a flashlight.

The **Tomb of Maya** (#1) was constructed for the superintendent of the royal harem. Its decorative reliefs depict King Akhnaton with his family and closest friends. On the entrance walls of the **Tomb of Ahmose** (#3), the deceased can be seen worshiping the sun. Ahmose was royal fan-bearer to Akhnaton, and is most often depicted praying in his official costume, carrying a fan and an axe. The **Tomb of Meri-Re** (#4), the high priest of Aton, is one of the largest and best preserved of the group, with vibrant colors still remaining. Plans of the temples and palaces of Akhnaton adorn the walls of the tomb's hypostyle hall, enabling Egyptologists to deduce the appearance of the ancient city's official buildings. One wall of the tomb features an ornately decorated chariot, glowing with color. The famous profile of Nefertiti is identifiable in several places, but has been chipped away by thieves. Her famous bust-with-crown was discovered here, but kept hidden by its German discoverers for years and then taken to the Berlin Museum. The **Tomb of Pentu** (#5), chief physician to the royal family, has been badly damaged, as has the **Tomb of Panhesy** (#6), 1km to the south. Panhesy was the Servant of Aton, observer of granaries and herds, and chancellor of Lower Egypt. His tomb was converted into a church by early Christians, but its original decorative carvings survive in reasonably good condition, as does a fairly ordinary staircase.

If you make it to the southern tombs, two are worth touring. The **Tomb of Mahn** (#9), Akhnaton's chief of police, contains several levels of chambers, connected by a winding stairway and adorned with various scenes of the deceased with royal personages. The striking **Tomb of Ay** was constructed for the king's secretary and groom, Queen Nefertiti's nurse, and later Tut-Ankh-Amon's successor as pharaoh. Although Ay abandoned his designs here to excavate a more elaborate tomb for himself in the Valley of the Kings at Thebes, the structure was intended to be the finest in the necropolis at Tel el-Amarna. Its hypostyle hall is imposing. The wall inside the main entrance is covered with scenes depicting the bustling street life of the ancient city, complete with soldiers, visiting officials, and dancing women. On the way south, you'll glimpse the insubstantial ruins of Akhnaton's city, all but leveled by reactionaries after his death (at about the time of Tut-Ankh-Amon).

Assyut

The third-century philosopher Plotinus, Assyut's most famous native son, remarked that, "Every beautiful vision requires an eye that is able to see it." The eye that can appreciate the beauty of Assyut has been trained by time in the tourist whirlpools of Luxor and Aswan; when you become afraid your own reflection will try to sell you a souvenir, you are ready to appreciate Assyut. You may travel here for the same reason people have always come to Assyut: Here the road from the oases and the Western Desert reaches the Nile. Always an important market and commercial center, Assyut is today the most important city in Upper Egypt, with a large university and an economy that thrives on everything except tourism. It is big, fairly crowded, inexpensive, and authentic.

All transportation connects to and from the main square in front of the **train station.** More than a dozen trains per day travel to Cairo (375km, 2nd class A/C LE3.40, 7 hr.) via Mallawi (80km, 2 hr.). A half-dozen air-conditioned trains shuttle daily to southern cities, including Sohag (92km, 2 hr.), Qena (230km, 4-5 hr.), Luxor (300km, 6-7 hr.), and Aswan (500km, 12 hr.). **Buses** are more convenient to the closer cities; the station lies just south of the train station. Three buses daily pass through Assyut en route from Cairo to Kharga Oasis (LE4, 4-5 hr.) and Dakhla Oasis (LE5, 8 hr.), but not all stop in the city center each day. A surer way to reach the oases is to grab a **service taxi** from the stand 100m south of the train station (only to Kharga, LE4.50). The wait shouldn't be more than an hour or two. Service taxis also provide convenient, though dangerous, transportation to other Nile cities. Stands for various destinations spread out to the west and south of the train station.

For budget accommodation, the best value in town is **el-Haramein Hotel,** 1 block east of the train station on the road to the Nile. It's brand spanking-new, spotless, and has sparkling bathrooms. The proprietors serve delicious lime cocktails (30pt) and Ceylon tea (20pt) all day. (Singles LE4, doubles LE6.50, triples LE7.50. Fans 50pt.) The **Zamzam Hotel,** a few doors east of el-Haramein, is older but still comfortable, despite lacking fans. (Singles LE3, doubles LE6.) The **Hotel Assoiut de Tourism,** right across from the station, has slightly cheaper prices but far grungier rooms and toilets. (Singles LE2.60, doubles LE5.) The price includes breakfast in their restaurant on the second floor, which also serves decent kebab, chicken, and *kufte* dinners for about LE2-3. Martyrs in search of the IYHF youth hostel (Lux Houses, Building #503; tel. 48 46) should walk south from the train station to the small square (10 min.) and ask for a shared taxi to al-Walidiya (10pt). Dorm beds in stuffy 6-person rooms are LE1 (nonmembers pay LE1 one-time registration fee). There are kitchen facilities and a Ping Pong table. In the middle range, **Akhenaten Hotel** (tel. 32 77 23) is the best value, with a valiant attempt at elegance with modern beds and shining toilets. (Singles LE10, with shower LE13. Doubles LE13, with shower LE16.58. A/C and TV LE2 each.) Wave your *Let's Go* and receive a 10% discount. To get there, walk 2 blocks north from the station and turn left.

A favorite restaurant with locals is the **Mattam al-Azhar,** where you can get a delicious, crispy whole chicken, big enough for three or four people, for LE4, as well as other less massive but affordable fare. Walk down Sa'ad Zahgoul St. from the south end of the station square, leading away from the Nile, and it's 100m in a new building to the left. No English sign, so look for the ornate wooden screen above the door. **Express Restaurant,** in the heart of commercial Assyut, is a spotless and lively place which serves tiny but tasty hamburgers (40pt) and *shwarma* or kebab sandwiches (40pt). The non-alcoholic Birell beer (40pt) will taste more authentic if you add a pinch of salt. From the second floor you can observe the "Times Square" of Assyut while listening to American top-40 music. To reach the restaurant, walk 200m north along the train tracks from the station, then turn left onto July 26 St. The restaurant is 100m past the underpass. You can buy local produce in the **market** by the train station. **Alexandria Bank,** in the square 200m west of the train station, will change traveler's checks. (Open daily 8:30am-2pm and 5-8pm.)

There are few **sights** of interest in Assyut. The *souk* is unspectacular but untouristed. If you turn north from the *souk's* central intersection, and continue for 50m, you will find on your right the courtyard of an old inn where the caravan camels were stabled. Farther along is an old Turkish bath with a beautiful marble fountain; ask the custodian to admit you. The Nile bank of Assyut is leafy and pleasant, with a view of the British-built Assyut Barrages to the north. The entire tourism industry of Assyut is represented by one man, Saber, whose small shop in the Zamzam Hotel sells quality handmade folk clothing and crafts. Saber can lead tours through what he calls the "true heart of Assyut," including *felucca* trips to a sandy island on the Nile and a visit to the small village where Nasser was born. Find Saber at his shop, **Open Sesame.** He's the one wearing a genuine Lee cap.

Service taxis (25pt) from Assyut run 8km to Dir Drunka, home of the **Convent of Saint Mary,** a pharaonic quarry sanctified by the Coptic Church. Mary and Jesus are thought to have stayed here. The convent has numerous icons and a baptismal chamber. In August the Copts arrive here on their pilgrimages. The service taxi will drop you off at a road leading to the convent, a 15-minute uphill walk.

Sohag

A bustling city of 75,000 inhabitants, Sohag is the commercial center for a large surrounding agricultural area. The backbones of the local economy are onion packing and soa, not tourism. This is a city where the taxi drivers prowl around in 35-year-old Ford Deluxes, not modern Mercedes. Sohag is practically unknown among foreign visitors, so you'll be extended hospitality seen only in smaller villages.

Sohag is situated on the west side of the Nile, 467km south of Cairo, 92km south of Assyut, and 204km north of Luxor. Sohag is the nearest city to Abydos, at 50km away. There is the usual Nilonic plethora of transportation. The **train station** is in the center of town in the middle of al-Mahatta St. Frequent trains head both north and south. The train to Luxor takes four hours and costs LE2.60 in air-conditioned second class. The **bus station** lies 300m south of the train station. Buses leave frequently, especially in the morning, to Assyut (2 hr.), Qena (LE1.75, 3 hr.), and al-Balyana, near the ruins of Abydos (1 hr.). **Northbound service taxis** can be caught 200m north of the train station, just west of al-Mahatta St. (Assyut LE2, 1½ hr.) **Southbound** service taxis stop by the bus station and depart every 20 minutes in the morning to Qena and al-Balyana (LE1, 1 hr.), where you can connect with a service taxi to Abydos for 25pt. **Local taxis** leave from 200m west of the bus station to Dayr Amba Shenouda (25pt), or you can hire a private taxi to the sights for LE5-6 round-trip.

The three hotels in Sohag are strung like beads next to each other, across from the train station. **Andalos Hotel** (tel. 23 43 28), just north of the train station on al-Mahatta, is the best value, with clean, spacious rooms and fans. (Singles LE4, doubles LE6. *Fuul* breakfast included.) **El-Salaam Hotel** (tel. 32 33 17) is similar to the Andalos, with fans and a TV lounge. (Singles LE5, with bath LE8. Doubles LE10.) **Ramses Hotel,** next to el-Salaam, has adequate but run-down rooms without fans. (Singles LE4, doubles LE6.) A cheap option is the **IYHF Youth Hostel** (tel. 32 43 95), across the river in Akhmim at 5 Port Said St. (members LE1). The town of Akhmim is a Coptic community renowned for its cotton weavings, shawls, and batik crafts.

Dozens of *fuul* and *tamiya* joints dot the area around the station. For crusty fresh bread, spicy *tahina,* and ½ roast chicken (LE2.50), stop in at the **El Eman for Roast Grill** a few doors north of Andalos Hotel.

About 10km northwest of Sohag, on the edge of the desert, are two of the finest Coptic monuments in Upper Egypt. The **Dayr Amba Shenouda (White Monastery)** is named for its white limestone blocks, many of which originally belonged to a pharaonic temple and sport hieroglyphic inscriptions. The monastery was founded in 400 C.E. by the St. Shenoudi. You can enter the carpeted church within the monastery complex; remove your shoes and be sensitive to the pilgrims who stay there with their families. As you enter you'll be greeted by a bethroned Jesus, balancing an eroded globe in his right hand and the Bible in his left. To the right in an inner room, you'll find the oft-used baptismal chamber. Between July 15 and 30, the monastery attracts 1000 to 2000 Coptic pilgrims daily. During that period, childless women often get into sacks and roll down a hill in hopes of obtaining divine intervention.

The smaller **Dayr Amba Bishoi (Red Monastery)** is named in Arabic after its founder, St. Bishoi, a thief who converted to Christianity and repented through fasting and prayer. You can discern the outlines of a tenth-century fresco of the Pantocrator on the apse of the central altar. During the pilgrimage period, you can visit both sites from Sohag by bus for 40pt.

Abydos

Abydos, one of the most ancient cities in Egypt, has all but vanished, except for the imposing Temple of Osiris built by the Nineteenth-Dynasty Pharaoh Seti I. Although not as imposing as its gargantuan cousins at Luxor and Karnak, the temple is the greatest work of the New Kingdom, and is noted for its delicately painted murals and magnificent bas-reliefs. Abydos was a cult-center for Osiris, one of the most important and popular deities of the Egyptian pantheon. Egyptians of the New Kingdom hoped to make the pilgrimage to the temple, either in this life or the after-life.

Practical Information

Since there are no accommodations in the area, most people visit Abydos as a long daytrip from Luxor (LE30-40 in combination with Dendera Temple). You can also stop en route between Luxor and points farther north. The closest town to the ruins is **al-Balyana,** on the main north-south rail line and easily accessible. Eight of the 10 daily Luxor-Cairo **trains** stop at al-Balyana. From Cairo, it's best to take the train (11 hr.). From Luxor, it's much faster to go by service taxi to Qena (LE1.25) and change for al-Balyana (LE1.50). For the return trip, take a service taxi to Nag Hammadi (LE1), where you can usually catch a taxi to Qena. Another strategy is to stay in Sohag, the nearest city, and come to al-Balyana by service taxi (LE1). The **service taxi station** in al-Balyana is 1 block east of the railway station. From here you can also catch a service taxi to Abydos (35pt). An infrequent and crowded bus also runs from town to the ruins (10pt). The proper fare for a private taxi to Abydos is LE3, though it requires some hard bargaining. The only accommodations in al-Balyana are at the **Hotel Wadi** next to the train station. The rooms look like they haven't been cleaned since the hotel was built, and the bathrooms are no treat either (dorm beds LF1.50, singles LE3). Try to stay elsewhere. There is no restaurant in town.

Sights

In Egyptian mythology, Osiris, the god of the Nile, was slain by his evil brother Seth, dismembered, and scattered throughout the land. Although Osiris' sister and consort Isis recovered all but one of the pieces and reconstituted his body, Osiris was in no condition to reign over the land of the living, so he reconciled himself to being lord of the afterlife. Osiris' resurrection was his greatest achievement, and dead pharaohs throughout Egypt's history came to be identified with him. Abydos became the site for the cult of Osiris because, according to legend, his head was buried here. The myth of Osiris was once reenacted annually at Abydos, including a simulation of his death and dismemberment.

The great **Temple of Seti I** is constructed in three stages: The visitor passes first from light into semi-darkness, and finally into the dark interior where the gods were said to dwell and mortals forbidden to set foot. During the approach, the ceiling becomes lower and the floor slopes gently upward, in order to create the effects of depth and isolation from the world of light.

Approach the temple through the rubble of the first court, once planted with trees and flowers. Only three of the original seven doors remain to the **Portico of Twelve Pillars,** which guarded the entrance into the temple proper. The central doorway leads to the first hypostyle hall, lined with 24 colossal papyriform columns. This grandiose entrance gives way to the magnificent second hypostyle hall, which contains some of the finest bas-reliefs ever carved in Egypt, colorfully illuminated in striking tones of orange and blue. On the right-hand wall as you enter, Seti I is displayed offering incense to Osiris and other deities. At the opposite end of the second hypostyle hall, a long, narrow corridor known as the **Gallery of the Kings** leads toward the southeast. This simple passage houses one of Egyptology's most treasured finds, the **Kings' List,** which mentions the names of 76 Egyptian rulers from

Menes of Memphis to Seti I, though it misses a few. Correlating this list with prior knowledge, scholars were able to pinpoint the sequence of the Egyptian dynasties. The Gallery of Kings ends in a series of small unfinished chambers, probably used as storerooms and sacrifice areas.

The remains of the **Osireion,** a great cenotaph for Seti I, lie below the main temple in a swampy depression. (The actual tomb of Seti I is in the Valley of the Kings in West Thebes.) The interior is closed to visitors because of the sodden earth. The best you can do is climb up to the roof of the neighboring main temple and look down. Nearby is the largely destroyed **Temple of Ramses II,** built by the braggart son of Seti I.

Retrace your steps to the temple's second hypostyle hall, through the Gallery of the Kings, to view the southern wing of the Temple of Abydos. Beside the entrance to the Gallery of the Kings is another doorway, yielding to a chamber with two tiny chapels adjoining it. The right-hand chapel contains a graphic relief showing the mummy of Osiris impregnating Isis, who has transformed herself into a falcon.

Return to the second hypostyle hall before proceeding into the temple's interior. Sanctuaries dedicated to Horus, Isis, Osiris, Amun, Horakhti, Ptah, and the patron Pharaoh Seti I line the hallway. In a number of the small sanctuaries and throughout the rear portion of the temple many of the figures have been defaced. Osiris' sanctuary is more elaborate than the others, opening into the **Inner Sanctuary of Osiris,** a chamber still possessing most of the original painted scenes of Osiris' life. Only a few of the fine reliefs adorning the walls have suffered abuse by thoughtless travelers. The sanctuary is flanked by three small chapels housing the best preserved reliefs in the temple, which depict brilliantly colored scenes of rituals. (Site open 7am-5pm. Admission LE1, students 50pt. Ticket covers everything so there's no need to fork over *baksheesh.*)

Qena and Dendera

Qena, the provincial capital of the region north of Luxor, is a nice place to live but you wouldn't want to visit. The streets are lined with trees and prosperous shops, and minarets and white church steeples adorn the town center. But in a town where foreigners still attract surprised stares, there are predictably few tourist facilities. Hours spent in Qena can be a pleasant pit stop from the tourist track, but it's a good idea to take a quick look around and keep going, as you will only stop here on the way to or from Hurghada or the temple at Dendera 9km to the north. It's easy enough to meet the locals. Just ask for directions and you may well be invited to tea, especially if you're a student. Though few speak English, the friendly people of Qena are generally genuinely happy to help, and will rarely overcharge you.

Practical Information

For a medium-sized city, Qena couldn't possibly have a more complex transportation system, with its three important transit centers in three different parts of town. The best way to get from one train, bus, or taxi terminal to another is to hail a horse carriage (20pt per person for more than 3 people).

Train Station: Near the center of town, at the end of prosperous al-Mahatta St. 6 trains with A/C run in either direction daily. To Cairo (600km, 2nd-class A/C LE6, 12-13 hr.), to Luxor (68km, LE1, 2 hr.; inconvenient), to Aswan (270km, LE3.50, 6½ hr.).

Bus Station: From the train station, head down Qena's main street toward the Nile, turn right at a large intersection, and walk past the mosques. The station will be on your left. Buses are often slow and crowded; recommended only for the Qena-Hurghada run. Buses to Hurghada come from Luxor, at around 7am and 1pm daily (LE7).

Service Taxis: Northbound: Next to the bus station. To Dendera, 25pt per person. For Abydos, say you want to go to al-Balyana (LE1.50); if you mention Abydos, which is only 3km farther, you'll have to refuse offers for a special taxi. Sohag is the northernmost destination.

Southbound: From the train station, cross the canal and walk along its eastern bank to the square with a mosque. Frequent connections to Luxor (LE1.25) and Aswan (LE5). To reach Esna, change at Luxor. To reach Edfu or Kom Ombo, you'll have to pay the full fare to Aswan. **To Hurghada:** At the far right corner of the square beyond the canal and train station, as you walk away from the center of town, passing the square's mosque (LE8). Hairpin turns near the sea are usually taken at top speed. Hang on.

Local Taxis: Departures from an alley near the bus station and between Qena's two largest mosques. To Dendera LE3 round-trip with earnest bargaining. If you plan to keep the driver waiting several hours, pay him LE4.

Police: In the train station (tel. 32 57 24). Open 24 hours.

An interesting excursion is to **Naqada,** about a half-hour south of Qena by taxi. Around the turn-of-the-century, a monk built the **Pigeon Palace** there. This ornate palace houses 30,000 pigeons in comfort. Naqada is equally accessible from Luxor.

Accommodations and Food

Try not to spend the night in Qena. Luxor, with its bevy of cheap, comfortable hotels, is only an hour away. For those who must, there are two bearable hotels in town. The most comfortable option in summer is to take a room with a bath at the slowly disintegrating **New Palace Hotel** (tel. 25 09), where at least the rooms have fans. (Singles LE3.50, with bath LE5. Doubles LE5, with bath LE7.) Hot water is sporadic. The hotel is directly across from the train station, behind the Mobil Station. **Hotel al-Salaam** is not significantly worse, although there are no fans. To get there, walk down the main street from the station, go through the intersection and under the blue-green squared archway, and then bear left. (Singles LE2.25, doubles LE3.25.)

The most accessible restaurant in Qena is **el-Prince Restaurant,** on the corner of the major intersection ½km west of the station. Look for the white sign on your right. The usual Egyptian specialties—kebab, *kufte,* chicken—are available (LE3-5). **Hamdy Restaurant,** 100m down the street from el-Prince and north of the square, serves complete meals of chicken, rice, ladyfingers, and salad for LE2.50. The streets running north and east (back to the station) from that intersection are lined with stands selling fresh produce, *fuul, kushari,* and *tamiya,* as well as a few shops selling canned goods and staples.

If you are stuck in Qena for more than an hour, head to the Nile, about 1km from the central mosques. The view is spectacular, especially at sunset, and you can sit in a cafe in front of the cruise boat landing and watch the Egyptians watching the foreigners.

Sights at Dendera

The cheapest way to reach the antiquities at **Dendera** (8km from Qena) is to take a service taxi (25pt) that will drop you off at a fork in the road just 1km from the site. Follow the paved road to the left through the lovely green field, and you'll see the well-preserved ruins looming ahead. The roof, walls, and inner sanctuary of the **Temple of Hathor** remain largely intact. Only the colossal Temple of Horus at Edfu is better preserved. Hathor, the city's patron deity, was worshiped as early as the Old Kingdom, but this temple dates only from the first century B.C.E. The late Ptolemies and the Romans found it politically expedient to associate themselves with the worship of Hathor, and Cleopatra, Augustus, Claudius, and Nero all sponsored the decoration of the temple. A benevolent goddess, Hathor was usually depicted as cow-headed, or shown wearing a crown of two horns cradling Ra, the sun disk. Because of her patronage of love and joy, Hathor, the "Golden One," was identified by the Greeks as Aphrodite. During an annual festival, a statue of Hathor was conveyed in a sacred procession down the Nile to meet Horus of Edfu.

During the summer, a large colony of bats inhabits the more secluded portions of the temple. Glance up at the ceiling before entering some of the temple's smaller chambers. A flashlight will come in handy as a supplement to the weak interior illumination.

Approaching the temple from the main entrance to the site, the magnificent facade of the **Great Hypostyle Hall** looms before you. Eighteen columns are surmounted by haunting but battered capitals in the form of cow-goddesses' heads. The pharaohs merged three goddesses during the later years of the New Kingdom: Hathor, Sekhmet the lioness, and Bastet the cat. A feline quality comes through Hathor's bovine features. On the ceiling, the protective vulture of Upper Egypt and the winged disk of Lower Egypt are drawn in bold patterns. Farther into the temple's inner sanctum, wall paintings portray the embalmer's art, while the ceiling is decorated with pictures of Nut, the sky goddess. In the second hypostyle hall, also known as the **Hall of Appearances,** six columns march in double formation up the central aisle of the temple, complemented by six small chambers on either side. The function of these chapels, aside from providing spacious bat nests, is indicated in their frescoes: Perfumes used during sacred rituals were kept in the laboratory and across the hall in the temple's treasury. The second hypostyle hall gives way to the **Hall of Offerings,** where the daily rites were performed. A staircase leading up to the roof is decorated with processional figures carved in elegant relief. From the top, enjoy the view of farmland and desert. In the kiosk in the southwest corner of the roof, priests performed the ceremony of "touching the disk," in which the soul of the sun god Ra appeared in the form of light.

Return to the Hall of Offerings via the second staircase, running down the eastern side of the temple, and proceed into the **Hall of the Ennead,** immediately preceding the inner sanctuary. The chamber to your left is the wardrobe, and opposite, a doorway leads through a small treasury into the **Court of the New Year,** where sacrifices were performed during the festival of the New Year. On the ceiling of the colorful portico, the goddess Nut gives birth to the sun, whose rays shine upon the head of Hathor. Retracing your steps to the main temple, proceed to the **Sanctuary,** the most sacred portion of the temple that was once the site of the cult statue of Hathor. Its interior is carved with scenes of offerings. The exterior surface of the Sanctuary is decorated with a frieze of ninety squatting divinities just below the upper cornice. The **Mysterious Corridor** surrounds the sanctuary on three sides, and 11 chapels, each with a distinct religious function, open off of it. The **Per Naser Chapel** is dedicated to Hathor in her terrifying lioness incarnation. A small chamber known as the **Throne of Ra** adjoins the chapel. A minuscule opening in its floor leads to the crypt (#7), a fascinating subterranean hallway embellished with colorful reliefs. The crypt is unofficially closed to the public, but the guard will be happy to give you a guided tour in exchange for a little *baksheesh.*

The most notable scene of the temple's exterior relief work portrays Cleopatra and her son making offerings to the gods. The lions' heads on the outside walls once spouted water. To the southwest of the temple, stone steps lead down to the enclosed, overgrown **Sacred Lake.** Around the corner, directly south of the temple, are the scanty remains of the **Temple of Isis,** built by Augustus to commemorate the birth of the pharaoh. Festivals celebrating a god's or pharaoh's birth took place at these *mammisi* (birth houses). Just southwest of the temple's main entrance gate are two other *mammisi.* Although the *mammisis* of Nectanebo is in ruins, the Roman *mammisis,* built during the reign of Nero, displays Hathor in various poses on both the interior and exterior walls. To its north, pieces of an interesting cobrahead frieze lie on the ground. (Admission LE2, students LE1. Open daily 6am-6pm.)

Luxor

Luxor's relationship with its illustrious past is not so much reverent as parasitic. Never have so many come so far to see so much that is dead. Hundreds of thousands of visitors every year from all over the world descend like locusts to tour the spectacular remnants of the ancient capital of Thebes. Greeting them is an energetic mod-

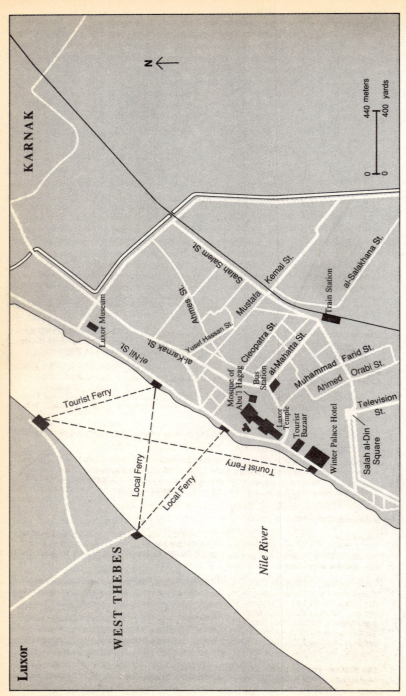

Luxor

KARNAK

N ←

440 meters
400 yards

Salah Salem St.

Kemal St.

al-Salakhana St.

Ahmes St.

Mustafa

Train Station

Luxor Museum

Yusef Hassan St.

Cleopatra St.

al-Karnak St.

el-Nil St.

al-Mahatta St.

Muhammad Farid St.

Tourist Ferry

Mosque of Abu'l Haggag

Bus Station

Ahmed

Orabi St.

Luxor Temple

Tourist Bazaar

Television St.

Winter Palace Hotel

Local Ferry

Tourist Ferry

Salah al-Din Square

Local Ferry

Nile River

WEST THEBES

ern city devoted to fun and profit, filled with hotels, souvenir shops, and smiling dragomen willing to perform any service for as much as they can get. Fortunately, as the city is completely dependent on tourism, it's a buyer's market, particularly during the slow summer season. And though you may be nearly driven mad by the constant pestering of salesmen and beggars of every description, Luxor is a terrific town for the budget traveler: A few dollars per day will buy comfortable accommodations, good food, and access to unforgettable sights.

Built on the site of Thebes, capital of united Egypt during the New Kingdom (Eighteenth to Twentieth Dynasties, 1555-1090 B.C.E.), the town is custodian of some impressive monuments. The Temples of Karnak and Luxor right in the town move even jaded travelers with their overwhelming array of gateways and towering masses supported by forests of gigantic columns. Luxor's historic and artistic wealth spills over to the other side of the Nile, where fabulous tombs and temples fringe the West Theban plain. In the barren Valley of the Kings beyond, pharaohs such as Tut-Ankh-Amon achieved the immortality they sought: If their desired, supernatural methods did not work, the international fame of their exquisite rock-hewn tombs has done the job. Luxor is also well-suited to daytrips encompassing the antiquities at Abydos, Dendera, Edfu, or Esna.

Practical Information

Tourist Office: At the front of the tourist bazaar next to the New Winter Palace Hotel, just south of Luxor Temple on the Nile (tel. 822 15). Helpful, honest, English-speaking staff can tell you what the official rates should be for every service offered in Luxor—familiarize yourself with the price ranges. The free *Upper Egypt Night and Day* offers a limited train schedule. Flight information available. Open daily (including Ramadan) 8am-2pm and 3-8pm. Also in the **tourist bazaar** and at the **airport** (tel. 823 06). Open daily 8am-8pm.

Passport Office: el-Nil St. (tel. 823 18), 1 door south of the ETAP Hotel, on the north side of the Luxor City Council Building. Register your passport or extend your visa here in the foreigners office. Visa business in morning only. Open daily 9am-3pm and 6-9pm.

Banks: Misr Bank, al-Karnak St., next to Philip Hotel. Open daily 10am-1:30pm and 5-8pm. **Cairo Bank** in the lobby of ETAP hotel has longest hours, open 8am-10pm.

American Express: Old Winter Palace Hotel on el-Nil St. (tel. 828 62), south of Luxor Temple. Holds all mail. Traveler's checks sold to cardholders. No money wired. Open daily 8am-8pm.

Post Office: Main office (for Poste Restante), halfway down al-Mahatta St. Another branch in the bazaar near the tourist office. Both open Sun.-Thurs. 8am-2pm.

Telephones: Next to EgyptAir, in front of the Old Winter Palace Hotel off Nile St. **Central Telephone Office** is on al-Karnak St. behind ETAP Hotel. International and national calls (to Cairo LE1 minimum). Better, more expensive service at luxury hotels along the Nile, including the Savoy and ETAP (to Cairo LE1.50). **Telegrams** can be sent from the main post office or telephone offices, above.

Telephone Code: 095.

Airport: 5km northeast of town (tel. 820 77 or 848 72). Take a taxi. Served only by **EgyptAir** (tel. 820 40), next to the entrance of the Old Winter Palace Hotel. In summer, to Cairo (6 per day, LE89), to Aswan (3 per day, LE38). More flights in winter. Also to Abu Simbel—book 4 days ahead.

Train Station: At the head of al-Mahatta St. (Station St.), ¾ km inland from Luxor Temple. The station looks like a temple. If you're returning by train to Cairo, make reservations the day you arrive in Luxor. Trains to Cairo are very unreliable. With A/C: Recommended. 6 per day, 1st class LE12.55, 2nd class LE5.85, 12-13 hr.; regular: 6 additional per day, 2nd class LE3.45, 18 hr.). Also sleepers to Cairo (2 per day, 1st class LE124, 2nd class LE78). To Aswan (with A/C: 4 per day, 1st class LE8, 2nd class LE4, 5 hr.; regular: 2 additional per day, 2nd class LE2, 7 hr.). It's possible to pay a walk-on fee and travel without a guaranteed seat, but the trip to Cairo is too long to risk standing.

Bus Station: The most popular central station is at the intersection of al-Karnak and al-Mahatta St., by the mosque and the Horus Hotel. All buses stop here. Main Luxor terminal is on Television St. off Salah al-Din Sq., 4 blocks southwest of the train station. To Cairo

(2 express buses per day, non-A/C 5:15am, LE9, A/C 4pm, LE13; 13 hr.). From 6am to 3:30pm, buses run about every hour to Esna (LE1), Edfu (LE1.50), Kom Ombo (LE1.75), and Aswan (LE3); most buses to south are without A/C. To Qena (LE1) and northern Nile towns every 2 hr. 6am-3pm. To Hurghada (6am and noon, LE4, 4 hr.).

Service Taxis: al-Karnak St., 1 block inland from the Luxor Museum on the Nile. During early morning and late afternoon, service taxis leave every 15 min. for Qena (LE1.25, 1 hr.), Esna (LE1, 45 min.), Edfu (LE2, 1½ hr.), Kom Ombo (LE2.50, 2-3 hr.), and Aswan (LE4, 3-4 hr.).

English Bookstores: Aboudi Bookstore, in the tourist bazaar a few doors down from the tourist office, has a large selection. **Hachette Bookshop,** in the arcade of ETAP Hotel, has books on ancient Egypt as well as maps. A variety of publications can be bought at the kiosk in the train station.

Swimming Pools: Pools at several luxury hotels offer the best way to survive a summer afternoon in Luxor. The **Old Winter Palace Hotel** charges LE5 for a dip in a nice pool with water that occasionally tints your hair green (open daily 7am-sunset). The **ETAP Hotel,** 3 blocks north of Luxor Temple, charges LE6 for a swim.

24-Hour Pharmacy: Ahsraf pharmacy (tel. 828 34). Walk 200m on al-Karnak from intersection with al-Mahatta, turn right and then left on the next block. English spoken.

Hospital: el-Amiri Hospital, el-Nil St. (tel. 820 25), north of Luxor Museum near the youth hostel. English spoken. Open 24 hours.

Medical Emergency: Tel. 123.

Tourist Police: el-Nil St. (tel. 821 20), in the tourist bazaar. Also in train station (tel. 820 18). Both open 24 hours. Regular police (tel. 820 06), just west of al-Karnak St.

The town of Luxor simmers on the banks of the Nile, 670km upstream from Cairo and 220km downstream from Aswan. Surrounded by a heavily cultivated floodplain, Luxor is an agricultural center, with a weekly **vegetable market** (*souk*) in central Luxor on el-Souk St., and a weekly **camel market** in nearby el-Mesha village, both on Tuesdays. But it's the tourist industry that dominates life in Luxor. The scramble for tourist dollars reaches a fevered pitch on the streets around Luxor's three main landmarks: **Luxor Temple,** on the Nile at the center of town; the **train station,** ¾ km inland on the eastern edge of Luxor; and **Karnak Temple,** 3km northeast of the first two at the northern fringe of town.

Although there are only a few street signs and even fewer maps in town, you should not have any trouble finding your way around Luxor as long as you know the three main thoroughfares: **al-Mahatta Street** ("Station") runs perpendicular to the Nile; **el-Nil Street** along the Nile; and **al-Karnak Street** runs parallel to el-Nil.

Since Luxor is a small town, you can easily get around by foot. **Horse-drawn carriages** (*kalishes*) will pester you as you walk along the Nile. A carriage ride can be worthwhile for transport of baggage, for the trip out to Karnak Temple, or for romance. Don't pay more than LE1 for a trip in town and LE2 for the trip to Karnak. Renting a **bicycle,** a wise move in Luxor, is inexpensive. Bike shops are everywhere in central Luxor, and the competition keeps rates down to LE1.50-3 for a full day. Hotels are usually the best place to ask—for example the New Karnak Hotel rents bikes for LE2 and obliges early morning requests. Places on the main street charge LE3, and that is the maximum you should pay. Locks are included. Nothing feels better than to speed by the *kalishes* on their way to Karnak Temple, and you're less likely to be pestered on a bike.

Luxor moves at a frenetic pace. Hotels and pensions go up and come down, opening and closing with alarming frequency: Be sure your chosen abode still exists. On a grander scale, teams of Egyptians and Chinese work to transform Luxor's central riverfront. By 1989, locals brag, el-Nil Street will rival Aswan's corniche in Nile-side elegance. As the completion date keeps floating downriver, the site remains an eyesore. A good sense of humor is a must if you're planning to stay here, and *La, Shokran* (no thank you) a necessary ammunition against the pharaonic armies of pestering salespeople and carriage drivers.

Accommodations and Camping

Choose your hotel carefully in Luxor. Most of the budget hotels cluster around the train station, lining al-Mahatta St. and the streets immediately to the north and south. Cheap, comfortable pensions are grouped mostly around Television St., off Salah al-Din Sq. As you exit the station you will be approached by hawkers offering you hotel rooms; often these are comfortable but small pensions and hotels with no other way to attract customers. Many people follow the hawkers back to surprisingly pleasant rooms; a few are surprised in a more nasty manner. Once you are at their hotel they will do almost anything to keep you; waving your *Let's Go* and naming some other hotel you intend to visit might knock a pound off the price. The budget hotel owners of Luxor will climb all over each other in their competition for guests. Usually the traveler benefits, but some very slippery characters are out there. See the room before you take it and make sure the price you're offered is inclusive.

Virtually every hotel charges its maximum official rate in winter, but shaves off taxes, service fees, and another pound or two in the off-season. The result: Prices in summer may be up to 50% lower than in winter, making even some luxury hotels a bargain. "Summer" generally means mid-April through the end of October. The cheapest hotels often raise their rates only in December and January. Competition is usually fierce, and starving student types can shave some piasters or pounds off almost any price at any time of year. At many inexpensive hotels, you can sleep on a roof or a terrace for LE2 per person. In most hotels listed, hot water and fans are the rule.

Youth Hostel, 16 al-Karnak St. (tel. 821 39), 200m north of the service taxi station, halfway between Karnak and Luxor Temples, across from the YMCA camp. Modern and relatively clean, but inconveniently located. Grimy bathrooms. Lockers for backpacks. Flexible lock-out. Dorm beds LE3, doubles LE8. Nonmembers required to purchase a guest card for LE1.

New Karnak Hotel, opposite the train station (tel. 824 27). Justifiably popular—tidy and comfortable, with friendly management. Fills up any time of year. Singles LE4.50. Doubles LE6, with bath LE8.

Negem El-Din Pension, Ramses St. (tel. 823 52), next to the railway tracks. If you are wondering why such a pleasant place, with a kitchen, washing machine, and tropical garden with restaurant is so cheap, wait for the first midnight train to roar by your window. LE2 per person; in winter LE3-4. A few rooms with A/C LE3.50 per person. Omelette breakfast LE1.

Sphinx Hotel, Yusef Hasan St. (tel. 828 30). From the train station head 3 blocks north to the end of Ramses St., then 3 blocks west on Yusef Hasan. Comfortable rooms are cleaned daily. Amiable staff creates a homey atmosphere. Fans in every room. Singles LE5, doubles LE7, triples LE10.50; in winter singles LE7, doubles LE9, triples LE11. In both seasons, LE1 extra for private bath. Complete meals LE3.50.

Akhnaton Hotel, al-Manshiya St. (tel. 839 79), on the second sidestreet to the right as you head south on al-Manshiya from the train station square. Attractive and nice, with carpets, a TV lounge, restaurant, and tacky party decorations in lobby. Some rooms with private showers. Singles LE5, doubles LE9, triples LE13. Breakfast included.

Salah el Din, al-Manshiya Sq. A 10-min. walk from the train station, south on al-Manshiya to Salah al-Din Sq. Pleasant, with some balconies overlooking the square. Fans in every room. Singles LE4, with bath LE5. Doubles LE8, with bath LE10.

Sinai Hotel, Gesr al-Awamia St. (tel. 847 52), off Television St. From the train station, follow al-Manshiya St. south to Salah al-Din Sq., and continue south to Television Sq. (300m total). From the small market area at the base of Television St., angle off to the right up Gesr al-Awamia (heading south). The hotel's red sign is 150m down the street. Simple, spotless, and silent. Worth the walk to its inconvenient location. Big rooms with fans and good-hearted management. Singles LE6, with shower LE9. Doubles LE10, with shower LE15. Triples LE15, with shower LE20. Breakfast included.

Atlas Hotel, Ahmed Orabi St. (tel. 835 14), a long 300m west of Salah al-Din Sq. A bit run-down; its only highlights are three of the cheapest A/C rooms in town. Enterprising owner "Dr." Ahmed, who has his eyes set squarely on your wallet, offers overpriced tours. In summer singles LE6, with A/C LE9. Doubles LE10, with A/C LE12. Breakfast included.

Ramoza Hotel, al-Mahatta St. (tel. 822 70), on your right as you walk toward Luxor Temple from the station. Near all the train station area cafes. Spotless. A/C. Hot private showers. Singles LE16.65, doubles LE19.40, triples LE24. Management might shave off a pound or two in the summer. Breakfast included.

Nile Hotel, Nefertiti St. (tel. 828 59), just in from the Nile, 200m north of Luxor Temple. Near the ETAP hotel. A classy but slightly impersonal Nile-side retreat with reasonable prices. Sparsely furnished but immaculate rooms with carpets and A/C. Singles LE14, doubles LE20, triples LE25; in winter singles LE16, doubles LE22, triples LE27. Prices lower for groups and longer stays. Continental breakfast included. The **Hotel Phillipe** next door is nearly identical and a few pounds more expensive.

Grand Hotel, Muhammad Farid St. (tel. 841 86). Walk down al-Manshiya from the train station; turn left after 200m. Not sparkling, and a bit smelly, but the most caring management in Luxor. Fans in each of the small rooms, yet it still overheats in the summer. A bargain. Singles LE2.50, doubles LE5. Breakfast LE1.

Pensions: Luxor offers several very small, homey, inexpensive hotels. Most are clustered around Television St., 300m southwest of the train station off al-Manshiya St. Intimate atmosphere, eccentric management, and unusual decor are the rule.

> **Nubia Home,** off Gesr al-Awamia. On the way to Sinai Hotel, look right to the alley beyond the market area. Lives up to the name with its Nubian élan. Friendly and mellow managers look after their guests, sometimes providing free meals and arranging free seats on bus tours. Refrigerator, kitchen, TV, and a washing machine at your service. Singles LE3, doubles LE6, spacious quad LE8.
>
> **Titi Hotel** (tel. 838 03), off Television St. 1 block past the bus station and to the right. Spotless, classy, and well-managed. Owner Ahmed seems to care for his guests and speaks superb English as well. Rates negotiable, starting with LE3 for a bed. Home-cooked meals available and highly praised.
>
> **Princess Pension** (tel. 839 97), off Television St. behind the bus station. You won't be treated like a princess, but it's clean and homey, with refrigerator and washing machine. Beds LE3.50; in winter LE4.50. Breakfast included. Bike rental LE2.
>
> **Happy Home,** near the station, down the first street to the left as you walk down al-Mahatta St. Friendly manager Muhammad Esnawi keeps a small, clean establishment with hot water, fans in each room, kitchen, and refrigerator. LE3 per person, doubles LE5.
>
> **Pension Roma,** Sidi Abu al-Haggag St., north of the corner cafe, off Television St. The current home of ever-popular proprietor Michael Jackson and his precocious younger brother. Very small and intimate—perhaps uncomfortably so. Beds LE3. Breakfast LE1.50.

The **YMCA Day-Camp,** on al-Karnak St. (tel. 824 25) offers a flat, grassy area for tents and caravans. During the summer, the grounds are bright and noisy with Egyptians frolicking until midnight or later. Still, you can use the hot shower and the somewhat filthy toilets, and the walled camp is guarded all day and night. (LE2 per person, vehicles 50pt-LE1.) The camp is about 1½km from Luxor Temple on the east side of al-Karnak St., roughly halfway to Karnak Temple, just north of the service taxi station.

Food

Luxor's inexpensive restaurants huddle around the train station. The cheapest filling meal in town can be purchased at the *kushari* joint on your left as you walk down al-Mahatta St. from the station (20pt per plate). If you arrive in the middle of the night, the only place open will be the outdoor *kufte* grill to the right as you walk out of the train station. *Kufte,* salad, bread, and *tahina* sell for LE2.50. On al-Mahatta St., **Mensa** restaurant on the right as you walk toward Luxor Temple has great shish kebab for LE3.50.

Luxor's market street intersects with al-Mahatta St. Most of the vegetable and fruit stalls lie between al-Mahatta and Yusef Hasan St. Tuesday, market day, draws farmers and shoppers from the surrounding region. Beat the summer heat with a cool, juicy watermelon (about LE1.50 for a medium-sized one). Along al-Mahatta St. and on al-Karnak St. where it meets Luxor Temple, you can cool off with fresh juices from numerous **juice stalls** (15-50pt per glass). Tamarind, coconut, mango, and strawberry are local favorites. On the southern side of al-Mahatta St., about halfway down the street, you'll find one of the half-dozen sugar cane juice stalls, where a great cubic machine takes in fresh stalks through its square mouth, spitting pulverized husks out the back, and squirting sweet, delicious juice out the front.

New Karnak Student Restaurant, next to the hotel of the same name. Great snacks, prompt service, unbeatable student prices. Eggs (scrambled, fried, or boiled) 75pt, rice or potatoes with tomato sauce 50pt, spaghetti with tomato sauce 50pt, chicken soup 30pt, ¼ roast chicken LE1.25, commercial ice cream 50pt, and excellent eggplant 50pt.

Amoun Restaurant, al-Karnak St., just north of Luxor Temple. Good bargain. Large meal of chicken, fish, or beef kebab with potatoes, rice, salad and bread, LE4. Cafe next door. The **El Patio** restaurant, on the same street nearer the temple, is similar.

Marhaba, overlooking Luxor Temple near the New Winter Palace Hotel. Brash young waiters in fake Arab garb. Great views. On the expensive side, LE5.20 for shish kebab, grilled pigeon, or fish. Prices do not include 20% tax and service.

Restaurant Limpy, al-Mahatta St., next to the New Karnak Hotel. Not the most gracious place, but a comfortable outdoor terrace and decent food. A good place to meet travelers for *felucca* excursions and trips to Thebes. Full meal with chicken or kebab LE2.75. Yogurt 30pt. Breakfast LE1.

Sights

Luxor itself offers only three tourist sights. You can visit Luxor Temple, Karnak Temple, and the Luxor Museum in one day, but most visitors prefer to visit them on separate afternoons or evenings, after spending the cool morning in West Thebes.

Luxor Temple

The graceful columns of Luxor Temple, visible from al-Mahatta St., rise in the heart of modern Luxor on the east bank of the Nile. The first work on the temple was done under the New Kingdom Pharaoh Amenhotep III, who built on the site of a small Middle Kingdom temple to Amon-Ra and rededicated it to Amon, his wife Mut, and their son, the moon god Khonsu. The unfinished work of Amenhotap was completed under Tut-Ankh-Amon. The most significant later contributions were those of Ramses II, among which are the six large statues of himself that guard the entrance. The sanctuary was later restored under Alexander the Great. When Christianity came to Luxor, part of the complex was used as a church. Only an altar and a few mosaics are left from this period, but the **Mosque of Abu'l-Haggag,** added by the Fatimids, still stands in the temple court. It remains in active use, and in 1968 it was even expanded by local Muslims while the Egyptologists were away on summer vacation.

The doorway to the temple's interior is cut through the enormous **Pylon of Ramses II,** nearly 24m tall. Flanking the main doorway are two of the six original **Colossi of Ramses II,** as well as a pink granite obelisk with four praying baboons on one side. The obelisk's identical twin was removed in 1836 and stands in the Place de la Concorde in Paris. Carved reliefs on the pylon describe Ramses' battles against the Hittites. Double rows of monumental papyriform columns with lotus-bud capitals surround the open **Court of Ramses II,** with its huge statues of Ramses II. The more sacred **Temple of Amon, Mut, and Khonsu** lies to the right of the court.

Continue through the court to reach the **Colonnade of Amenhotap III,** with its fourteen pillars crowned by Egyptian lotus-bud capitals. From here, proceed into the **Court of Amenhotap III.** Notice the traces of the original coloring on the architraves; it is likely that much of the temple complex was originally painted in this manner. Beyond this second court rises the hypostyle hall, or antechamber, with its 32 enormous columns set in four rows. Latin inscriptions to Julius Caesar adorn an altar in one of the rooms to the left of the pillared hall. Alexander appears before Amon and other deities in some bas-reliefs in the **Sanctuary of Alexander the Great** at the end of the corridor.

Daytime temperatures can be unbearable, so visit at night if possible, when the dark silky Nile flows by the illuminated interior. Bats dart about, an eerie flutter of wings in the almost deserted temple. An early-morning visit will complement the nocturnal one, revealing details of the temple as well as its overall structure.

(Temple open in summer daily 6am-10pm; in winter daily 6am-9pm; during Ramadan, 6am-6:30pm and 8-11pm. The lights go on year-round at 7:30pm. Admission LE2, students with ISIC LE1.)

Karnak Temple

Overwhelming in its complexity and its mammoth proportions, Karnak Temple stuns visitors. Every major period in the ancient history of Egypt is represented by its additions to this complex of shrines dedicated to Amon and his family. Karnak came to represent the power of Amon and the importance of his cult throughout the Egyptian world, as well as to testify to the greatness of the Theban rulers.

On the way from Luxor Temple to Karnak, recall that Luxor was the site of an annual festival honoring the god Amon. A great procession accompanied a statue of the deity from Karnak Temple along the river to Luxor Temple. The entire 3km distance between the two great temples was connected by the sacred **Avenue of the Sphinxes**—a paved boulevard lined on both sides with hundreds of majestic, human-headed lions, each holding a statuette of Ramses II between its paws. The final stretch of the avenue remains, complete with two rows of sphinxes. You'll find the sphinxes at the northern end of al-Karnak St. by the **Temple of Khonsu** to the right of the main entry to Karnak Temple.

Enter **Karnak Temple** from the west with the Nile at your back, and pass through a double row of ram-headed sphinxes (unrelated to the avenue described above). The temple is a melange of additions and alterations spanning millennia, but because of the traditionalism of pharaonic architecture, the different pieces hold together as a whole. The deeper you proceed from the entrance on the west, the farther back in time you go.

From the Ptolemaic and Roman outer gate and wall you gaze down a sacred boulevard, past pylons and doorways from every era, straight into the holiest of holies—the inner sanctuary of Amon. The first pylon is Ptolemaic (second century B.C.E.), and the eighth is the contribution of Queen Hatshepsut (fifteenth century B.C.E.). The tenth-century B.C.E. **Great Court,** the area before you as you emerge from the first pylon, is the largest single portion of the complex at Karnak. Chambers on the left are dedicated to the Theban Triad of Amon, Mut, and Khonsu. They were built during the Twenty-ninth Dynasty and adorned with bas-reliefs depicting the deities. On the right is a temple built by Ramses III; the three chapels behind its inner court are also dedicated to the Theban Triad.

Return to the Great Court and continue to the right into the **Great Hypostyle Hall,** one of the pinnacles of pharaonic architecture, with its sandstone forest of 134 colossal papyrus columns. Many of the pillars still wear bright paint, and every square centimeter of the ceiling, walls, and columns is carved with inscriptions. Note the abundance of boastful depictions of the fertility god, Nim, with spectacular erections.

Beyond the Great Hypostyle Hall lies the **Central Hall,** where you can make a foray through the fourth, fifth, and sixth pylons, or turn south toward the seventh through tenth pylons. Next to the seventh pylon are statues of Thutmosis III and several other royal personages carved in limestone and granite. The ninth and tenth pylons are officially closed for excavation but *baksheesh* usually reopens them.

Walking east toward the fourth pylon, you will find the **Obelisk of Queen Hatshepsut,** carved in pink granite, at the center of a small colonnade. Passing through the rubble of the fifth pylon and the granite sixth pylon, enter the **Hall of Records,** where two elegantly proportioned granite pillars stand, one decorated with carvings of the lotus of Upper Egypt, the other with the papyrus of Lower Egypt. Behind the hall, the **Sanctuary of the Sacred Boats** is a double-chambered chapel famous for its exquisite carvings, many of which still retain their original color. The chapel's ceilings are adorned with the stars of the night sky. The building is open on both ends, and the outside southern wall is particularly well-preserved, with scenes of the sacred boats of Amon's annual procession.

Straight ahead, the **Festival Hall of Thutmose III** dominates the eastern edge of the Karnak complex. The roof survives intact, supported by 52 tapering pillars.

Some of the bases were actually whittled down to make room for large processions. In Christian times, the hall was converted into a church; frescoes of haloed saints still adorn the interior walls and column shafts. Beyond a low wall to the east, the **Gate of Nectanebo** marks an early entrance to the complex.

Retrace your steps to the great court, turn left and walk 50m to glimpse, on your left and south of the Festival Hall, the limpid waters of **Birket al-Mallaha** (Sacred Lake). Priests purified themselves in the holy waters of this rectangular pool before performing ceremonies within the temple. At the northwest corner, an enormous rose-colored granite scarab, a symbol of the rising sun, sits atop a stone. The scarab was dedicated by Amenhotap III to the sun god Atum-Khepri. A small cafe next to the lake offers refreshments at outlandish prices.

It will take at least one and a half hours to see the entire complex, so in summer it is advisable to bring bottled water and come early. Equip yourself with Jill Kamil's excellent paperback guide *Luxor,* or tag along with a tour group. The temple lies 3km north of Luxor Temple at the end of al-Karnak St., 1 block east of el-Nil St. (Admission LE3, students LE1.50. Temple open daily sunrise-6pm; in mid-summer sunrise-7pm; and in mid-winter sunrise-5pm.) Walk or bike along the Nile or take a horse-drawn carriage. With a lot of bargaining, you can cut the standard tourist price of LE2-3 down to LE1. A local service taxi runs between Karnak and the station (20pt).

If you space out during the nightly 90-minute **sound and light show** at Karnak Temple, you're in the correct state of mind. Most of the narration is uninspired and melodramatic, but the pharaonic ruins take nicely to illumination. Throngs of noisy shutterbugs will probably keep you from getting full value from your LE10 payment. (Shows in English Mon., Wed., and Sat. at 8pm, Fri. at 10pm.)

Luxor Museum

The Luxor Museum, facing the Nile midway between Luxor and Karnak Temples, has a small, high-quality collection. Beautiful treasures from the neighboring temple complexes and the Valley of the Kings, including the celebrated tomb of King Tut-Ankh-Amon, beckon visitors away from the outdoor sites. The stunning gold-inlaid wooden bust of Hathor, the cow goddess that welcomed Tut to the underworld, welcomes you as you enter the museum. In the main hall straight ahead, you will see the exquisite statue of King Thutmose III (1490-1436 B.C.E.). His sculpted image conveys youth, majesty, and unimaginable power. To the right is an unforgettable glowing duo of Sobek and Amenhotap III (1403-1362 B.C.E.) set in alabaster—sort of an "Ancient Egyptian Gothic." On the highest level, two haunting busts of Amenhotap IV exhibit unusual elongated features. This humanistic depiction contrasts with the idealized style favored by the pharaonic artisans. Amenhotap squints across the hall at a large case containing arrows and model funeral boats from Tut-Ankh-Amon's tomb, and the astonishingly brilliant mummy casing of Shepenkhonsu, a tenth-century B.C.E. noblewoman buried in the Asasif tombs. The museum has taken several statues of Sakhmet from Karnak's Temple of Mut. The image of this cold-eyed, strangely buxom lion-goddess may haunt you for days.

The museum is within easy walking distance (1½km) of both Luxor and Karnak Temples. Its hours are daily 4-10pm in summer, daily 4-9pm in winter. (Admission LE2, students LE1.)

Entertainment

Late afternoons in Luxor, especially in summer, are most pleasantly spent relaxing aboard a *felucca* on the Nile. **Banana Island** is a popular destination: Two miles upriver, it is a small peninsula studded with palms and fruit trees where you can eat small, green, tasty bananas for LE1. The souvenir stands and overpriced soft drinks detract from the experience. The round-trip to Banana Island takes two to three hours; for a group of four people, a fair price is LE5 per person plus tip. For other excursions you should pay no more than LE10 per hour; in the summer bargaining can save you half that. *Feluccas* are prohibited from sailing after 8pm.

Escape from Luxor's heat and tourist farmers by swimming at the ETAP and Winter Palace Hotels. The ETAP pool is open late at night and the poolside Egyptian band plays '50s music. If you look like you belong, you may not be charged. Most of the large hotels along the Nile open their doors to casual visitors, offering nightclubs and bars to those willing to part with their pounds. A low-budget alternative, Luxor's numerous **sidewalk cafes** buzz with flies and the nightly conversations of the town's male population. Try challenging one of the locals to a game of dominos. Foreign women won't necessarily feel uncomfortable at a cafe, but a woman sitting alone is sure to attract lots of attention.

West Thebes

The rulers of Thebes spent their days grandly on the east bank of the Nile, then after their deaths grandly occupied the west bank. The ancient kings apparently all aspired to a tomb with a view on the Nile's western shore, which consequently overflows with tombs, temples, and treasures. The necropolis of Thebes is possibly the world's most richly endowed graveyard. Over the course of centuries, robbers and archeologists have pilfered much of the treasure, but the necropolis features an unparalleled collection of Egyptian funerary art.

Security was the main concern of the Middle Kingdom rulers who built the Theban tombs. Thieves had become so adept at entering the pyramids of Memphis, the capital of the Old Kingdom, and making off with the articles meant to accompany the pharaohs into the afterlife, that the royal mummies had barely been wrapped up before their precious belongings—and sometimes even their bandages—were ripped off. A radical change in burial practices was essential to ensure proper treatment of the dead.

The western edge of Thebes, capital city of the New Kingdom, was selected as the site for all subsequent tombs. In order to conceal the location, contents, and design of the tombs, the work was carried out in utmost secrecy by a team of laborers who dwelt within the necropolis itself. Perfecting techniques of tomb construction, decoration, and mummification, this community of 300 craftspeople devoted themselves to the City of the Dead over the course of generations, handing their knowledge down through their families. (Remains of the workers' walled city have been excavated near the Temple of Dayr al-Medina.) Tomb design reflected the new emphasis on secrecy. Instead of a single ostentatious pyramid, there were pairs of funerary monuments: an underground grave, lavishly outfitted with the articles needed for the afterlife and sequestered in an obscure recess of the desert, and a grandiose mortuary temple where the monarch could be worshiped for eternity. False passages, fake sarcophagi, hidden doorways, and deep shafts, were designed to foil even the most cunning robbers. Once a deceased pharaoh was safely stowed, workers immediately began to construct the tomb destined for his successor.

One area in particular seemed ideal for entombment: a narrow, winding valley ringed on three sides by jagged limestone cliffs and approached by a single rocky footpath. This isolated canyon, known as the **Valley of the Kings,** became the burial place of New Kingdom pharaohs. Although it looked great on the drawing board, it failed to deter the grave-robbers. Few of the tombs managed to escape vandalism.

Queens and favored consorts were accorded ceremonial burial with full honors and security precautions in a separate corner of West Thebes, the **Valley of the Queens.** The highest members of the Theban aristocracy also practiced the elaborate burial customs. Numbering over 300 in all, several of the **Tombs of the Nobles** rival the royal burial chambers in quality of craft and design. There are over 400 tombs in all of West Thebes. While the hot, dry climate preserved the painted walls from the elements, the elaborate subterfuges managed to save some of the tombs from the burglars.

Practical Information

If you visit West Thebes in the summer, take the following advice to heart: Start early in the morning, preferably with the sun at 5am. Summer afternoons on the west bank of the Nile are brutally hot, and most of the guards close up the antiquities and head home after 2pm. Explore during a series of early morning visits. The sun cooks visitors after 9am, which is also when most tourists finish breakfast and invade. All sites open at 6am, offering about three hours of peace and pleasant temperatures. The sites officially close at 4pm in winter, and at 5pm in summer. Drinks are sold at some of the ruins but usually at high prices—bring plenty of water.

To reach West Thebes from Luxor, take one of the ferries. **Tourist ferries** operate frequently for 35pt round-trip (ask for a return voucher; bikes 25pt), more often than the local ferries. One tourist ferry docks next to the Savoy Hotel, 300m north of the temple. The other docks in front of the Winter Palace Hotel, 200m south of Luxor Temple (closed in the summer of 1988 due to corniche construction). Both tourist ferries shuttle you to the main (non-student) ticketing office on the west bank. (Ferries operate daily 6am-6pm.)

Two **local ferries** (10pt each, bicycles 15pt) run frequently as well, and are more picturesque, though they sometimes wait as long as 30 minutes before leaving. One docks next to the Mena Palace Hotel, just north of Luxor Temple; the other, which carries cars, docks at a well-marked spot near the ETAP hotel, 300m north of Luxor Temple. Both local ferries take you to the southern dock on the west bank. From the dock, head inland to the student ticket kiosk, where non-students may also purchase tickets (see below). Modest dress is *de rigeur* on the local ferries, which are intended primarily for the *fellaheen* (peasant farmers) of the West Theban Plain. (Ferries operate daily 6am-midnight.)

Once on the west bank, car-free travelers have three transportation options: bicycle, taxi, or donkey. In winter, **bicycles** are the most practical and economical choice. Rent before crossing the river, since bikes are harder to find on the west bank. (See Practical Information above.) Bicyclists will find little traffic on the well-paved roads. Still, moto-cross skills will come in handy at some sites, particularly in the unpaved area around the Tombs of the Nobles.

A typical day in West Thebes might involve 20km to 30km of cycling. In winter, cycling allows you to determine your own pace and routes. In summer, however, when temperatures approach 46°C, bike riding can be hazardous even in the early morning. The ride to the main complex is uphill, and the road to the Valley of the Kings is a low-grade but relentless climb. Do the tough haul during the cool early morning, and the downhill return in the afternoon.

Hiring a **taxi** for the day is surprisingly economical and allows you to cover the most ground. The fare for a small cab (1 to 4 passengers) should be LE12, for a large cab (5 to 8 passengers) LE15. Approach tourists in Luxor (try the New Karnak Student Restaurant), and ask if they would like to share the cost of a taxi. Then come early and bargain hard with the drivers who wait at both the northern (tourist) and southern (local) ferry docks. Ignore any prattle about government rates and per-person charges. You must state not only your price, but also the period of time for which you will require the driver's services. At the end of the trip, *baksheesh* of LE1-2 is in order, unless the driver was incompetent.

Mark Twain wrote that riding a **donkey** in Egypt "was a fresh, new exhilirating sensation, this donkey riding, and worth a hundred worn and threadbare pleasures." Regardless, don't pay more than LE5 for three hours on even the best-looking of these plodding beasts. You will, however, have to pay extra for a guide, so the bigger your party, the better. (The price should be the same—approximately LE2 for the guide and another LE2 for his donkey—regardless of how many are in his charge.) Make sure you like your guide; some of Luxor's less charming donkey guides may attempt to extort money from tourists and knock them off their donkeys if they don't pay. Although slow, the donkeys offer more versatility than bikes or taxis, since they can take the spectacular, if precipitous, paths that crisscross the limestone ridges on which the various sights are scattered. The traverse from the Valley of the Queens or Dayr el-Bahri over the ridges to the Valley of the Kings makes an especially fun donkey trip.

In the winter, hardy souls with time to spare can get around **by foot.** You might want to hitchhike to the student ticket kiosk (3km from the ferry dock) or take a local taxi there (about 25pt). Most of the Theban Necropolis and the Valley of the Queens lies within 3km of the kiosk. The Valley of the Kings lies an easy 8km away by road, or a few strenuous ones by donkey path.

Guided tours in air-conditioned coaches with English-speaking guides can be arranged through the various corniche travel agents and cost LE30-40 per person including admission. Most tours visit Valley of the Kings, Valley of the Queens, Collossi of Memnon, and Hatshepsut Temple. The larger your group, the better your bargaining power. Often the travel agencies will have prearranged tours and you can tag along for under LE20. Isis Travel and Misr Travel on the corniche are good ones to start with, but shop around. The loss of spontaneity, adventure, and independence may be balanced by the gain of convenient transportation and a more thorough description of the sights.

Try to bring a **flashlight** when visiting West Thebes. In the Tombs of the Nobles, and to a lesser extent elsewhere, a flashlight will save you the necessity of paying *baksheesh* to guards and will enable you to see much more. Photography is prohibited at all sites, and the regulation is enforced with a vengeance, since flashes spoil the paintings.

Although most travelers receive their fill of West Theban sights in two or three days' worth of excursion, the wealth of ancient relics could occupy even a casual Egyptologist for weeks. The best inexpensive specialized guidebook to the area is Jill Kamil's paperback *Luxor* (LE8-12), available at bookstores in town. The most thorough, though far more expensive, coverage readily available in English is Nagel's *Encyclopedic Guide to Egypt.*

Accommodations and Food

Only a few hotels are located on the west bank, and with one exception they are not as comfortable as those in Luxor. However, by staying here you can be at the sights as early as possible, and the tranquil settings are a respite from the bustle of Luxor. The five hotels listed are within ½km of the student kiosk, convenient to all the sights. A taxi from the ferry docks should cost LE1. If you intend to bike here, try to arrange a two or three day rental in Luxor through one of the hotels before you cross the river.

Food is available from the hotels, as indicated below. The official **rest houses** by the Ramasseum and in the Valley of the Kings serve drinks year-round and offer meals in the winter season. Both close at around 1:30pm in the summer. All the hotels offer the use of refrigerators to their guests.

Queens Hotel, near Medinat Habu Temple. Pleasant and hospitable, with a colorful interior and a rooftop terrace. The friendly elderly manager, Hag Ali, will be proud to show you a copy of the portrait of himself in the Brooklyn Academy of Art or the letters of recommendation written for him by archeologists. LE3 per person, with breakfast LE3.50. Complete and plentiful meals of beef or chicken LE4, arranged upon request.

Hotel Habou, facing Medinat Habu Temple (tel. 824 77 or 826 77 in Luxor), ½km southwest of the student kiosk. Nubian style domed roofs keep the air cool in summer, warm in winter. Simple, clean, colorful rooms. Shared baths and fans. Run by a charming family. Singles LE6, doubles LE10; cheaper in summer. Sleep on terrace, or in winter only, **camp** in guarded backyard for LE1-1.50 per person. Standard **meals** for guests or travelers in pleasant blue restaurant or leafy patio: breakfast LE1.50, lunch or dinner LE5. Mineral water, tea, coffee, or *karkaday* available anytime.

Pharaoh's Hotel, 100m due south of the student kiosk along an unpaved road. Has the aura of a Greek villa. New, stylishly decorated, and very comfortable: the height of luxury in the area. All rooms with A/C. Singles LE15, doubles LE25; in winter singles LE35, dougles LE45. Breakfast included.

Hotel Marsam, across the road from the student kiosk (tel. 824 03). Rustic and exotic setting—Spanish style adobe with surroundig lush fields. Dine with the resident Italian archeologists on duck, rice, and eggplant for LE4-5. Rooms LE8. Breakfast included. Bike rental LE2.

Hotel Memnon, next to the Colossi of Memnon (tel. 860 05), ½ km southeast of student kiosk. Monastic: Hard beds and bare rooms, offset by an atmosphere of peace and calm. Beds LE5, breakfast included. Complete lunch or dinner LE5. **Camping** in the shade LE2 per person. Campers have access to facilities, including a kitchen of sorts.

Tickets

Buying tickets to the tombs and temples can be a complicated affair. There are two ticket kiosks. The one for non-students is on the west bank of the Nile next to the tourist ferry dock. The student kiosk is 3km farther inland, just beyond the Colossi of Memnon. Non-students can also use this ticket kiosk. Both kiosks are open daily 6am-4pm.) Decide which antiquities you want to visit and buy the appropriate numbered tickets. Non-student prices are as follows (student discount is 50%, ISIC required):

#1	Valley of the Kings	LE5
#2	Dayr al-Bahri (Temple of Hatshepsut)	LE2
#3	Medinat Habu (Temple of Ramses III)	LE2
#4	Ramasseum	LE1
#5	Asasif Tombs	LE1
#6	Tombs of Nakht and Mena (closed for restoration in 1988)	LE1
#7	Tombs of Rekhmire and Sennofer	LE1
#8	Tombs of Ramose, Userhet, and Khaemt	LE1
#9	Dayr al-Medina (Temple and Tombs)	LE1
#10	Valley of the Queens (Tomb of Nefertari closed for restoration in 1988.)	LE1
#11	Seti Temple	LE1

You really must plan ahead if you don't want to join the masses who buy more than they can use. A ticket is valid only for the day of purchase, and there is no refund for unused tickets. Furthermore, it is impossible to buy tickets anywhere except at the ticket kiosks, or to enter a site without an admission ticket. You probably will not be permitted to buy, nor have time to use, more than five separate tickets. If you're staying for more than a day, break your visit to West Thebes into geographical segments that eliminate doubling back. A logical, if incredibly crammed, morning itinerary would cover the Valley of the Kings, Dayr al-Bahri, Valley of the Queens, and lastly Medinat Habu. The Tombs of the Nobles and the Ramasseum are less frequented, though by no means deserted. There is no need to shy away from the pages of description following. The sights are divided into four sections: Valley of the Kings (ticket #1); Mortuary Temples (tickets #2, 3, 4, and 11); Tombs of the Nobles (tickets #5-9); and the Valley of the Queens (ticket #10). The crucial sights are listed at the beginning of each section.

Valley of the Kings

Seen from the town of Luxor, the sun sets behind a barren limestone ridge on the far side of the Theban Plain. The Valley of the Kings, tucked in behind this ridge, lies only 5km from the Nile, yet is accessible only via long, circuitous routes. From either ferry dock, head inland toward the ridge and the temples of the Necropolis of Thebes. There are two possible routes to the beginning of the Valley road. Students must head 3km straight inland past the Colossi of Memnon, to the student kiosk, then northeast past the sites of the necropolis to the beginning of the Valley road. Non-students with tickets from the Nile-side office can turn right (northeast) at the canal (follow the signs), and go 2km along the canal, then turn west by the Abul Kasem Hotel and go 1½ km to the base of the Valley road. The well-paved, gently sloping road winds for 5km into desolate, sweltering mountain valleys. The Valley of the Kings itself, no more than 400m long and 200m wide, can easily be toured by foot with the aid of clearly marked, well-groomed gravel paths. Over 64 known and numbered tombs honeycomb the valley. Many of them are not open to the public, but the best-known tombs are almost always accessible. Some are kept locked and can be opened only by a guard. All tombs listed are illuminated with fluorescent lights, but a flashlight reveals dark side chambers.

Below are described the tombs that attract the most people; there are many others that are still worth exploring. If you are pressed for time, and want just the greatest hits, visit #6, 17, and 35.

Just around the corner, in front of the Rest House, is West Thebes' most renowned and, to those who don't see it first, most anticlimactic tourist attraction: the **Tomb of Tut-Ankh-Amon (#62).** Its celebrated discovery in 1922 unearthed a cache of priceless pharaonic treasures that has toured the world several times and is now resides permanently in the Egyptian Museum in Cairo. Archeologist Howard Carter, convinced that the young pharaoh Tut-Ankh-Amon had been buried near his ancestors in a splendidly outfitted tomb, set out to uncover "King Tut's" grave. Egyptologists had expected that the tomb would contain little of interest because the pharaoh reigned only a short time before he died. The determined archeologist, ignoring professional censure, toiled for six seasons in the Valley of the Kings. Finally, after more than 200,000 tons of rubble had been moved, Carter began to lose heart. Even his sympathetic patron, the wealthy Lord Carnarvon, reluctantly decided to cut off funding for the project. But before admitting failure, Carter made one last attempt. The final unexplored possibility was a site beneath the tomb of Ramses VI, in an area covered with workers' huts. Beneath these shanties an ancient door was found. Carter wired Lord Carnarvon in London, who journeyed to Egypt for the tomb's opening. This sensational event revealed a breathtaking store of riches, vindicating Carter beyond his wildest dreams. The tomb had remained almost intact, barely disturbed by robbers for centuries; it was crammed with decorated furniture, wheat, vegetables, wine, clothing, canopic jars, jewelry, and utensils—even several royal walking sticks—and three mummies, including that of King Tut himself. Carter, under-employed for so long, was kept busy for 10 years cataloging the contents.

Tut's mummy was encased in close fitting, superbly-decorated coffins that closed around each other like Russian wooden dolls. The most famous is currently in the Cairo Museum, but the breathtaking innermost mummy case of solid gold, studded with decorative jewels, remains *in situ,* along with Tut's exquisitely carved sarcophagus. Of all the pharaohs buried in the Valley of the Kings, only Tut retains the privilege of resting here in peace.

King Tut's tomb may seem miniature because he reigned as pharaoh for only two years. The interior walls of the burial chamber, perfectly preserved, depict colorful scenes from the *Book of the Dead.* One wall is covered with representations of baboons, placed there to guard Tut in the afterlife. On the back wall, post-mortem scenes are portrayed: Priests carry the king to his tomb, and the high priest who succeeded him marries Tut's wife. A goddess wearing a leopard skin blesses the king from the right-hand side of the wall.

The twelfth-century B.C.E. **Tomb of Ramses IX (#6),** on the left upon entering the valley, features fantastic ceiling murals of gold figures doing funky things against a deep blue background. As in many tomb decorations, the bodily distortions and topsy-turvy orientations will seem nightmarish to unaccustomed Western eyes. Most of the decorative carving adorning the interior walls depicts the spirit's journey to the underworld after death. A lengthy corridor slopes down to a large anteroom, covered with a proliferation of demons, serpents, and wild animals. Beyond, through a pillared room and corridor, a pit in the burial chamber once held Ramses IX's sarcophagus. Nut, goddess of morning and evening, embellishes the ceiling, soaring above constellations and boats full of stars.

The **Tomb of Ramses VI (#9),** closed in 1988 for restoration, directly behind and above the Tomb of Tut-Ankh-Amon, is best known for its unusual ceiling. An elongated gold portrait of the goddess Nut extends along the ceiling from the third main corridor and through a fourth hallway, curving around into a pillared chamber. On the ceiling of the tomb chamber Nut is pictured again, in figures symbolizing the morning and evening skies. Bizarre images of men with snake's heads, little naked figures riding cobras like camels, and people with elongated limbs and torsos dance off the walls and ceilings. Below, the remains of Ramses VI's sarcophagus have been smashed to pieces by grave-robbers. The tomb was begun by Ramses V, but usurped by Ramses VI in a common maneuver of the pharaohs to save time and money.

From Ramses VI's Tomb, walk east up the hill behind the Rest House to reach the **Tomb of Seti I** (#17;), which is closed in 1988 for restoration. This is the Theban necropolis' largest and most finely decorated shrine. Three long corridors decorated with poorly preserved scenes from the underworld give way to a pillared chamber adorned with an enchanting mural depicting the pharaoh with deities. In the adjoining room, portions of the relief work remain unfinished, though the sketched outlines were doubtlessly applied by a master carver. Descend the staircase to a series of sloping hallways terminating in a large chamber; from here a short ramp leads to the burial area of Seti I. The pharaoh's mummy was found in the front chamber, inside a remarkable sarcophagus carved from a single piece of alabaster (since removed to London). In the rear portion of the richly decorated burial chamber, the vaulted ceiling is embellished with a group of astrological figures on a deep blue background and in an unusually asymmetrical arrangement. These inner chambers have exquisite, well-preserved paintings on all available surfaces. Look for the contrasting images of cows—a side chamber to the right contains the image of a golden Hathor with little humans beneath her belly; the final corridor graphically depicts a slaughter. On the lower rear wall, the opening to another shaft has been blocked off. This passage reputedly terminates in another chamber, but has never been fully excavated. Archeologists uncovered 90m of undecorated passageway before abandoning the project, afraid that the hundreds of workers needed to haul out rubble would damage the interior.

The steep entrance next to the Tomb of Seti I descends into the **Tomb of Ramses I** (#16), a single burial chamber dominated by Ramses' pink granite sarcophagus. The tomb walls, some of the most colorful in the valley, are painted with scenes of Ramses hobnobbing with the likes of Maat, Ptah, Nefartum, Annubis, Atum, and Osiris. The first corridor is the shortest of any royal tomb in the valley, and only the burial chamber is painted—no wonder, since this Ramses ruled for only two years (1320-1318 B.C.E.).

Known as the "Tomb of the Harp Players" after a pair of musicians adorning one of its interior chambers, the **Tomb of Ramses III** (#11) is just west of the Rest House. The tomb was discovered in 1769 by a traveler. All along its second corridor, tiny alcoves are decorated with pictures of the room's former contents. The fourth chamber on the left contains the sadly damaged paintings of bald and burly harp players. The third corridor of this otherwise perfectly linear tomb ends abruptly, turning sharply to the right to avoid intersecting the adjacent tomb of Amenneses. Despite its flawed layout, however, the tomb of Ramses III features an interesting interior. Scenes of slaves holding immense, writhing snakes cover the walls of the pillared hall. On the lower left wall, representatives of African and Asian nations parade with tribute. The burial chamber itself remains unexcavated and closed.

West Thebes' most dramatically situated burial site is the cliff-side **Tomb of Thutmose III** (#34), reached via a long, steep staircase that ascends a precipitous ravine sandwiched between towering limestone cliffs. To reach the tomb, follow the dirt road, marked with signs, that begins next to the Tomb of Ramses III, leading southwest up the hill. Make certain that the door will be unlocked for you before you trek up to the tomb. Thutmose III's primary concern was secrecy. In no other tomb was greater care taken to camouflage the grave's location—subsequent pharaohs learned that such precautions were futile. Instead of hauling stones up and over cliffs, they located all tombs in one heavily guarded area. Measures taken to increase security include having passages adjoin one another at odd angles and an astonishingly sudden and deep rectangular shaft, now traversed by a small footbridge.

Thutmose III's burial chamber is an oval room with innovative yet restrained ornamentation. The light, salmon-colored interior is varied only with touches of black. Two square pillars are adorned with drawings of the pharaoh and Isis in a boat. This pharaoh, who ruled Egypt when the empire was at its largest, was interred in the red sandstone sarcophagus that remains in the tomb. Simplified hieroglyphic writing, in imitation of the style of the *Book of the Dead,* complements elegant human figures drawn only in outline.

In 1898, local Egyptian farmers directed France's most eminent archeologist, Victor Loret, to the **Tomb of Amenhotap II** (#35). The names of these *fellaheen* have been forgotten, but they catapulted Loret to international recognition. The tomb lies past the Tomb of Ramses III, west of the Rest House. From the path leading up the western hill to the Tomb of Thutmose III, bear right and go to the northern cliff face. Although thieves had stolen its most valuable riches, the interior was essentially undisturbed, and contained the untouched mummy of Amenhotap II, as well as nine other sacred mummies. The Cairo Museum now has custody of these royal mummies, including Thutmose IV, Amenophis III, and Seti II. One red sarcophagus remains. The burial chamber, decorated with a complete set of texts from the *Book of the Dead,* is one of the most beautiful in the Valley of the Kings. Only rare touches of bright color enliven the figures of deities that adorn its muted yellow walls. Stars cover the entire ceiling. The decorators apparently intended to create the effect of wallpaper, since the coloring closely resembles that of papyrus. A footbridge spans the deep pit used to protect the burial chamber from thieves.

Next door, the **Tomb of Harmhab** (#57) has an unimpressive entrance opening up into a small well chamber covered with a series of festive reliefs. This room leads into a false burial chamber, its roof supported by two pillars. But the grave-robbers were not fooled—they unearthed the stairway leading down from this room into the real tomb and made off with the pharaoh's stock of articles for the afterlife. Only a handsome red granite sarcophagus remains. The decorations in Harmhab's burial chambers were never finished.

The **Tomb of Seti II** (#15) is southwest of the Rest House. Take the road leading uphill toward Thutmose III's Tomb and then the first right after the path to the Tomb of Amenhotap II. The grave consists of a series of long, descending corridors culminating in a small burial chamber that houses a statue of the pharaoh. On one side of the statue is the pharaoh, on the other, his consort. Near the tomb entrance is the mummy of an unknown person; Seti II's mummy has been transferred to the Egyptian Museum in Cairo. Although the painted decorations and bas-reliefs on the corridor walls are fairly well-preserved, their crafting is inferior to that of the neighboring tombs. The tomb ends abruptly, as the king died before it could be completed.

Next door, the **Tomb of Tausert and Seth Nakht** (#14) reveals the thievery of the pharaohs themselves. Queen Tausert reigned in 1215 B.C.E.; upon her death, successor Seth Nakht usurped her tomb, superimposing his own drawings and inscriptions over the earlier, carefully painted images. In the first chamber, Queen Tausert can be seen with her two husbands, Septah and Seti II. Even here, Seth Nakht changed the inscription to make the drawings represent himself. Double images represent the dual human-divine role of the pharaoh. The large central vaulted chamber is covered with luxurious bas-reliefs. The identical burial chamber is also vaulted, but the images on its walls have been defaced.

The **Tomb of Ramses IV** (#2) is outside the main entrance to the Valley of the Kings. Walk 100m down the paved road away from the entrance booth; the tomb is on the left. Because it is seldom visited, you may have to ask the guard to turn on the lights. The painted carvings retain most of their original color, but lack the vitality and expressiveness in many of the other tombs. The descent into the **Tomb of Merneptah** (#8) stretches about 80m, and the burial chambers contain a number of huge granite sarcophagus lids. The tomb lies just inside the main gate, across from the Rest House to the west.

The prominently located **Rest House** serves expensive refreshments and closes at around 1 or 1:30pm in summer. Only drinks are available during the summer (mineral water LE1.25, soda a steep LE1.70). In winter they serve meals. Public toilets add some popular appeal.

Mortuary Temples

As if gorgeous rock-hewn tombs weren't spectacular enough to attract anyone interested in antiquities, West Thebes boasts some of the finest **mortuary temples** ever built. Treated as gods while living, the pharaohs continued to be worshiped after death in their mortuary temples. Though overshadowed by Luxor's Karnak in scale and historical importance, the West Theban temples of Hatshepsut, Ramses III, and Ramses II are true gems. Other mortuary temples such as Seti I's and the lesser-known, unticketed temples on the necropolis beckon those visitors with a surplus of time and interest. The mortuary temples of the Necropolis of Thebes, all accessible from one road that runs parallel to the Nile, are described from south to north. From the ferry docks, head inland 3km past the Colossi of Memnon until you come to an intersection. A road to the left leads to the temple of Ramses III at Medinat Habu, ½km to the southwest. With the exception of Dayr al-Bahri, the mortuary temples afford little shade; during the summer months they are best visited before the onslaught of the afternoon sun.

The largest mortuary temple, that of Amenhotap III, has been destroyed, except for the **Colossi of Memnon,** an impressive pair of statues seated in magnificent isolation on the northern side of the entrance road to the necropolis. Towering to a height of 20m, the figures of Amenhotap III were Thebes' greatest tourist attraction during the Roman era. At night, an eerie whistling sound emanated from the stones, which the Romans interpreted as the voice of Memnon, legendary son of Aurora, the goddess of dawn. The sound, according to scientists, was actually produced by grains of sand splitting off from the statues as the sunbaked rocks contracted in the cool night air. Unfortunately, the Colossi ceased to sing after repairs during the reign of Septimus Severus. Nowadays, the Colossi stand as welcoming sentinels to visitors coming up from the Nile. (Free.)

Left, at the end of the road after the Colossi, stand **Medinat Habu,** a series of well-preserved edifices constructed in several stages by various pharaohs. The largest, most impressive structure in the complex is the **Mortuary Temple of Ramses III,** decorated with reliefs of the pharaoh's numerous successful military campaigns. The immense wealth of Ramses III, the richest pharaoh of all time, is evident throughout. The temple is approached through an elaborate pavilion. Two small watchtowers and a massive battlement guard the first doorway, leading through a single gate into an outer courtyard. To the north lie ruins of the original temple complex, constructed by Amenhotep I and Queen Hatshepsut, and beyond can be found the remains of a sacred lake. On the court's southern side is the Shrine of Amenertais.

As you enter the Temple of Ramses III through the imposing first pylon, you will reach the first court, where a series of columns runs the length of the south side. Column-figures representing the king once supported the roof to the north. On the walls of the inner court, carvings depict Ramses' workers tallying the severed hands, tongues, penises, and huge testicles of slain enemies. As in Karnak, the fertility god Nim is occasionally pictured with an arm-length erection. Early Christians converted the second court into a church, covering the walls with a layer of mud to obscure the representations of gods and pharaohs, and, ironically, preserving them. The Great Hypostyle Hall adjoins this courtyard, bordered by small chambers originally used to store jewels. Beyond the hall lie three chambers in varying states of deterioration, surrounded by small chapels dedicated to various deities. At the southwestern side of the temple, you can see the main pylon's delightful relief of Ramses and a cornucopia of cattle, corn, and carefully drawn fish. The low ruins just to the southwest were once administrative and living areas. The guards call one small building "Ramses' toilet."

Ramasseum

The first stop as you turn right after the Colossi of Memnon is the Mortuary Temple of Ramses II, better known as the Ramasseum. You can visit it most conveniently in conjunction with the nearby Tombs of the Nobles. Ramses II, who reigned for 67 years during the thirteenth century B.C.E., was an admirer of sculpture. His favorite statues were those of himself. He also prized magnitude, especially in his sculptures. This is the pharaoh who ordered up Abu Simbel; the Ramasseum as well once housed two of his mammoth exercises in narcissism. Though only the chest, shoulder, and one foot remain of its original 17m, 1000-ton bulk, the **Colossus of Ramses II** is still awesome. Located in the scanty remains of the Temple's first court, the beautifully-carved ancient torso looms forcefully, dwarfing the neighboring statues of Osiris. The forefingers alone measure over 1m long. This monolith was transported in one piece from the pharaoh's granite quarries at Aswan to Thebes. Originally, this colossus and its twin flanked the passageway leading into the second court, a colonnaded square whose pillars were carved with representations of Osiris. The second court is reputedly that identified by the Roman historian Diodorus as the Tomb of Ozymandias. The connection with this pharaoh arises from speculation that Ramses's second name, "User-ma-re," sounds like Ozymandias when corrupted. This story inspired Shelley to pen his famous poem "Ozymandias," about fallen imperial power. The westernmost portion of the temple is completely ruined, though bits of relief work, expertly sculpted, still poke through the rubble.

Dayr al-Bahri

Just north of the Ramasseum, a paved road leaves the main north-south thoroughfare and heads straight for the cliffside **Mortuary Temple of Hatshepsut,** known in Arabic as Dayr al-Bahri. Located in the center of the necropolis, the temple is 500m north of the Tombs of the Nobles. Hatshepsut's masterpiece rises in three broad, columned terraces from the desert floor against a backdrop of sheer limestone cliffs. The Temple's Arabic name means "most splendid of all," and, indeed, the architecture blends spectacularly with the landscape. From a distance, the majestic geometric porticos of the structure have an almost modern look.

Queen Hatshepsut spared no expense in the construction of her mortuary temple, and may have helped to design it as well. After the death of her father Thutmose II, Hatshepsut assumed the role of monarch. Of the four women known to have ruled in ancient Egypt, the most information is available about her. Her temple, currently under excavation by a team of Polish archeologists, has been restored with modern materials, yet retains much of its original grandeur. You'll be hard-pressed to find any intact images of Hatshepsut anywhere; after her death, the soon-to-be-great Thutmose III defaced virtually all of them. He probably was sore that his step-mother and aunt, Hatshepsut, had cleverly displaced him and ruled in his stead.

You enter the complex from the southeast, walking across the barren lower court. On this first level, the heavily restored colonnades and back wall show little of their original reliefs. Walk up the ramp, big enough for a two-lane highway, to the central court. This level is the most interesting. The colonnaded back wall contains, from left to right, the Shrine of Hathor, Colonnade of the Expedition of Punt, Birth Colonnade, and Shrine to Annubis. (See below.) Another huge ramp leads to the upper court. This third level, set up against the cliff, contained a complex of shrines to Hatshepsut, on the left; to Amon-Re, in the center; and to the solar cult, on the right. Badly ruined, and sadly defaced by Christians, this upper court is currently undergoing restoration and is closed to the public. Assorted pieces of the upper complexes fill portions of the central court.

At the left (southwest) side of the central court's magnificent portico is the lovely **Shrine of Hathor,** entered through two colonnades with Hathor-headed columns. The chapel's interior, closed in 1988, is not illuminated, so you'll need a flashlight or candle. In the first chamber, Hatshepsut is depicted with several deities, and the ceiling is painted a rich shade of blue speckled with tiny stars. Though the figure of Hatshepsut was scraped off by her brother, the relief picturing the queen making offerings to Hathor in the second chamber remains. You can see Hatshepsut drinking from the udder of the cow-goddess Hathor in the shrine's innermost room. In the outer portion of the shrine, a relief on the southwest wall depicts a similar scene.

Images of Hathor's husband, the falcon-god Horus, decorate the columns and walls. Throughout the shrine, you sense the intimacy between the Queen and her favorite deity, the distinctly feminine goddess of music and dance.

Reliefs in the adjacent **Colonnade of the Expedition to Punt** mingle accurate portrayals of an Egyptian trading venture with fanciful, paradisiacal images of legendary Punt. The three-sided relief commemorates an expedition organized by Hatshepsut to this African kingdom to procure valuable myrrh and incense trees. The trees, featured prominently on the reliefs, were to be planted in front of the temple. The naturalistic reliefs depict fully-rigged galleys, and traders with stores of skins, henna, and the trees. On the left-hand wall, scenes from Punt include an idealized African village and a small relief of the eccentric Queen of Punt herself. Legs swollen with elephantiasis, she greets Hatshepsut's Egyptian envoys.

Moving to the right-hand (northeast) side of the ramp, you'll find the badly damaged **Birth Colonnade.** The series of reliefs narrating the birth of Hatshepsut were intended to counter opposition to her rule. The queen is depicted as a boy, and gods bless the mother before recording her divine birth.

Continuing to the right, you'll come upon the **Shrine of Annubis.** Here the jackal-headed god of mummification presents himself in full morbid splendor. The brilliant and well-preserved painted reliefs of the inner court and chambers depict Annubis and Amon-Re receiving tasty-looking offerings of food. Dazzling gold, red, and blue cobras line the top of the inner court walls. A series of inner chambers angle into the cliffside, their walls and arched ceiling still covered in colorful sacred paintings. The shrine has a curious Greek ambience, produced by a combination of fluted white columns, delicate artwork, and overall airiness.

The **Shaft of Dayr al-Bahri,** north of the Temple of Hatshepsut at the foot of the towering cliffs, was the site of the greatest mummy find in history. In 1876, the local director of antiquities began receiving reports of a steady flow of unknown ancient artifacts appearing on the Luxor market, and became convinced that a pharaonic tomb was being plundered. Later, the eldest brother of Luxor's most prominent antiquities merchant, after fighting with his sibling, admitted to the authorities that a grave had been found, and directed them to the spot where a shaft descended 12m into the earth. Amenhotap I, Thutmose II, Thutmose III, Seti I, Ramses I, and Ramses III were all laid to rest in this single shaft along with a host of other royal mummies. Apparently the high priests, realizing that even the most elaborate precautions failed to prevent grave robbers from disturbing the bodies of deceased pharaohs, made a final and successful attempt to hide the mummies by moving their remains to this secret communal grave. The 40 mummies unearthed at Dayr al-Bahri now rest in the Egyptian Museum in Cairo. Strangely, the body of Hatshepsut is not among them. Though the queen constructed two tombs for herself, one in the Valley of the Kings, and the other south of Dayr al-Bahri, her remains have never been found. Currently, the top two levels of Dayr al-Bahri are closed for renovation.

Temple of Seti I

From Dayr al-Bahri, return to the main road, turn north and follow it to the end. Turn right to visit what remains of the **Mortuary Temple of Seti I,** father of Ramses II, a warrior who enlarged the Egyptian empire to include the island of Cyprus and parts of Mesopotamia. The mortuary temple contained some of the priceless treasure brought back by Seti I from his successful campaigns, as well as some of the finest relief work ever executed in ancient Egypt. Though the treasure is gone, the carvings remain, despite the ill-preservation of the temple itself. The best-preserved section of the edifice is the hypostyle hall, its roof ornamented with winged sun disks. Eight small chambers open onto the hall: Here Seti I is depicted before various deities, offering incense and performing sacred rites. At the west end, the goddesses Mut and Hathor suckle the infant pharaoh. Beyond the hypostyle hall is a sanctuary where the sacred boat of Amon was housed. The sanctuary's walls are ornamented with equally splendid reliefs of Seti I. The overall structure of the temple is imposing.

Tombs of the Nobles

Just a few hundred meters southeast of Dayr al-Bahri is West Thebes' most crowded burial site. There are over 400 Tombs of the Nobles. Although many of these aristocratic graves are closed, even commoners can visit a good number of them. The area is divided into five regions: the Tombs of Rekhmire and Sennofer (ticket #7); the Tombs of Ramose, Userhet the Scribe, and Khaemt (ticket #8); the Tombs of Nakht and Menna (ticket #6); the Asasif Tombs (ticket #5); the Temple and Tombs at Dayr al-Medina (ticket #9). You must buy a separate ticket for each. Tickets #6, 7, and 8 will give you access to some of the most highly regarded tombs. At each site look for nearby but less famous tombs that may also be open. As in the rest of West Thebes, it is wise to come equipped with a flashlight or candle, since many graves are unlighted. A guide is unnecessary because the sites are scattered through a village full of local Egyptians who will point out the way for you. A map of the area, if you can get your hands on one, will be useful.

Throughout the New Kingdom, Theban aristocrats held *de facto* control over much of the pharaoh's empire, serving as advisers on matters of state. The pharaoh often remained ignorant of the most crucial political developments, as individual members of the elite fought among themselves for control of the kingdom. Some aristocrats affected pharaonic status by amply providing themselves with luxuries for the afterlife and devising well-hidden underground tombs. Unlike the divine pharaoh, who would live among the gods after his death, the Theban aristocrats needed more assurance that a comfortable existence awaited them in the afterlife. Accordingly, every facet of their earthly lives was carefully recorded on the walls of their tombs. The decoration is thus more naturalistic than the reliefs found in the tombs of pharaohs. Artists freely followed their inclinations and painted scenes of everyday Egyptian life, providing a copious archeological record. Because the limestone in this portion of the necropolis was inferior, artisans could not carve in relief. Instead, they painted intricately detailed murals on a whitewashed stone surface.

Tombs of Rekhmire and Sennofer

Starting at the northwest portion of the site, tomb #100 belongs to Rekhmire, a governor of Thebes who advised Thutmose III and prided himself on his administrative genius. A historian's delight, the **Tomb of Rekhmire** is comprised of biographical narratives. Large, well-preserved murals depict the full range of activities Rekhmire oversaw. This tomb, which consists of two chambers designed in an unusual T-shape, is perhaps the most absorbing of all the tombs in West Thebes. The roof of the rear chamber slopes up into the limestone, creating triangular walls, 2m high at the entrance and 10m high at the far end.

In the first chamber, you'll see a trial of tax evaders by Rekhmire, who sits with a set of rolled papyrus texts strewn at the foot of his judgment throne, proving that written law existed as early as 1500 B.C.E. On the inner, left-hand wall, the finely detailed mural depicts a procession of tributaries from Crete (top), Syria (middle), and African Kingdoms (bottom). The handsomely dressed envoys bring amphoras of Aegean wine, Arabian horses and an Asian bear, and African animals, skins and ivory, respectively.

Near the middle of the furiously active murals of the second chamber, you'll see, on the left wall, an array of artisans and farm laborers. Opposite, on the right wall, female courtiers pamper noblewomen and play various instruments; their male counterparts engage in similar activities below them. The immense innermost murals show, on the left, a procession bearing funerary art to a tomb and irrigation projects, and, on the right, a charming, two-meter-square representation of irrigated farmland. The niche at the top of the rear wall was meant to contain a statue of Rekhmire himself. From this lofty perch, the governor could continue in death, as in life, to survey all the activities of Thebes.

Trek 50m up the hill to the south of Rekhmire's tomb to reach the **Tomb of Sennofer (#96).** This bright, festive tomb is known as "Tomb of the Vines," after the filigree grapevine that spreads all over the ceiling. A delightful lattice of purple and green simulates a shady arbor for Sennofer, overseer of the royal gardens of Amon under Amenhotap II. The plan of the tomb is as unusual as its decor: A curving wall leads into the first room, which in turn leads straight on into the pillared burial chamber. In the rear right-hand corner as you enter, a priest robed in leopard skin purifies Sennofer and his wife as they make offerings to the gods of the underworld. The big, wet eyes of Hathor follow you around the tomb from the tops of the columns. The superb condition of the paintings and their remarkable expressiveness make this small tomb worth a major detour. You will need a flashlight here; otherwise, the guard will show you around with a portable electric light or lantern.

Tombs of Ramose, Userhet, and Khaemt

The **Tomb of Ramose** (#55), southeast of the tombs of Rekhmire and Sennofer down a short dirt road, was built during a period of transition from the polytheism of the Old Kingdom to monotheistic worship of Aton-Ra, the sun god. Ramose was preeminent during the reigns of Amenhotap III and Akhnaton, and was apparently one of the first converts to the latter's monotheism. The sun-worship introduced by Akhnaton was briefly popular, and greatly increased the prestige of Aton into nothing more than a local deity.

On the right-hand rear wall of the columned first chamber, all of Egypt bows down to the solar disk. Aton's rays end in small hands, some holding the key of life. This main hypostyle chamber remains unfinished, and is decorated in both the old and new styles. On the wall through which you enter, the images carved in unpainted relief reflect the traditional, stylized tastes of the Old Kingdom, with scenes of Ramose resting with his fashionably decked-out family. In contrast, the wall to the left as you enter the displays the expressive and realistic "Amarna style" in scenes of a mourning procession.

Continue on from the Tomb of Ramose to the **Tomb of Userhet the Scribe** (#56), only a few meters to the south. Although an early Christian monk destroyed most of the female figures adorning the walls, after making his home within the confines of its burial chamber, the tomb's decor still has a festive quality due to the unusual pink tones of the interior frescoes. Userhet, Amenhotap II's royal scribe, had his resting place painted with scenes from everyday life. The left-hand entrance wall narrates scenes from rural life, showing farmers branding their cattle, and grain being collected for the royal storehouse. The refined figures are executed in remarkable detail. On the right-hand side, a barber carefully trims the locks of a customer, while a line of men await their turns.

Just south of this tomb, off the main dirt road, is the fourteenth-century **Tomb of Khaemt,** superintendent of the granaries of Upper and Lower Egypt during the reign of Amenhotap III. Many of the murals in his funeral chamber reflect his important occupation. On the wall through which you enter there is an exquisite portrait of Renenet, snake goddess of the granaries, and farther along a depiction of corn-laden boats docking at the busy port of Thebes. The subjects are carved in extraordinary detail. The third chamber contains a plaster cast of a bust of Khaemt—the original is now in Berlin.

Tombs of Nakht and Menna

Slightly north of the Tomb of Ramose, a trail leads off the main dirt road, winding east a short distance to the **Tomb of Nakht.** The warm, vivid paintings in its interior chamber memorialize the life of Nakht, scribe of the royal granaries under Thutmose IV. Notice the portrait of Nakht and his wife at the rear of the first chamber. Their son presents them with geese and flowers, and below Nakht's chair, a large cat eats contentedly. An aging photograph on display in the second chamber is all that remains of an exquisite statue of Nakht lost at sea on its way to the U.S. during World War I.

From the Tomb of Nakht, head north a short way and bear west toward the **Tomb of Menna,** mainly of interest for the frescoes of wildlife. Menna, land steward of Thutmose IV, is seen fishing and fowling. Birds take flight from the swaying papyrus thickets, while crocodiles and fish swim in the waters below. The tomb did not originally belong to Menna; in the first corridor to the right as you enter the tomb, a patch of stucco has flaked off, revealing an older set of decorations. Apparently, Menna stole his burial place from another noble.

The tombs of both Nakht and Menna have been closed for restoration. Ask at one of the kiosks about their reopenings.

Walk south from the Tomb of Nakht along the dirt road to see if the **Tomb of Userhet the Prophet** is open. Though the tomb is in poor condition, it contains a fine painting of Userhet with his wife and sister, seated beneath a fig tree drinking the water of life from a golden vessel. Before them, reflected in a small pond, the souls of Userhet and his spouse, represented as human-headed birds, also sip the precious fluid.

Asasif Tombs

Southwest of Dayr al-Bahri, east of the Tombs of Nakht and Menna lies **Asasif**, a region of the Tombs of the Nobles that is currently a hotspot of archeology, with several research projects digging. Asasif became the most popular aristocratic burial area during the Twenty-fifth and Twenty-sixth Dynasties (about the tenth century B.C.E.). The **Tomb of Kheruef** (#192), constructed during the fourteenth century B.C.E. for one of Amenophis III's most influential stewards is the finest in this portion of the necropolis. Enter the burial site through an outer courtyard containing other tombs, where a series of well-wrought reliefs stands against a protecting wall. Note the ceremonial dance in which a jumping bird and monkey are accompanied by flutists and drummers, to the left of the doorway as you enter. On the right is a striking portrait of Amenhotap III surrounded by 16 princesses.

Also noteworthy are the **Tomb of Pabasa** (#279), with a grand staircase leading down to the first chamber and the **Tomb of Pedmenopet** (#33), the largest tomb in the Theban necropolis. You'll need a good flashlight or the assistance of a guide to negotiate the ladders. In the **Tomb of Ibi** (#36), a steep staircase descends to a number of austere chambers. Several of these tombs, which are erratically open to the public, are kept locked. Hunt down the guard to admit you. A single admission ticket allows you entrance to all the Asasif tombs.

Dayr al-Medina

To reach the scanty remains of the **Tomb Workers' Walled City**, start from the Ramasseum and follow the small road west to Dayr al-Medina. Nearby stands the small **Temple of Dayr al-Medina** (Monastery of the Town), an elegant shrine dating from the Ptolemaic era. Dedicated to Hathor, the goddess of love, and Maat, the deity of justice, the temple was named during Christian times, when monks constructed a monastery next door. Enter the temple through a vestibule adorned with two palm columns. The doorway leading into the center chapel is flanked by seven heads of Hathor. Inside, each shrine is enhanced by relief carvings depicting scenes from the *Book of the Dead*. A number of aristocratic tombs are situated near the temple, the finest of which is the **Tomb of Sennutem** (#36). This prominent noble held the esteemed title of "Servant in the Place of Truth." His oval burial chamber is enlivened by a well-preserved mural that shows Osiris embalming Sennutem's mummy. Across the room are scenes of wheatfields, flowers, and fruit. Scenes from Sennutem's journey to the underworld, including the opening of his tomb, ornament the unusually low, curved ceiling. One admission ticket allows you entrance to the Temple and Tombs of Dayr al-Medina and the Workers' Walled City.

Valley of the Queens

During the later years of the New Kingdom, a special burial area was chosen for the wives and children of the pharaohs. Traditionally, the pharaoh's closest relations were buried beside the monarch, but this arrangement changed during the reign of Ramses I (fourteenth century B.C.E.), when princes, consorts, and wives were buried in the Valley of the Queens. In the southwest corner of West Thebes, directly west of the Colossi of Memnon at the end of the main road, the Valley of the Queens contains fewer than 30 royal tombs. The quality of the tombs of these ancient Nile Valley Girls varies enormously. Some are little more than large holes in the ground, while others sparkle with well-preserved ornaments that make them definitely worth visiting. If the most interesting tombs are closed, make the Valley of the Queens a low priority. Check at the ticket kiosks to find out which are open. If you do come, bring a flashlight. As in the Valley of the Kings, tombs here lie within easy walking distance of one another and are connected by gravel pathways. In case you see some Egyptians painting the walls don't be alarmed. They are preserving the pigments with a special fixative: No new colors are added.

The **Tomb of Amon-Hir Khopshef** (#55) is richly bedecked with bas-relief carvings. Father Ramses III introduces the young prince, as a nine-year-old boy, to each of the major deities. Amon-Hir Khopshef wears the groomed topknot of a pharaonic prince. The colored scenes of deities and farmers fill entire walls—a rare sight in Theban tombs. In the rear burial chamber, you'll see the poignantly short sarcophagus that held the prince's mummy. A mysterious desiccated fetus lies curled in a small glass display next to the sarcophagus.

The **Tomb of Queen Nefertari** (#66) is the most beautiful tomb in the Valley of the Queens. Nefertari (Arabic for "beautiful companion"), favorite consort of Ramses II, was provided with a sumptuous place of rest. The pharaoh devoted considerable attention to provisioning her afterlife. In the entrance hall, to the left as you enter, the soul of Nefertari worships the sun rising between two lions, symbols of the past and future. This tomb has been closed, and may not reopen for several years.

The **Tomb of Titi** (#52) belonged to a queen of the Ramesside Era. The most memorable of the brightly colored scenes from the afterlife are in the burial chamber. These scenes depict the 16 stripe-shirted bodies of what might have been the members of the Theban rugby team. The **Tomb of Kha Em Wast** (#44), memorable for its exquisite, bright paintings, was built for another son of Ramses III. Handsome portraits of Anubis and images of lions guard the entrance to the rear burial chamber. Along the entrance corridor, the pharaoh and his son are shrouded in wispy, diaphanous garments.

Between Luxor and Aswan

The 220km stretch of the Nile containing the sleepy rural towns of Esna, Edfu, and Kom Ombo provides a welcome relief from Luxor's chaos. The area is a cultural melting pot—many Nubians displaced from their flooded homes behind the High Dam now mix with Arab *fellaheen* (peasants) in transplanted communities. In addition, each of the towns is graced by an outstanding Ptolemaic temple.

Whether you go by taxi, bus, or train, you'll have no difficulty stopping in Esna, Edfu, and Kom Ombo during a day's journey between Luxor and Aswan. Each lies on the main transportation lines. These towns and their temples also make excellent day trips: Esna and Edfu from Luxor; Edfu, Kom Ombo, and the camel market at Daraw (near Kom Ombo) from Aswan.

If you've got a little extra time and a little extra cash, put yourself on a *felucca* for a leisurely, low-budget sail between the two cities. The traditional three-day *felucca* trip in either direction includes Esna, Edfu, and Kom Ombo as ports of call. If you have a whole lot of extra time and want to savor the best in Egyptian hospitality, buy a **donkey** for LE50 and set off downriver. (Unfortunately, this is not a viable option for solo women.)

By Taxi, Bus, or Train

Traveling by **service taxi** (*taxi ugra*) is the most efficient and sensible option for shuttling between the river towns at almost any time of day. It's also cheap—prices per person approximate bus and train fares. Find the local taxi stand, get in a taxi going to your destination, wait for it to fill, and pay upon arrival. Be sure to pay what your fellow passengers pay—watch them or ask them. Representative fares per person and estimated travel-times:

Luxor-Aswan: LE3.50, 3-4 hr.   **Luxor-Edfu:** LE2, 1½ hr.
Luxor-Esna: LE1.25, 1 hr.   **Luxor-Kom Ombo:** LE2.50, 2-3 hr.
Esna-Edfu: LE1.50, 1 hr.   **Aswan-Esna:** LE2.50, 2-3 hr.
Edfu-Kom Ombo: LE1.50, 45 min.   **Aswan-Edfu:** LE1.50, 1½ hr.
Aswan-Kom Ombo or Daraw: 75pt, 40 min.**Kom Ombo-Daraw:** 10pt, 5 min.

The two potential drawbacks to travel by service taxi are that you must wait an unpredictable (though usually short) time for a taxi to fill, and that taxi travel is dangerous. Although the Nile road is good, drivers tend to speed. Twisted Peugeot carcasses in roadside ditches testify to the occasional result.

A group of five to seven people may want to hire a **private taxi.** Expect to pay LE50 for the trip from Luxor to Aswan with one hour stops in Esna, Edfu, and Kom Ombo.

Buses can be convenient because they are frequent (12 per day in both directions) and do not require advance purchase of tickets. Simply climb aboard and pay the conductor when he comes by. Two disadvantages to bus travel are that buses stop early (last service out of Luxor or Aswan around 3pm), and most lack air conditioning. A bus is a more viable option for traveling out of Luxor or Aswan; you may find no seats available when you try to board in one of the towns in between. Buses cost roughly the same as service taxis, but take somewhat longer to reach their destination (5-6 hr. between Luxor and Aswan).

Last and least, the seven daily **trains** present more hassle than they are worth on short runs. Air conditioning is a plus, but one probably outweighed by the headache of purchasing a ticket and waiting for a delayed train. Fortunately, you can usually get a seat in an air-conditioned car between Luxor and Aswan without advance booking—simply walk on and pay the LE1 surcharge. Second-class air-conditioned travel is slightly cheaper than a service taxi (Luxor to Aswan LE3), while second-class non-air-conditioned is a very cheap alternative (Luxor to Aswan LE1.50). In summary, go ahead and take the train for the longer rides such as Luxor to Kom Ombo or Aswan, and Aswan to Esna or Luxor, but consider a taxi or bus for shorter trips.

Consult the Practical Information sections of the Luxor and Aswan chapters for more information on buses, taxis, and trains. The following sections also contain additional information.

By Felucca

Hiring a *felucca* is a fairly simple affair. First gather a group of travelers who would like to spend a few days together drifting along the Nile, then stroll along the waterfront in Luxor or Aswan and bargain with the *felucca* pilots. Set the price, length of the trip, and meeting time, and you're on your way. Pay the captain when you reach your destination, since otherwise the boat might "break down" halfway there. The typical large *felucca* sleeps up to eight people, displays a single tall sail, and is piloted by an English-speaking Nubian. Police regulations forbid sailing after 8pm, so passengers either sleep on wooden slats in the docked *felucca* or on the river bank next to the boat. While you can negotiate to pay for food en route, many travelers pack their own supplies or make stops for food along the way. Food will cost LE5 per person for a typical trip. Another good idea is to bring bottled water.

Ignore the extravagant official rates for *felucca* trips quoted at the tourist office (LE35 per person from Esna to Aswan, LE40 per person from Luxor to Aswan, 6 people minimum, registration fee included); everyone else does. In the summer of 1988, when business was slow, pilots were generally accepting LE150 total for a three-night, six-to-eight-person sail between Luxor and Aswan, with stops in Kom Ombo, Edfu, and Esna. The trip upstream takes at least a day longer and costs LE20-40 more.

When you begin the *felucca* trip in Aswan, you will be asked to fork over a LE5 per person registration fee and to register your passport. Apparently, the government requires a travel agency to insure passengers. In Aswan, **Seven Tours**, on the central corniche (tel. 32 36 79), handles nearly all the *felucca* business. Curiously enough, the registration is not enforced for trips beginning in Luxor. The Aswan or Luxor tourist offices can explain the latest developments in the *felucca* scene.

Note that the standard *felucca* trip between Luxor and Aswan actually involves taking a taxi between Esna and Luxor. *Felucca* pilots give different explanations for this detour, including the drawbridge at Esna, rough river currents between Esna and Luxor, and rivalry between pilots from Aswan and those from Luxor. At any rate, you will have to pay extra (perhaps LE5 per person) to make the entire trip in a *felucca*.

Esna

The Great Hypostyle Hall, built during the reign of the Roman Emperor Claudius, is all that remains of the magnificent **Temple of Khnum** at Esna. The temple lies nearly 10m below street level in an open pit in the middle of the busy agricultural community of Esna. On Thursdays, early in the morning, there's a camel market here. The short walk through town to the site passes some beautiful *mashrabiya* (wooden screen) windows and small medieval mosques. To reach the temple from the service taxi station, walk south along the main street for about 10 minutes. Cross a small bridge over a canal. Hang a left toward the Nile and walk for about 10 minutes until you reach the temple ticket office. The temple is about 50m inland through a street packed with tourist kiosks. Horse-drawn carriages can get you to the temple for 50-75pt.

Khnum was a ram-headed creator god who is said to have molded the first human on a potter's wheel. Although begun in the Eighteenth Dynasty, the Temple of Khnum is largely a Roman creation and is in many ways a feeble imitation of inherited technical and artistic achievements. Esna was an important regional center for the area south of Luxor, and the pharaohs of the Eighteenth Dynasty, desiring stronger popular support, sanctified this temple to the local deity. The temple was later covered with sand, and became the foundation for peasant homes. Archeologists discovered the magnificent hallway in excellent condition. Today the temple forms an incongruous spectacle in Esna, threatening to engulf the tiny houses.

Many of the interior carvings are of inferior quality. The Romans, in an effort to decorate the temple in a traditional pharaonic manner, produced forced and uncomfortable results. A procession of stiff, strangely deformed figures marches solemnly across the walls of the hallway. On the outside walls, the king grabs dozens of enemies by the hair, ready to finish them off with a deadly blow, while Khnum and Menhyt look on. The height of the massive columns inside a relatively small space produces an effect of grandeur and enormity. Compare this feeling with the temple's appearance from the outside: It will look a lot smaller. Some faint blues and reds on the tops of the 24 columns hint at how brilliant the inside of the temple must have looked.

The temple is open daily from 7am to 6pm. (Admission LE1, students 50pt). Esna lies on the west bank of the Nile, connected to the main highway and rail line on the eastern side by a bridge. A smaller highway runs along the western bank to West Thebes. Luxor is 70km downstream; Edfu lies 50km and Aswan 155km upstream. Esna can be reached by taxi, train, bus, or *felucca;* see above for details. Along the road there are numerous fruit and vegetable stands. A small grocery store on the left sells yogurt (70pt), crackers, and cheese. Or share a watermelon (about LE1.50). Avoid the restaurant halfway to the temple from the Nile, which charges LE5 for a complete but unsanitary meal. The town offers nothing but miserable accommodations—stay in Luxor, Edfu, or Aswan.

Edfu

As a first time visitor here, you may walk the unpaved streets, watch a water buffalo cooling off in the Nile, observe the local Nubians and Arabs going about their business in the modest market place, and wonder what all the fuss about Edfu is for. At the back of town, however, where garbage-strewn streets lose themselves in cropland and small barren hills, you'll discover the reason behind Edfu's fame. Here, silently oblivious to its surroundings and to the passage of two thousand years, stands an incredibly well-preserved ancient site—the mammoth and magnificent Temple of Horus. This labyrinth of dark chambers and towering pillars is almost perfectly intact. It stands with Karnak and Abu Simbel as one of the most impressive sights in Upper Egypt.

Practical Information

Like Esna, the town of Edfu is on the west bank of the Nile, connected by a bridge to the main highway and railroad on the east bank. Roughly halfway between Luxor (115km) and Aswan (105km), Edfu lies 50km south of Esna, and 65km north of Kom Ombo. You can easily reach Edfu from any of these other towns by taxi, bus, train, or *felucca*. (See Between Luxor and Aswan above.) The **bus station** on Tahrir St. is 100m north of central **Temple Square.** Tahrir St. runs parallel to the Nile about 1km inland. Wide al-Maglis St. links Temple Sq. with the Nile. The Edfu bridge, with the **train station** on its eastern end and the **service taxi station** near its western end, is 300m north of al-Maglis St., roughly 2km from the center of town. The last bus out of town in either direction leaves at around 6pm, the last trains pull out at around 9 or 10pm. To reach the **temple** from Temple Sq., follow the signs and head away from the Nile for 200m. Local pickup trucks can take you from the train station to the temple (25pt). A private taxi will make the trip to the temple for LE1.50-2. Edfu's horse-drawn **carriages** shuttle tourists between the Nile and the temple; although drivers ask LE1-2 for the trip, most passengers pay about 75pt.

Accommodations and Food

Unlike Esna and Kom Ombo, Edfu offers just enough amenities to warrant an overnight stay in a hotel. Of Edfu's four hotels, the **el-Madina Hotel** (tel. 70 13 26) offers the best deal. Just to the north of Temple Sq., this shabby but clean place offers rooms with fans and shared hot showers, and a few rooms with balconies. (Singles LE4, doubles LE7, triples LE9. Breakfast LE2. Dinner LE4.) Thrice-wedded owner Taha and his son love to engage travelers in lengthy conversations. **Hotel Dar el-Salaam** (tel. 70 17 27), 100m away from the temple on the left, has clean, if dingy, rooms with fans. (Dorm beds LE4, singles LE6, doubles LE8.) The name means "Port of Peace" and compared with the next two alternatives, it's just that. **Hotel Magdy** sits midway up al-Maglis St. The fanless rooms here look like POW cells. The toilets are abysmal, and water comes in one temperature: cold. No extra charge for filthy beds. (LE2 per night.) The **Sami Ramis,** several doors west, is slightly more pleasant, but can be hostile to foreigners. (Beds LE3.) No English is spoken at either the Hotel Magdy or the Sami Ramis. Across the street from Hotel Sami Ramis, **Restaurant Zahrat el-Medina** ("City Flower" in Arabic) is clean and pleasant, with complete chicken meals for LE2. Numerous cafes along the main streets offer mineral water, tea, and snacks. Gomhouriya St. (JAM-hor-rea), which parallels Tahrir St. 1 block to the west, is Edfu's *souk,* where local farmers bring their produce daily.

The Temple of Horus

Dedicated to Horus, this Ptolemaic structure took over 200 years to construct and was completed only in 57 B.C.E., making it one of the last great Egyptian monuments. The Ptolemaic designers conceived of this temple to Horus and the Temple at Dendera, dedicated to his wife Hathor, as a matched set. You'll be struck by their similarity if you visit both. Once per year, the image of Hathor was conveyed upstream in a sacred barge so that wife and husband could spend some time to-gether. Their reunion in midstream was an occasion for joyous celebration.

A number of other important religious festivals centering around the life and death of the falcon-god Horus were celebrated at Edfu. During the annual "Union with the Solar Disk," Horus' earthly form was brought to the roof of the temple to be rejuvenated by the rays of the sun. The rite was generally performed in con-junction with the New Year holiday. Another important ritual was the coronation festival, in which a falcon was selected from the sacred aviary to become the living symbol of Horus during the following year. After secret rites, the bird was crowned in the temple's main court and triumphantly paraded to the interior where it reigned in darkness for one year.

From the site's entrance by the ticket kiosk and tourist police station, walk the full length of the structure and enter the temple at the far end. The entire temple is surrounded by a massive exterior wall, closed off at one end by a colossal pylon through which you enter the temple proper. The main doorway through the pylon is flanked by two battlements rising to a height of 36m and guarded by a noble gran-ite falcon. Only a chunk of his co-sentinel on the right remains. Enter the temple through the 12 mammoth columns of the **Great Hypostyle Hall,** continuing on to the second Hypostyle Hall, outfitted with a similar arrangement of smaller pillars. Doorways on either side lead to the **Corridor of Victory,** a narrow exterior passage-way running between the temple and its protective wall. Note the progressive nar-rowing of the temple as you proceed toward the end containing the inner sanctum. Several elegant lions' heads jut from the otherwise smooth brick surface to survey the narrow corridor.

Two staircases lead up to the roof (closed to the public) from the Hall of Offer-ings, which follows the second Hypostyle Hall. The central hall is flanked on both sides by two chapels. To the right as you enter, a doorway leads to the **Court of the New Year,** where the sky goddess Nut curves into a slender L-shape on the ceiling. Beyond the central hallway is the sanctuary, where the cult statue of Horus was once housed. Only the foundations of the figure remain. Fully enclosed within the outer shell of the main temple and surrounded by a corridor on three sides, the sanctuary is inscribed with scenes depicting the revenge of Horus. The play-by-play account starts on the back of the left outside wall. The ancient legend is that Osiris was killed by his jealous brother Seth, who chopped Osiris into 14 pieces and scattered them all over Egypt. Osiris's wife Isis, grieving over her husband's death, searched out the pieces, reassembled them, and made love to them. As a result, Horus was born. Seth chaged himself into a hippopotamus to escape Horus' wrath, but this trick failed—in the last scene you see Seth butchered into 14 pieces of hippo meat. Eight smaller chambers open off the corridor. The central one at the rear of the temple houses a modern reconstruction of the sacred barge used to convey the cult statue.

Outside the temple, directly in front of the main entrance pylon, is a well-preserved Roman *mammisis* (birth house), where the birth of Horus was annually reenacted amid festive celebration.

The site is open daily from 6am to 5pm. (Admission LE2, students LE1.)

Near Edfu: el-Kab

If you're traveling by bus or private taxi on the main highway north of Edfu, consider a stop at **el-Kab,** 15km north of Edfu near the village of el-Mahamid. This religious center was dedicated to the goddess Nekhbet, and contains ruins from most eras in Ancient Egyptian history: an inscribed rock from the old Kingdom, tombs from the Middle and New Kingdoms, and a Ptolemaic temple. Most interest-ing are the **Temple of Nekhbet,** with its fanciful Hathoric columns, the historically important **Tomb of Admiral Ahmose (#5),** and the **Tomb of Pahert (#3).** The gov-ernment has only recently developed this complex for tourism, and although grow-ing in popularity, el-Kab remains an isolated set of ruins, displayed against the lonely desert landscape. (Open daily sunrise to 4 or 5pm; admission LE2, students LE1.)

Kom Ombo

Forty-five kilometers north of Aswan on the east bank of the Nile is Kom Ombo, the site of an Egyptian temple as renowned for its location as for its rigorously symmetrical construction. Unlike other temples in Egypt, Kom Ombo is still situated along the banks of the Nile, giving much the same visual impression today as it did when completed during Ptolemaic times. The sanctuary's real peculiarity, however, lies in the fact that every architectural element has a twin. Double doorways lead into double chambers and sanctuaries after passing through double halls and past double colonnades. The temple was dedicated to a pair of gods: Sobek, the toothy crocodile god, and Horus, the winged falcon or sky god. The priests were diplomatic and, so as not to offend either deity, ordered everything to be built in tandem. There is almost no shade at Kom Ombo, so be sure to bring plenty of water and a hat.

Although a temple has stood at Kom Ombo since the time of the Middle Kingdom, the oldest portions of its ruins have been removed to the Louvre in Paris and the Egyptian Museum in Cairo. What remains here dates from the Ptolemaic and Roman periods. The main temple dominates the site from a hill overlooking the Nile. After its abandonment during the decline of the Roman Empire, the rising waters of the river inundated the site and left the temple almost completely submerged in sand. In later years, the portions of the temple still above ground were used as a quarry for a neighboring edifice, and as a result the side walls have vanished. Nonetheless, the temple retains much of its original magnificence.

Enter through the paved court, whose columns still retain their original brilliant coloring. In the center sits the foundation of a granite altar. Pass from the court into the vestibule, with carvings strung across the far wall. The figures near the top were located above the concealing layer of sand and were consequently defaced by unappreciative Christians. In the interior of the temple are the less substantial remains of the Hall of Offerings and the inner sanctuaries dedicated to Sobek and Horus. On the rear walls, you'll find some particularly alluring shots of a semi-nude Cleopatra. Around on the northwestern side, the low outside walls exhibit fine reliefs of Sobek and Horus.

Adjoining the northern edge of the temple are the Roman water supply tanks, comprised of two wells joined to a stepped vat, and, to the west, the remains of a Roman *mammisis.* The guards at the site claim that crocodiles once lived in the well and that Cleopatra's bath is nearby. For a little *baksheesh,* they'll let you climb down the well and take a look for yourself. The **Chapel of Hathor,** directly south of the main temple, houses a remarkable collection of grimacing crocodile mummies unearthed near the road leading away from the site. You can see their noses pointing out into the sunlight through an iron grille at the entrance to the chapel. (Site open daily 6am-6pm. Admission LE1, students 50pt.)

The remains of the temple are 4km from the center of town. The bus, train, and service taxi stations in Kom Ombo are all next to each other along the main street. A covered pickup truck (10pt) runs all day between the river, near the ruins, and the center of town. The truck leaves from behind the large gray mosque with the minaret, 1 block off the main street. From where the truck lets you off, it's a 1km walk south (upriver) to the temple. If you wish to hire a private taxi, don't pay more than LE1 each way. If you're coming from Aswan by service taxi or bus, ask to be let off at the well-marked turn-off to the "tembel" 2km south of town. From the turn-off, walk 1½ km through sugar cane fields to the temple site. (See Between Luxor and Aswan for more information on transportation including *feluccas.*)

There is no point in staying at one of Kom Ombo's fleabag **hotels,** since Aswan lies only 50pt away by public transportation. It is better to stay with a local family, if you're invited, or to avoid spending the night at Kom Ombo altogether. The town offers nothing special in the way of **food;** stalls next to the temple charge high prices for cold mineral water.

Near Kom Ombo: Daraw

Sudanese merchants, Bishari tribespeople, and Egyptian *fellaheen* convene in Daraw every Tuesday morning for a **camel market.** The Sudanese purchase camels for the equivalent of LE200 each, march for one month through the desert to Daraw, and resell them at 4-500% profit. The Bishari are traditional Saharan nomads with a unique language and culture. Some of the men conduct business in full traditional dress: flowing pants, fighting sword and dagger, and a cloak draped over their shoulders. Typically, a Sudanese camel owner will pay a Sudanese or Bishari shepherd to drive his camels north to Egypt. The owner then flies up to oversee the selling. If you're interested, the going rate for a big male camel is LE1000-1200, which will save you close to LE1000 over prices in Cairo. Although the automobile has displaced the camel to some extent, *fellaheen* appreciate camels as carriers of sugar cane and as sources of cheap meat.

Tuesday is the only market day in the summer, but camels are sometimes also sold on Sundays and Mondays in the winter. On Tuesday, the camel market is flanked by a **livestock market** where cattle, water buffalo, sheep, and goats are sold. On market day, impromptu shaded *fuul* and tea stands serve the multitudes. The camel market runs 5am to 2pm, but peters out after about 11am. A good strategy is to rise very early in Aswan, visit the camel market, and move on to see the temple at Kom Ombo. To reach the camel market, you will walk through an equally large **fruit and vegetable market** where the Nubian women do their weekly shopping.

Service taxis go to Daraw from Kom Ombo, 8km to the north (10pt, 5 min.) and Aswan, 32km to the south (75pt, 1 hr.). All the trains and buses running between Luxor and Aswan stop in Daraw. The taxi stand, bus station, and train station all lie along the main highway. To reach the market from the taxi, bus, or train station, walk 300m toward the Nile, bearing left when the first street ends, then right. During the winter there may be another location for the market; ask around. The word for camel is *gamel,* and it may be helpful to draw a picture if you need help with directions.

Aswan

Downstream from the first cataracts of the Nile, the city of Aswan grew and flourished as Egypt's frontier town. Having prospered as the trading center between Egypt and the rest of Africa, Aswan remains a gateway to the plains of Sudan and Nubia. Aswan has emerged as Egypt's premier winter resort (mean maximum temperature in January is 24°C), offering a warm and dry climate with clean and comfortable living conditions. It is too early to know for sure what effect the High Dam south of town may have on the region; the immense and eerie Lake Nasser adds moisture to the air while the dam powers Aswan's burgeoning industry. For the time being, however, Aswan is small enough to be relaxed and pleasant.

Women will feel surprisingly comfortable in this laid-back city, where tourists are not the only show in town. The great numbers of Nubians in the city and its surrounding villages contribute to Aswan's warmhearted spirit and African élan. Their homes were inundated by the dam and relocated here.

Around Aswan, the Nile suddenly ceases to be sandwiched between green fields, and courses instead through a stark desert. The spotless corniche, perhaps Egypt's most elegant boulevard, slips along the Nile for the entire length of the city. Across from the corniche, an archipelago of lush islets adds to this soul-satisfying vista along the length of the Nile. Aswan also has one of the largest and most colorful markets south of Cairo, and visitors can browse here without being hounded by over-eager shopkeepers.

Practical Information

Tourist Office: Corniche al-Nil (tel. 32 32 97), 2 blocks toward the river from the train station and 1 block south, then ½ block inland from the corniche, obscured by a small park. English-speaking co-directors Mr. Farrag and Mr. Soukry are cheerful and helpful. They facilitate travel to Kalabsha and the Sudan and have official prices for *feluccas* and taxis. Open daily 9am-2pm and 6-8pm; in Ramadan daily 9am-3 or 4pm.

Passport Office: Corniche al-Nil (tel. 32 22 38), in the center of town. Look for the big yellow sign 3 doors south of the Continental Hotel. Register your passport or extend your visa here. Open daily 8am-2pm and 6-8pm. Reduced hours on Friday. Visa registration in morning only.

Banks: There are 4 banks on Corniche al-Nil. Banks open daily 9am-2pm and 6-8pm.

American Express: Tel. 232 22. In the lobby of the Old Cataract Hotel at the far southern end of the corniche. Will hold mail and hopes to introduce banking services (currently none). Open daily 8am-7pm; in Ramadan daily 8am-2pm.

Post Office: Corniche al-Nil, across from and just south of the Rowing Club Restaurant, toward the northern end of town. Open daily 9am-2pm. **Poste Restante** is 1 block off the corniche, in the center of town, behind the Bank of Alexandria. Open Sat.-Wed. 8-11am and 7-11pm, Thurs. 8-11am, Fri. 7-11pm. Your mail might fare better if sent from a major hotel.

Telephones, Telegrams, and Telex: Corniche al-Nil, 2 doors south of EgyptAir. Comparatively efficient for international calls. Open 24 hours. Also a telephone and telegraph office in the train station (open daily 8am-10pm).

Telephone code: 097.

Airport: 23km south of town (tel. 32 33 64), near High Dam. LE4 one-way by taxi. Served only by **EgyptAir,** Corniche al-Nil (tel. 32 24 00), at the southern end, before the Ferial Gardens and Cataract Hotels. In summer: To Cairo (2-4 per day, LE125.30, 2 hr.); to Luxor (2-4 per day, LE39.50, 40 min.); and to Abu Simbel (2-3 per day, LE110, 40 min.). Far more frequent service in winter (for example, to Abu Simbel up to 20 per day). Book several days in advance for Abu Simbel. Open daily 8am-6pm.

Train Station: Northern end of al-Souk St. (tel. 32 20 07), 2 blocks east of the corniche, at the northeast corner of Aswan. To Luxor (7 per day, 5:20am-8:30pm; 1st class A/C LE5, 2nd class non-A/C LE1.80, 3rd class non-A/C 60pt; 5 hr.). Reservations to Luxor not essential since walk-on seats are usually available for LE1.50 extra. All Luxor trains continue to Cairo (1st class A/C LE15.75, 2nd class A/C LE7.15, very uncomfortable 3rd class non-A/C LE1.80; 18 hr.). Also *wagon-lits* to Cairo (2 per day; 1st class, LE123.90; 2nd class, LE78). 2nd class *wagon-lits* are usually fully booked well in advance. Also trains to High Dam, most of which are continuations of runs from Luxor (8 per day; 6:30am-7:45pm, returning 8am-9:30pm; 20pt). Present your student ID for up to a 50% discount. Book all trains at least 3 days in advance, especially during high season.

Bus Station: Abtal al-Tahrir St., 3 blocks south and 1 block west of the train station, 1 block in from the Nile in the northern part of town. North to Nile Towns: Daraw, Kom Ombo, Edfu, Esna, and Luxor (13 per day, 5:45am-3pm; to Luxor, LE2.50, 5 hr.) and continuing to Qena (7 of the 13 per day, LE3.50, 6hr.) To Hurghada: connect from 6am bus to Qena or 7:30 and noon buses to Luxor. South to Hazan/Old Dam (#20 and 59, also from Corniche; 14 per day, 6am-9:30pm, 10pt). Also to Abu Simbel (A/C; daily at 8am, back in Aswan 5-6pm; LE8 each way; 3 hr.). No bus service to High Dam.

Ferry to Sudan: Nile Navigation Company: To Wadi Halfa on eastern shore of Lake Nasser. Office next to tourist office (tel. 32 33 48; open Sat.-Thurs. 8am-2pm). Boats on Mon. and Thurs., possibly another in summer. 1 day trip, but may take up to 3 days. Ferry connects with train to Khartoum. (1st class LE69, 2nd class LE42.)

Local Ferries: 3 options daily. To Elephantine Island from either el-Shati Restaurant on central corniche or EgyptAir at the south end of the corniche (6am-9pm, every 15 min., 25pt for foreigners). To West Bank tombs and villages from Seti Tours, opposite tourist office (6am-6pm every 30 min.; 6pm-9pm, every 1 hr., 25pt).

Service Taxis: Taxis leave from the roofed station 1km south of the train station on the east side of the tracks, next to the large underpass. To Daraw or Kom Ombo (75pt), to Edfu (LE1.50), to Esna (LE2.50), and to Luxor (LE3.50). For taxis south and to Aswan environs, wait in the square at the corner of Mahmoud Yakoub St. and Abtal al-Tahrir, next to Happi Hotel, 2 blocks south of the bus station. To Hazan/Old Dam (25pt). You can arrange special trips with taxis anywhere in Aswan. See the Aswan sights and South of Aswan or Abu Simbel sections for details about taxis to High Dam, Kalabsha, Philae, and Abu Simbel. 7-person taxis cost 40% more than 4-person taxis.

Bike Rental: Nahas Yahia, near Bata Shoes Store, 1½ blocks off central corniche from Aswan Moon Restaurant, on southern fringe of the *souk*. Bikes with rear brakes only, and locks. Rates negotiable: around LE1 per hour, LE4 per day. Must leave passport, student ID, or other collateral. Another bike shop is 100m south of Ramses Hotel on Abtal al-Tahrir St. LE1 per hour, LE10 per day. Aswan is ideal for bike travel.

Swimming Pools: at the following hotels: **New Cataract** (LE7) at the southern end of the corniche, **Isis** (LE5) in the north central segment, and **Oberoi** (LE7) on the northern half of Elephantine Island (hotel ferry is free). Admission fee includes one complimentary non-alcoholic beverage. Attendants are not always present to enforce the admission fees, especially by the end of the afternoon. All pools open daily 9am-6pm. Municipal Pool no longer admits foreigners.

Bookstores: No real English bookstores in Aswan, just hotel gift shops.

Photo Developing: King Aswan Lab, on Matar St. (tel. 32 31 24), will print 36 color prints in 1 hr. for LE21.80 or in 24 hours for LE21. Open Sat.-Thurs. 9am-10pm.

Pharmacies: el-Nile Pharmacy, Corniche al-Nil, across from Isis hotel in the central part of the corniche. **Atlas Pharmacy,** next to Mena Hotel on Atlas St. (tel. 32 43 00). Both open 9am-2:30pm and 5-11pm. Both stock a variety of over-the-counter drugs, including contraceptives. Each night, one pharmacy in town is open 24 hours.

Hospital: German Hospital, near the Grand Hotel or southern corniche (tel. 32 21 76 or call tourist office). Quality care. Treat now, pay later with insurance. Open 24 hours.

Tourist Police: Tel. 32 43 93 or 32 31 63. Main office above the tourist office. Also in the train station on the south side. Friendly, helpful, English-speaking staff. Open 24 hours.

Aswan, the southernmost city in Egypt, is 890km upstream from Cairo and 220km south of Luxor. Frequent taxi, bus, and train service connects Aswan with Luxor. A great way to travel between these two cities is to sail on the Nile in a *felucca*. The trip takes 3-5 days and costs LE110-150 for a group of six, depending on your bargaining skills (see Between Luxor and Aswan). Aswan functions as the base for exploring the farther reaches of southern Egypt—notably the High Dam and Nubian monuments such as the Philae and Abu Simbel Temples. Many travelers make the mistake of scheduling too little time in Aswan. Rushed sight-seers should plan on three days at the very least: one for Aswan, one for Philae and the Dam, and one for a round-trip excursion to Abu Simbel.

You are almost never more than 2 blocks from the river in Aswan, so it's hard to get lost. The northern half of Aswan lies along three long avenues running parallel to the bank of the Nile. By far the most handsome and prominent of the trio is the riverside **Corniche al-Nil,** featuring most of the fancy hotels, travel agencies, public services, restaurants, and banks. Two blocks in, Aswan's busiest and most picturesque lane, **al-Souk Street** (Market St., also known as Sa'ad Zaghloul St.), features everything from merchants with towering aromatic mounds of spices to tacky tourist trinket stands with pseudo-marble busts of Queen Nefertiti. This street begins at the train station at the northeast corner of town and runs 2km south, ending at the *souk*.

In the southern half of town, the corniche continues for another 2km, ending at the **Ferial Gardens,** just downriver from some of Aswan's poshest hotels. The northern grid pattern becomes confused when it reaches the central market. South of the *souk*, inland streets form a dusty labyrinth of narrow alleys and cul-de-sacs. Last and perhaps least, running in between the corniche and the market street, **Abtal al-Tahrir Street** starts at the youth hostel and culminates in its own little cluster of overpriced tourist bazaars.

Most tourists find that walking is the best means of transportation in Aswan. Rent a bike to cruise at a faster pace. The white local taxis charge about LE1 to travel the length of the city.

Accommodations and Camping

Nowhere in Egypt is the difference between high season and low season so pronounced as in Aswan. During high season (Oct.-April), expect to pay 10% to 50%

extra. In low season, luxury hotels sit empty, desperate for business, and sometimes lower their rates by as much as 60%. There are fewer dirt cheap hotels in Aswan than in Luxor, but the city's many comfortable middle-class hotels with fans and air-conditioning often have reasonable prices. During the summer months, when temperatures in Aswan soar as high as 48°C (120°F), air-conditioning is practically a necessity. The **Mena, Ramses, Abu Simbel,** and **Hathor** hotels are all reasonably priced and air-conditioned. If you get a group of travelers together, you can drop the price to LE5-6 per night for a spotless room with air-conditioning and private bath. Don't be concerned if the locale of your hotel looks down-at-the-heels. Like all Egyptian cities, Aswan is remarkably safe, day and night. All places listed provide showers. Rates listed here are low season prices.

Youth Hostel (IYHF), 96 Abtal al-Tahrir St., 1 block west and 1 block south of the train station (tel. 32 23 13). Entrance to the section for foreigners on the side of the building. Dirty, crowded, large rooms. Filthy toilets. Difficult to sleep—people wake at all hours to catch trains. Exceedingly hot in summer. Dorm beds. Lockout 10am-2pm. Curfew 11pm. Members LE2. Nonmembers may purchase membership for LE18, but requirement may be overlooked when hostel is empty.

Marwa Hotel, Abtal al-Tahrir St., across from the hostel. Shabby but adequate rooms. Friendly place, with hot water, fans in every room, and free use of refrigerator. Dorm beds LE2-3.

Aswan Palace Hotel, 17 Mahmoud Yakoub St. (tel. 32 26 56), centrally located by the vegetable *souk,* 1 block west of al-Souk St. From Misr Bank on the corniche, walk past the shared taxi stop and look left. Energetic management. Spacious, simple rooms with fans and hot showers on each floor. Cafe and free refrigerator use. Year-round low prices: singles LE2.20, doubles LE4.10, triples LE6, quads LE7. Extra beds LE1.

Mena Hotel (tel. 32 43 88), 200m north of the train station. Follow the tracks past 2 gas stations, walk 100m, then turn left. The best value in town, despite inconvenient location in extreme northeastern corner of tourist's Aswan. Immaculate, well-furnished rooms, some with double beds, most with A/C, all with faultless baths. Excellent service, rooms cleaned each day, and manager Mr. Adel is extremely helpful. A good place for women. Singles LE8, doubles LE10, five-person suite LE25. In winter: singles LE10, doubles LE15, five-person suite LE35. Discount for students. Large breakfast included.

Molla Hotel, Kelanie St. (tel. 32 22 78), 3 blocks in from the Aswan Moon Restaurant and the corniche, up the hill and around the corner from Bata Shoes, 3 blocks south of the central *souk.* Surprisingly tidy and comfortable for the price. Conscientious management. Fans in every room and free use of refrigerator and stove. Dorm beds LE2.90, with shower LE3.50. Singles LE6. Doubles LE7, with bath LE8.20. Quad with bath LE14. Breakfast included.

Hotel Continental Aswan, Corniche al-Nil (tel. 32 23 11), next to the blue archway over the corniche. Long on funky, informal atmosphere: crumbling floors, balconies overlooking the Nile, cafe on the sidewalk outside. Short on amenities—wear shoes to the bathroom. Cold water only. Central location. Simple rooms for one or two LE3, triples LE4, quads LE5.

El-Amin Hotel, Abtal al-Tahrir St. (tel. 32 31 89), 3 blocks south and 1 block west of train station; follow the sign. Another face in Aswan's crowd of reasonably clean and pleasant, yet inexpensive hotels. Amiable management. Fans in each room. Singles LE4.50, doubles LE8. Prices negotiable.

Rosewan Hotel (tel. 32 44 97). Turn right as you leave the train station, head past a gas station, and take the next left. The hotel is on the right, in the middle of the next block. Neat and hospitable. Owner-manager Farouk Nasser is friendly and looks after his guests. Large rooms, all with fans. Convenient store next to lobby. Year-round: singles LE5.66, with shower LE7. Doubles LE9, with shower LE11.50. Triples LE14.70, with shower LE16. If full, try the **Saffa Hotel** next door (tel. 32 21 72), which is dark and dingy but has fans and sinks in each room. Singles LE2.25, doubles LE4, triples LE4.35. Breakfast included.

El Salaam Hotel, Corniche al-Nil (tel. 32 26 51), 25m south of the Isis Hotel on the opposite side of the north-central corniche. Spotless, carpeted rooms, some with balconies overlooking the river. Sterile, but secure and comfortable. All rooms with bath. Restaurant adjacent. Singles LE10, doubles LE14, triples LE21, extra bed in triple LE3. Breakfast included.

Hathor Hotel, Corniche al-Nil (tel. 32 25 90), next to el-Salaam. Clean, bright rooms overlooking the Nile. Fans and cramped baths in every room. Singles LE10.75. Doubles LE16, with A/C LE18. Triples LE21, with A/C LE24. Back rooms discounted LE2-3. Breakfast included.

Ramses Hotel, Abtal al-Tahrir St. (tel. 32 40 00), 1 block west and 2 blocks south of train station. Off-season rates are low for large, immaculate rooms (sheets changed daily) with good bathrooms and A/C. Singles LE8, doubles LE14, triples LE17. In winter: singles LE12.35, doubles LE17.30. Breakfast included. TV LE1.

Aswan's **campground,** a magnet for cross-Africa safari groups, also welcomes independent campers. For LE1 you can pitch a tent on the grass in this spacious, walled campground. Facilities include showers, water, and adequate toilets. You'll be charged extra for a motorcycle (50pt), car (LE1.50), or caravan (LE2). You can purchase firewood from local wood sellers. The campground, adjacent to the Unfinished Obelisk (see South of Aswan), lies 2km south of town on Sharq el-Bandar St. Take the main road running south of Aswan from the EgyptAir office on the southern corniche. The signpost is 400m off the main road to the northeast. The campground is inconvenient without motorized transport.

Food, Shopping, and Entertainment

Numerous cheap *fuul* and *taamiya* places cluster to the south of the train station. The **riverside restaurants** have great scenery, relaxed atmospheres, relatively low prices, and terraces by the Nile. At sunset, the **outdoor cafe** atop the rock outcropping in the Ferial Garden rivals even these restaurants in tranquility and inspirational scenery.

Monnalisa, on the corniche. Superb food on a lovely stone terrace overlooking the Nile. A non-profit favorite of the folks at the tourist office. You may hear imitation reggae. Baked fish with tomato sauce, rice, and salad for LE2.75. Kebab LE2.50. Breakfast LE1. Try the Monnalisa cocktail of blended fruit juices for 40pt.

El-Madina Restaurant, on al-Souk St., 2½ blocks south of the train station, across from the Cleopatra Hotel. Lightning service, fresh bread, and Egyptian food everyone can enjoy. You may share a table with local merchants. Chicken or meat with rice, potatoes in sauce, salad, bread, and zesty *tahina* for LE2.25.

Aswan Moon Restaurant, next to the Monnalisa and across from the National Bank of Egypt. Cozy up to *feluccas* on the river while listening to Nubian favorites. Shines as a nighttime cafe. Has excellent ice cream, flown in from Cairo, and many Egyptian specialties, like *mahalabiyah* (rice pudding). ½ roast chicken LE3.50. Lunchtime service painfully slow. 10% service charge.

El-Shati Restaurant, on the corniche, right across from the Hotel Continental. A delicious selection of fruit juices: banana (35pt), mango (65pt), lemon, grape, or guava juice or *karkaday* (25pt). Decent full-course menu with choice of beef, chicken, or steak entree (LE2.85). Complete menu with spicy roast fish entree (LE3.50). Modest breakfast (LE1). Ice cream (60pt). 10% service charge.

Restaurant el-Nil, across from El Shati 2 doors down from the Continental Hotel. Very clean with excellent *tahina*, salad (50pt), full menu of rice with fish or meat entree (LE4). Share a huge roasted chicken with your friends (LE4.50).

Masry, 50m up Aswan Matar St. from al-Souk St. Slightly more expensive than the corniche restaurants but attentive service in a fancy atmosphere. A bit hot and stuffy in the summertime. Try their roast pigeon special with rice, *tahina*, and salad (LE4.50).

For cheap eats, buy fresh fruit, vegetables, and bread in Aswan's markets. The main *souk* spills up streets and down alleyways in the center of town. The highest concentration of shops and street hawkers is at the southern end of al-Souk St., where it intersects al-Sayyida Nafisa St., Aswan's older market street. This area lies 3 blocks in from the Isis Hotel on the corniche. The vegetable markets lie to the north. A small concentration of produce stands fills the streets next to the Aswan Palace Hotel, a few blocks north of the main market intersection. A larger vegetable *souk* is tucked away near the train station, on the northeast edge of al-Souk St. Shop in the morning for the best produce; prices and quality drop as the day progresses.

The trade in nonperishables heats up in the evenings, especially from 8 to 10pm, when all of the shops and cafes are open. Stroll through the *souk* then, and you'll see well-dressed Egyptians shopping with their families. From among the market's many cloth merchants, seek out **Barakat Nadir Kaldas,** whose shop is in the alleyway 50m up al-Sayyida Nafisa St. from the corniche. Select one of his colorful, high-quality Egyptian cotton prints, and he'll cut and sew you a garment on the spot (trousers LE3-10, tank tops LE4-7, shirts LE8-12, dresses LE5-12, gorgeous *galabiyas,* the traditional dress of the Nubian people, LE15-25). Egypt's self-styled goodwill ambassadors, Barakat and his demure assistants, show off recommended patterns in many languages as they ply customers with tea.

Sip coffee in the evening and watch the heart of market life from **Al-Nasa Club** on al-Souk St., 3 blocks north of Barakat's shop. A few doors south look for delectable chocolate delights at the **Karmi Nuts Oven** under the Mickey Mouse sign. The *fondam* may remind you of marzipan.

The **nightclubs** in the Kalabsha and Oberoi Hotels are not worth the expense. The latter is on Elephantine Island, and the routine usually features Nubian music and a nubile belly dancer. Cover charges vary according to season; drinks are very expensive. In the winter season, the **Ramses Hotel Disco** bops nightly (LE5 admission, on Abtal al-Tahrir St., 1 block west and 2 blocks south of train station), while the **Aswan Cultural Center,** on Corniche al-Nil between the Abu Simbel and Philae Hotels, features genuine Nubian dancing and sells handicrafts. (Dancing Sat.-Thurs. 9:30-11pm during winter only. Admission LE3.10.)

Sights

Be aware from the start: Aswan is not a city of great historical treasures. Although there are pharaonic, Coptic, Islamic, and modern monuments, none of these attractions is outstanding. Aswan's real charm lies in its inviting market streets and its beautiful location on the Nile. On the west bank, directly across from the city, the wind-blown sand forms dunes with razor-sharp edges and sweeping contours. In the middle of the river floats a host of small islands where most of the city's official attractions can be found. The largest of these, **Elephantine Island,** is connected by regular ferries to the mainland (see Practical Information). As you disembark, you'll see the entertaining **Aswan Archeological Museum,** with its modest collection of local finds, on the left. The museum has a nice garden, and the guard may show you a mummy. (Open daily 8am-4pm; in summer until 5pm. Admission LE1, students 50pt to see the island whether you are interested in the museum or not.)

Past the museum's entrance at the water's edge stands a sycamore tree. Directly beneath the tree and carved into a rock by the water is the celebrated **Nilometer,** a long cylindrical shaft that measured the height of the Nile. In ancient times nothing was of greater practical significance than the testimony of the Nilometer. When it proclaimed that the river was high, the annual flooding would be profuse and the harvest correspondingly bountiful. When the Nilometer indicated a dearth of water, it foretold times of hunger and misery. The Nilometer is hollowed out from the stones of an ancient harbor quay, best viewed by *felucca* from the water. The upper stones date from the Roman period, while the lower stones, from pharaonic times, still bear inscriptions and cartouches from the reigns of Thutmose III and Amenophis III.

Elephantine Island was the original site of the settlement of Aswan. The only surviving remains have been excavated on the southeast corner of the island, directly behind the museum. The comparatively uninteresting ruins consist of traces of the ancient city, including the remains of a large **Temple of Khnum** and a small stone **Temple of Heqa-Ib,** dedicated to one of the island's ancient rulers. On the other side of the ruined city, at the southeastern tip of the island (particularly delightful when viewed from the Nile) is a little Ptolemaic temple reconstructed by German archeologists. The colors of the fragmented bas-reliefs are well-preserved.

Most visitors confine themselves to a brief tour of the ruins at the southeastern end of Elephantine Island. The central section of Elephantine, however, has three **Nubian villages,** where you'll find friendly residents and interesting alleys. The Nubians prefer that you be escorted by one of the villagers and be discreet about photography. You can often see and hear their boisterous wedding parties from the mainland. The entire northern half of Elephantine Island is taken up by the Oberoi Hotel, surrounded by a tall *cordon sanitaire* that keeps the tourists away from the Nubians. To reach the hotel, take their private ferry from the Aswan corniche; to reach the Nubians, skip the hotel.

Behind Elephantine Island and not visible from central Aswan, **Geziret al-Nabatat** ("Island of the Plants," or Kitchener's Island) is Aswan's most enchanting spot. The entire island is a botanical garden where African and Asian species grow and blossom in profusion. The bizarre plant life also attracts a variety of exotic and flamboyant birds. Lord Kitchener, the British general of both the Sudan and the Boer War who served at the turn of the century as Her Majesty's Consul-General in Egypt, lived here. Kitchener pursued his hobby of botany with fanatical passion. White ducks inhabit a lake at the southern end of the island, which belongs to a biological research station. Also at this end of the island is an overpriced **cafe** that provides a wonderful spot to rest and an exquisite view. Mineral water goes for a steep LE1.25; the cheapest offering is a glass of tea for 50pt. To reach Kitchener's Island, you can rent a *felucca* and combine an island visit with stops along the west bank. It is also possible to hire a rowboat from the west side of Elephantine Island. Nubian boys of elephantine strength spend much of their days bathing on the river on the western shore of the island. Without too much negotiation you can arrange for them to take you over to Kitchener's Island for about 75pt for one to five passengers. If you wait until 7pm, when all the Egyptians who work on the island head home, you can catch a rowboat back for 50pt. (The island is open to tourists 8am-sunset. Admission 50pt.)

To reach the sights on the west bank of the Nile, hire a *felucca.* You'll have to negotiate with the pilots, most of whom are free-spirited Nubians. The official government rate for a four-hour trip to Kitchener's Island, the west bank, and Elephantine is LE8 for a small boat regardless of the number of passengers. If you include a visit to St. Simeon's Monastery, add LE2. In practice, it often takes shrewd bargaining to get such a rate. Be very explicit in advance about where you want to go, especially if you visit St. Simeon's Monastery, and how much time you plan to take. Make an effort to meet other tourists who wish to share a *felucca.* Try the restaurants along the corniche or the cafes in front of the Hotel Continental. If you wish to visit the Tombs of the Nobles in addition to the usual itinerary, plan on at least a five-hour trip and two more pounds for the *felucca.* Ferries run to and from the tombs and the east bank for 25pt, so you're better off visiting them separately.

The most accessible attraction on the west bank of the Nile is the **Mausoleum of Agha Khan,** just a short climb from where the *felucca* docks. Agha Khan is the hereditary title of the ruler of the Ismaili Muslims. The Ismaili believe that the Agha Khan is the direct descendent of Muhammad and inheritor of his spiritual responsibilities of guidance. The Agha Khans used to rule from Pakistan, but political exile has since compelled them to take up residence elsewhere. Aswan became the favorite winter retreat of Muhammad Shah Agha Khan (1899-1957), the 48th Imam of the Ismaili. Upon his death, the Begum (Agha Khan's wife) oversaw the construction of the mausoleum, where she is also buried. The exterior of the shrine is less impressive than its interior, modeled after the traditional Fatimid tombs of Cairo. Enter the mausoleum through a massive pair of brass doors. At the opposite end of the structure in the small domed chamber stands the marble sarcophagus inscribed with passages from the Koran. Each day a red rose is laid upon the sarcophagus; contemporary legends tell of the distances across which a red rose has been flown when there was none available in the area. (Open Tues.-Sun. 9am-5pm. Free. *Baksheesh* for the guards is forbidden. Friendly caretaker will show you around. Men and women are occasionally refused entrance if they are wearing shorts.)

Standing isolated and majestic in the desert, 1km directly inland from the mausoleum, is **Dayr Amba Samaan** (Monastery of St. Simeon). Built in the sixth and seventh centuries C.E. and abandoned in the thirteenth, the monastery sits on a terrace carved into the steep hills clearly visible from the Mausoleum of the Agha Kahn. No one around is really quite sure who St. Simeon was or what he did. With its turreted walls rising to a height of 6m, the monastery has more the appearance of a fortress than of a religious sanctuary. Indeed, it was eventually abandoned, due in part to repeated attacks by Bedouin, and in part to the difficulty of maintaining a water supply. The original walls of the complex stood 10m high, and enclosed a community of 300 resident monks. Upstairs, the monks' cells with their stone beds are currently occupied by bats. In the courtyard you can still see the remains of a primitive bread oven. The monastery also had a church, and accommodations sufficient for several hundred pilgrims. Some of the original frescoes of the church are still visible. (Open 9am-6pm. Admission LE1, students 50pt.) To reach the monastery, follow the paved path which starts from behind Agha Khan Mausoleum (15-20 min., bring water) or hire a camel near the *felucca* stop. (LE2 per camel; two people fit on one camel.) Get the finances straight with your guide before he leads you out into the desert.

The **Tombs of the Nobles** are skipped by most visitors to Aswan. They lie farther north along the west bank of the Nile, honeycombed into the face of the desert cliffs and beautifully illuminated at night. These tombs of governors and dignitaries date primarily from the end of the Old Kingdom and the First Intermediate Period. Unfortunately, most of the tombs are in sad disrepair. The bright color and detail of the reliefs in **The Tomb of Sarenput II (#31),** from about 1920 B.C.E., make this tomb worth the easy trip across the Nile. Six lifesize stone sarcophagi stand guard over the inner chamber. Scenes on the rear wall depict the nobleman hunting and fishing. Farther south on the mountain ridge are the interconnected and unattractive Sixth-Dynasty tombs of Nikhu and Sabni (#25 and 26), a father and son. Take a moment to appreciate an aerial view of Aswan from the tombs. The **Tomb of Heqa-ib** (unmarked, just north of #35) boasts an attractive facade and some excavated relief work in the interior. (Open daily 8am-4pm. Admission LE1, students 50pt. Ferries for the tombs leave from in front of the tourist office on the east bank of the Nile, 25pt.)

Perhaps the most worthwhile excursion in the Aswan area is to any of the numerous **Nubian villages** in the surrounding region, particularly on the occasion of a wedding. You may be invited to join the celebrations as the dancing and music build in intensity; the villagers consider it a mark of honor to have guests from far away villages and nations attend their weddings. Nubian weddings traditionally involved 15 days of partying, but the demands of modern life have cut the festivities down to three or four.

You may spot the traditional domed roofs of Nubian buildings. Their large houses made of Nile mud consist of a half dozen rooms around a courtyard. Each cluster of rooms has its own dome or cylindrical roof. While the disruption wrought by the High Dam has threatened to destroy this traditional architecture, Egyptian architect Hasan Fatry has brought it international recognition.

The Nubians have a long history as an advanced culture. Nubian kingdoms flourished on trade and agriculture during pharaonic times. The Nubians retain many characteristics that set them apart from other Egyptians; besides their African racial features, they speak their own language and have a remarkably strong set of kinship ties. The women dress colorfully, although Muslim standards of modesty require them to wrap a thin black robe over their clothes. Close ties with the Sudan remain, despite the international boundary and the monstrous lake that threatens to cut off Egyptian Nubians from their Sudanese kin.

Because the villages on Elephantine Island are readily accessible, they are visited more frequently by tourists. The ferry to the west bank tombs will bring you to **Garb Aswan,** another series of Nubian villages. From the ferry dock, you can walk or catch a taxi north to the villages. There you can readily meet the locals, observe the traditional houses, and purchase handicrafts, such as baskets, woven hats, and necklaces. The villagers are open and friendly, and you will undoubtedly be asked to join them for a cup of tea or a game of backgammon during the heat of the afternoon. If you are going to Elephantine or the west bank, ask your *felucca* captain to show you around the village.

South of Aswan

Aswan itself may lack spectacular antiquities, but the emerald 15km stretch of the Nile south of town more than compensates. This region of the First Cataract includes both the **Old Dam** (5km south of Aswan), built in the early twentieth century by the British, and the enormous **High Dam** (15km south of Aswan), whose construction in the early 1960s created Lake Nasser. On an island in the lake between the two dams, the exquisite **Philae Temple** still proclaims the glory of Isis. Just beyond the west side of the High Dam, the lonely **Temple of Kalabsha** stands guard over brooding Lake Nasser and the surrounding desert. The pharaoh's granite quarries lie on the southern border of Aswan and contain the famous **Unfinished Obelisk.** The area invites daytrips from the comfortable base of Aswan.

Getting Around

Fortunately, many convenient modes of public transportation reach these sights. An excellent road follows the Nile from Aswan to the village of **Hazan,** site of both the Old Dam and the motorboat launch to Philae. The road crosses the dam and continues for 10km along the west side of the Nile to reach the High Dam. Getting from Aswan to Hazan is simple, as the route is served by **service taxis** (25pt per person) and by **public bus** (#20 and 59 from corniche; 14 per day, 6am-9:30pm; 5pt). To reach the High Dam by road, hire a **special taxi.** Typically, a group of travelers hires a taxi to take them to the Philae launch, then to the Old Dam and on to the High Dam, returning after three or four hours to Aswan. With a little bargaining, up to four people can hire a small taxi for four or five hours for LE12, or up to eight people can hire a large taxi for LE16. A full itinerary for this fare includes the High Dam, the Old Dam, Philae Temple, and the nearby Unfinished Obelisk and ancient granite quarries. The trip can be a relaxed 7am to 1pm tour. The best place to meet tourists for such a venture is in one of the cafes on the corniche. Try the cafes in front of the Hotel Continental.

If you don't mind spending a little more, another way to see all the sights except the Temple of Kalabsha is to take one of the **taxi tours** occasionally organized by the youth hostel upon special request (approximately LE4 per person). Though you'd save money by getting your own group together, the tour has the advantage of leaving at 5am sharp, allowing you to be the first to reach all the sights. The driver is taciturn, and the group rarely grows larger than four. Inquire at the hostel at least two nights before you want to go. The tours usually operate in the busier winter months only. Hotel managers at such places as the Marwa, Mena, and Ramses Hotels also organize tours. Ask at the hotel reception desk or tourist office. Less reliable are the illegal tours arranged by private operators. You can arrange tours of all the sights around Aswan for as many days as you wish, but be sure to settle where you are going and how much it will cost before you agree to anything. The outdoor cafe at the **Abu Simbel** hotel is a favorite hangout of self-styled tour guides.

The Dams and Quarries

The most notorious of the attractions in the area is Egypt's contemporary attempt at monumentality, the **High Dam (Sadd al-Ali),** completed in 1971. A kilometer thick at its base, 3.6km long, and 110m high, the dam has inundated Nubia with waters as deep as 200m, wiping out 45 villages and requiring the relocation of thousands of people, as well as the removal of numerous ancient monuments to high ground by UNESCO. The dam also interrupts the flow of silt, depriving Egypt's farmlands of their traditional, rejuvenating natural fertilizer, and the croplands now become saltier with each passing year. Should the dam ever break, the consequences would be horrendous: Most of the population would swirl away into the Mediterranean. After the 1967 war, Egyptians feared that the Israelis would destroy the dam, and in 1984, Libya threatened to bomb it.

On the other hand, the dam's 12 turbines produces over 2 megawatts of electricity. Agricultural productivity has been greatly enhanced, and the surface area of Egypt's arable soil has been increased by 30%. The dam enabled Egypt to enjoy an undiminished water supply during the drought of this past decade, while the Sudan and East African countries starved. In August 1988, however, the dam saved Egypt from the flood suffered by Sudan when the Nile overflowed after heavy rains. The consequences of the massive project are still unfolding: For example, a rise in the Sahara's water table has been noticed as far away as Algeria. Archeologists suspect that the high water table has damaged the tombs at Luxor.

The most conspicuous consequence of the High Dam is **Lake Nasser,** the world's largest artificial lake, which stretches 500km across the Tropic of Cancer and into the Sudan. The beauty of the lake—long slender fingers probing into the desert—is tempered by an awareness of its effects: the dispersion of an entire people, followed by the slow death of their culture, and the loss of priceless antiquities beneath the waters.

The High Dam at Aswan has had significant international repercussions as well. Plans for the construction were unveiled after World War II when it became apparent that Egypt had achieved maximum agricultural output and could no longer feed its rapidly increasing population. When the United States offered and then refused to provide loans for the High Dam project in 1956, President Nasser ordered the seizure and nationalization of the Suez Canal, allegedly as a means of generating the necessary hard currency. This triggered the Suez Crisis, in which France, Britain, and Israel invaded Egypt and were restrained by the United Nations. The Soviet Union decided to provide the necessary loans and technology, and work began on the dam in 1960.

On the east bank, just before the dam, the **Visitors Pavilion** features plaques and sculptures blending Soviet socialist-realist motifs with traditional pharaonic figures and symbols. Plans for the construction of the dam—written in Russian and Arabic—include a map with the names of the 45 Nubian villages the engineers knew would be washed away. At the center of the pavilion is a 15m model of the High Dam and the surrounding environs, minus the water. Another display gives a photographic description of the dismantling of Abu Simbel. (Museum open 7am-5pm. Free, but the guard will expect some *baksheesh* for opening the place.)

A towering stone monument at the foot of the dam on the west bank is another remnant of Soviet cooperation. Shaped as a stylized lotus blossom, it was intended as a symbol of Soviet-Egyptian friendship. Shortly after the completion of the dam, when Anwar Sadat came to power, Egypt severed relations with the Soviet Union and turned back to the United States. The top of the dam features excellent views of the islands to the north and Lake Nasser to the south. (Admission to the top LE1.50.)

Eight trains per day travel to the eastern end of the High Dam (see Practical Information), but you'll have to hitchhike or walk the several kilometers across the dam to see the sights. Take the train to the High Dam only if you plan to catch the boat to Wadi Halfa in the Sudan. The train station usually presents a colorful spectacle, crowded with Sudanese tribespeople (largely Bishari) camping out while they wait for the next boat home. Otherwise take a taxi. Note that the dam closes to traffic at 5pm on most days.

Less spectacular than the High Dam but more scenic, the **Old Dam,** a few kilometers to the north, merits a brief visit. Built by the British between 1898 and 1902, the dam supplied most of Egypt's power for many years. The Old Dam can be reached by bus from the Aswan bus station (see Getting Around). The area known as the **First Cataract** is extremely fertile, and one of the most pleasant spots in the Aswan area. In the picturesque village of **Hazan,** 70-year-old British villas snooze peacefully in walled gardens. When the Nile is high, water gushes forth dramatically from sluices on this east bank. It fills the air with cool spray, while the surrounding trees grow heavy with peaches and mangoes. Situated just below the waters of the First Cataract, **Sehel Island** attracts remarkably few tourists. Its claim to fame lies in a hospitable Nubian village, some scanty ruins, and a variety of inscriptions ranging from the Fourth Dynasty to the Ptolemaic period. If you're interested in a longer *felucca* ride from Aswan, this island makes a perfect destination. (LE10-15 for a 3-hr. tour.)

If you're traveling by taxi back to Aswan after touring the High Dam or Philae, ask the driver to stop at the Fatimid Tombs, the adjacent Unfinished Obelisk, and the nearby granite quarries. They all lie near the camping area, 300m east of the main road at a turn-off 1km south of Aswan. The **Fatimid Tombs,** low, stone buildings with crescents on their roofs, are small but typical early Islamic shrines. They are easily spotted on the left side of the road. The tombs have been more or less abandoned; it can be spooky wandering around the dark cemetery, which is frequented by semi-wild packs of dogs who look right at home amidst the doghouse-sized tombs. The **Unfinished Obelisk** was abandoned at its site because of a flaw in the granite; it was to have stood a whopping 41.7m high on a base 4.2m on each side. Its sides and top were already carved and polished before the designers abandoned the project. The **granite quarries** here supplied most of ancient Egypt with the raw material for pyramids and temples. One method of stone cutting involved the insertion of wooden wedges into slits made with quartz tools. The wedges were then moistened and their expansion split the rock. Such simple technologies—and lots of muscle—substituted for dynamite and jackhammers. (Obelisk and quarries open daily 6am to 5 or 6pm. Admission 50pt, students 25pt.)

Philae

Circumstances have conspired to perpetuate the aura of romance that has surrounded the temples of Philae since their construction in Ptolemaic times. Philae Island's isolation and the majesty of its position at the frontiers of Nubia, overlooking an unusually fertile region, have long attracted visitors. In the Greek and Roman eras, the temples of the cult of Isis drew the pious and the curious alike. Rediscovered by modern Europeans, Philae remained a popular tourist destination even after 1902, when the construction of the Old Dam partially submerged the temples. When the Dam was enlarged in 1912, archeologists feared that the temple would eventually be destroyed by the Nile's strong currents. Philae was finally saved only after the construction of the High Dam alerted the world to the watery plight of Nubia's monuments. Between 1972 and 1980, UNESCO and the Egyptian Antiquities Department labored to transfer the complex of temples from Philae Island to higher ground on nearby Agilka Island. In 1980, the new site of the ancient temples was opened to a fresh flood of tourism. Today, motorboats shuttle visitors past eerie rock outcrops while white ibises glide across the desert sky.

The well-preserved **Temple of Isis** dominates the island's western edge. The goddess Isis was the mother of nature, protector of humans, goddess of purity and sexuality, and sister-wife of the legendary hero Osiris. Her following was so strong that the cult of Isis continued long after the establishment of Christianity, dying out only in the sixth century during the reign of Emperor Justinian. Nearly all the structures on Philae date from the Ptolemaic and Roman eras, after the beginning of artistic decline in Egypt. Hence the quality of their decorative relief work is comparatively poor. Nevertheless, all buildings display the influence of the Greco-Roman style, and blend classicism with pharaonic traditionalism. A fascinating collection of antique graffiti is inscribed on the ancient walls, testifying to Philae's long history of tourism. The birds have also left their mark on the outer western wall of the temple, which is splattered with their droppings.

From the landing at the southern tip of the island, climb the short slope leading to the temple complex past Philae's oldest structure, the **Portico of Nectanebo.** The paved portico once formed the vestibule of an ancient temple, but the larger edifice has been washed away. The eastern side of the colonnade remains unfinished, and the capitals crowning its handsome columns are each unique. At the first pylon, towers rise to a height of 18m on either side of the main entrance into the temple. Through this entrance is the central court, on whose western edge sits a Roman *mammisis,* its elegant columns emblazoned with the head of the cow-goddess Hathor. To the north is the slightly off-center second pylon, marking the way to the temple's inner sanctum. The *pronaos* (vestibule) was converted into a church by early Christians, who inscribed Byzantine crosses on the chamber walls and added a small altar. Proceed on to the *naos,* the temple's innermost sanctuary. Just inside the doorway is an amusing piece of ancient graffiti etched into the granite wall in capital letters: "B. Mure Stultus Est" ("B. Mure is stupid"). The *naos* terminates in three small chapels, decorated with representations of Isis and other deities. A staircase leads from the western side up to the **Osiris chambers,** a set of apartments containing excellent reliefs depicting Osiris' mourners.

Retrace your steps to the second court to explore the island's western edge. Beyond the Roman *mammisis* are a series of ruined structures, and at the foot of the quay an ancient **Nilometer.** Slightly to the north is **Hadrian's Gateway,** with a relief showing the Nile god, wrapped in the coils of a serpent, pouring water from two vessels below the solemn gazes of a vulture and a falcon. At the northern tip of the island are the **Temple of Augustus** and the **Roman Gate.** Nearby is a somewhat grimy restroom (bring your own toilet paper). Return to the landing via the island's eastern edge. About half-way down, directly east of the temple's second pylon, is the charming **Temple of Hathor;** fanciful representations of flutists, harp players, and lyre-playing monkeys adorn its columns. Farther south, clinging to a steep slope leading down to the water's edge, is the enchanting **Kiosk of Trajan.**

The nightly one-hour **sound and light show** at Philae may enhance your appreciation of the temples. There are shows in English every night except Thursday and Sunday. (Showtimes 8:30pm and 9:30pm, LE10; buy tickets at Philae.)

You can visit Philae by **taxi** as part of an itinerary including the High Dam, or reach the island using public transportation by taking a **bus** to the Old Dam from the Aswan bus station. From the last bus stop, walk west to the boat dock either along the main paved desert road, or through the lake-side village (about 2km either way). Whether you come by bus or by taxi, you have to hire a motorboat to reach the island. The proper round-trip fee for a small **motorboat** is LE6 for one to eight people, and 75pt per person for eight or more people. It is normally easy to find other visitors to join in a rental on the motorboat docks at any time of year, since Philae is a popular tourist destination. The boat pilot is obliged to wait for you as you tour the site, so you needn't rush. If you linger for more than an hour, though, some additional *baksheesh* is in order. Don't pay the driver his fare until you're back on the east bank. (Open daily 7am-6pm; in Ramadan daily 7am-4pm. Admission LE3, students LE1.50. Purchase tickets by the dock.)

Kalabsha

The enormous **Temple of Kalabsha,** dramatically situated above the sparkling waters of Lake Nasser at the top of the High Dam, is one of the best pharaonic ruins in the Aswan area. Dedicated to the Nubian god Mandulis, the temple was begun by Amenhotes II, erected primarily during the reign of Augustus, and served as a church during the Christian era. The West German government paid to have the entire temple dismantled and transported in 13,000 pieces to its present site, 50km north of its original home, which was overwhelmed by Lake Nasser. The Germans had modern machinery, but you'll probably wonder how the ancient Egyptians managed without it. Of all the Nubian monuments rescued from the encroaching waters, many Egyptologists consider well-preserved Kalabsha to be second only to the treasures of Abu Simbel. Military restrictions protected the Temple of Kalabsha from the usual tourist traffic found at Egypt's other antiquities until recently.

New steps are under construction from the temple to the water's edge, and Kalabsha's halls may become more crowded.

You no longer need a permit to enter the Kalabsha Temple area; you simply pay a 25pt toll at a military checkpoint. The temple is located on the west bank of the Nile, just south of the High Dam and a few hundred meters past the checkpoint. The most convenient way to reach Kalabsha is by **taxi**. A taxi can bring you from Aswan (official rates LE10 for 1-4 persons, LE10-15 for a 7 person taxi). You can also reach the road to Kalabsha independently by taking the **train** to the eastern end of the High Dam (20pt; see above), and then hitchhiking or walking across the dam. As a foreigner, you may be charged a LE1.50 toll; don't forget that the dam closes at 5pm. Unless the water level in Lake Nasser has risen dramatically (which would make Kalabsha an island accessible by boat only), you will walk the 2km to the temple, passing abandoned hulls of a marooned fishing fleet along the dusty way. Don't try to walk in the summer heat. The site is officially open from 6am to 5pm, but the guard may be so surprised to have visitors that he'll let you stay past 5pm. (Admission LE2, students LE1).

An immense causeway of dressed stone leads from the water to the temple's main entrance, and the first pylon is off-center from both the causeway and the inner gateways of the temple itself. Notice the sun disk and cobra symbol over each successive entrance. A carving of St. George and inscriptions in Coptic survive from early Christian times. The grand forecourt between the pylon and the vestibule is surrounded by 14 columns, each with a unique capital. Stairs lead up from a small room just beyond the vestibule to the roof, where you can look over the entire forecourt and vestibule. From the roof you will get a fantastic view of the temple, the columns, Lake Nasser to the south, and the High Dam to the north. Styles have changed, but the lotus-shaped sculpture at the dam shows how monument-making has continued.

Because the temple faces east, light flows into the **Holy of Holies,** or innermost chamber, in the early morning hours. Bring a flashlight if you want to explore at other times, and beware of bats—they're everywhere. A passageway leads north through the vestibule to an inner encircling wall; follow the wall around to the south until you find the well-preserved **Nilometer.** Extraordinary carvings of Mandulis, Isis, Horus, and Osiris cover the outside walls. To the west, beautifully carved bas-reliefs depict Amenophis II in the presence of the gods.

Outside the huge fortress-like wall, the remains of a small **shrine** are visible to the southeast. The present structure is largely a reconstructed facade. Piles and crates of stones litter the ground to the south of the main temple. This catch-all of Nubian remains includes some predynastic elephants and miscellaneous reliefs of Nubian wildlife. The carvings and cartouches on the fallen obelisks retain significant traces of their original colors. The detail on some of the slabs reveals fine artisanry. The double-image technique, characteristic of Nubian temples, is used to portray motion in some of the drawings.

Slightly removed from Kalabsha Temple, to the southwest, are ruins of the **Temple of Kertassi.** Two Hathor columns remain, as well as four other columns with elaborate floral capitals and a single monolithic architrave. Up the hill to the northwest is the **Rock Temple of Beit al-Wali** (House of the Holy Man), rescued from the rising waters of Lake Nasser with the aid of the U.S. government. One of many Nubian temples constructed by Ramses II, it features the typical poses of Ramses smiting enemies, and Ramses receiving prisoners. Like a miniature Abu Simbel, this cave-temple was hewn from solid rock. Brilliantly colored bas-reliefs adorn the walls of the temple's outer and inner chambers. Examine the scenes closely: Both political and social history are shown in everything from graphic chariot battles to household toil.

Abu Simbel

At the southernmost end of the Nile in Egypt lie the most awe-inspiring monuments in the country. Four 22m-tall statues of Ramses II, carved out of a single slab of rock, greet the sunrise over Lake Nasser from the massive Great Temple of Abu Simbel. Ramses II had this grand sanctuary and the nearby Temple of Hathor built more than 3500 years ago to impress the Nubians with the power and glory of Egyptian rule; Abu Simbel still serves its purpose, leaving no visitor unmoved. For a sneak preview of the site, look at the back of any Egyptian one pound note.

Practical Information

Abu Simbel is 274km south of Aswan and 50km from the Sudanese border. An excellent paved road through the desert has opened the way for land vehicles. Every morning air-conditioned **buses** leave from the Aswan bus station at 8am and arrive at the temple at 11:30am. The same bus brings you back, leaving from the Hotel Nefertari near the site at 1:30pm and arriving in Aswan at about 5pm (LE8 each way). Purchase your tickets to Abu Simbel at the bus station at least one day in advance. You buy your return ticket on the bus when you come back. Note that tourist bus companies offer luxury tours at LE50 per head; don't confuse these with the public transport. Bring snacks and water for the trip.

The proprietors of Mena, Ramses, el-Amin, and Marwa hotels organize taxi tours to Abu Simbel and the High Dam for LE15-18 per person. You will generally leave at 4am and be back in Aswan by 1-2pm. The advantage of these tours is that you will arrive early at Abu Simbel when there are fewer tourists and when the summer desert heat is still bearable. In the summer, however, you'll be scorched by the non-air-conditioned taxis. A private taxi trip arranged on your own will save a few pounds in a group of seven. The Hotel Continental is a good place to make arrangements. If you plan to make the trip by taxi, you will need to have your passport registered with the Aswan police office. The drivers will handle this service for you. Keep your passports during the length of the trip regardless of whether you're traveling by bus or taxi, as they are occasionally checked by the border police.

In summer, three **flights** per day from Cairo and Aswan serve Abu Simbel (round-trip from Aswan LE110, from Cairo LE248). In winter, there are several additional daily flights. EgyptAir provides its passengers with free bus service to the temple. After a whirlwind tour, you'll be driven back to the airport for the return flight.

During the winter, you can stay overnight in Abu Simbel at the **Nefertari Hotel,** 100m away from the temple down the main road. **Camping** in the surrounding desert presents no problem. The best sites are next to the police station (for safety) or next to the hotel (for comfort). The **police station** is 400m away from the temple along the road. Those who arrive by bus and decide to stay the night on impulse should have little difficulty finding a hospitable villager. The **town** of Abu Simbel, a determined but small and displaced version of its former self, lies about 2km from the temple site.

The site of Abu Simbel is open daily from 6am to 6pm, later if planes fly in during the evening. While the interior of the temple remains closed at other times, you can view the exterior at odd hours if you are friendly to the guards. (Admission including obligatory guide fee, LE6.50, students LE3.50).

Sights

When the rising waters of Lake Nasser threatened to engulf one of Egypt's greatest treasures, nations joined together and moved the two great temples at Abu Simbel 200m to higher ground. At a cost of $36 million, teams of engineers from five countries painstakingly cut the temples, which were hewn out of solid rock, into 3000 pieces weighing between 10 and 40 tons each. The pieces were moved, the temples reconstructed, and in 1968 a hollow mountain was built around the two structures. They were carefully oriented to face their original directions, and the surrounding landscape was recreated. All in all, 11 temples were moved. Some were placed in Egypt, others were given to the U.S., Spain, Italy, and Holland. (The Temple of Dendar is now sheltered in New York's Metropolitan Museum of Art.)

The **Great Temple of Abu Simbel** is Ramses II's masterwork. This energetic builder effectively dedicated the temple to himself, although the great god Ra-Hurakhti is paid lip service. As you progress through the temple, the artwork depicts Ramses first as great king, then as servant of the gods, next as companion of the gods, and finally, in the inner sanctuary, as a card-carrying deity. It is the representation of Ramses as a great king that is most impressive. The seated **Colossi of Ramses,** four 20m statues of the king at the front of the great temple, wear both the New and Old Kingdom versions of the crowns of Upper and Lower Egypt. An earthquake in 27 B.C.E. crumbled the upper body of one of the Colossi. Modern engineers were not able to put it back together, so they left it in its original faceless state. The relatively small figures standing between Ramses' legs represent the royal family. A row of praying baboons tops the entrance; the ancient Egyptians admired the baboons' natural habit of greeting the rising sun.

From the interior of the **Great Hypostyle Hall,** eight more statues of Ramses stare ominously out from under artificial light. The god Osiris, in the form of a vulture, adorns the ceiling to protect the statues of the king. Etched on the walls are some of Egypt's most beautiful murals. Note the artist's double-image technique to portray motion in the dramatized Battle of Kadesh, fought between Ramses and the Hittites of Northern Syria. On the entire northern wall of the hypostyle hall, Ramses retells this story, his favorite since he won, with a richly detailed mural.

Farther into the rock-hewn temple are antechambers that once stored objects of worship. In the vestibule, Ramses is depicted embracing the gods. On the walls, sacred white barques carry the dead to the underworld. In the inner sanctum, four statues depict Ramses and the gods Ra-Hurakhti, Amon, and Ptah (the Theban god of darkness). Originally encased in gold, the statues now wait with divine patience for February 22 and October 22, when the first rays of the sun reach 100m into the temple to bathe all except Ptah in light. February 21 was Ramses' birthday and October 21 his coronation date, but when the temple was moved, the timing of these great moments was shifted by one day.

At the smaller **Temple of Hathor,** six 10m standing statues of King Ramses and Queen Nefertari (as the goddess Hathor) adorn the facade. Nefertari's is one of Egypt's two great temples dedicated to women; the Temple of Hatshepsut in West Thebes is the other. Scenes on the walls depict Ramses' coronation, with the god Horus placing the crown of Upper and Lower Egypt on his head. The temple was constructed in the traditional three-room fashion: The first chamber containing six columns was open to the public, the second chamber was open to nobles and priests, and the inner sanctuary reserved for the pharaoh and the high priest.

Alexandria

> *If a man make a pilgrimage round Alexandria in the morning, God will make for him a golden crown set with pearls.*
> —*ibn Dukmak*

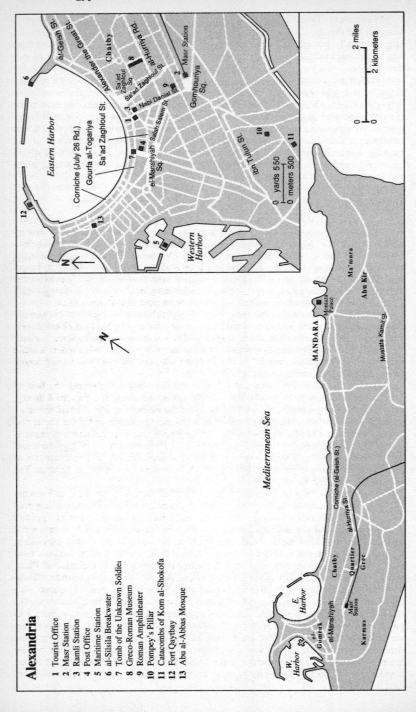

Alexandria

1 Tourist Office
2 Masr Station
3 Ramli Station
4 Post Office
5 Maritime Station
6 al-Silsila Breakwater
7 Tomb of the Unknown Soldier
8 Greco-Roman Museum
9 Roman Amphitheater
10 Pompey's Pillar
11 Catacombs of Kom al-Shokofa
12 Fort Qaytbay
13 Abu al-Abbas Mosque

Not any more. The wonders of Alexandria—the world's greatest library, the monumental lighthouse, the tomb of Alexander the Great—are all gone. The Hellenistic city is literally buried under the new metropolis, and Cleopatra doesn't live here any more. Alexandria does have one crown left to it—the seashore and line of golden beaches.

Alexandria, ancient and modern, has been shaped by the Mediterranean. Although the city shares the problems of excessive dirt, overcrowding, noise, and poverty with Cairo, there is a different spirit here. Perhaps the endless blue sea cools the city's temperament as well as the air's temperature. In any case, for both Europeans and Egyptians, Alexandria is a haven from the pressure-cooker that Cairo becomes in the summer. During the day, hundreds of thousands splash at the beaches, while at night they stroll along the corniche, joining the throngs at nightclubs and restaurants. If *al-Qahirah* is "The Conqueror," then *al-Iskandaria* is the spoils.

History

In 332 B.C.E., **Alexander the Great** was sitting pretty. In that year, the overachieving young emperor had wrenched Egypt from the Persians. After a triumphant reception at Memphis, he set off for the Oracle of Amun at the distant Siwa Oasis to discover if he was the son of the god. On the way down the seacoast, he came across a small fishing village facing a natural harbor. Liking the spot, he ordered a city to be built there. Following the great tradition of Ramses, he dedicated it to himself, something he did dozens of times during his conquests. Leaving architects behind to start construction, he left for Siwa and never came back.

Upon Alexander's death nine years later, Egypt fell into the hands of his general **Ptolemy Soter.** Ptolemy truly created the new city, glorifying his former employer. Ptolemy even hijacked Alexander's corpse—which was on his way to Siwa, according to his last wishes—and interred it with great pomp under Alexandria's main square. The body and its tomb, like all of the Ptolemaic city, is now buried somewhere under the downtown maze.

Ptolemy and his descendants dedicated themselves to transplanting the best of Hellenic civilization to Egyptian soil. The *Museion,* including the famous **Library,** soon became the greatest center of learning in the ancient world. **Euclid** invented geometry here, while other great minds determined the diameter of the earth and the exact duration of the earth's revolution. To satisfy the spiritual needs of his subjects, Ptolemy imported an Asian god, **Serapis.** With a committee of Egyptian and Greek theologians, he came up with a popular syncretic faith in which aspects of the Hellenic Zeus and of the Pharaonic Apis bull were combined in Serapis. The new cult was a big hit.

The wondrous city soon became the site of one of the seven wonders, as Ptolemy II built the great **Lighthouse of Pharos Island.** Its immense 400 foot tower featured a beacon of flame and mirrors. The once-unused harbor was increasingly packed with ships, and Alexandria traded its way into becoming the richest commercial center of the east. It attracted many peoples to its bountiful culture, and, inevitably, it attracted the attention of the Romans. In 48 B.C.E., **Julius Caesar** and his rival **Pompey** fought to determine who would control the new empire. Defeated at Pharsalus, Pompey fled to Egypt, with Caesar in close pursuit. There they found a fifteen-year-old king, **Ptolemy XIV,** fighting a civil war with a twenty-year-old queen—his sister and wife—by the name of **Cleopatra.** From Shakespeare to Hollywood, the story is familiar. Ptolemy tried to charm Caesar by assassinating Pompey, but Cleopatra tried more intimate tactics. She won his favor, and bore his child. After Caesar's death, she and **Mark Antony,** two happy-go-lucky kids, got together and dreamed of ruling the known world together. But it was not to be: Defeated by **Octavian** (soon to be the Emperor Augustus Caesar) at the Battle of Actium, the lovers committed suicide and their city became the capital of a brand new imperial province.

The fortunes of the city rose and fell with the empire. It remained a great center of learning and culture. Here the first Greek translation of the Hebrew Bible, the **Septuagint,** was written for the expatriate Jewish population after the destruction of the Temple in Jerusalem. The translation is named for the 70 scholars who, according to legend, each labored in isolation, and yet produced precisely the same text.

According to tradition, **St. Mark** introduced Christianity here in 62 C.E., founding what was to become the **Coptic Church.** In the third century, mass conversions made Alexandria a Christian spiritual center, but Roman persecutions increased as well. Their atrocities reached a bloody height under **Diocletian,** who murdered so many Christians that the Copts date their calendar from the beginning of his reign, calling it the Martyr's Calendar.

But the **Christians** had their vengeance. Once they were officially recognized by the Emperor Constantine, their influence grew, and they turned on their pagan neighbors with vengeful fury. The last remnant of the Great Library was burned during anti-Roman riots in 309. Harmony did not come with conversion, for the Egyptian Church differed with the Byzantines on matters of theology. In challenge to the authority of the Byzantine Church they set up a Patriarchate of their own in Alexandria. The Byzantines persecuted the schismatics to such an extent that when the **Persians** came as conquerors in the seventh century, quickly followed by the **Arabs,** they were received as liberators.

Alexandria was still a great city when the Arabs found it, but its fortunes quickly waned. The new capital in Cairo eclipsed its glory, while a series of earthquakes shook its structure, finally reducing the immense lighthouse to rubble in the thirteenth century. Pharos Island itself gradually became a peninsula, attached by an hourglass-shaped isthmus. The **Mamluks** exiled political opponents here, and when the canal from the Nile dried up, the city literally became a backwater.

The **modern city** began when **Muhammad Ali** decided he needed it as a port for his navy; by redigging a canal to the Nile, he immediately rejuvenated the city. Over the course of the nineteenth century, it became the favorite haven of expatriate Europeans as well as wealthy Turks and Egyptians. The entire colonial government migrated here from Cairo for the summer. This was the city that Lawrence Durrell and E.M. Forster documented in their novels and histories. After the Revolution of 1952, Alexandria saw heavy building and heavy crowding. It is now Egypt's biggest port, its second-largest city (population 4 million), and its summer capital.

Orientation

Alexandria's 10- and 15-story buildings parade down 20km of Mediterranean beachfront, on a strip at most 3km wide. The city's industrial, commercial, and residential sectors jostle for space along the main arteries, which parallel the coast. Ancient Alexandria, on the now-tranquil Eastern Harbor, remains the heart of the modern city. This downtown commercial district, called **el-Manshiya,** is the hub of Alexandria's transportation network, nightlife, and tourist trade. Just west of downtown lie **el-Gumruk** and **el-Anfushi,** the colorful, aged residential neighborhoods of ancient Pharos Island. A nightmarish gray tangle of factories and port facilities sprawls along the Western Harbor. Immediately southeast of el-Manshiya, the so-called **Quartier Grec** encompasses **Masr Railway Station,** the city's main depot, and numerous foreign consulates. South of el-Manshiya and Masr Station, the dusty streets of **Karmus** overflow with students, workers, and many of Alexandria's poorest citizens. The **corniche** is Alexandria's celebrated four-lane highway, pedestrian promenade, and sea wall. **Montaza Palace,** an 18m drive from el-Manshiya, pins down the far eastern boundary of Alexandria. Note that the corniche is also called **July 26 Road** along the Eastern Harbor, and **al-Geish Road** between al-Silsila breakwater and Montaza. The posh Western-style resort village of **Ma'mura** lies just east of the Montaza garden wall.

The best place from which to orient yourself downtown is **Sa'ad Zaghloul Square,** on the waterfront with a massive statue of Sa'ad Zaghloul in the center; he was an Egyptian nationalist who opposed British rule. You should become familiar with the four streets that border the square: Along the western edge runs **Nabi Danial Street;** along the waterfront is the **corniche;** the square's eastern border is formed by **Safia Zaghloul Street;** and **Alexander the Great Street** is the thoroughfare on the south. Alexandria actually has two central squares: **Ramli Station Square** occasionally confuses visitors since it borders **Sa'ad Zaghloul Square** on the southeast corner. Safia Zaghloul Street, which bisects the two squares, is Alexandria's principal north-south boulevard. Bordering Ramli Station Sq. on the south side is **Sa'ad Zaghloul Street,** which does *not* border Sa'ad Zaghloul Sq.). In addition to their central locations, the two squares serve as transportation ganglions for the city. Intercity buses run from the station on the corner of Nabi Danial St. in Sa'ad Zaghloul Sq., and many municipal buses serve the big stop in front of the square on the corniche.

El-Manshiya Square is on the Eastern Harbor. It combines rectangular Orabi Square, an important interchange for local buses, and smaller Tahrir Square (Midan Tahrir), which centers on the **Tomb of the Unknown Soldier,** a neoclassical monument facing the corniche. El-Manshiya Square lies about 5 blocks west of Sa'ad Zaghloul Sq. at the intersection of al-Sabaa Banat St. with Salah Salem and Orabi St. Another main thoroughfare is **al-Hurriya Road,** which runs east-west about 5 blocks south of Sa'ad Zaghloul Sq. Lined with banks and travel agencies, al-Hurriya runs all the way to Montaza. A detailed, though hard-to-find *Tourist Map* of Alexandria (LE3) covers all of the city to Montaza and Abu Kir, and shows tram lines as well. Try the **El Ma'aref Bookstore,** 44 Sa'ad Zaghloul St., which has an entrance on the south side of Sa'ad Zaghloul Sq.

Transportation

Intercity

Alexandria rises where the lush greens of Delta farmlands meet the barren tans of the Western Desert and the cool azure blues of the Mediterranean. Cairo is a three-and-a-quarter-hour drive to the southeast on either of two 225km roads. The boring desert road passes through Giza and brushes Wadi al-Natrun, while the more interesting Delta road crosses both branches of the Nile and passes through Tanta.

You may choose from among several inexpensive, reasonable options for travel between Cairo and Alexandria. Convenient **inter-city buses** come in two varieties: The red-and-gold Golden Rocket Buses (which offer A/C, a movie, and even "in-flight" refreshments!), and the pleasant blue buses of the West Delta Bus Company, not all of which are air-conditioned. Both bus lines connect Alexandria's Sa'ad Zaghloul Sq., via the desert road, to Cairo's Giza Sq. and Tahrir Sq. All Golden Rockets and some of the blue buses (which don't seem to have an English name) also connect Tahrir Sq. with Heliopolis and the Cairo Airport. The **Golden Rocket buses** run hourly, in both directions, between 6am and 6:30pm. Golden Rocket tickets cost LE7 to Cairo, and should be booked a day or two in advance during the busy summer season. Look for the red booths in Tahrir across from the Nile Hilton; in Alexandria within the southwest corner of Sa'ad Zaghoul Sq.

The **blue buses** run from 5:30am to 7pm, nine times daily (roughly every second hour) and cost between LE3 and LE6, depending on whether you travel in the non-air-conditioned, the well-ventilated, or the air-conditioned buses—you have to ask when each type runs. Only the air-conditioned buses go to the airport (LE2 extra), but the non-air-conditioned cheapos stop at Wadi al-Natrun for a 10-minute rest. The ticket counter for the blue buses in Alexandria's Sa'ad Zaghloul Sq. is 2 doors west of the southwest corner of the square, opposite the tourist information office.

For those who need to catch an early morning flight, both lines offer special middle-of-the-night runs to the Cairo Airport. The Golden Rocket leaves at 1am and costs LE13, while the blue line leaves at 12:30am and costs LE9. It's wise to buy a ticket well in advance for trips on Fridays, Saturdays, and holidays, the peak times. Remember that traffic from Cairo to Alexandria is heavy from mid-June to mid-September. Even on normal days during this period, the morning's first and the evening's last buses are usually full.

Of the two major bus companies, only the blue line connects Alexandria with cities in the **Delta** and along the **Suez Canal.** One run links Alexandria with Tanta, al-Mansura, Damietta, and Port Said (4 daily, 7am-1pm, LE5-6, 5½ hr.). Another run links Alexandria and Ismailia (2 daily, LE3.50, 5 hr.). A third option, seldom used by vacationers of the foreign or Egyptian varieties, is the uncomfortable **Delta bus.** This miserable milk route stops in every Delta town on the highway and becomes a virtual sweatbath in summer. Buses serve Alexandria's Masr Train Station Sq. (daily 7am-4pm about every hour, LE1.10-1.50). Those who must scrimp each pound and are willing to make a significant sacrifice in comfort will get a close-up view of Delta life. (See Marsa Matruuh for details on the frequent bus service from Alexandria to points west.)

Trains between Alexandria and Cairo are frequent and generally speedy (nearly 30 per day, 2½-3 hr.). The main line connects Cairo's Ramses Station with Alexandria's Masr Station via the Delta cities and Alexandria's Sidi Gabr Station (5km east of Masr, on al-Hurriya Rd.). Roughly 16 trains are air-conditioned and offer advance reservations (1st class LE5.15, 2nd class LE2.65). The rest are unreserved regular trains with no air-conditioning (2nd class LE1.40, 3rd class 65pt) or slower third-class only trains (4 per day, 65pt, 4 hr.). Most of the trains with air-conditioned cars also have regular cars, with corresponding lower rates. The first train leaves around 6am in both directions—check at the train stations for schedules. The last train from Alexandria leaves at 9:40pm in summer and 8pm in winter; Cairo's last is 9:30pm in summer and 8:25pm in winter. The summer season, July through September, sees the heaviest traffic, and seats in an air-conditioned car then should probably be reserved a day or two in advance. Traveling without reservations presents few problems. Usually enough room remains for you to climb aboard and wait for the ticket collector, while at worst you'll have to stand or sit in a corridor for three hours.

If cost-cutting is your primary concern, third-class trains are absolutely the cheapest way to go between the two cities. **Hitchhiking** is impossible and, in any case, might cost you the price of a taxi. **Intercity taxis** are an inexpensive and generally comfortable alternative to bus or train travel. Shared Peugeot taxis (*taxi ugra*) shuttle between Alexandria's Masr Station and Ramses Station in Cairo. From Cairo, look for taxis in Ahmed Himli Sq., which is behind and north of Ramses Station; in Kolali Sq., which is across the street and west of Ramses Station; or in Tahrir Sq., along the access road that runs in front of the Nile Hilton and the Arab League Building. In Alexandria, look for taxis by Masr Station, at the southern end of Nabi Danial St. A taxi should cost LE4 per person in summer and about LE3 in winter. The risk of an accident is a serious drawback to taxi travel. A taxi ride on the Delta highway can be a hair-raising experience at best.

EgyptAir flies several times daily between Cairo and Alexandria (LE52, 30 min.). Alexandria's small airport lies several kilometers southeast of downtown. Air France plans to begin flights between Paris and Alexandria in late 1988. To travel from the airport to el-Manshiya Sq., take local bus #203 or a taxi.

There are some limited options for traveling to Europe from Alexandria by **passenger ferry.** (See Getting There By Sea in the General Introduction.)

Within Alexandria

Feet serve well in downtown Alexandria. The main squares, the train station, and the corniche all lie within walking distance on streets bristling with shops, cafes, and foodstalls. A brisk half-hour's walk will take you from old Pharos Island to al-Silsila along the corniche—an especially enjoyable trip at night. Though Alexandria, like any port, has its share of hustlers and hawkers, the city is remarkably safe. Pedestrians should feel comfortable day or night.

To visit outlying districts, you'll need to take a tram, bus, or taxi. Note that tram and bus numbers are in Arabic only. **Trams** run virtually all the time and are a steal at 5pt per ride. Ramli Station, 1 block east of Sa'ad Zaghloul Sq., is the main terminus. Hop on the tram at any stop and pay the conductor. Avoid the trams at rush hours, when they are packed. The following are some important tram lines:

#1-5: East from Ramli to the beaches.

#1 and 2: To Sidi Bishr (10km east).

#15: Through el-Gumruk and el-Anfushi to Pharos.

#16: From el-Manshiya Sq. south to Karmus and Pompey's Pillar.

City buses zip through three main terminals—Sa'ad Zaghloul Sq., el-Manshiya Sq., and Masr Train Station. Buses run from approximately 5:30am to midnight or 1am, and cost only 5-20pt. The following are some noteworthy bus lines:

#129: From el-Manshiya Sq. to Montaza and Abu Kir.

#220 and 300: Along the corniche.

#209: From Ramli Station to Pompey's Pillar.
For a more comfortable ride to the eastern beaches, look for the deluxe double-decker buses that run along the corniche (25pt).

A **local taxi** ride in Alexandria is likely to be less death-defying than in Cairo. The normal red-and-black taxis are everywhere; the deluxe, monochrome Peugeot taxis charge much more. Pay the price on the meter plus 25-50pt *baksheesh;* more late at night or for a long trip. A typical trip within the confines of downtown should cost 60-80pt, while a trek to Montaza or Abu Kir might run LE4-5. (See the Egypt Introduction for more advice on taxi travel.)

Finally, if you're in no hurry, hail one of the many horse-drawn carriages that wait along the corniche. Depending on your bargaining ability, this will cost LE1-3 per hour.

Practical Information

Tourist Office: Main office, Nabi Danial St., at the southwest corner of Sa'ad Zaghloul Sq. (tel. 80 76 11). Fluent English spoken, uncrowded, and extremely helpful. Open daily 8am-6pm, during Ramadan 9am-4pm. Well-informed and helpful branch offices at **Masr Station** (tel. 492 59 85; open 8am-6pm) and the **port** (tel. 492 59 86). Pick up a free copy of *Alexandria by Night and Day,* which lists restaurants, hotels, travel agents, and other useful information; it includes a train schedule to Cairo, and a fine map of central Alexandria. The Masr Station office can help you get an English train timetable for all of Egypt (50pt).

Passport Office, 28 Talaat Harb St. (tel. 482 43 66 or 483 71 72). Walk west on Sa'ad Zaghloul St. from Ramli Station, and bear left on Falaki St. when Sa'ad Zaghloul begins to curve toward the sea. Talaat Harb will be your first left and the office is on the corner of Falaki St. on the western side of Talaat Harb. Register your passport here. Open Sat.-Thurs. 8am-1pm and (theoretically) 7-9pm, Fri. 10am-1pm and 7-9pm.

Consulates: U.S., 110 al-Hurriya St. (tel. 482 19 11), 2km east of downtown, 1 block west of a rotary and parks. Can replace passports, but other important business should be transacted in Cairo. Open Sun.-Thurs. 8am-4:30pm. **U.K.,** 3 Mena Kafr Abdu St., Roushdy (tel. 84 71 66), 6km east of downtown, several blocks south of al-Hurriya. Open Mon.-Fri. 8am-1pm. **Israel,** 453 al-Hurriya St., Roushdy (tel. 84 09 33). There are no Canadian, Australian, or New Zealand consulates.

Banks: Most convenient is **Misr Bank,** in the Cecil Hotel, Sa'ad Zaghloul Sq. (tel. 80 70 55). Open daily 8am-noon and 5-8pm. **Bank of America** (tel. 492 12 65), across from the football stadium on Lomomba St., 1 block south of al-Hurriya Rd., and **Barclay's,** 10 Fawoteur St. (tel. 492 13 07) are both open Sun.-Thurs. 9am-2pm.

American Express: A small branch office is in **Eyress Travel,** 26 al-Hurriya Rd. (tel. 483 00 84), 5 blocks south of Sa'ad Zaghloul Sq. No financial services (they'll refer you to Cairo). Client letters held. Open Mon.-Thurs. 8:30am-1pm and 5-6:30pm, Fri.-Sat. 8:30am-1pm.

Post Office: On Alexander the Great St., 3 blocks west of Orabi Sq. in a grimy 1-story building with the entrance in back. Also a branch in Masr Station, and beside Ramli Station. All open daily 8am-8pm. For **Poste Restante,** just wander around the Alexander the Great office shouting "Poste Restante" until someone appears. Open daily 9am-3pm. **Postal Code:** 21519.

Telephone Office: Ramli Station. Open 24 hours. Also at Masr Station and at the west end of Sa'ad Zaghloul Blvd. (Both open to 11pm.) For overseas calls the 4-star hotels in town are more reliable: Best of all is the Cecil in Sa'ad Zaghloul Sq., whose operators can often put through an overseas call within 5 or 10 min. Bring plenty of cash since it's impossible to make collect calls. Calls cost LE6-8 per min. at the hotels and LE4-5 per min. at the phone offices.

Telephone Code: 03.

Car Rental: Avis, in the Cecil Hotel, Sa'ad Zaghloul Sq. (tel. 80 75 32), rents Fiat 127s for LE42 per day, 100km free. Must be over 25. **Budget,** 59 al-Geish St., Chatby (tel. 597 12 73). Similar rates. Must be over 20.

English Bookstores: The pickings are surprisingly slim in a city whose cosmopolitanism seems to have peaked a generation or two ago. **El-Ma'aref** (see Orientation) has a few English selections; **Book Center,** 49 Sa'ad Zaghloul has a good selection of English literature in paperback and some books on Egypt; **Library Mustakbal,** 32 Safia Zaghloul St. has a fair selection and may be the only place in town that stocks Durrell's classic *Alexandria Quartet.*

Cultural Centers: U.S., 3 Pharana St. (tel. 482 10 09). A fine library here. Open Mon.-Fri. 8am-4pm. **U.K.,** 9 Ptolemies St. (tel. 482 01 99). Open Mon.-Fri. 9am-4pm.

Swimming Pool: It is *usually* possible, for a small fee, to swim at the posh hotels in Montaza. Call ahead to avoid disappointment. Try the Sheraton (tel. 96 92 20), the Summer Moon (tel. 430 03 67), the Ramada Renaissance (tel. 86 61 11), or the Agami Palace (tel. 430 02 30).

Photography and Film Developing: Kodak, on Safia Zaghloul St. across from the Rialto Cinema, has a large selection of Kodak film for sale, around LE6 each. Developing LE1, plus 35pt per print. Open Mon.-Sat. 10am-11pm. There are also a number of smaller photo accessory and film shops along Sa'ad Zaghloul St.

Late-night Pharmacy: Khalid, 3 doors west of Sa'ad Zaghloul Sq. on Alexander the Great St. Open daily 9am-10pm. Many others are located along Sa'ad Zaghloul St.

Hospital: al-Moassa (tel. 421 66 64), on al-Hurriya St. For most illnesses, ask for help at a 5-star hotel or, presuming you can make it, at your consulate. The **Medical Care Advisory Team (MCAT),** 97 Abel Salam Aref St. (tel. 586 23 23), 8km east of downtown in Gleem Beach, is accustomed to dealing with foreigners.

Police: Emergency, tel. 123. **City Police** (tel. 122) are available 24 hours, but if possible contact the **Tourist Police,** Montaza Palace (tel. 86 38 04), in Montaza. Branch office upstairs from the tourist office in Sa'ad Zaghloul Sq. (tel. 80 76 11). Both open Sat.-Thurs. 8am-8pm, Fri. 8am-2pm.

Accommodations

For those who want a cheap room with a view of the sea, there are a number of small hotels on the streets running south from the corniche near **Ramli Station.** The crowds and dirt might be tolerable at LE2-3 per night, but the insects, ranging from tiny ticks and fleas to armor-plated, three-inch cockroaches, can be intolerable. These beasties are common in the dives near the waterfront. The places listed below are relatively clean and cheap, and all except the hostel lie within walking distance from the two main squares.

Streets in **el-Manshiya Sq.** likewise bristle with budget hotels. Many Egyptian vacationers prefer to stay in the hotels near the corniche beaches. Short-term foreign visitors seem to prefer accommodations near the center of town. Those who insist on a beachside retreat should head out toward Montaza (18km) at least as far as Sidi Bishr (14km), where the amenities begin to balance the inconvenience of staying so far from the center of town. For those really pinching pennies, it is possible to camp by the beach at Abu Kir for 25pt (see Abu Kir below).

Youth Hostel (IYHF), 32 Port Said St., Chatby (tel. 597 54 59), just off the corniche. Take an eastbound tram (5pt) from Ramli Station until you see the large red and white dome of St. Mark's College on the left side. The hostel lies opposite. Fly-infested, crowded, colorless, and near an unappealing beach. Overflowing with bored Egyptian teenagers. Lunch and dinner served. Often fills, reserve in advance. Open daily 8-10am and 2-11pm. Strict curfew. Members LE2.05, nonmembers LE5.05.

Hotel Acropole, 1 Gamal al-Din Yassin St., 5th floor (tel. 80 59 80), 1 block west of Sa'ad Zaghloul Sq., just off the corniche. The closest cheap hotel to the bus station. One of the best deals in town. Clean and comfortable, though the grimy entrance may lead you to expect otherwise. TV lounge. Fills fast. Reserve 5 days in advance during the summer. Dorm beds LE5, singles LE8. Breakfast included.

Hotel Triomphe (tel. 80 75 85), across from the Acropole, but a significant step down in quality and cleanliness. Also fills quickly. Singles and doubles LE6.

Hotel Marhaba (tel. 80 09 57), on the northwest side of Orabi Sq. Large, tidy, centrally located. Many of the rooms have glorious ocean vistas. Singles LE13, with bath LE15. Doubles LE18, with bath LE21. Breakfast included.

Ailema Hotel, 21 Amin Fakri St., 8th floor (tel. 493 29 16). From Ramli, walk east 3 blocks and turn right. The revolving door is somewhat elegant; the rooms are not, although some have nice views. Fairly clean. Singles LE9, doubles LE14. Breakfast and taxes included. Upstairs is the **Hyde Park** (tel. 493 56 66), with similar rooms for about a pound more.

Admiral Hotel, across from the Ailema (tel. 483 23 88). Spotless, tastefully decorated, and comfortable rooms. Fancy lounge/lobby and restaurant. Singles LE15, with bath LE20. Doubles LE25, with bath LE30. Breakfast and taxes included.

Hotel Picadilly, 11 al-Hurriya St., 9th floor (tel. 493 48 02). At the intersection with Nabi Danial St., on the southeastern corner. Halfway between the corniche and Gomhuriya Sq., which is next to Masr Station. The elevator works, despite appearances. While the rooms are a bit decrepit, the staff is friendly, and it usually has vacancies. Closest decent place to the train station. No breakfast served. Singles LE5, doubles LE8.

Hotel Leroy, 25 Talaat Harb St. (tel. 483 34 39), across from the passport office. Now dusty and dilapidated, this must once have been a magnificent place, with its art-deco bar and lounge area. Rooms and toilets a little dirty. Usually deserted, so solo women might feel uncomfortable. Singles LE11, doubles LE16.50. Breakfast included.

Corail Hotel, 802 al-Geish St. (tel. 96 89 96), 2½ blocks west of Montaza, overlooking the corniche and Mandara Beach. Take a corniche bus. Orderly and bright. Biggest advantage is proximity to the romantic Montaza Palace and Gardens. All rooms with bath and phone. Seldom booked up. Singles LE26, doubles LE42. In winter prices are about LE10 lower. Breakfast and lunch included.

Food

As elsewhere in Egypt, the cheapest food in Alexandria is sold in the *fuul* and *tamiya* stands throughout the city. Some of the tastiest offerings are found around the cloth market between Pompey's Pillar and Masr Station, and on the western side of the peninsula, where 15pt will buy a huge sandwich, salad, and *tahina*. Since most of these places are a bit grimy, they are recommended only for those with a strong palate, strong stomach, and little objection to flies. Those who have a gut feeling that Alexandria is a threat to their health should stick to restaurants, where they may be in for a pleasant surprise.

Muhammad Ahmed Fuul, 2 blocks south of Sa'ad Zaghloul Sq. and a street west of Safia Zaghloul St. Across from an 8-ft. stone wall, off Sa'ad Zaghloul St. No English sign, but you'll recognize it by the gaudy, gold Arabic letters over the door. Don't let their advertisements in magazines mislead you (they read "Foul Mohamed Ahmed"). There are those who consider this the best *fuul* and *tamiya* joint in Egypt. The food is excellent, and the price unbeatable for a sit-down restaurant. *Fuul* 40pt; *tamiya*, salad, pickles, and bread make a good light meal for 36pt. Especially good is the *arroz bi khalto* (literally, "rice with everything") for 75pt.

Restaurant Denis, 1 Ibn Basaam St., 4 blocks east of Sa'ad Zaghloul Sq. This neat little Greek joint, just off the corniche, serves up the best budget seafood in Alexandria. Pick out your fish in the kitchen (LE10-20 per kilo, ½ kilo per person is plenty) and they'll bring out loads of salads, dips, and bread; you can stuff yourself silly for LE10. Beer and wine served. Open daily noon-2am.

Restaurant Elite, 43 Safia Zaghloul St., directly across from Santa Lucia. Run by a pair of Greeks, this place has cosmopolitan charm. Large, light, and airy, with checkered tablecloths and Picasso prints on the walls. Try the canneloni (LE2.40), pizza (LE2), or great *moussaka* (LE5). Open 11am-midnight (sometimes later).

Tikka Grill, jutting into the Eastern Harbor on the waterfront near Abu al-Abbas Mosque, 1½ km west of Sa'ad Zaghloul Sq. A bit of a hike, but one you won't regret. Excellent Indian food, impeccable service, and a sweeping view of the corniche at this classy place. Dishes LE9-12, including the unlimited salad bar and a bottle of mineral water. Full meals LE10-15. Liquor served. Open daily 1-4:30pm and 8pm-1am.

Santa Lucia, 40 Safia Zaghloul St., 5 blocks from the corniche. One of the fanciest places in town. While full meals (at LE25-30) are out of the budget range, you can get a huge plate of great *taramasalata* (cod-roe, a poor man's caviar) and bread for LE6, almost a meal in itself. Open daily noon-4pm and 7pm-1am.

Cafeteria Asteria, 40 Safia Zaghloul St., several doors down from Santa Lucia. This clean cafeteria serves a variety of cheap, light meals. The pizza is particularly good (LE3.40).

New China Chinese Restaurant, 802 al-Guesh St., Mandara (tel. 96 89 96), in the Corail Hotel, 3 blocks west of Montaza Palace. Despite a sleazy atmosphere, this place has the best (and possibly the only) Chinese food in Alexandria. Dishes around LE8.50. Try the delicious fried chicken in lemon sauce, or the *leung chow* fried rice, crammed full of seafood (LE3). Liquor served. Open daily noon-11pm.

For desserts, the **Delices** and **Trianon** Patisseries serve expensive pastries in a setting redolent with expatriate ease. Cafes line the corniche on both sides of Sa'ad Zaghloul Sq., along with restaurants where you can pay LE10 for a meal of grilled meat or fish and watch the people go by. More inexpensive cafes, or *ahwas,* are located in the neighborhood streets south of the waterfront. And for liquid refreshment of the holistic kind, the best **juice bars** are located on Safia Zaghoul St., 1 block south of Ramli Sq.

Sights

Very little remains of ancient Alexandria, since the modern city has been built on top of the old one. While the city lacks impressive ruins, the excellent **Greco-Roman Museum** introduces visitors to ancient Alexandria and its Hellenistic civilization. The cult of Serapis is well-depicted: Look for the handsome sculptures of Zeus and Apis, and for the Greek youth Harpocrates, finger-in-mouth. Galleries abound with Greek alabaster head casts and impressive arrays of larger-than-life sculptures. One of the most fascinating of these is a huge statue of Diocletian seated in his throne in the center gallery, the largest extant sculpture of red porphyry. The museum also houses an interesting exhibit of terra-cotta figurines depicting Greeks in everyday life. In room #9 you'll find a mummified crocodile and other relics from the cult of Phepheros, the crocodile god worshiped in ancient Fayyum. The museum's courtyard holds an intriguing crocodile temple, also attributed to the cult of Phepheros, as well as numerous structures from Egypt's Greco-Roman past; make sure to step out into the courtyard to observe these finds. To reach the museum, walk south from the corniche along Safia Zaghloul St., turn left on al-Hurriya St., and walk until the sign for the museum directs you to the left again. (Open Sun.-Thurs. and Sat. 9am-4pm, Fri. 9-11:30am and 1:30-4pm. Admission LE1, students 50pt.)

After a visit to the museum, it's easy to trek to the three major ancient sites, all of which lie within a few kilometers of downtown. Near Masr Station is the beautifully preserved white marble **Roman Amphitheater,** the only one of its kind ever discovered in Egypt. Behind the 13-tiered theater sit the ruins of a Roman bath (to the left) and of a Roman villa and cistern (to the right). The Polish team that made these excavations is now uncovering the Ptolemaic streets and shops of Kom el-Dik on the same site. These other ruins are closed to the public. Self-styled guides may offer to sneak you in for a fee, but since almost everything of interest is visible from the theater, it's not worth it. To get here from Sa'ad Zaghloul Sq., walk down Nabi Danial St. and take the second left after al-Hurriya St.; the entrance will be on your left. (Open daily 9am-4pm, during Ramadan 9am-2pm. Admission LE1, students 50pt.)

The most famous ancient monument is **Pompey's Pillar,** a single granite column 25m high named by the Crusaders, who mistakenly imagined that it had some connection with Pompey. In fact, it dates from the time of Diocletian, several centuries later, and was part of the Serapium, a religious center in which the rites of the cult of the bull god Serapis were celebrated. Not surprisingly, the temple was leveled once the Roman Empire became Christian. The pillar, transported from Aswan, was raised by the Roman provincial governor in honor of the emperor Diocletian's role in quieting an Alexandrian revolt. Apparently, the temperamental emperor swore that he would massacre the rebellious people until blood stained the knees of his horse; however, as he entered the cowering town his mount stumbled into a pool of blood, fulfilling Diocletian's oath prematurely. The emperor did not sack the city, and the lone pillar remains to mark the people's gratitude to him and his clumsy horse. The ruins of the Serapium around the pillar have been excavated and the best finds moved to the Greco-Roman museum. Now only a few sphinxes and statues are lying about, which may barely lessen the sense of disappointment in this scene. To reach the site, take bus #209 from Ramli and get off on Karmus St. when you see the pillar. Alternatively, take tram #16. (Admission 50pt, students 25pt; the pillar alone is free. Site open daily 9am-4pm, during Ramadan 9am-2pm.) The pillar lies at the northeast corner of the ruins park. Nearby is Alexandria's *cloth market,* where crowds of women inspect the bales of brightly colored cloth scattered around the street.

If you walk past the entrance to the Serapium (in the direction the bus travels), take your first right, and follow it about ½km, you will arrive at the eerie **Catacombs of Kom al-Shokafa.** These Roman tombs descend in three levels down to a depth of about 35m and are remarkable for the bits of sculpture and reliefs depicting Egyptian gods with unmistakably Roman bodies. Don't miss the jackel-headed Anubis with a torso like Charles Atlas; he's by the entrance to the innermost burial chamber. As you enter the central rotunda, the large room to your left is where the funeral feasts were held, a creepy place for a meal if there ever was one. The hall of the goddess Nemesis, farther down and to the left, is, appropriately, flooded. (Admission LE1, students 50pt. Open daily 9am-4pm, during Ramadan 9am-2pm.)

Kom al-Shokafa is located in one of Alexandria's slums. As you walk by, dozens of Egyptian kids will run after you screaming, "Hello," "Good Morning," "What's your name," and "What time is it now?" They just want some attention and to hear you speak English. The garbage-strewn streets around Kom al-Shokafa can be very depressing, but if you want to see real third-world poverty, walk north of the street leading to the catacombs between Amud al-Sawari and al-Rahma St. These turn into dirt paths leading through a housing development and a shantytown of corrugated metal.

The neighborhoods of Alexandria lying west and north of the central square reward backstreet wanderings. Dilapidated el-Gomrok and breezy Anfushi are crowded with old mosques, Coptic churches, and finely decorated nineteenth-century buildings. A few sights here cannot be missed. The Islamic **Fort Qaytbay** commands the ancient island of Pharos, now the tip of the peninsula separating eastern and western harbors. The fort symbolizes "the big one that got away": It was built in the fifteenth century by the Mamluk Sultan Qaytbay from the ruins of one of the seven ancient wonders, the Lighthouse of Pharos. Inside, a naval museum features an exhibition of artifacts salvaged from the sunken French fleet, destroyed by Nelson at the Battle of the Nile. Note the small mosque in the center of tower; the entire fortress is aligned so that a wall will face Mecca. (Admission LE1, students 50pt. Fort open daily 9am-3pm.) There is a cafeteria-restaurant beneath the northern battlements serving sandwiches (70pt) and soft drinks (50pt). The fort's imposing white walls set against the ocean draw the eyes of every stroller in the corniche. You can get a wonderful view of it from the harbor walls just outside. Across from the fort is a rather pathetic **aquarium.** (Open daily 9am-2pm. Free.) To reach the fort, take tram #15 west from Ramli Station and get off when it makes a sharp left turn. You will find yourself in the middle of an open-air **fish market,** and lo, it stinketh. At the point where the tram turned left, you should turn right on the road between the Kuwait Airlines sign and the mosque; the fort is at the end of this road. The first entrance you will see upon approaching the fort is an oceanographic museum just as pathetic as the aquarium opposite. Keep going another 30m until you reach the fort's ticket booth and gate.

The **Mosque of Abu al-Abbas,** with its four domes and tall minarets, is located about 1km south of the fort along the corniche and is Alexandria's most prominent and elaborate example of Islamic architecture. The holy man Abu al-Abbas came from Andalusia, Spain, and settled in the Delta. His tomb rests to one side of the mosque. Legend has it that he rose from his tomb to catch bombs falling on Alexandria during WWII raids. Inside is a peaceful oasis where Muslims relax and pray all day long. If you don't speak Arabic (i.e., you're not Muslim), you may be refused entrance. Women enter from the back, at the *harim.*

Another attraction in central Alexandria, the **Fine Arts Museum,** at 18 Menasha St., contains a small but interesting collection of modern Egyptian art as well as Alexandria's public library. From Masr Station, walk east on Mahmoud Bey Salama St., which runs along the southern side of the railroad tracks. The museum is on the right at the first major intersection. (Open Sun.-Thurs. and Sat. 8am-2pm, Wed. 4am-2pm and 7-9pm. Free.)

Alexandrians buy their produce and fish in an **open air market** running north of el-Gomhouriya Sq. in el-Gomrok. Between el-Gomhouriya Sq. and the corniche is a bazaar with hundreds of stalls, selling souvenirs, jewelry, fabric, and household goods, packed into a tight grid just a few blocks long.

Those who plan to spend more than a day or two in Alexandria should travel at least once to the eastern beaches. This district's highlight is **Montaza Palace and Gardens.** Formerly King Farouk's summer retreat, the huge complex includes gardens as well as beaches. Nowadays, modern hotels, too, gleam amidst the palms. The palace and its museum have been closed to the public, but the gardens and groves are open and are a favorite picnic spot for Alexandrians. You could easily spend a whole day here. (Admission to the gardens 80pt, holidays LE10. Semi-private beach west of the palace LE1.)

Entertainment

Alexandria's most popular (read unbelievably crowded) attractions are its **beaches.** During the hot summer months, Cairenes flock here by the thousands to escape from the noise, dirt, and heat of the capital. The masses will daunt all but the most fanatical sun-worshipers: It's possible to ride up and down the entire 18km without seeing a single square yard of uninhabited sand. Add the effects of ever-increasing erosion and pollution (the net weight of the litter nearly exceeds that of the bathers), and the whole idea of hitting the beach may seem repulsive unless you've just come from Cairo or Upper Egypt. The beaches along the corniche are the most crowded and family-oriented. Women bathe fully clothed or, occasionally, in very modest one-piece bathing suits. Westernized Egyptians tend to congregate at the slightly less crowded beaches at Mandara, Montaza, and Ma'mura. Mandara is simply another in a long series of beaches along the corniche, but Ma'mura is an enclave tucked against the eastern wall of Montaza. Its relative isolation and popularity with affluent Cairenes lend it the swank, glittery atmosphere of a French beach resort, and European standards of beachwear apply. Ma'mura, just east of Montaza, can be reached by a Montaza bus (#129).

Most of Alexandria's nighttime entertainment centers around the string of night-clubs along the corniche. In summer you'll see wedding parties wherever you go along the corniche, and foreigners are often invited to share the fun. Clubs, often family-oriented, jut out above the beaches. Most require patrons to drink (LE5-10 worth), but have no cover charge. **Crazy Horse,** in Ramli Station, is the best known. Away from the corniche, **Santa Lucia Restaurant** has a low-key bar that features live music (see Food), and nightclubs are also attached to **Au Privé Restaurant,** 14 al-Hurriya St., and the **Hotel Alexandria,** 23 el-Nasr St., near the port. **The Spit-fire Bar,** off Gourfa el-Togariya St., 2 blocks west of Sa'ad Zaghoul Sq., has a Western atmosphere and funky decor.

Also extremely popular are Alexandria's **cinemas.** English-language films usually play at the Amir, Royal, al-Hurriya, and Zaghloul theaters (all on or just off Safia Zaghloul St.). Shows are usually at 3, 6, and 9pm, but there's about an hour of ads and newsreels before the main feature. (Tickets LE1.) Scan the billboards for details. In late summer, an **international film festival** presents uncensored films in all the city's theaters; ask at the tourist information office.

During the high season, the **Reda Dance Company** performs nightly at the Firquit Reda Theater in the Chatby district. If you want to provide your own theatrics, the Cecil and Palestine Hotels both have **casinos,** where you can gamble away your foreign currency at an alarming speed. Thriftier travelers can join the majority of Alexandrians for an evening stroll down the crowded downtown streets or a drink at one of the **seaside cafes.**

Near Alexandria

The fishing village of **Abu Kir** (commonly pronounced "Abu'EER") lies on a peninsula 5km past Montaza. The village has yet to be absorbed by Alexandria's relentless eastward expansion, and remains dusty and rural. Abu Kir is famous as the site of Nelson's 1798 naval victory over Napoleon, foiling the little Frenchman's dream of Egyptian conquest. More importantly to the traveler, however, Abu Kir is a great place to sample Mediterranean seafood. It is far superior to that in Alexandria, and it's worth the short evening's excursion to dine here.

There are two options for eating fish (*samak*) in Abu Kir. If it is daytime and money is short, try eating on the beach: As you step off the train or bus (see below), walk east to the waterfront. On the beach stands a row of tables. Anglers will come in from the boats anchored offshore and cook the fish you select right at your table.

The second option is a seafood restaurant. Try the **Zephyrion** (tel. 97 13 19), an Abu Kir landmark since 1929. The blue and white pavilion has expanded in girth as its popularity has grown. Typically, a full dinner of fresh fish with beer and a salad runs LE8. Cooked fish will cost roughly LE14 per kilo (more for shrimp and other exotica). In the end, appetite dictates financial damage; however, it's possible to binge for LE16. Brave visitors sometimes try the octopus plate (LE2.50). The man who may come to your table and offer a plate of oysters on the half-shell is not from the restaurant, and accepting his food will cost you a whopping LE12-15. Next door to Zephyrion is another, nameless seafood place, not as nice but with slightly lower prices. To reach either of these places, head north to the waterfront from the main mosque; they're right on the beach. Both are open noon to midnight, until 2am in the summer.

Abu Kir offers little except fish and is best visited as a daytrip from Alexandria. The town is a haven for campers, though, since **Abu Kir Camp** (tel. 97 14 24) offers the only consistently available camping in the Alexandria area. You can rent a 7-person tent for about LE1.50 per night, or pitch your own tent for 25pt. Alternatively, with permission from the local police, you can camp for free on the beach at Abu Kir. You can reach Abu Kir by **local bus** #129 from Orabi Sq. (daily 8am-1:30am, 30pt), by **train** from Masr Station (daily 4am-1am, every 15 min., third class 8pt), or by **local taxi** from downtown (LE3-5).

For generations, many of the wealthiest Egyptian vacationers in Alexandria have been avoiding the crowded city beaches by setting up at **Agami,** a resort town 20km west of el-Manshiya. Long famous for its white sand and turquoise waters, Agami lies where Alexandria meets the Western Desert. In recent years, pollution from the city's Western Harbor has dirtied some of Agami's beaches, and the crowds have grown. A bevy of hotels and villas fringe the choppy waters of **Agami Beach** and adjacent **Hannoville Beach.** The resort, easily accessible from downtown Alexandria, makes a worthwhile daytrip or overnight excursion. Buses #500 and 600 leave Masr Station, Ramli, and el-Manshiya Sq. for Agami (daily 6am-midnight, 20pt). In Agami, you'll have several comfortable and inexpensive options for accommodations. Try the **New Admiral** (tel. 80 00 79; singles LE7-10, doubles LE10-12) or the slightly upscale **Costa Planca Hotel** (tel. 494 01 06 or 401 06; similar prices).

Mediterranean Coast

Sea meets sand along Egypt's coast in a 400km stretch of untouched shoreline. In some places the transition from desert to sea is gentle; elsewhere rugged cliffs mark the change. Legends of Cleopatra, Alexander, Rommel, and Montgomery—and their favorite beaches—abound. While opportunities for free secluded camping are virtually unlimited (simply check in with the nearest police or military office), most of the gleaming coastline remains tantalizingly inaccessible to budget travelers. The coastal highway between Alexandria and Libya bisects this junction between the Mediterranean and the Western Desert. Buses, trains, and service taxis make regular runs between Alexandria and Marsa Matruuh, the coast's only sizable town. The 290km of coastline in between, however, are not served by public transportation. Consequently, you must have a private car, or risk very long walks across the desert to reach resort villages such as **Sidi Abd al-Rahman,** 44km west of al-Alamein. Fortunately, Marsa Matruuh, a delightfully low-key resort town, offers enough variety of coastal scenery to satisfy the most demanding of beach bums.

A detailed, scholarly map of Egypt will tell you that seven or eight towns line the coast between Sidi Abd al-Rahman and Marsa Matruuh. Experience will tell you otherwise. For the names of these towns the cartographers could have substituted the names of their residents; the ratio approaches one to one.

You can pass the time on the bus contemplating the grandiose dream of the Qattara Depression Project. Desperate to increase the amount of their country's arable land, Egyptian planners have long dreamed of bringing water to the nutrient-rich but bone-dry soils of the Western Desert's **Qattara Depression.** Covering a region the size of the Delta, and dipping well below sea level, the depression lies 100km inland. The dream is to take water from the Mediterranean Sea, desalinate it, and send it coursing past al-Alamein to irrigate huge new tracts of farmland. Initial steps were taken with Soviet aid during Nasser's rule, but early optimism was disappointed by shifting political alliances and burgeoning costs. The Egyptians still seek enormous foreign aid for the project, but definite plans for a massive reworking of the desert landscape seem unlikely in the near future.

Marsa Matruuh is the jumping-off point for trips to unforgettable **Siwa Oasis.** Immortalized by its ancient Temple of Amun, once visited by Alexander the Great, this oasis has a venerable history of trade with the coast. An excellent road now links the oasis with Marsa Matruuh. An easily obtainable pass to visit Siwa and a five-hour bus or taxi journey are all that stand between the traveler in Marsa Matruuh and this miracle in the desert.

Marsa Matruuh

Spreading out from a perfect turquoise-blue bay, the resort city of Marsa Matruuh looks like it was built yesterday. Dozens of mold-and-pour style concrete villas accommodate the thousands of Egyptians who fall victim to the universal human urge to go to the beach. The natural harbor here has served travelers, merchants, and soldiers from Alexander to Rommel—but now the majority of sea vessels here are rented by the hour, and the major military presence is at the holiday resorts maintained for Air Force and Navy officers. As Alexandria's beaches grow polluted and crowded, more and more upper-crust Egyptians and expatriates come to Marsa Matruuh for their summer holidays. Few foreigners make it out here; those who do are rewarded by the finest beaches in Egypt and a relaxed, holiday atmosphere. This is as close as Egypt gets to pure hedonism.

Practical Information

The best way to reach Marsa Matruuh is to take a **bus** from Alexandria. The blue buses leaving Sa'ad Zaghloul Sq. are convenient and inexpensive (about 5 per day, 7am-4pm; with A/C LE9, non-A/C LE6; 5 hr.). The plush Golden Rocket Line now serves Matruuh several times per day (4 hr., LE10). Both companies connect from Tahrir Sq. in Cairo (blue buses: A/C LE12, non-A/C LE7.50; Golden Rocket: LE20; both 8 hr.; book a day or two in advance at the booths in front of the Nile Hilton). In Marsa Matruuh, blue buses arrive and depart from the **bus station,** about 7 blocks inland, 3 blocks west of Alexandria St. Golden Rocket buses continue to the parking lot beside the tourist office, on the corniche.

Marsa Matruuh's **train station** is perched at the top of Alexandria St., about 2km from the corniche, and 3 blocks east of the bus station. Trains run several times daily to and from Cairo's Ramses Station (1st class LE10, 2nd class LE6, 3rd class LE2, *wagon-lit* 3 times per week LE16) and from Alexandria's Masr Station (1st class LE5, 2nd class LE4, 3rd class LE1.50, *wagon-lit* 3 times per week LE10). Contact Egyptian Railways for exact times; *wagon-lit* reservations should be made well in advance.

Shared **service taxis** (*taxi ugra*) shuttle between the bus station in Marsa Matruuh, Alexandria's Masr Station, and Cairo's Ahmed Himli Sq. or Kolali Sq. (both adjacent to Ramses Station). In Marsa, you'll find the taxis at the southern side of the bus station. If you travel by shared taxi, you won't have to wait in line for a ticket to Alexandria or Cairo, you won't have to come days in advance, and you'll be guaranteed a seat (albeit a tight one). Moreover, a service taxi will cost the same, or only slightly more than the bus. Best of all, you'll travel at a breakneck pace. A shared taxi to Alexandria should cost about LE7, and to Cairo about LE11.

EgyptAir flies to Marsa from Cairo (2 flights per week, LE97). Their office is on Galeh St., 3 blocks west of Alexandria St.

You need to know only two streets to find your way around Marsa Matruuh: the lively **corniche,** which stretches the length of the bay, and busy **Alexandria Street,** which runs perpendicular to the corniche from the Marsa Matruuh Governate inland to the hill north of town. Most of the hotels and government offices are clustered along the corniche and the three streets that run parallel to it. Restaurants and cafes line lower Alexandria St.

Once you've arrived in Marsa Matruuh, getting around is a sea breeze. At the bus or train station, scores of donkey commanders will besiege you. Don't turn them away. Although the covered donkey carts (called *carettas*) never reach first gear, they are cheap (50pt-LE1 for most rides), ubiquitous (they nearly outnumber the cars), and fun to ride. If you're in a hurry, select a gray or white donkey—the little brown ones must be genetically inferior. Agree on a price before you set off; with a little encouragement, the drivers will bargain each other down. For most destinations in town you don't even need a donkey—you can get there with a 10-minute walk. To travel farther afield, rent a **bicycle** from the shop next to the Riviera Palace Hotel, 1 block from the corniche on Alexandria St. (LE1 per hr., open 24 hours).

Marsa Matruuh's **tourist office,** located where Alexandria St. meets the corniche, is a pretty hopeless set-up. The manager speaks little English, seems uninterested, and is hardly ever around. No map available. (Open, hypothetically, daily 9am-2pm and 8-10pm.) Otherwise, the place to obtain information is at one of the fancy hotels along the corniche; just act like you're a guest, and they'll be very helpful.

The manager of the tourist office is also head of the **tourist police** (and possibly its only officer). If you have trouble tracking him down, go to the **Police Station** on the first street south of the corniche, 2 blocks east of Alexandria St (open 24 hours). Next door is Marsa Matruuh's **Post Office** (open Sat.-Thurs. 8am-3pm), and across the street is the **Telephone Office** (open 24hours). At the easternmost end of this street, about a 10-minute walk from the tourist office, is the fortress-like **Military Investigations Office,** where you must go to receive permission to camp on the beach, visit Siwi Oasis, or register your passport (if you did not do so in

Cairo). Bang on the green metal door and someone will eventually let you in. The staff is efficient, helpful, and English-speaking. (Open daily 8am-2pm and 8-11pm.)

The town **hospital** is located at the top of Alexandria St., near the train station. Facilities here are more limited than those in the large cities, and it's probably a good idea, if condition permits, to catch the next flight to Cairo. For less-serious ailments, **M.M. Pharmacy** is located on the east side of Alexandria St., 2 blocks south of the corniche. (Open daily 9am-2pm and 5pm-midnight.)

Because Marsa Matruuh is so close to Libya, there is a noticeable military presence in the surrounding areas. While unnecessary within the city limits, it's a good idea to carry your passport with you outside of town and on the more obscure beaches to avoid being hassled by officers on power trips. There may also be a passport check on the road into town.

Accommodations

Hotel prices in Marsa Matruuh have skyrocketed in recent years. The tourist season lasts from the beginning of May to the end of October, though July and August are the peak months. The month of Ramadan (April 6-May 7 in 1989) brings crowds of Copts and Muslims alike to Marsa Matruuh. In the mild but generally sunny off-season, many hotels either close entirely or slash their rates and the luxurious new hotels along the corniche become affordable. For example, the government-run, two-star **Arous el-Baha** (tel. 94 24 20) on the corniche drops its full board requirements and its prices, between October and May (in winter singles LE10, doubles LE12.50).

Small, very inexpensive hotels can be found along and nearby Alexandria St., 3 or 4 blocks inland. However, these are frequented only by Egyptians—many of them have no English signs—and therefore some foreigners, especially women, might find a stay here unpleasant. Men with small budgets and open minds can rent a bed in a crowded room for LE1-2, but guard your belongings. The hotels listed below are accustomed to foreigners and are safer for women.

IYHF Youth Hostel, (tel. 23 31). Very difficult to find: Walk west from Alexandria St. on Galeh St. until you pass the Omar Effendi Store. Follow the street angling off to your right toward the beach. The Youth Hostel is a two-story concrete cube behind similar 3-story buildings along an unnamed street that juts off to the left about ½km north of Omar Effendi. Ask for the *bayt al-shibab.* If you make it, you'll find a very pleasant warden and not very pleasant shared rooms. Kitchen available. Members LE1 per night, non-members LE4.

Ghazala Hotel, Alma Rum St. (tel. 94 35 19), a 3-story yellow building just east of Alexandria St., about 6 blocks from the corniche. Large, comfortable, and very clean rooms. Best budget bed in town, but call ahead, as it sometimes fills with groups (expecially July-Aug.). LE4 per person. Doubles LE10.

Hotel des Roses, Galeh St. (tel. 94 27 55), 5 blocks east of Alexandria St. Cool, neat, and quiet rooms. Slightly overpriced but rarely fills. Open June 1-Sept. 30. Singles LE13, doubles LE25. Breakfast and dinner included.

Rio Hotel, Galeh St. (tel. 94 20 23), on the corner of Alexandria St. Spic-and-span but bare rooms, many with balconies, are pleasant during the day but hot and noisy at night. Mosquitoes are a problem. Singles LE6.50, doubles LE7.

Hotel Beau Site (tel. 94 20 66 or 94 33 19), on the far western edge of the corniche, 2km from Alexandria St. Really classy: excellent service, tasteful decor, relaxed atmosphere, comfortable rooms with fans, and a well-kept beach. Many Egyptians consider it the best hotel in Egypt. Owner Demetrius and brother Tony take interest in their guests' welfare. Very expensive, but a bargain for what it offers. Reserve well in advance at the Osman Ahmed Osman Building, Roxy, Heliopolis, Cairo (tel. 259 94 80). Open May 1-Oct. 31. Singles LE33, Doubles LE41. Superb compulsory full board LE21.75 per person. Three tents, sleeping two, on the beach are available for LE25.

Cairo Hotel, Tahrir St. (tel. 94 26 48), 3 blocks east of Alexandria St. in a quiet neighborhood. Small place. Low-slung, colorfully painted, with a grape arbor. Very simple rooms with sinks. Singles LE3, doubles LE5. The **Hotel Mena House** across the street has similar rates; both can fill up with Egyptian families. Both are also populated with mosquitoes.

New Lido (tel. 94 45 15), on the corniche 1km west of Alexandria St. Rents 4-room flats (including kitchen, bath, and balcony) that accommodate 4 comfortably, and 5 or 6 in a squeeze, for LE46 per night. Alternatively, 4 can fit in the beach bungalows farther down the beach for LE25 per night (no kitchen, but a private bath).

Campers have two options. You can receive permission to camp for free on the beach by the bay from the military investigations office (see Practical Information). The law against camping without a permit is strictly enforced. You could also take a bus to Ubayyad Beach and rent a tent from the **Badr Camp** (open sided *tuf-tuf* in summer 50pt, microbus LE1-2). At Badr, two people get a beachside tent with carpet-cots, plus three meals for LE16.·

Food and Entertainment

The cheapest way for a group to eat in Marsa Matruuh is to shop *en masse* at the local market and divide the cost by the number of mouths. The vegetable *souk* is located about 3 blocks east of Alexandria St., north of Tahrir St.

While many inexpensive restaurants vie for customers on Alexandria St., the champion must be the **Hani el-Onda,** 2 doors east of Alexandria St. on the south side of Tahrir St., 3 blocks south of the corniche. Their Faustian bargain: You agree to eat three meals in this dimly lit, but cool and clean, hole-in-the-wall. They serve you in return a breakfast of beans, eggs, jam, bread, and tea; a lunch of macaroni, chicken, vegetable, salad and dessert; and a dinner of beans, sliced beef, bread, jam, and cheese—all for only LE6. They also serve individual meals for LE2-4. (Open 24 hours.) Runner up is the **Alexandria Tourist Restaurant,** on the east side of Alexandria St. 2 blocks south of the corniche, where a meal costs LE3-4. They'll also prepare chicken, rice, salad, and macaroni for a picnic on the beach.

The **Mattam Shatti Matruuh** (Matruuh Coast Restaurant) serves good chicken, soup, and potatoes for LE2-3. No English sign, but you will find it 4 blocks up Alexandria St. on the east side; identify it by the white tile with red lettering around the door. The "Greek Restaurant" directly across the street is not recognizably Greek; servings are meager, and service is slow.

For a treat, head out to the **Hotel Beau Site,** on the western end of the corniche (see Accommodations). Sumptuous, well-prepared buffet meals are served here in an elegant porch restaurant (breakfast buffet LE8, lunch LE11, dinner LE12). Every night after dinner Demetrius and Tony turn on the disco music in the Bamboo Bar. Go wild. Once per week they have a "special party" with some theme: a costume ball or a beauty contest. Non-guests must buy drinks to attend. There is also a weekly "kiddie party."

Most of the fancy hotels along the corniche open their bars or nightclubs to all those who wish to lose sobriety. Small independent nightclubs along the bay attract reserved crowds of young Egyptians on every summer night. Try the **J.R. Club,** ¾km west of Alexandria St., or **Disco 54,** in the Radi Hotel, on the corniche 4 blocks east of Alexandria St.

Sights

Marsa Matruuh offers no sights other than its **beaches,** but they are magnificent enough. All the beaches are closed to swimmers after sunset. As part of a government effort to control drug trafficking, soldiers are on patrol along the coast throughout the night.

Five kilometers of soft sand rim the crescent-shaped bay of Marsa Matruuh. From the town's small port on the east to Lido Beach on the west, this stretch of beach attracts the summer crowds. As in Alexandria, some women here swim fully clothed; as is the case throughout Egypt, bikinis and revealing one-piece suits can make the onlookers and the wearer uncomfortable. The Beau Suite Hotel has a private beach which is cleaner, less crowded, and more liberal (some bikinis can be spotted) than the public beaches. There is no charge for non-guests, but they encourage you to rent an umbrella (LE1 per hour) or a surf kayak (LE6 per hour).

East of the port, the shoreline arcs around into a peninsula that faces the town from across the bay. Hire a donkey cart, rent a bike, or hire a boat from the port to take you over to the peninsula, called Rommel's Isle. The **Rommel Museum** (closed in the summer of 1988, but due to reopen by 1989) contains a mediocre exhibit built into a series of cool caves that Rommel used as his headquarters in the North African campaign. (Admission 50pt. Open daily 9am-3pm.) Around to the ocean side of the peninsula, just past the marine Fouad Hotel, is **Rommel's Beach,** where, according to legend, he swam each day. On the ocean side of the isle, the wreck of an old U-boat juts out of the water. You can rent a surf kayak to paddle out to the wreck. Head straight to the red buoy on your left. The sub lies parallel to the beach 20m toward the mosque from the red buoy; you'll need a diving mask to see it under 3m of water. **Alam al-Rum** and **Hashiisha** beaches both lie farther east.

To the west of the main town beach, the **Beach of Lovers** caps the western horn of the bay. You can easily reach this beach by foot or by surf kayak. Inconsiderate visitors have recently begun to desecrate the sand while worshiping the sun, and the heaps of litter grow daily. Farther west on the ocean side of the bay, you will encounter more wind, less trash, and **Cleopatra's Beach,** on the far right hand side of which lies a little cove called **Cleopatra's Bath.** Reputedly, the queen and Marc Antony frolicked here. About another 5km down the coast lies a wide, flat sand beach called **Ubayyad.** Unfortunately, it is scarred by the barbed wire and tented villages of Cairo bureaucrats. **Badr Camp** is here (see Accommodations). The farthest and most spectacular spot of all is **Agiiba,** about 20km from Marsa Matruuh. Stop along the way at the ruins of the tiny **Temple to Ramses II,** which lie neglected in the sand. Agiiba, which means "wonderful," is an inlet in a series of rocky cliffs peppered with caves. The view of the Mediterranean from the cliff tops is fantastic, and below, **Agiiba Beach** waits seductively.

To reach these western beaches, either take a shared **taxi** or **microbus** from the bus station (LE2-3 per person to Agiiba), or catch the open-sided *tuf-tuf* bus (50pt to Cleopatra, Ubayyad, or Agiiba). The bus shuttles back and forth from the bus station every 15 minutes from 8am to about 5pm (summer only).

Alternatively, you can join one of the Hotel Beau Site's **excursions.** Anyone can take part in these weekly car or boat tours to the more distant beaches. The fee of LE8 includes transportation, a guide, umbrellas, and refreshments. Every now and then the hotel will sail a boat to Cleopatra's Beach (LE4). Finally, you can try to **hitchhike.** Since vacationing Egyptians tend to be kind to the rare foreigners here, this last option is quite feasible.

Rumor has it that there is a sunken Roman or Ptolemaic fleet somewhere near Marsa Matruuh. Ask the tourist office for details.

Al-Alamein

Al-Alamein means "two worlds," and history and geography have conspired to allow this town to live up to its name. It is a minute village set in a broad and barren desert plain slightly too distant from the water to attract beach-going tourists. But as students and veterans of World War II well know, there was a time when al-Alamein was far less quiet, far less out-of-the-way, and far less empty. In November, 1942, the Allied forces under the command of the British General Montgomery halted the advance of the Nazi Afrika Corps here. Al-Alamein had seemed to the Germans a gateway to Alexandria and a key to the control of the continent. The Allied victory here marked the beginning of the end for the Axis Powers in North Africa and simultaneously crushed the mystique surrounding the "Desert Fox," German Field Marshal Rommel, whose force of Panzer tanks had previously proved invincible. The Battle of al-Alamein was not only one of the war's most important confrontations, it was also one of the most violent: Nearly 10,000 soldiers lost their lives and 70,000 were wounded.

On the east side of town toward Alexandria lies the **British War Cemetery,** the resting place of 7,367 men, 815 of whose headstones bear only the terse and sad inscription "Known Unto God." Wreathed in purple flowers and set against the seemingly interminable desert, the excruciatingly neat rows provide a scene at once staggering, poignant, and eerily beautiful. Be sure to read the plaque and inscriptions within the shaded alcove; they explain the battle's significance as well as the diverse origins of the victims here (Britain, New Zealand, Australia, east and west Africa, South Africa, Greece, France, India, Malaysia and the Pacific Islands). Maintained by the British War Graves Commission, the cemetery is almost always open.

The **War Museum** at the west side of the village is within a pistol shot of the bus stop and main square. It contains displays of weaponry, military attire, and descriptions of the actions of Rommel, Montgomery, and the other participants in the battle. The room dedicated to Egypt's 1973 war with Israel is somewhat anomalous. Although not a victory for Egypt, the smashing of the Bar Lev Line along the Suez remains a point of great pride for all Egyptians. (Admission LE1. Open daily 9am-6pm; during Ramadan 9am-3pm.) Eight kilometers west of town, up on a small peninsula overlooking the sea, are the smaller and less frequently visited **German** and **Italian Cemeteries.** Both are large, fortress-like edifices, resting on desert swells overlooking the distant sea. Without a private car or specially hired taxi, it will be difficult to visit these last two monuments. Try hitching along the main road.

Look for the small marker about 3km west of the town center marking the farthest Axis advance, with an arrow pointing east: "Il Fortuna, Non Il Valore: Alexandria, 111km."

Getting to al-Alamein is easy. Leaving is the hard part. All of the buses that run between Marsa Matruuh and Alexandria or Cairo make a half-hour rest stop at al-Alamein. You can disembark, but may find it difficult to board a later bus unless you have already purchased a separate, full ticket at your point of departure. The buses are usually already packed when they get here.

The only other sure way to visit al-Alamein without your own car is to hire a **service taxi** to make the trip. This means you have to find six other people who want either to take a long rest in al-Alamein on a cross-desert run, or to make a special, round-trip excursion from Alexandria (about LE60 for the taxi with either option).

Another possibility for leaving al-Alamein, though it's a miserable one, is to catch one of the four daily **trains** that pull through al-Alamein (2 each way, under LE1 to Matruuh or Alexandria). All the trains arrive in the late morning or early afternoon. Inquire at Masr Station in Alexandria or at the station in Matruuh for schedule information. The disadvantages of train travel are that only third class is available and that the al-Alamein stop is 2km across the sweltering desert from the village. **Hitchhiking** may be the best option. Try arranging a ride with one of the drivers taking a rest stop in al-Alamein by offering to pay a few pounds for the trip.

For those who wish to spend the night in the dusty little village (not recommended), there is essentially one option: the **al-Alamein Rest House,** with singles for LE15 and doubles for LE19. The Rest House is attached to the restaurant, which is also the bus stop. The restaurant itself serves good food (meals LE3-5) and ice-cold drinks.

Siwa Oasis

Siwa Oasis is a tropical island in a great, endless sea of sand dunes. Completely isolated from the rest of Egypt, Siwa's history and culture are unique. Amidst groves of date palms and dark, cool natural springs, the Siwans live as they have for a thousand years. But as the outside world makes inroads into the oasis, the native way of life has begun to adapt to the demands and rewards of modern consumer culture. Even so, Siwa Oasis is a calm, beautiful, and almost otherworldly respite from the world to which you are accustomed. Like Alexander the Great, who made Siwa famous by his pilgrimage to the Oracle of Amun here in 331 B.C.E., the modern visitor will be richly rewarded, even if you are not declared to be godly.

A taxi or bus from Marsa Matruuh takes you through a completely barren landscape on much the same path followed by Alexander's camel caravan. Today, a paved road cuts through the desert like a tendril of modernity, and the 300km trip takes only five hours; the caravans needed eight days to make the trip—if they made it. But even until 1984, when the new road was completed, the trip by truck or car required 12 hours; every so often a foolhardy driver would leave the line of telephone poles and vanish into the wastes. Siwa's isolation has made it legendary in the annals of Egypt. Ancient historians told odd tales of strange cities and mysterious kingdoms in the desert. Nature defeated most attempts to ascertain the truth; in 500 B.C.E. an entire Persian army was swallowed up by a desert sandstorm. This suited the Siwans, who have always resented any outsiders meddling in their lives, particularly those who wanted them to pay taxes.

The rare European travelers who stopped here in the eighteenth and nineteenth centuries used to meet with hostile receptions from the Siwans, who would occasionally kill the intruders. The Khedive in Cairo had to cope with armed rebellions throughout the nineteenth century; when the Axis powers arrived during the Second World War, the Siwans had no problems accepting their generous gifts. Today, the Siwans are a reserved people, less likely to seek out contact with strangers, although the increasing influx of tourists and television signals has made them more receptive to what the outside world has to offer.

Everything seems different in Siwa. The Siwan language, for example, which is not written, is a dialect of Berber related to the Moroccan Tuareg language. It is barely influenced by Arabic, although most Siwans do speak Arabic. In Siwan, *mashi* is "yes," and *oola* is "no". The Siwans live in cool mud houses of local design that are made from salty clay supported by palm logs. This primitive-looking architecture is better adapted to the desert climate than modern stone buildings.

In scholarly circles, Siwan culture is best known for its tradition of folktales and its repressive customs concerning women. The Siwan women wear brightly colored garments in the fashion of the Berbers of the Saharan plains in Libya, Tunisia, and Algeria. They adorn their necks, heads, and limbs with heavy silver jewelry and braid their hair in elaborate styles. Visitors will probably have only fleeting encounters with the women, who are expected to remain hidden indoors. When they do go out, the women shroud themselves in a gray-blue cloth that they close around their faces at the sight of a stranger. Upon the death of her husband, a woman must spend many weeks in solitary confinement to protect others from her temporary "evil eye." Siwan marriage customs, famous for their complexity, include a series of visits by various participants, a mock struggle for the bride, bathing in a special spring, and a huge feast. The bride wears a fantastic array of colorfully embroidered shawls, dresses and skirts; cascades of silver ornaments tumble from her forehead and wrists. Only before her marriage, between the ages of 12 and 16, is a Siwan girl free to play in the streets in brilliantly hued dresses.

The sexual conservatism of Siwa pervades every aspect of life here. For example, only male donkeys are used to prevent the corruption of women by scenes of donkey-love. Up until last year, when a special facility was completed, women were never taken to the hospital—no man will allow a fellow Siwan to see his wife's body. Very ill Siwan women were taken to Marsa Matruuh to be treated by strangers, if they survived the trip. Because of these very conservative attitudes, foreign visitors (particularly women) should dress modestly. For men, this means not wearing shorts in town; for women, no bare arms or legs. The simplest solution is to invest in a cotton *galabiya* (the ankle-length shirts worn by Egyptians). They're cheap (LE10-15), cool in the summer heat, and you will be much more readily received and befriended by native Siwans if you wear one.

Despite lingering traditional values, modern times have brought sudden change. In recent years, the national government has been working overtime to make up for long years of neglect. The new road, completed four years ago, will mean an increased number of well-stocked stores and a growing stream of tourists. Universal education, a new quarry, a new desalination plant, and modern agricultural projects are altering the ways Siwans experience daily life. The Siwans seem to welcome the changes—a thousand televisions were ordered the first week after electricity was introduced—but most seem determined to keep the old ways flourishing. In the next decade, the oasis will probably lose much of its distinctive character. But for now, travelers find Siwa both readily accessible and unique.

Those planning to spend more than a day in Siwa should make an effort to acquire a copy of the late Ahmed Fakhry's superb, 200-page guide to Siwa. The author, a renowned Egyptologist, conveys his love for Siwa through detailed descriptions of its history, culture, and geography. It is written in an informative, journalistic style, and contains lots of entertaining anecdotes. Published by the American University in Cairo, Fakhry's *The Oases of Egypt: Volume I, Siwa* is available at the AUC's bookstore for LE9 in hardcover, or 95pt for the paperback edition. The Hotel Arous el-Waha usually has a copy or two on hand for the use of their guests, or you can purchase a paperback copy at Mahdi's shop near the hotel.

Practical Information

Siwa Oasis hides in a desert depression about 300km southwest of Marsa Matruuh, a coastal town 290km west of Alexandria. Siwa's western edge comes within 50km of the closed Libyan border. The only practical way to reach Siwa is by road from Marsa Matruuh. Alternatively, you can hire a camel in the Nile Valley, brave 20 days of sandstorms and endless possibilities for death, and break every Egyptian travel restriction law on a trek across the Western Desert. Now that the procedure for acquiring a Siwa permit has been simplified, you can reach Siwa from Cairo or Alexandria in a single day—but allow some time for exhaustion and unpredictable bureaucratic hassles. Sane travelers will allow at least five days, if not a week, to fully enjoy and explore Siwa.

The new road from Marsa Matruuh is well-paved but infrequently used. You can travel its length on a crowded, non-air-conditioned **bus** from the main station in Marsa Matruuh (daily 7:30am and 3pm, LE3, 5hr.). It's a good idea to take the morning bus, since the one in the afternoon originates in Alexandria and has only standing room left by the time it reaches Marsa Matruuh. (Both buses arrive at the station 30 min. before the departure time.) The buses return at 5am and 2pm, and go on to Alexandria (LE6) after the stop in Marsa Matruuh. Although it is possible to catch the bus in front of the Arous el-Waha Hotel, you should board it in the town square if you want a seat.

A more comfortable option is to share a **service taxi** from Marsa Matruuh (4 hr., LE6-7 per person). They leave from the northwest side of the bus station square, with departures in early morning and late afternoon—the only times when eight people at once want to go to Siwa. Catching a taxi at other times is possible—but the hotter it is when you travel, the longer the trip will take. Taxis leave Siwa more sporadically; again, the best times are early morning and late afternoon. Wait for taxis in the Siwa town market, by the Abduh Restaurant. If you despair of finding a taxi, you might try to hitch a ride with someone; offer the equivalent taxi fare for the service. Both taxis and buses stop at a simple desert **Rest House** halfway between Marsa Matruuh and Siwa. You can get soft drinks and *fuul* here, but probably not bottled water. There is an outhouse out back.

Because Siwa, so close to Libya, is a "militarily sensitive area," visitors must acquire a special permit to visit the oasis. The authorities have recently streamlined the procedure to facilitate tourism; if all goes well it can take as little as 10 minutes. However, in Egypt, all bureaucratic matters are unpredictable, so be prepared to spend some time in Marsa Matruuh if need be—not an unpleasant fate by any standards. Your first stop should be at the small photocopy shop on Galeh St., 1 block east of Alexandria St. and opposite the mosque, and make a photocopy of your passport photograph and Egyptian visa (50pt). Next, walk over to the military investigations office, at the eastern end of the first street north of Galeh St. (about a 10-min.

walk). Bang on the green metal door to be admitted. The helpful staff, growing more and more accustomed to Siwa-bound tourists, will probably be able to issue a permit while you wait.

Your pass will be issued for a specific, limited period of time. Ask for more time than you think you'll need, since you will not be able to extend the pass once in Siwa. Visas of more than one week might be difficult to obtain. The standard pass gives you access to "The Amun temples, Cleopatra bath, the town of Siwa, and agricultural areas." That last term is interpreted to include the area near Siwa town, including the western village of al-Maraqi. If you want to visit places farther afield, such as the salt lake and small temples near Ayn Qurayshat, you will have to ask for special permission in Marsa Matruuh. In general, these and the other undeveloped regions in the eastern oasis are off-limits to foreigners, as are the Ghara Oasis and the uninhabited oases east of Siwa. Keep the pass and your passport readily accessible during the journey to Siwa, since soldiers at a couple of military checkpoints will ask to see them. (The bus driver may take them from you at the start of the trip, and show them to the officers himself. Don't forget to take them back afterwards.)

Once in Siwa, you'll find that getting around is easy. The oasis fills a depression that stretches for 82km west to east, and between 3 and 30km north to south, but most visitors concern themselves only with the **town of Siwa** and the nearby villages and ancient sites. About 6000 people live in the town; 2000 other Siwans plus a few hundred Bedouin live in villages scattered elsewhere in the oasis. The paved road from Marsa Matruuh ends at the **New Mosque.** The dusty main north-south road in town continues past the mosque into the two squares of the **town market.** The ruined houses of **ancient Siwa** rise in eerie geometric forms above the market on a rock acropolis. The narrow streets of Siwa town radiate from the market and the acropolis. The town is broken by a swath of palm trees on its eastern side, and fringed by palms on all but the southern side, which merges gently into the desert.

The **police station, the telephone office** (which can handle **international calls,** and the **post office** are all located in modern buildings just west of the New Mosque, across from the government hotel. The complex also includes the brand new **tourist information office,** the domain of the very competent Mr. Mahdi Muhammad Ali Hweiti. A sociology major at the University of Alexandria, fluent speaker of English, and native Siwan, Mahdi is the official host to all visitors in Siwa. He can arrange sightseeing expeditions, provide maps and information on Siwan festivities and events, and generally make your stay a pleasant one. Congratulate him on his marriage last year.

Siwa has recently introduced covered donkey carts (*carettas*) which can take you outside of town for LE1-2 per hour. You can rent **bicycles** for LE1 per hour or LE5 per day in the market. The one **local bus** crawls west from Siwa town to al-Maraqi making a 50km loop. Round-trip fare 50pt; ask Mahdi for times. Siwa town has no banking services or travel agencies. Aside from the main telephone office, **telephones,** too, are unheard of here, but the **postal service** seems reliable.

The climate in Siwa is similar to that in Aswan and the other oases. Winter is pleasantly warm, with cool nights. Summer is hot; the city lies somnolent under the afternoon sun in July and August. Electric power only lasts from 8pm to 3am, and air-conditioning and even fans are just a sweaty fantasy. The natural springs, however, work wonders for fevered brows. The mild weather, and the many local festivals connected to the harvest, make fall and winter the best times by far to come.

Accommodations and Food

Although far from a resort town—that's not what you come here for, anyway—Siwa offers decent lodging and plentiful, clean food. The government's new, three-story **Hotel Arous el-Waha** (Worthy Bride Hotel) stands right at the end of the road from Matruuh. By Siwan standards, the carpeted, clean rooms with private bath are the height of luxury. Every evening, the mayor of Siwa appears to chat with guests while the helpful staff looks after their comfort. If you find the rooms uncomfortably hot (very likely in the summer), you can drag your mattress out onto the large, breezy terrace. (Singles LE8.50, doubles LE11.40, extra beds LE2.50. Breakfast of eggs, cheese, jam and bread LE2, lunch and dinner LE5; request it the night before. Tea, coffee, and warm water available anytime.) The government also runs the newly renovated **Social Rest House,** just down the street toward the market, where you can get a bed in a shared room for LE3. Two private hotels, the slightly decrepit **Hotel Medina** just north of the main market square, and the small, cramped **New Siwa Hotel** across the street from the military intelligence office, both charge LE1.50 per person, shared bath only.

In the summer of 1988 it was possible to **camp** without permission in Siwa town and in nearby areas, but this policy is apt to change depending on relations with Libya, so check with Mahdi before pitching your tent.

Several cafes and small, simple restaurants line the two market squares, established for the small population of transient workers. What you order often bears little resemblance to what you receive: basically, whatever is in stock that day. Standard offerings are rice, fresh chicken, and *fuul,* all for LE2-3. The Restaurant Kelani Sons, on the inside northern corner, serves consistently decent food, but you can never predict who'll run out of what when. The local stores, well-stocked with canned goods, offer fresh and dried Siwan dates, figs, and other fruits in season, as well as soda and mineral water. One of the stores on the north side of the southern square, to the right of a shop selling clothing, has its own generator, so it can sell cold drinks throughout the day. Because Siwans tend to be more reserved and conservative than residents of most Egyptian towns, the traveler will be lucky to receive an invitation to eat or stay with a local family. Women will be allowed to enter a home much more readily than men.

Sights

Siwa Oasis, a tapestry woven in dusty browns and tangled greens, is regarded by most as the most beautiful of Egypt's oases. From atop the ruins of **ancient Siwa,** built on a rocky hill, you can look out on the quiet streets of Siwa town, which wind from the cluster of mud houses into luxuriant palm gardens. From here you will also see the Sahara: black gashes of rock to the north, waves of sand to the south, and the relentlessly blue desert sky all around. Weird geometric profiles of crumbling walls loom about you. These are the remains of the romantic medieval fortress-town of Shali, described by eighteenth-century European visitors. Its encircling wall once protected the Siwans from marauding Berbers and Bedouin. As you descend on the paths leading back to the market, you can imagine the Siwans slowly abandoning their acropolis for the more spacious settlement at its base. The descent began when Muhammad Ali conquered Siwa in 1820 and protected the inhabitants from attacks. The heavy rains, that occur only once every two decades but disastrously melt the Siwan houses, encouraged migration to the new town. By 1930, the ancient city had become a ghost town. The most recent rains were in 1985, but because of the rise of concrete buildings, damage was limited. Leave your raincoat behind.

A second acropolis rises 1km to the northeast of ancient Siwa. During the bombing of Siwa town by the Italians during World War II, its caves and ancient tombs sheltered the Siwans from the modern marauders. During this period, the local people discovered several more Ptolemaic- and Roman-era decorated tombs. Called the **Tombs of Jabal al-Mawta,** they merit a visit by every traveler to Siwa. Arrange a visit through the tourist office; Mahdi will arrange for one of the three custodians to meet you there to unlock the most important tombs. Remember to bring a flashlight. Don't miss the **Tomb of Si-Amun.** Although damaged by Allied and Egyptian soldiers during the war, it contains a beautifully painted ceiling depicting the six boats of the sun's journey across the sky. Damaged murals on the walls show bearded, Greek-looking nobleman Si-Amun and his sons worshiping Egyptian deities. The tomb opens north and dates from the third century B.C.E., when Siwa enjoyed a position as an important trading post for the Hellenic city of Cyrene on the Libyan coast. The **Tomb of the Crocodile** features a fanciful cartoon of a grimacing Nile Valley crocodile, but is otherwise uninteresting. The larger **Tomb of Niperpathot** was built by a nobleman during the last pharaonic dynasty, the twenty-sixth. It is the oldest tomb in Siwa, yet altogether unmemorable. The whole sight is littered with bones, and if you look carefully you can see human skulls and mummy wrappings poking up out of the sand. The acropolis commands exhilarating views of Siwa town and the oasis, although the summit, now a military look-out post, is off-limits. Wave to the friendly soldiers, but don't take pictures of them. And reward your guide with LE1-2 *baksheesh* for his pains.

In Siwa town, hail a *carreta* and rattle off through the palm groves to the village of **Aghurmi.** Like Siwa town, Aghurmi rests peacefully at the foot of a once-inhabited acropolis. To ascend the acropolis, you pass through an old gate made of palm logs, and then underneath a weatherbeaten but still sturdy old mud **mosque.** As you climb to the open center of the acropolis, the ruins of ancient Aghurmi surround you. Up ahead, perched dramatically at the cliff-edge of the acropolis, looms the well-preserved **Oracle of Amun,** small but imposing. Now imagine that you are Alexander, come to consult the internationally famous priests of Amun. You pass through the stone temple's simple gateway into the outer, then the inner court. The silent, uninscribed gray walls whisper with the echoes of bygone rituals. Accounts of ancient Greek and Roman historians paint the scene: Priests carry the sacred boat containing the image of Amun as women sing and dance in procession. Enter the inner sanctuary, the only decorated chamber, and speak with Amun. The oracle of Amun is said to have confirmed everyone's suspicion that Alexander was a god-king, proclaiming him the "son of Amun." However, Alexander never told anyone what he asked the oracle in private, nor what the answer was. The secret died with him within 10 years.

The temple of the Oracle of Amun is thought to date from the Twenty-First Dynasty (c. 1000 B.C.E.). It became widely celebrated in later dynasties, and was well known to the ancient Greeks, who constructed many shrines to the sun-god Amun in their own country. Modern-day visitors enjoy unrestricted access to the temple and the Aghurmi acropolis—no guards, no fees. You can look around the acropolis, peer down the sacred well where offerings were purified (next to the mosque), and climb the mosque's minaret for a superb view of the town and the astonishing sunsets.

Below, the village of Aghurmi welcomes foreign visitors. The local men and children sell **Siwan handicrafts** on behalf of the hidden women. Aghurmi is an excellent place to purchase fine baskets and intricately embroidered wedding clothes. Ask to see a *margunah,* the large, handsomely decorated basket that graces every Siwan household. The mayor of Siwa states emphatically that tourist dollars help to maintain the handicraft tradition in Siwa.

A number of independent dealers have sprung up and will approach you with invitations to "special exhibitions" of handicrafts. Although small, these are mostly reputable, and a pleasant evening can be spent sipping *chai* and examining the goods. Mahdi of the tourist office acts as a broker for many families, operating a small shop near the Arous el-Waha Hotel with a good selection of decorated clothing, *margunahs,* and heavy silver-alloy ornaments and jewelry, which the Siwan women traditionally wear by the kilo.

If you follow the road heading southeast of Aghurmi, after 1km you'll stumble onto the meager remains of the **Temple of Amun,** also known as Umm 'Ubaydah. Time has not been kind to this once-great companion of the oracle temple. In 1897, a government official of Siwa (the *Marmur*) blew up the temple for materials to be used in the construction of a police station and the modern mosque in Siwa town. All that is left is a single inscribed, broken wall, sitting forlornly amidst the palms.

Beyond the temple on the same road, about 2km to the south, glistens the cool and mossy **Pool of Cleopatra.** Like many of the approximately 200 natural springs in Siwa, this one has been encircled with a stone pool. An irrigation duct runs out one end of the silky pool. Known to Herodotus as the "Spring of the Sun," this pool is popular with local men and boys, who swim and splash about in their undershorts. Modestly dressed women should feel comfortable swimming here as well. On the other side of town, the **Pool of Fatnus,** on an island in the middle of a salt lake (accessible by a small causeway), provides a spectacular setting for an afternoon swim. Some local new tour guides haved dubbed this "Fantasy Island." Interpret this oracle yourself.

Siwa is blessed with many such pools, which provide water for crops and recreation for sweaty Siwans. In fact, Siwa, like all the oases, suffers from too much of a good thing. Water drainage is poor in the desert depressions, where salt lakes form as unused water collects and evaporates. Over the years, Siwa has lost a good deal of farmland to the growing deposits.

You can get a good look at a salt lake to the west of Siwa town, where you'll find dramatic desert vistas. On the road to **al-Maraqi,** which traverses a low desert pass, you will observe craggy yellow buttes honeycombed with caves and Roman tombs. The village of al-Maraqi lies in its own lush oasis, virtually severed from the rest of Siwa by fingers of the desert. Several dozen Bedouin families inhabit this western fringe of Siwa: Conservatively dressed Bedouin women seem ostentatious in contrast to their Siwan sisters. Al-Maraqi makes a pleasant daytrip from Siwa town. From Siwa you can catch a local bus to al-Maraqi. After two hours on a twisting road, the bus will stop in al-Maraqi and then turn around for the return trip. The round-trip fare is 50pt. (Contact Mahdi at the tourist office for precise times.)

The village of **Abu Shruf,** 35km to the east, is a Bedouin encampment surrounding a small, 2000 year-old stone temple. The road to Abu Shruf passes Ain Qurayshat, the largest spring in Siwa. All the water flowing from this spring goes to waste; the least you can do is swim in it. This, however, is outside the limits of the standard permit.

Every October, the Siwans gather for a huge feast at the rocks of Dakrur. A "chief of the feast" oversees the distribution of food to the small groups spread over the plain, and none may begin to eat until the chief climbs to the top of the rock and shouts "Bismillah!" ("In the name of God.") Tourists are invited to attend, and it is an experience not to be missed. Dakrur, 1km south of the Pool of Cleopatra, is also an excellent site for **camping.** Mahdi at the tourist office can arrange car trips to Abu Shruf and Dakrur; he will also have information on festivals and the harvest.

Sinai

Caught between pale red rocks and bright blue water, the Sinai Peninsula is naturally and strategically blessed. Sinai is the end result of millennia of tectonic friction between the Asian and African continents. In the twentieth century, the political friction between Egypt and Israel caused the peninsula to become a battleground. However, it is not military forces, but natural ones that have caused extraterrestial desolation of the desert mountains of Sinai's southern interior. The jagged mountain ridges with their bizarre lithology contrast spectacularly with the lush and lively scenery underwater along the coast of the Gulf of Aqaba. Exquisite coral gardens teem with brilliantly colored fish in what is widely acclaimed as the world's greatest diving area. Sun-worshipers gather on beaches by luxury hotels. In the center of the southern desert pilgrims climb the peak said to be Mount Sinai, where God's name and law were revealed to Moses.

Four wars have been fought between Israel and Egypt in the Sinai, and minefields, trenches, and twisted fuselages still litter parts of the desert. In 1903, the British drew the borders of the Sinai from Rafiah on the Mediterranean coast to Eilat in an attempt to keep the Turks and Germans a safe distance from the Suez Canal. During the British Mandate, the Rafiah-Eilat line became the international boundary; after the 1948 war between the Arabs and Israel, it became the armistice line between Israel and Egypt. In 1956, Egypt blocked the Straits of Tiran off the Sinai coast, thus cutting off Israeli access to the Red Sea, Africa, and Asia. This move helped to trigger the 1956 fighting, in which Israel captured all of the Sinai. Foreign pressure and a United Nations pledge to keep the straits open to Israeli shipping persuaded Israel to return the Sinai to Egypt five months later.

In 1967 the scenario was repeated. Egypt called for the withdrawal of U.N. troops stationed in the Sinai, and the troops were withdrawn. Amidst Soviet and Syrian allegations that Israel was preparing a major attack, Egypt again blocked the straits. Israel launched a preventive attack. By the fourth day of the conflict, two days before the war ended, Israel had recaptured the Sinai. This time Israel ignored foreign pleas to accept peace terms that involved returning the Sinai, and held on to the territory as a buffer against Egyptian attack. In 1973, Egyptian forces crossed the Canal in a surprise offensive to recapture the Sinai. The Egyptians smashed the Israeli Bar-Lev defense line in six hours. However, Israel's forces regrouped and recaptured the peninsula. Israel retained the Sinai until, under the terms of the 1978 peace treaty, the land was returned to Egypt in two stages: the first half in 1979, the second in 1982. US troops stationed in the Sinai monitor the treaty, most visibly at the MFO base in Sharm el-Sheikh.

When Israel returned the Sinai, thousands of Israeli settlers were forcibly uprooted as their towns were bulldozed. Today, the Sinai is populated primarily by nomadic Bedouin, the majority of whom are descendents of Arabs from the Arabian peninsula. The 12-year Israeli occupation irreversibly changed the nature of Bedouin culture. Previously isolated from the rest of the world, the Bedouin had developed their own tribal practices. Under Israeli rule, the Bedouin began to supplement their income by catering to the influx of tourists. Modernity lifted the restrictions that the desert climate placed on their lifestyle.

The southern half of the Sinai contains the Aqaba coast, a snorkeler's paradise stretching from Taba on the Israeli border to Ras Muhammad at the peninsula's southern tip; Mount Sinai; and the only parts of the spectacular desert interior open to tourists.

Sinai Bureaucracy

You'll need a **visa** to visit the Sinai. A regular Egyptian visa is fine as long as it's obtained in advance. Egypt issues a **Sinai-only visa,** on the spot at the Israeli border at Taba (valid for one week). This visa limits travel to the Aqaba Coast and the St. Catherine's area. Unlike normal one-month Egyptian visas, the Sinai-only visa comes without a grace period. Overextend your stay, and you'll have to pay a hefty fine. But the procedure at the border, unlike almost everything else in Egypt, is simple. After you pay the NIS12.50 Israeli departure tax and have your passport stamped, the Israelis will drive you past the Sonesta Hotel to the Egyptian checkpoint. Here, a number of Egyptian officials will examine and stamp your passport and grant a Sinai visa, if necessary. The next official will collect the tourist tax. After one more official looks at your passport, you wait for the next bus south.

Buses run to Sharm el-Sheikh, via Nuweiba, Dahab, and Na'ama at 7am, 9am, 1pm, and 3pm (LE10, 4 hr.). Buses to Cairo (LE20, 9 hr.). and St. Catherine's (LE11) via Nuweiba (LE5) leave at 10am. A small shop by the checkpoint provides cheap refreshments and shade.

A number of **regulations** govern travelers to the Sinai. Travel is officially restricted to main roads and settlements, but in practice you can obtain permission from the police to visit parts of the desert interior with a Bedouin guide. Never leave the main roads by yourself. Sleeping on the beach is prohibited in some areas (notably Na'ama Bay), and the police often have nothing better to do than harass sleeping backpackers. Since these areas are not always marked, ask around before unrolling your sleeping bag. Nude sunbathing is illegal, as is smoking the hash that many will try to sell you. You cannot bring a rented car or any four-wheel drive vehicle into the Sinai. If you hold a standard, one-month Egyptian visa, you must register your passport with the police in any town within seven days of your arrival in Egypt. Don't wait until Sharm el-Sheikh to do this, since the passport office there sits several kilometers south of the town itself. Virtually none of the police in the Sinai speaks English. Because the police may not understand you, even if a Bedouin translates, they may try to cover themselves by inventing new regulations on the spot. If they're not sure whether you've registered (and they may overlook the rather obvious triangular registration stamp on your passport), they may insist that you have to register in every town you visit. If you ask any procedural question they can't answer, you may be ordered to go to the main police station at Taba or Sharm el-Sheikh, no matter how inconvenient this may be from your point of view. This is often a way of passing the buck to their superiors. Don't disregard police orders, but remember that they may not understand your situation or their own regulations. Any Arabic you know goes a long way with the police and other officials.

Getting There

The Sinai is most easily approached on the way to or from Israel. Several buses each day leave the Egyptian/Israeli border at Taba, 6km southwest of Eilat, between 7am and 3pm and travel the full length of the Aqaba Coast to Sharm el-Sheikh. Buses from Taba to Cairo also stop in Nuweiba and St. Catherine's. Bus #15 leaves from opposite Eilat's central bus station for the border. It is impractical to come through Rafiah and Gaza unless you are going to al-Arish.

Coming from Egypt, either Cairo or Suez is the departure points for the Sinai. In **Cairo,** buses leave Abbassiya Station, also known as Sinai Station, which lies at the northeast end of Ramses St., 5km from Ramses Station, in the al-Abbassiya district of Cairo. (Local buses from Ramses and Tahrir Stations include #56, 54, and the Talaba bus. From the Nile Hilton in Tahrir Sq., look for the yellow ticket booth with the green stripe. Fare is 50pt.) The daily Sinai buses from Cairo go to Sharm el-Sheikh (7am, LE13.50; 10am, 1pm, 11:30pm, and 12:30am, LE10.50) and St. Catherine's, Nuweiba, and on to Taba (7am; LE10, 15, and 20, respectively). One bus per day travels directly to Nuweiba via the new road across the northern Sinai (11pm, LE15, 7 hr.). A direct bus runs to Dahab, which may stop in St. Catherine's if it's not full (8am, 8pm, LE16.50, 7 hr.).

The city of **Suez** is another transit option, especially for travelers coming up from Hurghada. Buses from Suez's Arba'iin Bus Station, off Sa'ad Zaghloul St. 1500m from the bay, run to the following locations once per day: To St. Catherine's (LE7, 4½ hr.); to Sharm el-Sheikh (2pm, 10:30pm, LE6.50, 5½ hr.); and continuing to Dahab (LE6, 6½ hr.); direct to Nuweiba (1:30pm, LE10, 4½ hr.); and to Taba (9:30am, LE10, 5½ hr.). Note that most buses from Cairo to the Sinai bypass Suez, passing through the tunnel north of town. For travel to the Sinai from Hurghada, see the Hurghada section below.

Planes fly to all regions of the Sinai. **Air Sinai** charges steep prices for its flights from Cairo to al-Arish ($46), St. Catherine's ($46), and Sharm el-Sheikh ($58), from Luxor to St. Catherine's ($66) and Sharm el-Sheikh ($54), from Hurghada to St. Catherine's ($54) and Sharm el-Sheikh ($40), and for flights between Sharm el-Sheikh and St. Catherine's ($38). Despite the expense, some budget travelers pay the money to enjoy the magnificent sight of the Sinai Desert from the air. If you fly, pay in pounds. You can contact Air Sinai in Cairo (at the Nile Hilton courtyard), in Tel Aviv, or through EgyptAir in any smaller Egyptian city. Most flights operate only a couple of times per week.

Getting Around

Well-paved roads connect the Sinai's handful of permanent settlements. New roads might not appear on your map of Egypt. In addition to the schedules mentioned above, the following daily **buses** run within the Sinai: from Sharm el-Sheikh to Dahab, Nuweiba and Taba and from St. Catherine's to Nuweiba and Taba. To get to al-Arish, your best bet is to go to Rafiah and find a taxi. Buses in the Sinai are notoriously idiosyncratic, often arriving and departing late—or even early. Be skeptical about any bus information you receive. The conductors are usually honest, and sometimes genuinely forget to give you change.

The **taxi** situation in the Sinai is not much more sensible than the buses. Taxis have the annoying tendency to just follow buses and try to persuade travelers as they step off to get in and go one town farther. Taxis are relatively scarce, but when you can find one, they are usually a good deal. Taxi fares go up at night and when you are alone, so plan any nighttime jaunts around the bus schedules. As always, bargain, bargain, bargain!

Infrequent traffic and blistering heat make **hitchhiking** a dubious idea at best. Don't hitch unless someone offers you a ride to your destination or to a place where you can wait in the shade for a bus. Women should never hitch alone; if your ride gives you trouble and you ask to be let off, you could find yourself on a deserted road in blistering heat with nothing but parched rocks for hours around.

Practical Information

Money is a problem in the Sinai. Foreign currency in any form other than U.S. cash can be exchanged only at the banks in Taba, Sharm el-Sheikh, and al-Arish. Elsewhere in the Sinai, the banks are essentially worthless. If you're coming from elsewhere in Egypt, change your money beforehand since exchange rates are better. Prices for everyday items in the Sinai are more expensive than elsewhere in Egypt, but lower than in Israel. American cash is often accepted by storekeepers, including renters of scuba equipment.

Food in the Sinai is best described by the Rolling Stones song about not getting what you want, but getting what you need. Each town has a few safe, affordable restaurants as well as supermarkets that stock at least a meager variety of canned goods. Inexpensive, fresh pita bread (ask for *khoubz* if the vendor is confused) is found everywhere.

Budget accommodations are usually only a step above sleeping outside, and many travelers find the latter option cheaper and more pleasant. Camping equipment is not widely available in the Sinai. Bring along a sleep sack, warm clothes, or a sleeping bag (in winter months), and plan to keep a close watch on your belongings. Inquire at police stations and diving shops about storage—they will often provide this favor. Toilets, showers, and even running water are few and far between; toilet paper and tampons are obtainable only in Na'ama and possibly Nuweiba. Stock up before you leave, and guard them with your life.

Snorkeling equipment should be purchased in Cairo or Israel. The diving shops charge outrageous rental fees (LE9 per day for mask, fins, and snorkel) for equipment of varying quality, and sometimes close unpredictably. The Aqaba coast has some of the most spectacular reefs in the world; you don't want to see them through leaky, filthy masks, or to spend a day or two stewing on the beach waiting for the only diving shop in town to reopen. Since decent equipment can't be bought anywhere in the Sinai, you should have little trouble reselling your gear before you leave.

Red Sea snorkeling is such an exciting experience that it's easy to abandon all caution. Wear sneakers or fins at all times: The coral can rip your feet to shreds, and various fish with painful or lethal stings lurk on the bottom. (The black sea urchin likes to hide in holes and crevices in the coral, and its long, black spikes are extremely painful. The gnarled stonefish, camouflaged as a stone, sits quietly on the bottom—though less common than the sea urchin, its bite is lethal.) Sharks are attracted by blood, so never enter the water with an open wound or if you are menstruating. Panicking and thrashing tend to excite sharks—if you see one, climb calmly out of the water and spread the word. Finally, remember the Sinai sun is brutal. Though you may feel cool in the water, the sun is still doing its best to burn you to a crisp. Wear a shirt while snorkeling, and use a waterproof sunscreen.

You must be certified to rent scuba equipment in the Sinai, but diving shops will take you on a safe, shallow introductory dive with a guide for $40 (all diving shops quote prices in dollars), or give you a full certification course for about $150. If you have an accident while diving, the diving shops at Dahab and Na'ama have decompression chambers. If you are certified but you haven't logged a dive in the past three months, most diving shops will require a checkout dive.

Prepare yourself for the **climate** in the Sinai. Temperatures can reach 50°C (120°F). As in all of Egypt, wear a hat and avoid strenuous activity in the midday heat. On summer nights, the temperature drops to about 30°C (80°F), and lower at St. Catherine's; winter nights can be downright cold. Keep guzzling water even when you're not thirsty, up to as much as five or six liters per day, or more if you're trekking. Although Egyptians say the water is potable in the Sinai, stick to bottled mineral water. At 75-90pt for a liter and a half, it may be your major expense. If you become seriously dehydrated or develop other medical problems, go to the **hospitals** in Sharm el-Sheikh and St. Catherine's.

Except for al-Arish, there are no private **telephones** anywhere in the Sinai. You can phone elsewhere in Egypt from the telephone offices in Sharm el-Sheikh and St. Catherine's, and the phone office will also send telegrams. **Mail** is very slow.

Mount Sinai and St. Catherine's Monastery

If you didn't know its history, you'd probably call this remote, bone-dry mountain region "God-forsaken." Jews and Christians would beg to differ. To them Mt. Sinai is the site of God's greatest revelation to Moses. "And the LORD came down upon Mount Sinai, to the top of the mountain; and the LORD called to Moses at the top of the mountain and Moses went up." (Exodus 19:20). Muslims also accept the prophethood of Moses, although they believe the revelation to him was superseded by one to Muhammad. Gebel Musa is regarded as the mountain where, according to Exodus, Moses ascended, met with God face to face, and returned with the most influential tablets ever carved. The area's religious importance was increased by the legend that identified the valley at the mountain's base as the site of the burning bush, through which God called upon Moses to rescue his people from slavery in Egypt.

In the early Christian era, religious hermits began to congregate around this site, living in nearby caves. The monastery of St. Catherine's had its beginnings in their rudimentary communal life, and in a small chapel built by Helena, the converted mother of Emperor Constantine. In 342 C.E., Emperor Justinian ordered the construction of a splendid basilica and monastery on the same site. He set these within the walls of a fortress to enable Christians to live in the desert without fear of persecution. The monastery and the mountain then became perennially popular destinations for Christian pilgrims. In the present day, secular travelers mob Mt. Sinai all year long.

Practical Information and Food

The village of St. Catherine's is tucked away in the mountainous interior of the southern Sinai. Excellent roads run west to the Gulf of Suez, and east to the Gulf of Aqaba, both about 100km away. If you come from the west, you'll pass through the lush **Oasis of Feiran**, where Islamic tradition holds that Hagar fled in banishment from her husband Abraham. One kilometer before you reach the village, you'll see the spur road leading to St. Catherine's Monastery and the base of Mt. Sinai on the left. The monastery is about 1km up this road. Buses make the trip from Cairo and Suez (see Getting There, above), but not directly from Sharm el-Sheikh. Leaving St. Catherine's, you can catch the unreliable buses of the East Delta Bus Company to Cairo (6am and 1:30pm, LE11), to Suez (7:30am and 8:30am, LE6.50), to Dahab and Sharm-el-Sheikh (12:30pm, LE4 and LE6 respectively), and to Nuweiba and Taba (1:30pm, LE6 and LE11 respectively). Arrive early at the bus station, as buses often leave ahead of schedule. Don't count on catching any buses to the east after the 1:30pm run. Service taxis occasionally fill up for runs to Dahab (about LE5 per person) and elsewhere.

The bus will leave you in the village (tell the driver if you want to get off at the road to the monastery), an appealing cluster of new stone buildings. The building next to the bus stop contains a small **restaurant** (open 7am-10pm) and a **bakery** (fresh pita 10pt), located painfully near the **toilet.** Near the bus station, two small **supermarkets,** the better of which is Supermarket Katreen, overflow with useful things such as flashlights and canned food. Clear English signs mark the village's **hospital, gas station, police station,** and **post office** (open daily 8am-midnight). The phones at the post office cannot be used for international calls. A new shopping center with a **bank** and a **market** is located on the way to the police station.

Accommodations

For lack of better alternatives, most visitors to St. Catherine's sleep on the summit of Mt. Sinai. If you don't have a sleeping bag or enough warm clothing to withstand the chilly nighttime temperatures on the mountain (10°C in June), you don't have to be left out in the cold. The monastery's **youth hostel** rents bunk beds in hot rooms for LE5 (check-in 5-7pm; you'll have to wait for the monks to finish praying). The gates to the monastery close at 9:30pm. Showers are no longer available. The Tourism Village where the spur road meets the highway is not a budget option (LE80 and up), but the adjacent compound offers beds in stone huts for LE4.50. The toilets are in a separate building; no showers are available. Five kilometers from St. Catherine's on the road to Nuweiba lies **Zeitouna Camping** (tent sites LE5 per person).

Sights

Tradition has it that Emperor Justinian ordered the execution of the architect of **St. Catherine's Monastery** when he learned that it had not been built on the summit of the mountain. In a way, it was fortunate that the architect ignored the emperor's directions and chose the foot of Mount Sinai—the monastery is not only well-protected but also close to an abundant water supply. St. Catherine's is believed to be the oldest unrestored example of Byzantine architecture in the world. The monastery once housed hundreds of Orthodox monks, but its population has now dwindled to 17, all of Greek descent. Though linked with Mt. Sinai and the burning bush, the monastery is officially dedicated to St. Catherine. She was a stubborn evangelist to members of the Roman emperor's family who was martyred in Alexandria.

The monastery possesses many treasures, including jewel-studded crosses, hand-carved wooden furniture, and exquisite icons dating to the fourth century. One of the finest libraries of ancient manuscripts in the world can also be found here. Unfortunately only the splendid **chapel,** which contains a fascinating portion of the monastery's collection of icons, is open to the public. With special permission, you can visit shrines at the rear of the chapel, including the **Shrine of the Burning Bush.** The altar supposedly contains part of the root; a transplanted shoot of the original wonder-plant flourishes behind the chapel, out of public view. The Ottoman **mosque** within the fortress represents Egypt's "spirit of brotherliness" to the Ministry of Tourism, but not to the Orthodox Church. Don't miss the gruesome **Ossary,** a separate building outside the walls, where the bones of all the monastery's former residents lie in great heaps (bishops have special niches in the wall). A **gift shop** offers books on the monastery's history. The Ossary and the enclosed part of the monastery are open Monday through Thursday and Saturday, from 9:30am to 12:30pm (free, modest dress required).

The Sinai Peninsula owes its name to the towering 2285m peak of Mount Sinai (*Gebel Musa* in Arabic). Religious scholars speculate that this peak could not be the biblical peak, but it looks the part. You can climb Mount Sinai by either of two ascents. The shorter of the two, the **Steps of Repentance,** is actually the harder route. It is said that the 3000 steps were built by a single monk in order to fulfill his pledge of penitence. The steps are treacherous by night. Take them during the day while wearing a hairshirt and fulfill your own vows of repentance (about 75 minutes). The other route, the **camel path** (2-2½ hr. by foot), begins directly behind the monastery. About two-thirds of the way up, and directly below the path's juncture with the steps, is a 500-year-old cypress tree, which dominates a depressional plain known as **Elijah's Hollow.** Here the prophet Elijah is said to have heard the voice of God (I Kings 19:9-18). Two small chapels now occupy the site, one dedicated to Elijah and the other to his successor Elisha.

The best time to start the journey is about 5pm—late enough to avoid the blazing heat, but early enough to climb by sunlight. The alternative, taken by many travelers, is to hike at night, but the going is rougher (even with a flashlight and the glow of the moon) and the temperature is chilly. In any event, try to spend the night on the summit. You will awake to the sunrise and Mount Sinai's unforgettable view, extending to the mountains of Africa and Saudi Arabia, the Red Sea, and the Gulf of Aqaba. Sleeping bags form a nocturnal assembly on the mount's peak, so those who seek a more spiritual experience should sleep in Elijah's Hollow and be sure to rise before the sun does. The summit holds a small chapel, built in 1937 over the remains of a Byzantine church. In the cave below, Moses supposedly hid himself when he first came face-to-face with God. The chapel is almost always unattended and closed, but if you're thin you can climb through the loosely barred windows on the south side.

A few preparations are in order for a night trek. Dress warmly and bring a sleeping bag; there's no room to pitch a tent. If you don't have a flashlight, wait at the start of the path for someone who does. The overtaxed but always hospitable monks will allow you to leave your bags in a room at the monastery for the night for LE1 per piece. You don't need a guide—the path is easy to follow, the way is safe, and the self-professed escorts know nothing about the history of the mountain. The camel path begins 50m up the valley from the monastery's rear wall. This wide path is not difficult to find; it makes switchbacks up the right side of the far end of the valley. One point that causes most hikers a moment of confusion is the path's juncture with the steps, which occurs soon after you pass through the camel trail's narrow, steep-walled stone corridor. After passing through the corridor, head left, and follow the steps up the last one-third of the ascent. Those who decide to negotiate the steps up can find their origin at the far corner of the monastery's right wall. They are marked by a sign reading "To Moses Mountain."

Six kilometers to the south of Sinai looms **Gebel Katherina (Mount Catherine),** the highest mountain in Egypt (2642m). It is named after the saint, whose remains were reportedly discovered on its summit in the seventh century by monks. The path to the top, more secluded and beautiful than the Sinai highway, begins in the village itself and takes five to six hours to ascend. A chapel with water sits at the summit.

Locals recommend taking **camel trips** from Dahab and Nuweiba, and not Saint Catherine's. If you insist, a man will let you sit on a camel and have a quick ride for LE1. Rides up to a day long are available. Ask around the Cafeteria Catherine, on the outskirts of town.

Sharm el-Sheikh

Like the military commanders during the Egyptian-Israeli conflicts, travelers will be interested in Sharm el-Sheikh only for its strategic position. Commanding the southernmost point of the Sinai Peninsula, Sharm el-Sheikh is an important transportation interchange. To enjoy the Aqaba Coast's reefs and beaches, head up the spectacular twisting road to Na'ama Bay (6km), to Dahab (100km), to Nuweiba (170km), or to Taba (240km).

Buses leave from the bus station in Sharm el-Sheikh for Cairo every day at 6am, 10am, 1pm, 11:30pm, and midnight (LE14). A more popular bus—so popular that you'll feel like a sardine—leaves Sharm el-Sheikh for Taba between 9-9:30am, with stops at Na'ama, Dahab, and Nuweiba. The fare all the way to Taba is LE5; LE3.50

gets you to Nuweiba, and LE2.50 to Dahab. A bus to St. Catherine's (LE6), stopping at Dahab (LE3), leaves at 8am. Another bus heads directly and only to Nuweiba at 5pm. **Taxi** service out of both Sharm el-Sheikh and Na'ama Bay is rare and difficult to arrange.

Ask the bus driver to let you off at Sharm el-Sheikh's excellent **IYHF youth hostel** (tel. 637), which admits only IYHF members, and prohibits card playing and alcohol. To reach here from the bus stop in Sharm el-Sheikh, cross the street and walk up the hill opposite. The hostel is up top on the left; you'll see the red Arabic letters on the fence of the hostel's unexpected basketball court. The hostel has airconditioning and showers, and breakfast is included in the LE6 price. It's a great place to meet Egyptian teenagers. The price of tentsites and bungalows in Na'ama Bay makes this hostel an excellent option for travelers to Na'ama. There is an 11:30pm curfew. (Open in summer 6:30-9am and 2-11pm; in winter 2-10pm.)

Coming down the hill from the youth hostel, you will pass the **tourist police** and the **bus station,** where tickets to Cairo can be reserved (definitely recommended). Look for the green metal fence (the bus station is behind it) and the "City Council" sign (the bus station is beneath it). However, the place to catch the bus to Dahab is at the metal bus stop on the highway to Taba. Continuing south at the bottom of the hill, you will come to a **hospital,** and a **police station** (look for the fluttering Egyptian flag). To register, which you'll have to do if you have a standard Egyptian visa and want to stay in the youth hostel, follow the road from Na'ama about 1km farther south to the main police station at the port. Down the road south on the right is Sharm el-Sheikh's only decent restaurant, the **Sandy Palace** (pizza LE4, chicken or fish LE6, salad 75pt). There is no need to visit the restaurants farther south unless you enjoy brains and other such delicacies.

If you follow the road all the way up the hill, and turn right at the top, you'll find the town's main square, which contains three **banks** (open Mon.-Sat. 8am-2pm, Sun. 10am-noon, and evenings), a **post office** (open daily 9am-3pm), and a **telephone office** from which you can only make phone calls within Egypt (open 24 hours). Beyond these, around to the right, are a few pathetic **cafes,** and several so-called **supermarkets,** which stock biscuits, milk, cheese, about 10 different kinds of canned goods arranged in pyramids, and occasionally fresh produce.

To travel between Na'ama and Sharm el-Sheikh, try hitching, or take the yellow, open-sided *tof-tof,* which runs about every hour from the square until 7pm (50pt one way). Since the bus is unreliable and hitching easy (low volume but high yield), a good strategy is to begin thumbing and flag the bus down if it happens to come by. If you are American and decide to hitch, don't curse compatriots for not giving you a lift—MFO personnel are forbidden to pick up civilians. Taxis also run between Na'ama and Sharm el-Sheikh. In a group, the fare should be 50pt; traveling alone at night, the fare jumps to LE3-5.

Na'ama Bay

As you step off the bus in Na'ama Bay, you may not be tempted by the prospect of yet another beach and resort. Stick your head under the surface of the Red Sea and you may stay a few days. Venture to Ras Muhammad and Tiran Island and you may never leave.

The bus stop at Na'ama Bay is in front of the Marina Sharm Hotel. Incidentally, don't be alarmed if you hear locals and travelers alike referring to the bay as "Marina" or "Marina Sharm." These are the Hebrew names for Na'ama Bay, which is a resort built by Israelis. Buses that leave from Sharm el-Sheikh nearly always call at Na'ama, 6km to the north, a few minutes later; the stop at Na'ama is behind the cafe-bar and in front of the Marina Sharm Hotel.

Sleeping on the beach is illegal at Na'ama, and the police are strict. But if you hike south over the hill to the beach below the MFO base, chances are better that you will not be hassled. Alternatively, you can negotiate the rocks to the north and sleep above the beach. The latter may be the best idea since you can slumber right beside some fantastic reefs and swim through them at sunrise. Both of these free campsites are a bit of a hike from Na'ama. To avoid the walk, rent a big tent for LE6 or a small tent for LE4.50 from **Gafy Camping**, halfway up the cove. A campsite costs LE2 (you supply the tent). A bed in an air-conditioned bungalow at the **Aquamarine Hotel** on the north side of the bay costs LE17 (breakfast included). If you arrive in Na'ama without a tent, you may want to head to the IYHF hostel in Sharm el-Sheikh.

The best place to buy food is the **supermarket** in Na'ama, off the beach road just south of the Aquanaut diving shop. The building is marked "Shopping Center" on the side. The supermarket has an extraordinary variety of food (for the Sinai, including fresh produce, cheese, yogurt, and canned goods. You can also find such rarities as suntan and after-sun lotion, sanitary napkins, and rudimentary snorkeling equipment. The **snack bar** next door sells spaghetti (LE1.65), omelettes (LE1.40), and a fish dinner with rice, *tahina,* and salad (LE6.50). Avoid the tiny hamburgers. The **Wrecker's Den,** next to the Aquamarine Hotel, serves full meals with fish, chicken, or kebab for LE8. If stray cats bother you at your table, don't be afraid to throw them over the wall. The white, stone building across from the Marina Sharm Hotel has a dance band at night on the upper level. On the bottom floor is a cafe-bar that sells baked goods for 10-50pt. Across from the bar are **public showers** and the **tourist police.** Money can be changed at the Hilton from 5-8pm.

Serious divers should head for the **Camel Dive Club,** behind and to the north of the tourist police. If you rent their equipment, you can camp in back of the shop for free. Na'ama's three other **diving shops** (Red Sea Divers, at the southern end of the bay; Aquamarine, at the Aquamarine Hotel; and Aquanaut, midway between them) rent snorkeling and scuba equipment at almost identical prices. (Mask, fins, and snorkel $5 per day, introductory dives $40, regular dives $35. A five day diving course is $150.) Red Sea Divers also offers windsurfing for $5 per hour and night dives for $20. All diving shops take LE2 for $1, so try to pay in pounds. Most dive shops require a check-out dive if you haven't been diving in three months. These shops also have showers for customers. From the beach in front of the Hilton, you can bicycle (LE5 per hour), waterski (LE25 for 15 minutes), and windsurf (LE50 per half day).

Though Na'ama Bay itself does not have any good reefs, two excellent dive sites are within walking distance. Coral, undersea foliage, and gorgeous fish await divers in the seductive **Near** and **Far Gardens** to the north. To reach the Near Gardens, walk north from Na'ama until you reach the point at the end of the bay (about 30 min.); the Far Gardens are about a half hour walk beyond them. Bring water, since there's no shade along the way, and wear tennis shoes—sandals are tough to manage on the rocks. Red Sea Diving, on the southern end of Na'ama Bay, runs glass-bottomed boats daily to both sites for LE4.

When you've had enough of these sights (this may take several months), take one of the diving shops' daily trips to more distant, and even more beautiful, sites. **Tiran Island** and **Ras Muhammad** are the most spectacular: Fish of virtually every imaginable size, shape, and incandescent color cavort about the labyrinthine coral gardens, while manta rays, hammerhead sharks, and other exotica lurk in the depths. On clear days, Ras Muhammad offers a spectacular view of Asia to the east and Africa to the south. Unfortunately, these trips are the most expensive: $45 per day including equipment and meals. For $35 per day, thriftier souls can visit the reefs at **Ras Masrani, Ras Umm Sidd,** and other nearby sites. Though Jacques Cousteau might rate these a tad below Tiran and Ras Muhammad, their aquatic splendors should keep you gaping for hours.

Dahab

Dahab has two personalities. One half of the village resembles a small scale Na'ama Bay: Its beach, lined with tents and shade ramparts, is a tourist outpost beside splendid reefs in the desert. Yet, only 3km away, the other personality shows:

an indisputably traditional Bedouin village, with palm trees and thatch huts, skirted by meandering goats and chickens. Dahab's village residents live, for the most part, off the fish they catch, the few livestock they tend, and the dates they harvest from the palms. Behind the village are ridges of stupendous mountains, and the glittering blue ocean conceals even more startling scenery.

Modern Dahab offers three budget options: sleep on the hotel beach in a thatched hut (LE2, no mattresses, blankets, or sheets), stay in a brand-new bungalow (LE15 per person with breakfast), or sleep in the tents (LE10 per person). The **kiosk** where the bus unloads sells standard canned Sinai fare. Behind the kiosk is the very upscale hotel **restaurant,** which serves breakfast (7-9am) for LE3, and lunch (1-3pm) for LE9, and dinner (8-10pm) for LE12. There is also an overpriced **cafeteria** on the beach.

Buses run from Dahab's resort area to Sharm el-Sheikh (via Na'ama Bay) at 8am, 2:30pm, 5pm, and 8pm (LE2.50); to St. Catherine's at 4am and 9:30am (LE5); to Taba (LE3.50) via Nuweiba (LE2.50) at 8:30am and 10:30am; and directly to Nuweiba at 6:30pm. Finally, a bus leaves at 8pm to Cairo (LE16.50), but it is not recommended: Unless you have a prearranged place to stay in Cairo, you may have trouble finding a bed at the hour when you arrive. If you stay in the Bedouin village, keep in mind that at least two of the Bedouin in the village own **shared taxis.** Since they usually spend the night at home, you can often arrange for a trip with them in the morning. If you do, haggle! If someone's going to work that day, the taxi has to leave sometime, with or without you.

To really enjoy Dahab, head north by taxi to the Bedouin village. The 50pt one-way fare is a small price to pay to avoid lugging your pack the 3km in the hot Sinai sun. If you can't find a taxi, walk back across the parking lot and head for the two white water towers of the MFO base. Just inside the base the asphalt road ends, and a rough dirt track leads to the village—follow this and aim for the far palm grove, which is barely visible from the base. Going back to the bus station, drivers may try to charge more, up to LE3 if you are alone. Avoid this by bargaining and recruiting others to share your cab.

The main option for accommodations in the Bedouin village is a thatched or stone hut (either is LE2 per night and holds two people comfortably). The stone huts all have locks, and are much more carefully guarded than the thatched huts. Some of the best stone huts are at the **Star of Sinai** campground, just south of the cove; there are toilets and the truthfully advertised "best showers in Dahab." Don't get railroaded into the first huts you are taken to when you leave the taxi. If no one greets you, just find yourself an empty hut and move in. It may be difficult to tell who really owns the huts—beware of con artists. You can also sleep on the narrow strip of beach in front of the huts, but the wind and sun can make outdoor snoozing uncomfortable.

Eating in Dahab is surprisingly good. The **Fighting Kangaroo,** run by a former Australian, specializes in vegetarian food. He serves amazing pita pizza (small LE1.50) as well as salads (LE1.50), spring rolls (LE3), and combination fried rice (LE3). The restaurant will provide a hut and three meals for LE9 per day. Try the specials at **Aly Baba** (chicken LE3, felafel LE2) which include salad, chips, cheese, and *tahina*. The **Happy Camel Cafe** serves *fuul* (LE1.50), and one of the best tuna pizzas you'll ever have (small LE1.50). For light snacks and drinks, just pick the restaurant that is playing your favorite music. Children run through the village selling fresh pita (20pt each) that contains only a few stones and insects and is generally quite good. The sweet pita is generally a ticket to diarrhea. Buy your mineral water at the supermarkets (80-90pt).

The modern section of Dahab near the bus station still has a number of conveniences. The **diving shop,** the white building near the sea, rents masks, snorkel, and fins for $5. Sailboard rental is $5, and an introductory dive costs $40. Scuba excursions to Ras Muhummad cost $45 for equipment, transportation, and guide—less if you pay in pounds. The adjacent restroom pavilion is no longer functional, but the dive center allows customers to use their facilities. The official showers and restrooms are in the holiday village. The hotel charges 50pt per use, but the facilities are never attended.

The best of Dahab's reefs begins at the northern and southern ends of the cove on which the village is built. Walk either north or south until you see the waves breaking over the coral, and plunge in. To find reefs closer to the modern village, check the map in the diving shop. Some of the cafe owners in the Bedouin village rent low quality masks, fins, and snorkels. Use them if you're desperate, but be prepared to surface every few minutes to empty the water from your mask.

Crazy House, halfway up the cove in the Bedouin village, runs the popular **Blue Hole Lobster** tours. Blue Hole, 2km north of the village, features rugged mountain scenery and is an excellent dive site. The trip, which leaves at 5pm and lasts until morning, culminates in a lobster feast (LE20 to dive, LE15 to eat). Ask around the Bedouin supermarket about trips to **Wadi Gnay,** an oasis with a small, brackish spring and a Bedouin village. The trip takes one day by camel, and costs LE22, including the LE2 tax. Agree on the route before you set off, and *pay afterwards*. The police station at which your guide must obtain permission, and at which you can register, is in the Bedouin village next to the palm huts.

If you do stay in the Bedouin village, be respectful of your neighbors. The moment you see the Bedouin men in their long, flowing white robes and the women in their austere, black garb you will want to take a picture of them, but Bedouin religion prohibits making images of people. Always ask before you try to take a picture, and though some don't mind, take any "no" as final.

Nuweiba

Under Israeli occupation, Nuweiba was a famed and crowded meeting point of hippies and international backpackers. The Israelis are gone, and so is much of the clientele, leaving the marvelous beach and coral reefs. Unlike in Dahab, the local Bedouin live in fenced-off villages where tourists are discouraged from sleeping (though they may visit).

The bus to Nuweiba stops in front of a cafeteria on the beach. Make sure you get off here, and not at the busy ferry port 8km to the south (see below).

Daily **buses** arrive in Nuweiba from Sharm el-Sheikh and Dahab, from Taba, from Cairo or Suez via Sharm el-Sheikh or St. Catherine's, and directly from Cairo. (See Sinai Getting There and Getting Around, and village sections above.) Leaving Nuweiba, you can go to Dahab(LE2.50, 70 min.) and Sharm el-Sheikh (8am, 10am, 2pm, and 4pm, LE7, 3 hr.), to Taba (10am, noon, and 3:30pm, LE2, 1 hr.), to St. Catherine's (11am and midnight, LE6, 1½ hr.) and on to Cairo (11am and 11pm, LE16). The bus to Cairo may leave from the port, so ask at the cafeteria.

Next to the cafeteria's picnic tables is the reception desk for the lowbrow section of the tourist village. A bed in a thatched bungalow or in a three-person tent costs LE12.50. A better alternative is to sleep on the beach or pitch your own tent for LE2. Diehards can leave the compound and crash on the beaches to the south for free without hassle. If you stay in the lowbrow village, you are entitled to use the toilet and salt-water shower facilities, open from 7am to 3pm and 5 to 7pm (non-residents must pay 20pt per trip). Nearby restrooms are open 24 hours.

Near the back of the lowbrow compound you'll find a **police station,** where you can usually register during the day. Continuing to the north, past the Bedouin huts, is the highbrow village (singles LE48, doubles LE50). For a taste of the high life, explore their terrace bar and overpriced restaurant, where sun-worshipers have no need to leave the beach. For more contact with the rich and famous, head to **Macondo's,** the fish restaurant at the rear of the cafeteria. All the fresh fish, salad, rice, melon, *tahina,* and bread you can eat is LE10. The restaurant is open for lunch (2-5pm) and dinner (8-12pm). The **fish-and chips stands** on the southern end of the beach sell fish, french fries, and salad for LE3.50. The quality varies enormously with the day's catch. The cafeteria serves light meals and stocks canned goods, but is an expensive alternative (beer LE3.50, mineral water LE1, canned *fuul* 70pt).

Better to head to the more prosperous of the Bedouin villages. Walk out of the bus lot, turn right, and follow the road through sharp corners. You will be greeted with cries of "welcome" and will find several reasonably-priced, popular cafe-restaurants, fruit and vegetable stands, and an excellent **supermarket.** This clean establishment stocks a wide range of essentials including sanitary napkins and toilet paper.

For reef exploration, rent equipment from the **diving shop** on the cheap beach (mask, fins, and snorkel $4.50; full day scuba packages $35; snorkel trips $10 with a speedboat, with a jeep $40). Try to pay in pounds. To reach the **sailing club,** go around the fence to the highbrow beach (windsurfing LE8 per hour, glass-bottom boat rides LE4 per person, and canoes LE4 per hour). The diving shop and sailing club sometimes close for no apparent reason during the summer. To reach the best reefs, walk south along the beach until you see the waves breaking over the coral. For more secluded diving, walk 500m beyond the visible point south of the main beach to what locals call "The Stone House."

Nuweiba makes an excellent base for a **camel trip** into the desert interior. You can arrange a trip directly with a Bedouin guide (ask around the fish stands or at the cafeteria's picnic tables). A popular excursion from Nuweiba is the one-day trek along a wadi cut in the mountains to a freshwater spring to the lush oasis of **Ayn Furtaga.** The trip past Ayn Furtaga to **Ayn Hudra** takes two days by camel or one by car. Both treks lead through spectacular desert scenery and are well worth the time and the LE25 per person per day cost. Abd El-Hamid of South Sinai Travel (tel. 76 88 32 at the village reception desk) organizes expertly run safaris of 5-7 days, usually in the mountains near St. Catherine's for LE90 per person per day. These winter-only safaris feature land rovers, knowledgeable Bedouin guides, and authentic cuisine.

Because the desert, St. Catherine's Monastery, and Mt. Sinai are technically off-limits to tourists, your Bedouin guide will have to take your passport to the police the day before and receive permission to make this trip. Unfortunately, some of the best treks are completely illegal. Don't pressure your guide to take you off the agreed-upon route; he risks serious trouble with the police while you, as a tourist, risk nothing.

The Ferry from Nuweiba to Aqaba, Jordan

Traveling from Nuweiba into Israel couldn't be simpler. You just take the bus to Taba, pass through customs no matter what's in your passport, and continue to Eilat. Getting from Nuweiba into Jordan by passenger ferry is more complicated, especially for those who have ever visited Israel. There are two **daily ferries.** The first departs between 10am-noon, the second 2-4pm. One-way passage on the deck costs LE45. Sailing time is about three hours. Show up at or before 9am and 1pm, respectively, to deal with customs, ticketing, Egyptian bank hassles, and very long lines.

Any Nuweiba bus can leave you at the terminal, or at least at the turn-off, which is 8km south of town (bus fare 50pt, taxis LE1). The morning bus from Taba comes by at 8am and is convenient for catching the morning ferry. You can also catch a direct bus from Cairo to the ferry, leaving from Abbassiya Station at 11pm and arriving at about 6am. The bus, like everything concerning the ferry, will be crowded with Egyptian workers bound for jobs in Jordan, Iraq, Saudi Arabia, and the Gulf States. At times when the Egyptians are traveling for their holidays—especially during some weeks in August and September—all the space may be taken. Normally, you can buy a ticket when you arrive at the port.

As a foreigner, you will be whisked through the gate and into the customs building on the right, where you can proceed to the head of the line. Here you'll fill out a form for the Egyptian authorities and receive an exit stamp in your passport. You will not have to pay an exit fee. From customs, you can proceed north across the lot to enter the poorly marked **ticket office.** Officially, the regulations requiring you to prove that you have legally exchanged the fare have been scrapped.

Entering the ferry, you'll be searched perfunctorily, then asked to hand over your passport. During the trip, or immediately after you disembark, a Jordanian visa (valid for one month or two weeks) and an entry stamp will be entered into your passport. While it's best to come to Nuweiba with a Jordanian visa already in your passport, you can obtain one en route. American, Canadian, Australian, New Zealander, and British travelers should have no difficulty obtaining this visa. Travelers from the Eastern Bloc nations and some other countries are better off obtaining a visa beforehand. Your passport will be returned at Jordanian customs in Aqaba, or, if you go searching for it, on the boat. Passports are returned to Egyptian workers on the boat in the craziest display of bureaucratic inefficiency you'll ever see. In Aqaba, you'll have to endure a long wait, then pass through a painless customs search, and finally be free to catch a taxi or minibus into Aqaba center, 10km north (the drivers will probably accept Egyptian currency).

Travelers with **evidence of a visit to Israel** in their passports might be allowed to board the ferry, but will not be allowed to disembark. An Egyptian Taba entry stamp has been known to pass through, and will probably not cause problems. (Don't stake your whole trip on this flimsy guarantee.) Clever types who have two passports *must* be sure to get the Nuweiba exit stamp in the passport that has no sign of Israel in it.

Some manage to travel from Israel through the West Bank into Jordan, and then on to **Syria,** through ingenious use of the Nuweiba-Aqaba ferry. The Syrians assume that those without a Jordanian entry stamp entered Jordan through the West Bank. Those willing to spend the extra time and money can cross from Aqaba to Nuweiba and return to Aqaba, thereby picking up the required Jordanian entry stamp. You could travel even around Egypt between ferries.

al-Arish

Al-Arish, the only significant settlement in the northern Sinai, has little in common with other Egyptian cities. Lacking the isolation of the desert, the flowing waters of the Nile, and the natural splendor of the Aqaba Coast, al-Arish is a rather uninteresting city of 30,000 inhabitants. Because there is hardly a sight in sight in al-Arish, few tourists bother to visit. By the same token, however, the city shows what Egyptian life is like without the distortions of the tourist trade. You may, in fact, be the only Westerner around, and in cafes, you will rival the TV as a topic of conversation.

Believe it or not, al-Arish is trying to turn itself into a beach resort, and an equal surprise is that it looks set to succeed. A number of luxury hotels are under construction alongside the small holiday villas which line the wide, sandy beach, and more and more Egyptian families are coming to frolic amid the sand, palm trees, and burnt-out anti-aircraft guns which dot the beach. It will be several seasons, however, before these facilities are open for business and the tourist army begins its invasion.

Al-Arish's **bus station** is at the southeast corner of Baladiya Sq. From there, the town's main thoroughfare, July 23 St., runs north to the ocean, where it meets Fouad Zakry St. The **police station** (tel. 120, 121, or 122) and **hospital** (tel. 77) are on Gish St., east of Souk Sq.—the first square inland on July 23 St. The **post office** (open Sat.-Thurs. 9am-3pm) and **telecommunications office** (open 24 hours, international call possible) are in the same building east of July 23 St., 3 blocks north of Baladiya Sq. Most of the town's shops and restaurants are located on July 23 St. **Pharmacy Fouad,** 2 blocks north of Baladiya Sq., on the west side of the street, is open daily until midnight, and can put you in touch with a local doctor. The easiest way to reach the beach from the middle of town is to take a minibus (15pt) or taxi (50-75pt) from the bus station.

Budget accommodations are scarce in al-Arish. A clean bed and a roof over your head is about the best you'll get here. The **el-Salaam Hotel** (tel. 219), 1 block north of Baladiya Sq. on July 23 St., has clean rooms of varying size for between LE4-

8; you can pack in extra people for free. The **Moonlight Hotel** (tel. 362), down July 23 St. near the beach, has similar rooms and similar rates, but a quieter location. The best bargain in town is **al-Arish Camping**, 7km west of town along Fouad Zakry St. (LE5.50 for 2 beds in a spacious lit tent; LE1.50 if you bring your own equipment). It's also possible to camp for free on the beaches near town, but permission (not automatically granted) is necessary from the police station in town.

Groceries are easier to find here than in the rest of the Sinai, and the town has two excellent restaurants. The **Aziz Restaurant,** under the el-Salaam Hotel, serves delicious kebab, *kufte,* and salad for LE5, macaroni for LE1.50, and a big breakfast for LE1.75. About 300m down the right side of the street is the **Sammar Restaurant,** which has great chicken and chips for LE3.50. On the way, have a look at the bizarre, multi-colored brick minaret on your left, al-Arish's only tourist sight. July 23 St. is lined with small cafes and restaurants where you can get a cup of *chai* or a *fuul* sandwich for a few piastres.

Direct **buses** run to al-Arish daily from Cairo's Kolali Sq., behind Ramses Station (LE6, 6 hr.), Suez (LE3.50, 4½ hr.), and Ismailia (LE2.50, 3½ hr.). From Port Said, it is necessary to change buses and cross the Suez Canal by the small, free passenger ferry at **Qantara,** about 50km south of Port Said. Service taxis run direct from all the above locations for LE2-3 extra. There are no trains or transport across the peninsula to the Aqaba coast.

Suez Canal and Red Sea Coast

Suez Canal

Cutting between Asia and Africa, the strategic Suez Canal is a miracle of nineteenth century engineering, although not an exciting tourist attraction. It stretches, without locks and at a depth of up to 15m, for 112km, from Port Said on the Mediterranean, past Ismailiya, to Suez on the Red Sea. Construction began in 1859 under the direction of Ferdinand de Lesseps, and the canal opened 10 years later. The canal made rapid travel from Europe to the Indian Ocean possible, and as such became a crucial element in the infrastructure of the British Empire. In 1956 the canal was abruptly nationalized 12 years ahead of schedule by General Nasser to pay for the Aswan Dam, precipitating a British-French "peacekeeping" invasion. In 1967, with Israeli troops on the Sinai side of the canal, Nasser blocked it with sunken ships; it remained closed through the 1973 War. While it was closed, supertankers were built to travel around Africa, and these big ships cannot pass through the canal. The result is that the canal's business has never fully recovered, and neither have the canal cities.

The Suez Canal is not a sight—it's a business. Port Said, Ismailiya, and Suez live off laden ships of commerce, not buses of tourists. All three cities have suffered heavy war-damages and the only reconstruction evident is Ismailiya's newly paved streets and neat parks. In a nation as richly endowed with sights as Egypt, this region should rank low on the itinerary.

Port Said (Bur Sa'id)

Gateway for the canal and, conversely, for the Mediterranean Sea, Port Said (*Bur Said*) is the northeasternmost point on the African continent and the busiest and most interesting of the Suez Canal cities. Rows of tankers, freighters, and cruise ships dock next to the white colonnade of the port authority here, where the canal widens to meet the Mediterranean. At night the lights of the ships form a long string that stretches far out into the sea. Port Said is currently under development as a beach resort, an alternative to the increasingly crowded shores of Alexandria. While better beaches exist in Egypt, Port Said's proximity to Cairo and its current relative obscurity make it an appealing daytrip.

You'll find most important services along the canal or along the beach at right angles to the canal. **Palestine Street** follows the canal; 2 blocks from its southwestern end is the shiny new **tourist office** (tel. 22 38 68), with a helpful staff and an excellent free map. (Open Sat.-Thurs. 8am-8pm.) The **tourist police**(tel. 22 85 70) are located in the customs building, at the southwest end of Palestine St., and also at a branch office in the train station. (Both open 24 hours.)

Port Said's **post office** for Poste Restante is at the southeast corner of Ferial Gardens. (**Postal code** is 42511. Open daily 7am-5pm.) The **telephone office** is about halfway up Palestine St., and is open 24 hours. Port Said's most modern hospital is **el-Mabarrah Hospital** at the western end of July 23 St. **El-Isaaf Pharmacy,** located on Safia Zaghloul St. near the intersection with Shohada St. (tel. 22 88 88), is open all night. There are a number of small, reputable **currency exchange** offices around town (sporadic hours). The most convenient place to change money is **Thomas Cook,** on Gomhouriya St., 3 blocks from July 23 St. (Open daily 9am-6pm.) A number of countries (including the U.S. and U.K.) have **consulates** in Port Said, and the tourist office or tourist police can provide addresses and phone numbers.

Most of the better accommodations in town are either on or just off Gomhouriya St., which parallels Palestine St., 2 blocks inland. About halfway up Gomhouriya St. is the enormous **Hotel de la Poste,** which has small, clean rooms with private shower and fan for LE8 (singles) and LE10 (doubles). Three blocks north is the **Regent Hotel** (tel. 22 38 02), which has huge, spic-and-span rooms with balconies and shared bath. (Singles LE10, doubles LE14. Breakfast included.) One block south of the post office is the **Abu Simbel Hotel** (tel. 22 11 50), a modern and luxurious establishment for the price, with singles at LE17 and doubles LE27 (breakfast included). All rooms have private bath, fan, refrigerator, TV, and balcony. The **Akri Hotel** (tel. 22 10 13), 2 blocks from the southern end of Gomhouriya St., has singles for LE5-7 and doubles for LE8-9, breakfast included. In the Sea Rangers' building near the Timsah Lake Beach on the corner of New Corniche and al-Amin St. is an **IYHF youth hostel** (tel. 22 32 02) which admits members only (dorm beds 80pt).

Port Said has a limited selection of restaurants. Try **Soufar,** on the corner of Degla and Gomhouriya, or **Seahorse,** on New Corniche. Both charge LE6-8 for dinner. For excellent seafood, try the small, unnamed restaurant on New Corniche St. near the ETAP Hotel. LE6 buys a ¼ kilo of fine shrimp. **Popeye's Cafe** is a also a good bet—right across from the Hotel de la Poste (meals LE5-6; no spinach).

The best way to see the canal is from the **Noras** floating restaurant; there is a one-hour cruise daily at 6:30pm, which costs LE3 (including a drink). Also pleasant, but expensive, are the lunch and dinner cruises. (Daily 3pm and 9:30pm, LE12-20.) The boat departs from Palestine St., at the corner of July 23 St. Otherwise, take advantage of the free **ferry ride** across the canal to **Port Fouad.** The crossing gives you a good view and the chance to wander around the less touristy shops of the smaller port. To catch the ferry, walk to the canal end of Palestine St. Port Said's **Military Museum,** west of the obelisk on July 23 St., holds displays depicting ancient pharaonic and Islamic battles, but concentrates on the victories of the 1973 War. Maps show how the nearby Bar Lev Line was smashed in six hours. (Open daily 8am-3pm. Admission LE1.) In front of the museum, the **beach** runs east to the canal. Access to the beach is free. Beach chairs and umbrellas are available for rental, and fresh showers are spaced every 100m along the beach.

Lying 350km east of Alexandria and 230km from Cairo, Port Said pins down the northeastern corner of the Delta region. Buses run from Cairo's Kolali Sq. in front of Ramses Station to Port Said several times daily. (Golden Rocket LE6, A/C blue bus LE4. 3 hr.) One bus also runs daily from Sa'ad Zaghloul Sq. in Alexandria, via Cairo. (Golden Rocket LE9, A/C blue bus LE5. (6 hr.) Port Said's bus depot is on the northeast side of Ferial Gardens, 2 blocks west of Gomhouriya St. Service taxis as well run from Cairo's Kolali Sq. (LE5-6). To reach the **service taxi stand** in Port Said, take a municipal taxi (LE1-1.50), and ask for a *taxi ugra* to the city you wish to reach. You can also reach Port Said by **train** from Cairo: Five trains leave Ramses Station daily for the trip (4½ hr., second class A/C LE3.35 or LE1.95). The railway station in Port Said is just below Mustafa Kemal St., which runs northwest from the bottom of Gomhouriya St. Trains from Cairo pass through Mansoura in the Delta, then stop in Ismailiya before proceeding along the canal to Port Said.

Ismailiya

When you arrive in Ismailiya, you'll find it hard to believe that this town of narrow, shady streets, and quiet, tree-lined boulevards is home to a bustling canal trade and 50,000 people. You can walk from one end of Ismailia to the other in 10 minutes, and the town moves at a mellow rate that is a refreshing change from the frenetic pace of other Egyptian cities. Heavily damaged during the wars of 1967 and 1973, Ismailiya has been almost completely rebuilt. Great care was taken to retain the provincial charm which has attracted visitors since the town's founding during the construction of the canal. Wander through the silent avenues, lounge in the sprawling gardens in the middle of town, or hit the beaches at nearby **Lake Timsah** (Crocodile Lake—just a name, not a warning). Ismailiya is a decent place to soothe shattered nerves and recover from the rigors of Egyptian travel.

The city's main artery runs diagonally from the **train station** at Orabi Sq. to the Ismailiya Canal, via Gomhourriya Sq. Many of Ismailiya's restaurants, hotels, and shops are on Sultan Hussein St., which runs north-south, about 5 blocks east of Orabi Sq. The **bus station** is at the northwest corner of town, west of the train station. The **post office** (open Sat.-Thurs. 9am-3pm) and the **telecommunications office** (open 24 hours) are both on Orabi Sq., and the **police station** (tel. 270 08) is in the Governorate Building along the canal, 2 blocks south of Gomhouriya Sq.

The **museum,** by the canal at the northern end of town, displays local history from ancient times to the present. Here you can learn that the canal now runs over parts of the course of a navigable waterway to the Nile, expanded by Ramses II to a width of 50m and a depth of 5m. Darius and Napoleon were among those preoccupied with the construction of canals in this area. Stelae commemorating Darius' success in reopening the canal to the Nile are on display. Napoleon gave up his dreams of a similar project when a civil engineer miscalculated the Mediterranean to be some 50m higher than the Red Sea and predicted a disaster (open daily 8:30am-1:30pm, admission 50pt). Near the museum, the **Garden of the Stelae** contains sphinxes from the age of Ramses II. (Inquire at the museum entrance for permission to visit.) The **House of Ferdinand de Lesseps,** on Muhammad Ali Quay, is named for the director of the Suez Canal's construction, and will complete your introduction to canal history (open Wed.-Mon. 9am-4pm, free). Otherwise, spend the day relaxing on the beaches. Unfortunately, access to some resort clubs requires payment of a stiff LE5-10, though the price does include buffet meals.

The best lodgings in town are at the **Nefertari Hotel** (tel. 228 22), 41 Sultan Hussein St., which has tidy and comfortable rooms. (Singles with bath LE9. Doubles with bath LE13. Breakfast included. A/C LE3.) Also pleasant is the **Isis Hotel,** at Orabi Sq. (Singles LE5, with bath LE12. Doubles LE8, with bath LE14.) One block east is the upmarket **Ramses Hotel,** which has singles with A/C, private bath, TV, and telephone for LE20 and similar doubles for LE25. Buy your food from street vendors, or try **Nefertiti's** on Sultan Hussein St. down from the Nefertari Hotel, which serves meals for LE3-5, and a great omelette and fries for LE3.50. Next door is **George's,** which has Egyptian and Western meals for around LE5. For dessert, **Groppi's** across the street serves delicious pastries for about 70pt.

Midway along the Suez Canal, Ismailiya is linked by road and the Ismailiya Canal to the Delta, and by highway and railroad to Cairo (160km) and Alexandria (280km). From Cairo, catch one of the frequent buses or service taxis from Kolali Sq. in front of Ramses Station (each LE3-4). There are seven **trains** per day (3½ hr., second class A/C LE2-2.20).

Suez

Where the Red Sea meets the Suez Canal, the city of Suez sprawls like a sluggish animal. Its oil refineries and myriad ships spew out smoke and fumes like a beast's malodorous breath. Through the dust and smog, red cliffs behind the city contrast with the blue bay. Suez has very few hotels or restaurants and little to attract the tourist—most travelers simply pass through the city en route to the Sinai by way of the new tunnel under the canal 30km north of town or on their way south along the Red Sea coast. The only sights in Suez are the canal and the gulf. About the only monuments in town are three American tanks on the corniche captured from Israel in 1973. A trip to the beach at **Ain Sukhna**, 60km south along the Red Sea, can be arranged with some ingenuity; getting there is easy, as buses and service taxis run down the coast from Suez, but unless you have your own car or a hired taxi, it will be difficult to get away. Decent reefs near the shore make this the only snorkeling spot convenient to Cairo, but don't wander into the old minefields back under the cliffs. There are no restrooms, restaurants, or showers. All in all, it's probably worth traveling the extra several hours to Hurghada for superior reefs and amenities.

The few hotels and restaurants in Suez are on al-Gaysh St., the wide, dusty, garbage-strewn thoroughfare that runs east-west from the **bus station** to the seashore. The **Misr Palace** (tel. 230 31), just off al-Gaysh St., 6 blocks east of the bus station and across from the luxury Bel Air Hotel, has unblemished, comfortable rooms. (Singles LE8, with shower LE10. Doubles LE12, with shower LE20. Breakfast included. Fans LE1.) One block east at the deluxe **White House Hotel** (singles LE21, doubles LE26), rooms include private shower, TV, air-conditioning, and breakfast. While expensive, it's a breath of comfort in an uncomfortable town. The **IYHF youth hostel** (tel. 31 45), on Tarik al-Hurriya St. across from the stadium, is a hike from the station, and you'll get beds in crowded dormitories for LE1. The hostel often fills with pilgrims during the *haj* season (early July) as Suez is a departure point for Mecca. For food there are two good choices. The **Magharbel Restaurant**, several doors down from the White House Hotel, serves decent, yet slightly overpriced, Egyptian meals (LE6-8) in an air-conditioned dining room. Across the street is the **St. James Restaurant,** which has good fresh fish (LE3), shrimp (LE9), and other Egyptian dishes (LE3-4). Also try the newly rebuilt **Champs Elysées,** two doors down from the Magharbel. The **tourist police** station is in the **bus station,** just off al-Gaysh St. The **telecommunications office** is on the north side of al-Gaysh St., 4 blocks east of the bus station (open 24 hours). The **post office** is on Hoda Sharawi St., parallel to al-Gaysh St. and 1 block north (open Sat.-Thurs. 9am-3pm).

Suez can be reached by **bus** from Kolali Sq. in Cairo (LE5), or from Ismailiya (LE1.25). **Service taxis** run from Kolali Sq. and Ismailiya at slightly higher prices. Two **train** routes link Cairo and Suez: A slow one via Ismailiya (5 per day, 6-7 hr.), and an express train (4 per day, 3 hr.). Only two of the slow trains have air-conditioning; second-class seats cost LE1.10. Once per day, buses run from Suez to Alexandria (LE6). Three buses per day run to Hurghada on the lonely Red Sea Hwy (6am, 7am, and 7pm; LE8; 6 hr.). Tickets to Hurghada should be reserved a couple of days in advance. Since you won't want to stay in Suez that length of time, either take a **service taxi** (6-7 hr., LE10-12), or travel to Hurghada from Cairo by bus and avoid Suez altogether. Suez is the main jumping-off point for forays into the wilds of the Sinai. Buses run daily to Sharm el-Sheikh (LE6.50), St. Catherine's (LE8), Dahab (LE8), Nuweiba (LE9.50), and Taba (LE11.50). Times vary, so you should plan to arrive in Suez early in the morning and be prepared to spend several hours sipping tea until your bus leaves.

Monasteries of St. Paul and St. Anthony

Two isolated outposts, the monasteries of St. Paul and St. Anthony, lie 30km apart (82km by road) near the edge of the Red Sea. These centers of faith, dating from the beginning of the Christian monastic tradition, house monks and novices who lead a monastic life similar to that of their predecessors through the last 16 centuries.

St. Anthony, who grew up in the Nile Valley, turned his back on worldly concerns and retreated into the Eastern Desert, where he became the first renowned ascetic of the Christian Church. Anthony's dramatic move reflected the restlessness that overtook Christians in the fourth century C.E. when Constantine made Christianity the official religion of the Roman Empire. The Church lost its position as a bold group of outsiders. This was a disturbing development for many earnest followers of Christ, who felt that the church had gained worldly security and wealth at the expense of its otherworldly focus. In Egypt, some of these restless Christians, mostly educated middle-class men, sought to escape this world by going to the deserts, where they could pray in solitude and dedicate their lives to God and not to Caesar. Among them, St. Anthony suffered a paradoxical popularity: His desert hermitages became popular pilgrimage sites, and crowds of the pious and the curious gave the recluse little peace. You'll see icons of longhaired, barefoot Antonius, with a long white beard and animal skins for clothes, adorning the walls of many Coptic churches in Egypt. Even a century after the saint's death, the Greek scholar Athanasius told the story of his choice of poverty and hardship, his wild battles with demons, and his wise counsel to monks and layfolk. Athanasius' *Life of Anthony* became the prototype for most later Christian hagiography.

A few years after the death of St. Anthony, his monastic followers settled at the present site and constructed the basic buildings. The **Monastery of St. Anthony** served as a refuge for some of the monks of Wadi al-Natrun when their own monasteries were attacked by Bedouin tribes in the sixth century. During the seventh and eighth centuries, the monastery was occupied by Melkite monks, and in the eleventh century it was pillaged by the army of Nasr ad-Dawla. About 100 years after the sack, it was restored and came into Coptic hands. The Church of St. Anthony and the southern walls are among the few remains that date from before the construction of the present monastery in the sixteenth century.

The Church of St. Anthony is divided into five parts: the haikal, the passage in front of the haikal, the nave, the narthex, and the small chapel at the southwest corner of the church. Each section has its own set of wall-paintings. East of the Church of St. Anthony, the Church of the Apostles contains three haikals. During Lent, the monks celebrate the liturgy in the eighteenth-century Church of St. Mark. As in the Wadi al-Natrun monasteries, the Chapel of St. Michael is on the top floor of the keep. The impressive monastic library contains more than 1700 manuscripts.

The major religious attraction in the vicinity of the church is the **Cave of St. Anthony.** The one- to two-hour expedition to the cave, 680m above the Red Sea and 276m above the monastery, is definitely worth the effort. The best time to climb the mountain is in the early morning before 6am, or after 4pm. Try to return before dark, and remember to bring water. On the south wall of the cave, you'll find interesting medieval graffiti.

The **Monastery of St. Paul** has four churches, the most important of which is **Church of St. Paul,** built in the cave where St. Paul is said to have lived for 90 years. Many of the frescoes date from the fourth and seventh centuries. Ostrich eggs, symbolizing the Resurrection, hang from the roof. Above the church is the fortress to which the monks retreated when the Bedouin attacked. A secret canal from the spring ensured their survival through long sieges.

You may have to endure the hardships of a pilgrim to reach these monasteries. Direct access is limited to private cars and tour buses from Cairo. The Cairo-

Hurghada bus crosses the Eastern Desert from a point in the Nile Valley north of Beni Suef to **Ras Za'farna** on the Red Sea; it passes the turn-off to St. Anthony's 33km west of Ras Za'farna. From this desolate spot, it's a potentially dangerous 10km uphill trek south in the desert heat to St. Anthony's monastery. This bus, and the bus running between Hurghada and Suez, pass by the turn-off to St. Paul's. The turn-off lies 25km south of Ras Za'farna, 145km south of Suez, and 266km north of Hurghada. St. Paul's monastery hides in the mountains, 12km inland from the coastal road, about a one-and-a-half-hour drive from St. Anthony's. If you have the patience of a monk, you can catch a ride with one of the passing brethren.

Perhaps the easiest way to reach the monasteries is to join a church group expedition. For further information in Cairo, contact the Coptic Church of St. Peter and Paul (al-Batrussiya), 22 Ramses St., Abassiya, or the YMCA at 27 al-Gomhouriya St. (tel. 91 73 60). A group of seven could hire a service taxi from Suez or Hurghada. It's an unusual trip, with no fixed price, but LE10 per person for a full day's round-trip excursion seems reasonable.

You can spend the night at St. Paul's if you have a letter of recommendation from the Patriarch in Cairo, obtainable at St. Mark's Church, Ramses St., south Abassiya Sq. Remember to bring all your own food. Drinking water is supplied by the monks at both monasteries, but there are no showers or cooking facilities.

Hurghada (Ghardaka)

In the fleabag hotels and second-class train compartments of budget travelers' Egypt, a great debate rages. The issue: Is Hurghada worth the effort? The affirmative team consists of temple-weary snorkeling enthusiasts, who flee Upper Egypt on the fairly painless bus ride from Qena. These folks appreciate the town's relaxed character and its low prices, and they can't get enough of Hurghada's colorful coral reefs teeming with life. The negative team contends that a town lying several kilometers removed from its port, whose public beaches are rocky and windblown, whose buildings are universally charmless or still under construction, should never be called a seaside resort. It's true that sun and sand worshipers would do better to make a pilgrimage to Marsa Matruuh on the Western Mediterranean Coast, while many travelers prefer the Sinai's combination of legend, Bedouin hospitality, sandy beaches, and equally splendid coral reefs. Perhaps only the wealthy scuba diver can unequivocally proclaim devotion to Hurghada. This Red Sea town deserves its explosive new popularity in some ways; yet the wise budget traveler should do some headscratching before putting Hurghada on the Egypt itinerary.

Practical Information

Although paved highways link Hurghada with the main population centers, the town is remote by any standard. From Qena, 70km north of Luxor in the Nile Valley, it's 160 barren, mountainous kilometers to Port Safaga on the Red Sea coast, and another 50km of empty coastline north to Hurghada. And that's the short way: Suez lies 410km north at the far end of the Gulf of Suez, and Cairo is another 130km (or 500km from Hurghada, via a desert shortcut to Ras Za'farna). Wealthy folk can cover these distances by **airplane.** EgyptAir flies daily from Cairo to Hurghada at 7:15am, and returns from Hurghada at 8:30am (LE97). In the winter, EgyptAir has flown from Luxor to Hurghada; ask if this service is continuing. The **EgyptAir/Air Sinai office** (tel. 407 88) in Hurghada is in the tourist bazaar opposite the big mosque on the northern end of the main road through town. (Open Sat.-Thurs. 9am-2pm and 6-8pm; partial service Fri. 9am-2pm. Busy in winter.)

Those not among the jet-set will have to stay down to earth on the way to Hurghada. **Buses** tend to be crowded and hot, with pseudo-air-conditioning. If the trips seem long, it's only because of the distance; maniacal drivers and high quality roads make for high speed transit. It's necessary to book seats on any bus to or from Hurghada at least one day in advance. Standing room may be available at the last minute. From **Cairo,** three buses per day leave Ahmed Himli Station, that confused beehive of buses behind Ramses Train Station. The buses usually run in the early morning and late evening, but this varies; find out exact times when you book your seats. Prices run from LE8 (non-A/C, crowded) to LE15 (A/C, luxury buses), and the trip takes about six hours. The buses return from Hurghada via Suez at similar times and again, tickets should be bought a day or two in advance. In Suez you can connect with buses to the Sinai. Buses to Hurghada leave from Luxor daily at 6am and noon, stopping in Qena about an hour later (unless they are full). Returning from Hurghada, there are two buses per day to Luxor and another to Qena. These buses take between five and six hours and cost LE8 to Luxor, LE7 to Qena. The Hurghada **bus station,** basically a parking lot, lies on the southern side of town, 100m down the main road to the port.

Service taxis also run from all of the above towns. Prices per person are comparable to bus fares (perhaps 15% higher). The **service taxi stand** in Hurghada lies in the center of town, 1 block east of the main street to the port, a five-minute walk uphill from the bus station. Taxis fill up frequently for runs to Suez and Qena, especially in the morning.

In reaching the **Sinai** from Hurghada, a common goal of visitors here, the rich go quickly and the poor suffer. If you reach Suez early enough by bus or taxi, you can catch another bus or taxi to Sharm el-Sheikh, St. Catherine's, or other destinations (see under Suez). The threat of spending 12½ hours on buses and a night in Suez may prompt you to hire a seven-person service taxi to make the entire trip (e.g. Hurghada to St. Catherine's, 5am-4pm, LE25-30 per person). **Air Sinai,** EgyptAir's diplomatic stepchild, flies on Friday to Sharm el-Sheikh (9am, return 10am, LE70, 35 min.) and on Monday to St. Catherine's (9am, return noon, LE96, 50 min., LE96). Otherwise, you can catch the ferry, which leaves at 8am every Saturday, Monday, and Wednesday for the five-hour trip to Sharm el-Sheikh. Tickets cost LE45, and should be purchased at least a day in advance, from **Les Voyages** (tel. 401 84), across from the Red Sea Restaurant in the middle of town.

The main **town** of Hurghada, a cluster of hotels, restaurants, shops, and residences, lies 2km north of the **port** of Hurghada. A busy highway connects the town with the port, which boasts diving shops and a couple of cafes, but virtually no hotels. If you follow the coastal road south from the port, you'll pass Moon Valley resort (4km) and the Sheraton Hotel (6km), which overlook the ocean. The Magawish Club Med (8km) seems to be the last in a long string of tourist resorts up the coast. Local buses (25pt) run between the town and port, and out to the resorts. Convenient minibuses also shuttle back and forth frequently (50pt-LE1), and taxis will make the trip as well (LE4-5). Strong headwinds make this route quite difficult for bicyclists.

Although the town lacks street signs, finding your way around should present no problems. Barren, rocky, and well-named **Ugly Mountain** pokes up on the southeastern side of town, blocking it from the nearby sea. The main avenue that comes up from the port skirts the western edge of the town. From south to north, along a 2km stretch of this street, you'll find all the important points in town. First is the inter-city bus station, followed by the busy blocks of hotels and restaurants. Next comes a stretch containing the police station, the telephone office, the post office, the tourist police, and tourist offices. Opposite the large mosque on the north end of town sits the tourist bazaar, which contains travel agencies and the EgyptAir office. Visitors may want to hold on to their mail until they reach Suez or Cairo. The **telephone office** (open Sat.-Thurs. 24 hours) resembles a local social club on Fridays. The **tourist office** is not yet ready to cope with tourists, so the best sources of information are the owners of the tourist flats in town. (See below.) There is a **Misr Bank** on the main street 1 block from the Red Sea Restaurant (open daily 8:30am-2pm and 5-8pm). You can rent **bikes** for LE1 per hour from a shop just north of al-Dhar Mosque, on the eastern side of town. (Return at 7-9pm.)

Accommodations

Although it is no longer an isolated fishing village and is sprouting fancy resorts with a fertility rivaling that of the reefs, Hurghada remains far enough off the beaten track to deter most tourists. This keeps prices affordable even to those on the tightest budget. The cheapest place to **camp** is on the beach, although you'll have to trek quite a way from town in either direction to find a secluded spot. You must acquire permission to sleep on the beach at the **Frontiers Office,** near the large mosque and the EgyptAir office at the north end of town. You must present your passport and two 20pt stamps. (Office open Sat.-Thurs. 10:30am-2pm and 7-9:30pm, Fri. noon-2pm and 7-9:30pm.) LE6 per person buys campers a bureaucracy-free site near the beach at the **Moon Valley** budgeteer's resort; toilet and shower are included. (See below for directions and details.) In general, the beaches along the Red Sea coast are risky for campers. Though many are sandy and inviting, the military takes a dim view of unofficial crashers and, more importantly, many still have minefields.

The cheapest and most popular places to stay in Hurghada are the **tourist flats** clustered along the few busy streets in the town, but absent from the port area. Most offer a homey, if cramped congeniality, fairly clean rooms and shared baths, kitchen facilities for guests, and friendly personal service from the management. They typically accommodate only a dozen people.

Hurghada Happy House (tel. 405 40), between al-Dhar Mosque Sq. and the main avenue. From the bus station, walk 50m uphill, turn right, and walk toward the small mosque. A perennial favorite because of the ever-smiling Captain Muhammad Awad. (See Sights for more on his helpfulness and reef trips.) Clean bathrooms, large rooms with fans. Also under his command are the nearby **Happy House II** and **Happy Home.** LE3 per person at each.

Luxor Tourist Flat on the main avenue, 1 block form the Happy Houses. Run by part-time philosopher and full-time buffoon Muḥammad Youneas. Clean and comfortable (but lacking fans), with a helpful and friendly staff; youngest brother Freds will arrange bus and boat tickets and sight-seeing. LE3 per person.

Sunshine House Hotel, across from the Luxor Tourist Flat. Operated by the Captain's kind-hearted nephew, Emad. Spotless, with fans, loads of rooms, and a roof where you can crash for free if the rest of the town is full (sometimes happens Oct.-Nov.). Emad's diving shop is downstairs, and a restaurant is promised. LE3 per person.

Nefertiti House (tel. 400 83), near the Red Sea Museum and Gobal Hotel in the northeast corner of town. Manager Abdel Shazly is a foil to the Captain: He's young, intense, and operates a rival reef trip. Friendly and helpful nonetheless. Despite what other hotel owners may tell you, he is probably not dead. Inquire about his new budget hotel. LE3 per person.

Gobal Hotel (tel. 406 23), on Naqib Mubarak St., in the northeast corner of town, is Hurghada's only mid-range hotel. Rooms are very clean, all have fans, and the hotel is large and comfortable. Friendly staff. Singles LE11, doubles LE17. Breakfast included.

The only budget accommodations near the beach are the small, primitive bungalows at **Moon Valley** (tel. 400 74), 4km southwest of the port on the coastal highway. The accommodations are adequate, though minimalist and hot. The main attraction here is the sea; a sandy beach is under development, and snorkeling or wading in the turquoise water is a great way to pass time. Tasty meals served in a colorful airy restaurant add to the overall appeal. (Bungalows with private bath and 2 beds LE20; grubby bungalows without bath LE8 per person. Breakfast and dinner included.) To reach Moon Valley, take a minibus or local bus from town.

Food

The three square blocks of the central town really come alive at night. Roam the streets, browsing at the vegetable stands, bakery, and prosperous shops, or stop in at the numerous cafeterias, food stalls, and restaurants. Two adjectives that apply to most restaurants in Hurghada are "cheap" and "good." The popular and delightful rooftop garden at the **Red Sea Restaurant** is just off the main avenue, 1 block north of the Happy House. Though the food is surprisingly below average and the service stinks, all the tourists and all the boat captains gather here at night. (Fish

LE3-4, chicken LE3.50, complete meals LE5-7, beer LE2.20.) Not quite as popular, but a much better bet on food and prices, is the outdoor **Weshahy Restaurant,** just east of the main drag, down the street from the Happy House. Its huge menu includes barracuda, turtle, or shark steaks (LE3), as well as the more conventional kebab (LE4), chicken (LE2.50), and great macaroni in tomato sauce (almost a meal in itself, 60pt). Also serves a good breakfast of egg, cheese, bread, jam, yogurt, and tea, or felafel, *fuul,* cheese, bread, and tea, for LE2.

For romantic seaside dining, head out to **Moon Valley** (see above), where Egyptian-style dinners of fresh seafood, vegetable, salad, bread, fruit, and dessert go for LE5-6. Alternatively, take a 15-minute walk to the beach on the far side of Ugly Mountain and head past the Gobal Hotel on a winding tarmac road to the **Restaurant Gaysoum,** near the hospital. Spacious, clean, but rather unimaginative, this restaurant offers a seaside porch and a video machine. (Overpriced breakfast LE1.50, lunch LE4, dinner LE5, service charge extra. Open daily 7am-1am.) You can also shop for food at the **Express Supermarket,** across from the Red Sea Restaurant, in the middle of town.

Sights

All of Hurghada's main attractions are, of course, underwater. Red Sea creatures come in a dazzling array of colors, shapes, and sizes. Buck-toothed trigger fish, iridescent parrot fish, rays with blue polka dots, sea cucumbers, giant clams, and a million others perform in this briny circus. Always warm and crystal clear, the sparkling water seduces even the most ardent landlubber.

To enjoy the beach in safety you'll need to take a few precautions, however. The desert sun can give you a painful burn: Wear protective sunscreen, or clothing. To walk near the reefs, you'll need shoes—the coral can easily make shish kebab out of your feet. If you see something that looks like an aquatic pin cushion, it's probably a sea urchin or blowfish, both of which are better left alone. Avoid the feathery lionfish as well—its harmless-looking spines can deliver a paralyzing sting. Last, but not least, is the well-named fire coral, which can bloat a leg to mammoth proportions, leaving welts resembling red golf balls. Before plunging in, look at one of the plastic cards that pictorially identifies these nautical nasties—most guides and diving shops carry these cards.

You can reach some reefs without the aid of a boat. One interesting body of coral lies off the beach to the left of the Sheraton; another, which is rarely explored, parallels the coast off the northern end of town on the far side of Ugly Mountain. But to reach Hurghada's most brilliant scenery you must take a boat. The trip to **Geftun Island,** the most popular excursion, costs LE15 per person including lunch. The all-day affair allows you to snorkel around some spectacular reefs. The trip includes two one-hour snorkeling stops near the island and a fish meal, prepared on the boat during the trip and eaten on the soft, sandy island beach. Make arrangements the night before with the manager of a hotel or tourist flat, since the port authorities maintain the policy of reserving divers' passports and visas prior to all dives. Make sure your hotelier copies your name and passport number correctly for the form. If he makes a mistake, they won't just fix it at the dock, they'll haul you off the boat and send you back to town. Be sure to take along a hat, suntan lotion, and bottled water, or you'll be miserable.

The standard Geftun Island trip takes one full day; the tricky thing for budget travelers is planning for more days of underwater sight-seeing. If you make arrangements with a hotelier or boat-owner, you can take another trip to Geftun and see two different reefs. Better yet, inquire about excursions to other locales. Captain Muhammad of Happy House may very well be the best source of travel information in town. He knows and loves the reefs, the water, and the fish. Even if you don't want to buy any of the stuffed sharks (LE20) or nautical knick-knacks in his Red Sea Wonderland shop (or stay at his place), stop by for a chat. Both the Captain and Adel Shazly of the Nefertiti House organize trips to the **House of Sharks,** a wondrous off-shore reef, accessible by road and located 21km south of Hurghada.

Here you can stick to the inside reefs, or venture with the captain and his guides to the outside reefs, where you'll almost certainly see good-sized reef sharks, stonefish, lionfish, moray eels, and other dangerous beasties. Muhammad Emad (from the Sunshine House), and Adel all claim they've never had a serious accident. The House of Sharks trips start at 10am and return at 5pm, and cost about LE3 per person for the minibus, LE4 if there are fewer than 10 people. True enthusiasts can tag along on trips to reefs north of Hurghada. The Captain sometimes takes on snorkelers with his scuba diving clients for the price of equipment rental. When there's little wind, trips to northern reefs such as **Abu Ramada** can top anything else in Hurghada's water. Adel Shazly also runs overnight snorkling trips to **Gobal Island**, a three-hour boat ride away. The excursion usually lasts three days, and the price of LE10 per day includes food, sleeping bags, and transportation.

On any snorkeling trip you can bring your own **equipment** or rent from the guides. Adel Shazly has the best rates, with mask and snorkel for LE1 per day, and flippers for another LE1. The Captain and his relatives also rent the aquatic bits and pieces from a shop adjoining the Sunshine House—mask and snorkel, LE2 per day, flippers another LE2. The Sheraton rents the same stuff to *khoagas* (dumb tourists) for LE11 per day. If you're interested in **scuba diving**, check with the **Dolphin Aqua Center** in the Gobal Hotel. Individual dives cost LE40-50, and full certification courses will set you back LE350 plus $50.

Beach bums will beg for more than Hurghada has to offer. There is a **free public beach** beside the Sheraton Hotel, 7km southwest of town, but Western bathers (particularly women) may feel uncomfortable here. Much better is the semi-private **Shelighada Beach,** just before the Sheraton, where LE3 will buy you a day on their soft, clean sand, free soft drinks up to that value, fresh water showers, and more liberal bathing fashions. Finally, you can use the beach (but not the pool) at the Sheraton for LE5 per day. Minibuses (50pt), local buses (25pt), and taxis (LE5) shuttle between the center of town and the Sheraton all day. (Inquire in town about a new beach on the other side of Ugly Mountain, scheduled for completion in 1989.)

The rocky, windy coast by the Gaysoum Restaurant nearer to town offers vistas of fishing boats and bright blue water, but no natural sand. It's worth taking the snorkeling boat trip to Geftun Island, if only to enjoy the leisurely visit to its wide, soft, coral-sand beaches.

Four kilometers north of town, the mediocre (but free) **museum and aquarium** will introduce you to Red Sea marine life. The reefs offshore are said to be fascinating. Bus fare is 25pt; catch a ride going north from the main avenue in Hurghada town or at the traffic circle in the port.

Western Desert Oases

Springing from the Western Desert with their groves of palm trees, the oases are perfect oases from the chaos of Cairo and the unmatched tourist exploitation of Upper Egypt. The oases are the only fertile land away from the Nile, and the only inhabited places in the desert. Delicious spring water, luxuriant groves, and fields of watermelons and cucumbers all stand against the dramatic, dry landscape. Ruins from all periods in Egyptian history nestle among the native mud houses. Although isolated and seemingly on the edge of modern civilization, the oases may be the highlight of the trip for hardy travelers. The Bedouin and Egyptian *fellaheen* who dwell beside the green fields treat strangers with warm hospitality traditionally extended to desert voyagers.

This is an adventure for the rugged: Getting around entails a variety of unusual risks, tourist facilities are few, and almost no one speaks anything but Arabic.

The series of oases scattered throughout the Sahara—**Kharga, Dakhla, Farafra,** and **Bahariya**—marks the trail of a prehistoric branch of the Nile. Their aquifers are thought to be replenished by an annual flow of water from the Sudan. This bounty of water has been an impetus for development in crowded and mainly water-starved Egypt. In 1958, the government released studies that showed considerable stores of water below the desert floor, accessible with new techniques of drilling deeper wells. The government's New Valley Project was designed to fully exploit this underground water to irrigate and fertilize the desert. A mass relocation of land-less peasants from the Delta to the New Valley was also planned. However, the hypothesis that the underground water is recharged by seepage from the more humid parts of Africa has been questioned. New estimates indicate that the supply could last only another 100 to 700 years, and that it is not replenished yearly. Rather it has been left over from 6000 to 12,000 years ago.

These ups and downs in the water supply and fortunes of the people in the oases are not new. Periods of prosperity have been rare. The Romans, who brought water-wheels and aqueducts, were able to tap deeper water and push back the desert. The population burgeoned and prospered for about 300 years. But overirrigation and abandonment of fallow methods of farming eventually cut down productivity. The oases were in a long, slow decline from then until the 1970s, when Sadat targeted the New Valley for development. The plans proved far too ambitious and expensive, though new desert wells have opened vast regions around the oases for cultivation. Government attention has meant sudden change for the oasians. Travelers will appreciate the excellent new roads and other recently introduced conveniences, but may be saddened by the rapid depletion of cultural distinctiveness and natural beauty.

In general, the oases share the climate of Nile Valley cities on the same latitude—Bahariya is like Cairo, Kharga is like Luxor. But the air is fresher in the oases, and breezes are more common. October through April is unquestionably the best time to visit. It is not unusual for summer temperatures, especially at Kharga, to soar as high as 50°C. Even at night, summer temperatures persist in the upper-20s. There is no air-conditioning anywhere. If you go in summer, accommodations will be a snap to find and bargaining for lower prices easy.

Don't leave Cairo for the desert without a copy of Dr. Ahmed Fakhry's guide to the oases. *Bahariya and Farafra Oases* provides an extremely readable introduction to the life and history of these oases. Dr. Fakhry made many important discoveries in his beloved oases, but died before completing his guides to Kharga and Dakhla. The volume, along with Fakhry's *Siwa Oasis,* is published by the American University in Cairo Press and is available in the university bookstore on the Old Campus and at several of Cairo's English language bookstores (LE9-10 paperback). The university library on the New Campus also has both volumes for consultation.

Getting Around

The car-free budget traveler should be able to reach every oasis with little difficulty. Daily **buses** run from the al-Azhar bus station in Cairo to Bahariya, Kharga, and Dakhla, and thrice-weekly to Farafra (due to become daily). A special air-conditioned bus runs from Ataba Sq. in Cairo to Kharga and Dakhla every morning. Inexpensive buses also run from the town of Assyut, halfway down the Nile, to Kharga and Dakhla. Kharga is also served by **plane** from Cairo every Wednesday and Sunday. **Service taxis** travel to Bahariya from Cairo, and to Kharga from Assyut. (See the individual chapters on the oases, Cairo, and Assyut for detailed transportation information.) You can also **hitchhike** from one oasis to the next, but you may have to wait a day or so for a ride, especially between Farafra and Dakhla. The military checkpoints outside each oasis make good hitching spots.

Car rental is convenient and comfortable for desert travel, though rather expensive. The car must be in excellent condition to survive the long, hot, poorly maintained desert roads—which rules out most of the cars rented to tourists in Cairo. Four-wheel drive is highly recommended. Renting a caravan (mobile home) can solve a lot of problems, including the tricky matter of transporting food, water, and extra gas, as well as providing a comfortable place to sleep every night of the trip.

If the cost (LE100 per day plus a steep mileage charge) is split among several people, caravans become economical.

If you have the time and energy, visit all four oases in the Western Desert by making a giant loop along the Great Desert Road and the Lower Nile Valley in either direction. Beginning in Cairo, the best place to rent a car, travel to Kharga via Assyut and proceed north from there. Or drive through the desert to Bahariya and continue to the southern oases; then return via Assyut along the Nile, passing by the archeological sites near Minya and Mallawi. The entire trip is about 1700km.

A number of caveats are in order concerning **desert travel.** There are still no gas (petrol) stations anywhere between Bahariya and Dakhla. The only gasoline in the tiny oasis of Farafra is in the hands of the military, who may be reluctant to sell it to tourists. Buy jerry-cans in Cairo or Assyut, and fill them with enough gas to cover the vast distances between stations. A caravan consumes amazing quantities of fuel; buy enough extra to fill an entire tank. Several large containers filled with drinking water are also essential in case an accident leaves you stranded.

Foreigners are wisely prohibited by the military from leaving the main road. Remember that desert roads are long, uneventful affairs stretching straight ahead for hundreds of kilometers. The monotony of the driving makes it easy to lose concentration and flip over into the desert. Try to drive in the cool of the morning. Finally, never drive at night—the chances of getting lost are much greater and the potholes become invisible.

The best alternative to hosteling in the oases is **camping.** Most fertile land here belongs to farmers, who'll usually permit you to pitch your tent. The ideal spot is just outside the main town of an oasis, where it's quieter and you can usually find a small pool of water. Each oasis offers one or more bearable and cheap **hotels** or **rest houses.** Stockpiling **water** is a bright idea, as occasionally the filter and pump systems break down and water is cut off for between an hour and a day. Some **food** staples are available at all of the oases; food is most difficult to obtain at Farafra. If you are renting a vehicle, bring along food as well as drinking water.

Note that the requirement that foreigners obtain permission to visit the oases was lifted in 1985-86. Despite what out-of-date sources will tell you, you need only flash a passport at the numerous military checkpoints en route—keep it handy. In Dakhla or Kharga, you'll be asked to pay a LE4.10 per person **tourism development tax.** The receipt is your admission slip to all the ancient sites in the New Valley. If you pay at a hotel, be sure to keep the receipt as proof; otherwise you'll probably have to pay at a roadblock. Fees pay for the new rest houses and tourist offices.

Bahariya

This small oasis has long been an important stopover for caravans traveling between the Nile Valley and the rest of North Africa. Since pharaonic times, the arrival of merchants and their heavily laden camels was a major event in Bahariya. For many centuries, pilgrims on their way to Mecca would join the traders on the cross-desert trek, and enjoy an enthusiastic welcome by the Bahariyan faithful. Nowadays, it's the caravans of gung-ho European adventurers, roaring through the oasis in landrovers, that cause the most excitement in Bahariya. This oasis has delighted each generation of desert travelers with its delicious bubbling springs, lush gardens of date palms and lemon trees, and genuine hospitality. Bahariya's ancient ruins are scanty and largely inaccessible, and **Bawiti** (pop. 24,000), its main village, unattractive; however, nearby gardens and springs more than compensate. The town offers several food stores, a gas station, a market, and two or three coffee shops, so it is a good place to refuel your vehicle and your body if you're heading to Farafra. If you're ill, the **Mushtashfa Hospital,** 200m north of Hotel Alpenblick, can take care of you.

The budget traveler should jump into the welcoming arms of the **Hotel Alpenblick** as soon as possible after arrival in Bawiti. Bahariya's hotel-cum-restaurant-cum-tourist information office has cheap, adequate accommodations (LE2-2.50 per person, no fans), inexpensive meals (¼ chicken LE3), and drinks (tea or coffee 25pt, bottled water 60pt). Though some toilets don't flush and the bedsprings creak, the hotel does offer the warm, easygoing hospitality of honest proprietor Salah Sherif and his buddies. Salah can be a big help for carless travelers, and is sympathetic to starving student types. He arranges cheap sight-seeing expeditions to Bahariya's main attractions, lurching around the oasis with foreigners spilling out the back of his pickup truck, and Crazy Max, his mutt, tagging along behind. Salah's unmistakable hotel awaits you just off the main road through the oasis, several blocks uphill from central Bawiti. The next best option is the colorful **Oasis Hotel,** where you can sleep in one of its four rooms, all with fans, for LE2 per bed. The friendly proprietor, Muhammad, arranges trips to the nearby springs and gardens as well. The hotel is 1 block uphill from the bus stop. Muhammad also runs **Oasis Restaurant,** just off the main street, 2 blocks from the bus stop, where you can get an adequate breakfast, lunch, or dinner (LE3). For piaster-pinchers, the **Lamey Hotel** on Bawiti's main street offers shared rooms with soldiers and truck drivers for LE1 (probably not an option for women).

Even if you're just passing through Bahariya, don't pass up a dip in the **Bir Mathar,** a gushing spring 6km from Bawiti. The slightly sulphurous water pours out of a viaduct into a small shaded cement pool surrounded by a tranquil landscape of velvet greens and desert browns. Unfortunately, women are forbidden to swim here during the daytime when the men swim. At night, a dip is not a problem for women. Salah charges LE1.50 per person for the Bir Mathar trip. From Bawiti, head east a couple of kilometers, then turn north off the main road to cut between the barren rock outcrops and the lush gardens. At the far (north) side of the gardens, turn west and head for the cluster of abandoned villas near the well. En route, you can climb the outcrops for a view of the green carpet of Bahariya's date palms spreading into the desert. Salah will take you to the nearby gardens for a pound or two. The road to Bir Mathar continues southeast through the desert to **Bir al-Ghaba,** which lies 15km from Bawiti. Here you'll find both a hot and cold spring in another beautiful oasis landscape. Both men and women can swim in this deserted spot. Salah makes a daytrip to Bir Ghaba for LE2 per person; his overnight excursion costs LE5, including food. There is also a very hot spring 2½km out of the town center, south along the main road.

Archeological sites of interest cluster around Bawiti and al-Qasr, the older city adjacent to Bawiti in the west. The **Tomb of Bannentiu,** on the eastern outskirts of Bawiti, was discovered by Ahmed Fakhry and dates from the Twenty-sixth Dynasty. Its central and burial chambers are decorated with fairly well-preserved painted reliefs, including murals of the journeys of the sun and moon. The tomb is currently closed for restoration and preservation work. Ask locally about when the tomb will be reopened. Bahariya's resident Egyptologist, Muhammad at the Bahariya Department of Antiquities, is the best-informed source. Fakhry also discovered a many-chambered **ibis burial,** 500m south of Bawiti, where sacred ibises, falcons, and quails were interred in jars. This tomb also dates from late pharaonic times, and was used into the Roman era. The burial chamber cannot be visited, but there's not much left to see, anyhow. **Al-Qasr** itself, the ancient capital of Bahariya, hides scanty Roman remains among its mud brick dwellings.

Getting There

Next to Kharga, Bahariya ranks as the most accessible of the oases in Egypt's Western Desert. From Cairo, a 350km road leads past the pyramids of Giza and southwest across the desert to Bawiti. The distance can be covered in five or six hours by private car. At least one **bus** per day leaves from al-Azhar Station in Cairo early in the morning. (LE4, LE6 for A/C buses; 7-8 hr.) On Monday and Thursday, another bus departs at 1pm. Book one to two days in advance to guarantee yourself a seat. The morning bus returns at 7 or 8am from Bahariya to Cairo. The bus to Cairo from Dakhla, which picks up passengers at Bahariya at 1:30pm, is usually full, so you may have to stand for seven hours (Mon., Thurs., and Sat. only). Service may increase to two buses every day within the coming year. Each day, a few **service**

taxis travel between Cairo and Bahariya (normally in evenings only, LE7). The departure point in Cairo is an obscure cafe in the el-Saiyida district, west of the Citadel, south of Port Said St. Taxis leave from the inconspicuous Bahariya Cafe, which inhabits a corner of Sharia Qadry, a few blocks south of Port Said St. Social history explains the obscure location: Bahariyans immigrated to this seedy Cairo neighborhood during the hard times of the 1940s and '50s.

The Roads from Cairo and to Farafra

As you leave metropolitan Cairo, you'll pass just north of the pyramids of Giza. Beyond lies one of Egypt's new planned cities, designed to accommodate some of the country's burgeoning population. If your taxi driver gets lost on the eerie streets-without-houses of **October 6th City,** you may gaze at the distant pyramids and think of Matthew Arnold's line about being trapped between two worlds—one dead and the other struggling to be born. Halfway to Bahariya, taxis and buses alike stop at the unassuming rest house. Rejuvenate your weary bones here with *fuul,* pita, and mineral water. Approaching Bahariya, notice how the entire landscape becomes drenched in a dark, reddish color. Vast deposits of iron here are quarried by a huge iron mine just off the highway 40km before Bawiti. A freight train transports the ore to Cairo, but not passengers. The mine has a gas station.

Heading southwest toward Farafra, you leave the fertility of Bawiti behind. Look for the tiny oasis of **al-Hayz,** 40km to the southwest. The modern settlement (lying 5km east of the main road on a gravel track) is a puny remnant of the large, prosperous community that flourished at al-Hayz in early Christian times. About 2km down the gravel track from the main road lie the picturesque and substantial remains of an early **church** and **military camp.** You'll need permission from Bahariya to approach or enter these ruins: The guard won't take *baksheesh.*

A trip from Bawiti to Farafra Oasis (180km) will enable you to experience the varied beauty of the desert. The paved road features spectacular canyons, windswept mesas, and rugged desertscape. The precipitous eastern and western escarpments of the Bahariyan depression meet at a point about 60km south of Bawiti. The road winds up through this pass and onto a brief plateau, then drops into the Farafra depression. Soon you'll enter the fantastic **White Desert,** where the wind has shaped mountains of chalk into giant white mushrooms, lions, and camels. The Hotel Alpenblick in Bawiti arranges camping trips to the White Desert which leave in the afternoon from Bahariya and continue to Farafra after an evening amid sandy weirdness. (LE70 for 1-8 people; difficult to gather a group in summer.)

Farafra

Farafra remains isolated and remarkably unspoiled; after a decade of access by paved road, still only a few vehicles venture out here. With a population of 1500, Farafra is the smallest of Egypt's major oases, barely big enough to support one cafe. The oasis is also one of the most picturesque in all of Egypt: The compact explosion of lush foliage perches on a sloping hill like a bright green fortress. Tiny dirt paths lead through the gardens behind Farafra's single immaculate settlement; nearby you can bathe in hot springs that bubble up through the desert floor. In *The Oases of Egypt,* Ahmed Fakhry repeats an often-told story about Farafra's isolated existence. Once upon a time, the good people of Farafra lost track of the day of the week; with Friday prayers at risk, they had to send a reliable messenger by camel to Dakhla (230km away) to end the confusion.

Two government **rest houses** will put up foreigners in Farafra. Both offer spartan accommodations, including a small kitchen, for LE2.20 per person. You should bring your own sheets and drinking water. The first rest house is the conspicuous yellow building by the military checkpoint; the second is 2km north of town. If both are full (a rather unlikely event), someone in town will house the overflow for the same price. The **Hotel President Sadat,** west of the main road on the outskirts of

Farafra town, offers slightly better rooms for LE2.15—when it's open. Buy **food** at two shops in town, or at the **cafe,** which is on the main road through town. Another small kitchen/restaurant across from the cafe and the bus stop will make meals upon request. Bread, canned food, and mineral water are available at the shops, but supplies are limited. Local farmers can sell you fresh produce. There is electricity from 7pm until midnight; a wireless telephone in town provides Farafra's only communication with the outside world.

In the town of Farafra, don't miss the **Art Museum,** the brainchild of local artist Badr. His colorful museum displays his expressive sculptures and paintings, many depicting life in Farafra. Mounted local wildlife and an exhibit of Farafran artifacts round out the collection. (Open sporadically. Contributions welcome.) Many of Badr's murals adorn the outside walls of local houses. In the middle of the village, 800m west of the cafe and the main road, a cool spring bubbles into a pool. You can refresh yourself here, or wash your laundry amid fantastic views of the stars at night. **Well #6,** 4km west of the Farafra town, is an idyllic spot to swim and camp. It is accessible only by unmarked desert roads, however, so be sure to ask a villager or one of the soldiers stationed near the town to show you the way.

Getting There

Three weekly buses (Sat., Mon., and Thurs.) stop in Farafra at 10am on their way from Dakhla to Bahariya (1pm, LE5) and eventually arrive at Cairo (6pm). On Sunday, Tuesday, and Friday, the bus returns from al-Azhar via Bahariya, and on to Dakhla (LE5). The bus service is projected, on an Egyptian schedule, to eventually become daily, with the addition of a fleet of new air-conditioned coaches. One caveat: The buses may be standing room only by the time they reach Farafra. **Service taxis** from Bahariya shuttle to Farafra every few days (LE4-5). The **Hotel Alpenblick** is a good place to wait for rides; it also organizes trips to Farafra (see above). To return, you will have to wait a few more days. However, if you scout around in Farafra you may be able to find drivers to take you to Dakhla or Bahariya for under LE20, with a detour into the White Desert along the way. **Hitchhiking** is a viable option: Wait near the military checkpoint outside of Dakhla, Farafra, or Bahariya and be sure your ride is traveling the entire route. If you have the bucks, the best way to reach here is probably to rent a car or van in Cairo.

The Road to Dakhla

The 310km road to Dakhla was constructed in 1982 but is fast deteriorating. Much of its foundation is made of chalky rock, heaped up to prevent the road and the vehicles on it from slipping into the quicksand on either side. Be careful about where you step off the road if you stop. Moving dunes obscured the southern part of this road for years, making travel between Dakhla and Farafra an unpredictable undertaking. Nowadays, the road is kept clear. The road sees so little traffic that you will feel that you have reached the Earth's end.

Ten kilometers south of Farafra, you'll come to a tiny, uninhabited oasis officially considered part of that town. The land here is cultivated by the villagers; occasionally a handful of farmers can be seen. Otherwise, the spot is deserted and quiet, and the best place in the area to pitch a tent. Nearby, in the desert, is an ancient well—don't drink the water.

Still farther down the road toward Dakhla, about 50km from Farafra, is the tiny, sparsely inhabited **Oasis of Sheikh Merzuq,** where you'll find a sulphur spring with a viaduct carrying water into a concrete pool. The pool is a refreshing spot for men to take a dip, but women are strongly advised not to swim here. The local Bedouin will show you the way to an ancient **Roman well,** which has delicious fresh water bubbling up from a deep spring.

Just north of **Bir Abu Minqar,** about one-third of the way to Dakhla, you come to a pass and look south upon a sea of golden sand. In contrast to this vision, your experience with the bored soldiers posted at Abu Minqar can be uncomfortably down to earth. From here the road skirts the western edge of the escarpment, flanked by dunes, all the way to Dakhla.

Dakhla

Dakhla is nicknamed the "pink oasis," after the pink cliffs that line the horizon, but what surprises the visitor is its extraordinary greenness. It's hard to imagine how Dakhla's lush fields and luxurious fruit orchards can so successfully defy the harsh surrounding desert. On Dakhla's western edge, sand dunes seem to threaten to engulf the road and passing vehicles. At two places, the desert overwhelms the greenery, breaking Dakhla into three separate oases.

Yet the 65,000 Dakhlans are the clear victors in the struggle of water versus stone and farmer versus dune. Basking in government attention, the people of Dakhla have reclaimed wasteland, planting peanuts and rice before introducing more fragile crops. The New Valley Project may have rendered the town of Kharga unappealing to visitors, but in Dakhla something of the opposite has occurred. While in oases such as Siwa and Farafra, development seems to be dampening local culture, here residents in Mexican-looking straw hats share an infectious, optimistic enthusiasm with visitors. In Dakhla, the ancient hamlets retain their distinctiveness, while verdant new fields fringe a modern highway.

The town of **Mut,** the major settlement in Dakhla, was named for the Egyptian goddess of the queen. People in Mut are generally kind without expecting hefty returns, with the possible exception of an occasional kid pestering you for *baksheesh*.

Practical Information

Tourist Information Office: 2nd floor of Tourist Rest Home (tel. 407; home tel. 758), in New Mosque Sq., Mut. Helpful, energetic, and philosophical Ibrahim Muhammad Hassan speaks excellent English. Good maps and information on Dakhla. Ibrahim also supervises the government rest houses here. Open daily 8am-2pm, sometimes 9-11pm, in winter 8-11pm.

Bank: Misr Bank, in Liberty Sq., opposite the police station. Will not change traveler's checks, but does exchange foreign cash. Open Sun.-Thurs. 8am-2pm and 5-8pm, Fri.-Sat. 10am-1:30pm; in summer Sun.-Thurs. 8am-2pm and 8-10pm, Fri.-Sat. 10am-1:30pm.

Telephone Office: In central New Mut, 500m west of New Valley St., about 1km northeast of New Mosque Sq. International and outside-the-oasis calls. Open 24 hours. To reach Dakhla from other Egyptian cities, dial the **telephone code** of 088 and then the telephone office at 90 11 01, 90 11 02, 90 11 03, or 90 11 04; they will connect you to the local number.

Intercity Buses: Main station in New Mosque Sq., Mut. To Kharga (4 per day, LE2.50, 3½ hr.), with connections to Assyut (LE5, 8 hr.) and Cairo (LE15, 14 hr.). Early morning bus to Cairo (Mon., Thurs., and Sat. 6am; LE15, 14 hr.) with stops in Farafra (LE5, 4½ hr.) and Bahariya (LE10, 7½ hr.). Intercity buses also stop in both the Eastern and Western Villages. Check the schedule at the bus station or the tourist office and book 1 day in advance. About half of the buses from Dakhla without A/C, and frequently late. A/C LE1.50-3.50.

Local buses: From New Mosque Sq., Mut to the Eastern Villages (6 per day, 6am-4pm, Balaat and Bashendi 25pt, return to Mut 1 hr. later) and Western Villages (3 per day, 6am-2pm, al-Qasr 25pt, return to Mut ½ hr. later).

Taxis: Special sight-seeing tours LE10-15 for one day, LE6-8 for a trip to east or west Dakhla. Ask around New Mosque Sq. in Mut and bargain. Special to Kharga LE30-40. Local covered pickup trucks shuttle frequently between the intersection of Liberty Sq. and the Eastern and Western Villages (25pt for the full trip). Best time to catch them is in early morning; a trickle at night.

Bicycle Rental: Sporadic service from workshop in Mut's New Mosque Sq. LE2-3 per day. Bargain.

Gas Station: On the outskirts of eastern Mut on main road to Kharga. Open 24 hours. Last gas until Bahariya, 500km away.

Hospitals: Tel. 332. Ambulance tel. 333. On the edge of Mut next to the gas station, and small ones in each village.

Post Office: In New Mosque Sq., Mut. Open Sat.-Thurs. 8am-3pm.

Police Station: Tel. 500. In Liberty Sq., on the Kharga-Farafra main road. You must register here on your first night in Dakhla if your hotel proprietor will not do this for you. Open daily 8am-2pm and 7-9pm.

Dakhla, farthest from Cairo of all the oases, lies 310km from Farafra and 700km from Kharga. The center of the oasis is at **Mut,** a built-up modern capital. At **West Mawhub,** 80km west of Mut, and **Tineida,** 45km east of Mut, you'll find patches of green. The cultivated regions dot the main, well-paved highway. These areas are centered at **al-Qasr,** 32km west of Mut; at the capital itself; and at **Balaat** and **Bashendi,** 35-40km east of Mut.

The concrete squalor of New Mut centers around **Liberty Square** (Midan Tahrir), 1km north of New Mosque Sq., at the intersection of the Kharga-Farafra Hwy. From Liberty Sq., **New Valley Street** winds south 2km to modest **New Mosque Square,** center of Old Mut and the focus of transportation and commerce in all Dakhla.

Accommodations and Food

Three hotels will keep you based in Mut, but two outlying rest houses make overnight trips to Balaat and Bashendi an option. Visit the tourist office for information about government rest houses. You could also camp in the desert away from roads or far from Dakhla proper.

Tourist Rest House, in New Mosque Sq. (tel. 407), conveniently next to the bus station. Small, deteriorating rooms without fans, extremely hot in the summer and with armies of marauding flies. Ibrahim of the tourist office runs this place personally. To be repainted and repaired by 1989 and carpets added. Dorm beds LE1.30, in rooms with private bath LE2.40.

Tourist Wells Rest Houses: Two government-run hotels lie near the hot springs 3km west of Mut. Follow the sign on the main road. You should have no problem catching a ride (10pt), otherwise take the enjoyable walk through the countryside. Both are more tranquil than the centrally-located Tourist Rest House.

The Roadside Rest House, also known as the "Villa," 50m from the springs. Bright, clean rooms with screens and fans. Kitchen available. LE3.50 per bed.
Poolside Rest House, also known as the "Bungalows." Six doubles facing the hot spring's swimming pool. Rooms cramped, with screens, no fans, and private bath. LE3.50 per bed.
Camping facilities are planned nearby, but that's a Mut point because you can camp here now. Reasonably priced meals can be reserved with the proprietors in the morning.

Dar al-Wafden, in eastern New Mut (tel. 778), 200m northeast of telephone office. Spacious and modern, but poorly cleaned. Occasional cockroaches feasting on your toilet. Singles LE1.50, LE2 for more appealing rooms.

Balaat Rest House (35km east of Mut) and **Bashendi Rest House** (40km east of Mut), both within easy walking distance of the respective villages. These simple government rest houses, although new and fairly clean, are quickly deteriorating. Occasionally closed to accommodate groups of teachers. Beds LE2.30.

Don't come to Dakhla for the food. Mut has the monopoly on restaurants, and the **Shehaab Restaurant,** 50m west of Liberty Sq. on the main highway, is consistently cheap. (Miserly chicken or sinewy beef with local rice and salad LE1.65.) **Restaurant,** under the same large sign, halfway between Liberty and New Mosque Sq. by the main road, has complete meals of even chewier beef for LE3. The roadside television here attracts loyal soccer fans from the neighborhood. **Pastry and Sweets** bakery next to Shehaab bakes foot-long, extremely sweet apple *fatirs* for 50pt. Shops and cheap food stalls cluster in New Mosque Sq. near the bus station and 100m to the north on New Valley St. The daily produce market in New Mosque Sq. offers a limited selection. Many shops in Mut can provide you with staples and bottled water. A **bakery** on New Valley St., midway between Mut's two squares, offers fresh pita (2pt) and fancier breads (5-10pt).

Sights

Don't linger in unattractive Mut. The only sight is the **Dakhla Ethnographic Museum.** The exhibits explain traditional oasis culture by reconstructing a typical Dakhlan family dwelling. The bulky wooden lock on the palm-wood door would defeat a veteran lock-picker; you can examine the intricate mechanism in the display case. Household objects from daily Dakhla life adorn the walls of the museum, including a gazelle-hide container for transporting fat on long camel trips. Next to it is an ingenious gazelle trap, with a barbed basket hidden in the sand. Clay figurines lodged in seven rooms within the house recreate scenes of village life, including the preparation of a bride for marriage and the celebration of a pilgrim's return from the *haj.* The museum is located next to Hotel Dar al-Wafden in eastern Mut. At this time, visits can only be arranged through the tourist office, but regular hours are planned in the future (admission LE1).

Use the capital as a base for travel to the outlying villages (see Practical Information for bus schedules). The highest priority daytrip is to **al-Qasr,** 32km northwest of Mut on the main highway. The charming modern mud-brick town was built in and around the substantial remains of Dakhla's medieval Islamic capital. Mud is the building material of choice, because it keeps houses cool in summer and warm in winter. Al-Qasr is known for the wealth of ornate **wooden lintels** adorning many of the old doorways. The lintels are of acacia, and commemorate the owner, the builder, and date of construction. Climb the minaret of the old mosque, or the stairwell of the *madrasa* (now a courtroom, formerly an Islamic school) to view ancient mud rooftops sprouting TV antennas. Nearby you will find a pharaonic arch, once used to support the entrance to a house, and a Roman doorway a few doors away. On the fringes of the Old Town you can see a functioning **pottery works,** where the natives churn out everything from ashtrays to chamberpots. If you walk a while around the **old village,** about ½km north of the east-west road, you'll stumble onto one of the two caretakers who will show you about.

From al-Qasr, head 5km west on the main highway, traversing some sand dunes, to reach the turn-off for **al-Mousawaka Tombs.** The local bus to west Mawhub can drop you here. Head 3km south on the well-marked gravel track to reach the guarded tombs, hewn into a rock outcropping. The **Tomb of Petosiris** features brightly painted funerary scenes with a cast of characters that's half ancient Egyptian, half Greco-Roman. The ceiling blazes with Greek-looking angels, portraits of the deceased, and a full-blown zodiac. The adjacent **Tomb of Sadosiris,** whose paintings are primitive, features unusual images of a two-faced man, looking back at life and toward the afterlife, and of a mummy carrier with wooden wheels. These tombs are only the two most interesting of hundreds of Greco-Roman tombs sprinkled around the immediate area. You can visit the tombs at any time; just ask the guard to open them for you.

On the return trip to Mut, take time to enjoy the beauty of this part of Dakhla. From inside a cathedral of arched eucalyptus trees, you'll look out on rice fields with straw-hatted Dakhlan farmers and snowy white ibises. Beyond the palm groves and villages loom the pink cliffs or gleaming sand dunes of the desert. At **el-Drous** village, where settled Bedouin still tend their camel herds, you might take a 5km detour east to a picturesque **Islamic Cemetery.** Three kilometers before Mut, stop for a dip at the so-called **Tourism Wells.** Here hot spring water (42°C) has been tapped to fill two swimming pools before flowing into irrigation channels (25pt admission, free with New Valley tourism development tax). The water in the two pools is almost stagnant, but a new cold spring is soon to be tapped nearby, since the old one died recently.

On the eastern side of Mut, two historic, well-kept villages may restore your faith in rural living. In the crowded old section of **Balaat** (pop. 5000), you wander through long, dark passageways to come upon a burst of palm fronds and grape vines in someone's inner courtyard. Note how the large palm-log doors open with slender, pegged wooden keys.

At **Bashendi,** 5km farther east (and 40km from Mut), the proud accomplishments of a "model village" will rival Roman tombs for your attention. Walk straight up the clean village streets, past the cool curves of houses and walls to find the **Tomb of Ketemus.** This large stone edifice contains four rooms, including one decorated with scenes of its second century Roman owner mingling with the desert gods Min, Seth, and Shu. Outside, eight more tombs with sarcophagi lie open to the sun. Next door, the prominent **Tomb of Bash Endi,** the base of which is Roman but whose domed roof is distinctly Islamic, commemorates the village's beloved namesake. If you've lost something on your travels, you might join locals to decorate the holy man's tomb with henna in hopes of finding missing objects. The village leaders will eagerly bring you to visit the Bashendi **carpetworks,** where local youths are trained in weaving on looms. Many carpets, which you can buy, depict scenes of Dakhlan life in desert hues. An unusually ornamented Muslim cemetery marks the end of the village.

Except for some natural pyramids, the section of desert along the **road to Kharga** has unusually little to stir the imagination. The rest house, midway, doesn't even offer food. Just before you reach Kharga, crescent-shaped sand dunes march across the road, necessitating occasional detours.

Kharga

The most accessible and developed of the oases, the city of Kharga is the closest thing in Egypt to a desert boomtown. With the New Valley Project, Kharga's population has mushroomed to nearly 60,000, including 1000 Nubians who settled here after the waters of Lake Nasser washed away their villages. Model villages have sprung up all over the oasis to begin work on the new fields. Kharga's ugly boomtown neighborhoods are not particularly interesting to the traveler, but Old Kharga and the surrounding villages warrant a visit. Superb pharaonic, Christian, and Islamic ruins are scattered throughout the oasis, and Kharga's hot sulphur springs are great places to soak off desert dust.

Practical Information

Tourist Information Office: In an igloo-like white building opposite the Kharga Oasis Hotel (tel. 90 12 05 or 90 12 06). Manager Mr. Tawfik diligently digs up the latest information. Open Sun.-Thurs. 10am-3pm and 7-10pm; in Ramadan Sun.-Thurs. 10am-5pm and 8-11pm.

Banks: Misr Bank, opposite Cinema Hibis. Exchanges cash but not traveler's checks. Open Sun.-Thurs. 8am-2pm and 5-8pm, Fri.-Sat. 10:30am-1:30pm and 5-8pm. The manager of the Kharga Oasis Hotel will also change hard currency.

Post Office: Main office on Gamel Abd al-Nasser St., behind the Cinema Hibis. Another in Old Kharga's Showla Sq. Both open Sat.-Thurs. 9am-3pm.

Telephone and Telegram Office: Opposite the main post office. Sporadic international service. Open 24 hours. **Telephone code** is 088.

Planes: On Sun. and Wed., from Cairo (dep. 5:30am) via Luxor to Kharga and back to Cairo (dep. 8am). Cairo-Kharga LE98. Airport turn-off is 3km north of town on Assyut Rd., then 2km southeast; minibus or shared taxi from governate on Nasser St. (50pt).

Buses: Station in Showla Sq. To Assyut (6 per day 6am-3:30pm, 7pm, and 8pm; LE2, 4 hr.), to Cairo (6am, 9am, 7pm, and 8pm; morning buses LE6.50, evening buses LE9; 9 hr.), to Dakhla (6am and 5pm; also 2 of the afternoon buses from Assyut and Cairo also stop in Kharga on way to Dakhla, LE2.50, most buses not A/C, 3½ hr.), and to Baris (noon and 2pm, LE1, 2 hr.).

Service Taxis: Opposite bus station. Fairly frequent to Assyut (LE4). Possible to Baris (LE1). Rare to Dakhla or Cairo except at festivals. Special (unshared) to Dakhla, total LE40. For local sight-seeing, LE10-15 per day. All the sights including Baris and Dush LE30.

Hospital: Tel. 90 07 77. Main branch just off Nasser St. Open 24 hours.

Tourist Police: Tel. 90 15 02. In police station, across from new tourist office building. Open daily 8am-2pm.

Of all the oases in Egypt's Western Desert, Kharga lies closest to the Nile Valley—240km from Assyut via an excellent road. The greenery begins about 20km north of the town of Kharga, which is the capital of the New Valley. A picturesque, newly paved road heads south from Kharga, skirting sand dunes and small oases en route to **Bulaq,** 15km south, and **Baris,** 90km away. In sprawling, spacious Kharga town, **Gabel Abd al-Nasser Street** is the main drag. This street becomes the road to Assyut at its northern end, and intersects with the road to Dakhla near the landmark Cinema Hibis. **El-Showla Square,** the focus of Old Kharga, lies roughly 3km southeast of this intersection. Convenient **covered truck-taxis** shuttle between Showla Sq. and the Kharga Oasis Hotel, at the northern end of Nasser St. (5pt).

Accommodations and Food

There are two places stay in Kharga. The **New Valley Tourist Homes** (tel. 90 07 28), next to a large church, 200m west of Nasser St. The turn-off is about 200m north of the new mosque, which is just north of the Cinema Hibis. Known only as "Metalco" to locals, this hotel's 14 bungalows resemble barracks for migrant workers. Simple rooms with semi-private baths come in two varieties. (Regular singles LE2.30, nicer singles LE3.50. Doubles LE5.10.) The **Waha Hotel** (tel. 90 03 93), an even match with the Tourist Homes, rises four stories above the southern base of Nasser St. The adequate hotel has new sheets and friendly management. (Singles LE2.50-3, doubles LE5-6, triples LE6; 10% service charge extra.)

Despite its size, Kharga town offers no more interesting or tasty food than the other oases. The large, colorful *souk* adjacent to Showla Sq. can satisfy a craving for fresh produce. Otherwise, try the hotels: Metalco serves fine meals under its huge straw igloos if there are enough people (breakfast LE1, dinner LE3); a friendly cafe beneath the Waha offers standard inexpensive Egyptian fare (open daily from 1:30pm); and the fancy Kharga Oasis Hotel has overpriced meals and Stella beer (LE2.50).

Sights

In contrast to the sterile modernity of boulevards in New Kharga, life spills out the windows and doorways along the narrow streets of Old Kharga. Sky blue and mud brick brown comprise the main color scheme here. Palm trunks and fronds keep passageways in perpetual shade. You can buy locally made ceramics and carpets in the *souk.* Those with delicate stomachs may not appreciate the thriving trade in assorted beef entrails.

Kharga's important ruins cluster at the northern end of town. A shared covered taxi will take you as far as the Kharga Oasis Hotel, and from there you can walk to the sites. The **Temple of Hibis,** 1km north of the Kharga Oasis Hotel and visible from the road, was built by the Persian emperor Darius I (c. 500 B.C.E.). The temple is one of only a few surviving monuments of the Persian period. It was later dedicated to the Egyptian god Amun. The second entrance features colored bas-reliefs, and the entire building is rich with inscriptions. On the fourth arch, a nineteenth-century French traveler carefully carved his name and recorded his status as the first European to visit the temple. Across the road, to the southeast, you can see the **Temple of Nadura** crowning a hill.

The eerie above-ground tombs of the Christian **Necropolis of al-Bagawat** stand at the desert's edge, 500m past Hibis Temple on the road to Assyut. From the third to the eighth centuries C.E., a sizable Christian community inhabited Kharga. The domed, mud-brick mausolea here are the only surviving traces. The necropolis is visible from the road. A vehicle with four-wheel drive can manage the dirt road, or you can hike the distance. For a little *baksheesh,* the caretaker in the mud hut near the cemetery will unlock the doors of the most colorful tombs. The interior frescoes of biblical scenes are excellent examples of Coptic painting in the early Alexandrian style. Greek inscriptions identify Adam and Eve, Noah's Ark, and the Virgin Mary. In the Chapel of the Exodus, an unforgettable ceiling mural depicts Pharaoh's Roman-looking army pursuing the Jews as they flee from Egypt. Atop the cemetery's central hill are the remains of a fourth-century mud-brick basilica.

On your way back to town, take a look at Kharga's newest and noisiest tourists at **"Tourism Duck Lake,"** the most picturesque of Kharga's new duck farms.

The Roads to Baris and to Assyut

If you've got time to spare, take the road along the old 40-day camel trail south to Baris. This legendary caravan route went from western Sudan all the way to the Egyptian Nile Valley. The numerous ancient ruins in the small oases south of Kharga demonstrate that Egypt's current rulers are not the first to take special interest in this remote district.

Leaving Kharga town, you'll cross sandy desertscapes until you reach the **Khwita Temple,** 17km to the south. The impressive, 10m walls of the temple-cum-fortress command a hill 2km east of the road. The Amun temple rises above a complex of adobe and sandstone—remnants of a once-flourishing Ptolemaic settlement. The **Zayan Temple,** with its mud-brick architecture, lies 5km south, also to the east. At the 25km mark, you'll come across shaded **Nasser Wells,** and, farther on, better-developed **Bulaq Wells.** Soak your body in the hot springs here, and decide whether to stay at the spartan government **rest houses** (beds LE2.30).

The secluded and picturesque village of Baris lies 90km south of Kharga. Two buses run daily from Kharga to Baris. Since there are no hotels, the only option for staying overnight in Baris is to camp. Otherwise, take the bus back (departs Kharga at noon and 2pm, returns at 6am and 4pm; LE1 each way, 2 hr.). Fortunately, you won't starve in Baris, as a half-dozen small kiosks sell soda, mineral water, and canned goods. The blue structure resembling a doghouse sells kebab, *fuul,* and tamiya every day except Friday. You may be asked to join villagers for a meal.

A sturdy vehicle will be able to manage the 23km trek southeast to the **Dush Temple,** which feels like the hottest and most isolated place in Egypt. The temple, originally built for the worship of Serapis and Isis, dates back to the Roman emperors Justinian, Trajan, and Hadrian. The temple is in the process of excavation. Sand is slowly being removed, revealing a church and a well with clay pipes leading to an underground city. Pottery shards litter the site. All signs indicate that Dush was once a prosperous area, eventually abandoned as a result of its wells drying up. Once you're on the roof of the temple, you'll realize that the temple was the highest structure for miles around. To reach the temple, take the road east upon reaching Baris.

The 240km **road to Assyut** passes through plenty of inspirational desert scenery. The town of Kharga is surrounded by a moonscape of dunes and rock outcroppings. As you leave, it becomes clear that the oasis sits in the middle of a 200 square kilometer depression; the road ascends the escarpment in a dozen switchbacks, presenting unforgettable vistas of desert emptiness. The al-Obbur Rest House, offering water and refreshments, is the only building along the way. Beyond the rest house, the road passes through the "sea of melons," where wind-resistant silica nodules litter the landscape. After the long desert silences, the descent into the Nile Valley's confusion of color and noise brings both relief and sadness.

JORDAN

US $1 = 0.37 dinar (JD)   JD1 = US $2.69
CDN $1 = JD0.31   JD1 = CDN $3.25
UK £1 = JD0.63   JD1 = UK £ 1.59
AUS $1 = JD0.30   JD1 = AUS $3.36
NZ $1 = JD0.25   JD1 = NZ $4.07

For important information on Documents and Formalities, Money, Safety and Security, Climate Concerns, Border Crossings, Travel Etiquette, Accommodations, History, and Religion, see the General Introduction to this book.

Jordan is a land of warm temperatures and even warmer welcomes. Although tourists have tended to let the political heat scare them away, Jordanian hospitality will soothe the weary traveler's soul. If tourists really went to where the good things are, Jordan would be packed full.

The cost of travel in Jordan is relatively high, but you won't be peering through crowds of tourists to see glass-enclosed sights with English labels. You can travel in Jordan on the back of a camel, or snorkel among the brilliant coral reefs of the Gulf of Aqaba. To those willing to sacrifice a few dollars or pounds on the altar of the desert sands, Jordan offers an unparalleled array of historic monuments, from Crusader castles to desert palaces, from Roman ruins to the rose-hued remnants of Petra. The country remains largely untouched by Western wanderers, and the startling lack of such traffic here makes any Jordanian expedition an exotic adventure.

Tension between Israel and Jordan runs deep. Technically, the two countries remain at war. Much of the Jordanian population is of Palestinian descent, and the *intifadah* (uprising) on the West Bank has brought the conflict back to center stage as well as aggravating internal disputes. Although you should be sensitive to political concerns, ill feelings are not taken out on tourists, and you will be treated as an honored guest. Jordanians have yet to become blasé about Western tourists.

Planning Your Trip

If your passport contains an Israeli stamp, you will be denied entry into Jordan. Anyone crossing the King Hussein/Allenby Bridge is *not* legally permitted to return by the bridge.

Work, Apprenticeship, and Archeological Digs

It is hard for foreigners to find jobs. Formal positions must be arranged before arrival, and you must name your employer to obtain a work visa. **Work permits** can be secured from the Ministry of Labor. **Residence permits** are also required for stays of more than three months.

Some apprenticeships are available for science students through the **International Association for the Exchange of Students with Technical Experience (IAESTE).** (See General Introduction for address.) Applicants must be college juniors or seniors majoring in the sciences. The application deadline is December 10.

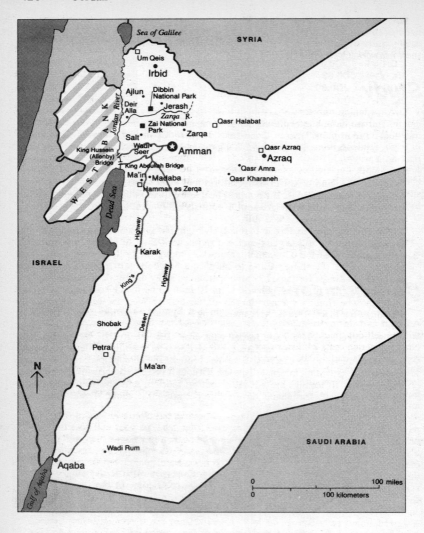

Volunteers for **archeological digs** are also in demand. Most archeological journals list digs abroad; *Biblical Archeology* is an excellent source. Also try The Archeological Institute of America (see General Introduction for address), which publishes the *Fieldwork Opportunities Bulletin*.

Study

Two Jordanian universities are open to foreign students. **The University of Jordan** in Amman has a liberal atmosphere in which American and European students may feel more at home than in the conservative, traditional **Yarmoukh University** in Irbid. Students interested in Islamic culture, however, may enjoy the more rapid pace at Yarmoukh. Both schools offer a wide range of courses and run summer schools. Both universities guarantee dormitory housing for women. A Jordanian embassy or consulate can provide further information on either school. The University of Jordan has a special foreign students program. For more information, write to the **Ministry of Education,** P.O. Box 1646, Amman, Jordan (tel. 691 81 91).

Once There

Communication

Stamps may be purchased between 8am and 8pm at the main post office in Amman and during regular business hours elsewhere. Stamps and aerogrammes tend to sell out quickly, so try to buy them early in the day. An **air mail letter** to North America costs 240fils, an aerogramme or postcard is 150fils; the cost for Europe is 160fils and 120fils, repectively. Mail from Jordan to North America and Europe takes one to two weeks. **Packages** may be sent through the parcel office, located behind the main post office. **Poste Restante** operates at the central post office in Amman and in the larger cities. American Express offices, located in Amman and Aqaba, also hold mail.

The **telephone system** is functional and automatic, but often overloaded. The rare pay phones are particularly poor and require 50fils whether your call goes through or not. If you ask shop owners where to find the nearest pay phone, they will probably invite you to use theirs. Most shops are equipped with phones, but they can only make local calls. Another option is to use a hotel phone, but be sure to find out about surcharges ahead of time. Both push-button phones and rotary dials should be operated slowly for the correct number to be registered. Keep trying after the first unanswered ring or busy signal. The dial tone sounds like the U.S. busy signal.

International calls can be made in Amman from the telephone center around the corner and up the hill from the main post office on Prince Muhammad St. (See Amman Practical Information.) When calling North America, the first three minutes will cost about JD4; you pay at the desk after the call is made. In other parts of Jordan, international calls must be made at fancy hotels, where service will be faster, clearer, and more expensive. Late night and early morning are the best times to dial overseas. The best option is to use a private phone and reimburse the owner. You can dial directly to the U.S., Europe, and Australia (875fils per minute between midnight and 8am; JD1.250 otherwise; to the U.S. dial 00 and international code). Neither phone nor mail service extends to Israel. For an international operator, dial 17. Call 63 93 61 for information on local codes. For other information, dial 12. **Collect calls** cannot be made from government telephone offices.

The **international phone code** for calling to Jordan is 962.

Telegrams can be sent to North America for under 200fils from larger post offices and some hotels. Telegrams can also be placed over the phone by dialing 18.

Currency and Exchange

The **Jordanian Dinar (JD)** is a decimal currency, divided into 1000fils. Prices are always labeled in fils, but the usual spoken practice is to call 10fils a piastre (pt). Thus, 500fils will be written as 500fils, but referred to as 50pts. A piastre is also sometimes called a "girsh" and a ½pt is a "tarifeh." Bills come in denominations of JD50, 20, 10, 5, 1, and 500fils. Coins are silver for 250fils, 100, 50, and 25, and copper for 10 and 5. Confusingly, the numerals that Westerners call "Arabic" are not used in the Arab world, so it's a good idea to learn the Arab forms (see Arabic Numerals in the General Introduction and look at car license plates that are in both scripts). Denominations on currency are also written in Arabic and modern Arab numerals.

Currency exchange is easy to find in Amman, but harder elsewhere. Bank exchange hours are 9:30am-12:30pm. Official money-changers offer slightly better rates and have longer hours, as late as 9pm and on Fridays. The national Housing Banks are the best bets outside of Amman. Queen Alia Airport has exchange facilities for incoming planes. A passport is always required to change traveler's checks. Credit cards are not accepted except in expensive hotels.

Tipping

Tips are expected in restaurants, unless "service included" appears on the menu. Taxi drivers do not expect tips. If you are with a large sightseeing group, tip the bus driver about 500fils. A small tip to the room cleaners in hotels is appropriate.

Business Hours

Jordan's business timetable has been shaped by the various natural, religious, and economic forces at work in the country. The desert sun forces the lunchtime hours to be a time of rest. Most stores and offices open between 8 and 9:30am, close from 1pm to 3 or 4pm, and reopen in the afternoon. In Amman, retail stores often close as late as 8 or 9pm, when the transportation system winds down. Banks and government offices, however, retain only a skeleton staff in the afternoon, so try to complete all your important business in the morning. Government offices are open Sat.-Thurs. 8am-2pm. Money changers are open all day.

Friday is a holiday throughout the Muslim world, although perhaps less so in Amman and Aqaba, where some stores stay open seven days per week to keep up with the competition. Foreign banks and offices generally observe both Friday and Saturday as weekday holidays, though they may keep longer hours during the rest of the week. Museums are closed on Tuesdays. The only consistent daily schedule is the Islamic call to prayer. Five times per day, the faithful turn from the material world to kneel facing the holy city of Mecca. Non-Muslim travelers should not visit mosques during prayer sessions.

Accommodations

Though the Jordanian government has gone to great lengths to establish adequate, regulated accommodations for tourists, the budget traveler has been left out of the planning. Regulated tourist hotels charge prices as high as Jordan's temperatures. Jordan has no IYHF hostels.

Hotels

Jordanian hotels are inspected annually and regulated by the government according to a five-star system. Bargaining is difficult; hotel owners may be more flexible in the off-season winter and summer months. Fall and spring are the busiest times throughout Jordan, though sunny Aqaba sees the most activity during the winter season. Single women may feel uncomfortable at some of the cheaper hotels, and may on occasion be excluded. Remember also that Jordanian law forbids unmarried couples from sharing a room. Cheap hotels usually don't have double beds. Parents and children share rooms, but otherwise you may be asked to split up. The price is usually per bed (not per room) in cheap hotels, so you won't lose out—at least not financially.

The Ministry of Tourism provides a comprehensive list of classified hotels and their prices (available at the Ministry's Public Relations Office in Amman). Below is a table of the approximate rates set by the government.

Class	Singles	Doubles
Five-star	JD28	JD31
Four-star	JD21	JD15
Three-star	JD4	JD7
Two-star	JD3	JD5
One-star	JD2	JD3.500

Most hotels add a 10% service charge. Ask whether it's included in the quoted price. If business is slow, use the surcharge as a bargaining chip. Some of the cheaper places charge an extra 250fils for a hot shower; many have European-style toilets, but some don't. The unclassified places usually have clean beds, but washing facilities are often dreadful. Hotel owners will often ask to hold your passport for the length of your stay.

Alternate Accommodations

Hotels are rare outside Amman and the handful in Aqaba. The primary alternatives elsewhere are the government **Rest Houses** in Petra, Karak, Azraq, and Dibbin National Park. The clean, simple Rest Houses charge about JD6.600 for singles and JD9.200 for doubles. If you plan to stay at one, especially in the spring or fall, reserve a room in advance with the **Hotel and Rest House Corporation**, P.O. Box 2863, Amman, Jordan (tel. 81 32 43).

Camping

Camping is possible virtually everywhere in the country, although organized facilities are nonexistent. Favorite sites include the beach north of Aqaba, the caves and ledges at Petra, and Dibbin National Park. You'll need a sleeping bag for the cool summer nights, while winter evenings can bring sub-freezing temperatures. Remember to drink plenty of water to offset the effects of the dry air. There are very few insects at night, and sleeping out is not uncomfortable. Many hotels will let you spread a bag out on the roof for a small fee.

Far more interesting than camping is spending a night with the Bedouin. Throughout the country, their black tents still represent oases of hospitality to strangers. Tea, Arab coffee, and meals always accompany an invitation, although showers and toilets rarely do. While the Bedouin would never accept money, the gift of a pack of Marlboros will be appreciated.

Transportation

Most visitors to Jordan stay long enough to see the major sites at Petra and Jerash, yet not long enough to master the transportation system. Organized bus tours and private taxis can easily cost JD5-10 per day, but cheaper, if slower, modes of transportation are readily available. The country has a fine train system, which unfortunately is only for freight, and the only reliable long-distance bus company, JETT, offers a limited number of routes. However, fleets of shared taxis (called *service*) and collective minibuses shuttle between all cities, towns, and villages. Hitchhiking is a common practice among Jordanians and is generally a viable option, though more so in the north than in the south, where the wagging thumb gesture is often mistaken for a friendly wave.

All of Jordan's roads are currently open to unrestricted travel, with the possible exception of the militarily sensitive highway along the Jordan Valley from Aqaba to the Dead Sea. Travel to the **West Bank** requires a special, hand-held permit available only at the Ministry of Interior in Amman. (See Border Crossings in the General Introduction as well as Practical Information in Amman for details.) Travel restrictions change with the political climate; check with the Ministry of Tourism or travel agencies for the latest developments.

Taxis and Service

Private taxis, useful mainly in Amman, are yellow and have "taxi" written in Roman letters on them. Jordanian taxi drivers take their horns seriously, their fares a little less so, and the law hardly at all. Insist that the driver use the meter: It's the law, and it will keep the price down. The starting fare is 150fils. Drivers may also charge extra (again, illegally) for large amounts of baggage.

Service taxis, (pronounced sairVEEce) are shared taxis, usually white or gray Mercedes with a white sign written in Arabic on their roofs. The front doors have the route and number (again in Arabic letters only). This is the best way to travel, and people will always help you out. *Service* can be hailed en route. Payment takes place whenever the rider feels like it—usually just as the cab is negotiating a sharp curve. *Service* rides tend to be hair-raising experiences, as most drivers consider their routes to be race courses. Travel within Amman is generally easier on foot, but the service taxis are invaluable for inter-city travel. There are specific *service* routes in Amman and between the central transport terminals in the larger cities. In Amman, *service* cost between 60 and 100fils; a ride may cost up to JD2.650 from Amman to Aqaba. Shared taxis rarely run in the evenings and the long-distance ones may make only two or three trips per day. Schedules are irregular—they leave when all five seats are full. Don't get into one alone, or you will pay for all the seats.

Service to the northern part of the country depart from the cluster of depots in **Abdali Station** (North Station) on King Hussein St. The fare is 420fils to Jerash, 650fils to Ajlun, 870fils to Irbid, 270fils to Salt, and JD1.100 to the King Hussein/Allenby Bridge. From Irbid, it's 260fils to Um Qeis and 420fils to al-Hemma. *Service* to the southern part of Jordan leave Amman from **Wahadat Station** (South Station) in Jebel Ashrafieh. The station is several kilometers from downtown Amman between the Abu Darwish Mosque and the Wahadat Refugee Camp. *Service* leave from Wahadat Station to Madaba (300fils), to Karak (JD1.700) down the Kings' Hwy., and to Ma'an (JD1.350) via the newer Desert Hwy. At Ma'an you can transfer for service to Wadi Musa (Petra) and Aqaba (430fils and JD1.300, respectively). All these prices are government-regulated, but drivers occasionally hike the fares. See if other passengers accept an impromptu increase—they won't unless it's justified.

Buses

Public buses supplement the service taxi system in Amman. The intercity bus network is sparse due to the monopoly granted by the government to the **Jordan Express Tourist Transport (JETT)** company. Private buses, however, cover the most popular routes, and private minibuses travel to more remote areas. Regular service on JETT buses is limited to daily schedules from Amman to Aqaba, Petra, and the King Hussein/Allenby Bridge, from Amman to Damascus, Syria, and to Cairo via Aqaba and the Sinai. (See Amman Practical Information for details about schedules and the station.) The **Arabella** and **Hijazi** bus companies travel to Jerash and Irbid. Minibuses operate widely as well; destinations are written only in Arabic, so you have to ask (unless, of course, you read Arabic).

Bus fares are slightly lower than *service* rates, but buses travel more slowly. The JETT luxury coaches cost more than regular buses, but are usually air-conditioned, and come with hostesses and even videos. They also leave more or less on schedule, rather than when seats are filled. Booking ahead is a good idea and often necessary. Most towns have one main terminal shared by intercity buses and service taxis; Amman and Irbid have several. In Amman, buses follow the pattern of *service,* with traffic to the north leaving from Abdali Station and buses to the south leaving from Wahadat Station. There are some exceptions; for example, bus #31 to Madaba and the Kings' Highway leaves from Abdali via the Seventh Circle.

Cars

Some of Jordan's greatest attractions are barely served by the public transportation system. For groups of four to six, renting a car can be an affordable, efficient way to reach less accessible sights. With a car, for example, the round-trip to Azraq via four or five desert castles can be done in eight to 12 hours. The magnificent Kings' Highway route, hardly served by other modes of transportation, can be seen from a private car in another full day. At least one rental agency will let you return a car rented in Amman at an office in Aqaba, but you must pay for the car to be returned to Amman.

If you don't split the costs, car rental in Jordan can break your budget. Most rental agencies charge about JD8 per day, including insurance, plus 40fils per kilometer. The unlimited mileage deals are cheaper (JD12-14 per day), but you must rent the car for at least a week. (See Amman and Aqaba Practical Information sections for details.) Always ask whether the car has a fire extinguisher. The desert heat may demand it and the police require it. The four-wheel-drive cars the companies push are unnecessary except to reach Qasr Touba, south of Azraq. Even at Wadi Rum, ordinary cars are adequate, and can be supplemented by camel.

Gas costs 180fils per liter. The law requires seatbelts to be worn (JD5 fine for infraction), and speeding tickets can run to an exorbitant JD50. Many rental companies like an International Driver's License but others will accept a valid national license if you're over 18. **Road accidents** should be reported to tel. 89 63 90, and an **ambulance** can be called at tel. 77 51 11 or 77 51 19.

Hitchhiking

Hitchhiking experiences in Jordan are generally good, but *service* and minibuses are cheap enough to make hitching unnecessary except in remote areas like along the King's Highway. Rides between small towns (Jordan Valley, Amman environs, Irbid area) come fast, and drivers are usually friendly. Be careful in the desert and the city: Even short waits in the sun can be dangerous. Bring lots of water and cover your head with a broad-brimmed hat. Try not to be let off where sand dunes will be your only companions.

When hitchhiking within a city (Amman, Irbid, Jerash, Ajlun), empty taxis will pester you as they pass by. The profusion of rich tourists and transient workers in urban areas makes it nearly impossible to hitch a ride from private cars. The steady stream of trucks serving the port facilities compensates, with many drivers eager for company on their long trans-Jordan hauls. It is so rare for women to hitchhike alone that misunderstandings easily develop. It is strongly advised that women travel in pairs or with a male companion if hitchhiking.

Dress Codes

Jordan is predominantly Muslim and socially conservative, so modest dress is a must; besides, suntanning is a low priority for Jordanians. Tourists—men or women—who dress like exhibitionists will certainly have trouble. You will not be arrested, but inappropriate dress will alienate you from the very people you have come to meet. The same modesty is required of men and women. The code is simple:

Do not wear shorts. Your pants should come down to at least mid-shin (women may wear pants). Shirts should cover the shoulders and upper arms. Women should wear head scarves in mosques. Feet, however, can be exposed freely.

A mosque is a place of worship and should therefore be treated with the utmost respect. When entering a mosque, shoes must be removed and left at the door. You should not lean or sit (except on the floor), and do not sleep in mosques. Photos may be taken of the building, but it may be thought rude to photograph the people. Don't visit mosques after the call to prayer.

Life in Jordan

Economy

Unlike its Arab neighbors, Jordan has not been blessed with oil reserves or other significant natural resources. The West Bank had been some of Jordan's most productive land. Because of its dearth of natural resources, Jordan remains dependent on Arab financial aid. Remittances from Jordanian workers in the Gulf States constitute another important addition to the Jordanian economy. With the outbreak of the Iran-Iraq War in 1980, Iraq became a major importer of Jordanian goods and services and relied on Jordan's highways as its lifeline. In 1981, Jordan's exports to Iraq jumped to $186 million—more than a 400% increase from just two years before.

Recently, Jordan's economic fortunes have begun to turn sour. At its current 2-3% growth rate, Jordan's economy is failing to keep pace with its burgeoning population. With the ongoing oil glut, Jordan's Arab benefactors are less able and willing to pump petrodollars into Jordan's coffers. Workers' remittances have also dwindled due to the plunge in oil prices. Jordanian exporters are facing a financial crisis as Iraq sinks deeper and deeper into debt, amassing a mountain of IOUs to the Jordanian government. With the end of the war appearing to approach, the prospects for repayment are brightening, but Iraq may well reduce its imports when it rebuilds industries.

Festivals and Holidays

The most important festivals of the year are Islamic celebrations, including the holy month of **Ramadan** (April 7-May 6 in 1989) and the four-day **Id al-Adha** (Feast of Sacrifice, July 19-24 in 1989). Jordan's other major holidays are **New Year's Day, Mullid al-Nabi** (Muhammad's Birthday), the feast of **al-Miraj** (commemorating Muhammad's Night Journey), and **Arab Renaissance Day,** in late April, marking the Arab Revolt of 1916. Government offices and banks close on the national holidays of the **King's Birthday** (Nov. 11), his **Ascension to the Throne** (Aug. 11), **Independence Day** (May 25), **Labor Day** (May 1), and **Arab League Day** (March 22). Muslim holidays are determined according to the lunar calendar and differ from year to year. Expect difficulties in making international flights between Muslim countries during Ramadan and Id al-Adha. Note also that traditionally Muslims count years beginning with the Hejira, or Muhammad's emigration from Mecca to Medina. Therefore 1989 is 1409 A.H. in the Muslim world. However, the Western calender is used in daily life.

For the Christian community, the **Easter Celebrations** (some following the Gregorian calendar, others the Julian) are the most spectacular of the year. **Christmas** is a smaller feast, especially for the Coptic and Abyssinian Churches, which celebrate it during the second week of January rather than on December 25.

Literature

There is little or no Jordanian literature as such. The Arabic language is shared by many nations, and Arabic literature from various countries serves the whole of the Arab world. Jordan has an ancient heritage of literature: The oldest example of a Semitic script was found in Karak (the Mesha Stele, now in Paris).

Among English travel accounts, C. M. Doughty's *Arabia Deserta* and Wilfred Thesiger's more recent *Arabian Sands* are powerful adventure stories inspired by a romanticized version of Bedouin lifestyle. T.E. Lawrence's *Seven Pillars of Wisdom* contains vivid descriptions of the battles fought and the territory explored during the Arab Revolt of 1916-18; even if you don't reach Wadi Rum in the Jordanian desert, see *Lawrence of Arabia* on the big screen. The Arab Legion chief of the 1940s and 1950s, John B. Glubb, wrote *A Soldier with the Arabs* and several books based on his life. A little less adventurous, but more erudite, is Jonathan Raban's *Arabia: A Journey through the Labyrinth.* Gertrude Bell, one of the first Western female travelers in the region, writes of her adventures in her travels through Jordan and Syria in *The Desert and the Sown.*

For the archeologically and historically inclined, there are G.L. Harding's *Antiquities of Jordan* and Julian Huxley's *From an Antique Land.* Ian Browning's *Petra* is wonderfully comprehensive. Finally, Agatha Christie's *Argument with Death* makes a light introduction to the power of Petra.

Food

Jordanian cuisine has evolved through centuries of Bedouin cooking. The national dish, *mensaf,* consists of eight to 10 kilos of rice on a tray at least a meter across, topped with pine nuts and the stew of an entire lamb or goat. The Bedouin still serve the head of the lamb on top, reserving the prize delicacies—eyes and tongue—for the tongue-tied and goggle-eyed guests. The right hand is used to ball the rice, and flat bread to pull off chunks of meat and dip them into the *jamid* (sweet yogurt).

Most other dishes include the main ingredients of *mensaf.* Traditional dinners, served between 2 and 3pm, are rarely as spicy as those in other Arab countries. Popular dinners are *musukhan,* boiled chicken with olive oil and a delicious spice called *sumac,* served with *khoubz* (bread); *yakhne,* a meat casserole with small onions, cabbage, and tomatoes; and *mahshi,* a tray of vine leaves, squash, or eggplant stuffed with mincemeat, rice, and onions. *Mezze,* loosely translated as hors d'oeuvres, encompasses a wide range of dishes which include *hoummus* with olive oil, *mutabal* (an eggplant dip), *labneh* (thickened yogurt), cucumbers, tomatoes, and pickles. Supper is usually a smaller meal; *fuul* (fava beans) is a standard breakfast.

Traditionally, a guest receives *qahwa sada* (bitter coffee) both as a greeting and as a farewell. When visiting the Bedouin, a complete ritual accompanies the coffee. When the guest first arrives, the roasted beans are ground in a carved wooden *mihbash* (mortar and pestle). Its strong rhythmic pounding announces to neighbors that a meal is being prepared for guests, and during the feast of *Id al-Fitr,* a symphony of the *mihbash* sounds through many Bedouin valleys. Once ground, the coffee beans are boiled in a large brass pot, then poured through ground cardamon pods into a smaller brass pot, and finally poured through tamarisk twigs to a third pot, from which the coffee is served. The coffee, always poured with the left hand into one of a stack of tiny cups, is gone at a sip, but you'll be offered refills; three is the polite number of cups to accept. Shake the cup when you've had enough. There is also the more familiar Arab (or "Turkish") coffee made sweet with the grounds in the cup.

Restaurants abound in Jordan, but if you can read the menu, you usually can't afford the food. Luckily, street food is plentiful. Kebabs and *shwarma* are skewered lamb or chicken. *Fuul* (pronounced fuhl) is cheap: Pulped beans in olive oil scooped up with bread. Fresh *ka'ik*, a bread ring with sesame seeds, is a street treat, and you'll see long lines at the market for *knaffeh*, a delicious creamy confection made of cream of wheat. Follow the crowds and explore.

Water in Amman is piped in from Azraq Oasis and the Euphrates River (in Iraq). Although certainly drinkable, it is hardly pure. For the fastidious, bottled water (200fils) or iodine tablets are a good idea. As the desert recedes, more vegetables enter the country's diet, but raw salads and fruits may be a problem for your stomach if not washed properly—fruits and vegetables that can be peeled are best. Watermelons are cheap in season.

Amman

Like Rome, Amman is built on seven hills, called *jebels*. Unlike Rome, it *was* built in a day—almost. Just before 1948 Amman was a tiny Jordanian village, much reduced from its former position as the Ammonite capital in biblical times and the city of Philadelphia in Roman times. Amman's population ballooned when the wars of 1948 and 1967 brought a flood of Palestinian refugees. Most Palestinians in Jordan live in and around Amman; overall, they make up over half of the country's population. Egyptian workers, attracted by the dinar's strength and by the availability of jobs in Amman, also constitute an important segment of the city's population. Recession in the Persian (Arabian) Gulf, however, has caused many guest workers to return home. Bedouin tents on the city's outskirts, Iraqi truckdrivers, and Saudi businesspeople all add to Amman's cosmopolitan yet Arabian character. The sum is a burgeoning collage of hectic markets and gleaming boulevards and bureaucratic monoliths next to tourist hotels. The generosity of the residents here is a godsend in a city as expensive as it is modern.

For travelers, Amman is a useful base to explore the rest of Jordan. Many of Jordan's best sights are daytrips from here. The country's transportation hub, Amman also offers cheap accommodations, government services, and the embassies or consulates of the countries you may plan to visit next. However, don't sacrifice time here that would be better spent enjoying Petra, Jerash, and Jordan's rural landscapes.

Orientation

Al-Balad, the downtown district of Amman, lies in a valley neatly framed by several *jebels*. Streets from the city's disproportionately large western districts pour off the *jebels* into **King Faisal Street,** the ever-crowded heart of the downtown commercial communities. Faisal St. runs into the **al-Husseini Mosque** (also spelled al-Husyni), the center of modern Amman. A colorful **market** several blocks southwest, the spacious **Roman Amphitheater** and the new piazza beyond, several blocks northeast, roughly mark the limits of this area of downtown. The shops in the city center, as numerous as grains of desert sand, sell everything imaginable for negotiable prices.

The steep hills of Amman surround the downtown area. Though distances between *jebels* appear short on a map, traversing these slopes is a pedestrian's nightmare. **Jebel Amman,** along whose summit you can see the neon signatures of fancy hotels, is the governmental and diplomatic core of the city. Its eight **numbered traffic circles** follow a line leading westward out of town, although traffic circles beyond Fourth Circle have been replaced by busy intersections that are still called "circles." From Seventh Circle, traffic heads south to Queen Alia International Airport and the Desert Highway (Aqaba 335km), to the Kings' Highway via Madaba (35km; Karak 125km; Petra 260km), and via Na'ur to the Dead Sea and to Jerusalem (90km). From the Eighth Circle, you can continue west to Wadi Seer, or head north to Jerash (50km).

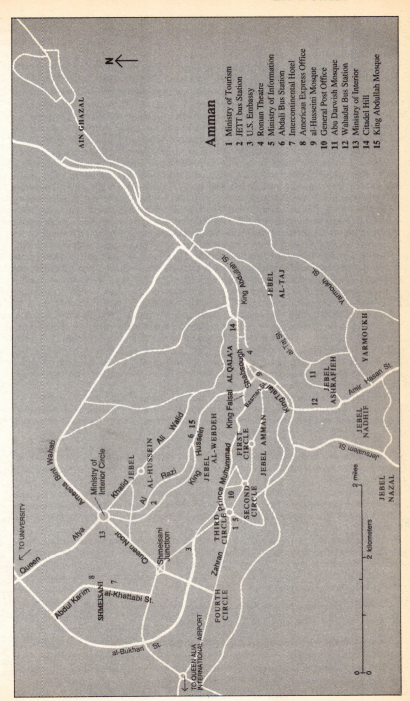

Amman

1 Ministry of Tourism
2 JETT bus Station
3 U.S. Embassy
4 Roman Theatre
5 Ministry of Information
6 Abdali Bus Station
7 Intercontinental Hotel
8 American Express Office
9 al-Husseini Mosque
10 General Post Office
11 Abu Darwish Mosque
12 Wahadat Bus Station
13 Ministry of Interior
14 Citadel Hill
15 King Abdullah Mosque

Sloping to the northwest of Jebel Amman lies the ritzy suburb of **Shmeisani,** with its vibrant nightlife. **Jebel al-Weibdeh,** across the wadi to the north of Jebel Amman, is a quiet residential district spotted with fine hotels. Its northern slope descends to **King Hussein Street,** where the JETT and Abdali (north) Bus Stations have attracted a swarm of street food stands and busy hotels. Beside Abdali Station, the blue dome and octagonal minaret of the enormous new **King Abdullah Mosque** is visible from the surrounding jebels. The mosque was positioned so as to dominate the two churches in the district (the nearer of which is worth a visit). Across the mosque stands the **National Parliament** building. **Jebel Hussein,** up the slope to the northeast, is residential as far as its northern boundary at the **Ministry of Interior Circle,** also known as Gamal 'Abd an-Nasser Square. Passes to the West Bank are obtained here. From this circle, traffic heads northwest to Jerash (50km).

Across from the Roman Theater towers rocky **Jebel Qala'a** (Citadel Hill), where the Archeological Museum sits among the excavated remains of Roman and Umayyad palaces, temples, and hilltop fortifications. To the south, in the direction of the airport, rises **Jebel Ashrafieh;** its ornate Abu Darwish Mosque can be seen above the Wahadat (south) Bus Station and the Wahadat Palestinian refugee camp. Beyond the other residential *jebels,* the city recedes into the surrounding desert sands.

The names of the streets in downtown Amman are better preserved in the collective memories of the people than in street signs. Most streets elsewhere are clearly marked in English. Even still, you will need to learn some of the landmarks to find your way around. Good orientation points are the various *jebels* and the major hotels, banks, and monuments on them.

Getting Around

Buses and service taxis to the north central and northwestern parts of the country, including the Jordan Valley, leave from **Abdali Bus Station** on King Hussein St. on Jebel al-Weibdeh. **Hashemi Street Station,** near the Roman amphitheater, serves traffic to the northeast, including Zarqa, Mafraq, and points east of Irbid. Traffic to and from the south is based at **Wahadat Station** near the Abu Darwish Mosque on Jebel Ashrafieh. Service taxis (called simply *service,* pronounced sair-VEEce) are six-seater shared cars that run along fixed routes.

To reach locations within the city or to find the starting point for buses and *service,* ask a downtown shopkeeper—at least you'll be pointed in the right direction, and quite possibly, you'll be escorted there. Buses and *service* can also be flagged down anywhere along their routes, but a longish wait for a vehicle with space for another passenger is common. Public transportation stops around 8 or 9pm, and a couple of hours earlier on Fridays; after that, walking is the only alternative to the expensive regular taxis. These yellow, metered cabs patrol the streets in search of fares until 11pm, sometimes later. Cabs charge 150fils plus about 100fils per kilometer. The approximate cost to travel from downtown to Abdali or Third Circle, or from Third to Sixth Circle, is 500fils. A taxi between the two bus/*service* stations (Abdali and Wahadat) should cost 800fils. (See Transportation in the Jordan Introduction.)

To leave Amman, *service* are the best bet, but within Amman **buses** radiate from the downtown area and cost 60-70fils for city trips, 100 fils to areas just outside Amman. Be warned, however, that buses going on different routes may display the same number. Wave down any bus traveling in your direction and ask the driver if he stops where you want to go.

#53-61: Passes Abdali Station, the JETT offices, and the Ministry of Interior Circle.

#39: Climbs Jebel Amman to the numbered circles.

#41-45: Heads directly to Third Circle before passing Fourth, Fifth, Sixth, and Seventh Circles.

#10 and 59: Goes to the Sports City (north of Shmeisani).

#10 and 53: Travels to the university and the American and British Institutes.

#61: Travels Jebel Hussein to Duwar Firas.

#61-63A: Passes the Archeological Museum on the Citadel.

#21, 23, and 24: Passes the Armenian Quarter and the Abu Darwish Mosque on the way to Wahadat Station.

#31B: Runs to Queen Alia Airport. You must buy a ticket at the hut in the center of Abdali Station.

Service provide good, inexpensive transportation to the various sectors of this hilly city, and are a bit quicker than the buses. The long lines at major intersections are for these taxis. Identify them by the white blobs on their doors that say "service" in Arabic letters. The cars are usually old white Mercedes with their route numbers on the front doors (again in Arabic). Fares are the same no matter how far along a particular route you go. The following are the most useful routes in Amman:

#1: Travels on Jebel Amman between Center City and Third Circle, passing First and Second Circles. 70fils.

#2: Starts downtown on Basman St. (look for the Basman Theater), and travels on Jebel Amman to Malik Abd Ribiya St. between Second and Third Circles. 60fils.

#3: Starts downtown on Kureisha St., and travels on Jebel Amman to Fourth Circle. 70fils.

#4: Runs from Basman St. to al-Amaneh Circle and gardens passing near all points of interest on Jebel Weibdeh. 60fils.

#5: From Basman St., travels up Jebel Weibdeh to Queen Alia Institute, just uphill from Abdali Station. 70fils.

#6: Starts downtown at terminus on Malik Razi St. (better known as Cinema al-Hussein St.) then travels along Kings Faisal and Hussein St. to Gamal 'Abd an-Nasser Circle passing Abdali and JETT Stations. 70fils.

#7: Starts by Cinema al-Hussein St., and runs past Abdali Station to Shmeisani near the Ambassador Hotel and the Gallery Alia. 70fils.

Service and minibuses to Wahadat Station start at Kureisha St. (also called Sakfi Seil) near Petra Bank and pass near Abu Darwish Mosque on Jebel Ashrafieh. From the same area, *service* head west to Middle East Circle, far out in Shmeisani (100fils). Another route starts at Shabsough St. near the Gold Market in Center City, and passes Abdali Station and Jebel Hussein to Ministry of Interior Circle (100fils). Between here and Third Circle, *service* cost 60fils.

Practical Information

Ministry of Tourism: P.O. Box 224 (tel. 64 23 11). From Third Circle on Jebel Amman, walk south past the American Cultural Center and take your first right. The Ministry is a few hundred meters farther on the right hand side. The English-speaking public relations office distributes adequate free maps of Amman, and an indispensable free map of Amman and Jordan. Hotel price listings, tourist literature, and free posters also provided. A good first stop. Open Sat.-Thurs. 8am-2pm.

American Express: International Traders, Abd al-Karim Khattabi St. (tel. 66 10 14 or 66 10 15), opposite Ambassador Hotel in Shmeisani. Holds mail. Obtains foreign (particularly Egyptian) visas at no charge for card holders, though the process may take longer than usual. Open Sat.-Thurs. 8am-1pm and 3-6pm. Often open later.

Ministry of Interior, southwest side of Ministry of Interior Circle (Gamal 'Abd an-Nasser) Sq., Jebel Hussein (tel. 66 31 11 or 63 88 49). 3½km northwest of downtown, about 2km northwest of Abdali bus station on King Hussein St., at intersection with Queen Noor St. Permits to visit the West Bank and Jerusalem issued here. Bring two photographs and passport three days in advance of your trip. Permit is free.

Banks and Currency Exchange: Banks are open to change currency Sat.-Thurs. 9:30am-12:30pm; foreign banks sometimes open later. Authorized money changers on the street give similar rates, and are open daily until 8 or 9pm. Some changers remain open on holidays, but often not for traveler's checks. Most change traveler's checks at about the same rate as cash. The nationwide **Housing Bank** is your best bet in small towns. Passports must be shown when cashing traveler's checks. **Citibank** on Prince Muhammad Street off Third Circle (tel. 64 46 13), offers the full range of banking services.

Central Post Office: Prince Muhammad St., downtown at the bottom of the staircase where the *service* to Center City let you off. Stamps and Poste Restante open 8am-8pm. Cables can be sent from this office. Branch office at Intercontinental Hotel open 7:30am-8pm. For International Registered Express Mail, go to international office at intersection of King Hussein St. and Bir al-Saba St., near Nasser Circle. Office is a low building near radio tower to the northeast. 72 hr. to USA; very expensive.

Telephone Office: Follow the road behind the post office, and it's up the hill 300m to the left. Open daily 8am-midnight. Rate for 3 minutes to the U.S. JD3.750, to Great Britain JD3. Overseas calls can be made from most hotels at anytime for a surcharge. Collect calls not possible at telephone office or hotels. A directory is available in English and in Arabic. It is cheapest to dial direct from a private phone and pay the owner back, if you meet someone willing. For telephone and postal information, dial 12. Remember neither phone calls nor mail to Israel is possible. **Airport: Queen Alia International Airport,** 35km south of Amman. Buses leave from the airport for Abdali Bus Station every ½ hr., 500fils (5:30am-8pm). Bank and tourist office (tel. 53 070; open 24 hours) in the airport. Jordanian visas available at the airport. There is a JD7 exit fee.

Buses: JETT Bus Station, King Hussein St. (tel. 66 41 46 or 66 41 47), 600m northwest (up-hill) from Abdali Station, and 500m southeast (downhill) from pyramidal Housing Bank Building on Queen Noor St. Look for small office with blue sign on north side of the street. Air-conditioned buses to King Hussein/Allenby Bridge (Sun.-Fri. 6:30am, 1 hr., JD2.500); to Petra (6:30am, 3½ hr., JD3; round-trip tour including guide, horse, lunch at Petra, back in Amman 7pm, JD14); to Aqaba (7 and 9am, 2:30, 3:30, and 4pm, JD3). Also to Damascus, Syria (7am and 3pm, 5 hr., JD3). To Cairo (3am, JD16). Possible service to Baghdad (10pm, JD10 plus JD3 departure tax). Reserve at least a day in advance, especially to bridge and Aqaba; you can reserve by phone. Office open daily 6:30am-8pm. **Minibuses** to Jordanian towns from various points in Amman (See Jordan Introduction.)

Service Taxis: To Jordanian towns and King Hussein/Allenby Bridge from Abdali and Wahadat Bus Stations. (See Jordan Introduction.)

Car Rental: Lots of possibilities, most very expensive. Local agencies, rather than worldwide agencies have the best deals. The unlimited mileage option is best for longer excursions. *Your Guide to Amman* has some deals including JD16 for car and four-star hotel for two. International drivers license is often required. **Arabian Rent-a-Car (ARAC),** Intercontinental Hotel (tel. 64 13 50). Cheapest for unlimited mileage among the established agencies: Honda Civics JD24 for 2 days, JD31.50 for 3 days, including insurance; credit card required. Also, try **Golden Wings** (tel. 68 17 48), opposite the Commodore Hotel in Shmeisani or **Dirani Rent-a-Car** (tel. 66 06 01), behind the Hiya Arts Center in Shmeisani.

English Bookstores: University Bookstore (tel. 63 63 39), Jebel Weibdeh, near Khalaf Circle. A good selection of paperbacks and books on the archeology of Jordan. Open 8am-7pm. **Amman Bookstore,** on Prince Muhammad St., near Third Circle, and the more expensive bookstores in the **Marriott** and **Intercontinental** hotels carry an excellent selection of books on the Middle East as well as maps and guides to Jordan's sights. The Intercontinental also carries a good selection of books on Palestinians. **InterBooks,** off Second Circle, carries local English-language news papers. Foreign papers can be found in any large hotel or on any of the numerous stands along Prince Muhammad St.

Publications: The *Jordan Times* lists useful telephone numbers, museum hours, and cultural events in Amman, and current government prices for fruits and vegetables (helpful for bargaining in the market). *Jerusalem Star,* published weekly, lists cultural events. *Your Guide to Amman,* published monthly and available for free at larger hotels and travel agencies, has a more complete listing of similar information.

Department of Antiquities: Tel. 64 44 82. Research office and library with updated information on digs. From Third Circle, walk toward the Holiday Inn on Hussein Bin Ali St. Turn left at the traffic light, then immediately right. The department is a few hundred meters along, on the left. Distributes books and detailed maps of the country's 3 regions (Amman/Irbid, Karak, and Ma'an) highlighting archeological sites (JD2.500). Open Sat.-Thurs. 8am-2pm.

American Center for Oriental Research (ACOR): P.O. Box 2470 (tel. 84 61 17). In northwestern Amman, across from Jordan University, in a modern white building set on a forested hill. Take university-bound bus #53 from the Roman Nymphaeceum or King Hussein St. and get off at the last stop before the university. You'll see ACOR 150m up the hill to your left. Excellent source of information and referrals on Jordan's history and on current archeological work. You may be able to hitch a ride with ACOR associates to remote sites. Also possible to stay here, although priority is given to scholars and archeologists (see Accommodations). Library open daily, including holidays, 9am-7pm.

Friends of Archeology: P.O. Box 2640. A private local organization sponsoring weekly automobile field trips to historical sites. Travelers can hitch a ride on some trips. Call ACOR for information, or read their newsletter posted at cultural centers. Field trips usually leave from Department of Antiquities (free). Trips depend on the interests of the scholars in residence.

Laundry: No public laundry facilities. Better hotels have services, and in cheaper places you can negotiate the price. Handwashed clothes dry instantly in the sun.

Emergency: It's best to call the American Embassy 24-hour hotline (tel. 64 43 71) and ask them to call the police or ambulance. **Police:** Tel. 63 91 41. **Medical Emergencies:** Tel. 63 03 41, 62 11 11, or 637 17. **Ambulance:** Tel. 195 or 77 51 11. **Traffic Accidents:** Tel. 89 63 90. *Your Guide to Amman* contains list of doctors and hospitals.

24-Hour Pharmacies: The *Jordan Times*, Jordan's English daily paper, has a listing of all-night pharmacies.

Diplomatic Missions

United States: Midway between Second and Third Circles on Jebel Amman across from the Intercontinental Hotel (tel. 64 43 71). Not able to help much with West Bank permits. Consular division open Sun.-Thurs. 8am-4pm. Observes all Jordanian holidays plus most American ones.

Canada: Off Abd al-Karim al-Khattabi St. in Shmeisani (tel. 66 61 24). Open Sun.-Thurs. 8:30am-2pm.

Britain: Abdoun, near the Greek Orthodox Church (tel. 82 31 00). Consular division open Sun.-Thurs. 8:30am-1:30pm.

Australia: Fourth Circle on Jebel Amman (tel. 67 32 46). Open Sun.-Thurs. 8:30am-2:30pm. Friendly and helpful with foreign visas.

Egypt: Jebel Amman (tel. 62 95 26). Just west of the U.S. Embassy before Third Circle. For visas, bring 1 photo and JD4.500. Due to long lines of Egyptian guest workers, it's better to obtain an Egyptian visa at the Cairo airport if you are traveling by plane; you cannot obtain visas at the Aqaba consulate.

Iraq: Between First and Second Circles on Jebel Amman (tel. 62 31 75). Visas require a letter from your embassy. Tourist or transit visas must be cleared through Baghdad, and are nearly impossible to obtain unless you are with a tour.

Lebanon: Second Circle on Jebel Amman (tel. 64 13 18). Temporarily closed to the public because of war. Prospective adventurers are advised that it's illegal for Americans to visit anyway. Normally open 8-10am.

Syria: Jebel Amman, up from Third Circle toward the Holiday Inn (tel. 64 10 76). Take a left at the 5-way intersection, then your first right. Also near (north) of Fourth Circle. For a visa, bring JD2 and 2 photos. You must have a Jordanian entry stamp on your passport, and have no evidence of visits to the West Bank or Israel. British nationals are not admitted to Syria. Open for visas Sun.-Thurs. 9am-1:30pm.

Saudi Arabia: First Circle, Jebel Amman (tel. 81 41 54). Essentially closed to travelers—there are no tourist visas to Saudi Arabia, only business visas.

American Cultural Center: Jebel Amman just south off Third Circle (tel. 64 15 20). Library open Sun. 8am-5pm, Mon.-Thurs. 8am-7pm. Free American feature films 2-3 times per week. Occasional lectures on Jordan.

British Council: Rainbow St. (tel. 63 61 47). From First Circle walk 200m (away from Second Circle) along the right-hand branch of the fork. It's on the right. Air-conditioned library. Sponsors films and lectures during winter. Library open Sat.-Thurs. 8:30am-1:30pm and 4-6pm.

Accommodations

The cleanest and most reputable hotels can be found **near Abdali Bus Station** in Jebel Weideh. The location is accessible to the city center and to transport out of Amman. It is also the safest area for female budget travelers. Just beyond Jebel Weibdeh lies the posh **Shmeisani** district, with a few reasonable accommodations. This area is less accessible, but is the center of Amman's meager nightlife.

The **city center** is chock full of small seedy hotels. Every block has three or four, every alley at least one. Look into a few before you start to rejoice: Chances are they're all-male, not too clean, and a little intimidating, though cheap (generally singles JD1.250, doubles JD2.500). Under no circumstances should solo woman travelers stay in this area. The area around **Wahadat bus station** also has hotels, but they are generally awful and should be avoided unless you plan a crack-of-dawn start from that part of town.

Most prices are set by the government, but during slow times, especially summer, it's often possible to bargain. Many of the cheaper places cater to foreign workers, but owners like to accommodate tourists. Your passport will usually be demanded by the owner. Make sure you remember to ask for it back. Beds with clean sheets can be found everywhere, but washing facilities are usually less satisfactory. The rule is BYOPT (Bring Your Own Toilet Paper).

Near Abdali Station

Remal Hotel Sa'id Bin al-Harith St. (tel. 63 06 70), across from the *service* station. Pleasant rooms with balconies and spotless bathrooms. Singles JD3.500, doubles JD5.

Al-Monzer Hotel, King Hussein St. (tel. 63 32 77), across from the northwest corner of Abdali Bus Station. Large, bare, clean rooms with private baths and lukewarm water. Comfortable dining and TV rooms. Popular with foreigners and families. Singles JD3, doubles JD5. Laundry service available. The **Cleopatra Hotel,** across the stairwell (tel. 63 69 59), is a step down in quality and price. Singles JD2, doubles JD3.500.

Canary Hotel, Jebel Weibdeh (tel. 63 83 53), near Terra Sancta College. From Abdali, walk 1½ blocks down King Hussein St. to the fork at the base of Jebel Weibdeh, bear right, then take the first right after the fork up a sidewalk staircase. A convivial, family-like atmosphere in this 3-star hotel. The extra dinars go for rooms with A/C, and breakfast in the outdoor garden. Will store luggage. Singles JD4.500, doubles JD7, but subject to bargaining. 10% service charge.

Sunrise Hotel, down the hill from the Al-Monzer Hotel (tel. 62 18 41). Small rooms with tidy bathrooms. Singles JD3.500, doubles JD5.

City Center/Al-Husseini Mosque Area

Cliff Hotel, King Faisal St. (tel. 62 42 73), at the top of the street across from the "Seiko" Fork, at the base of King Hussein St. On the third floor, above a cafe. Cheap, small, friendly, and surprisingly pleasant. Sinks in each room and reliable luggage storage. Good deal. Often full. Singles JD1.500, doubles JD2.500. Beds in a shared room JD1.350. Hot shower 250fils.

Haifa Hotel, King Faisal St. (tel. 65 44 55), near the large Arab Bank, across and just down from Cliff Hotel. You may forget that you're in one of Amman's cheapest hotels. Rooms clean and airy, some with tall windows and balconies reflect a long-gone elegance Dirty bathroom with pit toilet and no hot water. Public telephone just outside. Fills early. JD1.250 per person.

Bader Hotel, Prince Muhammad St. (tel. 63 76 02), near King Faisal St., a few blocks down from the post office. A no-frills place with clean, quiet rooms but dingy bathrooms. Small valuables can be locked in a safe, free luggage storage. Singles JD2.200, doubles JD3.850.

Palace Hotel, King Faisal St. (tel. 62 43 26), 1½ blocks up from al-Husseini Mosque. Turn left into a small alley with clothing stores. Genteel, with colorful posters and almost elegant TV lounge. Well-kept rooms with private bath. Top rooms breezier with less street noise. Great deal. Singles JD4, doubles JD6. Try to bargain down JD1.

Khayyam Hotel, Hashemi St. (tel. 63 83 29), opposite the Roman Amphitheater. Unassuming, noisy little place with dirty toilets, but clean airy rooms with fans. Most rooms overlook the amphitheater. Jug of wine not included. Dorm beds JD1.250, singles JD2-2.500, doubles JD2.750. Bargain for a lower rate. Showers 250fils.

Outlying Districts

Nefertiti, 26 al-Jahed St. (tel. 60 38 65), in Shmeisani, behind the American Express office. An excellent treat. 13-min. by foot from Abdali. Quiet and comfortable, on a tree-lined street. Laundry available. Singles with shower JD4.500, doubles JD7.

YWCA Hostel, Jebel Amman (tel. 62 14 88). From Second Circle, head downhill from Rosenthal about 500m. Look for a sign and 3-story hotel on right. Quiet and clean. Women only. An excellent way to meet Jordanians and learn about the culture first-hand. Often nearly full with residents. Curfew 11pm in summer, 10:30pm in winter. Dorm beds JD3, semi-private rooms for 1 or 2 JD4. Breakfast and kitchen use included.

American Center for Oriental Research (ACOR) (tel. 84 61 17), near Jordan University in northwestern Amman. (See Practical Information for directions.) Home base for field workers in Jordan. Family atmosphere. English and archeology spoken here. Room and big Arabic-American lunch including brownies and pecan pie JD7 (sometimes JD5 for students). Private showers, laundry (500fils). Priority given to scholars. Backpackers should call first to see if room is available. Better yet, write ahead to make a reservation if you know when you'll be in Amman.

Food

Amman's cuisine draws on a Bedouin and Palestinian heritage. Amman's better sit-down restaurants cluster near Third Circle and in Shmeisani; these places usually add a 10% service charge to the bill. A low-budget stomach may be easily satiated by a variety of dishes in Amman, but stick to the main streets and busy places.

Shwarma is always available for about 170fils, but if it remains in the heat all day, you may be sharing your meal with Amman's winged or crawling critters. The stand on Prince Muhammad St., just downhill from Third Circle, and the one on the Second Circle, near the Lebanese Embassy, offer exceptionally succulent *shwarma*, and the fast pace of the business ensures fresh meat. Felafel and corn on the cob for 100fils are staples. Common additions include *hummus* plates and various salads for 150fils. Bread, however, is the essential ingredient. *Khoubz* (flatbread), is the most convenient; *ka'ik* (sesame rings), the most tasty. Both kinds are available at almost any stand for 50fils. Be sure to ask for *za'atar* (dried thyme) to sprinkle on top. For greater variety, try cheese or meat *sfiehah* (Arabic pizzas) or *manaish* (bread baked with olive oil, thyme, and other spices).

In the **downtown** area, rolled felafel sandwiches are a budgeter's dream. Take a fresh pita, squash in some felafel, throw in *tahina* (sauce) and salad, toss in a half dozen greasy french fries, and bingo!—you have a meal for 100fils. Two busy stands opposite and in front of al-Husseini Mosque are open late. You can shop at the **vegetable market** and street stalls several blocks southeast of the mosque to supplement your diet (bananas and plums 70fils per kilo; watermelons, cantaloupes, and grapes are cheap). You'll find a cleaner **market** on Jebel Amman, 1½ blocks south of the area between First and Second Circles. The market around Abdali Station is small and rather dirty. The one around Wahadat Station is enormous and equally dirty. A treat not to be missed are the freshly squeezed **juices** found in stands throughout Amman. Depending on the season, you can get fresh orange, grapefruit, melon, banana, or carrot juices. Prices range from 100-170fils.

If you're in the Shmeisani district, ask for directions to the **Ata Ali Cafe,** a hot spot for wealthy Amman teenagers. Ice cream flavors range from mango and kiwi and back to chocolate. It's not like home, but it is ice cream. Americans who are truly homesick should head furtively to the expensive **Pizza Hut** in Shmeisani. After a long day trekking to dusty ruins, stop in at **Zalatimo Sweets,** across from Abdali Station. Here you will find a treasure-trove of Arabic sweets. Try the *kunafi* (cream of wheat type of dessert) and raise your blood sugar.

Cairo Restaurant, between King Talal St. and Omar al-Mukhtar St., the 2 broad avenues heading southwest from al-Husseini Mosque. Walk about 100m from the mosque toward the market, and look left for a side street full of golden roasting chickens. Among the many inexpensive restaurants here, the Cairo is big, bright, and orange, on the mosque side of the street. All the waiters and most customers are Egyptian. Service is quick and efficient. The food is satisfying and inexpensive: ½ roast chicken 600fils, *fasula* (bean soup) 400fils, in the morning *fuul* plates (Egyptian-style fava beans) 200fils, salad 150fils, lots of rice 100fils, tea 50fils. Bread, lemons, and peppers on the house. Open 5am-11 or 11:30pm.

Salaam Restaurant, a ½ block away from al-Husseini Mosque on the left-hand side of King Faisal St. No English sign, but look for spitted chickens grilling in the window. The colorful crowd, good food, and air-conditioning outweigh the gloomy interior. About JD1 buys you bread, bird, fries, and salad. Menu is written in Arabic, but waiters can describe the other dishes. Open daily 7am-10pm.

India Chicken Tikka Inn, Prince Muhammad St., just downhill from Third Circle. Features Tandoori chicken, among many excellent dishes; ½ bird costs 900fils.

Golden Chicken Restaurant, at the corner of Ahmed Shawqi St. and al-Azraq St., Jebel Weib-deh (tel. 62 11 49). Across the park from the Jordan National Gallery. Neat and comfortable. (*Mezze* dishes 200fils each, ½ grilled chicken 770fils, beer 710fils). Open daily 11am-11pm.

Sights

Though Amman often serves as a transit center between Jordan's major attractions, it has several worthwhile sights of its own. The **Roman Theater,** downtown on Jebel al-Qala'a, is Amman's best-known sight. The theater, built by Antoninus Pius (138-61 C.E.), could accommodate 6,000 spectators. (Free.) In front stands a colonnade. At the out-of-town end of the colonnade is the **Odeon,** a smaller, covered Roman theater used for musical concerts (closed for restoration). Beyond the Odeon is a new **piazza** (opened 1987) where people rollerskate, and entire families promenade in their fanciest clothes as the sun sets (everyone leaves by about 10pm). Enjoy an evening's stroll between **al-Husseini Mosque** and the **Nymphaeum** (a vast Roman public fountain, once decorated with nymphs—they have disappeared underground, as has the water supply).

Built into the foundations of the theater on either side of the stage area, two colorful museums deserve a visit. The **Folklore Museum** (tel. 65 17 42) consists of two rooms filled with mannequins impersonating an entertaining cast of Jordanian characters, as well as smaller rooms displaying Palestinian embroidery. Take note of the *mihbash,* the roast coffee grinder. (Open Wed.-Mon. 9am-5pm; holidays 10am-4pm. Admission 250fils.) The **Museum of Costumes and Jewelry** (Popular Life of Jordan Museum; tel. 65 17 60) highlights and explains current attire and jewelry in Jordan. You can learn about the origins of regional embroidery, and why the white shawl is called "the thrilling of the soul." The gallery to the right of the entrance displays sixth-century mosaics from Madaba and Jerash. (Admission 250fils. Open Wed.-Mon. 9am-5pm.)

From the Roman Amphitheater, or any downtown locale, you can climb the steep steps and streets to the flat top of **Citadel Hill.** On the southern slope of Jebel al-Qala'a, the citadel is the site of ancient Amman, called Rabbath-Ammon, or the "Great City of the Ammonites." Neighbors of the Israelites, the Ammonites appear many times in the Bible. Travelers sleeping in the rough may recall King Og of Bashan: A neighboring kingdom boasted the world's first iron bedstead—which the Ammonite promptly stole (Deut. 3). Later King David beseiged the city twice, the second time assuring his chance of marrying Bathsheba by putting her husband Uriah in the front line of battle. A few Byzantine and Umayyad ruins remain. To reach the summit from the Roman Theater, cross Hashemi St. and pick your way to the top, up narrow stairways and through mounds of backyard garbage (about 20 min.). Taxis also make the climb, and bus #63 passes nearby. At the top, the view of the Roman Theater is superb. The wadi below and to the right is Center City; across from it is Jebel Ashrafieh and the black-and-white checkerboard dome of the **Abu Darwish Mosque,** built in the 1940s by emigrée Circassians. To the east, you'll see the **Royal Palace** at Raghadan, although you'll have to get a little closer to see the red and black regalia of the Circassian guards.

Apart from the sweeping view, the main attraction on Citadel Hill is the **Archeological Museum,** (tel. 63 87 95) which contains a chronological series of finds from ancient sites all over Jordan. Displays range from 200,000-year-old dinner leftovers, to Iron Age anthropomorphic sarcophagi, minimalist Nabatean portraits, and

Roman marble statuary. (Admission 250fils. Open Sat.-Mon. and Wed.-Thurs. 9am-5pm, Fri. and holidays 10am-4pm.) In front of the museum are the foundations of a second-century Roman temple, which once housed a 10m statue of Hercules, to whom the temple was probably dedicated. Three giant marble fingers beside the museum steps and ponderous column segments scattered about the site hint at the shrine's former magnificence.

The best preserved and most intriguing ruins lurk behind the museum. Vaulted chambers tower 10m over a spacious courtyard where elaborate floral decorations can still be traced in the stonework. The seventh-century structure once supported a huge stone dome, but the building's function, as a mosque, audience hall, or living quarters, remains unknown. Below the Roman walls directly north, an open pit leads into the underground passageway that connected the fortified city to a hidden water supply. With a flashlight and careful footwork you can enter the cavernous rock-hewn **cistern** by this route. The more conventional approach is from the gate on the street below.

The Citadel was the heart of ancient Amman; today the pulse beats downtown, in and around the **al-Husseini Mosque.** The Ottoman-style structure was built in 1924 on the site of an ancient mosque, probably also the site of the Old Cathedral of Philadelphia. The area around the mosque is full of second-hand shoeshops—keep your footwear in sight if you go inside. In the bustling market area surrounding the mosque, food and merchandise compete for space, children learn business administration, and the old men absorb themselves in a game of tric-trac or smoking the *nargileh* (water pipe). The glittering shops in downtown's **Gold Market,** between King Faisal and Shabsough St., are crowded with awestruck browsers.

For a more manageable selection of indigenous products, search through the **Jordan Craft Center** (tel. 64 45 55), between Second and Third Circles, and to the left off Zahran St. This is a non-profit exhibition of jewelry, embroidery, caftans, and pottery (open Sat.-Thurs. 9am-1:30pm and 4:30-7pm; in winter Sun.-Thurs. 9am-1pm and 3-6pm). Amman also features a number of galleries that display national and regional art. These are found in the ministry and luxury-hotel districts. The **Jordan National Gallery,** on Jebel Weibdeh (tel. 63 01 28), at Muntazah, displays contemporary artwork from around the Muslim world as well as nineteenth-century paintings of the Middle East by European artists. (Open Wed.-Mon. 9am-6pm and in winter Wed.-Mon. 9am-5pm.)

Amman's finest Byzantine artifact is the sixth-century **Suwaiffiyeh mosaic,** unearthed during construction at the western edge of the city. Ask the caretaker to hose down the floor for a better look at the design of weird creatures, which include leaf-bearded men and eagles with ears. To reach the site, follow the signs from the first left on the way from Sixth Circle to Seventh. (Open Sat.-Thurs. 8am-4pm., Fri. 9am-2pm.) The **Martyr's Monument** and **Military Museum** (tel. 66 42 40) is housed in an odd square building overlooking the Hussein Sports City (open Sun.-Fri. 9am-4pm).

In the late afternoon, stimulate your senses by walking along the jasmine-scented Second and Third Circles, near the old government and embassy district.

Entertainment

Amman is not known for its rocking nightlife—to say the least. The cool evening air usually lures people to bed for a comfortable night's sleep. Night owls will find sustenance for their souls on dance floors or in the restaurants. Most of Amman's major hotels cater to tourists with late-night discos. On the far side of the Shmeisani (about twice as far as the Ambassador Hotel, on the same road—a 40-min. walk) is the **Middle East Hotel,** which hosts an excellent disco on Friday and Sunday nights. The crowd is mostly foreign, and the tunes often turn to reggae. Out by Sixth Circle, the **Amra Hotel** also has a fairly lively nightclub on Fridays and Saturdays. Cover charge at these places is usually JD2 and drinks will cost you JD1. The El

Cesar Restaurant on Jebel Weibdeh offers more traditional Jordanian music and dancing, but few affordable edibles.

At first glance, the city center seems to lack the traditional Middle Eastern constellation of cafes and tea houses. Look again. They're mostly up on the second floors. One of these is the downtown **Hilton Cafe,** overlooking the intersection of King Hussein and King Faisal St. (above the Seiko watch sign). There is a colorful open-air local hangout on the second floor. You can learn the local card games over a cup of Amman's thickest Arabic coffee (150fils) and entertain your quickly acquired friends by choking on the dense charcoal and tobacco smoke of a *nargileh* (300fils). There is a "men's club" atmosphere, however, and even women accompanied by men are likely to cause a stir. **Babiche Cafe** in Shmeisani is a good choice for coffee or drinks. Facing the Ata Ali Cafe, turn right, and it's down the street.

During the late afternoon and early evening, Amman's central *souk* (market) becomes the city's most entertaining spot. The *souk* lies southwest of al-Husseini Mosque, encompassing several blocks. Here, the press of pedestrians spills into jammed streets. Most people rest between 2-4pm (*service* and buses become scarce), but for the homeless budget traveler, several cafes allow you to linger over a coffee in the shade for a couple of hours. Try **Maatouk's** on Third Circle (coffee 200fils).

Near Amman

Salt

During Turkish times, Salt (pronounced sult) was the chief administrative center of the surrounding area, and in the 1920s it seemed a likely choice for the newly independent state of Jordan. Fortunately, Salt was bypassed in favor of the smaller but more centrally located village of Amman. While development obliterated Amman's rural charm, Salt has retained its original character. The pride of Salt is the mosque on Jebel Yushah, which, according to Muslim legend, covers the site of the tomb of the prophet Hosea (Yushah). The panorama of the Jordan Valley stretches below. A stroll through the hilly streets where every block reveals another jewel in Jordan's finest treasury of Ottoman architecture can be the most rewarding part of a visit to this sleepy town. Many of the yellow-stone buildings date from the late nineteenth century. The Ottoman barracks, still intact, were built over a thirteenth-century fortress that was destroyed to prevent its falling into Crusader hands. Salt is also known for its large Christian community, reflected in the churches dotting the hillsides.

Salt caps several steep hills at the top of Wadi Shueib. The lush, terraced farmlands and eucalyptus groves of the wadi tumble just to the southwest of town and descend to Shuneh Nimrin on the Jordan Valley highway. Hitching or taking a minibus up the wadi is the most dramatic way to approach Salt. Shuneh Nimrin lies on the busy route from Amman to the Allenby Bridge. From King Abdullah St. on the east side of Amman, bus #57 slowly makes the 30km trip northwest to Salt, stopping at Fifth Circle and the town of Suweileh en route. A *service* from Abdali Station is similarly priced (270fils). Salt has no tourist restaurants, but food stands and shops are plentiful.

Wadi Seer

Burgeoning Amman spreads its urban tentacles westward to Wadi Seer, however, this small town stubbornly holds on to a rural personality. Wadi Seer, like much of the fertile hill country to the north and west of Amman, was settled by Circassians. These fair-skinned Muslims came from Russia during the Czarist persecutions of the 1870s and account for blond-haired Jordanians. Amman's Folklore Museum displays the traditional Circassian costume—very Russian-looking with cylindrical fur cap, black waistcoat, and red trim.

At Wadi Seer, the high desert plateau falls precipitously toward the Jordan Valley. The town's namesake stream snakes through exhilirating, leafy countryside on its way to the Dead Sea. The narrow asphalt road that follows this valley out of town seems designed for daytripping motorists or tramping backpackers. It's a half-hour hitch from Amman, and *service* also make the trip. Minibuses rouse dust down a serpentine road.

Only the rare greenery of tobacco plants and olive trees breaks the 12km stretch southwest to the ruins at **Iraq al-Emir** and the nearby grottoes. The hospitable villagers of Wadi Seer believe that the secret to the sight's history is encoded in the carvings on the huge blocks of brown stone that stand between the town and the caves. The only clue offered by the caves themselves, which form two unimpressive rows in the brown limestone mountainside, is the Aramaic inscription "Tobiah" near two of the cave windows. You can still see rock-cut water troughs and tethering rings in a couple of the chambers that were apparently used as stables.

Local legend holds that the castle was built by a love-struck slave named Tobiah. While his master was away on a journey, Tobiah built a palace and carved lions, panthers, and eagles into its walls to gain the hand of the master's daughter. Unfortunately, the master returned before Tobiah could finish the work, and the slave went unrewarded. Historians prefer to explain the inscription and the castle remains with reference to Tobiah the Ammonite Servant. Although Tobiah was a rich priest in Jerusalem, the name of the castle refers to his occupation as a servant of God. Josephus, the first-century historian, also records the wealth of a Tobiah family and the exploits of their young son Hyrcanus who "built a strong fortress, which was constructed entirely of white marble up to the very roof and had beasts of gigantic size carved on it, and he enclosed it with a wide and deep moat." The ruins (restored in 1987) are called **Qasr al-Abd** (Castle of the Slave), but it more resembles a Hellenistic palace than a defensive fort. Several red stone lions are still visible; the one on the pediment farthest from the entry gate is still intact. The nearer one has a hole in its throat and must have been a fountain. A dip in the terrain indicates where the moat was.

At the bridge on the way from Wadi Seer, you pass **al-Bassa springs,** the source of the valley's lushness. Beside the bridge are an ancient mill and aqueduct. Above the left bank of the wadi, you'll see **el-Deir,** a monastery carved into the face of the cliff. This extraordinary building deserves the 20-minute scramble, even if you don't find any of the Roman gold that villagers claim is buried under the floor. The walls inside are covered with thousands of triangular niches, each of which once cradled a grinning skull: The chamber is an ossuary which stored relics of monks.

The *service* to the municipality of Wadi Seer leaves from Third Circle and costs about 150fils. A minibus leaves from Abdali Station for the same price and will let you off either in Wadi Seer, at the al-Bassa springs, or at Iraq al-Emir, the village named for the caves. The village store provides supplies. Past the castle the road disappears, making passage to the Jordan Valley impossible for normal vehicles. To reach the Dead Sea, you'll have to backtrack to Amman.

Ain Ghazal

In the mid-1970s, bulldozers preparing a new highway north of Amman unexpectedly revealed traces of one of the largest Neolithic settlements in the Middle East. Since then, more delicate excavations at Ain Ghazal (Spring of the Gazelle), have unearthed two caches of plaster figures from the seventh millenium B.C.E., which are among the oldest human statues ever found. Archeologists hope that other Pre-Pottery Neolithic artifacts from the site will provide the first continuous record of a community's transition from nomadic to city life.

You can check on the progress of the excavation and get an interesting introduction to archeology at the American Center for Oriental Research in Amman (see Amman Practical Information). To reach Ain Ghazal, take bus #67 from Center City to Marka; get off at the stop after the First Circle in Marka (Duwar Marka).

Turn right at the corner by the bus stop and walk to the schoolhouse ahead on the right.

Northern Jordan

Jordan Valley and Dead Sea

From the beginning of civilization, the Jordan River has brought this desert valley to life. Its cool swath cuts through the shimmering heat of the flatlands. In the shadow of the steep bluffs on either side lie the ancient remains at Deir Allah and Pella. And at the end of the bounty in the valley lies the Dead Sea.

The challenge in reaching Deir Alla, Pella, and the Dead Sea is getting to the highway that follows the contours of the Jordan River along the length of the valley. Once there, hop on one of the many buses or *service* shuttling up and down the road, or you should be able to hitch. Perhaps the simplest method is to begin by heading west from Amman to South Shuna (Shuneh Nimrin), a busy village on the Jordan Valley Highway. You can take one of the frequent *service*. A bus also runs to South Shuna from the Ras al 'Ain area in southern Amman, near the intersection of Ali Bin Abi Taleb St. and Jerusalem St. near Jebel Nadhif (200fils). From South Shuna buses travel north to Deir Alla, via Karemah where you transfer buses, or south to Suweilah and the Dead Sea Rest House (120fils). Bring a hat and plenty of water as daytime temperatures soar.

Dead Sea

The only stretch of sand along the **Dead Sea** that is open to visitors lies along its northern shore, an hour and a half from Amman or Deir Alla. During the middle of the day, the sun reflects off the still surface of the Dead Sea, creating the illusion that the entire body of water is about to spill over the Jordan Valley. The peculiar buoyancy of this briny water, which forces even the most ambitious swimmer into a back float, attracts many Jordanians. As these are family outings, there is almost never room for hitchhikers in the cars that head south from the King Hussein/Allenby Bridge or South Shuneh. You'll regret entering the water with even the slightest scratch, as the salt water will sting painfully. No settlements or accommodations exist along the Dead Sea coast, but the **Dead Sea Rest House** (tel. (05) 57 29 01) offers showers (250fils) to relieve the burning sensation of a thick crust of salt. Unless you swim around the barrier on the north, which closes off the nicest section of beach, you'll have to pay 250fils to enter the resort enclave. The complex contains the showers, the air-conditioned Rest House, and an overpriced restaurant (pizza JD1, fish JD1.750, banana split 950fils, beer 750fils). The Rest House beach is rock-hard and the local dogs noisy, but if you miss the last bus at around 5pm and can't get a ride, it's safe to sleep here. The sunset almost makes it worth getting stuck.

Within 30km south on the highway to Aqaba (Rte. 65; accessible in this stretch) is **Zarqa Ma'in**, a cascading hot spring. (See Madaba, Kings' Highway for details.)

Deir Alla and Pella

Deir Alla, 50km north of the Dead Sea, today appears as nothing more than a sleepy little town. The only clue to its long-lived past is the huge, dusty mound towering over the bus stop. On and around the sandy *tel* overlooking the modern town, archeologists have collected Bronze Age, Iron Age, Roman, and Islamic artifacts documenting over 20 centuries of human occupation. Two temples dating as far back as 1300 B.C.E. have been excavated. To the sight-seer, however, the *tel* tells no tales: Baked mud walls of ancient temples and shrines blend into the top of the sun-tanned mound, only vaguely suggesting the former structures. For elucidation, consult the exhibit at the dig headquarters, stationed on the left at the end of the dirt road, as you pass by the foot of the *tel.* A map, explanation of the excavation, and an extensive sampling of its spoils are on display here. Deir Alla is said to be the spot where Jacob rested after wrestling with the angel as well as the site of the ancient city of Succot.

The best way to reach Deir Alla is to take a minibus from South Shuna (see above). *Service* also run sporadically from Amman's Abdali Station to Deir Alla village next to the site (600fils). From Salt you can hitch to Deir Alla, but it's a long, lonely trek, since few cars pass. You do, however, pass through **Zai National Park,** about 5km beyond Salt, where there are perfectly good abandoned camping grounds.

A 30km ride north of Deir Alla lands you in the serene surroundings of **Tabaqat Fahl,** or the biblical **Pella.** A thriving city during the first century C.E. as a member of the Decapolis commercial league, Pella is gradually being reawakened by American and Australian archeologists. On the high bank of a tortuous wadi, a stark row of Roman pillars frames bald hills and gaping ancient tombs. Far below, a Byzantine amphitheater opens onto green lawns and cool springs at the wadi's mouth. Locals have dammed the spring to create pools. These are great for splashing, but not for drinking; make certain to bring plenty of the wet stuff. Across from the Archeological Station stand the ruins of an Umayyad mosque and cemetery. Renovations to the church and civic center behind the theater uncovered the skeletons of camels and their keeper buried since an earthquake in 747 C.E. destroyed the town. To reach the site from the main road, hike or hitch 2km up the paved turn-off to Tabaqat Fahl (Pella). The trail will take you to the Australian compound on the hill to the right.

The trip from Deir Alla to Pella (Tabaqat Fahl) takes about an hour by bus (200fils). Pella is also accessible by bus from Irbid's North Station (1 hr., 200fils).

Jerash

Called Gerasa in ancient times, Jerash is one of the most extensive provincial Roman cities extant. Gerasa was a member of the Decapolis, a commercial league of cities in Rome's Asian Province, which included Pella as well. Because of its isolation in a remote valley among the mountains of Gilead, Jerash has survived long after the other nine cities were destroyed.

Unlike the other great cities of the classical period left in this area, Jerash is typically Roman in design. The city expanded over earlier settlements and little evidence of pre-Roman days remains. Inscriptions calling the town Antioch reveal that the Seleucid king of that name had a prominent outpost here, but Jerash began its golden age only after its conquest by the Roman Emperor Pompey in 63 B.C.E. For the next three centuries, Jerash prospered: Granite was brought from as far away as Aswan, and old temples were razed and rebuilt according to the latest architectural fashions. The Emperor Trajan annexed the Nabatean lands in 106 C.E. and built a highway from Damascus to Aqaba, passing through Jerash. Hadrian visited the town in 129; the Triumphal Arch built for the occasion still stands. The town was converted to Christianity and had a bishop by the mid-fourth century. Following the destruction of the Syrian trading center at Palmyra and the decline of the Nabatean kingdom, however, trade routes shifted from the desert to the sea. Frantic construction continued through the sixth century. Without their former wealth, however, Jerash's citizens could only replace the older monuments with flashy, inferior structures, and these were mutilated by invading Persians in 635 C.E. The great earthquake of 747 C.E. left little in the hands of the Muslim Arabs, who by then controlled the city. The Crusaders described Jerash as uninhabited, and it remained abandoned until its rediscovery in the nineteenth century. After the invasion of the Ottoman Turks, Circassians built the modern town on the eastern slope of the stream valley, in what used to be the main residential area of Jerash.

Practical Information and Food

From the South Gate down the Street of Columns to the North Gate, the entire city of Jerash is barely 1km long. The tiny Chrysoras River (Golden River) separates the ancient ruins on the west bank from the new town on the east. The **Visitors Information Center** is on the left of the main road entering the city from the south, about 400m north of the Triumphal Arch. Here groups of any size may hire guides for JD2. The useful booklet *Jerash: A Brief History* (500fils), which includes a map and explanation of the sights, enables you to make a cheaper and more leisurely exploration. The detailed scale model of Jerash on display here will orient you to the ancient city. (Open daily 7:30am-7:30pm.)

From the town's **bus station,** buses travel to Amman's Abdali Station (300fils), Ajlun (200fils), and Irbid (250fils). *Service* for the same destinations leave from the bus station, but cost about 125fils more. Public transportation shuts down around 7pm. Driving from Amman to Jerash takes about 45 minutes. If you're **hitching** to Amman, Dibbin, or Ajlun, walk south from the visitors center to the major intersection less than 1km away. The right turn leads to Ajlun and Dibbin National Forest, with its new camping facilities. The straight road heads south toward Amman. You can flag down buses here. The main road through town continues north to Irbid. The best place to hitch to Irbid is at the northern edge of town, just behind the major branch that splits off to the left. It's an easy hitch to and from Amman.

Because Jerash makes such an easy daytrip from Amman, there are **no accommodations** in the town; however, there is plenty of room for discreet camping along the western edge of the enclosed site. You might also consider camping at Dibbin National Park about 8km away. The government **Rest House,** to the left of South Gate, overlooks the ruins, and serves traditional Jordanian food as well as burgers à la air-conditioning. (Kebabs JD1, *hummus* 220fils. Open daily 8am-9pm.)

At the **Al Khayyam Restaurant,** just past the visitors center, JD1 buys bread, salad, and grilled meat (open daily 8am-10pm). Street stands surrounding the bus station in town sell cheap felafel and *fuul.* Several shops near the intersection of the Ajlun and Amman highways can supply you with water and food staples for a trip to Ajlun. There's a petrol station here, too. No banking, telephone, or postal facilities exist.

Sights

Excavations have uncovered so much that a visit to Jerash is a complete immersion in a Roman bath of antiquities. While your imagination is fired by columns, theaters, temples, and gates, remember that 90% of ancient Jerash still lies buried beneath your feet. Admission to the site is 500fils at the entrance by the visitors center, and the ruins are open daily from 9am to 7pm. The following paragraphs describe the ruins from south to north.

The **Triumphal (or Hadrianic) Arch,** 400m south of the ancient walls, honors the arrival of Emperor Hadrian in the winter of 129 C.E. Walking from that monument to the main entrance, you'll pass the extensive remains of the **Hippodrome,** including stables and spectator's seats. From the entrance, the **Forum of Ionian Columns** opens up into a main street intersected by two perpendicular avenues. The odd shape of the forum remains a mystery, as does the reason why the surrounding colonnade was built on a foundation 11m deep. Roman markets and exhibitions must have made the enclosed paved area one of the liveliest spots in the city.

A footpath leads from the forum up to the breathtaking **South Theater.** Greek numerals reveal that the 4000 seats here could be reserved by Jerash's wealthy citizens. The two-story backstage, still complete with curtains and marble statues, once dominated the setting. The ruined **Temple of Zeus** stands behind the theater's seats. Even today, visitors enjoy scrambling up to the second-floor chambers unchecked by the authorities. The **Street of Columns** runs the distance between the forum and the North Gate. Its 260 pairs of columns are Corinthian replacements for earlier Ionic columns and were once topped by aqueducts carrying water throughout the ancient city. The huge paving stones still show the grooves worn by the chariots that raced through the streets. The occasional holes were designed for the drainage of rain water into a main sewage system. Pedestrians were protected under massive sidewalk coverings, of which only a few traces remain.

Walking through the first intersection, (named **South Tetrapylon** for its four slabs), look left to see the **Cathedral** and **Nymphaeum.** The "crow-step" designs on these buildings and the Nabatean coins found here bear witness to the strong commercial links with the desert kingdom at Petra. The ornamental fountains of the Nymphaeum were used in an annual reenactment of the Miracle at Cana, where Jesus changed water into wine. The bishop sat in the large stone chair between the staircases. Several hundred meters behind the cathedral, three churches possess the finest mosaics to escape Caliph Yazid II's order to destroy all "images and likenesses" in 720 C.E. You can view the mosaics by climbing the bank that abuts the northernmost wall and peering down at the cavorting animals and geometric designs that cover the floor of **Saints Cosmas and Damian's Church.**

Farther down the Street of Columns, before the second intersection with the four arches (which used to support a central dome), you can ascend two sets of restored stairs to the **Propylea** and the massive **Temple of Artemis.** In honor of Hadrian's visit, Corinthian capitals also replaced their Ionian predecessors on these 13m columns. The temple of the patron goddess of Jerash was part of a complex of buildings and courtyards with a magnificent view of the city. The **East Baths** are across the wadi, just north of the mosque in the new town. Scattered around the western part of the city are the ruins of some 13 churches of more recent vintage. They're of little interest today; even when first built, the stones were pillaged from the larger monuments and ornamentation was carelessly executed. The **Northern Gate** was built in the second century C.E. to open onto the newly completed road to Pella in the Jordan Valley. One of the springs that supplied the city's water lies a short way out. The pool that remains was the site of the annual Maiumas water festival, a coed swimming party that persisted late into the sixth century, much to the consternation of the conservative Christian community.

Each evening following sunset there is a 90-minute **sound and light show** among the ruins (JD1). Shortly afterward, the gates close for the night. A special **JETT bus** used to leave for Jerash at 4:30pm and return to Amman after the show (JD1). During the busy tourist season, check with the JETT office to see if they still offer this service.

Jerash is permanently undergoing restoration, partly due to a government attempt to raise its profile in the world. The **Jerash Festival** (now in its eighth year) takes place every summer in late July under royal patronage. Check with the Ministry of Tourism for details (tel. 64 14 67); the *Jordan Times* also has full coverage. The ruins provide a dramatic setting for musical, theatrical, and dance groups from Arab and Western countries. The Royal Jordanian Bagpipes Regiment sends the sounds of Old Scotland pealing between the columns, recalling the days of the British Mandate. The festival draws thousands of spectators; shows begin about 7pm each evening except Fridays. Tickets to most events cost JD2-4, and a simple admission to the grounds to wander among the booths and stands costs JD1. You will be searched on entry, and may be required to hire a guide (JD2) if you arrive during the day. An international telephone exchange is set up in the grounds, charging normal fees.

Transport in Jerash during the festival is crowded. Do not expect to hitch unless you are leaving town before 4pm. *Service* are also crowded. Coming home at about 10pm is less of a problem, though most cars are full of families and do not stop for hitchers.

Near Jerash

Ajlun

A massive stone castle commands the summit of a bulging hill, whose arid slopes are blanketed with pine forests, wild oaks, fig trees, and olive groves. Grapes are grown and wine is made locally, though drunk only in winter. The village is partly Christian, and the name of the next town, Kafranjah, indicates that the Crusaders (Franks, *Franjis* in Arabic) spent some time here—if only as prisoners. The Crusaders were never able to capture the castle or nearby village. The square tower of the village mosque in the main square is from no later than the fourteenth century; the minaret is more recent. New houses are being built everywhere, and the dusty character of this place may soon be lost.

The main sight is **Qalat al-Rabadh,** a huge Arab castle built between 1184 and 1185 by Azz al-Din Ausama, a commander of Salah al-Din. Although an earthquake has damaged the castle, from the top you can still see Jerusalem on a clear day. After the Crusader threat subsided, the Mamluks used the castle to transmit messages by beacon and by pigeon: From Baghdad to Cairo, day or night, the relay could be made in 12 hours. (Open daily 8am-6pm. Free.)

Ajlun lies a hilly 24km west of Jerash, an easy hitch or minibus ride from that town, from Amman (73km), or from Irbid (88km). *Service* from Amman takes 75 minutes (650fils). From Ajlun's main traffic circle, which revolves around a shabby henna tree, it's 4km to the summit. The excellent road slopes fairly gently, and allows an easy one-hour hike up from the town's circle. You can also catch a taxi there for JD1 round-trip, if it makes it. Ajlun has a post office and there are two banks on the square.

The only lodgings are the luxury **Rabadh Hotel** (tel. 46 22 02) between Ajlun and the castle (singles JD7.600, doubles JD9.800), but if you've got a sleeping bag, head for the peak. Although the castle is closed after dark, you can camp along the eastern slope and wake to a spectacular sunrise.

The Rabadh Hotel's terrace restaurant charges a premium for its view of the fortress and valley: shish kebab for JD1.300, a full breakfast for 600fils. However, if you stick to *mezze* dishes at 200fils per plate, you can have an enjoyable light lunch. Those who prefer to fill their stomachs rather than feast their eyes should stop in Ajlun at the **Green Mountain Restaurant** in the town's center circle. A half-chicken costs 600fils, *hummus* and *fuul* 170fils, and 800fils buys a feast.

Dibbin National Park

The Aleppo pines and oaks of the fertile woodland are an incredible sight in a country which is largely desert. Located in the hills 10km southwest of Jerash and lying only 65km north of Amman, Dibbin National Park attracts crowds of Jordanian nature lovers. The park encompasses some 20km of forest stretching south from the town of Dibbin.

The government provides refreshments, shaded bungalows (doubles about JD7), and camping facilities (about JD1). On the old road to Jerash near Dibbin you'll find a government **Rest House** with singles for JD5.500 and doubles for JD6.600; extra beds cost JD3. The access road leaves the Amman-Jerash Hwy. about 2km south of Jerash, winds up to the park, then parallels the highway for a while before returning to it, 25km south of Jerash (and 25km north of Amman). Look for the signs. You'll need to hitch or take a car, as there are no buses or *service* to the park.

Irbid

North of Jerash, the main road slices through Jordan's most fertile region to the industrial center of Irbid at its core. Like Amman, the modern city has burgeoned over the site of an ancient Decapolis town (Arbila). But while Amman's expansion generated an almost sterile spaciousness, Irbid's narrow streets thicken with clamor and commerce as development flows back into the heart of the city. Activity is more subdued on the modern campus of **Yarmoukh University** at the outskirts of town. Irbid offers little else for the traveler except that it is a convenient base for exploring nearby Um Qeis and al-Hemma.

Minibuses from Amman, Jerash, and Ajlun stop at Irbid's South Station. From here you can take a *service* downtown (60fils) where you'll find taxis to the North Station (50fils), taxis to Yarmoukh (150fils), and Irbid's cheap accommodations. You should have little difficulty hitchhiking the 88km from Amman via Jerash (which is 40km from Irbid). **Al-Amin Al-Kabir Hotel** (tel. 24 23 84) is on the left, 1 block downhill from the city center and the Ministry of Antiquities building. The rooms are clean and airy with ceiling fans, but close to traffic on the main drag. (Singles JD1.150, doubles JD2.500.) For a more communal atmosphere and a nice view, try the **Abu Bakr Hotel** near the city center (tel. 24 26 95). Irbid's nicer hotels are near Yarmoukh, which is inconvenient. The **al-Nasim Hotel,** on the other side of the campus (tel. 743 10), has clean singles for JD4.500 and doubles for JD7. The **al-Razi Hotel Restaurant** offers delicious Jordanian food, but the hotel itself is out of budget range. Sitting outside among veiled students and waterpipes, you can order great pizzas for under JD1 or a mini *mensaf* for JD1.500. The **Um Keis Restaurant** on campus is a good place to meet students over a cheap meal. The quickest way from Amman to Irbid is by the Arabella or Hijazi Bus Companies (1½ hr.; 700fils). The buses are luxurious and cool, and high enough to give breathtaking views along the route. Irbid has a good **post office** in the central square (ask for Grindley's Bank), well-supplied with aerograms and stamps, but no international telephone.

Near Irbid: Um Qeis and al-Hemma

Um Qeis was the biblical Gadara, where Jesus exorcised a sinner's demons and transferred them to a herd of pigs (Mark 5:1-20), known as the Gadarene Swine. As a thriving Decapolis city and huge resort for Romans who wanted to be near al-Hemma's therapeutic hot springs, Gadara had several theaters and outnumbered Jerash in temples. You can see the Sea of Galilee on clear days; greater Gadara once extended to those distant, verdant shores. Black blocks from the site checker the stone walls of the modern village—the latest evidence of the pillage and plunder that obliterated Gadara's former grandeur. In ancient times Gadara was renowned for its writers, philosophers, and good government. The city was probably founded in fourth century B.C.E.; Caesar Augustus ceded the town to Herod the Great, but it was destroyed in the Jewish Rebellion of 66-70 C.E. Today, much of the **Roman amphitheater** survives with covered passageways around the back. At the foot where the stage sits a six-foot, headless, marble goddess with a cornucopia. Nearby, squat, square pillars litter the ruins of the bathhouse; at one time they elevated the bath floors to allow steam to circulate underneath. In front of the theater are the standing columns of a Byzantine Church, a double square of white pillars and a circle of black ones within. The white columns may have been part of the original Roman street. An office of the Department of Antiquities is useful only for providing shade—it is never open. There is nowhere to stay in town, although you will find good campsites. There is a post office, and plenty of shops supply necessary food and drink.

Head to **al-Hemma** for the beautiful ride below the Golan Heights. From Um Qeis you can hitch or wait for the next minibus from Irbid to al-Hemma. If you decide to hike the 10km, choose your shortcuts with caution: The skull and bones signs mark mine fields, and should be heeded. A mine explosion would change your positive impression of the Jordanians. Shortly beyond Um Qeis, a soldier will ask to see your passport. Just after the military roadblock, the valley of the Yarmoukh River opens below. The high plateau across it—surprisingly near—is the Golan Heights.

Arriving in the tiny village of al-Hemma, you will quickly resolve not to stay overnight in the bright pink staircase-shaped hotel which charges JD4.500 for a small room. Although the sulfurous odor comes from the mineral springs, it seems to be just as strong at the hotel. At the springs compound, a kiosk on the right sells tickets; the nearby cafe sells sandwiches and watermelon.

Men swim on Fridays in the outdoor pool, despite rumors of tiny biting bugs lurking within. During the rest of the week, 500fils buys entrance to the separate men's or women's indoor pools whose stench makes swimming a rather uninviting option. You may prefer a refreshing stroll through the picturesque village where mud huts, lush pomegranate groves, and banana palms create a tropical atmosphere.

Buses (150fils) and *service* (400fils) run to Um Qeis and al-Hemma from Irbid's North Station. The last minibus back to Irbid leaves around 5pm and sometimes allows enough time to catch an Arabella or Hijazi bus back to Amman.

Azraq and Desert Castles

After hours of driving through desert lava fields, a vast patch of dusty green appears as a heavenly relief. As Lawrence of Arabia, the British World War I leader of Bedouin troops, noted, *"Numen in est"*—the Spirit of God is here. The springs at Azraq are the only permanent body of water in over 2500 square kilometers. Consequently, the oasis serves as a resting stop for hundreds of species of exotic birds, and truck drivers from three continents, as they pass on their respective migrations through Jordan's desert.

The discovery of an enormous cache of flint hand-axes indicates that paleolithic settlers hunted in the area 500,000 years ago. Yet, the most remarkable records of human habitation are the scattered Umayyad castles. Jordan's slice of the Arabian Desert preserves the finest of a group of structures that originally formed a chain from the north of Damascus to Khirbet al-Mafjar near Jericho. Built in the seventh and eighth centuries by the caliphs of the first Muslim dynasty, the Umayyads, the castles were mysteriously abandoned a century later. The imposing stonework of **Qasr Kharaneh** and strategic location of **Qasr Azraq** and **Qasr Mushatta** support speculations that the castles sheltered caravans plying the trade route between Syria, Arabia and the Far East. The baths near **Qasr al-Hallabat** and the magnificent frescoes at **Qasr Amra** reveal a setting of transplanted urban comforts in the desert, where days spent hunting slipped into evenings of poetry, music, and dance.

Practical Information

A trip to Azraq Oasis and the Desert Castles is a journey filled with uncertainty. There is no public transportation to the area, so you'll have to figure out a way to travel the 100km from Azraq and Amman by car. Excluding Qasr al-Touba, which lies far to the south and is accessible only by four-wheel drive vehicle, the castles lie on a paved highway loop, with the western end touching Amman and the eastern end at Azraq. It is possible to reach the area by **hitchhiking,** but a **car rental** in Amman and with the costs split among several people is a wiser way to make the trip. Unlike the caravans of yore, Jordan's modern highway system allows you to visit all of the castles in one day. You might be able to find a Jordanian traveling companion.

Hitchhikers will need a huge supply of food and water and a taste for adventure. Think long and hard before you undertake this extraordinary challenge. There is a lot of traffic on the Damascus highway from Amman to **Zarqa** (30km), which can also be reached by *service* from the downtown station near the Roman Theater. The road to Azraq turns right at a military checkpoint just north of Zarqa, where there is usually a fairly long line of Jordanian thumbers. Be careful about accepting rides from military vehicles, since most of these will take you only as far as some lonely desert junction. The Iran-Iraq War filled the highways with commercial trucks heading for Baghdad. Many of these also pause at a truckstop 2km east of the Damascus highway. The highway out to Azraq passes right by Qasr al-Hallabat

(30km from Zarqa) before reaching Azraq (87km from Zarq
tion, you'll have to hitch 13km north to reach Qasr Azraq, th
If you take the southern highway back to Amman, you will pa
(25km from Azraq), then Qasr Kharaneh (40km from Azraq),
Mushatta (about 90km from Azraq and 40km from Amman).

A Clockwise Tour

The following description of the castles and Azraq details a road trip
the northern route from Amman to Azraq, and the southern highway on the
trip—a clockwise tour. This direction is simpler for hitchhikers; drivers cou
as easily make a counterclockwise tour. The road from Amman to Zarqa pa
through Jordan's worst speed trap. The fine for exceeding the posted speed lin
is a whopping JD50, and Westerners will not receive special treatment.

Approximately 30km east into the desert from Zarqa, **Qasr al-Hallabat** comes
into view. Make the right turn onto the paved road and turn left up the track to
the gate. The Bedouin gatekeeper's tent is the one nearest to the entrance. The gate
is never locked, but a few wild dogs roam in the area. The strategy is to hurl rocks
in their direction long before they even approach. The castle lies in heaps all over
the large site making it difficult to distinguish Nabatean ruins from Roman ones
and the Byzantine monastery from the Arab mosque. Down the hill you can see
the snaking remains of a wall that was part of the castle's outer defenses.

Back on the main highway, you can see the difference between the sand and limestone desert to the south and the volcanic desert to the north. Just off the road to
the south is the **Hammam Sarah,** the ruined bathhouse modeled after Amra. The
many stones thrown into the well over the last 1000 years have not made it any
shallower.

On the long and lonesome highway east of Hallabat you can listen to the engine,
but you'll hear nothing else. After the desert stillness, you'll come upon the 12
square kilometers of lush parklands, pools, and green gardens of the **Azraq Oasis.**
These wetlands constitute Jordan's only permanent body of fresh water. Azraq
makes a perfect resting place. You may want to relax and find your bearings at
Azraq Junction, where the highway to the northeast heads off for Iraq, and the
southeastern road leads to the southern castles and into Saudi Arabia. The government **Rest House** lies about 5km north of here. Singles cost JD 6.600 and doubles
JD10, including use of the heavenly coed swimming pool in the back. If you just
want to swim in the pool, it's JD1 for the day. Meals cost JD2. During the summer,
almost no one stays here, so don't expect any hitches.

About 13km north of Azraq junction on the highway to Iraq, you'll find **Qasr
Azraq.** On the edge of a lava field, its blocks of dark basalt have remained piled
one on top of another long after the mortar weathered away. The Druze gatekeeper
will swing open the three-ton portals of the castle or show you his Lawrence of Arabia postcard collection. The most interesting attractions lie within a few meters of
the entrance, although most of the castle is in excellent condition because of restoration. Carved in the pavement behind the main gate is a Roman board game, and
the gatekeeper may play a round or two if you express interest. Right above the
entrance, you'll find the room used by Lawrence of Arabia during his short stay
on the premises—it is no longer the fetid dungeon where he sought to punish himself
for the failure of one of his missions. (Azraq sees a lot of strange ducks.) The castle,
which was first built by the Romans as a fort around 300 C.E. and later rebuilt
in 1237 by the Ayyubids, used to rise over three levels. Only parts of the second
level remain, with a ceiling that exposes an intricate web of basalt beams.

Throughout the trip, keep an eye out for desert wildlife. The Jordanian government tries to protect varied desert habitats, since many indigenous species are disappearing. In the **Shaumari Wildlife Preserve,** southwest of Azraq near Qasr Amra,
the government is reintroducing the gazelle, the ostrich, and the Arabian oryx. A
magnificent and endangered species, the oryx has two long, black horns. In remote

regions to the northeast and southwest of Azraq, cheetah and even desert wes may be reintroduced.

Even from a distance, the bath complex of **Qasr Amra** captivates with the elegant plicity of its design. The interior is also the best preserved of the desert palaces. The vaulted ceilings are covered with colorful frescoes, and mosaics grace most of the floors. These ancient works have been restored and freed from the soot left by centuries of Bedouin camp fires to unveil a portrait of Umayyad culture. Men return from the hunt laden with gazelle, oryx, and deer. Musicians and dancers run out to greet them. The naked frolicking women in the *hammam* (baths) become more serious as they prepare the spit for the evening roast. An early portrayal of the zodiac covers the domed ceiling of the *caldarium* (hot room). The frescoes are all the more fascinating since they date from the earliest days of Muslim culture, when human and animal depictions were permitted. You can reach Qasr Amra on the road heading southwest of Azraq Junction; it lies about 28km from Qasr Azraq.

On the road west from Qasr Amra, waves of heat shimmering above the sand create the illusion of huge swamps, called Lake Mirage, which seem to slide to the left as the day progresses from morning to afternoon. Wadi Butm (Valley of the Pistachio) is named for the groves of trees that once grew here.

Qasr Kharaneh remains somewhat of a mystery. Some experts explain that it was a defensive fort, while others argue that it was a caravanserai. The latest interpretation holds that it served as a retreat where Umayyad leaders discussed matters of state. A painted dedication in a second story room of the well-preserved castle dates its construction 92 years after the Prophet's flight from Mecca to Medina (711 C.E.). The "defensive" theory on Kharaneh is supported by the four corner towers and the solid square plan of a Roman fortress but the lack of narrowly slit windows from which guards could fire arrows down at attackers casts doubt. Note the Greek inscription in the doorjambs: Its presence implies that the Umayyads built upon an earlier structure.

Continuing west, you'll come into less harsh expanses of desert, and Bedouin tents will become more plentiful. To reach **Qasr Mushatta,** take the highway or a turn-off to Queen Alia International Airport. You may want to hire a *service* from the village of Muwaqaar, in the north, to reach the castle. The castle is on the left as you approach the airport from the north, but the public access road turns off to the right and loops all the way around the airport, about 4km. If you're walking from the airport, don't take this marked turn-off. Instead, continue on the left of the airport, past the Alia cargo terminal, until Mushatta appears on the left (a half-hr. walk). The facade of the eighth-century castle sits by the entrance with wonderfully carved floral designs; most of it was delivered to Kaiser Wilhelm as a gift from Ottoman Sultan Abdul Hamid, so only fragments remain. From Qasr Mushatta and the airport, it's simple to hitchhike back to Amman or catch a taxi or bus into the city.

Kings' Highway (Al-Mujeeb)

Three roads link Amman and Aqaba: the **Wadi Araba Highway,** the **Desert Highway,** and the **Kings' Highway.** The Wadi Araba Highway hugs the Dead Sea Coast. Due to its proximity to Israel, the highway serves as a military road; a permit from the police is required for civilian use. By contrast, heavily laden trucks rumble stolidly around the clock along the Desert Highway, the umbilical cord that ties the cities of the north to Aqaba's port. Since the Iran-Iraq War, the Desert Highway has become the chief link from Europe and Turkey to the Persian (Arabian) Gulf. Major roadworks will soon make the highway smooth and swift, but the government can do little about the scenery—three hours of desert to Petra and five hours of the same to Aqaba. Only the antics of swifter drivers who impatiently drive on the shoulder or squeeze between oncoming cars break the monotony of the desert flatness. Gas and telephones along the way are scarce. Hitching is good.

Unless you are a hurried vacationer rushing from Amman to Aqaba or want to spend all your three days in Jordan at Petra, the Kings' Highway is the way to travel the length of Jordan. This ancient route meanders through spectacular canyons, crisscrossing numerous historical sites along the way. Known by the same name in biblical times, this road was traveled by the Israelites during their exodus from Egypt (Numbers 21-22). Caravans filled with spices and perfumes made their long way from Arabia to Palestine and Syria by the Kings' Highway before being shipped to Europe. Old Testament sites, Byzantine churches and mosaics, Crusader castles, and stunning scenery await you on your journey here.

Service run most of the way from Amman to Petra, as do **minibuses,** but generally in the mornings only. Karak is a good overnight stop. Nothing leaves Tafilah after 4pm except *service,* so get an early start. Because many drivers shun the Kings' Highway, hitchhiking is poor. Drivers tend to head for the first entrance to the Desert Highway—check that they intend to stay on the Kings' before climbing in. The highway is called the **Wadi Mujeeb Road** in Arabic (pronounced MU-jeeb). Because roadside bystanders often wave at passing cars in salutation, you should point at the curb beside your feet—the gesture used for hailing buses. A light pack and lots of water are key.

The distances are manageable: Amman to Madaba 33km; Madaba to Karak 98km; Karak to Petra 150km. The total distance from Amman to Petra is 282km along the Kings' Highway, or 262km along the Desert Highway. If you can't reach Petra in a day, it's easy to find good sites for **camping,** particularly in the wadis north of Karak or in the desert regions between Karak and Petra. A Rest House and a couple of hotels in Karak provide the only indoor accommodations.

To take the Desert Highway from downtown Amman, you can catch a ride south on Jerusalem Street (in Jebel Nadhif across Wadi Abdoun), which turns into the Desert Highway (Rte. 15). To set off on the Kings' Highway, it's easiest to take a *service* from Amman's Wahadat Station all the way to Madaba (250fils), then try to get a ride on the road to Karak which passes out of Madaba by the Apostles' Church. Alternatively, you can head south toward Queen Alia International Airport. Eighteen kilometers south of Amman, you'll come to the intersection of Highway 49, the Kings' Highway, and Highway 15, the Desert Highway. By the mini-obelisk marking the Kings' Highway-Desert Highway fork, a small group of hitchhikers often waits to see if the first offer will take them to Wadi Rum and Aqaba or Madaba, Karak, Shobak, and Petra. You can reach the junction by taking the Madaba-bound *service* from Wahadat Station, or by hitching south from Seventh Circle.

Madaba

Located on a plateau of orange groves overlooking the Jordan Valley, Madaba is a pleasant, sleepy town. The scanty Roman remains surrounding the government Rest House do not evoke visions of Madaba in its heyday as a flourishing trade center the size of Jerash. Yet the elaborate mosaics scattered throughout the town recapture Madaba's importance as a Byzantine ecclesiastical center. Leveled by an earthquake in the eighth century C.E., Madaba lay untouched for nearly 1100 years until Christian clans from Karak reinhabited the city in the late 1800s.

The prominent, yellow-brick Greek Orthodox **Church of St. George** stands in the center of town. Inside, parts of the sixth-century Map of Palestine, originally composed of 2.3 million tiles, remain intact. The map pictures the Palestinian cities of Byzantium, including Nablus, Hebron, and Jericho. The map at one time pictured the whole of the Middle East, as evidenced by the few remaining tiles of Turkey, Lebanon, and Egypt. A map of Jerusalem, with representations of the buildings existing in the sixth century including the Church of the Holy Sepulchre, is the most interesting and renowned section. The church is not known by local Christians and Muslims for the map, however, but for an appearance of the Virgin Mary in 1980. A small shrine in the crypt pictures Mary as she purportedly appeared, with a green "healing hand." (Church open daily 7am-7pm, except at lunch time; ask around for the caretaker. A 250fils donation is requested.)

Madaba's ramshackle **museum** houses the town's most extensive collection of mosaics, including a well-preserved depiction of the Garden of Eden. The museum's prominent sign greets you at the southern edge of town. (Admission 250fils. Open Sat.-Mon. and Wed.-Thurs. 9am-5pm, Fri. and holidays 10am-4pm.) The admission ticket is also good for entrance to the **Apostles' Church** on the left, at the bottom of the second right uphill from the museum. Use your imagination here to unravel the arcane symbolism embedded in the town's largest intact mosaic, which depicts a woman surrounded by mythical sea creatures in the center of a field of parrots. The church, built in 578, is gone, but the mosaics are perfectly preserved under a modern hangar. Ask the guardian to spray water on the stones to make them shine (a good practice when viewing mosaics).

Madaba has a **hospital** (Nadim Hospital), a **currency exchange,** and a **post office,** but no accommodations. The **tourist office** (open Sat.-Thurs. 8am-2pm), across from St. George's, deals with both Madaba and the surrounding sites.

Service (400fils) and buses (250fils) run to Madaba from Wahadat Station in southern Amman every half hour until around 6pm. The **Rest House,** next door to the tourist office, serves kebab and chips (JD1) as well as other snacks and soft drinks (open daily 8am-11pm).

Near Madaba: Mount Nebo and Zarqa Ma'in

Moses' last request to God was for a view from **Mount Nebo.** No wonder. On a clear day, you can see all across the Jordan Valley to the glistening Dead Sea, and beyond that to Jericho. The Bible says "no man knows the place of his burial to this day," but Moses' grave is said to be in a secret cave somewhere along the **Ain Musa.** On Nebo itself, there are only a few tombs, but on the higher Mount Pisgah stands an enigmatic serpentine cross, next to the **Memorial of Moses.** The memorial houses the baptismal fonts and well-preserved "Mosaic" mosaics of a Byzantine church dedicated to Moses. It also contains restored mosaic panels unearthed by an Italian archeological team and Franciscan monks, whose mountaintop excavations have uncovered monasteries dating back to the third century C.E. The buildings close at 6pm, but walk on for a view of the Dead Sea. Families come here to picnic and watch the sunset.

Traffic is too light for convenient hitching from Madaba to the mountaintop, but you can catch a **bus** to Faysalieh (50fils) from the traffic circle near St. George's and the Rest House. From Faysalieh it's a 40-minute walk to the peak. Just beyond Faysalieh, a marked turnoff leads to **Khirbet al Mukhaiyat.** Mosaic fiends will want to make the one-hour detour (round-trip) to see the secular scenes of fishing, hunting, and wine-making that decorate yet another well-preserved floor in a Byzantine church. Cigarettes are the preferred form of *baksheesh* for the Bedouin gatekeeper who lives next to the mosaic on the hill at the end of the paved road.

Herod the Great, Governor of Judea in 40 B.C.E., frequently visited the hot mineral springs at **Zarqa Ma'in** to relieve his rheumatism. As he lay dying, he was carried here from his fortress at nearby Mukawir—the place where John the Baptist was beheaded (Matthew 14:1-12). The road from Madaba descends southeast from a high escarpment to the Zarqa Ma'in River, into which spring water cascades from the low cliffs. From here you can see the hills of the West Bank rising across the Dead Sea. For 250fils both men and women can swim in **Hamman es-Zarqa,** the hot indoor pool sunk in the cliff face, or bathe under the wonderful torrents of hot waterfalls. The road farther south overflows with free pools where the water temperature ranges from tepid to boiling. Reach Zarqa Ma'in by bus from Madaba. JETT Bus Company in Amman offers day trips to the springs for JD2 round-trip, leaving at 8am and returning at 6pm.

The Kings' Highway from Madaba to Karak rises and falls over plateaus and wadis. Forty kilometers south of Madaba you descend into the vast **Wadi Mujeeb,** Jordan's Grand Canyon, 4km across and 1100m deep. On one escarpment lies the biblical **Dibon** where the Mesha Stele was found in 1868. (The original huge tablet, engraved by King Mesha with the earliest Hebrew script found up to that time, is now in the Louvre.) An ancient Roman mile marker appears on the road approaching the modern town of Dhiban, and after the town disappears from view, the great Wadi Mujeeb opens up.

Few direct buses run from Madaba to Karak along the highway. The easiest way is to hitch or catch a minibus to *el-Qasr,* which has a ruined Roman temple (c. 350 C.E.) and a bus to Karak (250fils).

Karak

Karak, ancient capital of Moab, is dominated by **Karak Castle,** the largest in the line of mountaintop Crusader castles stretching from Turkey to southern Jordan. In 1132 C.E., Baldwin I built the castle as the precise midpoint between Shobak and Jerusalem. Although the fortress wall is virtually destroyed, its building blocks remain large enough to make you gasp. Inside, the vaulted stone ceilings conveniently span only a few meters, resulting in a network of long narrow audience halls and barracks. You can still see the bolt holes for mammoth stone doors that have since turned to dust or, worse, souvenirs. The castle is chock-full of secret passageways and hidden rooms, and it's great fun to explore. To the west across the moat, you can see battlements from which prisoners were cast to their deaths. The tower in the northwest corner was added in the thirteenth century. Beneath it, a 50m tunnel leads out of the town through an arched gateway. To the right of the castle entrance, you can descend a stone staircase to the **museum,** which holds Nabatean and Roman coins, Mamluk pottery, dry descriptions of the spine-tingling archeological site of Bab al-Dhira and of the biblical cities of Buseirah and Rabbah, and a plaster copy of Dhiban's Mesha Stele. (Open Sat.-Thurs. 9am-5pm, Fri. and holidays 10am-4pm. Admission 250fils, no fee to enter site.)

The prosperous modern town of Karak falls away from the castle to the north and east. Karak town makes a good resting place for travelers on the Kings' Highway. Have a snack or meal at the government **Rest House** (beer 735fils, *ḥummus* 250fils; lunch or dinner JD1.750), and take in the view of Jordan descending toward the Dead Sea. The restaurant looks across the Jordan Valley to Jerusalem, whose lights sparkle during the starry nights. To avoid the Rest House's inflated prices and mediocre service, pick up provisions in town and have a picnic amidst the ruins. The rooms here are fine and have private baths, but without fans or air-conditioning it's not worth shelling out JD6.600 for a single, JD9.900 for a double, or JD14 for a triple, plus a 10% service charge. The best cheap lodging is the clean and friendly **Castle Hotel** (tel. 15 24 89), adjacent to the Rest House. (JD2 per bed in doubles and triples, showers included. Good for solo women.) Above the hotel is the friendly but useless tourism office. The main street runs downhill from here through the **market,** where you can buy fresh fruit, cheap chickens (50fils a kilo, still clucking), and more felafel and kebabs. You'll find plenty of cheap food places. An impromptu **money exchange** operates in front of the castle entrance. Karak also has a **hospital** in the northwest end of town. The **police station** is immediately uphill from the minibus station.

Occasional minibuses make the trip to Karak from Madaba or Wadi Musa (near Petra) for a few hundred fils. *Service* from Wadahat Station in Amman are more reliable but offer less scenic traveling. They run directly from Wahadat Station to Karak (JD1.900), traveling via the Desert Highway; unfortunately this approach skirts the fantastic wadis north of Karak. You can hitch in and out of town. There are several ways to get from Karak to Petra: You can continue down the Kings' Highway to Tafilah by bus (76km, 300fils) and see more stunning scenery, or you can catch a quicker bus to Ma'an via the Desert Highway (and a *service* from there to Petra). If you're going as far as Aqaba, you can take the Wadi Araba (Jordan

Valley) Highway (bus from Karak leaves at 2:30, JD3, 3½ hr.). You must receive permission to use the highway from the police in Karak by presenting your passport (if you are driving, it is done while you wait). No hitching is allowed. The road offers fine views of the Dead Sea and the West Bank. It is possible to make it back to Petra from Aqaba by nightfall. Tafilah has no lodgings, and the local cab drivers know you can be trapped. Bargain down to JD10 for the scenic two-hour ride to Petra.

Near Karak

Highway 80 west from Karak leaves the Kings' Highway to drop for 20km until it reaches the Dead Sea "port" of Mazra'ah and the al-Lisan (tongue) Peninsula. About 5km before reaching Mazra'ah and the Wadi Araba Highway to Aqaba, Route 80 passes **Bab ed-Dhira.** The cemeteries at this ancient site have held some 20,000 shaft tombs containing an unbelievable 500,000 bodies and well over 3,000,000 pottery vessels. The size of the long bones indicate that average height in Bab ed-Dhira was a healthy 2m. Whether you're thumbing between here and Karak or on the Wadi Araba Highway along the Dead Sea to Aqaba, expect very little traffic. Stop in at the **Mazra'ah Police Post** 5km north of the junction if you need assistance. The Wadi Araba highway, running close to Israel, is militarily sensitive and may be closed to civilian travel.

Traveling east on Highway 80 toward Qatrana on the Desert Highway, you'll pass the turn-off for **al-Lejjun,** where archeologists have excavated the Roman Empire's southeasternmost frontier post. Streets, barracks, tower, church, and *principium,* which date from 30 C.E. and were destroyed by an earthquake in 551, have all been unearthed. The major remains are 2km north of the turn-off, below the Turkish barracks on the hill (now used as stables), which were built with stone pillaged from the site in order to defend the nearby railway against T.E. Lawrence and his cohorts. Take a *service* toward Qatrana and get out at the "Lajjun" sign.

Tremendous hospitality is assured in towns just north of Karak on the Kings' Highway (Rabbah, Qasr) and just to the south (Mazar, Tafilah). The mosques at Mu'tah and at the nearby village of Mazar commemorate the Islamic generals who died in the first great battles between the forces of Islam and Byzantium in 632. The green-domed mosque in Mazar houses a small Islamic museum on the first floor.

Only after you pass Mazar and begin the descent into the great Wadi Hasa does Karak Castle (20km north) fade from view.

Shobak

As the desert becomes more desolate, and Petra beckons only 25km farther south, you'll come upon the village of Shobak (*Nijil-Shobak*). From the marked turn-off at the northern edge of town, travel 4km to **Shobak Castle,** the first of seven castles built by King Baldwin I of Jerusalem in 1115 to control the triangular trade between Syria, Egypt, and Saudi Arabia. The castle fell to Salah al-Din in 1189. Although most of the castle is gone, the view from the approach road across the natural moat is outstanding, with the huge white stones silhouetted against the sky and the desert brush. Villagers who lived inside the castle walls and depended on the water from the rock-hewn well, 375 steps deep, have recently abandoned the area, leaving a secluded spot for camping. (Free; no closing hours.)

Shobak town can sometimes be reached in a shared minibus from Karak and Wadi Musa (near Petra), although much of the traffic between those towns takes the Desert Highway. If you hire a taxi, make sure the driver will not charge exorbitantly to wait while you look around.

Petra

The lost city of Petra can now easily be found, but that does not lessen its impact. After hiking for more than a mile through a natural 3m-wide fissure, you face a towering sculpture, raw mountains fashioned by human hands into impossibly delicate structures. It is Khazneh, the Treasury, Petra's finest monument to the watchful gods of the dead. Petra, meaning "stone" in ancient Greek, is perhaps the most astonishing ancient city in the modern world. It's worth changing your travel plans just to explore this Nabatean city carved to match the imposing proportions of the mountains.

For 700 years, Petra was lost to all but the few hundred members of the Bedouin tribe who guarded their treasure from outsiders. In the nineteenth century, the Swiss explorer Johann Burkhardt heard some Bedouins speaking of the "lost city" and vowed to find it. At first he was unable to find a guide, but he knew that if this was the Petra of legend, the biblical Sela, then it must be close to Mount Hor, the site of Aaron's tomb. Impersonating a devout pilgrim, Burkhardt found a guide and, on August 22, 1812, walked between the cliffs of Petra's *siq* (entrance). Awestruck, and driven to sketch the monuments and write down his thoughts, he aroused the suspicion of his Bedouin guide. The ancient rocks were carved by a divine magician, warned the guide, urging the visitor to consummate his sacrifice and leave. Since Burkhardt left, others have never stopped arriving.

At the area's principal water source, Ein Musa (Spring of Moses), Moses supposedly struck a rock with his staff and demanded water (Exodus 17). By the eighth millenium B.C.E., farmers settled in the vicinity of Wadi Musa, the Valley of Moses, with the newly discovered art of cultivation. By the sixth century B.C.E., the Nabateans, a nomadic Arab tribe, had quietly moved onto land controlled by the Edomites, and begun to profit from the trade between lower Arabia and the Fertile Crescent. Over the next three centuries, the Nabatean kingdom flourished and grew, secure in its easily defended capital. During this era, the Nabateans carved their huge temples out of the mountains, drawing on Egyptian, Greek, and Roman architecture as inspiration for their own style. Unique to the Nabateans are the crow-step (staircase) patterns that grace the foreheads of many of the monuments.

In 63 B.C.E., the Nabatean King Aretas defeated Pompey's Roman Legions. However, the Romans controlled the entire area around Nabatea, prompting the later King Rabel III to strike a deal: As long as the Romans did not attack during his lifetime, they would be permitted to enter after he died. Thus, in 106 C.E. the Romans claimed the Nabatean kingdom, and together began to improve further upon the city of rose-colored Nubian sandstone.

At its height, Petra may have housed 20-30,000 people. But after an earthquake in 363 C.E., the shifting of the trade routes to Palmyra (Tadmor) in Syria, the expansion of the sea trade around Arabia, and then another earthquake in 747 C.E., Petra declined. All but the rock-hewn tombs was reduced to rubble, as it remains today. The city fell under Byzantine and then Arab control for a few centuries before the Crusaders tried unsuccessfully to resurrect it by constructing a new fortress. By then it had lost so much of its importance that even its location was forgotten. Petra slowly decayed thereafter. It was sought unsuccessfully by a few explorers, but not until Burkhardt schemed his way in did the rose-colored city again reveal itself to the West.

For decades, the resident Bedouin successfully adapted to the influx of tourists; food and accommodations inside Petra became their province. In 1984-85, however, in its concern for the fragility of the monuments, the government removed this element of Petra's attractions. Now virtually all of Petra's Bedouin and their colorful presence have been relocated to a housing project near Wadi Musa.

Practical Information

Petra awaits you in the rocky wilderness near the southern end of the Kings' Highway about 280km from Amman, or 260km via the speedy Desert Highway.

It is possible to do the distance by donkey, but air-conditioned JETT coaches leave Amman daily at 6:30am and arrive about three and a half hours later; they return at 3pm from Petra (one-way JD3). JETT offers additional daytrips to Petra as well. Reservations can be made at JETT stations. JETT also offers an overpriced daytrip package, with round-trip passage, horse, guide, admission ticket, and lunch in Petra for JD13—not a great deal. Make reservations for any JETT bus to Petra well ahead of time to be assured a seat during the busy fall and spring seasons. The buses pull up to the visitors center at Petra.

Service to Petra from Wahadat Station takes about five hours, if the wait in Ma'an isn't too long (JD2 or more per person). From Aqaba, the two-hour trip costs JD1.500 per person by *service* and about JD1 by minibus. Start early in the morning to make any of these connections. Leaving Petra, you can catch minibuses or *service* from the center of Wadi Musa, near the post office. They leave for Aqaba, Ma'an, or Amman between 5:30 and 6am. A local bus to Ma'an leaves at 6am, returns at 2pm, and costs 500fils one-way.

To reach Petra from the Kings' Highway, take the well-marked turn-off and head west into the colorful, steep-sided town of Wadi Musa. Pass the main traffic circle and travel through the main market area of Wadi Musa. After a tortuous 5km, the spur road leaves town and soon ends at the entrance to Petra. The cluster of buildings here includes the visitors center, the government Rest House, the lavish Forum Hotel, and the gatehouse to the valley that leads to the *siq* and Petra proper.

At the **Petra Visitors Center,** the tourist police are helpful, and you can engage an official guide for JD3 per trip. It's easy to tag along behind a group with a guide or to form a group of your own. The various guidebooks available at the visitors center are helpful, but there's no substitute for the expertise of a Bedouin guide for trips to the more remote sites of al-Barid or al-Madras. At the Nabatean shop inside Petra you ought to be able to hire a guide for a full day's excursion (about JD3-4 with bargaining). On the other side of the visitors center are the **Rest House** and the swinging gate at the beginning of the trail down to the *siq*. Here you can rent a horse for the short ride (JD2), but it's more interesting to walk, keeping your eyes up on the tower cliffs of Jebel Khubtha to the right and Jebel Madras to the left, and on the monuments that begin to appear all around you.

Although you'll probably want to spend most of your time in Petra itself, the village of **Elji** is just a few minutes uphill from the visitors center. At the top of the hill, on the other side of the village, is the intersection leading south to the Desert Highway and Aqaba, and north up the Kings' Highway back to Amman.

Admission to the ancient city is JD1 for adults, 100fils for children. Petra is open daily from 5am to 6pm, but these hours are poorly enforced. The guard at the entrance to the *siq* will admit people as late as 8pm.

Accommodations, Camping, and Food

The recently refurbished **Rest House** (tel. 830 11 or 830 14), beside the entrance to the site, charges JD6.600 for singles, JD9.900 for doubles, and JD14 for triples. Much better deals are available up the hill in Wadi Musa at the **Musa Spring Hotel and Restaurant** (tel. 833 04) and the **Alanbat Hotel, Restaurant, and Student House.** The Musa Spring is marginally farther out of town and marginally cheaper. The genial owners (three brothers) have to be persuaded to let you pay the full bill. (Doubles JD4.500. Roof beds JD1. Meals JD1.250. Free tea and hot showers.) A free shuttle bus takes guests down to the Petra *siq* (1 hr. on foot) at 8am and returns at 6:30pm. Cheap deals back to Amman can be arranged through the hotel. The **Alanbat** (tel. 832 65) has doubles with a nice view for JD5, and offers most of the same services.

For **camping** nearer to Petra, the fancy **Forum Hotel** (four-star, takes credit cards), near the Rest House, charges JD1.500 per person for a patch of relatively soft sand illuminated by glaring hotel lights. A tent is sometimes available for a few extra dinars, and campers have access to toilets and showers. If you don't need a shower, the tourist police or the friendly manager of the Rest House will suggest safe places to roll out your bag on the hard ground nearby. Technically, it's not allowed, but many travelers do camp. The area is patrolled all night by guards and is safe.

The best place to camp is inside Petra itself. Unfortunately, you now need a permit from the Ministry of Antiquities, although enforcement is lax. Hundreds of vacant caves lie far away from the theater area where you can safely stash luggage for weeks on end. The guard at the entrance to the *siq* will admit people with backpacks blatantly bulging with camping gear.

The **Rest House Restaurant** is worth a visit only because it was built over one of Petra's Nabatean tombs; have a drink in the tomb's inner chamber, now a bar (beer 710fils, soda 150fils). In the separate restaurant, a filling meal of chicken or shish kebab, fries, *hummus,* salad, and bread costs JD2.200. (Open daily 6:30am-11pm.) At the **New Petra Restaurant,** adjoining the Alanbat Hotel, you can get grilled meat and salad for JD1.300, or a breakfast of eggs, *hummus,* and tea for 750fils. (Meals JD3.500, beer JD1.100, mineral water 350fils.) The only place to grab a bite in Petra itself is a small sandwich shop below the museum. The town has a **post office,** numerous stores, and a **health center,** as well as ordinary cheap restaurants.

Sights

The Red Sea is not red; Petra assuredly is. Whether or not the Red Sea parted, the walls of Petra's *siq* (entrance) did, and you can still walk through the canyon's breach.

Aside from a number of revered monarchs, the Nabateans worshiped only two deities: Dushara, the god of strength, symbolized by hard, sculptured rock, and al-Uzza (or Atargatis), the goddess of water and fertility. Yet the number of temples and tombs in Petra seems infinite. These structures, with the colors and shapes of the rock mountains, and the caves are Petra's enticements. Although cars now occasionally squeeze through the *siq,* it requires only a little climbing to escape the tour groups that have begun to flock to the Khazneh and the inner valley. A few of the spectacular monuments are close enough to be glimpsed on a one-day jaunt, but the majority require a little sweaty exploration. Spend enough time in Petra to immerse yourself in its wonders.

Even before you pass through the *siq,* caves stare at you from distant mountain faces, and large *sahrij* monuments (box tombs) call for your attention. Whether these huge cubes were tombs or sacrificial altars is unclear. On the left, built high into the cliff, is the **Obelisk Tomb.** Closer to the entrance of the *siq,* rock-cut channels once held ceramic pipes bringing the Ein Musa's waters to the inner city as well as to the surrounding farm country. A nearby modern dam burst in 1963 and the resulting flash flood killed 28 tourists in the *siq.* While designing a new dam, excavators uncovered the ancient Nabatean dam. Builders used it as a model for the new one.

As you enter the *siq,* walls towering 200m on either side begin to block out the light, casting shadows on the niches in the amber-hued rock that once held icons of the gods to protect the entrance and welcome visitors. The *siq* winds along for 1½ km, and then slowly admits a faint pink glow as it widens at the **Khazneh** (Treasury), standing guard over the exit. At 90m wide and 130m tall, it is the best preserved of Petra's monuments, although bullet holes are clearly visible on the upper urn. Believing the urn to be hollow and filled with ancient pharaonic treasures, Bedouin periodically fired at it, hoping to burst this impervious piñata. Actually, the treasury was a royal tomb and, like almost everything else at Petra, is solid rock. In the morning, the sun's rays give the monument a rich peach color, while in late afternoon it glistens rose until the sun drops, creating eerie red.

To the right of the Khazneh, Wadi Musa opens up and presents the large **Roman Theater** (ahead to the left) and the long row of Royal Tombs on the face of Jebel Khubtha (to the right). The Romans built their theater under and into the red stone Nabatean necropolis, whose caves can still be seen above it. The theater seats some

3000 people and is being restored to its second-century appearance. Appreciative audiences are returning for the first time in over 1500 years, and, after hiding for centuries in curtained chambers beneath the stage, a marble Hercules (now in the museum) emerged to greet them a few years ago. Traditional Bedouin dances are slated for performance here in future seasons.

Across the Wadi are the **Royal Tombs.** The **Urn Tomb,** with its unmistakable recessed facade, commands a splendid view of the still-widening valley from a high portico. Nearby is the **Corinthian Tomb,** allegedly a close copy of Nero's Golden Palace in Rome. The **Palace Tomb** (or the Tomb in Two Stories) is so broad that it juts out from the mountainside. The tomb had to be completed by attaching pre-assembled stones to its upper left-hand corner. Around the corner, to the right, is the **Tomb of Sextus Florentinus,** who was so enamored of these hewn heights that he asked his son to bury him in this last outpost of the Roman Empire. A legend explains the "crow-step" decoration on top of each building. The crow-steps look so much like inverted stairways that the people of Meda'in Salih (a miniature Petra in Saudi Arabia), claim that to punish Petra's wickedness, Allah threw Petra upside down and turned it to stone. Whatever their origin, these crow-steps endure as the single exclusively Nabatean aspect of Petra's amalgam of architectural styles.

Around the bend to the left, several restored columns dot either side of the paved **Roman main street.** Two thousand years ago, columns lined the full length of the street, while markets and apartments branched off it. The ancient public fountain nearby is suggested by the raised **Nymphaeum** ruins near its base. Farther along is the triple-arched **Temenos Gate,** formerly thought to have been constructed to herald a visiting emperor who never actually appeared. Recent excavations reveal that it was actually the front gate of the **Qasr Bint Faroan** (Palace of the Pharaoh's Daughter). This was a Nabatean temple built to honor the god Dushara. Its Arabic-sounding name underscores the linguistic link between early Aramaic, which the ancient Nabateans spoke, and Arabic. Across the road to the right, recent excavations have uncovered the **Temple of al-Uzza (Atargatis),** also called the **Temple of the Winged Lions.** In season, you can watch the progress of the American-sponsored excavations here, which have already uncovered several workshops and some fine Nabatean pottery. On the trail leading off to the left of the Nabatean temple, a single column stands proudly beside its two fallen comrades: The **Zib Faroan** (Pharoah's Phallus) marks the entrance to the ancient Roman city. To the right of the Nabatean temple, a rock-hewn staircase leads to a small archeological **museum,** which holds the spoils of the Winged Lions dig, as well as carved stone figures from elsewhere in Petra. (Open Sun.-Thurs. 9am-4pm, Fri. and holidays 10am-4pm.)

Hikes

Up to this point, particularly if you're visiting Petra during the peak spring and fall seasons, you'll have shared this splendor with a flock of tour-group shutterbugs. Many people, content with this daytrip dosage, will go home raving about Petra's first ten percent. It's only the tip of an inverted iceberg: The magnificent rest of Petra is nestled in dozens of high places scattered over a vast area. You may ask yourself why you would want to stay longer. Well, these monuments reward the climber with fascinating stone sculptures, the same as they ever were, spectacular natural beauty, water flowing underground, and once-in-a-lifetime vistas. At least two days are necessary for the following four treks and another two or three days if you venture beyond Petra proper—assuming you do not afford yourself the luxury of getting severely lost a few times. The Bedouin say you must stay long enough to watch your nails grow long—that is, to absorb the redness of the dirt firsthand.

The shortest and easiest of the hikes leads down the wadi to the left of and behind the Temple of the Winged Lions. Fifteen minutes of strolling down the road that runs through the rich green gardens of **Wadi Turkimaniya** leads you to the only tomb at Petra with a Nabatean inscription: The lengthy invocation above the entrance beseeches the god Dushara to safeguard the tomb and to protect its contents from violation. It didn't work. The chamber has been stripped bare.

A second, more interesting climb begins at the end of the road that leads from the Zib Faroan to the cliff face a few hundred meters left of the museum. The trail winds its way up to the **Qasr Habis** (Crusader Castle), outclassed by so much else at Petra. But the steps have been recently restored, and the 10-minute climb to the top is rewarded by a spectacular panorama. The round-trip takes under an an hour.

Jebel Harun and Jebel Umm al-Biyara

The third climb begins just to the right of Jebel Habis below the museum. A sign points to **el-Deir** (the Monastery) and leads northwest, across Wadi Siyah, past the Forum Restaurant to Wadi Deir, with its fragrant oleander. As you squeeze through the narrowing canyon, you confront a human-shaped hole in the facade of the **Lion's Tomb.** A hidden tomb awaits the daredevils who try to climb the cleft to the right of the tomb; less intrepid wanderers can backtrack to the right and find it a few minutes later. On the path again, veer left and eventually stone steps lead high up, past a providential Pepsi stand (tea 100fils, soda 150fils, water 200fils), to Petra's largest monument. El-Deir, 50m wide and 45m tall, was begun in the first century C.E. but never really completed, and is less ornate than the Khazneh. On the left, a lone tree popping through a crack in the rock leads you to more ancient steps, which continue all the way up to the rim of the urn, atop the monastery. To the west, through an opening in the mountains, you can see the Wadi Araba stretching from the Dead Sea all the way to the Gulf of Aqaba. Straight across the wadi looms the highest peak in the area, **Jebel Harun** (Aaron's Mountain or Mount Hor). On top of the mountain, a white church reportedly houses the **Tomb of Aaron.** If you have iodine tablets and a canteen, you can pull cold water out of a well some 100m east of the monastery clearing and drink it. From the well, an elaborate system of stone pipes and ducts is visible on the facing mountain. The whole trip takes a couple of hours, and a few more if you detour into **Wadi Siyah** and its seasonal waterfall on the way back.

The fourth hike climbs Jebel **Umm al-Biyara** (Mother of Cisterns), which towers over the Crusader castle on Jebel Habis. Follow the trail from the left of the Nabatean temple past the Zib Faroan and down into the wadi to the right. Bear uphill to the largest tomb facade on the right and the small blue sign. If you scramble 50m up the rock chute, to the left of the sign, you'll reach the beginning of a stone ramp and stairway that leads to the top. It was here, at the site of Petra's original acropolis and the biblical city of Sela, that a Judean king supposedly threw thousands of Edomites over the cliff's edge. The huge piles of shards, over 8000 years old, are the only remnants of the mountains' first inhabitants. Later, residents carved the four great cisterns and drainage channels. This excursion lasts three grueling hours.

If instead of climbing Umm al-Biyara, you continue south along Wadi Tughra, which runs by its foot, you eventually reach the **Snake Monument,** one of the earliest Nabatean religious shrines. From here it's about two hours to Aaron's Tomb on Jebel Harun. The path meanders around Mount Hor before ascending it from the south. When it disappears on the rocks, follow the donkey droppings. As you start to climb Jebel Harun, you'll see a lone tent. A Bedouin inside, the official holder of the keys, will escort you the rest of the way and open the building for you to explore. The entire trek takes five to six hours.

The High Place

One of the most popular hikes is the circular route to the **High Place** on Jebel al-Madbah, a place of sacrifice. It gives a full view over the remains of Petra. Just as the Roman Theater comes into view, a staircase cut in the rock leads to the left. When the trail levels and forks at the top of the stairs, take the right branch. On the left, **Obelisk Ridge** presents one obelisk to Dushara and another to al-Uzza. On the peak to the right, the Great High Place supports a powerful string of grisly sights: Two neatly cut altars, an ablution cistern, gutters for draining away sacrificial blood, and cliff-hewn bleachers for a bird's eye view of the slaughter. A magnificent view of the whole Wadi Musa valley stretches below. To mollify acrophobic nerves, head downhill, leaving the obelisks on your left, and double back under the western face of the Great High Place. If you hunt around, you'll find a staircase leading down to a sculptured **Lion Fountain.** The first grotto complex beyond it is the **Garden Tomb.** Below it is the **Tomb of the Roman Soldier,** a well-proportioned structure with an elegant facade, and across from it, a rock **triclinium** (feast hall), which has the only decorated interior in Petra. The trail then leads into Wadi Farasa by the Katute site, the dwelling of a merchant apparently driven away by the Romans' nearby waste disposal site. You'll leave the trail near the Zib Faroan. The circle, followed either way, takes about one and a half hours.

Al-Madras and al-Barid

The region around Petra sparkles with lesser archeological gems, but you can only investigate those places within walking or donkey-riding distance. All roads in this isolated area lead back to the Kings' Highway, not to outlying sites. The protected position of the sites is partly a blessing. Outside Petra, imported commercialism has not altered the Bedouin lifestyle. Wildlife is easier to spot, and you may find yourself alone.

Before the entrance to the *siq,* a trail to the left of the Obelisk Tomb climbs to **al-Madras,** an ancient Petran suburb with nearly as many monuments as Petra itself. On the way, watch for the short-eared desert hare and a full spectrum of long skinny lizards—red, brown, and even pastel blue. Bring plenty of water, some food, and a Bedouin guide. The round-trip takes four to eight hours, depending on how much of al-Madras you want to see.

If you continue past the Tomb of Sextus Florentinus to the **Mughar al-Nasara** (Caves of the Christians), you will find a trail cut into the rock leading to the northern suburb of **al-Barid.** A road passing the new hotel in Wadi Musa also approaches this archeological site. Al-Barid is a curious miniature of Petra, complete with a short *siq,* many carved tombs and caves, and inscriptions on high places. There's even a painted house, something Petra can't claim. Also off the new road past the hotel is **al-Beidha.** Excitement runs high among the members of the excavating expedition here because they have uncovered traces of a Pre-Pottery Neolithic village, a sedentary society dating to the eighth century B.C.E. This finding would make it one of the earliest known farming communities in the world, along with Jericho on the West Bank of the Jordan. A Bedouin guide can lead you here over an easy trail taking about three hours each way. Again, bring food, water, and an extra JD2-3 or some of your own native trinkets—a blues harp, pocket calculator, or a frisbee.

Southern Jordan

Aqaba

Aqaba is perfectly set in a sweeping natural amphitheater beneath a curtain of rugged brown hills. Aqaba is Jordan's sole access to the sea. An even more spectacular world awaits beneath the water: Legions of brilliantly colored creatures flit through a fantasy land of coral, each a different shape and hue. As Jordan's only seaport, Aqaba is an important trade and military center. As a swinging resort, Aqaba is the darling of the Arab elite in need of a periodic escape from the dry cityscapes. The budget traveler may feel like a tropical fish out of water among expensive accommodations and food.

With its strategic and commercial potential, Aqaba has never suffered neglect. In biblical times, Solomon's copper-laden ships sailed for Ophir from the port of Etzion-Geber. The Romans stationed their famous Tenth Legion here, the Crusaders fortified the port and the little Isle of Greye, 7km off the coast, and the successors of Salah al-Din built the fort, whose remains grace a waterfront park today. In 1917 during the Arab Revolt, Faisal of Saudi Arabia and T.E. Lawrence staged a brilliant desert raid on the Ottomans' fortifications and captured the port (an awesome if drawn-out scene in the film *Lawrence of Arabia*). In 1965, King Hussein traded the Saudis 600km square of southeastern desert for 13km of coastline. Aqaba was given the space to develop into a wealthy tourist's paradise, and the port facilities quickly expanded into the new territory. With the reopening of the Suez Canal in 1975 and the increased traffic caused by the Iran-Iraq War, the harbor is now packed with solemn-looking mammoths and will soon be dominated by a military watchtower.

If you don't find this sight intriguing, simply keep your head underwater, where all this commotion has had little effect on the fish, who continue their play undisturbed. Although Aqaba's sunny climate makes it a popular winter resort, summer days can be pleasant too—if you observe the customary afternoon siesta.

Practical Information

Tourist Office: In Salah al-Din's fort on southern waterfront. Rudimentary.

American Express: International Traders Travel Agency Office, 1 block west of Municipality Sq. (tel. 31 37 57), a few doors from the Ali Baba Restaurant. Holds mail and will cash traveler's checks in building next door, but all other services only at office in Amman. Open Sat.-Thurs. 8am-1pm and 4-7pm, Fri. 8am-1pm; in winter Sat.-Thurs. 8am-1pm and 3-6pm.

Central Post Office: 2 blocks north of Municipality Sq. **Poste Restante, international telephones** and **telegrams** are here. Open daily 8am-11pm, except for post office, which is closed Fri.

Air Travel: Alia has regular flights to and from Amman (JD13 one-way, JD18 round-trip, about ½ hr.). Flights to Cairo from July 1-Aug. 15 JD25 one-way. JD7 departure tax. Bus available from Aqaba Airport to city center (7km, 250fils).

JETT Bus Station: From Municipality Sq. area, head 1km west on corniche, past the Miramar Hotel. Office on corner of office building, facing palm grove. Only regular bus service to Amman (5 daily: 7am, 8am, 9am, 1:30pm, and 4pm, JD4, 4½ hr). No other routes. JETT buses are luxury class, with hostess service, A/C, and sometimes videos. Good views and rest for weary or burnt limbs.

Bus and Service Station: 2 blocks southeast (uphill) of Municipality Sq. Serves points north of Aqaba. 1 minibus per day Sat.-Thurs. to Petra when full (at around 10-11am, inexpensive). Regular taxis offer groups quick transport to Petra (JD20), or take a *service* to Ma'an (daily, JD2), then transfer to a minibus or taxi for Wadi Musa (Petra) and other points north. Taxis to Aqaba ferry terminal (10km, 500fils after bargaining).

Ferries to Egypt: Jordanian National Lines, to Nuweiba in the Sinai (daily, 11am and 4pm, second-class JD7.500, first-class JD11.250, 3 hr. Departure tax JD5 (from port), cars JD21, not including driver). Overnight facilities at Nuweiba (hotels and camping) if you arrive late. Tours of the Sinai available from Nuweiba (LE15). Travelers' reports differ about this trip: 8-hr. waits are not uncommon. Buses from Nuweiba to Cairo meet the boats (LE20, 6-10hr.). Ferry to Suez, Egypt (at least one per day, deck-class JD17.5, third-class JD19, second-class JD21, first-class JD31, 17hr.). A cabin bed is a wise investment on these tightly packed ships. Trip to Nuweiba much preferred. Possible to purchase tickets on the day of departure (difficult during Ramadan) and not necessary to arrive at the port more than 1 hr. before departure. In Aqaba purchase tickets from any agency; in Amman at the JETT Station or Za'artarah Shipping on Prince Muhammed St., off Third Circle (open Sat.-Thurs. 8:30am-7pm, Fri. 8:30am-noon). Jordan National Lines headquarters are in Amman (tel. 78 27 82).

Visas: Egyptian visas cannot be obtained in Aqaba. You must get one in Amman, or better still, before leaving home.

Car Rental: Kada Rent-a-Car, in the lobby of the Aqaba Tourist House, east of the JETT station, 500m from Municipality Sq. **Khaled El-Qedreh Rent-a-Car** (tel. 48 18), 500m north of the east side of the post office. Cheapest daily rates—convenient for Wadi Rum jaunts. JD4.500 per 24 hours, plus 725fils per extra hour. 36fils per km. Open daily 8:30am-1:30pm, 7:30-5:30pm.

Medical Emergency: Princess Haya el-Hussein Hospital, near the JETT Station on the way into town (tel. 31 41 11 or 31 41 12). One of Jordan's best hospitals, with decompression chambers and a staff capable of dealing with diving accidents.

Police: Down the steps and 100m to the right of the Palm Beach Hotel (tel. 31 24 11, or 31 24 12). Camping permits.

Between King Hussein's villa on the border with Israel and the huge, fenced-in port facilities 4km down the arcing **corniche** to the southeast, Aqaba is one long beach. Luxury hotels and military complexes have gobbled up a good part of the beach near town.

Assorted shops line the streets of central Aqaba, which focuses on **Municipality Square.** South of the port and 10km from central Aqaba, the **ferry dock** handles the thousands of Egyptian workers and occasional foreign travelers who cross the Gulf of Aqaba to Nuweiba or Suez in Egypt (see above). If you'll be taking the ferry, be sure to arrive with an Egyptian visa already in hand, as you cannot get an Egyptian visa in Aqaba. (See the Nuweiba Ferry section in the Sinai chapter for information on arriving in Aqaba from Egypt.)

One kilometer past the ferry port, you'll come to the Marine Research Center building, just past which you'll find Aqaba's finest coral reefs and a sandy beach that stretches south to a factory and the Saudi border. From the beach or from a ferry coming into Aqaba, you can marvel at the way four countries come together in the small northern tip of the Gulf of Aqaba: Egypt meets Israel near the conspicuous resort hotels at Taba, glittering Eilat faces Jordan's Aqaba across an eerie no-man's-land, and Saudi Arabia glowers on the southeast horizon.

Hitchhiking in and around Aqaba can be easy, because there is an abundance of trucks that serve the port. Herds of six-wheeled beasts cover huge areas along the highway 2km north of town. These truck stops make strategic starting points for hitching trips to the north. Taxi fare out to the truck stops is about 500fils; the road to the port, which skirts the eastern side of town, offers closer hitching points.

Accommodations and Camping

A question has long circulated among budget travelers: Which is higher in Aqaba—temperatures, tan lines, or prices? Sleeping near the beach or in an air-conditioned room will set you back several dinars. Aqaba's cheapest hotels cluster on the streets near Municipality Sq. There are no laundry facilities outside hotels.

Jerusalem Hotel (tel. 31 48 15), on the second floor of the busy block running south from the southwest corner of Municipality Sq. Park. A well-kept place with friendly management. Clean rooms and shared bathrooms. The spacious, clean roof offers a great view of the sea-coast, and has its own bathroom, mattresses, and blankets—the best deal in Aqaba at 700-750fils per person. Singles JD1.500, doubles JD2.500.

Red Sea Hotel, in a tall building just off the northwest corner of Municipality Sq. (tel. 31 21 56). Fans blessed with a crosswind. Fills up quickly, and safe. Singles with bath JD3. Doubles with bath JD4. A/C and TV for JD3.

Aqaba Hotel, on the corniche (tel. 31 40 91), 1500m west of Municipality Sq. past the JETT station. The best place for air-conditioned indulgence by the beach. Singles JD8, doubles JD9.200, and you can sometimes put four or five people in a cottage for JD12 (official price JD25 for 4).

Hotel Palace Nile, at the northeast corner of Municipality Sq. Park (tel. 51 77 or 51 78), opposite the post office. Interior is altogether clean, bright, and pleasant, with psychedelic wall murals. Overhead fans in each room. Grimy bathrooms. Singles JD1.500, doubles JD3.

Al-Samakeh Hotel (Fish Hotel, no telephone), on the corniche 500m east of Municipality Sq., set back from the road, by the beach. Tiny rooms with little light. Men only. Singles JD1.500, doubles JD2.500.

The only legal **camping** north of the port is in the lots beside some of the larger hotels. The **Aqaba Hotel** has hard ground (it's basically a parking lot), but the JD2 fee also admits you to the private beach and showers. The best place to camp is beyond the ferry port, but you must be careful with your belongings. Until camping facilities (under construction) are completed, the nearest water source is at the Marine Research Center, just beyond the ferry. It's a good idea to acquire a camping permit from the police station by the Palm Beach Hotel, though permits are rarely checked.

Food

The fare in Aqaba is only fair. Fresh fish would be a welcome and obvious addition to the menu, but it's actually difficult to find here. Because of the low plankton content in the clear northern waters of the Gulf of Aqaba, there are few edible sea creatures around, and Jordanians are not permitted to fish richer Saudi waters farther south. There is a **market** just up from Municipality Sq. where you can fill up on fresh fruit, bread, and cheese. Shops on the streets surrounding the square sell delicacies from dates to ice cream, all at high prices.

Cafeteria Mohandes, 250m northwest of Municipality Sq., on the main north-south avenue. You can't miss the flashing lights, brightly lit, festive interiors, and the crowds of Egyptian workers. Arabic pop music spills across the street to the outdoor TV patio. Cheapest eats in Aqaba: plates of filling *hummus ma lahme* (with meat, tomatoes, and cucumber) 820fils, ½ chicken 650fils, *fuul* with *tahina* 180fils, and inexpensive felafel and salads. Open daily 6am to 1-2am.

Ali Baba Restaurant, by the corniche, 2 blocks west of Municipality Sq., 100m south of the Cafeteria Mohandes. Aqaba's "in" hangout. Slow service, but a colorful patio with a wonderfully tacky fish fountain dedicated to King Hussein. Tasty, filling spaghetti and meat sauce (770fils), soups (200-300fils), kebab JD(1.250). Tea, fresh juice (250 fils), and large beer (850fils) available all day. Open daily 6am-1pm.

Pakistani Restaurant, turn right into the alley 1 block downhill from the post office, then left to the restaurant's green sign. Adequate vegetarian dishes, cheap and filling. Curried scrawny chicken and rice 560fils. Open daily 7am-10pm.

Sinbad's Fish Restaurant, and next to it **al-Samakeh,** on the beach next to the al-Samakeh Hotel, serve good fish along with salad, *hummus,* tea, and coffee for JD2. Local wine JD1.500.

Sights

You'll be making the best use of your time in Aqaba if you do no more than stick your be-snorkeled head underwater. **Yemenieh Reef,** just south of the Marine Research Station beyond the port, ranks among the world's best, and can offer enough surprises for weeks of exploration. Most fancy hotels rent the necessary equipment and also organize outings. With a mask, snorkel, and pair of fins, you can wander off on your own to some of the more isolated spots near the Saudi border where the fish run on super-octane. Always wear foot covering, as the coral can slice your feet at the lightest touch, and be careful about what you poke: Urchins, fire coral, chicken fish, and stone fish might poke back. All are painful and the latter two sometimes deadly. (Emergency medical help, tel. 31 41 11.)

The **Aquamarina Club** (tel. 43 33), next to the Aqaba Hotel, runs two dives Saturday through Thursday at 9:30am and 2:30pm for JD5 (scuba) or JD2.500 (snorkeling), including equipment and transportation. They also offer a crash certification course for those whose diving skills are shaky or non-existent (JD20). Rental fees for snorkeling equipment alone are about JD2 per day. If you plan more than a few days diving, you may want to invest in your own equipment. The **Yamani Bookstore** across from the post office has the biggest selection of masks (JD4 and up) and fins (JD7 and up).

You can become acquainted with some of the sea's residents without getting wet by visiting the excellent **aquarium** at the Marine Research Center, just beyond the port. (Admission 250fils. Open daily 9am-1pm and 2-4pm.) Another option is a costly **glass-bottom boat ride,** available up and down the coast. If you've never been to a tropical fish pet-store, the trip is worthwhile. The fare is about JD6 whether your group is two or 12. Make sure you ask the captain to locate a small shipwreck.

In early mornings and late afternoons, the winds are strong enough to make **wind-surfing** and **sailing** possible; the Aquamarina Club charges JD2 per hour for a board, JD3 for a boat. Make sure you aren't blown illegally across the border into Eilat as you swerve between tankers.

The Aqaba Hotel will let you pay JD1 for the privilege of burning your feet on its white sands. The best **beaches** are free but distant. Indignant sun and coral worshipers often choose to walk southeast to the free pebble beach behind a "Restricted Area—No Camping" sign. The trek out past the port on the 10km strip leading to Saudi Arabia is long and the hitch difficult, but with a whole day to kill and a huge picnic, this is the place to go. Come prepared to fend off the very hot sun. A hat and sunscreen are necessities even if you feel pretty tanned.

Aqaba should thank its lucky starfish for aquatic splendors, because interesting sites above sea level don't hold water. The ruins of Solomon's Etzion-Geber, with its remnants of copper smelting furnaces, have been excavated but remain inaccessible just near the Israeli border, along with the old biblical city of Eilat. Even those not worn out from snorkeling or boozing in exclusive clubs will probably want to skip the **Medieval Fort,** located in a palm grove on the south central beach. The fort is almost always closed and even when open is no more than an empty shell. The only piece of ornamentation left is the Hashemite Coat of Arms on the double-arched portico.

An accord between the Jordanian and Egyptian goverments has recently opened up the Egyptian Isle of Greye (7km off shore) to tourists with Jordanian visas. Day passes can be obtained in Aqaba, and the boat ride takes about 45 minutes. There is stupendous swimming and snorkeling (bring your own equipment) around the island (known in Arabic as *Djezirat Faraum,* Pharaoh's Isle), and on it are a modest restaurant and shop. It's better to bring your own food and water. On the island stand the ruins of a castle that originally guarded this extreme end of the Crusader Kingdom of Jerusalem. Salah al-Din took it in 1171, and after counterattacks by the Europeans abandoned it in 1183. Extensive restoration has been carried out recently.

Wadi Rum

Those who most appreciate the majestic grandeur of Wadi Rum revel in its inaccessibility. No buses or *service* come here, and most Jordanians have never been to this area, located nearly 300km south of Amman. Buses and *service* along the Desert Highway can drop you off 25km north of Aqaba at the turn-off marked "Rum-30km." From here it is fairly easy (easier in spring than summer) to hitch a ride east and south to the **Desert Police Headquarters** in the heart of Wadi Rum. The fare from Aqaba to Ma'an or Petra is JD1, but you may be able to pay only 500fils for this part of the journey. The only other option is to rent a car—cheaper from Aqaba than from Amman if you're only visiting Wadi Rum. The journey is only 1½ hours from Aqaba. Some of the more expensive Aqaba hotels organize their own trips. This might make spending extra to stay in one worthwhile, but ask in advance.

Two tectonic plates have parted to create a wide desert valley. At sunset the cliffs are split into eerie worlds of darkness and light. At the southern end of the valley is the fort of the Desert Camel Corps, the descendants of the British-trained Arab Legion. In *Seven Pillars of Wisdom,* T.E. Lawrence wrote of his passage between these rusty crags when his "little caravan fell quiet, ashamed to flaunt itself in the presence of such stupendous hills." The distinguished-looking members of the Desert Patrol, however, are proud to be photographed on their ornamented camels. When not posing for visitors, they chase smugglers and renegade Bedouin. Their full-length *zabouns* are crisscrossed by camel-leather cartridge straps and graced by bright red bandoliers, daggers and pistols—stay on their good side. The red and white checked *kaffiyeh* with *egal* (black cord) is worn by all male Howeitat Bedouin here, and the women embroider intricate, colorful patterns on their long black dresses. Many of the men wear a *thobe,* a Bedouin version of the *jalabeya,* and camel-skin thonged sandals. If all this looks strangely familiar, you probably saw some of these Bedouin in *Lawrence of Arabia,* which was filmed here.

Beyond the ruins of the Nabatean temple behind the Bedouin tents, the great massif of Jebel Rum shoots up to 1754m. A jeep, or better yet, a camel, can take you farther through the sheer rust cliffs towering above the mudflats. These monstrous slabs of granite and sandstone erupted through the desert floor millions of years ago, and their striations in the bays and grottos point toward magnificent vistas down the 30km-long wadi. The pale, almost purple mountains cast against a deep blue sky have inspired the name **Valley of the Moon.** For JD2-5, a Bedouin will lead you on a camel to a crack in the rocks where the springs that support all the wadi's life begin. Dark stains point out the conduits carved by the ancient Nabateans to conserve their precious water. You may also be shown Lawrence's Well, where T.E. used to take a nap. The Bedouin can point to many places where huge boulders are inscribed with Thamudic graffiti thousands of years old. Such script, which evolved into modern Ethiopic, can be seen from Mada'in Salih in Saudi Arabia to Ma'an.

Only Jeeps or camels can continue through Wadi al-Yutm al-Umran to Khirbet Kithara back on the Desert Highway near Aqaba. From the desert fort, a jeep makes a four-hour trip into this area for about JD10. Be sure to leave yourself plenty of time to enjoy the fantastic Bedouin hospitality, especially if you opt for the camel ride. At the Desert Patrol headquarters, ask for Sabbah, the representative for the Ministry of Tourism. He speaks little English, but can help arrange camel tours (JD7 per person) or Jeep tours (JD8 for 10km, split between six people) to various destinations.

So far, the government **Rest House,** at the right just before the Desert Patrol outpost, maintains a monopoly on refreshments. (Beer 770fils, bottled water or Pepsi 300fils.) There are no beds, but the comfortable cushions are good for a shaded siesta during the afternoon heat. If you chat with the proprietor, he may let you spend the night. The Rest House will soon be rebuilt, and showers and cooking facilities will be added. The Jordanian government has decided to push Wadi Rum as a tourist attraction—Douglas Scott climbed it in 1975, and they feel you should too. Advertisements of the Wadi have appeared on Australian television. Fearful that tourists might hop the border, the Saudis have constructed an embankment at the end of the Wadi, so a quick dash into Arabia proper is no longer possible. **Camping** is easy and free: If the Bedouin don't extend an invitation, the Desert Police will suggest places to camp.

The night skies are bright with meteorites over the desert. Enjoy.

INDEX